Social Psychology

Social Psychology

Second Edition

John C. Brigham
Florida State University

HarperCollins*Publishers*

To the newest Brigham, Jason Beck, and to his sisters and brother, Tracy, Suzi, and David, who have shared in our delight at his long-awaited arrival.

Sponsoring Editor: Laura Pearson
Project Coordination, Text and Cover Design: The Wheetley Co., Inc.
Photo Research: Rosemary Hunter
Cover Art: "The Sensation of Crossing the Street, The West End, Edinburgh" by
          Stanley Cursiter, 1913. Private Collection.
Production: Michael Weinstein
Compositor: Pam Frye Typesetting, Inc.
Printer and Binder: R. R. Donnelley & Sons Company
Cover Printer: The Lehigh Press, Inc.

For permission to use copyrighted material, grateful acknowledgment is made to the copyright holders on p. 791, which is hereby made part of this copyright page.

Social Psychology, Second Edition

Library of Congress Cataloging-in-Publication Data

Brigham, John Carl, 1942–
    Social psychology / John C. Brigham. — 2nd ed.
        p.   cm.
    Includes bibliographical references and indexes.
    ISBN 0-673-52064-1
    1. Social psychology.   I. Title.
HM251.B647   1991
302—dc20   90-24657
                                                      CIP

91 92 93 9 8 7 6 5 4 3 2 1

BRIEF CONTENTS

CONTENTS

PREFACE

To the Instructor

I believe that social psychology is a fascinating field of inquiry and I have attempted to convey the excitement and challenge of the field through the pages of this book, to portray accurately and clearly the state of social psychology as we enter the 1990s. I don't feel that there must be a dichotomy between interest and readability, on one hand, and scholarship and professional "respectability" on the other. I have been guided by the belief that both of these criteria can be well satisfied. Accordingly, I have blended analyses of the most current research findings with coverage of the "classic" studies and theories underlying them, and continually linked applications of these findings and theories to students' everyday lives. Maintaining clarity and high interest level has been a constant focus of my writing. My aim has been, quite simply, to create a textbook that I would have liked to have read during my student years.

The subject matter is presented in five sections. The introductory section discusses the history of social psychology, outlines basic methodologies, and briefly discusses some pertinent general issues such as deception and research ethics. I also preview about a dozen general theoretical issues that are basic to social psychology. Recurring attention to these issues in subsequent chapters helps provide an integrative and coherent focus. The next two chapters fall under the broad heading of social cognition, as I cover research and theory concerning perceptions of others and of ourselves, and the process of observing behavior and making attributions (Chapter 2). The social self is analyzed in detail in Chapter 3. Part III deals with social influence, as we consider attitudes and persuasion (Chapter 4), behavior change, compliance, and conformity (Chapter 5), and the influence of groups on the individual (Chapter 6).

Social relations are the focus of Part IV. Positive relations are covered first: prosocial behavior and altruism (Chapter 7), attraction, liking, and loving (Chapter 8), and long-term relationships (Chapter 9). Many social psychology texts discuss initial contacts and attractions between people but pay little attention to the maintenance and enhancement of relationships or to the important concerns of breakups, divorce, and post-breakup adjustment. In my experience, these issues are of major interest to students, so they are examined in some detail in Chapter 9. The focus then shifts to negative social relations: aggression (Chapter 10) and prejudice and discrimination (Chapter 11).

The final section analyzes three areas where social psychological theory and findings have been applied in contemporary society: analyzing the effect of the environment on behavior (Chapter 12), applying social psychological analyses to the law and the criminal justice system (Chapter 13), and studying the social psychology of health (Chapter 14). Included in this last chapter is research on preventing self-destructive behaviors (smoking, drinking, overeating, nonuse of auto seat belts, unsafe sex), ways of increasing adherence to medical recommendations, and behaviors that may be causal factors in disease (coping styles, optimism/pessimism, Type A/Type B behavior patterns, and hostility).

This has been a very thorough revision, and users of the first edition will notice numerous changes. I have benefited greatly from the comments and suggestions of many students and professors who used the first edition. Every aspect of the first edition has been carefully evaluated, sentence by sentence, revised, and updated. Over seven hundred reference citations are new to this edition. The number of chapters is reduced from sixteen to fourteen, and Chapter 3, The Social Self, is entirely new. Self-relevant research and theoretical approaches that were scattered through several chapters in the first edition are now integrated into Chapter 3, organized in terms of three central issues: the self-concept, self-esteem, and self-presentations. Material on race, gender, and age effects have been combined into a single chapter on Prejudice and Discrimination (Chapter 11), which focuses on commonalities in the ways that we tend to perceive people in groups, causes of prejudice and stereotypes, and possible ways to reduce intergroup prejudice and discrimination. Material on the history of social psychology, discussion of recurring issues and themes in social psychology, and some speculations on the value of knowing social psychology, which comprised the final chapter of the first edition, now are included in the first chapter.

An INSTRUCTOR'S MANUAL, written by Fred Whitford of Montana State University, contains a wealth of teaching aids for each chapter: learning objectives, activities, and lecture modules, all keyed to chapter outlines. In addition, the manual includes general teaching strategies, guided lab experiments, student worksheets and "Teacher-to-Teacher," a section that highlights typical problem areas for students, offers suggestions for teaching those areas, and includes an integrated class plan incorporating many of the text's supplements.

Over 1,500 test items are featured in the *Test Bank*, written by the author in conjunction with Jane E. Jacobi of Clemson University. It offers questions that test conceptual knowledge and are referenced by learning objectives, cognition type, and difficulty level. A set of 25 preselected items from each chapter is also provided for use as a review quiz. The test bank is also available in a computerized version for IBM, IBM-compatible, and MacIntosh systems.

A number of people have made crucial contributions to this book in various ways. Dr. Karol Brigham, therapist and Associate Director of the FSU Student Counseling Center, authored Chapter 9 on long-term relationships. I am indebted to many of my colleagues who graciously granted my requests for reprints and preprints of their current work. Over a hundred undergraduate and graduate students gave me valuable feedback on the various revised chapters as they evolved. I am particularly lucky to have worked with a group of remarkably thorough, creative, and knowledgeable reviewers who provided insightful and valuable suggestions and criticisms of the first edition and/or earlier drafts of the revised chapters. I wish to thank the following people for reading and commenting on various parts of the revised edition: Bem Allen, Western Illinois University; Robin Akert, Wellesley College; William A. Barnard, University of Northern Colorado; G. Dale Baskett, Tuskegee University; Paul A. Bell, Colorado State University; Robert Bothwell, University of Southwestern Louisiana; Fred Bryant, Loyola University of Chicago; Margaret Clark, Carnegie Mellon University; Russell D. Clark, III, University of North Texas; Mark Covey, Concordia College; Jack Croxton, SUNY-Fredonia, Donald G. Dutton, University of British Columbia; Jeffrey D. Fisher, University of Connecticut; Robert Hays, University of California-San Francisco; Jon Krosnick, Ohio State University; Mark Leary, Wake Forest University; Charles Lord, Texas Christian University; Michele Y. Martel, Northeast Missouri State University; Sharon Presley, California State University-Long Beach; Carolyn Showers, Barnard College; James M. Weyant, University of San Diego; Carol Woodward, Moorpark College.

I also wish to thank the following people for reading and commenting on various parts of the manuscript for the first edition of this text: Teresa M. Amabile, Brandeis University; Ellen Berscheid, University of Minnesota; Eugene Borgida, University of Minnesota; Martin M. Chemers, The University of Utah; Edward Donnerstein, University of Wisconsin—Madison; John F. Dovidio, Colgate University; Richard I. Evans, University of Houston; Samuel Gaertner, University of Delaware; Sara Gutierres, Arizona State University; Irwin A. Horowitz, The University of Toledo; Janet Shibley Hyde, Denison University; Edward E. Jones, Princeton University; Katherine W. Klein, North Carolina State University; Thomas F. Pettigrew, University of California, Santa Cruz; Ronald W. Rogers, The University of Alabama; William Samuel, California State University, Sacramento; K. Warner Schaie, The Pennsylvania State University; David A. Schroeder, The University of Arkansas; Richard C. Sherman, Miami University; Daniel Stokols, University of California, Irvine; Valda Thompson, The University of North Carolina at Chapel Hill; and Russell H. Weigel, Amherst College.

I am also grateful to Tom Pavela, formerly of Little, Brown, for his initial enthusiasm and support for this project, to Molly Faulkner and Mylan Jaixen at Little, Brown for their continuing editorial support as the first edition developed, and to Don Hull at Scott, Foresman, for his support and friendship through the development of the second edition. Elizabeth Gabbard at The Wheetley Company, Inc., Laura Pearson at HarperCollins, and Rosemary Hunter at Scott, Foresman also played crucial roles. In Tallahassee, I was fortunate to have the services of several dedicated typists and word-processor operators: Mari Figueroa, Carmen Lamas, Sandra Rich, and Sharon Wittig. They will be almost as happy as I when this book sees the light of day. A special debt of gratitude goes to my wife, Karol, and to Jason, David, Tracy, and Suzi, who were constant sources of support, ideas, inspiration, and sometimes welcome distraction, throughout this lengthy journey.

To the Student

You may not know it, but you act as an amateur social psychologist every day, as you interact with other people and analyze their social behavior, as well as your own. "Why did he do that?" "What does she see in him?" "How can I convince him?" "What will happen when they meet?" People usually don't treat such questions as scientific issues, but social psychologists do; they study human social behavior in a scientific manner. Finding the causes for people's behavior; learning how people influence and are influenced by others; understanding positive behaviors such as altruism, liking, and loving; analyzing negative behaviors such as aggression and prejudice; and ascertaining how people behave as members of groups in contrast to their behavior as isolated individuals are major areas of concern in social psychology. We deal with these issues constantly, and their relevance to our daily lives represents, to me, the excitement of social psychology. Through these pages, I hope to communicate some of that excitement to you.

Human behavior is complex—this is part of the fascination of studying it, though it is also sometimes a source of frustration to those who seek oversimple answers and explanations. I'm going to tell it to you straight: I won't patronize you by pretending we have all the answers or glossing over inconsistencies, but neither will I try to dazzle you with jargon or get bogged down in trivialities. To the best of my ability, I'm going to put you on the cutting edge, aware of just what it is that we now know about social behavior.

In recent decades a series of calamitous events have raised painful questions about our society, its institutions, and human social behavior. The assassinations of such prominent figures as John F. Kennedy, Martin Luther King, Jr., Robert Kennedy, and John Lennon and the attempted assassinations of George Wallace, Gerald Ford, Ronald Reagan, and Pope John Paul II made people acutely aware of the role of aggression and violence in contemporary society. News accounts describing deplorable cases in which people were harmed because no one came forth to help them raise other disturbing questions about the behavior of our fellow citizens. Vietnam brought the realities of war to the forefront of national consciousness. More recently, the so-called best and brightest minds in the U.S. government conceived and approved the disastrous attempt to rescue the American hostages in Iran in 1980 and the abortive arms-for-hostages deal with Iran later in the 1980s.

Major social movements, likely to have a great influence on the restructuring of contemporary society, have also arisen in the United States and Canada in recent years. In particular, the civil rights movement, the separatist movement in Quebec, and the women's movement have had dramatic impacts on the attitudes and behavior of men and women, majority- and minority-group members alike.

The concepts of conformity, compliance, and attitude change have become particularly prominent in the political and governmental realm. Scandals involving powerful government and business officials brought the notions of conformity and obedience into sharp focus. The question has been asked again and again: How can intelligent, hard-working people be drawn into disastrous activities such as the Watergate scandal of the 1970s or the defense-contracting scandals and the Iran-Contra affair of the 1980s? The use of increasingly sophisticated persuasion techniques in mass-media advertising campaigns and the "selling" of political candidates has raised new questions about the efficacy and morality of persuasion techniques. "Brainwashing" of political and military prisoners illustrates a more frightening sense of attitude change. The tragic explosion of the space shuttle *Challenger* in 1986 sparked renewed interest in how groups make decisions (in this case, the decision to launch the shuttle in unfavorable conditions) while under stress.

These are some of the many interesting issues that social psychology tackles in a scientific manner. Social psychologists go beyond the casual, unsystematic, individual observations that we usually rely on when we attempt to understand our everyday world. Social psychologists carefully gather information through research to answer the questions about human behavior that bewilder most of us. Why do people do what they do? How can you influence other people effectively or resist people's attempts to influence you? What factors cause people to be more helpful, more loving, or more aggressive? How can prejudice and discrimination be combated? Why do some relationships last while others fail? How do social power and situational influences affect our actions? What makes people behave differently in groups than they do as individuals?

I believe that the most important contribution of social psychology is to provide information that increases human understanding and helps improve the overall quality of life. Hence, I have blended coverage of the most current and important research findings with the application of these findings to understanding our lives and the events that surround us. These issues include politics; international affairs; marriage and divorce; televised violence; advertising; "brainwashing" attempts; psychological, legal, and political issues dealing with race and gender and aspects of the legal and health care systems; group decision-making; and reactions to emergency situations.

Particularly provocative studies or research discussions are set off from the text and presented in Focuses, to highlight them for your attention. Each chapter begins with a preview of what will be covered and ends with a summary section reviewing the most important points. These features are designed to make learning easier and more interesting. Central terms are highlighted in the text and defined in the margins; there is also a complete glossary at the end of the book. A **Study Guide** is available to help you further your study of social psychology and master its important principles and concepts. Written by Michele Martel of Northeast Missouri State University, this guide includes learning objectives, annotated chapter outlines, a glossary of key terms, and a self-test with answers.

One of my goals is to enable you to see the world as a social psychologist sees it, to understand the social psychological vantage point. Even if you never take another social psychology course, I will have attained this goal if years from now you are able to look back and see that some of the principles and theories that you learned have proven valuable to you in dealing with the world. And, I must admit, I have a second goal as well. I hope that a few of you will be as excited and stimulated by this material as I was during my first social psychology course, and will decide to make a career of helping us improve our understanding of human behavior.

Your reactions can help achieve these goals. I will appreciate knowing what you liked and didn't like about the book, what you found valuable or not-so-valuable. I encourage you to write me at the Department of Psychology, Florida State University, Tallahassee, Florida 32306, and give me your comments and suggestions.

In the first chapter I propose that there are several advantages to knowing social psychology. First, the knowledge can help you better understand human behavior, making you less susceptible to the biases, stereotypes, and prejudices that commonly affect people's social perceptions. Increased social knowledge expands your alternatives and choices in life. Second, you can become an "informed consumer" of psychological research. After you leave school, most of your exposure to research findings will be through newspapers, magazines, television, and conversation. Many times, research findings are misrepresented or misinterpreted in these portrayals. With some knowledge of research techniques, methodology, and interpretation, you can avoid being misled by these (intentional or unintentional) misrepresentations. Further, I think it's just plain interesting and fun to find out what makes us tick.

Obviously, no single book can cover exhaustively everything that we know about social behavior. But I hope that after plowing through this text you will find that your understanding of the human condition is a little deeper than it was before. If so, I'm gratified.

John C. (Jack) Brigham

PART ONE

Introduction

CHAPTER 1

Social Psychology: The Study of Human Behavior

The mission of the U.S. space shuttle *Challenger* in January 1986 was to be a glittering tribute to the triumphs of U.S. space technology, given an added down-to-earth human touch by the presence of school teacher Christa McAuliffe, representing the "Teacher in Space" program. The tragic explosion just seventy-three seconds after lift-off stunned the nation. Was the disaster a result of a technological failure that could not have been anticipated? Or, in retrospect, were there crucial social psychological factors that heavily influenced officials' prior judgements that the space shuttle was so safe that a civilian, Ms. McAuliffe, could safely go along for the ride? More immediately, did social psychological factors also influence the fatal decision to go ahead with the launch on that cold January morning, even though several rocket engineers were alarmed that a cold-weather launch could be disastrous? Did a kind of psychological "go fever," a fervent desire to keep the space program on schedule, infect the decision making process in the crucial hours before the launch? Can research on decision making under pressure help us understand what happened and perhaps avoid similar disaster in the future? ❖

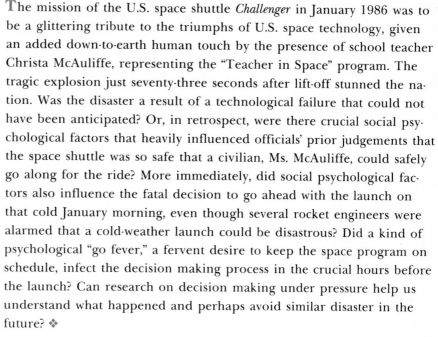

A month before Rod Matthews bludgeoned a fourteen-year-old classmate to death, he watched a videotape docudrama, "Faces of Death," that portrayed a series of brutal killings. At Matthews's murder trial in 1988, a psychiatrist testified that the video might have inspired the fifteen-year-old youth to "see what it was like to kill someone." Police in Greenfield, Massachusetts, believed that Mark Branch, suspected of having stabbed an eighteen-year-old female college student to death, may have been similarly inspired. Police found dozens of extremely violent films, including "Faces of Death," in the nineteen-year-old's home. They also found a machete and goalie masks like those used by Jason, the gruesome film character in the horror movie series, *Friday the 13th*. Branch hung himself a few days after the murder (Bass, 1989). In 1977, fifteen-year-old Ronny Zamora, pictured at left, killed an eighty-two-year-old neighbor during an attempted burglary. The manner of slaying resembled an episode of "Kojak," Zamora's favorite TV program. The boy's lawyer entered a plea of innocent by virtue of "television intoxication," but a jury nonetheless found him guilty of murder. Can social psychology help us understand incidents such as these? ❖

WHAT IS SOCIAL PSYCHOLOGY?

The Lure of Social Psychology

Concerns about violent events that seem to stimulate aggression have become commonplace in today's news media, while the *Challenger* disaster was the most memorable event of the 1980s for many of us. What these events have in common is that each can be better understood through social psychological knowledge. The application of social psychological knowledge to decision-making processes and social policies might enable us to make such tragedies less prevalent in the future. This is the excitement of social psychology: its theories, concepts, and research findings provide critically valuable information about the central issues and problems of modern life.

What Is Social Psychology?

social psychology:
The scientific study of the behavior of an individual (or groups of individuals) as he or she influences, and is influenced by, other persons.

empirical:
Pertaining to facts, experimentation, observation, or data.

Social psychology involves the scientific study of human social behavior. Years ago Floyd Allport (1924, p.12) defined social psychology as "the science which studies the behavior of the individual insofar as his [or her] behavior stimulates other individuals or is itself a reaction to their behavior." From a social psychological perspective, an individual's behavior can properly be understood only when one knows how that individual views his or her environment (Cartwright, 1979). Social psychologists' scientific training gives them an objective frame of reference about human social behavior, enabling them to find **empirical** answers to important questions through well-conducted research.

Social psychological research on the "overconfidence effect" in human judgments (to be discussed in Chapter 2) shows why the overconfident estimates given to Congress by officials of the National Aeronautics and Space Administration (NASA) should have been examined more critically. NASA officials had estimated that the chances of an engine failure during launch were only 1 in 100,000 (Feynman, 1988). By this estimate, a space shuttle could be launched each day for 300 years with the expectation that only one would be lost during this entire period! Social psychological analyses of conformity, compliance, and group decision-making processes, especially the concept of "groupthink" (to be analyzed in Chapters 5 and 6), can help us understand how the critical decision to launch was made, despite misgivings by many of those involved. Awareness of this concept may also help people avoid falling into the "groupthink" trap in the future.

The possible effect of media violence on aggressive behavior, as exemplified by the brutal murders allegedly committed by Rod Matthews, Mark Branch, and Ronny Zamora, is another issue investigated by social psychologists. I will briefly touch upon this issue later in this chapter and it will be discussed in detail in Chapter 10.

Social psychological concepts are just as relevant to the events of our everyday lives as they are to the more spectacular occurrences depicted in the media. Consider Jay, a hypothetical friend of yours who is a fellow college student. In the next few days he may encounter situations that involve virtually all of the central concepts analyzed in this book. For example, tomorrow Jay has a job interview for a summer job as a camp counselor. One of his first decisions of the day is whether he should wear a suit or dress casually. What are the social norms (conformity pressures, Chapter 5) for such interview situations? What assumptions might the interviewer make about him, depending on how he's dressed (social perception and attributions, Chapter 2)? Choosing a middle ground (sport coat, no tie), Jay emerges from his room to find that, once again, his roommate Bob has left clothes and dirty dishes strewn about the apartment. How can he get his roommate to appreciate a clean apartment (attitude change, Chapter 4)? Are there ways to bribe or force Bob to quit leaving his stuff around everywhere (social influence, Chapter 5)?

While Jay is walking to class, a student in front of him drops her armload of books. Should he help her pick them up—will she see him as helpful or as paternalistic or sexist (prosocial behavior, Chapter 7)? Arriving at class, he sits beside an interesting-looking woman he hasn't seen before. Finding himself tongue-tied and unable to make the usual pre-class small talk, Jay wonders why this woman is affecting him so. What might be the costs and potential rewards in trying to get to know her better (attraction, relationships, Chapters 7 and 8)? After class Jay has a spirited discussion with Bill about whom to vote for in the upcoming student government elections (attitude change again). Bill says he won't vote for one party because they have put forth a woman candidate for student body president; Jay argues that Bill is being sexist (prejudice and discrimination, Chapter 11). Arriving back at his apartment, Jay finds Bob watching an R-rated "slasher" video that combines sex and violence, Bob's favorite kind of movie. Jay wonders what effect the video might have on Bob or others who watch such films (aggression, Chapter 10).

I could go on and on, but I hope you get my point by now. Part of the excitement in learning about social psychological concepts comes from their pertinence and usefulness—social psychology studies the social phenomena that influence us every day of our lives. Through these pages, you will become familiar with the scientific theories that have been developed to understand, predict, and (sometimes) control human social behavior. We will also analyze the research studies designed to test these theories.

What Is Ahead

The first chapter lays the groundwork by examining research methodology and theoretical perspectives on which social psychology relies. In subsequent chapters we will look at the wide variety of important human social behaviors that have been studied by social psychologists. One set of chapters analyzes *social cognition* — the way that we perceive ourselves and others. We will look at how people perceive others and attempt to understand their behaviors by making attributions. Then, the concept of self will be evaluated. The next several chapters cover *social influence* — how people attempt to change others' attitudes and behaviors. These factors include persuasion and attitude change, obedience and compliance, and the effects of groups on individuals' behavior.

Our attention will turn next to *social relations* between individuals. I will describe scientific investigations of the positive relations between people (prosocial behavior, attraction, love, long-term relationships) as well as negative relations (aggression, prejudice, sexism, racism). Finally, I will discuss areas of *applied social psychology* where social psychological research and theorizing have been used to evaluate the effect of the physical environment on social behavior and to study the legal system and the social psychological aspects of health care.

The first chapter has three major sections intended to provide you with a frame of reference for interpreting social psychological knowledge. First I will define the field of social psychology, review its history, and discuss the role of theory. In the second section, I will discuss the scientific method as it is applied within social psychology, focusing especially on correlational and experimental studies. Research ethics and the use of deception in research will also be discussed.

The final segment briefly analyzes important recurring themes that will constantly surface as we analyze various types of social behavior. To whet your appetite, four sets of themes are discussed: (1) the determinants of social behavior; (2) important principles in understanding one's own behavior; (3) central principles in understanding other people's behavior; and (4) basic issues in how behaviors are changed. Finally, I'll present some personal views on how knowledge gained from social psychology can be valuable in everyday life.

How Social Psychology Differs from Other Fields

Many other fields also study human behavior. Sociology, economics, anthropology, criminology, political science, and several other subareas of psychology (e.g., clinical, personality, developmental, experimental) examine many of the same general issues. But each field has a different focus and level of analysis. Sociology, anthropology, criminology, history, economics, and political science usually involve a societal level of analysis, focusing on group cultural, historical, or economic factors. Other subareas of psychology, in contrast, use an individual level of analysis, seeking to understand behavior in terms of a person's individual characteristics (e.g., one's personality traits, one's unique learning history). A clinical psychologist might, for example, closely examine the personalities of Rod Matthews, Mark Branch, and Ronny

interpersonal focus:
Social psychology's focus that analyzes individuals' behavior in terms of the social factors and social situations people often deal with.

Zamora, attempting to identify unique traits that led to their homicidal behavior.

Social psychologists adopt a level of analysis somewhere in between these extremes, involving an **interpersonal focus.** They analyze individuals' social behavior in terms of the social factors and social situations that people continually deal with. Social psychology studies individuals' behaviors within various social systems in particular societies. As we will see shortly, social psychologists rely more heavily on experiments as a way of gathering information than do sociologists or other social scientists. Because social systems differ across societies and change as time passes, the particular behaviors that social psychologists study change as well. The focus of attention for social psychology has changed considerably over the years as unfolding events have brought different concepts into public awareness.

The History of Social Psychology

The Early Years
Social psychology is a very young and growing field. In 1979 Cartwright estimated that 90 percent of all social psychologists who had ever lived were alive at that time. The Society of Personality and Social Psychology is one of the largest and most active divisions of the American Psychological Association, with over 4,500 members in the late 1980s. The roots of social psychology can be seen in the writings of nineteenth-century European philosophers such as Hegel, Compte, Spencer, Le Bon, and Tarde, who were concerned with the relation of people to their society. During the same period, scientists in Britain and Germany began to conduct empirical research to answer psychological questions. The first research usually classed as an empirical social psychological study was published by Norman Triplett in 1898. Triplett, a British bicycle-racing enthusiast, observed that cyclists seemed to ride much faster when racing or when being paced by a teammate than when racing alone against the clock. Apparently the presence of other people had an impact on performance. To test this hypothesis scientifically, Triplett gave children the task of winding fishing line on a reel as fast as possible, either alone or with other children. As he suspected, the children worked faster with other children than when working alone. This effect produced by the presence of others was later labeled **social facilitation**; we will encounter more recent research on this concept in Chapter 6.

social facilitation:
Stimulation merely from seeing or hearing the similar movements of other people. This may improve performance in some situations.

The first textbooks in social psychology were published in 1908. Edward Ross's *Social Psychology* had a sociological orientation, including chapters on the "mob mind," customs, fashion, public opinion, and social conflicts. The concepts of imitation and suggestibility provided unifying themes. In contrast, William McDougall's *An Introduction to Social Psychology* had a more biological and psychological tone, focusing on instincts as the major determinants of human behavior.

Though both were original and creative contributions, neither textbook shaped the emerging field of social psychology. (Curiously, neither cited Triplett's pioneering research of a decade earlier.) Ross's central concepts were too global to be very useful, while McDougall's approach did not fit the image of humanity that was emerging from Sigmund Freud's psycholoanalytic approach or the behavioristic approach popularized by John B. Watson. Many felt that McDougall's instinct approach did not give sufficient attention to the effects of the environment on behavior. Further, he seemed to imply that humans could not easily change and were all very similar to each other, ideas that were not closely associated with the American experience (Pepitone, 1981).

In the 1920s social psychology began to take on a more modern form. Floyd Allport's *Social Psychology* (1924) covered many concepts that have remained at the core of social psychology. Arguing against the sociological approach, Allport (1924, p. 4) maintained that "There is no psychology of groups which is not essentially and entirely a psychology of the individual." Allport was more empirical and less philosophical than Ross or McDougall had been, discussing experimental work on social facilitation, social influence, conformity, and emotions. The first *Handbook of Social Psychology,* edited by Murchison, was published in 1935, an event that marked the end of the "pre-experimental era" in social psychology, according to one analyst (Jones, 1985).

A contributor to American social psychology? Cartwright (1979) named Adolf Hitler as the one person who had the greatest impact on American social psychology, because Hitler's Nazi movement drove many talented European social psychologists to the U.S.

Social psychology truly became a field of its own after World War II, when it exploded into prominence in America at a time when universities in Europe and Asia were still trying to recover from the ravages of war (Cartwright, 1979). Although present-day social psychology is based mostly on American models and methods, many of the early giants in the field were Europeans who fled to America prior to World War II (e.g., Lewin, Heider, Lazarsfeld, Adorno). The benefits of this emigration for American social psychology led Cartwright (1979) to name Adolf Hitler as the one person who had the greatest impact on the development of American social psychology.

Social psychology courses are taught both in psychology and sociology departments, though more often in psychology. Through the 1940s there were almost as many sociologists as psychologists who authored social psychology textbooks. But in recent years over 75 percent of the social psychology textbooks, including this one, have been authored by psychologists. Textbooks in social psychology accomplish far more than just summarizing previous work. Jones (1985, p. 4) asserted that "It is hard to think of another field in which textbooks have served as such an important vehicle for theorizing about, and generating influential distinctions within, its subject matter."

Social Psychological Theories and the *Zeitgeist*

Every science, but especially social psychology, is affected by events in the world around it. The major sociopolitical events and social movements of

zeitgeist:
The social and political "spirit of the times"; social psychological theories and research directions are heavily influenced by the prevalent *zeitgeist*.

the twentieth century have had a substantial impact in determining the issues and problems that social psychologists have chosen to study. The shape of American social psychology has been dramatically affected by the social and political **zeitgeist**, or "spirit of the times." This is more influential in social psychology than in most other sciences because of the close relationship between social psychological interests and social events. Social psychology depends on society for data and its findings may be used to influence the course of societal events. Thus, in the 1960s and 1970s the assassinations of public figures and a number of widely publicized other murders stimulated a great deal of research interest in the social determinants of aggression. The study of attitude change and prejudice received enormous impetus from World War II, which brought concerns about propaganda and morale in the military and the potential integration of ethnic minorities into established military units. Studies of racial prejudice were also common during the civil rights movement of the 1960s. Research on the authoritarian personality and obedience studies in the 1950s and 1960s grew out of reactions to the Nazi experience. Jones (1985) noted that it seems more than a coincidence that the widespread interest in the determinants of conformity reached a peak in the mid-1950s shortly after the rise of Senator Joseph McCarthy and his hysterical attacks on social deviance and "card-carrying Communists."

The assassination of President John F. Kennedy and civil rights leader Martin Luther King Jr. in the 1960s motivated many social psychologists to study the causes of violent behavior in individuals and in society.

Much of the scientific interest in bargaining and negotiation may have come from concerns about international disarmament negotiations in our nuclear age. Interest in bystander intervention research was nurtured both by a widely publicized urban murder in 1964 and a broader public concern in the 1960s with urban alienation and apathy. The Vietnam War, the Watergate scandal in the 1970s, and the Iran-Contra affair in the late 1980s spurred renewed interest in conformity and compliance pressures.

The personal concerns of researchers are important as well. Victims of prejudice may be more likely than nonvictims to study prejudice. Many female psychologists have been drawn to the study of sexism and sex-role socialization. Some social psychologists who were particularly bothered by high levels of violence in modern society have chosen to study the social determinants of human aggression. Several important sociopolitical events of the past half-century are listed in Table 1-1, along with the theoretical issues and scientific questions they stimulated.

Why Research Areas Become Popular

In addition to the *zeitgeist*, the popularity of a research area can derive from its theoretical power. A provocative theory that generates many interesting and testable propositions will stimulate a great deal of research. Another factor is the prestige of creative researchers and their institutions. If a particularly well-respected professional embarks on a new research direction, a number of "disciples" may follow in the same path.

The availability of research funds also influences research directions. As society's concerns and political philosophies change, so does the willingness to grant research funds for particular topics. In the 1970s, those applying for support to do research on alcoholism or drug abuse tended to receive a warm reception. In the 1980s, research on health-related factors was "hot" and well funded. In contrast, research funds for many other social psychological topics were cut drastically in the conservative political climate. Governmental funding policies may have a powerful impact on the directions in which research proceeds.

Finally, scholars are attracted by the freedom and opportunities available at the frontiers of unexplored scientific territory. Social psychologists' curiosity about new areas of inquiry may lead them to be impatient and dissatisfied with existing research directions as they seek out new directions to explore.

Why Research Areas Become Less Popular

There are several reasons why research areas become less popular. Government funding for particular areas may be cut as values and political orientations change. Sometimes scientists may conclude that all the important questions in a particular area have been answered. In other cases, research in a particular area leads to a dead end as subsequent research may fail to replicate the original provocative finding. A research area also may become unpopular when later studies reveal that the earlier promising findings were due to methodological flaws or artifacts. Finally, changes in ethical standards may mean that some kinds of research can no longer be carried out. For example, in the past high-risk research on experimental drugs was sometimes

TABLE 1-1

Critical Events	Theoretical Concepts Involved	Central Research Issues, Goals
World War II (1940s)	Attitude change	— Learning how best to use propaganda
	Leadership	— Improving morale and leadership within the military
	Prejudice	— Improving intergroup relations in the military
Nazi atrocities (early 1940s)	Authoritarianism	— Understanding a personality style that could support Fascism
"McCarthyism," anti-Communist hysteria (early 1950s)	Conformity	— Understanding why so many people followed Senator Joseph McCarthy
Civil rights movement (1960s)	Prejudice, racism	— Developing ways to reduce racial prejudice and discrimination
Widely publicized murders where bystanders didn't help; concern with urban alienation. (1960s, 1970s)	Altruism, helping behavior	— Identifying reasons why people don't help
Assassinations of John F. Kennedy, Martin Luther King, Jr., Robert Kennedy; urban riots (1960s)	Aggression, media violence	— Studying how levels of aggression and violence can be reduced in individuals and in society
Vietnam War, Watergate scandal, student activism (late 1960s–early 1970s)	Conformity, compliance	— Understanding powerful situational pressures that may compel someone (a soldier, a prisoner of war, a government official, a protesting student) to do something he/she strongly disapproves of
Feminist movement (1970s)	Sexism	— Developing ways of combating sexism and the exploitation of women
Energy crisis (1970s)	Attitude and behavior change	— Finding the best ways to change attitudes and behaviors regarding energy conservation
Threat of nuclear war (1970s, 1980s)	Bargaining, negotiation	— Investigating ways of increasing international communication and agreement
Emergence of the elderly as a powerful minority group (1980s)	Ageism, prejudice	— Developing ways to reduce age-related prejudice and discrimination

carried out on prison "volunteers." In recent years such studies have not been permitted due to ethical concerns about health risks to the participants and the feeling that prisoners do not truly have a free choice about volunteering in such situations.

Theories in Social Psychology

"Commonsense" Beliefs

implicit personality theories:
Our implicit and often unrecognized theories about what traits tend to go together in others.

You probably think that you have a good idea of why people behave as they do. Your knowledge about people is organized into **implicit personality theories.** Implicit personality theories involve generalizations that seem to be supported by common sense. This is all well and good, as such theories often have some basis in reality and may seem useful for making predictions. But they may also be quite misleading. Many generalizations are so widespread that they have become a part of our common cultural folklore:

> "Absence makes the heart grow fonder."
> "Too many cooks spoil the broth."
> "Birds of a feather flock together."
> "Out of sight, out of mind."
> "Two heads are better than one."
> "Opposites attract."

commonsense beliefs:
Generalizations that are widely shared within a culture, but are often inadequate and inaccurate in describing things as they really are.

What is the truth of these generalizations? You may have already noticed that some sayings seem to contradict others. Does "absence make the heart grow fonder," or is "out of sight, out of mind" a more accurate statement? The beliefs we hold about the world are formed by information from others as well as our own experiences. People recall their own experiences (though their memories may be inaccurate, as we will see later), watch how others behave, and form their attitudes and values accordingly. Together, these sources of information yield what are sometimes termed **"commonsense beliefs."** Commonsense beliefs are those that people accept because they seem to be correct, because many other people also believe in them, and because they seem useful for understanding what is happening.

Our society highly values commonsense generalizations, but they are often inadequate and misleading. Most people do not test their beliefs systematically, especially when everyone believes the same premises, such as the once-popular belief that the Earth was the center of the universe. Further, even when common sense does contain a germ of truth, we don't know under what conditions it applies. You might agree that absence sometimes seems to make the heart grow fonder. But there are also times when separation apparently has a negative effect on a relationship (seeming to indicate "Out of sight, out of mind"). What determines the applicability of each maxim?

Research can supply the answers. For example, the quality of the relationship may be important—perhaps absence makes the heart grow fonder only when the love bond was strong to begin with. Another factor might be the social opportunities available—if Bill is stationed at an isolated all-male military outpost and Debbie is a student at a large coeducational university, we might hypothesize that Debbie will have a more difficult time remaining faithful than Bill.

There are other dangers in accepting commonsense information. Much conventional wisdom that shapes our beliefs comes from authoritative sources such as government, parents, mass media, teachers, and friends. Accepting the opinions of experts can be risky because their opinions can be biased by their own interests and by the information they pay attention to, as we will see in Chapters 2 and 3. It is important not to accept any belief without carefully analyzing the evidence for and against it. Even "unbiased experts" have their own pet theories and are likely to display the all-too-human tendency to forget or underemphasize facts that do not support their particular views. Finally, information obtained from authoritative sources may lull people into the secure but incorrect belief that they already have all the answers, lessening the chances of further investigation and discovery.

Good Theories/Bad Theories

A **theory** is an organized system of ideas that allows us to explain and predict behavior. A good theory summarizes what is known about a phenomenon, and also permits **hypotheses** (predictions) about future occurrences. Theories provide a way of organizing the voluminous facts that people observe (whether they be scientists or laypersons) every day. They are invaluable for organizing our knowledge and helping us make sense of it all. For

theory:
An organized system of ideas that summarizes current knowledge and allows predictions of future occurrences.

hypothesis:
A prediction that is derived from a more general theory and can be tested by research.

Does absence make the heart grow fonder? This soldier may be professing his undying love to his girlfriend back home. Is she likely to wait faithfully for him, or might the adage, "out of sight, out of mind" be more applicable to her situation?

example, in the 1960s many tragic cases were reported in the media where bystanders did not help victims in emergencies. Especially troubling was the case of Kitty Genovese, who was brutally murdered in New York City in 1964. Her assailant took over one-half hour to murder her and her screams were heard by at least thirty-eight of her neighbors, none of whom even called the police. (This case will be described in some detail in Focus 7-2). The media labeled such cases "bystander apathy," but two social psychologists, Bibb Latané and John Darley (1969) reasoned that the bystanders' nonresponsiveness may have resulted from situational and social factors, rather than apathy. Drawing on the facts available to them, Latané and Darley developed a theory that bystanders' nonhelpful responses to emergency situations were produced by social reactions to other bystanders: assuming that other bystanders would help or using other bystanders' nonhelpful reactions as a cue in deciding that the situation was not an emergency. The series of studies that Latané and Darley designed to test this theory will be discussed in Chapter 7. The results of each study led them to revise their theory slightly, which, in turn, led to new predictions and to new studies to test the new predictions.

In ordinary language, people sometimes use the term *theoretical* to mean the opposite of *practical*. But as pioneering social psychologist Kurt Lewin once observed, "There is nothing so practical as a good theory." Without theories, we would be overwhelmed by the amount of information that we need to know, and the prediction of future events would be impossible. Theories, these systematic ideas that summarize and explain facts, are invaluable for conducting the everyday business of life, as well as for stimulating empirical research that increases our scientific knowledge.

Not all theories are created equal. The value of a theory depends on a number of qualities (Ryckman, 1985; Shaw & Constanzo, 1982). First, a theory should be in *agreement with known data*, fitting the facts that are already known. Second, a good theory is *comprehensive*, explaining a wide range of behaviors. Third, a good theory is *parsimonious* (economical), containing only those concepts necessary to explain its subject matter. A theory cluttered with unnecessary or repetitive concepts is not parsimonious. A fourth, and crucial, criterion for a good theory is whether it is *testable*, providing means by which specific hypotheses and predictions can be derived and subsequently tested by research. If a theory does not allow one to derive testable predictions, then its empirical validity can never be satisfactorily assessed. Most social psychological theories are less comprehensive but more testable than personality theories such as Freud's.

heuristic value:
The degree to which a theory stimulates thought and research and challenges others to develop opposing theories.

A fifth criterion for a theory is its **heuristic value,** the degree to which it stimulates thought and research and challenges others to develop and test opposing theories. Finally, the usefulness, or *applied value*, of a theory is an important attribute. Many social psychological theories have had considerable application in areas as diverse as advertising, political campaigns, ther-

---

FOCUS 1-1

Theories in Social Psychology

A GOOD THEORY

1. is *in agreement with known facts;* it incorporates what has been found about human behavior.
2. is *comprehensive* in its domain, attempting to understand and explain a wide range of human behavior.
3. is *parsimonious,* not using any more concepts or propositions than are necessary to explain its subject matter.
4. is *testable;* includes concepts that can be described and measured sufficiently clearly so that specific hypotheses can be derived and tested by research.
5. has high *heuristic value,* stimulating further thought, theorizing, and research.
6. has *applied value* and is *useful* for predicting, understanding, changing, and controlling behavior in real-life situations.

A POOR THEORY

1. ignores or contradicts what has been found about human behavior.
2. is limited in its domain, attempting to explain only a small range of behavior.
3. is cluttered with many unnecessary or repetitive concepts or propositions.
4. has concepts that are so unclear or unmeasurable that specific hypotheses cannot be derived and tested.
5. does not excite or stimulate people into further thought or research.
6. has little application or usefulness for people's everyday lives. ❖

---

apy techniques, media relations, health care procedures, prejudice-reduction programs, affirmative action policies, and prison reform. A theory that is applicable to a wide range of people and situations is more valuable than one that has a limited range of applicability. Focus 1-1 summarizes these characteristics of good and poor theories. Let's turn now to how social psychologists go about testing the theories they create.

RESEARCH IN SOCIAL PSYCHOLOGY

Social Psychological Research Methods

In recent years there has been much concern about the possible effect of movie and TV violence on the aggressiveness of viewers, particularly children. One theoretical position, popularized by Sigmund Freud and some ethologists (scientists who study animal behavior), holds that viewing vio-

catharsis:
The theory that by acting out or observing others, people are able to release or drain off their pent-up emotions.

lence is likely to cause **catharsis**, reducing aggressiveness in viewers who could "drain off" their aggressive energy by identifying with the aggressive characters in the show. A contrasting theoretical position holds that *social learning* is likely to take place, producing the opposite effect. Social learning theorists propose that viewers of aggressive material are likely to become more aggressive themselves, modeling their behavior after what is seen on the movie or TV screen. Since many people are deeply troubled by the levels of violence in our present society, the issue is an important one. Both theories are testable, as they lead to competing hypotheses about the effects of viewing media aggression. How might a social psychologist try to discover the actual effect of viewed aggression?

Testing Theories via the Scientific Method
Gathering information by means of the scientific method enables one to answer questions that are open to scientific analysis. Figure 1-1 illustrates the way science proceeds. We begin with facts (in the lower left-hand portion of the figure). A **fact** is a logical conclusion, based on observation, about which virtually everyone who observes the same situation would agree. It is a fact that the young men described at the begining of the chapter were accused of brutal murders. It is a fact that as I write this page, it is raining outside (yes, in sunny Florida). If I ask all those I will meet today whether it is raining, presumably they will all agree that it is. Observations on which there is some disagreement, on the other hand, would be categorized as opinions. My view of whether or not it is a nice day would be an opinion, since persons who like or dislike rainy weather would have different views.

fact:
A logical conclusion based on observation, about which virtually everyone would agree.

Sigmund Freud observed his patients, listened to their attempts to deal with their innermost feelings and emotions, read what others had written about the effects of observing violence, and developed his theory of catharsis. Social scientists (e.g., Bandura, 1973) derived social learning theory from the analysis of existing research findings; then they observed children in controlled research situations as they tested hypotheses derived from the theory. The results of hypothesis testing are themselves facts and are the raw materials from which this book (and the field of social psychology) are created. If testing is done well, research results can be relied upon. If research is done poorly, the resulting "facts" are likely to be incorrect and would lead to erroneous generalizations about behavior. Assuming that the research has been done well, the new facts (research results) can be used to revise or create new theories which, once again, can lead to additional hypotheses that can be tested — and the process repeats itself. Thus, there is an ongoing cycle of research as theories are tested and revised continually.

There are three general types of research methods that social psychologists sometimes use. I will briefly mention an infrequently used technique, the case history method, before analyzing correlational and experimental methodology.

FIGURE 1-1

The Scientific Method

A scientist begins with facts about the world. Through induction, *or moving from specific to general statements, theories are constructed. Predictions are derived on the basis of* deductive *reasoning from theories, starting with general propositions and creating specific hypotheses from them. These hypotheses are then tested to determine if the facts support or refute them.*

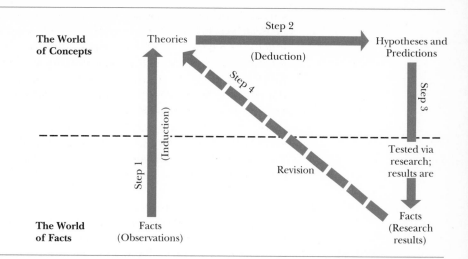

The Case History Method

One might try to discover the relationship between media violence and aggression by analyzing individual case histories such as the three murders described at the beginning of the chapter. Although one could cite a number of cases that seem to show a relationship between aggression and viewing media violence, these examples do not provide clear causal evidence that viewing violence incites aggression in the viewer. A critic might point out that thousands of other people saw the same videos and TV programs and did not act aggressively afterward.

The case history method has some usefulness in social psychology because one can study events that are uncommon, complex, or uncontrollable, such as riots, wars, and political movements. But case history information is not strong evidence in the scientific sense. First, researchers are limited to events that occur naturally; if these events are uncommon, there may not be much basic information. Second, and more importantly, the researchers are limited to their own perceptions in evaluating the information. Our perceptions of events and people are often biased by our own needs and expectations. Even though researchers may be more aware of such biases than most people, they are still not immune to them, and the commonalities and similarities that researchers *think* are present may not really exist.

Correlational Studies

A second research technique assesses the relationship between two or more **variables** that are not controlled by the experimenter. (A variable is anything that changes and can be measured.) One could use the correlational technique to analyze the relationship between children's TV viewing habits (one

variable:
Any factor that changes and can be measured.

variable) and their aggressiveness (the other variable). The first step would be to study a group of children and measure the two variables. For example, after TV programs have been rated according to the average number of violent acts per episode, children could be asked what their three favorite TV programs are. Each child would be assigned a score denoting the sum of the violence levels of his or her three favorite programs. The children's aggressiveness could be assessed by getting ratings from people who know them — their teachers, parents, or classmates — or the researcher could observe each child for a period of time and rate the child on aggressiveness. The ratings might include questions about fighting, verbal aggressiveness, and threats, bullying, and so forth.

The direction and strength of the relationship between two variables is described by the **correlation coefficient** (r). A correlation near zero indicates that there is no linear relationship between the two variables; a correlation near 1.00 (i.e., $r = .60, .75, .83$, etc.) describes a positive relationship between the two variables; the closer to 1.00, the stronger the relationship. If the correlation is negative, it indicates an inverse relationship between the two variables: high scores on one variable were associated with low scores on the other variable.

A correlational study on viewing aggression was carried out in rural New York State by Eron (1963). Selecting a community where only one TV channel could be received, he gathered two items of information on eight- and nine-year-old boys: the violence level of their three favorite programs, and their aggressiveness (as rated by their teachers and classmates). Eron found a small positive correlation, $r = .21$, between the two variables. On the average, the aggressive children preferred more violent programs than the nonaggressive children did. It would be tempting to conclude from this study that viewing violent TV leads to increased aggression in boys. However, such a conclusion is not justified, as we will see below. The advantage of a correlational study over a case history is that the precise strength of a relationship can be described by the correlation coefficient. The major limitation of a correlational study is that it cannot say anything definitive about the **cause** of the relationship. The finding that two variables are related to each other does not tell you whether the first variable caused the second, the second caused the first, whether they both affect each other or, as is often the case, they are both affected by additional variables. In short, *correlation does not imply causation*. With correlational studies, one must be very cautious in talking about the meaning of the results. Correlational studies are valuable, but always keep in mind that they do not provide direct evidence about causality.

Eron's finding can be interpreted in several ways. Perhaps viewing violent TV caused boys to become more aggressive. But perhaps the opposite was the case — boys who were already aggressive came later to prefer violent TV programs (i.e., aggressiveness caused TV-viewing preferences). A third possibility is that the type of home environment that produced aggressiveness in boys also encouraged them to watch violent TV programs (that is,

correlation coefficient:
A statistic that describes the strength of a relationship between two variables. The statistic can range from − 1.00 (a perfect inverse relationship) through 0 to + 1.00 (a perfect positive relationship).

cause:
The condition that produces a particular behavior.

a third variable, home environment, influenced both aggressiveness and TV-viewing preferences).

What Causes What?

Focus 1-2 describes the results of several correlational studies. The first one describes a negative correlation (inverse relationship) between hours of sleep per night and overall adjustment. The second vignette describes a negative correlation between number of football games and temperature: During the year as the number of football games increases, the temperature goes down. The third piece describes a correlation between type of occupation (bus driver or conductor) and susceptibility to coronary heart disease.

You can probably think of other factors that could cause the negative correlation between the number of football games played and the temperature. But what about the other two studies? The implication of the first piece is that we need less sleep, and if we slept less we would be happier. This is the classic error: The writer has inferred causation from correlation, assuming that sleeping less will lead to (cause) better adjustment. The data can't tell us whether or not this is true. Perhaps people who are already depressed sleep longer as a way of avoiding contact with others. If so, then their adjustment level would be causing their sleep habits, rather than vice versa, and sleeping less would not help them become less depressed. Or perhaps biochemical or social factors are determinants both of sleeping habits and overall adjustment. If this is the case, changing one's sleeping habits would not lead to changes in adjustment.

The third study is widely viewed as a classic by people concerned with preventing heart disease and is still widely cited by many health professionals today. Researchers in England (Morris et al., 1953) found a significant relationship between type of job — driver or conductor (ticket-taker) in double-decker buses — and rate of heart disease. Ever since, many have cited this study as strong evidence that lack of exercise (more characteristic of the drivers) increases chances of heart disease. But this is *not* a legitimate conclusion from this study. Bus drivers and conductors could choose their occupation — they were not randomly assigned to one job or the other (a crucial requirement of an experiment, as will be discussed later). Hence there could have been many pre-existing differences between the two groups of men. And indeed there were — subsequent study (Morris & Crawford, 1958) showed that the drivers were more likely to be overweight than the conductors. It is quite possible that obesity, rather than a difference in exercise, led to the differences in rate of heart disease. There might also have been other important pre-existing differences between drivers and conductors. But many health professionals were so eager to find scientific evidence that lack of exercise increased the risk of heart disease that they incorrectly interpreted the correlation from the 1953 study as causal evidence. (Of course, there is now other evidence, derived from more recent well-controlled experimental studies, that exercise *can* play a causal role in reducing the risk of heart disease.)

FOCUS 1-2

Correlation and Causation

SLEEP LESS—FEEL BETTER?

Question
Has anyone ever figured how much sleep is really needed?

Answer
New studies say almost everyone sleeps too much and that those who sleep less than six hours are happier with themselves, more energetic and efficient, nonworriers, and political conformists. Long sleepers—over nine hours—were found to be depressed, critical complainers, and nonconformists. (newspaper article based on research by Hartmann, 1973.)

FOOTBALL AND THE WEATHER

Now here's something that certainly makes a great deal of sense. In a letter to the *Chicago Tribune*, Alan L. Benjamin propounded a theory that football causes winter. "You may have noticed that when the season starts, the weather is always warm and sunny," Benjamin wrote. "But after the fullbacks, halfbacks, quarterbacks and any other fraction-backs have thundered from goalpost to goalpost a few times nature gets upset, and cold weather begins. You may also have noticed that countries where football isn't played, such as Mexico, Jamaica and Egypt, do not have cold weather.

In Canada, on the other hand, where they have one additional player on each side, winters are worse than here." "Small wonder," Benjamin concludes, "that during the NFL strike we had freakishly mild weather across much of the northern U.S. And have you noticed how much colder it's turned since the strike ended?"

TRANSPORT WORKERS, EXERCISE, AND HEART DISEASE

In the early 1950s Jeremy Morris and his colleagues (Morris et al., 1953) studied the health records of 31,000 male transport workers aged thirty-five to sixty-four in Great Britain. They compared the death rates due to coronary heart disease of drivers and conductors on double-decker busses. Conductors had the far more active job, jumping off and on the bus at each stop and walking up the bus stairs many times each day to punch tickets of passengers sitting on the upper deck. Morris found that the conductors had lesser incidence of coronary heart disease than the drivers. Also, when the disease did appear, it was usually less severe in the conductors. ❖

Source: The excerpt above is reprinted courtesy of SPORTS ILLUSTRATED from the December 6, 1982 issue. Copyright © 1982, Time, Inc. *Scorecard,* edited by Robert W. Creamer. "Scholarly Research Department." All rights reserved.

The point is, when you find that two factors are related (correlated) to each other, even when it seems logical that one factor must have caused the other, don't be seduced. Don't fall into the trap of assuming causation from correlation, even if the results fit your preconceived stereotypes. Empirical evidence from well-conducted experiments is needed to unravel the mystery of what causes what.

The Experiment

experiment:
Research study in which at least one independent variable is manipulated by the experimenter to evaluate its effect on one or more dependent variables.

independent variable:
A factor that is varied by the experimenter to assess its effect on a dependent variable.

dependent variable:
A behavior that is measured in an experiment to see whether it has been affected by the independent variable.

random assignment:
A crucial part of an experiment wherein each subject is randomly assigned to one condition (or level) of the independent variable.

subjects:
Individuals whose thoughts, feelings, or behaviors are studied in research.

Characteristics of Experiments. In social psychology the term **experiment** is used to describe a particular kind of research methodology. Experiments have become an increasingly popular method within social psychology. Before 1950 less than 30 percent of the articles published in the leading social psychology journal were based on experiments. By 1979 that figure had risen to almost 90 percent (Higbee et al., 1982).

Experiments differ from other research methods because they demand greater control by the experimenter. An experiment contains at least one **independent variable**, an experimental factor that is manipulated or controlled by the experimenter, and at least one **dependent variable**, a factor that may be affected by the independent variable. An experiment is designed to see whether the dependent variable is affected by (depends on) changes in the independent variable. The dependent variable is the behavior that is measured in the experiment. The experimenter controls the independent variable, creating two or more levels (also called *conditions*) to see what impact these levels of the independent variable have on the dependent variable. This may sound confusing, but don't despair. I'll work through an example of an experiment below.

Another critical characteristic of an experiment is the **random assignment** of **subjects** to conditions, which means that the subjects have no choice about what condition (level of the independent variable) they are exposed to. The experimenter, by some random procedure, decides which subjects are exposed to which level of the independent variable. The outcome of this procedure is that there will be no pre-existing average differences between the groups of subjects exposed to each level of the independent variable. One can be confident, based upon probability theory, that the experimental groups (one group for each level of the independent variable) are about the same in average intelligence, physical condition, motivation, personality, and any other characteristics that might be important. The 1953 British bus driver/conductor study (Focus 1-2) lacked this crucial feature.

The experimenter must have a great deal of control over the situation to carry out random assignment and to manipulate the independent variable. Therefore it is difficult, if not impossible, to study some complex or uncommon events, such as natural disasters, by the experimental method. One often has to try to create a situation similar to the one of interest in a setting in which sufficient control is possible.

An Experiment on TV Viewing and Aggression. How might one design an experiment to see whether viewing violent TV causes increased aggression? The dependent variable (the behavior in which the researcher is interested) would be aggression; the independent variable would be the type of TV material viewed (violent or nonviolent). Bandura, Ross, and Ross (1963) studied forty-eight boys and forty-eight girls, ages three to five, who were randomly assigned to view one of three types of aggression (the experimental groups) or no aggression at all (the control group). Children in the experimental groups saw an adult model hit, beat, kick, and stomp on a large, inflated, clownlike "Bobo doll." The four levels of the independent variable were: (1) view aggression by a live model, (2) view filmed aggression by the same adult model, (3) view filmed aggression by the adult dressed like a cat in cartoon-like surroundings, or (4) view no aggression at all. After this, each child was left in a playroom containing a Bobo doll and several potentially aggressive toys (a dart gun, a mallet). Hidden researchers (who did not know which type of stimulus each child had viewed) observed the child for twenty minutes and coded the child's level of aggressive behavior, both imitative (aggression toward the Bobo doll) and nonimitative (aggression involving other toys). As Figure 1-2 indicates, children who viewed any of the three violent stimuli behaved considerably more aggressively in the playroom, on the average, than did children who saw no violent stimulus.

Because the experimenters randomly assigned the children to conditions (determining which stimulus each child saw), we can be confident that before they viewed the stimuli the four groups of children were about equal in their average level of aggressiveness. It follows that the difference in subsequent aggressiveness must be due to what was viewed (the independent

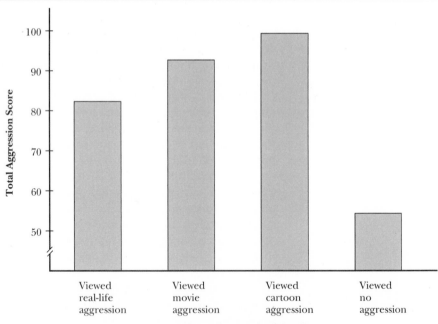

FIGURE 1-2

An Experimental Study of Viewed Aggression

Level of aggression shown by boys and girls ages 3 to 5 after viewing one of three types of aggressive stimuli or no aggressive stimulus.

Source: Data from Bandura, A., Ross, D., & Ross, S.A. (1963). Imitation of film-mediated aggressive models. *Journal of Abnormal and Social Psychology, 66,* 3–11.

An experiment on observing aggressive models. Children in the Bandura et al. (1963) study who saw an adult or a cartoon character behave aggressively toward a Bobo doll were likely to behave aggressively themselves. (Photos from Bandura, A., Ross, D., & Ross, S. A. (1963) Imitation of film-mediated aggressive models. Journal of Abnormal and Social Psychology, 66, 8.)

variable), as this is the only factor that differed between the groups. Unlike a correlational study, a well-designed experiment can provide information about one variable causing changes in another. The experimental study provided evidence that viewing aggression (the independent variable) caused differences in children's aggressiveness (the dependent variable).

Control Groups. Many experiments, including the one we just analyzed, make use of a **control group** — a group that does not receive an experimental treatment. But not all experimental designs need a control group. Consider an industrial psychologist who wishes to assess the effects of different levels of lighting on worker performance. Different workers could be randomly assigned to work under conditions of high illumination, moderate illumination, and low illumination. The independent variable (level of illumination) would have three levels. But the notion of a control group makes no sense in this case, because it would be meaningless to have a group work in total darkness. This experiment is still legitimate, even without a control group. As long as an independent variable can be manipulated so that it has at least two levels, an experiment can be carried out.

Advantages and Disadvantages of Experiments. In an experiment, the experimenter needs to have enough control over the situation to manipulate the independent variable and to eliminate the effects of **extraneous variables** (other variables that might affect the dependent variable). This is accomplished by randomly assigning subjects to conditions. The major difficulties with an experiment, compared to other research methods, are the amount of time and effort involved to achieve the necessary control and the fact that many naturally occurring situations cannot be studied directly by the experimental method. A researcher interested in violence against spouses clearly cannot (and would not) randomly assign some people to be abused by their spouses. One could do a correlational study (what personality profile is typical of people who abuse their spouses, for example), but

control group:
A group that does not receive an experimental treatment.

extraneous variables:
Variables other than the independent variable that might influence the dependent variable in an experiment.

not an experiment. The advantages of an experiment are that one can gain unequivocal evidence of causation, achieve better control over extraneous variables, and explore the dimensions of a complex variable in a controlled setting (Aronson et al., 1990). Important steps in correlational and experimental studies are summarized in Table 1-2.

Evaluating Research Studies

There are several important standards for evaluating the worth of a study. The first, internal validity, assesses whether the study has been done correctly, according to the scientific method. If so, then we can pay attention to more esoteric issues such as how far to generalize the findings, the study's impact on the participants, and the similarity of the research setting to real life (Aronson et al., 1985; 1990; Campbell & Stanley, 1966). After analyzing these criteria, we'll turn our attention to another crucial factor—the way that the research sample is gathered.

Internal Validity

internal validity:
The extent to which a study is well designed and carried out.

The most important criterion is **internal validity**, which basically means: was the study done right? If it is an experiment, were subjects randomly assigned to conditions? Did the researcher successfully manipulate the independent variable? Was the dependent variable measured appropriately? Were the correct statistical analyses carried out? If the answer to these questions is yes, then the study has internal validity and we can turn to the other criteria. If the study has poor internal validity, in contrast, nothing else really matters because the study is flawed from the start.

confounding:
The degree to which an extraneous variable is unintentionally varied along with the independent variable.

Confounding in Experiments. In an experiment one must make sure that the manipulation affects only the independent variable and nothing else. If another (extraneous) variable is unintentionally varied along with the independent variable, the extraneous variable is said to be **confounded** with the independent variable. This can be a major problem. In our earlier example, Bandura and his coworkers manipulated the type of aggresssive stimulus the children saw. But suppose that the children who saw the aggressive stimuli were excited by any variation in their daily routine and it was this excitement, rather than the aggression shown by the models, that made them more active and aggressive in the free-play situation. In this case, aggression and excitement are confounded. A way to avoid the problem might have been to have a different kind of control group where the children watched a film of an event such as a track meet that was equally exciting but not violent. If this control group showed a low level of later aggressiveness, then one could be more confident that the higher levels of aggression shown by the groups that observed the aggressive models were not due merely to differences in levels of excitement. Researchers typically go to great lengths to minimize the chances that confounding will occur.

TABLE 1-2   IMPORTANT STEPS IN THE RESEARCH PROCESS

	Preliminary Steps	Data Collection	Data Analysis
Correlational study	Selection of the two variables of interest	Measurement of the two variables	Calculation of a correlation coefficient between scores on the two measures
	Development of measures of the two variables		
	Selection of sample to be assessed		
Experimental study	Selection of one or more independent variables (IV) to be manipulated and one or more dependent variables (DV) to be measured	Exposure of subjects to one level of the IV(s); measurement of the DV(s)	Comparison between the mean (average) scores of the different groups on the DV(s)
	Development of measures of the DV(s)		
	Manipulation check for the effectiveness of the manipulation of the IV(s)		
	Random assignment of people to conditions (creating groups)		

experimenter effects:
Changes in a subject's responses unwittingly caused by reactions to the experimenter's behavior or expectations.

interviewer bias:
When an interviewer's expectations or preferences for a particular answer influence the respondent's reply.

Experimenter Effects. **Experimenter effects** occur when an experimenter unwittingly affects the phenomena that are being studied. She or he might behave more warmly toward some subjects than others, or give unintentional cues about what responses are expected. **Interviewer bias**, in which an interviewer's expectations or preferences for a particular answer influence the respondent's reply, is a type of experimenter effect. Experimenter effects have been studied most thoroughly by Rosenthal (1966). He conducted studies showing that when inexperienced experimenters (such as undergraduate volunteers) were asked to conduct studies and also were told of the results their supervisor expected to achieve, often the results reflected these expectations to a degree that suggested systematic bias. In contrast, experienced researchers take considerable pains to make sure that their own expectations do not affect the results of studies they conduct. It may involve the use of more than one experimenter; the one who interacts directly with the subjects is kept "blind" as to the hypotheses of the study or the particular condition that each subject is in. In this way the experimenter's expectations will not systematically affect the data.

Experimental Realism

experimental realism:
The amount of impact that a research situation has on the participants.

Experimental realism describes the impact that a research situation has on the participants. Studies that expose subjects to highly involving events have high experimental realism. In contrast, filling out a long, boring questionnaire on a topic of little interest creates low experimental realism. The Bandura, Ross, and Ross (1963) study was moderately high in experimental realism, since the events (real-life and filmed aggression) were probably interesting and involving to the children. High experimental realism is desirable because when subjects are highly involved in the situation, irrelevant factors such as fatigue, distraction, and boredom will be less likely to interfere with honest responding (Berkowitz & Donnerstein, 1982).

Mundane Realism

mundane realism:
The degree of similarity between the research situation and real-world situations to which it is intended to relate.

laboratory studies:
Studies conducted in designated research areas, often with students as subjects.

field studies:
Studies that take place in natural settings that are not specifically designed for research.

The similarity between the research situation and the real-world situation to which it is intended to relate is called **mundane realism**. In discussing mundane realism, we can distinguish between laboratory studies and field studies. **Laboratory studies** are conducted in designated research areas, often on college campuses with students as subjects. **Field studies** take place in natural settings such as shopping centers, sporting events, street corners, and so forth. An advantage of field studies is that they have more mundane realism than do laboratory studies. Another benefit of field studies is that often the participants do not know that they are being studied and are simply behaving in an everyday manner; therefore the researcher doesn't have to worry about them behaving unnaturally as they might if they knew they were being observed by an experimenter. Also, a wider range of behaviors can be studied in field settings than in a laboratory situation. The advantage of laboratory-based research is that the experimenter has control over what happens and usually can more easily manipulate independent variables and measure dependent variables. In a field study it may be impossible to eliminate all extraneous variables or to manipulate an independent variable to do a true experiment. Despite these difficulties, however, we will encounter many instances of successful field experiments in the chapters ahead.

High mundane realism is desirable because it allows for easier generalization to theories that apply to real-world situations. Situations of low mundane realism are problematic, as it is risky to generalize from these situations to the external world. The Bandura et al.(1963) study was fairly high in mundane realism; watching films and having the opportunity to play with aggressive toys are events that most children encounter in their everyday lives.

External Validity

external validity:
The degree to which one can generalize the research finding of a study.

External validity refers to the generalizability of a finding, to the range of populations and settings to which it can be applied (Aronson et al., 1990). Would the same finding be obtained using a different sample of subjects, different ways of manipulating the independent variable, or different ways of measuring the dependent variable? External validity can be enhanced by using a heterogeneous sample, one that contains persons of different ages, genders, educational levels, race, and so forth. In contrast, if a study involves only college introductory psychology students (a homogeneous sample), as many do, the external validity of the finding is limited because the sample is restricted in terms of age and level of education. If the study were a survey of attitudes about sex or drugs, for example, one would not want to generalize student survey findings to "people in general," since college students' attitudes may differ considerably from those of people of other ages or educational levels. Despite this limitation, many researchers continue to use college students as subjects for two reasons: (1) they may want to compare their results with other studies that have also used college students, and (2) it is usually much easier to obtain a sample of college students than to study a more heterogeneous sample.

The external validity of a finding is enhanced when it can be shown that the same finding occurs even when different samples are studied, or when different ways of manipulating the independent variable or measuring the dependent variable are employed. The findings of the Bandura et al. (1963) study—that children who watched the aggressive models acted more aggressively themselves,—supported the social learning theory of modeling aggression. But no single study alone can provide unequivocal support for a general theory. The external validity of Bandura's findings was limited because they studied only one type of subject (nursery-school-aged children) and measured aggression in only one way (observers' ratings). The fact that the researchers used three different types of aggressive stimulus (live, movie, and cartoon-like movie) increases external validity on that dimension.

This study alone can't be said to establish the validity of social learning theory, but the theory has gotten impressive support over the years as other studies have found the same effect using other samples (older children, adolescents, college students, older adults), other ways of presenting aggressive stimuli to the subjects (real TV programs, violent movies, violent sports events, etc.), and other ways of measuring subsequent aggression (questionnaires, ratings by friends, teachers, or parents, willingness to deliver electric shock to a fellow subject, etc.). As we will see in Chapter 10, when the same general finding occurs in many different research settings and procedures, this is the hallmark of external validity and indicates a significant contribution to the advancement of scientific knowledge.

Sampling

Representativeness

The **sample** is the group of people on which the research is conducted. If a **sample** is **representative** of the larger **population** from which it is drawn, one can generalize the research results obtained from the sample back to

sample:
The group of subjects, taken from the population, on which a study is conducted.

representative sample:
A sample whose members show the same distribution of characteristics as the population from which it was drawn.

population:
The larger group from which a research sample is drawn.

the population. As noted, research samples often are taken from the population of undergraduate introductory psychology students, which limits external validity. Since enrollment in introductory psychology courses is generally drawn from all segments of the undergraduate community, researchers often assume that these students are representative of college students in general. Are college students representative of adults in general? The answer depends on the variables that are being investigated. As noted, if the variables are ones on which age or education could be expected to have a strong impact, one would hesitate to generalize from a college student sample to people in general. If the variables represent more basic processes, such as physiological responses, one might feel more comfortable generalizing from college students' responses to people in general.

Biased Samples

biased sample:
A sample of subjects that is not representative of the population from which it was drawn.

If a sample is gathered in a biased manner, the research results will be biased. The presidential election poll taken by *Literary Digest* magazine in 1936 provides a painful example of what happens with **biased sampling**. *Literary Digest* had successfully predicted the results of the 1932 presidential election. In 1936 they gathered a huge sample of over two million ballots (remember, this was before the age of computers) by sending sample ballots to people included on auto registration lists and in the telephone book, and by including ballots in copies of the magazine. This is perhaps the largest survey research sample ever used, before or since. The magazine confidently predicted that Alf Landon would achieve an easy victory over Franklin D. Roosevelt. In actuality, Roosevelt scored a landslide victory over Landon, winning 46 states and 523 of the 531 electoral votes. *Literary Digest*, stunned by its massive misprediction, stopped election polling the next year and went out of

Source: From *Penguin Dreams and Stranger Things: A Bloom County Book* by Berke Breathed. Copyright © 1985 by The Washington Post Company.

Some public-opinion polling techniques such as exit polls, in which voters are interviewed immediately after they have voted, are considered controversial because of their intrusiveness.

business in 1938. A young pollster who utilized a sample only about 1 percent the size of the Digest's sample (30,000 prospective voters) correctly predicted the results of that same election. That pollster was George Gallup, president of what was later to become the nation's largest political polling company.

What was wrong with the *Literary Digest's* giant sample of voters? Remember that 1936 was the midst of the Great Depression; a great number of people had neither automobiles nor telephones, and they certainly weren't reading *Literary Digest*. These poorer people (most of them Democrats) never got a sample ballot and therefore couldn't vote in the poll, whereas the richer people (most of them Republicans), who had phones or cars and might read literary magazines, received sample ballots. As a result, *Literary Digest* vastly oversampled Republicans and undersampled Democrats. Since then, public opinion pollsters have taken extreme steps to try to avoid similar mistakes and to gather samples that are representative of the voting population in general.

Probability Sampling

probability sample:
A type of representative sample in which every individual in a population has known probability, usually an equal probability, of being chosen as a respondent.

Today's pollsters use **probability sampling** methods, wherein every individual in the population has a known probability (usually an equal probability) of being chosen as a respondent. In probability sampling the expected amount of sampling error (the degree to which the sample's responses are likely to differ from the entire population's response) can be calculated exactly. The bigger the sample, the smaller the sampling error. A representative sample of 1,500 respondents will estimate the views of a whole nation just as accurately as it will estimate the views of a single city's residents. A properly chosen sample of 1,500 cases should not miss the true population value by more than 2.5 percent in either direction (Oskamp, 1977, p. 75). Polls that appear in newspapers and magazines often involve smaller sample sizes (500 to 800 people) and, hence, have larger amounts of sampling error (4 to 5 percentage points). Table 1-3 presents the accuracy of the Gallup Poll in predicting the winner's share of the vote in U.S. presidential elections from 1936 to 1988.

THE SOCIAL PSYCHOLOGY OF THE RESEARCH SETTING

Research from the Subject's Perspective

Demand Characteristics

In any research study there are potentially two studies: the study planned by the investigator and the study as perceived by the subjects (Adair, 1984). It is the subjects' perceptions that determine how they respond. The

TABLE 1-3   RECORD OF GALLUP POLL ACCURACY IN PREDICTING THE PERCENTAGE OF THE POPULAR VOTE IN U.S. PRESIDENTIAL ELECTIONS

Year	Predicted Winner: Gallup Final Survey[a]		Winner: Election Results[a]	
1988	56.0%	Bush	53.4%	Bush
1984	59.0	Reagan	58.9	Reagan
1980	47.0	Reagan	51.0	Reagan
1976	48.0	Carter	50.0	Carter
1972	62.0	Nixon	61.8	Nixon
1968	43.0	Nixon	43.5	Nixon
1964	64.0	Johnson	61.3	Johnson
1960	51.0	Kennedy	50.1	Kennedy
1956	59.5	Eisenhower	57.8	Eisenhower
1952	51.0	Eisenhower	55.4	Eisenhower
1948	44.5	Truman	49.9	Truman
1944	51.5	Roosevelt	53.3	Roosevelt
1940	52.0	Roosevelt	55.0	Roosevelt
1936	55.7	Roosevelt	62.5	Roosevelt

[a]The figure shown is the winner's percentage of the Democratic-Republican vote except in the elections of 1948, 1968, and 1976. Because the Thurmond and Wallace voters in 1948 were largely split-offs from the normally Democratic vote, they were made a part of the final Gallup Poll pre-election estimate of the division of the vote. In 1968 Wallace's candidacy was supported by such a large minority that he was clearly a major candidate, and the 1968 percentages are based on the total Nixon/Humphrey/Wallace vote. In 1976, because of interest in McCarthy's candidacy and its potential effect on the Carter vote, the final Gallup Poll estimate included Carter, Ford, McCarthy, and all other candidates as a group.

researcher must understand how the situation is perceived in order to draw valid inferences from the subjects' responses.

If the children in Bandura's study had somehow perceived that the experimenters were interested in whether they would play with aggressive toys after watching the violent film, this perception could have modified their behavior. For example, they might have tried extra hard to be "good kids" or they might have tried to behave in other ways that they thought the experimenters expected. There are perceived pressures inherent in any situation that seem to demand certain kinds of behavior; these have been labeled as **demand characteristics** (Orne, 1962). Most of the time, demand characteristics call for socially desirable behavior that fits the norms of the situation. But research situations may have special kinds of demand characteristics that can interfere with the honesty of responding. Knowing that one is being studied may cause a person to adopt a particular role, rather than to behave naturally. Several possible roles that research subjects may adopt are discussed below.

demand characteristics: Perceived pressures in a situation that seem to demand certain kinds of behavior; research situations have unique demand characteristics.

Roles Subjects Play

When people know that they are participating in a research study, they may be more concerned with behaving in a particular role than with behaving naturally (Christensen, 1982; Weber & Cook, 1972). A person playing the *good subject role* might attempt to give responses that will validate the perceived research hypothesis. A subject who chooses to play a *negativistic role*, in contrast, will try to screw up the researcher by giving responses opposite or unrelated to the perceived research hypothesis. Those adopting the *faithful subject role* believe that being docile and following the experimental instructions scrupulously is most important. Where norms for appropriate behavior are strong (e.g., intelligence, prejudice, sexual behavior, drug use), subjects who know they are being observed may feel **evaluation apprehension**, leading to the *apprehensive subject role*. They try to act in ways that will present them in a socially desirable light.

If subjects adopt any of these roles, there is a problem in interpreting the research results, since researchers usually want to generalize their findings to situations where people are behaving naturally. In many of the studies that we will review, you will see how experimenters have taken elaborate steps to minimize the likelihood that demand characteristics and role-playing would be a problem.

evaluation apprehension: Apprehension about being evaluated negatively by someone else.

The Importance of Feeling Special: The Hawthorne Effect

In the 1920s some industrial psychologists (then called "efficiency experts") from Harvard were hired to evaluate worker performance in a plant in Hawthorne, Illinois (Roethlisberger & Dickson, 1939; Mayo, 1933). Six women who worked assembling telephone relays were called into the supervisor's office and asked if they would participate in an experiment on evaluating new working conditions. After establishing a baseline measure of how many relays per day the women usually assembled, the researchers began to change the working conditions to see what effect this would have on the women's job performances. First they changed the payment system and the women's performance improved. Then they introduced rest periods during the day and performance improved still more. The efficiency experts then reduced the work day by one-half hour, and then by one hour, and performance continued to improve. This would seem to show that the new job procedures were all very beneficial for production. But the researchers were smart enough to switch back to the original conditions as well, to see what the impact of this change would be. They found that the workers' performance continued to improve.

Apparently the changes in working conditions were largely irrelevant to the women's performance. The women were working harder because they had been given extra privileges and attention. They felt special because their advice was sought throughout the study, a very unusual experience in assembly plants in those days. As was later noted, "the experiment [the researchers] had planned to conduct was quite different from the experi-

Hawthorne effect:
The finding that making people feel special and important may have a more significant impact on their performance than the experimental manipulation that the researchers think is important.

ınent they had actually performed" (Roethlisberger & Dickson, 1939, p. 183). The intended manipulations (changes in working conditions) were confounded with changes in the women's perceptions of how they were treated. The phenomenon has come to be known as the **Hawthorne effect**, the notion that making people feel special and important may have a significant impact on their performance (Adair, 1984). Researchers need to take this factor into account when designing studies; for example, by having a control group that is also made to feel special but does not have the changed working conditions.

Deception, Stress, and Research Ethics

Why Deception Is Sometimes Used

Psychologists generally agree that, whenever possible, research techniques should not involve deception. However, social psychology investigates many highly important issues (such as altruism, aggression, prejudice) that involve strong norms. People are often motivated to give a socially desirable impression (as an altruistic, nonaggressive, unprejudiced person) if they know a researcher is watching. Hence, in these areas there may be no obvious alternative to deception if one wants to study how people really behave. Some amount of deception may be necessary to increase the chances that people will behave naturally.

Because of the ethical issues involved in research, universities and government agencies that grant money for research have Institutional Review Boards (IRBs) that evaluate proposed research and decide whether or not it should be allowed to proceed. Many federal agencies and IRBs have specified that all research participants should read and sign an informed consent form that describes in detail the research procedures and states that the individual is free to withdraw from the study at any time. But studies have shown that in some situations people behave quite differently after exposure to informed consent forms (Dill et al., 1982; Gardner, 1978). The forms detract from mundane realism (in real life we don't usually sign forms before venturing into a situation) and may decrease the experimental realism (impact) of the situation or add new demand characteristics. Strange or uninformative research results can be produced when subjects are fully informed about the nature of the research in which they are participating (Resnick & Schwartz, 1973). Psychologists and IRBs tend to be more bothered about research ethics than are subjects themselves. In surveys, undergraduates tend to rate ethically questionable research situations as more acceptable than psychologists do (Farr & Seaver, 1975; Smith & Berard, 1982).

Protecting Human Subjects

All researchers must carefully follow guidelines for the protection of their subjects. The American Psychological Association (APA, 1982) drafted a set of ethical principles for the conduct of research with human participants.

risk/benefit ratio:
The proposition that all research must be evaluated in terms of the risks to potential subjects and the benefits to society of the research; research should be carried out only when the benefits substantially outweigh the risks and risks are not too high.

These principles focus on the **risk/benefit ratio**, the relationship between the potential risks to research participants and the benefits that such research may have for advancing knowledge about humanity. The APA guidelines indicate that priority must always be given to the research participants' welfare. The participants should emerge from the research experience unharmed; or, at least, the risks should be minimal, understood by the participants, and accepted as reasonable. "In general, after research participation, the participants' feelings about the experience should be such that the participants would willingly take part in further research" (APA, 1982, p. 18).

Ethical issues arise when a study employs deception or when subjects feel that their privacy is being invaded. A basic tension often exists between belief in the value of free scientific inquiry and belief in the dignity of humanity and people's right to privacy. The more socially sensitive the research topic (e.g., sexual behavior, drug use), the greater may be people's desire to protect their privacy by refusing to participate.

Most cases involving deception seem harmless. A questionnaire has a misleading title, a subject is observed from behind a one-way mirror, a subject believes he is watching a real incident via closed-circuit television when actually it is a videotape, and so forth. The major ethical questions are raised by the few experiments that involve situations so powerful (high experimental realism) that observers have worried about subjects' welfare. Some research areas in social psychology use deception more than others. A survey of almost 1,200 research articles published in social psychology journals between 1959 and 1979 found that over half of the studies (58 percent) used some form of deception (Gross & Fleming, 1982). Over 90 percent of the studies of compliance/conformity, altruism, and aggression used deception of some sort, while in other areas (e.g., group processes) researchers were less likely to use deception (Figure 1-3).

The Effects of Deception

A powerful research situation may induce people to behave in a negative manner (e.g., aggressively) that conflicts with their self-concept. Might this have a devastating effect on individuals' self-concepts? Are social psychologists justified in providing such threatening knowledge to subjects when the subjects didn't ask for it? Some social psychologists have argued that such self-knowledge can be very valuable (McGuire, 1967; Mills, 1969). But in such situations there is also a particularly strong need for very sensitive debriefing and for follow-up studies to make sure that long-term negative effects do not occur (Cook, 1975).

How you evaluate deception studies may depend to a large extent on your general view of human nature. Vocal critics of deception studies (Baumrind, 1985; Ring, 1967) tend to have a "humanistic" orientation, feeling that humans are relatively fragile creatures who can experience long-term posi-

FIGURE 1-3

Percentage of Published Studies in Social Psychology That Used Deception, 1959–1979

A total of 1,188 articles were surveyed.

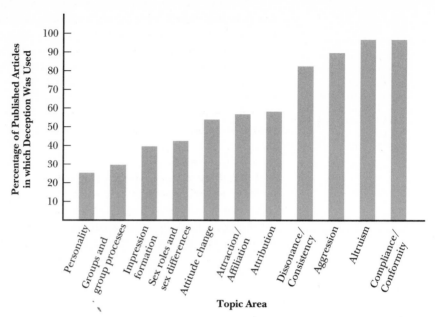

Source: Data from Gross, A. E., & Fleming, I. (1982). Twenty years of deception in social psychology. *Personality and Social Psychology Bulletin, 8,* 402–408.

tive growth only as a result of positive experiences. From this orientation, powerful deception studies are seen as having negative effects on the participants. Most experimental psychologists would not endorse this orientation. Rather, they believe that people are well able to handle, and may even benefit from, short-term stress (such as that caused by some studies) if the tensions are subsequently reduced by sensitive debriefing (West & Gunn, 1978).

debriefing:
The experimenter explains to subjects what was done, why it was done, and what it means.

Debriefing is a particularly important aspect of a study involving deception. After the experiment is over, the experimenter explains to the subjects what was done, why it was done, and what it means. The experimenter should also communicate his or her own sincerity as a scientist and discomfort over the fact that deception had to be used. When the subject has been taken in by an effective cover story, it is important to point out that it is not the subject's gullibility, but rather the credibility of the cover story (on which the experimenter has worked long and hard), that made the deception effective. The experimenter can also ask for the subject's aid in improving the experiment and making the situation more realistic and less stressful (Aronson et al., 1985).

As far as we can tell, deception studies have not produced widespread trauma to participants. One reviewer concluded "Although the evidence is not definitive, there appear to be fewer problems resulting from deception than some persons had feared, especially with respect to harm to subjects, involuntary self-knowledge, and damage to trust" (C. Smith, 1983, p. 323). In a survey of introductory psychology students who had served as research subjects (Smith & Richardson, 1983), 20 percent said they felt harmed by the experience (had felt nervous, humiliated, deceived, angry, or physically discomforted). While those who had participated in deception studies were slightly more likely to have felt harmed than those in nondeception studies, students in deception studies rated their experience as significantly more enjoyable, perceived more educational benefit, and felt that they had received a better debriefing, than did students in nondeception studies. Smith and Richardson concluded that while deception in research is perceived as harmful by a minority of subjects, potential harmful effects of deception can be eliminated by careful, sensitive debriefing. Continuing attention and sensitivity to the welfare of subjects in research situations is of the utmost importance.

RECURRING ISSUES AND THEMES

As we review the theories that have sought to predict, understand, and control human social behavior, several basic issues will recur frequently. I've divided these issues into four categories: (1) determinants of social behavior; (2) understanding one's own behavior; (3) understanding others' behavior; (4) ways of changing behavior. Because this is a preview, many of the concepts will not be familiar to you at this point. Not to worry; this brief overview is meant simply to whet your appetite for what's ahead and to provide you with frames of reference for understanding the social psychological information you will encounter. In the final section I will give some personal opinions about why I think it is quite valuable to know social psychology.

What Determines Human Social Behavior?

Genetic/Biological vs. Social Factors

The extent to which human social behavior is determined by biological or genetic factors has been debated intensely in recent years, particularly in the areas of altruism and helping behavior, aggression and violence, and gender differences. We will see in Chapter 6 that the controversial field of sociobiology recently has arisen as a means of explaining many types of social behavior in biological terms. Whereas social psychologists tend to focus less on biological and hereditary factors than sociobiologists or behavioral geneticists do, remember that behavior is determined by a combination of factors, including one's genetic/biological heritage. In the future we can expect to see greater communication between social and biological approaches.

Egoistic vs. Altruistic Motives

A second issue in the question of what determines behavior is whether human behavior is basically egoistically or altruistically motivated. Philosophers have debated this issue for centuries, of course, and you won't get any easy answers here, but in Chapter 7 I will review research that addresses this thorny issue. Our analyses of ingroup-outgroup relations and prejudice (Chapter 11) will also touch upon this question.

Personality vs. Situational Forces

At a more immediate level, is our behavior determined more by our internal attributes (personality traits, attitudes, beliefs, values, self-concept) or by situational forces? While many people assume that their behavior is largely determined by their internal attributes, social psychological research, with its interpersonal orientation, demonstrates that situational factors often have a very powerful effect on what we do. Situational forces are particularly visible in studies of helping in emergencies, conformity, and pressure to comply with orders to behave in hurtful ways.

Three general conclusions can be drawn from these studies. First, our behavior is dramatically influenced by what other people do in the same situation; they serve as models and provide information about how to interpret the situation and what the consequences of various behaviors are. Second, most people are genuinely unaware of how strongly their behavior has been influenced by the behavior of others. And third, it is very difficult for the average person to resist pressures to comply to the wishes of others.

Understanding One's Own Behavior

Causes vs. Reasons

reason:
The purposes or goals of a behavior as the actor understands them.

On the surface it seems so simple. We think we know who we are and why we do things. But as any psychotherapist could tell you, it's not that simple. Social psychologists distinguish between *causes* and **reasons**. If asked why you did something, you will give your reason—the purposes or goals of the behavior as you understand them. But people are often unaware of the true causes of their behaviors—the condition that produces the behavior. Your reason may or may not be the same as the cause of your behavior. Social psychological research investigates the causes of social behavior.

Self-Presentations and Self-Concept

Each of us seeks to present ourself in particular ways to others. In Chapter 3, I will evaluate the strategies that people use to create their self-presentation. We will see how people incorporate new information about themselves (sometimes perceived in a biased way) into their self-concept. We will also analyze the subtle ways in which people protect or enhance their self-esteem by comparing themselves with less-fortunate others.

Adaptive Illusions

We are accustomed to thinking that an accurate perception of the world is essential to a well-adjusted personality. But recent research suggests that there are several illusions that characterize the way "normal" people think about themselves. Unlike most illusions, these may be beneficial for psychological well-being, as long as they are not too extreme. People tend to be unrealistically optimistic, to have exaggerated perceptions of competence or mastery, and have overly positive self-evaluations. In addition, people want to feel that they control their own destinies. People who sense a lack of control are likely to suffer from depression and what has been termed "mindlessness." They are also likely to give up, to stop trying to control their outcomes, even when circumstances have changed and efforts to control things would be effective. Most people maintain an illusion of control, convincing themselves that they have more control over their outcomes than they really do.

Understanding Others' Behavior

Biases in Processing Social Information

Our personal theories about people are based on our observation and interpretation of others' behavior. Our observations of people are often inaccurate because we interpret their behaviors in terms of our existing attitudes and tend to remember best behaviors that fit our pre-existing generalizations. In Chapter 2 we will study these biases in detail. Among other things, people tend to overgeneralize from vivid personal experiences and to ignore statistical base-rate information. Also, individuals see past events as more predictable than they were at the time and often remember their own predictions as being more accurate than they really were. Additionally, people tend to be overconfident of the accuracy of their judgments, past and present, and think that others agree with their own perspective more than is actually the case.

The Impact of Expectations

self-fulfilling prophecy: A type of behavioral confirmation bias in which one's expectations (the prophecy) set in motion a behavioral sequence that ends up seeming to confirm (fulfill) the expectations.

Our expectations and stereotypes about people not only affect our perceptions of others; they also mold and channel our interactions with them. For example, teachers' expectations about students can affect students' performance in expected directions, thereby setting in motion a **self-fulfilling prophecy**, a chain of events that results in an apparent confirmation of the expectations. In Chapters 2 and 7 I will review several examples of this tendency, as when attractive people are treated differently than are unattractive people. An awareness of the way this process works may help you avoid falling so easily into the expectancy-confirmation trap.

Social Categorization

Stereotypes of minority groups are pervasive in our society. Scientific analyses of how we categorize people suggest four important points. First, social factors (race, gender, age, etc.) have a *powerful attributional impact*. When no additional information is available, or in some cases despite additional information, people are willing to make attributions to others based largely on stereotypes about their race, gender, or age. In many instances, these attributions may, over time, be believed by the target group themselves. Second, people tend to *prefer their own group*, the ingroup, which they perceive as better, more heterogeneous, and less extreme. A third factor, already noted above, is the occurrence of *expectancy confirmation effects*. A person's behavior toward another individual may channel their interactions so that the outgroup member behaves as expected (behavioral confirmation) or, in the absence of any interaction, people may selectively interpret, attribute, or remember aspects of the outgroup's behavior in ways that are consistent with the ingroup member's expectations (cognitive confirmation). A fourth point concerns the *pervasiveness of social barriers* against outgroup members. These barriers are sometimes quite obvious, such as laws or social policies that discriminate on the basis of sex, race, and age. But the barriers may also be much less direct, as with negative reactions to affirmative action programs and reduced funding for programs to help the elderly.

The Fundamental Attribution Error

fundamental attribution error:
The widespread tendency to make dispositional attributions for other people's behaviors but environmental attributions for our own behaviors.

The **fundamental attribution error**, discussed in Chapter 2, occurs when people (actors) make situational attributions to explain their own behavior but make dispositional (personality) attributions to explain the same behavior by someone else. For example, in attempting to explain why someone complied with authority pressure, the casual observer is apt to make a dispositional attribution: the person who complied must have been weak-willed, or sadistic, or a conformist. The complier, on the other hand, is more likely to attribute his compliance to aspects of the situation, especially to the external pressure placed on him. In short, we may recognize the influence of environmental forces in determining our own behavior, but we tend to forget this when judging others' behavior.

Changing Behaviors

Social Power

One theme that recurs throughout social psychology is the importance of social power and its uses and abuses. The distinction between traditional reward-based power (coercive and reward power), power due to one's role or status (expert, legitimate, and informational power), and power derived from the degree to which one is admired or liked (referent power) is critical. Referent power is usually more effective than the others because it does not require surveillance to be effective and is likely to lead to internalization (private acceptance) and permanent behavior change. Referent power is relevant to a host of situations, including groups such as Alcoholics Anonymous and Weight Watchers.

Referent power in operation. The Alcoholics Anonymous program for combating alcoholism relies heavily on the referent power of leaders and fellow AA members.

Social Learning from Models

Throughout this book we will see evidence of the critical importance of models in affecting people's behavior, whether it be aggression, helping in emergencies, conformity and compliance, or the ability to resist conformity and compliance pressures. Although modeling behavior is most visible in children, it continues throughout life. Each day we serve as models for other people and observe others as models for our own behavior. Consequently, you may influence other people's behavior more than you realize, simply through your status as a model. One criterion of a well-adjusted personality, by some analyses, is the ability to identify and constructively utilize appropriate models.

Changing Situations vs. Changing Individuals

Social psychologists' interpersonal orientation and their awareness of the strong influence of situational pressures on behavior make them particularly sensitive to social programs that change behavior by changing situations. As Pettigrew (1988, p. 207) noted, "it is far easier and more ethical to alter situations than to alter people." This doesn't mean that working with individuals is ineffective—we will see, for example, that special training in refocusing attributions for failure may be valuable for some people. But a more powerful approach may be to identify situations that elicit specific behaviors from individuals and seek to modify those situations. Social policies based on research on the effects of media violence and prejudice-reduction programs that focus on equal-status contact between antagonistic ethnic groups illustrate this approach.

THE VALUE OF SOCIAL PSYCHOLOGY

Applying Social Psychological Knowledge

Knowledge-Driven vs. Decision-Driven Research

Inasmuch as social psychologists study human behavior within the social context, issues of public policy often are directly relevant. Research programs can be seen as **knowledge-driven** (basic) or **decision-driven** (applied) (Masters, 1984). Most of the studies discussed in the upcoming chapters are knowledge-driven, a product of the researcher's desire to increase general knowledge about human social behavior. In many areas, earlier basic research has led to decision-driven research concerned with specific policy-related decisions. These include laws meant to induce helping in emergencies, legislation to desegregate schools, to eradicate sexism, and to improve legal decision making, policies concerning violence and violent sexuality in the media, procedures to improve health care, and ways of improving the quality of decisions reached by policymaking groups.

Decision-driven research can have shortcomings. It may narrow the range of problems seen as worthy of study, it may reduce concern for learning about important mediating processes which eventually affect behavior, and it may increase "research faddism," as researchers flock toward assessing factors most relevant to today's decisions and ignore other important issues (Mark & Bryant, 1984).

Social Psychology and Public Policy

Should social psychologists actively try to apply their research findings to social problems and public policies? Some say a resounding "yes!" Two presidents of the American Psychological Association (Bevan, 1976; Miller, 1969) suggested that psychologists should actively attempt to "give away" their accumulated knowledge to the public to promote human welfare. Another APA president, Albert Bandura (1974, p. 859), stated "As a science concerned about social consequences of its applications, psychology must also fulfill a broader obligation to society by bringing influence to bear on public policies to ensure that its findings are used in the service of human betterment."

Yet not all psychologists agree. Richard Atkinson (1977, p. 207), while director of the National Science Foundation, argued, "The psychologist's job

knowledge-driven research:
Basic research designed to increase general knowledge about human social behavior.

decision-driven research:
Research designed to assess the effect of various policy-related decisions, such as legislation or social programs.

activist/collaborator role:
A scientiest advocates social policies and solutions that seem appropriate and tries to influence legislation in order to promote human welfare.

is to search for data, principles and laws . . . There is no reason why psychologists should not advocate political viewpoints, but they should advocate them only as individual citizens. The psychologist's role as a scientist is to set forth the facts, and to set forth these facts in as value-free a fashion as possible." Social psychologists disagree whether or not scientists should take an **activist/collaborator role**, advocating social policies and solutions that seem appropriate and attempting to influence policies and legislation perceived as promoting human welfare. For what it's worth, I think that these are appropriate goals.

Understanding Behavior and Making Choices

I would like to begin our journey by pointing out some potential advantages of knowing social psychology. Social psychological knowledge can help you better understand behavior and make you less susceptible to the biases and prejudices that color most people's social perceptions. Moreover, it can be invaluable in enabling you to make free, fully informed choices about your own behavior. Further, social psychological knowledge can aid you in becoming an "informed consumer" of scientific research.

Knowledge increases one's alternatives and choices. Understanding subtle psychological principles can liberate persons from being tied to their influences (Gergen, 1973). Becoming sensitive to these influences may enable you to make choices based on your own personality and values rather than subtle social forces. In general, it is adaptive to pay careful attention to how other people behave, to use them as models, and to learn from other people's experiences. Beware, however, of being so strongly influenced by others that you do not make a clear choice yourself but allow their behavior to dictate your interpretation of the situation and your subsequent actions. As expressed by humanist Rollo May (1971, p. 100), "Each of us inherits from society a burden of tendencies which shapes us willy-nilly; but our capacity to be conscious of this fact saves us from being strictly determined." For freedom of action to be more than just an illusion, we must understand the social influences that normally shape our behavior; then we can decide how to react to those influences. None of us will always make the wisest behavioral choice, but an awareness of social psychology can enlighten us to the range of social psychological factors that may infringe on our free choice in any social situation.

Becoming an "Informed Consumer" of Research Findings

Unless you decide to become a scientific researcher yourself, most of your exposure to research findings after leaving college will be through newspapers, magazines, television, and conversations. Often, research findings are overcondensed, misapplied, or misrepresented by the media. With your background in social psychology, you may be able to avoid falling prey to these misrepresentations. When a study is reported, the first question to ask is: Was the study an experiment or not? Remember that a true experiment involves the random assignment of subjects to conditions (levels of the independent variable), the manipulation of the independent variable (into two or more levels) by the experimenter, and control of other extraneous sources of variance. One can make causal conclusions only from an experiment. Correlational studies are valuable too, and in some areas are the only type of study possible, but one must be cautious not to imply causation from correlation (Focus 1-2).

Issues of sampling are critical, especially for opinion poll results. If the sample is representative, then it is proper to generalize the findings back to the larger population from which the sample was taken. Another important issue is the task faced by the subjects. Did the research situation appear to "demand" certain responses (demand characteristics) from subjects? Were they likely to feel apprehensive about being evaluated by the researcher? If so, then the research consumer needs to treat the research results with appropriate skepticism.

Awareness of these factors enables you to be a well-informed consumer of research results from properly conducted research studies and to not be misled by poorly done research. Naturally, those of us who have chosen to devote our professional lives to social psychology think of it as an interest-

SYLVIA

Source: *Chicago Tribune*, May 17, 1990.

ing and exciting field. I hope I'll be able to communicate some of that excitement to you through the pages of this book. Not everyone will find the quest as fascinating as a social psychologist does, but perhaps your understanding of the human condition will become a bit broader and deeper.

SUMMARY

Social psychology involves the scientific study of human behavior. By means of the scientific method, researchers study the behavior of individuals or groups of individuals as it influences, and is influenced by, other people. The case history method is used infrequently in social psychology. Correlational and experimental research methods are used most often. In an experiment the researcher manipulates one or more independent variables and subjects are randomly assigned to levels of the independent variables. An experiment has several advantages over a correlational study. Experiments allow better control over extraneous variables, permit the exploration of the dimensions of a complex variable and, most importantly, can provide unequivocal evidence of causation. Even though experiments provide powerful information, there are many situations in which experiments cannot be carried out because the researcher cannot control the independent variable or randomly assign subjects to conditions. In these cases, correlational studies are most appropriate.

An acceptable study must have internal validity: it must be well designed and include appropriate analyses. It is desirable that a study also be high in experimental realism (having a strong impact on the participants), mundane realism (be similar to real-world situations), and external validity (the results can be generalized widely). Any factors that interfere with the spontaneity of a subject's behavior detract from the worth of a study. Subjects who are playing a role, or feel special because they are being studied, or react to demand characteristics are not behaving spontaneously, and it would be risky to generalize from their responses. Because people are often sensitive to others' expectations and social desirability pressures, the only viable way to elicit spontaneous behavior in some situations is through the use of deception, which involves a number of important ethical issues.

Several central issues that will recur frequently in analyses of social behavior were briefly previewed. Questions concerning the determinants of social behavior were presented: genetic/biological vs. social determinants, egoistic vs. altruistic motives, and personality vs. situational forces. Analyses of how people understand their own behavior include the distinction between causes and reasons, various types of self-presentations, and the adaptive nature of several illusions. Recurring themes in understanding others' behavior include common biases in how people process social information, the importance of expectations, social categorization, and the fundamental attribution error. Central themes in changing behaviors include social power, social learning from models, and the issue of whether to change situations or individuals.

The value of social psychology was briefly discussed in terms of the types of research programs (knowledge-driven and decision-driven) and the applications of research outcomes to public policy. We also looked at the relevance of research findings for understanding behavior, making informed choices, and becoming an "informed consumer" of reported research findings.

PART TWO
Social Cognition

CHAPTER 2

Perceiving and Understanding People

. . . the first step towards the intellectual mastery of the world in which we live is the discovery of general principles, rules, and laws which bring order into chaos. By such mental operations we simplify the world of phenomena, but we cannot avoid falsifying it in doing so, especially when we are dealing with processes of development and change.   Sigmund Freud ❖

PREVIEW

An understanding of the processes by which individuals observe, interpret, and attempt to understand behavior is basic to social psychology. This chapter will analyze the way people perceive behavior, how they process social information about others, how they make attributions, and the manner in which attributional concepts help people understand human actions.

Our analysis begins with the study of *social cognition*, the processes involved in perceiving, evaluating, and categorizing other people. We will analyze common biases and errors in the ways that people process social information. First, I will review general errors in information processing, such as common tendencies to overgeneralize and to hang on to discomfirmed beliefs. Next, biases that are related to schemas will be discussed. Then we'll look at how people overvalue their own beliefs and behaviors and, finally, at the tendency to process information "mindlessly." Two comprehensive theories about how people make causal attributions about others' behaviors, correspondent inference theory and Kelley's "social scientist" model, will be reviewed in some detail, as will a model of attributions in success-failure situations. Additional biases that often affect causal attributions, in particular actor-observer differences, will also be analyzed. The concepts and theories covered in this chapter will prove useful for our analysis of social behavior throughout this book.

PROCESSING SOCIAL INFORMATION

Schemas as Cognitive Organizers

Cognitive Schemas

The ability to perceive others accurately and interpret their behavior is a vital human skill. But none of us has the unlimited time (or energy) to carefully evaluate each new individual we meet. Because of the complexity of the social environment, we all have to be selective in what we notice, learn, and remember. Social psychologists have developed the concept of *schema* (plural, *schemas* or *schemata*) to describe how social information is selectively perceived and organized in memory. Categorizing objects, experiences, and people is a basic human process (Anderson, 1982). There are two distinct processes in evaluating another person: evaluating his or her attributes as an individual (to be analyzed in Chapter 8), and social categorization (Pavelchak, 1989). Theorists have suggested that people prefer to categorize others whenever possible because it is simpler and more efficient than trying to understand others attribute by attribute (Fiske et al., 1987). We are all "cognitive misers," making the best of our limited mental capacities by using schemas to categorize and understand our world.

Our categorizations of people (person schemas) most often are based on visible characteristics such as gender, age, race, appearance, group membership, occupation, or behavior. Every individual probably has a favorite dimension on which they initially categorize others. Some people categorize others initially in terms of gender, others may pay particular attention to ethnic group membership, educational level, or physical attractiveness (Higgins et al., 1982). Schemas are crucial in the categorization process, directing our attention to relevant information, giving us a structure for evaluating information, and providing categories for memory. When thinking about the world, people will "pick up only what they have schemata for and willynilly ignore the rest" (Neisser, 1976, p. 80). Schemas provide an efficient (but not always accurate) way of understanding the environment.

Four main types of schemas have been described. **Self schemas** contain information about one's own characteristics. We will analyze self schemas in the next chapter. **Person schemas** contain information about typical people and are useful for categorizing others and remembering their schema-relevant behaviors. One's person schemas contain **prototypes** (Cantor, 1981), sets of features that one associates with members of a category with varying probabilities. When you envision a prototypical football lineman, rock star, or college professor, different sets of features come to mind. Suppose a casually dressed young woman walks into the campus bookstore and says to the older man behind the desk, "I'd like to order the books for a course."

self schema:
A schema containing information about one's own characteristics.

person schema:
A schema containing assumptions about typical people and prototypes.

prototypes:
Sets of features that one associates with members of a category with varying probabilities.

Person schemas. What assumptions would you make, based on your person schemas, about what these young women are like?

The older man replies, "The books aren't in yet for next semester." "I know," the young woman replies, "I'd like to order the books for the course." "Oh, certainly, what books does the professor want?" "I am the professor," is the young woman's frustrated reply. The bookstore clerk's prototype for a professor probably included the following attributes: older, male, orders books, and has a female secretary (who may do his book ordering for him). The clerk had difficulty dealing with a person who was a poor match for his prototype of a professor (Fiske & Taylor, 1984).

role schema:
A schema containing concepts of appropriate norms and behaviors for people in various social categories.

event schema:
A schema containing knowledge about typical sequences of events or social occasions.

Role schemas involve concepts of appropriate norms and behavior for various social categories based on race, gender, age, occupation, and so forth. These schemas involve the way we expect people to act while they are playing a certain role. When you ask a question during class, you and your professor probably interact in terms of your role expectations—student and professor. Should you run into your professor later at a local bar, your interaction might be quite different, since the student and professor roles are less relevant in that setting. Finally, **event schemas** or *scripts* (Abelson, 1981) contain knowledge of the typical sequence of events or social occasions (a party, a football game, a job interview); they help in understanding and remembering such events. Since our focus in this chapter is on how people perceive and understand others, we will pay most attention to person schemas. The next chapter will focus on self schemas; while role schemas will be particularly relevant to our analyses of prejudice (Chapter 11), and event schemas will be salient at many points during our social psychological

Individuals don't always fit our person schemas very well.

analysis of human behavior. We expect people to act in accordance with our schemas and we behave accordingly. If the person behaves in an unexpected manner or doesn't "follow the script" that we think applies to a particular situation, we may be surprised and upset.

Implicit Personality Theories

Taken together, your schemas about other people constitute an **implicit personality theory**, guiding your expectations, perceptions, and behaviors toward different types of people. Schemas form the backbone of our implicit personality theories, our implicit assumptions (which we may not recognize) about how people's personalities are structured. Suppose you are about to meet your roommate's father for the first time. You know that he is forty-five years old, divorced, a lawyer, played football in college, and drives a Porsche. What will you anticipate about his personality, based on this initial information? What person schema is activated?

Schema-related assumptions affect how we view other people, how we treat them, and what we remember about them (Cantor & Mischel, 1979). If one's implicit personality theory is a fairly accurate reflection of the world, few problems will arise. If one's theory is generally inaccurate, however, misjudgments about others may continually occur. Studies suggest that most people's implicit personality theories are somewhat valid (Lay & Jackson, 1969; Stricker et al., 1974). Now that you have a general notion of what is involved in processing social information, we can take a more in-depth look at how social cognition works.

Stages in Cognitive Processing

Attention. There are three main stages in cognitive processing: attention, encoding, and retrieval. *Attention* refers to what you notice when you encounter a person or situation. Schemas influence our perceptions of incoming information, especially when they have been activated before the perception takes place (Bargh & Pietromonaco, 1985). Schemas tell you what to expect, thus things that violate these expectations tend to stand out and are noticed. A student who is doing something unusual in class — humming, writing a letter, sleeping — is likely to be noticed due to behavior that is inconsistent with most people's event schema (script) for a college class.

Encoding. Not everything that is noticed gets encoded and stored in memory. Much information is never encoded, going in one ear and out the other, so to speak. Information that is vivid and distinctive is most likely to be encoded. But even stimuli that are encoded may be processed in an inaccurate manner, as information is distorted, omitted, or invented. Schemas play a powerful role in determining which social information gets encoded. Generally, information that fits nicely into existing schemas is encoded best (Cohen, 1981; White & Carlston, 1983). However, information that blatantly contradicts a schema may also be remembered well (Hastie & Kumar, 1979). When a friend behaves in an unusual or bizarre way, this schema-inconsistent behavior is noteworthy and we are likely to remember it (Stern et al., 1984).

Basically, information that is *relevant* to a schema (whether supporting or contradicting it) is encoded better than material that is irrelevant to the schema. Congruent (schema-consistent) and incongruent (schema-inconsistent) information may stimulate different types of cognitive processing (Hastie, 1981). The congruent information can simply be incorporated into the existing schema, with little thought. In contrast, to deal with the incongruent information you have to think about how it relates to the rest of the items in your schema.

Despite the evidence that people pay attention to schema-inconsistent information and encode it, individuals often don't revise their schemas even after encountering contradictory evidence. Schemas may resist change for two reasons. First, the person may explain away the contradiction as the exception that proves the rule, as a unique aberration. Second, contradictory evidence may stimulate a mental review of past evidence that supported the schema (O'Sullivan & Durso, 1984). Ironically, this may make the schema even stronger. Suppose your schema of football players includes the trait "unintelligent" ("dumb jocks"), and you meet a football player who carries an A average in accounting. Instead of revising your schema to include a higher probability that football players are intelligent, you may mentally review all you've read and heard about "dumb jocks," thus reassuring yourself that the schema is accurate and doesn't need revision. You may also show a **contrast effect**, exaggerating the differences between the studious player and other football players (Manis et al., 1986).

contrast effect:
The tendency to support an existing schema by exaggerating its differences with contradictory evidence.

Retrieval. A schema that has been used recently is more accessible than other schemas that have not been recently used. This is known as the **priming** effect (Conway & Ross, 1984); schemas that are primed because they were used recently are likely to influence social cognition and memory in the future. One way to imagine the priming effect is to think of schemas as "content-labeled mental storage bins" (Wyer & Srull, 1981). When a piece of information is used it is deposited at the top of the bin. This recently deposited information is easily accessible and likely to be used again if a relevant situation arises. The accessibility of particular schemas also depends on individuals' attitudes and beliefs. If an issue is particularly important to you, that category of information will have been frequently utilized and will be more readily accessible in new situations (Higgins & King, 1981). For a militant feminist, gender-related schemas are likely to be primed by frequent use and by their importance to her. The accessibility of these schemas means that the interpretation of new events, as well as memory for past events, is likely to be processed first in terms of gender.

priming:
The effect of prior context on the retrieval of information.

What does your schema of a college football player contain? Gerry Gdowski quarterbacked his University of Nebraska football team to the 1990 Fiesta Bowl, passing and running for over 2200 yards during the 1989 season. He also carried a 3.56 grade point average in accounting. Does this information fit your schema of a football player? (As an FSU professor, I feel compelled to add that Gdowski's Nebraska team was beaten by Florida State in the Fiesta Bowl.)

Gender-related schemas in action. This woman's gender-related schemas probably are central determinants of her opposition to the Equal Rights Amendment.

Heuristics: Mental Shortcuts

Advantages of Heuristics

Heuristics are mental shortcuts and strategies that people use to make sense out of their complex environments. The advantage of using these mental rules of thumb is that we can process information quickly and efficiently. If we couldn't, we would succumb to **cognitive overload** (Milgram, 1970), being overwhelmed by the avalanche of perceptual stimuli that bombard us each day. Our heuristic strategies make it easier for us to invoke relevant schemas to process complex, incomplete, or ambiguous information. To be most useful, these strategies should be reasonably accurate processes that permit quick and simple ways of dealing with social information. In many cases, however, our heuristic strategies encourage biased and inaccurate information processing.

Types of Heuristic Strategies

The Representativeness Heuristic. We often judge whether or not someone belongs to a certain group by how similar he or she is to our schema of the typical group member (prototype). We match information from the environment (the person's appearance) against our schema to determine whether the person is representative of that schema (Tversky & Kahneman, 1974). While at a party Tracy notices Matt, a man she has not met before, talking with some of her friends. She wonders whether Matt is in a fraternity. She may check out his visible characteristics—his appearance and behavior—against her schema of fraternity men. If there is a match, the fraternity-man schema will be invoked and she is likely to assume that Matt has other characteristics contained in her schema. The representativeness heuristic allows us to classify people quickly and painlessly, but it can lead to mistakes. Perhaps Matt does not belong to a fraternity and it is only coincidence that his appearance fits Tracy's schema of a fraternity man, or per-

heuristics:
Mental shortcuts and strategies that people use to make sense out of their complex environments.

cognitive overload:
Being overwhelmed by the volume of perceptual stimuli that are encountered each day.

Cognitive overload. City-dwellers are often faced with so many rapidly arriving cognitive inputs that they must use heuristic strategies to simplify their cognitive environment so that they can deal with it efficiently.

haps he is in a fraternity but does not have most of the other characteristics included in Tracy's schema. Overuse of the representativeness schema can lead to stereotyping.

The Availability Heuristic. The availability heuristic is used to estimate the likelihood of events. When answering the questions "How often?" or "How many?" we quickly sample the information that is readily accessible in our memory to see how many examples come to mind. If you are considering a ski holiday and worrying about the possibility of breaking a leg, you are likely to mentally review the experiences of your acquaintances who have gone skiing. You will estimate your chances of getting hurt based upon their experiences.

This process will produce accurate answers as long as the information in memory is reasonably representative. But if you happen to have an unusually reckless or unlucky set of friends, 80 percent of whom have returned from ski trips wearing casts, then your mental estimate of the likelihood of a skier getting injured (80 percent) will be inaccurate. Or if your previously existing schema of skiing includes high injury potential as a central component, then you may have encoded and remembered schema-consistent instances where skiers were hurt better than you remembered the more numerous (but schema-inconsistent) instances where skiers did not get hurt. The schema-consistent information would be more available to you, leading to a biased estimate of your own level of risk.

Another important factor is the range of information originally available to an individual. Suppose you are trying to estimate what proportion of families in the U.S. owns home computers. If you grew up in a well-to-do neighborhood where all of your friends' families owned home computers, then your schema of the "average family" is likely to contain the element "owns a home computer." As a result, you may greatly overestimate the proportion of U.S. familes that have home computers.

The Anchoring Heuristic.　When faced with the need to make a judgment about an unfamiliar event, people often use available information about a similar event as an anchor or frame of reference, then adjust their judgment if the situation seems to warrant it (Tversky & Kahneman, 1974). For social perceptions, the self is often used as an anchor. Is your friend Roger popular? The easiest way to make this judgment is to compare his popularity with your own, using your own popularity as an anchor. If you think he is about as popular as you are (equal to the anchor), and you consider yourself popular, then you will place Roger into the "popular" category. This process doesn't always yield accurate judgments, however. Research indicates that once people have established an anchor point, they generally do not adjust their social judgments away from the anchor point as far as they should for the sake of accuracy (Quattrone, 1985). For example, Cervone and Peak (1986) asked college students to predict how well they would do in solving twenty anagrams (jumbled word problems). Some were asked whether they would solve more or less than four problems (low anchor point) while others were asked if they would solve more or less than eighteen problems (high anchor point). The students were told that the comparison level (anchor point of four or eighteen) had been randomly selected. As Figure 2-1 indicates, those exposed to the low anchor expected to do less well themselves, even though they knew that the comparison point was randomly chosen. Further, they didn't work as long on the problems as the high-anchor or the control (no anchor) subjects did. Hence, an anchoring bias affected both judgments of self-efficacy and subsequent behavior.

Disadvantages of Heuristics: Biases and Errors

Our mental shortcuts for processing social information do not always serve us well. Sometimes they lead us to process information inappropriately. There are several general categories of errors dealing with social information that we humans tend to make. First, we make general mistakes— overgeneralizing from single incidents, being oversusceptible to first impressions, holding onto our beliefs even when they have been disconfirmed, sometimes processing information "mindlessly." Second, our schemas bias our information processing. We remember schema-relevant information better, and interpret it differently, than information that does not fit our schemas. We also channel our thinking and our interactions in ways that seem to confirm our schemas and may perpetuate our stereotypes. Third, we overvalue our own beliefs and attitudes. We think they are correct and widely shared (normative), and we tend to think that we knew the answers all along (hindsight bias).

General Errors in Processing Social Information

Generalization Fallacies.　There are many potential sources of information about people: personal experiences, observations of friends, and information from large groups of individuals gathered through surveys and

FIGURE 2-1

The Impact of Anchoring on Self-Efficacy and Task Persistence

Mean level of self-efficacy (the number of anagrams subjects judged themselves capable of solving) and task persistence (the number of trials subjects worked on the first task) were lower when subjects were given a low anchor (comparing themselves with someone who got four of twenty anagrams right) than when given no anchor or a high anchor (comparing themselves with someone who solved eighteen of twenty anagrams).

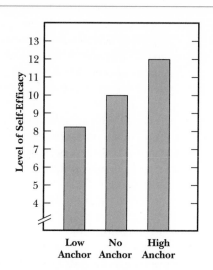
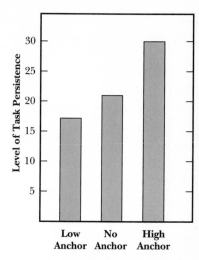

Source: From Cervone, D., & Peake, P. K. (1986). Anchoring, efficacy, judgements and behavior. *Journal of Personality and Social Psychology, 50,* 495. Copyright © 1986 by the American Psychological Association. Reprinted by permission.

research. Logically, data obtained from many individuals ought to provide more accurate information about behavior than data obtained from just a few (oneself or one's friends). Thus, you ought to be more influenced by the behavioral information conveyed by this book, based on research involving thousands of people, than on your own experiences or observation of your friends. But this is not likely to be the case.

Information about personal experiences (e.g., personal anecdotes) is cognitively accessible, more vivid, concrete, and easily usable. Statistical or "base-rate" information, in contrast, is more abstract and may seem less relevant or more difficult to apply. Research has shown that, perhaps because they use the availability heuristic, people tend to overvalue information about individual cases and undervalue general statistical information (Borgida & Brekke, 1981). Most people are prone to a **generalization fallacy**, a tendency to overgeneralize from individual cases (Slovic & Fischhoff, 1977), from small samples (Tversky & Kahneman, 1971), and from personal experience (Nisbett & Ross, 1980). Though people may be quite accurate when specifically asked to make a statistical probability judgment, most people do not use statistical or probability information (a statistical heuristic) very efficiently for everyday problems (Nisbett & Kunda, 1985). As we might expect, people who have had formal statistical training do better than those who have not had such training (Nisbett et al., 1983).

generalization fallacy: The tendency to be heavily influenced by vivid, concrete, easily usable information based on personal experience, and less influenced by statistical base-rate data.

Perceptual Errors. Even under the best of conditions human perception and memory are fallible. We are constantly bombarded by perceptual stimuli and even if one is using appropriate heuristics, some information is likely to get encoded incorrectly. This is especially true if the event is complex and fast-moving, as is the case for a crime. Research shows that the error rate among eyewitnesses (false identifications) is distressingly high (Brigham, 1989). An overconfidence effect is also evident. Eyewitnesses' confidence in the correctness of their identification is generally high and only weakly related to actual accuracy (Bothwell, Deffenbacher, & Brigham, 1987).

The Primacy Effect. First impressions can bias the way later information is interpreted. In a clever study, Jones and his colleagues (Jones et al., 1968) had subjects watch a film of a person attempting to solve a series of problems. Each observer saw one of three patterns of performance. The actor's rate of correct answering either: (1) declined from an initial high rate to a low rate, (2) improved throughout the period observed, or (3) remained at the same level. Although the stimulus person's overall rate of performance was the same in all three conditions, persons who had watched the declining rate of performance rated the actor as more intelligent and more likely to perform well in the future than did subjects who had watched the other two patterns of performance.

The observers apparently established an expectancy early in the experiment, attributing a high level of intelligence to the stimulus person who started out very well. Once they included "high intelligence" in their schema for that person, they were reluctant to change it, even in the face of later conflicting evidence. You can imagine how this tendency might apply to a class in which college students are evaluated on several noncumulative exams during a semester. A primacy effect does not always occur, however. If the new information makes the order of events important, modifying the schema and weakening memory for the earlier information (as a cumulative exam might), then the opposite tendency, a recency effect, may occur (Anderson & Hubert, 1963). Otherwise, when the attribution involves a stable characteristic (such as ability or intelligence) and subsequent information does not modify the schema, a primacy effect is more likely.

belief perseverance:
The tendency to persevere in our beliefs even when the original basis for these beliefs has been disconfirmed.

Belief Perseverance. Our initial beliefs about other people sometimes persevere even when the original basis for those beliefs has been completely disconfirmed (Ross et al., 1977). One reason is that people often invent additional reasons to support their cherished beliefs. Then, even if the original basis for the belief is later discredited, the additional, invented reasons supporting the belief remain (Ross & Anderson, 1982). A practical demonstration of belief perseverance was provided in a study of voters' beliefs about Richard Nixon at three points during the U.S. Senate's 1974 Watergate hearings. Voters who had supported Nixon in 1972 persevered in their positive beliefs about him despite all the damaging evidence that emerged during the hearings. Voters who had supported McGovern in 1972, on the other hand, became increasingly negative toward Nixon as the hearings progressed and more damaging testimony emerged (Carretta & Moreland, 1982).

Central Traits. Our person schemas, organized into implicit personality theories, assume that a person who has one particular trait is likely to have certain other traits as well. In an early study, Asch (1946) created two descriptions of hypothetical persons differing on only one of seven traits—warm vs. cold. The difference on a single **central trait** (warm-cold) significantly affected subjects' predictions of several of the person's other traits such as generosity and sense of humor. In another study (Kelley, 1950), students evaluated a new instructor at the end of his lecture quite differently depending on whether he had been described previously as "a rather cold person" or "a rather warm person." Students informed that he was a rather warm person rated him as considerably more humorous, sociable, good-natured, considerate, and informal than did the other students, even though all students had heard the same lecture. In addition, most of the students who had received the warm description participated in the classroom discussion, but fewer than a third of the students who had read the cold description participated.

A particular trait may be central in some contexts but not in others, depending on what other characteristics are measured. Part of the reason that the warm-cold trait was so important in the Asch and Kelley studies is that in many of the subjects' implicit personality theories, it was related to some of the other traits (humorous, generous) on which ratings were made (Wishner, 1960).

The Halo Effect. We often have to make judgments of people we don't know well. Our vague general impression of the person may cause a **halo effect**, influencing our perceptions of many specific traits. For example, Nisbett and Wilson (1977) had people watch an interview with a Belgian professor who appeared likable or unlikable. Not only did subjects prefer the likable professor, they also rated his accent and his physical appearance as more pleasant. Apparently the subjects' overall evaluative response to the professor influenced their ratings of his accent and physical appearance. Not only can perceived physical attractiveness be influenced by a halo effect, as in this study, but physical attractiveness can also produce halo effects, as we will see in Chapter 8.

Schema-Related Biases

Seeing What We Expect: Cognitive Confirmatory Bias. Because our schemas guide the processing of social information, we tend to seek, interpret, and remember information in a biased way that confirms our preexisting schemas. This type of processing shows a **confirmatory bias** (Snyder & Swann, 1978). The scientific method, reviewed in Chapter 1, is designed to rule out the confirmatory bias in the testing of research hypotheses.

When we evaluate ambiguous evidence, we tend to slant our evaluations so that the material fits our schemas. This bias is particularly visible

central trait:
A trait that is of major importance in determining our reaction to someone, as it affects how they are evaluated on other supposedly related traits.

halo effect:
When we have only a vague, general impression of someone as good or bad, this may affect our perceptions of many of that person's other more specific traits.

confirmatory bias:
Since our attitudes and schemas guide the processing of social information and our behavior toward others, we tend to interpret and remember information in a biased way that conforms to our preexisting schemas.

in our evaluations of the degree to which two factors covary (are related). If we expect them to be related, we are more likely to notice and remember confirming instances (cases where they were related) than nonconfirming instances. This tendency has been labeled the **illusory correlation effect**. Because expectations bias our perceptions and memory, we perceive an expected relationship as much stronger than it actually is.

illusory correlation effect:
The tendency to perceive expected relationships as much stronger than they really are.

For example, some projective personality tests (measures such as the Rorschach Inkblots Test that assess people's responses to ambiguous stimuli) appear to have little or no validity when tested scientifically. Nevertheless many clinicians continue to use them as key elements in their diagnoses, claiming that they can see very consistent patterns of responses where certain responses indicate (covary with) particular psychological problems. But many studies have demonstrated that when shown random patterns of association between two factors, most people who expect them to be related will misperceive the events and see a clear relationship between the two factors. (Chapman & Chapman, 1967). Prejudiced people are particularly likely to perceive negative traits and behaviors as being correlated with membership in the disliked group even when no such pattern exists (Hamilton & Sherman, 1989). As Jennings et al. (1982, p. 215) put it, "In the realm of covariance assessment, the contest between expectations and evidence is apt to be an unequal one." Our expectations usually prevail.

Once we have determined, rightly or wrongly, that new information fits our schema, we turn to other matters. When a person behaves in a schema-consistent manner in an initial contact, we tend not to pay much subsequent attention to him, instead relying on the schema for further assumptions about his behavior. We are likely to pay attention only if he begins to behave in a way that is inconsistent with our schema (White & Carlston, 1983). Then we will probably struggle to interpret this new behavior in a way supporting our existing schema.

behavioral confirmatory bias:
When a person's behavior channels an interaction so that behaviors that seem to confirm the person's expectancies are elicited from the other individual.

*Causing Behaviors We Expect: **Behavioral Confirmatory Bias**.* Not only do we bias our perceptions to confirm our existing schemas, we also may slant our behaviors in ways that induce schema-confirming behaviors from others. For example, in a clever study Snyder, Tanke, and Berscheid (1977) had men talk on the phone to women they had not met. Each man had been led to believe that the woman he was talking to was either attractive or unattractive in appearance. Analysis of the women's comments showed that the women thought to be attractive spoke in a significantly warmer and more likable way than the women thought to be unattractive. The men's behavior (acting warmer and more likable themselves when they thought they were talking to an attractive woman) had caused the women to respond in a way that seemed to confirm the men's schema that attractive women are warm and likable. Another term for behavioral confirmatory bias is *self-fulfilling prophecy*. One's expectations (prophecy) set in motion a behavioral sequence that ends up seeming to confirm (fulfill) the expectations. One place this can be seen is in the classroom. Jussim (1989) found that when teachers had expectations about their students, it affected student achievement and motivation as well as the grades that teachers assigned to the students.

I have asserted that people generally perceive, interpret, and remember information in ways that confirm their preexisting schemas. You may find yourself objecting to such a blanket indictment of cognitive processing. Are there times when you are truly open to new information, evaluate it accurately, and test your personal hypotheses in a valid manner? Research suggests that there are. People often seek out schema-disconfirming data when trying for an in-depth understanding of a single individual (Stern et al., 1984) or when they feel that disconfirming evidence will provide important diagnostic information about someone (Trope & Bassok, 1982). In short, when we are strongly motivated to form a clear, unbiased impression of someone we may be able to overcome the biasing effect of heuristics and biases in cognitive processing (Erber & Fiske, 1984). But usually people are not on guard against bias, and biasing factors are likely to infiltrate their everyday evaluations and judgments about others.

stereotype:
A generalization that is considered unjustified by an observer.

The Perpetuation of Stereotypes. A **stereotype** can be conceptualized as a negative schema (generalization) about a group that is considered unjustified by an observer who labels it a stereotype (Brigham, 1971). One might consider the schema unjustified because its contents are untrue, or because it is rigid and doesn't change in the face of disconfirming evidence, or because it leads to unjust (stereotypical) treatment of group members. Not all group schemas are negative, of course, but the term *stereotype* has traditionally been reserved to apply only to negative schemas (Lippmann, 1922). We are likely to label someone's person schema as a stereotype when it is negative, oversimplified, rigid, and widely shared within the culture.

Suppose Bill encounters information about Debbie, a sorority member, that conflicts with his stereotype of sorority women. Cognitive biases

Person schemas as stereotypes. What assumption would you make about these men's personalities and behaviors, based on their appearance?

may allow him to hang on to his stereotype despite the disconfirming evidence. Further, due to the false consensus bias (discussed below) he may assume that his stereotypic view of sorority women is more widely shared than it really is, perceiving widespread social support for his viewpoint. Or, as noted earlier, he can rationalize away the inconsistent information about Debbie, deciding that she is the exception that proves the rule.

What if Bill encounters information about Debbie that seems to support negative aspects of his stereotype, although he suspects that the information may not be correct? He might engage in a two-stage expectancy-confirmation process. Initially, when he has reason to suspect that stereotypic information may not be valid, he will refrain from using it. His schematic expectancies function at this stage only as hypotheses about Debbie's likely characteristics (the representativeness heuristic). The second stage occurs when he has the opportunity to observe Debbie's actions and can then test his hypotheses against the behavioral evidence. He may use a biased "confirming strategy," leading him to find false support for his stereotypic hypothesis (schema). Darley and Gross (1983) found that people who had only a little information about a girl (her socioeconomic status) would not make stereotyped predictions about her probable ability level. Yet when people received the social class information and also saw a videotape of the child taking an academic test, those who believed that the child came from a high socioeconomic background rated her abilities well above grade level, whereas those who thought the child came from a lower-class background rated her abilities as below grade level. Apparently, people felt freer to stereotype when they could rationalize that their judgment was based on lots of information.

Overvaluing Our Own Beliefs and Attitudes

> To believe in your own thought, to believe that what is true for you in your private heart, is true for all men — that is genius.
> —Ralph Waldo Emerson

Assuming That Our Beliefs and Behaviors Are Widely Shared. People tend to overestimate how typical their own beliefs, values, attitudes, and judgments are (Ross et al., 1977). Further, individuals who engage in a behavior believe that the behavior is more prevalent than those who do not. They see their judgments and behaviors as relatively common and appropriate to the circumstances, while alternative responses are seen as uncommon, deviant, and inappropriate. A meta-analysis of 115 studies showed this general effect in many situations (Mullen et al., 1985). Further, subjects who succeed in a task give higher estimates of consensus (believing that others will succeed too) than those who fail at the task (Deutsch, 1989). People are particularly likely to overestimate the degree of consensus (agreement with their position) when they are a numerical minority in a group. Rebels and dissidents, for example, are likely to greatly overestimate the number of people in the society who support their minority position (Mullen & Hu, 1988).

false consensus bias:
People tend to overestimate how typical their own beliefs, judgments, and behaviors are.

The **false consensus bias** may have two sources: self-justification and selective exposure. By assuming that others think and behave as you do, you can justify your own actions, assuring yourself that your schemas are correct and lessening pressure to change them in the face of conflicting evidence. Selective exposure refers to the false impression of the commonness of our responses that we get (using the availability heuristic) because we tend to seek out the company of others whose schemas, values, and behaviors are similar to our own (Deutsch, 1989; Zuckerman et al., 1982). Unfortunately, relying too heavily on our own attitudes and behaviors as anchors may detract from our ability to understand and predict another person's behavior, especially when that person is from a group very different from our own (Hoch, 1987).

overconfidence effect:
People tend to be more confident in the accuracy of their judgments than they should be.

Overconfidence That Our Beliefs Are Correct. We tend to have more confidence in the accuracy of our judgments than we should. In one study, clinical psychologists, psychology graduate students, and undergraduates were asked to make psychological judgments about a number of therapy cases. Although the accuracy of judgments made by all three groups remained low throughout the study (about 28 percent), the judges' confidence in the accuracy of their judgments rose dramatically, from 33 percent to 53 percent, as they made more judgments (Oskamp, 1965). They weren't getting any better, but they certainly thought they were! You can imagine how this bias could affect the confidence of a psychologist or physician who has been making diagnoses for twenty or thirty years.

Experts, once forced to go beyond their data, may be as prone to overconfidence as nonexperts. This tendency has been shown not only with clin-

Attempting to clean up the 1989 Exxon oil spill in Alaska: A painful example of experts' overconfidence. Exxon officials showed the overconfidence bias, initially stating that Exxon could easily control the massive oil spill in the waters off Alaska.

ical psychologists but with professional auto mechanics (Fischhoff et al., 1978) and geotechnical engineers (Hynes & Vanmarche, 1976). The initial overconfidence by officials at Exxon that they could easily contain and clean up the disastrous oil spill in the waters off Alaska in 1989 is a painful case in point. This bias becomes particularly chilling if we consider "expert" judgments on issues such as the safety of nuclear reactors. A review of the multimillion-dollar Reactor Safety Study (U.S. Nuclear Regulatory Commission, 1975) concluded that the experts' judgments of the probability of a core meltdown were characterized by a high degree of overconfidence (Slovic et al., 1982).

Why does overconfidence occur? For one thing, people are often unaware of the true determinants of their behavior (Nisbett & Wilson, 1977). Therefore, they may not realize it when their judgments are based on faulty processes such as stereotypes or inappropriate heuristics. The human tendencies to interpret new information and remember past events as confirming our existing schemas (utilizing the availabilty schema) and the tendency to persevere in our beliefs despite conflicting evidence can give us a false impression of how accurate our judgments have been. The false impression of high past accuracy may lead us to assume that we will also be very accurate in subsequent judgments.

Overconfidence is particularly likely on tasks that are difficult, as people tend to remain highly confident even when increased caution would be prudent (Lichtenstein & Fischhoff, 1977). For example, how accurately can you predict what your best friend will do in a particular situation? Such social predictions also fall victim to the overconfidence effect, as people use their person schemas, stereotypes, and implicit personality theories as guides for predicting other's behaviors, underestimating how strongly situational forces influence behaviors (Dunning et al., 1990). People also tend to be overconfident in their ability to predict their *own* future behavior, again probably because they underestimate the impact of future situational forces (Vallone et al., 1990).

Thinking That We Knew All Along: The Hindsight Bias. When we look back (with hindsight) we tend to remember our past judgments as having been much more accurate than they really were. Fischhoff and Beyth (1975) had students predict the outcome of President Nixon's upcoming visits to China and the USSR. When asked after the visits to recall what they had predicted, most students remembered their predictions as being closer to what actually occurred than they really had been. Similarly, one day before the 1980 presidential election, Leary (1982) asked a group of students to predict the outcome of the election. A day after the election a second group of students were asked to estimate what their preelection predictions would have been. These students showed a clear **hindsight bias**, remembering their predictions as much closer to the actual election outcome than the preelection predictions of the other students had been. A similar finding was demonstrated for preelection and postelection estimates about a Hawaiian guber-

hindsight bias:
The tendency to remember past judgments as having been much more accurate than they really were, or to assume others should have known what would happen.

FOCUS 2-1

Overconfidence at NASA

The tragic 1986 explosion of the U.S. space shuttle *Challenger*, shortly after takeoff from Cape Canaveral, Florida, killed all seven astronauts aboard and shocked Americans who had grown accustomed to thinking that space launchings were routine, safe events. In the aftermath of the disaster Richard Feynman (1988), a winner of the Nobel Prize in physics, was appointed to a presidential commission to investigate what had gone so terribly wrong. In the course of his investigation, Feynman was astonished by the variation in the estimates that "experts" had previously made about the chances of disaster.

The explosion occurred because of the failure of the O-rings that held together the sections of the solid-fuel rocket booster engines. What had the experts earlier predicted about the chances of engine failure? An independent engineer consulting for NASA had thought one or two failures per 100 launches a reasonable estimate. Engineers at the Marshall Space Center in Alabama, where the engine was designed, estimated a one in 300 chance of failure. Engineers at Rocketdyne, the engine's manufacturer, claimed only a tiny chance

of failure, estimating the probability at 1/10,000. Management at the National Aeronautics and Space Administration (NASA) had testified to Congress that the chance of failure was only one in 100,000. By their estimate, one could launch a space shuttle each day for 300 years and expect to lose only one! Feynman (1988, p. 223) observed, "It would appear that, for whatever purpose—be it for internal or external consumption—the management of NASA exaggerates the reliability of the product to the point of fantasy."

This appears to be a tragic example of the overconfidence effect among experts. While some NASA officials might have deliberately exaggerated their safety estimates in order to increase public confidence and funding from Congress, it is clear in hindsight that all of the experts were woefully overconfident in the safety of space launches. Another important aspect of this disaster that is directly relevant to social psychological analysis, the inadequate decision-making processes that led up up to the launch, will be analyzed in Focus 6-1. ❖

natorial compaign (Synodinos, 1986). This "I knew it all along" effect can be demonstrated in other ways, too. In the week before football's 1985 Super Bowl, I asked a group of students to predict the outcome anonymously. Most (81 percent) predicted a Miami Dolphin victory. A week after the San Francisco 49ers' decisive victory, I asked another group to remember their pregame predictions. The majority (58 percent) remembered predicting that San Francisco would win.

We also fall prey to this bias in evaluating others' judgments. We not only think, "I knew it all along," we also think, "You should have known it all along." Thus, psychological or historical analyses of decision making in important events such as Pearl Harbor, the Vietnam War, Watergate, or the Iran-Contra scandal, may be affected by this bias, as later writers unfairly claim that the participants "should have known better" about the way events were to unfold (Chapter 6). As one historian noted, historians "play new tricks on the dead in every generation" (Becker, 1935). Hindsight is 20/20.

President and Mrs. Nixon on the Great Wall of China in 1972. After the president's visit, students showed a hindsight bias when recalling that their pre-visit predictions about Nixon's visit had been.

The hindsight bias probably results from a combination of cognitive and motivational factors (Hawkins & Hastie, 1990). People may have forgotten their original judgment entirely, or they may selectively recall only those aspects of their past behavior that are consistent with the outcome, or they may reinterpret their past actions in light of subsequent events. While these cognitive actions are not deliberate, in other cases individuals may be motivated to deliberately misconstrue their past judgments in order to manage the impression they give to others, so that they appear consistent and knowledgeable.

Mindless Information Processing

It should be abundantly clear by now that people often do not process social information accurately, relying instead on stereotypic schemas and simple heuristics. In the extreme, the tendency to respond in routinized, unthinking ways has been labeled **mindlessness** by Ellen Langer (1989). This describes a reduced level of cognitive activity in which a person responds unthinkingly to the environment, relying on old habits and schemas. Much of our typical day passes in mindless activities and "automatic" rituals (e.g., Two people passing on campus, each asking "How's it going?" and not waiting for an answer). We may become aware of our mindless information processing only when we do something unusually stupid (locking the keys in the car, putting the iron in the refrigerator, calling the wrong person on the phone, etc.).

While each of us runs on autopilot some of the time, the tendency to mindlessly operate in terms of schemas and stereotypes can have a number of negative effects, as Langer (1989) pointed out. If you mindlessly think of yourself solely in narrow, schematic terms (e.g., Mr. so-and-so's wife, a biology student), this narrows your self-image and makes it tougher to deal flexibly with the world. Narrow, schematic thinking also prevents people from making intelligent choices, as they cling to one perspective or one way of

mindlessness:
The tendency to respond in routinized, unthinking ways.

doing things. In a classic experiment, Luchins and Luchins (1942) showed that when students learned to perform a mathematical task in a particular way, most of them continued mindlessly to use the process they started with, even when a much simpler solution was available for the later problems. In a more general sense, people who cling to single-minded explanations for events (e.g., their divorce) seem to adjust more poorly than those who see many possible explanations for their situation (Langer & Newman, 1981). An example of lessened control that may result from mindlessness is learned helplessness, which will be discussed shortly.

Mindless information processing may also contribute to incidences of unintended cruelty. In a series of studies that will be discussed in detail in Chapter 5, Stanley Milgram found that most normal individuals could be induced to deliver apparently painful electric shocks to a fellow research subject when the experiment routine seemed to demand obedience to the experimenter. Most subjects mindlessly complied with the experimenter's statements that they had to continue in the study. Mindless information processing may also allow us to compartmentalize uncomfortable thoughts (e.g., Thinking "I'm just a subject pushing levers in an experiment," rather than "I'm hurting a fellow human being.").

Certain environments and roles can encourage mindlessness. Mindlessness might be especially detrimental to the elderly, because many elderly people live in very routinized environments that do not encourage creativity or thoughtfulness, decreasing the opportunity for active information processing (Langer et al., 1984). Langer (1982) proposed that prolonged mindlessness could be severely incapacitating and might even result in premature death. In recent years many creative programs have been established to reduce the mindlessness-inducing aspects of the environment in which elderly people live.

An environment that may encourage mindlessness. Elderly people often live in routinized, unstimulating environments that make mindless processing of information likely.

Debiasing: Attacking the Biases

We have seen that people often proceed mindlessly, not using information very accurately. They are prone to overgeneralize from specific, vivid cases and to underutilize statistical data, to persevere in their beliefs even when new information contradicts these beliefs, to reinterpret their memories in terms of a hindsight bias, to perceive a false consensus about their beliefs and actions, and to bias their processing of information or their interactions so that they confirm their existing schemas. This analysis of biases in social information processing paints a rather dismal picture. But I should note here that these biases are not always maladaptive. We will see in Chapter 3 that some biases may serve a valuable function in protecting self-esteem.

There are ways in which some biases can be corrected or avoided, though it's not easy. While attempts to reduce the hindsight bias by warning students about it beforehand did not reduce its occurrence (Fischhoff, 1977), the bias was reduced when people were induced to imagine the various other ways in which an event could have turned out (Slovic & Fischhoff, 1977). Belief perseverance can be reduced via explanations of its nature, its personal relevance, and costs (Ross et al., 1977). Generally, in order to reduce bias or error a person must recognize that bias exists, be motivated to reduce the bias, and have the means to do so (Neuberg & Fiske, 1987).

calibration training:
A way of reducing the overconfidence effect by giving people immediate and continuous feedback on the accuracy of their judgments.

Calibration training seems effective in reducing the tendency toward overconfidence. When people are given repeated immediate feedback about the accuracy of their judgments, they are able to better calibrate (adjust) their perception of accuracy and their overconfidence disappears (Fischhoff, 1982). Of course, in everyday life few of us get immediate, accurate feedback about our judgments. Another effective technique has been to have people list reasons why their preferred judgment might be wrong; after doing so they are less overconfident (Koriat et al., 1980). Calibration training is effective in reducing overconfidence, but formal education is not; highly educated people (physicians, for example) are just as susceptible to overconfidence as are less educated people (Detmer et al., 1978). Perhaps we ought to study ways of incorporating calibration training into our formal education system.

Individual Differences in Ability to Evaluate Others

Problems in Assessing Accuracy. Although people are susceptible to the numerous biases discussed above, some still seem to be better judges of people than others are. Social scientists have had a difficult time pinning down what makes this so. In part, the problem stems from lack of a good criterion of what one's "true" personality is. Most measures of personality are relatively imprecise and many are of dubious validity. Hence, researchers must look for criterion instruments (such as psychological tests) that have been validated under rigorous conditions and are quite sensitive to individual differences. Another complexity is that many assume that the people they observe (the target persons) are similar to themselves (Bender & Hastorf, 1953), using the self as an anchor. This assumption of similarity can lead to a research artifact, a finding that is not what it appears to be. Most raters evaluate others more in terms of the rater's own characteristics than those of the target person. Because some raters will happen to be similar to the target person, these raters will appear to be more accurate than raters who happen to be dissimilar to the target person.

stereotype accuracy: The ability to predict an individual's response based on knowledge of the social category to which the individual belongs.

differential accuracy: The ability to tell where each person stands in relation to others with respect to a particular characteristic.

Two Skills Involved in Evaluating People. Despite these complexities, social psychologists have been able to gather some evidence on the skills involved in judging others accurately. There appear to be two components that may be fairly independent of one another (Cronbach, 1955; Tagiuri, 1969). **Stereotype accuracy** is the ability to predict an individual's response based on knowledge of the group to which the individual belongs (e.g., race, gender, age). A person who has this skill would be good at judging what most people in a particular group are like.

However, one could have this general sense of what most people in the group are like, but still miss badly on judgments about specific individuals. The second component, **differential accuracy**, refers to the judging of specific individuals, which involves the ability to tell where each person stands in relation to others. Cline and Richards (1960) found that stereotype accuracy seemed to be the more powerful determinant of overall accuracy. Although research seems to indicate that the two skills are unrelated, another possibility is that there are people who are consistently good judges in both senses, but they are too few to be easily identified (Tagiuri, 1969).

Cognitive empathy, the ability to see things from another's "psychological point of view," seems to be related to the ability to judge others accurately (Bernstein & Davis, 1982). If we could develop more information on factors that enable people to make accurate personal judgments, we could turn our attention to training people to be better judges of others.

MAKING CAUSAL ATTRIBUTIONS

Suppose that Bob, a college student, continually arrives ten minutes late to his 9:00 A.M. history class. As a fellow student in the class, you may try to understand Bob's behavior. What kind of reasoning process are you likely to go through?

When events are happening around us, we are almost irresistibly drawn to seek their causes, to make *causal attributions.* In social situations we constantly attempt to understand the behaviors of others, and then infer from these behaviors the underlying characteristics of the other person. What does

dispositions:
Internal characteristics such as attitudes, beliefs, schemas, values, and personality traits.

Bob's behavior tell us about him? Each of us would like to be able to control things so that our interactions with others have favorable outcomes. Such control depends, at least in part, on our ability to figure out people's **dispositions** (their attitudes and personality traits) and to predict their behavior.

Our inferences about others' behavior can vary on three dimensions (Meyer & Koelbl, 1982; Weiner, 1979). The *locus* of the behavior can be seen as internal or external. Bob's lateness can be construed as stemming from his own personality characteristics (internal locus) or as determined by his environment (external locus). The *controllability* of the outcome can also vary. Can Bob control the outcome or is there nothing he can do about it? Finally, the dimension of *stability* refers to whether the behavior is typical for Bob (a stable occurrence, he is often late) or is unusual for him (unstable). It is easiest to make a dispositional attribution when the behavior is seen as internal and stable. I will discuss these dimensions in more detail later as they apply to success/failure situations.

Causes and Reasons

Why is Bob habitually late for class? There are two levels of explanation. If we ask Bob, he can give us *reasons* for his action, the purposes or goals of the behavior as he understands them ("It's a long walk from my eight o'clock class," or "Nothing important happens in the first ten minutes of class," and so on). Alternatively, we can objectively analyze the *cause* of his behavior. A cause can be defined as "that condition which is present when the effect [behavior] is present and which is absent when it is absent" (Kelley & Michela, 1980, p.462). Our analysis might indicate that the causes of his behavior (say, disliking the class or getting attention for arriving late) were quite different from the reasons he gave. People are aware of their reasons, but they may not be aware of the underlying causes of their behavior (Locke & Pennington, 1982).

Another important distinction is between actions (voluntary behaviors) and occurrences (nonvoluntary behaviors) (Kruglanski, 1979). Actions (Why did he do that?) can be explained by reasons or causes, but occurrences (Why did that happen to him?) can be explained only by causes. Outlined below are the two most influential theories about attributions. The correspondent inference model, which will be discussed first, deals only with actions, whereas Kelley's "social scientist" model covers both actions and occurrences.

When Causal Attributions Are Made

There are several situations in which causal reasoning is particularly likely. Sometimes an explicit causal question is posed, as in a courtroom. When an unexpected event occurs, people are especially motivated to seek its cause (Hastie, 1984). Dependence on another person for desired outcomes also stimulates causal reasoning. For example, researchers found that an individual about to go out on a blind date with a stranger was more likely to engage in causal reasoning (about the stranger's probable dispositions) than was an individual who did not expect to date the stranger (Berscheid et al., 1976). Finally, feelings of failure or loss of control increase the prevalence of causal reasoning (Alloy et al., 1984). For example, when people fail at an academic achievement task, they are more likely to use causal reasoning than when they do not fail (Wong & Weiner, 1981).

One typically goes through several steps in trying to understand a behavior (action): observing the action, making a judgment about the intentions underlying the action (What outcomes could the actor have been hoping for? How hard was she or he trying to achieve them?), and deciding what attribution to make. There are three general types of causal explanations that people can make (Hansen, 1980). They may decide that the behavior was caused by: (1) *dispositions* of the actor (traits, personality characteristics); (2) characteristics of the *stimulus* the actor was interacting with; or (3) the *circumstances* in which the behavior took place. When the event is observed, one of these three explanations is tentatively advanced. The confirmatory bias may affect the processing of causal information. As an example, behavior consistent with an observer's schema of the actor is generally attributed to the actor's dispositions; but the identical behavior, if inconsistent with the schema, is usually attributed to situational factors (Crocker et al., 1983; Kulik, 1983). In this way, the observer can continue to accept the schema as valid despite the conflicting evidence.

Models of the Attribution Process

Heider's Model

The first systematic analysis of how people interpret the causes of other's behaviors was carried out by Fritz Heider (1944; 1958). Heider proposed that each of us, motivated to understand other people's behaviors in day-to-day interactions, operates like a "naive scientist." People rely on intuitive causal principles and a "commonsense psychology" in deciding whether or not to attribute other people's behavior to their internal dispositions.

In Heider's (1958) model, a person's behavior is seen as caused by environmental forces plus personal forces (which include dispositions). Environmental forces are those factors in a situation which "press" for a specific type of behavior. Personal force is seen as the product of ability (or power) and the effort that one exerts. If either ability or effort is lacking, the strength of personal force will be zero (see Figure 2-2). Heider's general approach

---

FIGURE 2-2
Determinants of Behavior

According to Heider's (1944, 1958) Model

to the attribution process was extended by Edward E. Jones and his colleagues and by Harold Kelley. Because they provide valuable frameworks for understanding issues basic to human behavior, these more recent theories will be discussed in some detail.

Correspondent Inference Theory

Edward Jones and his coworkers (Jones, 1979; Jones & Davis, 1965; Jones & McGillis, 1976) studied the influence of dispositional forces and environmental forces on causal attributions. They analyzed the conditions that give rise to dispositional attributions, or what they called **correspondent inferences** — cases in which an observer judges that a particular disposition of a stimulus person (actor) is a sufficient explanation of the actor's behavior (e.g., "Bob is constantly late because he's an irresponsible person.") They identified four general classes of factors that affect an observer's attributional processes.

The Strength of Environmental Factors. The relative strength of environmental forces on the actor directly affects the type of attribution an observer will make. For example, Jones and Harris (1967) had subjects observe a debater delivering a speech supporting or criticizing Cuban Premier Fidel Castro. Subjects were told either that the debater had been free to choose which side of the topic to present (weak environmental pressure), or that the debater had been assigned to this side of the topic (strong environmental pressure).

As one might expect, subjects attributed more extreme pro- or anti-Castro attitudes to debaters who had a choice of which side to present than to debaters who had no choice. But even in the no-choice conditions, the debater's assigned position affected attributions made about him. Debaters assigned to the pro-Castro side were evaluated as more pro-Castro than the average student, while those assigned to the anti-Castro side were seen as much more anti-Castro than the average student. This effect has been termed **behavior engulfing the field**, illustrating that even when behavior occurs under strong environmental pressure, it can still influence observers' attributions.

The Effect of the Behavior on the Observer. The degree to which an observer is affected by a behavior will also influence the type of attribution made about the actor. **Hedonic relevance** describes the degree to which an action is gratifying or disappointing to the observer of the action. **Personalism** refers to the degree to which an observer perceives that action as directed specifically toward her (Jones & Davis, 1965). When the hedonic relevance and personalism of an action increase, the likelihood that which an observer will make dispositional attributions to the actor will also increase. The observer's confidence that she has made the "correct" attribution increases as well.

Consider how a psychology professor might react to the news that salaries of auto workers were going to be cut by 10 percent. The action has

---

correspondent inference theory:
A major theory of attribution that analyzes the factors that cause people to make dispositional attributions.

behavior engulfing the field:
The tendency for people to make dispositional attributions to an actor even when the actor's behavior was forced by environmental factors.

hedonic relevance:
The degree to which an action is gratifying or disappointing to the observer of that action.

personalism:
The degree to which an observer perceives an action as directed specifically toward her or him.

no hedonic relevance to the professor and hence she would be unlikely to infer anything much about the personality of the company president. Suppose, however, that the dean of the professor's college announced salary cuts of 10 percent for all college employees. This action is hedonically relevant to the professor and she would be more likely to make dispositional attributions about the dean. Yet she still might not be sure that her attribution is correct. But suppose that the dean called the professor's office and announced that only her salary would be cut. This action is hedonically relevant and also contains a high degree of personalism; the professor's attributions about the dean's dispositions would be strong (and negative).

The Expectedness of the Behavior. An action that is expected tells us less about the actor than an unexpected action does. Unexpected actions are those which are out-of-role, extreme, socially undesirable, or inconsistent with one's prior behaviors. We expect politicians to act in the ways that most politicians act (friendly and tactful for example), thereby fitting our schema of a politician. If they behave in an extreme or out-of-role manner, or inconsistently with their prior behavior, this behavior is unexpected and is perceived as providing a good deal of information about what they are really like (Jones, Davis, & Gergen, 1961).

When a person acts inconsistently with your schema of him, you are likely to make a dispositional attribution (Fiske & Ruscher, in press). Suppose a male politician cries. The out-of-role, extreme behavior may lead to negative dispositional attributions. In March 1972, Senator Edmund Muskie, then the heavily favored front-runner for the Democratic nomination for president, burst into tears while responding to a very hostile editorial during the campaign in the New Hampshire presidential primary. Many political analysts felt that the dispositional attributions that voters made to Muskie because he cried (that he was weak or unstable) doomed his chance to win the nomination.

When someone behaves in a socially undesirable fashion—such as a student walking out of a class in the middle of a professor's lecture or a professor reacting angrily to a legitimate question from a student—observers will quickly attribute a personality trait, such as rudeness, to the offender. Ironically, the effects of a series of socially desirable actions may be completely wiped out by the effect of one undesirable act. A socially undesirable action is treated as carrying far more information than is a desirable action in making attributions. This *negativity bias* is especially characteristic of morality judgments. We usually have positive expectancies about others' behaviors (that they will act in a moral way) and hence negative actions stand out in contrast (Skowronski & Carlston, 1989).

The Alternative Actions Available: Unique Outcomes. Suppose you find that your friend Ken is taking a statistics course next semester. To what do you attribute his action in choosing the course—his dispositions or the environment? If you find that this course is required for his major, is highly recommended for people wanting to go to graduate school, and satisfies several college requirements, you are likely to make an environmental attribution about Ken's behavior. Taking statistics had a number of *unique outcomes*, termed **noncommon effects** by Jones and Davis (1965), which could not have been achieved in any other way. Therefore, one is likely to attribute the behavior to these effects rather than to Ken's personality. If, on the other hand, you find that statistics is not required for Ken's major and satisfies no general college requirements, you are likely to make a dispositioned attribution. There must be something about Ken (intellectual curiosity, a liking for statistics, masochism) that caused him to make that choice.

noncommon effects:
Unique outcomes of a behavior that could not have been achieved in any other way.

Attributional Factors Applied. Let us return our attention to Bob, our often-late history student. What might lead the professor to attribute Bob's lateness to environmental forces or to underlying dispositions? Because the action probably violates norms for student behavior, it is likely that the action will be attributed to Bob's dispositions. If the action was extreme (twenty-five rather than two minutes late) the professor would be even more likely to make a dispositional attribution. In contrast, if she knows that Bob has a previous class far across campus, and that no one can make it to class on time from that distance (a strong environmental factor), she will be more apt to make an environmental attribution.

We can also look at the degree to which the action affects the observer (in this case, the professor). If the professor sees Bob's late appearance as detracting from the effectiveness of her lecture (high hedonic relevance), she will be more confident in attributing a dispositional cause to Bob's behavior. If she sees Bob's behavior as directed specifically toward her (high personalism), she will give even greater weight to dispositional forces "He's purposely trying to annoy me — he's not a nice person."

It is somewhat difficult in this case to speculate on any unique outcomes of Bob's behavior. Learning the course material or getting a good grade could be better achieved by an alternative behavior, coming to class on time. From this perspective, his behavior has no unique outcomes and one would be likely to make a dispositional attribution. However, if he has another outcome in mind that cannot be accomplished in any other way — being noticed by his classmates or by the professor, for example — this outcome may be seen (in Bob's eyes, at least) as a unique result of his action. If we had this information, we might make a dispositional attribution to Bob's inordinate need to be noticed.

In summary, the types of behavior most likely to lead observers to make a dispositional attribution are behaviors that: (1) occur in situations in which perceived environmental forces are not strong; (2) have consequences for the observer (hedonic relevance); (3) are perceived as directed intentionally toward the observer (personalism); (4) are seen as not caused by roles, social norms, or other social-desirability pressures; (5) are negative; (6) are extreme; and (7) have few unique outcomes.

Kelley's "Social Scientist" Theory

The Kelley Cube. Correspondent inference theory limits its analysis to a single action, but Harold Kelley's attribution theory (1967; 1973) takes additional information into account. It is focused on the actor, the situation in which actions or occurrences take place (time, modality, particular circumstances), and the stimulus—the object toward which the actor's behavior is directed. Like Heider, Kelley sees us acting as naive psychologists, using all of the information at our disposal to decide whether the locus of someone's behavior is internal or external. In order to make accurate attributions about an actor's behavior in a particular situation, we want to know: (1) how the actor behaves in other situations, (2) how the actor has behaved previously in this situation, and (3) how other people behave in this situation. Kelley sees observers as proceeding much like social scientists: analyzing data (on person, situation, and stimulus factors) and looking for the dimensions on which variation occurs. One can analyze the *distinctiveness* of the actor's behavior (Does the actor behave differently in other situations?), the *consistency* of the behavior (Has the actor behaved in the same way in this situation on other occasions?) and *consensus* (Do others behave in the same way in this situation?).

Let's take an example of how these factors are applied in interpreting behavior. Paula failed her calculus exam—to what do you attribute this action? If you find that this action is distinctive for Paula (it is unusual; she doesn't fail exams in other courses), consistent across situations (she has failed other calculus exams), and there is high consensus (many other students also fail calculus exams), this yields a *stimulus attribution*—there is something about this particular stimulus, the calculus course, that causes people to behave in this way (to fail exams). In contrast, if Paula's behavior is nondistinctive (she fails exams in other courses too), consistent, and has low consensus (others don't fail the calculus exams), then the observer is likely to make a *person attribution*—it is some characteristic of Paula that caused her to behave as she did. A *situation attribution* is most likely when the behavior is distinctive (Paula doesn't fail other exams), consensus is high (others also failed this calculus exam), but consistency across situations is low (Paula didn't fail other calculus exams). Perhaps this particular exam (this situation) was unusually tough.

As you might expect from our discussion of the biases that distort the processing of social information, the attribution process does not always proceed as rationally as this. People who function at relatively concrete levels of cognitive development (as opposed to higher abstract levels) are less able to make appropriate attributions based on Kelley's factors (Allen et al., 1987). There are also individual differences in the ways in which people use the three types of information (consensus, distinctiveness, consistency) in their attributions (Tukey & Borgida, 1983). People seem to give less emphasis to consensus information than to distinctiveness or consistency information when making attributions about actions (voluntary behaviors) (Kassin,

1979).When interpreting less voluntary actions (occurrences), however, people may look closely at consensus (Zuckerman & Feldman, 1984). Apparently consensus information is seen as useful (Did everyone react to the stimulus in the same way?) for insights into environmental conditions (e.g., powerful social norms) that may have provoked the behavior.

Applying Kelley's Theory. The three dimensions in Kelley's framework can be illustrated in cube format, with each dimension portrayed on one side of the cube (Figure 2-3). To gain enough information to interpret Bob's lateness to history class, we need to know: (1) how consistent is Bob's lateness to history, (2) how do other people (in our example, fellow students Suzi and Brad) behave toward the same stimulus (history class), and (3) how do the three of them behave toward different stimuli (say chemistry and psychology classes).

We know that Bob's behavior in history has high consistency (he's late to most of his history classes) and low consensus (others are not late to the history class). We then look to the distinctiveness dimension to try to understand the behavior better. Is Bob late to his other classes as well, or just to history? If Bob is late to all his other classes too, his behavior is stable and the distinctiveness of the present behavior is low, and the teacher will be likely to attribute his behavior to a stable disposition—say, laziness or irresponsibility (Figure 2-4).

If the teacher finds out that Bob is not usually late to his other classes, however, then the distinctiveness of his behavior in history class is high and the attributional process is more complex. The professor might attribute Bob's behavior to the particular context, such as a preceding class on the

---

FIGURE 2-3

Three Dimensions of Attributions Assessed in the Kelley Attributional Data Cube for Making Attributions about the Reasons for Someone's Behavior.

The shaded cell is the specific behavior for which an attribution is made (person 1 reacting to stimulus 1 in situation 1).

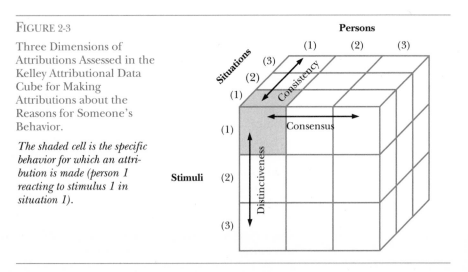

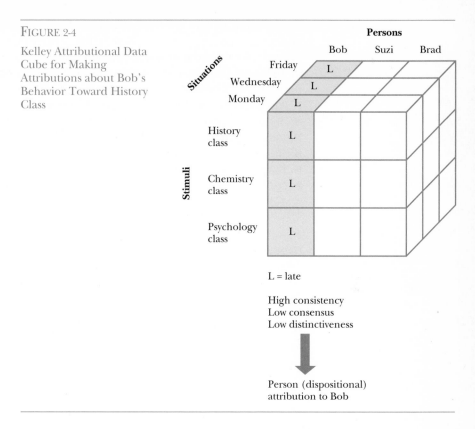

FIGURE 2-4

Kelley Attributional Data Cube for Making Attributions about Bob's Behavior Toward History Class

L = late

High consistency
Low consensus
Low distinctiveness

Person (dispositional) attribution to Bob

other side of campus. Or one might attribute his behavior to an interaction between actor and stimulus factors. Perhaps Bob simply doesn't like history or the professor's style of teaching, or perhaps their personalities clash. Or, as suggested earlier, perhaps Bob is trying to get another student's attention by sauntering in late every morning.

Kelley is attempting to describe the thought processes that we all use in our everyday lives. Kelley's theory stresses the *covariance* between causes and effects. Like social scientists, perceivers look for an association between a particular effect (e.g., Bob's lateness) and a particular cause across a number of different conditions. With which causal factor does the effect covary? As a naive psychologist you observe the effects that seem to regularly follow a particular stimulus—Bob's behavior.

discounting:
The role of a given factor in producing an effect will be discounted (seen as less important) if other causes are also present (such as status differences, role requirements, or unique outcomes).

Discounting. The role of a given factor (the person, the situation, the stimulus) in producing an effect will be **discounted** (seen as less important) if other possible causes are also present, such as status differences, role requirements, or unique outcomes. You are likely to discount the role of dispositional factors in Bob's lateness if you know that he has a prior class far across campus. For another example, if you see Linda help Jennifer, you might be tempted to make a dispositional attribution that Linda is a helpful person. If you know, however, that Jennifer is Linda's boss, you are likely to discount the role of dispositional factors for Linda's behavior because of the status difference between them: It is important to be nice to one's boss. If you feel that this is the only way Linda could make a good impression on Jennifer (a unique outcome), you would be even more likely to discount Linda's personal dispositions. On the other hand, if you saw Jennifer act helpful toward Linda, you would be likely to make a dispositional attribution to Jennifer (she is a helpful person), for there are no obvious status differences or role requirements that would force such behavior.

Attributions about Success and Failure

Causes of Successes or Failures. As you may have noticed after exam week, people search for the causes of success or failure in achievement situations. Three important dimensions have been identified: locus, stability, and controllability (Weiner, 1980). The locus of the behavior can be seen as internal (such as a disposition of the actor) or external (e.g., environmental pressure). Success or failure can be seen as a stable occurrence (one that is typical of the actor's experiences) or an unstable occurrence (one that is unusual in the actor's experiences). Finally, the behavior can be seen as controllable or uncontrollable by the actor.

An example is portrayed in Table 2-1. Let's look again at Paula's failure on her calculus exam. If Paula's failure is seen as stable and having an internal locus, then the failure will be attributed to her internal characteristics—say to a lack of ability if it was not controllable (in Kelley's terms, a person attribution) or a lack of effort if it was controllable (a person-by-situation interaction, in Kelley's framework). Or her failure could be perceived as having an external locus. Stable external factors might include the teacher's dislike for Paula (at least somewhat controllable by Paula's behavior in class, a person-by-stimulus interaction) or the difficulty of the exam (an uncontrollable situational factor). Unstable external factors might include interference from other students or bad luck (situational factors).

| TABLE 2-1 | POSSIBLE CAUSES OF ACHIEVEMENT OUTCOME: THE DIMENSIONS OF LOCUS, STABILITY, AND CONTROLLABILITY USED TO INTERPRET FAILURE ON AN EXAM |

	Internal Locus		External Locus	
	Stable	**Unstable**	**Stable**	**Unstable**
Controllable	Typical low effort	Temporary low effort	Teacher dislikes Paula	Unusual interference from other students
Uncontrollable	Lack of ability	Mood factors	Very difficult exam	Bad luck

Sources: Based on Weiner, B., (1979). A theory of motivation for some classroom experiences. *Journal of Educational Psychology, 71,* 3–25; Fiske, S. T., & Taylor, S. E. (1984). *Social cognition.* Reading, MA: Addison-Wesley.

Future Expectations. Future expectations are affected primarily by the stability of one's attributions. If performance is attributed to unstable factors (such as unusual effort, mood, or luck), then present success or failure will not strongly affect future expectations. If the performance is attributed to stable factors such as ability, on the other hand, then future expectations will be revised depending on whether one succeeds or fails.

Learned Helplessness

What happens when one experiences repeated failure? If he attributes the failure to unstable, noncontrollable, external factors (bad luck or an unusually tough task), there are no implications for future outcomes. But if he attributes the failures to a stable noncontrollable internal factor such as lack of ability, this attribution increases the chance that he will not try hard in subsequent situations, a condition that has been labeled **learned helplessness** (Abramson et al., 1978). Feeling a lack of control of one's environment can lead to giving up and to strong self-attributions about one's lack of ability.

learned helplessness: People who fail repeatedly may make a self-attribution to lack of ability, increasing the chance that they will not try hard subsequently even in situations where they would have been effective if they had tried.

The consequences of such self-attributions can be immense, since the passivity may carry over into new situations in which people might be able to control their environment if they tried (Tennen & Eller, 1977). Helplessness responses learned in one situation are likely to carry over into other situations when: (1) the person attributed the uncontrollable events in the original situation to internal, stable, global factors (Abramson et al., 1978); (2) the new situation is similar to the original situation (Pasahow, West, & Boroto, 1982); and (3) the individual has a general attributional style that attributes negative outcomes to broad, general factors. The latter two factors interact; people with this style will show learned helplessness in new situations even when they are not similar to the original situation (Mikulincer & Nizan, 1988). In contrast, people whose style is to attribute negative outcomes only to specific factors are likely to generalize feelings of helplessness only to situations similar to the original one (Alloy et al., 1984). Psychotherapists often focus on changing such destructive patterns of self-attributions that can produce pervasive learned helplessness in their clients.

Biases in Attribution

Attribution theories illustrate how people can behave rationally in deciding what attributions to make about others' behaviors. But as we saw earlier, people are not always rational in interpreting their behavior or others'. Below I will discuss several systematic biases that color how we make attributions about others, starting with a bias that is so pervasive it's been labeled the "fundamental attribution error."

Actor-Observer Differences

The Fundamental Attribution Error. Before reading further, take a moment to complete the rating scale in Focus 2-2. People often make different

---

FOCUS 2-2

Attributions to Oneself and to Others

First rate your best friend on the following characteristics, using the scale that follows. Then go back and do the same for yourself.

Rating Scale

-2 Definitely does not describe

-1 Usually does not describe

 0 Sometimes describes, sometimes not

+1 Usually describes

+2 Definitely describes

	Best Friend	Self
Aggressive	_____	_____
Introverted	_____	_____
Thoughtful	_____	_____
Warm	_____	_____
Outgoing	_____	_____
Hard-driving	_____	_____
Ambitious	_____	_____
Friendly	_____	_____
Total	_____ Total	_____

Now go back, ignore the pluses and minuses, and total the two columns. An interpretation of your scores will be given in the text. ❖

Source: From SOCIAL COGNITION by Susan T. Fiske and Shelly E. Taylor (1984). Copyright © by McGraw-Hill, Inc. Reprinted by permission.

---

attributions about the behavior of others than about their own. They tend to make dispositional attributions to others' behaviors and environmental attributions to their own behavior. This tendency of observers to underestimate the power of environmental forces on others' behavior is so widespread it has been labeled the *fundamental attribution error* (Ross, 1977). To investigate this phenomenon, several researchers (Nisbett et al., 1973) asked male college students to describe why they liked their current girlfriend, and to describe why their best friend liked his girlfriend. The students tended to attribute their best friend's choice of a girlfriend to dispositional qualities of their friend ("He's the kind of person who . . ."). In contrast, they described their own choice in terms of properties of the girlfriend ("She is very pretty/intelligent/lovable"). This is an environmental attribution, since the girlfriend is part of the student's environment. The students tended to assume their friend's future behavior would be consistent with his present behavior, but they did not feel this as strongly about their own behavior. Finally, the researchers presented a list of personality trait descriptions. Subjects were asked to judge how each trait applied to five people, including themselves. The students were quite willing to assign personality traits to others but were likely to use the "depends on the situation" category for themselves. Look back now at Focus 2-2. If you are like most of us, the total score for the best friend column was greater than for the self column, illustrating this tendency.

It appears that in each person's mind, personality traits are seen as factors that significantly affect other people's behavior, but affect our own behavior to a far lesser degree. Recall how behavior tends to "engulf the field"—we recognize the influence of environmental forces on our own behavior, but we tend to forget this when deciding why others behave as they do. This tendency is particularly relevant to evaluations of why someone committed a terrible act. To the perpetrator, the explanation "I had to do it; I had no choice" (high environmental forces) may seem extremely reasonable. To the observer, however, this environmental attribution may seem completely unacceptable.

Biases in attributions are affected not only by whether one is an actor or an observer, but also by whether one is an active or a passive participant in the interaction. *Active perceivers*, those who are interacting with the target person, must deal with a more complex situation than do *passive perceivers*, who are simply observing the target person. Active perceivers attempt to manage the impression they give (Chapter 3) while reacting to the other's behaviors and anticipating the future course of the interaction. Because they do not have as much cognitive energy left to correct for common cognitive/perceptual biases, active perceivers will usually be more susceptible to cognitive errors (Gilbert et al., 1988). For example, active perceivers usually show the fundamental attribution error more strongly than do passive perceivers (Gilbert et al., 1987).

In some situations, however, active perceivers may make more accurate attributions than passive perceivers do. Gilbert and Krull (1988) found that when exposed to a political speech unenthusiastically given by someone who had been forced to read it (recall the Jones and Harris political-speech study discussed earlier), active perceivers showed the fundamental attribution error less often than did passive perceivers. The researchers suggested that the busier active perceivers had less opportunity to pay attention to the verbal content of the speech and had to rely more on their "automatic" perception of nonverbal cues, such as the speaker's lack of enthusiasm. Since nonverbal cues often provide better evidence of lying than verbal cues do (Chapter 13), active perceivers (who are looking mostly at nonverbal cues) are less likely to be fooled by a liar. In the researchers' words, "In some cases, seeing less means knowing more" (Gilbert & Krull, 1988). This, to me, is a comforting finding. Since we are active perceivers in our important relationships, we may not be as vulnerable to some cognitive biases as other research might suggest.

Causes of Actor-Observer Differences. An actor has more precise information about her own emotional state, her intentions, and the past events that led up to the action, than an observer does. To the observer, the most salient information is the act itself, strengthening the observer's tendency to assume that a disposition led to it. For the actor, on the other hand, the most noticeable features are the environmental factors that are "out there." While the actor may also be aware of how her action appears to others, it does not have as powerful an impact on her perceptions as it does on an observer's perceptions (Jones & Nisbett, 1971). If the observer is given more information about the actor, the tendency toward the fundamental attribution error may be reduced (Miller & Lawson, 1989).

Since people believe that most trait labels do not apply to them, why is there still such a strong belief that others have stable traits? This difference may result from the way in which we process information. As observers, we see most people in relatively few roles, as a teacher or student, boss or employee, customer or salesperson. Because people tend to behave consistently when in a single role, we may assume that their overall behavior is more consistent than it really is. We tend to expect others to behave more consistently in the future than we expect ourselves to. In addition, because we impose structure on our environment via schemas, we may exaggerate the degree of consistency we see in others' behavior in order to make our cognitive world simpler (Jones & Pittman, 1982). Others' behaviors may appear more consistent than they really are, leading us to (often falsely) assume a constancy in their dispositions. In addition, so many trait labels are available to describe both behavior and dispositions (aggressive, friendly, helpful, and so on) that it is easy to fall into the habit of making dispositional attributions to others. There may be personality differences that make some people particularly susceptible to this tendency (Hicks, 1985). Croxton and Morrow (1984) found that people who had a more complex cognitive style were less susceptible to the fundamental attribution error than those who had simpler views of their environment.

The Role of Self-Awareness

Self-awareness, to be discussed in Chapter 3, also affects attributions. When people become more aware of their own appearance, as by sitting in front of a mirror or camera, causing them to focus their attention inward, they may make attributions differently from people whose attention is not as self-focused. For example, Duval and Wicklund (1973) had subjects imagine themselves going out on a blind date arranged by a friend. They were asked whether an enjoyable time would be attributable more to their own behavior or to their friend's actions in selecting a blind date appropriate for them. Subjects in a condition of high self-awareness were more likely to attribute the success to themselves (a dispositional attribution) than were subjects in the low self-awareness condition. The high self-awareness subjects behaved as observers do, showing a tendency to make dispositional attributions even when it was their own behavior that was being interpreted.

The Just World Assumption

There is a widespread tendency to blame innocent victims for the suffering they experience. This has been labeled the **just world assumption** (Lerner, 1980), the belief that the world is a just and fair place and thus victims of misfortune must have done something to deserve their fate. In part, this orientation may stem from the general tendency to make dispositional attributions about others' behaviors. Our Judeo-Christian religious heritage may also contribute, with its emphasis that "the meek will inherit the earth," that the good will be rewarded and the evil punished. The just world effect is particularly evident in the unfair harassment that rape victims often receive from police and in the courtroom (Jones & Aronson, 1973). In past years, many male police officers, judges, and attorneys seemed to believe that when a woman was raped she must have done something to encourage or permit the act. The just world assumption enables people to gain reassurance that they will not suffer misfortunes themselves (see Focus 2-3). If we convince ourselves that bad things happen only to bad people who deserve them, then we can maintain the illusion of control and reassure ourselves that we control our fate and can avoid misfortunes simply by refraining from the "bad" behaviors.

just world assumption: The tendency to believe that the world is a just and fair place, and thus victims of misfortune must have done something to deserve their fate.

Reattribution Training

Analyzing the ways in which people make attributions provides valuable insights into our perceptions and evaluations of others. Attributional analyses can yield important information for helping schoolchildren maintain intrinsic motivation, avoid failure, and make more productive self-attributions.

Children who consistently experience failure in school because of inappropriate learning materials or teacher prejudice may adopt a learned helplessness strategy, becoming passive and unresponsive. This passivity may continue even when conditions change and their responses would no longer be futile. In attempts to reverse such situations, psychologists have used **reattribution training** (Dweck, 1975). The focus of this training is on the importance of controllability and stability. Children are retrained to take responsibility for their failures, but are also encouraged to make more temporary self-attributions by attributing past failures to unstable, changeable conditions, rather than to lack of ability. If the children learn that they can control their outcomes, they may begin to try again (Wortman & Dinzer, 1978). This process can work for college students as well. College freshmen who were worried about their academic performance were given convincing evidence that college grades are quite unstable and usually improve considerably over the four years of college. The students receiving this information were less likely to leave college and improved their grades in the next year more than comparable students who did not receive such information (Wilson & Linville, 1982). However, since it turned out that the

reattribution training: A technique, used especially with children, to change the focus of attribution about failures to a more productive one.

FOCUS 2-3

When Bad Things Happen to Good People

In a best-selling book, *When Bad Things Happen to Good People,* Rabbi Harold Kushner, whose son died of progeria (rapid aging) at the age of 14, addressed the question "Why do bad things happen to good people?" (p. 6). Each day newspapers inform us of senseless murders, fatal practical jokes, young people killed in automobile accidents on the way to their wedding or coming home from their high school prom. Illness, misfortune, and death sometimes happen to people who seem to be leading good lives or are too young to deserve the harsh fate that befalls them. As we have seen, it is tempting to make the "just world" assumption, to believe that bad things happen only to bad people, especially other people, perhaps because God is a righteous judge who gives them exactly what they deserve. By accepting this image of a just world, we can keep things understandable and maintain an illusion of control.

Rabbi Kushner argued that nothing makes bad luck happen, it just happens. Bad things happen randomly to people independent of their own personal deservingness. "Life is not fair; the wrong people get sick and the wrong people get robbed and the wrong people get killed in wars and accidents" (p. 142). Attempts to justify a tragedy to the survivors by speaking of God's will or other justifying factors may simply make it harder for the survivors to deal with feelings of grief, anger, and outrage. "Vulnerability to death is one of the given conditions of life. We can't explain it any more than we can explain life itself. We can't control it or sometimes even postpone it. We can ask the question 'What do I do now that it has happened?'" (p. 71).

This image of randomness and lack of control does not coexist easily with the notion of an all-powerful all-knowing God. Rabbi Kushner stated,

"I believe in God, but I do not believe the same things about Him that I did years ago when I was growing up or when I was a theological student. I recognize His limitations. He is limited in what He can do by laws of nature and by the evolution of human nature and human moral freedom. . . . I can worship a God who hates suffering but cannot eliminate it more easily than I can worship a God who chooses to make children suffer and die, for whatever exalted reason. . . . God does not cause our misfortunes. Some are caused by bad luck, some are caused by bad people, some are simply an inevitable consequence of our being human and being mortal living in a world of inflexible natural laws" (p. 134).

There is no satisfying explanation that can easily make sense of it all. To Rabbi Kushner, the most adaptive response would be to forgive the world for not being perfect, to reach out to the people around us, and to go on living despite it all. In his words, "Are you capable of forgiving and accepting in love a world which has disappointed you by not being perfect, a world in which there is so much unfairness and cruelty, disease and crime, earthquake and accident? Can you forgive its imperfections and love it because it is capable of containing great beauty and goodness, and because it is the only world we have? Are you capable of forgiving and loving the people around you even if they have hurt you and let you down by not being perfect? Can you forgive them and love them because there aren't any perfect people around and because the penalty for not being able to love imperfect people is condemning oneself to loneliness?" (pp. 147-148) ❖

Source: From WHEN BAD THINGS HAPPEN TO GOOD PEOPLE by Harold S. Kushner. Copyright © 1981 by Harold S. Kushner. Reprinted by permission of Schocken Books, published by Pantheon Books, a division of Random House, Inc.

students who left college actually had higher GPAs than those who stayed, the overall effectiveness of this treatment needs further clarification (Block & Lanning, 1984).

SUMMARY

Understanding the processes by which people interpret behavior is basic to social psychology. Social information is selectively perceived and remembered in terms of one's schemas. Biases in the way people typically process social information include the tendency to overgeneralize and to retain disconfirmed beliefs. Of particular importance are the schema-related tendencies to see what we expect to see (cognitive confirmatory bias) and to cause other people to behave in ways that fit our expectations (behavioral confirmatory bias). People also tend to overvalue their own beliefs and behaviors, seeing them as common and accurate and thinking with hindsight that they knew all along what would happen. The ability to evaluate other people accurately involves two skills that are independent of each other: stereotype accuracy and differential accuracy.

The correspondent inference theory of Jones and his coworkers asserts that dispositional attributions are more likely when environmental forces are low, the behavior is unexpected, the behavior affects the observer, and the behavior had no unique outcomes. Kelley's social scientist theory asserts that people incorporate information about the consistency and distinctiveness of a behavior, as well as the degree of consensus, in reacting to a particular stimulus. People then make attributions to the person, to the stimulus (which can be another person), or to the situational context in which the behavior occurred. The most important dimensions for attributions in success-failure situations are the perceived locus of the behavior (internal or external), its controllability, and the stability of the outcome. Attributions can be biased by the fundamental attribution error, the widespread tendency to make dispositional attributions for other people's behaviors but situational attributions for our own.

Attributional approaches have proven useful in combating learned helplessness. The attributional concepts discussed in this chapter will serve us well in the chapters ahead. Our analysis of persuasion (Chapter 4) will highlight the attributions that people make to communicators (regarding expertise and trustworthiness). The actor-observer difference in attributions is particularly important when trying to understand cases of blind obedience such as the atrocities of Nazi Germany and Jonestown, Guyana (Chapter 5). Our analyses of altruism, attraction, love, and aggression all will utilize attributional concepts (Chapters 7–10). Schemas will be particularly relevant in the consideration of stereotypes and prejudice (Chapter 11). The distinction between dispositional and environmental attributions is highly applicable to the social psychology of the legal system (Chapter 13), since judges and jury members must often make attributions about the causes of a defendant's behavior.

CHAPTER 3

The Social Self

It is as hard to see one's self as to look backwards without turning around.   Henry David Thoreau

It is only through the approval of others that the self can tolerate the self.   Kingsley Davis

Consciousness of self gives us the power to stand outside the rigid chain of stimulus and response, to pause, and by this pause to throw some weight on either side, to cast some decision about what the response will be.   Rollo May ❖

PREVIEW

The concept of *self* is familiar to each of us as we struggle to understand who we are. Social psychologists have recently applied their skills to the investigation of this crucial but elusive concept; in this chapter I will review the fruits of their labors. I will begin with a short historical discussion of the concept of self in psychology, reviewing the "selves" identified by William James at the turn of the century and the more recent conceptualization of self as a cognitive schema.

How do you know what your "self" is like? You develop your cognitive sense of self, your self-concept, from how others react to you, from social comparison, from observing your own behavior (self-perception), and from your autobiographical memories of your past. But one can be mistaken in interpreting information about one's self, one's personality, and even one's emotions. I will discuss research evidence on the misattribution of emotions as well as the general biases in how we process information about ourselves.

Self-esteem denotes the emotional side of our self-concept. One's self-esteem is greatly affected by discrepancies between the actual self, the ideal self, and the "ought self" (feelings of duty and responsibility). Feelings about oneself are also affected by self-awareness, the degree to which one is looking inward introspectively. People often attempt to enhance their self-esteem by interpreting self-relevant information in a biased, self-serving manner that either makes them look good or avoids any responsibility for looking bad. We will examine these interesting cognitive "tricks" in some detail. I'll also discuss some illusions that people adopt to protect their self-esteem; some illusions are self-deceptive and maladaptive, but some may be valuable for adjusting to the world.

The final section will analyze the self in interaction with others, the authentic or strategically manipulated "face" that we choose to present to

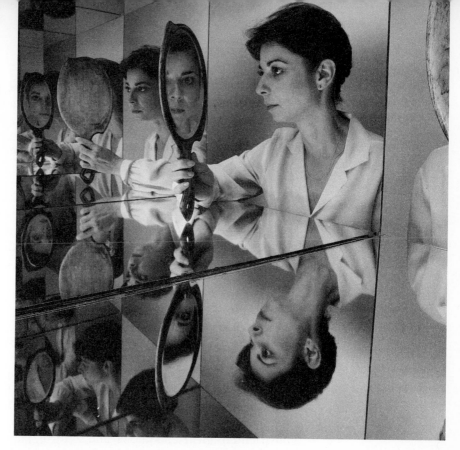

Each individual's personality has many facets.

others. I'll outline five types of strategic self-presentations, and we'll look at a personality style, self-monitoring, that differentiates between people who typically base their behavior on their own inner feelings and those who behave according to perceived social norms and the impression they want to make. Finally, we will look at deindividuation, which occurs when one's "sense of self" is reduced because of situational forces.

WHAT IS THE SELF?

spontaneous self-concept:
Those aspects of your self that are most salient to you.

Who are you? Take a few minutes and write down the features that would describe yourself. Your responses comprise your **spontaneous self-concept**, those aspects of your self that are most salient to you. When asked to describe themselves, people generally mention those attributes that are distinctive in relation to others. The "distinctiveness postulate" asserts that one tends to define oneself in terms of one's peculiarities, one's unique features (McGuire & McGuire, 1982). In describing yourself, in addition to basic factors like your name, age, and gender, you are likely to have mentioned those physical factors (e.g., height, weight, race, attractiveness) or personality traits that are unusual in the group you were comparing yourself with (e.g., fellow students). The more unusual or distinctive a factor, the more salient it is in one's spontaneous self-concept. As you change focus from one comparison group, such as your classmates, to another, such as your parents, the traits that you see as distinctive are likely to change. Your age, for example, is likely to be a more salient feature of your spontaneous self-concept when you are among people much younger or older than you.

The concept of *self* was discussed in detail by early personality theorists such as William James, Sigmund Freud, Alfred Adler, G. H. Mead, and C. H. Cooley. Self also plays a prominent role in more contemporary humanistic theories of personality development and functioning (e.g., Abraham Maslow, Carl Rogers). In the 1980s a growing number of social psychologists turned their attention to this concept. To give us a historical perspective before we get into contemporary theory and research, I will begin with William James's philosophical analysis of the self.

William James: Many Selves

A century ago William James, one of the first psychologists, proposed that the **known self** or the sense of "me," what we would now call the self-concept, has a number of components. There is the *material self*, your body and possessions. The *spiritual self* includes your personality traits, attitudes, values, and social perceptions. Finally, there are a number of *social selves*: the "me" that your friends know, the "me" that your parents know, the "me" that your boyfriend or girlfriend knows, and so forth. James suggested that there are as many social selves as there are classes of people who carry an image of you in their mind (James, 1890/1981).

Self-Schemas

We saw in Chapter 2 that *schemas* are cognitive generalizations that organize and guide the mental processing of information. The self acts as a schema for processing self-relevant information. Kihlstrom and Cantor (1984, p.2) suggested that the self exists as "one's mental representation of oneself, no

known self (sense of me): The characteristics that we believe we possess.

CATHY

Worrying about Cathy is a central part of her mother's self-schema and role schema.

FIGURE 3-1

The Known Self as
Conceptualized by
William James
(1890/1981)

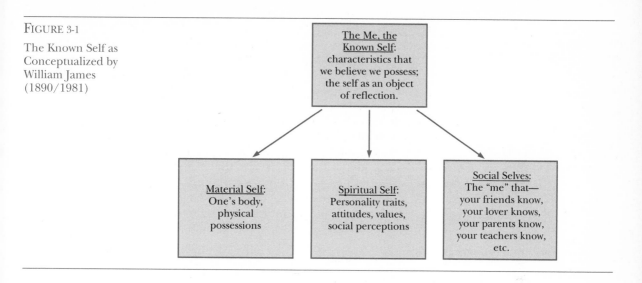

different in principle from mental representations that a person has concerning other ideas, objects and events and their attributes and implications. In other words, the self is a concept, not unlike other concepts, that is stored in memory as a knowledge structure." The self-schema (a) organizes abstract and concrete memories about the self, and (b) controls the processing of self-relevant information (Nasby, 1989a).

Because self-schemas determine how self-related information is learned and remembered (Markus et al., 1985), information processed with reference to the self (e.g., when you decide whether or not certain terms describe you) is more easily recalled than information processed by other means (Lord, 1980). Your well-organized self-schema processes information efficiently and hence it is readily accessible for subsequent recall (Hull et al., 1988); the **self-referent effect**.

self-referent effect:
Information processed
with reference to the self
is more easily recalled.

Look again at the way you described yourself. The traits that you listed are the traits that are most central to your self-schema (Markus et al., 1982). People tend to see themselves as having rich, well-developed, and adaptive personalities, possessing more traits than do other people and being less predictable than others are (Baxter & Goldberg, 1987; Sande et al., 1988). Characteristics that are central to one's own self-schema are valued more highly than are other characteristics. As an example, students who did well in a computer course later rated "computer skills" as a more important part of one's personality than did students who got poorer grades in the course (Hill et al., 1989). Furthermore, self-relevant traits are also used more often to judge others (Higgins et al., 1982). So if you wrote down "honest" as an important component of your self-schema, you are also probably very sensitive to other people's honesty.

THE SELF-CONCEPT

What Is the Self-Concept Based Upon?

Appraisal by Others

Our assumptions about our personal qualities, organized by self-schemas, comprise our **self-concept**. Our self-concept includes beliefs about our characteristics and an evaluation of each characteristic, whether it is one of our strong or weak points. Many of us wish that our self-concept was not so vulnerable to what others say, but input from others is a central source of information about the known self. As William James noted, our sense of "me" is derived largely from our social experiences. Other people are usually not shy in telling us what they think about us: about our personality, our attitudes and values, our appearance, and so forth. We pay close attention to what "significant others," such as friends, parents, teachers, and bosses, say about us. As a consequence, our judgment of ourselves in many ways reflects how we have been evaluated by others. Many years ago Charles Horton Cooley (1902) described the **looking-glass self**, our sense of self that evolves out of others' opinion of us through the process of *reflected appraisal*. People provide you with information about yourself directly by telling you what they think of you, and indirectly by how they react to you. If people seem entranced by what you say, you might consider yourself to be an interesting person; if they yawn and look elsewhere, you might decide that you are boring. We will see later that information from others is not always perceived in a totally accurate manner. Our own attitudes, values, and other parts of our self-schema may lead us to distort the information that we receive.

Social Comparison for Self-Evaluation

As a college student, your perceived level of intelligence may be an important part of your self-schema. How do you decide how intelligent you are? External sources may provide some information—what you've been told by your parents and teachers, how you scored on an intelligence test. A second way to assess your intelligence would be through **social comparison**, comparing your level of intelligence with that of your fellow students. Through social comparison you can evaluate your skills, thoughts, feelings, and traits by comparing yourself with others. There are three general goals that might be achieved via social comparison: self-evaluation, self-improvement, and self-enhancement (Wood, 1989).

The initial theory of social comparison, proposed by Leon Festinger in 1954, focused on self-evaluation. Festinger argued that people have a basic need for self evaluation. When physical reality cannot serve as a standard against which to evaluate one's feelings, skills, or beliefs, a person turns to other people, to *social reality*. For example, are you friendly? No physical standard can evaluate friendliness. It is necessary to compare yourself with others, to use them as an index of reality, in order to arrive at a conclusion.

self-concept:
Our assumptions about our personal qualities, organized by self-schemas.

looking-glass self:
Our sense of self that evolves out of others' opinions of us.

social comparison:
Comparison with other people in order to assess the appropriateness or validity of one's thoughts, behaviors, or feelings.

Social comparison for self-evaluation. There is an absolute standard for determining how good a golfer you are—your score for 18 holes. To ascertain how good a racketball player you are, in contrast, you need to use other players as standards for comparison. Who can you usually beat, and who usually defeats you?

Other theorists have pointed out that, in addition to the need to *evaluate* opinions and abilities, people also desire to *validate* them and to obtain evidence that their opinions are correct and their abilities are good (Goethals & Darley, 1977). People are most likely to engage in social comparison when they are uncertain about some aspect of themselves or when they find themselves in an unfamiliar or ambiguous situation (Cottrell & Epley, 1977).

Clearly, not every person or task can serve as a valid standard for social comparison. We generally compare ourselves only with those who are similar to us on related attributes such as age, sex, and experience (Goethals & Darley, 1987; Wheeler & Koestner, 1984). Recreational tennis players do not compare their ability and skills with tennis professionals; rather, they use other recreational tennis players as their yardstick. Individuals are generally interested in accurate self-evaluations and will seek out information that is the most useful. For example, when subjects are presented with a choice of tasks of differing capacity to diagnose their level of ability, they tend to select the task that will best diagnose their ability, even if the comparison is likely to be unfavorable (Trope, 1986).

The strong need for social comparison in unfamiliar situations was demonstrated by Stanley Schachter (1959). He conducted a series of studies in which female students were told that the experiment was investigating the effects of electric shocks. Women in the high-fear condition were told that the shocks would be painful. Other women (low-fear condition) were told only to expect mild shocks. The experimenter then left the room, giving the women the option of waiting alone in a spacious room equipped with books and magazines, or in a classroom with other women who were also participating in the experiement. As Figure 3-2 indicates, most of the women in the high-fear condition chose to wait with others. In the low-fear condition, however, most of the women didn't care whether they waited alone or with someone else. Subsequent studies showed that most women in the high-fear conditions wanted to wait with other women who were waiting for the same experiment, rather than women waiting for a different experiment.

FIGURE 3-2

The Impact of Fear on Affiliation

Decisions made by college women awaiting painful shocks (high fear) or mild shocks (low fear) about whether to wait alone or with others also in the same experiment.

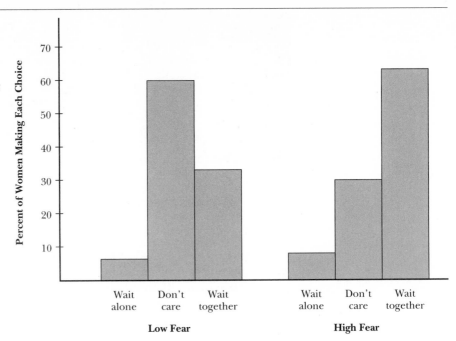

Source: Data from Schachter, S. (1959). *The psychology of affiliation.* Stanford, CA: Stanford University Press.

Seeking out others who are in the same boat as you has two general benefits: (1) general fear reduction (social comfort) from the presence of others, and (2) social comparison for self-evaluation. In high-fear conditions, people may wonder whether their feelings of arousal and anxiety are normal. To evaluate their reactions, individuals can seek out others in the same situation and compare their feelings to discover whether their own reactions are appropriate. As Schachter (1959) pointed out, the old saying "Misery loves company" could be revised to "Misery loves miserable company"—miserable people are valuable for social comparison.

Observing Our Own Behavior: Self-Perception

self-perception theory: Theory that we often infer what our attitudes are by observing our own behavior.

Your own behavior provides an important source of information about your self. Daryl Bem's **self-perception theory** proposes that people may "come to know their own attitudes, emotions, and other internal states, partially by inferring them from observations of their own overt behavior and/or the circumstances in which this behavior occurs" (Bem, 1972, p. 5). If you observe yourself reacting calmly to an emergency, you may decide that you are a calm person. If, on the other hand, you feel yourself gasping, sweating, and trembling in the same situation, you might decide that you are an excitable person. Bem proposed that you look at what you are doing and infer a reason for that behavior, just as an outside observer would infer your reasons from observing your behavior. Suppose Gary begins talking in a singles bar with Carolyn, whom he has never met before. If he observes himself getting tongue-tied, flustered, and embarrassed, he may think, "Based on the way I'm reacting, I must really like her." He has inferred his positive attitude (liking) from observing his behavior.

We do not have "privileged insights" in the causes of our own behavior, Bem asserted, but follow the same procedures in explaining our own behavior as in explaining the behavior of someone else. People observe their behavior and the situational context in which it occurs in much the same way that they might observe the behavior of another person. Not all self-information is treated equally, though. People seem more likely to infer characteristics about themselves on the basis of what they *did* than on the basis of things that they did *not* do (Fazio et al., 1982).

overjustification effect:
This occurs when an external reward leads people to discount the importance of internal factors in their self-attributions.

The Overjustification Effect. Suppose that you have been doing unpaid volunteer work for a campus agency. While working as a volunteer, you may attribute your behavior mostly to *intrinsic* motivators such as altruism or enjoyment of the work. If funds should become available and you can now be paid, your self-attributions are likely to shift to include the payment, an extrinsic motivator, as part of the reason for your behavior. External rewards lead people to discount the importance of internal factors in their self-attributions (Lepper et al., 1973). As a result, you may come to value the work itself less than you had before. If the salary is later removed, part of your justification for engaging in the work is removed also—and you might quit.

The effect of rewards on motivation depends on how they are perceived. Rewards can be seen as controlling or can provide information and support autonomy (Deci & Ryan, 1987). When used in a controlling fashion rewards decrease intrinsic (internal) motivation (Pittman & Heller, 1987). Teachers who use rewards controllingly cause their students to have relatively low intrinsic motivation and low self-esteem (Deci et al., 1981). The informational use of reward, in contrast, can increase feelings of competency and self-determination. If a reward is seen as a bonus (providing information about a job well done) rather than a bribe (to control your behavior), it can enhance intrinsic motivation instead of interfering with it (Rosenfield et al., 1980). Teachers, parents, and business managers should take note.

Unawareness of Why We Do Things. If we are accurate in pinpointing the causes of our own behaviors, then we should be able to see through false information about ourselves that others may try to give us. But researchers have shown that people are often mistaken about the causes of their behavior. People's explanations of their own behavior may be based not on access to private information, but rather on their intuitive theories about the likely causes of that behavior. To provide evidence on this issue, Nisbett and Wilson (1977) systematically manipulated factors that influenced subjects' behavior and then asked the subjects to report what caused them to behave as they did. For example, the researchers systematically reinforced (by saying "uh-huh" or "good") certain types of verbal responses made by subjects.

This generally increased the frequency of these responses but, when asked, the subjects were not aware of this influence on their behavior. In general, subjects' reports of what had influenced their behavior (their reasons) showed little relationship to the researchers' objective analysis of factors that had really affected the subjects' behavior (the causes). In later chapters we will encounter other examples of people's unawareness of powerful influences on their behavior.

Biases in Autobiographical Memory

The Self as a Totalitarian Ego

We constantly receive information about ourselves — we get compliments or "constructive criticism" from friends, we see ourselves succeed or fail at various tasks. Each of us interprets and remembers this self-relevant information in terms of our own unique set of self schemas. But there are certain consistencies in the ways that everyone processes and remembers self-relevant information. Greenwald (1980) proposed that the self acts as a totalitarian ego that processes social information in a biased manner. He identified three major biases: egocentricity, cognitive conservatism, and the self-serving bias. I'll discuss the first two biases here, postponing the discussion of self-serving biases until the next section.

egocentricity:
Greenwald's term for the tendency for judgment and memory to be focused on the self.

Egocentricity describes the tendency for judgment and memory to be focused on the self. Each of us perceives events from our own unique perspective. We tend to assume that others see things the way we do and think and feel the same way too. This has been labeled the *false consensus bias* (Ross, Greene, & House, 1977; van der Plight, 1984). It is comforting to think that most others react as we do. We also see ourselves as causing others to act as they do, perhaps exaggerating our role in affecting their behavior.

Another instance of egocentricity involves taking the credit for group tasks. Recall the last time you worked on a group project. Did you contribute more than the other group members did? If you're like most of us, you probably remember that you contributed more, whether or not that was really the case. Most people show an egocentric bias in evaluating group tasks, giving themselves more credit for the outcome and recalling more of their input into the project than their coworkers' input (Thompson & Kelley, 1981). Researchers (Ross & Sicoly, 1979) asked married couples how much each spouse contributed to caring for the children, solving conflicts, making important decisions, and cleaning house. On average, each spouse claimed to have made the major contribution about 70 percent of the time. This is a logical impossibility of course; it reflects the self-centered nature of the egocentric bias.

This general tendency may grow as time passes. Burger and Rodman (1983) found that immediately after successful completion of a task people assigned more responsibility to their partners than to themselves. Three days later, however, the pattern reversed itself; people attributed more responsibility to themselves than to their partners, reflecting an egocentric bias. Apparently memory for the partner's performance faded more rapidly than did memory for one's own performance.

Cognitive Conservatism and the Hindsight Bias

cognitive conservatism: The tendency of the self to resist cognitive change.

Cognitive conservatism means that our self-concepts are resistant to change. People most often put themselves in situations likely to reinforce their existing self-schemas, seeking confirming information and avoiding situations that might yield inconsistent information. Of course, despite this tendency to resist change, our self-concept, attitudes, and values *do* change over time. When this happens, people maintain their image of consistency by distorting their memory of their earlier attitudes, remembering them as closer to their present attitudes than was actually the case. In a set of studies, Ross and his colleagues (1981) found that we are revisionist historians with respect to our autobiographies. After changing their subjects' attitudes, the researchers asked the subjects to report how frequently they had engaged in attitude-relevant behavior in the recent past. Subjects' estimates, it turned out, were biased in the direction of supporting their new attitudes. We rewrite our personal history to make ourselves seem very consistent. This is a variant of the hindsight bias discussed in Chapter 2.

The **Barnum Effect**

Barnum effect: People are likely to interpret a fake general personality description as an accurate individual description of their own characteristics.

Circus showman P. T. Barnum remarked that his shows were so popular because they contained "a little something for everybody." He also asserted that "There's a sucker born every minute." Subsequent research has shown that people can easily be duped into believing that general personality descriptions (having high *stereotype accuracy*) apply specifically to them. Focus 3-1 presents a general personality description that has been used in many studies. People who think this description was prepared on the basis of their own questionnaire responses tend to see it as very accurate (Ulrich et al., 1963). Several studies have found that people rate its accuracy for them at about 4.5 on a 1-to-5 scale on which 5 means "excellent" (Snyder & Shenkel, 1975).

People may even prefer a fake general description to a description that is truly based on their own responses. Sundberg (1955) had clinical psychologists prepare personality descriptions of individuals derived from their responses to a lengthy psychological test, the Minnesota Multiphasic Personality Inventory (MMPI). When given a choice between the profile derived from their responses and a fake, general profile, the majority of people rated the general one as a more accurate description of themselves! Men and women are equally susceptible to the Barnum effect (Snyder et al., 1977), but people who have an external locus of control orientation (feeling that they do not control their destinies) and who are more concerned with social desirability pressures, tend to be most susceptible (Mosher, 1965; Snyder & Larson, 1972).

We are particularly likely to accept a general description as accurate if we believe it is based on a lot of information, such as a psychological test or even astrological information. Astrology is big business in America: about

FOCUS 3-1

A Description That Fits Everyone

You have a strong need for other people to like you and admire you. You have a tendency to be critical of yourself. You have a great deal of unused capacity, which you have not turned to your advantage. While you have some personality weaknesses, you are generally able to compensate for them. Your sexual adjustment has presented some problems for you. Disciplined and controlled on the outside, you tend to be worrisome and insecure on the inside. At times you have serious doubts as to whether you have made the right decision or done the right things. You prefer a certain amount of change and variety and become dissatisfied when hemmed in by restrictions and limitations. You pride yourself as being an independent thinker and do not accept others' opinions without satisfactory proof. You have found it unwise to be too frank in revealing yourself to others. At times you are extroverted affable, and sociable, while at other times you are introverted, wary, and reserved. Some of your aspirations tend to be pretty unrealistic.

How accurate is this as a description of your own personality? Most people rate it as an accurate description of themselves; it has high stereotype accuracy. Most of us have strong needs to be liked, are sometimes self-critical, have some problems with sexual adjustment, at times feel insecure, and so on. Yet we are generally unaware of how similar our worries and weaknesses are to those of others. This lack of awareness may be what keeps fortune-tellers, astrologers, and palm readers in business. ❖

70 percent of our daily newspapers carry astrological columns and there are about 200,000 practicing astrologists (Glick et al., 1988). Ronald and Nancy Reagan apparently paid close attention to astrological signs while he was governor of California and later U.S. president. General descriptions, when supposedly based on astrological data, can appear quite impressive. Researchers found that a fake general description that was seen as a moderately accurate description of oneself when presented as a general sketch, was seen as more accurate when it was said to be an astrological description based on the person's month and year of birth, and most accurate when said to be based on the day, month, and year of birth (Snyder et al., 1976; Snyder et al., 1975).

Would people who believe in astrology be more susceptible to the Barnum effect than who don't believe in it? Glick and his colleagues (1988) presented high school students with general positive or negative personal descriptions. The students were told either that the description was based on their astrological data or that it was simply a list of traits that might or might not apply to them. As Figure 3-3 indicates, in general the students saw the positive descriptions as more accurate than the negative ones. Believers were more likely to accept any description, astrological or nonastrological, than were skeptics. And, most interestingly, believers were just as willing to accept a negative as a positive description when said to be based on astrological data, perhaps demonstrating a strong need to validate the

FIGURE 3-3

Astrology: Believers and Skeptics

The self-accuracy of general personality sketches as perceived by high school students when the descriptions were said to be based on individual astrological information or to be general descriptions.

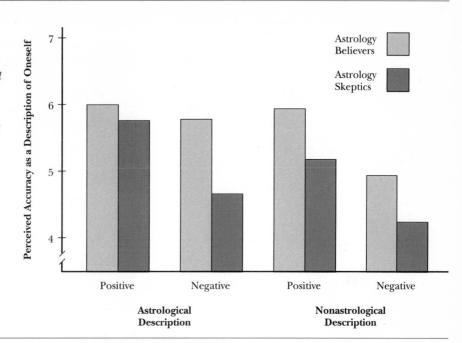

Source: Data from Glick, P. C., Gottesman, D., & Jolton, J. (1988). The fault is not in the stars: Susceptibility of skeptics and believers in astrology to the Barnum effect. *Personality and Social Psychology Bulletin, 15,* 572–583.

accuracy of astrology. An earlier study (Glick & Snyder, 1986) had found that believers judged target persons to be "very similar" to astrological horoscopes even after they had received disconfirming information indicating that this was not so. We see here a powerful example of a schema (a belief in astrology) distorting perception and memory in a schema-consistent manner.

A high level of stereotype accuracy is immensely valuable to fortune-tellers, palm readers, and astrologers (Hyman, 1981). If they know what most people who seek their services are like, then they are less apt to err in their evaluation of an individual. They can provide clients with general descriptions and clients who are believers are likely to interpret these as a specific description of themselves. For example, a French psychologist who posed as a mail-order astrologer and mailed out the identical general horoscope to everyone received more than two hundred "thank you's" praising his accuracy and perceptiveness (Snyder et al., 1977).

The Favorability Bias

Most people rate favorable self-descriptions as more accurate than unfavorable ones. But they also see favorable descriptions as more typical of "people in general" (Snyder & Schenkel, 1975). This tendency led one psychologist (O'Dell, 1972) to wonder whether the fake, favorable personality descriptions really are more accurate than descriptions derived from personality tests. As far as I know, no one has yet tested this possibility.

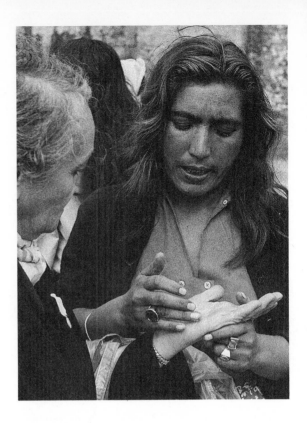

The social psychology of fortune telling. A fortune teller who has developed a high degree of stereotype accuracy and a confident manner is likely to appear quite insightful.

The Attribution of Emotions

Two Crucial Factors: Arousal and Cognitive Cues

You experience many different emotions: fear, love, hate, sorrow, joy, and so forth. How do you tell exactly which emotion you are experiencing? In particular, how do people interpret their emotional states in unusual situations when they can feel emotional physiological reactions but have no obvious label for the feelings?

During childhood, parents and others teach us to label our emotional states. Children learn to associate emotional terms with the psychological and physiological states they are experiencing at the time. Yet most research has indicated that there are more labels for emotion than there are different psychological states (Cannon, 1929), though some have questioned this assertion (Ekman et al., 1983). Under conditions of any strong emotion, physiological changes occur that are associated with the sympathetic nervous system. These include a slowing down of digestion, a diversion of more blood to the head and the extremities, pupil dilation, and a higher pulse rate. Given these general reactions, how do you decide exactly what emotion you are feeling?

Stanley Schachter (1964) proposed that the way we label our emotional states depends on two factors: (1) the existence of a general state of physiological arousal, and (2) cognitive cues in the environment that tell us how we should be feeling. In most everyday situations, these two pieces of information go hand in hand. We feel physiologically aroused and it is obvious to us what caused the arousal, so then we make an emotional self-attribution.

Suppose you walk into a yard and suddenly encounter a large, snarling dog. Physiological arousal occurs: Your heart pounds, your hands sweat, and your pupils dilate. What caused this arousal? The dog, of course. The environment provides a clear cue for the arousal, and you quickly label the state "fear." However, under some conditions of arousal the environment may provide no clear cues for why arousal occurs. What do we do then? If the situation is ambiguous, individuals may look to others or seek additional information to determine the correct label for their emotional state.

An experiment by Schachter and Singer (1962) illustrates how this process may work. In a study supposedly examining the effects of an injection of a vitamin supplement on vision, the researchers gave some subjects an injection of epinephrine, a synthetic form of adrenaline that produces physiological arousal, while the others received a placebo (having no physiological effect). Some subjects given the adrenaline were told that the vitamin supplement could produce arousal. They had a clear explanation (cue) for their arousal and did not have to search further for an explanation. Other subjects were given no explanation. These aroused subjects should have begun an attributional search, trying to identify the source of their arousal.

Some subjects were placed in the waiting room with another student who had supposedly been given the same injection (actually he was an accomplice of the experimenter) and acted euphoric—happy and silly. Aroused subjects who had no simple explanation for their own arousal behaved as if they, too, were euphoric; their interpretation of their own emotion was influenced by the behavior of the accomplice. However, subjects who had been told that the drug would produce arousal expressed less euphoria. They didn't need the cues provided by the accomplice because they had already used the cues provided by the experimenter. The subjects who had been injected with the placebo substances expressed intermediate degrees of euphoria.

In another phase of the experiment, different subjects received injections and had to fill out an annoying personal questionnaire while waiting with an accomplice who became furious, ripped up the questionnaire, and stormed out. The subjects who had received the injection of epinephrine and who were not told what physiological reactions to expect acted angrier than those who had received only the placebo injection. Hence, in ambiguous situations your interpretation of your own emotion may be influenced by how you see others react.

Other researchers have not always been able to replicate these findings. Marshall and Zimbardo (1979) found that subjects injected with epinephrine and exposed to a happy confederate did not feel happy. If anything, they felt slightly more unhappy than those who received the placebo. The results of this study and others (Maslach, 1979) suggest that unexplained

FIGURE 3-4

Basic Conditions of the
Schachter and Singer Study
on the Misattribution of
Emotion

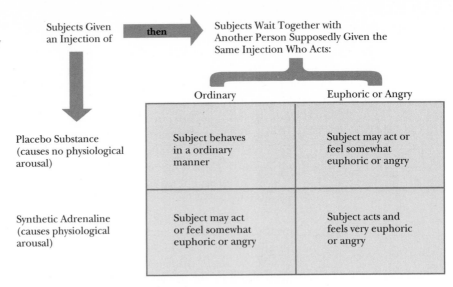

Source: Based upon Schachter, S., & Singer, J. E. (1962). Cognitive, social and physiological determinants of emotional state. *Psychological Review, 69.* 379–399.

arousal is a negative feeling and that people will search for information from which to make self-attributions. The resulting attributions are more likely to be negative than positive.

Even pain can be affected by cognitive cues. Nisbett and Schachter (1966) had college students undergo electric shocks. Some of them were told to expect side effects from a pill they had taken earlier. The side effects they were told to anticipate were all symptoms of general arousal. Actually, the pill was a placebo with no physiological effects. Subjects who could attribute their arousal to the pill rated the pain of the shocks as significantly less severe than subjects who were not told to expect side effects from the pill. Furthermore, several persons who expected the side effects were willing to take higher shock than the machine could deliver; none of the persons in the control condition were willing to do this. Hence, if a person can attribute arousal to a pill rather than to fear of shock, the shock itself becomes less feared and (apparently) less painful.

Clearly, what we believe affects how we feel and how we act. When confronted with an arousing situation, individuals who believe they are fearful are likely to label their arousal state as fear. Individuals who believe they are brave but somewhat excitable may label the same arousal state as excitement. The behaviors of these two persons will be different because their self-attributions differ. Cognitive processes can have a strong impact on our perceived emotions.

False Feedback about Emotional Reactions

False Feedback and Preferences. Difficulties in interpreting one's physiological reactions may be greater if a person receives false information about his bodily reactions. For example, Valins (1966) had male college students look at slides of naked women while their heartbeat rates were recorded. Subjects were told that their amplified heartbeat would be audible, but to pay no attention to it. The heartbeats that they heard were actually prerecorded, timed to increase in rate when they viewed certain slides. The bogus heart-rate feedback had a distinct effect on the subjects' judgments of attractiveness. Students rated as most attractive those slides toward which they thought their heartbeats had reacted by increasing. Valins ran another experiment in which subjects were led to believe that their heartbeats slowed down in response to certain slides. Here again, subjects rated as most attractive those slides toward which they thought their heartbeats had reacted, this time by slowing down.

Men who thought that their heartbeat rates changed in response to certain photos came to like those photos more than others. The subjects used their internal sensations—or what they *thought* were their internal sensations—as sources of information about the causes of their own behavior. We seek in this way to make sense out of our actions as well as our bodily states. A later study (cited in Valins, 1970) found that even after subjects had been debriefed and told that the heartbeats they heard were not their own, they continued to prefer the same photos. Apparently they had developed other reasons to justify their supposed preferences and these reasons continued to be influential.

Are some people more sensitive to internal cues than others? In another study, Valins (1967) found that men who were classified as unemotional by personality tests made less use of the information about their heartbeat rates than did men whose responses to the tests classified them as emotional. The more emotional subjects chose more of the pictures associated with the changed (either increased or decreased) heart rate. More recent research indicates that people who are more attentive to their internal bodily processes show a greater susceptibility to misattribution effects (Brockner & Swap, 1983).

misattribution therapy:
A therapeutic technique that changes the focus of a person's attributions in a self-enhancing way.

Misattribution Therapy

Changing the focus of someone's attributions (such as from an internal to an external may have considerable therapeutic value. The success of desensitization therapy may involve changing cognitions about one's internal state. For example, Valins and Ray (1967) conducted two experiments with subjects who were afraid of snakes. Their subjects were given sham (ineffective) "therapy" and also heard prerecorded heartbeats that they thought were their own. People who thought that they heard their hearts become calmer in the presence of snakes, supposedly because of the therapeutic techniques, were

Misattribution therapy for fear of snakes. Researchers found that people who were very afraid of snakes became more likely to approach and pick up snakes after they had received false feedback that their bodies were responding more calmly to the presence of snakes.

significantly more likely to approach and touch a snake than were subjects who did not hear their hearts apparently become calmer. More recent work suggests that the misattribution effect may work for people with relatively low fear levels but not for highly fearful people (Conger et al., 1976). This is a serious limitation, since people in therapy are often at high levels of emotion.

Attributions about what caused improvement in therapy can also change. After significant behavior change has been achieved through a combination of psychotherapy and drugs (such as tranquilizers or energizers), when the drugs are withdrawn the improvement in behavior also may disappear (perhaps to the surprise of the therapist). The therapist attributes the client's improvement to genuine change the client has made during therapy (stable internal factors), whereas the client may attribute at least part of the change to the drugs (unstable external factors). Hence, when the drugs are taken away, part of the reason for getting better is also removed. More lasting change could be achieved, we can predict, if the client makes internal self-attributions, perceiving the changes as internal and self-caused (not due to drugs or other external factors).

This proposition can be tested by giving people new information about what caused changes in their behavior. In one study, individuals who had originally been led to attribute changes to external factors (drugs taken in the experiment) later were told that the drugs were inactive placebos and the change had been due to their own efforts. These people maintained the changed behavior more strongly than did subjects who continued to attribute their changed behavior to the drugs (Davison et al., 1973). Although there is experimental evidence that changing the focus of attributions can lead to longer-lasting behavioral changes, the clinical significance of such effects needs to be more fully determined before actual treatment programs based on these attributional principles are developed (Harvey & Galvin, 1984).

In a related manner, emotional reactions to a stimulus can be reduced by giving people a neutral explanation for their arousal symptoms (e.g., that the symptoms were caused by a placebo pill). Olson (1988) had college students read a prepared speech in front of a video camera, a task that makes most students anxious. Some subjects were told that while they read the speech they would be receiving "subliminal noise" through earphones (noise outside the range of conscious hearing). They were told that the noise would make them feel somewhat tense or unpleasantly aroused, thus giving them a neutral explanation (the subliminal noise) for the arousal caused by making the speech. No subliminal noise was actually used but, as predicted, these subjects showed less anxiety (fewer speech errors, stammers, or stutters) during their speech than did subjects who had not been given this expectation about the noise. In a follow-up study Olson and Ross (1988) showed that subjects who thought the subliminal noise would have a strong impact on their arousal symptoms made fewer speech errors (showing a stronger misattribution effect) than did those who thought the noise would have a weaker impact.

Misattribution Effects: An Overview

Results of several decades of research indicate that the misattribution of emotions occurs, although our emotions may not be quite as pliable as Schachter (1964) suggested. Misattribution effects have been found for many emotions: anxiety, fear, pain, aggression, attraction, sexual responses, guilt, and humor (Cotton, 1981; Olson, 1988). The major research problem has been to create experimentally the necessary precondition for misattribution: high arousal, situational cues that lead people to misattributions about the source of the arousal, and a plausible misattribution source (Reisenzein, 1983).

Our analysis of social cognition and attribution in Chapter 2 emphasized that, at a very basic level, people are motivated to understand both themselves and their environment. To do so, one must make causal analyses of one's own feelings and behaviors. These attributional judgments have consequences not only for cognitive aspects of the self (for how one interprets one's actions, as we saw in Chapter 2), but also for affective aspects of the self, such as emotions (Olson, 1990)

SELF-ESTEEM

Self-Discrepancies

Earlier you wrote down those characteristics that most typified yourself: your actual self-concept. But there are several other senses of self as well. If you feel energetic, write down four more lists of characteristics: (1) The self that you would like to be, embodying all your hopes and goals (*ideal self*); (2) The characteristics that important others (e.g., your parents) wish you would attain (*ideal self-others*); (3) The characteristics that you feel you ought to have in terms of a sense of duty, responsibility, and obligations to others (*ought self*); and (4) The characteristics that important others feel you ought to have (*ought self-others*). These four lists represent your **self-guides**, or personal standards.

All of us have some discrepancy between our actual self-concept and our self-guides. E. Tory Higgins and his colleagues (Higgins et al., 1986; Hig-

self-guides:
The personal standards that we all possess: the ideal self, the ideal self-others, the ought self, and the ought self-others.

self-discrepancies:
Differences between one's self-concept and self-guides.

gins, 1989) have proposed that the amount of emotion caused by these **self-discrepancies** will depend on the magnitude of the discrepancy and your awareness of it (remember the availability heuristic in Chapter 2). Large actual/ideal discrepancy will batter one's self-esteem, leading to dejection, dissatisfaction, depression, and the like. A large actual/ought discrepancy is more likely to produce guilt, shame, anxiety, or resentment.

Most of the time people handle discrepancies between self-concept and self-guides pretty well. But if the discrepancy is too great, or the person's awareness of it is particularly acute, the result might be major clinical disorders centering around anxiety (actual/ought discrepancies) or depression (actual/ideal discrepancies).

Enhancing Self-Esteem

self-esteem:
The evaluative part of the self-concept.

The evaluative part of the self-concept is **self-esteem.** William James (1890/1981) defined self-esteem as one's successes divided by one's aspirations. We have already seen that while people are often motivated to obtain accurate information about themselves via social comparison processes or by observing their own behavior, at other times they may be motivated to strengthen their self-esteem by seeing themselves in a particularly positive light. As Markus (1980, p. 127) noted, the "notion that we will go to great lengths to protect our ego or preserve our self-esteem is . . . probably one of the great psychological truths." James suggested that one needs only to lower one's aspirations to increase self-esteem, but things are not that simple, as we will see (Goethals, 1986). Many cognitive operations actually serve two purposes: making one feel better about oneself (enhancing self-esteem) and improving the impression one gives to others (self-presentation). Though the dividing line between these motives is often not distinct, in this section I will discuss behaviors predominantly associated with self-esteem, while self-presentational motives will be analyzed in the next section.

Self-Enhancing vs. Self-Verifying Information

self-consistency theory:
The theory that people prefer social information that confirms their self-concept, providing self-verification.

self-enhancement theory:
The theory that people seek information that will enhance their self-concept.

People's self-concepts can affect the kind of social information they seek. It seems logical that people with positive self-concepts will seek out feedback that is positive and will see this information as accurate, fitting their positive view of themselves. But what about people with negative self-esteem? **Self-consistency theory** predicts that people prefer social information that confirms their self-concept, providing self-verification (Swann, 1987). Information that confirms one's self-conceptions is likely to be seen as especially trustworthy, diagnostic, and accurate. From this perspective, people with low self-esteem should be most comfortable with negative feedback that confirms their negative view of themselves. **Self-enhancement theory,** in contrast, argues that people seek information that will enhance their self-concept. This view proposes that people with low self-esteem will seek and prefer positive social feedback that may improve their self-concept, even though it may conflict with their current negative view of themselves.

Both theories may be partially correct. Swann and his co-workers (1987) found that cognitive reactions to self-feedback were driven mostly by a desire for self-verification, while emotional reactions to the feedback were related to how positive it was. College students were told that they were in a study of first impressions based on nonverbal information. Subjects were to be evaluated by another student who would observe them giving a speech behind a soundproof, one-way mirror. After giving the speech, half of the subjects (randomly determined) received positive feedback: they were told that the observer saw them as self-confident and competent. The remaining subjects received negative feedback: the observer noted that they did not appear self-confident, seemed to have some doubts about their social competence, and probably felt somewhat uncomfortable and anxious around other people. Each subject then evaluated the accuracy of the feedback and mood was assessed with a measure of depression, anxiety, and hostility.

The researchers predicted that cognitive reactions to the feedback would differ according to subjects' self-esteem (which had been measured earlier in a different setting). They predicted that high self-esteem subjects would rate positive feedback as most accurate but low self-esteem subjects who received negative feedback would rate it as most accurate. For emotional reactions, in contrast, all subjects who received the positive feedback should feel better, regardless of their level of self-esteem. As Figure 3-5 demonstrates, this is what occurred.

FIGURE 3-5

Cognitive and Affective Reactions to Positive and Negative Feedback about Oneself as a Function of Self-Esteem.

People with high self-esteem see positive feedback as more accurate, those with low self-esteem see negative feedback as more accurate. Regardless of self-esteem level, people feel better (positive affect) after receiving positive feedback.

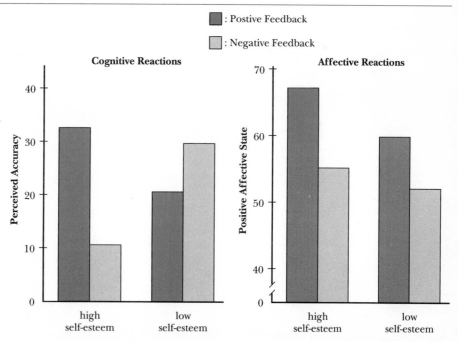

Source: Data from Swann, W. B. Jr., Griffin, J. J., Predmore, S. C., & Gaines, B. (1987). The cognitive affective crossfire: When self-consistency confronts self-enhancement. *Journal of Personality and Social Psychology, 52,* 881–889.

Thus, even though low self-esteem subjects saw negative self-feedback as accurate, they didn't like it: they became more depressed, anxious, and hostile after receiving it. Negative information that is expected is seen as valid, but self-enhancing information is more satisfying (Shrauger, 1975). These findings that cognitive and emotional reactions were independent of each other are provocative and merit further study.

Self-Serving Biases

self-serving bias:
The general tendency to interpret information in a way that supports a positive self-image.

Each of us is motivated to perceive himself or herself as a competent, helpful, good person. The **self-serving bias** (also called the ego-defensive bias) refers to the general tendency to interpret information in a way that supports this positive self-image. This bias is relevant both to one's view of oneself (self-concept) and to the impression one gives to others (self-presentation). Though these two aspects are often difficult to separate, I will focus mostly on self-concept aspects here and on self-presentations in the next section. One way to preserve one's self-image is to take credit for successes, making a self-attribution, and avoid blame for failures, attributing the failures to others or to bad luck. The self-serving bias may be particularly visible in sports, where successes (wins) are clear public events that are strongly reinforced with money, fame, and adulation (Carver et al., 1980). Self-serving defensive attributions are most likely to occur: (1) when an individual's behavior is public, observed by others; (2) when an individual had a free choice in deciding to act and feels responsible for the outcome of the action; and (3) when the person is highly involved in the activity (Weary, 1980).

In situations where a defensive attribution would be seen negatively by others (as accepting undue credit or unfairly avoiding blame), or would lead to unrealistic expectations about one's future behaviors, people may accept equal responsibility for positive and negative outcomes (Weary et al., 1982). These attributions are still self-serving in a self-presentational sense because they are attempts to make one look good (as modestly declining credit for success or bravely shouldering the responsibility for failure). However, privately people still accept more responsibility for positive than for negative outcomes (Figure 3-6). Research (reviewed by Greenwald & Pratkanis, 1984; Schlenker, 1985) suggests that private self-evaluations may be just as biased as public self-presentations are. For example, in Dutton's studies on reverse discrimination, which will be discussed in Chapter 11, people whose self-image of equalitarianism had been questioned were likely to take tokenistic actions to convince themselves, as well as others, that they were not really prejudiced. In effect, people's concerns about the impressions they give (self-presentations) bias the public causal attributions they make, while self-esteem needs bias their private attributions (Arkin et al., 1980).

self-esteem maintenance:
Maintaining positive self-esteem via processes of reflection and comparison.

Self-Esteem Maintenance

One's self-esteem can be maintained by reflection and comparison (Tesser, 1988). People can raise their self-esteem through **reflection** by pointing out

reflection:
A way of raising self-esteem by pointing out the outstanding accomplishments of others with whom one is associated.

self-evaluation maintenance model:
Tesser's model of how people maintain positive self-evaluations by comparing themselves with others who do less well or associating themselves with people who do very well.

the outstanding accomplishments of others with whom they are associated in some way (a classmate, a parent, one's children, a neighbor, a co-worker). People can enhance self-esteem through *comparison* by comparing their performance with others' performance on the same task.

What is the best way to maintain a positive self-evaluation? According to Tesser's (1988) **self-evaluation maintenance model,** the relevance of another's performance to one's self-definition (self-schema) determines the relative importance of the reflection and comparison processes. If the behavior is highly relevant to one's self-definition, then the comparison process will be most important. Positive self-esteem could be maintained by comparison with someone who does less well (downward social comparison). Suppose that you and your friend Casey take the Graduate Record Exam (GRE) in hopes of going to graduate school (highly relevant behavior). If Casey scores much higher than you, comparison with Casey threatens your self-esteem. To prevent this loss you can do a variety of things. You might reduce the closeness of your relationship with Casey or focus on ways the two of you are different. Or you could change your self-definition, deciding that grad school is not important to you, thereby reducing the relevance of Casey's performance for you. As self-relevance is reduced, the reflection process becomes more important and, as a consequence, you now might be able to gain in self-esteem through your association with Casey's achievement. Hence, being outperformed by a psychologically close other (e.g., a friend) can lower self-esteem when self-relevance is high (via the comparison process), but can also raise self-evaluation (via the reflection process) when self-relevance is low.

FIGURE 3-6

Self-Serving Attributions

Attributions of responsibility to oneself for positive and negative outcomes, as affected by whether the attribution will be public (known to others) or private.

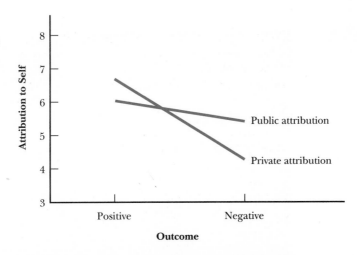

Source: From Weary, G., Harvey, J.H., Schwieger, P., Olson, C. T., Perloff, R., & Pritchard, S. (1982). Self-presentation and the moderation of self-serving attributional biases. *Social Cognition, 1,* 156. Copyright The Guilford Press. Reprinted by permission.

basking in reflected glory:
Through reflection, people attempt to raise their own self-evaluation by pointing out the outstanding accomplishments of others with whom they are associated in some way.

This type of reflection process has been referred to as *BIRGing*—**Basking In Reflected Glory** (Cialdini et al., 1976). For issues of low self-relevance, the better the performance and the closer the association with the person, the more powerful this reflection process will be. In a clever field study, researchers monitored the clothing worn by students in large introductory psychology courses in seven universities on the Mondays after Saturday college football games. They found that students were much more likely to wear school-identifying apparel after a win than after a loss. In addition, students used "we" much more often in describing wins ("we won") than in describing losses ("they lost"). BIRGing can occur even when the connection is a very superficial one: most college students do not contribute directly to their college football team's success. Even the coincidence of having the same month and day of birth as another person leads people to emphasize the connection if the other person is successful (Cialdini & DeNicholas, 1989). This tendency can be explained by *balance theory* (Chapter 8), which predicts that observers tend to evaluate "connected" or related objects similarly. The tendency to BIRG is an attempt to gain esteem from those who see the connection between you and the successful object.

As an example of these processes, Tesser, Campbell, and Smith (1984) found that children named as friends those classmates whose performance was better than their own on activities of little relevance to their self-concept, but was somewhat inferior to their own on more relevant activities. In a related vein, Tesser and Campbell (1982) found that college women evaluated a friend's performance most positively when it was on a task of low self-relevance (there was little need to make an unflattering comparison). A stranger's performance, in contrast, was regarded more positively when it occurred on a relevant task (Figure 3-7).

BIRGing after the Super Bowl. Fans of the San Francisco 49ers bask in the reflected glory of their team's victory in the 1990 Super Bowl.

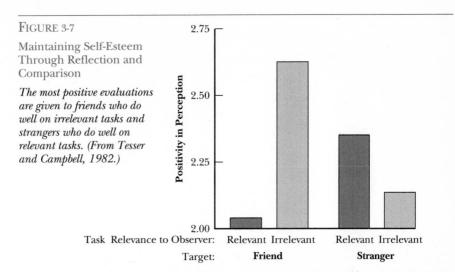

<figure>

FIGURE 3-7

Maintaining Self-Esteem Through Reflection and Comparison

The most positive evaluations are given to friends who do well on irrelevant tasks and strangers who do well on relevant tasks. (From Tesser and Campbell, 1982.)

Task Relevance to Observer: Relevant   Irrelevant   Relevant   Irrelevant

Target: **Friend**   **Stranger**

</figure>

Source: From A. Tesser & J. Campbell (1982). Self-evaluation maintenance and the perception of friends and strangers. *Journal of Personality, 50,* 261–279. Copyright © 1982 by Duke University Press. Reprinted by permission.

Upward Social Comparison for Self-Improvement

Individuals who are striving to improve themselves may compare themselves with others who are performing at higher levels (Wheeler et al., 1982). Though there is little research on upward social comparison, it appears that people who are hard-driving, competitive, and highly motivated to achieve a goal are particularly likely to make upward comparisons (Matthews & Siegel, 1983). Thus if you are eager to become a campus leader in the future, you are likely to compare yourself frequently with present campus leaders.

Downward Social Comparison for Self-Enhancement

We have seen that people can increase their feelings of well-being by comparing themselves with others less fortunate than they. Such downward comparisons are particularly likely to be made by individuals who feel threatened or who have low self-esteem (Wills, 1981). In some cases, individuals may try deliberately to decrease the well-being of others so that the individual can feel better in comparison. Patterns of scapegoating, the derogation of victims, prejudice, and aggression toward minority groups (Chapters 10 and 11), can all stem from downward social comparisons to protect self-image in threatening conditions. In Wills's (1981, p. 268) words, "People who are unhappy like to see others who are unhappy. They may not necessarily go out of their way to produce unhappiness in others, but sometimes they do." Other types of personal threat, including job disruption, marital conflict, and serious medical problems, can also motivate downward social comparison as people seek to compare themselves with others who are even more unfortunate than they are, thereby reducing their own distress (Menaghan, 1982; Wood et al., 1985; Wood, 1989).

Self-Handicapping

A story is told of the famous chess player Deschapelles. When he was no longer certain of beating all challengers, he refused to have a match at all unless his opponent would accept "pawn and move" (a one-piece advantage plus the opening gambit). Then, if Deschapelles lost he would claim it was because of the odds. This strategy came to be known as the "Deschapelles coup" (Berglas, 1985, p. 235).

The possibility of looking incompetent is ego-threatening to most of us. When people worry that their earlier successes were due to luck, they may fear failure at an important upcoming task. As a result, they may resort to a **self-handicapping** strategy (Jones & Berglas, 1978), acquiring a handicap (e.g., by not practicing, using drugs, getting drunk, not trying hard) before or during the ego-threatening event. Acquiring a handicap allows one to discount the role of low ability as a cause for failure because another possible cause, the handicap, is also present. For example, a student who is unsure how he will perform on the Graduate Record Examination might go out drinking the night before the exam. Then if he performs poorly the cause will be ambiguous: The outcome could be attributed to his hangover—an unstable factor—instead of his lack of ability, a stable factor (Harvey & Weary, 1984). The notion of self-handicapping blends concepts from attribution theory (Chapter 2) and the desire to manage the impressions we give to others (Arkin & Baumgardner, 1985). Our chess player Deschapelles was able to await challengers and then structure the terms of matches he would play. It seems as though he was able to "quit while he was ahead." He would compete, but only on his terms, and he was happy to rest on his laurels if potential challengers refused to accept those terms.

The development of a questionnaire measuring self-handicapping tendencies allowed researchers to study self-handicapping in some interesting situations. Rhodewalt et al. (1984) found evidence of self-handicapping among competitive athletes. Members of the Princeton swim team who were low and high on self-handicapping tendencies were found to practice about the same amount before an unimportant swim meet, but before a very important swim meet the high self-handicappers practiced much less than their low self-handicapping teammates. A similar effect on pre-tournament practice was found by studying pro golfers.

The data are not yet definitive on whether the motivation behind self-handicapping is only to give a better impression to others, or whether there is a motive to deceive oneself as well by avoiding blows to one's self-esteem. Jones and Berglas's (1978) pioneering study found that self-handicapping occurred in both public and private situations, suggesting that both types of motivation were present. Our current knowledge suggests that the main motivations are to protect the impression one gives to others (public) and to maintain our illusion of control over important life events (a private motivation) (Arkin & Baumgardner, 1985).

self-handicapping:
Acquiring a handicap before an ego-threatening event so that subsequent failure can be blamed on the handicap.

One could also try to protect one's image by claiming, after a failure occurred, to have been under a handicap such as suffering from depression or test anxiety. This is somewhat different from situations in which one actively acquires a handicap (by getting drunk, for example) before the event occurs. Smith, Snyder, and Handelsman (1982) found evidence of both processes. Test-anxious people reported high anxiety (an unstable factor) when it was a reasonable explanation for poor performance on an intelligence test. When anxiety was not a reasonable explanation, in contrast, test-anxious subjects reported reduced effort (again, an unstable factor) as the reason for their poor performance. The poor performances were blamed on psychological factors (test anxiety, low effort) in order to avoid stable negative self-attributions (lack of intelligence). Low effort during the exam is an instance of self-handicapping, while using test anxiety as a later excuse for poor performance can best be seen as a type of self-serving attribution (Leary & Sheppard, 1985). I'll have more to say about excuses later.

There are other possible self-serving attributions as well. The person may claim that the situation was unique and that his poor performanace should not be generalized to reflect his competence (Mehlman & Snyder, 1985). Or individuals may report more adversity in their background (a broken home, a difficult childhood) as a justification for failure (DeGree & Snyder, 1985).

What if self-handicapping becomes a prevalent life-style? Chronic drug abuse might be one consequence. Steven Berglas (1988), one of the originators of the concept, suggested that many patterns of alcohol abuse stem from a self-handicapping life-style typified by defense-oriented behavior aimed at preserving a tenuous sense of self-regard. "I could be a success and reach my great potential if it just wasn't for this drinking problem." Berglas proposed that if self-handicappers can be led to attribute their previous successful performances to internal factors such as ability, planning, or hard work, then the need for self-handicapping may decrease.

Denying Negative Information

People tend to remember information that fits their schemas and forget or distort conflicting information. If one's self-schemas contain mostly positive attributes, negative information doesn't fit well. Hence, past failures and shortcomings are likely to be forgotten and negative feedback is likely to be denied or distorted. This tendency will be strongest for people with positive self-concepts, those whose self-schema contains positive attributes. For people having negative self-concepts, in contrast, failure and negative feedback may fit quite nicely into their self-schema. For these people, success experiences would be schema-inconsistent and difficult to accept.

Though people are usually motivated to forget past failures, when they are trying to improve themselves they may exaggerate negative events in the past. Hoping that they have changed, these people are invested in remembering how bad off they used to be. For example, Conway and Ross (1985) found that students who had completed a study-skills program exaggerated how poorly they had studied before joining the program, thereby convincing themselves that the program had been worthwhile.

Self-Handicapping as a Life-style: Gary Hart and the "Self-Defeating Psychiatric Disorder"

"I'm a proud man and I'm proud of what I've accomplished . . . . I'm not a beaten man; I'm an angry and defiant man . . .(U)nder present circumstances [where the press is making me the issue] this campaign cannot go on. I refuse to submit my family . . . friends . . . and myself to further rumors and gossip. It's . . . an intolerable situation. I believe I would have been a successful candidate. And I know I could have been a very good President . . . But apparently now we'll never know."

Senator Gary Hart, May 8, 1987, upon withdrawing as a candidate for the Democratic presidential nomination.

Within weeks of defying a *New York Times* reporter to "put a tail on me" when asked about his alleged womanizing, Senator Gary Hart, the undisputed front-runner for the 1988 Democratic presidential nomination, canceled scheduled campaign stops and met Donna Rice in a Washington, D.C. townhouse. The liaison was observed by reporters and the furor that erupted forced Hart's defiant withdrawal from the campaign in May 1987. Months after his withdrawal Hart reentered the campaign, claiming that "I can't be hurt, and I know no fear." He also asserted "Just as challenge and insecurity frighten most people, security and safety frighten me."

Steven Berglas (1987; 1988) suggested that Hart's seemingly poor judgment might be an instance of a self-handicapping life-style. If Hart was frightened by security and, despite months of humiliation stemming from his involvement with Rice, was certain that he could not be hurt politically by the event, he must derive psychological benefits from being embroiled in controversy or beseiged by problems, Berglas proposed. The notion of self-handicapping demonstrates precisely how and why ostensibly self-defeating actions, problematic situations, and obvious impediments to success can, on occasion, protect and sustain a lofty, even arrogant, self-image for those who "suffer" them. By engaging in self-handicapping behaviors following success and prior to any further assessment of the attributes thought responsible for that success, the self-handicapper can protect a highly favorable but fragile self-image from the implications of negative feedback.

Berglas proposed that Hart's pattern of behaviors represented a variation of the diagnosis of "self-defeating personality disorder" (American Psychiatric Association, 1987). Hart demonstrated the "self-protective" subtype of this disorder, Berglas asserted, because of three factors. First, he chose a situation that would lead to failure and disappointment — the liaison with Ms. Rice in Washington as well as allowing himself to be photographed partying with her on the yacht *Monkey Business*. Second, the situation closely followed a personal achievement — the alleged affair occurred less than a week after a crucial poll had certified his front-runner status. Third, he failed as a result to accomplish a task (winning the nomination) despite a demonstrated ability to do so.

In his withdrawal speech, and in subsequent speeches, Hart claimed he was the victim of press harassment. By blaming a hostile press for his withdrawal, Berglas speculated, Hart secured the ultimate self-handicapping victory "quitting while ahead." Far from "self-destructing," Hart's withdrawal let him preserve the self-image of competence because he made it appear as though any problems he encountered were caused by an external handicap — journalistic harassment. He could argue that the press, not his character or lack of ability, cost him the nomination. And he could maintain unchallenged the self-image that "I would have been a successful candidate and . . . I could have been a very good President."

Clearly, Berglas's speculations do not *prove* that Hart was driven by self-handicapping motives. Nevertheless, they provide an interesting example of how this tendency may play an important role in one's life-style. ❖

Did Gary Hart demonstrate a self-defeating personality style?

excuses:
Explanations designed to maintain a positive self-image and a sense of control.

illusion of control:
People believe that they have more control over their destinies than is actually the case.

Compensating for Shortcomings

Another way to protect the self-concept is to compensate for one's shortcomings by de-emphasizing their importance while emphasizing the importance of areas in which one excels. The good athlete who is a poor student is likely to rate athletics high and academics low in importance to her. The good student who is a poor athlete is likely to see things just the opposite. People tend to rate as most important those positive traits they think characterize themselves (Lewicki, 1983). In a similar vein, when individuals rate how well or poorly they perform in various roles (as son or daughter, friend, student), those roles they see as most important are the ones in which they do well (Hoelter, 1983). If you experience failure in some roles, say as a student or an athlete, you can shore up your self-esteem by looking at other roles: "Well, at least I'm a nice person and a good friend and, after all, that's what's most important in life."

Making Excuses

When faced with a negative personal outcome (e.g., failure), people often make **excuses** that shift causal attributions to sources less central to their sense of self. C. R. Snyder and his co-workers (1983) identified three common types of excuses: (1) "I didn't do it"—using denial to lessen one's apparent responsibility for the outcome; (2) "It wasn't so bad"—reinterpreting the outcome in less negative terms; (3) "Yes, but . . ."—providing other reasons to explain the outcome. Excuses are designed to maintain a positive self-image and sense of control (Snyder & Higgins, 1988).

Looking back at the attributional theories discussed in the last chapter, we can see that excuse-makers often attempt to manipulate the central attributional concepts of locus, controllability, and intentionality (Weiner et al., 1987): It wasn't me; I couldn't help it; I didn't mean to. Kelley's dimensions of consensus, consistency, and distinctiveness (Figure 2-2) are also relevant. The excuse-maker can manipulate consensus by claiming that it happens to everyone else too (high consensus). He could lessen consistency attributions by asserting that he has succeeded at this task many other times (low consistency for failure in this situation). He might stress the high distinctiveness of this negative outcome by emphasizing his personal strengths in other areas (Snyder & Harris, 1987).

Do excuses work? Yes, they do, according to Snyder and Higgins (1988), at least when they do not become a prevalent life-style. Their review of the research literature led them to the conclusion that excuses are a "complex, serious, and demonstrably effective aspect" of the coping process.

Illusions: Adaptive and Maladaptive

The Illusion of Control

It is comforting to believe that we can control our own destinies. Perhaps as a consequence, people often deceive themselves into thinking that they have more control than they really do. Superstitious behavior during sporting events is one example. The habitual gambler who convinces himself he has figured out a "sure thing" and bets his whole paycheck on a horse race is a painful instance. We often use irrelevant information to increase our feelings of control. Thus, in games of pure chance people tend to bet more against a nervous opponent than a confident one, they value a lottery ticket they chose themselves more than one that was given to them, and they feel more confident and bet more when they have had prior practice in the game (Langer, 1975; 1977). In a game of pure chance, none of these factors can affect one's chances of winning, but people behave as if they do. The illusion of control is greater when more skill-related cues are present, even when they are irrelevant (Wortman, 1975).

Perceived Control and Depression

One of the major mental health problems in America today is depression. Estimates are that at any given time, about 15 percent of the U.S. population are experiencing some depressive symptoms such as sleep disturbances, loss of appetite, exhaustion, or an inability to function at one's usual level of enjoyment and energy (Rehm & O'Hara, 1979). Since a major component of depression is the way that one perceives oneself and others, attributional analyses may shed some light on this problem.

A prime reason for self-serving biases is to maintain a positive self-image and high self-esteem. While the term *bias* suggests that there is something undesirable about ego-defensiveness, ego-defensive biases may serve a valuable function. Nondepressed persons seem to avoid feelings of helplessness and maintain the illusion of control via ego-defensive attributions; chronically depressed persons do not (Abramson et al., in press). Alloy and Abramson (1982) found that nondepressed students overestimated how much control they had over desirable events (winning money, for example) that were actually uncontrollable; depressed students more accurately assessed their amount of control over the events.

The illusion of control in action. Many people have elaborate schemes for selecting the lottery numbers they play, hoping to establish some control over this random event.

A growing number of studies have investigated how comparison of oneself to others relates to depression. Depressed people, perhaps anxious because they feel a lack of control over life events, are highly motivated to engage in social comparison and are very sensitive to social-comparison feedback (Weary et al., 1987). This feedback is likely to be interpreted negatively, heightening the depressed person's sense of hopelessness and low self-esteem (Beck et al., 1979). Depressed people may also be less likely than others to utilize downward social comparison with less-fortunate others as a means of self-enhancement (Alloy & Ahrens, 1987), though other research suggests that if they do use downward social comparison, it may make them feel better (Gibbons, 1986). Depressed people also show less false consensus bias than nondepressed people do (Tabachnik et al., 1983). In general, then, depressed people fail to adopt illusions that would allow them to see themselves and their environment in a more positive light.

Analyzing college students' attributions about three everyday problems in living—depression, loneliness, and shyness, Anderson and Arnhoult (1985) found that two factors were most strongly related to college students' problems. *Controllability*, the extent to which the students felt that they would be able to control their outcomes in the future, was most directly related to the number of everyday problems students had. *Locus*, whether they saw their behavior as internally or externally determined, also was a significant factor. Depressed, lonely, and shy students felt that their outcomes were not controllable and believed that their behavior was determined mostly by external factors.

Several interventions involving self-attributions might combat depression. One could raise depressed people's expectations about the future outcomes of their behavior or improve their evaluations of existing outcomes (interpreting them as more positive). People could also be encouraged to see their outcomes as more controllable. One might encourage depressed people to engage in downward social comparison with less-fortunate others. Since chronically depressed people seem to adopt a "depressive self-focusing style," focusing negatively on themselves after failure experiences (Pyszczynski & Greenberg, 1987), one could work on changing attributions for failure from internal, stable, general factors (such as "I'm stupid") to external, unstable, specific factors (such as "It was a really difficult exam").

Some Illusions Are Adaptive

The past two chapters have presented considerable evidence of biases in the way that people process self-relevant information. We saw that people are overconfident about the accuracy of their own beliefs and assume that others think and behave as they do (false consensus bias). The present chapter has reviewed various ways that people distort threatening or personally unfavorable information in order to protect or enhance their self-esteem. Many prominent personality theorists (e.g., Gordon Allport, Erik Erikson, Erich Fromm, Abraham Maslow) have argued that accurate perceptions of the self and the world are essential for mental health. From their perspectives, these biases and illusions would appear to be maladaptive. But is this so?

In recent years several researchers have proposed that some information-processing biases may be adaptive for mental health. Three general **adaptive illusions** seem characteristic of normal human thought: overly positive self-evaluations, exaggerated perceptions of control or mastery, and unrealistic optimism about life's future events (Taylor & Brown, 1988). By definition, most people can't be above the average but, nevertheless, most of us see ourselves as well above average on many dimensions. We think of ourselves as safer drivers (Svenson, 1988), smarter (Wylie, 1979), and having more ability and better personalities than the average person has (Brown, 1988). College professors are not immune to this illusion—in one survey 90 percent of professors rated themselves superior to their average colleague (Blackburn et al., 1980). Research indicates that these illusions enhance the ability to care about others, the ability to be happy or contented, and the ability to engage in productive and creative work (Taylor & Brown, 1988). The strategies succeed in part by distorting incoming self-relevant information in a positive direction. Contradictory, negative, or ambiguous self-information may be assimilated into preexisting positive schemas about the self and the world with very little cognitive processing. Negative information is isolated and represented in as unthreatening a manner as possible. The illusions may be particularly valuable in dealing with depression, negative feedback, or threatening information about illness (Janoff-Bulman & Timko, 1987).

adaptive illusions:
Three widely held illusions seem adaptive for mental health: the illusion of control, overly positive self-evaluation, and unrealistic optimism about the future.

SELF-PRESENTATIONS

The Self in Social Interactions

We are usually acutely aware of the impressions we give to others by our appearance and behaviors. We care what others think of us and we usually seek to establish or maintain a positive image through a process called *self-presentation* or *impression management*. Several decades ago Erving Goffman (1959; 1967) suggested that social life is like a series of theatrical performances, where each participant's performance is designed as much for its effect on the audience as it is for honest and open expression of the self. The participants play roles and attempt to maintain their social identities through appropriate self-presentations. Goffman asserted that during interactions each person acts out a *line*, much like a part in a play, a pattern of verbal and nonverbal behaviors through which one expresses one's view of the situation and the participants, especially oneself. A major feature of one's line is the **face,** the positive social value the person claims for himself or herself, a public expression of self-worth.

We can identify two components of impression management:

face:
The positive social value claimed for oneself in social interactions.

impression-motivation:
How motivated you are to control how others see you, to create a particular impression in others' minds.

impression-construction:
Choosing the particular image one wishes to create and behaving in specific ways to achieve this goal.

impression-motivation and **impression-construction** (Leary & Kowalski, 1990). *Impression-motivation* describes how motivated you are to control how others see you, to create a particular impression in others' minds. *Impression-construction* involves choosing the particular image one wants to create and altering one's behavior in specific ways to achieve this goal. Leary and Kowalski (1990) proposed that impression motivation stems from three primary motives: the desire to obtain social and material rewards, to maintain or enhance self-esteem, and to facilitate the development of an identity. Conveying the right impression can provide social rewards such as approval, friendship, and power and may also lead to an increase in material rewards such as a raise in salary (Schlenker, 1986). We've already discussed the importance of the second factor, maintaining self-esteem. Making the right impression can elicit esteem-enhancing reactions (compliments, praise) from others. Self-presentation may also be a means of creating or reinforcing an identity, as when a new college freshman solidifies her identity as a college student by behaving as she thinks a college student "should" behave. These three general motives usually go together—self-presentational behaviors that obtain rewards also raise self-esteem and help establish desired identities. Occasionally they may conflict, though, as when a woman plays dumb to impress her chauvinistic date (Gove et al., 1980).

The motivation to manage the impression one gives is greatest in situations that involve important goals (such as friendship, approval, material rewards, etc.) where individuals feel dissatisfied with the image they currently project (self-discrepancy). Impression-motivation is even stronger when one feels dependent on a powerful person who controls important resources (e.g., one's boss) or after a failure or an embarrassing incident (Leary & Kowalski, 1990). Your motivation to present a positive, competent self-image would be very high, for example, if you had an interview for a job you really wanted (a valued goal), especially if you felt you had not made a good impression on a previous job interview. A model of self-presentations is depicted in Figure 3-8.

The State of Self-Awareness

self-awareness:
The degree to which attention is directed inward to focus on aspects of the self.

The state of **self-awareness** exists whenever you turn your attention inward to focus on the contents of the self (Carver & Scheier, 1981; Wicklund, 1975). Self-awareness is crucial for knowing one's self-concept and understanding what one's personal standards, values, and goals are. People in a state of high self-awareness generally behave in a manner more consistent with their attitudes and values (Gibbons, 1978; Wicklund, 1982). They may also feel emotions more intensely (Scheier & Carver, 1977) and show better memory for their personal experiences (Pryor et al., 1977). In attributions, self-directed attention increases the acceptance of personal responsibility for positive outcomes but may decrease the acceptance of responsibility for negative out-

FIGURE 3-8

The Motivation for Impression Management

Primary self-presentational motives and dispositional/situational antecedents that affect the degree to which people are motivated to control how others (the target) perceive them.

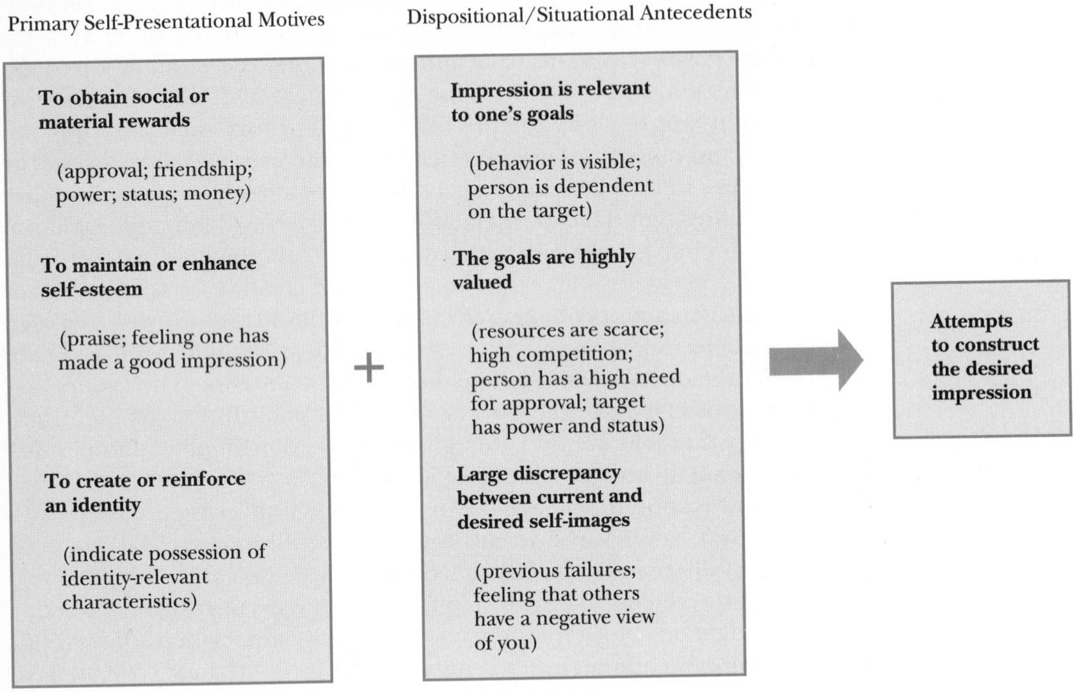

Primary Self-Presentational Motives   Dispositional/Situational Antecedents

| **To obtain social or material rewards** (approval; friendship; power; status; money) **To maintain or enhance self-esteem** (praise; feeling one has made a good impression) **To create or reinforce an identity** (indicate possession of identity-relevant characteristics) | **+** | **Impression is relevant to one's goals** (behavior is visible; person is dependent on the target) **The goals are highly valued** (resources are scarce; high competition; person has a high need for approval; target has power and status) **Large discrepancy between current and desired self-images** (previous failures; feeling that others have a negative view of you) | → | **Attempts to construct the desired impression** |

Source: Based upon Leary, M. R., & Kowalski, R. M. (1990). Impression management: A literature review and two-component model. *Psychological Bulletin, 107*, 34–47.

comes (Cohen et al., 1985). This is especially true for people with high self-esteem, as they show the greatest degree of self-serving bias in their attributions (Brown, 1988).

Self-focused people often compare their behaviors with ideal standards such as rules and social norms. In general, people who are made self-aware will perform in a socially desirable manner as they attempt to match their behavior to the relevant social standards. But comparing our behavior to ideal standards may be an unpleasant experience, because we may discover that we fall short of our ideal standards. Hence people will often avoid situations that are likely to increase self-awareness, fearing that they won't measure up to the standards (Mullen, 1983).

Public vs. Private Self-Awareness

When attention is directed toward the self, it may be focused on relatively private aspects not typically available to outside observers, such as moods,

private self-awareness: When attention is focused on relatively private aspects of the self not readily available to outside observers, such as moods, perceptions, and feelings.

public self-awareness: When attention is directed at the aspects of self that are visible to others, such as social appearance and actions.

perceptions, and feelings (**private self-awareness**) or on relatively public aspects observable to other people, such as social appearance and actions (**public self-awareness**) (Buss, 1980). Self-awareness has been conceptualized both as (a) a mental *state* influenced by environmental stimuli, and (b) an enduring personality *trait* describing which aspect of one's self-schema (public or private) is habitually activated. The state of private self-awareness is increased by a mirror, while cameras, recordings of one's own voice, and audiences increase the state of public self-awareness. A performer is generally in a state of public self-awareness, aware of the impression she is trying to convey to the audience by her behavior. Being a minority in a group also increases one's state of self-awareness. The more you feel you or your group is outnumbered, the more self-aware you become (Mullen, 1983).

People high in the trait of private self-awareness are continually concerned with their personal identity and are very attentive to their own thoughts and feelings. As a result, they process self-referent information more rapidly (Mueller, 1982) and their self-descriptions are more consistent over time (Nasby, 1989b). In contrast, people high in the trait of public self-awareness are most concerned with their social identity and other people's reaction to it (Fenigstein, 1979). People high in public self-awareness tend to conform more than those high in private self-awareness (Froming & Carver, 1981; Santee & Maslach, 1982). They are also more likely to use self-handicapping strategies (Shepperd & Arkin, 1989). As we might expect, they also tend to be more interested in clothing and fashion (Solomon & Schopler, 1982). [There is considerable debate about whether it is useful or confusing to conceptualize self-awareness as both a state and a trait variable (Carver & Scheier, 1987; Fenigstein, 1987; Wicklund & Gollwitzer, 1987). The term *self-consciousness* is sometimes used to describe the trait of self-awareness.]

The more attention one pays to any factor (whether another person, oneself, or the environment), the more it is perceived as a causal agent (Taylor & Fiske, 1978). Therefore, people high in private self-awareness, attentive to their own thoughts and feelings, are especially likely to see themselves as responsible (as causal agents) for things that happen to them (Fenigstein & Levine, 1984). Deindividuation, discussed below, results from reduced public and private self-awareness and can lead to antisocial behaviors.

High public self-awareness. Cameras, microphones, and an audience increase one's feeling of public self-awareness, making one aware of his social identity and other people'e reactions to it.

Strategic or Authentic Self-Presentation?

Acting out lines and claiming a particular face are central aspects of self-presentation. By controlling the face we present to others—our chosen social identity—we attempt to control their impressions of us. You can think of countless examples of *strategic self-presentations* where people deliberately strive to shape others' perceptions of them, as when a politician running for reelection dresses to create a particular impression and carefully says just what he thinks his audience wants to hear. Or consider how you might behave on a first date with someone you want to impress. Are you likely to change your appearance or modify your expressed attitudes to fit your date's preferences?

Although it is easiest to think of impression management as a strategy of deliberate manipulation, this is not necessarily so (Tetlock & Manstead, 1985). To extend William James's notion of self, in selecting a particular self to present in a situation, one may be choosing among several equally "true selves." In some interactions one's goal may not be impression management but **self-verification**—the authentic presentation of the self as one believes it to be (Schlenker et al., 1980; Swann, 1986).

As we attempt to influence others' perceptions of us, we often influence how we see ourselves as well (Schlenker, 1985). When you first meet an interesting person you may have two goals—to make a good imrpession and to let that person get to know the "real you." Given these goals, if you feel that the other person is forming the wrong impression of you despite your attempt at authentic self-presentation, you are likely to intensify your efforts to influence their perceptions of you, to show them the "real you" (Swann & Ely, 1984; Swann & Hill, 1982).

In many social situations there may be conflict between the goals of strategic and authentic self-presentation. During a job interview do you strategically try to present the "socially desirable you"—competent, likable, hardworking, responsible—or do you present the "real you," who might not always be so competent or hardworking? Your decision may depend partially on the situation (the desirability of the job, the attitude of the interviewer) and partially on your personality.

Conditions under Which Self-Presentation Occurs

Other people like to view you as having a consistent personality—it makes their social environment predictable by treating you as having a stable set of attributes. As a consequence, you learn to see yourself as a definable social object and you may become concerned with the consistency of your actions. Your self is not entirely constant, however; it shifts from moment to moment due to changing motivational states and situational cues. Further, the self is constantly evolving and changing to adjust to our behaviors and their outcomes.

self-verification:
The authentic presentation of the self as one believes it to be.

Self-presentation is an ongoing process, as we shape our responses to create a desired impression. I should note however, that there are a few situations where self-presentation may *not* be a primary concern (Jones & Pittman, 1982). First, when a person is highly involved in a task, absorbed by a physical or intellectual challenge, self-presentational concerns may be inhibited. Second, purely expressive behavior such as anger or joy may not be under self-presentational control at the moment it occurs. Third, many mindless, ritualized social interchanges, such as routine commercial transactions, often do not seem to involve self-presentational motives. Finally, on some occasions individuals are especially concerned with self-verification and the authenticity of their responses. During therapy sessions or intimate encounters individuals may want their actions to be maximally self-verifying, revealing their true feelings, beliefs, and values with no distortion or concealment. These situations, however, are the exception rather than the rule. The majority of time people are aware of the "face" they are projecting to others.

Strategies of Self-Presentation

Self-presentation can have several goals. One may wish to appear likable, competent, powerful, righteous, or to arouse sympathy. Each goal involves a different self-presentation strategy, as described by Edward Jones

Self-presentation in a job interview. Successful candidates must present themselves in a socially desirable light, attempting to fit the interviewer's schema of the ideal employee.

Self-presentation by intimidation. A football player may attempt to present himself as exceptionally tough by taunting his fallen opponent.

and his co-workers (Jones, 1965; Jones & Pittman, 1982). These goals are not mutually exclusive; a person may try to satisfy several of them at the same time.

ingratiation:
A self-presentational strategy with the goal of being seen as likable and attractive.

Ingratiation. The goal of ingratiation is to be perceived as a likable and attractive person. Common tactics include complimenting others, being a good listener, being friendly, doing favors, and conforming in attitudes or behaviors. The ingratiator assumes, correctly, that we tend to like people whose attitudes and values appear similar to our own (Chapter 8). Jones and Wortman (1973) labeled ingratiating actions as *illicit* because the actor's ulterior motivation is concealed. The ingratiator is highly concerned with establishing the *appearance* of sincerity and authenticity.

intimidation:
A self-presentational tactic of arousing fear and gaining power by convincing someone you are dangerous.

Intimidation. Another self-presentational goal may be to arouse fear and gain power by convincing someone you are dangerous. Unlike the ingratiator, the intimidator typically shows no interest in being liked; he wants to be feared. A strong-arm robber is the prototypical intimidator, but you can undoubtedly envision other situations involving attempts at intimidation: athletes on opposing teams, parents with children, perhaps professors with students. In many situations, a person with a short fuse can dominate a relationship or a group. Because threats may cause others to leave the situation if they can, the intimidation strategy may be used most often in situations from which escape is not easy.

self-promotion:
A self-presentational strategy in which one attempts to impress others with one's accomplishments.

Self-Promotion. When one's goal is to be seen as generally competent or skilled at a particular task, the self-promotional strategy is common. Self-promoters describe their strengths and attempt to impress others with their accomplishments. They may also describe minor unimportant flaws if this will make them seem more honest, but the self-promoter does not have an easy road. Most of us learn that others often exaggerate their abilities and therefore their claims to competence can be partially discounted. Self-promoters risk being seen as arrogant, untruthful, or insecure. Jones and Pittman (1982) labeled this the "self-promoter's paradox." In addition, in many areas competence can be objectively diagnosed and the self-promoter's claims can be debunked: "If you're so smart, how come you only have a C average?"

Aware of these problems, the gifted self-promoter will seek indirect ways to enable others to reach their own conclusion that she is competent in the desired respects rather than simply "blowing her own horn." Successful self-promotion may be quite important for achieving such goals as admission to a prestigious graduate school or getting a good job.

exemplification:
A self-presentational strategy where one attempts to project integrity and moral worthiness.

Exemplification. The exemplifier seeks to project integrity and moral worthiness. The exemplifier typically presents himself as honest, disciplined, and charitable, the saint who walks among us, the martyr who sacrifices for the cause. Jones and Pittman describe the typical exemplifier as manipulative and insincere; but it is important to remember that not every case of exemplary action is taken simply for its manipulative effect. There are "true

Self-presentation via exemplification. Mother Theresa exemplified her central values through her work with the poor in Calcutta, India, and elsewhere. She founded the Missionaries of Charity, which began work among the dying and destitute of Calcutta and has since spread around the world.

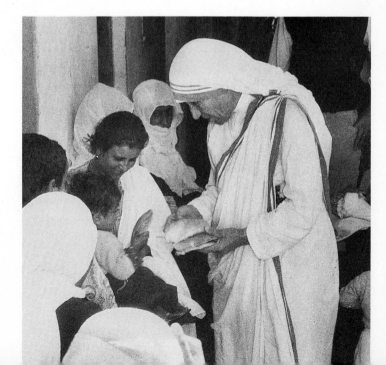

exemplars", people whose consistently virtuous behavior is internalized and unaffected by the responses of others, although such individuals are probably quite rare. More common is the self-presenter who is concerned that others perceive and are influenced by it, even though he might vigorously deny such manipulative motivation and might, indeed, be unaware of it. The exemplifier must be careful not to cross over the line from self-sacrifice to self-righteousness. Religious leaders who live lives of apparent virtue in return for persuasive power are examples of exemplifiers, as are parents who attempt to model the values of their culture in front of their children.

supplication:
A self-presentational strategey where one advertises one's weakness or dependence in order to solicit help or sympathy.

Supplication. This strategy advertises one's weakness or dependence to solicit help or sympathy. It may be the only strategy available to those who lack the resources needed for the preceding strategies (likability, power, apparent competence, apparent moral worthiness). By stressing personal weakness or dependence, the supplicant relies on societal norms of obligation or personal responsibility. These norms are most salient when the dependence appears not to be the responsibility of the supplicant—a person who was born handicapped, for example, as opposed to a person who became an alcoholic.

Supplication as a self-presentation strategy. If this woman acts helpless, it is likely a passerby (probably male) will stop and change the tire for her. However, using supplication can lower her own self-esteem.

Self-criticism is one behavior the supplicant may engage in. But research shows that although self-criticizers tend to receive support from others, privately they are perceived as poorly functioning individuals (Powers & Zuroff, 1988). Hence, though a self-critical style may elicit support early on, over the long run it is likely to produce negative reactions from others.

Though supplication may often be a tactic of last resort, in some cases it may be preferred. The bachelor who presents an image of incompetence in the kitchen may convince a kindhearted woman to cook dinner for him; the woman who appears unable to change a tire may find a willing male to help her out. I suspect, as do Jones and Pittman, that many children exaggerate their ineptitude at common household chores in hopes that their parents will continue to do them. Similarly, husbands often avoid learning how to sew, cook, or change diapers in order to ensure that their wives will continue to take responsibility for these tasks. One problem with supplication is the heavy cost to one's self-esteem of advertising one's incompetence or helplessness. In addition, the object of the supplication may grow tired of the tactic: "Hey, it's time you learned to do this yourself!"

Self-presentational strategies have the goal of influencing how others view you, but they may also change how you view yourself. There may be a *carryover effect*, influencing one's self-concept (Jones et al., 1981; Rhodewalt & Agustsdottir, 1986). In some cases, the chosen self-presentational strategy may make existing aspects of the self more salient and more likely to influence one's own future behavior. In other cases, engaging in strategic behavior that is discrepant with the existing sense of self may cause a change in the way the self is perceived. This reflects the more general tendency for attitudes to change to become consistent with counter-attitudinal behavior (Chapter 4).

Style of Self-Presentation: Self-Monitoring

self-monitoring:
The aspect of self that one typically focuses on. High self-monitors are concerned with the impression they give to others, while low self-monitors pay more attention to their inner feelings.

The concept of **self-monitoring** (M. Snyder, 1987) also utilizes the public/private distinction. People high in self-monitoring are concerned with what is socially appropriate and pay particular attention to how others behave in social settings. They use this information to guide their own behavior. High self-monitors are "skilled impression managers" (Snyder, 1981). Their behavior is determined more by what is situationally appropriate than by their true attitudes, feelings, and emotions. Low self-monitors, in contrast, tend to pay more attention to their inner feelings and are less concerned with situational cues indicating what behaviors are appropriate. High self-monitors respond to the social cues inherent in different situations and act like very different people according to the situation. Some representative items from Snyder's Self-Monitoring Scale are presented in Figure 3-9.

High self-monitors tend to be high in public self-awareness, while low self-monitors are high in private self-awareness (Tomarelli & Shaffer, 1985; Webb et al., 1989). As one might expect, high self-monitors possess greater social skills than do low self-monitors (Hamilton & Baumeister, 1984). They

FIGURE 3-9

Measuring Self-Monitoring

*Sample items from Snyder's
self-monitoring scale*

Source: From *Public Appearances,
Private Realities: The Psychology
of Self-Monitoring* by Mark
Snyder. Copyright © 1987 by
W. H. Freeman and Company.
Reprinted with permission.

People high in self-monitoring would agree:	Those low in self-monitoring would agree:
I guess I put on a show to impress or entertain people.	I find it hard to imitate the behavior of other people.
I'm not always the person I appear to be.	I can only argue for ideas I already believe.
I may deceive people by being friendly when I really dislike them.	In a group of people I am rarely the center of attention.
I sometimes appear to others to be experiencing deeper emotions than I actually am.	I have trouble changing my behavior to suit different people and different situations.
In different situations with different people, I often act like very different persons.	I am not particularly good at making other people like me.

appear more relaxed and friendly in social situations, are more likely to initiate social interactions, are more attentive to social cues in ambiguous situations, learn appropriate social behaviors more rapidly, and are better at understanding nonverbal behaviors. In Snyder's words, high self-monitors have a *pragmatic* sense of self, defining their identity largely in terms of social situations and roles that they play.

Will high self-monitors be seen by their acquaintances as "social phonies" who lack real values, character, or genuineness? Not necessarily, because high self-monitors segment their social world to a greater extent than do low self-monitors, engaging in different social activities with different sets of people. Therefore, inconsistencies in their behavior across two situations will not be readily recognized by others since the high self-monitoring person is with different people in the two situations (Snyder et al., 1982). William James's (1890/1981) notion that individuals have many social selves seems especially true of people high in self-monitoring.

There may be two different reasons why high self-monitors modify their behavior to fit others' expectations and situational pressures. Theorists have differentiated between avoidance/protective and acquisitive/aggressive strategies (Arkin et al., 1986), between "getting along" and "getting ahead" (Wolfe et al., 1986). High self-monitors who adopt an avoidance/protective orientation tend to be insecure, low in self-esteem, and shy; those who adopt the aggressive/acquisitional style are not (Briggs & Cheek, 1988; Wolfe et al., 1986). Thus, high self-monitoring behavior can be motivated either by avoidance or acquisition.

Reduced Self-Awareness and Deindividuation

People sometimes do things while members of a group that they never would do as individuals. Early social scientists (e.g., LeBon, 1895/1960) speculated

---

FOCUS 3-3

"The Who" Concert Stampede

The crowds started gathering outside Cincinnati's Riverfront Coliseum at two o'clock in the afternoon on December 3, 1979, six hours before the concert was scheduled to begin. They were waiting to see The Who, the high-voltage British rock group whose combination of controlled rage and frenetic music had electrified rock fans for more than a decade. The doors were supposed to open at 6 P.M., but the four-man band was late and needed more time to test the acoustics. By about 7:30 P.M., when the gates finally opened, there were close to 7,000 fans outside—most holding unreserved general admission tickets, all determined to get close to the stage and all forced to filter through just two banks of doors. As The Who were completing their acoustics check, the sound of their amplified instruments drifted out over the gates. The crowd surged forward, mistakenly believing the show had begun. Glass shattered as impatient fans battered open a locked door—and the stampede began.

"It was crazy," said one woman who had waited in line for hours. "Some guy reached out and grabbed my wrist and pulled me into the middle. Then I fell down. Then somebody grabbed me and pulled me up again. By then, my shoes and purse were gone. Then I fell down again. I fell over some guy and people were just walking over him. It felt like a lot of people stepped on me, but somebody grabbed me again. When I got up, I just ran."

The wild melee lasted only a few minutes. When it ended, 11 people ranging from age 15 to 22 were dead, suffocated in the crush. "Most of the people who died were very small," said Fire Chief Bert Luganni. More than 20 others were injured, and the white concrete outside the 18,000-capacity arena was piled ankle-high with purses, coats, shoes, and eyeglasses (*Newsweek,* December 17, 1979, p. 52).

Inside the coliseum, Cincinnati Fire Marshal Clifford Drury told Who Manager Bill Curbishley that the show should go on as scheduled. Drury reasoned that the crowd, most of whom did not know what had happened at the west gate, would not sit still for a cancellation. So The Who played its standard two-hour set, though they kept the encore short. When the four came offstage, Curbishley told them the news. Kenny Jones slumped against a wall. John Entwistle tried to light a cigarette, which shredded in his shaking hands. Roger Daltrey began to cry. Pete Townshend went ashen quiet. Daltrey thought the whole tour should be canceled. Then Townshend spoke up. He said, "If we don't play tomorrow, we'll never play again" (*Time,* December 17, 1979, pp. 86–87). ❖

deindividuation:
The loss of inner restraints that may occur when an individual feels submerged in a group.

about the "group mind" and "mob psychology" that seemed to encourage extreme behaviors by group members. The concept of **deindividuation** was later developed to describe the loss of inner restraints that may occur when an individual feels submerged in a group (Festinger et al., 1952).

Theorists have proposed that reduced self-awareness is the key factor producing this loss of restraint (Diener, 1980; Prentice-Dunn & Rogers, 1989). Group membership can have two major effects. When a group member feels anonymous and thinks that responsibility for his actions is shared with other group members, his public self-awareness is reduced. As a consequence, he feels less accountable for his actions, less concerned about others' disapproval or retaliation, and freer to engage in previously inhibited behaviors.

Being in a group can also have a second set of effects. When one feels immersed in a cohesive group and is physiologically aroused, this leads to reduced private self-awareness, producing the state of deindividuation. The individual's thinking and emotional patterns are disrupted; he is less attentive to his own internal standards and more affected by external cues such as the behavior of other group members. The two parallel paths that lead to disinhibited behavior are depicted in Figure 3-10.

Most researchers have focused on the disinhibition of negative behaviors such as violence but, in theory, prosocial behaviors (joy, celebration)

FIGURE 3-10

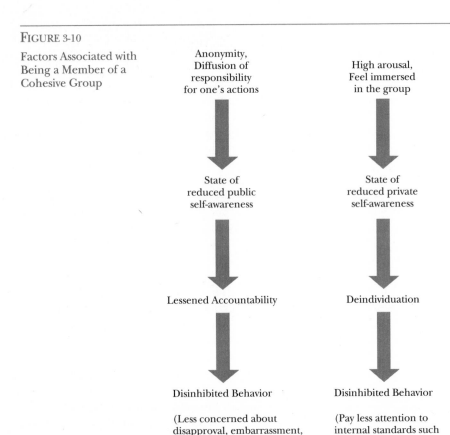

Factors Associated with Being a Member of a Cohesive Group

Anonymity, Diffusion of responsibility for one's actions

High arousal, Feel immersed in the group

State of reduced public self-awareness

State of reduced private self-awareness

Lessened Accountability

Deindividuation

Disinhibited Behavior

Disinhibited Behavior

(Less concerned about disapproval, embarrassment, or retaliation for one's actions)

(Pay less attention to internal standards such as conscience, moral code, values, attitudes; more affected by external cues)

Source: Based upon Prentice-Dunn, S., & Rogers, R. W. (1989). Deindividuation and the self-regulation of behavior. In P. B. Paulus (Ed.), *Psychology of group influence* (2nd ed., pp. 89–109). Hillsdale, NJ: Erlbaum.

Reduced public self-awareness at Halloween. Masks and costumes make children more anonymous, lessening public self-awareness and perhaps making them feel less accountable for their actions.

could also be increased if they were suggested by the external cues (Johnson & Downing, 1979). Spivey and Prentice-Dunn (1989) found that when the situational cues suggested that prosocial behavior was appropriate, deindividuated subjects behaved more prosocially (dispensed more money as a reward to a fellow subject) than did subjects who were not in a state of deindividuation. In contrast, when the situational cues suggested aggressive behavior (delivery of electric shocks to a fellow subject for poor performance), deindividuated subjects delivered stronger shocks than did other subjects.

An interesting cross-cultural study discovered a direct relationship between a tribe's warring and aggressive behavior and its costuming to achieve anonymity (Watson, 1973). Researchers found the degree of aggressiveness the tribe planned for any particular occasion was directly related to how carefully each warrior covered himself with paint, thereby becoming more anonymous. Sometimes anonymity alone may encourage deindividuated behavior. Other researchers took advantage of the custom of Halloween trick-or-treating to study the effects of anonymity on children's behavior. Half the children met at the door of a house were carefully identified by the adult answering the door; the other half were allowed to remain anonymous, hidden behind the cover of their costumes. The investigators were interested in what would happen when the children were left alone in the foyer of the house, with a bowl of candy and a bowl of pennies in clear view. They found that the anonymous group was prone to take more money and candy (Diener et al., 1976). Being anonymous and hidden in a crowd created a tempting situation for inappropriate behavior to occur.

Reduced self-awareness may permit the expression of all kinds of antisocial behavior. People can easily lose their individual identities in large crowds at sports stadiums and concert arenas. Tragic riots associated with important soccer matches throughout the world have produced many deaths and injuries. In one incident in 1985, 38 people were killed and over 400 were injured in Belgium in a riot that occurred before a soccer match between England and Italy had even begun. Sports crowds on the American sports scene—especially football, hockey, and baseball—have also shown the potential for violence. Most sports fans would probably not act violently unless they were part of an anonymous crowd. Another tragic example of crowd behavior is presented in Focus 3-3. We will encounter deindividuation again when analyzing behavior in prisons (Chapter 5) and aggression (Chapter 10).

SUMMARY

In the previous pages we have seen how the concept of self is viewed by social psychologists. Individuals' self-schemas affect the ways in which they interpret (or misinterpret) their own emotions. Self-schemas also affect our memory for, and interpretations of, information about ourselves. People generally interpret self-relevant information in ways that confirm their existing self-schema and maintain their level of self-esteem. If self-esteem is threatened, people may respond in several ways: by acquiring a handicap that can be used to explain away future failures, by denying or distorting the threatening information, by compensating for their shortcomings, or by making excuses. These biases may be adaptive in enabling people to maintain a positive self-image, a feeling of control over events in their lives, and an optimistic outlook.

Though people often try to present themselves in an authentic, straightforward manner, in many situations "strategic" motives underlie self-presentation strategies. There are a number of self-presentational strategies one can adopt in attempting to present oneself in a particular light, including ingratiation, intimidation, self-promotion, exemplification, and supplication.

Individuals differ on the degree to which they typically focus attention inward on the self (low self-monitoring, private self-awareness), as opposed to paying more attention to other people and the values and standards of society (high self-monitoring, public self-awareness). Being an anonymous member of a crowd, experiencing high emotional arousal, and feeling lessened responsibility for one's behavior can produce states of reduced private and public self-awareness. Under these conditions a state of deindividuation occurs, where people are likely to let their behavior be guided by what others are doing rather than by their inner standards or societal values.

PART THREE
Social Influence

CHAPTER 4

Attitudes and Persuasion

The concept of attitude is probably the most distinctive and indispensable concept in contemporary American social psychology. . . . This useful, one might almost say peaceful, concept has been so widely adopted that it has virtually established itself as the keystone in the edifice of American social psychology.   Gordon Allport, 1935

Most often people seek in life occasions for persisting in their opinions rather than for educating themselves. Each of us looks for justification in the event. The rest, which runs counter to that opinion, is overlooked.   Andre Gide ❖

PREVIEW

attitude:
has been defined as the amount of affect for or against a psychological object or, alternatively, as having three components: affect, behaviorial tendencies, and cognition.

Each of us has **attitudes** toward the important people, social objects, and issues in our lives. The complex series of decisions and behaviors you engage in every day is determined in part by your attitudes. Attitudes have long been a central concern of social psychology. One of the earliest scholarly books in social science (Thomas & Znaniecki, 1918) defined the entire field of social psychology as "the study of attitudes," and Gordon Allport (1935, p. 798) later defined attitude as "the most distinctive and indispensable concept in social psychology." The processes by which attitudes develop and change and their influences on our behavior have been the focus of thousands of social psychological studies.

Our analysis will begin by defining attitudes and describing how they are formed, their functions, and the ways they are measured. We will turn next to the conditions under which behavior can be predicted from attitudes. You will see that when attitudes and behaviors are conceptualized and measured appropriately, attitudes predict behavior quite well. The effectiveness of persuasive communication (political speeches, advertisements, or courtroom arguments, for example) for changing attitudes will be analyzed according to aspects of the source, the message, the audience, and the channel.

We will analyze the most important theories of attitude change: the theory of planned behavior, the elaboration likelihood model, cognitive dissonance theory, self-perception theory, and impression management theory. Then, we will look at the other side of the coin—ways to resist persuasion through defensive behaviors, forewarning, and inoculation.

THE IMPORTANCE OF ATTITUDES

What Are Attitudes?

There are two popular definitions of attitudes. Some theorists (Katz & Stotland, 1959; Rajecki, 1982) have proposed that attitudes have three components: affect, behavioral tendencies, and cognition (the A-B-C component model of attitudes). The division of human experience into thought, feeling, and action has a long history in Indo-European thought, being found in ancient Hellenic, Zoroastrian and Hindu philosophy (McGuire, 1989). The affective component of attitude describes one's emotional reactions toward the attitude object; the behavioral component includes the behaviors associated with the attitude object; and the cognitive component includes beliefs, facts, and information about the attitude object. An affective response (I like Karol), a behavior (I'll take Karol to a rock concert tonight), and a cognition (Karol is sexy) all relate to the same concept.

Other psychologists prefer to define attitude in terms of *affect* (feeling) or *evaluation* on a general good-bad dimension. These approaches see behavior and cognition as concepts that are closely related to attitudes but are not the same thing (Ajzen & Fishbein, 1980). Thus Thurstone (1946, p. 39) defined attitude as "the intensity of positive or negative affect for or against a psychological object," while Cacioppo et al. (1989) argued that evaluation, rather than affect, is the central feature of attitudes because some attitudes seem to evoke virtually no affect. I prefer to define an attitude as a schema, which usually includes affect, that is used to evaluate objects.

There are several basic characteristics of attitudes. First, attitudes are inferred from the way individuals behave (which could include the behavior of filling out an attitude questionnaire). Second, attitudes are directed toward a psychological object or category. People's schemas determine how they categorize the objects toward which attitudes are directed. Third, attitudes are learned. Because attitudes are learned, it follows that they can be changed. Finally, attitudes influence behavior. Holding an attitude toward an object gives one a reason to behave toward the object in a certain way.

How Attitudes Are Formed

Suppose that Staci is a candidate for student body president at your school. What factors are likely to determine your attitude toward her (and your subsequent willingness to vote for her)?

social learning:
A theory that stresses the impact of observational learning and reinforcement on human social behavior.

Learning by Observing Others
We learn many attitudes by **social learning** (discussed in detail in Chapter 10). Children observe how others (parents, peers, teachers, television characters) evaluate people, and model their own attitudes after those expressed by these important role models. If parents constantly express racial or reli-

gious prejudices, for example, their children are likely to develop similar attitudes unless other models (the media, peers, teachers) demonstrate different attitudes. But social learning is not limited to children. Your attitude toward Staci may be strongly influenced by what your role models (fellow students that you like and admire) think of her.

Learning through Reward: Instrumental Conditioning

We are rewarded (with praise, approval, friendship) for expressing some attitudes and punished for expressing others. Rewarded attitudes tend to be held more strongly; punished attitudes are weakened. If your friends ridicule you (punishment) when you say nice things about Staci, you may develop a more negative attitude in order to avoid their disapproval.

Learning through Association: Classical Conditioning

classical conditioning: Learning through association, when a neutral stimulus is consistently associated with a stimulus that produces an emotional response (an unconditioned stimulus).

When a neutral stimulus is consistently associated with a stimulus that produces an emotional response (an unconditioned stimulus), **classical conditioning** occurs. After repeated pairings of the stimuli, the previously neutral stimulus becomes a conditioned stimulus and elicits the same response that the unconditioned stimulus does. If you hear others continually refer to Staci or her political party in uncomplimentary terms, the negative affect associated with the terms will become associated with Staci as well. This process is often important in the development of ethnic prejudices. For example, an American child may hear his parents continually describe Arabs in derogatory terms: "dirty Arabs," "vicious Arabs," and so forth. Eventually, the negative emotion associated with the descriptions (dirty, vicious) becomes associated with the concept Arabs, and the groundwork for a prejudiced attitude has been laid (Zanna et al., 1970).

Learning by Direct Experience

Many of our attitudes are learned by direct experience with the attitude object. If you meet Staci, your attitude toward her will be strongly influenced by the impression you form. Our interactions with the attitude object, as well as our memory for these interactions, can be biased by our preexisting schemas and stereotypes, as we saw in Chapter 2. We may set in motion behavioral confirmation sequences, which channel our interactions in directions that seem to confirm our existing attitudes, schemas, and expectations. If you expect (perhaps based on your friends' negative attitudes toward her) that Staci will be unfriendly and distant, she may appear so when you meet her. But her apparent unfriendliness may actually be a reaction to your subtly expressed negative attitude, rather than an enduring trait of Staci's.

Observing Our Own Behavior

Although we are accustomed to seeing attitudes as causes of behavior, it is also true that behaviors can lead to changes in attitudes. Self-perception theory, discussed in Chapter 3, proposes that we often infer what our attitudes are by watching our own behavior. Suppose you realize that you are flustered and tongue-tied while talking with Staci, acting as if you really want to impress her. You also realize that you've been in an intense conversation with her for quite some time. Observing yourself, you may think, "Based on the way I am behaving, I must like her after all." You have inferred a positive attitude from observing your behavior.

Functions Attitudes May Serve

Understanding

Social scientists have described four functions that attitudes may serve (Katz, 1960; Smith, Bruner, & White, 1956). First, an attitude can act as a schema, a way to structure the world so that it makes sense, thus serving an understanding function. For example, your attitudes about political issues provide you with a frame of reference for evaluating political candidates. If candidates support issues toward which you have positive attitudes, you are likely to respond more favorably than if they argue against those issues.

Social Adjustment

In many cases, appropriate attitudes allow us to identify with, or gain approval from, those around us. The expression of certain attitudes may be rewarded (instrumental conditioning) by important persons such as parents, teachers, employers, and friends. Attitudes that allow a person to achieve rewards, identification, or approval are serving a social adjustment function. Focus 4-1 provides an example of a politician revising his expressed attitude to gain approval.

FOCUS 4-1

Social Adjustment and Expressed Attitudes

John Connally, a candidate for the Republican presidential nomination in 1980, glibly revises his position on the Equal Rights Amendment in order to impress a voter. Impression management in action:

> The Very Republican Lady from Columbus, Ohio looked sternly at former Texas Gov. John Connally and asked: "What are your views on the ERA?" "I'm for it," Connally shot back. "I've been for it since 1962." The Very Republican Lady, obviously no fan of the Equal Rights Amendment, glared.

After a short, pained silence, Connally began to revise and extend his remarks. "Actually, I have mixed feelings," he said. "If the amendment would weaken or destroy family life, I'd have to take another look.... I wouldn't have voted to extend the time for ratification. That was wrong.... So for all practical purposes I guess you could say I'm against it today." ❖

Source: Copyright 1980, *The Des Moines Register*. Reprinted with permission.

Ego Defense

An attitude that reflects a person's unresolved personality problems, such as unexpressed aggression or fear of losing status, is serving an ego-defensive function. As defense mechanisms, attitudes allow people to protect themselves from acknowledging uncomplimentary basic truths about themselves. Consider a white male who feels oppressed and mistreated by more powerful people. He sees others making more money and enjoying a larger share of the good things in life. One way to restore his tattered self-esteem would be to adopt a negative attitude toward minorities, considering himself superior to an entire segment of the population: anyone who is not a white male. His ethnocentric outlook seems to elevate him in the hierarchy of society, since a sizable portion of it must, by his definition, remain "below" him.

Expressing Values

terminal values:
Preferences for certain end-states such as equality or freedom.

instrumental values:
Preferences for certain broad modes of conduct such as honesty or courage.

Values are basic concepts of what is seen as desirable. **Terminal values** are preferences for certain end states, such as equality, freedom, or self-fulfillment. **Instrumental values** are preferences for broad modes of conduct, such as honesty, courage, chastity, or adherence to the Golden Rule (Rokeach, 1979). Attitudes can express a person's central values. For example, many people in recent years felt that their attitudes about abortion expressed deeply held values about life and about freedom of choice. Values differ from attitudes in that they are more deeply held and unquestioned, and do not have specific objects associated with them. Values are more general than attitudes; a person has many thousands of attitudes but only several dozen values.

How Functions Relate to Attitude Change

A rational, information-based message ought to be effective in changing an attitude that is serving an understanding function. If one's attitude was serving primarily a social adjustment function, however, change attempts could focus on rewards and on relationships with other people. The Very Republican Lady in Focus 4-1 quickly changed John Connally's expressed attitude toward the ERA by "punishing" his earlier statements with an angry glare.

An attitude that expresses deeply held values will be difficult to change, for values do not change easily. One possible technique would be to demonstrate that a different attitude more appropriately expresses other important values. Changing an attitude serving the ego-defensive function would be especially difficult, because the attitude stems more from the characteristics of the attitude holder than from the attitude object. One would have to change the personality of the attitude holder, through methods such as psychotherapy. Personality style may also affect which change techniques are effective. DeBono (1987) found that people high in self-monitoring (Chapter 3) held attitudes that served primarily a social adjustive function, while low self-monitoring individuals' attitudes were more likely to serve a value-expressive function.

Value-expressive attitudes. Demonstrators on both sides of the abortion issue express their feelings outside Florida's capitol in 1990. Many individuals' attitudes about abortion stem from strongly held values about freedom of choice, the origin of life, and so forth.

Measuring Attitudes

Self-Report Measures

The most widely used type of attitude measure is the self-report questionnaire, usually involving either agree/disagree responses or responses on five or seven Likert-scale categories, ranging from "strongly agree" to "strongly disagree." Self-report measures are easy to utilize, but they can have a number of problems stemming from ambiguity in the instrument and effects due to the presence of others (norms, expectations, and social desirability pressures). An ideal attitude questionnaire has clear, straightforward questions that are not all worded in the same direction. If the topic is interesting and good rapport is established with the respondents, the influence of nonattitudinal factors such as intelligence, boredom, and motivation will be minimized.

The presence of others can introduce systematic error. As noted in Chapter 1, respondents may feel pressure to play a role: they may be apprehensive or negativistic, or they may try to give the responses they think the experimenter wants. Evaluation apprehension pressures can be minimized by guaranteeing anonymity for the respondents; experimental demand can be controlled by not letting the respondents know what the researcher expects. Interviews represent another type of self-report measure. They may be structured (for each question a specific set of answers is provided, like a multiple-choice exam) or unstructured (a general question is asked and the respondent answers in as much detail as he or she wishes). Boredom or carelessness is less of a problem with interviews. Also, the respondent has a chance to clarify ambiguous answers. However, a major disadvantage is that the interviewer's own responses (intentional or unintentional cues) may affect the respondent's answers. To avoid this problem, interviewers are carefully trained not to react to respondents' answers.

FOCUS 4-2

A Subtle Way to Measure Sensitive Attitudes

People often don't feel comfortable responding honestly to questions about sensitive issues. Though respondents' evaluation apprehension can be reduced by establishing good rapport and guaranteeing anonymity, dishonest responding may still be a problem. The *randomized response technique* was developed as a clever way of getting an estimate of group responses while guaranteeing to each individual that no one will ever know how he or she answered the question.

The procedure depends on probability theory. Suppose, as part of a study on sexually-transmitted diseases (cf., Chapter 9), you want to know what proportion of college students have engaged in "unsafe sex" in the last month. Before responding to the question, each of the subjects flips a coin. If their coin lands heads they are to answer "yes," regardless of their actual behavior. If the coin lands tails, they are to answer truthfully. Hence, even if someone saw a person's "yes" response, there would be no way of knowing whether the answers represented a truthful response or a heads coin-flip.

How can the group's actual response rates be estimated? Suppose 80 of 100 respondents answered "yes." We know that roughly 50 of the 100 respondents would have answered "yes" because of the coin flip, regardless of their attitudes. Since 30 additional students also answered "yes," we can estimate that the overall prevalence of "yes" answers would have been 60 percent (30/50) if everyone had responded truthfully.

Two studies have illustrated the value of this technique. Himmelfarb and Lickteig (1982) found that a significantly greater proportion of respondents admitted to socially sensitive behaviors (such as cheating on taxes, using illegal drugs, reading soft-core pornography) when the randomized response technique was employed. Shotland and Yankowski (1982) found that the estimated rate of truthful responding to a sensitive question (whether students had received prior information about test questions) was 80 percent via the randomized response technique as compared to only 10 percent when the question was asked directly. This technique appears to be a valid way of gathering accurate group data on socially sensitive issues. ❖

Other Measurement Techniques

While self-report measures are most commonly used, researchers have investigated alternative measurement techniques as well. One alternative method is to observe overt behavior toward the attitude object. For example, people might be asked to donate money or sign a petition to support a particular cause.

Nonverbal behaviors such as head movements can also be indicators of attitudes. One study found that when students were listening to a message with which they agreed, 73 percent of their head movements were vertical (as in nodding "yes"); when they listened to a counterattitudinal message, only 47 percent of head movements were vertical (Wells & Petty, 1980). Another attitude-related behavior, as Sir Francis Galton (1884) observed over a century ago, is the distance people keep between each other. How far apart two people stand while talking can be used as an index of their liking for each other (Mehrabian, 1981). Using behavior to estimate attitudes is sometimes misleading, though, because other nonattitudinal factors (e.g., social norms, values, situational pressures) may strongly affect behavior.

Another possible way to measure attitudes is to find tasks in which people's performance is systematically biased by their attitudes. For example, some years ago we asked a number of students to play the part of a debate judge and impartially evaluate arguments concerning racial matters, without reference to their own attitudes (Brigham & Cook, 1970). We hypothesized that despite their attempts to be impartial, the students' evaluations would be so strongly affected by their attitudes that we could use these evaluations as indirect measures of their attitudes. As predicted, arguments that agreed with a person's racial attitude were evaluated as considerably more

Estimating attitudes from behaviors. How far apart people stand while talking may indicate their attitudes toward each other.

plausible than were those a person disagreed with, so that the patterns of judgments could be used as an accurate indirect measure of the subjects' racial attitudes.

One might also try to estimate attitudes from physiological reactions to attitudinal objects. Early research identified two types of physiological responses that seemed relevant to attitudes: a general measure of arousal, the galvanic skin response (GSR)(Porier & Lott, 1967; Westie & DeFleur, 1959) and changes in the size of the pupils of one's eyes while viewing the attitude object (Hess, 1965). But subsequent research indicated that GSR and pupil dilation seem to be related to interest, stimulus novelty, attention, or mental effort, rather than attitudes (Cacioppo & Sandman, 1981; Petty & Cacioppo, 1983).

Over a century ago, Charles Darwin (1872) noted that emotions have corresponding facial expressions. Can expressions serve as measures of attitudes? The contraction of facial muscles can be assessed by an electromyograph (EMG) which measures, via electrodes, the tiny electrical output of muscle groups. For example, people show significantly more EMG activity in the muscles associated with smiling while imagining positive events in their lives and more activity in the frowning muscles while imagining negative events (Schwartz et al., 1976). EMG measurement of the muscles in the brow region can differentiate between positive and negative emotional reactions (Cacioppo et al., 1986). Darwin called these the "grief muscles," whose actions pull the brows down and together. Recent research suggests that changes in brow activity may be associated with a number of different emotions (Cacioppo et al., 1988). At present this method can assess the direction (positive or negative) but not the intensity of an attitude. It remains to be seen whether this method proves useful as a measure of attitudes.

Attitudes and Behavior: When Do They Correspond?

Attitudes are assumed to be important determinants of behavior. Yet attitudes and behavior may not correspond perfectly. As Kurt Lewin (1951) noted, behavior (B) is a function of a person's (P) characteristics (which include attitudes) and the environment (E): $B = f(P, E)$. Attitudes interact with other personal characteristics (such as motives, values, other attitudes, and personality traits) which, in turn, interact with environmental factors to determine behavior. Hence, to predict behavior from a single attitude is risky. Suppose a student has positive attitudes toward performing well in school and also toward honesty. If he is failing biology and has the opportunity to see the test ahead of time, it is not clear which attitude will determine his behavior (to cheat or not to cheat).

Environmental forces also exert powerful influences on behavior. In many cases, situational pressures are powerful enough to determine behavior by themselves. For example, in several studies of obedience (discussed in the next chapter) situational pressures to obey were so strong that most subjects did so, even though they probably wanted to disobey. The subjects' attitudes and values about hurting people were not effective predictors of their behavior, because their attitudes toward obeying authority and the situational pressures had a greater impact.

The LaPiere Study

In the early 1930s there was strong anti-Oriental feeling in the United States. Sociologist Richard LaPiere (1934) traveled about ten thousand miles through the American West and Midwest from 1930 to 1932 in the company of a Chinese couple—a student and his wife—who were personable, charming, and "skillful smilers." The couple were generally treated well; they were served at every one of 184 restaurants and were turned away at only one of sixty-seven lodging places. Yet when LaPiere later wrote to each of these places asking if it would be all right for him and a Chinese couple to stop at their establishment, over 90 percent of the establishments that replied said no. Similar letters were sent to establishments they had not visited; the refusal rate among those who replied was also quite high (84 percent).

Some writers argued that LaPiere's findings indicated that there is no relationship between attitudes (here designated as the response to LaPiere's letter) and behavior (the acceptance of the Chinese couple in person). But, interesting as it is, this study actually tells us little about the relationship between attitudes and behaviors (Campbell, 1963; Dillehay, 1973). First, a yes or no answer to a letter is not a valid measure of one's attitude toward a group. Second, only about half the establishments responded to the letter. It seems reasonable to assume that the ones who responded were likely to be those who were most bothered by the possibility of the Chinese couple's visit. Hence the respondents constituted a biased sample. Third, consider the image to which the persons responded. The mental image of "a Chinese couple" may have been quite different from the friendly couple, accompanied by LaPiere, they met face to face. Fourth, it is likely that in many cases the people who dealt directly with LaPiere and his companions were not the same ones who responded to the letters. Finally, it is easy to reject someone by letter but much more difficult to reject them as they stand before you, particularly if they belong to a group whose reactions you cannot predict. For these reasons, LaPiere's study does not provide useful information on the relationship between attitudes and behaviors.

Measurement of Attitudes and Behaviors

The extent to which attitudes relate to behaviors depends on two sets of factors: the methodology by which the relationship is assessed (how the attitudes and behaviors are measured) and characteristics of the attitude itself.

Most older studies used only a single instance of behavior, such as the accept/reject standard used by LaPiere. You can improve prediction of behaviors from attitudes dramatically if you employ a more comprehensive behavioral index that measures several behaviors relevant to the attitude, rather than just one. People's behavior in many situations provides a more reliable indication of their overall behavioral tendencies than does behavior on a single occasion. For example, Weigel and Newman (1976) measured attitudes about environmental quality, conservation, and pollution issues. Over an eight-week period they also measured fourteen environmentally relevant behaviors such as circulating petitions, picking up litter, and recycling of paper and bottles. They found that the correlation of the environmental attitudes scale with any single behavior was only small to moderate, but the correlation of the attitude scale with the index of all fourteen behaviors was quite strong. These results are particularly compelling for several reasons. First, the researchers measured overt behavior, not just self-reports of past activity. Second, they used a field setting and noncollege-student subjects (increasing mundane realism and external validity). Third, the behavioral data were collected several months after the attitude scale was administered. These findings (Table 4-1) show that when attitudes and behaviors are measured appropriately, attitudes will exhibit a robust capacity to predict the direction that behavior will take.

The specificity of the attitude measure is also important. People's attitudes will predict their behavior most closely when they are asked about their attitudes toward that specific action (Ajzen & Timko, 1986). The results of studies that looked at two very different behaviors—buying lead-free gasoline and using birth control pills—are depicted in Figure 4-1. In both studies, the researchers asked questions about general attitudes (environmentalism, birth control) and attitudes toward more specific behaviors. Heberlein and Black (1976) looked at attitudes as predictors of whether motorists would buy lead-free gasoline or regular gasoline. Their study was carried out in 1973, when the decision whether to buy lead-free gas was voluntary. They found motorists' scores on a general environmentalism scale correlated only slightly with the amount of lead-free gasoline purchased. However, as they looked at attitudes that were more directly relevant to the specific behavior they were measuring, the relationship increased. Thus, motorists' attitudes toward buying lead-free gasoline correlated quite strongly with the amount of lead-free gasoline they actually bought.

Studying married women, researchers (Davidson & Jaccard, 1979) assessed the use of birth control pills two years after asking attitude questions about contraception. General attitudes toward birth control pills did not relate to the subsequent use of birth control pills. However, as attitudes more directly relevant to the behavior were measured, the relationship became stronger. Attitudes toward birth control pills correlated moderately with the use of birth control pills, and attitudes toward *using* birth control pills in the next two years correlated even more strongly with their later use. A further study (Davidson & Morrison, 1983) found that prediction of people's contraceptive use one year later was strongest when many different factors (beliefs, feelings, and behavioral tendencies regarding various contraceptive techniques) were taken into account.

TABLE 4-1   CORRELATIONS (*r*) BETWEEN SUBJECTS' ENVIRONMENTAL ATTITUDES AND BEHAVIORAL CRITERIA

Single Behaviors	r	Categories of Behavior	r	Behavioral Index	r
Offshore oil	.41[b]				
Nuclear power	.36[a]	Petitioning behavior	.50[b]		
Auto exhaust	.39[b]	scale (0–4)			
Circulate petitions	.27				
Individual participation	.34[a]	Litter pick-up scale			
Recruit friend	.22	(0–2)	.36[a]	Comprehensive behavioral index	.62[c]
Week 1	.34[a]				
Week 2	.57[c]				
Week 3	.34[a]				
Week 4	.33[a]	Recycling behavior	.39[b]		
Week 5	.12	scale (0–8)			
Week 6	.20				
Week 7	.20				
Week 8	.34[a]				

Note: $N = 44$

[a] $p < .05$

[b] $p < .01$

[c] $p < .001$

Source: Weigel, R. H. & Newman, L. S. (1976). Increasing attitude-behavior correspondence by broadening the scope of the behavioral measure. *Journal of Personality and Social Psychology, 33,* 799. Copyright 1976 by the American Psychological Association. Reprinted by permission of the publisher and authors.

Characteristics of Attitudes

Not all attitudes are equal in their ability to predict behavior. The way in which an attitude was initially formed affects the attitude-behavior relationship. Attitudes formed on the basis of direct behavioral interaction with the attitude object are likely to show greater consistency with behavior than attitudes formed by other means. There are two reasons for this. An attitude based on direct experience may be more closely tied to an individual's self-image (Fazio, 1986). In addition, the attitude is more cognitively accessible.

Recall the discussion of the availability heuristic (Chapter 2) often used in social information processing. Attitudes based on direct experience are more available, more cognitively accessible, and more likely to guide behavior. For example, Fazio and Williams (1986) studied the cognitive accessibility of voters' attitudes toward the candidates prior to the 1984 presidential election. Accessibility was defined by the amount of time it took each voter to respond to two questions about how good a president Ronald Reagan or Walter Mondale would be. Voters whose attitudes were more accessible (they

FIGURE 4-1

Can Attitudes Predict Behavior?

The ability of attitudes to predict behavior increases as the attitude measured is closer to the specific behavior.

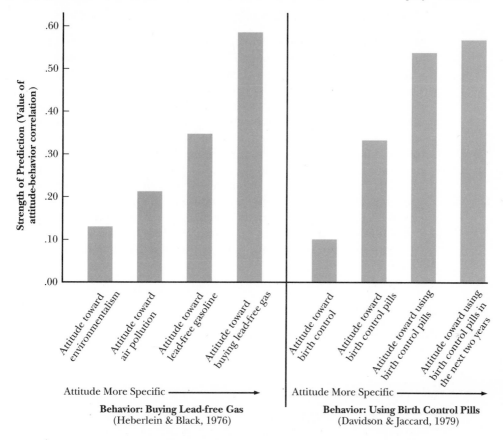

Behavior: Buying Lead-free Gas
(Heberlein & Black, 1976)

Behavior: Using Birth Control Pills
(Davidson & Jaccard, 1979)

Sources: Data from Heberlein, T.A., & Black, J. S. (1976). Attitudinal specificity and the prediction of behavior in a field setting. *Journal of Personality and Social Psychology, 33,* 474–479; Davidson, A. R., & Jaccard, J. J. (1979). Variables that moderate the attitude-behavior relation: Results of a longitudinal survey. *Journal of Personality and Social Psychology, 37,* 1364–1376.

took a shorter time to respond) showed a significantly stronger attitude-behavior relationship: Their attitudes toward Reagan and Mondale correlated more highly with their actual vote.

Attitudes that are more strongly held, as when someone has a vested interest in the issue, are also more cognitively accessible and more clearly related to behavior. Sivacek and Crano (1982) found that college students young enough to be directly affected by a proposed law to raise the drinking age to twenty were much more likely to campaign against the law than

theory of planned behavior:
Beliefs influence: (1) attitudes toward behavior, (2) subjective norms, and (3) perceived behavioral control.

subjective norm:
One's understanding of what others expect one to do an one's motivation to comply with these expectations.

perceived behavioral control:
One's beliefs about how difficult it would be to perform a given behavior.

were older students whose social lives would not be directly affected by the time the proposed law took effect. The older students were just as strongly opposed to the law as the younger students were, but they were less likely to act in accordance with their negative attitude.

Theory of Planned Behavior

Much work on attitude-behavior prediction has been stimulated by the theory of reasoned action developed by Icek Ajzen and Martin Fishbein (1980), which was later renamed the **theory of planned behavior** by Ajzen (1988). The theory describes the relationship between beliefs, attitudes, and behavior. Beliefs influence: (1) attitudes toward a particular behavior, (2) **subjective norms,** and (3) **perceived behavioral control.** These components influence behavioral intentions which, in turn, influence behavior. A person's attitude toward a behavior, the top box in Figure 4-2, is determined by beliefs that performing the behavior leads to various desirable or undesirable outcomes. Subjective norms involve (1) beliefs about what behaviors are normative (expected by others), and (2) one's motivation to comply with normative expectations. Perceived control is determined by one's past experiences and beliefs about how easy or difficult performance of the behavior is likely to be.

Suppose that you resolve halfway through the semester not to cut any

FIGURE 4-2

The Theory of Planned Behavior

Behaviors are predicted from attitudes, subjective norms, and perceived behavioral control.

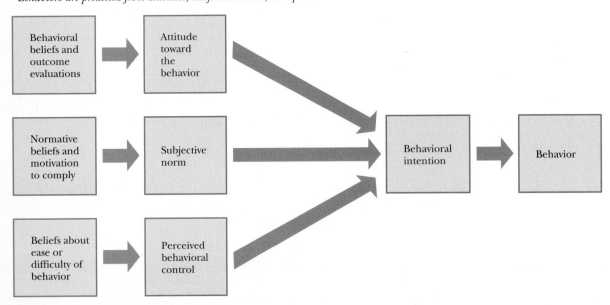

Sources: Based upon Ajzen, I. (1985). From intentions to actions: A theory of planned behavior. In J. Kuhl and J. Beckman (Eds.), *Action-control: From cognition to behavior* (pp. 11–39). New York: Springer. Ajzen, I., & Fishbein, M. (1980). *Understanding attitudes and predicting social behavior.* Englewood Cliffs, NJ: Prentice-Hall.

more social psychology courses and to get an A in the course. You think that it is desirable to attend class and to get an A (positive attitude toward the behaviors). Further, you feel that your friends will approve of these behaviors and you care what they think (supportive subjective norm). However, one goal (attending class) is much more easily achieved than the other. Motivation alone should enable you to make it to every class meeting, but additional factors such as knowledge and study skills will also affect whether you get your A. If you decide (perhaps based on past experience) that studying hard and learning enough will be very difficult for you (low perceived behavioral control), your intentions to achieve the A will be substantially weakened. Ajzen and Madden (1986) studied exactly this issue in two social psychology classes and found that all three factors—attitude toward the behavior, subjective norms, and perceived control—were predictors of intention to attend class and intention to get an A in the course. Amount of perceived behavioral control is particularly important in areas where people's self-confidence beliefs may be particularly weak, such as the ability to get an A, to lose weight, or to stop smoking. As Table 4-2 illustrates, students' intentions to engage in three behaviors (attending class, getting an A in the course, and losing weight) were related to all three predictors.

When people are motivated to be deceitful, this rational theory may not predict behavior as well. In a clever study of taxpayers and tax evaders in the Netherlands, Hessing, Elffers, and Weigel (1988) found that, as the theory asserts, attitude toward the act (of tax evasion) and subjective norms together predicted self-reports of whether or not the respondents had cheated on their taxes over a two-year period (the researchers did not measure perceived behavioral control). But none of these measures—attitude toward the act, subjective norms, or self-reports—were significantly related to the actual degree of tax evasion as established from government records for those two years.

TABLE 4-2   APPLYING THE THEORY OF PLANNED BEHAVIOR: PREDICTIONS OF INTENTIONS TO ENGAGE IN THREE BEHAVIORS

Correlations between intentions (I) and three central predictors: attitude toward the behavior (AB), subjective norm (SN), and perceived behavioral control (PBC).

Behavioral Goal	Correlation Between:		
	AB and I	SN and I	PBC and I
Attending class	.51*	.35*	.57*
Getting an A grade	.48*	.11	.44*
Losing weight	.62*	.44*	.36*

Note: Starred correlations mean that scores on these two factors (AB and I, SN and I, or PBC and I) were substantially related to each other (statistically significant) for this behavioral goal.

Sources: Data from Ajzen, I., & Madden, T. J. (1986). Prediction of goal-directed behavior: Attitudes, intentions and perceived behavioral control. *Journal of Experimental Social Psychology, 22,* 453–474. Schifter, D. B., & Ajzen, I. (1985). Intention, perceived control and weight loss: An application of the theory of planned behavior. *Journal of Personality and Social Psychology, 49,* 843–851.

There are other factors that also affect the attitude-behavior link. Some people are generally more consistent in their behavior and are more likely to show a stronger attitude-behavior relationship than others (Bem & Allen, 1974). Attitude-behavior correspondence is higher if the attitude is part of a general set of attitudes that are relatively stable within the individual (Schwartz, 1978). Correspondence is greater for active people, that is, those who are willing to disclose their feelings and act upon them: apathetic people may appear inconsistent due to their general inactivity. Also, people who think of themselves as practicing what they preach show greater attitude-behavior consistency. The degree to which people are sensitive to situational cues and influenced by them is also important. Individuals who rely on internal feelings rather than situational cues when making behavioral decisions (low self-monitors) show greater attitude-behavior correspondence (Zanna et al., 1980). These low self-monitors also show greater preference for situations that allow the open expression of attitudes (Snyder & Kendzierski, 1982). The major factors affecting the attitude-behavior relationship are summarized in Table 4-3.

Where is this research leading us? In past decades researchers began with the concern about *whether* attitudes could predict behavior, then progressed to studies of *when* attitudes predict behavior. In the 1990s scientists will be studying the *how* question. Through what processes do attitudes influence behavior? How are attitudes formed and how do they change? Reflecting increased concerns with social cognition (Chapter 2), cognitive processes will be closely studied. Scientists will also be looking at motivational factors (e.g., ego-defensiveness, the desire to manage impressions) that may also affect attitudes (Chaiken & Stangor, 1987).

TABLE 4-3	ATTITUDES AS PREDICTORS OF BEHAVIOR

Attitudes Will Predict Behaviors Best When:

The Attitude is:

Cognitively accessible
Based on direct experience with the attitude object
Part of a stable set of attitudes

The person is:

An active person (engaging in many behaviors)
A consistent person
Low in self-monitoring (relies on inner dispositions)
High in need for cognition

Measurements of the attitudes and the behaviors correspond:

To predict a specific behavior,
    measure attitude toward that act
To predict a general set of behaviors,
    measure general attitudes

HOW CAN ATTITUDES BE CHANGED? PERSUASIVE COMMUNICATIONS

Attitude Change Processes

Let's look again at your attitudes toward Staci, the candidate for student body president. She and her supporters will be eager to persuade their fellow students to vote for her. They want to change the attitudes of those students who are initially neutral or negative toward Staci. If they are to be successful, what process may be involved?

Three general change processes were identified by Kelman (1958). **Compliance** occurs when people accept influence because they hope to achieve a favorable reaction from a powerful person or group. The action will be performed only when under surveillance by the powerful agent. People change their behavior, but not the underlying attitude. If your boss at your campus job supports Staci, you may declare your support for her too, at least while the boss is listening. **Identification** occurs when one accepts influence in order to maintain a satisfying self-defining relationship with another person or group. Here the person actually believes in the new attitude, but its content is more or less irrelevant; the satisfaction comes from the act of conforming. If you were a fraternity or sorority pledge and discovered that most of the brothers or sisters supported Staci, you might become a supporter too, as this would be an additional way of identifying yourself with the desirable group. **Internalization** occurs when one accepts influence because the induced behavior is intrinsically rewarding (e.g., it feels right) and is congruent with one's value system. If you become convinced, through talking with Staci or her supporters, that she is the best-qualified candidate, then you will internalize a changed (positive) attitude. You will support her whether under surveillance by others or not. In most attitude change situations, it is internalization that the persuasive source hopes for. Another way of describing attitude change, proposed by Carl Hovland and his colleagues (Hovland, Janis, & Kelley, 1953; Hovland & Weiss, 1951), focuses on the steps people go through when they are persuaded: attention, comprehension, acceptance, and retention. In our example, *attention* refers to the degree to which you are aware of (attend to) Staci's messages. An attitude message cannot be effective unless the audience pays attention to it. Advertisers spend millions of dollars each year designing messages to catch audience attention. (Much has been written about the role of sex in advertising as an attentional gimmick.) If the audience attends to the message, the next necessary step is that they *comprehend* and understand it. Staci may find out what politicians, advertisers, and college professors are already aware of: audience comprehension is often difficult to achieve.

The third step involves *acceptance* of the message (yielding to it). If accepting Staci's message leads to social acceptance or approval, or to the feeling that your values are being clearly expressed, or would aid you in the task of ego-defense, then acceptance is more likely to occur. The fourth fac-

compliance:
When people accept influence in order to achieve a favorable reaction from a powerful person or group.

identification:
When one accepts influence in order to maintain a satisfying self-defining relationship with another person or group.

internalization:
When one accepts influence because the content of the induced behavior is intrinsically rewarding and is congruent with one's value system.

tor, *retention*, involves remembering and acting upon the major points of the communication. If the attitude change message is forgotten soon after it is perceived, little permanent attitude or behavior change will result. For these reasons, advertisers and politicians take great pains to repeat messages and phrase them in such a way that they are likely to be retained (see Figure 4-3).

Source Characteristics

The source, or origin, of a communication is an important determinant of whether the message will produce attitude change. Three characteristics of the source of a communication have been studied extensively: credibility, attractiveness, and power.

Credibility: Expertise and Trustworthiness

credibility:
The credibility of a communication source depends mainly on expertise and trustworthiness.

knowledge bias:
Biased reporting when the source has incorrect information

reporting bias:
Occurs when the source has correct information but fails to report it.

The **credibility,** or believability, of a source depends mainly on two factors: expertise and trustworthiness. Expertise is the extent of knowledge that a source appears to have; trustworthiness refers to the source's intentions. There are two types of bias a source may have: *knowledge bias* and *reporting bias* (Eagly, Wood, & Chaiken, 1978). **Knowledge bias** occurs when the source has incorrect information, whereas **reporting bias** occurs when the source has correct information but fails to report it. Knowledge bias is most relevant to expertise; reporting bias relates to trustworthiness. A trustworthy source seems sincere and appears to have no personal gain stemming from any attitude change that might occur.

FIGURE 4-3

Message-Learning Approach to Attitude Change

According to the message-learning approach, the fundamental processes in attitude change are attention, comprehension, acceptance/yielding, and retention. These processes are affected by source, message, audience, and channel factors.

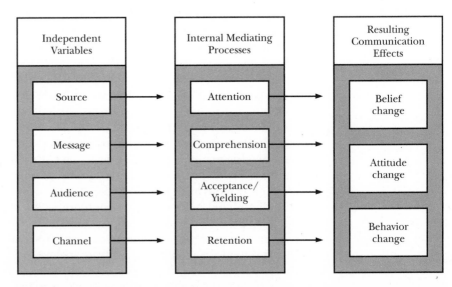

Source: From Petty, Richard E., and Cacioppo, John T., *Attitudes and Persuasions: Classic and Contemporary Approaches.* © 1981 Wm. C. Brown Publishers, Dubuque, Iowa. All Rights Reserved. Reprinted by permission.

Turning again to our campus election, your evaluation of Staci's knowledge about campus problems and student government will determine her expertise in your eyes. Her perceived trustworthiness will be high if you see her as telling the truth about what she believes. If you think she is being deceptive and running largely because of self-interest, in contrast, her trustworthiness is low. The greater a source's perceived expertise and trustworthiness, the greater the attitude change it can produce (Aronson et al., 1963).

Audience members make attributions regarding the reasons why a communicator advocates a particular position (Eagly, 1981). The listener may attribute the source's behavior to dispositional factors (this is what Staci really believes), to situational factors (Staci has a lot to gain by advocating this position), or to the "rightness" of the message itself. If the content of a message confirms your expectations about what Staci would say, you are likely to attribute Staci's position to dispositional factors ("It's what she believes") or situational factors ("She was under pressure to say that"). On the other hand, suppose the content of the message disconfirms your expectations. Suppose Staci belongs to a sorority but takes the position that more campus resources should go to independents, rather than sororities or fraternities. Now the attributional task is more difficult. You might decide that the compelling rightness of the message's position (the needs of campus independents) overcame Staci's tendency to say what you expected (advocating support for sororities). If you make this attribution, you are particularly likely to accept her message.

Illustrating this effect, a criminal who argued that police should have greater power in dealing with crime produced more attitude change in an audience than a criminal who argued that police power should be decreased (Walster et al., 1966). Similarly, observers were more convinced by a speaker who gave a proenvironmental speech despite having a probusiness back-

Credible communicators? Evangelists Jimmy Swaggart and Jim Bakker were highly credible, attractive, and powerful sources of information to their followers. Their involvement in widely-publicized sex scandals in the 1980s had a devastating effect on their trustworthiness (a central component of communicator credibility) in the eyes of many of their former followers.

Can a Soviet leader be a credible communicator in the U.S.? During his visit to the American Midwest in 1990, Soviet Premier Gorbachev was perceived as a highly credible communicator by many Americans.

ground, or one who gave a proenvironmental speech in front of a probusiness audience, than by speakers who gave speeches fitting their background or the audience's preferences (Eagly et al., 1978).

Generally, as a source's trustworthiness increases, so does the attitude change obtained (Cooper & Croyle, 1984). Yet other factors may mediate this relationship. *Forewarning* the audience about a source's persuasive intent will inhibit attitude change when the issue is a personally important one (Petty & Cacioppo, 1979). Although forewarning may suppress immediate attitude change, delayed influence can still occur (Watts & Holt, 1979).

"Overheard" conversations are more effective in changing attitudes than are messages explicitly directed to an audience. For example, subjects who overheard a telephone conversation (which they thought they were not supposed to hear) were more persuaded than were subjects who heard the same message delivered as a speech (Walster & Festinger, 1962).

The Sleeper Effect

Even though the level of a communicator's credibility can produce vast differences in attitude change, over time the enhancing effect of a highly credible communicator may be lost as the source of the message is forgotten (Figure 4-4). We all have bits and pieces of information floating around in our heads for which we've forgotten the source: "Somebody said that . . . ." or "I heard somewhere . . . ." Some of this information may have come from highly credible sources, but we've forgotten what came from where. During the campus election, you may recall various proposals but forget which candidate said what.

The decrease in the impact of communicator credibility over time has been called the **sleeper effect**, as it happens after an audience "sleeps on" a message. When people forget that the source was highly credible, some of the attitude change that had occurred is lost (line A in Figure 4-4). The noncredible source is ineffective initially, and it may stay ineffective over time, as depicted by line C.

sleeper effect:
The impact of a communicator's credibility may lessen as time passes and the audience forgets who the source was.

FIGURE 4-4

The Sleeper Effect in Attitude Change: The Differential Effects of Communicator Credibility May Dissipate over Time

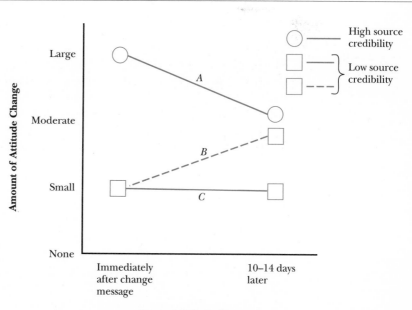

A source's low credibility is a *discounting cue* that causes the audience to reject the message. However, when the discounting cue was not received until after the message was heard, sometimes there is an increase in attitude change over time for messages from low-credibility sources (line B in Figure 4-4)(Greenwald et al., 1985). The suppressing effect of low credibility lessened as time passed, either because the discounting cue became dissociated from the message (Cook et al., 1979; Gruder et al., 1978) or because the discounting cue was forgotten at a more rapid rate than was the message (Pratkanis et al., 1988). Hence, even if Staci has low credibility in her audience's eyes (a discounting cue), she may be able to achieve some attitude change if they later forget that the message came from her.

It is difficult to produce long-lasting attitude change from just one exposure to a persuasive message, even when delivered by a highly credible source. Advertisers and politicians recognize this, as they air the same commercials day after day, month after month, hoping to reinstate the source of the communication. If the identity of the communicator is reinstated, the differential effects of communicator credibility also reappear (Kelman & Hovland, 1953).

Attractiveness of the Communicator

A communicator's attractiveness to an audience is based on several factors, including physical appearance, pleasantness, likableness, and similarity to the audience. These aspects are closely related, as each aspect of attractiveness influences perceptions of the other aspects. If you look at the photos on posters of candidates running for campus offices, as a group they are likely to be better-looking than average. People tend to like good-looking people more, as we will see in Chapter 7; physically attractive people are also perceived as more likable and capable than are less attractive people. In addition, we tend to see people whom we like as more similar to us than those whom we dislike. A disliked communicator is usually ineffective in changing people's attitudes. In fact, disliked individuals sometimes produce a **boomerang effect;** the audience changes its attitudes in a direction opposite to what the disliked source advocated (Abelson & Miller, 1967). Conversely, likable communicators produce attitude change. Those who are similar to their audience in terms of attitudes, skills, and abilities are more effective persuaders than those who are dissimilar. The impact of attractiveness depends to some extent on the type of message. Communicator likability affects persuasion for videotaped and audiotaped messages (which make the communicator especially noticeable) more than for written messages (Chaiken & Eagly, 1983).

Effective communicators must walk a fine line between expertise and similarity. They must be perceived as experts (to some degree) or the audience will dismiss the message. But they must not seem too dissimilar to the audience. Similarity to the audience is most important if values are central to the issue; if the issue is more factual, similarity is not as important

boomerang effect:
If a message is delivered by a highly disliked source, the audience may change their attitudes in a direction opposite to what the disliked source advocated.

Ronald Reagan, the "consummate communicator"? Much of Reagan's success as a politician was due to his effective communication style, his skill in presenting himself to the American people as highly trustworthy and attractive.

(Goethals & Nelson, 1973). On a related note, an attractive source may be effective regardless of the number of arguments used, but the effectiveness of a less attractive source is more strongly related to the number of arguments used (Norman, 1976). To be an effective communicator, Staci must establish her expertise, but she must do it in such a way that she seems to have the same basic values, needs, problems, and desires as other students. Then she will seem attractive as well as expert.

Power

If the source has power to reward or punish the target, wants the target to agree, and will find out if the target did agree, then the target is likely to be influenced (McGuire, 1969). Consider the degree of conformity in a large corporation. Junior executives may express opinions that are remarkably similar to those of the boss; the boss's social power has molded the subordinate's attitudes. But is this really attitude change, or is this merely compliance to the boss's opinions without any internalization? It probably starts out as only compliance but research evidence suggests that, over time, attitudes that initially reflect compliance can become internalized and accepted privately. Later in this chapter we'll analyze how this happens.

Message Characteristics

The Position Advocated in a Message

The amount of discrepancy between the message and the target's views is very important. For example, we can portray a student's attitude toward a campus issue (say that more student fees should be used to improve parking

FOCUS 4-3

Can a Newscaster's Smile Help Elect a President?

In recent years many observers have complained of a "hostile media," claiming that network news coverage was biased against their preferred political party or candidate (Vallone, Ross & Lepper, 1985). Since network news commentators could serve as highly credible attitude-change communicators who have a chance to address millions of viewers nightly, this charge is a serious one. Contrary to these complaints, however, careful analyses (Clancey & Robinson, 1985) found no evidence of systematic verbal bias among the networks or among the network commentators.

But attitudes can be conveyed by nonverbal means as well. Recall that Cacioppo and his associates (1988) were able to measure attitudes accurately via EMG analyses of movement in the brow muscle. At a less subtle level, if a parent consistently smiles while talking about one of her children, Lori, but frowns while talking about the other, Nancy, aren't we likely to assume that she prefers Lori over Nancy? Further, might people assume that Lori is a more likable child? Brian Mullen and his colleagues (1986) reasoned that news commentators might show bias through their expressions when discussing politicians. During the 1984 presidential election campaign they videotaped newscasts on the three major networks, selecting segments in which each newscaster was talking about the two candidates, Ronald Reagan or Walter Mondale. They showed these segments without sound to a number of observers who rated the newscaster's expression for each segment. No differences were found for ratings of Dan Rather (CBS) or Tom Brokaw (NBC), but Peter Jennings of ABC had a pleasant expression significantly more often when he talked about Reagan than when he talked about Mondale.

Did Jennings' bias have an effect on ABC's viewers? Perhaps so. The researchers found that over 75 percent of ABC news viewers in four cities intended to vote for Reagan while only 62.5 percent of NBC and CBS viewers had similar intentions. This difference might occur because viewers who were already pro-Reagan chose to view ABC news because they were aware of Jennings' bias, but other analyses done by Mullen and his co-workers cast doubt on this possibility. Instead, their data suggested a subtle type of persuasion via classical conditioning, where a conditioned stimulus (Reagan's name) was repeatedly associated with a positive stimulus (a pleasant facial expression). Alternatively, repeated smiling when mentioning Reagan's name might be construed by viewers as a form of political endorsement by a highly credible communicator. The researchers concluded (p. 295) that, "the selection of the president by the electorate may itself be influenced by which candidate the newscasters smile upon." A sobering thought, indeed. ❖

facilities) along a continuum ranging from extremely negative affect (– 10) to extremely positive affect (+ 10) (Figure 4-5). Suppose Staci wants to convince Dave, whose attitude toward using the fees in this manner is moderately negative (– 4), to support it. How strong a position should Staci take?

It has been proposed that for each individual's attitude, three distinct regions exist (M. Sherif & Hovland, 1961). Surrounding one's own position is the **latitude of acceptance,** within which attitude-relevant statements are seen as acceptable. For example, Dave might basically accept negative statements ranging from – 7 to – 1. The latitude of noncommitment includes statements that are neither acceptable nor unacceptable to the audience. Finally, the latitude of rejection includes positions unacceptable to the person. Attitude change is most likely to occur when the message falls within the audience's latitude of acceptance (Atkins, Deaux, & Bieri, 1967). If the discrepancy between the message and the audience's position is too great, the communication will be dismissed. But if the discrepancy is very small, the target might assimilate the message and fail to notice any difference of opinion (Hovland et al., 1957). Hence, we can expect that the greatest attitude change will occur at moderate levels of discrepancy. In our example, Staci might present a message at – 1 (point B in Figure 4-5), arguing that the idea is not quite as bad as Dave thinks it is.

Involvement, Credibility, and Discrepancy

Latitudes of acceptance, noncommitment, and rejection are influenced by perceived source credibility and attractiveness and by the audience's degree

latitude of acceptance:
That area centered around one's own position within which attitude relevant statements are seen as acceptable.

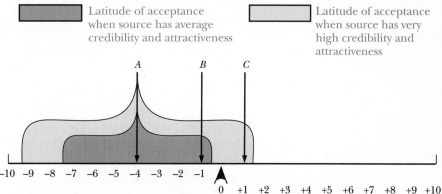

FIGURE 4-5

Discrepancy and Credibility: The Credibility and Attractiveness of a Source Interacting with Discrepancy

Latitude of acceptance when source has average credibility and attractiveness

Latitude of acceptance when source has very high credibility and attractiveness

A = Target's initial attitude (moderately negative: –4)
B = Effective position for a message from a source having average
 credibility and attractiveness
C = Effective position for a message from a source having very high
 credibility and attractiveness

of involvement with the issue. If Dave sees Staci as a highly credible communicator, this widens his latitude of acceptance (e.g., from − 9 to + 1 in Figure 4·5) and Staci can achieve attitude change with a message (e.g., point C) that would be too discrepant if presented by a less credible communicator (Aronson, et al., 1963; Bochner & Insko, 1966).

Dave's level of involvement is also important. If an issue has a high level of value-relevant involvement for an individual (it is linked to important values), the individual's latitude of rejection will be wide and the latitude of noncommitment will be very narrow. Also he may attribute less credibility to a communicator. Hence, it will be difficult to change his views. Johnson and Eagly (1989) conducted a *meta-analysis* of fifteen studies that analyzed involvement. **Meta-analysis** is a sophisticated statistical technique for combining the results of many separate studies to assess their overall findings. The meta-analysis found that high value-relevant involvement was associated with less persuasion. If Dave feels that campus parking issues are related to his values (personal freedom, ability to get an education, etc.), then Staci will have a hard time persuading him to change his views. She would have to use a message fairly close to Dave's initial attitude to avoid falling within his latitude of rejection (C. Sherif et al., 1973).

meta-analysis:
A statistical technique for combining the results of separate studies into a single analysis.

Changing Attitudes in Natural Settings

Changing attitudes in natural settings is complicated, since a communicator must establish high credibility and also estimate the audience's position and level of involvement. A nice example of step-by-step attitude change comes from a study of women attending Bennington College from 1935 to 1939 (Newcomb, 1958). At the time of the study, Bennington was a new, rather expensive women's college. Most students came from well-to-do families with Republican backgrounds. The faculty, on the other hand, tended to support Democratic candidates and programs. The older students and faculty gave liberal political information to the younger women and a group norm toward liberal political attitudes developed, placing conformity pressures on the younger women. A dramatic change occurred in most students' political attitudes over their four years of college—they became more liberal each year. In a straw vote prior to the 1936 presidential election, most of the freshmen (62 percent) voted Republican, but very few of the juniors and seniors (16 percent) did. A follow-up study twenty-five years later indicated that most of the college-liberalized women had retained their liberalism (Newcomb et al., 1967). Most had married men with similar liberal views. Those few who had moved back toward conservatism were likely to have married men with conservative views.

The "Sidedness" of a Message

Should a communicator mention only one side of the issue or should both sides be mentioned, with the favored side stressed? The answer depends on the audience's characteristics. If an audience already agrees with the position of the communicator, and the communicator's task is simply to make them agree more strongly, or if the audience is poorly educated, a one-sided message is likely to be more effective. If an audience initially disagrees with the issue or is well educated or knowledgeable, a two-sided message will work better (Lumsdaine & Janis, 1953). In Staci's case, since Dave is well educated and opposes her position, she had better start with a two-sided message. By presenting both sides, Staci is apt to be perceived as more trustworthy and expert. In fact, merely mentioning to a skeptical audience that there are two sides to an issue, even without explaining the other side, can increase a communicator's influence (Jones & Brehm, 1970).

Drawing a Conclusion

Should a communicator draw conclusions for an audience? Again, characteristics of the audience can be the deciding factor. When an audience is unintelligent and/or uneducated, or when a message is complex, it is best for the speaker to draw conclusions. Otherwise, the audience may not realize what the communicator wants. However, when it is clear that an audience will be able to draw the desired conclusion—when it is intelligent and/or educated and knowledgeable about a topic or when a message is simple—it is best to leave the conclusions unstated (Linder & Worchel, 1970; McGuire, 1969). Probably Staci should let Dave draw his own conclusions.

Ordering of Messages

Communicators such as politicians, advertisers, and lawyers, who know that their audience will be exposed to conflicting messages, face another question: Is it better to present your message first or last? Research indicates there is no simple answer; it depends on the length of time between the two messages and the length of time between the second message and the attitude measurement situation (the election, the visit to the store, the jury's deliberation). If the messages are close together and there is a long delay afterward, a **primacy effect** is likely to occur—it's better to have your message first. On the other hand, if the two messages occur far apart and attitudes are measured shortly after the second message, a **recency effect** is more likely—the second message is more effective (Miller & Campbell, 1959; Wilson & Miller, 1968).

primacy effect:
In some persuasion situations, a person who argues first has the most impact on an audience.

recency effect:
The second of two opposing arguments is likely to have a greater effect when there is a long interval between messages and attitudes are measured shortly after the second message is delivered.

Audience Characteristics

De Facto Selective Exposure

In natural settings it is often difficult to deliver a message to the intended audience. A Democratic candidate for political office may create a special message to convince Republicans to vote for her. But when the message is aired, 90 percent of the people who tune in and stay tuned in are likely to be Democrats. While people may not go out of their way to avoid information inconsistent with their own views, because of the subculture to which they belong they come into contact mostly with messages that support their

de facto selective exposure:

People tend to come into contact with messages that support their existing opinions, because of the subcultures to which they belong and the materials that they encounter.

existing opinions, a phenomenon labeled **de facto selective exposure** (Sears, 1968). To illustrate, business-minded people might read the *Wall Street Journal* or *Barron's* because they want up-to-date information about the business world. Because many of the articles and advertisements adopt a probusiness orientation, readers end up exposing themselves to ideas that support their existing attitudes. Thus, behaviors that begin with one goal in mind (learning about current business trends) have an additional result: People end up exposing themselves to information that is consistent with their existing attitudes.

Personality Factors

People who have learned that they can rely on the word of others tend to be trusting and are more likely to be affected by persuasive communications. Self-esteem also relates to attitude change. People with high self-esteem are generally less likely to yield to persuasion, because they have confidence in their opinions (Cook, 1970). Their self-evaluation is high enough to make a credible communicator less credible in comparison; they may think they know as much as the communicator does.

Intelligence and self-esteem may differentially affect one's ability to comprehend a message and one's willingness to yield to it (Figure 4-6). Highly intelligent people are better able to comprehend a complex message but may be less willing to yield to it. McGuire (1968a) hypothesized that since attitude change depends on both comprehension and acceptance, the likelihood of attitude change is greatest when the audience members are at an intermediate level in the relevant personal characteristics, where the probability of comprehension of the message is high enough and the probability of yielding is still relatively high as well (point A in Figure 4-6). Although McGuire's model has considerable logical appeal, thus far it has received only mixed research support (Eagly, 1981)

De facto selective exposure. People most often come into contact with messages that support their existing attitudes (in this case, a probusiness orientation).

FIGURE 4-6

The Theoretical Relation-
ship between Audience
Factors (Such as Self-
Esteem or Intelligence)
and Attitude Change

*Attitude change cannot be
greater than level of reception
(attention, comprehension, and
retention) or level of yielding.*

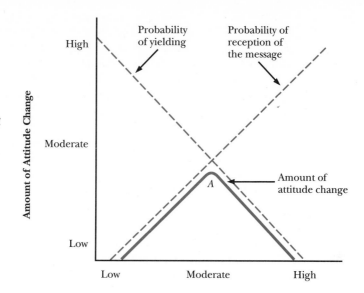

**Audience Characteristic
(such as intelligence or self-esteem)**

Source: Based on McGuire, W. J. (1968a). Personality and susceptibility to social influence. In
E. F. Borgatta & W. W. Lambert (eds.), *Handbook of personality theory and research.* Chicago:
Rand McNally.

Age

Are young people more or less persuasible than older folks? An "impressionable years" hypothesis would propose that individuals are highly susceptible to attitude change during late adolescence and early adulthood and
that susceptibility drops precipitously thereafter and remains low for the
rest of one's life. An "increasing persistence" hypothesis, in contrast, proposes
that people become gradually more resistant to change throughout their lives.
Analyzing survey data from national elections between 1956 and 1980,
wherein each individual's attitudes toward several issues were measured at
several points over a four-year period, Krosnick and Alwin (1989) found support for the "impressionable years" hypothesis. The eighteen to twenty-five-
year-olds showed significantly more attitude change than did the older
groups. The twenty-six to thirty-three-year-olds showed the next most change,
but there were no age-related differences among older groups (up to age
eighty-three). Harkening back to the issue of external validity (generalizability) discussed in Chapter 1, these results suggest that attitude-change studies
that utilize college students may yield an exaggerated impression of how easily attitudes can be changed.

Channel Factors

Communications can be transmitted through several channels: print media (newspapers, magazines, books), audio media (radio, telephone, audiotapes), or audiovisual media (television, movies, videotapes). Persuasive communications are most effective when tailored to the channel. For instance, complex messages are comprehended better from print than from audio or audiovisual channels. Yet once comprehension has been achieved, yielding is greatest for audiovisual channels and least through print (Chaiken & Eagly, 1976). Hence, an easy-to-comprehend message will be most effective when presented via the audiovisual media, but a hard-to-comprehend message may be most effective when presented first in print (so that it can be comprehended) and then through audiovisual channels.

THEORIES OF ATTITUDE CHANGE

Central and Peripheral Routes to Persuasion

Now that we have analyzed what factors lead to attitude change (characteristics of the source, message, audience, and channel), we can turn to the *how* and *why* of it. Several important theories have emerged in recent years that predict and explain attitude change.

There may be two basic routes to attitude change—a *central route* characterized by careful, systematic processing of information, and a *peripheral route* wherein simpler heuristics are used for quick and efficient (but not necessarily accurate) evaluation of the message. Thinking about (elaborating on) the issue requires considerable effort. In their **elaboration likelihood model,** Petty and Cacioppo (1986) theorized that people will choose the central route only when they are motivated to think about the issue and have the ability to understand the arguments. Ability to process the communication is better when it is repeated, there are no distractions, the message is simple, and the audience is intelligent. Attitude change that results from the central route should be relatively enduring.

elaboration likelihood model:

Model describing the central route to attitude change (long-lasting change resulting from thinking about the issue) and the peripheral route (temporary change from non-issue relevant factors).

When the audience's motivation or ability to think about the issue is limited, they are likely to choose the peripheral route, using simple heuristics that associate certain persuasion cues (such as perceived consensus, source expertise, or source attractiveness) with message validity. They accept the assumption that if everyone else agrees (consensus), it must be right; or, if that expert communicator says it's so, it must be so. Change through the peripheral route is less enduring and will usually persist only as long as the relevant persuasion cues remain salient.

People are most likely to choose the central route when they are motivated by a desire to hold a valid, accurate attitude (when the attitude serves a knowledge function) and the issue is relevant to important goals or outcomes (Johnson & Eagly, 1989). If people's reactions to persuasion are motivated more by defensiveness (ego-defensive function) or the desire to manage the impression they give (social adjustment function), they are likely to make use of peripheral heuristics in responding to the message (Chaiken, Liberman, & Eagly, 1989).

The model implies that it is quite difficult to produce enduring attitude change, because the recipient must have the ability and the motivation to process the information and must find the message convincing. In politics and advertising the central route to persuasion may be too difficult to manage, making the peripheral route more effective. Often advertisers use no arguments at all, relying instead on repeated exposure, classical conditioning (association of the product with attractive people or a catchy jingle), and the availability heuristic. Although these factors may lead to attitude change, it is not likely to be permanent, for the audience has not been convinced by the arguments themselves.

Because peripheral-route change is temporary, advertisers continually repeat the message to remind the audience of the expertise or attractiveness of the source. A moderate level of repetition enhances central processing and analysis of arguments; if your arguments are good ones, then attitude change will occur. But repetition is not always helpful. If your arguments are weak, it is better not to repeat them so that the audience members do not analyze them too closely (Cacioppo & Petty, 1989).

Peripheral route change can still lead indirectly to more permanent change in some cases. Once the temporary behavior change has occurred,

The peripheral route to attitude change. Advertisers who use celebrities as spokespersons are aiming to change consumers' attitudes via the peripheral route.

FIGURE 4-7

Two Routes to Attitude Change

The elaboration likelihood model developed by Petty and Cacioppo.

If audience member has:	High motivation to systematically think about the issue	Low motivation to systematically think about the issue
	High ability to think about the issue	Low ability to think about the issue
	High need for cognition	Low need for cognition
Audience will evaluate the message via the:	Direct route	Peripheral route
Audience's reaction to the message is mediated by:	Systematic information processing	Simple heuristics
Amount of attitude change will depend on:	Quality of the arguments	Peripheral factors such as: source characteristics, perceived consensus, message length

Sources: Based upon Petty, R. E., & Cacioppo, J. T. (1986). *Communication and persuasion: Central and peripheral routes to attitude change.* New York: Springer-Verlag. Chaiken, S., Liberman, A., & Eagly, A. H. (1989). Heuristic and systematic information processing within and beyond the persuasion context. In J. S. Uleman & J. A. Bargh (Eds.), *Unintended thought* (pp. 212–252). New York: Guilford.

audience members may then think favorably about the issues and generate bolstering (supportive) cognitions on their own, leading to more permanent attitude change. Hence, what begins as a temporary attitude change via the peripheral route may end up being a more permanent change via the central route.

In summary, this model suggests that if the audience is motivated and able to think about the message, and convincing arguments are available, then the central route is the best strategy to pursue. On the other hand, if the arguments are weak or the audience is unable or unwilling to understand them, then the peripheral route will be a more promising strategy.

Individuals differ in their *need for cognition*, the enjoyment derived from effortful information processing. People with a high need for cognition are motivated to take the central route, analyzing arguments and thinking about important issues. They tend also to show greater attitude-behavior consistency. Those low in need for cognition, in contrast, are more likely to pay attention to peripheral factors such as an attractive or prestigious communicator (Cacioppo et al., 1986). I pointed out earlier that all of us are "cognitive misers," using schemas and other cognitive heuristics to simplify our complex cognitive environments. People low in need for cognition are the most miserly. If Staci has crafted a persuasive appeal that contains effective arguments, it will have the greatest impact on an audience high in need for cognition, who will carefully evaluate the arguments. If facing an audience whose members are low in need for cognition, however, she'd be better off stressing peripheral factors such as endorsements from other popular students (Haugtvedt et al., 1988). Sample items from the Need for Cognition Scale appear in Table 4-4 (Cacioppo & Petty, 1982). Now that we have covered the elaboration likelihood model of attitude change, we can turn to a theory that has stimulated more social psychological research than any other: cognitive dissonance theory.

Cognitive Dissonance Theory

Basics of Cognitive Dissonance

cognitive dissonance theory:
Attitude or behavior change is likely when two cognitive elements are in a dissonant relationship to one another.

The most influential theory of attitude change has been **cognitive dissonance theory.** Leon Festinger (1957) proposed that any two *cognitive elements* (knowledge, opinions, or beliefs about the world, about oneself, or about one's behavior) can exist in one of three general relationships: irrelevant (no relationship to each other), consonant (consistent with each another), or dissonant (incompatible with each another). To illustrate, consider the cognitive elements "Cigarette smoking seems to cause serious illness and shortened life expectancy" and "I smoke." Assuming a person has no suicidal tendencies, these cognitions are incompatible. This incompatibility produces psychological tension, or dissonance, motivating the person to do something

---

TABLE 4-4	MEASURING THE NEED FOR COGNITION

People with a Low Need for Cognition Will Agree:

Learning new ways to think doesn't excite me very much.

I prefer just to let things happen rather than try to understand why they turned out that way.

I like tasks that require little thought once I've learned them.

I find little satisfaction is deliberating hard and for long hours.

Thinking is not my idea of fun.

Simply knowing the answer rather than understanding the reasons for the answer to a problem is fine with me.

People with a High Need for Cognition Will Agree

I would prefer a task that is intellectual, difficult, and important to one that is somewhat important but does not require much thought.

I tend to set goals that can be accomplished only be expending considerable mental effort.

I prefer watching educational to entertainment programs.

I would prefer complex to simple problems.

I enjoy thinking about an issue even when the results of my thought will have no effect on the outcome of the issue.

I really enjoy a task that involves coming up with new solutions to problems.

Source: From Cacioppo, J. T., & Petty, R. E. (1982). The need for cognition. *Journal of Personality and Social Psychology, 42,* 116–131. Copyright © 1982 by the American Psychological Association. Reprinted by permission.

to reduce the dissonance. The more important the two cognitions are, or the greater the ratio of dissonant to consonant cognitions on a specific topic, the greater the amount of dissonance.

To reduce dissonance, an individual may change an attitude, change the dissonant behavior, or seek new information or social support to strengthen one of the cognitive elements. As an example, cigarette smokers might change their attitude toward medical research, refusing to believe in its findings. Or they might alter their behavior: stopping smoking, or cutting down, or moving to a low-tar brand. At a more devious level, smokers might change their perceptions of the behavior by deciding that they really don't smoke very much or don't inhale very deeply. To strengthen one of the cognitive elements, smokers might reaffirm all the supposedly positive aspects of smoking (relaxation, social poise, etc.).

Research has led to two major modifications to cognitive dissonance theory. In 1969 Aronson pointed out that it makes most theoretical sense to speak of inconsistency between a *self-concept* and cognitions about a behavior that violates the self-concept. In the case of smoking, for example, dissonance arises between the self-concept "I am a reasonable, sensible person" and the cognition "Smoking is a behavior that is likely to shorten my life and is therefore unreasonable." Second, dissonance is greatest when a person feels *personal responsibility* for the elements causing the dissonance (Wicklund & Brehm, 1976). Dissonant cognitive elements (which include a self-concept belief and personal responsibility) produce psychological tension that must be reduced. Five related areas of dissonance research are reviewed below.

Cigarette smoking can be a source of cognitive dissonance. To reduce dissonance smokers might quit, change their attitudes about the risks of smoking, or change their perception of their behavior.

Free Choice between Alternatives

A person who makes a free choice between two equally attractive alternatives has to deal with some possibly negative aspects of the item chosen and some possibly positive aspects of the item rejected. (If you've ever bought a car, you know how this works.) The situation can produce dissonance since the cognitions, "I am a reasonable, intelligent person" and "I have chosen a product that may be the poorer of the two," are in conflict. People can justify their decisions to themselves by increasing the evaluations of the attractiveness of the chosen object and/or by deciding that the rejected object was less attractive than they had thought previously.

In one of the earliest dissonance experiments, Brehm (1956) let college women choose one of two household products as a reward for participation in a market research study. Unknown to each woman, these two products had been selected by the experimenter specifically because she had rated them earlier as being equally attractive. When the women were given the opportunity to rerate the items later, the products they had chosen were rated as more attractive, whereas the unchosen products were seen as less attractive. This overvaluing process occurs only when an individual has a free choice between the alternatives. If a person is simply given one object or if the individual is told which object must be picked, no dissonance arises and no attitude change takes place.

Free choice can produce cognitive dissonance. Choosing between two equally attractive alternatives (compact discs) can cause cognitive dissonance, which can be reduced by overvaluing the chosen object and devaluing the unchosen one.

Many later studies have also shown that people tend to overvalue things they choose and to undervalue things they reject—even for behavior such as placing bets at the racetrack (Knox & Inkster, 1968). There is also some evidence (Walster, 1964) that a regret phase occasionally occurs immediately after the decision is made, in which the chosen alternative is not overvalued and the person seems to regret his or her choice. But this phase, if it occurs at all, is short-lived and is quickly replaced by overvaluing one's choice.

Induced Compliance

What will be the impact of counterattitudinal behaviors, actions that are in conflict with a person's attitudes and preferences? For example, what happens when a person lies (a counterattitudinal behavior, assuming that the person values honesty)? In a classic experiment, college men were given several boring tasks to do for an hour (Festinger & Carlsmith, 1959). Afterward, the men were asked to help out the experimenter and convey false information to the next subject, telling her the study was interesting and enjoyable. Some men were told they would be paid one dollar for doing this, while others were told they would get twenty dollars. The next participant (actually, an experimental accomplice) acted hesitant and the subject had to convince her that the tasks were enjoyable. After this, subjects were interviewed by a different experimenter and asked to evaluate the study. Other participants, the control group, simply completed the boring task and then gave their opinions to the interviewer.

Subjects offered only a small incentive (one dollar) for lying changed their attitudes toward the task, later saying that they found it somewhat interesting and enjoyable. Subjects in the control condition and those who had told the lie for a large incentive (twenty dollars) rated the task as uninteresting and unenjoyable.

Why did the counterattitudinal behavior (in this case, lying) produce attitude change in the small-incentive group? After telling the lie, the men were confronted with the cognitions "I am a moral, decent human being" and "I just told a lie and misled someone." Some subjects could deal with the dissonance by pointing to aspects of the situation (twenty dollars) that partly justified the decision to lie. But subjects who accepted one dollar to lie had less justifiction for their action; hence, they should have experienced more dissonance. To reduce it, they could convince themselves that the behavior wasn't really a lie by evaluating the task more positively.

The extent to which attitude change follows counterattitudinal behavior is related to two additional factors: *responsibility* and *consequences*. People feel more responsible for their counterattitudinal actions when they had a high degree of choice whether to perform the behavior. The consequences of the counterattitudinal behavior are also important. If the consequences seem minor or unforeseen, they can be dismissed easily. Otherwise, the behavior can't be so easily dismissed and dissonance is greater, leading to more attitude change (Goethals et al., 1979; Wicklund & Brehm, 1976).

In fact, some theorists (Cooper & Fazio, 1984; Scher & Cooper, 1989) have recently asserted that dissonance in these situations is caused not by feelings of inconsistency but rather by an awareness that one has caused an aversive event. Scher and Cooper (1989) had students write an essay supporting an increase in student fees (a counterattituindal position) or opposing such an increase (proattuitudinal). The students were told that their essays would be shown to the Dean's Policy Committee; some were led to believe that, because of the order in which essays would be shown to the committee, their essay would probably have a "boomerang effect," persuading the committee to take the side opposite the one advocated in the essay. From the students' point of view, an aversive outcome would be if they convinced committee members to support an increase in student fees. This could happen by writing a counterattitudinal essay (pro-fees) that was persuasive or a proattitudinal essay that had a boomerang effect. As Figure 4-8 shows, it was students in these two conditions who showed the most attitude change, indicating that the aversive outcome, rather than just writing a counterattitudinal essay, was the crucial factor.

In practical terms, to get the greatest attitude change from a counterattitudinal behavior, you should apply just enough pressure to get the person to perform the behavior, so that he feels he had a choice (and therefore feels responsible). You should also convince him that his behavior had significant aversive consequences.

Counterattitudinal behavior can be caused by one's expectations, as well as by more direct pressures. For example, people often modify their behavior

---

FIGURE 4-8

Aversive Consequences
May Cause Dissonance

Amount of atttitude change in students who wrote a counterattitudinal essay supporting an increase in student fees. Half of the students were told that the essay would affect the audience in the direction opposite from the one in which it was written (boomerang condition).

Source: From Scher, S. J., & Cooper, J. (1989). Motivational basis of dissonance: The singular role of behavioral consequences. *Journal of Personality and Social Psychology, 56,* 904. Copyright © 1989 by the American Psychological Association. Reprinted by permission.

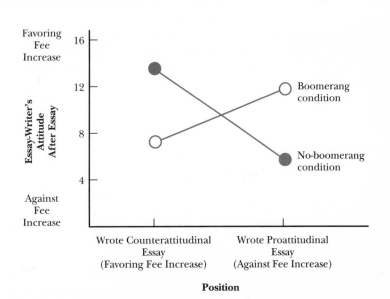

depending on what their audience expects. We tell "white lies" to avoid insulting someone; we tell our boss or our parents what they want to hear. Professors are not immune to this bias; they write more positive letters of recommendation about graduate school-bound seniors when they are told the senior will see the letter than when they are told that the senior will not see it (Ceci & Peters, 1984). People high in the trait of authoritarianism (Chapter 10) are particularly likely to modify their behavior to match the expectations of an audience composed of high-status persons (Higgins & McCann, 1984). These instances of counterattitudinal behavior may seem harmless enough but, to corrupt an old phrase, "saying is believing" (Higgins & Rholes, 1978). People's attitudes are likely to change to more closely reflect their new behavior.

Justification of Effort

Suppose you have put a lot of effort into gaining membership in a fraternity or a sorority. You were admitted only after a strenuous period of initiation as a pledge. After finally being accepted, you discover that you don't like the people or their activities very much. Your expectations of the group's worth have been disconfirmed. The more effort you put into gaining membership, the greater will be the amount of dissonance you feel. You might reduce the dissonance by deciding that the group is pretty good after all, thereby justifying your efforts to join it.

To investigate this process, Aronson and Mills (1959) had college women sign up for group discussions on the psychology of sex. Each prospective member was given an easy or difficult "screening test" (initiation) to determine her "suitability" for the group. Each woman was told that she had passed the test and was eligible to join the group. Another group of subjects was given no initiation at all.

For the first meeting of the group, the women listened to a dull, boring discussion of sexual behavior in lower animals. This disconfirmed the women's expectations that the group would be interesting and worthwhile, producing dissonance. Women in the difficult-initiation condition should have experienced the most dissonance, since they had worked hardest to gain entrance to the group. They could rationalize their behavior by seeing the discussions as relatively worthwhile. As predicted, they rated the group discussions more positively than did women in either the mild-initiation or no-initiation conditions. This general finding was replicated in a study that used mild or severe electric shock as the initiation and cheating as the discussion topic (Gerard & Mathewson, 1966). This **suffering-leads-to-liking effect** may be particularly relevant to the severe initiation procedures sometimes used by college fraternities and the rigors of military boot camp.

suffering-leads-to-liking effect: People who put forth great effort or endure suffering to join a group may value the group highly in order to justify their behavior.

Disconfirmed Expectations

In the 1950s a woman (given the pseudonym Mrs. Keech) in a midwestern town apparently began receiving messages from the planet Clarion by means

Does suffering lead to liking? Severe initiations into a group, such as military "boot camp," may cause people to like the group more, in order to justify having gone through the initiation.

of "automatic writing"; her hand wrote out messages that she felt were sent to her by other beings. Mrs. Keech and her followers, mostly college students, studied the messages—a mixture of mysticism, science fiction, and Christianity. In September Mrs. Keech received a prediction that the world would be destroyed on December 21 by flood and earthquake, but that a flying saucer would land on the evening of December 20 to rescue her small group. Several social psychologists and graduate students joined the group, concealing their true identities from the others (raising ethical questions about such an infiltration). They wanted to observe what would happen when Mrs. Keech's prediction of doom was disconfirmed (Festinger, Riecken & Schachter, 1956).

On the night of December 20, most of the group assembled at Mrs. Keech's house, in order to be picked up by the flying saucer at midnight. After the hour had passed and it became clear that the saucer was not going to arrive, shock and frozen disbelief gripped the adherents. Presumably, dissonance was rampant. At 4:45 A.M. Mrs. Keech announced that she had just received a new message—the rulers of Clarion had decided to spare the earth from the cataclysm because of the impressive faith of this small group of followers. If we look upon this message with a cold and cynical eye, we must have the greatest respect for Mrs. Keech. What an effective way to rationalize the behavior of the group members!

What else did the group do after this disconfirmation? Prior to the disconfirmation the group had avoided publicity, but afterward they telephoned wire services and newspapers to publicize their explanation of the prophecy and tried diligently to recruit new members, thus increasing the amount of social support for their interpretation of events. The group gradually broke up months later.

Around 1960, a fundamentalist religious group built fallout shelters near a small town in the Southwest. They spent forty-two days and nights in the fallout shelters in the expectation that the world would be decimated by nuclear war. Fortunately, their expectations were not met. After the 103 faithful received the word to come out of the shelter, they held a joyous reunion in the church. The group reinterpreted their biblical sources and a leader spoke of how their faith had not been shaken. Many church members gave testimony that their stay in the shelters had strengthened their Christian fellowship.

Unlike Mrs. Keech's group, however, the fundamentalists did not try to recruit new members. Perhaps this can be explained by the fact that the church group was considerably larger than Mrs. Keech's group. Adequate social support may have already been available within the group itself, making a drive for increased membership to gain social support unnecessary. Furthermore, the church group was not subjected to much ridicule. The Civil Defense officials in the area even presented the group with an award, and the mayor said, "I sincerely hope no one ridicules them for their beliefs" (Hardyck & Braden, 1962). Thus, the church members probably did not feel as much need to rationalize as did the members of Mrs. Keech's group.

Some scholars believe that Jesus Christ predicted the coming of a Kingdom of Heaven on Earth within the lifetime of his followers. If his followers thought this prediction had been made, could Christian evangelism in its early days have been actually an attempt to rationalize disappointment in the wake of a disconfirmed prediction (Carmichael, 1962)? Similar predictions occur today as well. In the 1980s two spokesmen, one in Florida and one in Arizona, received national attention for their scripture-based predictions that the beginning of the end of the world was at hand. After the due date had passed uneventfully, one man explained that further study of the scriptures had revealed that the world was still on the brink of disaster, but "we have a few days left" (Pugh, 1981). Thank goodness!

Insufficient Deterrence

Thus far we have analyzed dissonance-producing situations in which people acted in a way that they did not want to (induced compliance) or that they later regretted (disconfirmed expectations). Dissonance can also occur when people are deterred from doing what they wanted to. Dissonance ought to be greatest when a minimal amount of pressure is used to deter them from the desired activity. The dissonance could be reduced by decreasing their liking for the activity.

This supposition was tested with nursery school children aged four and five who were asked to rank five toys in attractiveness and were then left alone by the experimenter for ten minutes (Aronson & Carlsmith, 1963). In a no-temptation condition, the experimenter took the toy rated as second-most desirable with him. In the temptation-plus-mild-threat condition, the experimenter left the toy but asked the child not to play with it, saying that he would be annoyed if the child did. In the temptation-plus-severe-threat condition, the experimenter told the child not to play with the toy and said he would be very angry and take away all the toys if the child did. None of the children actually played with the toy. After the experimenter returned, the children were then asked once again to rank the attractiveness of all five toys.

As dissonance theory predicts, the perceived attractiveness of the forbidden toy increased in the severe-threat and no-temptation conditions, and decreased in the mild-threat condition. Apparently the children in the mild-threat condition had the weakest external justification for not playing with the forbidden toy; they could reduce the dissonance by devaluing the toy and deciding that they didn't want to play with it anyway.

This devaluing effect can be long-lasting; it was still visible in a follow-up study three to nine weeks later (Freedman, 1965). When given the opportunity to play with the same five toys, without instructions about avoiding any toy, two-thirds of the children in the severe-threat condition played with the previously-forbidden toy, but only 29 percent of the children from the mild-threat condition played with it.

Evidence for the Existence of Dissonance

It is difficult to measure dissonance directly, but a clever study by Zanna and Cooper (1974) provides us with indirect evidence of how dissonance feels. The researchers had people write counterattitudinal essays under low or high-choice conditions. We have seen that induced compliance generally leads to the greatest attitude change under conditions of high choice. The researchers also gave the subjects a pill: some were told that the pill might make them feel tense, others were told it might make them feel relaxed, and still others were told that the drug would have no side effects. In actuality, the pill was a placebo having no physiological effects.

Dissonance should have been greatest in two of the three high-choice conditions: relaxation and no side-effects instructions. Conversely, in the third high-choice condition (tense instructions) subjects could attribute their tense feelings to the pill ("That's why I feel this way") rather than to the counterattitudinal behavior, reducing the need to change their attitudes to reduce dissonance. Subjects in the low-choice conditions should feel little pressure to change their attitudes. As Figure 4-9 illustrates, these predictions were confirmed.

There is also more direct evidence of physiological arousal from writing counterattitudinal essays. Under high-choice conditions people showed more skin conduction responses (a reliable indicator of heightened physiological arousal) than did writers under low-choice conditions (Croyle & Cooper, 1983). Dissonance apparently feels generally like an unpleasant, stresslike state (Fazio & Cooper, 1983; Higgins et al., 1979).

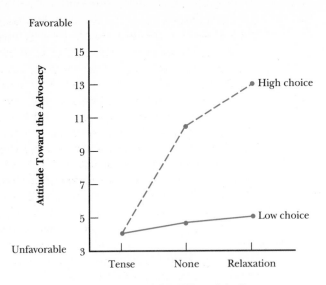

FIGURE 4-9

Effect of Choice and
Anticipated Side Effects
of a Drug on Attitude
Change

Supposed Side Effect of the Drug

Source: Data from Zanna M. P., & Cooper, J. (1974). © 1981 Wm. C. Brown Publishers, Dubuque, Iowa. All Rights Reserved. Reprinted by permission.

While the findings discussed in this section have been interpreted in terms of cognitive dissonance theory, two other theoretical approaches have also been put forth to explain the same findings. We can now take a look at these alternative explanations.

Alternative Interpretations

Self-Perceptions

As discussed in Chapter 3, *self-perception theory* (Bem, 1972) proposes that we often infer what our attitudes are by observing our own behavior. When we see ourselves doing something unusual (such as telling a lie or behaving in a counterattitudinal manner) we may use this information to revise our estimate of what our attitudes must be. In the Festinger and Carlsmith (1959) experiment, subjects who lied for twenty dollars had an external reason for the behavior; they could tell themselves that they behaved as they did to get the money, and not because they liked the boring task. Subjects who received only one dollar, however, could not easily explain their behavior by pointing to the small amount of money. Instead, they inferred that they must have liked the task.

Instead of the state of psychological unpleasantness that dissonance theory suggests, self-perception theory describes a more neutral, passive process wherein individuals simply change their perceptions of their attitudes.

If an external reason for a behavior is obvious, people infer that they engaged in the behavior for that reason. If no such cause is present, people infer that their attitude must be consistent with the behavior, since there is no other apparent cause for the behavior.

Self-Presentation

We also saw in Chapter 3 that individuals strive to present themselves to others in a socially desirable light, and strive to see themselves positively as well. From a self-presentational position, we could predict that the findings discussed above could result from the desire to present a positive image (e.g., as a consistent person) to others (Tedeschi & Rosenfeld, 1981), or to maintain a positive view of themselves (Schlenker, 1985). Behaving inconsistently with their attitudes is probably discrepant with most people's self-concepts. Claude Steele's (1988) **self-affirmation theory** proposes that people have a need to validate important aspects of their self-concept, especially when the self-concept has been threatened. In a dissonance-producing situation, Steele argued, the disturbing thing about the dissonant behavior is its negative reflection on the self-concept, rather than cognitive inconsistency per se.

After writing a counterattitudinal essay, for example, people might affirm their self-concept by changing their attitudes to reflect their behavior, as dissonance theory predicts. Alternatively, however, some people might choose to affirm valued aspects of the self through other behaviors that have nothing to do with the essay. To illustrate, Steele and Liu (1981) found that most students who wrote a counterattitudinal essay opposing increased funding for the handicapped changed their attitudes in the direction of the essay, *except* for subjects who expected to be able to do a self-affirming behavior later on—helping blind students. These latter subjects had no need to change their attitudes because they had the opportunity to affirm a valued aspect of the self in a different way.

From a self-presentation perspective, in contrast to dissonance theory and self-perception theory, individuals are seen neither as being upset by psychological unpleasantness nor as passively inferring their attitudes from their behaviors, but as actively managing their own self-image or the impression they give to others.

Relationships between the Three Approaches

The processes described by self-perception and cognitive dissonance theory may occur under different conditions. Self-perception may apply more to the acquisition of attitude-congruent behavior, that is, change stemming from messages that would fall within the person's latitude of acceptance. Dissonance theory, on the other hand, may be more applicable to changes caused by attitude-discrepant behavior, namely, behavior that would fall within the person's latitude of rejection (Fazio et al., 1977). When an attitude is first

self-affirmation theory: Steele's theory that people are motivated to take actions to affirm important aspects of their self-concept.

being formed, the issue is probably not very important and latitudes of acceptance are likely to be wide; hence, self-perception may be the dominant process. For firmly held attitudes, latitudes of acceptance are narrower because importance is greater, and cognitive dissonance may be the dominant process involved.

Research has shown that the relationship between dissonance and self-presentation may be closer than previously realized. Schlenker (1985) asserted that dissonance theory could be seen as a special case of concern about self-presentation. Self-presentation responses are directed toward an audience, whereas dissonance-reduction responses are directed toward oneself (Tesser & Paulhus, 1983). Experiments suggest that the effect of counterattitudinal behaviors may result either from cognitive dissonance, or from self-presentation pressures, or both (Paulhus, 1982). Either high choice or concern with self-presentation can produce dissonance and lead to attitude change (Baumeister & Tice, 1984). While additional research will be needed to further untangle the effects of these powerful forces, it is clear that both dissonance and self-presentation concerns are important factors in producing changes in attitudes and behaviors.

RESISTING PERSUASION

Defensive Behaviors

So far we have been concerned with factors leading to attitude change. What about the other side of the coin? What makes attitude change less likely? One way to resist persuasion is to derogate the source of the communication, another way is to refute the arguments made by the persuasive source. This is difficult to do because persuasive arguments are often designed to resist refutation. Still another way to resist persuasion is to reject the persuasive arguments. In this case, a target does not try to refute the arguments logically; instead, the arguments are dismissed as being not worthy of comment.

Less visible defensive procedures also exist. Drinking alcohol may allow one to reduce dissonance, thereby reducing attitude change that might otherwise occur in dissonance-producing situations. Steele, Southwick, and Critchlow (1981) found that subjects induced to drink alcohol (supposedly as a taste test) after writing a counterattitudinal essay showed less subsequent attitude change than subjects induced to drink water or coffee. Another process, often visible in therapy cases, occurs when Freudian defense mechanisms such as denial are used to resist persuasive attempts, even when the attempts (by a therapist, for instance) are intended to help a person's psychological adjustment. We often see the operation of rationalization and distortion in people's perceptions of others' arguments. There are innumerable ways to distort, misperceive, and deny information when faced with persuasive communications.

Forewarning

Sometimes forewarning people about an attitude change attempt can help them resist the message. When forewarned that a message is coming, an individual may become more resistant to persuasion if the issue is personally important and relevant. If the issue is relatively unimportant, forewarning has little effect (Petty & Cacioppo, 1979). When people are forewarned about the content of the message as well, they tend to think about the issue and develop counterarguments, becoming more extreme in their preferred position. This has been labeled the **anticipatory polarization effect** (Cialdini & Petty, 1981).

Inoculation

Drawing an analogy from medical practices, William McGuire (1964) proposed that just as people are most susceptible to infections against which they have not built up an immunity, they will be most susceptible to persuasive arguments against which they have not built up defenses. McGuire proposed that training people to defend their positions can inoculate them, rendering them less susceptible to later attitude-change pressures. Working with health "truisms" seldom questioned in our culture (such as the merits of penicillin and the value of frequent toothbrushing), McGuire gave subjects one of four types of defensive training. Training was either refutational (learning to refute persuasive communications) or supportive (creating arguments to support positions one holds). Some early research indicated that refutational training was more effective than supportive training in inoculating people against counterarguments (McGuire & Papageorgis, 1961; Suedfeld & Borrie, 1978). However, two other studies found that refutational and supportive defenses were equally powerful in increasing resistance (Adams & Beatty, 1977; Pryor & Steinfatt, 1978). Hence, though we can conclude that defensive training is effective in resisting attitude change, at this point we cannot say whether one method is superior to the other.

OVERVIEW

Several major trends were evident in attitude change research during the 1970s and 1980s. First, many studies yielded insights into why and how attitudes predict behavior. Second, theorists focused on the cognitive processes that mediate attitude change, as illustrated by the elaboration likelihood model and the theory of planned action. A third trend was a renewed interest in consistency, either the desire to be consistent (dissonance theory) or the desire to look consistent (self-presentation). Current researchers are working to differentiate situations in which attitude change occurs because of an uncomfortable tension state (dissonance) from those in which change results from self-presentational motives.

---

anticipatory polarization effect:
When people are forewarned that they will encounter a persuasive message, they tend to develop counterarguments and become more extreme in their preferred position.

inoculation theory:
Training people to defend their position can make them less susceptible to persuasion.

SUMMARY

For many years the study of attitudes has enjoyed a central place in social psychology. Attitudes may serve several functions: understanding, social adjustment, ego defense, and expression of values. Attitudes are potent predictors of behavior when the attitudes and behaviors are appropriately measured. The effectiveness of persuasion depends on the source, the message, the audience, and the channel. Important source characteristics are credibility (expertise and trustworthiness), attractiveness, and social power. A key aspect of the message is the amount of discrepancy between the position advocated and the audience's initial position. When the communicator is very credible or the issue is not related to the audience members' values, the audience members' latitudes of rejection are narrower and they are more likely to be persuaded.

The theory of planned action proposes that behavior is a function of one's attitude toward the act, subjective norms (perceived norms and one's motivation to comply with them), and perceived behavioral control. The elaboration likelihood model, in contrast, distinguishes between the central route and the peripheral route to attitude change. The central route produces the most permanent change and will be effective when the audience members have the ability and motivation to think carefully about the arguments. Under other conditions, the peripheral route produces more attitude change. Cognitive dissonance theory focuses on the relationship between cognitive elements. When the relationship is dissonant, the person will be motivated to change attitudes or behaviors. Dissonance effects have been studied in situations involving free choice between alternatives, induced compliance (counterattitudinal behavior), justification of effort, disconfirmed expectations, and insufficient deterrence from desired behavior. Self-perception theory and impression management theory have been proposed as alternative ways of interpreting the research findings. Recent work on methods of self-presentation has identified common themes that cut across the dissonance, self-perception, and impression management approaches.

CHAPTER 5

Influencing Others: Changing Behaviors

I have never been a quitter. To leave office before my term is completed is abhorrent to every instinct in my body. But as President, I must put the interest of America first. America needs a full-time President and a full-time Congress, particularly at this time with problems we face at home and abroad. To continue to fight through the months ahead for my personal vindication would almost totally absorb the time and attention of both the President and the Congress.... Therefore, I shall resign the Presidency at noon tomorrow....

Richard M. Nixon, 1974

I have regret and condemnation for the extermination of the Jewish people, which was ordered by the German rulers, but I myself could not have done anything against it. I was a tool in the hands of the strong and powerful and in the hands of fate itself.... Where there is no responsibility, there can be no guilt.... I was only receiving and carrying out orders.   Adolf Eichmann, 1961

A foolish consistency is the hobgoblin of little minds.

Ralph Waldo Emerson

I was a pawn in a chess game being played by giants.

Lt. Col. Oliver North, 1989 ❖

Richard Nixon resigns the U.S. presidency. The Watergate scandal, which culminated in Nixon's resignation in 1974, involved many unfortunate incidences of conformity and compliance by presidential aides and reelection committee staffers.

PREVIEW

Social influence occurs whenever you do something because of the presence (real or imagined) of other people. Humans are social creatures and each of us is continually influenced by others. Chapter 4 analyzed the way that attitudes and behaviors are influenced by persuasive messages. In this chapter we will investigate social influence that is related to social power. In the language of attribution theory, we will be studying the environmental factors that interact with dispositional factors in determining behavior.

To begin, we will analyze the different bases of social power involved in social influence. The psychological processes underlying social influence will then be evaluated: reciprocity, commitment and pressure toward consistency, liking, scarcity, social proof, and authority. The latter two processes will be analyzed in greatest detail because they are especially relevant to conformity and compliance, as exemplified in Milgram's hurting-on-command studies. Social influence will also be evaluated in several controversial events from recent history, including wartime atrocities such as the My Lai massacre, the brainwashing of prisoners of war, national scandals that involved strong pressures to conform (the Iran-Contra affair, Watergate), the tragedy in Jonestown, Guyana, conversions to unusual religious cults, and attempts to "deprogram" religious converts.

Although most social psychological research in this area has focused on how conformity or compliance can be increased by social pressure, there is another equally important and interesting question: How do people resist social influence pressures? Recent studies of minority influence have identified the ways in which minorities can influence the majority, sometimes in dramatic ways. How much obedience, conformity, independence, and nonconformity is good for our society? You won't get a definitive answer to this complex and value-laden question, but you can acquire some understanding of the important psychological factors that are involved.

SOCIAL INFLUENCE

Social Influence in Historical Context

Strong social influence pressures on many of President Nixon's colleagues played a major role in the Watergate scandal and coverup. Less than two years after he had been reelected by the largest margin in history, Richard Nixon resigned in 1974 in the face of almost certain impeachment and conviction by Congress. Obedience pressures have been crucial features of many other vitally important events in recent history.

Adolf Eichmann on trial. Eichmann, chief of the Jewish Affairs section of the Gestapo in Nazi Germany during World War II, was tried for murder in Israel in 1961. His defense was that he had been "just following orders."

Field Marshal Keitel was one of twenty-two important Nazi German military and civilian officials tried for murder at the Nuremberg War Crime Trials in 1946. During his trial, Keitel stated, "It is tragic to realize that the best I had to give as a soldier—obedience and loyalty—was exploited for intentions which could not be recognized and that I did not understand the limit which is set even for a soldier in the performance of his duty." Nineteen of the twenty-two Nazi defendants were convicted and ten, including Keitel, were hanged.

Adolf Eichmann held the position of chief of the Jewish Affairs Section of the Gestapo, which coordinated the sending of Jews to Nazi concentration camps during World War II (see Focus 5-1). He was regarded as the "Jew specialist" of the Gestapo (Heydecker & Leeb, 1958). Eichmann was both architect and chief executor of the policy that led to the deaths of almost six million persons (Woetzel, 1972). He escaped from Germany after the war and was located in Argentina by Israeli secret agents in 1960. Eichmann was abducted to Israel, where he was tried and convicted of murder in 1961 and executed in 1962.

First Lieutenant (Lt.) William Calley was an American soldier tried for the murder of 104 civilians in the Vietnam hamlets of My Lai and Song My in 1968. From all accounts, Calley's Charlie Company killed virtually every inhabitant on whom they could lay hands: about 500 men, women, and children, regardless of age or sex, and despite the fact that no opposition was encountered. The pilot of one American observation helicopter was so shocked by what he saw that he reported the killings to brigade headquarters and repeatedly put his helicopter down to rescue wounded women and children (Taylor, 1970).

FOCUS 5-1

Was Adolf Eichmann "Normal"?

Debate continues to this day about whether Adolf Eichmann was a "helpless cog" in the German war machine, as he later claimed, or a dedicated, fanatical murderer. In 1983 the TV series *60 Minutes* analyzed this man once again (Moses, 1983). Gideon Hausner, the prosecutor at Eichmann's 1961 trial, noted that Eichmann had been a perfect gentleman during his imprisonment, even giving his captors advice on how prison security could be tightened. The Israeli psychiatrist who examined Eichmann prior to his trial had stated, "This man is entirely normal, more normal than I feel myself after this examination" (Papadatos, 1964, p. 28). In 1943 Yahiel Dinur had seen his visa to leave Poland torn to shreds by an SS officer, Eichmann, sending him instead to Auschwitz. At Eichmann's trial almost twenty years later, Dinur collapsed—from the realization that Eichmann was not a godlike army officer but an ordinary, unremarkable man. And if this Eichmann was so ordinary, Dinur thought, then what Eichmann had done, any other man might also be capable of doing. In Dinur's words, "Then came everything. Then I saw I am capable to do this. I am capable exactly like he. It's not a god, it's not a Hitler, it's not a Heydrich, it's not Adolf Eichmann ... it's me" (Moses, 1983, p. 17).

But was Eichmann really just like you and me? In 1961 a psychiatrist asked him whether he had ever had a guilt feeling. Eichmann replied, "Yes, once or twice, because of skipping school." After a particularly gruesome scene in which hundreds of Jews were executed, Eichmann was distraught and reported to his superiors, "This can't go on like this. Our poor boys! How can they stand the strain?" He was concerned about the German soldiers' reactions to the massacres they conducted, but he apparently never gave even a passing thought to the victims. Eichmann considered the extermination of Jews the one great achievement of his life, according to one of his fellow officers, Wilhelm Hoettl. In 1944, Hoettl recalled later, "Eichmann said, 'We exterminated so many millions of Jews.' He said it with pride, and he said it so proudly because it was yet another achievement for him. 'You know I, this little Eichmann, managed to fulfill my task in such a thorough way. I achieved it—I, the one who was ridiculed by everyone.'" According to another observer, "He was obsessed with the idea that at least as many Jews as he could put his hands on should perish, because this was his victory and Germany's victory. If they couldn't win on the battlefield, at least they won the war against the Jews" (Moses, 1983, p. 16).

A monster or an ordinary man? Are there many people who, put in a similar situation and ordered or encouraged to commit atrocities, would follow those orders? We can only hope not, but the question is a chilling one. Was Shakespeare right when, in *King Lear*, he wrote, "The devil is a gentleman"? ❖

Lt. Calley describes his perception of the situation he faced in Focus 5-2. Although many others in the military chain of command were accused of involvement, Calley was the only officer brought to trial before a military court-martial for his part in the massacre. There he stated that "I felt then and I still do that I acted as I was directed. I carried out the orders I was given and I do not feel wrong in doing so." Nevertheless, he was convicted

---

FOCUS 5-2

Lieutenant William Calley's Impression of the My Lai Massacre: Compliance, Behavioral Contagion, or Murder?

I didn't know if a VC squad, or platoon, or company—what was in Mylai Four. Or the goddamn battalion even. I only knew, It is shooting at us: I got that from the chopper pilot. He brought her in and shouted at me, "A hot one!" It meant, "We are under fire!" It meant a lot more, though, "I hope you'll make it. I hope I'll make it. I am not staying here! Get out!" I thought, Well, here we go, I got up, I jumped—I didn't move. I tried, I just forced myself, I jumped a few meters into the paddies under me. The troops jumped out of the chopper behind me. Ahead of us: Mylai Four.

I'm going to die sometime: I had always known it. Ignored it, and knocked on the door of death today, and I couldn't ignore it. The fear now: I was saturated with it. I felt it, I kept running but it took extra effort to. A bullet: a pretty good way to go, I knew. No fuss. No muss, I wouldn't even know it was hitting me. A mine: that's worse, to wake up and think, Now, what did I lose? My legs: I still have my arms, though. I would try to think positively. Of the great guys who run around, jump out of planes, hop up a mountainside with

an artificial leg. I would think, I'm out, I don't have to worry anymore. I had that mechanism: and I kept running to Mylai Four. It whirled, it was like seeing a bomb burst or a person blow up.

The fear: nearly everyone had it. And everyone had to destroy it: Mylai, the source of it. And everyone moved into Mylai firing automatic. And went rapidly, and the GIs shot people rapidly. Or grenaded them. Or just bayoneted them: to stab, to throw someone aside, to go on. Supposedly, the GIs said, "Chalk one up," "Hey, I got another one," "Did you see the fucker die?" I didn't hear it: I just heard Medina telling me, "Keep going," and I said, "Keep going! Keep going! Keep—"

"God," people say. "But these were old men, and women, and children." I tell you: I didn't see it. I had this mission, and I was intent upon it. I only saw, they're enemy. Of course, I still was in South Vietnam. I knew, There are old men, women, and children in South Vietnam. It was common sense, sure, but in combat there is damn little common sense. ❖

Source: Calley (1972).

---

of premeditated murder and sentenced to life imprisonment. The sentence was reduced a few months later to twenty years and he was later pardoned.

Lieutenant Colonel (Lt. Col.) Oliver North was convicted of illegally destroying documents and lying to members of Congress who were investigating his role in the Iran-Contra affair in the late 1980s. Lt. Col. North's defense, like that of Eichmann and Lt. Calley, was that he had merely been following the orders of his superiors. North's case is described later in Focus 5-5. In this chapter we will examine the social processes that can induce people to commit such acts as these that are later widely deplored.

Bases of Social Power

social power:
A person's capacity to alter the actions of others.

Every day you attempt to influence countless other people and, in turn, are yourself a target of numerous influence attempts. Many of these are obvious, such as advertisements in the media or personal requests from friends, while others are more subtle. People who believe they possess **social power**, defined as the capacity to alter the actions of others (Kelman, 1974), will often use this power to influence others. Social power is derived from having access to resources (rewards, punishments, information, expertise), from one's position or role (legitimate power), or from being liked and admired (referent power). I will briefly discuss the varieties of social power that have been identified (French & Raven, 1959; Pruitt, 1976), then we will turn to the strategies and principles that underlie most influence attempts.

Coercive Power

coercive power:
The ability to force another person to change his or her behavior by threats or punishments.

Coercive power involves the ability to force other people to change their behavior by threats or punishments. During Watergate, President Nixon was well aware of the coercive power that the Congress and the U.S. Supreme Court held over him: the threat of impeachment and conviction for malfeasance if he remained in office. Similarly, Eichmann, Field Marshal Keitel, Lt. Calley, and Lt. Col. North were aware that their superior officers could punish them severely if they disobeyed orders. This does not mean that coercive power was the strongest force or the only factor determining their behavior (see Focus 5-1), but it may have played a role.

Although coercive power is widely used, it is often ineffective, especially when utilized against groups. When a group is threatened with coercion, the threat may actually bring the group closer together (Tedeschi, 1974). Knowing this, national leaders sometimes exaggerate the extent of the military threat from nearby countries or from rebels in their own country in order to unite the populace behind them. As cognitive dissonance theory would suggest, coercion may increase the value placed on the threatened activity. If a group is threatened, it may respond with countercoercion, producing an upward spiral of aggression (Tedeschi et al., 1974). Coercive power also requires surveillance to make sure that the changed behavior persists. The low-power person is likely to attribute his behavior to the surveillance rather than to the worth of the behavior itself (no private acceptance); hence, the behavior change is unlikely to continue once surveillance has been lifted. Thus, in terms of the concepts discussed in Chapter 4, coercive power may be effective in causing compliance, but it is not likely to lead to identification or to private acceptance (Kelman, 1958).

Legitimate Power

legitimate power:
Power derived from being in a particular role or position.

Those who have **legitimate power**, derived from being in a particular role or position, do not have to justify their actions. In the military, officers have legitimate power over enlisted men. In the classroom, your professor has legitimate power. Experimenters have legitimate power over subjects in a research situation.

reward power:
Power gained by giving positive reinforcements such as money, praise, or prestige to others.

expert power:
Power deriving from specialized knowledge that one has.

expert witness:
A person certified by the trial judge as having expertise in a particular area that is likely to be of relevance and value to the jury.

referent power:
Power derived from the degree to which one is admired and liked.

informational power:
Power that exists when an individual has information that others do not have.

Reward Power

Giving positive reinforcement such as money, praise, or prestige demonstrates **reward power**. In the past few years, we have become more aware of the potential abuses of reward power in politics and government. Special interest groups, lobbyists, political action committees (PACs), and wealthy campaign contributors can wield great reward power over legislators. Reward power can easily lead to compliance, but it may not lead to private acceptance. If the reward is removed, the new behavior may disappear. As we saw in Chapter 4, a reward may actually decrease the likelihood that the behavior will continue after the reward is removed, because individuals may attribute their behavior to the reward rather than to any benefits of the behavior itself (the overjustification effect).

Expert Power

If you have important knowledge that others do not, you have **expert power** over them. Medical doctors and college professors have expert power as reflected in their M.D. and Ph.D. degrees. In the American system of law, ordinary witnesses can testify only to facts they have observed. In contrast, an **expert witness** is a person certified by the trial judge as having expertise in a particular area of relevance to the jury. An expert witness can give opinions and answer hypothetical questions, something ordinary witnesses are not allowed to do.

Referent Power

Power derived from the degree to which one is admired and liked is called **referent power.** People want to identify with others whom they consider admirable and likable. Hence, people have referent power over those who wish to identify with them. In the military situation, a superior officer who is liked and respected by his men has referent power in addition to the legitimate power that his rank denotes. His orders are more likely to be followed than are orders from a disliked officer who has legitimate power but little referent power. Unlike reward or coercive power, referent power does not require surveillance to be effective since the motivation to comply is not dependent on external rewards or punishments.

Informational Power

An individual who has information that others do not possess has **informational power** (Raven & Kruglanski, 1970). The eyewitness to a crime has the power to influence a jury because of the information that he or she has. Someone who knows a secret has informational power over those who would like to know it. Informational power is limited to situations for which the information is relevant, though some information has wide relevance. During recent years many people have become increasingly concerned over the informational power wielded by TV newscasters and their staffs. In selecting which thirty-second sound bites are shown to audiences of millions, they may have a dramatic influence on viewers who may derive their sociopolitical views from the TV newscasts.

The most likely influences of the various types of social power are depicted in Table 5-1. A number of studies of bases of social power have been conducted over the past twenty-five years. Most of the studies, however, have suffered from major methodological shortcomings, making it difficult to draw many firm conclusions about the relationship between power bases and outcomes (Podsakoff & Schriesheim, 1985).

BASIC PSYCHOLOGICAL PROCESSES IN SOCIAL INFLUENCE

Each of us is continually faced with pressures to comply with many different, and sometimes conflicting, norms and standards. We often feel internal pressures to "fit in with the crowd," to be accepted by doing what is expected of us. Countless times we are urged to comply with requests or to obey commands from another person (our boss, parent, lover or spouse, college professor, salesperson, commanding officer in the Army, experimenter in a psychological study). There are a number of techniques that are used by those who seek to influence people. Robert Cialdini (1988) described six

TABLE 5-1	TYPES OF SOCIAL POWER AND THEIR EFFECTS			
Type of Social Power	Origin	Leads to Compliance?	Leads to Private Acceptance?	Limitations
Coercive	Strength, ability to back up threats	Yes	No	Requires surveillance; leads to dislike of source
Legitimate	Role or position	Yes	Perhaps	Affects only behavior relevant to the role
Reward	Access to desired reinforcers	Yes	No	Requires surveillance and access to reinforcers
Expert	Knowledge others do not have	Yes	Yes	Affects only behavior relevant to area of expertise
Informational	Information others do not have	Yes	Perhaps	Power reduced after information is dispensed
Referent	Being admired or liked	Yes	Yes	Fewer limitations than other types

techniques that are commonly employed by would-be influencers, those who do it for a living, such as salesmen, advertisers, and people soliciting donations, as well as the rest of us who attempt to influence our acquaintances in our everyday interactions.

We are influenced by what others do for us. Social pressure to return a favor *(reciprocity)* is normative in our society. Most of us also want to remain consistent with our earlier behaviors *(commitment and consistency)*. We tend to be influenced by people we *like*, who have referent power. If a product is hard to get because of its popularity (the *scarcity principle*) we may desire it all the more. We often use others' behaviors to guide our own. If a product is quite popular we may want it ourselves, using others' preferences as *social proof* of its worth. Finally, we are often influenced by people in *authority* who may have coercive, reward, or legitimate power. I will discuss each of these factors in turn, paying the most attention to social proof and authority pressure, which probably have the greatest impact in our lives.

Reciprocity

reciprocity:
Social pressure to return a favor.

You tear open the envelope and discover 1,000 address labels preprinted with your name, courtesy of the charitable organization that is soliciting a donation from you. In the airport a young woman thrusts a flower or religious book into your hands, despite your protests. She then asks for a donation to her religious group. The man at the booth in the supermarket hands you a free sample of a new product. Each of these people is depending on the principle of **reciprocity**. We have been taught to return favors and obey the Golden Rule. Once they have accepted something, even completely unsolicited, most people find it very difficult to resist the ensuing request for a donation or purchase of a product. "She gave something to me, so I feel obligated to give something back to her." It's difficult not to feel caught in a web of indebtedness.

Guilt

If you feel guilty because you have done something wrong, you are likely to take action to reduce the guilt. You may perform a good act to balance the bad guilt-inducing act, or you may let yourself in for some (reciprocal) unpleasantness and thereby punish yourself for the bad act. In several experiments, college students were led to believe that through carelessness they damaged expensive research equipment. Afterward they were more likely to comply with a request to volunteer for another experiment than were students who did not think they had broken the equipment. Subjects who thought they had done a great deal of damage to the equipment were more likely to volunteer for a future experiment than were students who thought they had done a small amount of damage to the same equipment (Brock & Becker, 1966).

A guilty person is often torn between two considerations: (1) reduction of guilt, and (2) a desire to avoid confronting the person who has been harmed. Greatest compliance is obtained when adherence to the request does not require further interaction with the victim. If the request requires a person to work closely with the victim of the guilt-inducing action (an uncomfortable situation), guilty persons are no more likely to agree to participate than are nonguilty ones (Carlsmith & Gross, 1969; Freedman et al., 1967).

Another important factor is the ease with which one can make reparations to a victim. If the guilty person cannot repay the victim fully or if the cost of repaying is too great (in terms of time, inconvenience, money, or discomfort), the guilty person may react by endorsing the just world assumption (Chapter 2) and devaluing the victim ("Well, she deserved it. It was her own fault for letting it happen."). The guilty person might also decide that the harm was caused for good reason (such as for the sake of science) or because one was under orders and had no choice. Cognitively, guilt can be reduced by changing one's perception of the victim or of the act itself.

The Door-in-the-Face Effect

You may feel somewhat guilty if you reject a request by a door-to-door salesperson, perhaps by slamming the door in her face. Investigating the so-called **door-in-the-face effect** (also called the *rejection-then-retreat* tactic), researchers have found that if a person first asks for a very large favor and is refused, and then asks for a smaller favor, compliance with the smaller favor is more likely than if that individual had asked solely for the smaller favor (Cialdini et al., 1975).

The effectiveness of the door-in-the-face technique depends upon three factors: self-presentation, reciprocal concessions, and perceptual contrast. We prefer to be seen in a favorable light by others, and people may believe that others would see them as unconcerned and unfriendly if they refused

door-in-the-face effect:
If a person asks first for a very large favor and is refused, and then asks for a smaller favor, compliance with the smaller favor is more likely than if that individual had asked solely for the smaller favor.

This cartoon shows the "door-in-the-face" effect in action.

two requests (Pendleton & Batson, 1979). Hence, in order to maintain a positive self-presentation, they feel pressure to agree to at least one of the two requests. Additionally, scaling down a request from a large to a moderate level can be seen as a concession. Then the person who refused the large request may feel some pressure to compromise by making a concession as well, agreeing to the moderate request. People may think that because the requester backed down and compromised, they ought to meet the requester halfway. Perceptual contrast comes into play because the second request may seem smaller in comparison with the large initial request.

that's-not-all technique: Inducing compliance by adding a benefit or dropping the price while the customer is considering the deal.

Implied compromise also underlies another compliance strategy, dubbed the **that's-not-all technique**. Here the salesperson offers the customer a deal at a fairly high price. While the customer is thinking about it, the salesperson either adds another product to the deal ("That's not all, I'll also include . . .") or lowers the price. Studies show that people are more likely to accept this better deal, perhaps due to feeling of reciprocity, than if the same deal was offered originally (Burger, 1986).

Commitment and Pressures toward Consistency

We saw in Chapter 4 that people feel internal pressure to remain consistent, thereby avoiding feelings of cognitive dissonance. Appearing consistent to others is also an important component of our self-presentations. We want to appear consistent, both to others and to ourselves.

Salespeople are well aware of this human tendency. Some years ago a personable young man, supposedly a medical student, appeared at my door and asked if he could chat with me for a while as part of a class project to help medical students develop a better "bedside manner." After some small talk he asked me if I would vote for him in a contest among his medical school class for "most sociable." I readily agreed, as he seemed friendly and engaging. Only after I had made this public commitment did he inform me that voting was done by subscribing to magazines—the more I subscribed to, the more votes he got. Sadly, this deceptive sales tactic is often effective, largely because of consistency and commitment pressures. After all, I had said I would vote for him, so to go back on my word, even though it was given before I knew about the magazines, seemed to be breaking a commitment. I argued silently with myself as I wrote out the check, but I just couldn't bear to be seen as breaking my word, even though I had been deceived into giving it. Another effective sales technique is to have the customer, rather than the salesperson, fill out the sales contract. This is designed to increase the customer's feelings of public commitment to the contract, making it psychologically even more difficult to back out.

The Foot-in-the-Door Effect
Salespeople have long known that if customers can be made to comply with a small request (e.g., a vote as "most sociable"), chances are improved that they will later comply with a larger request (e.g., buy magazines). The effec-

foot-in-the-door effect:
If one complies with a small request, the chances are improved that he or she will later comply with a larger request.

tiveness of this **foot-in-the-door** *(foot)* technique was demonstrated by Freedman and Fraser (1966). The experimenters went from door to door, asking housewives to sign a petition sponsored by the Committee for Safe Driving, which asked their senators to work for legislation to encourage safe driving. Almost all the housewives signed the petition. Several weeks later, different experimenters went from door to door in the same neighborhood, asking housewives to agree to put a large, unattractive sign saying "Drive Carefully" in their front yards. More than half the women who had previously agreed to sign the petition (the small request) agreed to post the sign (the larger request). In contrast, only 17 percent of the women who had not been approached earlier with the petition agreed to post the sign. Thus, making a small request before asking for a larger favor increased the likelihood that the larger favor would be granted.

A meta-analysis of 120 experimental groups exposed to the foot procedure indicated the effect is replicable (Beaman et al., 1983). It doesn't always work, though. If people reject the small request, they are even less likely to grant the larger favor than are those who were not asked the small favor (Snyder & Cunningham, 1975). Other studies suggest that the foot technique may not be effective for very large requests. Foss and Dempsey (1979) attempted to use the foot-in-the-door technique to get donations in a blood drive. Contrary to the hypothesis, those who had agreed to a small request several days earlier (to place on their dormitory doors a poster advertising a blood drive) did not agree to give blood more frequently than those who were presented only with the larger request to donate blood. It appears that if there is a great deal of perceptual contrast between the two requests, the effect may be inhibited (Shanab & Isonio, 1982; Shanab & O'Neill, 1982).

The foot-in-the-door effect causes a change in self-perception. People observe their compliance to the first request and decide that they are the type of people who willingly agree to those kinds of requests. As a result, the probability of their future compliance with similar requests is increased (DeJong & Musilli, 1982). Changes in people's perception of the situation, such as finding that helping is not unpleasant, can also occur (Rittle, 1981). The importance of self-perceptions is illustrated by a study of Israeli housewives (Hornik, 1988). The housewives were originally asked to allow a sticker to be placed on their apartment doors supporting the Israel Cancer Association (ICA). Half of the stickers implied that the resident had fulfilled her obligation ("I have already contributed . . .") while the other stickers implied continuous involvement ("I care—I contribute . . .") and presumably affected self-attributions. As predicted, when contacted a week later by different ICA volunteers, women whose doors had the "continuous involvement" stickers more often contributed to the ICA.

low-balling:
Once a person has made a decision to engage in a behavior, the cost of that behavior can be raised and the person may still feel committed to the action and engage in it.

The Low-Ball Procedure
Another method of inducing compliance has apparently been known to car salesmen for a long time. The technique, called **low-balling**, swings into action after a customer has decided to buy the product. Once the customer

Low-balling in operation? Many car salespeople use the low-balling technique, getting customers to commit to purchase a particular car, and then raising the cost.

has made the decision, say to buy a car for a very low price, the salesperson ups the price. The customer may be told that the original price did not include an expensive option that the customer assumed was part of the offer, or that the salesperson's boss has now vetoed the deal. The reason that the customer decided to make the purchase — the low price — has been removed and the performance of the decided-upon behavior — buying that car — is now more costly. The salesperson knows that once the customer has decided to make the purchase, he may go ahead and buy the car, even though it is now more costly.

In three studies, Cialdini and his co-workers (1978) found the low-ball procedure effective in getting compliance to a more costly behavior when the initial decision had been made with a high degree of choice. In one study, introductory psychology students were called by an experimenter who asked them to participate in an experiment on thinking processes. Some of the subjects were told, before answering the request, that the experiment would take place at 7 A.M.— presumably an unpleasant bit of information. The other subjects were simply asked if they would agree to participate in the study, and only after they had agreed to participate were they told the experiment would take place at 7 A.M. (low-balling). More than half of the subjects in the low-ball condition made an appointment to participate, but fewer than one-third of the control condition subjects did so. In addition, more than half of the low-ball condition subjects actually showed up, as opposed to just 24 percent of the control condition subjects.

Why does low-balling work? One important factor is commitment. A person who freely chooses to perform an action feels some responsibility for the action (Kiesler, 1971). Changing a decision may result in a variety of negative self-perceptions such as hastiness, lack of judgment, inconsistency, or lack of intelligence. A second reason is that choice situations are often stressful. Once the stress has been reduced by making a choice, we may find ourselves reluctant to destroy the sense of completion and to begin again the stressful task of making a new choice. A third reason is that people may feel a personal obligation to the requester (Burger & Petty, 1981).

Comparing and Combining Influence Techniques

The foot-in-the-door technique (*foot*), the door-in-the-face tactic (*face*), and low-balling are all widely used by salespeople. A question of both practical and theoretical interest is: Which is likely to work best and under what conditions?

Using college professors as subjects, Harari and his associates (1980) conducted a clever study to compare the effectiveness of the face and foot techniques. Individual students approached the unsuspecting professors and made one of the following requests. The large request involved asking the professor to meet with the student for two hours a week for the remainder of the semester to discuss the role of the professor's department in the university system. The moderate request was to meet with the student once for several hours to discuss the same topic, and the small request was to meet with the student once for fifteen to twenty minutes to discuss the same topic. In large- and small-request conditions, the student made the moderate request either after the small request had been granted or after the large request had been turned down. Professors were significantly more likely to comply to the moderate request when the initial request had been larger (78 percent complied) than when it had been smaller (33 percent complied), or when no initial request had been made (56 percent complied). These findings demonstrate the effectiveness of the face technique as a way of getting someone to comply with a moderate request.

The face and foot techniques work in some situations but not in others. Two factors need to be present for the face approach to work. First, the interval between the first and second requests must be relatively short so that the feeling of obligation is still salient. Second, the two requests must be made by the same person, since the idea of concessions or compromise with this person is important. In contrast, a longer interval (weeks, months) between the first and second requests can still be effective for the foot technique (Beaman et al., 1983). Also, for the foot technique, the requests do not have to be from the same person, because it is the recipient's self-image that has changed. Hence, the foot technique is applicable to a somewhat wider range of circumstances (requests from two different people, requests separated by a longer time period), though it may not be applicable to particularly costly situations.

It is possible to combine the foot and face conditions. Goldman (1986) had telephone interviewers ask people if they would be willing to stuff and address seventy-five envelopes containing material supporting the Kansas City Zoo (the target request). Some (face condition), were given a large request first (to call 150 people and conduct a survey about the zoo), which almost everyone declined. Others (foot) were given a small request first— to answer a few questions about the zoo. Still other subjects were given a combination of requests — first the large request and then a moderate request to be interviewed for about twenty-five minutes. Most people exposed to these two requests declined the large one but agreed to the moderate request. Most of these folks then agreed to a third request, the target request, while fewer than half of those in the foot or face conditions agreed to it (Figure 5-1).

The three compliance techniques are summarized in Table 5-2. All involve two messages: two requests in the foot and face techniques and, in low-balling, a second message that the behavior is more costly than previously believed.

Liking

We are more easily influenced by people we like than by those we don't. The most successful salespersons are often those who appear especially likable to their customers. A liked person has referent power, the most widely applicable variety of social power (Table 5-1). Joe Girard, a Chevrolet sales-

---

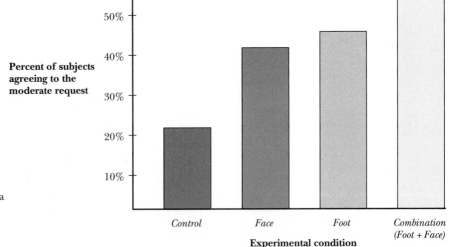

FIGURE 5-1

Compliance Techniques: Combining the Foot-in-the door (*Foot*) and Door-in-the-face (*Face*) procedures

Proportion of subjects agreeing to a moderate request to stuff and send 75 envelopes in support of the Kansas City Zoo

Percent of subjects agreeing to the moderate request

Experimental condition

Source: Data from Goldman, M. (1986). Compliance employing a combined foot-in-the-door and door-in-the-face procedure. *Journal of Social Psychology, 126,* 111–116.

TABLE 5-2	COMPLIANCE TECHNIQUES: FOOT-IN-THE-DOOR *(FOOT)*, DOOR-IN-THE-FACE *(FACE)*, AND LOW-BALLING		
	Foot	**Face**	**Low-Balling**
Basis of the technique	Small request (granted) followed by a moderate request	Large request (turned down) followed by a moderate request	Commitment to a decision is followed by information that the behavior is more costly than previously thought
Goal of the compliance technique	Compliance with a moderate request	Compliance with a moderate request	Commitment to the more costly behavior
Do the messages have to come from the same person?	No	Yes	No
What is the best interval between the two messages?	Short or long	Short	Short(?)
Is it effective in "costly" situations?	Perhaps not	Yes	Yes

man in Detroit, won the title of "number one car salesman" every year from 1966 to 1977, even being listed in the *Guinness Book of World Records*. When asked his secret, he claimed he gave people two things: a fair price and someone they liked to buy from. Presumably, Mr. Girard had a likable personality. But he went beyond that. Every month he sent every one of his more than 13,000 former customers a greeting card with a simple message: "I like you" (Cialdini, 1988). Did this tactic increase his influencibility for future sales? We can't know for sure; we saw earlier that compliments are not effective when they are perceived as ingratiating, insincere, and manipulative (Jones & Wortman, 1973). But when coupled with Girard's likable personality, his card-a-month technique might have been very effective.

Scarcity

scarcity principle:
When a resource is in low supply, desire for it may increase.

Scarcity is often related to value, as collectors of everything from baseball cards to coins know. Salespeople often attempt to use this principle by manipulating real or apparent scarcity even when availability is not limited. Advertisers often create artificial impressions of scarcity to boost sales of their products through limited-supply offers and impending deadlines ("Hurry, only two days left."). Further, salespeople may attempt to stimulate competition between buyers for a scarce resource, driving the price higher. If you have attended a lively auction, you have seen this in action. Cialdini (1988) described a student who, when selling a used car via a newspaper ad, would schedule the same appointment time for all of the interested buyers. When a customer saw all of the other potential buyers, his eagerness to get the car before "the other guys" did often resulted in a quick sale.

psychological reactance:
People who feel that their freedom of choice is under attack will attempt to reestablish freedom directly by performing the threatened behavior and may aggress toward the influence source.

Scarcity can stimulate **psychological reactance** when one's freedom of choice (e.g., freedom to buy the car) is threatened. People who feel reactance often attempt to reestablish this freedom by performing the threatened behavior. In addition, the threatened option is likely to seem more desirable (Brehm & Brehm, 1981). For example, consider consumers' evaluations of the attractiveness of laundry soaps containing phosphates in an area where sale of such soaps had been banned by law (Dade County, Florida), and in an area where sales were allowed (Tampa, Florida). Consumers in Dade County, who may have felt reactance from being denied the choice to purchase the detergent, evaluated phosphate detergents as much more effective than did Tampa consumers (Mazis, 1975). Reactions to censorship may also involve feelings of scarcity and reactance. College students who believed that their dean had interfered with their freedom to listen to a speech changed their attitudes in the direction of the speech (Ashmore et al., 1971). Censoring a communication also increases people's desire to obtain the communication (Worchel et al., 1975).

Reactance increases the attractiveness of a fobidden action.

DENNIS the MENACE ®

"I DON'T *WANTA* GO OUTSIDE AN' PLAY...   UNLESS SHE SAYS I *CAN'T*."

Source: Dennis the Menace® used by permission of Hank Ketcham and © by News American Syndicate.

Social Proof: Using Others as Social Standards

social proof:
Using other people's behavior as social standards for evaluating one's own behavior

We saw earlier that people often use others' behavior as social standards to evaluate their own, via social comparison. When a company advertises its product as the fastest-growing or best-selling item, it is drawing on this principle. People tend to think, "If so many other people buy it, it must be pretty good." In Chapter 7 we will see that this tendency to use the behavior of others as standards for our own actions can have tragic consequences in situations in which someone needs help in an emergency. Bystanders may not help because each has been influenced by the inaction of other nonresponsive bystanders into deciding that help is not needed.

Conformity

conformity:
Yielding to perceived group pressure; behaving according to perceived group norms that are contrary to one's private preferences.

People feel pressure to fit in with the crowd and to be accepted by doing what is expected of them. For example, a male first-year law student shows up for his first class at the State University School of Law dressed in a T-shirt, jeans, and sneakers. To his surprise, he sees that every other male in the class is wearing a coat and tie. Although no one says anything to him, he feels quite out of place and at the next class he, too, is dressed in a coat and tie. This is an instance of **conformity**; he is yielding to perceived group pressure. He behaves according to the perceived group norms (for appropriate dress), which are contrary to his private preferences. He has used the other students as social standards for appropriate dress.

Many of the events that contributed to the Watergate fiasco involved conformity. Presidential Counsel John Dean III had as his credo, "To get along, you go along" (*Newsweek*, May 21, 1973, p. 28). Perhaps the clearest evidence of the general conformist atmosphere was revealed in the Senate testimony of Herbert L. Porter, an official on the Committee to Re-Elect the President (*New York Times* staff, 1973, p. 227).

> PORTER: I was not the one to stand up in a meeting and say that this should be stopped, either. . . . I kind of drifted along.
> SENATOR HOWARD BAKER: At any time, did you ever think of saying, "I do not think this is quite right, this is not the way it ought to be?" Did you ever think of that?
> PORTER: Yes, I did.
> SENATOR BAKER: What did you do about it?
> PORTER: I did not do anything.
> SENATOR BAKER: Why didn't you?
> PORTER: In all honesty, probably because of the fear of group pressure that would ensue, of not being a team player.

Independence

During the Korean war, approximately 3,600 American soldiers were captured and imprisoned in China. While in prison, they were subjected to constant pressure to change their attitudes and adopt the standards and group norms repeatedly stressed by the Red Chinese. Most of the American war prisoners resisted these attempts and did not conform. Later interviews indicated that there were two very different reasons why they resisted conformity pressures (Schein, 1956). Most resisted because they simply felt it would be wrong to collaborate with the enemy. These prisoners held to the standards they believed in. This is an example of **independence**, behavior that ignores group pressures and norms. Still another group of resisters were characterized by a long history of unwillingness to accept any authority; they had not conformed well to the norms of the U.S. Army and neither did they obey their Red Chinese captors. These men were showing **anticonformity**, an active attempt to contradict group pressures. Anticonformists feel reactance; they are just as concerned with norms as conformists are, but their behavior is in the opposite direction, toward resisting the norms. "Nobody can tell me what to do!" Independent people, in contrast, pay no attention to the norms in the first place.

Why Does Conformity Occur?

Each of us possesses two types of information about the world. *Personal information* is grounded in physical reality and one's own experiences; our knowledge about our own life and behaviors is personal knowledge. *Social information* is supplied by others. By observing others you gain two types of social information: normative (what behaviors are expected, accepted, and rewarded), and informational (evidence about reality). **Normative social influence** occurs when one changes behavior in order to gain acceptance and approval from others. **Informational social influence** occurs when one changes behavior in order to be more accurate or correct (Deutsch & Gerard, 1955).

independence:
Behavior that ignores group pressures and norms.

anticonformity:
An active attempt to contradict group pressures and behave in the opposite manner.

normative social influence:
Occurs when one changes behavior in order to gain acceptance and approval from others.

Conformity on the street-corner. Do these similarly dressed pedestrians feel group pressure to obey the "Don't Walk" signal?

informational social influence:
Occurs when one changes behavior because of the information that the behavior of others provides.

Suppose you were a tourist in a foreign country. When you first arrive, you are likely to observe the local people carefully as sources of factual information (How do you buy a train ticket? Where can you change money?) as well as normative expectations (What actions are approved of? What clothing seems popular?). In our law school example, the dress of other students provided normative information about what type of clothing was appropriate. Cohesive groups tend to reject people who deviate from the group's normative standards and our law student could anticipate rejection or ridicule if he continued to dress inappropriately. However, if individuals begin by deviating, as our law student did in his first class, but then conform, they are likely to be accepted by the group (Schachter, 1951). Research also indicates that if a person feels like a deviate (not accepted by the ingroup) and is given an opportunity to behave negatively (to deliver an electric shock, for example) to ingroup members or to a fellow deviate, that person will choose to shock the ingroup members. If the ingroup members are given the same choice, on the other hand, they will choose to shock the deviate (Freedman & Doob, 1968). A group thus has two sources of pressure for conformity: providing normative information about how one is expected to act, and having the reward power to reject people who do not behave in the appropriate manner.

Early Studies of Conformity

autokinetic effect:
An illusion that occurs when a person looks at a stationary pinpoint of light in an otherwise completely dark room and the point appears to move.

If a person looks at a stationary pinpoint of light in an otherwise completely dark room, the point of light will appear to move. Sherif (1935) used this **autokinetic effect** (Luchins & Luchins, 1963) to measure conformity by having college students view the light and make judgments alone and then in pairs. When subjects were alone, they developed a stable frame of reference rather quickly, and judgments of the light's apparent movement were within a relatively small range. In two-person groups, one member's report of the light's movement affected the other member's report, presumably because there were no other sources of information available. The responses of the co-subject had informational social influence (though most subjects later claimed that their judgments had not been influenced by the other subject). The changed frame of reference that developed from the other's influence was very stable; when subjects returned the next day to make judgments alone, the influence of the other subject was still apparent in their responses. Indeed, a later study found that the changed frame of reference persisted for as long as a year (Rohrer et al., 1954).

Solomon Asch (1956) set up a conformity situation that had stronger normative pressures. Seven college men were seated at a circular table and given the task of judging which of three lines on one board appeared to be the same length as a single line on another board. The task was quite easy and over 90 percent of the subjects had made correct judgments when alone. The subjects stated their choice one at a time. Actually, all but one of them were accomplices of the experimenter. On the first few trials, everyone made the correct response. But then the first subject made an incorrect response

The Asch conformity study. The subject (number 6) in Asch's study faces a difficult situation. The first five subjects (all accomplices of the experimenter) have given the same incorrect answer to the visual discrimination problem. Should he conform to the norm that they have just established?

and the next three subjects agreed. The real subject, responding fifth, was in a difficult situation. Should he conform to the group norm and make an incorrect response or should he remain independent and give the answer he saw as correct?

Conformity is not an all-or-none response. Asch (1956; 1958) found that about 30 percent of his subjects never conformed on the critical trials (those on which the majority gave an incorrect answer). A small number (about 15 percent) conformed on three-fourths or more of the critical trials, though none conformed on every critical trial. The remaining 55 percent of subjects conformed on at least one trial but resisted conformity pressures on the majority of critical trials. Averaging across all subjects, conforming responses were given about one-third of the time on the critical trials.

One interpretation of agreement with the incorrect group response is the "tyranny of the group" in putting conformity pressures on individuals. But an attributional analysis suggests the lone subject has two attributional questions to answer: (1) To what can I attribute the other subjects' responses? and (2) What attributions will they make about me if I don't agree with them (Ross, Bierbrauer, & Hoffman, 1976)? The Asch studies were deliberately structured so that the first question had no clear answer. Concerning the second question, the subject might feel that dissent would be seen as questioning the other subjects' competence, leading them to make negative attributions to him. In this tough situation, the conforming response may seem the most adaptive one.

Would Asch's results occur today? Perhaps not; times and behavior patterns change. Perrin and Spencer (1981) carried out a conceptual replication of Asch's study in Great Britain in 1980 and found almost no conformity (less than 1 percent on the critical trials). They suggested that the personal costs of deviating from the group were much higher in the 1950s than later; the attributions made about nonconformity in the 1950s may have been far different from attributions in the 1980s. Supporting this conjecture, when they increased the personal costs of nonconformity by using youths on probation as the real subjects and probation officers as the rest of the group, conformity rose to a level similar to that found by Asch. The study does not mean that overall levels of conformity are necessarily any lower today than in past years; rather, people may be conforming in different situations or in different ways today than in the past.

Factors Affecting Conformity

In the Asch paradigm, as group size increases to six or eight people (with only one person being the real subject), the likelihood of conforming behavior by lone subjects also increases (Gerard et al., 1968). Increasing group size affects normative more than informational social influence. After a point the factual information provided by each additional group member becomes redundant, but the expectation of group disapproval for a deviate continues to get stronger as the group grows larger. Hence increasing majority group size will increase conformity more when the advocated group norm could not be correct (as in the Asch paradigm) and normative social influence is therefore paramount, than when the group's norm *might* be correct and informational social influence is involved (Campbell & Fairey, 1989).

The status, similarity, and apparent expertise of group members also affect the amount of conformity. The higher the status other group members have (referent power, possible reward power) or the more similar to the subject (referent power) they appear to be, the more normative social influence they have. Expertise (expert power) increases their informational influence (Kiesler & Kiesler, 1969).

Recall that in Asch's basic study, the rest of the group was unanimous against a lone subject. It makes a drastic difference if a second group member also disagrees with the majority. In Asch's setup, when there was a second deviate, the amount of conforming behavior by the real subject was cut to about one-fourth of the level found with a single dissenter (Asch, 1956). Interestingly, the other dissenter need not be correct in his responses. Even when another dissenter gives a different incorrect answer, the likelihood of conformity by the real subject is reduced (Allen & Levine, 1971). Here the other dissenter would not be serving as a source of informational influence, since he was wrong too, but would be providing evidence that it is all right to disagree with the group norm.

The recent performance of the group also has an effect. When the group began by agreeing with the subject for many trials and then suddenly disagreed, as in Asch's study, the subject was more likely to conform than if the group began by disagreeing. Also, subjects who have evidence that they did well on the task individually are more likely to resist conformity pressures in a group situation (Mausner, 1954). The easier the problem or the more competent the person feels, the less conformity is likely to occur (Hollander & Willis, 1967). More conformity is also likely to occur when the response must be made publicly (stated aloud) rather than privately (Deutsch & Gerard, 1955).

Personality and Conformity

Is there a particular type of person who is likely to conform? One series of studies found that people who conformed on one type of situation tended to conform in other situations too, but the degree of consistency across situations was not very strong. People who conformed were likely to have more negative self-concepts and to score low on measures of leadership ability and high on measures of authoritarianism (Chapter 11). However, no overall difference in degree of psychological adjustment was found (Crutchfield, 1955). Some evidence exists that people with lower intelligence are more likely to conform (Nord, 1969), perhaps because they feel less expert than others. People with low self-esteem and low feelings of personal worth conform more than those with higher self-esteem (Santee & Maslach, 1982).

Resistance to conformity pressure can serve a value-expressive function (Chapter 4). People high in public self-awareness, those concerned with their social identity and other people's reaction to it, tend to conform more than those high in private self-awareness, who focus inward on their personal values (Froming & Carver, 1981; Santee & Maslach, 1982). Persons high in "need for control" are more likely to resist conformity pressures (Burger, 1987).

Conformity and Reduced Self-Awareness

Though social programs or institutions are not designed to create antisocial behavior, research suggests that one social institution, prisons, may do just that. Researchers (Zimbardo et al., 1982) did their best to psychologically simulate the characteristics of a real prison in a role-playing study. Half of the volunteer subjects (young men) were randomly assigned roles as prisoners, the other half as guards. All were paid $15 a day for the two-week study. The prisoners were rounded up on the first morning, taken in squad cars to the police station where they were processed (searched, handcuffed, fingerprinted, and booked), and taken blindfolded to the "prison" (the basement of the psychology building at Stanford University). Prisoners were identified only by numbers and had to wear identical open-backed hospital gowns (to cause feelings of vulnerability). They wore stocking caps on their heads to reduce the identifiability and individuality of hairstyles. The guards were given identical khaki uniforms, billyclubs, whistles, keys to the cells, handcuffs, and reflecting sunglasses. Prisoners and guards could hide behind their uniforms and lose their individuality, reducing both public and private self-awareness. These factors are summarized in Table 5-3.

Guards were instructed to "maintain law and order" and take responsibility for whatever problems arose during the two weeks. Prisoners became passive, helpless, and depressed. Some guards became aggressive and abusive to the prisoners. The experience was, in fact, all too real; after six days the experiment had to be terminated. Already five of the nine original prisoners had been released because of extreme emotional depression or acute anxiety attacks.

The Stanford prison study. Anonymity, high arousal, and immersion in the group led to reduced self-awareness and the disinhibition of negative behaviors.

The strangest aspect of this experiment was that the effects were obtained in a group of normal young men participating in a simulated study. Loss of personal identity and reduced feelings of self-awareness had dramatic impacts on behavior. Zimbardo and his co-workers carried out a full-day debriefing session at the end of the simulation to make sure they had not caused lasting psychological harm to their participants. Annual follow-ups indicated that the mental anguish of the participants dissipated soon after the end of the study, but the self-knowledge gained in the study persisted. This study vividly illustrates the strong effect of role schemas that reduce self-awareness.

People who succumb to conformity pressure end up doing things that they would rather not do. But there is another way in which lowered self-awareness can lead to changed behavior—individuals may feel freer to do things they always wanted to do but were previously inhibited from. This disinhibition effect has been termed **behavioral contagion** (Wheeler, 1966). The looting that sometimes accompanies urban riots is an example. City dwellers who have long desired better possessions see others looting stores

behavioral contagion: Disinhibited behavior; because of lowered self-awareness individuals engage in previously inhibited behaviors.

TABLE 5-3   CONFORMITY AND DISINHIBITION STEMMING FROM
                     REDUCED SELF-AWARENESS

Routes by which the situational pressures and role schemas in the Zimbardo et al. (1982) "prison study"
elicited negative behaviors from the participants

Situational Factors	Resulting Psychological State	Behavioral Outcomes
Anonymity, Shared responsibility →	Reduced public self-awareness ⟶	Disinhibition of negative behaviors
Guards: Identical uniforms, reflector sunglasses, addressed only as "Mr. Corrections Officer"		Reduced concern about disapproval from others (experimenters, prisoners, other guards) for mistreating prisoners
Prisoners: Identical hospital gowns, hair covered, referred to only by prisoner number		Reduced concern about disapproval from others (experimenters, guards, other prisoners) for rebelling or giving up
High arousal, immersion in group →	Reduced private self-awareness ⟶	Pay less attention to internal standards, more attention to external cues. Conformity or behavioral contagion likely
Guards: Unusual, highly arousing situation; group identity as guards		Increased likelihood of conforming to norms set by other guards (abuse of prisoners)
Prisoners: Unusual, highly arousing situation; group identity as prisoners		Increased likelihood of conforming to norms set by other prisoners (rebellion, giving up, emotional outbursts)

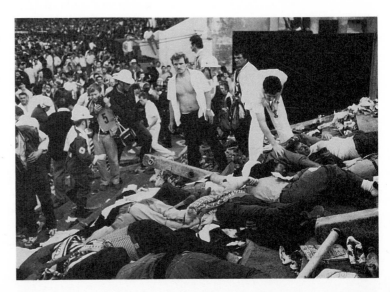

Behavioral contagion and sports violence. A riot that preceded a scheduled 1985 Italy vs. England soccer match in Belgium killed 38 fans and injured over 400 more. The riot stemmed in part from reduced self-awareness, deindividuation, and behavioral contagion among members of the crowd.

FOCUS 5-3

Behavioral Contagion on Campus: Binge Eating

Many observers have warned that bulimia is becoming the women's psychological disease of our time, rivaling depression in its prevalence. Bulimia is an eating pattern characterized by episodes of uncontrolled binge eating alternating with periods of fasting, strict dieting, or purging via diuretics, laxatives, or vomiting. Nearly all of those affected are women (Gandour, 1984).

Estimates in the 1980s were that 4 percent to 15 percent of college women had serious problems with bulimia (Sinoway et al., 1985), yet the disorder was almost unheard of before the 1970s (Rosenzweig & Spruill, 1986). The rapidity with which the disorder has spread in recent years suggests that social influence might play an important role. Bulimia is especially prevalent in women's groups such as cheerleaders, athletes,

dance camps, and sororities. All of these are highly cohesive groups where group members could have strong social influence over each other.

To investigate this issue, Crandall (1988) studied two popular university sororities over a two-year period. Sorority members filled out several questionnaires assessing their eating habits, height and weight, friendship patterns, and popularity. In both sororities, clear norms about appropriate binge-eating behavior were found. In one sorority, the more one binged, the more popular one was. In the other sorority, popularity was associated with binging the right amount: Those who binged too much or too little were less popular than those who binged an average amount. ❖

and getting away with it. The highly arousing nature of the riot and their identification with group membership produce lowered private self-awareness, leading to deindividuation and less attention to internal standards such as conscience. The anonymity of the riot reduces the participants' public self-awareness, minimizing fears about being caught.

The 1968 My Lai massacre in Vietnam may have involved behavioral contagion, as well as compliance to Lt. Calley's orders (Focus 5-2). If some of Lt. Calley's men were happy to have an excuse to kill indiscriminately, their participation in the massacre was an instance of behavioral contagion. Seeing other soldiers firing at the villagers without being punished may have lowered their internal restraints against doing the same thing. An interesting example of behavioral contagion on the college campus is described in Focus 5-3.

Authority Pressure

A final principle of social influence is *obedience to authority*. Every modern society has a complex and widely accepted system of authority; otherwise anarchy would rule. We are brought up to obey, more or less, our parents, teachers, police officers, and others in positions of authority. People most

compliance:
Changing one's behavior to fit someone's request or order.

often speak of **compliance** to a request and *obedience* to an order, but I will treat the concepts as interchangeable. Basically, they refer to changing one's behavior to fit someone's request or order. If the law professor had bellowed, "Don't you ever come to my class dressed like that again!" our casually dressed student probably would have been dressed in a coat and tie for the next class. This would be a case of compliance, rather than conformity, because he was complying to an expressed demand.

During the Watergate cover-up, acting FBI Director L. Patrick Gray, who had spent twenty-six years in the Navy, obeyed several dubious orders from above without question. "Mr. Gray conceded that he sent raw FBI reports to the White House, for example, but explained that he had been acting on the belief that there should be a 'presumption of regularity' about the men close to the president, and that he had simply followed their orders, which had come to him 'down the chain of command.' It was the old submarine captain speaking" (*New York Times* staff, 1973, p. 625). Gray also destroyed two boxes of files given to him by presidential advisors John Dean III and John Ehrlichman. When asked at the Senate hearings why he hadn't refused to destroy the files, Gray replied, "I don't think the thought ever entered my mind to do that. . . . I was receiving orders from the Counsel to the President and one of two top assistants to the President and I was not about to question these" (*New York Times* staff, 1973, p. 632).

Hurting on Command: Milgram's Studies

The Basic Setup. Stanley Milgram (1963; 1964; 1965a; 1974) carried out a series of studies to investigate how far people would go in obeying orders. In the basic study, men were paid to participate in a study of memory and learning at Yale University. The experimenter, an impassive and rather stern man, explains that the study investigates the effect of punishment, electric shock of increasing intensity, on learning. The subject's task, as a "teacher," is to administer a learning task to another subject, the "learner." The learner, actually an accomplice of the experimenter, is strapped into a chair in an adjoining room with an electrode attached to his wrist by electrode paste "in order to avoid blisters and burns." The experimenter has assured the learner that although the shocks can be extremely painful, they cause no permanent tissue damage.

After the training trials, the teacher's task is to administer a shock, moving one level higher on the shock generator each time the learner makes a wrong answer. The shock generator has thirty levers in a horizontal line, ranging from 15 to 450 volts in 15-volt increments. Labels above each group of four levers range from *Slight Shock* to *Danger: Severe Shock* up to *XXX*. The teacher is given a sample shock of 45 volts, which stings considerably.

The learner does not do very well, missing about three-quarters of the items, and the teacher has to deliver stronger and stronger shocks. When the teacher pushes the 300-volt lever, the learner pounds on the wall of the room but doesn't answer at all. The experimenter tells the teacher that failure to answer is an error and he should shock the learner according to the

Hurting on command. In Milgram's basic setup, the subject (the "teacher") was seated in front of a shock generator (upper left) while the "learner" was strapped into a chair to receive shocks (upper right). The experimenter explained the teacher's duties (lower left), and the teacher was later faced with the difficult decision of whether to obey or defy the experimenter (lower right).

usual schedule. On the next item, the 315-volt level, the learner again pounds on the wall but for the remainder of the experiment, he does not answer.

Most teachers indicated that they wanted to end the experiment and spare the learner further pain. But the experimenter made it rough for them. If the subject suggested that they stop (this often happened at the 300-volt level), the experimenter would reply, "Please continue." If the teacher protested, the experimenter would say, "The experiment requires that you continue," "It is absolutely essential that you continue," or, finally, "You have no other choice, you must go on." (Of course, the subjects *did* have a choice; they could have walked out at any time.) The experimenter assured the subject that he, the experimenter, would take all responsibility for any injury to the learner. After the teacher refused to continue or delivered the highest shock possible, the true purpose of the study was explained to him. He was shown that the shock generator was fake and that the learner did not actually receive any shocks.

How many people obeyed the experimenter all the way to the end? Forty psychiatrists at a medical school predicted that fewer than 1 percent of the subjects would deliver the highest shock possible (450 volts). A sample of college undergraduates made similar predictions (Milgram, 1965b). The general expectation was that only the most sadistic or unusual subjects would continue to deliver shocks. This illustrates the fundamental attribution error (Chapter 2)—the tendency to attribute other people's behavior to dispositional factors rather than situational forces. Yet in the original study, every one of the subjects obeyed up to the 300-volt level and 65 percent of the subjects went all the way to the end of the scale, the 450-volt level.

Why did most subjects continue to deliver shocks that seemed to be causing pain to another person? Situational forces were strong. The teacher, in the role of research subject (Chapter 1), had been assured that he was helping to obtain valuable scientific knowledge. The fact that the designations of teacher and learner were (supposedly) random may have made it easier for the teacher to justify his behavior. Prods and assurances from the experimenter also played a major role in eliciting maximum cooperation. Both low-balling and the foot-in-the-door effect are also relevant. The subjects had committed themselves to a situation that proved far more costly than they had expected. They had agreed to a series of smaller requests to participate in the experiment, and were put under pressure to comply with a larger request, to continue even after the learner wanted to stop. In addition, there was no clear breakpoint at which the teacher could easily quit (Gilbert, 1981).

Variations on a Theme. In later studies Milgram (1974) varied aspects of the experimental situation. One factor was the proximity of the victim. In a proximity condition, the learner was placed one and a half feet from the subject in the same room. Both visual and audible cues to the victim's pain were available to the subject. The touch-proximity condition was identical to the proximity condition, except that beyond the 150-volt level the victim refused to put his hand on a shock plate to receive the shock. Thus, on every subsequent trial, the experimenter ordered the teacher to force the victim's hand onto the shock plate. A plastic shield prevented the teacher from receiving the shock. When the victim was closer, more subjects refused to obey. Forty percent administered the highest shock in the proximity condition and 30 percent in the touch-proximity condition. As many have reported, it is much easier to drop bombs on an unseen enemy than to have to kill an individual enemy soldier.

Closeness of the authority figure was also varied. When the experimenter was present at the beginning to give initial instructions but then left the room, using a telephone for further instructions, obedience was only one-third as frequent as when the experimenter remained physically present. Moreover, when the experimenter was absent, several subjects administered shocks of a lower voltage than they were supposed to. Perhaps it was easier for subjects to handle conflict in this way than to openly defy the experimenter.

Milgram hypothesized that the prestige of the sponsoring institution (Yale) might have been important. To check this possibility, the study was conducted in a three-room office in a somewhat run-down commercial building in downtown Bridgeport, Connecticut. The sponsor of the study was supposedly Research Associates of Bridgeport. Almost half (48 percent) of the subjects delivered the maximum shock possible (Milgram, 1965b) — not quite as many as had done so at Yale, but close enough to suggest that the prestige of the sponsoring institution was not crucially important.

Finally, Milgram looked at the effect of group pressure. Another setup had three teachers (two of them accomplices). The real subject "by chance" became the one who actually pushed the shock lever. In one study both accomplice-teachers followed the experimenter's commands and did not show any sympathy for the learner. These obedient models did not strongly affect the behavior of the real subjects, as the compliance rate was only slightly greater (72 percent) than in the original study. In a second variation, the two teacher-accomplices were defiant. One accomplice refused to continue after the 150-volt level and the other quit at the 210-volt level. This defiance had a major impact on the real subjects, as only 10 percent of them continued all the way to the maximum shock.

The defiant teachers served as social models, demonstrating that it was possible to disobey the experimenter without facing severe consequences. They showed that the experimenter's social power was not so strong that it couldn't be resisted. Yet three-fourths of the subjects who refused to go all the way claimed that they would have stopped even without the other teachers' examples. The results from the other conditions strongly suggest that this is not so, although the subjects may have honestly believed that it was. As we saw earlier (Chapter 2), people are often unaware of what factors determine their behavior.

In still another condition, the teacher could choose the level of shock to deliver. Only one of forty subjects used the 450-volt level at all. In still another variation the subject was assigned to a subsidiary role and did not have to press the shock lever himself. Here 92.5 percent of the subjects stayed with the experiment through the 450-volt level. Most men seem willing to participate in a situation involving pain, as long as they are not the ones who inflict it (Milgram, 1974). Figure 5-2 summarizes the results of many of Milgram's studies.

Although Milgram's studies highlight the situational factors that may increase or decrease the overall rate of obedience, they unfortunately do not provide many insights on a conceptual or theoretical level (Wrightsman, 1974). Why do some subjects obey in the same situation in which others are defiant? Why do some situational factors have a stronger effect on obedience than others? Answers to these questions must await future research.

Watergate on Campus

The power of authority pressure was further demonstrated in a controversial study by West, Gunn, and Chernicky (1975) in which college students were asked by a private investigator to consider being part of a four-person team that would break into an advertising firm. The student's role would be to microfilm the advertising agency records. The situation contained powerful pressures toward compliance. Each student was first induced to attend the preliminary meeting (foot-in-the-door) and was faced with a unanimous majority (the private investigator and his assistant) that had expert power (detailed plans and knowledge).

Students were given one of four descriptions of the operation's origin. Some were told that the burglary was secretly sponsored by the Internal Revenue Service, which promised them total immunity from prosecution if they were caught — a situation designed to parallel the Watergate circumstances

FIGURE 5-2

Degree of Compliance under Different Conditions in Milgram's Studies

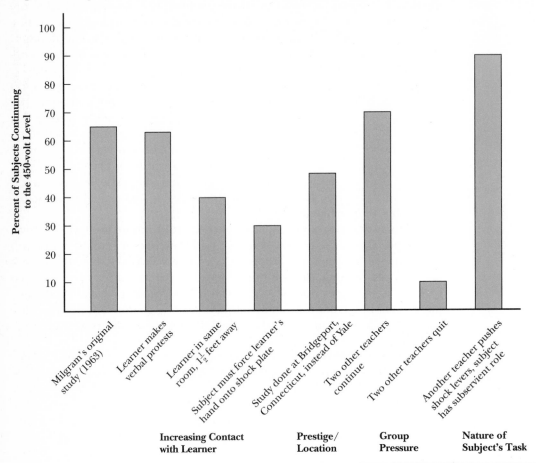

as closely as possible. A second set of students were given the same explanation, except that no mention of immunity from prosecution was made. The break-in was described to a third set of students as sponsored by another advertising firm. These students were told they would get $2,000 for participating. Finally, a fourth group of students was told that the break-in was merely to see whether the private investigator's plans would really work.

Each subject was asked to agree to attend a final planning meeting. When immunity was promised, almost half of the students (45 percent) agreed to attend. In the other three conditions, few students (5 percent to 20 percent) agreed to the meeting. After each subject had either accepted or rejected this request, the purpose of the experiment and the reasons for the deception were explained to them. Thus, no one actually engaged in illegal activities (Cook, 1975). The results suggest that in a situation that encourages compliance, many presumably law-abiding citizens can be induced to consider illegal activities when they are apparently sponsored by the government and immunity from prosecution is promised.

West and his co-workers also described each of the four situations in detail to a different sample of students and asked them why people might agree to come to the final meeting. The students showed the fundamental attribution error. They tended to attribute subjects' agreement to participate to dispositional factors (greed, irresponsibility, a conformist personality). Other students, asked what would determine their *own* behavior in such a situation, were more likely to refer to situational factors.

Processes Involved in Compliance to Authority

What is it about some situations that enables socially reprehensible behavior to occur? Kelman (1973) identified three important psychological processes. **Authorization**, sanction given by the authority figures, allows people to claim little responsibility for their actions. They may believe that they are helping their leaders in a crucially important mission. Milgram (1974) described his subjects as being in an **agentic state**, seeing themselves as mere agents of the experimenter. They felt little responsibility for their actions, allowed the experimenter to define the situation, and tried to ignore extraneous stimuli (such as the learner's signs of distress). A second process, **routinization,** transforms the behavior into routine, mechanical operations. People can concentrate on the details of the job, thereby avoiding thinking about the implications of what they are doing. (Recall the discussion of "mindless" information processing in Chapter 2.) Finally, through the process of **dehumanization**, the victims are robbed of their humanity and individuality, making it easier to act against them. Derogatory group terms (*gooks, commies, Japs, niggers, spics, dirty Jews,* etc.) define people as inferior and limit empathy for them.

Important Issues in Obedience Studies

Ethical Considerations. Participation in an obedience study is a very powerful experience. Subjects generally are expecting much less, emotionally, than they receive. For example, subjects in the Stanford prison experiment were unprepared for the intensity of the experiences that followed. The framework of Milgram's study was not described until after the subject had arrived at the laboratory and accepted money for his participation. In the "Watergate study," subjects had no idea they were to be pressured into considering illegal behavior.

Surveys show that virtually no one thinks that he or she would go all the way in the original Milgram experiment. Probably few if any of the "guards" in the prison experiment expected that they would engage in abusive, sadistic behavior, which is alien to a healthy self-concept. Yet many subjects found that they engaged in socially undesirable behavior when under

authorization:
Sanction given by authority figures which allows people to claim little responsibility for their actions.

agentic state:
When people see themselves as mere agents of an authority figure and deny responsibility for their own actions.

routinization:
transformation of behavior into routine, mechanical operations.

dehumanization:
The process through which victims are robbed of their humanity and individuality, making it easier to aggress against them.

authority pressures. The effect of such knowledge on one's self-concept might be devastating. When they agreed to participate, subjects did not ask for drastic or depressing insights into their own psyches. Because of this, some have argued that obedience research is unfair to subjects (Baumrind, 1964; 1985).

On the other hand, such self-knowledge can be valuable. It may give subjects a greater understanding of human behavior, particularly their own. Some participants in the Stanford prison study later volunteered vacation time to work in local prisons, and most became advocates of prison reform as a result of their "prison" experience. Extensive follow-up surveys found no evidence of harm from participating in Milgram's studies (Milgram, 1964; 1965b). Some caution should be used in interpreting the survey results, however. People who have done something unpleasant (such as administering shocks) may be motivated later to justify their behavior to themselves, especially when asked by the same experimenter. Ambivalent or neutral subjects may decide that it was a valuable experience, perhaps as a way of reducing dissonant feelings about their participation.

Generalizability of Results. Do findings from obedience studies enable us to better understand events such as Watergate or the Iran-Contra scandal, or atrocities such as those in Nazi Germany, the My Lai massacre in Vietnam, and the mass suicide of the followers of the Reverend Jim Jones in Guyana? The research situations are different in many ways from real-life situations in which, for example, orders are filtered down through a chain of command while many other confusing and frightening things are going on (Allen, 1978). In contrast, obedience is expected behavior for research subjects. People take seriously their responsibilities as participants in a scientific study, in which—contrary to real life—their behavior is closely monitored by an authority figure. Therefore, some have proposed there may be little similarity between behavior in obedience studies and behavior of, say, Nazi German officers (Baumrind, 1964; Orne & Holland, 1968).

Others have argued that obedience research findings are both relevant and generalizable. Etzioni (1968) suggested that Milgram's research illuminated the "latent Eichmann" that resides in most of us. Allen (1978) suggested that perhaps Lt. William Calley "is really not much different from you and me." Karnow (1971) suggested that Milgram's research "demonstrated in the laboratory what Lt. William Calley and his unit would later dramatize at My Lai—that man's behavior is almost invariably dominated by authority rather than by his own sense of morality." Milgram argued, "If we now recoil at our own conduct, it is because we are just as capable as the Nazis of committing crimes in the name of obedience" (Karnow, 1971).

Some additional evidence suggests that obedience findings can be generalized. In a study of former Nazi SS concentration camp personnel and members of Gestapo units, Dicks (1972) noted many of the same psychological processes that Milgram's subjects showed, for example, feelings of being a "helpless cog" who is required to follow orders. Milgram (1963, p. 371) commented, "Gas chambers were built, death camps were guarded, daily quotas of corpses were produced with the same efficiency as the manufacture of appliances. These inhumane policies may have originated in the mind of a single person, but they could only be carried out on a massive scale if a very large number of persons obeyed orders."

Is Everyone a Potential Eichmann? Eichmann, Field Marshal Keitel, Lt. Col. North, and Lt. Calley all gave "following orders" as the explanation for their behavior. Historically, such explanations have usually been rejected by others as self-serving rationalizations. But research evidence suggests that such rejection may not be entirely fair. Perhaps many men in such situations *really were* just following orders. Perhaps many of us might have behaved similarly if we were in a situation that seemed to demand such behavior. This might be all the more likely if we have been brought up in a culture where strict obedience to authority was stressed, such as post–World World I Germany. Novelist Kurt Vonnegut, Jr., (1966) has written, "If I'd been born in Germany I suppose I would have been a Nazi, bopping Jews and gypsies and Poles around, leaving boots sticking out of snow-banks, warming myself with my sweetly virtuous insides." Nevertheless, a United Nations report declared, "The fact that a person acted pursuant to order of his government or superior does not relieve him of responsibility under international law, provided a moral choice was in fact possible to him" (*Time*, December 5, 1969, p. 32).

Does Personality Make a Difference? Although research indicates that situational pressures and social power are prime factors in compliance, this does not mean that one's personality is irrelevant. As Focus 5-1 illustrated, there is evidence that Eichmann was overzealous even for a Nazi, that he truly "loved his work" and saw as his goal the death of as many Jews as possible. Field Marshal Keitel and Lieutenant Calley, in contrast, more easily fit the picture of men who were truly just following orders. As noted earlier, most attempts to identify personality factors that relate to susceptibility to authority pressures have been unsuccessful. However, there have been a few significant findings.

Lt. Col. Oliver North testifies to Congress. Lt. Col. North claimed that his illegal actions resulted from "just following orders" from President Reagan and other high government and military officials.

Prisoners high in authoritarianism, a personality style that includes a tendency to obey authority (to be discussed in Chapter 11) were more likely to have lasted the six days in the Stanford prison study than were low-authoritarian prisoners (Zimbardo et al., 1982). People high in authoritarianism were also more likely to go all the way in Milgram's obedience experiments (Elms & Milgram, 1966). Level of moral development, as measured by Kohlberg's (1969) scale, also made a difference. A study using thirty-four of Milgram's former subjects found that over 85 percent of the subjects in the middle stages of moral development had gone all the way in the Milgram setup but only 25 percent of the people at the highest levels of moral development had done so (Kohlberg, 1969) . Although this study was based on a very small sample, the results are intriguing. The studies show that personality can affect susceptibility to authority pressures for compliance.

A more broad-based view of orientation to authority comes from Kelman and Hamilton (1989), who conducted in-depth surveys of adults across the nation. They identified three general orientations toward authority: *rule* orientation, *role* orientation, and *value* orientation. Some general characteristics of each orientation are summarized in Table 5-4. How would you think each orientation would respond to situations where someone claims to have been "just following orders," as in the trial of Lt. Calley? The researchers found that those endorsing the rule and role orientations showed little disapproval of Lt. Calley for his actions and did not think he should have been convicted. Most value-oriented people, in contrast, approved of Calley's conviction, feeling that he should have refused to follow the order to shoot. It would be interesting to know whether a similar pattern of viewpoints would have been found in reaction to the trial of Lt. Colonel North.

Impact of the Situation: There but for the Grace of God Go I

Research illustrates the tremendous impact of situational forces (forces leading to obedience to authority or forces that place people in specific roles) on human behavior. Situational pressures are more important than most of us like to think. As noted above, though, situational factors do not completely control our behaviors. One study (Funder & Ozer, 1983) found a mean correlation of about .40 between situational factors and behavior in several types of studies (including Milgram's).

Although we all like to think of ourselves as free souls who are independent of situational restraints, this is often not the case. Zimbardo and his co-workers (1982, p. 242) proposed:

> Therefore, it is time psychologists stopped offering legislators, lawmen, and lay people "traits," "dispositions," and "individual differences" as reasonable solutions to existing problems in our society. To change behavior we must discover the institutional supports which maintain the existing undesirable behavior and then design programs to alter these environments.

TABLE 5-4	ORIENTATIONS TO AUTHORITY		

General characteristics of the three broad types of orientation to society identified by Kelman and Hamilton

	Rule Orientation	**Role Orientation**	**Value Orientation**
Expectation from citizen	Follow rules; avoid trouble	Meet citizen obligation to obey and support the government	Take active part in formulating, evaluating, and questioning policies
Expectation from government	Uphold rules; assure security and order	Uphold roles; assure national and personal status	Uphold values; pursue policies reflecting national principles
Participation in duties	Passive: minimal compliance (as necessary to protect interests)	Supportive: active part in carrying out policies	Evaluative: active part in formulating and assessing policies
Socialization process	Compliance	Identification	Internalization
Role of morality in citizen action	Moral principles irrelevant	Moral obligation to government overrides personal morality	Personal moral principles must enter into consideration
Nature of support to government	Compliant	Reliable, enthusiastic	Firm but conditional

Source: From CRIMES OF OBEDIENCE by Herbert C. Kelman and V. Lee Hamilton, p. 269. Copyright © by Yale University Press. Reprinted by permission.

Coerced Attitude and Behavior Change: Brainwashing?

brainwashing:
A popularized term for attitude and behavior change that takes place under extreme authority pressure and control.

DDD syndrome:
Conditions facing prisoners of war that make it particularly hard to resist compliance pressures: dread, dependency, and debility.

Indoctrination of War Prisoners. About 3,600 Americans were taken prisoner during the Korean war in the early 1950s. Most of them were subjected to indoctrination or **brainwashing** pressures by their captors. Popular hysteria in the U.S. suggested that a diabolical new technique had been developed through which anyone could be made to comply with the wishes of the brainwasher (Brinkley, 1953).

The prisoners of war (POWs) were under stressful physical and psychological conditions that made it difficult for them to resist compliance pressures. These conditions have been labeled the **DDD syndrome**, including the factors of debility (from semistarvation, fatigue, wounds, and disease), dependency (the POW's total dependency on his captors), and dread (fear of death, fear of pain, fear of nonrepatriation). "Among the POWs pressured by the Chinese Communists, the DDD syndrome in its full-blown form constituted a state of discomfort that was well-nigh intolerable" (Farber et al., 1956, p. 273).

The Chinese indoctrination program was based on four major factors (Schein et al., 1961). The first centered on the *removal of supports* for existing beliefs, attitudes, and values. All the prisoners' usual sources of information about the world were cut off by the Chinese. The prisoners were segregated by rank in order to undermine the internal structure of the group by removing its leaders. Emotional isolation prevented prisoners from validating their attitudes and values through interaction with others (using others as social standards).

A second phase of the indoctrination involved *direct attacks* on attitudes and values. Although the anti-American material in daily lectures was naive and often incorrect, the constant hammering at certain points made it likely that some Chinese arguments would filter through. Most effective was the use of "testimonials" by other prisoners who apparently supported Communist enterprises (Schein, 1956). Such testimonials had a double effect: they further weakened group ties among the POWs while at the same time presenting pro-Communist arguments (Lifton, 1961).

A third procedure used *indirect attacks* on attitudes and values. After lectures, for example, the prisoners might have to give written answers to questions about the lecture. Prisoners also had to confess publicly to wrongdoings and to criticize themselves when they broke any of the camp rules. Though initial confessions seemed relatively harmless, eventually a prisoner would break another camp rule, leading to demands for more confession and stronger self-criticism. After a prisoner had been "trained" to speak or write out trivia, statements about more important issues were demanded (the foot-in-the-door technique).

The use of *reward* and *coercive power* was the fourth characteristic of the indoctrination program. Medication, clothing, food, better conditions, and promises of early repatriation were powerful incentives. Perhaps the most important privilege was freedom of movement; cooperative POWs had free access to Chinese headquarters and could go wherever they wished at any time of the day or night. At the other extreme, threats of death, nonrepatriation, torture, reprisals against families, and reduction in food and medication were all used.

How effective are these techniques? It is hard to tell exactly, because a prisoner could collaborate with the enemy without altering his beliefs, or could be converted to communism to some degree and still not collaborate. Psychologists estimated that 15 percent of the POWs cooperated with their Communist Chinese captors to some degree (Schein et al., 1961). Twenty-one of the 3,600 POWs chose to remain in China or North Korea after repatriation to America became possible. These twenty-one POWs were dishonorably discharged from the Army in absentia in 1954, and none were ever prosecuted for their actions while a prisoner of war. All but two of the twenty-one men left China over the next two decades.

Given what we know about the power of situational pressures, what should be done about POWs who crack under these intense pressures? The American Armed Forces Code of Conduct (1955) seems clear. A prisoner of war:

> should not take part in any action which might be harmful to his comrades. When questioned, the POW is bound to give only his name, rank, serial number, and date of birth. He should evade answering further ques-

tions to the utmost of his ability. He should make no oral or written statements disloyal to his country and its allies.

If this code is strictly interpreted, then a number of American POWs in Korea and later in Vietnam were guilty of violations. But is it reasonable to expect people to resist such powerful pressures? Military and legal experts themselves are unsure. Although the U.S. government brought charges against some Vietnam and Korean War POWs for collaboration, all charges were subsequently dropped except for the case of Private Robert Garwood (Focus 5-4).

FOCUS 5-4

The Case of Bobby Garwood

In February 1979, in Hanoi, Vietnam, a man passed a note to a Finnish economist with the United Nations. The note identified the man as Bobby Garwood, a U.S. Marine who wanted to go home. Several weeks later, after the U.S. State Department had interceded, Garwood was on his way back to America. Garwood was a tenth grade dropout who had been abandoned in childhood and raised by his father and stepmother. He joined the Marines in 1963 and in 1965 he was a nineteen-year-old jeep driver in Vietnam, ten days away from rotating home, when he was captured. Hence, when he reappeared in 1979, Garwood had spent almost half of his life in Vietnam.

Garwood returned to the United States to face charges of extreme misconduct while he had been a prisoner of war in Vietnam. Nine American former POWs who had spent time in several jungle prison camps with Garwood testified that he had served as an interpreter at political indoctrination classes and had suggested that they cross over to the North Vietnamese side. They testified that he had interrogated POWs new to the camp and had served as a camp guard, carrying an AK-47 assault rifle. He also ate well while they starved. A former American POW said, "He was squatting like them, walking like them, and giggling like them. In my opinion, he was a white Vietnamese" (*The Washington Post*, February 6, 1981, p. A1).

Garwood had already been a captive for two years by the time the first American POW encountered him.

Garwood's defense attorneys in his 1980–81 court-martial disputed little of the POWs' testimony. However, they asserted that he had been broken and driven insane by torture. According to his attorney, Garwood twice attempted to escape. Recaptured both times, he was beaten, stripped naked, and kept for a month in a bamboo cage with little food or water, growing weaker and suffering from exposure, leeches, and tropical disease. His captors forced him to watch their games of Russian Roulette with captured South Vietnamese soldiers.

The five-man jury of Marine Corps officials, all decorated Vietnam veterans, found Garwood guilty of collaborating with the enemy in Vietnam. Garwood was the only U.S. Vietnam-era serviceman to be found guilty of actions taken while he was a POW. Similar charges against eight other POWs were dropped in 1973 by the Pentagon under White House pressure soon after one of the men in the group committed suicide (*The Washington Post*, February 6, 1981, pp. A1, A30). In Garwood's case the Marine Corps jury ordered a dishonorable discharge, reduction to the lowest pay grade, and forfeiture of pay from the date of his imprisonment, but no prison term. ❖

Religious Cults. The growth of religious cults in America in recent years stimulated renewed concern about forced changes in attitudes and behaviors. People who define themselves as religious seekers and encounter a cult member at a turning point in their lives are most likely to be converted (Lofland & Stark, 1965). Cults can provide the seeker with consensus, support, and social reinforcers. The use of reward power can be particularly effective, as a new member may receive an outpouring of affection from cult members. Coercive power and deceit may also be used, preventing members from leaving when they wish, allowing no access to usual sources of information, and using threats for failure to conform (see Focus 5-5).

In recent years some cult members were forcibly removed from their group and **deprogrammed,** put under intense pressure to reestablish their old, more traditional beliefs. Several organizations, many staffed by ex-cult members, carried out deprogramming for fees ranging up to $25,000 (Bromley & Shupe, 1981). Under some temporary conservatorship laws, adults may be declared legally incompetent and forcibly held, with the approval of their "guardians," until the presumed effects of the group's influence are undone (until they recant their new faith). In the meantime, the legal rights of the alleged incompetent can be suspended. The legalities of such procedures are dubious; some deprogrammers served prison time for their activities. Some social scientists suggested that deprogramming is similar to brainwashing, or even to exorcism. Observers noted, "It is ironic that while modern anticultists perceive commitment to cults' doctrines as the result of brainwashing, their own attempts to restore their loved ones to 'normality' closely resemble the very phenomena they profess to despise" (Shupe et al., 1977, p. 952).

deprogramming:
A procedure in which members of unpopular groups are put under intense pressure to recant and reestablish their older and more traditionl beliefs.

The Jonestown tragedy. Over 900 people died, most by voluntarily swallowing cyanide-laced Kool-Aid, at the orders of the Reverend Jim Jones in the jungles of Guyana.

RESISTING COMPLIANCE PRESSURES: THE POWER OF A MINORITY

Psychological Reactance

I noted earlier that people may show psychological reactance when their freedom of choice is under attack (Brehm & Brehm, 1981). Their sense of being consistent with past behaviors and values is threatened and they may attempt to reestablish freedom by performing the threatened behavior. Aggression may be aimed at the source that threatened the freedom of action. Further, the threatened behavior may appear more attractive. People feeling reactance will be unlikely to comply because compliance requires giving up even more freedom. Reactance increases when the threat is perceived as more arbitrary or unreasonable, when the threatener is less attractive, and when the actor places a high value on self-reliance and autonomy (Grabitz-Gniech, 1971).

FOCUS 5-5

The Jonestown Tragedy

Perhaps the most chilling example of conformity and compliance to authority in recent years was the mass suicides of the followers of the Reverend Jim Jones in Guyana in 1978. Jones, whose People's Temple had moved to South America from the U.S. a few years before, apparently weilded an enormous amount of social power over his followers. We would suspect that many of those followers were "seekers" who were eager to find someone in whom to put their absolute faith. The Jonestown massacre has been compared to the tragedy in Masada in A.D. 73, when numerous Jews killed themselves rather than face prosecution under the Romans, or the episode in World War II when 1,000 Japanese hurled themselves from a cliff in Saipan as American troops took control of the island (Wooden, 1981).

The episode began when Leo Ryan, destined to become the first U.S. congressman killed in the line of duty, heard many stories about strange happenings within the temple. The colony's former financial secretary said Jones was collecting $65,000 a month in social security checks from older commune members. Ryan and an entourage of people, including nine newsmen and four relatives of commune members, went to Guyana to investigate the temple. At first Ryan was impressed by what he saw. The people seemed happy and not under force. He was even treated to a chorus of "America the Beautiful." Later the facade that had been built up for him began to break down. He was handed a note by someone saying that he wanted to leave. When shown the note, Jones said that he felt betrayed but tried to convince Ryan that people were free to come and go. Ryan told Jones that he wasn't going to do anything against the temple because he felt satisfied with what he had seen.

When Ryan was ready to go home, he traveled to the Port Kaituma airstrip along with the reporters and a few people from the commune who had expressed the desire to return home. One of the members of the commune who had pretended to be a defector began shooting, wounding two other defectors. At the same time, a tractor pulling a trailer came up the runway. Men with automatic pistols, semiautomatic rifles, and shotguns began shooting. Only eight people survived the shots and Ryan wasn't one of the fortunate ones.

Back at the camp, Jones told his two lawyers that some of the people who had left with Ryan had no intention of leaving. "They want to kill somebody." Jones told the two lawyers to wait at a guest cottage while he ordered a revolutionary suicide to protest racism and fascism. The lawyers were able to escape into the jungle. Two of Jones's lieutenants returned from the airstrip and told Jones about the killings.

Jones began to act quickly. The camp doctor prepared a vat of strawberry-flavored Kool-Aid, added painkillers and tranquilizers, and then put in half a gallon of cyanide. Parents and nurses used syringes to squirt the mixture onto the tongues of the babies while the rest drank the mixture. Some of the people weren't quite so willing, but the guards forced them to drink, shooting some in the process. A few people were able to escape into the jungle. The water supply was also poisoned to kill the camp's cattle, chickens, and pigs. The camp's monkey mascot was shot. Jones later put a gun to his head and shot himself. It took authorities more than twelve hours to reach the few survivors. The Guyanese troops found 803 passports, over a million dollars in cash, and over 900 bodies (Kerns & Wead, 1979; *Newsweek*, December 4, 1978; *Time*, December 4, 1978; Wooden, 1981). ❖

Minority Influence

The Impact of a Consistent Minority

Generally, as we have seen from conformity research, majorities exert more influence than minorities do. But history describes many unusual individuals (e.g., Christ, Muhammed, Galileo, Freud) who, despite all of the conformity-compliance pressures they encountered, steadfastly refused to conform and instead stuck to their beliefs. Though they stood alone (at least initially), these individuals had a dramatic impact on others and on the course of events. What enabled these people to convince many others to follow in their path? Research indicates that a minority's style is a critical feature. To illustrate, several researchers reversed the usual conformity setup by having a minority of two people (accomplices) in a group of six subjects give consistently incorrect public responses, mislabeling blue slides as green (Moscovici et al., 1969). This (incorrect) minority had a substantial influence on the behavior of the majority group (the four real subjects). About one-third of the majority group members reported seeing a green slide at least once, something that never happened when there was no dissenting minority.

minority influence: The process by which a consistent, firm minority may alter the beliefs and behaviors of the majority.

Minority influence is most likely to occur when the minority is consistent, firm, and uncompromising, but not unnecessarily rigid, in holding to their initially unpopular view. In this case, the minority is likely to be seen as competent and certain. If there is time enough for the minority's position to be debated and understood by the majority, other group members may move toward the stable position endorsed by the minority (Moscovici & Nemeth, 1974; Moscovici & Personnaz, 1980).

Minority influence is most powerful when the minority takes a position in the direction that the general norms are moving (e.g., arguing for civil rights in the 1960s or feminism in the 1970s). When arguing against

A lone protester stopped a line of tanks for several minutes as the Chinese Army moved to crush protests in Tienamen Square in Beijing in 1989. He tried unsuccessfully to persuade them to turn around.

Minority influence can shape history. Jesus Christ, Charles Darwin, and Sigmund Freud steadfastly adhered to their initially unpopular views and eventually convinced many others to follow in their path.

the evolving norms, a minority is not effective (Maass et al., 1982). This explains why minority groups such as the Ku Klux Klan and the John Birch Society had minimal impact in the United States in the 1960s and 1970s, when norms were moving away from a white supremacy ideology, while women and blacks gained considerable influence (Maass & Clark, 1984). More generally, members of a cultural outgroup (e.g., homosexuals, racial minorities) who are also a numerical minority within the group (a "double minority") will not exert as much influence as majority-group members do when they are in the minority (Clark & Maass, 1988).

It appears that exposure to a minority view has a different cognitive impact than does exposure to the majority view. The majority view fits the schemas of most group members and they can accept the information easily, without much thought. The minority's view, in contrast, is likely to be subjected to relentless criticism. This criticism is likely to stimulate cognitive conflict among group members, resulting in **divergent thinking**, a process that involves considering the problem from varying viewpoints. In the course of the discussions some of the minority's adversaries may be converted. This may lead to better decision making (Nemeth, 1986).

divergent thinking: Considering a problem from varying viewpoints, usually resulting in better decision making.

Moscovici (1980) asserted that majority influence (conformity) leads only to public compliance whereas minority influence produces internalization (private acceptance), sometimes even when people fail to show public compliance (Maass & Clark, 1983). Interpreted in terms of the elaboration likelihood model of attitude change (Chapter 4), minority influence produces enduring change via the central route rather than temporary change via the peripheral route. To summarize, minority influence occurs when a minority displays a consistent behavioral style and has enough time for its position to be understood, leading majority group members to attribute certainty and competence to the minority.

idiosyncrasy credits:
A person who has
demonstrated compe-
tence and has achieved
status in the group builds
up idiosyncrasy credits
and will be permitted (up
to a point) to deviate
from group standards.

Idiosyncrasy Credits

A person who has demonstrated competence and has achieved status in a group through initial conformity to the group's norms builds up **idiosyncrasy credits** in the group (Hollander, 1964). As these credits accumulate, this individual will be permitted (up to a point) not to conform, that is, to innovate and to depart from group norms without being rejected. Therefore, a dissenter will be most influential when he or she has conformed to group norms on previous occasions, thus building up idiosyncrasy credits. In contrast, the minority influence model suggests that influence will be greatest when the individual maintains a nonconformist orientation from the outset, showing a consistent behavioral style. One study compared the influence of a minority who dissented on every one of four problems to the influence of a minority who dissented on only the last problem, and found that both procedures had an impact. For male subjects, dissenting only on the last problem had the most effect (supporting the idiosyncrasy credit model), but for females, both procedures were equally effective (Bray et al., 1982).

Making Obedience a Thoughtful Process

More than seventy years ago, Harold Laski (1919) wrote:

> Civilization means, above all, an unwillingness to inflict unnecessary pain. Within the ambit of that definition, those of us who heedlessly accept the comments of authority cannot yet claim to be civilized.
>
> Our business, if we desire to live a life not utterly devoid of meaning and significance, is to accept nothing which contradicts our basic experience merely because it comes to us from tradition or authority. It may well be that we shall be wrong; but our self-expression is thwarted at the root unless the certainties we are asked to accept coincide with the certainties we experience. That is why the condition of freedom in any state is always a widespread and consistent skepticism of the canons upon which power insists.

Historian C. P. Snow has written (1961, p. 24):

> When you think of the long and gloomy history of man you will find more hideous crimes have been committed in the name of obedience than have ever been committed in the name of rebellion.

The lessons from war, Jonestown, and recent government scandals, as well as from the psychological laboratory, point to a basic facet of human behavior: We are all susceptible to pressures, direct or subtle, to conform or comply with the wishes of others. The choice of whether to accede to these pressures is still ours, but is often a difficult one. As you can see from these thoughts of a U.S. Vietnam veteran in 1972 (Severy et al., 1976, p. 320), the choices can be agonizing:

I was there a year, and I never had the courage to say that was wrong. I condoned that. I watched it go on. Now I'm home. Sometimes I, my heart, it bothers me inside, because I remember all that, and I didn't have the courage to say it was wrong.... You say it's right because they are the enemy, and then when you come home, you can't believe that you didn't have the courage to open your mouth against that kind of mur- der, that kind of devastation over people, over animals.

FOCUS 5-6

Lieutenant Colonel Oliver North and the Iran-Contra Scandal

In May 1989, after 3 months of trial, Lieutenant Colonel (Lt. Col.) Oliver North, the Marine at the shadowy center of the Reagan administration's se- cret effort in the mid-1980s to arm the Nicaraguan Contras with the proceeds from secret arms sales to Iran, was convicted in federal court of illegally altering and shredding documents and obstruct- ing Congress. Lt. Col. North was the point man for the secret plan hatched by the National Secu- rity Council to divert tens of millions of dollars derived from secret sales of U.S. arms to Iran to support the Contra rebels in Nicaragua. North had admitted in court that he misled members of Congress about his Iran-Contra activities. But, he claimed, he had done so under orders from his superiors.

North's defense was that he had been a good soldier loyally carrying out what he knew his Commander-in-Chief, President Reagan, wanted. "If the Commander-in-Chief tells his Lieutenant Colonel to go stand in the corner and sit on his head," he declared, "I will do so." North described himself as "a pawn in a chess game being played by giants." Early in the scandal President Reagan had praised North as a "national hero"; two years later Reagan, then out of office, had no immedi- ate comment on North's conviction.

North's dilemma echoed, in some ways, the plight of Lt. Calley and of the Watergate defen- dants of fifteen years earlier. North, like some of the Watergate defendants and Lt. Calley, claimed that he was simply following the orders of his su- periors. North's trial judge instructed the jury, be- fore they began their deliberations, that nobody had the power to order North to break laws and that even if he were authorized to do what he did, he had to have "clear, direct instructions . . . not simply a general admonition or vague expression of preference." Was North merely a sacrificial lamb, a scapegoat who enabled his superiors to evade responsibility, as his defense lawyer claimed? Or was he a habitual liar who followed Adolph Hitler's maxim that "the victor will never be asked if he told the truth," as the prosecutor argued? The jurors had a difficult time deciding North's fate. After days of deliberation they found him guilty on three counts but not guilty on nine others. Public opinion was divided, too. A *Newsweek* poll found that 39% of Americans thought the verdict was too harsh, while 31% thought it was fair and 19% believed that North got off too easy (Martz, 1989a). ❖

Sources: Alterman (1987); Ledeen (1988); Martz (1989a; 1989b); "Jury Finds North Guilty" (1989).

Research has provided a new and sobering frame of reference for the evaluation of human behavior under conditions of extreme authority pressure. Most people remain unaware of what these pressures can do. For instance, observers who witness a reenactment of the Milgram experiment invariably fail to appreciate the magnitude of the situational forces operating upon the teacher in that situation (Bierbrauer, 1979). The lessons of Nazi Germany, Vietnam, and Watergate seem not to have been learned very well. The answer is not simply to stop obeying orders but to make obedience a *thoughtful process* (Allen, 1978). In order to do so, one must have a conception of what is reasonable, moral, and legitimate. If you have carefully thought about these concepts and are aware of the human tendency to be controlled by others, the likelihood of being caught by controlling situations may be considerably lessened. Lt. Colonel Oliver North's interpretation of obedience is portrayed in Focus 5-6. Clearly, for North, obedience was not a "thoughtful process." We can draw some comfort from the findings that people who stick to their guns and consistently resist social pressures can have a strong impact on the attitudes and behaviors of others around them.

SUMMARY

We are constantly trying to influence other people, while also dealing with their attempts to influence us. Much social influence involves the use of social power. Though we are most familar with reward and coercive power, referent power (derived from respect and liking) is likely to have the most effect. Referent power does not require surveillance, access to rewards or punishments, or special status. Several psychological factors underlie social influence: feelings of reciprocation, desire to remain consistent, liking, reactions to apparent scarcity, using others as social standards, and obedience to authority. Studies of conformity have demonstrated how people are heavily influenced by norms and the behavior of others.

Our susceptibility to strong authority pressures has been vividly illustrated in Milgram's shock/obedience studies. Debate continues about the ethical issues involved and the extent to which we should generalize from such studies. Studies of brainwashing and religious conversions also illustrate the power of situational factors in determining our attitudes and behavior. If people believe that their freedom of action is being threatened by an influence attempt, they experience psychological reactance and are likely to do something to restore their perceived freedom of action. Recent research shows that social influence can also flow from a minority to the majority. Minority influence is most likely to occur when the minority is consistent and firm but not rigid and when there is enough time for the minority's position to be debated and understood by the majority.

CHAPTER 6

The Group and the Individual

I must follow the people. Am I not their leader?

Benjamin Disraeli

The competent leader of men cares little for the interior niceties of other people's characters: He cares much—everything—for the external uses to which they may be put.   Woodrow Wilson

Nine top executives of the Cureall Drug Company are meeting to decide whether or not to go forward with marketing a potentially popular but possibly dangerous male contraceptive drug. They believe they can get approval from the U.S. Food and Drug Administration (FDA), although the drug is entirely new and has never before been used on humans. Data from animal research are mixed; some studies have suggested a danger of harmful side effects for human use, and nothing is known about the possible negative effects of long-term usage. The marketing decision is crucial for Cureall. Potential for profits is huge, given the widespread use of contraception and dissatisfaction with other methods. But if the drug should prove to have negative side effects or cause long-term harm, the potential for human suffering, and financial disaster for the company through lawsuits would be immense. ❖

PREVIEW

Up to now we have focused on the behavior of individuals within the general social context. In this chapter we examine the behavior of people in groups and collectives. I will begin by discussing the nature of groups: what they are and why people join them. We will then look at how groups affect individuals' behavior. We will evaluate the reasons why individuals sometimes perform better, and sometimes perform more poorly, when in the presence of other people.

Groups such as committees, juries, legislatures, and military chiefs of staff, are often called upon to make vitally important decisions. We will analyze the psychological factors that affect these decisions and techniques for avoiding poor decisions. Interactions between groups will be analyzed from the perspectives of bargaining, negotiation, cooperation, and conflict. Our analysis will cover groups of many sizes, from small laboratory groups to nations. Leadership will be examined from several standpoints, including the "great person" theory of leadership and recent contingency theories that focus on the interaction between the orientation of the leader and the amount of situational control he or she has.

THE NATURE OF GROUPS

What Is a Group?

group:
Two or more people who interact with and influence each other and are held together by common interests or goals.

A **group** can be described as two or more people who interact with and influence each other (Shaw, 1981). The group is held together by the common interests or goals of its members. The Cureall Drug Company executives are a group because they have common interests and are interacting with each other. **Group behavior** refers to group members' responses to the social structure of the group and to the norms it adopts. In contrast, **collective behavior** refers to actions of people who, simply because they are in the same place at the same time, behave in a similar manner: victims fleeing from a natural disaster, fans attending a rock concert, or commuters trying to make their way home through rush-hour traffic. We will analyze both group and collective behavior in this chapter. Social facilitation and deindividuation are most relevant to collective behavior; group decision making, groupthink, and leadership styles are most relevant to group behavior.

group behavior:
Group members' responses to the social structure of the group and to the norms it adopts.

collective behavior:
Actions of people who, simply because they are in the same place at the same time, behave in a similar manner.

Why Do People Join Groups?

Why should one join a group? There are two general reasons (Schachter, 1959). First, a person may join a group in order to *reach goals* not achievable by working alone, such as community improvement projects, preserving national defense, or maintaining various government services. Second, groups may represent ways of *satisfying human needs* and obtaining social rewards, such as approval, belonging, prestige, praise, love, or friendship.

The size of a group can affect the type of interactions that occur and the decisions that a group makes. For example, Osborn (1963), who popularized the concept of brainstorming to solve problems, suggested that the optimal size of brainstorming groups was from five to ten members. Juries in the United States typically contain twelve members, although in recent years the size of some juries has been reduced to six. As noted in Chapter 5, the larger the group the greater the likelihood that a lone dissenting member will conform to group norms. A Cureall executive would be less likely to dissent openly from the prevailing group view of eight other executives than if the group contained only three or four people.

group cohesiveness:
The degree to which group members like each other, have similar goals, and want to remain in one another's presence.

Another important factor is **group cohesiveness**, the degree to which group members like each other, have similar goals, and want to remain in one another's presence. Cohesiveness usually leads to higher productivity, as members who like one another and want to remain together are likely to work harder toward a group goal. Cohesiveness does not always have positive results, however, because members are especially likely to feel pressure to conform to the group norms. If the Cureall executives formed a cohesive group, as they probably would, it would be very difficult for a dissenter to hold out against the views of her colleagues and friends. As we will see, in some situations cohesiveness can have a negative impact as people conform to support a poor decision.

THE INFLUENCE OF OTHERS ON INDIVIDUALS' BEHAVIORS

The Influence of Others on Performance

We often perform important tasks in the presence of other people. Sometimes they are working with us cooperatively or against us competitively; at other times they may be behaving independently of us (co-actors) or simply watching (an audience). One of the earliest questions asked by social psychologists was: What is the effect of the presence of others on individuals' behavior? As you will see, the answer is not a simple one. Sometimes people do better when others are around, while at other times they do worse. The presence of others can affect performance in three general ways: by influencing the amount of *effort* put forth, by increasing *arousal,* and by influencing *cognitive factors* such as distraction and apprehension about being evaluated. We'll take a look at each of these factors below.

The Presence of Others Affects Effort

co-actors:
Fellow participants in an activity who are nearby.

One of the first social psychologists, Norman Triplett (1898), was interested in bicycle racing. He noticed that bicycle racers usually went faster when they were racing an opponent or being paced by a teammate than when they were racing alone against the clock. To experimentally test the effect of the presence of others on performance, Triplett gave children the task of winding fishing line on a reel as fast as possible, either alone or with other children. As he suspected, the children worked faster with other children (**co-actors**) than when working alone. Subsequent research with other animal species has revealed that many animals will perform differently when other members of their species are nearby performing the same task. For example, rats and fish will eat more (Harlow, 1932; Welty, 1934), cockroaches and dogs will run faster (Vogel et al., 1950; Zajonc, 1965), and chickens will peck more rapidly (Rajecki et al., 1976). Getting back to humans, an observational study found that male and female solitary joggers in a park significantly increased their speed when running past a woman seated on a park bench (Worringham & Messick, 1983). The influence of an audience depends on its size, its proximity, and the status of its members (Latané, 1981). As the number of people in an audience increases, so does their influence. As with conformity, however, increases in influence tend to be smaller as the number of people increases. Audiences that are close by have more impact than those that are at some distance.

rivalry:
Increased motivation and effort due to competition.

social facilitation:
Stimulation merely from seeing or hearing the similar movements of other people.

social loafing:
When members of a group work less hard than they would individually.

Floyd Allport (1924) suggested that increased activity in the presence of co-acting others was due to two factors: **rivalry** and **social facilitation**. Rivalry refers to increased motivation and effort due to competition—certainly a central factor in a bicycle race—and social facilitation refers to stimulation merely from seeing or hearing the similar movements of other people—as might be the case when being paced by a teammate during training.

Although groups may accomplish more than individuals, sometimes members of a group may put forth less effort than they would individually. Latané and his colleagues (Latané et al., 1979) termed this effect **social loafing**. Social loafing is more likely if the task is unappealing (Zaccaro, 1984) and when one's individual efforts cannot be evaluated by others or by the individual (Harkins, 1987). This leads to diffusion of responsibility (no one will know if I don't work very hard) and increased temptation to be lazy, as there is no causal relationship between an individual's effort and the outcome. However, if the entire group's performance can be evaluated, social loafing may disappear (Harkins & Szymanski, 1989).

Social loafing may even occur on the national level. The economic problems that plagued communist governments in the U.S.S.R., China, and Eastern Europe in recent decades may have resulted partially from widespread social loafing by their citizens, because workers and farmers were not rewarded directly for their individual efforts under the communist system. Experiments with limited private ownership of property and a free market economy in these countries often led to greatly improved productivity (Latané et al., 1979), increasing pressures toward the abandonment of the communist system in the late 1980s and 1990s. These experiments don't mean that social loafing *inevitably* occurs in group-production systems since, for example, Israeli communal kibbitz farms actually outproduced Israel's non-collective farms (Latané et al., 1979). But, in general, social loafing is a likely outcome when people's individual efforts on well-learned tasks are pooled and cannot be separately evaluated.

Social facilitation in action. Research has shown that joggers run faster when they think someone is watching them than when they think they are unobserved.

The Presence of Others Increases Arousal

We have seen that many animals become more active in the presence of others. But it is important to distinguish between working hard and performing well. Research shows that individuals will work hard when others are present and the individual's contribution can be identified. But hard work doesn't guarantee a successful outcome. Robert Zajonc (1968) pointed out that the presence of others increases one's *drive* or *level of arousal,* which leads to a greater tendency to perform simple, well-learned, or dominant responses. If the dominant responses are appropriate for the situation, then performance will be improved. If, on the other hand, one is trying to perform a complex response that is not dominant or well-learned, performance will be poorer. Thus, Zajonc argued, the factors that determine whether social facilitation or inhibition will take place are the complexity of the task and how well-learned the response is. A meta-analysis of 241 studies (Bond & Titus, 1983) found partial support for Zajonc's theory.

Consider a college professor giving her first lecture of the year (a complex task) before a large social psychology class. If she is experienced and knows the material well, her lecture will be stimulated by the presence of a large audience and she probably will do an excellent job. If, on the other hand, this is the first class she has ever taught and the material is relatively unfamiliar, her lecture performance is likely to be inhibited by the presence of a large class. People become most aroused when they expect that the audience will be judging their performance, as students judge the quality of a lecture (Sasfy & Okun, 1974). Additionally, people who expect to perform before a high-status audience tend to be more nervous than those who expect to perform in front of a low-status audience (Latané & Harkins, 1976).

The social facilitation effect has been found even in a situation as mundane as a poolroom. Several researchers (Michaels et al., 1982) studied students playing pool at a university union. After establishing by observation which players were above average and which were below average, the researchers had teams of four observers stand next to the table where players were playing and observe the next several rounds of play. As Zajonc's theory would predict, the presence of the observers had different effects on the players' scores depending on their general level of ability. The above-average players became somewhat more accurate in their shots (80 percent versus 71 percent previously) and the below-average players became even worse when watched by others (their accuracy dropped from 36 percent to 25 percent.)

The Presence of Others Can Cause Distraction and Evaluation Apprehension

Imagine that you are one of the pool players described above. When you become aware that you have an audience, you might feel two conflicting tendencies: to pay attention to the task (the pool game) or to your audience. This conflict itself may increase arousal which, in turn, can enhance the ten-

A good lecture or a poor lecture? The presence of a large audience may improve the quality of the professor's lecture, via social facilitation, or it might result in a poorer lecture due to distraction or evaluation apprehension.

dency to perform the dominant response, as predicted by Zajonc. In support of this proposition, research has shown that many nonsocial forms of distraction, such as flashing lights or loud noises, can produce increased arousal and can affect task performance (Sanders & Baron, 1975). Also, people report that they experience greater distraction when they perform complex tasks in front of an audience than when alone (Baron et al., 1978). An individual can be affected by the presence of others even when the others are not visible and when they lack the potential to evaluate the person. Perhaps the presence of others creates uncertainty and arouses an individual's alertness for the unexpected (Zajonc, 1980b). An audience can evaluate your performance, which is not only distracting but can also cause *evaluation apprehension* (discussed in Chapters 1 and 3), self-presentational concerns about how your performance will be evaluated by the audience members. An audience may exert stronger effects on people's behavior when the people know that the audience is evaluating them than when they do not know. The knowledge that others are evaluating you can cause you to direct more attention to the audience, thus intensifying the conflict between paying attention to the audience and paying attention to the task at hand.

Tying It All Together

Recent theoretical propositions by Harkins and Szymanski (1988; Harkins, 1987; Szymanski & Harkins, 1987) provide a creative integration of the disparate findings on effort, arousal, and distraction. They theorized that task complexity interacts with evaluation apprehension in the ways depicted in Figure 6-1. When people feel that their individual performance can be evaluated, this is likely to improve performance on simple tasks (social facilitation) but impair performance on complex tasks (due to distraction or evaluation apprehension). In contrast, when individual contributions cannot be evaluated by others because everyone's contributions are pooled, performance is impaired on simple tasks (social loafing) but improved on complex tasks, as people can rise to the challenge without worrying that others will know if they fail at the complex task.

It is clear that even after nine decades of research and several hundred studies, we still need to delve further into the deceptively simple issue of the effect of the presence of others on human behavior. To summarize what we know this far, one's performance in a group is affected by the effort put forth (social loafing), arousal (related to task complexity and the presence of others), and cognitive activities such as distraction and worry about being evaluated (Paulus, 1983). The presence of other people sometimes improves an individual's performance on a task, due to social facilitation, rivalry, or challenge, while in other situations the presence of other people interferes with performance, because of social loafing, distraction, or evaluation apprehension. Initial research supports the integrated model depicted in Figure 6-1 (Bartis et al., 1988), but more studies will be needed to see if the disparate findings can be tied together this neatly.

Behavior in Groups

Group Performance vs. Individuals' Performance

Suppose that the probationary period for your new job is almost over; it's time for you to be evaluated for a permanent position. Would you want this crucial task to be done by an individual (your boss) or by a group (a personnel committee)? More generally, do groups make better or poorer decisions than do individuals? A general belief in the adage "two heads are better than one" can be seen in the acceptance of juries for legal decision making and the widespread use of committees. Having issues resolved by small groups, rather than by individuals, can have several advantages. It gives an aura of fairness because many opinions are considered. Information may be shared and combined in creative ways and group members may feel more committed to their final decision than if the decision had been made by a single individual (Stasser & Titus, 1987).

Early research (Shaw, 1932) seemed to show that group problem solving was superior to individuals' abilities to solve problems. Such findings

FIGURE 6-1

The Key Role of Evaluation Apprehension in Social Facilitation and Social Loafing

When people feel that their individual performance can be evaluated this is likely to improve their performance on simple tasks and impair performance on complex tasks (left side of Figure 6-1). When individual contributions cannot be identified, in contrast, the presence of others is likely to impair performance on simple tasks and improve it on complex tasks. (Based on Harkins, 1987; Harkins & Szymanski, 1988)

	When the Presence of Others:	
	Increases likelihood that individual performance can be evaluated	Decreases likelihood that individual performance can be evaluated (pooled contributions)
Simple or Well Learned Task	Performance enhanced (social facilitation, rivalry)	Performance impaired (social loafing)
Complex or Poorly Learned Task	Performance impaired (distraction, evaluation apprehension)	Performance enhanced (challenge)

led to the popularity of "group brainstorming" (Osborn, 1963). But subsequent research has indicated that comparing group and individual decision making is a complex issue. One finding is clear: Group performance generally is superior to the average individual's performance (Hill, 1982; Shaw, 1981). In addition, interactions within a group may produce new ideas or solutions. The group has the advantage of a wider range of knowledge and the greater probability that someone in the group will have the specific knowledge relevant to the question at hand.

On the other hand, groups do not always produce better decisions. In a group not everyone can contribute at once; individuals must wait their turn. This may cause *production blocking*, disrupting their thinking or diminishing their motivation to participate (Diehl & Stroebe, 1987). Another potential problem is that although individuals may bring "unshared" information to the group (information that is not known to other group members), not all of the unshared information may be brought to the attention of the other group members. Group discussion could serve an educational function when unshared information exists, because each group member could inform others of new information of which they were previously unaware. But research suggests that unshared information doesn't get used very frequently unless little other information is available. Otherwise, members tend simply to reiterate already-shared information, providing only a limited, biased sample of all the information that could have been available (Stasser & Titus, 1987).

Though a group's performance is usually better than the average individual's performance, it is often inferior to the performance of the best individual, especially when the group contains many low-ability members and is faced with a complex problem (Hill, 1982). The performance of one exceptional individual may be superior to that of a committee. But sometimes a group will be led astray by a strong persuasive individual whose ideas are not accurate.

Social impact:
A faction's ability to exert influence on a group depends on the faction's size.

The **social impact** of a faction, its ability to exert influence on a group, depends on its size (Latané & Nida, 1981). Both majorities and minorities in a decision-making group may exert influence, but majorities are potentially more effective because of their superior numbers. Several potentially problematic social processes can take place in groups. I have already mentioned social loafing; below we will analyze other processes—group polarization, the tendency to diffuse responsibility across the group members, and groupthink.

Factors Affecting Group Decision Making

Composition of the Group
Many critical decisions are made in meetings of groups such as legislatures, boards of directors, committees, or cabinet ministers. We can identify four principal factors that may affect the quality of a group's decision. First is the *acceptance of common goals*. When members of a group accept a common goal, then coordination and exchange of information among group members will be easier and more complete. Second is the *divisibility of the group's task*. Some tasks can be readily subdivided and others cannot. The best use of group members can be made when the task can be divided up. A third factor is *communication and status structure*. Research shows that when there is status discrepancy in a problem-solving group, the higher-status people will speak more and have more influence, whereas the lower-status people tend to defer to those with higher status (Hurwitz et al., 1953). Of course, differences in status are not always counterproductive; in some cases, an effective leader making quick decisions is necessary. A final factor is *group size*. Although a larger group is likely to contain a greater range of opinions and information, there is less participation by each person and therefore less efficiency. Those who tend to dominate or who have a clear stake in the outcome often are able to take over a large meeting, whereas they might be less able to do so in a smaller gathering.

Similarity of Group Members to Each Other
Group decision making is apt to be faster and easier when group members are similar to each other, but the absence of competing viewpoints means

that alternative decisions are less likely to be considered. Historically, many groups that made important decisions affecting the lives of women or minority groups have been criticized because the group was homogeneous (all white males, for example). They were able to reach a decision easily because all shared the same social background and gender socialization, but the decisions reached often were not the best ones for the people affected. Hence, heterogeneous groups are sometimes more effective than homogeneous ones (Hoffman, 1965) because there is greater diversity of information and individual members are more likely to question the assumptions and opinions of one another. But if the differences between group members are so great that hostilities and stereotyped attitudes take over, then effective group functioning may become impossible.

Group Polarization Effects

group polarization effect: Decisions made within a group are likely to be more extreme than decisions made by individuals working separately.

Decision making is the major task faced by many groups. An important question is: Are the decisions made by groups likely to be different from those made by comparable individuals? Some writers have assumed that group decisions are likely to be more conservative. Whyte (1956) argued that a decision resulting from the team approach in business enterprises would result in a conservative course of action. Yet recent research indicates that this is not usually the case. In fact, group decisions are often likely to be more extreme than decisions made by comparable individuals who are working separately—an effect labeled the **group polarization effect**. Laboratory studies involving simulated juries of college students have found that individuals become more extreme in their views about a defendant's guilt or innocence after a group decision (Myers & Kaplan, 1976). There is indirect evidence that judges may show the same tendencies. A study comparing the decisions made by individual judges with those made by panels of three judges in civil liberties cases found that the panel decisions tended to be more extreme (in a pro-civil liberties direction) than were the individual judges' decisions (Walker & Main, 1973).

Why should the group polarization effect occur? One possibility is that social comparison (Chapter 3) leads to polarization. By definition, only half of us can be above average, but we have seen that most of us like to think we are. To the extent that we can compare ourselves with others and conclude that we are better than average, our self-image is enhanced. Perhaps most people believe that they are above average in attitudes, in terms of holding attitudes that are more extreme in the more appropriate, highly valued direction. During group discussion a person may find that her attitudes are less extreme and more average (or moderate) than she had believed. In order to maintain her positive self-image of holding above-average views, she might shift her attitudes to a more extreme position in the valued direction (Brown, 1974; Clark, 1971). One piece of evidence supporting this position is that shifts toward extremity can occur when people are provided with information on the relative position of their own views even when there is no group discussion (Myers, 1978).

A second factor may be the persuasiveness of the arguments used in group discussions. The group will shift toward the point of view that is supported by the largest number of convincing arguments during discussion. The greater the proportion of arguments favoring a point of view, the greater the shift in the direction of that point of view (Burnstein & Vinokur, 1977). A meta-analysis of twenty-one studies (Isenberg, 1986) found that both of these factors contribute to group polarization, with arguments usually having the stronger effect.

social categorization: When people perceive themselves as members of a group, they distinguish themselves from people outside of the group and adopt the characteristics seen as typical of their group.

Social categorization may also contribute to the group polarization effect. When people perceive themselves as members of a group, they distinguish themselves from people outside of the group and adopt the characteristics seen as typical of their own group (Turner, 1987; Turner & Oakes, 1989). During group discussion the perceived group norms that emerge may be stereotypically extreme. Group members may adopt this "extremized" norm as a way of reinforcing their social identity and their social concept via self-categorization, thereby resulting in attitude polarization (Mackie, 1986; Turner & Oakes, 1989).

Groupthink

Facing Stressful Decisions

A group faced with an important decision is in a difficult position. Information is often scarce or contradictory, time may be short, and the consequences are high. Political or military decisions with national or international repercussions often are made by groups. The executives of the Cureall Drug Company face a decision that could affect thousands of people. How do group members cope with stressful situations?

defensive avoidance: A coping strategy by which people try to avoid information that might stimulate anxiety or reveal the shortcomings of their chosen course of action.

groupthink: The process through which groups faced with an important stressful decision may be more concerned with reaching unanimous agreement than with evaluating the facts of the situation.

concurrence seeking: Trying to get everyone in a group to agree to a decision.

One way is by **defensive avoidance**, trying to avoid information that might stimulate anxiety or reveal the shortcomings of the chosen course of action (Janis & Mann, 1977). Defensive avoidance can lead to **groupthink** (Janis, 1982). Groupthink is most likely to occur when: (1) the decision makers are a cohesive group; (2) there are structural faults in the organization (such as insulation from outside information or a "promotional" leadership style in which the leader actively promotes his or her own ideas); and (3) there is a "provocative situation" involving high stress from external sources and low self-esteem among group members. In such situations, **concurrence seeking** — trying to get everyone to agree to a decision, any decision — may be a stronger motivating factor than is the search for the decision that best fits the facts.

Symptoms of Groupthink

Janis (1982) described eight primary "symptoms" of groupthink (Figure 6-2). These constitute three types: *overestimating one's own group, closed-mindedness,* and *pressures toward uniformity.* Groupthink represents a way to maintain the self-esteem of group members by striving for consensus and unanimity in order to feel more secure in their decision. Unfortunately, this striving rules

FIGURE 6-2

Symptoms of Groupthink (from Janis, 1982)

<u>Overestimating one's own group</u>

> The illusion that the group is invulnerable
>
> Belief that the group is inherently moral

<u>Closed-mindedness</u>

> Collective rationalizations
>
> Stereotyped views of outgroups and their leaders

<u>Pressures toward uniformity</u>

> Self-censorship of group member's own doubts and misgivings
>
> Direct pressure on dissenters to conform
>
> Self-appointed "mindguards" who try to "protect" the group from adverse information
>
> The illusion that group members agree unanimously

Source: Based upon Janis, I. (1982). *Groupthink* (2nd ed.). Boston: Houghton Mifflin.

out such critical factors as independent thinking, checking of information, attention to moral concerns, and self-doubts about the wisdom of the group's decision. The processes of groupthink and group polarization may interact. Once a group has decided on a more extreme decision than they would have advocated as individuals, groupthink may operate as a way of justifying the extreme decision.

Might the marketing decision made by the Cureall executives result from groupthink? Their decision is an important one, and the group is cohesive (the executives have common goals and probably like and respect each other). There are possible structural flaws present as well. The group might be isolated from outside information (such as research findings that the new drug is not as safe as they would like to think) and may have a strong leader (perhaps the company president or marketing director). Under these conditions, we could expect the executives to rationalize any worries about negative outcomes, such as side effects or lawsuits, through the illusion of the company's invulnerability and inherent morality ("We never have marketed an unsuccessful or harmful product, and we never will!"). Executives who have some doubts about marketing the contraceptive without further research and testing may censor themselves, not wanting to appear uncooperative or overcautious, or they might subtly be discouraged from protesting by other executives (acting as mindguards).

Many major decisions of recent history seem, in retrospect, to bear the imprint of groupthink (but we should beware of the hindsight bias in our tendency to think that the participants should have known that their deci-

*Pressure toward unanimity:
self-censorship*

Source: Drawing by H. Martin: © 1979 The New Yorker Magazine, Inc.

sions would turn out disastrously). Janis (1982) argued that American unpreparedness for the Japanese sneak attack at Pearl Harbor, Hawaii, in 1941, the decision to invade North Korea during the Korean War in 1950, the disastrous decision by the U.S. government to sponsor an invasion of Cuba at the Bay of Pigs in 1961, the escalation of the Vietnam War during the 1960s, and the Watergate cover-up in the 1970s, all resulted in part from groupthink. Janis contrasted these five "groupthink decisions" with two other policy decisions that did not show the imprint of groupthink — the Marshall Plan that aided European countries after World War II and the Cuban missile crisis in 1962, when the U.S. naval blockade forced the Soviets to withdraw offensive missiles from Cuba.

A more recent analysis of these important decisions (McCauley, 1989) suggested that four structural conditions are particularly important in distinguishing groupthink decisions from nongroupthink decisions: promotional leadership, group insulation, pressure to comply to the group norms, and group homogeneity. As Figure 6-3 indicates, the other factors proposed by Janis (1982) did not distinguish as well between good and bad decisions (nongroupthink/groupthink) as clearly as Janis's theory asserts. While it's true that groupthink decisions were made by cohesive groups facing external threat, as Janis theorized, so were the nongroupthink decisions. McCauley's analysis is summarized in Figure 6-3. Focus 6-1 describes another tragic case where groupthink may have been involved—the explosion of the space shuttle *Challenger* in 1986. How would you evaluate that situation in terms of the conditions listed in Figure 6-3?

It is difficult to carry out research on decision-making processes in important groups because researchers are not present at the meetings. Neverthe-

FIGURE 6-3

The Lessons of History:
Groupthink and Nongroupthink Decisions

McCauley's (1989) analysis of seven important historical decisions, based on historical accounts provided by Janis (1982) and others.

Condition: Was It Present?	Pearl Harbor Unpreparedness	Groupthink (Poor) Decisions				Nongroupthink (Good) Decisions	
		North Korea Invasion	Invasion of Cuba at Bay of Pigs	Escalation in Vietnam	Watergate Cover-up	Marshall Plan	Cuban Missle Crisis
Promotional leadership	No	Yes	Yes	Yes	Yes	No	No
Group is insulated	No	Yes	Yes	No	Yes	No	No
Homogeneous group	Yes	Yes	No	No	Yes	No	No
Compliance pressure	No	No	Yes	Yes	No	No	No
Cohesive group	Yes	Yes	Yes	Yes	Yes	Yes	Yes
External threat	Yes	Yes	Yes	Yes	Yes	Yes	Yes
Crisis (time pressure)	No	No	No	Yes	Yes	Yes	Yes
Perceived difficult decision	No	No	Yes	Yes	Yes	Yes	Yes
Recent group failure	No	No	No	Yes	Yes	Yes	No

Source: From McCauley, C. (1989). The nature of social influence on groupthink: Compliance and internalization. *Journal of Personality and Social Psychology, 57,* 250–260. Copyright © 1989 by the American Psychological Association. Reprinted by permission.

FOCUS 6-1

The *Challenger* Disaster and Groupthink

Could the tragic explosion that destroyed the U.S. space shuttle *Challenger* in 1986 be related to the decision-making process that preceded the fateful takeoff? In hindsight, it appears that the seven astronauts who perished were victims of poor decision making that could have been avoided. Tragic mistakes in judgment were made, but they were not the product of individual stupidity. Rather, it appears that officials at the National Aeronautics and Space Administration (NASA) and scientific experts surrendered to strong psychological pressure to launch the shuttle that cold morning. The forces confronting NASA included a perceived need to secure greater congressional funding, the desire to initiate the popular "Teacher in Space" program, and the desire to demonstrate NASA technology to the world. It was those pressures that permitted groupthink symptoms to become involved and placed NASA officials in a potent "psychological pressure cooker" (Kruglanski, 1986).

NASA and top management at Thiokol, the company that designed the space shuttle, rationalized their decision to launch the *Challenger* and disregarded potential problems that might have caused the mission to be delayed. Objections from engineers and other experts were ignored and kept from top decision makers. Some engineers realized that the O-ring seals would not function properly due to the presence of ice on the launch pad from extreme weather conditions the night before; the seals could do extensive damage to the orbiter. Arnold Thompson, one engineer, recalled pleading with the officials: "They wouldn't listen. I couldn't make them listen." When lift-off finally came, Thompson was in his office with other engineers, trying "to ignore the dread, but unable to avoid the awful news." The officials at NASA and Thiokol ignored several warnings from their own experts; had they known about the concept of groupthink, they might not have done so.

Everyone involved in the mission wanted desperately to launch the *Challenger* and, while unknowingly experiencing many of the symptoms of groupthink, they convinced themselves that it was perfectly safe to do so. Tremendous psychological pressures caused a severe distortion in the decision-making process. Because there was no definitive evidence to prove to the management that disaster was likely to occur, NASA officials appeared to take comfort in a sense of inherent morality and accepted the illusion that they were invulnerable to disaster (McConnell, 1987). When asked why no one had done something to correct the O-ring problem, Lawrence Mulley, chief of the booster rocket project, replied: "We at NASA got into a groupthink about this problem. We saw it, we recognized it, and concluded it was an acceptable risk." Richard Feynman (1988, p. 236), the Nobel Prize–winning physicist we met in Focus 2-1, commented on the "almost incredible lack of communication between the managers and their working engineers."

Several groupthink symptoms were visible in the way that officials at Thiokol and NASA reacted to the pressures. Most obvious, in hindsight, were the illusions of invulnerability and unanimity, a belief in the group's morality, suppression of dissent within the group, and collective efforts to rationalize perceptions of danger. When disaster happens, everyone looks for someone else to blame. In the case of the space shuttle *Challenger*, however, there was not a single "person" on whom blame could be laid. Instead, the insidious groupthink process led to an extremely poor group decision. The overruled recommendations, the breakdown in management communication, and the pressures from outside sources affected NASA in a way in which neither they nor the American public will forget. ❖

less, some evidence has been obtained from records, recollections, and public statements of decision makers involved in five crucial international decisions. Tetlock (1979) analyzed the same two nongroupthink decisions (the Marshall Plan and the Cuban missile crisis) and three groupthink decisions: the Bay of Pigs invasion, the decision to invade North Korea, and decisions to escalate the Vietnam War in 1964 and 1965. Consistent with the theory, leaders in the groupthink decisions were more simplistic in their perception of policy issues and made more positive references to the United States and its allies (their own group) than did the decision makers in the nongroupthink decisions.

Preventing Groupthink

A group can take two general steps to reduce the probability that groupthink will occur: *discouraging leader bias* and *preventing group isolation*. The leader should be impartial rather than stating his or her preferences and expectations at the outset—this will lessen the tendency of group members to conform to what they think the leader wants. The leader also should encourage each group member to be a critical evaluator and should give high priority to objections and doubts. At every meeting, at least one member should be assigned the role of "devil's advocate", questioning and probing the direction in which the group is moving. Someone might be asked to prepare a worst-case scenario, describing in detail what conceivably could happen if everything went wrong. For example, what will happen to Cureall Drugs and its contraceptive customers if the most negative possible interpretation of present research turns out to be true? Unless time pressures prevent it, after an initial consensus about the decision, the group should hold a second-chance meeting at which each member is expected to express any residual doubts and rethink the entire issue.

To prevent group isolation, the policy-planning group could, from time to time, divide into subgroups and meet separately under different leaders, then come together to hammer out their differences. Each group member should periodically discuss the group's deliberations with trusted associates in his own unit of the organization and report back their reactions. Input from independent outside experts should be sought. For example, Cureall could bring in research scientists not associated with the company to present their research findings and scientific opinions. If these steps are taken, the resulting decision is more likely to accurately reflect the facts of the situation instead of group members' needs to reach agreement and rationalize their decision.

Limitations of the Groupthink Concept

In some situations pressure toward concurrence may be a positive factor, as when decisions are simple or routine. Hence groupthink might be better defined as *inappropriate* concurrence seeking that occurs too soon when groups are faced with important dilemmas. Longley and Pruitt (1980) suggested that only four of the processes listed in Figure 6-2 are really manifestations of concurrence-seeking tendencies: pressures on dissenters, self-censorship, mindguarding, and collective rationalization. The illusions of invulnerability and unanimity, in contrast, are present before concurrence seeking begins; and the remaining two processes—belief in the inherent morality of the group and stereotypes of outgroups—are general characteristics of the way that ingroups view outgroups (Chapter 11), rather than factors specifically related to concurrence seeking. The groupthink notion has much intuitive appeal, but more work is needed to clarify the concept and the limits of its applicability.

BARGAINING, COOPERATION, AND CONFLICT

Any time two individuals, or two groups, must come to a joint decision, the potential for conflict exists. We can identify four overlapping sources of conflict. Conflict can be produced by the *context of the current interaction,* as when two sides are in competition for scarce resources or one side seeks to exploit the other. In general, groups are more likely to adopt a competitive orientation and end up in conflict than are individuals (McCallum et al., 1985). The more resources a side has (e.g., a union with a large strike fund; an athlete who can choose between several teams), the more it is likely to engage in conflict (Martin, 1986). Conflict can also be a product of the *history of prior interactions,* as when one group has made poor decisions, perhaps due to groupthink or the group polarization effect. Or one side might become entrapped in a failing course of action, a possibility I will discuss a little later. A third contributing factor is the *personality and needs* of the individuals involved, such as fear or the need for dominance or power. Finally, *perceptions and misperceptions of the other side* can be important. Prejudice, stereotypes, and group misperceptions can set conflict in motion and can derail attempts at reconciliation. I will discuss misperceptions between nations later in this chapter, while individual prejudice and stereotypes will be covered in detail in Chapter 11. When conflict arises or is anticipated, people may turn to bargaining or negotiation. The strategies and likely outcomes of bargaining and negotiation are analyzed below.

Bargaining and Negotiation

Bargaining and negotiation are pervasive in modern life. At the individual level, divorcing spouses must negotiate a settlement, professional athletes' agents negotiate contracts with team management, individuals negotiate the sale of a house, and so forth. At a group level, negotiation ranges from union-management collective bargaining to treaty negotiations between nations.

Individuals or their representatives engage in offers, counteroffers, challenges, and concessions. If the process is successful, an agreement acceptable to both sides is achieved. If the parties cannot or will not cooperate, then negotiations may never get off the ground or may be broken off, or one party may capitulate to the other, or conflict may escalate (Pruitt & Rubin, 1986). A host of social psychological factors are important in bargaining—compliance techniques, social influence processes, attitude-change strategies, and attraction to, or dislike of, one's opponent. Stereotypes and preconceived attitudes such as racism or sexism may also have a strong influence. A variety of possible strategies are summarized in Table 6-1 in the section on leadership. I will first analyze interactions between individuals and small groups and then turn to group interactions at a much larger level—the relations between nations.

Bargaining Strategies

Suppose you are representing a union in union-management contract negotiations. Should you begin by making a moderate offer, thereby increasing your attractiveness in the eyes of your opponent? Or should you begin with an extreme, unreasonable offer, expecting that you will then compromise toward a more reasonable position? Several studies suggest that the second process will be more effective. Persons using extreme initial offers generally do better in terms of final outcome than persons with more moderate initial offers (Benton, 1971; Yukl, 1974). This approach is a variation of the door-in-the-face process discussed in Chapter 5. Making an extreme initial offer and later a more reasonable one seems to have two effects: (1) The extremity of the initial offer may cause one's opponents to reevaluate their stance and to lower their expectations of the final outcome; (2) when one backs off from an extreme offer in further negotiations and moves to a more

When bargaining and negotiation break down. When negotiation fails to resolve a union-management conflict a strike may result.

reasonable one, it may be seen as a concession and may stimulate similar concessions from the opponents. Effective bargainers, therefore, are those who start with offers that are extreme enough to shake up their opponents' preconceptions but are not so extreme that the opponents break off the negotiations or become angry and defensive.

Bargainers often seem unwilling to grant seemingly reasonable concessions. There may be several reasons for this. First, there is no guarantee that their opponents will reciprocate, and people are unwilling to give up something without the guarantee of getting something in return. Second, in making concessions one may come to be perceived as weak or ineffective by one's followers. For political leaders and labor leaders this perception can be damaging to their future effectiveness, and public embarrassment would be costly. Research suggests that people who grant only a few small concessions do better than those who offer more concessions (Komorita & Brenner, 1968). Third, the presence of alternative courses of action is desirable; those who have a reasonable alternative deal at their disposal (more resources) have an important edge in bargaining over those who do not (Komorita & Kravitz, 1979). If you are bargaining to buy a used car and the dealer realizes that there are equally attractive cars at a competitor's lot, you are likely to get a better deal than if his is the only lot in town.

If individuals believe the other side respects them and sees them as competent, they are likely to be more open to negotiations. Conversely, if individuals believe their competence is being questioned, they are likely to get defensive and stubborn (Pruitt, 1981). Starting out with a tough bargaining position and then gradually softening one's stance may convey to the other side that their opponent is a competent bargainer, which can lead to conciliatory behavior. Persons behave more cooperatively when they play against an adversary who moves from competition to cooperation, based on the other person's responses, than an adversary who is either consistently cooperative or consistently competitive (McNeel, 1973; Oskamp, 1974).

It is also important to pay attention to the other person's overall cooperativeness or competitiveness. Many of the procedures that lead fundamentally cooperative persons to behave even more cooperatively have exactly the opposite effect on competitive people; they become even more competitive and resistant than before. For example, the effect of an audience (such as TV cameras or reporters present at a labor-management negotiation) may increase self-awareness, making cooperatively disposed negotiators even more cooperative but causing the negotiator who is concerned with appearing tough to behave in an even tougher and less cooperative manner (Forsyth, 1990).

Cooperation or Competition?

The "Prisoner's Dilemma." Imagine that two men are apprehended as suspects in a burglary case. Although there is some evidence to connect each to the crime, it is not strong enough to guarantee his conviction. Each of

prisoner's dilemma:
A research game where if both partners cooperate, they both win; if one attempts to cooperate while the other competes, the competitive partner wins and the cooperative partner loses; if both partners attempt to compete, they both lose.

the suspects is isolated in a room and is told, "Look, we know we may not have the evidence to convict you, but we're questioning your partner too. We'll make it worth his while to squeal on you. If he does, you'll get five years for burglary and he'll get off scot-free. But you can make it easier on yourself by talking first. If you talk and he does not, we'll let you go free for turning state's evidence. If you both confess, we'll make sure the judge gives each of you a reduced sentence of only two years. If neither you nor your partner confesses, we'll still get you both on a vagrancy charge, which will keep you in jail for six months." As the top part of Figure 6-4 illustrates, both prisoners are put in a difficult situation, particularly because they cannot communicate with one another.

This dilemma embodies the strain between cooperation and competition that underlies many conflict situations. Considering both partners, the best overall outcome is for neither of them to talk, for then they both receive just a six-month sentence for vagrancy. If one talks and the other does not, the squealer goes free and the victim gets a five-year sentence. If they both squeal, each gets a two-year sentence. The problem is that you cannot tell what your partner is going to do. If you respond cooperatively (with your partner) by remaining silent, but he does not, you become the victim and he goes free. If the two prisoners are interested only in saving their own skins and getting the best possible deals for themselves, they probably will both choose to squeal and thus end up with two years each in jail when each could have gotten away with six months. The prosecutor's job has been made easier. The prisoner's dilemma game also has been used as a research tool with varying degrees of money substituting for jail terms (bottom part of Figure 6-4).

social dilemma:
A situation in which there is a higher individual payoff for the selfish response but lower overall payoffs if both sides consistently make the selfish response.

Social Dilemmas. The prisoners' dilemma situation contains a mixture of cooperative and competitive motives. In more general terms, it is a type of **social dilemma** (Samuelson & Messick, 1986), involving a higher possible individual payoff for the selfish response but lower overall payoffs if both sides consistently make the selfish responses. The conservation of scarce natural resources is an important social dilemma that will be analyzed in Chapter 12. When college students play a social dilemma game, often an initial trusting interaction dissolves into mistrust as soon as one person decides to exploit the other. Whether or not this happens depends on the instructions players are given. When told they are in a competitive game where their goal is to try to get a higher score than their partner, participants almost invariably take the noncooperative course (Red in Figure 6-4) and both lose. On the other hand, when the situation is presented as a cooperative game in which each player is supposed to help the other beat the bank and win as much total money as possible, players generally behave in a cooperative manner (choosing the Black response in Figure 6-4). Finally, when the game is presented as an individualistic endeavor in which each person is supposed to get the highest score without regard to the other's performance, there is greater variability in behavior (Bixenstine et al., 1981). When players

FIGURE 6-4

The Prisoner's Dilemma

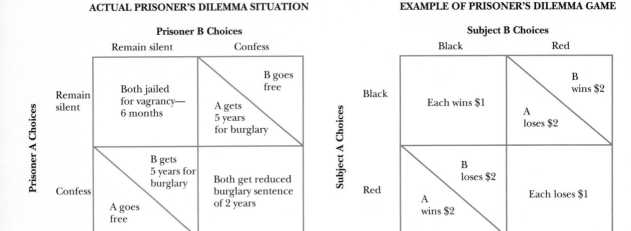

ACTUAL PRISONER'S DILEMMA SITUATION

EXAMPLE OF PRISONER'S DILEMMA GAME

are allowed to communicate with one another, cooperation is more likely and the overall outcome is more positive (Deutsch, 1960).

In general, a "tit-for-tat strategy" is most effective in such situations (Axelrod & Dion, 1988), where I always respond to you with the same move you just made to me. If you make the cooperative response, so do I; if you respond competitively, I do too. In this way, you are likely to see me as nice (I will not be the first to defect from a coopertive course of action) but provokable (your competitive move is met by a competitive move), forgiving (I'll cooperate again when you do), and easy to understand.

Personality Differences

You have undoubtedly noticed that individuals differ from one another in the extent to which they cooperate or compete. Some seem ready to compete on any issue at the drop of a hat, others go out of their way to be cooperative (Kramer et al., 1986). Researchers have suggested the existence of three general orientations (Blascovich et al., 1978). *Competitors* are those who seek to maximize their own gains in comparison to others. They are more concerned with beating others than obtaining positive outcomes for themselves and so may settle for negative results, as long as they surpass those of the competition. *Cooperators* want to equalize their own gains and the gains of others and tend to be most satisfied when the outcome is positive and equal for everyone. Finally, *individualists* are concerned primarily with maximizing their own gains, regardless of how other people do; they are concerned with their own outcomes and pay little attention to the outcomes of the others. In the prisoner's dilemma game, competitors usually try to exploit their opponent whereas cooperators usually seek to cooperate with this person. Individualists, as we would expect, adopt whatever strategy will give them the most positive outcomes.

People high in *need for power* are especially likely to perceive conflict in a situation (Fodor, 1985). This may set a self-fulfilling prophecy in motion, as they may become competitive or aggressive and stimulate competitiveness from others, although they perceive their behavior as merely self-defense (Winter, 1987a).

Becoming Trapped in an Interaction

social traps:
Situations in which short-run, self-serving behaviors create long-run losses.

Have you ever found yourself committed to a course of action that seemed like a good idea when you started but is now increasingly unrewarding, yet you can't see a way out of it? If so, you are in a **social trap** (Platt, 1973). Entrapment occurs when an individual or group becomes overly committed to a course of action as a result of having invested time, energy, self-esteem, or pride in the action. During a conflict both sides may become entrapped as each invests more and more of its resources and as each becomes increasingly concerned about losing face in the eyes of the other. You can illustrate this process via the "dollar auction." Gather a bunch of friends and offer to auction off a dollar bill to the highest bidder; the only catch is that the second-highest bidder must pay his or her bid but receive nothing. Often the bidding is very spirited and the "winner" ends up paying well over a dollar, sometimes as much as twenty dollars, as he and the eventual second-place bidder compete to avoid the costly second-place finish (Teger, 1980). In general, pressures that drive each party to remain in a social trap are: (1) the reward associated with obtaining the goal, (2) the presumed closeness of the goal, and (3) the cost associated with giving up the investment.

Consider America's increasing involvement in the Vietnam War during the late 1960s. The same resources (time, money, human lives) may be viewed both as an investment and an expense. As more resources become involved, they can be viewed as investments that increase the chances of reaching the goal, but they can also be seen as expenses that can be compared with the cost involved in withdrawing from the situation. In addition, the more resources are spent, the closer people believe they are to the goal in question. The greater the conflict, the greater the pressure to act decisively — either by quitting before it's too late or committing oneself totally and seeing the conflict through to the end. As Vietnam demonstrated so tragically, the more one has invested in an entrapping situation, the more one is likely to continue to invest in it. The information-processing biases analyzed in Chapter 2 can play a crucial role, as participants interpret and remember information in a biased format that supports their side. Participants also tend to be overconfident that the other side's negotiations will collapse or that they will accept the negotiator's offer (Bazerman, 1986).

Social traps can occur at the individual level and at the group level (Messick & McClelland, 1983). The prisoner's dilemma game (like the dollar auction) can become a social trap if the two participants become locked into a competitive, we-both-lose pattern of responding. U.S. government and military officials demonstrated this tendency during America's escalating involvement in the Vietnam War. Research indicates that persons who, in advance, set a limit to the extent of their involvement are less likely to become entrapped, particularly if the limit has been set publicly (Brockner et al., 1979). Individuals are more likely to become entrapped when they strongly fear losing face, as union leaders and national leaders often do (Brockner et al., 1981), and when they are distracted from paying attention to the costs of their continued involvement (Rubin, 1981). Given the power of entrapment in escalating conflicts and the broad range of situations in which it seems to occur, further research on factors increasing and decreasing its likelihood would be valuable.

International Relations

Thus far, you have been reading mostly about interactions between individuals or small groups of people. Now it is time to focus our attention on interactions between much larger groups — between nations. Many social psychological concepts are relevant to the arena of international relationships.

International Perceptions: Common Delusions and Misconceptions

A number of delusions and misconceptions can lead to poor decision making and lack of cooperation between nations, as well as between individuals or small groups. Some of the misconceptions were previewed in our discussion of groupthink. Ralph White, a psychologist with a long career in international affairs (he worked for the Central Intelligence Agency, the Voice of America, and the U.S. Information Agency), described a number of problems. Focusing on the difficulties in international communication, White (1969) called attention to the frequent existence of a "mirror image" in the way people of different nations view one another (Bronfenbrenner, 1961). The people of nation A often see nation B in precisely the same way that the people of nation B see nation A. The people of both nations may assert that the other side is the aggressor whose government deludes its people and adopts policies verging on madness, and so forth. The mirror image is reflected in **value-guided patterns of attributions,** wherein actions by one's own country are attributed to altruistic motives while similar actions by other countries are attributed to self-serving motives (Sande et al., 1989). Such attributions may produce a self-fulfilling prophecy culminating in a "mirror image war," as discussed in Focus 6-2.

Analyses of the Vietnam War (White, 1969) and the continuing Arab-Israeli conflict (White, 1977) illustrate that such misperceptions occur in many

value-guided attributions:

Actions by one's own country are attributed to altruistic motives while similar actions by other countries are attributed to self-serving motives.

conflicts. Common misperceptions are: (1) seeing the other side as totally evil, the *diabolical enemy image*; (2) feeling that "God is on our side," the *moral self-image*; (3) trying to seem tough and "manly" at all costs, the *macho self-image*; (4) unwillingness or inability to understand how the other side may feel, *absence of empathy*; (5) the tendency to see people in another country as more friendly to one's own side than they actually are, the *"pro-us illusion,"*; and (6) *overconfidence by military leaders*, as was so painfully evident during the early part of U.S. involvement in Vietnam.

All of these tendencies reduce the likelihood that the two sides will be able to communicate effectively, and the resulting disruption of communication is likely to have negative results. First, the amount of overt communication between the parties decreases, making it far more difficult for one to discover what the other really thinks. Second, the limited communication that remains tends to be distorted. Hostility also may help to create a self-fulfilling prophecy, in which one side's distrust of the other leads it to behave in ways that cause the other side to respond in a manner that can be conveniently interpreted by the first side as justifying its distrust.

Third, escalating conflict may lead to considerable stereotypic distortion in the kinds of judgments that each side forms of the other. Research demonstrates that the information-processing biases covered in Chapter 2 are particularly likely to occur in perceptions of individuals or groups categorized as "the enemy" (Silverstein & Flamenbaum, 1989). Studies of prejudice (Chapter 11) have noted the tendency to categorize one's own group in favorable terms and outgroups in negative terms. As conflict between groups escalates, the tendency may become even stronger. In addition, the tendency to make value-related defensive attributions also may become stronger; desirable or charitable acts are attributed to kindness if practiced by our side, but to necessity or manipulativeness if practiced by the other side.

Reducing International Conflict

Improving International Communications. How can the leaders of nations communicate more effectively? White (1969) suggested three general social psychological principles which, if understood by national leaders, might reduce the likelihood of misconceptions and misperceptions: (1) **Mirror-image wars**. If leaders can understand the development of mirror-image wars, as described in Focus 6-2, they may be able to resist pressures to let their country become involved in one.

(2) **Two-sided communications**. In Chapter 4 we saw that two-sided communications are more effective than one-sided communications when the audience is well educated, highly involved, and intelligent, and initially disagrees with the speaker's position. International situations often fit this mold, so international communicators (propagandists, negotiators) ought to increase their use of two-sided communications. ("We realize that your side has some important and valid points too.") Communication is easier if the two sides can find some common ground. Back in 1969, White proposed

mirror-image wars: Wars in which both sides genuinely believe that the other side is the true aggressor.

two-sided communications: Messages that acknowledge that there are two sides to the issue; effective when the audience is well-educated, involved, intelligent, and initially disagrees.

FOCUS 6-2

Mirror-Image Wars

How frequent are mirror-image wars? White (1969) suggested that they are quite common. He categorized each of thirty-seven wars that occurred between 1913 and 1968 and concluded that a little over half (twenty-one of thirty-seven) could be classed as mirror-image wars. They would include the Vietnam War, World War I (but not World War II), the Israeli-Arab conflicts, and the Korean War. White (1969, p. 30) continued, "There is a supreme irony in this type of war. It seems utterly ridiculous that *both* sides should be fighting because of real fear, imagining the enemy to be a brutal, arrogant aggressor, when actually the enemy is nerving himself to fight a war that he too thinks is in self-defense."

Drawing partly from the research of ethologists (Chapter 8) on the territorial fighting of animals (Ardrey, 1966; Lorenz, 1966), White suggested that the majority of mirror-image wars have evolved from national *territorial self-images* — rigid, emotional claims to a piece of territory by both sides. The territory may be along a disputed border, as in the China-India and Germany-France disputes, or it may be a larger area such as Taiwan, Israel, Northern Ireland, Algeria, South Korea, or South Vietnam. Usually each side positively refuses to grant that there could be any validity to the other side's claim. In each side's reality-world that land just *is* its own and that's all there is to it.

In many cases these overlapping territorial self-images become entangled with each side's virile self-image. The Vietnam War provides a classic example, White (1969, p. 33) proposed. "Each side feels that it *must* expel the alien intruders. On both sides ideology is to a large extent rationalization; the chief underlying psychological factor is pride — the virile self-image — defined as having the courage to defend one's 'own' land when foreigners are perceived as attacking it. In a sense you could say that fear is a fundamental emotion in wars of this type, but it is important to recognize that the fear is mobilized by cognitive distortion." Some of White's suggestions for avoiding such cognitive distortions are discussed in the text. ❖

---

that the sociopolitical philosophies of the East and West were converging, and that a common ground of a "modal world philosophy," attractive to most people of the world, was visible. This philosophy included: a preference for private ownership and free enterprise; a belief in political democracy and free speech; and an emphasis on social welfare and helping the poor. The apparent collapse of communism in Eastern Europe in 1989 and 1990 makes White's speculations look pretty prophetic. International communications that stress this (or other sources of) common ground are likely to be more effective than those that don't.

"pro-us" illusion:
The general tendency to see people in another country as more friendly to one's own side than they actually are.

A third factor is the **"pro-us" illusion** mentioned above. There is a general tendency to see the people in another country as more friendly to one's own side than they actually are, White asserted. National wishful thinking is painfully evident, in retrospect, in the U.S. decision to sponsor the invasion of Cuba at the Bay of Pigs in 1961 and in the growing U.S. involvement in Vietnam in the 1960s. In both cases American policymakers expected the local populace (Cubans, South Vietnamese) to rise up and support the foreign troops on their soil; in both cases, the expectations were wrong. If policymakers could be made aware of this common illusion, such tragically unfounded expectations might become less likely.

GRIT plan:
A plan to free ourselves from "psychological vicious circles" of military arms development, wherein one party makes a unilateral conciliatory gesture which may lead to conciliatory gestures by the other side.

Conciliatory Actions: The GRIT Plan. Mutual hostility between the Soviet Union and the U.S. nurtured an arms race that had cost U.S. citizens an average $4,700 per household by 1987 (Union of Concerned Scientists, 1987). Are there ways to free our nations from these "psychological vicious circles" (White's term)? A process labeled **GRIT**, for *graduated and reciprocated initiatives in tension reduction*, shows promise. Developed by Osgood (1962), the plan calls for one party, such as a nation, to announce in advance its intention to make a cooperative conciliatory policy. This is followed by a series of conciliatory acts—for example, reduced production of arms or withdrawal of troops. The first gesture should be relatively small so that if it is exploited by the other side, the first side will suffer no serious harm. Conciliation is temporarily abandoned if the conciliatory acts are exploited, but the initiator persistently renews conciliatory acts after retaliating for any exploitation that occurred. The hope is that when the opponent is provided with an opportunity to reciprocate with a cooperative gesture, a step-by-step process evolves in which each side makes increasingly cooperative gestures. The first steps taken by each side might be viewed with suspicion by the other, but if several such tension-reducing steps take place, the seeds of trust might be planted and the process might escalate until large-scale acts of cooperation and disarmament occur.

Laboratory studies of conflict situations suggest that the GRIT procedures will be effective. Research by Lindskold and his associates has provided consistent support for GRIT as a strategy for inducing conciliation in such situations (Lindskold & Aronoff, 1980; Lindskold & Finch, 1981). Several studies of U.S./Soviet relationships in the 1950s and 1960s suggested that this principle held in real-life situations as well. One study of U.S./Soviet relationships between 1946 and 1963 found that each conciliatory move made by one side was followed shortly thereafter by a conciliatory move on the part of the other side (Gamson & Modigliani, 1971). Analysis of the policies of the John F. Kennedy administration after the Cuban missile crisis suggested that the U.S. government's efforts to reduce tensions led to some

International cooperation. Soviet Premier Mikhail Gorbachev and President George Bush sign a series of accords between the U.S. and the U.S.S.R. in 1990.

reciprocations of cooperative gestures between the United States and the Soviet Union, but Kennedy's assassination brought an end to the experiment (Etzioni, 1967). The detente policies of the Nixon and Ford administrations in the 1970s also seemed to contain elements of GRIT.

The world climate in 1990 seems the most promising in decades for meaningful steps toward world peace and better international understanding, thanks in part to the *glasnost* policy initiated by Soviet Premier Gorbachev in 1988. A number of remarkable changes have taken place in recent months, including the dismantling of the Berlin Wall, increased freedom in several countries in Eastern Europe, and the *perestroika* liberalization movement in the Soviet Union. Many of Premier Gorbachev's actions (such as unilateral withdrawals of Soviet troops from Eastern Europe) seemed to fit into the GRIT framework. Hopefully, we are entering a historical phase where many of the principles discussed in these pages will be applied.

The Threat of Nuclear War. Still, the spectre of nuclear war hangs over all of us. The Stockholm International Peace Research Institute calculated that by 1985 the Western powers and the Soviet bloc would be capable of destroying each other a hundred times over (Myrdal, 1976). The American Psychological Association in 1982 called for a "halt to the nuclear arms race" and "an immediate nuclear freeze" (Abeles, 1983). Important questions for which we do not yet have answers are: How do leaders evaluate nuclear risks? What psychological factors affect how leaders balance the perceived risk of nuclear war versus the risk of not achieving ends seen as vital to national interests (Blight, 1987)? Many of the concepts discussed earlier are relevant. Mutual ignorance, groupthink, derogatory national and ethnic stereotypes, and the tendency to dehumanize the enemy affect peacetime perceptions about arms control just as they influence wartime views (Klineberg, 1984). Use of techniques such as GRIT and an emphasis on superordinate goals (goals that affect everyone, such as the survival of humanity) might reduce tensions. Also relevant is the notion of self-fulfilling prophecy — treating a group as trustworthy may increase the likelihood its members will behave in a trustworthy manner. These steps might lead to more accurate interna-

The Berlin Wall falls in 1989. The dismantling of the Berlin Wall symbolized the remarkable thaw that occurred in 1989–90 between countries in Eastern and Western Europe.

tional perceptions, increased understanding, and decreased suspiciousness, defensiveness, and hostility, producing a lessening of international tensions, of mistrust, and of the terrible threat to ourselves and our world (Intriligator & Brito, 1988; Markey, 1985; Wagner, 1985).

A growing body of theory and research demonstrates that social psychologists possess skills and information (such as an understanding of attitude change, compliance tactics, intergroup perceptions, and negotiation and bargaining strategies) that may yield valuable insights into interactions between nations and their leaders (Smith, 1986; Tetlock, 1986). Focus 6-3 describes ten possible applications of social psychological knowledge toward the prevention of nuclear war.

LEADERSHIP

What Is a Leader?

Former U.S. President Harry Truman defined a leader as "someone who has the ability to get other people to do what they don't want to do and like it." I will define a **leader** as someone who: (1) can influence successfully the direction of a group by influencing its attitudes and behaviors, and (2) maintains the image of having the group's best interests in mind. Being a leader involves reciprocal transactions between the leader and followers. The leader directs, guides, and influences, and the followers give the leader status, self-esteem, and their willingness to respond to influence (Hollander, 1986). In most instances, the right to lead is voluntarily conferred upon the leader by the group members. Leadership is thus a *social role* involving legitimate influence, rather than a unique quality of an individual.

We can analyze leadership behavior more closely by looking at the functions a leader may serve for the group (Forsyth, 1990; Lord, 1977), among the most important of which are:

1. Helping to define and reach group goals. The leader may serve as a policymaker and formulate a plan.
2. Maintaining the group. A leader may be able to reduce tensions, arbitrate differences, and keep the group together.
3. Providing a symbol for identification. By identifying with the leader as a symbol, a group may be able to maintain its unity. Government leaders and union leaders often serve this function.
4. Representing the group to others. The leader may represent the group and its relationships and negotiations with other groups.

leader:
A person who can influence the direction of the group by influencing its attitudes and behaviors, and maintaining the image of having the group's best interests in mind.

Possible Social Psychological Contributions to the Prevention of Nuclear War

Ten ways in which social psychological knowledge can contribute to preventing the outbreak of nuclear war, according to Ralph White (1985).

Government and military policymakers can be made aware of the *dangers* of:

(1) *The mirror image*

White (1984) found much contemporary and historical evidence that the three chief war-promoting motives in the Soviet Union—exaggerated fear, macho pride, and anger—resembled the same three war-promoting motives in the United States. Realistic empathy is urgently needed on both sides to counteract these motives.

(2) *Macho pride*

A major motive behind actions that lead to war, macho pride stimulates the upward spiral in the arms race. In a crisis it may be important to offer the opponent a "face-saving way out," as President Kennedy did for the Soviets during the Cuban missile crisis.

(3) *Misperceptions*

Unconsciously motivated processes (denial, rationalization, selective inattention) as well as more cognitive factors such as those covered in Chapter 2 (belief perseverance, overgeneralization, overconfidence in the accuracy of one's beliefs, the fundamental attribution error) can cause distorted perceptions and beliefs, increasing hostility. If people are aware of these biases, they may avoid being influenced by them.

(4) *Impaired rationality in a crisis*

Stress, time pressures, and information overload interfere with the ability to think rationally and realistically. Groupthink processes are one possible result. As noted in the text, there are effective ways of reducing the likelihood that groupthink will occur.

(5) *The malignant process of hostile interaction*

A suspicious, hostile attitude increases one's sensitivity to real or perceivd differences and threats. A "vicious cycle" of interactions develops in which each side justifies the other's fears and anger, via a self-fulfilling prophecy. Leaders may feel that the solution to the conflict can only be imposed by means of deception or superior force (Deutsch, 1983). Awareness of this process may promote conflict resolution by directly combating a "good guys-bad guys" conception of the conflict.

(6) *Armed deterrence is only effective sometimes*

Armed deterrence sometimes works but, for psychological reasons, often does not. Deterrence is often misinterpreted as preparation for war. Evidence from psychological research, as well as from historical events, is mixed regarding the positive (peace-promoting) or negative (war-promoting) effect of a strong deterrence capability.

(7) *Psychic numbing*

People often react to overwhelming threat with psychological defense mechanisms such as repression, denial, projection, and selective inattention. The threat of nuclear war may stimulate "psychic numbing" wherein people fail to face the issues or to take actions that might reduce the chances of war. Government officials could adopt public-information policies that might reduce the chances of pyschic numbing.

Government and military policymakers can be made aware of the *benefits* of:

(8) *Reversing the malignant spiral process*

As noted in the text, the GRIT strategy may be effective in reversing the upward spiral of tensions and arms and leading instead to increased trust and reduced hostilities.

(9) *Flexibility in negotiations*

Research shows that negotiators are much more effective when they adopt a flexible, non-defensive orientation. Public opinion poll data indicated that by the mid-1980s most Americans were strongly in favor of U.S. flexibility in arms control negotiations (Yankelovich & Doble, 1984)

(10) *Integrative bargaining*

An integrative bargaining style involves firmness about the ends one seeks, along with flexibility on means (Pruitt, 1981). The values as well as the goals of both sides need to be appreciated. Conflicts can often be solved by appealing to values that are, at least in theory, held by both sides. ❖

5. Transforming the group. In some cases a leader may be able to perform a *transforming function*, where group members are helped to transcend their ordinary roles as followers and become agents of moral leadership themselves (Burns, 1978). Mohandas K. Gandhi's role in achieving independence for India is an example.

The "Great Person" Theory

"great person" theory of leadership:
The theory that people are effective leaders because of unique personality traits they possess.

One of the first proponents of the **"great person" theory of leadership** was Thomas Carlyle (1841–1907), who asserted that great leaders are successful because of certain unique personality characteristics. Inspired to search for unique features of successful leaders, much early research on leadership proceeded on the premise that those who became leaders were different from those who became followers. Hundreds of leaders were compared with many hundreds of followers, but early reviews of such studies concluded that no reliable and coherent pattern of results existed (Mann, 1959; Stogdill, 1948). The research results led a generation of textbook authors to assure students that personality traits were not strongly related to leadership.

Nelson Mandela: A transformational leader.

leadership emergence:
The process by which one gets chosen to be a leader.

leadership effectiveness:
Determined by how well a group performs under one's leadership.

Personality and Emergence as a Leader

Recently, however, the picture has changed. First, researchers (Lord et al., 1986) have pointed out that earlier reviews have confused **leadership emergence** (who gets chosen as a leader) with **leadership effectiveness** (how the group performs under his or her leadership). Many political analysts have bemoaned the fact that the characteristics that may be crucial in enabling one to get elected as president (e.g., good looks, money for advertising, a persuasive speaking style) may have little or nothing to do with one's ability to govern effectively. Most early leadership studies focused on leader emergence, but were incorrectly generalized to the issue of leader effectiveness.

Second, more recent studies plus reanalyses of older studies have indicated that there are several traits that are reliably linked to leadership emergence. A meta-analysis of twenty-seven studies by Robert Lord and his co-workers (1986) found three traits strongly related to leadership emergence: *intelligence*, *dominance*, and stereotypically *masculine personality characteristics* (aggressive, decisive, unemotional). *Personal adjustment* is a fourth trait that may be related (Gibb, 1969). Why these traits? Recall the notion of implicit personality theories discussed in Chapter 2. Lord et al. (1984) suggested that people have implicit leadership theories, traits that form their prototype of the ideal leader. When a potential leader matches the leadership prototype held by most followers, he or she is likely to be perceived as a leader and to emerge as one.

Another study, reanalyzing data from an earlier study on leadership emergence done by Barnlund, (1962), found that the same people tended to emerge as leaders in many different types of experimental situations. In their reanalysis, Kenny and Zaccaro (1983) speculated the important characteristic of those who emerged as leaders was not a traditional personality trait, but the ability to perceive the needs and goals of the group and to adjust one's personal approach accordingly.

Another set of researchers obtained personality test scores from over two thousand American political leaders, delegates, or alternate delegates to their party's presidential conventions. The political leaders, both males and females, scored higher than average on measures of *self-confidence*, *need for achievement*, and *dominance*. The leaders scored lower than average on measures of the tendency to elicit sympathy or emotional support from others, to express self-criticism or guilt, and to be deferent (to subordinate oneself) to others (Costantini & Craik, 1980).

Personality and Leadership Effectiveness

We know considerably less about traits that may relate to how well one performs as a leader. In a classic study of leadership styles, Lewin, Lippett, and White (1939) trained graduate students in behaviors indicative of three leadership styles: *democratic*, *autocratic*, and *laissez-faire*. The democratic style emphasized group participation and majority rule, the autocratic style in-

Contemporary leaders: Do they have similar personality characteristics? Do British Prime Minister Margaret Thatcher, South African leader Nelson Mandela, New York Governor Mario Cuomo, and civil rights activist Jesse Jackson appear to share many of the same personality characteristics?

volved tight control of group activities where decisions were made by the leader, and the laissez-faire style involved very low levels of any kind of activity by the leader. Results indicated that the democratic style had a somewhat more positive impact on group processes than did the other two styles, but the differences were not clear-cut. In general, we can say that democratic leadership style leads to greater member satisfaction but does not always lead to better productivity (Shaw, 1981).

It appears that the intelligence of a leader is most important for leadership effectiveness if the leader has a directive style and is working in a stress-free environment with a supportive group. In some situations, however, if the leader has a nondirective style, high intelligence may be a drawback. The leader may provide group members with more ideas than they can handle, or members may feel let down that their intelligent leader spends too much time listening and does not give them enough guidance (Fiedler, 1987).

In other situations, the ability and willingness to take risks may be important leadership qualities. Studies of military combat leaders and leadership in a large urban fire department concluded that men who showed more bravery and took more risks were consistently seen as more effective leaders (Frost et al., 1983). These risk-taking leaders also were more experienced and more satisfied with their jobs than were less effective leaders.

What do these recent studies tell us about the validity of the "great person" theory of leadership? Certainly there may be a kernel of truth to the theory. Although no specific set of traits consistently differentiates successful leaders from unsuccessful ones in all situations, some traits are related to leadership emergence or to leadership effectiveness.

Wielding Social Power

A leader can use his or her power in many ways; a number of possible power tactics are listed in Table 6-1 (Forsyth, 1990). Given this wide range of possible behaviors, why should power corrupt and absolute power corrupt absolutely, as British Lord John Acton asserted? Kipnis (1976) suggested a number of reasons. First, powerholders have access to social power and can use it to influence others. Persons in power tend to assume a right to use their position to get what they want, especially if they wield coercive, reward, or legitimate power. Second, powerholders with a strong power base tend to believe that they, rather than the target, control the target's behavior and they will take it as a personal insult (or worse) if their orders are not followed. Military officers or bosses (in some cases, parents) may become very upset if their orders are not followed. Focus 6-4 describes tragic situations in which aircraft crews did not dare question the leadership of the captain.

Third, to the extent that the powerholder's influence has been successful, she may feel superior to the target, thereby increasing her psychological distance from the target. For example, a mother who is able to control her teenage daughter's behavior through coercion may derive some satisfaction from feeling superior to, and different from, the teenager. But using coercive power may reduce the mother's potential for later using referent power, which depends on similarity and identification. As a result, future communication between the two is likely to be minimal.

Imagine yourself as an employee: which power bases would you prefer that your boss use when interacting with you? To answer this question, Hinkin and Schriesheim (1989) developed questionnaires measuring five bases of social power and satisfaction with supervision. The questionnaires were given to several samples of people — undergraduates in business courses, part-time MBA students, and employees at a psychiatric hospital. As Figure 6-5 indi-

	POWER TACTICS	
TABLE 6-1	TACTICS THAT PEOPLE MAY USE TO INFLUENCE OTHERS IN BUSINESS, GROUP, AND INTERPERSONAL SETTINGS	

Tactic	Definition	Example
Discussion	Using rational argument or explanation	• I give her supporting reasons. • I explain why I favor the plan. • We talk it over.
Request	Stating what should be done or asking for compliance	• I say what I want. • I tell her what I expect. • I ask her to do it.
Demand	Forcefully asserting oneself; insisting on compliance	• I demand that she do it. • I insist that he stop. • I give the order.
Instruction	Teaching; demonstrating by example	• I explain how to do it. • I set an example.
Persuasion	Using coaxing, convincing arguments	• I talk him out of it. • I persuade her to do it. • I develop a strong presentation.
Negotiation	Bargaining; making compromises; trading favors	• I work out a deal. • We compromise. • I drop a demand if she does.
Pressure	Using group influence	• I appeal to the boss. • I turn the group against her. • I get others to take my side.
Claiming expertise	Demonstrating or claiming superior knowledge or skill	• I rely on my experience. • I let them know I'm an expert. • I bury them in technical details.
Persistence	Continuing in one's influence attempts or repeating a point	• I reiterate my point. • I don't give up. • I don't take no for an answer.
Manipulation	Lying; hinting; deceiving	• I lie about it. • I get her to think it's her idea. • I drop a hint.
Supplication	Entreating; asking humbly or earnestly	• I plead. • I cry. • I act helpless.
Ingratiation	Deliberately increasing one's attractiveness	• I try to seem cooperative. • I flatter him. • I try to be seductive.
Disengagement	Withdrawing from the setting; breaking off the interaction	• I go on strike. • I ignore him until he does it. • I leave.
Reward	Providing valued reinforcers	• I increase his pay. • I give her the day off. • I shower him with praise.
Threat	Warning of negative consequences in the future	• I threaten to cut her pay. • I tell him he might be fired. • I threaten legal action.
Punishment	Imposing negative consequences	• I cut her pay. • I reprimand her. • I punch him.

Source: From Forsyth, D. R. (1990). *Group dynamics* (2nd ed.). Pacific Grove, CA: Brooks/Cole. Copyright © 1990 by Brooks/Cole Publishing Co. Reprinted by permission.

FOCUS 6-4

Leadership in the Cockpit

It is difficult to question, psychologically, a leader's decisions. This understandable reluctance can have tragic consequences. It has been estimated that 65 percent of aircraft accidents result from human error, often when one crew member has adequate information but does not provide it to other crew members (Foushee, 1984). For example, in January 1977 a Japan Airlines transport crashed shortly after takeoff in Alaska, killing three crew members and two cargo handlers. Extensive investigation by the National Transportation Safety Board (NTSB) revealed that the American captain had a blood alcohol level more than double that considered legally intoxicating for Alaskan automobile drivers. The taxi driver who drove the captain and his two Japanese crew members to the airport later stated that the captain acted jerky, unstable, and drunk. Several other persons who were not personal acquaintances of the captain said that he had been drinking and showed signs of being drunk, yet they had said and done nothing about it. Once on board the aircraft, the pilot got lost while taxiing to the runway and initially selected the wrong runway for takeoff, yet still nothing was said to him. The NTSB report commented, "It is extremely difficult for crew members to challenge a captain even when the captain offers a threat to the safety of the flight. The concept of command authority and its inviolate nature, except

in the case of incapacitation, has become a practice without exception. As a result, second-in-command pilots react indifferently in circumstances where they should be more assertive. Rather than submitting passively to this concept, second-in-command pilots should be encouraged to affirmatively advise the pilot in command that a dangerous situation exists" (National Transportation Safety Board, 1979).

Recorded cockpit conversations revealed that during takeoff of an Air Florida plane in a heavy snowstorm in Washington, D.C., in January 1982, the pilot failed to react to the copilot's repeated subtle advisories that all was not normal during takeoff. Minutes later the plane plunged into the Potomac River, killing seventy-eight passengers (Foushee, 1984).

Laboratory research has provided further evidence of the difficulties in questioning a superior's behavior. In a study of behavior of airline crews in a flight simulator, experimenters had the captain fake subtle incapacitation to see how the crew would react. In one-quarter of the cases, the simulated flights would have "crashed" because the copilot did not react assertively and take control in time (Harper, Kidera, & Cullen, 1971). Assertiveness training for copilots and other crew members should have high priority, so that they will feel comfortable challenging a captain who, for whatever reason, is unable to function well. ❖

Debris from the 1982 Air Florida crash in the Potomac River.

cates, for all samples combined, satisfaction was strongly related to supervisors' use of expert and referent power and less strongly to legitimate and reward power. People responded negatively to the use of coercive power.

Leadership in Sports

Baseball managers and basketball and football coaches are in visible leadership roles. The success of their leadership is usually measured by the team's won-lost record and possibly also by the amount of money earned by the team. The high salaries paid to successful coaches implies that their employers see them as having valuable leadership traits or abilities. Yet the same coaches have widely differing records in different situations.

A number of highly successful college football coaches did very poorly when they took coaching jobs in the pros. Or take the case of baseball manager Billy Martin, whose managerial career vacillated like a yo-yo. Martin was hired and fired by major league clubs a remarkable number of times in the 1970s and 1980s. Was Martin an effective or ineffective leader? The judgment of his superiors, who hired and fired him, seems contradictory. Perhaps the answer lies in the interaction between Martin's skills and liabilities and the requirements of the situation. The skills necessary to turn a nonwinning team into a winning one (which Martin seemed to do very well) may be different from the skills necessary to keep a winning team successful and productive. These case histories illustrate the relevance of contingency theories of leadership, which emphasize the interactions and transactions between characteristics of the leader and characteristics of the situation.

FIGURE 6-5

Social Power and Satisfaction

Subordinates' Satisfaction With Supervisor's Use of Different Bases of Social Power.

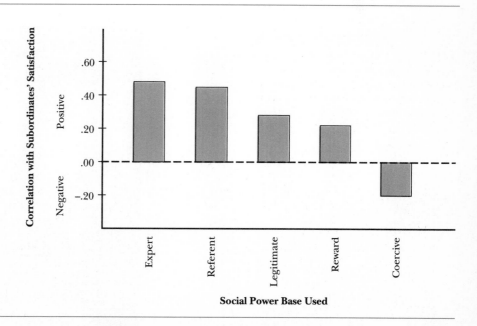

Source: Data from Hinkin, T. R., & Schriesheim, C. A. (1989). Development and application of new scales to measure the French and Raven (1959) bases of social power. *Journal of Applied Psychology, 74,* 561–567.

Personality, Power, and Politics

Although the "great person" theory of leadership has been challenged by social scientists, it is clear that personal appeal and having "an attractive forceful personality" (in the language of the Harris Poll) is of enormous concern to campaign strategists and journalists during U.S. presidential campaigns.

How might a presidential candidate's personal characteristics interact with changing issues and the ever-shifting tide of public opinion? One possibility is that a potential leader's appeal depends on a *match* with the requirements of the situation (Bem & Funder, 1978). For example, David Barber (1980) argued that American presidential elections follow a regular cyclical course: first, there is a focus on *conflict*, then a concern for *conscience*, and finally a need for *conciliation* to bring all the parties together again. This leads, in turn, to a renewed conflict orientation and the cycle is repeated. For each election, the type of personal appeal that is most effective will vary—in a conflict year, a "fighter" is likely to be victorious, while a candidate who pledges to "bring us together" may succeed in a conciliation year.

Another perspective focuses on the *transactions* between a leader and followers, on the match between the characteristics of the leader and the followers. Erik Erikson's psychobiographies of Adolf Hitler, Martin Luther, and Mohandas Gandhi (Erikson, 1950; 1958; 1969) stressed that these leaders, with their own identities, conflicts, and needs, were chosen by their contemporaries who had corresponding conflicts and needs. The success of these leaders depended, in Erikson's view, on the match between their own personal characteristics and the historically conditioned characteristics of their potential followers. This theoretical perspective is supported by experimental

Mohandas K. Ghandi: Did his characteristics match his followers' needs and implicit leadership theories? Gandhi's success in leading India to independence from Great Britain may have been made possible by the match between his personality and needs and the corresponding needs and conflicts of his followers.

work that finds leader success to be related to a kind of match between leaders' and followers' characteristics or between their implicit leadership theories (Bass, 1981; Lord et al., 1986).

It is difficult to assess U.S. presidents' personal characteristics in order to evaluate this theory, but a couple of interesting attempts have been made. Barber (1977) differentiated American presidents in terms of two dimensions: level of activity (active or passive) and reaction toward the activity (positive or negative). This typology is summarized in Focus 6-5.

Self-presentation strategies are an important part of leaders' transactions with their followers. This is especially true for leaders who are elected, since the followers are the source of the leader's legitimacy (Elgie et al., 1988). A leader has many potential tasks: director of activity, problem solver, planner, communicator, advocate, external liaison, and mediator of within-group conflict. No one person can do it all, but leaders must convince their fol-

---

FOCUS 6-5

The Character of Twentieth-Century U.S. Presidents

Political scientist James David Barber (1977) asserted that orientations of U.S. presidents vary on two important dimensions: *active-passive* and *positive-negative*. The four combinations of these factors, and the twentieth-century presidents who fit into each typology (according to Barber), are given below. What orientations have more recent presidents shown?

Active-positive. These people are very active as leaders and seem to enjoy their role. This suggests relatively high self-esteem and relative success in relating to the environment.

    Theodore Roosevelt (1901–1909)
    Franklin D. Roosevelt (1933–1945)
    Harry S Truman (1945–1953)
    John F. Kennedy (1961–1963)
    Gerald Ford (1974–1977)

Active-negative. There is a contradiction here between relatively intense effort and relatively low emotional reward for the effort.

    Woodrow Wilson (1913–1921)
    Herbert Hoover (1929–1933)
    Lyndon B. Johnson (1963–1969)
    Richard Nixon (1969–1974)

Passive-positive. This is the receptive, compliant other-directed character whose life is a search for affection as a reward for being agreeable. Such a person is cooperative rather than personally assertive.

    William H. Taft (1909–1913)
    Warren G. Harding (1921–1923)

Passive-negative. Someone who does little in politics and enjoys it even less. There is an orientation toward dutiful service.

    Calvin Coolidge (1923–1929)
    Dwight D. Eisenhower (1953–1961) ❖

Source: Barber, J. D. (1977). *The presidential character.* Englewood Cliffs, NJ: Prentice-Hall.

lowers that they have "leadership qualities." The leader may try to behave in ways that correspond to the followers' implicit leadership theory, their prototype of leader. Gary Hart's involvement with Donna Rice in 1988 and Edmund Muskie's crying during the 1972 campaign (Chapter 2) violated voters' prototypes of leader behavior and crippled the candidates' chances for the presidential nomination. Leaders may also try to convey expressions that enhance their influence and effectiveness (Leary, in press). They may act warm and friendly when seeking loyalty, or gruff and intolerant when seeking compliance. Each of the self-presentation strategies discussed in Chapter 3 may be used by leaders: ingratiation, intimidation, exemplification, self-promotion, and supplication.

American Presidents and U.S. Society: Do Their Motive Profiles Match?

Can greatness and appeal among political leaders be analyzed in psychological terms? David Winter (1987b) set out to answer this question by analyzing the content of inaugural addresses made by every elected U.S. president from George Washington to Ronald Reagan. Each president's "motive profile" was derived from scores on measures of three important social motives: achievement motivation, affiliation-intimacy motive (concern for close relations with others), and power motive (a concern for impact and prestige). For each decade, Winter also calculated society's motive profile for the same three motives. These were estimated from content analyses of "cultural documents"— popular novels, children's readers, and hymns, through a procedure developed by McClelland (1975).

A significant degree of leader-situation match was found across the 180 years of U.S. history. Those presidents who were most successful (defined in terms of percentage of the popular vote when first elected president and whether or not they won if ran for reelection) had motive profiles that more closely matched the society's motive profile (the prevalent implicit leadership theory?) for that decade. So, to get elected president, it appears important that a candidate's expressed motives match the dominant themes of the decade.

Presidential performance, however, was a different story. Historians' average ratings of presidential "greatness" were *negatively* related to president-society congruence in motives. Many presidents who are rated very highly by most historians (e.g., Washington, Lincoln, Theodore Roosevelt, Truman, Kennedy) had motive patterns quite discrepant from those of American society at the time. Historians' evaluations were more related to the leader's attributes (especially power motivation) than to the degree of leader-situation match. As Winter (1987b) noted, we may vote for the candidate who feels most "comfortable" or congruent to us, who best fits our implicit leadership theory or our dimly perceived motives. But often the "uncomfortable" leader, discrepant in motive from the larger contemporary society, turns out to be regarded later as the great leader.

"Uncomfortable" leaders may be great leaders. These American presidents, whose personal motive patterns did not match society's prevailing motive pattern at the time, have been rated by many historians as among our greatest presidents.

Contingency Theory

The Transactional View of Leadership

transactional view of leadership:
A view that sees leadership as a reciprocal process of social influence between leader and followers.

To be considered a leader, one must be able to affect the behaviors of his or her followers. But social influence works both ways—a leader's behavior often is strongly affected by the actions and demands of the other group members (Hollander & Offerman, 1990). The **transactional view** sees leadership as a reciprocal process of social influence between leader and followers.

consideration behavior:
Leader behavior that includes interpersonal warmth, concern for the feeling of subordinates, and two-way communication.

intitiation of structure:
Leader behavior involving directedness, goal facilitation, and task-related feedback.

task-motivated:
Leadership style focusing mainly on task achievement, on getting the job done.

relationship-oriented:
Open and participatory leadership style concerned with interpersonal relations.

One set of studies has identified two types of behaviors that seemed the most important. **Consideration behavior** includes interpersonal warmth, concern for the feelings of subordinates, and the use of two-way communication. **Initiation of structure** refers to directiveness, goal facilitation, and task-related feedback (Stogdill & Coons, 1957). In the business world these two styles might be labeled employee-oriented and production-oriented (Kahn & Katz, 1953) or *socioemotional* and *task-oriented* (Bales & Slater, 1955). Yet it has been proven quite difficult to relate these behavioral factors to group outcomes. The relationship between leader structuring behavior and group productivity has revealed few consistent patterns (Chemers, 1983).

Situational Favorableness

The interaction between characteristics of the leader and the situation in which the leader functions has been closely studied by Fred Fiedler and his co-workers (Fiedler, 1978; Fiedler et al., 1976). Fiedler developed the "Esteem for Least Preferred Co-worker" (LPC) scale on which a leader is asked to rate the individual with whom the leader had the most difficulty accomplishing an assigned task (Rice, 1978). A leader who gives a very negative rating for this co-worker (low LPC) is thought to be the kind of person for whom task success is very important and such a person is likely to be **task-motivated**. A leader who gives the least preferred co-worker a relatively positive rating (high LPC) would be more concerned with the interpersonal situation than with the task aspects and is called **relationship-oriented**.

The three dimensions of a leadership situation focused on by Fiedler were, in descending order of importance: (1) *group atmosphere* or *leader-member relations*, the degree of trust and support that followers give the leader; (2) *task structure*, the degree to which the goals and procedures for accomplishing the group's task are clearly specified; and (3) *position power*, the degree to which the leader has formal authority to reward and punish followers. The most favorable situation for a leader involves positive leader-member relations, clear task structure, and strong position power, all of which give the leader the greatest amount of situational control.

Research has indicated that neither general leadership style, task-motivated or relationship-oriented, is effective in all situations. In favorable, high-control situations involving clear tasks and a cooperative group, a task-motivated leader can be very effective. Under conditions of moderate favorableness and control involving an ambiguous task or an uncooperative group, the task-motivated leader may become anxious, overconcerned with a quick solution, or overly critical and punitive. The more open, considerate, and participative style of the relationship-oriented leader is likely to be more effective. In contrast, the crisis nature of the unfavorable low-control situation calls for a firm and directive leadership style, which is supplied by the task-motivated leader. The combinations of these factors are depicted in Table 6-2 and Figure 6-6. A task-oriented leader is apt to be most effective in the more extreme situations 1, 2, 7, and 8, and a relationship-oriented leader more effective in the intermediate situations 3 to 6.

contingency theory of leadership:
The theory that a leader's effectiveness is contingent on the relationship between the leader's style and characteristics of the situation in which the leader functions.

Fiedler's **contingency theory** has been the subject of considerable research and controversy. A meta-analysis of over 150 studies ascertained that the predictions of the theory were strongly supported by data from both laboratory and organizational studies (Strube & Garcia, 1981). The effectiveness of a leader can be predicted from the favorableness of the situation and the leader's primary orientation—to the task or to relationships within the group. Probably the weakest part of the theory concerns the difficulty in measuring situation favorableness (Rice & Kastenbaum, 1983).

The approach can be useful not only for analyzing leadership situations but also in learning to be a better leader. The Leader Match training program developed by Fiedler (Fiedler & Mahar, 1979) consists of three parts. Leaders are first taught how to analyze their own leadership style (task-oriented or relationship-oriented); then to analyze their leadership environment in terms of situational favorableness; and, finally, to consider ways of altering the situation to improve the match between leader and situation. The program assumes that for a leader, changing the situation is less difficult than changing the leader's style (personality). Fiedler and Mahar analyzed fifteen studies involving Leader Match and found that trained leaders scored consistently higher on measures of leadership effectiveness than did leaders not receiving such training. Although the increase in leadership effectiveness is impressive, the success of Leader Match training does not pro-

---

TABLE 6-2   CLASSIFICATION OF SITUATIONAL CONTROL AND FAVORABLENESS OF SITUATION ACCORDING TO FIEDLER'S CONTINGENCY THEORY OF LEADERSHIP

Situational Variable	Classification							
Group atmosphere	Positive (High)				Negative (Low)			
Task structure	High		Low		High		Low	
Position power	High	Low	High	Low	High	Low	High	Low
Situation Categorization	1	2	3	4	5	6	7	8
Situational control	High				Moderate			Low
Favorableness of situation for leader	High				Moderate			Low
	Best for leader						Worst for leader	

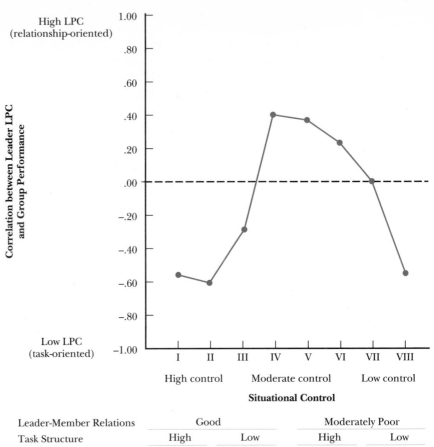

FIGURE 6-6

Empirical Support for Fiedler's Contingency Model

Summary of research findings on the correlation between leadership style (LPC) and group performance under different levels of situational control.

Leader-Member Relations	Good				Moderately Poor			
Task Structure	High		Low		High		Low	
Leader Position Power	Strong	Weak	Strong	Weak	Strong	Weak	Strong	Weak

Source: From Chemers, M. M. (1983). Leadership theory and research: A systems-process integration. In P. B. Paulus (Ed.), *Basic group processes* (p. 13). New York: Springer-Verlag. Reprinted by permission.

vide *direct* support for Fiedler's contingency theory. It is conceivable that the program's success may occur because leaders become sensitized to the general possibilities of changing their situation (Rice & Kastenbaum, 1983) or because the program simply bolsters the confidence of leaders (Csoka & Bons, 1978).

Development of Leadership Styles

Assumptions about Human Nature

Having analyzed the various leadership styles, we can now look at how they develop. Fiedler asserted that leadership styles rise out of stable, enduring, well-learned personality attributes, which are quite difficult to change

(Chemers, 1984). One basis from which leaders may develop their style of leadership is their assumptions about human nature, which Wrightsman (1974) measured in a series of studies. He identified two major dimensions on which people's views of human nature differ: an **evaluative dimension** and a **multiplexity dimension**. People who score high on the evaluative dimension believe that most other people are trustworthy, rational, altruistic, and independent. People scoring high on the multiplexity dimension believe that most other people are complex and differ widely from each other.

Effective Leadership Styles

For decades, industrial-organizational psychologists have investigated leadership styles most effective in employment situations. The Theory X/Theory Y approach developed by Douglas McGregor (1966) focuses on assumptions about human nature that might be held by managers in a job situation. One prevalent viewpoint, **Theory X**, assumes that most people prefer to be directed, are not interested in assuming responsibility, and want safety above all. It assumes that workers are motivated mostly by money, fringe benefits, and the threat of punishment. Managers who make such assumptions attempt to control and closely supervise their employees. The managers believe that external control clearly is appropriate for dealing with people, for most are seen as unreliable, irresponsible, and immature. In contrast, the **Theory Y** view assumes that people can be self-directed and creative at work if properly motivated and that it is the task of management to unleash the potential in individuals. Properly motivated people then can achieve their own goals best by directing their own efforts toward accomplishing the organization's goals.

In twenty-eight studies of functioning industrial groups, Argyris (1969) found that by far the most common behavior pattern stemmed from Theory X. Theory X behavior led to relatively ineffectual interpersonal relationships and ineffectual problem solving on issues that were important and loaded with feelings. When solutions were achieved, they did not tend to be lasting ones and the problems seemed to recur continually. Finally, members seemed to be blind to the negative influence they sometimes had on others. Leaders of groups were unable to predict the feelings that their subordinates had about them and were unable to predict accurately their influence on their subordinates.

Since Theory Y more closely fits many modern, humanistically oriented theories of personality, it would be easy to fall into the trap of thinking that Theory Y thinking is good and Theory X thinking is bad. McGregor was not implying, however, that everyone is mature, independent, and self-motivated, rather, that most people have the *potential* to be mature and self-motivated. Although a manager's best assumption usually is Theory Y, he asserted, managers may find it necessary to behave in a directive, controlling manner (as if they had Theory X assumptions) with some people in the short run to help them "grow up" (mature) until they are truly Theory Y people (Hersey & Blanchard, 1982).

---

evaluative dimension:
One of two major dimensions on which people's views of human nature differ. The degree to which people are seen as trustworthy, rational, altruistic, and independent.

multiplexity dimension:
One of two major dimensions in which people's views of human nature differ. The degree to which people are seen as complex and differing widely from each other.

Theory X:
Viewpoint that most people prefer to be directed, want safety, and don't want to assume responsibility.

Theory Y:
Viewpoint that most people can be self-directed and creative if properly motivated.

self-determination theory:

The proposition that the way a leader provides feedback to her followers is critical.

The impact of a leader's style is the focus of **self-determination theory**, developed by Deci and Ryan (1985), which asserts that the way that a leader (e.g., a manager) provides feedback to her followers (e.g., employees) is critical. She can foster self-determination by giving feedback in an informational way that supports individual autonomy and promotes competence. Or the feedback may be given in a controlling way that limits autonomy and decreases intrinsic motivation. Research indicates that three aspects of the leader's style of communication can promote self-determination: (1) allowing followers to make choices; (2) using noncontrolling positive feedback; and (3) acknowledging the other's perspective (Deci et al., 1989).

Self-determination enhances creativity, conceptual learning, self-esteem, and general well-being among workers, research shows (Deci & Ryan, 1985). For example, in a study involving nearly one thousand employees of a major office machine company, Deci, Connell, and Ryan (1989) found that subordinates whose managers were trained in a self-determination orientation showed higher general job satisfaction and more trust in the corporation than did subordinates of controlling managers.

Contingency theories of leadership point out that there is no single leadership style that is best for all situations. An effective leader will be aware of significant aspects of the situation and the characteristics of the people involved, and take them into account in planning her leadership strategy. Some might ask, "But isn't a leader being inconsistent if she uses one style in one situation and another style in another situation?" Not really. The important point is that effective leaders are those who are *consistent in adapting* their leadership style to the particular characteristics of any situation.

Leadership: Tying It All Together

You have just learned about the important aspects of leaders, followers, and situations that are likely to determine the effectiveness of a leader's behavior and the group's performance. Figure 6-7 summarizes these findings. There are three centrally important variables in a leadership situation: characteristics of the leader, of the followers, and of the situation. The leader's personal characteristics, such as motives, assumptions about human nature, task or relationship orientation, and leadership style, will affect the leader's expectations and behaviors. The characteristics of the situation, such as the amount of position power, clarity of the task, and quality of leader-member relations, will also affect expectations and behavior. The followers' personal characteristics, such as their motives, knowledge, maturity, and needs, will affect their expectations and their feelings of satisfaction. The behavior of followers will be determined by social norms, their expectations, their satisfaction, and situational factors. The transactional relationship between leaders' and followers' behaviors is represented by the two-headed arrow. Finally, the overall performance of the group is determined by the interaction between the leader's behavior and the followers' behavior.

FIGURE 6-7

The Influence of Leaders' and Followers' Behavior on Performance of a Task.

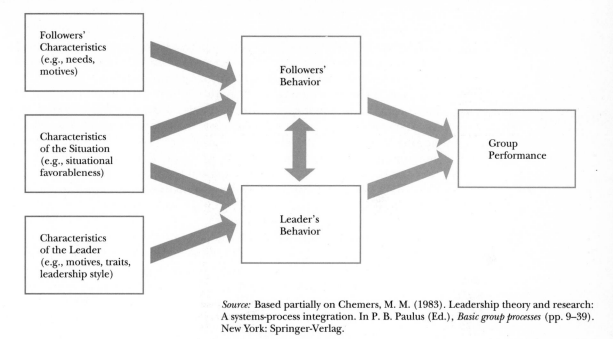

Source: Based partially on Chemers, M. M. (1983). Leadership theory and research: A systems-process integration. In P. B. Paulus (Ed.), *Basic group processes* (pp. 9–39). New York: Springer-Verlag.

To be an effective leader, therefore, you need to be aware of many factors. Awareness of your own assumptions about people and your usual style of leadership, sensitivity to group members' needs and expectations, and the ability to assess the amount of situational control that exists are crucial, as is knowledge of how to change a situation to match your leadership style. Perhaps it is this combination of skills and sensitivity, rather than more simplified notions such as charisma, intelligence, or oratory skills, that separate "great leaders" from the rest of us.

SUMMARY

This chapter has focused on group behavior as affected by the social structure of a group to which one belongs, and on collective behavior—responses to the presence of others in the same situation. The presence of others can improve performance on a task through social facilitation, challenges, and rivalry, or interfere with performance on a task through social inhibition, distraction, or social loafing. People in groups may make decisions in a different manner from single individuals. Judgments may become more extreme, or polarized, in a group. Moreover, if the situation is stressful and an isolated, cohesive group with a strong leader is faced with an important decision, groupthink may occur: Shared illusions of the group's invulnerability and unanimity develop as the group members strive to reach agreement on a decision, any decision. The tendency toward groupthink can be reduced by preventing leader bias and preventing group isolation.

The "prisoner's dilemma" situation has been used to study bargaining and negotiation. Starting out with a tough bargaining position and then gradually softening one's stance is often the most effective tactic. During negotiations or conflict, individuals or groups can become entrapped, overly committed to an unproductive course of action. Research findings on conflict and bargaining also have been applied to international relations. Theorists have described ways to improve international communications, such as developing an awareness of mirror-image wars, the GRIT plan, and common illusions and misperceptions.

The "great person" theory of leadership focuses on identifying traits of effective leaders. In contrast, the contingency theory of leadership asserts that the effectivenesss of one's leadership style depends on three aspects of situational control: leader-member relations, task structure, and the leader's position power. In general, a task-motivated leader is more effective in situations of very high or very low situational control and a relationship-oriented leader is more apt to be effective in intermediate situations. People's basic assumptions about human nature are likely to affect the leadership style they adopt.

PART FOUR

Social Relations

CHAPTER 7

Behaving Positively Toward Others: Prosocial Behavior and Altruism

PREVIEW

Open your eyes and look for some man, or some work for the sake of men, which needs a little time, a little friendship, a little sympathy, a little sociability, a little human toil.   Albert Schweitzer

A large part of altruism, even when it is perfectly honest, is grounded upon the fact that it is uncomfortable to have unhappy people about one.   H. L. Mencken

Suppose you are strolling out of the campus library when a student in front of you drops an armload of books. What factors might affect your decision whether to help pick up the books: your personality? your mood? the presence of others? whether you are in a hurry? the norms (expectations) for the situation?

You are walking back to campus at midnight with a friend after an enjoyable evening at a local bar. Suddenly you hear a scuffling sound and see two figures wrestling in a poorly lit parking lot nearby. One of them makes some grunting sounds, but it's not clear what they mean. How would you interpret what's going on? What would you do? Unlike the preceding scene, this situation is ambiguous—it's not clear whether help is needed or desired. Would you rush in to help, taking a chance that you'll be attacked or embarrassed? Would you shout to the people, asking if anyone needs help? Would you try to get someone else to help? Would you shrug your shoulders and walk on, figuring it's none of your business? Would you be strongly affected by how other bystanders (your friend and others walking by) react? ❖

PREVIEW

In this chapter we will be concerned with prosocial behavior. In discussing the origins of prosocial behavior, we will focus on social factors (childhood socialization and reinforcement from others) and possible biological origins. During the past two decades, debate has been intense as to whether human prosocial behavior has an inherited genetic base. There has also been spirited

Is this an emergency? Many situations are ambiguous to bystanders. Are these people just playing around or is this a mugging or an assault?

debate about whether prosocial behavior is often altruistic, stimulated by empathy for the person in need, or stems instead from egoistic motivations such as the desire to change a bad mood, to enhance a good mood, to reduce unpleasant arousal, or to avoid social disapproval or guilt for not helping. We'll review the creative research studies that have tested these possibilities. I will also discuss the personality and situational factors that affect prosocial behavior. Being helped does not always produce gratitude and positive reactions in the recipients; I will analyze several theories of why there are different reactions to being helped.

Researchers studying emergency situations have focused on the processes involved when a person decides to help someone. Some have investigated the impact of the presence of bystanders on the likelihood of helping, whereas others have zeroed in on the costs and rewards involved in helping in emergency situations. After evaluating research bearing on these theoretical orientations, we will turn briefly to the legal issues involved when one decides whether or not to help someone in an emergency. By the time you finish this chapter, you may find that your own responses to ambiguous emergency situations are somewhat different than before.

CAUSES OF PROSOCIAL BEHAVIOR

prosocial behavior:
Behavior intended to contribute to the well-being of another person.

altruism:
Selfless behavior that has the goal of increasing the recipient's welfare.

helping behavior:
Behavior designed to help another individual, regardless of the reason.

Behavior that is intended to contribute to the physical or psychological well-being of another person is called **prosocial behavior** (Wispé, 1972). We live in a society whose values require people to help and cooperate with others. Without such cooperation, society as we know it would not exist. Parents help children through the process of socialization and, on a broader level, we have a series of formal laws and less formal norms that define acceptable and unacceptable behavior among members of society. Concepts such as **altruism**, charity, friendship, cooperation, helping, rescuing, bystander intervention, sacrificing, and sharing all involve prosocial behavior.

Most of the research described in this chapter will deal with **helping behavior**, that is, behavior designed to help another individual, regardless of the reason. We will be concerned with a basic question: What factors determine whether or not a person decides to help? This question relates to a central question about human nature noted in Chapter 1: Are people basically altruistic or selfish?

Learning to Act Prosocially

Childhood Socialization

socialization:
The process of molding an individual's social behavior to fit the expectations of the culture in which he or she lives.

Much of social behavior is learned from one's parents during childhood. **Socialization** refers to the process of molding an individual's social behavior to fit the expectations of the culture in which he or she lives. Some of the values taught in childhood involve prosocial behavior. The Judeo-Christian ethic, with its emphasis on the concept of brotherhood, the Golden Rule, and the parable of the Good Samaritan, values helping others. Parents often urge their children to share, to help others, and to be unselfish. Parents are, of course, crucial factors in the socialization process through their social power (reward, coercive, legitimate, and expert), their ability to teach their children desired behavior, and their status as models. Siblings (brothers and sisters) and peers (same-aged children) are also powerful influences on socialization. The schools also may perform vital roles.

Another source for socialization is the media: television, movies, radio, written materials. Much interest has been stirred by the role of television in the socialization of children, particularly as it relates to prosocial and **antisocial behavior**. There are many more vivid portrayals of antisocial behavior (aggression, murder, violence) than prosocial behavior on television, and televised antisocial behavior has received much more research interest than has prosocial behavior. The impact of televised antisocial behavior will be discussed in Chapter 10.

antisocial behavior:
Behavior that is not condoned by society, such as aggression, murder, and violence.

Considerable evidence exists that televised prosocial behavior may have a significant impact on the behavior of children who watch it (see Focus 7-1). Over three dozen laboratory and field studies have demonstrated that

Socialization of prosocial behavior. Many children are taught to share with others, to help others, and to be unselfish.

children who are exposed to altruistic models act more helpfully themselves (Ahammer & Murray, 1979; Liebert & Sprafkin, 1988). The qualities of generosity, helping, cooperation, friendliness, adhering to rules, delaying gratification, and the ability to cope with fears can all be increased by prosocial television material (Rushton, 1982). Television can be a major source of observational learning experiences and a setter of norms.

There are two reasons for this: First, people, especially children, model much of their behavior after what they see others do. (Modeling will be discussed in more detail in Chapter 10.) Second, observing prosocial behavior may have a **priming effect**, activating positive thoughts related to prosocial behavior and human nature (Berkowitz, 1984). This possibility is supported by research showing that people who have just heard "good news" on the radio not only are more likely to be helpful to others but also seem to adopt a more positive view of human nature, assuming that other people are helpful as well (Blackman & Hornstein, 1977; Holloway et al., 1977).

priming effect:
The process by which observing a particular kind of behavior, or hearing about it, can activate thoughts related to other incidences of this behavior, making similar behavior more likely.

Reinforcement from Others

Children are often rewarded for being helpful and cooperative and for sharing with others. Such reinforcement of prosocial behavior is effective in adulthood as well, as illustrated in a field experiment conducted by Moss and Page (1972). Pedestrians in Dayton, Ohio, were approached by a woman who asked for directions to a local department store. After the pedestrian explained the store's location, the woman responded in a positive, neutral, or negative manner. In the positive condition, she smiled and said, "Thank you very much, I really appreciate this." In the neutral condition she said, "Okay," while in the negative one she interrupted rudely and said, "I can't understand what you're saying. Never mind, I'll ask someone else." Farther down the street a second woman waited until the pedestrian was six feet away, then began walking toward him, dropped a small bag, and continued walking. The pedestrians were much more likely to help this second woman by picking up the bag and returning it to her (80 percent to 90 percent helped) if they had been positively reinforced earlier or responded to in a neutral manner, than if they had received negative reinforcement for their earlier attempt at helping (only 40 percent helped). People high in need for approval are most strongly influenced by being reinforced for helping (Deutsch & Lamberti, 1986).

FOCUS 7-1

"Mister Rogers' Neighborhood" and Prosocial Behavior

Helpfulness, sharing, cooperation, and empathy are often stressed in the popular children's TV program, "Mister Rogers' Neighborhood." Since the early 1970s, researchers have tried to assess the impact of this program on young viewers. In one study, Friedrich and Stein (1973) controlled nursery school children's TV "diet" for four weeks. They found that after watching "Mister Rogers," children from lower socioeconomic families became more prosocial. However, the effect was short-lived; it was not visible in a retest two weeks later. Another study by the same investigators (1975) found that children who watched a series of four "Mister Rogers" programs responded more prosocially than children who did not see the shows. In addition, children who saw the programs and also were given direct prosocial training by role playing were more helpful than children who received only the training or saw only the prosocial programs. In still another study, children watched four fifteen-minute segments from "Sesame Street" or "Mister Rogers' Neighborhood" over a four-day period. Those children who watched "Mister Rogers" gave more positive reinforcement to other children and adults and had more social contact with them. For "Sesame Street," similar effects were found only for children who had low initial levels of these behaviors (Coates, Pusser, & Goodman, 1976).

The studies show that prosocial behavior can be affected by television viewing, especially if linked with other prosocial training. The importance of this linkage is further demonstrated by the finding that poor urban children who merely looked at prosocial television for eight weeks did not become more prosocial. However, if they also acted out plays from "Mister Rogers," they became much more prosocial (Friedrich-Cofer et al., 1979). The power of television to educate and stimulate viewers, especially children, to prosocial or to antisocial activities should not be underestimated (Rushton, 1982). ❖

Is Prosocial Behavior Biologically Predetermined?

Could traits such as altruism or empathy be inherited characteristics? A tough question to answer, but progress is being made. Rushton and his co-workers (1986) compared identical twins with same-sex fraternal twins on questionnaire measures of altruism and empathy. Because the identical twins responded more similarly on the measures, the researchers concluded that both traits were, to some degree, inherited. This interpretation has been disputed by other researchers (Mealey, 1985) and the question remains controversial and unresolved.

People often respond helpfully, in a rapid and impulsive manner, to others who are in a clear and unambiguous distress state. Clark and Word (1972), for example, found that the average time it took subjects to help a man who fell and cried out in pain was less than nine seconds. Such quick reactions suggest a basic helping tendency that is triggered by the awareness of distress in another individual.

Being upset by others' distress starts very early in life. Young children appear to become upset by distress in others. As early as the age of one, some babies actually try to comfort people who are crying or in pain; they snuggle up to them, pat them, or hug them. By eighteen months of age, children imitate other people's laughter, crying, or grimaces (Zahn-Waxler, Radke-Yarrow, & King, 1979). One researcher reported that "Some of these imitations seem almost reflexive. They are much like our definition of empathy . . . others appear more deliberate and studied, as if the child were 'trying on' an emotional expression to see how it feels" (Radke-Yarrow, quoted in Pines, 1979, p. 68). Other research shows that toddlers aged sixteen to thirty-three months respond more prosocially to friends' cries than to the cries of a toddler they don't know as well (Howes & Farver, 1987). Such studies suggest that the capacity for empathy and altruism exists at a remarkably early age.

Very young infants become distressed when they hear other infants cry. Martin and Clark (1982) exposed infants who were only eighteen hours old to four-minute tape recordings of themselves or another infant crying. As Figure 7-1 indicates, infants who heard another infant cry were likely to cry a great deal themselves. A second (unexpected) finding was that infants behaved very differently when hearing a tape of themselves crying; this apparently had a calming rather than alarming effect. Infants cried very little upon hearing their own cry, as the left side of Figure 7-1 indicates. A second study with infants showed that crying increased when a tape was played of an infant their own age crying, but not when they heard a tape of an older (eleven-month old) child crying or a tape of a crying sixteen-day-old chimpanzee. Martin and Clark noted that when adult observers listened to the three tapes, they rated the tapes of the crying chimp and the older child as more disturbing than that of the younger child. In contrast, infants were most upset by the tape of another infant crying. Hence this alarm reaction to others' crying appears to be both age-specific and species-specific. Very young infants can make discriminations between similar auditory stimuli; they can

FIGURE 7-1

Distress at an Early Age

Mean seconds of vocalization (crying) for eighteen-hour-old infants for the eight-minute period during and immediately after hearing a four-minute audiotape of a crying infant.

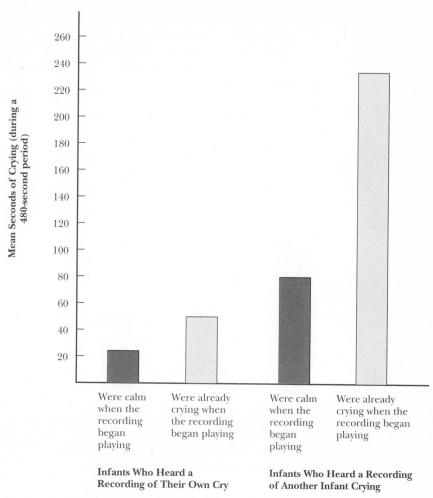

Source: Data from Martin, G. B., & Clark, R. D., III. (1982). Distress crying in neonates: Species and peer specificity. *Developmental Psychology, 18,* 3–9.

differentiate between their own cry and the cry of other newborns, older children, and other animals.

Sociobiology as an Explanation

The controversial field of **sociobiology** has recently arisen as a means of explaining many types of social behavior. Sociobiologists such as Edward 0. Wilson (1975; 1978) have argued that much of human social behavior is biologically determined. Sociobiology rests on two basic assumptions (Cunning-

sociobiology:
A controversial approach that argues that much of human social behavior is biologically determined.

ham, 1981): (1) a large number of social behaviors are partly determined by genetic factors; (2) genetically based behaviors will be passed on to future generations if they increase the "genetic fitness" (reproductive success) of the individual or close relatives who also carry genes for the behavior. While the sociobiological approach has been applied to many human behaviors such as attraction, aggression, sexual behavior, and gender differences, it has been particularly controversial when applied to helping behavior and altruism.

The traditional Darwinian theory of evolution emphasizes that genes that contribute to an organism's survival are more likely to be passed on to future generations, because the organism with these genes is more likely to survive long enough to reproduce itself. On the surface, it would seem that a genetic tendency toward altruism would probably not be passed on to future generations, for altruistic animals would be more likely to die early (by sacrificing their lives to save another animal), thus cutting short their ability to pass on their genes. In Wilson's (1978, p. 152) words, "Fallen heroes do not have children." However, sociobiologists have an answer to this apparent contradiction. They claim that **biological fitness** is not just the ability to survive, but rather the ability to get *genes like yours* into the gene pool for future generations. Hence, if an animal sacrifices its life to save its pregnant mate or its offspring, it would be increasing the chances that genes like its own (its offspring's) would be carried on through future generations.

biological fitness:
The ability to get genes like yours into the gene pool for future generations.

kin selection:
A theory that animals sharing a high percentage of genes by common descent will be altruistic toward each other.

This emphasis on **kin selection** is currently a highly influential model among evolutionary biologists, probably because it provides a parsimonious explanation of factors such as altruism and, at the same time, is consistent with the more traditional view that each organism functions to maximize its own survival. In theory, the nearer the kin (the greater the percentage of genes shared by common descent), the greater will be the readiness to sacrifice (Hoffman, 1981). In support of this general position, Wilson (1975) pointed out that hive animals, in which all individuals share a high percentage of the same genes, are more altruistic than other animals. Much of Wilson's evidence from animal altruism originates from studies of bees, termites, and other hive insects. As an example of how the logic of kin selection altruism might be applied to humans, potential blood donors might be reminded that their blood type ensures that their plasma will ultimately help those who are their relatives (same blood type), albeit distant ones (Cunningham, 1986).

reciprocal altruism:
This sociobiological model suggests that it is in your long-term selfish interest to help others because this increases the chance that others will help you in the future.

A different approach is Robert Trivers's (1971) model of **reciprocal altruism**. He suggested that natural selection favors altruism because it is in the long-term selfish interest of individuals to help others, thereby increasing the chance that others will help them when they need it in the future. Reciprocal altruism is especially relevant when the situation involves: (1) low risk for the help, (2) high benefit for the recipient, (3) high expectation that the situation will be reversed, and (4) recognition between helper and recipient so that the favor can be returned later.

Is the distress shown by infants and children who see another person in pain evidence of an inherited altruistic or empathic response? Some analysts think so. Hoffman (1981, p. 130) suggested that "it seems reasonable to conclude that the newborn's reflexive cry may be an early, possibly innate precursor of empathic arousal, although it is obviously not a mature empathic response." Modern evolutionary biology calls for a biological basis for altruism, he argued, since humans who have been socialized in a highly individualistic society still respond altruistically to others in distress.

At a more general level, Rushton (1989) developed "genetic similarity theory," proposing that genetically similar people tend to seek each other out (as friends, spouses, in social groups, as people to help). This proposal that humans somehow can detect genetic similarity in others, and react to it, is very controversial. The journal in which Rushton published his 1989 article also contained commentaries on the theory by thirty-three other scientists. Many strongly disputed the data on which Rushton based his theoretical claims, but some (e.g., Kenrick, 1989) suggested that some of Rushton's theoretical positions are supported by social psychological research findings.

Criticisms of Sociobiological Explanations

Like many common sense generalizations, sociobiology can be used in hindsight to explain almost any behavior (Chapter 2). The theory may seem remarkably sensible; but remember (from Chapter 1) that the real test for a good theory is whether it enables us to derive hypotheses and predict future behavior, not just to explain what has already occurred. The predictive power of sociobiology is questionable at this time.

Critics call attention to the fact that no genes for altruism have ever been identified and that there are important differences between humans and the social insects, on which many of the altruism suppositions have been based. Cultural influences and learning clearly play a major role in the evolution of human prosocial behavior (Campbell, 1978; Cohen, 1978; Sahlins, 1976). At present, the evidence for and against genetic determinants of altruism in humans is mixed, so we should reserve judgment on the role of genetic determinants until more clear-cut research evidence is available.

Psychological States That Lead to Prosocial Behavior

We can differentiate between behavior that appears altruistically motivated and that which appears egoistically motivated. *Altruistically motivated helping* has the goal of increasing the recipient's welfare, and *egoistically motivated helping* is directed toward increasing the helper's own welfare. Many actions are a mixture of the two motives. Are humans or other animals ever truly altruistic, willingly sacrificing their welfare for someone else? There is no simple answer to that question. Suffice it to say that philosophers have been debating the issue for over two thousand years, since the time of Plato, without arriving at a consensus.

Empathy

Seeing another person suffer is quite unpleasant. Daniel Batson and his co-workers asserted that there are two distinct emotional responses to seeing another person suffer: personal distress and empathy. Personal distress leads to egoistic (selfish) motivation, Batson proposed, and **empathy** leads to altruistically motivated helping.

empathy:
An emotional state elicited by and congruent with the perceived welfare of someone else.

Empathy can be defined as "an emotional state elicited by and congruent with the perceived welfare of someone else" (Batson & Coke, 1983, p. 419). Empathy involves feeling positive emotion when the other person's situation is desirable and negative emotion when it is undesirable. Researchers suggest a two-stage model of the impact of empathy on helping. Assuming the perspective of a person in need and viewing the world as he or she views it increases one's empathic emotional response. This heightened emotion, in turn, increases one's motivation to help. Whether the origin of this empathic emotion is more a product of our genes (as the sociobiologist would assert) or of socialization is open to question.

Many studies have found that empathy generally leads to prosocial behavior (Eisenberg & Miller, 1987). But is the prosocial behavior egoistically or altruistically motivated? To test the link between empathy and altruism, Toi and Batson (1982) had subjects observe a victim in distress. They were instructed either to observe the victim's reactions (thought to produce low empathy) or to imagine the victim's feelings (thought to lead to high empathy). The researchers made it easy or difficult for the subject to escape the situation without helping. Toi and Batson reasoned that people who are egoistically motivated will help only when they cannot easily escape without helping. However, people who are altruistically motivated should help regardless of how easy or difficult it is to escape the situation. The results supported such an analysis. As Figure 7-2 indicates, most subjects in the low-empathy condition helped only when escape from the situation was difficult. In contrast, most subjects in the high-empathy condition helped regardless of the ease of escape. These results provide considerable evidence that altruism can be motivated by empathy.

Further supporting this distinction, a series of studies found that individuals who reported experiencing mostly personal distress helped less when it was easy to escape without helping, suggesting that their underlying emotion was an egoistic desire to reduce their own distress. In contrast, those who reported feeling empathy were as likely to help when escaping was easy as when it was difficult, suggesting that their underlying motivation was an altruistic desire to reduce the distress of the person in need (Batson et al., 1983).

Where does empathy come from? Batson (1983) attempted to incorporate a sociobiological perspective. He proposed that there is a genetic predisposition to respond to the distress of others—especially close kin—with empathic emotion, which may lead to altruistic behaviors. This analysis suggests why we help our close relatives (parents, children, siblings) but does not explain how more general altruism develops. Some social scien-

FIGURE 7-2

Empathy and Altruistic
Helping

*Percentage of subjects helping
another person as a function of
empathy and ease-of-escape
from the situation.*

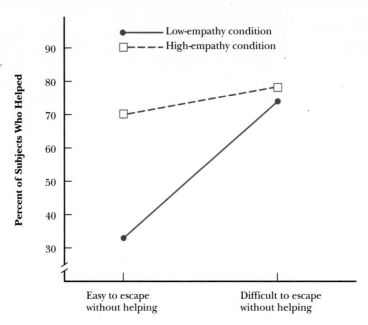

Source: Data from Toi, M., & Batson, C. D. (1982). More evidence that empathy is a
source of altruistic motivation. *Journal of Personality and Social Psychology, 43,* 281–292.

tists (Campbell, 1975) suggested that social institutions, especially religion, may broaden human empathic and altruistic responses. Batson (1983) proposed that religious imagery may extend kin-specific altruism to nonkin as well by extending the range of people we care for as "family" with kinship imagery, such as an emphasis on "brotherly love" and "we are all children of God." While this analysis is purely speculative at present, it provides an intriguing perspective on one possible role of religion in human society.

States Associated with Egoistic Helping

Guilt and Sympathy. In Chapter 5 we saw that guilt can influence a person to comply with a request. But while inducing guilt may be effective in getting someone to help, the recipient of help is seen as less likable and less respected than if the request for help elicited altruism instead (Rubin & Shaffer, 1987). Guilt may also have a general effect even when no specific request for helping is involved. We may experience guilt about some personal issue and then go out of our way to help someone else not at all connected with the events causing our guilt (Carlsmith et al., 1968). We may also be more likely to help someone when we feel sympathy for him because he has been mistreated by someone else (Eisenberg et al., 1989).

A Good Mood. A number of studies have investigated the impact on help-ing of a potential helper's mood. Studies have indicated that people who are in a good mood may be more generous and helpful to others than those who are not. For example, as a way of manipulating mood in a field experi-ment, Isen and Levin (1972) placed a dime in the coin return slot of a num-ber of phone booths so that the next telephone user would find it. A female confederate then waited near the phone booth until someone had gone into the booth, found the dime, and made his or her call. When the caller left the booth the confederate dropped a folder full of papers directly in the subject's path. As Figure 7-3 indicates, subjects who had found a dime in the phone booth (and were presumably in a better mood because of this small windfall) were much more likely to help the person pick up the papers than were those who had not found a dime.

In another study, Levin and Isen (1975) used the "lost letter" technique. They left a sealed, addressed envelope on the shelf in the phone booth. Once again, subjects who had found a dime were much more likely to help, this time by mailing the letter, than were subjects who had not found a dime. Other research indicates that this "mood effect" may not be very long-lasting. Isen et al. (1976) concluded that being put into a good mood increased sub-sequent helping initially, but as the good mood dissipated (after about twenty minutes), helpfulness decreased too.

FIGURE 7-3

The Impact of Mood on Helping

Percentage of people who help another person depending on whether the potential helper is in a good mood (just found a dime in the coin-return slot of a public telephone) or a neutral mood (did not find a dime).

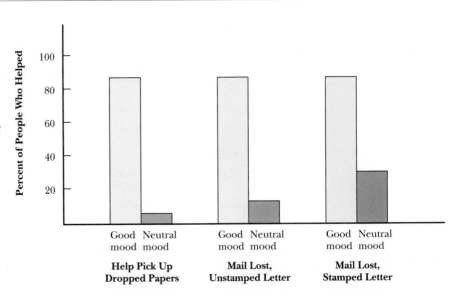

Source: Based on Levin, P. F., & Isen, A. M. (1975). Further studies on the effect of feeling good on helping. *Sociometry, 38,* 141–147; Isen, A., & Levin, P. (1972). The effect of feeling good on helping: Cookies and kindness. *Journal of Personality and Social Psychology, 21,* 384–388.

Even the weather can affect helping. Cunningham (1979) discovered that people generally are in better moods and more likely to help in nice weather. In both summer and winter the amount of sunshine (according to weather records) was positively associated with the amount of helping behavior. Cunningham labeled this the "Sunshine Samaritan effect." People even left larger tips in restaurants on a sunny day than on a cloudy, rainy one.

There are several reasons why good moods may increase helping. A pleasant mood may activate pleasant thoughts and memories (priming). As a consequence, happy people may feel more favorably toward those asking for help (Carlson et al., 1988). Helping others may also be a way to prolong one's good mood. Supporting this interpretation, people who don't expect their good mood to last are more helpful than those who expect their good mood to be long lasting (Yinon & Landau, 1987). Happy people whose attention is self-focused (Chapter 2) are especially likely to help (Berkowitz, 1987; Isen et al., 1978). Further, individuals in good moods are generally more active and thus are more likely to engage in a whole range of behaviors, including helping (Batson et al., 1979).

A Bad Mood. Bad moods lead to a wider variety of behaviors than do good moods (Isen, 1984). A number of studies have found that people in bad moods help more than those in good moods, but other studies have found conflicting results. Why might people in bad moods help more? One reason might be to "get out of the dumps," to make themselves feel better. The **negative state relief model** developed by Cialdini and his associates (Cialdini & Kenrick, 1976) asserts that helping others may be one means of relieving an unpleasant (negative) state. If the perceived benefits for helping are high and the costs are low, the perceived *reward value* for helping is high, and individuals in a bad mood should be quite likely to help, in order to improve their mood. Thus, negative mood may increase helping when helping is easy and highly rewarding, but it also may inhibit helping when helping would be difficult and not very rewarding (Weyant, 1978). A person will help when: (1) the helping is perceived as a pleasant experience; (2) the helper thinks that his or her bad mood is changeable; and (3) the helper believes that helping will be effective in improving the bad mood (Carlson & Miller, 1987).

negative state relief model:
A model suggesting that helping others may be a way to relieve the unpleasant state of a bad mood if the perceived reward value for helping is high and costs are low.

Who will be more helpful? Research shows that people in good moods are usualy helpful. Those in bad moods are sometimes helpful, too, if they feel that helping may get them into a better mood.

Most studies that found that bad moods increased helping have been conducted with adult subjects. Studies with children, on the other hand (Underwood et al., 1977), have often found that bad moods did not increase helping. Perhaps children have not yet learned that helping can be a way of pulling oneself out of a bad mood.

Focus of attention is important, too. Millar et al. (1988) proposed that helping will strengthen a mood if it shifts attention toward the cause of a mood but weaken the mood if it shifts attention away from the mood's source. Hence, if you are in a self-focused bad mood (e.g., moping about a personal failure), helping others will be effective in relieving the bad mood by changing your focus of attention. If your bad mood is other-focused, in contrast (e.g., a result of your roommate's slovenly habits), helping yourself, rather than others, should work best as a mood-improver.

Focus of attention also makes a difference in a more general way. People in bad moods may be less likely to notice the need for help and may be more helpful only if the need is clearly pointed out to them (McMillen et al., 1977). People in negative states who are focusing their attention on the problems of others are very helpful. However, negative-mood people whose attention is focused on their own needs, concerns, and losses, are not as likely to help (Thompson et al., 1980). Finally, there is evidence that helping is a more effective means of ending a bad mood when it is done publicly than when it is done privately (Kenrick et al., 1979).

Empathy vs. Egoistic Motives. We have seen that the likelihood of helping is greater from people in negative or positive moods than from those in neutral moods. Do these findings indicate that altruism in adults is actually a form of hedonism, equivalent to self-gratification? Baumann and associates (1981) asserted that we are socialized to find altruistic behavior self-gratifying, and that we therefore behave charitably in order to provide ourselves with reward (self-gratification).

Motivation for helping might be different for people in good or bad moods. Enhanced helping might be a direct effect of a bad mood (attempted self-reward), but an indirect effect of a good mood (from increased liking for others, activity, pleasant thoughts, equity considerations). In support of this interpretation, Manucia et al. (1984) found that when given an opportunity to be helpful, most sad subjects were helpful only when they believed that their mood was changeable. In contrast, most happy subjects helped regardless of whether or not they believed that their present mood could be changed.

Cialdini and his co-workers (1987) attempted to explain the empathy findings in terms of the negative state relief model. They argued that empathy produces helping because a person who responds empathically to someone in distress feels saddened and is motivated to help in order to elevate his or her *own* mood. As support for this interpretation, Schaller and Cialdini (1988) found that high-empathy people helped much more often than low-empathy people when no other opportunity to improve their mood was

FIGURE 7-4

Empathy and the Negative State Relief Model

People feeling high empathy are more helpful when no other way to change their sad mood is available (left side of figure). If other means of mood elevation are available (center and right of figure), high-empathy people do not help significantly more than low-empathy people.

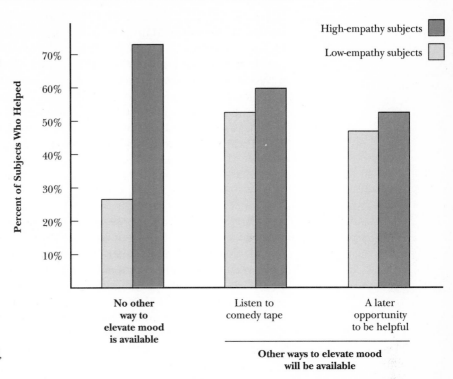

Source: Data from Schaller, M., & Cialdini, R. B. (1988). The economics of empathic helping: Support for a mood management motive. *Journal of Experimental Social Psychology, 24,* 163–181.

available (left side of Figure 7-4). However, when other ways to lose their sadness were available (knowing that they were going to listen to a comedy tape or would have the opportunity later to help a third person), high-empathy people were not significantly more helpful than low-empathy people. So even empathy-based helping may be egoistic, viewed from this perspective. Batson and his co-workers (1988; 1989) disagreed with this interpretation on the basis of their own research findings that the rate of helping among high-empathy subjects was no lower when they already anticipated mood enhancement (so there would be no need to be helpful if one's goal was only to improve one's mood) than when they did not.

Batson, Cialdini, and others have designed ever-more-intricate studies intended to test the two competing models and have continued to find conflicting results (e.g., Cialdini & Fultz, 1990; Miller & Carlson, 1990). Batson (1990, p. 344) commented, "I believe that an objective assessment of the evidence to date suggests that this [negative state relief] explanation is probably wrong, but of course I may be the one who is wrong." Stay tuned.

Unpleasant Arousal. Observing someone in need can be unpleasantly arousing to the observer, especially in intense situations such as emergencies. Jane Piliavin and her co-workers (1981) proposed that witnessing an emergency is physiologically and emotionally arousing. The level of arousal is greater: (1) when the emergency is perceived as severe, (2) when the bystander feels emotional involvement, empathy, or similarity with the victim, (3) when the victim is physically close to the bystander, and (4) when considerable time has elapsed without the victim's receiving help. In most cases, a bystander will respond in a way that reduces the arousal as rapidly and completely as possible, Piliavin theorized, with the least possible cost to himself or herself. If helping is to occur, it is important that the bystander interpret the arousal as caused by the victim's distress, rather than by something else. I will have more to say about this model when we look specifically at helping in emergency situations.

Helping: Altruism or Hedonism?

The five psychological states theorized to lead to prosocial behavior are summarized in Figure 7-5. As you have undoubtedly noticed, all but one refer to egoistic, rather than altruistic, motives. This may seem a familiar orientation; we saw in Chapter 3 that many recent social psychological theories emphasize a kind of "social egoism" (Batson, 1990) in social motives: self-presentation, self-enhancement, self-handicapping, self-evaluation maintenance, self-affirmation, self-discrepancy, and so forth. Each of these theories assumes egoistic motivation with the self-serving goal of maintaining or enhancing a positive self-image. To return to our question raised in Chapter 1, does this mean that most (or all) prosocial behavior is egoistically motivated? Let's look further.

Personality and Prosocial Behavior

The Ability to Self-Reward

We have seen that people who have learned that helping behavior is desirable can reward themselves if they help, enabling them to feel good about themselves (Bandura, 1977). It should be easier to engage in self-reward if one can attribute the helpfulness to an internal disposition (such as altruism, compassion, and goodness) than if the helpfulness is attributed to an external situational factor. As an example, Batson, Harris, and their colleagues (1979) arranged situations in which their subjects helped another person and subsequently were led to attribute their helpfulness either to compassion (a disposition) or to being forced to help (an external factor). When given another opportunity to be helpful, 60 percent of those who were led to attribute their earlier helping to compassion helped again; only 25 percent of those who had attributed their earlier helping to the external factor helped again. In a similar vein, individuals who agree to help because of the norm of reciprocity (you should help those who have helped you) tend to perceive themselves as less altruistic than people who help when reciprocity was not a factor (Thomas & Batson, 1981).

A paragon of helpfulness: pioneering nurse Florence Nightengale.

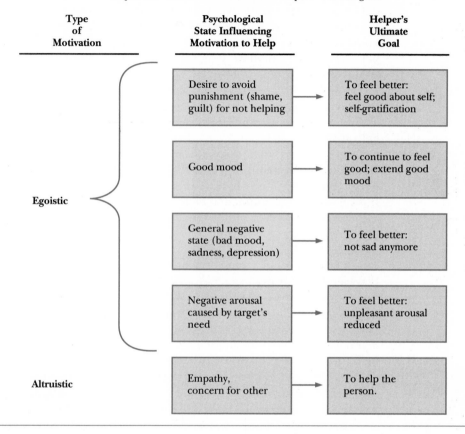

FIGURE 7-5

Psychological States That May Lead to Prosocial Behavior in Potential Helpers

General psychological states that may determine whether or not a person will be motivated to help someone who is in need, and the helper's ultimate goal.

Type of Motivation	Psychological State Influencing Motivation to Help	Helper's Ultimate Goal
Egoistic	Desire to avoid punishment (shame, guilt) for not helping	To feel better: feel good about self; self-gratification
	Good mood	To continue to feel good; extend good mood
	General negative state (bad mood, sadness, depression)	To feel better: not sad anymore
	Negative arousal caused by target's need	To feel better: unpleasant arousal reduced
Altruistic	Empathy, concern for other	To help the person.

A paragon of helpfulness: Swiss humanitarian Dr. Albert Schweitzer.

It is widely assumed that telling people about helpful models such as the Good Samaritan, Florence Nightingale, and Albert Schweitzer will encourage them to become more helpful individuals. But applying self-perception theory, one could hypothesize that being told about such helpful models could actually lessen people's motivation to help. They might feel that their own helpful behavior was caused by an external factor—the example of the helpful models. If this is so, people would be less likely to make a dispositional attribution for their own helpfulness, and as a result would be unable to reward themselves for helping. Thomas, Batson, and Coke (1981) found empirical evidence of this process. Thus, exposure to paragons of helpfulness may not have the desired effect of increasing helping behavior in the future.

Relationships between People

We tend to feel the most empathy toward those with whom we have a close relationship, such as friends, family, and lovers, because we are especially sensitive to their needs. Margaret Clark and her co-workers (1987) found that potential helpers were much more affected by a recipient's sadness when the helper had a "communal relationship" to the recipient (e.g., friends, family), than when they had an "exchange relationship" (e.g., strangers, business associates). Helping someone in a communal relationship improves the helper's mood more than helping someone in an exchange relationship does (Williamson & Clark, 1989).

People who grew up in small towns are more likely to be helpful than those who grew up in cities (Amato, 1983; House & Wolf, 1978). Further, analysis of sixty-five studies showed that people are more likely to receive help if they are in a rural area than in an urban area (Steblay, 1987). Perhaps one reason is that small-town residents have had more experiences with communal relationships. This regional variation is not due just to different personalities or values of the people who live in cities or rural areas, though. It is related to environmental factors in cities that discourage helping, such as noise, traffic levels, and population density, and social factors like perceived vulnerability to crime and the presence of different ethnic groups (Steblay, 1987).

Growing up in a small town does not always make one more helpful, however. Political and social factors may work against helping behavior. Hansson and Slade (1977) found that small-town dwellers were less likely to help in some situations, because they were less tolerant of deviance. When apparently lost letters were addressed to ordinary people (such as M. J. Davis at a post office box), small-town residents were slightly more likely to help by returning the lost letter than were city dwellers. However, when the letter was addressed to the Friends of the Communist Party, small-town dwellers were significantly less likely to help by mailing it than were city dwellers. The town dwellers were more choosy about whom they would help.

Recall that Piliavin et al. (1981) theorized that much helping in emergencies may be motivated by the desire to reduce the unpleasant arousal that the potential helper feels. They proposed further that arousal will be greater (and the motivation to help will be greater as well) when the helper has a feeling of "we-ness" with the person needing help. Friendship, similar backgrounds, and similarity in appearance, race, or gender can all affect feelings of "we-ness." I'll return to this issue later when analyzing emergency helping.

Personality Traits

A number of researchers have tried to identify personality characteristics that may make some individuals more likely to help than others. Studies have identified several personality factors that seem to be related to a prosocial personality. These include high self-esteem, the belief that one has control

of belief in a just world helped others to a greater degree than did those who scored low (Zuckerman, 1975). After the exam was over, though, there were no differences in helping behavior. Zuckerman speculated that those who held a strong belief in a just world helped more before the exam in order to make themselves more "deserving" of a good grade on the exam.

norm of social responsibility:
A social norm that we should help people in need when they are dependent upon us.

Also relevant is the **norm of social responsibility**, which suggests that we should help people in need when they are dependent upon us. It has been surprisingly difficult, however, to demonstrate any relationship between belief in such a norm and helping behavior. After a decade of research in this effort, Berkowitz (1972) suggested that the potency of a social responsibility norm had been greatly exaggerated. One explanation for its being so hard to pin down is that it may be too general. If everyone in our society adheres to the norm, then it will not be effective in accounting for why one person helps and another does not.

Even the way a request for help is phrased can make a difference. Several studies (Cialdini & Schroeder, 1976; Weyant, 1984) found that when asking for contributions, simply adding the phrase, "Even a penny will help", significantly increased the amount of donations. Perhaps legitimizing small donations takes away the commonly used excuse about being short of money. In contrast, asking for very large donations reduces the likelihood that people will contribute at all (Weyant & Smith, 1987).

Social Norms Discouraging Helping

norm of noninvolvement:
A social norm, often prevalent in urban areas, that people should not involve themselves in other people's affairs.

One reason that city dwellers are usually less helpful than small-town residents is that a **norm of noninvolvement** is often prevalent in urban areas. The norm may develop because everyone realizes that in cities people cannot continually involve themselves in each other's affairs; to do so would create conditions of continually frustrating distraction. Because population density is high, inputs from the environment may be too numerous to cope with or may arrive too rapidly. This overabundance of stimulation can lead to conditions that Milgram (1970) called **cognitive overload**. When overload is present, adaptations must occur. The human system must set priorities and make choices.

cognitive overload:
When inputs from the environment are too numerous to cope with or arrive too rapidly.

A number of adaptive responses to overload might be made by city dwellers. One adaptation is to give less time to each input; interactions are more brief and superficial. A second adaptive response is to disregard low-priority inputs. Time and energy are reserved for carefully defined goals (for example, the urbanite disregards the needs of others as he navigates purposefully through a crowded sidewalk). A third adaptation is to block off reception of inputs. City dwellers increasingly use unlisted telephone numbers to prevent strangers from calling them. More subtly, they block inputs by assuming an unfriendly expression, which discourages others from making contact. Less time given to each input means less opportunity for a potential helper to become familiar with the problem and feel empathy

The norm of noninvolvement. Passengers in a subway car carefully try not to pay attention to each other.

for the distressed person. Since low-priority inputs are disregarded, if the person needing help is not a central feature in the cognitive world of others, he may never be noticed and, thus, will not be helped. Each of these adaptions would make helping less frequent in urban situations, even though more potential helpers are around.

Helper-Recipient Interactions

Gender

Women generally receive help more often than men do, and men help in more situations than women do, according to a meta-analysis of 172 different studies (Eagly & Crowley, 1986). Why do these gender differences exist? One reason, undoubtedly, is the male gender role in our culture, which stresses chivalry, heroism, and assertiveness (cf. Chapter 11). In support of this interpretation, studies have found that gender differences are particularly large when the recipient is a woman and there are onlookers (who presumably make the gender roles more salient). Men may also be more likely to have the acquired skills necessary to help (e.g., knowing how to fix a flat tire) or the size and strength to make them less vulnerable in potentially dangerous helping situations. Thus, for example, researchers found that when a female motorist appeared to need help (she was in the process of jacking up the car to change a tire), about one car out of every four stopped to offer assistance. When the victim was male, only one car out of fifty stopped, and the drivers who did were almost all males (Pomazal & Clore, 1973; West et al., 1975). Pomazal and Clore also found that female hitchhikers were much more likely than male hitchhikers to be picked up. Again, as with the tire-changing study, almost all who offered rides were males.

When will a stranded motorist be helped? Research shows that female motorists are more likely to be helped than are males, and most helpers will be men.

Race

Given the levels of interracial hostility prevalent in our culture (Chapter 11), one might expect that people would be relatively unlikely to help others of a different race. Some research evidence supports this assumption. Gaertner and Bickman (1971) carried out a "wrong number study" to see how often residents would help a stranded motorist who had mistakenly called their number. The stranded motorist was helped significantly more often by male subjects (67 percent of the time) than by female subjects (55 percent). They also discovered that white respondents helped white motorists (who had a "white accent" on the phone) somewhat more often than black motorists (who had a "black accent"), but black respondents helped white and black motorists with about equal frequency. Hence, there appeared to be some racial distinction on the part of white subjects but not on the part of black subjects.

The impact of race and sex on helping was also investigated by Brigham and Richardson (1979), who organized almost a hundred visits to convenience stores (Figure 7-6). Their "customer" would bring a product costing between $1.15 and $1.50 up to the counter, and then discover that he or she had only a dollar. The customer asked the clerk to help by allowing the purchase of the product for a dollar. In 55 percent of the visits, the clerk helped. Both race and gender affected how often the customers were helped by white clerks. Whites and black females were all helped to an approximately equal degree (about 60 to 70 percent), but black males were helped considerably less often (33 percent). Several students of each race and sex served as customers, so the reaction toward any one race/sex category could not have been due to a personal characteristic of any single customer.

Reverse Discrimination

While discrimination against minority-group members in helping occurs, there also are situations where reverse discrimination may take place. Donald Dutton focused on the need in many whites to maintain an egalitarian self-image and avoid appearing prejudiced. If, for instance, a white woman denies a request made by a black (whose group has historically suffered from widespread discrimination), she may worry that her own behavior represents yet another instance of discrimination. If she considers herself egalitarian, this possibility may be quite threatening to her self-image, and so she may seek out opportunities to reinstate her egalitarian self-image. Helping a person of another race can provide one such opportunity.

In a pair of field studies, Dutton demonstrated the existence of a **reverse discrimination effect,** where whites behaved more favorably to blacks than to other whites in the same situation. In a restaurant with a dress code (coat and tie for males), blacks who were not dressed according to the code were more likely to be admitted than were improperly dressed whites (Dutton, 1971). In another study, greater donations were given to a black pan-

reverse discrimination effect:

When majority-group members behave more favorably to racial minority-group members than to majority-group members.

FIGURE 7-6

Impact of Race and Sex on Helping Behavior

Likelihood of receiving help from white convenience store clerks by being allowed to purchase for $1.00 a product costing from $1.15 to $1.50.

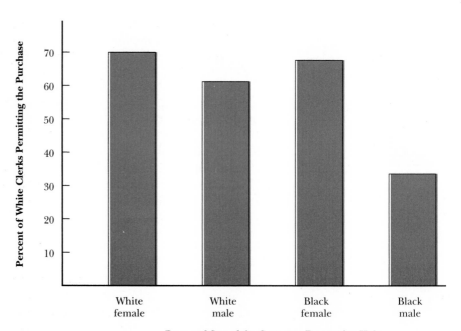

Source: Data from Brigham, J. C., & Richardson, C. B. (1979). Race, sex, and helping in the marketplace. *Journal of Applied Social Psychology, 9,* 314–322.

handler than to a white panhandler by white subjects who had previously been led to believe that they might be racially prejudiced (Dutton & Lake, 1973). These subjects avoided threats to their egalitarian self-image by over-compensating in their behavior toward blacks, thus convincing themselves that they really weren't racially prejudiced.

These studies involved somewhat trivial or token situations that had few costs for helping. If helping a minority-group member in such a token situation serves to reaffirm the white's egalitarian self-image, the white may feel no special pressure to be helpful in another situation — she has already "paid her dues." From this reasoning, Dutton and Lennox (1974) predicted that whites who had already given token help to a black would be less likely to help blacks later in more costly situations than would whites who had not had the opportunity to be helpful in the token situation. Supporting this hypothesis, they found that whites who had been told they might be prejudiced and then had the opportunity to contribute to a black panhandler (84 percent contributed) were less likely to volunteer later for Brotherhood Week activities than did whites who had encountered a white

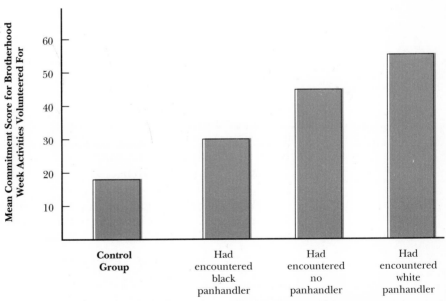

FIGURE 7-7

The Effect of "Token" Compliance on Subsequent Interracial Behavior

Average commitment score for Brotherhood Week activities endorsed on a commitment form by white subjects.

Source: Data from Dutton, D. G., & Lennox, V. L. (1974). Effect of prior "token" compliance on subsequent interracial behavior. *Journal of Personality and Social Psychology, 29,* 65–71.

panhandler or no panhandler. The subjects who had already given money to the black panhandler, having demonstrated their lack of prejudice, felt no need to engage in further activity to convince themselves and others that they were not prejudiced. Those who had not had the opportunity to engage in this token behavior (had encountered the white panhandler or no panhandler) were more likely to volunteer for Brotherhood Week activities (Figure 7-7).

There is an alternative way to interpret these findings. Encountering a black panhandler might have led to negative feelings toward blacks, perhaps reinforcing some of the prejudiced subjects' stereotype or schema of blacks as lazy or lacking ambition. These negative feelings could make later helping less likely. This interpretation received support from a study by Rosenfield and his co-workers (1982), who replicated the Dutton-Lennox procedures, except that subjects encountered either a black graduate student asking for signatures on a petition supporting more research on sickle-cell anemia, or a black panhandler. Subjects who encountered the black panhandler were less likely to help blacks later on, as Dutton and Lennox (1974) had found; but those who had encountered the black graduate student were just as likely later to help blacks as those who did not encounter a black person. These results suggest that negative feelings or apparent confirmation of stereotypes can also suppress helping toward minority-group members.

REACTIONS TO BEING HELPED

It is often difficult to ask for help. To do so may indicate that you can't handle the situation, threatening your self-esteem and leading to embarrassment or feelings of incompetence. Shy people, for example, ask for help less often from those of the opposite sex than do non-shy people (De Paulo et al., 1989). In addition, one may not wish to feel indebted to the helper (Williams & Williams, 1983). Hence, once help is offered, whether requested or not, the recipient's reaction may not be very grateful. An Indian proverb asks, "Why do you hate me? I've never even helped you" (Nadler & Fisher, 1986, p. 82). Why might recipients of help react this way?

Equity and Reactance Theory Predictions

Both equity theory (to be discussed in more detail in Chapter 9) and reactance theory (introduced in Chapter 5) predict that the reaction to helping will sometimes be negative. Equity theory asserts that individuals desire to maintain equity in their relationships, receiving a level of benefits they feel entitled to, and feel discomfort when a relationship becomes inequitable. From this view, receiving help might lead to feelings of inequity and indebtedness. One might try to restore equity by refusing the aid, derogating the helper and/or the aid, or helping the helper in return (Greenberg, 1980). People will avoid seeking help if they anticipate that it will be difficult to reciprocate in order to restore equity (Riley & Eckenrode, 1986).

Reactance theory asserts that any perceived loss of freedom results in a negative psychological state (reactance), which motivates people to restore their lost freedom. Receiving aid can restrict one's freedom in some situations such as welfare, hospitalization, and old-age homes. If the donors restrict the way in which aid can be used, the recipients may resent the help and the donor. Other nations' reactions to U.S. foreign aid (Gergen & Gergen, 1974) and the reactions of minority groups within the United States to some attempts at aid are examples of such reactions.

Threat-to-Self-Esteem Model

A more broadly based model for predicting reactions to aid has been developed by Jeffrey Fisher and Ari Nadler (Nadler & Fisher, 1986). They proposed that a negative response to aid is likely when the aid contains a negative self-message for the recipient, conflicts with the recipient's values (independence, self-reliance, dealing fairly with others, being treated fairly by others), or is not effective.

threat-to-self-esteem model:
Proposes that a negative response to aid is likely when the aid contains a negative self-message for the recipient, conflicts with the recipient's values, or is not effective.

An overview of the **threat-to-self-esteem model** is presented in Figure 7-8. The key factor is whether the aid is seen as *self-threatening* or *self-supporting* by the recipient. This is determined by: (1) the effectiveness of the aid, (2) characteristics of the donor (such as similarity to the recipient), and (3) characteristics of the recipient (such as self-esteem). The recipient will react positively if the aid is seen as self-supporting, and negatively if it is perceived as self-threatening. When the help threatens the recipient's self-esteem, her overall reaction will depend on whether she views her future outcomes as largely controllable or uncontrollable. If the future outcomes are viewed as controllable, the recipient is likely to feel short-term psychological distress (negative affect, negative evaluation of donor and aid) but will make positive instrumental responses (efforts to help herself). After the threat has been handled by self-help, she will feel good about her newly gained independence. An example might be an immigrant physician who needs short-term help getting settled in the U.S., but is able to make it on her own (self-help) once she has gotten established.

People who feel that their outcomes are not controllable, in contrast, don't make self-help responses. They continue to feel bad about the help they receive and are likely to sink into a state of dependency or learned helplessness (Chapter 3). An example might be a long-term welfare recipient who has concluded that she has no hope of getting off welfare because of racial discrimination.

Many needy persons who receive help are at a physical, psychological, or financial low point in their lives. At this point they may not view themselves as able to control their environment. Help under those conditions is

FIGURE 7-8

Reactions to Help

The threat-to-self-esteem model predicts whether an offer of help will be perceived favorably or unfavorably by the recipient (based on Nadler & Fisher, 1986).

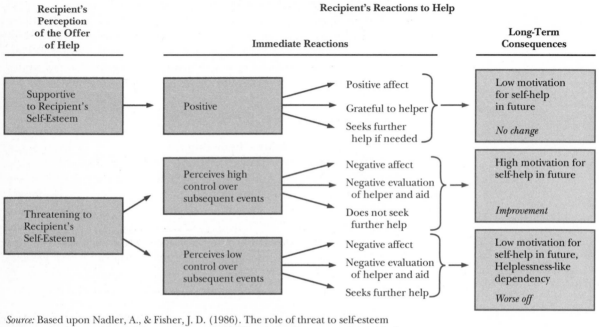

Source: Based upon Nadler, A., & Fisher, J. D. (1986). The role of threat to self-esteem and perceived control in recipient reaction to help: Theory development and empirical validation. In L. Berkowitz (Ed.), *Advances in experimental social psychology* (Vol. 19, pp. 81–122). Orlando, FL: Academic Press.

likely to yield helplessness-like passivity. Hence, paradoxically, at points of greatest need, help may be ineffective. What can be done to resolve this paradox? Helpers can take steps to increase the recipient's motivation for control or perceived ability to achieve control (recall our discussion of *reattribution training* in Chapter 3). Helpers might, for example, give specific behavioral coping suggestions designed to raise motivation or increase perceptions of control.

While high self-esteem is usually seen as a good thing, it may be a handicap when help is needed. Persons with high self-esteem (e.g., leaders) often feel threatened by aid from similar others (e.g., other leaders) on an important issue, finding it inconsistent with their view of themselves as strong and independent. How can people help leaders without threatening them? Researchers suggest that one could offer the leader a choice of helpers varying in similarity, or stress the special expertise of the helper and the benefits the recipient would derive (Fisher & Nadler, 1982).

HELPING IN EMERGENCY SITUATIONS

The Latané and Darley Model

Much recent attention in social psychology has focused on helping behavior within the context of an emergency situation. This research interest has stemmed from the grave concern and puzzlement produced by reports of seemingly bizarre events—tragic cases in which individuals in dire need of help have gone unaided, even as dozens of people witnessed their plight. The end result of this failure to give aid has often been the further injury, or even death, of the person in the emergency situation. Do occurrences such as this reflect apathy, callousness, and lack of concern for others in modern urban society? Do they illustrate the norm of noninvolvement? Or are there other factors that may explain such an appalling lack of response?

Bibb Latané and John Darley initiated a program of research to answer such questions. They began by identifying the special characteristics that differentiate an emergency situation from a nonemergency situation (Latané & Darley, 1969; 1970): (1) An emergency involves *threat or harm.* There are relatively few positive payoffs for the witness who takes a successful action in an emergency; usually the best that can be hoped for is a return to the status quo. (2) Emergencies are unusual and *rare events* and people will have had little personal experience in handling such situations. (3) Emergencies *differ widely* from one another. Each emergency (a drowning, a fire, an assault) presents a different type of problem, and each requires a different type of action by the witness. (4) Emergencies are *unforeseen;* they emerge suddenly and without warning and hence must be handled without benefit of forethought or planning. (5) An emergency requires *instant action.* The witness must make a decision before he or she has had time to consider the alternatives, which places the witness in a condition of stress. All of these characteristics provide good reasons for a person not to intervene. As Latané and Darley (1969) commented, "The bystander to an emergency situation is in an unenviable position. It is perhaps surprising that anyone should intervene at all."

Latané and Darley proposed that when a person is confronted with an emergency situation (defined in terms of the unique characteristics outlined above), there is a series of *decision points* through which that person must pass if he or she is going to intervene. These points are depicted in Figure 7-9. Only one specific set of choices will lead the person to take action in the situation.

First, the bystander must *notice the situation.* If bystanders are so lost in their own thoughts or so concerned with minding their own business that the event is not noticed, obviously they are not going to intervene. If the person does notice the event, he must then *interpret* it. In the example that

FOCUS 7-2

The Kitty Genovese Case: Stimulus to Research

Perhaps the best-known incident of bystander nonintervention concerned Kitty Genovese, a young woman living in the Kew Gardens section of New York City. At 3:30 A.M. on the morning of March 31, 1964, Ms. Genovese was returning home from her job as manager of a bar. She parked her car in the parking lot and headed for her apartment. Noticing a man at the far end of the lot and becoming nervous, she headed toward a nearby police call box but got only as far as the streetlights before the man grabbed her. She screamed, "Oh, my God! He stabbed me. Please help me!" Later investigators discovered that at least thirty-eight of Ms. Genovese's neighbors went to their windows to see what was happening. One, in fact, shouted, "Let that girl alone!" However, moments later, the man returned to Ms. Genovese and stabbed her once again. Lights went on again in many apartments, and the assailant got into his car and drove away.

Incredibly, the assailant returned again. One neighbor was watching out his window and picked up the phone to call the police, "Don't," his wife said, "thirty people have probably called by now." By then it was 3:45 A.M. and Kitty had crawled to the back of her building looking for safety. The killer found her there, slumped against the stairs. He stabbed her again, this time fatally. One-half hour and thirty-eight witnesses later, Kitty Genovese was dead. At 3:50 A.M. the police received the first call and were at the scene in two minutes. It later turned out that the neighbor who made the call, a "friend" of Kitty's, had crossed the roof of the building to the apartment of an elderly woman to ask her to make the call. Before he had even done that, he had phoned a friend in Nassau County for advice. By the time police questioned him, he was drunk, guilt-ridden, and distraught (Allen, 1978; *New York Times*, March 28, 1964; Rosenthal, 1964).

Ironically, the murderer was caught some time later by two bystanders who *did* intervene. One man saw him carrying a TV out of a neighbor's apartment. When asked what he was doing, he calmly replied, "Oh, I'm just helping these people move." The neighbor consulted a friend who lived nearby and they agreed that it was probably a theft. When the thief returned to the apartment, one man called the police while the other ripped the distributor from the thief's car, disabling it. After he was apprehended, the thief confessed to the Genovese murder and several other assaults.

Why were these neighbors so helpful while Kitty's neighbors had been so meek? Perhaps one reason is that they did not know that this petty thief was also a vicious killer (Allen, 1978). In addition, the robbery was a less ambiguous situation, and diffusion of responsibility is less likely to occur among friends than among strangers. ❖

The Intervention Process

Steps a bystander (potential helper) must go through if he or she is to help in an emergency situation.

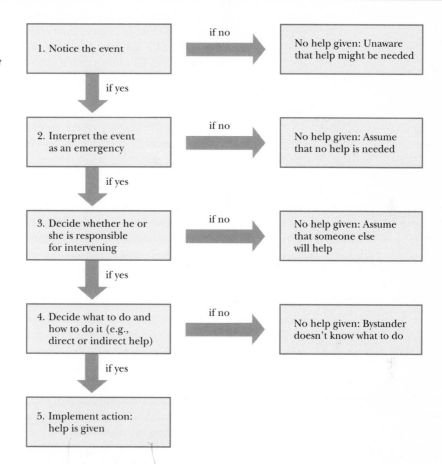

1. Notice the event	if no →	No help given: Unaware that help might be needed

if yes ↓

2. Interpret the event as an emergency	if no →	No help given: Assume that no help is needed

if yes ↓

3. Decide whether he or she is responsible for intervening	if no →	No help given: Assume that someone else will help

if yes ↓

4. Decide what to do and how to do it (e.g., direct or indirect help)	if no →	No help given: Bystander doesn't know what to do

if yes ↓

5. Implement action: help is given

Source: Based on Latané, B., & Darley, J. M. (1969). Bystander apathy. *American Scientist, 57,* 224–268; Latané, B., & Darley, J. M. (1970). *The unresponsive bystander: Why doesn't he help?* New York: Appleton-Century-Crofts.

began this chapter, are the two people in the parking lot friends or strangers? Is the scuffle an assault or playful tussling? In other words, is the situation an emergency or not? The third step involves deciding whether one has a *responsibility to act* in the emergency situation. Perhaps assistance is already on the way, or someone else may be better qualified to help. Or perhaps the bystander will decide that the emergency is simply none of his business.

According to the model, bystanders who have made the intervention choice at each of the three points above will have noticed the event, interpreted it as an emergency, and accepted personal responsibility to take action. The next step in this sequence involves more practical questions: *what* to do and *how* to do it. The bystander may take either of two courses of action at this point. He may undertake *direct intervention*: swimming out to someone who is drowning, grabbing an extinguisher to put out a fire, fighting off a mugger; or he may choose *indirect intervention*: attempting to report the emergency to the relevant authority (a lifeguard, the fire department, the police) rather than trying to cope with it directly. The amount of danger facing the bystander and his degree of skill or power may be major determinants as to which course of action to take. Witnesses to the Kitty Genovese murder did not take either step until it was too late (Focus 7-2).

Latané and Darley proposed that the intervention process is most likely to break down at the second or third stage — in interpreting the situation as an emergency, or in deciding whether one is responsible for intervention. Latané and Darley identified three social processes that could interfere with a bystander's decision to help when others are present. The first, **diffusion of responsibility**, occurs because the bystander feels incompetent to help, the victim is viewed as undeserving of help, or the individual thinks others are present and available to help (Latané & Nida, 1981). If responsibility is shared with others who are present, the more bystanders, the less responsibility for each individual. Bystanders may assume that someone else has already helped (say, by calling the police or an ambulance) or that other bystanders are bound to have more relevant skills (first-aid training, strength) than they. The costs for not helping (blame, guilt) can be reduced for any individual by assuming (or rationalizing) that responsibility for helping is shared by all of the bystanders.

Two social influence processes may also play a role. One process is **pluralistic ignorance**. If an emergency is ambiguous, each bystander initially is likely to appear unconcerned. But, in fact, each has not yet decided whether there is cause for concern. Until someone acts, each bystander sees only seemingly calm, nonresponding bystanders around. The other bystanders are serving as sources of normative influence (the normative behavior is to act unconcerned) and informational influence (it seems not to be an emergency) for each bystander. As a result, each bystander may decide, "Well, everyone else looks as though they're not worried, so it must not be an emergency." Each bystander is ignorant of the fact that the others may actually be just as uncertain or worried as he. The result is that no one interprets the event as an emergency and no one helps.

Fellow bystanders also increase the potential cost of making an inappropriate response. The fear of being evaluated negatively for helping leads to an **audience inhibition effect**. In ambiguous situations potential helpers may not be sure how other bystanders will view their attempts to help. Potential helpers will be inhibited when they fear that others see helping as inappropriate (Schwartz & Gottlieb, 1980). People who are especially sensitive to embarrassment and loss of poise are the most likely to be inhibited (Tice & Baumeister, 1985). Further, if other bystanders arrive only after the at-

diffusion of responsibility:
In emergency situations, the more bystanders present, the less responsibility each individual bystander feels.

pluralistic ignorance:
Bystanders to an emergency may interpret the situation as a nonemergency due to the apparently calm reaction of other bystanders.

audience inhibition effect:
People are inhibited from helping by fear of embarrassment and negative evaluations from other bystanders.

tempt to help has begun, they may mistakenly assume that the helper was responsible for harming the person needing help (Cacioppo, Petty, & Losch, 1986). Interestingly, most people believe that fear of embarrassment is a more potent determinant of their own behavior than of the behavior of others (Miller & McFarland, 1987).

Research on Helping in Emergencies

The Number of Bystanders

The steps taken by Latané and Darley provide a markedly clear instance of the scientific procedures depicted in Figure 1-1 in Chapter 1. The Kitty Geno-vese case (Focus 7-2) provided the initial facts that motivated Latané and Darley. From these facts and from their analysis of the factors unique to emergency situations, they developed a theory that the influence of other bystanders might have a dramatic effect on whether or not a person helps in an emergency. This theory produced the hypothesis that in an emergency situation, the greater the number of bystanders, the less the likelihood that a victim will receive help. Latané and Darley then carried out a series of studies to test this hypothesis.

In a "woman in distress" study, Latané and Rodin (1969) had subjects come to the laboratory to participate in a survey. Upon arrival, they were met at the door by an attractive young woman and taken to the testing room. Through an open door they were able to see a desk, filing cabinets, and a bookcase piled high with papers. The young woman then closed a collapsi-ble curtain between the waiting room and her office and stayed in her of-fice shuffling papers, opening and closing drawers, and making enough noise to remind the subjects of her presence. Four minutes later she turned on a tape recorder, which made it sound as though she had climbed up on a chair to reach a stack of papers on the bookcase. Subjects then heard a loud crash and a scream as the chair apparently collapsed, and she fell to the floor. "Oh my God, my foot ... I ... I ... can't move ... it. Oh, my ankle," she moaned, "I ... can't get this ... thing ... off me."

Seventy percent of the students waiting alone tried to help by pulling open the curtain or running out the other door looking for help. When two strangers were waiting together, only 40 percent of the time did either of them help. In a third condition, two friends had signed up and were waiting together; 70 percent of the time at least one of the friends helped. A final condition involved a subject and an experimental confederate trained to act unconcerned and nonchalant about the event. In this case, only 7 percent of the time did the subject go for help. In a second study (Latané & Darley, 1968), college students were alone or in groups of three, waiting to be called for an interview, when smoke began to leak into the room through a wall vent. Here again, unaccompanied subjects were much more likely to help (75 percent) by looking for the experimenters than were the three-person groups (38 percent). When two of the three people in the group were con-federates who acted unconcerned, only 10 percent of the time did the real subject go for help. Hence, in both studies the presence of others and their behavior dramatically affected the likelihood of helping. When questioned later, those who had not intervened claimed that they were unsure of what had occurred, that the situation did not seem too serious (pluralistic ignorance), or that they thought other people would help (diffusion of responsibility). Few people recognized the impact of the other bystanders' actions on their own behavior.

Ambiguity of the Situation

You might still wonder why more people did not help. One reason might be because Latané and Rodin used a tape-recorded situation. Although the subjects could hear the fall and screams, they could not feel the thud of a body hitting the floor. Thus, the situation was still somewhat ambiguous. In a replication of this paradigm, Clark and Word (1972) had a technician pass through the waiting room, carrying an aluminum stepladder and some venetian blinds. He closed the door to an adjoining room, climbed up the stepladder, dropped the blinds, jumped to the floor, and pulled the stepladder over on top of him. This situation was much less ambiguous because the subject could both hear and feel the fall.

Depending on the condition, either one, two, or five persons witnessed the fall. In the low-ambiguity situation the man also cried out in agony after the fall; in the high-ambiguity condition he made no verbal sounds. Every subject in the low-ambiguity situation helped, regardless of the number of bystanders. In the high-ambiguity condition, helping occurred only about 30 percent of the time. Here subjects in the two- and five-person groups were less likely to help than would have been expected on the basis of the alone subjects' responses, a result parallel to what Latané and Rodin had found.

In another study, Clark and Word (1974) varied the ambiguity of a potentially dangerous situation. Subjects, either alone or in groups of two, walked by a room while a technician was working on some electrical equipment. A serious shock was simulated by a flash of light and a dull buzzing sound that emanated from the equipment. In the low-ambiguity condition, the subjects observed the victim stiffen his body while giving out a sharp cry of pain, upset the apparatus and his tools, and collapse in a prone position on the floor, apparently unconscious. The victim appeared to be in contact with the equipment and wires, so helping could be potentially dangerous for the helper. In the moderate-ambiguity condition, the same scenario was acted out, except that the victim was in a corner of the laboratory not directly visible to the subjects. They would have had to step into the room and look around the corner to observe him unconscious on the floor. The high-ambiguity situation was similar to this, except that the victim did not give out a sharp cry of pain. Once again, in the low-ambiguity situation almost everyone helped by rushing into the room or running off to find the experimenter, and three-quarters of the persons helped in the moderate-ambiguity situation. In the high-ambiguity situation, on the other hand, help was given only about 25 percent of the time.

In another situation involving a victim's welfare, Darley and Latané (1968) invited college students to participate in discussions about the kinds of personal problems that are faced by normal college students in a high-pressure urban environment (New York City). To avoid embarrassment, subjects were told, they would remain anonymous and would be placed in individual rooms. In addition, the experimenter said he would not listen to the initial discussion himself, but would get the subjects' reactions later by questionnaire. Each person would talk in turn for two minutes to present his problems to the group. Next, each person in turn would comment on what the others had said, and finally there would be a free discussion. Subjects believed that they were part of two-, three-, or six-person discussion groups. In actuality, all of the persons except the subject were merely tape recordings. The real subject was always the last to speak. The first speaker mentioned that he was prone to seizures, particularly when studying hard or when taking exams. After everyone else had given their initial talk, he spoke again and seemed to be having a seizure as he spoke. His talk became increasingly loud and incoherent, culminating in, "I'm gonna die, er, er, I'm . . . gonna die, er, help, er, er, seizure!" When subjects thought that they were part of a two-person group, i.e., the only bystander, everyone helped. When subjects thought they were one of five bystanders (the six-person group), they helped only 62 percent of the time.

Why didn't the rest of these subjects help? Latané and Darley (1970) suggested that the widely used label of "apathy" was inappropriate for this behavior. Many of the nonhelping subjects showed physical signs of nervousness and seemed emotionally aroused while listening to the apparent seizure. Latané and Darley suggested that subjects were in an *avoidance/avoidance* type of conflict situation. On one hand, they worried about the guilt and shame they would feel if they did not help. On the other hand, they were concerned about making fools of themselves by overreacting or ruining an ongoing experiment by leaving their intercoms. Latané and Darley gave measures of a number of personality characteristics to subjects in this experiment and correlated their responses with their speed-of-helping scores; none were related significantly to speed of helping. The one factor that did relate significantly to helping was the size of the town in which persons had grown up. The smaller the size of the community in which the subject grew up, the greater the likelihood of that person helping the seizure victim.

Competence of the Bystanders

In the Clark and Word (1974) "electrocution study," subjects who had had formal training or experience with electrical equipment helped more (90 percent helped) than did those who were unfamiliar with electrical equipment (58 percent helped). In another study, bystanders who had taken a Red Cross course on first-aid and emergency care were much more likely to give direct help to someone who was apparently bleeding heavily from an accident (almost 50 percent helped directly) than were bystanders who had not had such training (only about 5 percent helped directly) (Shotland & Heinold,

Training in emergency care (such as CPR) makes a difference. Research shows that bystanders who have taken a course on first aid and emergency care are much more likely to give direct help if they encounter an emergency.

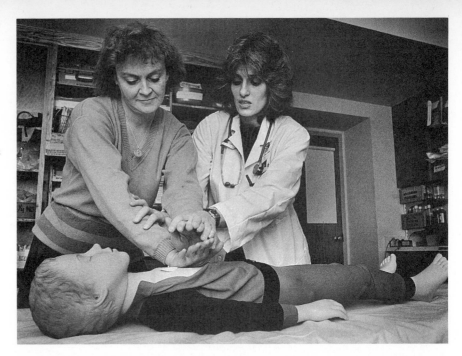

1985). Other researchers found that highly competent bystanders (registered nurses) who, along with another bystander, heard a workman fall from a ladder, helped just as frequently as people who witnessed the emergency alone (Cramer et al., 1988). In later interviews the nurses said they helped because they were confident in their ability and knew what steps to take.

We see that preexisting competence affects the likelihood of helping—does short-term training affect it as well? Pantin and Carver (1982) replicated the Darley and Latané (1968) seizure experiment with female subjects. Some of the subjects had three weeks earlier seen movies describing the importance of providing immediate first aid when an emergency occurs and detailing several first-aid procedures; the others had not. The women who had not viewed the film were slower to respond if they believed themselves to be in six-member groups than if they believed themselves to be in two-member groups, replicating the Darley and Latané (1968) finding. However, women who had viewed the films responded quickly regardless of perceived group size. Feelings of competence, which had been increased by viewing the films, significantly increased the likelihood that the women would help the victim of the seizure. It appears that increasing peoples' competence will reduce the likelihood they will be inhibited by other bystanders. This effect may not be long lasting, however, as Pantin and Carver found that these differences were not present in a follow-up six weeks later.

If bystanders already know about the psychological factors that can interfere with helping, such as pluralistic ignorance and diffusion of responsibility, are they more likely to overcome the inhibiting effect of these factors? In other words, are people more likely to help others because of information gained through the study of social psychology? Beaman and his coworkers (1978) conducted two studies to find out. Supposedly as part of research on college lectures, college students in introductory psychology heard a fifty-minute lecture, which described how pluralistic ignorance, diffusion of responsibility, and evaluation apprehension (fear of looking foolish) may cause bystanders not to help in emergency situations. A second group of students did not hear this lecture. The second part of the study was conducted in another building on campus. While walking to the other building, the same students passed a man who apparently was the victim of a bicycle accident. A female student (a confederate of the experimenter) always accompanied the subject and acted unconcerned about the accident, in order to make the situation a little more ambiguous.

The researchers wanted to see whether the students who had heard the helping lecture would be more likely to help than those who had not heard the lecture. As Figure 7-10 indicates, this is what they found. In a second study, subjects heard a lecture on helping, or saw a movie on the helping model of Latané and Darley, or were exposed to a lecture or film on a topic irrelevant to helping. Two weeks later the subjects, while on their way to participate in another experiment, passed a man partially sprawled against the wall in the hallway. As in the first study, students who had been exposed

FIGURE 7-10

Knowledge of Helping
Research Increases the
Likelihood of Helping

*Likelihood of helping in an
ambiguous emergency situation
as a function of whether or not
people have been exposed to
information on psychological
factors affecting helping behavior.*

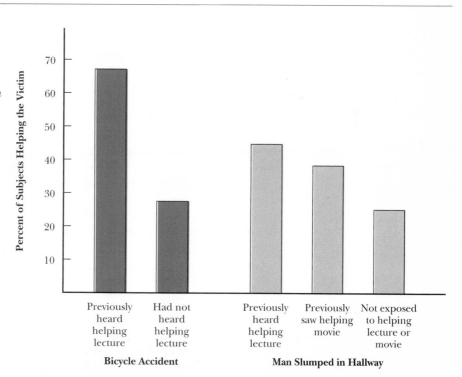

Source: Data from Beaman, A. L., Barnes, P. J., Klentz, B., & McQuirk, B. (1978). Increasing helping rates through information dissemination: Teaching pays. *Personality and Social Psychology Bulletin, 4,* 406–411.

to the helping movie or lecture were more likely to help than those who had not been. These results suggest that you are now more likely to help in an emergency situation than you were before you read this chapter.

It is important to remember that Beaman and his co-workers had a non-reactive bystander present in both studies. Otherwise, as we have seen, helping rates in clear, nonambiguous situations are usually close to 100 percent. Recall that Latané and Darley proposed that the presence of other persons can reduce the cost of not helping by diffusion of responsibility, reducing the guilt or blame that might be directed at any one individual for inaction. In addition, if others are present, a bystander might assume that someone else has already initiated action to help in the emergency.

The Impact of Race

Earlier we saw that individuals tend to be most helpful to those of their own race in nonemergency situations, except when their self-image of being unprejudiced has been threatened. How might racial biases affect helping in emergencies? Gaertner and Dovidio (1977) reasoned that the race of the person needing help (the victim) might interact with the general tendency for less helping when there are more bystanders present. They hypothesized that virtually every bystander would help, regardless of the victim's race, when just a single bystander was present. When there were several bystanders, on the other hand, the victim's race might become more important, as prejudiced bystanders might assume (or rationalize) that somebody else would be likely to help the victim (Figure 7-11).

Gaertner and Dovidio staged an emergency where several chairs seemed to fall on a white female or a black female victim. As predicted, they found that alone white female bystanders were about as likely to help a black victim as a white victim. However, when the bystanders thought there were other bystanders around, they were much less likely to help a black victim than a white victim, regardless of their level of prejudice. The researchers argued that these whites were not intentionally discriminating against blacks. Rather, they failed to help blacks when they could attribute their noninvolvement to the assumption that others would help. In this way they could maintain an egalitarian, nonprejudiced self-image.

The Arousal Cost/Reward Model

Arousal and Costs

Other theorists have focused on arousal and the costs and rewards for helping and for not helping. The *costs for helping* a victim might include danger, effort, time loss, embarrassment, and feelings of inadequacy if the help is ineffective. The *costs for not helping* might include self-blame for inaction, public disapproval, and loss of possible rewards (such as thanks from the victim or feelings of competence). If the costs for helping are low and the costs for not helping are high, direct intervention should occur. If the costs for help-

FIGURE 7-11

Impact of Race on Helping in an Emergency Situation

The percentage of white female bystanders who helped a female victim, depending on the victim's race and the number of bystanders present.

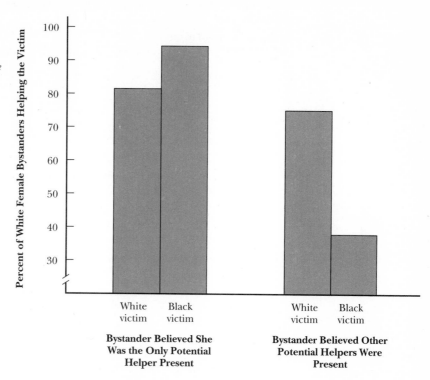

Source: Data from Gaertner, S. L., & Dovidio, J. F. (1977). The subtlety of white racism, arousal, and helping behavior. *Journal of Personality and Social Psychology, 35,* 691–707.

ing are high and the costs for not helping are low, the bystander is likely to leave the scene or to ignore or deny the existence of an emergency. If both types of costs are low, however, whether a bystander helps may depend on perceived norms in the situation: on perceptions of whether or not one *should* help (Figure 7-12). The dropped-books example at the beginning of the chapter depicts a low-cost, low-reward situation.

When the costs for helping and for not helping are both high, the bystander is in a difficult spot. The arousal cost/reward model suggests that either of two courses of action is likely. The bystander may intervene indirectly—for example, by calling a doctor, the police, or the fire department. Or the bystander may *cognitively reinterpret* the situation by deciding that help is really not needed or that others will probably help (diffusion of responsibility), or by derogating the victim—that is, deciding that the victim deserved her fate (the just world assumption). By making a reinterpretation, the costs for not helping are reduced and the bystander feels freer to leave the scene or ignore the emergency.

FIGURE 7-12

The Influence of Costs and
Rewards on Direct Helping

*The theoretical impact of per-
ceived costs for direct helping
and costs for no help in an
emergency situation, for a
moderately aroused observer.*

Potential Helper's Likely Behavior

Costs for Direct Helping

	Low	High
Low	Behavior; will be largely a function of *perceived norms* in the situation	Leaving the scene, ignoring, denial
High	Direct intervention	Reinterpretation, of the situation or disparagement of the victim, lowering the costs for not helping, leading to *or* Indirect intervention

(Left axis label: **Costs for Not Helping**)

Source: Adapted from Piliavin, J. A., & Piliavin, I. M. (1972).
The effect of blood on reactions to a victim. *Journal of Person-
sonality and Social Psychology, 23,* 253–261. Copyright 1972
by the American Psychological Association. Reprinted by
permission of the publisher and author.

Feelings of "We-ness" with the Victim

As noted earlier, Piliavin et al. (1981) suggested that three general factors affect the likelihood of the occurrence of helping: (1) situational characteristics (such as situation ambiguity and the number of bystanders present), (2) bystander characteristics (such as age, gender, race, competence to help), and (3) victim characteristics (such as gender, race, attractiveness). These factors affect the bystander's feeling of we-ness with the victim. The feeling of we-ness, in conjunction with the three general factors mentioned above, determines the amount of arousal that occurs, the extent to which the arousal is attributed to the victim's distress, and the bystander's perception of the costs for helping and for not helping. The arousal and the perceived costs, finally, determine which response the bystander will make: direct help, indirect help, or no help at all.

This arousal cost/reward model can be applied to many studies already reviewed in this chapter. Consider a study that compares helping by people who are alone or in two-person groups, and where the victim is of the same race or a different race from the bystander (e.g., Gaertner & Dovidio, 1977). The fact that there is only one bystander should increase the bystander's feelings of we-ness with the victim ("There are only the two of us"), and if the bystander is of the same race as the victim, this should increase feelings of we-ness still more, consequently producing greater arousal in the bystander. These feelings should also increase the perceived costs for not helping, thereby decreasing the relative costs for intervention. The combination of these factors would lead to the prediction that the same-race bystander will be most likely to intervene. Indeed, this is what the study found (Gaertner & Dovidio, 1977). You may wish to go back and see if you can reinterpret the other studies discussed in the chapter in terms of the arousal cost/reward model .

Legal Issues in Emergency Helping

In addition to psychological factors, crucial legal questions arise whenever someone is faced with an emergency situation. What can happen to you, legally, if you decide to help someone in an emergency? What can happen to you if you decide not to help? In other words, what are the potential legal costs or rewards?

It is extremely difficult to provide legal punishments for failure to help. Kaplan (1978) asserted that, "In fact, the law in the United States does not do very well in preventing armed robbery, burglary, drunken driving, and a host of other offenses in which people harm other people, and it seems to do appallingly badly at preventing people from harming themselves through drug use, gambling, or the like. It is arguable, then, that the law shows a wise economy avoiding the temptation to try to force people to be good to each other."

principle of individualism:
The argument that the law should not interfere with people's freedom to behave as they wish, as long as they do not harm anyone.

"why me" principle:
This principle focuses on the enormous difficulty in deciding who should be prosecuted for failure to help.

Two legal principles have often been cited as reasons why laws requiring people to help may not work well. The first is the **principle of individualism**, which asserts that the law should not interfere with people's freedom to behave as they wish, as long as they do not harm anyone. Applied to emergency situations, it suggests that one should not be forced to help (which would interfere with their freedom to not help) merely because of the carelessness or bad luck of someone else (the victim). The second factor is the **"why me?" principle**. This focuses on the enormous difficulty in creating standards for acceptable behavior in an emergency. If, for instance, a number of bystanders did not help in an emergency situation, which ones should be prosecuted for failure to help? Those who were prosecuted might very well be able to claim, "Why me, and not all those other bystanders?" Which of the thirty-eight bystanders in the Kitty Genovese murder should have been prosecuted for their failure to intervene? Although over a dozen countries (including France, Germany, Italy, Poland, and the U.S.S.R.) have "duty to rescue" laws, very few U.S. states have adopted such laws, making "failure to help" a misdemeanor (Woozley, 1983).

There is one exception to this general reluctance to penalize people for failing to help—cases of child abuse. Because people outside a family who suspect that child abuse is occurring may be reluctant to get involved in "family matters" involving someone else's child, many states have recently passed laws requiring citizens to report suspected cases of child abuse to the authorities.

Looking again at medical emergencies, there is another important issue. Suppose you come upon an automobile accident in which the victim

"Good Samaritan" statute:
A statute that protects those who try in good faith to help in an emergency situation.

needs immediate medical aid. You stop and try to help, but your help turns out to be ineffective or harmful. Can you be sued by the victim? The fear of being sued may be a powerful perceived cost for helping. **"Good Samaritan" statutes** have been passed in recent years throughout the United States to protect those who try in good faith to help in an emergency such as an automobile accident. In some states the laws apply only to physicians or licensed medical personnel; in others the law applies to everyone.

Florida's Good Samaritan law, for example, states:

> Any person, including those licensed to practice medicine, who gratuitously and in good faith renders emergency care or treatment at the scene of an emergency outside of a hospital, doctor's office, or other place having proper medical equipment, without objection of the injured victim or victims thereof, shall not be held liable for any civil damages as a result of such care or treatment or as a result of any act or failure to act in providing or arranging further medical treatment where the person acts as an ordinary reasonably prudent man would have acted under the same or similar circumstances.

In Florida, if someone wanted to sue you because your attempt to help turned out disastrously, the victim would have to prove that you acted differently from the way "an ordinary reasonably prudent man would have acted under the same or similar circumstances." The law applies only when the injured victim does not object; the interpretation in Florida has been that a victim who is unconscious does not have an objection. You may wish to check with your local police department, bar association, or law school to see what the Good Samaritan law says in your state.

Although Kaplan (1978) suggested that laws are not very effective tools for stimulating prosocial behaviors such as helping in emergencies, research has shown that helping is more likely if potential helpers are aware of the factors that often inhibit helping. The spread of such knowledge, plus the legal protection afforded by Good Samaritan laws and similar statutes, may increase the likelihood that, in the future, bystanders will help in emergencies. Let us hope so.

How can prosocial behavior be increased?

In the first chapter I wrote about "giving away psychology," using psychological knowledge for the benefit of society. Research on prosocial behavior is one area where this goal seems particularly relevant—if the prevalence of prosocial behavior can be increased, then social psychology will have made a substantial contribution indeed. As I briefly summarize what we currently know, you will notice considerable overlap with the factors I discussed in

Chapter 6 as relevant to conflict reduction. There is also a good deal in common with methods to reduce aggression (discussed in Chapter 10) and ways of lowering levels of prejudice and discrimination (Chapter 11).

First, the media can make a major contribution through *showing prosocial models*, as research shows that through social learning children exposed to such models become more helpful, cooperative, friendly, and so forth. In addition, observing prosocial behavior may "prime" positive thoughts related to human nature. A second general way to increase prosocial behavior is to *create a superordinate identity*, a view of all people as being part of the human family. Religious imagery, with its emphasis on brotherhood embodies this approach. From a sociobiological perspective, one may extend kinship-based altruism beyond the kinship group. The arousal/cost-reward model's emphasis on we-ness is also pertinent. As we saw with relation to conflict reduction, creating a superordinate identity reduces conflict and increases prosocial behaviors within the (larger) group. Feelings of *empathy* with other group members may become more likely.

Increasing attention to *prosocial norms*, such as the norms of reciprocity and social responsibility, may also make a difference. Similarly, reduced acceptance of norms that discourage altruism, such as the norm of noninvolvement, is also relevant. Many parents try to pass on the appropriate norms to their children and, through media messages, community leaders and religious groups sometimes attempt to get adults to pay more attention to prosocial norms. Community leaders and legislators may also try to *reduce costs and increase rewards for helping* via legislation and community projects. We saw how Good Samaritan laws are designed to protect people who help in good faith, while "duty to help" laws exist in a couple of U.S. states and many other countries. Various awards for heroism or community service provide reinforcement for helpful actions.

People are more likely to help if they feel they have the appropriate *skills and abilities*. People who are trained in first aid, lifesaving, CPR, or other relevant skills are likely to feel more competent when exposed to an emergency, and are therefore more likely to help. And the help they give is likely to be effective and not risky to themselves. Increasing people's *knowledge about the factors affecting prosocial behavior* can also have an impact. We saw that students who were knowledgeable about the Latané-Darley research were more likely to help in a subsequent situation than were others. Bystanders who know that situation ambiguity deters emergency helping may be more likely to ask questions to clarify an ambiguous situation, thereby negating the destructive effect of pluralistic ignorance. People aware of Good Samaritan statutes may be less likely to be deterred from helping due to fear of a lawsuit.

In sum, there are many things that can be done, as a society and as individuals, to increase the prevalence of prosocial behavior in our world.

Public recognition—a powerful reward.
The Honorary Fire Chief Award for Heroism was presented by Houston's Mayor Whitmire and the Fire Dept. to Van A. Vick for his successful rescue of Jesse Owens trapped under a bridge by rising flood waters.

SUMMARY

Prosocial behavior forms a cornerstone for modern society. During childhood we are taught to be helpful and considerate of others and we continue to be intermittently reinforced for prosocial behavior throughout our lives. Scientists disagree whether human prosocial behavior has an inherited component, as some sociobiologists assert, or whether it is entirely learned. People are more likely to behave prosocially for egoistic reasons when they are in a good mood, in a bad mood (when helping is seen as a way of changing the bad mood), when they fear punishment for not helping, or when they are unpleasantly aroused by the other person's need. Altruistically based helping may depend on the state of empathy. Theorists continue to debate the prevalence of egoistic vs. altruistic behaviors. Prosocial behavior is also related to being esteem-oriented rather than safety-oriented, to one's ability to reward oneself for being helpful, and to supportive social norms. The threat-to-self-esteem model notes that recipients of help respond negatively if the help is threatening to their self-esteem.

Helping in emergency situations is affected by the number of bystanders, their knowledge and competence to help, and the ambiguity of the situation. In ambiguous situations where several bystanders are present, the processes of pluralistic ignorance (being led by others' reactions to interpret it as a nonemergency) and diffusion of responsibility (deciding it is someone else's responsibility to help) can inhibit helping. From a different perspective, a person's feeling of we-ness with the victim will influence that person's arousal level and the perceived costs and rewards for direct intervention. Helping is most likely when a bystander's arousal is high, and perceived costs for helping are low and rewards are for helping are high. Though a few attempts have been made to pass laws requiring bystanders to help, the principle of individualism and the "why me?" principle have been cited as arguments against such laws. Levels of prosocial behavior in our society could be increased via media attention to prosocial models, an emphasis on superordinate identities, stressing prosocial norms, increased rewards and decreasing costs for helping, developing skills and abilities that enhance potential helpers' feelings of competence, and educating people about the situational factors that often prevent people from helping others.

CHAPTER 8
Attraction: Liking and Loving

Shared joys make a friend, not shared sufferings.   Nietzsche

True love is like seeing ghosts: We all talk about it, but few of us have ever seen one.   La Rochefoucauld

It's the first day of a new semester and you slide into your seat in the sociology classroom, ready for boredom or enlightenment. You are casually looking through the local paper when you sense someone settling into the seat next to you. Looking up, you are startled to see an unusual-looking person of the opposite sex whom you've never seen before. To your surprise, you feel yourself reacting physically to the person's presence. You're breathing a little faster, your heart seems to be racing, your palms feel sweaty, you fear you may even be blushing. What are you feeling? Why is this person having such an impact on you? Are you turned off or turned on? Might you be feeling love? lust? dislike? disgust?

Your friend Tracy always seems to shine in social situations. She's not strikingly beautiful, yet many people seem to want to monopolize her time. As you observe her surrounded by attentive people at a party, you wonder, "What does she have? What is it about her that makes her so attractive to others?" ❖

PREVIEW

interpersonal relationships:
The ongoing interactions between two or more people.

Whether we talk about togetherness or loneliness, friendship or unfriendliness, love or hate, we are talking about **interpersonal relationships**, the interactions between two or more people. Chapters 8 and 9 explore the most important psychological aspects of interpersonal relationships. The first relevant question is: Why do people affiliate with others? After briefly addressing this issue, I will focus on the factors that are most important in determining how much we like someone: propinquity (nearness), similarity, maintaining balance, and physical attractiveness. I will also touch on other important factors, such as positive emotional arousal, ability, reciprocal liking, and complementarity. Then we will briefly look at the other side of the coin: reactions to people who are unattractive, disfigured, or disabled.

Proceeding from liking to loving, we begin with an overview of definitions of love and possible styles of loving. I'll then review research and theory relevant to several compelling questions: How can you tell if someone loves you? How can you tell if you love someone? What is the difference between love and infatuation? We will also analyze research on misattribution and negative reinforcement as causes of love. By the end of this chapter you will be aware of what we currently know about love and how much more there is to learn. Chapter 9 will delve more deeply into affiliation and attraction, analyzing long-term relationships, marriage, and divorce.

AFFILIATION: WHY DO PEOPLE NEED PEOPLE?

In modern society most of our waking hours are spent in interaction with other people. The range of interactions is vast: Talking, making love, working cooperatively, arguing, listening, playing competitively, and fighting are just a few. People are truly social animals. But why do we affiliate with others?

Several types of social rewards are particularly relevant to the desire for social contact (Hill, 1987). We analyzed two of these, *social comparison* and *emotional support,* in Chapters 2 and 3. Recall that in order to evaluate their own abilities, attitudes, traits, values, and emotions, people often compare themselves with similar others. Social comparison uses others as social reality, a standard against which to compare one's own characteristics. While people usually compare themselves with others who are similar to them, we saw that in some situations they may compare themselves with others who are less fortunate than they, thereby enhancing self-esteem via downward social comparison. Affiliation can also provide emotional support. People often feel less fearful or lonely when others are around, as Schachter's (1959) "mad scientist" studies (Figure 3-2) demonstrated, especially when the others are in the same situation.

In this chapter and the next we will look at two additional types of social rewards that other people can provide. First, they can give us *positive feelings* associated with interpersonal closeness, friendship, affection, communication, and love. Second, others can give various types of *attention* to us: praise, recognition, status, and the like.

LIKING OTHERS: IMPORTANT FACTORS

Interpersonal attraction is related to one's attitude toward another person or group. When we are attracted to others, we evaluate them positively, tend to approach them, and behave positively toward them. In our examination of interpersonal attraction, I will highlight those factors that have been shown to affect the degree of attraction between people. Before reading further, take a few minutes to list those factors you think are most important in answering two questions: (l) What would determine how much you liked a room-

interpersonal attraction:
The tendency to evaluate a person or group positively, to approach them, and to behave positively toward them.

mate of your own sex? (2) What would determine how much you liked someone of the opposite sex? You will then be in a good position to compare your self-insights with the research findings on these questions.

Propinquity

propinquity:
An individual's proximity to others.

Suppose you live in an apartment complex near campus and a team of social psychologists gives everyone in your complex a series of questionnaires asking about personality characteristics, attitudes, abilities, values, and so forth. They also ask each of you to name your best friends within the apartment complex. What factor do you think would predict most accurately the friendship patterns in the complex? It turns out that the single characteristic from which friendship can be predicted most accurately in a situation such as this is **propinquity**, or nearness. We can most accurately predict whom you will like best by knowing who lives nearest to you. The same is true for other persons' opinions of you; those liking you best are likely to be those living near you. Of course, we can all think of specific cases in which this is not true, as in lengthy feuds between neighbors. Nevertheless, the general finding that nearness breeds liking has been noted again and again. For example, in a study of friendships at the married student apartments at MIT, Festinger and his co-workers (1950) discovered that the person most often named as a wife's best friend was her next-door neighbor. There are several reasons why propinquity influences attraction.

Availability
People who live close to us are more available and there are more opportunities to get to know them. The costs of getting to know each other, in terms of time and effort, are relatively small when a person lives close by.

The Expectation of Continued Interaction
People expect to interact more often, whether or not they want to, with those living nearest to them. This being the case, people tend to accentuate the positive and minimize the negative aspects of the relationship so that future interactions will be pleasant and agreeable (Knight & Vallacher, 1981). Indeed, Tyler and Sears (1977) titled their research study of this phenomenon, "Coming to like obnoxious people when we must live with them."

Predictability
As you become better acquainted with your neighbors, you are better able to predict how they will react. Hence, you can elicit positive reactions from them and arrange rewarding situations. Persons who are too unpredictable are usually disliked. On the other hand, some people are so predictable as to be boring. It appears that we are most attracted to people who are predictable, but not *too* predictable (Bramel, 1969).

Familiarity

mere exposure effect:
People develop more
positive feelings toward
objects and individuals
they see often.

Familiarity may lead to increased liking. Robert Zajonc (1968) pioneered research on the **mere exposure effect**. People develop more positive feelings toward objects and individuals they see often; they dislike the unfamiliar and the unexpected. "Comfortable" people and things (those with which we are familiar) elicit positive feelings. The more we are exposed to objects (such as unusual patterns, letters from foreign alphabets, photos of people) or other individuals, the more attracted toward them we become. This effect is strongest when somewhat positive feelings toward the stimulus already exist (Smith & Dorfman, 1975). In a meta-analysis of 208 experiments, Bornstein (1989) noted that the mere exposure effect is found under a variety of conditions.

A clever demonstration of this familiarity effect was provided by Mita, Dermer, and Knight (1977). Undergraduate women were asked to come to the laboratory and to bring a close female friend. Researchers then took frontal facial photographs of each subject. Two prints were made of each photograph: one a regular photograph, the other a reversed print, as one's face would appear if viewed in a mirror. The pair of photographs were shown to the subject and to her friend and each was asked to say which photo looked more attractive. Most of the friends chose the regular photo as more attractive. The subject, on the other hand, was more likely to choose the reversed photo. Of course, the reversed photo bore the image with which she was most familiar—she saw it in the mirror every day.

Familiarity increases perceived attractiveness. Most people think that a reversed photo of themselves (as they see in a mirror) is more attractive. In contrast, their friends find a regular photo of them (matching the image they see) to be more attractive.

You may already be protesting that there are some limitations to this exposure effect. Indeed there are: Constant, incessant repetitions are less effective in increasing attraction than repetitions that are mixed in among other experiences (Harrison, 1977). The effect usually levels off after ten to twenty exposures to the stimulus, as boredom begins to replace interest or novelty (Bornstein, 1989). Boredom may set in sooner when people's initial reactions to the stimulus were already negative (Grush, 1976). Children don't show this effect as much as adults do, perhaps because they are more curious about new stimuli and more easily bored (Hunter et al., 1983). Nevertheless, the overall effect of familiarity is a strong one. Why should this occur? A sociobiological analysis can provide a possible explanation. Bornstein (1989) argued that preferring familiar, safe stimuli has evolutionary advantages. In his words: "Who was likely to survive longer, reproduce, and pass on genetic material (and inherited traits) to future generations, the cave dweller who had a healthy fear of the strange and unfamiliar beasts lurking outside, or the more risk-taking (albeit short-lived) fellow who, on spying an unfamiliar animal in the distance, decided that he wanted a closer look?" (Bornstein, 1989, p. 282).

One modern-day application of this phenomenon is to political campaigning. Politicians spend huge amounts of money to gain exposure to the public. Although it is hard to separate the effects of exposure from the effects of all the other events in a campaign, analyses indicate that those candidates who gain the most media exposure usually win (Patterson, 1980; Schaffner et al., 1981). A study of U.S. Congressional primaries, for example, concluded that the winners tended to be either big spenders (which presumably increased their exposure) or incumbents (who had already enjoyed media exposure for several years) (Grush et al., 1978).

Similarity

> And they are friends who have come to regard the same things as good
> and the same things as evil. . . . We like those who resemble us, and are
> engaged in the same pursuits. . . . We like those who desire the same things
> as we, if the case is such that we and they can share the things together.
> —Aristotle, Rhetoric

law of attraction:
One's attraction toward a person depends directly on the proportion of positive reinforcement received from that person.

As Aristotle suggested, similarity is an important factor in determining liking, particularly similarity in attitudes and values. Donn Byrne and his colleagues (Byrne, 1971; Clore & Byrne, 1974) proposed a **law of attraction**, stating that one's attraction toward a person depends directly on the proportion of positive reinforcement received from that person. Similarity in attitudes and values can be a potent predictor of attraction and friendship. We tend to like people with similar attitudes and dislike people whose attitudes are dissimilar to our own (Rosenbaum, 1986; Smeaton et al., 1989). Though similarity in attitudes and values has been most widely studied, attraction is also affected by similarity in economic background (Byrne et al., 1966), personality characteristics (Byrne et al., 1967), and self-esteem (Hendrick & Page, 1970). Not only are we attracted to people with attitudes similar to our own, but also we assume that they will be highly attracted to us (Gonzales et al., 1983). Similarity in preferred activities, pastimes, and interests is especially important for same-sex friends (Werner & Parmalee, 1979).

Why is similarity so important? First, interacting with a person similar to yourself may be directly reinforcing. Second, if another person holds the same attitudes and values as you, the person validates your version of social reality, bolstering your self-concept and sense of rightness. Third, knowing that the other is similar to you may cause you to anticipate that future interactions will be positive and rewarding (Huston & Levinger, 1978). Finally, similarity may be related to familiarity. Since we tend to interact most closely with those similar to us, they will also become more familiar to us.

Personality differences can moderate the similarity effect. Leonard (1975) found that similarity actually decreased attraction when people had an unfavorable self-concept. Those with low self-concepts were actually more attracted to people dissimilar to them than to those who were similar. If you don't think much of yourself, then someone who is similar to you may not seem all that great. Jamieson, Lydon, and Zanna (1987) found that low self-monitors, people who are concerned with acting consistently with their own attitudes and values (cf., Chapter 3), were most influenced by attitude similarity. High self-monitors, in contrast, were attracted to others who had similar activity preferences, rather than similar attitudes and values.

Similarity in preferred activities and interests is especially important for same-sex friends.

There is an important distinction between *actual similarity* (how similar two people are) and *perceived similarity* (how similar two people think they are). Most of the similarity studies have not distinguished between the two, because the information on similarity has been presented by the experimenter. These experimental studies can be interpreted as measuring the effects of perceived, rather than actual, similarity. Research suggests that perceived similarity is more important than actual similarity in determining liking (Hill & Stull, 1981).

Though attitude similarity is important, its impact may be overwhelmed when romance beckons. Gold, Ryckman, and Mosley (1984) found that when an attractive woman showed possible romantic interest in them, men tended to misperceive her other attitudes as being more similar to their own than they actually were. The researchers suggested that this provides some support for the old adage that "Love is blind," as romantically inclined individuals may fail to accurately evaluate their potential partner on many dimensions, including attitude similarity.

Maintaining Balance

balance theory:
A theory that evaluates the balance between feelings involving a person (P), another person (O), and an issue, impersonal object, or third person (X).

Balance theory, as developed by Fritz Heider (1958), looks at the balance or imbalance between one's feelings toward several objects or people. Heider focused on triads involving a person *(P)*, another person *(0)*, and an issue, impersonal object, or third person *(X)*. A situation is balanced if the relationship among elements is harmonious and nonstressful. For example, if you *(P)* like Frank *(O)* and you both like liberal political ideas *(X)*, the situation is balanced. As a general rule, a triad is unbalanced when there are one or three negative relations (e.g., you like Frank and you like liberal ideas, but he is a strong conservative). When there is imbalance, something has to give. You could become negative in your attitude toward Frank, or change your attitude toward politics (becoming more conservative), or try to change Frank's political attitude in a liberal direction.

The same principles apply when *X* is a third person. Aronson and Cope (1968) demonstrated that research subjects were relatively willing to help a supervisor (left-hand side of Figure 8-1) when the supervisor had: (l) praised an experimenter who had been pleasant to the subjects, or (2) criticized an experimenter who had been harsh to the subjects. In other words, "My friend's friend is my friend" (all positive relations in the triad) and "My enemy's enemy is my friend" (one positive relation in the triad). When the situation was initially unbalanced (right-hand side of Figure 8-1), the subjects restored balance by disliking the supervisor and being less helpful to him.

Physical Attractiveness

The Central Importance of Physical Attractiveness
Take a moment and look back at those characteristics you listed as important in affecting your liking for a member of the opposite sex. If you are

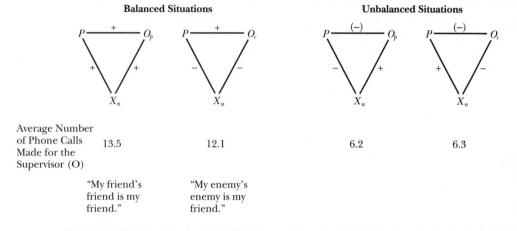

FIGURE 8-1

Helping in Balanced and Unbalanced Relationships

The subject's (P) likelihood of helping an experimental supervisor (O) by making phone calls was greater in balanced situations than in unbalanced situations.

Balanced Situations	**Unbalanced Situations**

Average Number of Phone Calls Made for the Supervisor (O)

13.5   12.1   6.2   6.3

"My friend's friend is my friend."   "My enemy's enemy is my friend."

Positive *P-O* Relations Lead to Much Helping   **Negative *P-O* Relations Lead to Only a Little Helping**

X_n = Nice experimenter
X_u = Unpleasant experimenter
O_c = Supervisor who criticized the experimenter
O_p = Supervisor who praised the experimenter

Source: From Aronson, E., & Cope, V. (1968). My enemy's enemy is my friend. *Journal of Personality and Social Psychology, 8,* 8–12.

like most college students, you listed attributes such as sincerity, intelligence, honesty, sensitivity, and perhaps even similarity in values and attitudes (Vreeland, 1972). But research suggests that there is one factor you may not have mentioned, which often far outweighs all the others in determining a person's reaction—*physical attractiveness*. This may sound like a simple overgeneralization. Surely educated persons have gone beyond the level of "judging a book by its cover"; surely we all have heard that "beauty is only skin deep." But judging from research results, very few of us really believe it.

Some researchers in the 1960s and early 1970s focused on "computer dances" where strangers were brought together and paired with one another for an evening. Studies (Walster et al., 1966) found that by far the most potent predictor of liking for one's computer dance date was the date's physical attractiveness. Other studies also found that attractiveness far outweighed other factors such as independence, honesty, and trustworthiness as a criterion for dating choices (Allen, 1978). The only factor that was as powerful as attractiveness, especially for women's dating choices, was race (Allen,

1976). More generally, physical attractiveness is related to dating popularity for both men and women, but more so for women (Reis et al., 1980), perhaps because men more often do the asking. The salience of attractiveness has also been demonstrated in analysis of responses to a commercial video-dating service. Women tended to choose men who were attractive, older than them, and of high status, while men chose women who were attractive and younger than them, but were not as concerned with status (Green et al., 1984).

Matching According to Attractiveness

matching:
People tend to pair off with others who are at about the same level of physical attractiveness.

Might one's own social desirability (which includes physical attractiveness) influence one's perception of the probability of attaining an attractive partner? Does it seem to you that all of the good-looking guys are usually with the good-looking women and vice versa? It's true; research illustrates a **matching** process by which people tend to pair off with others who are at about the same level of physical attractiveness. Matching is especially important in relationships where the partners are committed to each other. When photographs of couples who were engaged or going together were compared with a control group of couples formed by randomly matching pictures of men and women, the engaged-dating couples were more similar in attractiveness than were the randomly matched couples (Murstein, 1972). Matching in terms of attractiveness was also found in middle-aged married couples (Murstein & Christy, 1976; Price & Vandenberg, 1979). Even a study of same-sex friends concluded that for both sexes, friends were more similar in attractiveness than were randomly formed pairs (Cash & Derlega, 1978).

Not only do people marry others of equivalent attractiveness, there is also evidence to support the popular perception that people tend to marry others who look like themselves. Hinsz (1989) speculated that people may develop an attraction to faces similar to their own through the mere exposure effect, due to repeated exposure to their own face and faces of others genetically similar to them (their relatives).

Matching may also be related to the quality of a relationship. A study of dating couples at UCLA (White, 1980) found that those who were most similar in physical attractiveness were more likely to fall in love in the ensuing months than were couples who were dissimilar in attractiveness. Married couples tended to be more similar in attractiveness, on the average, than casually dating couples. Although a matching effect is visible in couples, this doesn't mean that individuals deliberately seek out partners of equivalent attractiveness. A meta-analysis of seventeen studies (Feingold, 1988) found that most individuals *seek* highly attractive partners but end up with partners that match their own attractiveness because less attractive people are forced to select less attractive partners due to social competition (Kalick & Hamilton, 1986).

The Importance of Attractiveness Over Time

You may be thinking, okay, perhaps physical attractiveness is important in the initial phases of a relationship, but surely it becomes less important as time passes. Over time, shouldn't similarity of attitudes and values plus other factors become more relevant? Logical thinking, but the research does not clearly support such a view. Mathes (1975) asked college-age men and women to sign a contract to go out on five dates with someone during the course of an experiment. He then assigned the men and women to date each other so that all possible combinations of physical attractiveness levels were created. Mathes hypothesized that attractiveness would be less important in later dates. Surprisingly, instead of becoming less important across five dates, attractiveness actually increased in importance from the first date to later ones.

Factors Affecting the Perception of Attractiveness

One's attractiveness to others is determined not only by physical features, but also by factors such as mood and facial expression. For example, even when told to compensate for expression, raters see photos of people with sad expressions as less attractive than those with neutral or happy expressions (Mueser et al., 1984). To some extent, you are as attractive as you feel.

As Focus 8-1 illustrates, one's evaluation of others' attractiveness can also be strongly affected by needs and motivations, such as the desire not to leave a bar alone at closing time. The attractiveness of one's partner can also affect perceptions of one's *own* attractiveness. Sigall and Landy (1973) found that a man was seen as more attractive when he was with a good-looking woman than when he was with an unattractive woman; the researchers labeled this the "radiating effect of beauty." Later research (Bar-Tal & Saxe, 1976) also found the radiating effect from females to males, but it was much weaker—a male's attractiveness did not have as strong an impact on evaluations of his female partner's attractiveness.

contrast effect:
A person who is surrounded by "beautiful people" may seem less attractive in comparison, due to a contrast effect.

But it is not always beneficial to be around attractive people. A person who is surrounded by "beautiful people" may seem less attractive in comparison, due to a **contrast effect**. Kenrick and Gutierres (1980) contacted one sample of men just after they had been watching a TV program featuring several beautiful actresses while others were contacted at a different time. The men who had just finished watching the beautiful actresses rated the attractiveness of a young woman's photo as significantly less attractive than those who had not been watching the show. To the extent that we are constantly exposed to beautiful people by the media, the contrast between them and the more ordinary-looking people we tend to date and marry may increase the likelihood of dissatisfaction in our relationships.

The overemphasis our culture places on physical beauty may have several negative consequences. It can lead to considerable personal unhappiness if individuals attempt unsuccessfully to capture the illusion of beauty. Few of us look like glamorous movie stars, but a lot of us may be frustrated because we have tried and failed to look as good. In addition, an overemphasis on physical beauty may strain long-term relationships. The choice of a marital partner might be made in terms of beauty rather than personality

FOCUS 8-1

"Don't the Girls (and Guys) All Get Prettier at Closing Time": Country and Western Psychology

A clever study has illustrated the effect of needs and perceptions on attractiveness. According to a country and western song by Mickey Gilley (1975), the girls in a bar "all get prettier at closing time." Part of the song goes:

> Now ain't it funny, ain't it strange
> the way a man's opinions change
> when he starts to face that lonely night.
> Oh, the girls all get prettier at closing time.
> They all get to look like movie stars.*

A daring group of researchers found empirical support for Gilley's observation (Pennebaker et al. 1979).

At three points during the evening, 9 P.M., 10:30 P.M., and midnight, the researchers obtained ratings on a ten-point scale of the attractiveness of male and female patrons from the men and women at three drinking establishments within walking distance of the University of Virginia. (Gilley sings, "If I could rate them on a scale from 1 to 10, looking for a 9 but 8 would fit right in . . . ") They found that the girls (and guys) did get prettier as closing time approached—in the eyes of the members of the opposite sex. Since ratings of the same sex did not change much over this same time period, it seems unlikely that inebriation or the early departure of the more attractive patrons could explain the change in ratings of the opposite sex.

Another study found an interesting variation of this effect. Nida and Koon (1983) repeated the Virginia reasearchers' procedures in a student-oriented bar and a blue-collar country and western bar (known as "Cowboy Bill's") in a small Georgia town. They found that the effect was evident at the country and western bar, replicating the earlier findings, but not at the student-oriented bar.

Either reactance theory or dissonance theory can explain this general effect. Reactance theory (Brehm, 1966) would assert that when one's freedom to select a partner is threatened (due to the approach of closing time), the attractiveness of the threatened alternatives (in this case, the available people of the opposite sex) should increase. Alternatively, if the patrons are psychologically committed to going home with a person of the opposite sex, then it would cause dissonance to decide that the available partners were unattractive. One way to reduce such dissonance would be to increase one's impression of the attractiveness of the potentially available partners. ❖

* From "Don't the Girls Get Prettier at Closing Time." Writer: Baker Knight. © 1975 Singletree Music (BMI) a division of Merit Music Corporation.

and background characteristics that might have a more positive impact on future happiness. Mismatches may occur between people who are similar in attractiveness but dissimilar in personality, attitudes, values, or other important factors.

Do attractive TV stars cause a contrast effect among viewers? Leading characters in TV soap operas (in this example, Dak Rambo of "Another World") are generally very attractive. Might long-time viewers grow to see their more ordinary-looking friends and lovers as unattractive in contrast?

Why Is Attractiveness So Important?

Visibility

One reason attractiveness is so important is that, like race and gender, it is a readily available, visible source of information about a person. If other personal characteristics such as intelligence or niceness were equally visible, they might have equally strong impacts.

Achieving Equity

equity theory:
Equity exists when each person in a relationship receives the same relative outcome compared to how much they have invested in the relationship.

distributive justice:
A basic component of the equity theory, which describes the balance of rewards and costs for two people involved in a relationsip.

Equity theory (Walster, Walster, & Berscheid, 1978) is derived from Homans' (1961) concept of **distributive justice**, describing the balance of rewards and costs for two people (P and O). Distributive justice prevails when:

$$\frac{P\text{'s rewards} - P\text{'s costs}}{P\text{'s investments}} = \frac{O\text{'s rewards} - O\text{'s costs}}{O\text{'s investments}}$$

Basically, equity is present when each person receives the same relative outcome compared to how much each invested in the relationship. Equity theory proposes that everyone is motivated by self-interest, seeking to maximize rewards and minimize costs. However, society teaches us that if we constantly act selfish by seizing more benefits than we deserve, we will be punished. "We soon learn that the most profitable way to be selfish is to be fair" (Walster et al., 1978, p. 15). The romantic choices of individuals are influenced by equity considerations, as illustrated by matching. Yet individuals also persist in trying to form relationships with partners who are somewhat more desirable than themselves. Our romantic choices thus seem to be a delicate compromise between the realization that we must accept what we "deserve" and our insistent demand for an ideal partner.

equitable relationship:
A relationship that would lead an observer to believe that the participants were receiving equal relative gains from the relationship.

Equity theory asserts that individuals are most content when they are in an **equitable relationship**. An equitable relationship is defined as one that would lead an observer to conclude that the participants were receiving equal relative gains from the relationship; in other words, there is distributive justice. People who are in an inequitable relationship will become distressed and consequently will attempt to restore actual equity, restore psychological equity (convince themselves and others that it really is "perfectly fair"), or terminate the relationship. Partners who think they are getting more than they deserve *(overbenefited)* tend to be less content and less happy and to feel considerably more guilty than those in equitable relationships. Partners who think they are getting less than they deserve *(underbenefited)* are less content, less happy, and more angry than those in equitable relationships. Physical attractiveness is one of the factors utilized by people to decide whether a relationship is equitable. Couples who match each other in physical attractiveness have equity in this important characteristic. Liking appears to result from a combination of equity and positive outcomes. People like their partners the most when the relationship is equitable *and* rewarding (Snell & Belk, 1985).

Social Competition

competitive marketplace analogy:
The idea that if one partner is more attractive than the other, the more attractive partner will more often be the target of the competitive affections of others.

The **competitive marketplace analogy** (Murstein, 1976; White, 1980) suggests that if one partner is more attractive than the other, the more attractive partner will more often be the target of the competitive affections of others. For example, people expect that more attractive spouses will have more opportunity and temptations to have extramarital affairs (Brigham, 1980). People expect that the more attractive partner is more likely to leave a relationship in search of greater reward, and the less attractive partner is more likely to worry about such a possibility.

The Physical Attractiveness Stereotype

physical attractiveness stereotype:
The widely shared belief that "what is beautiful is good," that physically attractive people also have other desirable characteristics.

In our culture there is a **physical attractiveness stereotype**, which assumes that "what is beautiful is good." Given only a brief look at someone, people are willing to make a number of assumptions about that person's personality and competencies, based solely on appearance. Dion et al. (1972) showed photos of three persons to college students and asked them to judge each person on personality traits, occupational status, and social and professional happiness. One of those pictured was quite attractive, one of average attractiveness, and one quite unattractive. As Focus 8-2 indicates, the students' judgments were heavily influenced by the facial attractiveness of the person pictured. Physically attractive people were expected to have more socially desirable personalities, to attain more prestigious occupations, and to have better prospects for happy social and professional lives.

The stereotype applies to body build as well as to facial attractiveness. College students tend to assume that people with athletic builds (mesomorphs) have desirable personality traits, while overweight people (endomorphs) have unfavorable characteristics—they are seen as lazy, sloppy, dirty, slow, physically unhealthy, and unattractive (Ryckman et al., 1989). Older studies had also found negative stereotypes of thin people (ectomorphs) but Ryckman and his co-workers found that thin people were seen in a generally positive light, as neat, happy, clean, fast, and intelligent. The researchers speculated that this change in the cultural stereotype of thin people might be a result of modern society's health-consciousness and emphasis on becoming thin for health reasons.

Even in a situation as serious as divorce, attractiveness of the partners may play a major role in how they are seen by others. College students' evaluations of the personalities of two people who were divorcing because of repeated adultery by the husband, repeated adultery by the wife, or mutual incompatibility, were more strongly affected by attractiveness than by what the person had done. Attractive men and women were rated as having far more attractive personalities than were unattractive men and women, regardless of whether they were adulterers, married to an adulterer, or simply incompatible with the spouse (Brigham, 1980). The only exception to this trend was that attractive women were rated as more vain than unattractive women. The factors that people assume are related to physical attractiveness are summarized in Focus 8-2.

Assumptions about Similarity

Physical attractiveness affects assumptions about belief and value similarity. People tend to assume that those whom they consider physically attractive also hold beliefs and values similar to their own (Marks et al., 1981). Because it is rewarding to associate with someone holding similar beliefs and values, this implies that people will expect attractive others to be more rewarding to them. Hence, these factors may interact with each other in determining overall attractiveness.

The Impact of Attractiveness on Personality

The "Social Psychology of Beauty"

We can identify three important social factors related to attractiveness (Adams, 1977). First, people have *different expectations* about attractive and unattractive individuals. The research on the "what is beautiful is good" stereotype clearly supports this assumption. Second, physically attractive people *receive different treatment and more favorable social exchanges.* For example, more attractive people are in greater demand as dating partners (Tesser & Brodie, 1971). Third, this different treatment may lead to *different personalities and social skills,* perhaps due to a self-fulfilling prophecy.

The influence of attractiveness begins early, reaching as far back as the maternity ward of the hospital. Nurses in charge of the care of premature infants gave a higher intellectual prognosis to those infants they perceived to be physically attractive (Corter et al., 1978). College students and teachers looked at attractive infants longer than unattractive infants (Hildebrandt & Fitzgerald, 1978), and there is evidence that attractive and unattractive in-

FOCUS 8-2

Some Assumptions About Physical Appearance

Compared to less attractive *persons*, more attractive persons are expected to:

Have more socially desirable personality traits (e.g., Dion et al., 1972, Brigham, 1980).

Be more likely to marry (Dion et al., 1972).

Be more likely to remarry if divorced (Brigham, 1980).

Attain more prestigious occupations (Dion et al., 1972).

Have better prospects for happy social and professional lives (Dion et al., 1972).

Be better able to reward you (Byrne, 1971).

Have beliefs and values similar to your own (Marks, Miller, & Maruyama, 1981).

As children, have higher educational potential and IQ (Clifford & Walster, 1973)

Be more responsible for good things that happen

to them and less responsible for bad things that happen to them (Seligman, Paschall, & Takata, 1974).

Show greater "marital competence" (Dion et al., 1972).

Compared to less attractive *women*, more attractive women are expected to:

Be more likely to request a divorce (Dermer & Thiel, 1975).

Be more likely to have an extramarital affair (Dermer & Thiel, 1975).

Have more opportunities and temptations to have an extramarital affair (Brigham, 1980).

Be more vain (Dermer & Thiel, 1975; Brigham, 1980).

Be more sexually warm (Dion et al., 1972; Brigham, 1980). ❖

fants receive different treatment from their mothers (Langlois & Stephan, 1981). Adult observers are less likely to attribute a chronic antisocial personality style to attractive children than to unattractive children who committed the same transgressions. Moreover, the transgression was rated as less undesirable when committed by an attractive child (Dion, 1972).

Physical attractiveness may influence teachers' evaluations of children, too. Fifth-grade schoolteachers were asked to examine the information given on a report card and estimate each student's IQ and potential future educational accomplishments. The teachers, who represented four hundred schools in Missouri, all received the same report card to evaluate. The only difference between report cards was in the student's picture—either one of six attractive boys and girls or one of six unattractive boys and girls—which was pasted on the corner of the report card. Researchers found that the more attractive the child (whether male or female), the higher educational potential and IQ that teachers assumed the child to have (Clifford & Walster, 1973).

This is a remarkable finding, particularly since evidence shows that a teacher's attitude toward a student can have a significant effect on the student's performance (Harris & Rosenthal, 1985; Rosenthal & Jacobson, 1968). Teachers also give attractive children more information, better evaluations, more opportunity to perform, and are more supportive of the child's educational endeavors (Adams & LaVoie, 1977). Basically, physically attractive children live in a different social world than their unattractive counterparts (Berscheid & Gangestad, 1982).

Differences in Personality and Skills

If attractive people encounter different expectations and treatment than do unattractive individuals, might different personalities develop as a result? Research indicates that facial attractiveness is quite stable through childhood (Sussman et al., 1983), so that any attractiveness-related treatment children receive is probably fairly consistent.

Some small differences in personality and skills have been identified. Physically attractive children tend to have higher self-esteem than unattractive children (Maruyama & Miller, 1981) and tend to be less aggressive than unattractive children (Langlois & Downs, 1979). Another study found that attractive fourth- and sixth-graders had higher grades, had better relationships with their classmates, and were perceived by their teachers as having higher academic ability (Lerner & Lerner, 1977). Both attractive children and attractive adults appear to be more assertive and self-confident than their unattractive peers (Dion & Stein, 1978; Jackson & Huston, 1975). Dominance, a concept closely related to assertiveness, appears to affect the perceived attractiveness of men but not of women. In a series of four studies, Sadalla et al. (1987) found that men portrayed as high in dominance (competitive, authoritative, masterful, athletic, high in control) were perceived as much higher in sexual attractiveness (by both men and women) than low-dominance men were. The researchers hypothesized that dominant women would be seen as significantly less sexually attractive than low-dominance women, due to sex-role stereotypes, but this did not occur—across the four studies, low-dominance and high-dominance women were rated equally in sexual attractiveness. The related trait of domineering behavior (excessive attempts to control the behavior of others) was not related to sexual attractiveness for men or women.

Attractive college students tend to have more sexual experience and less anxiety about dates than their less attractive counterparts (Curran & Lippold, 1975), and attractive college students were judged (by people who heard but did not see them) to have better social skills than were unattractive students (Goldman & Lewis, 1977). Thus, it appears that if individuals are treated in terms of a stereotype, actual differences in their personalities may develop in line with that stereotype—a self-fulfilling prophecy.

There is a downside as well to being attractive. Attractive people may become so accustomed to receiving insincere flattery or praise that they learn to discount praise, not trusting it even when it's genuine (DePaulo et al., 1987).

FIGURE 8-2

Dominance and Sexual
Attractiveness in Males

*High-dominance behavior
enhances the perceived sexual
attractiveness of males, but
not of females. In contrast, high-
domineering behaviors do not
significantly increase perceived
sexual attractiveness of either
sex.*

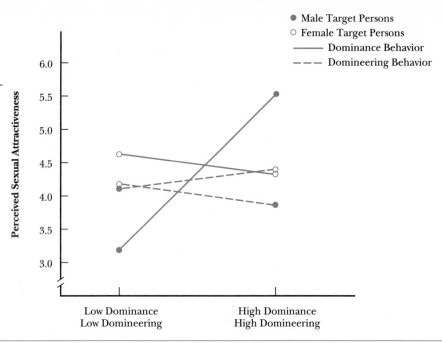

Source: Data from Sadalla, E. K.,
Kenrick, D. T., & Vershure, B.
(1987). Dominance and heterosexual attraction. *Journal of Personality and Social Psychology, 52,*
730–738.

Thus, Major and her co-workers (1984) found that physically attractive people were more likely to believe a positive evaluation of an essay they wrote
when it came from an evaluator who had not seen them than when it came
from someone who had seen them (and might have been biased by their attractiveness). Unattractive people, in contrast, showed the opposite pattern
of responses. Attractive people may also feel more social pressure to maintain their appearance (recall the discussion of bulimia in Focus 5-3), may
be stereotyped as conceited (Brigham, 1980), and may be the object of envy
or hostility from their less-attractive peers (Krebs & Aldofini, 1975).

The Role of Attractiveness in Relationships

Romantic love plays an important part in our evaluation of marriage. Physical attractiveness plays an important part in romantic love. As females and
males have more freedom in choosing marriage partners, the relative impact of important but "frivolous" factors such as physical attractiveness may
increase still further. Physical attractiveness of a potential lover is more important to some people than to others. People high in self-monitoring pay
particular attention to the physical attractiveness of a potential partner, while
low self-monitors pay relatively more attention to the potential partner's personality characteristics (Glick, 1985).

To assess the day-to-day impact of attractiveness, Reis and his co-workers (1980) had first-year college students complete an "interaction form" each day for forty days, describing every interaction with another person that lasted ten minutes or longer. They established that physical attractiveness of the male students was strongly related to the quantity of their social interaction with females. To the surprise of the experimenters, attractiveness of the female students was not consistently related to quantity of their social interactions. Attractive women did report more date/party interactions than did less attractive women, but this difference did not carry over into other areas of their social lives. For both sexes, particularly with opposite-sex interactions, satisfaction showed an increasing tendency over time to be positively correlated with one's attractiveness.

Not everyone is equally affected by the physical attractiveness stereotype. Andersen and Bem (1981) had college students converse by microphone with another student (partner) they could not see. Half of the students were led to believe (by a photo) that their partner was physically attractive, while the other half believed their partner was unattractive. The conversations were tape-recorded and judges later listened to each conversation and rated the participants on a number of traits, including how interested, animated, and enthusiastic they were. They found, as had Snyder, Tanke, and Berscheid (1977), that persons who thought they were talking to an attractive person were generally more responsive (animated, interested, and enthusiastic) than were those who thought they were talking to an unattractive person (Figure 8-3). This tendency was much stronger in sex-typed individuals (persons who are inclined to process information in terms of gender) than in nonsextyped individuals (people not predisposed to process social information according to gender).

The belief in a just world (Chapter 2) could contribute to physical attractiveness stereotyping. People who believe in a just world might be especially likely to feel that attractive individuals are "winners" who have desirable personalities as well. Dion and Dion (1987) found this to be true for perceptions of men: people with a strong belief in a just world were more likely to think that physically attractive men had attractive personalities and would have happier lives.

We have seen that attractiveness plays an important role in relationships. We can speculate that it may matter even more in the future than it does now. Because of increased mobility, the greater divorce rate, and the increasing number of remarriages, stepparents, and step-siblings in our current society, people must constantly be assessed very quickly by others. These quick judgments may often be made simply on the basis of people's appearance. Hence, attractiveness may have an increasingly powerful impact on our lives. In Berscheid's (1982, p. 21) words, it is very unlikely that prospective partners will be "judged just as dogs and cats and very small children judge us, simply on the basis of our behavior."

FIGURE 8-3

Sex-Typing and the Physical Attractiveness Stereotype

Judges' ratings of conversational responsiveness toward allegedly attractive and unattractive targets in same-sex and cross-sex dyads for sex-typed and adrogynous perceivers.

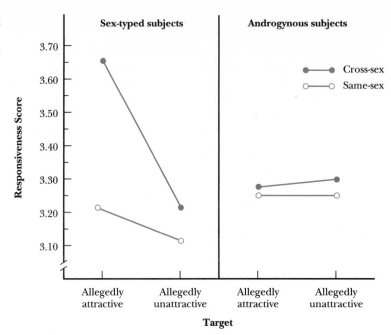

Source: From Andersen, S. M., & Bem, S. L. (1981). Sex typing and androgyny in dyadic interaction: Individual differences in responsiveness to physical attractiveness. *Journal of Personality and Social Psychology, 41,* 74–86. Copyright 1981 by the American Psychological Association. Reprinted by permission of the publisher and author.

Other Determinants of Liking

Positive Emotional Arousal

We tend to be attracted to people in whose presence we feel good, even if our feelings have nothing to do with their behavior. We find people more attractive when we meet them in pleasant surroundings. For example, people rated another person more positively when they were sitting in a room with a pleasant temperature than when they were in a hot room (Griffitt, 1970). In contrast, attraction to others is reduced when the surroundings are crowded, noisy, or polluted (Rotton et al., 1978; Glass & Singer, 1972). Recall from the last chapter that people are more helpful when in a good mood; those in a good mood also see others as more attractive.

Ability

As social exchange theory and reinforcement theory suggest, when other people are rewarding, we affiliate with them and like them. People who are able,

Fun increases liking. We tend to like people in whose presence we feel good.

competent, and intelligent can provide many rewards. They can help us solve problems, give us advice, help us interpret world events, and so forth. It follows that competent, intelligent people are liked more than are incompetent, unintelligent people. Yet this proposition has a major limitation. If a person is too perfect, we may feel uncomfortable or threatened. A too-perfect person also may be viewed as very dissimilar to ourselves in terms of attitudes, values, and so on, and this perceived dissimilarity might decrease their attractiveness to us. Hence, persons who are extremely competent and intelligent might be liked more when they show a few human frailties than when they appear to be perfect (Aronson, Willerman, & Floyd, 1966). This may explain why President John F. Kennedy became more popular with the American people after his blunder in sponsoring the attempt to invade Cuba at the Bay of Pigs in 1961. Most research has indicated, however, that a blunder decreases attraction for even the highly competent person (Deaux, 1972; Mettee & Wilkins, 1972). If the blunder makes one appear to be not only highly competent but also somewhat more similar to the audience, the increased-liking effect may occur. Otherwise, it will simply decrease one's appearance of competence and thereby decrease attraction.

Reciprocal Liking

When we know other persons like us, we can expect to be rewarded by them. Therefore, knowing we are liked is a powerful reward. We can expect that the other will help us in the future, and we also will feel good about the fact that another person thinks enough of us to be a friend (increasing our self-esteem). Therefore, liking begets liking. Friendship given usually means that friendship will be returned.

perceived reciprocity:
How much we think someone likes us.

actual reciprocity:
How much someone actually does like us.

The reciprocity relationship is somewhat more complicated, however. Several studies have suggested (Newcomb, 1961; Walster et al., 1966) that **perceived reciprocity** (how much we think someone likes us) is more important than **actual reciprocity** (how much someone actually does like us). When we look carefully at *relative liking* (how much does Tom like Sue compared to how much Tom likes other people, and compared to how much other people like Sue; and how much does Sue like Tom compared to how much Sue likes other people, and compared to how much other people like Tom?), strong evidence for actual reciprocity is also found (Kenny & Nasby, 1980). Other studies indicate that people generally like someone who likes others, even when the liking is not directly reciprocated (Folkes & Sears, 1977).

Why does everybody seem to like a "liker"? Perhaps because of expectancy confirmation (discussed in detail in Chapter 3). If you think of yourself as generally likable, you will believe that I like you, regardless of whether I really do. This belief may cause you to behave in a likable way to me, perhaps causing me to like you after all — a self-fulfilling prophecy. Illustrating this process, Curtis and Miller (1986) found that people who were falsely led to believe another subject liked them agreed more with the other subject, self-disclosed more, and had a more positive tone of voice and general attitude than did subjects who were not led to believe they were liked. These behaviors led to reciprocal positive behaviors by the other subject and to increased liking between them.

Reward Value of Positive Approval

There are limitations to the general power of reinforcement. The reward value of a compliment from another person greatly depends on who gives it and why the person seems to be giving it. If a person who compliments you seems to have ulterior motives and to expect something in return, the compliment will not increase your liking for the person. You may think of the compliment as dishonest and are likely to dislike the person you think is trying to con you (Jones & Wortman, 1973). Effective compliments are those that appear genuine, with no strings attached. Compliments received from individuals who have high status, who are very popular, and who are powerful are usually much more effective in increasing liking toward them than are compliments received from low-status, powerless, unpopular subordinates. The subordinate may have something to gain from the compliment, whereas the high-status person has less to gain and hence appears more sincere.

gain/loss theory:
Gain (or loss) of esteem from someone else has a more potent effect on liking (or disliking) than does constant praise or criticism.

The reward value of a compliment also depends on how often one has been praised by that person before. A compliment is usually most effective when it comes from someone who has previously acted neutral or negative, representing a "gain effect." **Gain/loss theory** (Aronson, 1969) proposes that gain (or loss) of esteem from someone else has a more potent effect on liking (or disliking) than does constant praise or criticism. The gain effect may occur because the compliment *reduced anxiety* associated with previous negative evaluations, or because the recipient believes that she has now *demonstrated her competence* and the evaluator realized this. Also, the positive evaluation may seem especially positive *in contrast* with the previous negative evaluations. Research has generally indicated that the gain effect is more potent than the loss effect (Clore et al., 1975).

FOCUS 8-3

Opening Gambits: What Works?

Many young people have spent a lot of time theorizing about which opening lines may be most effective in stimulating an attractive opposite-sex stranger to respond positively in a social situation (a party, a bar, at the beach). You may have done personal research yourself, testing the effectiveness of various lines. Systematic analysis of a hundred lines reported by college students revealed three basic types: direct, innocuous, and cute-flippant (Kleinke et al., 1986).

To scientifically assess reactions to such opening gambits, Cunningham (1989) had a male of medium attractiveness go into three bars and approach unaccompanied females with a direct approach ("I feel a little embarrassed about this, but I'd like to meet you, so can I at least ask what your name is?"), or an innocuous approach ("Hi" or "What do you think of the band?"), or a cute-flippant approach ("You remind me of someone I used to date" or "Bet I can outdrink you"). Observers coded each woman's response as positive (smiled, maintained eye contact, answered in a friendly fashion) or negative. The direct and innocuous lines were about equally effective (67 percent and 62 percent positive responses), while the cute-flippant lines were a disaster (19 percent positive responses).

A second study used both male and female experimenters who delivered one of the three types of lines to opposite-sex bar patrons. As you may have guessed, women responded much more selectively to the various approaches than men did. As in the first study, the direct and innocuous lines were moderately effective with women (about 70 percent positive response), but the cute-flippant lines were not (24% positive responses). Men, on the other hand, tended to respond positively (91 percent of the time) regardles of which of the three approaches the woman took.

A third study showed that males and females made very different attributions to someone using a cute-flippant line. Many women attributed dullness, irresponsibility, and a desire for dominance to cute-flippant men. Most men, in contrast, did not make negative attributions to women who used this approach. Does all this mean that no sensible man would ever use a cute-flippant approach? Not necessarily. Cunningham pointed out that such lines may be used to downplay the seriousness of the approach and protect the ego from rejection. This could represent a form of self-handicapping. ("It's not me she rejected, just that silly line. If I'd used a different line, she'd have liked me.") ❖

What's a good "opening line"? Intrepid researchers have identified some gambits that are more effective than others.

The Selectively Hard-to-Get Person

The reward value of approval also can depend on how often one appears to spread it around. It is well-established folklore that the woman (or man?) who plays hard to get will be seen as more desirable and presumably enjoy more success than the "easy" woman. The Roman poet Ovid, writing two thousand years ago, argued that:

> Fool, if you feel no need to guard your girl for her own sake, see that you guard her for mine, so I may want her the more. Easy things nobody wants, but what is forbidden is tempting. . . . Anyone who can love the wife of an indolent cuckold, I should suppose, would steal buckets of sand from the shore.

Being selectively hard-to-get (hard for others but easy for *you*) is likely to make someone especially attractive to you. In a computer-matching study (Walster et al., 1973), college men were invited to choose a date from a set of five candidates, described in folders, who had also evaluated them. One of the five women had indicated that though she was willing to date any of the men assigned to her, she was not enthusiastic about any of them (uniformly hard-to-get woman). A second woman appeared to be uniformly easy-to-get, as she indicated that she was enthusiastic about dating any of the five men assigned to her. The selectively hard-to-get woman had indicated only small enthusiasm for four of her date choices but extreme enthusiasm for the subject. The remaining two women had not filled out the forms. More men (59 percent) chose to date the selectively hard-to-get woman than any of the other types. They expressed greater liking for her and perceived her as both popular and friendly. The selectively hard-to-get person appears to represent the best of both possible worlds: popularity and niceness. Being chosen by a selectively hard-to-get person also raises one's self-esteem (Matthews et al., 1979).

When Opposites Do Attract: Complementarity

We have seen that similarity of attitudes and values leads to increased attraction. But what about a sadist and a masochist? On the surface, these two appear to be quite dissimilar. One likes to inflict pain whereas the other likes to receive it. Here it appears that opposites attract. In a similar vein, an individual who has a domineering personality would not get along very well with another domineering person. The dominant individual requires a submissive partner who will help fulfill both their needs between them. Complementarity of behaviors is particularly likely for dominance-submission behaviors (Strong et al., 1988).

complementary needs theory:
In selecting a partner, individuals may look for others who are similar with regard to some factors and then select as a partner the one who will best complement their personal needs.

Complementary needs theory asserts that many types of close relationships, particularly marriage, may require such complementarity of need systems in order to be successful (Winch, 1958). But in relationships like these, even though the needs are different (one has dominance needs, the other submission needs), it can still be viewed as a special case of similarity, since both partners agree on the roles that each will fulfill. They have similar attitudes about how their relationship should proceed; they may become good friends, since they need each other to satisfy their desires. Complementarity may be important in short-term interchanges under certain conditions, such as when people do not clearly understand what they are supposed to do. To get new ideas, they may prefer to interact with dissimilar people who see things differently and who may be able to give them a new interpretation to the puzzling events (Russ et al., 1980).

Liking can be affected by one's association with positive or negative outcomes.

Tying It Together

Many of the characteristics discussed thus far can be subsumed under the heading of *reinforcement* and *reward*. Proximity is important because it is less costly to interact with people who are nearby and one can get the benefits of friendship more easily. Physical attractiveness is important because attractive people are aesthetically pleasing (perhaps), we assume that they have desirable and potentially rewarding personalities, and it makes us look good to associate with them. Attitude and value similarity is important because it is rewarding to hear our own attitudes and values supported by someone else. In addition, similar people like the same things we do, are familiar, and know the same people as we do.

A study of previously unacquainted college roommates (Berg, 1984) found that satisfaction with one's roommate over a year's time and the decision whether or not to room together again the next year were significantly related to: (1) rewards received from the roommate (help, favors done), (2) the availability of other housing arrangements (i.e., costs), and (3) perceived similarity. Dale Carnegie's book *How to Win Friends and Influence People* (originally published in 1936 and one of the best-selling books ever) focused primarily on four factors. In order to win friends and influence people, Carnegie asserted: (1) one ought to be pleasant (deliver reinforcement), (2) one ought to like them (reciprocity), (3) one ought to find persons with similar interests (similarity), and (4) one ought to give praise to others (reinforcement again). The popularity of Carnegie's book (and of its many imitators) is not surprising, for he correctly identified four of the most important factors in attraction and friendship.

THE OTHER SIDE OF THE COIN: SOCIAL STIGMA

The Impact of Being Stigmatized

Just as people are attracted to those who are physically attractive, they tend to be repelled by persons who are very unattractive, disfigured, or disabled. The sight of someone who is disfigured or disabled evokes discomfort and a desire to avoid contact. People who deviate noticeably from norms of appearance or behavior—the retarded, the blind, the crippled, the former mental patient, the ex-convict, members of disliked ethnic groups—are **stigmatized.** "It is the dramatic essence of the stigmatization process that a label marking the deviant status is applied, and this marking process typically has devastating consequences for emotion, thought, and behavior" (Jones et al., 1984, p. 4). By stigmatizing another individual, people may enhance their own feelings of superiority and ingroup solidarity at the expense of the stigmatized (outgroup) person.

stigmatization: People who deviate noticeably from norms of appearance or behavior are usually avoided or treated in a negative manner.

Stigmatization and isolation. People who are stigmatized, as by being crippled, may be avoided or rejected by others.

Disfigured or disabled persons may remind us of our own vulnerability and the possibility that we could end up in such a plight. By avoiding these persons and minimizing contact, we may avoid having to think about such possibilities. Another way of protecting ourselves from acknowledging our vulnerability is to blame the victims for their fate, a variant of the just world assumption.

In addition to a tendency to avoid contact with stigmatized persons, there is also evidence of a "norm-to-be-kind to the disadvantaged." Hastorf, Northcraft, and Picciotto (1979) found that when performance on a task was being evaluated, handicapped persons received more positive feedback from others than did nonhandicapped persons, regardless of how well or poorly they did on the task. The implications of continually receiving feedback that is positive but often inaccurate are far-reaching. For example, handicapped persons might learn to ignore or discount all positive feedback from others because they have learned that it is often unrealistic. Recall that people who are very attractive may also learn to mistrust positive feedback, in their case because it may be insincere flattery.

Several years ago I was subjected to a demonstration of the effects of stigma after tearing knee ligaments in a softball game. I was put in a thigh-to-ankle cast and given short forearm metal crutches of the kind that crippled persons often use. As I limped through my daily life, I noticed a dramatic difference in how strangers reacted to me, depending on whether I was wearing long pants or shorts. When I was wearing shorts and the cast was clearly visible, people were friendly, often asking me what had happened or telling me about their own problems with casts and crutches. In contrast, when I was in long pants there seemed to be a decided tendency for people to avoid me and to avoid eye contact, perhaps not wanting to seem as if they were staring. Apparently I was perceived as having some permanent disability and people were noticeably uncomfortable about it. I found their discomfort very difficult to deal with.

Combatting Stigmatization

What can a stigmatized person do to combat such reactions? It helps us to acknowledge the handicap and bring the stressful issue out into the open. Hastorf and his co-workers (1979) found that when given a choice between working with a handicapped person who acknowledged his handicap and one who did not discuss it, most people chose to work with the person who acknowledged the handicap. It is helpful, too, if the stigmatized person gives others the opportunity to "prepare themselves" to deal with the uncomfortable problem (Gibbons et al., 1980). Research also suggests that nondisabled persons are more willing to interact with a disabled person who doesn't appear preoccupied with the disability, who demonstrates an interest in others, and who participates in typical social and athletic activities (Belgrave, 1984).

Because physical appearance makes such a drastic difference in the way people are perceived and treated, what about those whose appearance is very unpleasant or unattractive? Generally, most of us believe that there is nothing much we can do about our appearance, other than to control our weight and spend a great deal of money on hairstyles and grooming products. Yet there is another alternative: aesthetic or plastic surgery. For years physicians have debated about whether surgery on an otherwise healthy person is desirable or unnecessary and unethical (Goldwyn, 1972). Proponents of such surgery argue that it may have two effects: (1) increasing the self-esteem and self-image of the recipient, and (2) improving the way that others react to the person.

Recent studies show that people do react differently when a person's appearance is made more attractive. Kalick (1977; 1978) had college students view photos of people and rate them on appearance and various personality scales. Included among the photos were pre- and post-operative photos of eight young women who had had aesthetic surgery of the nose, the chin, or both. No subject saw a pre- and post-operative photo of the same woman. After-surgery photos were judged as significantly more attractive and also as kinder, more sensitive, more sexually warm and responsive, and more likable than were the pre-operative photos of the same women. Another study (Korabik, 1981) found that students rated girls as more intelligent and better adjusted, based on photos taken after they had completed orthodontic treatment, than when they saw photos taken before the treatment. These pictures were taken with the mouths closed and teeth not showing; apparently orthodontic treatment affects facial structure as well as teeth, and the raters must have been responding to the subtle facial changes. Berscheid (1981) noted that the dramatic change in others' reactions to one who has had aesthetic surgery, while generally leading to more positive treatment, may also be unsettling. It provides us with compelling evidence of the importance of physical attractiveness in determining our reactions to people.

LOVE

What Is Love?

Are Liking and Loving the Same?

Is love just intense liking or is it something else altogether? This question has intrigued people for centuries. The most basic distinction is that between **companionate love** and **passionate (romantic) love**. Companionate love is the affection we feel for those with whom our lives are deeply intertwined. The only real difference between liking and companionate love may be the depth of our feelings and the degree of our involvement with the other person.

Passionate love is something else again. Theorists (Berscheid et al., 1989a; Hatfield & Walster, 1978) have suggested that passionate love differs from liking in several major ways. First, although liking seems to relate strongly to rewards, passionate love seems to stimulate fantasy and imagined gratifications that may occur out of all proportion to the actual rewards received. Second, whereas liking and friendship often grow over time, passionate love often seems to become diluted with the passage of time. In contrast to liking, romantic love seems to thrive on novelty and uncertainty, rather than familiarity and predictability. Finally, liking seems consistently associated with good thoughts and feelings, but passionate love is often associated with conflicting emotions, as shown by teenagers' frequent question of whether it's possible to love and hate someone at the same time. To summarize, reinforcement concepts seem to account fairly well for liking and for companionate love, but passionate love seems to include a strong mix of rewards and punishments. New concepts may be necessary if we are to understand passionate love.

Rubin (1973; 1974) developed questionnaires to measure liking and loving and found that there was only a modest relationship ($r = .39$) between a woman's liking and loving scale score for the same man. Men's liking and loving scale scores were more strongly related ($r = .60$), leading Rubin to suggest that women may distinguish more sharply between liking and loving than do men. Passionate love, as defined by Hatfield and her co-workers (Hatfield & Rapson, 1987; Hatfield & Sprecher, 1986) has cognitive, emotional, and behavioral components. These are summarized in Table 8-1.

Definitions of Love

Books of famous quotations generally include more quotations about love than almost any other topic, superficial evidence of human interest in the

companionate love: The affection we feel for those with whom our lives are deeply intertwined; similar to very deep friendship.

passionate love: Romantic love that has cognitive, behavioral, and emotional components; seems not as directly related to rewards as is liking.

Passionate love. Romance novels and magazines help popularize the concept of passionate love in our culture.

TABLE 8-1   THE COMPONENTS OF PASSIONATE LOVE

Items measured on the Passionate Love Scale developed by Hatfield and Sprecher (1986) and Hatfield and Rapson (1987).

Cognitive Components

Preoccupation with one's partner
Idealization of the partner or the relationship
Desire to know the partner well and be known

Behavioral Components

Actions to determine the partner's feelings
Studying the other person
Serving and helping the partner

Emotional Components

Attraction to the partner, especially sexual attraction
Positive feelings when things go well
Negative feelings when things go awry
Desire for complete and permanent union
Physiological arousal
Longing for reciprocity

triangular theory of love:

Sternberg's theory that love has three central components: intimacy, passion, and commitment.

nature of love. It is ironic that Sigmund Freud, who had so many insights on so many other topics, had relatively little to say about love. Early in his career, Freud commented in a letter to Einstein, "Up to the present, I have not found the courage to make any broad statements on the essence of love, and I think that our knowledge is not sufficient to do so" (quoted in Reik, 1944, p. 9). Much later, near the end of his career, Freud lamented, "We really know very little about love."

Recently, social scientists have surveyed the vast writings on love to attempt to unmask its essence. As shown in Focus 8-4, even the government has gotten in on the act. Dozens of definitions have been proposed in the past two decades; I'll review only a central few. After digesting what the poets, philosophers, and songwriters had to say, Rubin (1973) suggested that the concept of romantic love had three characteristics: (1) a physical and emotional *attachment*—a need for another person, the passionate desire to possess and be fulfilled by that person; (2) *caring;* the giving of oneself to another person; and (3) *intimacy;* an intense bond between two people. Reanalyzing Rubin's Love Scale, Harold Kelley (1983) identified four main components: *caring, needing, trust,* and *tolerance for another's faults.* Kelley found that undergraduates saw caring as the most important factor in love, with needing the next most important. Trust was seen as less important for love, but just as central as caring and needing when describing friendships. Still another research program (Davis, 1985) found data suggesting that friendship and love have many characteristics in common, but two clusters of factors were more typical of love than friendship: a *passion cluster* (fascination, sexual desire, exclusivity) and a *caring cluster* (championing each other's interests, "giving the utmost").

Another way to conceptualize love is depicted in Figure 8-4. Robert Sternberg (1987; 1988) proposed a **triangular theory of love,** holding that love has three central components: *intimacy, passion,* and *commitment.* The intimacy component contains feelings that create the experience of warmth

---

FOCUS 8-4

The Politics of Studying Love

It is only within your lifetime that social scientists have begun to study love seriously. Before that, the study of love had been limited to general surveys, and to the observations of philosophers such as Plato and Ovid and personality theorists such as Freud, Reik, Fromm, Rogers, and others. As research grants were awarded for the study of love in the 1970s, the popular reaction to this expendature of money varied greatly. At one extreme, Senator William Proxmire in 1975 gave one of his "Golden Fleece Awards" to the National Science Foundation for, in his eyes, wasting taxpayers' money by supporting research on love. His press release stated that "even if they spend eighty-four million or eighty-four billion dollars, they wouldn't get an answer that anyone would believe. I'm also against it because I don't want the answer. I believe that two hundred million other Americans want to leave some things in life a mystery, and right at the top of things we don't want to know is why a man falls in love with a woman and vice versa . . . So, National Science Foundation—get out of the love racket. Leave that

to Elizabeth Barret Browning and Irving Berlin. Here if anywhere, Alexander Pope was right when he observed, 'If ignorance is bliss, 'tis folly to be wise.' "

Many people, as you might imagine, reacted angrily to Proxmire's potshot. An effective rejoinder was provided by *New York Times* columnist James Reston, who wrote that while love might always be a mystery, "if the sociologists and psychologists can get even a suggestion of the answer to our pattern of romantic love, marriage, disillusionment, divorce—and the children left behind—it would be the best investment of federal money since Jefferson made the Louisiana Purchase" (Reston, 1975). One leading researcher, Ellen Berscheid (1988), estimated that it cost her, at a minimum, two years from her personal and professional life to deal with the publicity, debate, and controversy that surrounded her work on love. The scientific study of love is still in its infancy, but I agree with Reston that it may be one of the most important social psychological research areas of our time. ❖

---

in a relationship (sharing, mutual understanding, emotional support), while passion refers to the drives that lead to romance, physical attraction, and sexual behaviors. While sexual needs may be paramount, other needs may also contribute to the experience of passion—needs for self-esteem, for dominance or submission, for affiliation. The commitment component involves a short-term decision that one loves someone and a long-term commitment to maintain that love.

Various combinations of those three components produce the seven varieties of love depicted in Figure 8-4. Most of the terms are self-explanatory; I'll comment on a couple that are less so. **Infatuation** (passion alone) is "love at first sight" or, in general, love that involves an obsession with an idealized partner. Infatuated relationships tend to involve unequal involvements and are very unstable. In contrast, *empty love* may occur in long-term, stagnant relationships, perhaps a marriage held together for convenience, habit, fear of change, or "for the children's sake." When all that's left is a commitment,

infatuation:
In Sternberg's theory, passion without commitment or intimacy.

As sex roles change, will men suffer more of the indignities traditionally reserved for women?

it is very difficult to restore the other elements to renew the marriage and make the magic return.

Fatuous love involves commitment made on the basis of passion without the stabilizing element of intimate involvement, which takes time to develop. It is the kind of love we sometimes associate with whirlwind Hollywood courtships and marriages. "When the passion fades—as it almost inevitably

FIGURE 8-4

Sternberg's Triangular Theory of Love

Varieties of Loving as Different Combinations of the Three Components of Love.

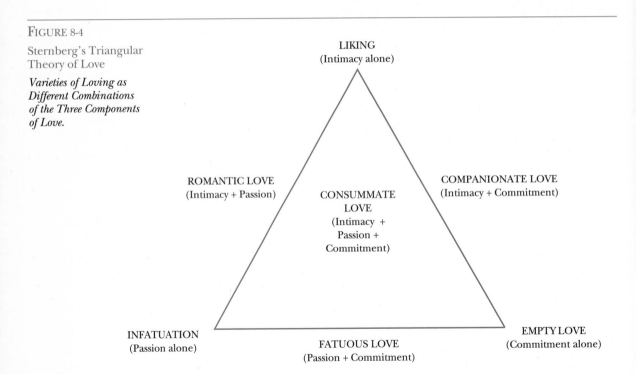

Source: From *The Psychology of Love,* edited by Robert J. Sternberg and Michael L. Barnes, p. 122. Copyright © 1988 by Yale University Press. Reprinted by permission.

does—all that is left is the commitment. . . . They feel shortchanged—they have gotten much less than they bargained for. The problem, of course, is that they bargained for too much of one thing (passion) and not enough of another (intimacy)" (Sternberg, 1988, p. 128).

Is commitment an integral part of love? Sternberg's model says so, but other research suggests that though the concepts of love and commitment overlap (Kelley, 1983), they are different. Figure 8-5 shows what college students listed as central features of love and of commitment (Fehr, 1988). There was little overlap between the central features most commonly listed: only trust, sacrifice, caring, and honesty were listed by over 10 percent of the respondents as central to both love and commitment.

How can we reconcile all these different conceptualizations of love? Clyde and Susan Hendrick (1989) provided a statistical solution. They gave five widely used measures of love to a sample of college undergraduates and then factor analyzed the students' responses to see which items from the var-

---

FIGURE 8-5

Do Commitment and Love Differ?

Percentages of college students who listed various characteristics as central facets of love and of commitment.

LOVE		COMMITMENT	
feature	% of subjects	feature	% of subjects
* Caring	44%	Perseverence	35%
Happiness	29%	Responsibility	28%
Want to be with other	28%	Living up to your word	24%
Friendship	23%	Devotion	21%
Feel free to talk about anything	20%	Faithfulness	19%
Warm feelings	17%	Obligation	18%
Accept another the way he/she is	16%	* Sacrifice	16%
* Trust	15%	* Honesty	15%
Commitment	14%	Love	15%
Sharing	14%	* Trust	13%
Think about the other all the time	14%	* Helping	12%
* Sacrifice	14%	Loyalty	12%
Understanding	13%	A promise	12%
		Being there for the other in good and bad times	11%
* Honesty	11%		
Respect	11%	* Mutual Agreement	11%
Contentment	10%	Caring	10%
Euphoria	10%	Give your best effort	10%

Source: From Fehr, B. (1988). Prototype analysis of the concepts of love and commitment. *Journal of Personality and Social Psychology, 55,* 557–579. Copyright © 1988 by the American Psychological Association. Reprinted by permission.

*Features listed by over 10% of respondents as characteristic of both love and commitment

ious questionnaires clustered together statistically. This resulted in five factors, which they labeled: passionate love, closeness, ambivalence, secure attachment, and practicality.

Why these somewhat different pictures? In part, the outcome of each study depends on exactly what questions are asked. Beyond this, the varied findings indicate we still have a way to go in pinning down an adequate definition of love. There are as many definitions of love as there are poets, philosophers, songwriters, and social scientists to write about it.

Styles of Loving

After surveying adults in the U.S., Canada, and Great Britain, Lee (1988) proposed that there were six basic *styles* of loving:

1. *Erotic or romantic love.* This kind of love reflects an immediate powerful physical attraction to someone else. Based on the sparse research available at the time, Hatfield and Walster (1978) suggested that usually such love burns intensely and then dies. Only rarely, they suggested, does the initial rapture blossom into a more lasting love. However, reviewing recent research just three years later, Traupmann and Hatfield (1981) proposed that both passionate and companionate love may be far hardier than earlier researchers had assumed.

self-centered love:
Love that is used as a game. Partners tend to not become too attached while the other person's affection grows.

2. *Playful or* **self-centered love**. The Roman poet Ovid developed the idea of playful love as a game. Persons who adopt this style tend not to become attached to their partners or allow their partners to become too attached to them. They see love as a series of challenges and puzzles to solve and may avoid becoming committed.

3. *Companionate love.* The companionate style of loving is less tumultuous than the obsessive or erotic styles. Cases of companionate love may occur when a couple begins as friends who share a common interest and enjoy doing things together. Gradually, perhaps to their surprise, the friendship may blossom into love. Unlike other couples, if these couples decide to separate as lovers, they may still be able to remain friends.

obsessive or insecure love:
Love that is characterized by obsession with the loved one and anxiety.

4. **Obsessive** or **insecure love**. Ancient Greek philosophers Sappho and Plato, among others, wrote of the agitation, fever, loss of appetite, sleeplessness, and heartache that obsessed lovers often feel. Such a style often leads to furious jealousy, helpless obsessions, and tragic endings, as the obsessive lover alternates between the peaks of ecstasy and the depths of despair. In a recent book, Hindy, Schwarz, and Brodsky (1989) described the "anxious romantic attachment" people may feel, the "he loves me, he loves me not" sensation of being kept constantly on edge by a fickle loved one.

practical love:
Where one searches for a partner who is an appropriate match in terms of personality and background. The hope is that they will develop a deeper bond.

5. **Practical love**. In this style of love, the lover searches for an appropriate match in terms of personality, religion, interests, background, and so forth. Lovers who endorse this style often hope that once an appropriate partner is found, more intense feelings may develop between the partners. The extreme of this orientation is reflected in cultures in which marriages

are arranged by the parents. The cultural expectation is that once the appropriately matched youths get to know each other, they will develop a deeper bond.

6. *Agape or* **altruistic love**. This is the classical Judeo-Christian concept of love, which is patient, kind, and does not demand reciprocity. Despite the attention given to this concept of love in religious and philosophical writings, it is apparently very uncommon. Lee (1974, p. 50) commented that, "I found no saints in my sample. I have yet to interview an unqualified example of agape, although a few respondents had brief agapic episodes in relationships otherwise tinged with selfishness."

Cultures and subcultures differ widely in which styles of love are deemed most appropriate. An anthropologist (Levy, 1973) reported that when Tahitians were asked to describe their feelings of passionate love, they were incredulous, for they could not imagine people having such emotions. Apparently, this style of loving did not exist in their culture. The American culture, on the other hand, seems particularly fascinated with the passionate side of love and its relationship to marriage. A half-century ago, another anthropologist asserted that "All societies recognize that there are occasional violent emotional attachments between persons of the opposite sex, but our present American culture is practically the only one that has attempted to capitalize on these and make them the basis of marriage" (Linton, 1936, p. 175).

What is the most important message in these observations? Probably that there is no one best style of love or loving. The happiness of a loving couple may be related to the match between their styles of loving. If the partners share the same approach to loving and the same definition of love, they share a common language and set of assumptions. If they hold two very different concepts (say, an obsessive lover and a playful lover) it seems unlikely that the relationship will be a lasting one; indeed, a great deal of pain may lie ahead.

How might different styles of loving develop? The **attachment style** that develops in infancy may be an important source. Hazen and Shaver (1987; Shaver et al., 1988) proposed that infants adopt one of three dominant attachment styles toward their parents: *secure, avoidant,* or *anxious/ambivalent.* The researchers argued that people tend to repeat their characteristic attachment style in adult romantic relationships. Some people are trusting and stable (secure attachment style), some are detached and unresponsive lovers (avoidant style), while others are anxious and uncertain (anxious/ambivalent style). In proposing this link between infancy and adulthood, Hazen and Shaver (1987) pointed out that the frequency of the different styles is about the same among infants (Campos et al., 1983) and among adults: about 60% show a secure attachment style, 20 to 25% are avoidant, and 15 to 20% are anxious/ambivalent. Of course, many other factors such as sex-role socialization and experiences in previous relationships will also affect the style of loving adopted as an adult.

altruistic love:
Love which is patient, kind, and does not demand reciprocity; very uncommon.

attachment style:
Characteristic way of relating to others that develops in infancy and may affect adult romantic relationships. Three major types are: secure, avoidant, and anxious/ambivalent.

Love versus Infatuation

The widely differing definitions and styles of love vividly illustrate the difficulty in pinning down this thing called love. Feelings that I label as love (e.g., playfulness, or passion, or friendly affection) may not be the ones that you would label as love. Similarly, behaviors that I define as loving may not appear loving to you. There is one question that many of us have spent much time and energy contemplating: Is it really love or just infatuation? What is the difference between these two widely discussed states? Some have argued that there is no difference. Hatfield and Walster (1978, p. 52) were skeptical that passionate love and infatuation differ in any way—*at the time one is experiencing them.* They suggested that the two terms are used most often when looking back at a relationship. If it has gone well, we decide that it was true love. Conversely, if the relationship dies, we conclude in hindsight that it must have been merely infatuation. Sternberg (1988), as we have seen, disagrees. He sees infatuation as passion without commitment or intimacy.

The situation becomes even more ambiguous when you try to analyze how other people (say your friends or your parents) decide whether your relationship is love or infatuation. In such cases, they may not really be commenting on the quality of your feelings at all. Instead, your friends or parents may be telling you whether or not they *approve* of your relationship. If they approve, they are likely to agree that it may be love; if they don't approve, they are likely to insist that it is only infatuation.

Factors Related to Love

Rewards

Perhaps each of us has a favorite style or styles of loving. Some people fly to the heights of ecstasy and crash into the depths of despair; others never experience such extremes and may even view such behaviors as more than a little strange (Tennov, 1979). Although liking and loving may differ considerably, many of the rewarding factors that increase liking are likely to increase the chances of loving as well: propinquity, similarity in attitudes and values, physical attractiveness, reciprocal loving. People who have socially desirable characteristics such as attractiveness, sociability, or high ability, and who behave in a rewarding way by being pleasant, attentive, or loving are more likely to become objects of someone's love.

Is it love or infatuation? Some researchers suggest that it's hard to tell.

Gender Differences

As Focus 8-5 illustrates, there is a stereotype in our culture that women fall in love more often than men. In actuality, research has indicated that men score higher on romanticism scales than women do (Dion & Dion, 1973; Hobart, 1958). Other research indicates that men fall in love faster (after a fewer number of dates) than women do (Kanin et al., 1970). Men and women also react differently to the breakup of a relationship. Research on college students indicates that women decide to end the relationship more often than do men. Perhaps as a consequence of this, men are more depressed,

FOCUS 8-5

Men and Women in Love

Please take a minute and answer the following questions:

1. How many times have you been in love? (By this I mean romantic love, not family love, etc.): _____ times.

2. When college sophomores and juniors are asked the same question, what will the average woman answer (in terms of how many times she has been in love)? Women will say _____ times.

3. What will the average sophomore or junior man answer (about how many times he has been in love)? Men will say _____ times.

I have asked these same questions to hundreds of students in psychology classes over the past few years. The answers given by men and women in the classes have been remarkably stable over the years. The number of times that men and women report being in romantic love are almost identical (the most common responses are 1, 2, and 0, in that order). Yet both men and women *predict* that women will report having been in love more than will men. This is an interesting stereotype which, according to the actual responses of the women and men, has no basis in reality. Women's predictions have generally been closer to the actual rates of reporting than were the men's. ❖

lonely, and unhappy after terminated relationships than are women, and have more difficulty accepting the end of the relationship (Hill et al., 1976). Men are three times as likely as women to commit suicide after a disastrous love affair (Hatfield & Walster, 1978). Kanin and his co-workers (1970) found that women tended to report more physical symptoms associated with intense love (feelings such as insomnia, cold hands, "butterflies" in the stomach, trouble concentrating, feeling like "I was floating on a cloud," etc.) than did men. It seems clear that the idea that women are generally more romantic than men isn't true. Men show stronger indications of some types of romanticism; women show stronger evidence of others.

Systematic sex differences in style of loving, however, may exist. Surveys of hundreds of adults indicate that men are more likely to adopt romantic, playful, or self-centered styles of loving, while women more often show companionate, obsessive/insecure, or practical styles (Hatkoff & Lasswell, 1979; Hendrick et al., 1984). No one seemed to be very altruistic. In general, women appeared to feel more of the "friendly" kinds of love (companionate, practical) than men did (Hatfield, 1982). Traupmann and Hatfield (1981) asked dating, newlywed, and older people how companionately they loved their partners and how much they were loved in return. While dating and early in marriage, most women felt that they gave their partners more companionate love than they received in return. Researchers found little difference in the degree to which men and women were willing to confide in their partners, but they differed in the types of information they shared. Men are

TABLE 8-2   WOMEN AND MEN IN LOVE

Reliable gender differences in the characteristic ways that men and women behave in loving relationships.

Women	Men

Prevalent sytles of loving are:
   companionate
   practical
   obsessive/insecure
	Prevalent styles of loving are:
	   romantic
	   self-centered
	   playful

Willing to self-disclose, talk of fears and feelings	Not willing to self-disclose, will talk about political views and perceived strengths
Often want more intimacy than they are receiving	May want less intimacy than they are receiving
Feel more physical symptoms associated with intense love	Score higher on measures of romanticism
More often the one who decides to end the relationship	More depressed, lonely, and unhappy after a relationship has ended
	Fall in love faster

more willing to talk about their political views and pride in their strengths, whereas women are more likely to disclose feelings about other people and their fears (Rubin et al., 1980). Women often may want more intimacy than they are receiving, and men may want far less (Chaiken & Derlega, 1974). These gender differences are summarized in Table 8-2.

How Can One Identify Love?

Figuring Out Whether Someone Loves You

Does he love me? Does she love me? That is a hard-to-answer question! Think back to the material on attributions covered in Chapters 2 and 3. Research indicates that, when making self-attributions about our emotions, we pay attention not only to our own physiological arousal, but also to factors in the environment. This implies that you can "help" someone decide that she loves you by acting as if you assume that you are loved. Note, this is quite different from taking the other person for granted. If you act as if you know (and appreciate) that your partner loves you, you are providing the other person with evidence that her behavior is perceived as loving. Your partner may use this evidence, along with whatever other evidence is available, to decide whether or not it's love. If you have treated it as love, that may increase the chance that your partner will treat it the same way. Of course, one could also set the opposite process in motion, too. A clever description of such a self-defeating tactic is presented in Focus 8-6.

Figuring Out Whether You're in Love

How do you know whether you're in love? This may be just as difficult a question as deciding whether or not someone loves you—there is no easy answer. After reviewing much of the research on this topic, Hatfield and Walster (1978) were left with the conclusion that the best guess is, "You're in love when you think you are." I have asked hundreds of college students how they have known when they were in love. A sampling of their answers appears in Focus 8-7. As other research would lead us to predict, women have been much more likely to mention physical sensations than men have been.

FOCUS 8-6

How to Make Yourself Miserable:
A Relationship-Destroying Maneuver

Reject-me move #1:

You: Do you love me?

Mate: "Yes, *of course* I love you."

Reject-me move #2:

You: "Do you *really* love me?"

Mate: "Yes, I really love you."

You: "You really really love me?"

Mate: "Yes, I really really love you."

You: "You're *sure* you love me—you're absolutely sure?"

Mate: "Yes, I'm absolutely sure."
(*pause*)

You: "Do you know the meaning of the word *love*?"
(*pause*)

Mate: "I don't know."

You: "Then how can you be so sure you love me?"
(*pause*)

Mate: "I don't know. Perhaps I can't."

Reject-me move #3:

You: "You can't, eh? I see. Well, since you can't even be sure you love me, I can't really see much point in our remaining together. Can you?"
(*pause*)

Mate: "I don't know. Perhaps not."
(*pause*)

You: "You've been leading up to this for a pretty long time, haven't you?" ❖

Source: From *How to Make Yourself Miserable,* by Dan Greenberg with Marcia Jacobs. Copyright © 1966 by Dan Greenberg. Reprinted by permission of Random House, Inc.

How Do You Know When You're in Love?
College Students' Views

Some undergraduates' anonymous responses to the question: "How do you know when you're in love?"

Female, age 21

I get a silly grin on my face. I feel warm inside. Sometimes its hard to breathe, like I'm on the verge of hyperventilating or something. I feel brave enough to stare in that person's eyes for hours.

Male, age 22

I feel that it really depends on the person. Some say they hear bells, see rockets, or feel the earth move. For me, it is an undescribable feeling of wholeness or completeness that seems to grow as time goes on. The more I get to know about my girlfriend, the more of a bonding there is between the two of us.

Female, age 19

I really truly care how the person feels, what will hurt them really matters. They are my best friend, I want to tell them everything that happens to me every day and to hear everything about their day. I love to hear everything about them; their thoughts, their dreams, their disappointments, how they were as a child. And I love to be with them always and be able to touch them always.

Male, age 20

When you are with the person you "love" and are unafraid to share with that person and give of yourself to that person unselfishly. You know you are in love when you feel this type of security within and have a need to express it to the person who is associated with the feelings.

Female, age 19

I can be myself around this person (happy, sad, grumpy, mature, immature, etc.) and he still treats me the same. This person makes me happy, he brings out the good in me and a lot of times gives me strength. I feel a secure bond between us. He's my best friend and my boyfriend. He makes me feel good about myself, and my life. I feel he admires me for the person I am, and he sees special characteristics about me that other people overlook.

Male, age 20

I knew I was in love when I felt that that person had become incorporated into my life so deeply that I felt like that person was a real growing part of me . . .like an arm or leg. When that person was in pain, I was in pain, when excited or happy, I was happy.

Female, age 19

I know when I'm in love when I care deeply for another person, love spending time with him, am able to share anything openly and honestly with him, and trust him completely. He also is my best friend. I also know I'm in love when I can disagree or argue but still care enough to accept the other person's view as their own.

Male, age 19

I feel I need the other person. When I'm not around her I miss her and feel a sense of emptiness. I feel I trust her and her love for me is always present. Any kind of "token" or reminder of her is special. I feel I can tell her anything.

Female, age 18

Because I stop eating and run on reserve energy.

Male, age 21

I know that I am in love when after a few months into the relationship, I regard that person highly enough to want to *work* on the relationship. ❖

Labeling One's Own Love: Self-Attributions

Deciding that you are in love can involve schemas, prototypes, and self-attributions of emotion. Recall our discussion of schemas and prototypes in Chapter 2. In attempting to answer this thorny question, you will compare the features of your relationship with your mental representation (schema) of "love." If there is a match, it must be love. Once you perceive a match, you are likely to assume that the relationship or your partner has all of the *other* features comprising your schema of love (see Figure 8-4), whether or not this is actually so.

Turning to emotional self-attributions, we saw in Chapter 3 that there are many factors that determine the self-attribution of emotion. Schachter's (1964) two-factor theory of emotion asserts that any particular feeling of an emotion is dependent on (1) a state of physiological arousal, and (2) cognitive cues available in the environment as to what caused the arousal. In most cases, these two items of information are very clear; we feel physiologically aroused and the cause of the arousal is obvious to us—an attractive person of the opposite sex.

In cases where the cognitive cues are somewhat mixed or ambiguous, a person may be uncertain as to what emotion she is feeling. Recall the classroom example that began this chapter. In these cases, arousal of one sort (fear or anxiety) might be interpreted as representing an emotion of quite a different sort (say, love). Walster and Berscheid (1971) suggested that the physiological arousal necessary for feeling an emotion such as love could stem from many causes. Obviously, sexual arousal is one; but other seemingly irrelevant emotional states, such as anxiety, guilt, loneliness, hatred, jealousy, or even confusion, may also lead to physiological arousal and, hence, to the increased probability of labeling one's state as love. Misattribution does not always occur, but numerous studies have demonstrated that under the right condition, a variety of awkward and painful experiences can deepen passion; these include anxiety, fear, embarrassment, loneliness, grief, and anger at parental attempts to break up an affair (Hatfield & Rapson, 1987).

This idea of the *misattribution of love* is not new. Writing in the *Art of Love*, Ovid suggested that an excellent time to arouse passion in a woman was while she was watching Roman gladiators fight. Centuries later, in the late 1800s, Horwicz (cited in Rubin, 1973, p. 6) suggested that "Love can only be excited by strong and vivid emotion, and it is almost immaterial whether these emotions are agreeable or disagreeable." Thus, Horwicz proposed, by taking one's partner to a place where strong emotions of excitement or fear would probably be aroused (such as watching gladiators), arousal of love might be facilitated as well.

Following the lead of Ovid and Horwicz, it can be predicted that if a state of emotional arousal exists *for any reason*, and if the cognitive situation suggests that passionate love would be an appropriate state to be feeling, then feelings of passionate love are likely to increase. If this is so, even negative experiences can induce love, for they still would intensify arousal. Love does not exist unless the lover defines it as such; therefore, if the appropriate cognitions are present, almost any form of arousal may lead a person to label the emotion as love. As poets have said, love may not be very different from hate after all.

Although research is far from complete, some evidence supports the application of this theory of emotion to the area of love. For example, very passionate love affairs appear most likely to occur during wartime. Perhaps these feelings of passion are intensified by the heightened general levels of emotional arousal that are common during wartime.

Dutton and Aron (1974) performed several experiments to test the misattribution interpretation of romantic love. In one field study, an attractive female or male interviewer approached solitary male hikers just after they had crossed a 5-foot-wide, 450-foot-long suspension bridge (which had a frightening tendency to tilt, sway, and wobble) 250 feet above rocks and rapids. Other subjects were interviewed by one of the same interviewers after crossing a sturdy bridge over a mere ten-foot drop. After the interview, the interviewer offered each subject a phone number in case he wanted to find out more about the research. The researchers hypothesized that men who had just crossed the frightening bridge might misattribute some of the emotion they were feeling (fear, anxiety, relief, etc.) as attraction, if a suitably attractive female were present. Dutton and Aron were interested in whether the respondents would be attracted enough to the female to call her later. Sure enough, men in the high-fear condition (high, swaying bridge) were more likely to call the attractive female interviewer later than were men in the low-fear (low, sturdy bridge) condition.

Other research has given renewed support to the notion that arousal can lead to misattributions of romantic love. White, Fishbein, and Rutstein (1981) used three different audiotapes to cause either (1) high negative arousal (a grisly description of a missionary being killed and mutilated while his family watched), (2) high positive arousal (recorded selections by comedian Steve Martin), or (3) neutral low arousal (a description of a frog's circulatory system taken from a biology text). Subjects then watched a five-minute videotape of a female college student talking about a variety of topics, including hobbies, family, career interests, and her favorite dating activities. For half the subjects she was made up to look very attractive; for the other half she appeared in unattractive clothing and makeup. After viewing the tape, subjects rated the woman on a number of items.

As Figure 8-6 indicates, when the woman was attractive, the males felt more romantic attraction to her when they were highly aroused in a positive or negative direction than when they were less aroused. The woman also was seen as having more positive traits when she was attractive and the men had been aroused (in either a positive or negative direction) than when arousal was low or she was unattractive. Analyses indicated that subjects who heard the arousing tapes paid more attention to the woman than did unaroused subjects, perhaps increasing the impact of her attractiveness. Misat-

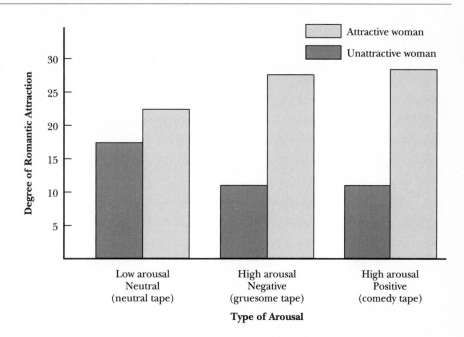

FIGURE 8-6

Misattribution of Romantic
Attraction

*College males' degree of roman-
tic attraction to an attractive
or unattractive woman,
depending on the amount of
arousal they felt.*

Source: Data from White, G. L., Fishbein, S., & Rutstein, J. (1981). Passionate love and the
misattribution of arousal. *Journal of Personality and Social Psychology, 41,* 56–62.

tribution effects are likely to the extent that possible alternative causes of
arousal (attractiveness) are more salient than the true causes of the arousal
(Murstein, 1986).

Labeling One's Own Love: Negative Reinforcement

Other researchers suggest that although misattribution is possible, it is rare.
Kenrick and Cialdini (1977) argued that a more economical explanation is
provided by extending reinforcement theory to include both negative and
positive reinforcement. If a person becomes associated with the termination
or reduction of aversive stimuli (negative reinforcement), then attraction for
that person should be strengthened. This explanation may provide a simpler way to understand many situations that have been classed as misattributions. In the Dutton and Aron (1974) experiment, for example, the
attractive female interviewer may have been associated with the relief that
the hikers felt after having crossed the scary bridge. Such a *reduction of aversive arousal* may serve to strengthen interpersonal bonds between persons
in the situation, increasing attraction. To the extent that fear or other aversive states are present in the context of a heterosexual relationship, Kenrick
and Cialdini (1977) argued, the reduction of relatively high levels of such

arousal will lead to increased attraction. Reductions in arousal may be caused by social acceptance, physical caresses, sexual release, and many other factors. They noted that lovers are sometimes heard to report that a lover's quarrel was almost worth it, because making up later was so much fun. Such an event would be especially rewarding because it embodies both types of reinforcement: the removal of a noxious state (the quarrel) and the substitution of a pleasant one.

In subsequent research, Kenrick and his co-workers (1979) conducted four studies that attempted to determine whether negatively induced arousal would, through misattribution, increase males' feelings of attraction for a nearby female. Misattribution did not occur in any of the four studies, supporting their idea that reduction of aversive arousal is the more important factor. However, these researchers do not go so far as to claim that misattribution of negative arousal would never occur. In their words, "Given a situation involving a highly ambiguous and diffuse state of arousal, for which there is no clear and salient cause, and given the presence of an individual of the opposite sex who meets all the standards for a romantic label . . . a misattribution of arousal along romantic lines would be quite possible" (Kenrick & Cialdini, 1977, p. 389).

Reprise

Hatfield and Walster (1978) asserted that the best answer to an extremely difficult question is: You're in love when you think you are. Perhaps this statement should be qualified a little. It is possible to be fooled — to mislabel arousal that is really caused by some other factor, even a negative one, as love. Misattribution of negative emotion may be uncommon, as Kenrick and Cialdini suggested, but it does occur. Misattribution of arousal is most likely to occur when a person is in an ambiguous state of arousal that has no clear cause, and also in the presence of a person of the opposite sex who meets all the standards (especially physical attractiveness) for a romantic attribution.

One aspect of romantic love that has not been closely studied is the sexual component (Rubin, 1988). Obviously, this is a difficult issue to study with questionnaires. But one leading researcher, when addressing the question "What is love?", admitted "I don't really know — but, if forced against a brick wall to face a firing squad who would shoot if not given the correct answer, I would whisper, 'It's about 90 percent sexual desire not yet sated'" (Berscheid, 1988, p. 373). If this is so, then researchers had better start figuring out how to incorporate sexuality into their conceptions of love.

SUMMARY

We can identify four major reasons why people affiliate with each other: First, affiliation permits social comparison with others, which can be useful for self-evaluation or be used in a self-enhancing way. Second, affiliation can provide emotional support (reduction of fear, loneliness, anxiety). Third, affiliation can produce positive affect (liking, love) from interpersonal closeness and communication. Finally, affiliation provides attention from others (praise, status, admiration, appreciation, and so forth). The most important factors determining liking are propinquity (nearness), similarity, maintaining balance, and physical attractiveness. Propinquity is important because nearby people are more available, more predictable (after continued interactions), and more familiar. Morever, we tend to stress the positive aspects of persons with whom we must continue to interact. Physical attractiveness is highly valued socially, and persons assume that physically attractive people have more attractive personalities. Other factors related to liking include positive emotional arousal, high ability, reciprocated liking and, occasionally, complementarity. On the other hand, being stigmatized can have a strong negative impact on one's well-being.

A number of different conceptualizations of love have been developed by social psychologists in recent years. Several styles of loving have been identified; finding someone with a style similar to your own may be critically important. It is not easy to figure out whether one is in love, that is, to make a self-attribution of love. One can be misled by the misattribution of arousal and by factors associated with negative reinforcement. Some have argued that an understanding of love is not appropriate or desirable. I (and the vast majority of social psychologists) disagree. If we can increase our understanding of the happiness that love can bring, and the ways in which sorrow, heartbreak, separation, and divorce can be reduced, we will have made a valuable contribution indeed. We will delve more deeply into an analysis of long-term relationships in the next chapter.

CHAPTER 9
Long-Term Relationships

by Karol Solomon Brigham

PREVIEW

In past years, most social psychologists interested in understanding relationships studied the factors that influence attraction in initial encounters. The study of the psychological dynamics of long-term close relationships has become a focus of social psychological research only in the past few years (Holmes & Boon, 1990). In this chapter we will go beyond the initial encounters and have a look at what happens over a longer period of time.

A variety of interactions characterize the close relationships that may exist between husbands and wives, friends, lovers, parents and children, and even employers and employees. In this chapter, we will focus primarily on adult heterosexual long-term relationships. Social exchange theory will provide a continuing frame of reference for our discussion. Several aspects of relationships will be analyzed, beginning with dating. We will examine the factors involved in relationship stability as well as reactions to "breaking up." We will then see what cohabiting relationships are like.

Most everyone in the United States will be married at least once. People have to deal with sexuality, jealousy, uses of power, and other commonly experienced relationship problems. Though every couple experiences their own unique course of relationship development and duration, many of the generalizations proposed in this chapter are relevant to any couple. And, as you know, things do not always work out. When this happens, people go through the difficult processes of breaking up, separating, or divorcing. We will look at how these decisions are made and how the balances of costs and rewards may determine certain outcomes in relationship decline and termination.

EVALUATING RELATIONSHIPS

How Relationships Develop

The process of establishing a long-term relationship is never exactly the same for any two couples. Yet certain generalities can be identified. No one theory can adequately explain relationship development, but several interesting ones have been proposed.

Complementary Needs Theory
Complementary needs theory, introduced in Chapter 8, proposes that in selecting a partner, individuals look for others who are similar with regard to factors such as age, race, religion, social class, residence, and even previous marital status (Winch, 1958). From this "field of eligibles," individuals select as a partner the one who will best complement their personal needs. Complementarity suggests a partner is different or opposite from them in some way. As a couple, the two people would form a more complete and satisfied

social unit. A filtering process in relationships was subsequently identified by Kerchkoff and Davis (1962), who suggested that value similarity and need complementarity are important at different points in a couple's relationship. Initially, similarity of social attributes of the couple are important, and only as the relationship progresses do personal and family values become important to a couple's permanence. Later, **need complementarity** might be the cohesive factor for couples whose relationships have progressed for a considerable amount of time.

Stimulus-Value-Role Model

The **stimulus-value-role model** (Murstein, 1987) suggests that mate selection occurs in three stages. In the stimulus stage, two people are attracted to one another. Often the stimulus is physical appearance. Next is the value stage, in which two people discover the extent to which they are alike in values and attitudes. Finally, in the role stage, a couple begins to act out their relationship roles. As a series of interactions takes place, decisions are made to maintain, deepen, or end the relationship.

Social Penetration Theory

Another stage theory of relationship development, **social penetration theory** (Altman & Taylor, 1973), focuses on the personality factors that affect the course of a given relationship. Social penetration theory analyzes the self-disclosures that take place in a relationship as the people reveal information about themselves. How does one learn enough about another person to evaluate the relationship? Altman and Taylor described the *breadth* and *depth* dimensions through which areas of personality are revealed. Breadth refers to the number of different areas about oneself that a person is willing to make accessible to another; depth refers to the level of personality that is revealed.

As people continue to interact in a relationship, they gradually move toward deeper areas of their personalities—from superficial to intimate levels of exchange (Focus 9-1). The process is accompanied by an increase in the areas of personality exchange (breadth) at a level of more intimate detail (depth). The process of social penetration is never complete and rarely proceeds in a smooth fashion; there may be spurts, plateaus, or long periods of stability. Many relationships never move beyond the exploratory stages.

A Theory of Relatedness

In their **theory of relatedness**, Levinger & Snoek (1972) described the developmental levels of long-term relationships. They described several levels of contact, beginning with awareness and surface contact and, if all goes well, deepening to interdependence and finally mutuality. In 1983, Levinger carried this work further and described an ABCDE model of sequential phases of relationship development. Levinger proposed the following five potential phases:

---

need complementarity:
The idea that people will like others whose needs are the opposite of their own.

stimulus-value-role model:
Murstein's suggestion that mate selection occurs in three stages: the stimulus stage, the value stage, and the role stage.

social penetraton theory:
Theory that focuses on the breadth and depth of self-disclosure in developing relationships.

theory of relatedness:
Theory that describes long-term relationships in five stages: awareness, build-up, continuation, deterioration, and ending.

Focus 9-1

Stages in Altman and Taylor's Social Penetration Theory

The social penetration process proceeds from superficial to intimate levels of exchange between two people. Although relationships do not always follow this exact course, there is usually a step-by-step progression. As the two people move closer together, there is an increase in the areas of personality exchange (breadth) at a level of more intimate detail (depth). The process is never really complete and it doesn't always proceed in a smooth fashion.

1. *Orientation Stage.* Interaction is largely limited to small talk, surface level clichés, and polite nonpersonal conversation. People are often very cautious and tentative in this stage.
2. *Exploratory Affective Exchanges.* There is a willingness to begin to allow the other person to know you better. Casual acquaintances and neighborly conversations would best describe this stage. Many of our interpersonal relationships do not pass beyond this point.

3. *Affective Exchange.* Interaction involves many facets of personality in this stage. Close friendships or dating relationships where people know one another well and have a fairly extensive history of association would be described by this stage. It is here that displays of intimate affection, such as kissing and intimate touching, are frequent. Also, there is an increase in communication concerning the private areas of personality.
4. *Stable Exchange.* The stable exchange stage is said to be achieved only in a few relationships. Partners who know each other well can now readily interpret and predict the feelings and behavior of the other. ❖

Source: Altman, I., & Taylor, D. A. (1973). *Social penetration: The development of interpersonal relationships.* New York: Holt, Rinehart & Winston.

A. AWARENESS or aquaintance with another person. This phase may last indefinitely.
B. BUILD-UP—interpersonal relations become increasingly interdependent. The partners explore the extent to which their compatible interactions exceed their incompatible interactions.
C. CONTINUATION—Consolidation of the relationship in a relatively durable commitment (marriage for many couples).
D. DETERIORATION—decline of the interconnection.
E. ENDING of the relationship, either through death or some form of separation.

Levinger noted that few relationships actually pass through all five stages. Most pairs never get beyond phase A, aquaintanceship. Of those who do, most are likely to terminate during phase B.

Interestingly, Levinger pointed out that different specialists have typically focused their attention on different parts of the sequence and have neglected others. For example, social psychologists have typically focused on phase A, initial attraction and impression formation (Chapter 8). Only recently have they turned their attention to B, C, and E (build-up, continuation, and ending). Clinicians (psychologists, marriage and family therapists) have concentrated on phase D, deteriorating relationships. Knowledge about the phase-to-phase transition or change processes has remained fragmentary.

Social Exchange Theory

Social exchange theory may be the perspective that best enables us to explain how and why people move through the various phases of relationships. Social scientists and philosophers have long known that many of the prime needs of human beings—for approval, love, friendship, and so forth—are satisfied by human interactions. Without others, such rewards could not be achieved. Approval, praise, love, and friendship can be bestowed only by other persons. Yet receiving rewards is only part of the story; giving is also rewarding.

social exchange theory: A theory that analyzes human interaction in terms of costs and rewards.

We often speak of conversation as an exchange of ideas. Our human interactions can involve the exchange of many things in addition to just ideas. To analyze human interactions in terms of what is exchanged, Harold Kelley, John Thibaut, and George Homans developed **social exchange theory** (Homans, 1961; Kelley & Thibaut, 1978; Thibaut & Kelley, 1959). According to the theory, any activity that leads to the gratification of a person's needs can be described as rewarding. The cost of engaging in an activity depends on the degree of effort, unpleasantness, and difficulty involved, and on rewards from other possible activities that are rejected in order to participate in the present one. Applying such an economic analysis to social relationships, one can speak of the *outcome* of an interaction in terms of overall rewards and costs. An activity provides one with a *profit* if the outcome is rewarding, or with *loss* if the outcome is negative. The theory assumes that we operate according to a **minimax strategy**, attempting to minimize costs and maximize rewards. Ultimately people tend to stay in relationships that are perceived as rewarding and move away from relationships that are perceived as too costly.

minimax strategy: The social exchange theory assumption that people attempt to minimize the costs and maximize the rewards of relationships.

Comparison Level: What We Expect

We can all think of many relationships that have had positive outcomes for us and many that have had negative ones, but the proportion of outcomes that have shown profits or losses differs among us. Some people have had high success interpersonally, with many profitable relationships; others have received less overall profit. Based on these differences, individuals develop expectations about the kind of outcome they are likely to receive from a particular relationship. Thibaut and Kelley (1959) described this general ex-

comparison level:
People's judgments as to the kind of outcome they expect to receive from a particular relationship.

pectation as a person's **comparison level** (CL). In general, an outcome that meets or exceeds one's expectations (CL) leads to feelings of satisfaction, while an outcome below one's expectation is related to dissatisfaction.

Individuals' comparison levels depend on their past experiences in relationships with others and their judgment of what outcomes people like themselves usually receive. One's self-esteem is closely related to comparison level. People with high self-esteem have a relatively high comparison level for interpersonal relationships; they expect to have relationships that provide a good profit level. People with low self-esteem (and hence a lower comparison level) may be satisfied with relationships that show little profit, or even a loss, if that is what they are used to receiving or think they deserve.

Comparison Level for Alternatives: The Next Best Thing

comparison level for alternatives:
The value of the next best alternative interaction a person could enter into.

Closely related to comparison level is **comparison level for alternatives** (CL_{ALT}), which refers to the value of the next best alternative interaction a person could enter. If the rewards available from an alternative relationship are high, a person may be less committed to a current relationship. For example, if Gina is stopped after class by an acquaintance who begins a conversation, the length of time Gina spends talking will depend on what alternative activities are possible. If she was going to the library to study when the acquaintance popped up, she might spend a longer time in conversation (assuming that studying in the library is not a very appealing alternative activity); her CL_{ALT} is low. If, on the other hand, she was on the way to meet an important date, the interaction with her acquaintance might be quite brief, since her CL_{ALT} would be high. The CL_{ALT} determines a person's *dependence* on a particular relationship, because it affects whether the person will sustain a particular interaction or reject it for an alternative. If outcomes drop below CL_{ALT}, the person may decide to terminate an existing relationship.

Satisfaction and Commitment

In order to understand why people stay together for a long time, we have to analyze both satisfaction and commitment. The satisfaction part is straightforward: we feel satisfied when perceived rewards are greater than costs. Commitment (a feeling of attachment and an intent to maintain the relationship) is more complex. Duffy and Rusbult (1986) theorized that people will be more committed to a relationship when: (1) they are satisfied with their outcomes; (2) there are no viable alternatives to the relationship; and (3) they have invested sizable resources in the relationship (such as time, effort, self-disclosure, emotional energy, mutual friends, shared possessions).

Utilizing a social exchange perspective, we will examine the development of romantic relationships: dating, cohabitation, and marriage. But do keep in mind that each individual will have a different perception about what is rewarding and what is costly, and it is unlikely that complex interpersonal relationships can be solely explained by this economic framework.

Theories of relationship development systematically analyze the exchanges between people in the process of forming relationships. Our focus on theories and stages doesn't mean that relationships always develop and proceed in predictable ways, as you may already know from personal experience. For one thing, chance often plays a vital role. As Bandura (1982) pointed out, chance encounters often strongly affect the course of life events—even in the formation of partnerships and marriage. He cautioned us to remember that "some of the most important determinants of life paths often arise through the most trivial circumstances." The theories of relationship development give us an important research and practical guide, but we should remember that life circumstances and chance encounters may have profound impacts on our relationships. If you ask a number of married couples how they met, you'll get varied stories. While social psychological analyses can provide valuable insights about the likely course of a relationship after two people meet, it is often chance or coincidence that determined whether the two ever met in the first place.

INTIMATE RELATIONSHIPS: DATING, COHABITATION, AND MARRIAGE

A relationship, once developed, can take many forms, from friendship to marriage. Although friendship is certainly relevant to romantic relationships, it will not be our central focus here. Rather, we will briefly review some relevant studies of dating and then move on to cohabitation and marriage, analyzing why couples stay together and how relationships usually end.

Dating

In North America, dating is the process through which much interpersonal interaction takes place in developing relationships. Dating is recreational as well as functional in meeting the needs of single people. Once a dating relationship begins, many factors will affect the course and progress—moving toward a more permanent commitment or breaking up. Why do certain dating relationships last, and what happens when they don't? One in-depth study of premarital relationships provided some answers. Hill, Rubin, and Peplau (1976) studied the course of the relationships of 231 unmarried couples. The couples were primarily white college students who had been dating for one to five months before their first contact with the researchers. An initial questionnaire was followed up at six months, one year, and two years.

About 45 percent of the couples had broken up by the end of the first year. One clear influence on these relationships was external circumstance; many relationships broke up at key turning points of the school year such as vacations. Factors external to a relationship may interact with internal factors to cause relationships to end at certain times. Within the relation-

Long-term commitment to a relationship can be a frightening prospect.
Source: From *Penguin Dreams and Stranger Things: A Bloom County Book* by Berke Breathed. Copyright © 1985 by The
Washington Post Company.

ship, closeness, amount of love, perceived probability of marriage, and equality of involvement were significant predictors of the relationship's stability.
Women appeared more sensitive than men to these factors and to problems
they were experiencing in the relationship. Women were also more likely
than men to compare their current relationships to other alternatives
(CL_{ALT}). Given this, it is not surprising to find that the women broke up dating relationships more frequently than did the men. We saw in the last chapter that men are generally more distressed about relationship breakups than
women are.

In a similar longitudinal study of shorter duration, Berg and McQuinn
(1986) found that couples still dating after four months were initially different than couples who broke up. They demonstrated greater love, they talked
more intimately, and they showed a greater willingness to change their behavior toward their partner.

Ellen Berscheid and her co-workers (1989a; 1989b) studied college students' romantic relationships across a nine-month period. To assess these
relationships they first developed a Relationship Closeness Inventory (RCI).
This inventory measures the frequency, diversity, and strength of interactions within relationships (Focus 9-2). Interestingly, when undergradutes were
asked to describe their "closest, most involved, most intimate relationship,"
only about half of them described a romantic relationship. Others described
a friendship or family relationship (Figure 9-1). Romantic couples who were
very close, according to RCI scores, were less likely to break up in the ensuing nine-months than were couples who initially scored as less close. The
likelihood of breakup was not related to how long the couple had already
been together, to their prior ratings of happiness, or even to their estimate
of how long the relationship would last. When close relationships did break
up, the partners felt greater emotional distress than those in less close relationships that ended. Simpson (1987) also found that closeness was related
to how much emotional distress individuals felt when a relationship broke

FOCUS 9-2

The Relationship Closeness Index

Components of the Relationship Closeness Index developed by Berscheid and her co-workers (Berscheid, Snyder, & Omoto, 1989a; 1989b), which assesses the frequency, diversity, and strength of interactions. Some sample items:

A. *Frequency of Interactions*
   During the past week, what is the average amount of time, per day, that you spent alone with this person in the
   morning, _____ ;
   in the afternoon _____ ;
   in the evening _____ ?

B. *Diversity of Interactions across Different Situations*
   For each of the following activities, check those that you have engaged in *alone* with this person in the past week (partial listing):

   Did laundry
   Prepared a meal
   Watched TV
   Went to a restaurant
   Went for a walk/drive
   Discussed personal things
   Went to a party/social event
   Attended class

   Went to church/religious function
   Worked on homework
   Engaged in sexual relations
   Cleaned house/apartment
   Went to a movie
   Exercised
   Went to a bar
   Visited friends

C. *Strength of Influence in Interactions*
   On a 7-point agree/disagree scale, indicate the amount of influence this person (X) has on your thoughts, feelings, and behavior.

   X influences the way I feel about the future.
   X does *not* influence how I choose to spend my money.
   X influences which parties and social events I attend.
   X influences the way I feel about myself.
   X does *not* influence my moods.
   X influences the basic values I hold.
   X does *not* influence the opinions that I have of other important people in my life.
   X influences how I spend my free time.
   X does *not* influence how I dress.
   X influences what I watch on TV.
   X does *not* influence which of my friends I see. ❖

Sources: From Berscheid, E., Snyder, M., & Omoto, A. M. (1989a). Issues in studying close relationships: Conceptualizing and measuring closeness. In C. Hendrick (Ed.), *Close relationships* (pp. 63–91). Newbury Park, CA: Sage. Berscheid, E., Snyder, M., & Omoto, A. M. (1989b). The relationship closeness inventory: Assessing the closeness of interpersonal relationships. *Journal of Personality and Social Psychology, 57,* 792–807.

up, though he found that distress was also higher for people who had dated the former partner for a long time and who believed they could not easily acquire a new desirable partner.

reward level:
Degree to which an individual receives positive rewards such as love, status, services, money, and sexuality, from a relationship.

These studies suggest that relationships that are close tend to be more stable, a finding supported by another study (Cate et al., 1982) of individuals who were dating one person exclusively. This study examined relationship stability considering the theoretical frameworks of equity and reward level. Contrary to predictions of equity theory (Walster, Walster, & Berscheid, 1978), **reward level** — the degree to which a person got positive rewards in the rela-

FIGURE 9-1

College Students' Closest
Relationships

*Percentage of students naming
each relationship type when
asked to describe the closest
relationship they have had
(from Berscheid, Snyder, &
Omoto, 1989a, p. 74).*

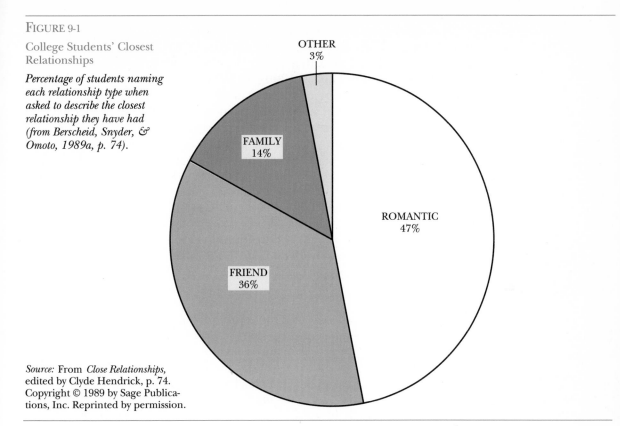

OTHER
3%

FAMILY
14%

ROMANTIC
47%

FRIEND
36%

Source: From *Close Relationships,*
edited by Clyde Hendrick, p. 74.
Copyright © 1989 by Sage Publications, Inc. Reprinted by permission.

tionship, such as love, status, services, goods, money, and information—was
a better predictor of relationship satisfaction than was equity. A further study
(Lloyd et al., 1984) found that involvement, reward level, and perceived
chance of marriage were all significant predictors of the stability of a premarital relationship, both at three and at seven months after the relationship began.

Continuing their investigations, Cate and his co-workers (1985) examined the ability of equity, equality, and reward levels to discriminate between
stable and unstable dating relationships. Participants in the study rated the
perceived level of equity (whether their proportionate outcomes were equitable relative to their inputs), equality (whether allocation of rewards was made
equally), and reward level of the relationship. When the participants were
contacted again three and seven months later, reward level was found to be
a better predictor of stability than equity or equality. Further study (Cate
et al., 1988) also demonstrated that level of rewards was equal or better than
equity in predicting satisfaction and involvement in premarital relationships.

Two explanations for these findings seem possible. If rewards in a relationship are high, the partners may not even be paying attention to the level of inputs and outcomes that are received or contributed by the other person (as suggested by Huston & Burgess, 1979). Alternatively, equity and equality may represent different aspects of the relationship than does reward level; equity and equality are judged on a momentary basis, whereas reward level may represent the cumulative aspects of the relationship over time. Although the explanation is still unclear, the perceived reward level at the outset of the relationship is a better predictor of whether a premarital relationship will last than is equity or equality. Finally, recall Rusbult's ideas about satisfaction and commitment mentioned earlier. When she tested this model with one member of dating heterosexual couples, she found that relationship satisfaction increased as rewards increased over time. Commitment increased because of increases in satisfaction, declines in the quality of available alternatives, and increases in investment in the relationship.

Cohabitation

Do the same factors hold true for couples living in the same household as for dating couples? Many premarital relationships that move beyond the dating stage culminate in a formalized commitment in the same household. When a couple makes a decision to live together it can be through a legal arrangement (marriage) or through a social arrangement (**cohabitation**). In the 1980s we saw a tremendous increase in the number of Americans living in the same household without the legal sanctions of marriage. In fact, over two million unmarried American couples were cohabitating in 1990. Let's have a look at cohabitation and see how these relationships may be similar to or different from both dating and marriage.

cohabitation:
A premarital relationship that involves a decision to live in the same household without the legal ties of marriage.

We can identify several different types of cohabiting relationships (Macklin, 1983):

1. *Temporary or casual convenience relationship.* Two persons share the same living quarters because it is convenient to do so.
2. *Affectionate, dating, going-together type of relationship.* The couple stays together because they enjoy being with one another and will continue as long as they both prefer to do so.
3. *Trial marriage.* In the "engaged-to-be-engaged" relationship, partners are consciously trying out the arrangement before making a permanent commitment to marriage.
4. *Temporary alternative to marriage.* The individuals are committed to staying together but are waiting to get married.
5. *Permanent alternative to marriage.* A couple lives together in a long-term committed relationship similar to marriage but without the traditional religious or legal sanctions.

Prevalence of Cohabitation in the United States

The number of unmarried couples living together more than tripled between 1970 and 1990. Most of the information that we presently have about cohabitation comes from the college campus, as most of the research has been carried out with college student samples. College students may be different from those people who don't enroll in college or who experience cohabitation in some other environment. For this reason, we will examine the prevalence of cohabitation in the noncollege population as well.

In the early 1980s it was estimated that 25 percent of undergraduates had cohabited and that 50 percent or more would if they found themselves in a satisfactory relationship and in a situation where they could cohabit (Macklin, 1983). In the general population, it seems that rates of cohabitation are higher after, rather than before, a first marriage (Clayton & Voss, 1977) and are of short duration. Tanfer (1987) found that cohabiting relationships that didn't result in marriage ended in an average of eighteen months. The number of couples who cohabit who also have children is considerably smaller than the number of cohabiting couples without children (see Figure 9-2). Cohabitation is more likely when children are not anticipated than as a chosen "familylike" life-style. When cohabitors consider add-

FIGURE 9-2

Unmarried Couples Living Together in the United States

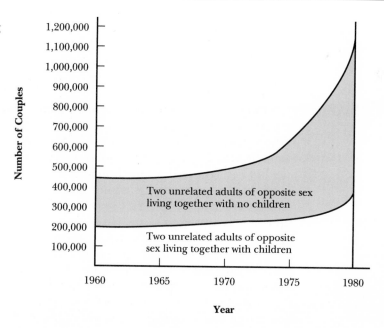

Source: Based on Glick, P. C., & Spanier, G. B. (1980). Married and unmarried cohabitation in the United States. *Journal of Marriage and the Family, 42,* 19–30.

ing children to their relationship, many are very reluctant to do so without first becoming legally married (Spanier, 1983).

What Cohabiting Relationships Are like

The internal dynamics for the process of forming cohabiting relationships are similar to those in the mate selection process previously described. One of the differences between cohabiting relationships and long-term marital relationships, however, is that cohabiting relationships operate with fewer *external support systems* (Macklin, 1983). As a result, the cohabiting couple may have to work more conscientiously at maintaining their relationship. Cohabitants may have to recognize more personal benefit from the relationship to continue the investment without external support and the social and legal sanctions of marriage. One of the personal benefits may be a hopeful marriage outcome. There do appear to be gender differences, however; on average, women cohabitors are more eager to marry their cohabiting partners than are male cohabitors (Blumstein & Schwartz, 1983).

Are cohabiting relationships any more equitable or satisfying than dating or marital relationships? Apparently not. Salce (1981) found no differences among married, cohabiting, and dating couples in equity, relationship satisfaction, partner satisfaction, or optimism for the relationship's future. However, in a more recent study of married couples, wives in couples who cohabited before marriage reported significantly lower perceived quality of communication, and both spouses reported significantly lower marital satisfaction, than did couples who had not cohabited before marriage (DeMaris & Leslie, 1985). The researchers concluded that preexisting differences between the kinds of people who do and do not choose to cohabit before marriage, rather than the experience of cohabitation itself, best accounted for their findings.

In general, studies that have attempted to examine the effects of premarital cohabitation on subsequent marital satisfaction have reported conflicting findings. Macklin summarized the existing research in 1983 and found little difference in marital happiness between couples who had lived together before marriage and those who had not. Watson and DeMeo (1987) found that the premarital relationship of the couple (cohabitation or traditional courtship) did not have an effect on marital adjustment of couples still married after four years. Crohan and Veroff (1989) found that living together before marriage was negatively related to happiness for blacks but not for whites in the early stages of marriage. Perhaps of greater importance, was the finding that *income* was significantly and positively related to marital happiness for both blacks and whites in the early stages of marriage. The living-together variable may be less important to overall marital happiness than the practical fact of how much money the couple earns.

From the standpoint of a cost and reward framework, it is probably the positive rewards (e.g., sufficient family income, feeling loved and appreciated by your mate) that determine marital happiness rather than the experience of living together before marriage in and of itself. As with dat-

FOCUS 9-3

Please answer true or false to each of these twenty questions before reading any further.

MARRIAGE QUIZ (circle one)

1. A husband's marital satisfaction is usually lower if his wife is employed full-time than if she is a full-time homemaker. T F

2. Today, most young, single, never-married people will eventually get married. T F

3. In most marriages, having a child improves marital satisfaction for both spouses. T F

4. The best single predictor of overall marital satisfaction is the quality of the couple's sex life. T F

5. The divorce rate in America increased from 1969 to 1980. T F

6. A greater percentage of wives are in the work force today than in 1970. T F

7. Marital satisfaction for a wife is usually lower if she is employed full-time than is she is a full-time homemaker. T F

8. If my spouse loves me, he/she should instinctively know what I want and need to be happy. T F

9. In a marriage in which the wife is employed full-time, the husband usually assumes an equal share of the housekeeping. T F

10. For most couples, marital satisfaction gradually increases from the first year of marriage through the child-bearing years, the teen years, the empty-nest period, and retirement. T F

11. No matter how I behave, my spouse should love me simply because he/she is my spouse. T F

12. One of the most frequent marital problems is poor communication. T F

13. Husbands usually make more lifestyle adjustments in marriage than wives. T F

14. Couples who cohabited before marriage usually report greater marital satisfaction than couples who did not. T F

15. I can change my spouse by pointing out his/her inadequacies, errors, etc. T F

16. Couples who marry when one or both partners are under the age of eighteen have more chance of eventually divorcing than those who marry when they are older. T F

17. Either my spouse loves me or does not love me; nothing I do will affect the way my spouse feels about me. T F

18. The more a spouse discloses positive and negative information to his/her partner, the greater the marital satisfaction of both partners. T F

19. I must feel better about my partner before I can change my behavior toward him/her. T F

20. Maintaining romantic love is the key to marital happiness over the life span for most couples. T F

The Marriage Quiz, developed by Jerry Larson (1988), is designed to measure college students' beliefs in selected *myths* about marriage. To find out your "myth acceptance score," ignore statements 2, 5, 6, 12, and 16. These are all true and not part of the myth. The remaining fifteen questions are all false, according to research findings. Score one point for each "true" answer you gave on these fifteen questions—the higher your score, the more you subscribe to the "marriage myths." The mean number of items missed on the quiz by a sample of college students with an average age of twenty was seven (Larson, 1988). Women missed significantly fewer items than did men, and students who had completed a marriage and family course missed significantly fewer items. Some of the items may also measure the romantic view of marriage. Answers of "true" to items 3, 4, 8, 9, 10, 11, and 20 would indicate that you have a romantic (and unrealistic) view of marriage. ❖

Source: From Larson, J. H. (1988). The marriage quiz: College students' beliefs in selected myths about marriage. *Family Relations, 37,* 3–12. Copyright © 1988 by the National Council on Family Relations. Reprinted by permission.

What are your expectations about marriage?
What "marriage myths" do you believe in?

ing, we can assume that in cohabitation, those who stay together and perhaps even marry are those in relationships in which commitment is high and the participants' evaluation of cost and reward benefits are positive, exceeding each individual's comparison level.

Marriage

In North America, there are many reasons why people marry: love, conformity, legitimation of sex, premarital pregnancy, legitimization and legal rights of children, emotional and/or financial security, companionship, protection, social expectations and, in the 1990s, the health security of a monogamous relationship. Many marriages are centered around emotional attachments—particularly love. We saw in Chapter 8 that there is considerable variation in the extent to which romantic love is seen as important in a culture, and the degree to which long-term relationships are based on some type of romantic attraction.

How crucial is romantic love for marriage? Attitudes have changed over the years, especially women's attitudes. Would you consider marrying a person who had all of the qualities you desired in a mate, except that you were not in love with her or him? Back in 1964, about 75 percent of women surveyed and 35 percent of men answered that they might consider it (Kephart, 1967). But by the mid-1980s, less than 20 percent of men and women said they might consider it. The gap between sexes had also disappeared (Simpson et al., 1986) (Figure 9-3).

Even when mate selection is formally the prerogative of the individuals who are to be married, parents and other adults in the culture exercise direct and indirect controls over the mate selection process. This might happen, for example, because parents play critical roles in selecting the child's neighborhood, social environment, and schools, and also in providing the value basis from which to select the long-term partner. In focusing on the social psychological perspective on long-term relationships, we will pay less attention to the cultural norms that would affect marital or long-term relationship choice (Lee, 1978). You should be aware, however, that these factors often affect the choice of whom one will marry.

Being married appears to be both psychologically and socially important to people. Although high rates of divorce in recent years may raise doubts in your mind that marriage is all that good a choice, the very high rates of marriage suggest that the marital state is desired by most Americans. In the United States, over 90 percent of men and women marry at least once in their lifetime, and most people (nearly 80 percent) who get divorced do, in fact, remarry.

For many people marriage is the ultimate legal and social commitment. What is it about marriage that is desirable for so many people? It had been found in many older studies that married people showed greater psychological well-being than unmarried people (Briscoe & Smith, 1974; Weiss, 1976). The positive effects of marital status were apparently greater for men

On average, people who are married are happier and psychologically healthier than are unmarried people.

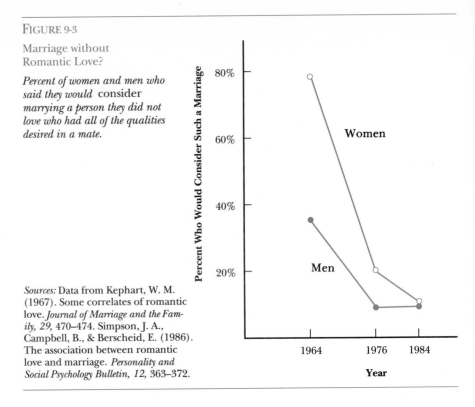

FIGURE 9-3

Marriage without Romantic Love?

Percent of women and men who said they would consider marrying a person they did not love who had all of the qualities desired in a mate.

Sources: Data from Kephart, W. M. (1967). Some correlates of romantic love. *Journal of Marriage and the Family, 29,* 470–474. Simpson, J. A., Campbell, B., & Berscheid, E. (1986). The association between romantic love and marriage. *Personality and Social Psychology Bulletin, 12,* 363–372.

than for women. Pearlin and Johnson (1977) interviewed over two thousand unmarried and married people to find out why marital status seemed to enhance psychological well-being. Unmarried people were found to be far more susceptible to depression than married people, and the unmarried experienced greater economic problems as well. Even when people with equal levels of economic hardship were compared, the unmarried were less able to cope and were more likely to experience depression; the pattern became even more pronounced as the hardships became worse. More recently, Wood et al. (1989) conducted a meta-analysis of seventy-nine studies that measured positive subjective well-being of men and women. They concluded that, in general, women reported greater happiness and life satisfaction than men. For both sexes, being married (as opposed to unmarried) was associated with favorable well-being. Contrary to earlier studies, happiness was more strongly related to being married for women than for men. Although there are conflicting data in these studies regarding which sex benefits more from marriage, we can conclude that people who are married are more satisfied with life, happier, and psychologically healthier than unmarrieds.

As demonstrated in Chapter 1, correlation does not imply causation. The fact that marriage, happiness, and psychological well-being are correlated does not necessarily mean that marriage *causes* psychological well-being. Perhaps persons who are already well adjusted are more likely to attract a marriage partner, or perhaps married persons have the advantage of being able to rely on their partners for emotional support and help when they need it. The results of many studies are confounded by the combining of two types of people into a single category of "unmarrieds": those who are single by choice and those who are single but don't want to be. It is important to remember that people who are single by choice may be quite different from those who would rather be in a relationship but are not.

Social contact can be important to a person's sense of well-being. Austrom (1984) compared large samples of single and married adults on several dimensions. In this particular study, social support was a better predictor of life satisfaction than was marital status. While the Wood et al. (1989) meta-analysis found that married people were, in general, happier than unmarried people, the results of recent national surveys suggest this may be changing, especially for men. The surveys found that the percentage of married people who rated themselves as "very happy" dropped from 38 percent to 29.5 percent between 1972 and 1986, while the percentage of "very happy" unmarried adults rose from 16 percent to 26.5 percent during the same period (Glenn & Weaver, 1988). Perhaps society's greater tolerance for the single life-style, a greater availability of sex without marriage, and modern society's emphasis on the value of individualism (Bellah et al., 1985) all contributed to this change. What appears important are close relationships rather than marriage *per se*.

One depiction of the relationship between love, relationship satisfaction, and mental and physical health is shown in Figure 9-4. Traupmann and

FIGURE 9-4

Hypothetical Relationship between Love and Mental and Physical Health

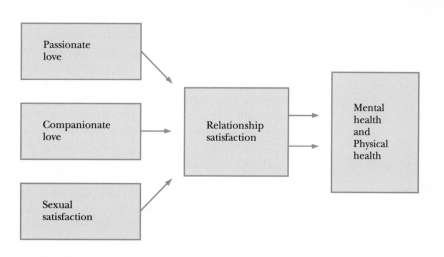

Source: From Traupmann, J., Eckels, E., & Hatfield, E. (1982). Intimacy in older women's lives. *The Gerontologist, 22,* 496. Reprinted by permission.

her co-workers (1981) proposed that love and sexual satisfaction lead to relationship satisfaction, which, in turn, affects both physical and mental health. This view is supported by Bloom et al. (1978), who found that widowed, separated, and divorced persons (victims of marital disruption) had higher rates of illness, accidents, and alcoholism than did presently married or never-married persons of the same ages. Since relationships themselves and satisfaction in relationships are so important to overall well-being, it would be valuable to examine in more detail what happens in a relationship over time.

Marital Satisfaction over Time

Many social observers have suggested that husbands and wives become less romantic and less satisfied with the quality of their relationships over the years of marriage. Is this true? To some extent, the answer appears to be yes. For example, Huston et al. (1984) examined the changes that take place in marital relationships during the first year. Data were gathered from 168 young couples shortly after their weddings and then again a year later. Several indicators of husbands' and wives' subjective evaluations of marriage showed a decrease in their satisfaction over the first year. Couples became increasingly dissatisfied with the amount of time they spent together (specifically, the extent to which their spouses initiated pleasurable activity) and showed dissatisfaction with the frequency with which they shared physical intimacy. Husbands and wives felt less "in love" a year after their marriage; it made no difference whether they had lived together before marriage or even whether they had become parents since their marriage.

Not only was there a decrease in love over the first year of marriage, but also an increase in ambivalence. In a measure of overall marital satisfaction, the couples reported significantly lower marital satisfaction between the time shortly after their marriage (the "honeymoon" period) and their first anniversary. Similar to the findings of Hill et al. (1976) with dating couples, the women reported more dissatisfaction with their interactions than did the men, both early in the marriage and a year later. Additionally, according to self-ratings, the husbands were more in love with their wives than their wives were with them, both early in marriage and a year later. Behaviorally, there was evidence that partners did things that brought each other pleasure less frequently a year into marriage, as the number of pleasurable activities shared by spouses declined. After just one year of marriage, husbands and wives were less affectionate, less approving, and talked to each other less than they had when first married. Be aware that these results do not necessarily mean that married couples are unhappy or dissatisfied generally. Although a year after marriage they were less happy than they were shortly after their marriage, their responses were still generally positive.

Other longitudinal studies have also documented changes in love over the course of a relationship. Traupmann, Eckels, and Hatfield (1982) interviewed college men and women who were dating someone casually or steadily, Utne (1978) studied newlywed couples shortly after their marriages and then again a year later, and Traupmann and Hatfield (1981) interviewed older women concerning their marriages and/or significant relationships. The researchers expected that, over time, passionate love would decline, but companionate love would not. Interestingly, they found that *both* passionate love and companionate love seemed to remain fairly high but declined slightly and equally. Other researchers have also found that most couples begin marriage very satisfied and show a decline in marital satisfaction over time (Rollins & Cannon, 1974; Spanier et al., 1975).

We saw earlier that women break up dating relationships more often than men do. Since women also tend to report more dissatisfaction in marriage than men do, it is hardly surprising that when U.S. marriages end in divorce, the wife is nearly twice as likely as the husband to initiate the process. In 1988, women filed 61.5 percent of the divorce petitions acted upon, while men filed 32.6 percent; the remaining petitions were filed jointly (National Center for Health Statistics, 1989a). (It may also be true that women are "expected" to file for divorce in our culture. If so, then even if the husband wants out of the marriage, the wife may still be the one who starts the legal proceedings).

The lowest point of satisfaction in a marriage is usually when there are teenaged children in the household (see Figure 9-5). Once they leave home, marital satisfaction tends to increase once again. The decline and subsequent increase in marital satisfaction appear greater for wives than husbands. Despite these findings, children probably are not the cause of marital dissatisfaction. Rather, marriage may have different meanings for husbands and wives, and different events (either inside or outside the marriage) affect the amount of satisfaction reported. In order to explore marital satisfaction further, researchers need to differentiate aspects of marriage that might lead to satisfaction, rather than simply measuring levels of satisfaction over time. For example, Lee (1988) found that the marital satisfaction of older wives was related to their spouses' employment status. If they were working and their husbands were not, wives tended to report lower levels of marital satisfaction. What initially appears to be a decrease in satisfaction over time may in fact be related to other circumstances, such as unemployment, economic resources, social support, or a change in the perceived balance of costs and rewards. Glenn (1989) suggested that an exchange perspective would lead one to predict some decline in marital satisfaction as duration of marriage increases. He pointed out that some of the valued characteristics that each spouse brings to the marriage, and on which the marital exchange is based, are likely to change as the spouses grow older. Examples would be youth, vitality, physical appearance, mutual liking, status, income, and goals. If the spouses' changes are not synchronized, the equity and reward level of the social exchange may be disrupted.

Social Exchange and Marital Satisfaction

Perhaps satisfaction in marriage can best be understood from a social exchange framework. As you remember, in dating and cohabiting relationships,

FIGURE 9-5

Satisfaction over the
Family Life Cycle

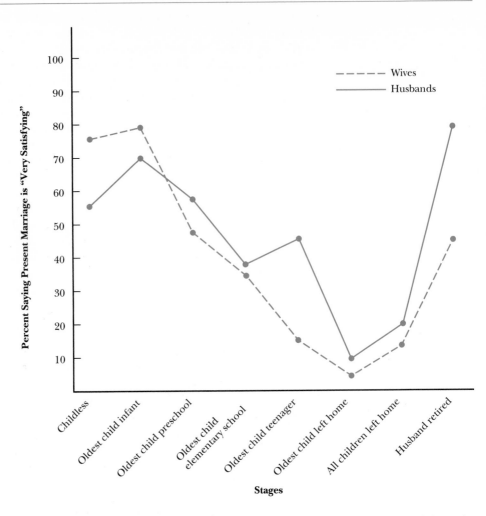

Source: From Rollins, B. C., & Feldman, H. (1970). Marital satisfaction over the family life cycle. *Journal of Marriage and the Family, 32,* 20–28. Copyright 1980 by the National Council on Family Relations. Reprinted by permission.

people stayed in those relationships that proved rewarding. We might expect that those marriages that endure are the ones in which rewards outweigh the identified problems (or costs). Further, equity theory would suggest that partners would be satisfied in a marriage if the balance between what each partner puts into the relationship and what they get out of it is relatively equal. When there is an imbalance, distress is often felt by both partners.

In marriages, research indicates that overbenefited and equitably treated partners are less likely to have (or at least to report having) extra-marital affairs than are underbenefited partners (Walster et al., 1978). Perceived equity also has psychological consequences. Interviewing newly wed couples, Traupmann et al. (1981) found that men and women who felt equitably treated were more content than those who felt either overbenefited or underbenefited. In another study, husbands and wives were asked to evaluate their own and their spouse's level of effort in different family roles: parent, cook, provider, housekeeper, and companion. Equity was determined by the difference in the scores of self-evaluation and evaluation of the partner. Husbands and wives who felt either overbenefited or underbenefited reported higher levels of depression than did equitably treated spouses (Schafer & Keith, 1980).

One interesting example of social exchange and marital adjustment centers on the important area of communication and self-disclosure. Couples who perceived relatively equal amounts of affective self-disclosure (talking about one's feelings and emotions) between themselves and their partners were more likely to be maritally satisfied (Davidson et al., 1983). The greater the discrepancy in the partners' affective self-disclosure, the lower the marital satisfaction. Marital partners seem to want as much from their partners as they feel they give in terms of affective communication. Partners who felt there was a big difference between their own and their partner's self-disclosure were unhappy. This finding was true for individuals who indicated receiving either more or less disclosure than they gave (people who felt either overbenefited or underbenefited).

Interestingly, individuals who indicated high levels of marital satisfaction were more likely to selectively *distort* their perceptions of disclosure received. Perhaps this is an attempt to eliminate distress from the relationship by overestimating or underestimating the partner's contributions in order to restore psychological equity. If the partners perceived they were exchanging at the same level, they were more likely to be satisfied. One couple's level of absolute exchange might be much higher or lower than another couple's level, but what is important is whether each partner feels an equal exchange with his or her spouse, not whether one couple actually discloses more or less than another couple.

The importance of perceived equity is further illustrated in a study of couples married an average of ten years (Matthews & Clark, 1982). The greatest amount of relationship satisfaction, stability, and sexual satisfaction was expressed by individuals who: (1) felt equitably treated, and (2) felt "validated" by their spouse, that is, felt accepted and appreciated by their spouse for simply "being themselves." This seems very similar to seeing one's spouse as a best friend. Feelings of equity and validation were also closely related to each other (Table 9-1). Seventy-three percent of the equitably treated individuals also felt validated by their spouse, but only 39 percent of the inequitably treated (overbenefited or underbenefited) individuals felt validated.

FOCUS 9-4

The Importance of Novelty: The "Coolidge Effect"

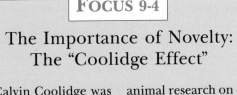

There is a story that when Calvin Coolidge was president, he and his wife visited a large chicken farm. Each was taken on a separate tour. Mrs. Coolidge noted a vigorous rooster mating with hen after hen. When told that the rooster had sex **dozens of times a day. Mrs. Coolidge replied, "Please tell that to the President."** Later, when President Coolidge arrived at the hen yard, he was told about the active rooster. "Same hen every time?" he asked. "Oh, no, Mr. President, a different hen each time." The President nodded and said, "Please tell that to Mrs. Coolidge."

This anecdote, labeled the "Coolidge Effect" by Wilson, Kuehn, and Beach (1963), described the effect of novelty on mating behavior of nonhuman animals. In a review of several decades of animal research on everything from rats and hamsters to sheep and cattle, Dewsbury (1981, p. 480) concluded that "novelty can be a great importance to sexual behavior [of nonhuman animals] under some conditions," although there is considerable inconsistency in the research results. How important is novelty for human attraction and sexual behavior? Obviously, we can't do the kinds of experimentation on humans that are possible with other species. Nevertheless, many theorists (e.g., Hatfield & Walster, 1978; Hendrick & Hendrick, 1983) have suggested that various kinds of novelty (of setting, of behavior, of stimuli, as well as of partner) can have significant impacts on human attraction, desire, and sexual behavior. ❖

Important Issues in Long-Term Relationships

As we have analyzed dating, cohabitation, and marriage, we have uncovered some similarities in forming and maintaining these relationships and suggested that they be viewed in a cost and reward framework. We can identify further important issues that will likely affect the participants' perceptions of whether their relationships are sufficiently rewarding to justify their continued emotional and practical investment.

Sexual Behaviors

Sexual behaviors play a major part in most romantic relationships. We will see that sex is one of the five most common marital problems, according to therapists' estimates (Figure 9-6), and pioneering sexuality researchers Masters and Johnson (1970) estimated that half of married couples suffered from some sort of sexual problem. Important issues can include what types of sexual behavior are seen as acceptable and the frequency and quality of sexual relations. Sexual exclusivity can be a major point of contention in many relationships as well. As described in Focus 9-5, concern about sexually transmitted diseases can affect both the sexual and the interpersonal nature of relationships.

Among dating couples, the traditional "double standard," the feeling that premarital sex was desirable for men but not for women, is not as strong

Increased fears about AIDS, herpes, and other sexually-transmitted diseases may have profound effects on sex roles and relationships in the 1990s.

as it used to be (Jacoby & Williams, 1985). But strong gender differences still exist, centering around the emotional quality of acceptable sexual relationships. For example, Carroll et al. (1984) found that when college students were asked how they felt about casual premarital sex, females were much less favorably inclined than were males. In a study conducted in the late 1970s (Clark & Hatfield, 1989), male and female college students were approached individually on campus by an attractive stranger of the other sex who said, "I've been noticing you around campus; I find you very attractive. Will you go out on a date with me?" Gender differences in accepting a date were not apparent (56 percent of the men and 50 percent of the women said yes). On the other hand, when confronted with the bold request, "Would you go to bed with me tonight?" 75 percent of the men said yes but not one of the women did. (After the student's response, he or she was debriefed and the request was not carried out. This study involves some interesting issues about research ethics).

One might suspect that these findings would no longer hold, since the potential costs of casual sex—sexually transmitted diseases such as AIDS and herpes—rose dramatically in the decade following the Clark and Hatfield study. Might this deter men today? Apparently not. Clark (1990) replicated the study in 1988 and found results almost identical to the earlier ones—not one of the college women but 69 percent of college men agreed to go to bed with an attractive stranger.

FOCUS 9-5

Relationships and Sexually Transmitted Disease: A New Intensity to an Old Problem

The sexual revolution that took place in the 1960s and 1970s brought with it dramatic changes in rates of sexually transmitted diseases (STDs). Some of the more common STDs of the 1960s and 1970s had been the deadly diseases of previous centuries (e.g., syphilis, gonorrhea). These former killers became treatable and/or curable in recent decades, but newer, more troubling diseases emerged. Herpes, the incurable but manageable viral infection, has received much attention as an estimated forty million Americans continue to deal with the physical, emotional, and relationship effects it can have. However, the most deadly STD of our time, Acquired Immune Deficiency Syndrome (AIDS), has far surpassed the others in level of potential danger.

Because there is no cure for AIDS, its prevention has gained more and more attention. The emergence of AIDS and concern about its spread may have a profound effect upon future sexual relations in dating and marriage, but thus far significant behavior changes in sexual relations among heterosexuals have not occurred.

Initially, people saw AIDS as striking only a certain population, male homosexuals. But the number of AIDS cases is increasing at a tremendous rate each year and amongst a wider population. As of 1989, more than eighty-six thousand people in the United States had been diagnosed as having AIDS (Centers for Disease Control, 1989) and several high-risk groups were identified: male homosexuals and bisexuals, intravenous drug users and their sexual partners, and infants of females who have AIDS. Recipients of blood transfusions before 1985 are also at risk. (Today, all donated blood in the U.S. is tested for AIDS and the blood supply in the U.S. is relatively safe.)

Although male homosexuals and intravenous drug users still account for the majority of AIDS cases, it is estimated that by 1991, heterosexuals will account for one in eleven new cases (McAuliffe et al., 1987). Masters, Johnson, and Kolodny (1988) expressed particular concern for the increase in heterosexual AIDS transmission among sexually active individuals who have many partners. All sexually active individuals are confronted with the possibility, however remote, of contracting this deadly sexually transmitted disease. There is no evidence that the virus is spread through casual nonsexual contact.

In spite of the deadly nature of AIDS and the prevalence of other bothersome STDs, several studies have found that dating and willingness to engage in sexual behaviors have not dramatically changed. One example is the Clark and Hatfield (1989) and Clark (1990) studies dicussed in the text. The females in those studies were unwilling to enage in casual sex, but apparently it was not due to concerns for personal safety. And college-age males' eagerness to engage in casual sex was apparently not changed over a ten-year period by the AIDS epidemic. In spite of the known risks O'Keeffe et al. (1990) reviewed several research studies that indicated many gay and bisexual men continued to practice high-risk behaviors associated with contraction of AIDS. A further discussion of the known risks of AIDS and behavior change by individuals can be found in Chapter 14. It seems thus far that knowledge and information about the nature of AIDS transmission has not been sufficient to ensure behavior change in many individuals and in relationships. ❖

In long-term relationships, researchers have noted a positive correlation between sexual adjustment and marital satisfaction — couples who have satisfying marriages also usually have satisfying sexual relations. But it is difficult to determine cause and effect here. Does good sex lead to satisfying relationships, or do good relationships produce good sex? There is no easy answer, though Sharon Brehm (1985) argued that the quality of sexual interactions will most often reflect the more general quality of the relationship.

The sexual aspect of a relationship is just one potential source of costs or rewards that a person might use to judge the worth of continued participation with a particular partner. Others would include jealousy and verbal, physical, and social abuse. Several types of abuse that may occur in relationships are further discussed in Chapter 10.

Jealousy

One problem common to many relationships is jealousy, an emotion that most of us have experienced. Think back and try to remember a relationship in which you felt jealous. Were your feelings rational (based on an accurate perception of reality) or irrational (the results of inaccurate perceptions)? Surprisingly, little empirical research is available concerning this important factor, which can greatly influence our feelings and our behavior. White (1980) speculated that jealousy describes the thoughts and feelings triggered by the loss (or anticipated loss) of a romantic partner to a rival. The loss of a romantic partner results in the loss of relationship rewards and a loss of self-esteem. Several tests of this model led White to the conclusion that men and women are equally likely to be jealous. Feelings of inadequacy as a partner, sexual exclusivity of the relationship, and the feeling of having put more effort into the relationship than one's partner (inequity) were all related to jealousy. Taking a more attributional approach, Berscheid (1983) proposed that jealousy is likely when: (1) there is an interruption (or threatened interruption) to the relationship; (2) the cause of the interruption is seen as outside the relationship (another person, an object, or an activity such as work or a hobby); and (3) one's partner is seen as having the power to change this cause. The more intense or exclusive the original relationship, the more jealousy is likely when the relationship is interrupted or threatened.

A troubled relationship can lead to loss of relationship rewards and also to loss of self-esteem to the partners. Mathes, Adams, and Davis (1985) found that the loss of relationship rewards leads to depression, while the loss of self-esteem leads to anger. When the loss is due to a romantic rival, as White had speculated, jealousy was the likely result. Their data showed that people higher in the trait of jealousy suffer more when a relationship ends in this way. Although White found no relationship between jealousy and self-esteem, Buunk (1982) found that low self-esteem was associated with higher anticipated jealousy in women, though not in men. The personality

FOCUS 9-6

Homosexual Relationships

Although our discussion of long-term relationships has primarily focused on heterosexuals, it is important to note that the long-term relationships of same-sex couples are most likely to follow the same general patterns. Homosexual relationships are often difficult to study, for many gay men and women are secretive about their sexual orientation and are not apt to volunteer as subjects for research studies. Those who do volunteer for research may not be representative of homosexuals in general (Gordon & Peplau, 1982). Despite these problems, studies of committed homosexual relationships have generally revealed similarities between these and committed heterosexual relationships (Bell & Weinberg, 1978; Peplau & Gordon, 1983). Research suggests that most gays desire steady love relationships rather than casual sex. Both heterosexuals and homosexuals attach greatest importance to "being able to talk about my most intimate feelings" with a partner (Peplau & Cochran, 1980). There was one major difference between the two groups: Sexual exclusivity in a relationship was reported to be much more important to heterosexuals than homosexuals. Note, however, that this research was completed prior to the general recognition of the outbreak of AIDS in the U.S. Since then, as noted in Chapter 14, the sexual behavior of many male homosexuals has changed dramatically.

Although many gay men and women form satisfactory long-term relationships, one problem faced by same-sex couples is the lack of social support or acceptance by heterosexuals. Many heterosexuals assume that homosexuals are less satisfied with their relationships than heterosexuals are. Illustrating this bias, Testa et al. (1987) gave heterosexuals identical information about a heterosexual couple, a lesbian couple, and a gay male couple. When the subjects rated the relationship, the gay and the lesbian couples were perceived as less satisfied with their relationship and less in love than was the heterosexual couple.

Satisfaction and commitment in homosexual and heterosexual relationships appear to be related to the same factors. Relationships that last, whether they be gay or heterosexual, are those where the participants report relatively high rewards, low costs, moderately unappealing alternatives, great investments, and very high levels of satisfaction and commitment (Duffy & Rusbult, 1986). Using Rusbult's investment model (described earlier in the chapter) to explore satisfaction and commitment in both heterosexual and homosexual relationships, Duffy and Rusbult (1986) found that greater satisfaction with relationships was associated with higher levels of rewards and lower levels of costs for all four groups of respondents (heterosexual males and females, and gay males and females). Gender appeared to be a more important predictor of individuals' behaviors than was sexual preference. Women, more than men, reported that they had invested more in their relationships and were more committed to maintaining their relationships. These are similar to other findings that, regardless of their sexual preference, women in general thought that emotional expressiveness and the sharing of feelings was of more importance than did men (Peplau & Cochran, 1980) Additionally, women thought it more important to have an egalitarian relationship than did men, again regardless of sexual preference. It appears that whatever their sexual orientation, most people want the same things from romantic relationships—affection and companionship (Peplau & Gordon, 1983), but men and women behave somewhat differently to get them. ❖

factor most strongly related to jealousy in Buunk's study was *emotional dependence* on the other person or the relationship.

In a nationwide study of nearly twenty-five thousand Americans, Salovey and Rodin (1985) found that certain personality characteristics made some people particularly prone to jealousy. They concluded that jealousy is rooted in low self-esteem and insecurities about self-worth. In further studies, Salovey and Rodin (1986) were able to distinguish reactions to romantic jealousy (where the desired object or goal was a person) and social comparison situations (e.g., of someone's status or possessions). When subjects were asked to react to stories evoking jealousy, romantic stories provoked more negative thoughts and feelings about the self and others than did social comparison stories. When jealousy is about another person, individuals with low self-esteem may be particularly vulnerable. For many couples, jealousy is a significant marital complication. Marriage generally implies sexual exclusivity and ongoing give and take — a natural setting for jealousy to develop. However, if one doesn't value exclusivity in one's own behavior (has been involved in, or intends to engage in, extramarital affairs), then a partner's exclusivity may not appear so important. Buunk (1982) found that people who had affairs were much less likely than most married people to express jealousy at their partner's possible extramarital involvement. Salovey and Rodin (1985) found similar results, but also added that the people who reported having affairs while in committed relationships were considerably more likely to look through their spouse's or lover's personal belongings for unfamiliar names and phone numbers. They also were likely to call their partners unexpectedly to check up on them, to follow them, or to question them about past relationships. Should we really believe that they were not very jealous? Jealousy may be just as powerful in dating as in marriage. Although separated and divorced people were much more likely than the married and widowed to *report* feeling or behaving jealously, unmarried cohabiting people may feel high levels of jealousy (Salovey & Rodin, 1985).

Happiness

What makes a happy relationship? One survey of men and women who said they were happily married (Lauer & Lauer, 1985) found strong agreement between husbands and wives about the reasons the marriage had lasted. For both men and women, "My spouse is my best friend" ranked number one, and "I like my spouse as a person" was mentioned next most often. The fifteen responses made most often by husbands and by wives are listed in Table 9-1.

Keep in mind that, like other studies, data from surveys such as these are influenced by the fact that intact marriages are studied; we lack data from separated or divorced couples. Also, even the longitudinal studies are typically of relatively short duration; following the same couples over several decades might produce different results. We can more fully understand marriage by examining data from unhappy couples as well. Studies of those who

TABLE 9-1	INGREDIENTS OF HAPPY MARRIAGES*

* REASONS THEIR MARRIAGE HAS LASTED, GIVEN BY HUSBANDS AND WIVES WHO SAY THEY HAVE A HAPPY MARRIAGE. REASONS ARE IN DESCENDING ORDER OF IMPORTANCE.

Reasons Given by Husbands	Reasons Given by Wives
1. My spouse is my best friend	1. My spouse is my best friend
2. I like my spouse as a person	2. I like my spouse as a person
3. Marriage is a long-term commitment	3. Marriage is a long-term commitment
4. Marriage is sacred	4. Marriage is sacred
5. We agree on aims and goals	5. We agree on aims and goals
6. My spouse has grown more interesting	6. My spouse has grown more interesting
7. I want the relationship to succeed	7. I want the relationship to succeed
8. An enduring marriage is important to social stability	8. We laugh together
9. We laugh together	9. We agree on a philosophy of life
10. I am proud of my spouse's achievements	10. We agree on how and how often to show affection
11. We agree on philosophy of life	11. An enduring marriage is important to social stability
12. We agree about our sex life	12. We have a stimulating exchange of ideas
13. We agree on how and how often to show affection	13. We discuss things calmly
14. I confide in my spouse	14. We agree about our sex life
15. We share outside hobbies and interests	15. I am proud of my spouse's achievements

Source: REPRINTED WITH PERMISSION FROM PSYCHOLOGY TODAY MAGAZINE. Copyright © 1985 (PT Partners, L.P.)

have sought professional help can provide valuable information about the kinds of problems people report experiencing in marriage. When marriage therapists were surveyed (Geiss & O'Leary, 1981), they reported problems in the following areas as having the most damaging effect on marital relationships, in order of importance:

1. communication
2. unrealistic expectations of marriage or spouse
3. power struggles
4. serious individual problems
5. role conflict
6. lack of loving feelings
7. demonstration of affection
8. alcoholism
9. extramarital sexual affairs
10. sex

Figure 9-6 addresses this issue from a different perspective — marriage therapists' views about the problems that have the most damaging effects on marriage. The percentage of couples seen in therapy who had expressed complaints in each of twenty-nine areas are listed. Here again, communication was identified as a problem for the greatest proportion of couples (84 percent). Six out of ten of the problems that therapists rated as having the

What problems most affect married couples? Therapists estimate that poor communication, unrealistic expectations, and power struggles are the most common problem areas.

most damaging effects on marriage were also complaints of over half of couples seeking help: communication, unrealistic expectations, demonstration of affection, lack of loving feelings, sex, and power struggles. So even though many married couples are relatively happy and remain in love throughout their marriages, several types of problems are quite common.

What Happens When People Do Not Perceive Equal Exchanges?

Uses of Power

Social power exists when a person is able to make demands on another and have those demands met. The amount of social power each member of a couple has in a relationship depends on social norms (such as sex-role expectations), the personal resources each brings (e.g., attractiveness, income, occupational skills), and the psychological dependency of each partner on the relationship. This latter factor involves the *principle of least interest* (Focus 9-7): The partner who is less involved psychologically in a relationship is likely to wield greater power.

When a partner would like to change the nature of a relationship, persuasion, negotiating, bargaining, or simply demanding a change may be involved. Interviews with over seven hundred husbands and wives indicated that referent and expert power were utilized most frequently and coercive power least frequently (Chapter 5) in discussions and arguments (Raven et

FIGURE 9-6

Marital Problem Areas

*Mean percentage of couples who identified problems in twenty-nine areas of marriage,
based on therapists' estimates.*

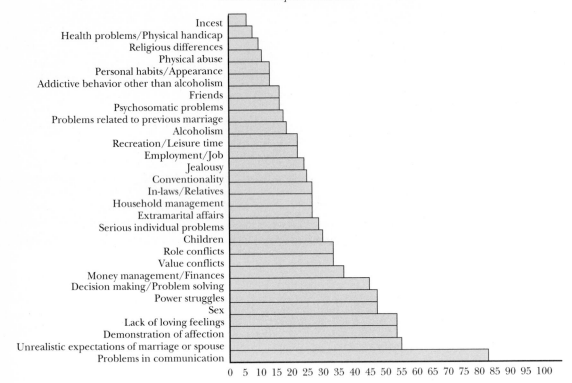

Percent

Source: Based on Geiss, S. K., & O'Leary, K. D. (1981). Therapist ratings of frequency and
severity of marital problems: Implications for research. *Journal of Marital and Family Therapy,
7(4),* 515–520.

al., 1975). Males tend to feel greater power than females and use power differently. Wives were most likely to attribute expert power to their husbands, and husbands thought their wives used referent power most often. Falbo and Peplau (1980) concluded that males tend to prefer direct and interactive strategies to get what they want, and females tend to use indirect and solitary strategies, such as withdrawal and negative affect. The direct interactive strategies were more likely to produce a satisfying relationship. The researchers suggested that because males expect compliance in their relationships, they have the luxury of being able to rely on direct methods; females, acting from a perspective of less power, must use strategies in which compliance is not expected. Males tend to rely more on logical arguments;

FOCUS 9-7

The Principle of Least Interest

Psychological dependency can involve the "principle of least interest" (Waller & Hill, 1951), wherein the partner who is less involved psychologically in the relationship wields more power. The degree to which a relationship itself is valued by the two partners may be one of the most crucial determinants of the way bargaining turns out. The principle of least interest suggests that the person who is least interested in continuing the relationship is able to have a greater influence on what happens. Also, the person who is least interested is far more likely to hold out for the greatest advantage. The person who most wants to continue the relationship has less influence, and is more likely to risk investing in the relationship with the hope of something positive happening.

Certainly, this principle could affect the exchange process. The partner who has the greater interest will probably try harder, giving more to the relationship and to the partner. Research findings would lead one to predict that these unequal relationships probably would not last. Hill et al. (1976) found that ending a dating relationship was desired more often by the partner who was less involved. Of couples who reported equal involvement, only 23 percent broke up in a year, compared with a 54 percent breakup rate in couples where at least one member reported initially that they were unequally involved.

An example of the principle at work comes from a survey of college-student couples (Peplau & Campbell, 1989) in which each member was asked who was the more involved member in the relationship and who had "more say" (social power) in the relationship. As Figure 9-7 indicates, when the man was less involved he had more say in 70 percent of the couples; men also had more say in most (54 percent) of the equally involved couples. In contrast, when the woman was the less involved partner, she had more social power over twice as often (49 percent of these couples) as the man did (23 percent). ❖

females are reported to use more indirect or emotional methods, such as pouting or becoming silent and withdrawn. Relying on displays of emotion is usually a tactic used by powerless people.

By virtue of the male's greater ascribed status in our society, in nearly every situation he has more legitimate power (power based solely on rank or position) than a woman does. Some will use their physical strength to control females (coercive power). Because males are more apt to control money and other valuable commodities, it follows that they are likely to have more reward power. Because of gender biases in educational training, males often have more expert power than females as well. A survey of heterosexual and homosexual men and women indicated that for men, having more power than their partner was more important, and having an **equalitarian relationship** less important, than for women (Peplau, 1981). As noted, there

egalitarian (or equalitarian) relationship
A relationship where each partner has equal power.

FIGURE 9-7

The Principle of Least
Interest in Dating Couples

*College students' reports of who
has more say (social power) in
their romantic relationship, as
related to which partner is
more involved in the relationship.*

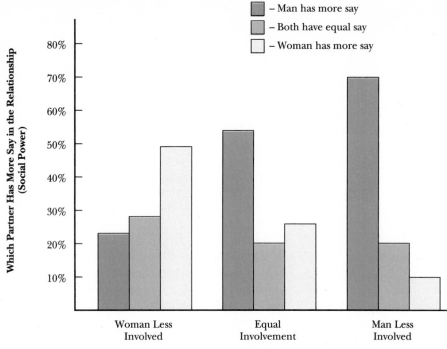

Legend:
- Man has more say
- Both have equal say
- Woman has more say

Y-axis: Which Partner Has More Say in the Relationship (Social Power)

X-axis: Psychological Involvement in the Relationship — Woman Less Involved, Equal Involvement, Man Less Involved

Source: Data from Peplau, L. A.,
& Campbell, S. M. (1989).
Power in dating and marriage.
In J. Freeman (Ed.), *Women: A
feminist perspective* (4th edi-
tion, pp. 121–137). Mountain
View, CA: Mayfield.

are three factors giving heterosexual males stronger power in intimate relationships than their wives. First, males, by social convention, have more power
by virtue of their higher status. Second, males generally have more resources
within their marriage (such as greater income and education) and this gives
them an additional edge. Third, females have tended to be more dependent
on their husbands for security than vice versa. Jesse Bernard poignantly
described the situation: "Take a young woman who has been trained for feminine dependencies, who wants to 'look up' to the man she marries, put her
at a disadvantage in the labor market, then marry her to a man who has a
slight initial advantage over her in age, income, and education, shored up
by an ideology with the male bias . . . and then expect an equalitarian relationship?" (quoted in Peplau & Gordon, 1983).

In Focus 9-8 Bem and Bem (1977) proposed that there was a simple
test for determining the truly egalitarian marriage. An equal-power relationship remains a desired but elusive goal. Over 90 percent of today's college
students say they desire a relationship where each partner has equal power,
but only 49 percent of young women and 42 percent of young men report
that their current relationship involves equal power (Peplau & Campbell,
1989). As we have already seen, men usually wield more power. Traditional
sex-role norms have ascribed more power to the male in making important

---

FOCUS 9-8

What Is an Equitable Relationship?

Consider the following example (from Bem & Bem, 1977, p. 181):

> Both my wife and I earned college degrees in our respective disciplines. I turned down a superior job offer in Oregon and accepted a slightly less desirable position in New York where my wife would have more opportunities for part-time work in her specialty. Although I would have preferred to live in a suburb, we purchased a home near my wife's job so that she could have an office at home where she would be when the children returned from school. Because my wife earns a good salary, she can easily afford to pay a housekeeper to do her major household chores. My wife and I share all other tasks around the house equally. For example, she cooks the meals, but I do the laundry for her and help her with many of her other household tasks.

Without questioning the basic happiness of such a marriage or its appropriateness for many couples, is it an *equal* marriage? Bem and Bem (1977) pointed out that there is a very simple test. If the marriage is truly egalitarian, then its description should retain the same flavor and tone even if the roles of the husband and wife are reversed.

> Both my husband and I earned college degrees in our respective disciplines. I turned down a superior job offer in Oregon and accepted a slightly less desirable position in New York where my husband would have more opportunities for part-time work in his specialty. Although I would have preferred to live in a suburb, we purchased a home near my husband's job so that he could have an office at home where he would be when the children returned from school. Because my husband earns a good salary, he can easily afford to pay a housekeeper to do his major household chores. My husband and I share all other tasks around the house equally. For example, he cooks the meals, but I do the laundry for him and help him with many of his other household tasks.

Somehow it sounds different, and yet only the pronouns have been changed to protect the powerful! It becomes apparent that the ideology about the woman's "natural" place unconsciously permeates the entire fabric of such "pseudo-egalitarian" marriages. It is true the wife gains some measure of equality when she can have a career rather than have a job, and when her career can influence the final place of residence. But why is it the unquestioned assumption that the husband's career solely determines the initial set of alternatives that are to be considered? Why is it the wife who automatically seeks the part-time position? Why is it *her* housekeeper rather than *their* housekeeper? Why *her* household tasks? ❖

Excerpts' source: Bem, S. L. & Bem, D. J. (1977). Homogenizing the American woman: The power of an unconscious ideology. Copyright © 1973 by Sandra and Daryl Bem. Reprinted by permission of the authors. In J. C. Brigham & L. S. Wrightsman (Eds.) *Contemporary issues in social psychology* (3rd ed.) (pp. 172–185). Monterey, CA: Brooks/Cole.

---

decisions (e.g., finance, career choices). In a study of students, those in female-dominant relationships (the least traditional and probably the most difficult to maintain) were less satisfied than those in male-dominated or equal-power relationships (Peplau & Campbell, 1989).

Bargaining and Negotiation

How people exert their power in a relationship depends upon many factors. One of these is the bargaining and negotiating skills of the individuals involved. Bargaining itself is the process by which the couple agrees on a certain outcome from among several alternative possibilities. How they negotiate a decision is based on their social power, communication skills, their history of interaction with each other, their degree of interest in the problem, the degree of interest in their partner, and their available resources.

An interesting perspective on bargaining and negotiating in marital relations was proposed by Scanzoni (1979). He suggested that as women gain resources (education, jobs, economic power, confidence, etc.) they are in a better position to bargain for satisfaction and rewards in their marital relationship. This is another variation of social exchange theory. Increased resources enhance a person's bargaining position in a relationship and will have an impact on both the bargaining style and the outcome of interpersonal exchanges or negotiations. One example of this can be found in a study by Maret and Finlay (1984). They found that women who had greater economic and educational resources had more power in their relationships.

One recently increased resource for many women has been the opportunity to pursue careers. Women who define work as a right, and for whom it has important consequences, are more likely to be effective negotiators and to have greater bargaining power with their husbands because of their increased access to tangible (money) and intangible (skills) resources. When Scanzoni (1979) studied women who filled traditional versus nontraditional sex roles, several differences were found in the way they solved problems and bargained with their spouses. Traditional women were defined as those who saw continued differentiation between husbands and wives in occupational, household, and marital roles, based on gender rather than on other factors such as interest, capabilities, or equality. Conversely, egalitarian women were those who shared equal rights and opportunities with their spouses. When these two groups of women were compared on problem solving and bargaining, traditional women tended to try to persuade their husbands by arguing on the basis of family or group well-being. In contrast, egalitarian women were more likely to argue for change on the basis of individualistic concerns or self-interest. Resources, too, had an impact on the bargaining style; the more resources, the more effective the woman's bargaining. In short, the more egalitarian wives, with greater resources, were more likely to bargain on the basis of self-interest. Such wives were likely to be better bargainers in terms of getting more of what they wanted in the marital relationship.

Bargaining doesn't always turn out well, and some individuals stay in relationships even though they are unhappy or their needs are not being met. Relationships that are stable over time are not necessarily characterized as "happy." Stability refers to whether a relationship lasts; satisfaction refers to the subjective evaluation of the couple's relationship. In exchange terms, stability might be as much related to perceived lack of alternatives (CL_{ALT}) as to the positive gratification within the relationship (Ross & Sawhill, 1975). Often couples maintain an unsatisfactory relationship because of lack of initiative, lack of alternatives, or the perception that staying is less costly (economically, socially, or emotionally) than leaving.

Consider the fear of contracting AIDS, for example. If a person is in an unsatisfactory relationship, he or she might stay due to the perceived high costs of leaving the relationship. One of the costs may be the idea of dating in an age of uncertainty with regard to sexually transmitted diseases such as herpes and AIDS, involving threats to physical as well as emotional health. To some individuals, an unsatisfactory monogamous relationship may be perceived as less costly than the alternative. The end result may be more people staying in unhappy relationships because they fear the alternatives. Researchers have not yet investigated this possibility closely, but results of an anonymous survey of two hundred undergraduates in 1989 found that roughly 20 percent of them said they had stayed longer in an unhappy relationship because of the fear of contracting a sexually transmitted disease from a new partner (J. Brigham, 1989).

The term "empty shell marriage" has been used to describe marriages that provide little in the way of positive satisfaction to the participants. They are held together for social or economic reasons, rather than by any intrinsic benefits from the relationship itself, and would be considered stable but not satisfying. If these marriages were not held together by legal and social sanctions, or psychological fears, would the relationships endure? Perhaps, but only for as long as the rewards (e.g., security, money, social acceptance) outweigh the emotional, financial, social, and legal costs.

RELATIONSHIP DECLINE AND TERMINATION

Declining Relationships

Conflict in any relationship is inevitable. Whether it be in marriage, cohabitation, friendship, or between parent and child, there are times when people simply don't get along. In long-term relationships where there is a legal or social commitment, people often stay together to work out their differences. Conflict is "managed" through an ongoing process of give and take. Using bargaining, compromise, mediation, and interpersonal skills, a couple tries to manage the conflict. The particular response that a person makes when conflict begins may depend on the quality of the relationship before the conflict arose.

Once a relationship is in trouble, the partners' interpretation of events may increase stress. In terms of the attribution dimensions discussed in Chapter 2, it has been found that spouses in troubled marriages tend to make causal attributions that are likely to increase the impact of negative events and decrease the impact of positive events. A review by Bradbury and Fincham (1990) found that the *globality* dimension was particularly salient, as distressed spouses view the causes of negative events as globally influential in the marriage, while positive events are seen only as specific to that incident. In terms of the dimensions described by Weiner (1980), causes of negative events in the marriage are likely to be seen as global (affecting many aspects of the relationship), stable (they are expected to happen again), and controllable (by the partner) (see Table 2-1). The focus of the event is seen as external: "It's his/her fault." Distressed spouses also tend to see their partner as selfishly motivated and behaving with negative intent. But which comes first, negative attributions or declining relationships? Do negative patterns of attributions harm relationships that were otherwise satisfactory, or does the realization that a relationship is already declining stimulate people to adopt a negative attributional view? After reviewing dozens of studies, Bradbury and Fincham (1990) concluded that it is more likely that changes in attributions occur first, making marital satisfaction worse.

Four primary reactions to relationship decline were described by Rusbult and Zembrodt (1983): **voice**, **loyalty**, **exit**, and **neglect** (Figure 9-8). These reactions vary on two dimensions—constructive/destructive and active/passive. Voice (expressing concerns) and loyalty (being supportive) are considered constructive responses, generally intended to maintain the relationship, whereas exit (leaving the relationship) and neglect (refusing to deal with problems) are destructive responses, tending to break up the relationship. *Destructive* refers to the fate of the relationship, not the individuals involved. For example, if a woman divorces an unloving husband who has been physically and emotionally abusive for many years, this may be a healthy and constructive response for her individual well-being, though a destructive response as far as the relationship goes.

On the active/passive dimension, exit and voice are active behaviors, whereas loyalty and neglect are more passive. As you may remember, Rusbult and Zembrodt (1983) identified three variables that might predict the degree of commitment to a relationship and also influence the choice of a response when a person was dissatisfied in a relationship: (1) the degree to which the individual was satisfied with the relationship prior to its decline, (2) the magnitude of the individual's investment of resources in the relationship, and (3) the quality of the individual's best alternative to the current relationship (CL_{ALT}). In general, high prior satisfaction and greater prior investment should promote constructive (voice and loyalty) rather than destructive (exit and neglect) responses. Available alternatives would promote active (exit and voice) rather than passive (loyalty and neglect) responses.

voice:

An active constructive reaction to problems in the relationship as the person takes action to improve things.

loyalty:

A passive constructive reaction to problems in the relationship as the person remains loyal and supportive.

exit:

An active destructive reaction to problems in the relationship as the person leaves the relationship.

neglect:

A passive destructive reaction to problems in the relationship as the person takes no action to improve things.

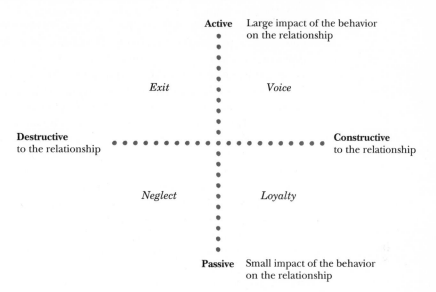

FIGURE 9-8

The Constructive/
Destructive and Active/
Passive Dimensions of
Exit, Voice, Loyalty,
and Neglect Behaviors

Exit—formally separating, moving out of a joint residence, threatening to end the relationship, deciding to "just be friends," thinking about breaking up, getting a divorce.

Voice—discussing problems, compromising, seeking help from a therapist or clergyman, suggesting solutions to problems, asking the partner what is bothering him/her, trying to change oneself or change the partner.

Loyalty—waiting and hoping that things will improve, "giving it some time," praying for improvement, forgiving and forgetting, supporting the partner in the face of criticism from others.

Neglect—ignoring the partner or spending less time together, refusing to discuss problems, treating the partner badly emotionally or physically, criticizing the partner for things unrelated to the real problem, "just letting things fall apart," (perhaps) developing extrarelationship sexual involvements.

Source: Rusbult, C. E. (1984). The constructive/destructive and active/passive dimensions of exit, voice, loyalty, and neglect behavior. Paper presented at Society of Southeastern Social Psychologists meeting, Atlanta. Reprinted by permission of the author.

Several aspects of this theory have been supported by research. In one set of studies, some subjects were asked to read essays describing a fictional situation, placing themselves in the position of the main character, while others based their responses on their own romantic involvements, focusing specifically on a time when they became dissatisfied with the relationship (Rusbult et al., 1982). In both situations, when there had been high prior satisfaction, voice and loyalty responses were the most likely response; high investment also encouraged voice and loyalty responses. In general, when subjects had more attractive alternatives, exit responses increased and loyalty responses decreased. Johnson, Rusbult, and Morrow (1983) found the same results when studying responses to dissatisfaction in long-standing relationships. When voice and loyalty had been chosen as the response to dissatisfaction, subjects reported more favorable outcomes; exit and neglect responses produced less favorable consequences.

Studying actual relationships, it was also possible to profile the person engaging in particular responses. There were no overall differences in the types of responses chosen by men and women. When dissatisfied, however, people with more education were slightly more likely to use a voice response, those with less education a loyalty or neglect response. Married persons were more inclined to use loyalty than were single persons (Johnson et al., 1983).

Gender differences in responding to dissatisfaction in marriage were found by White (1989). Men assumed a coercive stance (active response) toward their partners, while women took an affiliative position (passive response). There are times, of course, when a couple is either unable or unwilling to manage their conflict, and an exit response is chosen. We have already looked at breakups in dating and cohabiting relationships. As you remember, the relationships that endured were those in which the rewards were perceived as higher than the costs. Loyalty responses are less frequently used by single people. Instead, unhappy single people tend to leave relationships. Dating and cohabiting relationships are less bound by social norms and expectations for permanence than are marriages. As you can imagine, exiting a marital relationship can be a very difficult and painful process.

Divorce

Marital separation and divorce affect more than two million adults and more than one million children a year in the United States and it is estimated that if the current rate continues, half of all recent first marriages will end in divorce (London & Wilson, 1988). Divorce happens relatively early in most cases. In 1985 the median duration of marriages with children that ended in divorce was 6.8 years (U.S. Dept of Commerce, Bureau of Census, 1989). Many factors associated with marital satisfaction and divorce have been identified.

For example, marital stability is greatest for men who have graduated from college or who have gone on to graduate school. For women, however, those who have gone to graduate school experience below-average marital stability (Spanier & Glick, 1981). This information is interesting, but the data do not provide adequate information about the social psychological variables involved in the divorce process or the reasons people divorce. Let us examine these more closely, and then we may more fully understand these statistics.

Dimensions of Divorce

Divorce was described (Bohannon, 1971) as a process involving at least six dimensions: (1) the emotional divorce, (2) the legal divorce, (3) the economic divorce, (4) the co-parental divorce, (5) the community divorce, and (6) the psychic divorce. These six dimensions are not related sequentially and many may occur at the same time. Each one, however, does involve a distinctly

The emotions of divorce. Kathleen Turner and Michael Douglas depicted the raging emotions that sometimes consume divorcing people in the movie, "War of the Roses."

different task, and Bohannon asserted that people who successfully adjust to a divorce have to deal with each of the six dimensions. The *emotional divorce* occurs when the couple withdraw from one another (exit, neglect). Although they may appear on the outside to function adequately as a couple, they have experienced a decrease in their level of emotional intimacy. In the *legal divorce*, an emotionally divorced couple seeks a legal decree through the court system.

The *economic divorce* is closely related to the legal divorce in the sense that the divorce often involves a settlement of property. The assets of the couple must be divided and provisions made for adequate support of dependent children. In the *co-parental* dimension it is necessary that the divorcing couple determine custody, visitation rights, and the roles and expectations for further family involvement of each of the parents. Divorce also changes the status of the couple in the *community*. There is a change in status from married to divorced individuals. For some this means dating and relief, for others, isolation from family, former friends, and neighbors. Last is the *psychic divorce*. Bohannon suggested that this is the most difficult stage in the recovery from divorce, yet probably in the end the most rewarding. The main task is to regain autonomy and self-esteem that may have been lost either during the declining marriage or in the divorce process.

Although Bohannon focused on divorce, many of the processes he described would apply to cohabiting and dating relationships as well. Nonmarried couples probably go through emotional divorce, economic divorce (division of property if the couple have made purchases together or combined their assets), community divorce, and psychic divorce. Though there are exceptions, breaking up before marriage is generally seen as less stressful than marital breakups (Hill et al., 1976).

The Process of Divorce Decisions

How is the decision made to obtain a divorce? Social exchange theory has most often been used to describe the process of marital interactions and decisions to divorce. Levinger (1979; 1983) suggested that the determinants of relationship disruptions vary from voluntary to involuntary, with death being the extreme of involuntary dissolution. At the voluntary end, one or both partners may choose to leave the relationship through withdrawal, desertion, separation, or divorce. Intimate relationships are not easily broken; if they do break, the relationships must already have declined to a point where one or both of the partners see an alternative state that is more attractive than staying in the present marriage. The more attractive alternative is not necessarily another lover or another relationship; it may be just leaving the present relationship and being alone.

What appears important is that alternatives are being considered. These may be more or less satisfactory than the present relationship, depending on the person's comparison level for alternatives. The process, however, is not simple. Along with comparisons for alternatives, there are attractions and barriers that affect a person's choice in the dissolution decision. Levinger viewed a marriage as a two-person group (Chapter 6) and suggested that there are inducements to remain in the group, which include the attractiveness of the group itself and the strength of the restraints or barriers against leaving it (Table 9-2). Dissolution of an intimate relationship is often marked by a drastic change in perceived costs and rewards by one or both of the partners.

Alternatives for Women

Using a cost-reward framework, we can begin to explain some of the demographic facts about divorce. Recall that there is a substantial increase in separation and divorce rates as a wife's education increases and her annual income increases. Ross and Sawhill (1975) suggested two possible explanations: (1) that some wives are seeking employment in anticipation of divorce, and (2) that working causes marital strains. Others suggested that wives with income independent of their husbands' earnings are less likely to be tied to their marriages (Scanzoni, 1979; Levinger, 1979). There may be many more options for career development for those women. Moreover, using Scanzoni's suggestion of increased resources, it follows that as a woman increases the number of years of schooling, she develops more resources on which to base a decision to leave an unhappy marriage. With a good education she increases her likelihood of gaining a good job and reduces her dependence upon her husband and the marriage. It is not that higher education for women directly causes divorce, but more likely that higher education is a *resource* that provides the basis for more options when a marriage is unsatisfactory. Perhaps the increasing divorce rate is not an indication of greater dissatisfaction in

TABLE 9-2	FACTORS DIFFERENTIATING HIGH AND LOW COHESIVE MARRIAGES	
Attractions of Staying in a Relationship	**Barriers to leaving a Relationship**	**Alternative Attractions**
Rewards	Costs	Rewards
Material Family income Home ownership	**Material** Financial expenses of termination	**Material** For wife: Independent social and economic status
Symbolic Educational status Occupational status Social similarity	**Symbolic** Obligation toward marital bond Religious constraints Pressures from primary groups Pressures from the community	**Symbolic** Independence and self-actualization
Affectional Companionship and esteem Sexual enjoyment	**Affectional** Feelings toward independent children	**Affectional** Preferred alternative sex partner

Source: From DIVORCE AND SEPARATION: CONTEXT, CAUSES, AND CONSEQUENCES, edited by George Levinger and Oliver C. Moles. Copyright © 1979 by the Society for the Psychological Study of Social Issues. Reprinted by permission of Basic Books, Inc., Publishers, New York.

marriage, but an indication that individuals in unhappy marriages are more willing to explore various alternatives. Research by Houseknecht et al. (1984) adds another dimension. When surveying women with graduate degrees, they found a greater likelihood of divorce or separation for women who began graduate school *after* marriage than for those women who began graduate school before. How would you put this into a cost and reward framework? In addition to providing the woman with greater resources, going to school after marriage probably challenged some traditional family roles and placed more demands and stresses on the marital relationship.

Effects of Divorce on Children

It has been estimated that 60 percent of American children will live in a single-parent family before reaching the age of eighteen (Norton & Glick, 1986). In 1987, there were 7.25 million one-parent families in the United States (Glick, 1989), most of which were due to divorce and separation. In a thorough review of literature concerning the impact of divorce on children, Longfellow (1979) found that, in general, marital conflict itself had negative effects on children. "It doesn't seem to matter if the conflict leads to separation or divorce: The child who experiences his or her parents' marital discord is at greater psychiatric risk. Separation or divorce may well reduce the stress produced by marital conflict. On the other hand, if the conflict continues after the divorce, either openly or in more subtle loyalty battles, the child is likely to experience adjustment problems" (p. 305).

In a more recent review of the research literature, Demo and Acock (1988) concluded that the effects of divorce on personal adjustment are greater for younger children than for older children. However, on a long-term basis it appears that those individuals who experienced a parental divorce or separation are similar to others in their personal adjustment in adolescence and adulthood (Kulka & Weingarten, 1979; Acock & Kiecolt, 1988). For most children, the first few years after their parents' decision to divorce are the most difficult. Problems often occur in cognitive functioning, self-concept, and social interaction. Despite the problems following divorce, current research evidence suggests that these children will not suffer any more emotional problems in later life than will children from intact homes. If children maintain positive close relationships with both parents, they are likely to achieve successful academic and social adjustment (Hess & Camara, 1979; Peterson & Zill, 1986).

Remarriage

Marrying again after being divorced or widowed is becoming increasingly common in the United States. Although we hear so much about divorce, deaths cause almost half of all marital dissolutions (Thornton & Freedman, 1983). Death of a spouse is more likely to occur in marriages of long duration, whereas divorce is the common means of ending marriages of short duration. Remarriages have increased in recent decades and today compose a large proportion of all marriages. Approximately four out of five divorced persons remarry: 83 percent of all divorced men and 75 percent of all divorced women. Usually, remarriage takes place rather rapidly after termination of the previous relationship. Approximately one-half of those whose first marriages have ended in divorce remarry within three years and 80 percent of divorced men and 70 percent of divorced women are remarried within five years.

Divorced persons are much more likely to remarry than are widowed persons. The difference between the remarriage rates is not only due to the fact that the widowed are, on the average, older, but also that many persons divorce in order to marry someone else (they have a high CL_{ALT}). Although rates of remarriage among the divorced are quite high, second (or third or fourth) marriages are not always successful. The divorce rate of remarriage (44 percent) is actually slightly higher than that of first marriages (37 percent). Remarried men are more satisfied with their marriages than remarried women, but only slightly so (Verne et al., 1989). Similar to the patterns that characterize first marriages, there is a significant decline in satisfaction in remarriage for both spouses over the first three years of a remarriage. (Guisinger et al., 1989).

Stepfamilies

A potential problem in remarriage is that children from the previous marriage are often involved in the new one. Stepfamilies represent 17 percent of households with children under the age of eighteen, with approximately 5.2 million remarried-parent households in the United States today (Glick, 1989). Research on stepfamilies has generally indicated that the presence of children from a previous marriage increases the likelihood of marital unhappiness and the chance of divorce for a remarried couple. Several characteristics of the remarried or "blended" family are quite different from first-marriage families (Visher & Visher, 1979). First, virtually all of the members of the remarried family have suffered a loss of some relationship in the past. Second, one biological parent now resides outside of the family. Third, the relationship between the biological parent and his or her children precedes the relationship with the new spouse. Fourth, the role definitions for stepparents in our culture are poorly defined. Finally, because one biological parent lives outside the household, most children in blended families are members of more than one family. These circumstances can influence many family problems, ranging from jealousies and emotional upsets to practical problems of travel back and forth between households. Experiencing different sets of rules, discipline, and expectations in each of the two families can be very difficult for the children.

Stress in the Blended Family

Stepfamilies are perceived by adolescents as significantly more stressful than are natural-parent families. One survey (Colvin, 1981) found that one-third of adolescents in stepfather families and one-half of adolescents in stepmother families reported significant family relationship problems. In contrast, only one-fourth of the adolescents in natural-parent families reported similar levels of problems. Using the same research instrument, Pink and Wampler (1985) improved the research methodology by having all members of stepfamilies and first-marriage families respond. They also found lower quality, lower cohesion, and lower adaptability in stepfamilies as compared with first-marriage families.

Another factor leading to the higher divorce rate for remarriages is a consequence of the lack of shared standards for remarriage. The norms and social expectations that guide first marriages are virtually nonexistent in the remarriage situation. Family members in first marriages rely on a wide range of norms and expectations to assist in solving common problems of family life. Remarriage is not as clearly guided by such norms and expectations. For one thing, we lack proper kinship terms: What does a ten-year-old call his new stepmother, remembering that he already has one mother? Furthermore, who has the authority to discipline stepchildren? What is a stepparent's legal relationship to the child? The cultural stereotype of the "wicked stepmother" doesn't help either (Cherlin, 1983).

In spite of these stresses and the lack of shared standards, remarriages often are successful. Studying divorced fathers, Guisinger et al. (1989) suggested that the prognosis is good for remarriage when there is initially a good marital relationship, when the husband contributes equitably to child care, when the couple shares tasks and decisions, when stepmothers develop good relationships with children, and when the couple is not too negative about the former wife. From a cost and rewards perspective, the stable remarriages would be, as in first marriages, those where the rewards (love, affection, fulfillment, security, economic stability) outweigh the costs (such as unclear norms, conflicting social roles, jealousies, interference by former spouses).

Loneliness

Until now we have not paid attention to those times when individuals may not be involved in relationships at all, or may be lonely even though they are in a relationship. In spite of all the attention devoted to long-term relationships, many of us, at various times in our lives, suffer the unpleasant and often distressing experience of loneliness. Loneliness was defined by Perlman and Peplau (1982) as a "painful warning signal that a person's social relations are deficient in some important way" (p. 1). The deficiency may be present in either the quality or the quantity of social relationships. It is useful to distinguish between *predisposing* factors that make people vulnerable to loneliness (e.g., shyness, stigma, lack of social skills, social isolation, cultural norms like individualism), and *precipitating events* that trigger the onset of loneliness (e.g., divorce, going away to school, moving to a new community). As related specifically to long-term relationships (or the lack thereof), data from several studies suggest that loneliness is less common among married people than among nonmarrieds (Berg et al., 1981). Of the nonmarrieds, single people are the least lonely, divorced persons next, and the widowed the most lonely (Perlman & Peplau, 1982). It appears that there are gender differences regarding loneliness among the nonmarried. Cock-

Loneliness. Many of us, at various times in our lives, suffer the unpleasant, distressing experience of loneliness.

rum and White (1985) surveyed never-married men and women who were age twenty-seven to forty-six. For men, their life satisfaction was most influenced by their own self-esteem. Women's life satisfaction was influenced by very different things. Emotional loneliness was most important, followed by availability of attachment ("How available and accessible relationships are that provide a sense of security and peace"). For the unmarried, especially women, the absence of close relationships appears to have important implications for well-being. Loneliness is a powerful issue that has profound effects upon individuals.

Summary

Social psychological theories can provide valuable insights into the factors that affect satisfaction in long-term relationships. One idea common to many theories is the notion that people tend to stay in relationships that are perceived as rewarding and leave relationships that are perceived as too costly. Of course, there are many variations — not every person will perceive the same relationship in the same way, and some might remain in unhappy relationships because no better alternatives seem available. Although relationships can assume many forms — friendship, dating, cohabiting, marriage, and remarriage — it appears that the process of establishing and resolving relationships in each of these situations is similar. Important dimensions of a relationship include reward level, the perceived balance of cost and rewards, commitment, communication, the distribution of social power, sex, jealousy, and comparison levels for alternatives. A greater understanding of these issues and processes may assist individuals in maintaining satisfying and enduring relationships. In a similar vein, a better understanding of the common processes in relationship breakups and divorce may enable us to provide better assistance and comfort to people involved in these painful events.

CHAPTER 10

Aggression

No form of aggressive behavior or violence is so extreme or so bizarre that it has not been included within the latitude of acceptance of some culture, at some place, at some time.   Edwin Megargee

You can get much farther with a kind word and a gun than you can with a kind word alone.   Al Capone, on instrumental aggression ❖

PREVIEW

The last two chapters analyzed why people like and love each other. Now it's time to view the other side of the coin: the determinants of hostility and aggression. I will review the general views of aggression that are common today, covering the biological, psychological, and situational factors that affect aggression. The relevance of social learning theory will be evident at many points. Internal conditions that cause aggression include brain disorders, genetic abnormalities, general arousal, drug effects, and emotional reactions to aversive events. Inhibitions against aggression can be reduced by lowered self-awareness, dehumanizing the victim, and behavioral contagion. Central situational factors include threat or attack, instigation by others, exposure to aggressive stimulus cues, and characteristics of the target.

A central focus of this chapter is the effect of witnessing violent movies, sports events, and TV programs. Two major theoretical positions suggest radically different effects. The catharsis position, endorsed by many ethologists and by followers of Freud, asserts that viewing violence may lessen violent tendencies in the audience because aggressive energies may be "drained off" while watching the violence. The social learning position suggests just the opposite: aggressive behavior is likely to be learned and energized by viewing violent stimuli. Strongly held values and big money are involved in the contrast between these positions, as you will see. Values play an even stronger role in reactions when sexuality is combined with aggression, as in "slasher" films and violent pornography. Lastly, we will evaluate ways to control or reduce levels of aggression in society.

AGGRESSIVE BEHAVIOR: AN OVERVIEW

The Prevalence of Aggression in Our Society

Rising rates of violent crimes such as forcible rape and aggravated assault demonstrate the trend toward increased aggression in the United States. The murder rate in the U.S. is much higher than any other modern industrialized country. It is estimated that over 23,000 people will be murdered in the U.S. in 1990; a U.S. senator noted that, "1990 will be the bloodiest year in American history" (Flory, 1990). The U.S. murder rate was over *ten times* as great as the rate in Great Britain or Japan (Flory, 1990). Looking only at shootings, but including suicides and accidental shootings, it was estimated that over thirty thousand Americans were shot to death in 1989 (Magnuson, 1989). In the past decade many have become aware of the high levels of private aggression as well, as chilling statistics have surfaced on the frequency of child battering, spouse abuse, and sexual abuse of children and adults. If you are living in America, there is an 83% chance that someday you will be the victim of a violent crime such as murder, rape, kidnaping, assault, or robbery (Flanagan & Jamison, 1989, p. 250).

Definitions of Aggression

aggression:
Behavior intended to bring physical or psychological harm to a person who wishes not to be harmed.

Although aggression is a concept familiar to us all, it is not easily defined. **Aggression** is behavior intended to bring physical or psychological harm to a person who wishes not to be harmed. We must look closely at intentions (often hard to specify, as we saw in Chapter 2), and long-term benefit or harm (e.g., an injection involves short-term pain but is intended to improve the long-term welfare of the patient). Indirect acts, such as destroying someone's property or encouraging others to aggress against an individual or group, also qualify as acts of aggression. In societal terms, we are usually most concerned about **offensive aggression**, aggression not directly caused by someone else's behavior. Most research studies, in contrast, have looked at **retaliatory aggression**, aggression in response to someone else's provocation.

offensive aggression:
Aggression that is not directly in retaliation to someone else's behavior.

retaliatory aggression:
Aggression in response to someone else's provocation.

Another distinction concerns intentions. **Instrumental aggression** occurs when the aggression is a means to an end (as in a robbery), whereas **angry aggression** implies an emotional state of anger (as in a fight). In many experiments this distinction is not clear. For example, subjects may think they are delivering electric shocks to another student who has insulted them. They have been told that the purpose of the shocks is to serve as a stimulus to "help" the other student learn the task. Is the delivery of shock instrumental aggression (following the instructions to help) or angry aggression (getting back at an insulting person)? It's hard to say, since we don't know the subject's internal motivations.

instrumental aggression:
Aggression that occurs as a means to an end (as in a robbery).

angry aggression:
Aggression that involves an emotional state of anger; differentiated from instrumental aggression.

CAUSES OF HUMAN AGGRESSION

Aggression is an *overdetermined behavior* affected by genetic, constitutional, and environmental factors, individual learning histories, and specific situational events (Eron et al., 1987). I will discuss four general factors that influence human aggression: learned habits, internal conditions that instigate aggression, factors that reduce inhibitions, and situational factors (Megargee, 1984). These are summarized in Table 10-1.

TABLE 10-1	MAJOR FACTORS THAT DETERMINE AGGRESSION		
Learned Habits	**Internal Conditions That Instigate Aggression**	**Conditions That Reduce Inhibitions Against Aggression**	**Situational Factors That Increase the Probability of Aggression**
Direct experience	Human nature (?)	Low private self-awareness	Threat or attack
Social learning/Observational learning	Aggressive instincts (?)	Low public self-awareness	Instigation from others
Reinforcement for previous aggressive behavior	Genetic/physiological abnormalities	Dehumanizing the victim	Aggressive stimulus cues
Aggressive scripts	Emotional reactions to aversive events (frustration, anger, pain, fear)	Absence of empathy	Environmental stressors (excessive noise, heat, crowding)
	Aggression resulting from general arousal	Behavioral contagion	Characteristics of the potential target (cannot retaliate, member of disliked group)
	Drug effects		Ingroup-outgroup conflict

Learned Habits

Much of human aggression is learned. In Chapter 7 we saw how prosocial behavior can be learned either through direct reinforcement or by watching others behave. Aggression, like prosocial behavior, can also be learned. The question of whether human aggression is instinctive or learned is of great importance because of its implications for the effect that the observation of violence might have on aggressive behavior. Social learning theorists such as Albert Bandura (1983) asserted that human aggression originates from: (1) observational learning, (2) reinforcement for aggression, and (3) structural determinants such as physical size and biological factors. Individuals who are prone to behave aggressively because of previous observational learning, reinforcement, or personality characteristics are likely to react to emotional arousal with aggression (Figure 10-1).

instrumental motivation:
Instigation to aggression in which the violent behavior accomplishes a goal.

angry motivation:
Instigation to aggression in which injury to the victim is an end in itself.

Theorists have differentiated two broad types of instigation to aggression: **instrumental motivation**, in which the aggressive or violent behavior accomplishes a goal, such as economic gain, and **angry motivation**, in which injury to the victim is an end in itself. Instrumental aggression may have goals of acquisition (taking things that one wants), enhancement of one's self-concept by demonstrating courage and smartness, obtaining attention or seeking excitement, the need for affection, the use of violence to facilitate other crimes, the elimination of people who block goals, obtaining approval by the group (by one's gang, for example), and achieving power, control, or dominance over others.

People who have a particular personality style labeled the Type A coronary-prone behavior pattern (to be discussed in Chapter 14), are impatient, goal-directed, and have an exaggerated sense of time urgency. They are especially intolerant of delays or interference with their goal-directed behavior and hence are quite likely to feel frustrated and hostile. We will see later that this chronic hostility not only can produce aggression toward others but also may lead to an earlier death from heart disease.

Internal Conditions That Instigate Aggression

Aggression as a Part of Human Nature

Lord of the Flies, a novel written by Nobel Prize winner William Golding (1954), is a fictitious story of a group of English schoolboys who were shipwrecked on an island. The boys divided into factions, and violence and savagery quickly developed. The group was finally rescued after they had killed one boy and were hunting for another, dressed in primitive outfits with painted faces, chanting, "Kill the beast, cut his throat, spill his blood!" Peter Brook, the director of a movie that was made from the book, described the behavior of the young actors: "Many of their offscreen relationships completely paralleled the story, and one of our main problems was to encourage them to be uninhibited within shots but disciplined between them.... My experience showed me that the only falsification in Golding's fable is the length of time the descent to savagery takes. His action takes about three months. I believe that if the cork of continued adult presence were removed from the bottle, the complete catastrophe would occur in a long weekend" (Brook, 1964, p. 23).

Thanatos:
The "death instinct" or aggressive instinct described by Sigmund Freud.

Some social scientists have argued that human aggression results from an aggressive instinct. Appalled by the death and destruction of World War I, Sigmund Freud (1920/1959) theorized that every human being has an unconscious urge toward destruction. He labeled this drive **Thanatos**, the death instinct. According to Freud, these destructive aggressive urges can be released directly in aggressive behavior or may be displaced onto scapegoats or sublimated in more socially acceptable ways.

To what extent do inherited factors affect human aggression? For aggression, as with other traits, it is impossible to specify precisely the relative contributions of heredity, environment, and other factors. Some have suggested that we inherit temperamental differences that predispose people to be more or less restrained (Hogan, 1986). Studies have found consistent gender differences in aggression across cultures, suggesting that genetic factors may be involved. A meta-analysis of 143 studies (Hyde, 1984) found that gender differences in measured aggressiveness were larger than those found for any other behavioral characteristic. Another meta-analysis (Eagly & Steffen, 1986) found that gender differences were greater for aggression that produces pain or physical harm than for aggression that produces psychological or social harm.

Is aggression a basic part of human nature? The movie, Lord of the Flies, *depicted shipwrecked English schoolboys who quickly became aggressive toward each other once the constraints of civilization were removed.*

In almost all of the world's cultures men are expected to be more aggressive than women (Whiting & Edwards, 1973); these expectations could themselves produce consistent gender differences. Women feel more anxiety about aggression and more guilt and avoidance when faced with aggression (Frodi et al., 1977). Women's greater empathy (Hoffman, 1977) may also make them more sensitive to the negative consequences of aggression. Some research suggests that in situations where aggression is perceived as justified and empathy-arousing factors are controlled, women may act as aggressively as men do (Frodi et al., 1977; Frodi, 1978). If social disapproval about aggression in females were lessened, the sex differences in aggressiveness might be reduced as well (Richardson et al., 1979). Still, gender differences in aggressiveness may be partially biological, related to the effects of different hormones in males and females (White, 1983), though status differences and socialization undoubtedly play a role as well. Behavioral genetics research led one psychologist to argue that human aggressiveness is "deeply embedded in genetic history" (Rushton, 1988, p. 35).

Aggression as an Animal Instinct

ethologists:
Scientists who study animal behavior.

Many **ethologists** (scientists who study animal behavior) have argued that aggression is instinctual in humans (Ardrey, 1966; Lorenz, 1966; Morris, 1968; Storr, 1968). Yet they see it not as destructive or diabolical (as Freud did) but as natural and often beneficial. According to these ethologists, all species possess innate instinctive energies, which build up until discharged. Discharge is generally triggered or released by external cues, usually the behavior of another animal. Within-species aggression—**agonistic aggression**—may have beneficial effects for a species because it allows territorial spacing so that food supplies and shelter are not decimated. Agonistic aggression also creates dominance hierarchies where the most healthy animals are the ones who are able to mate and eat first and most.

agonistic aggression:
The ethological term for within-species aggression that allows the creation of dominance hierarchies and territorial spacing.

*Agnostic aggression.
Aggression within a species
may be beneficial because it
created territorial spacing
and dominance hierarchies.*

Ethologists also believe that most animals have an instinctive inhibition against killing other members of their species and that they fight only until one member has shown superiority over the other. Mankind, they suggest, is unique because we do not have this inhibition against killing members of our own species. Humans were originally a "flight species," they argue; primitive people didn't need the inhibitory mechanism against killing each other because they were scavengers, did not have fangs or claws, and could not easily kill one another. Now, unfortunately, humans have developed an awesome ability to kill one another simply by pushing a button or pulling a trigger. Without the inhibitory factors possessed by other species, we are in a uniquely perilous position. Some ethologists suggested that the solution to this situation is to develop events of "ritualized aggression," such as sports, where our aggressive energies can be released directly or indirectly.

Many social psychologists have criticized the ethological position, noting that often the ethologists failed to provide any empirical evidence to support their generalization and based their work on personal observations, which may often be incorrect (Berkowitz, 1969). Some ethologists have tended to indiscriminately generalize from other animals to humans, neglecting the role of learning. Human experience suggests that aggression does not always accumulate over time and demand release, as Mohandas K. Gandhi's life would seem to illustrate. The spiritual leader of India continually lived a policy of nonviolence in the struggle for independence from England, even while aggression was constantly directed at him.

If all humans have an aggressive instinct, then it should exist in all societies. Yet anthropologists have described several societies such as the Arapesh in New Guinea, the Lepchas in Sikkim, and the Pygmies in the Congo, which seem to be genuinely nonaggressive. Each of these societies is small, technologically weak, underdeveloped, and in an inaccessible place not coveted by other groups. Hence, it is possible for a nonaggressive society to exist (Gorer, 1968).

Despite criticisms from social psychologists, the ethological instinct position remains a popular one. The ethologists have made a plausible-sounding case for their position in the popular literature, despite a lack of strong supporting evidence. The commonsense notion of an "aggressive instinct" is easy to grasp and many people seem to prefer such a simplistic notion.

Genetic and Physiological Abnormalities

In 1966, Charles Whitman went to the top of a tower at the University of Texas and began firing at passersby below. Before he was finally killed by police, he had murdered sixteen people and injured twenty more. An autopsy revealed a walnut-size malignant tumor in his brain, leading many to wonder whether this tumor had led to his violent behavior.

Another biological abnormality possibly linked to aggression is the presence of an extra male chromosome. Research has shown that males with an extra Y chromosome (XYY males) are larger on the average than other males, are slightly less intelligent, and are fifteen to twenty times more frequent in prison populations than in the nonprison male population, although XYY males are rare even in prisons (less than 5 percent of male prisoners). Attempts to determine whether this chromosomal abnormality leads directly to violent behavior have not been very productive (Witkin et al., 1977). We do not yet know why it is more likely that XYY males will become imprisoned; perhaps they are in prison simply because their lower intelligence makes it more likely they will be caught when committing crimes. One recent review (Megargee, in press) argues that the XYY disorder has no direct relationship to violence.

Drug Effects

After drinking, many individuals become impulsive and less concerned with norms of conduct they usually obey. Distortions of judgment produced by alcohol may explain why many bars are closed on election day or during civil disturbances. A number of surveys have found a strong relationship between assaultive crime and alcohol. Overall, in about half of all violent crimes either the perpetrator, the victim, or both had been drinking (Pernanen, 1981).

Small doses of alcohol (the equivalent of one cocktail) may reduce the likelihood of an aggressive response to provocation (compared with people given no alcohol), but large doses of alcohol (the equivalent of three cocktails) substantially increase the likelihood of an aggressive response when someone is provoked (Pihl & Ross, 1987). What is it about drinking that increases aggression? The alcohol-aggression link cannot be due to solely pharmacological processes, since people who are not provoked do not show increased aggression even under high doses of alcohol (Taylor et al., 1979). Some drinkers' *expectations* about alcohol's effects may serve as a cue for aggressive behavior. Lang and his co-workers (1975) demonstrated that subjects in an experiment became more aggressive when they were led to believe they had received alcohol, regardless of whether they had really received any. This process does not occur in everybody, however, as there are wide individual differences in people's expectations about whether alcohol will stimulate aggressive behavior (Lang & Sibrel, 1989).

Aggressive behavior may be controlled to a great extent by situational factors: instigative cues such as threats, verbal insults, and pain, and inhibitory cues such as guilt, expectation of negative consequences, and the size of the potential target (Taylor & Leonard, 1983). High doses of alcohol impair complex cognitive processes and cause **cognitive disruption**, reducing one's ability to cope with difficult situations (Steele & Southwick, 1985). Cognitive disruption may especially affect reactions to subtle cues. Leonard (1989) found that alcohol did not affect responses to explicit aggression or nonaggressive cues in someone else's behavior, but interfered with understanding subtle nonaggressive cues. An intoxicated person is more likely to misinterpret another person's behavior as aggressive because he misses any subtle nonaggressive cues that may be present.

Finally, alcohol can serve as a basis for *rationalization or justification* of

cognitive disruption:
An interruption in normal thought process which reduces one's ability to cope with difficult situations.

behavior. Some husbands who are inclined toward spouse abuse blame their actions on alcohol (Leonard, 1988). Some of the political figures who were caught in the Abscam scandal in the late 1970s attempted to attribute their illegal or unethical behaviors solely to alcohol: "Don't blame me, I was drunk."

In contrast to alcohol, marijuana normally produces a pleasant, euphoric state and is seldom associated with violence. In fact, research by Taylor and his associates showed that persons who had received a high dose of THC, the major active ingredient in marijuana, were *less* likely to respond aggressively when provoked than people who had received no drug (Taylor et al., 1976). The contrasting effects of marijuana and alcohol on aggression after provocation are depicted in Figure 10-1.

Phencyclidine (PCP, or angel dust) seems to be directly connected with violence. Violent behavior may occur soon after taking the drug or during a PCP toxic psychosis, which may last several weeks (Mednick et al., 1982). Experiments have also demonstrated that barbiturates may elicit irritability, hostility, and overt aggression (Mednick et al., 1982). In recent years, rage reactions have been noted in some athletes who were taking massive doses of steroids to "bulk up" their muscles (Megargee, in press). The violence surrounding the "crack" cocaine epidemic also became vividly evident in the late 1980s. Much of this violence is instrumental, as users resort to violent crime to get money for the drug. But cocaine use can also produce paranoia and heightened aggressiveness in 15 to 25 percent of users, especially those who use it in conjunction with alcohol (Erickson et al., 1987). The associa-

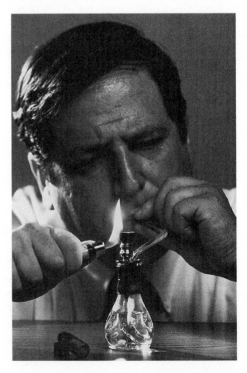

Cocaine and aggressiveness. Cocaine produces paranoia and increased aggressiveness in some users, especially if used in conjunction with alcohol.

FIGURE 10-1

Alcohol Increases
Aggression, Marijuana
Decreases It

*The effects of low and high
doses of alcohol and marijuana
on the amount of aggression
(electric shock) delivered to an
aggressive experimental
partner.*

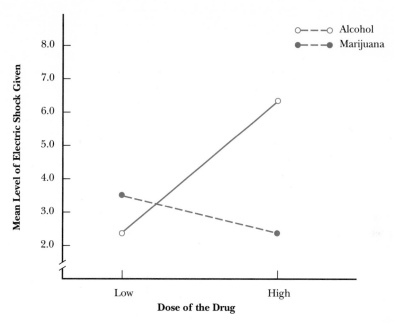

Sources: S. P. Taylor, R. M. Vardaris, A. C. Rawtich, C. B. Gammon, J. W. Cranston, & A. Lubetkin (1976). The effects of alcohol and Delta-9-Tetrahydrocan-Nabinol on human physical aggression. *Aggressive Behavior, 2* (2), 153–161. Copyright © 1976 Wiley-Liss, a division of John Wiley & Sons, Inc. Reprinted by permission.

tion of drug use with crime often indicates as much about our expectations and our social system as about the drugs themselves. Because most drugs are illegal and expensive, users often are forced to operate in a criminal subculture and may resort to instrumental aggression to get money for their habit.

Aggression as a Reaction to Aversive Events

Angry aggression is often produced by internal states, such as frustration or anger, that are a reaction to aversive events. The state of *frustration* and its relation to aggression have been widely studied. The concept of frustration is tricky; the term has been used to describe both an external instigating event, as when one's access to a desired goal has been blocked, and also the internal feeling that results from this external condition. The **frustration-aggression** theory was put forth by Dollard, Doob, Miller, Mowrer, and Sears in 1939. Originally they implied that every case of frustration results in aggression, but in 1941 Miller noted that frustration produces instigation to a number of different responses, only one of which is aggression.

frustration-aggression theory:
The theory that frustration instigates aggression and occurrences of aggression presuppose frustration.

Frustration is but one of many unpleasant events that stimulate negative affect (emotion). Berkowitz (1983, 1989a) theorized that aversive events activate rudimentary emotional responses associated with primitive fight (attack) or flight (avoidance/escape) reactions (Figure 10-2). These reactions can be stimulated by frustration, pain, depression, encountering disliked people or, as we will see in Chapter 12, environmental stressors (excessive heat, noise, air pollution). The relative strength of the fight and flight responses depends on the individual's genetic makeup, learning history, and situational factors. After the initial emotional reaction, the emotional experience (anger or fear) as well as the resulting behavior will be influenced by cognitive factors such as inhibitions against aggression, attributions about the cause of the aversive event (Weiner, 1985), instigation from others to aggress, and expected consequences.

FIGURE 10-2

Anger or Fear as Reactions to Aversive Events:
A model proposed by Leonard Berkowitz (1989b).

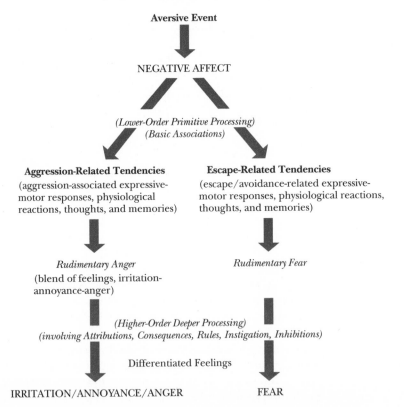

Source: From Berkowitz, L. (1986b). On the formation and regulation of anger and aggression: A cognitive-neoassociationistic analysis. Distinguished Scientist Award Lecture, American Psychological Association meeting, New Orleans. Reprinted by permission of the author.

A number of studies have shown that pain produces negative affect and angry aggression. People who are in pain from being forced to keep a hand in a tank of very cold water behave more aggressively and punitively than they would otherwise (Berkowitz et al., 1981; Berkowitz & Thome, 1987). Depression can also produce aggression. Although depressed people are often apathetic and passive (recall our discussion of learned helplessness in Chapter 2), there is considerable evidence that aggressive reactions can accompany depression too (Finman & Berkowitz, 1989; Miller & Norman, 1979).

Aggression Resulting from General Arousal

Schachter's (1964) two-factor theory of emotion, discussed in Chapter 3, asserted that experiencing an emotion is determined by the degree of physiological arousal (excitation) and the cognitive cues in the situation that suggest which emotional reaction is most appropriate. We know that cognition and arousal interact in the creation of emotion—but *how* do cognition and excitation affect each other? Zillmann (1988) proposed that excitation (arousal) can occur reflexlike with recognition that one is endangered, as the body prepares for vigorous fight or flight reactions. Excitation can also be modified by cognitions, as when one decides that an injustice has been committed. Excitation, in turn, can modify cognitions. Seemingly senseless behaviors, such as extreme domestic violence or other impulsive, violent behaviors, may occur when high levels of excitation interfere with cognitive functioning, Zillmann argued. When highly excited, people may also be more susceptible to illusions of power and invulnerability and more likely to fall back on well-established aggressive habits.

excitation-transfer theory:
The types of excitatory reactions caused by different stimuli may overlap with each other and this can lead to misattribution of excitation to aggression-related stimuli and to feeling higher levels of aggression.

An important part of Zillmann's theorizing, for our present purposes, is his **excitation-transfer theory**. Zillmann (1983) proposed that excitatory reactions caused by different stimuli overlap considerably with each other because intense excitatory reactions terminate gradually, not abruptly. Figure 10-3 illustrates a case in which a person has intense excitatory reactions to two stimuli: first to an erotic stimulus (A), and later to an aggression-producing stimulus (B). If asked at Point 1 to describe the level and source of his arousal, he would (accurately) attribute all of his arousal to the sexual stimulus. At Point 2 his level of excitation is higher because it is a combination of arousal produced by the aggressive stimulus and leftover arousal produced by the sexual stimulus. Zillmann argued that we are not good at differentiating between different *sources* of arousal; we tend to attribute our reactions to the most obvious prior condition. Thus at Point 2, the person feels highly aroused and is likely to attribute all of this arousal to the aggression-producing stimulus. As a result, he is more likely to behave aggressively than is someone who was exposed to the same aggression-producing stimulus but was not feeling any leftover excitation from a different source.

According to the excitation transfer model, then, when one is predisposed to aggress, arousal—even when caused by another source—may

FIGURE 10-3

An Illustration of
Excitation-Transfer Theory

Excitation caused by one stimulus (Stimulus A) may be interpreted as stemming from a second stimulus (Stimulus B), thereby increasing the likelihood of a strong response to the second stimulus.

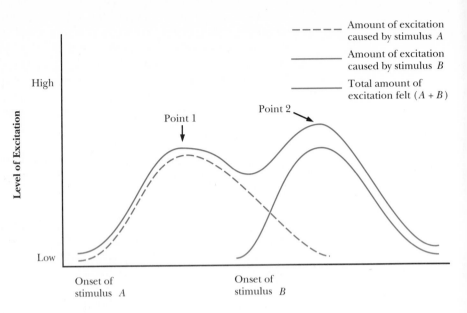

Source: Zillmann, D. (1978). Attribution and misattribution of excitatory reactions. In J. H. Harvey, W. J. Ickes, & R. F. Kidd (Eds.), *New directions in attribution research, Vol. 2.* Hillsdale, NJ: Erlbaum; Zillmann, D. (1983). Transfer of excitation in emotional behavior. In J. T. Cacioppo & R. E. Petty (Eds.), *Social Psychophysiology* (pp. 215–240). New York: Guilford Press.

facilitate aggression. Evidence for such a position has been demonstrated for violent material (Donnerstein et al., 1976), erotic material (Donnerstein et al., 1975), and humorous material (Mueller & Donnerstein, 1977). When an individual is predisposed to act in a prosocial manner, in contrast, further arousal should facilitate prosocial behavior (Mueller et al., 1983).

Factors That Reduce Inhibitions against Aggression

A third set of factors are those that *reduce inhibitions against aggression.* Inhibitions are learned, generally through punishment rather than reward. These include moral prohibitions, conscience, learned taboos, and values. Megargee (1982) suggested that there were four broad determinants of inhibitions against aggression: (1) *anxiety* or conditioned fear of punishment, (2) *learned values* and attitudes, (3) *empathy* or identification with the potential victim, and (4) *practical concerns.* Inhibitions may be raised by the presence of persons who arouse guilt over aggression, such as parents or clergy, or those who promise swift retributions for violent behavior, such as police, or those who may decrease aggressive instigation by pacifying an opponent or relieving tension through humor.

Lowered Self-Awareness

As noted in Chapter 3, lowered self-awareness can reduce inhibitions toward aggression. Anonymity, high emotional arousal, diffusion of responsibility, and membership in a cohesive group may lead to reduced public and private self-awareness (Figure 3-10). Low public self-awareness produces feelings that one is not accountable to others and does not need to fear censure or reprisals for one's behavior (disinhibition). Lowered private self-awareness leads to the state of deindividuation, resulting in lowered attention to one's own thoughts, feelings, values, and standards for behavior (Prentice-Dunn & Rogers, 1989). Since we usually have firm inhibitions against aggressive behavior, lowered self-awareness would increase the chances that aggression will occur, because ordinary restraints concerning aggression are weakened.

In support of these theoretical predictions, research has demonstrated that decreased self-awareness produces increases in verbal aggression (Festinger et al., 1952) and physical aggression (Zimbardo, 1970). Prentice-Dunn and Rogers (1980) manipulated three factors that should affect self awareness: anonymity to authority (the experimenter), anonymity to the victim (a fellow subject), and diffusion of responsibility. As predicted, people who were led to feel anonymous to the experimenter and to a fellow subject and to feel no responsibility for their behavior (the experimenter assured them that he would assume full responsibility for their fellow subject's well-being) were more aggressive — they delivered higher shock intensities for longer durations than did people not exposed to these conditions.

Lowered self-awareness. The hooded costumes worn by Ku Klux Klan members should produce very low levels of public and private self-awareness, disinhibiting behavior and increasing the liklihood of aggression.

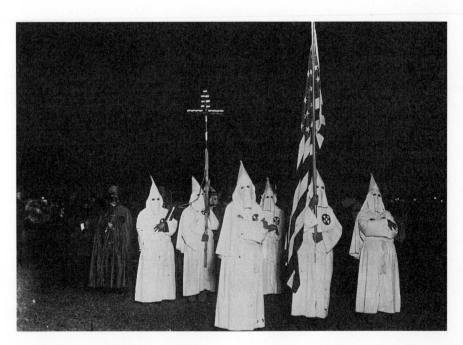

Merely being a member of a group, even without any direct instigation toward violence, may also increase aggression levels as self-awareness is lessened. Jaffe, Shapir, and Yinon (1981) placed four groups of Israeli citizens in a situation where they were to shock fellow subjects for every incorrect answer on a task. Subjects worked individually or in groups of three and could choose the level of shock to deliver. In the group condition, they were to reach a unanimous group decision about the level of punishment to be administered. Subjects in a group delivered considerably higher shocks than did subjects working individually. Furthermore, the intensity of shocks delivered by the group increased over time, a finding also reported by others (Buss et al., 1972; Goldstein et al., 1975). Group members reported feeling significantly less responsibility for delivering the shocks than did subjects working individually.

Dehumanizing the Victim

Inhibitions against harming another person are lowered if the person is *dehumanized*, not seen as a fellow human being. This lessens an aggressor's guilt and anxiety and may also imply that the victim is less sensitive to mistreatment (Kelman, 1973). Wartime propaganda often plays on these themes. Experiments (Bandura et al., 1975) show that students deliver higher shocks to members of a different group when they feel less responsibility (recall Milgram's shock-obedience studies in Chapter 5) and when the potential victims are dehumanized.

Chinese troops slaughtered thousands of protesting students in Beijing's Tiananmen Square in 1989. In retrospect, we can identify a number of ways in which the students were dehumanized and the troops' inhibitions against shooting civilians were reduced (Megargee, in press). The local army garrison, who might have felt liking, empathy, and sympathy for the students, was replaced by uneducated provincial troops who were told they were facing vicious counterrevolutionaries. It was nighttime and smoke further obscured the amorphous mob when the tanks were ordered to attack. Isolated inside their armored vehicles, the soldiers were probably unable to discern the effects of their fire on individual students. These conditions led not only to dehumanization of the victims, but also probably to deindividuation and low self-awareness among the soldiers.

Situational Factors That Stimulate Aggression

Threat or Attack

Threat or attack often produces a retaliatory aggressive response. There may be gender differences in retaliatory aggression. Hokanson and his colleagues (Hokanson & Burgess, 1962a, 1962b; Hokanson et al., 1963) found that males were more likely than females to respond to aggression with aggression of their own. These gender differences may reflect sex-role training, as men have been taught to "stand up for yourself" and "hit them back," whereas women are more likely to have been taught to "turn the other cheek" in the face of aggression.

Instigation by Others

The behavior of other people (instigators, observers, bystanders) can affect aggression, as pointed out while discussing behavioral contagion in Chapter 5. Instigation does not have to be direct. Borden (1975) found that male "teachers" in a Milgram-like shock study delivered higher shocks when they were being viewed by a male than when they were being viewed by a female observer. This may have occurred because the norms of society implicitly suggest that males approve of aggression but females disapprove. A second study supported the importance of perceived values—"teachers" observed by a karate club member showed greater aggression than those observed by a peace organization member.

Levels of aggressive behavior may also depend on whether one is a direct aggressor or an advisor. Gaebelein and Mander (1978) put college women in a situation where they were to deliver shocks to someone or advise another person on how many shocks to deliver. Subjects in an advisor role set significantly higher shock intensities than did subjects who were delivering the shocks directly. Do these results have implications for the behavior of military "advisors"?

Aggressive Stimulus Cues

When an aggressive cue, such as a gun or knife, is present, individuals may be more likely to behave aggressively than when such a cue is not present (Berkowitz & LePage, 1967; Leyens & Parke, 1975). This "weapons effect" has been found in some studies but not in others (Epstein et al., 1980). At this point it is safest to conclude that aggressive stimulus cues *can* increase aggressive behaviors but they do not always do so. If the mere visual presence of weapons does increase people's aggressive tendencies, this provides a compelling argument for stricter gun control, so that people's aggressive behaviors are not increased by the presence of aggressive stimulus cues (guns) in their homes.

Characteristics of the Target

Features of the potential target of the aggression are also important. Members of disliked, stereotyped groups are more likely to be targets of aggression (Chapter 11), as are people who are smaller or physically unattractive. In addition, potential targets receive more aggression if they do not have the potential to retaliate (Donnerstein et al., 1972), or to deliver censure (Donnerstein & Donnerstein, 1973), and if the target cannot tell who the aggressor is (Donnerstein et al., 1972).

FOCUS 10-1

All in the Family: Aggression in Intimate Relationships

Most researchers have studied aggression between strangers (research subjects) or between members of hostile groups (ingroup/outgroup distinctions to be analyzed in Chapter 11). But a great number of violent acts occur between intimates: 17 percent of homicides in the U.S. are within the family; in half of these one spouse killed the other (Uniform Crime Reports, 1983). About 10 percent of American wives say they have been assaulted by their husband some time during their marriage; about half of these cases involve repeated assaults (Straus et al., 1980). Surveys indicate that psychological and physical abuse is an all-too-common feature of college students' dating relationships as well (Laner & Thompson, 1982; Sigelman et al., 1984).

Wife abuse has a long history in Western culture. The Napoleonic code required husbands to physically punish their wives "for correction" (Davidson, 1977), and it was not until the 1980s that wife abuse became illegal in several New England states (Lehrman, 1981). Recent studies of men who have repeatedly assaulted their spouses suggest that they are likely to suffer from job stress, have a high need for power, have sexist attitudes about the woman's "role," and have an obsessive, dependent, controlling relationship style (Dutton, 1986). They are also more responsive to some environmental cues. Dutton and Browning (1984) showed videotapes of husband-wife arguments to men who had assaulted their wives and found that they became angrier than did men who were not wife-assaulters.

There is another side to this picture—women who kill their abusive partners. Less than 15 per-

cent of all homicides are committed by women, but they are seven times as likely to involve self-defense than are men's homicides (*Crimes of Violence*, 1969). A study in Chicago found that 40 percent of the women serving time for murder or manslaughter had killed husbands or lovers who had repeatedly beaten them (Lindsay, 1978). It appears that the factors usually portrayed as causes of aggression (Table 10-1) may not be relevant to this special group.

Comparing a sample of women who had killed or attempted to kill their spouses with a group of women were also in abusive relationships but had not attempted to kill their spouses, Browne (1986) found that personalities of the two groups did not differ, but the quality of the relationship did. The women who had attempted to kill their mates, in comparison to the other women, had been abused more frequently, had suffered more severe injuries, were more likely to have been threatened with death, had more sex acts threatened or forced upon them, had mates who were heavier drug users and more frequently intoxicated, and were themselves more likely to have made suicide threats. In brief, they were prisoners in intolerable relationships, usually threatened with harm or death if they tried to leave. In the language of social exchange theory (Chapter 9), they were "captive participants" in a relationship, where no alternative (a new relationship or no relationship) seemed possible. As Thibaut and Kelly (1959) noted years ago, people interacting in nonvoluntary relationships tend to focus more on cost (e.g., threats for leaving, harm) than on rewards. ❖

THE EFFECTS OF VIEWING AGGRESSION

Theoretical Viewpoints

The Instinct View

Ethologists such as Konrad Lorenz have defined aggression as the "fighting instinct" that is directed against members of one's own species. Freud and his followers conceptualized aggression as a destructive, instinctual urge that can be expressed in socially acceptable or unacceptable ways. Opinions about the origin of aggression directly affect assumptions about the effects of observing aggressive behavior in others.

If aggressive tendencies are innate and if each of us carries around a pool of aggressive impulses, then viewing the aggressive behavior of others could serve a valuable function. People might be able to vent their pent-up aggressive impulses while watching, and perhaps identifying with, the aggressive action. This idea goes all the way back to Aristotle, who wrote that drama is concerned with "incidents arousing pity and fear in such a way as to accomplish a purgation of such emotions" (in the audience members). The

Women who strike back. In the movie, "The Burning Bed", Farrah Fawcett portrayed a women who, after being savagely abused by her husband for years, finally set fire to his bed while he slept.

catharsis:
The theory that by acting out or observing others, people are able to release or drain off their pent-up emotions.

term **catharsis**, derived from the Greek word for purgation, describes this process of releasing aggressive tendencies through viewing the aggressive behavior of others. Alfred Hitchcock puckishly offered a defense of violent TV programs based upon this catharsis notion: "One of television's great contributions is that it brought murder back into the home where it belongs. Seeing a murder on television can be good therapy. It can help work off one's antagonisms. If you haven't any antagonisms, the commercials will give you some" (quoted in Schellenberg, 1970, p. 31).

Many popular ethological writers have propounded the notion of catharsis, asserting that animals (including humans) have innate instinctual energies that build up until they are triggered or released by external cues. However, Nobel Prize winner Konrad Lorenz later backed away from the catharsis notion he had supported in his influential 1966 book. Several years later, Lorenz (quoted in Evans, 1974, p. 90) remarked, "It's a very real question whether encouraging people to feel a vicarious destructive aggressivity increases the probability of such aggressivity, or whether the vicarious aggression acts as a catharsis. I think that the possible danger of removing inhibitions is much more important. If children are accustomed to seeing wars, murders, and fights on TV, their inhibitions against committing these violent acts may lessen." In another interview Lorenz admitted that, "I've written something . . . in my aggression book which I would qualify if I wrote it again. Nowadays, I have my strong doubts whether simply watching aggressive behavior has any cathartic effect at all" (quoted in Evans, 1975, p. 44).

Nevertheless, the catharsis position is often applied today as an explanation for the popularity—and perhaps the social value—of sports such as football in the United States. In essence, the argument holds that the typical football fan builds up a pool of aggressive potential over the week, having been frustrated and hassled at work and at home. The potentially harmful aggressiveness is released every weekend when the fan is able to identify with the institutionalized aggression of football. In theory, the fan walks away from the stadium or TV set a less aggressive person, ready to face the next week.

Institutionalized aggression. Is the institutionalized aggression in sports events likely to increase or decrease levels of aggressiveness in viewers?

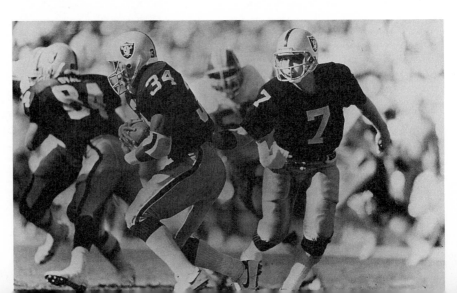

Focus 10-2 describes two attempts at applying the catharsis model to fans at college football and baseball games.

There is a second type of catharsis. People who are frustrated or angry and are able to aggress *directly* against the source of frustration may feel better afterward (Doob & Wood, 1972; Konecni, 1975). However, even this limited sense of catharsis has been questioned (Tavris, 1982), because it is not clear whether catharsis stems from a draining off of aggressive tendencies or from increases in guilt or anxiety over behaving aggressively.

FOCUS 10-2

Catharsis at the Stadium?

Several years ago, a cinderblock fence was installed around the outfield at the Florida State University baseball field. Prior to this time, a chainlink fence had surrounded the outfield, and FSU students and their friends would sit outside the fence watching the game and heckling opposing ball players. At times the heckling got vicious, spurring the sports editor of the campus newspaper to make the following observations:

> The standard cliché is that these people are envious of the ball players and since they can't put themselves in the athlete's shoes, they take out their frustrations on those lucky enough to be on the field. But I think the reasons go deeper than that. These people aren't frustrated athletes. Some (maybe most) wouldn't trade places with the guys on the field for anything.
>
> But they do get off on screaming at the ball players and the reason I believe says a lot about human nature. These people use the ball players as punching bags, pounding on them with their frustration and their pent-up anger. These people come out to the ball park and "hate" for two hours, then go home to their wives or girlfriends or fraternity brothers and are as nice and gentle and laid-back as a twenty-year junkie (*Florida Flambeau*, April 6, 1976. Reprinted by permission).

Here is a classic case of the catharsis hypothesis as applied to intercollegiate baseball. How likely is it that this view is an accurate one?

In recent years another custom developed around FSU sports—rowdy partying in and along the city's main street after home football games. When city police moved in to reopen the streets to traffic, a number of scuffles erupted and arrests were made. The campus newspaper editorialized:

> Above all, however, we are confused by the violence. We had been under the impression that football like most mass spectator sports is intended as a cathartic outlet—the mass of fans are supposed to sublimate their pent-up hostilities and frustrations in the play of the game. By the end of the game the fans should have been passive, their emotions spent. They were not. They became violent. We do not understand (*Florida Flambeau*. December 6, 1982, p. 4. Reprinted by permission).

Apparently catharsis theory still appeals to people as a plausible explanation for the effects of observing violence, even though research indicates that catharsis effects seldom occur. ❖

Social and Observational Learning

Humans are continually learning from their environment. When people witness acts of aggression, they are provided with models of one way to behave. If the aggression is succcessful—if the aggressive model obtains what he wants by the use of aggression—is it not possible that viewers will be more likely to become aggressive when they find themselves in similar situations? If children are constantly exposed to violence on television, will they come to believe that it is commonplace, acceptable, or even desirable? Psychology has accumulated a wealth of evidence that children learn from behaviors that they see other people perform. Will this imitation take place in regard to the aggression viewed on television? Proponents of the **modeling** position argue that it will.

modeling:
The social learning theory proposition that much of human learning takes place by observing other people (models) behave.

The Spread of Violence

If modeling has a major impact on violence, then we might expect the crime rate to rise after a well-publicized criminal event. This does occur, as shown by the significant rise in the crime rate after the assassination of President John F. Kennedy in November 1963 and after other widely publicized crimes (Phillips, 1983).

Other media-portrayed incidents, in addition to crimes, may also affect the death rate. Suicide rates increase significantly after widely publicized suicides (Phillips, 1974). The incidence of deaths in auto accidents (which may include disguised suicides) appears to rise shortly after widely-reported suicides (Phillips, 1979) and after suicides in episodes of soap operas (Phillips, 1982). Another study (Phillips & Hensley, 1984) reported a connection between the televising of heavyweight prizefights on closed-circuit TV and a higher homicide rate three to four days later. These researchers also found that the murder rate dropped somewhat several days after severe punishment (executions, life sentences) in specific murder cases had been widely publicized in the media.

The legacy of violent movies and TV programs is a grim one. The murder cases involving Rod Matthews, Mark Branch, and Ronny Zamora were described in Chapter 1. John W. Hinckley, Jr., the young man who shot President Reagan in 1981, admitted strongly identifying with Travis Bickle, the psychopathic cab driver in the film *Taxi Driver*, who set out to murder a political candidate. In 1984 in Wisconsin, a thirty-seven-year-old woman was hospitalized with burns over 95 percent of her body; her husband had splashed her with gasoline and set her afire. The man said he had gotten the idea from a TV movie, *The Burning Bed*, which dramatized the true story of a Michigan woman who killed her abusive husband by setting fire to his bed while he slept. Another example of the potentially tragic impact of modeling is provided by the "Tylenol murders" and their imitations in 1982 and 1986, and the series of "Deer Hunter deaths" that occurred after the depiction of Russian roulette in the award-winning movie *The Deer Hunter* (Focus 10-3).

FOCUS 10-3

Modeling Tragedies: "*Deer Hunter* Deaths" and Tylenol Poisonings

The Deer Hunter, an award-winning film about Americans in Vietnam, featured graphic portrayals of American prisoners being forced to play Russian roulette with loaded guns. By 1985, forty-one young people in the U.S. had shot themselves in the head, and thirty-four of them had died, from playing Russian roulette after watching *The Deer Hunter* in movie theaters or on cable TV (Deer Hunter Kills . . ., 1985).

Another tragic example of modeling occurred in 1982, when seven people in the Chicago area died after taking the painkiller Tylenol, which had been adulterated with cyanide. In the month after the Chicago deaths, the Food and Drug Administration in Washington counted 279 new incidents of suspected product tampering. The number of cases was undoubtedly inflated by the hysteria of consumers who blamed any nausea or headache on poisoned food or medicine but the FDA judged that at least thirty-six of the incidents were "hard-core true tamperings." Mercuric chloride was put into Excedrin extra-strength capsules in Colorado, rat poison was discovered in an Anacin capsule in another Colorado community, acid

was put in chocolate milk in Minnesota. One psychologist guessed that the possible motivation of the copycats was that it's "better to be wanted by the police than not to be wanted at all" (Church, 1982).

In response to the tamperings, the FDA passed regulations requiring tamper-resistant packaging of over-the-counter drugs. It was estimated that the new packaging would cost the industry between twenty million and thirty million dollars a year and would add from a penny to a dime to the cost of nonprescription drugs.

Another wave of product-tampering occurred in 1986, with another death from cyanide-contaminated Tylenol. After receiving only eighty-five tampering reports in all of 1985, the FDA logged up to three hundred a day in 1986 (O'Connor, 1986), though most turned out to be false alarms. In these incidents, the modeling behavior that occurred, given the tremendously heavy press coverage of the original Tylenol deaths, was another demonstration of a very basic principle of human behavior: modeling and social learning. ❖

priming effect:
concepts (e.g., aggression) presented in the media can stimulate related ideas, emotions, and behavioral tendencies that are associated with the concept in the viewer's mind.

Though the existence of modeling has been conclusively demonstrated, it does not easily account for the common finding that viewed aggression is often followed by aggressive behaviors different from those observed. Berkowitz (1987) asserted that media aggression can have a **priming effect** on related ideas, emotions, and behavioral tendencies that are associated with aggression in the viewer's mind. The reporting of violent events could produce a contagion of violence due to such cognitive priming effects, as the reports activate related ideas and memories that justify similar conduct. Berkowitz argued that realistic portrayals of violence are most likely to produce later aggression, particularly if they are vivid and capture the audience's full attention.

Aggression in Children

Individuals develop a characteristic level of aggression in childhood that remains relatively stable into adulthood (Huesmann et al., 1984). The National Commission on the Causes and Prevention of Violence issued an official statement saying, in part:

> Children begin to absorb the lessons of television before they can read or write.... . In a fundamental way, television helps to create what children expect of themselves and of others, and what constitutes the standards of civilized society (quoted in Siegel, 1970, p. 197).

In recent years researchers have carried out a great deal of experimental research on viewed aggression. The most common paradigm is to expose one group of people, often children, to an aggressive stimulus, usually a film or videotape, while another group is exposed to a nonaggressive film or to no film at all. If modeling theory is correct, the people who viewed the aggressive stimulus should later behave more aggressively than those in the other group. If catharsis takes place, however, the opposite should happen: people who viewed the aggressive film should subsequently behave less aggressively than those who did not view it. In Chapter 1 we analyzed a classic experiment on witnessed aggression. Recall that Bandura, Ross, and Ross (1963) exposed children ages three to five to "real-life" aggressive models, filmed aggressive models, an aggressive cartoon, or no aggressive model. Children who were exposed to any of the three types of aggressive models (real-life, movie, or cartoon) were considerably more likely to behave aggressively than children who had not seen any aggressive model (Figure 1-2), supporting the modeling view.

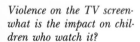

Violence on the TV screen-what is the impact on children who watch it?

If we look at the hundreds of studies on children's imitation of live, filmed, or videotaped models carried out over the past thirty-five years or so, the following points are established: (l) Nursery-school-age children imitate the aggressive behavior of adults or cartoon-type figures observed. (2) This imitation often is rather direct but may also involve the expression of more general aggressive patterns. (3) The observation of media aggression leads to imitation especially if: (a) the model is not punished, (b) the model is of the same sex as the child, (c) the child is moderately frustrated, and (d) no disapproval of the model's behavior is provided by adults in the child's presence (Geen & Thomas, 1986; Huesmann, 1986).

Long-Term Field Studies

Experimental Field Studies

Long-term naturalistic field studies of television viewing and aggression are vitally important, though they are difficult to carry out. To do an experiment, one must be able to control children's TV viewing, randomly assigning some to watch a schedule of violent TV programs while the rest watch nonviolent programs. Even if the researcher could exercise this much control, other problems arise. For example, some children on a "diet" of nonviolent television programs might become more aggressive because of their frustration at being deprived of their favorite (violent) programs. Further, if only part of children's TV viewing time is controlled, then children in the nonviolent TV group might be more likely to watch violent programs on their own time, to make up for the violent programs they had been "deprived" of.

Experimental field studies have found evidence that exposure to violent movies and TV does increase aggressive behavior, as social learning theory would predict (Leyens et al., 1975; Parke et al., 1977). Stein and Friedrich (1972) exposed children to four weeks of TV exposure and three weeks of follow-up measures. The children saw an aggressive diet (such as "Superman" and "Batman"), a neutral diet (a travelogue), or a prosocial diet ("Mister Rogers' Neighborhood"). They were then observed in their daily nursery school activities. Children who were already aggressive became more aggressive from watching the antisocial diet. As noted in Chapter 7, the children who watched the prosocial diet became significantly more cooperative with other children.

Correlational Studies

In two different correlational studies, Singer and Singer (1981) followed three- and four-year-old children over a year's time and correlated their television viewing at home with behavior during free-play periods at day-care centers. Both studies revealed consistent associations between heavy viewing of violent programs and unwarranted aggressive behavior in free play. Two other field studies compared aggressiveness in children before and after their communities had television (Granzberg & Steinbring, 1980; Williams, 1986) . One study found a significant increase in both verbal and physical aggression following the introduction of television. The other study found an increase in aggressiveness for those children who were heavy TV viewers. Finally, a study of teenaged boys in England found that, according to the teenagers' own accounts of their activities, they were more likely to engage in serious violence after being exposed to television violence (Belson, 1978).

In an in-depth longitudinal study, Singer, Singer, and Rapaczynski (1984) studied sixty-three children over a five-year period, beginning when they were four years old. Across the five years, later aggressiveness was strongly related to heavier viewing of TV violence and to parents' emphasis on physical punishment, even when initial levels of aggressiveness at age four were taken into account. Children who viewed much TV violence were also more likely to believe that the world was a "scary" place.

An ambitious attempt to assess the effect of TV viewing in the regular household situation over a twenty-two-year period was undertaken by Leonard Eron and his co-workers (1972). They contacted 211 young men (youths aged eighteen and nineteen) whose TV viewing behaviors and levels of aggressiveness had been measured ten years earlier (Eron, 1963). They assessed the TV viewing preferences of these young men (the rated violence level of their three favorite programs) and also their current levels of aggressiveness as rated by their peers and by self-ratings. As Figure 10-4 depicts, the violence level of their three favorite programs at ages eight and nine showed a significant relationship to how aggressive the young men were at age eighteen and nineteen. This relationship remained even when the effect of the relationship between aggressiveness at ages eight and nine and aggressiveness ten years later was controlled for statistically. The boys' view-

A successful, violent model. Research findings would lead to the prediction that children who viewed the popular "Rambo" movies would act more aggressively themselves afterwards, as Sylvester Stallone's Rambo provided an attractive, successful, violent model.

FIGURE 10-4

TV Viewing and Aggression
Across a Ten-Year Period

Correlation coefficients (r) between TV viewing preferences and aggression for 211 boys at ages 8–9 and viewing preferences and aggressive behavior of the same boys at ages 18–19. Solid lines denote relationships that were statistically significant, dotted lines denote the absence of any significant relationship.

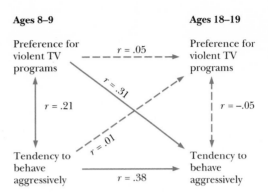

Source: Eron, L. D., Huesmann, L. R., Lefkowitz, M. M., & Walder, L. O. (1972). Does television violence cause aggression? *American Psychologist, 27,* 253–263. Copyright 1972 by the American Psychological Association. Reprinted by permission of the publisher and author.

ing preferences at ages eight and nine were a better predictor of how aggressive they would be ten years later than were many other factors also measured—including the parents' mobility, religiosity, punishment, aggressiveness toward their children, and occupational status; and the child's IQ, identification with the father and mother, or the total number of hours of TV watched.

Because the study is correlational in nature (the experimenters did not manipulate the kinds of TV programs the boys watched but, rather, the boys made the choices themselves), it cannot be said to provide unequivocal evidence that TV viewing preferences at ages eight and nine *caused* increases in aggressiveness ten years later. Nevertheless, Eron and his co-workers (1972) felt confident that their results strongly suggested a causal relationship.

Twelve years later the researchers contacted their subjects, now thirty-year-old men, once more. They found that the men's level of aggressiveness as adults—derived from self-ratings, wife's ratings, and crime records—was consistently related to their aggressiveness as eight- or nine-year-olds, thus indicating that aggression is a persistent trait in males (Huesmann et al., 1984). They also established that the men's aggressiveness could be predicted from their TV viewing habits as children, further supporting the hypothesis that violent TV may play an important role in the development of persistent aggressive habits (Huesmann, 1984; 1985). Men who had preferred violent TV as boys were much more likely to have been convicted of a serious criminal offense by the time they were thirty (Figure 10-5). These field studies show that long-term increases in aggression from viewing video violence has been conclusively demonstrated for boys; the evidence is not as clear for girls (Turner et al., 1986).

FIGURE 10-5

Seriousness of Criminal Convictions at Age Thirty as the Function of a Boy's Preference for TV Violence at Age Eight

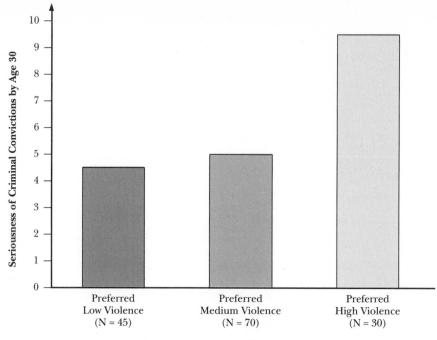

Source: From L. R. Huesmann (1986). The effects of film and television violence. In S. S. Katz and P. Yesin (Eds.), *Children and the media* (p. 114). Paris: Centre International de l'Enfance. Reprinted by permission.

Aggressive Cognitive Scripts

aggressive cognitive script:
A program for behavior that is developed early in life and is characterized by violence or aggression.

In a theoretical model of the development of aggression, Huesmann (1988) proposed that some children acquire **aggressive cognitive scripts**. A script is a "program" for behaviors, learned early in life, that is stored in memory and used as a guide for behavior and social problem solving (Huesmann, 1988). In term of the concepts discussed in Chapter 2, a script can be seen as an *event schema.* Observing media violence can induce aggressiveness in two ways. In the long term, by providing many examples of aggressive scripts, media violence has a cumulative effect on the development of the child's own aggressive script. In the short term, the observed violence serves as an environmental cue that can trigger the child's already-learned aggressive script.

The learning of an aggressive script, like other scripts, can involve observation of a model. The script may be strengthened and developed each time it is thought about, fantasized about, or acted out in play. The likelihood a child will use the script to guide his or her behavior depends both on the *strength* of the memory trace and on *environmental cues* that may cause the child to recall the script. Generally, the more the child's current situation matches the characteristics of the situations in memory, the more likely it is that the script will be used to guide behavior (Huesmann, 1986).

You might think that children who begin to develop aggressive scripts would learn that they don't work well, and would abandon them. Perhaps some do, but many children continue this behavior even when it is not rewarded by others. Why might they? Huesmann (1988) suggested several reasons. The child may misinterpret the outcome, focusing on the short-term gain (e.g., getting a toy) and ignoring more negative long-term effects (eventual punishment, unpopularity). The child may be unable to think of alternative scripts for achieving his goals. The child may choose an environment where aggression is more acceptable (e.g., playing only with other aggressive boys), or think in ways that make aggression acceptable ("Nice guys finish last").

Does Viewing Violence Cause Aggression?

Numerous laboratory and field studies on the effects of viewing aggression have supported the modeling position. Reviews of the many studies of the impact of TV violence have concluded that there is a consistent small positive correlation between viewing TV violence and later aggressiveness. Most social psychological researchers also believe that the cumulative experimental (laboratory and field) and correlational findings support the notion that viewed violence *causes* increases in aggressiveness (Geen & Thomas, 1986; Turner et al., 1986). Yet, not all scientists agree. Freedman (1984) argued that the causal evidence was not clear-cut. He suggested that an alternative hypothesis could not be ruled out — that people who prefer violent TV programs (due to personality, or environmental factors, or whatever) also tend to be aggressive. Nevertheless, it appears to me, as well as to many other social psychologists, that clear causal relationship between viewed violence and subsequent aggression *has* been demonstrated (Friedrich-Cofer & Huston, 1986).

Other Issues in Viewing Aggression

The Impact of Preferences, Attitudes, and Values

Viewing aggression may affect attitudes, preferences, and values, as well as behavior; viewers may become more tolerant of aggression in themselves and in others. Thomas and Drabman (1978) found that after viewing an aggressive film, third- and fifth-graders saw aggression as more commonplace and more typical of what "most kids" would do, than did children who had not seen the aggressive film. Other studies showed that after watching a violent film children were slower to summon adult aid to break up a fight — suggesting that they were more tolerant of aggression — after watching a violent film than after watching a nonviolent film (Drabman & Thomas, 1975).

In broader terms, television may provide viewers with the impression that the world is a violent place. Media violence communicates "facts" about social norms and relationships, about goals and means, about winners and losers, about the risks of life, and the price for breaking society's rules. Violence-laden drama illustrates who gets away with what. *Fear* may be an even more critical residue of a violent show than aggression, if this fear leads to reactive violence or to passivity in the face of injustice. Heavy television viewers are more likely to believe that most people just look out for themselves, take advantage of others, and cannot be trusted (Gerbner et al., 1980). Thus, a violent scenario may serve a double function. By demonstrating the apparent effectiveness of violence and social power, it may generate fear, insecurity, and dependence in its audience. In addition, the portrayed violence may incite destructive violence among some viewers.

A "Vicious Cycle": Aggressiveness and Preferences for Violent TV

As noted earlier, research suggests that aggressive children prefer to watch more and more violent television (Freedman, 1984). Hence, the process may be circular. Aggressive children are unpopular and because relations with their peers tend to be unsatisfying, they may spend more time watching television than their more popular peers do (Eron, 1982). The violence they see on television may reassure them that their own violent behavior is appropriate, while at the same time teaching them new coercive techniques that they may later use in their interactions with other children. In turn, their aggressive behavior might make them more unpopular and thus drive them back to television, and the circle continues. Aggression as measured by peer ratings increases significantly for both boys and girls from the first to the fifth grade, whereas the viewing of television violence increases up to the third grade and then starts to decline (Eron et al., 1983). Over the same period, the child's perception of television violence as realistic is decreasing. Thus, the third grade may be a period during which a number of factors converge, making the child unusually susceptible to television. Supporting this idea, the strongest relations between television violence and both simultaneous and later aggression have been reported for third-grade children.

Type of Aggression Viewed

Justifiability and Realism. Viewing aggression that is justified (the "good guy" triumphs) leads to more aggressive behavior among the audience than viewing aggression that is unjustified (Geen & Stonner, 1973). If the effects of aggression are depicted very graphically, some inhibitions against the modeling of aggression may occur (Goranson, 1970). However, inhibitions are weakened by repeated exposure to such films as the viewer becomes *desensitized* to the effects of violence. The inhibitions against modeling will be weaker in subsequent exposures to graphically portrayed aggression (Malamuth & Donnerstein, 1984).

Realism and televised violence.
Source: From *'Toons for Our Times: A Bloom County Book* by Berke Breathed. Copyright 1984 by The Washington Post Company.

ritualized aggression:
A release of violent behavior which is considered socially acceptable, such as a football game.

stylized aggression:
Apparent aggression seen as acting or a spoof.

Stylized aggression in pro wrestling. Spectators at aggressive athletic events, whether involving stylized or realistic aggression, tend to show higher levels of aggression afterwards.

Violent Sports Events. Some have proposed that viewing sports events, which can be seen as **ritualized aggression**, may serve a cathartic effect and decrease aggressive tendencies in the audience (see Focus 10-1). But social learning theory would predict just the opposite. Here, as elsewhere, the research evidence supports the social learning position. Goldstein and Arms (1971) studied males leaving the stadium after an Army-Navy football game. These fans scored significantly higher on a hostility scale than had an equivalent group of fans entering the stadium before the game. For male fans at an equally competitive but nonaggressive event (gymnastics), pre- and post-event measures of hostility did not differ. The finding of an overall increase in hostility of both Army (winners) and Navy (losers) fans supports a *general disinhibition* position that observing aggression weakens inhibitions against expressing aggression.

One could argue that exposure to **stylized aggression**—displays in which apparent aggression is seen as acting or a spoof—might have a different impact. Athletic events such as professional wrestling might be classed as stylized aggression. To see whether exposure to stylized aggression would differ in its effects from exposure to realistic aggression, Arms et al. (1979) studied spectators at a professional wrestling match (stylized aggression), a hockey game (realistic aggression), and a swimming meet (nonaggressive sport). The researchers randomly assigned a different sample of students to attend each of the various events so that preexisting preferences and aggression levels would not be different among the spectators they studied. Students at the hockey and wrestling matches significantly increased in some measures of aggression after the events, whereas spectators at the hotly contested swim meet showed no such increase. Hence, viewing stylized aggression appears to increase aggression just as much as does viewing realistic sports aggression.

Violent Videogames. As the videogame craze swept the nation in recent years, many wondered whether people who habitually played violent videogames might become more aggressive themselves, as they were repeatedly exposed to this variety of stylized aggression. Early research results have not been entirely consistent, but some studies have found that children who played violent videogames showed increases in minor antisocial aggressive behavior afterwards (Schutte et al., 1988; Silvern & Williamson, 1987). A survey of teenagers found that those who watched more TV violence also tended to spend more time playing more violent videogames (Dominick, 1984). So, while the evidence is still preliminary, it looks as if exposure to violent videogames may have the same kind of impact that exposure to violent TV and movies does.

Limitations of Aggression Research

Ethical and practical issues limit the external validity of much aggression research. First, in most studies, individuals may aggress in only one way—often a highly artificial one. In experiments subjects may be given the chance to deliver electric shocks to another person via an "aggression machine," or give another person negative ratings on a scale. With children, a common procedure has been to allow them to play with aggressive toys. In the real world, of course, aggression is much more likely to be produced by verbal abuse, guns, knives, and fists. Also, research subjects are given just one avenue to aggress, whereas in the real world people can choose their means of aggression, or they can choose to displace their aggression onto a target that cannot fight back. And, of course, there are restrictions on methods used to create anger, pain, or frustration in research subjects. Children or adults cannot be angered or frustrated in studies to the extent that they may be in real-life situations.

Keep in mind also that a one-shot viewing of an aggressive model on film in the laboratory differs from television viewing over an extended period of time. Not only is there a considerable difference in viewing time, but the complexity of the stimuli involved in television viewing is considerably greater than that in a controlled laboratory setting. Many messages come from television viewing; not all are violent, and some may even be antiviolent (see Focus 7-1). An additional issue concerns sampling and general application of findings. The subjects in most studies have been middle-class nursery school children or college students. Such samples differ greatly from the types of persons most often involved in aggression in the real world. Finally, researchers have usually studied retaliatory aggression rather than offensive aggression. In the criminal justice system, offensive aggression is of greatest concern. For all of these reasons, you should evaluate the research findings with some caution (Berkowitz & Donnerstein, 1982).

An Overview of the Effects of Televised Violence

Meta-analyses of hundreds of aggression studies lead to three general conclusions (Comstock, 1988; Hearold, 1986): (1) There is a positive association between exposure to media violence and subsequent aggressive behavior. (2) In studies with greater mundane realism (similarity to real-world events), the effect is smaller but still significant. (3) The reverse effect, an increase in prosocial behavior, occurs with exposure to prosocial models (as we saw in Chapter 7).

Progress has been made toward discovering the critical conditions under which certain filmed behavior (arousing action, justified aggression) in certain settings (with an approving peer or adult) by certain kinds of viewers (those predisposed to aggression) is associated with subsequent antisocial behavior. Several basic processes are relevant to the relationship between the viewing of violence and aggressive behavior. First, through the process of *modeling* and *observational learning,* viewers learn and imitate aggressive behaviors when portrayed by real or animated characters. Many studies have demonstrated that frustrated or aroused viewers, after watching a violent episode, behave more aggressively. Second, television viewing can cause *emotional or physiological arousal* that can affect aggressiveness, as Zillmann's work has shown. From a somewhat different perspective, Tannenbaum (1980) theorized that people seek an optimal level of overall arousal. If viewing aggression desensitizes viewers to arousal, then the desensitized-to-violence viewer might behave more aggressively in order to achieve the desired level of arousal. Third, viewing violence can cause *attitude change*. As we have seen, attitudes toward the use of violence, tolerance for aggressive behavior, preferences for viewing violence, fear of victimization, and reductions in inhibitions toward aggressive behavior are all influenced by viewing violence.

There have been two extensive government-sponsored investigations of the TV-violence link in recent years. The overall findings can be summarized in two quotations. During Senate hearings in the early 1970s, United States Surgeon General Jesse L. Steinfield stated: "Certainly my interpretation is that there is a causative relationship between television violence and subsequent antisocial behavior, and that the evidence is strong enough that it requires some action on the part of responsible authorities, the TV industry, the government, the citizens" (quoted in Liebert et al., 1982, p. 104). The summary to the government-sponsored study ten years later (Pearl et al., 1982, Vol. 1., p. 6) asserted that "In magnitude, television violence is as strongly correlated with aggressive behavior as any other behavioral variable that has been measured. The research question has moved from asking whether or not there is an effect to seeking explanations for the effect."

How strong is that effect? Speculating from his study of violence rates in South Africa, Canada, and the U.S. from 1945 to 1974, Centerwell (1989, p. 1) suggested that, "Television is a factor in approximately ten thousand homicides each year in the United States. While TV clearly is not the sole cause of violence in our society, and there are many other contributing factors, hypothetically if television did not exist there would be ten thousand fewer homicides per year" ("Thousands of homicides . . . ," 1989, p.1). This is only speculation on Centerwell's part, but it is troubling speculation, nonetheless.

Politics and Values in Studying Aggression

Politics, sociopolitical values, and vested interests are intimately involved in studies of media violence. The television and movie industries have millions of dollars invested in projects depicting violence in various forms. The level of violence in TV programming stayed roughly the same from the 1960s into the 1980s, with children's programs having the highest levels of violence (Comstock, 1982). The level of TV violence dropped somewhat between 1985 and 1990 (NCTV News, January 1990). Television and movie executives are naturally quite concerned with any research and theorizing that may threaten their livelihood. At the other extreme, abhorrence of violence in any form is an article of faith to many people. Each of these orientations is likely to give rise to prejudgments or to subjective interpretations of research findings. Sociopolitical values become even more strongly involved when media-depicted violence blends with media-depicted sexuality, as in violent pornography.

Does Violence "Sell"?

The Report of the Surgeon General's Advisory Committee, which advised reducing levels of aggression on TV, asserted that "violent material is popular. If our society changed in no other way than changing the balance of television offerings, people, to some degree, would still seek out violent material" (Surgeon General, 1972, p. 8). But, contrary to this assumption, research suggests that people don't prefer violent shows. Studies have found no relationship between the popularity of nonsports TV shows (Nielsen ratings) and the level of violence in the shows across a three-month period (Diener & DeFour, 1978) or over twenty-eight years of TV shows (Diener & Woody, 1980). Violent TV shows were generally liked *less* than were nonviolent shows when the two types of shows were equal on other dimensions such as realism, humor, romance, and conflict (Diener & Woody, 1981).

Hence, the argument that "violence sells" is not supported for nonsports shows, but violence may be related to enjoyment of sports events (Bryant & Zillmann, 1983). Researchers (Bryant, Comisky, & Zillmann, 1981) had viewers watch videotapes of plays from National Football League games. For male viewers, plays with a high degree of roughness/violence were rated as significantly more enjoyable than those with intermediate or low levels of violence (Figure 10-6).

What to Do?

The evidence from experimental laboratory studies is clear: Viewing aggression increases the probability of aggressive behavior over the short term. Findings from longer-term field studies suggest a similar trend.

From current evidence, should one conclude that violence must be banished from the movie and television screen? This question is hotly de-

FIGURE 10-6

Televised Football:
Roughness and Enjoyment

For males (triangles), violent play resulted in significantly greater enjoyment than play associated with lower levels of roughness. The corresponding trend in women's (circles) enjoyment of violent play was not significant, however.

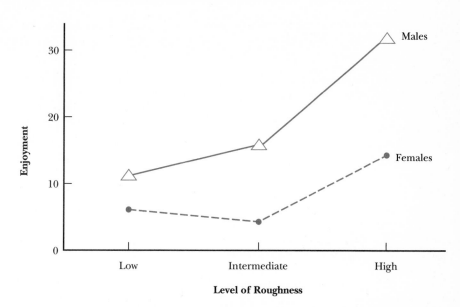

Source: Bryant, J., Comisky, P. & Zillmann, D. (1981). The appeal of rough-and-tumble play in televised professional football. *Communication Quarterly, 29,* 256–262. Copyright © 1981 by the Eastern Communication Association. Reprinted by permission.

bated (see Focus 10-3) and involves deeply held values about free speech, censorship, socialization of children, and the overall levels of aggression that may be desirable for society. About 90 percent of American TV programs cannot be shown on British TV without substantial editing, due to their level of violence (NCTV, 1989, p.3). To most Americans, total censorship would be intolerable, so there is no simple answer to the question of whether or how the government should control what can be shown on TV and in movies.

Another important, value-laden issue concerns the type of individual seen as best for our society. If the total elimination of aggression is our goal, then surely limits should be imposed on the amount of violence shown on television and in movies. On the other hand, is the complete elimination of aggression desirable? Most people probably feel that aggression and violence are necessary under some conditions, such as those involving self-defense. Thus, a fine balance must somehow be struck between the extremes of completely eliminating violence in the mass media and allowing unlimited exposure to it.

FOCUS 10-4

Violence on the Cable and in Music

The burgeoning popularity of cable TV and music videos in the 1980s added a new dimension to concerns about media violence. Of particular concern to some observers were Home Box Office (HBO) and the Movie Channel, cable TV channels on which the number of violent instances was more than double that of network television or PBS (NCTV News, 1982–1983). The National Coalition on Television Violence (NCTV) reported that the use of violent lyrics in popular rock music in 1963 was relatively infrequent and tame compared to more recent music. Violent lyrics had increased by 75 percent in 1973 and were more than twice as violent in 1984 as in 1963 (NCTV News, 1984). NCTV's monitoring of Music TV (MTV) music videos noted still larger amounts of violence and sexual violence—an average of 18.0 instances of violence or hostile action each hour on MTV, adding considerable violence to the song lyrics, which averaged 8.5 instances per hour. Over half of the MTV videos featured violence or strongly suggested violence. Phil Galli, NCTV's project director, stated, "Rock video's combination of lyrics and images adds a new dimension to television violence. Many of the videos added violent imagery that wasn't even present in the lyrics. We found large amounts of violence present in every viewing hour, with the exception of a fund-raising concert for Kampuchea."

In addition to depictions of violence, content analysis of MTV videos found that sexist, demeaning, and condescending portrayals of women were very common, though the degree of sexism decreased somewhat between 1987 and 1989 (Vincent, 1989). In the mid-1980s social scientists found an average of four sexual activities per MTV video; they described most of the depictions as "long on titillation and physical activity but devoid of emotional involvement" (Sherman & Dominick, 1986, p. 91).

Thomas Radecki, chairperson of NCTV, stated: "The heavy use of violence in a very appealing format by the leading rock movie stars clearly has a strong harmful effect on young American viewers. The message is that violence is normal and okay, that hostile sexual relations between men and women are common and acceptable, that heroes actively engage in torture and murder of others for fun." The NCTV spokesman argued that the MTV programming was very similar to the violent pornography studied by Donnerstein and his co-workers. If so, increases in desensitization toward violence in normal male viewers can be expected and, perhaps, increases in their willingness to rape women.

While MTV has proved highly popular with young people, feelings continue to run high. Radecki asserted that "Entertainment and real-life violence just keep growing." In recent years some legislatures have created laws banning music or performances classed as "obscene," while others have attempted to put warning labels on albums containing lyrics perceived as violent, degrading, or obscene. Of course, in all such efforts the toughest question is who decides what is "obscene" or "pornographic?" Our courts will continue to wrestle with this thorny issue. ❖

AGGRESSION AND SEXUALITY COMBINED: VIOLENT PORNOGRAPHY

Effects of Aggressively Toned Pornography

Many people have been concerned with the levels of sexual explicitness portrayed in the media. Sexuality and violence are the two main factors taken into account by the Motion Picture Association in deciding which rating to give a movie. A recent Gallup poll of American teenagers found that a large majority (84 percent) had seen an R-rated movie and one in seven had seen an X-rated movie (Linz & Donnerstein, 1989). The President's Commission on Obscenity and Pornography reported in 1971 that exposure of adults to explicit sexual materials had little or no effect upon patterns of sexual activity or attitudes about sexuality, and that such exposure apparently did not contribute to a decline in moral character or to an increase in either general crime rates or sexual crime (*Report*, 1971). Further, the commission noted that sexual offenders had generally been *less* exposed to sexually explicit materials and sexual knowledge during adolescence than had others. The majority of the commission recommended, therefore, the repeal of laws prohibiting adult exposure to explicit sexual materials and recommended increased exposure to sexual knowledge for young people through sex education.

Research shows that R-rated "slasher" movies may have a particularly negative effect on male viewers.

Although the President's Commission concluded that there was no direct relationship between exposure to pornography and subsequent sexual crimes, scientific criticisms of the Commission's conclusion (Dienstbier, 1977; Wills, 1977) led other investigators to reexamine this issue. Social and political concerns mounted throughout the 1970s and 1980s until a U.S. Attorney General's Commission on Pornography was created to study sexual explicitness in the media, sex-linked violence, and media degradation of women. Their report, released in 1986, noted the important distinction between violent and nonviolent sexuality. Nonviolent sexuality appears to have little or no negative impact on sexual behavior, as the earlier President's Commission had found. Nonviolent sexuality still may have negative effects in terms of attitudes, however. The 1986 Commission tentatively asserted that repeated exposure to nonviolent pornography that depicts scenes degrading to women will lead male viewers to more callous attitudes toward rape and toward women. At present, though, research findings on the attitudinal effects of nonviolent sexually explicit materials have been mixed, with some studies finding a negative impact on men's attitudes (Zillmann & Bryant, 1982) while others found no effect (Linz et al., 1988; Malamuth & Ceniti, 1986). Linz (1989) remarked that it was "unfortunate that the Attorney General chose to neglect these contradictions [in research results for nonviolent sexual material] in its rush to indict these materials (p.80)." For violent sexual portrayals (such as R-rated "slasher" films), in contrast, research

Sexuality and violence. Violence in relationships is disturbingly common, even on the college campus.

has yielded a consistent effect—male viewers show less sensitivity to rape victims after viewing these films.

Sexualized violence and degradation of women in the media can affect men's attitudes and behaviors in a number of ways. Figure 10-7, based on a model developed by Neil Malamuth (1986), illustrates factors that may interact to produce antisocial actions toward women. At the societal level, cultural factors (including sex-role training), exposure to sexual violent media, and a social network of aggression-supportive peers can contribute to sexist, proviolence attitudes. A particular individual's attitudes and values, dominance motives, sexual arousal to aggression, hostility toward women, and individual experiences (e.g., home environment, traumatic events) will further affect the likelihood that he adopts an antifemale orientation. In combination, these factors determine the likelihood that a man will behave antisocially toward women, either violently (stranger rape, "date rape," aggression in laboratory studies) or nonviolently (sexism, discrimination, verbal degradation). Such antisocial events are not as rare as one might think. A recent survey (Muelenhard & Linton, 1987) found that 78 percent of college women and 57 percent of college men had experienced some form of violence in a relationship. Fifteen percent of the women and 7 percent of the men said they had been involved in "unwanted sexual intercourse," that is, rape.

Exposure to violent pornography, particularly when it has a "positive" ending suggesting that the woman enjoyed the aggression, can affect male viewers' attitudes toward accepting violence toward women (Malamuth & Check, 1983). Donnerstein and Berkowitz (1981) showed one of four types of films to male undergraduates. The first, a neutral film, contained no aggressive or erotic content. The second, a purely erotic movie, depicted a young couple engaged in various stages of sexual intercourse. In the third

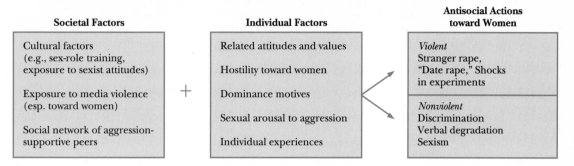

FIGURE 10-7

Factors Leading Men to Behave Antisocially to Women

Cultural, societal, and individual factors that may affect men's thought patterns about violence toward women.

Societal Factors		Individual Factors		Antisocial Actions toward Women
Cultural factors (e.g., sex-role training, exposure to sexist attitudes) Exposure to media violence (esp. toward women) Social network of aggression-supportive peers	+	Related attitudes and values Hostility toward women Dominance motives Sexual arousal to aggression Individual experiences		*Violent* Stranger rape, "Date rape," Shocks in experiments *Nonviolent* Discrimination Verbal degradation Sexism

Source: Based upon Malamuth, N. M. (1986). Predictors of naturalistic sexual aggression. *Journal of Personality and Social Psychology, 50,* 953–962.

film (positive-outcome aggressive-erotic), a young woman was stripped, tied up, slapped, and sexually attacked. But the movie ended with the woman smiling and in no way resisting. For the fourth film (negative-outcome aggressive-erotic) the scenario was the same, except that the last thirty seconds of the scene indicated that the woman was suffering and found the experience humiliating and disgusting.

After viewing one of the four films, the male subjects were put into a learning situation in which they were to deliver shocks to a partner (who had earlier angered them) if the partner answered incorrectly. As Figure 10-8(a) illustrates, aggression toward a female partner was greater when the men had watched the aggressive-erotic film that had the "positive" ending (the woman was no longer resisting). In a second study, Donnerstein and Berkowitz (1981) angered only half the males. Once again, the viewing of aggressive-erotic films increased levels of aggression to women, as Figure 10-8(b) illustrates. Note that when males were not angry and the film had a negative ending—the woman did not enjoy the experience—aggression was relatively low, about the same as for neutral and erotic films. However, when the subjects were angry, they were just as aggressive after viewing the negative ending as after viewing the positive ending. Hence, if a male is angry, then viewing aggressive-erotic material may increase his tendency to aggress toward females, regardless of whether or not the female depicted in the erotica appeared to be enjoying the aggression.

Written materials can also affect levels of aggression. Malamuth, Heim, and Feshbach (1980) had college students read stories that described either rape or sexual intercourse with mutual consent. Students who read the non-rape version of the story reported being more sexually aroused than those who had read the rape version. But stories that portrayed the rape victim as experiencing an involuntary orgasm apparently disinhibited subjects' sex-

FIGURE 10-8

Aggression, Sex of Target, and Violent Pornography

Males' level of aggression (shocks delivered) to men and women (a) and women alone (b) depending on type of film viewed.

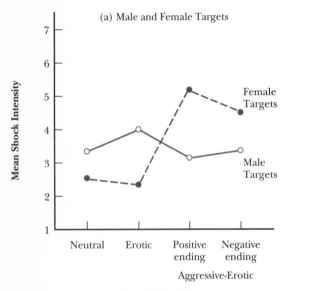

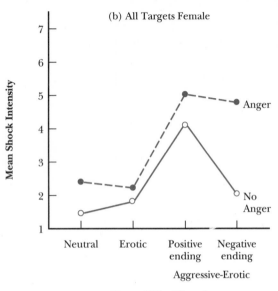

Source: Donnerstein, E., & Berkowitz, L. (1981). Victim reactions to aggressive erotic films as a factor in violence against women. *Journal of Personality and Social Psychology, 41,* 716, 720. Copyright 1981 by the American Psychological Association. Reprinted by permission of the publisher and author.

ual responsiveness and resulted in high levels of sexual arousal, comparable to those elicited by the description of mutually consenting sex. Surprisingly, males were most aroused when the victim experienced both an orgasm and pain (Figure 10-9). Many rapists strongly believe the myth that their victims derive pleasure from being assaulted (Clark & Lewis, 1977; Gager & Schurr, 1976).

Another effect of repeated exposure to sexually violent materials is a kind of psychological "numbing," as men who repeatedly view sexually violent films become less bothered by them and see them as less violent (Linz, 1985). Linz and his co-workers (1988) found that after viewing five sexually violent films in ten days, men saw the films more positively (as less depressing, less anxiety-producing, and less negatively arousing), than they had after viewing just one film. They also perceived the films as less violent and less degrading to women.

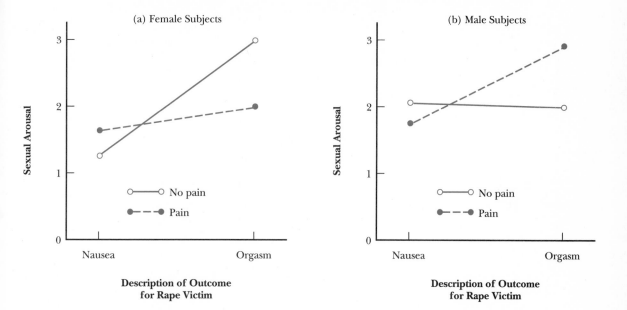

FIGURE 10-9

Sexual Arousal, Gender, and Outcome of Forced Sex

Sexual arousal as a function of subjects' gender and variations of (a) the pain to the female victim and (b) outcome (nausea or orgasm) of forced intercourse described in written materials.

Source: Malamuth, N. M., Heim, M., & Feshbach, S. (1980). Sexual responsiveness of college students to rape depictions: Inhibitory and disinhibitory effects. *Journal of Personality and Social Psychology, 38,* 404. Copyright 1980 by the American Psychological Association. Reprinted by permission of the publisher and author.

Scientific evidence on the second step in Figure 10-7, the link between negative attitudes and actual antisocial actions, is difficult to gather. Several laboratory studies have found that men with attitudes condoning violence toward women are more aggressive toward women (e.g., delivering loud noise as a "punishment") in an experimental setting (Malamuth, 1983; 1984) and men with such attitudes admit to more sexual aggression on self-report measures (Malamuth, 1986; Malamuth & Check, 1985). But these preliminary findings are only suggestive of a linkage in the real world. At present, we do not know whether or not this effect of media sexualized violence is long-lasting, since studies have generally measured aggression very shortly after exposure to the violent sexual depiction. In addition, as noted earlier, laboratory studies are limited in their external validity and mundane realism.

Is the Problem Sexuality or Violence?
Although the U.S. Attorney General's Commission on Pornography (1986) targeted sexually violent pornography as having particularly dangerous so-

FIGURE 10-10

Desensitization after Repeatedly Viewing Violent Sexual Films

Male college students' self-reported moods and evaluations of sexually violent films before and after viewing five films, one every other day.

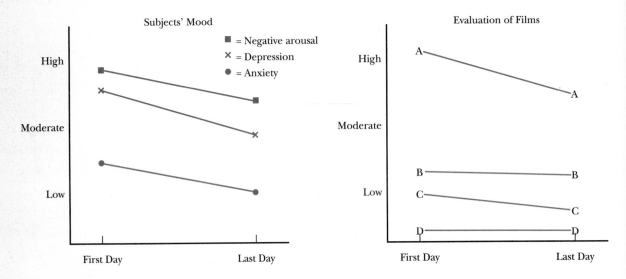

Source: Data from Linz, D. G., Donnerstein, E., & Penrod, S. (1988). Effects of long-term exposure to violent and sexually degrading depictions of women. *Journal of Personality and Social Psychology, 55,* 758–768.

A = Perception of nonsexual violence (8 questions)
B = Degrading to women (2 questions)
C = Extent sex & violence were combined (3 questions)
D = Enjoyment (2 questions)

cietal effects, several leading researchers have argued that it is the violence, not the sex, that produces the harmful effects. Studies have shown that R-rated "slasher" movies, which combine graphic violence (usually against women) with less sexuality than in X-rated films, show the most negative effects on male viewers. We have seen that men who view R-rated "slasher" films come to have fewer negative emotional reactions to the films, to perceive the films as less violent, and to consider them less degrading to women.

Normal sexuality and normal aggression are quite different in harm or deviance value. For most of us, exposure to extreme violence (killing) in the media is far greater than our exposure to extreme sexuality (intercourse) in the media. However, in real adult life, our relative degree of involvement with sexuality and violence is reversed. Few of us have ever seen an individual cause the violent death of another, but most adults consider themselves sexually sophisticated and are, or will be, involved in interpersonal relationships that include sexuality.

Notions of catharsis differ in the two realms as well. There is no persuasive evidence that media depictions of violence lead to cathartic release.

With explicit *nonviolent* sexuality, on the other hand, nonharmful cathartic effects are possible through sexual relations with a regular sexual partner or through masturbation (Dienstbier, 1977). Researchers have found that American male sex offenders, rapists, and child molesters had generally been exposed to less explicit sexuality as adolescents than had normal controls (Goldstein & Kant, 1973). Sexual offenders do not own or use more pornography as adults than do nonoffenders. Dienstbier (1977) argued that explicit nonviolent media sexuality which treats men and women in a humane egalitarian way, may provide needed sexual education and aid in the desensitization of deviance-producing tensions, allowing normal, healthy sexual patterns to emerge.

Studies consistently show that viewing aggression-but-no-sex films leads to more aggression toward women than does viewing films with explicit sex but no violence. Does adding sex to aggressive films increase their already-negative effect? Perhaps sometimes, but the increase may not be great (Linz et al., 1987). Donnerstein and Linz (1986, p. 59) remarked that the U.S. Surgeon General's Commission on Pornography "... has ignored the inescapable conclusion that it is violence, whether or not accompanied by sex, that has the most damaging effect on those who view it, hear it or read it." The researchers further concluded that it is violent images, rather than sexual ones, that are most responsible for people's attitudes about women and about rape.

Media degradation of women. A survey of detective magazines found that 76% of the covers depicted domination of women, with 38% depicting women in bondage.

Degrading images of women may be especially prevalent in some "non-pornographic" media. A survey of detective magazines, which have never legally been considered pornographic or obscene and have not been the target of censorship attempts, found that 76 percent of the covers depicted domination of women, with 38 percent depicting women in bondage (Dietz et al., 1986). Linz and Donnerstein (1988, p. 184) asserted that "Our research suggests that you need not look any further than the family's own television set to find demeaning depictions of women available to far more viewers than in pornographic material." Other researchers (Zillmann & Bryant, 1988) disputed this allegation, but it is an interesting point.

Clearly, more research is needed in this sensitive area. If researchers and legislators can rise above their preconceptions, values, and political agendas, we should be able to learn what media factors really affect violence and callous attitudes toward women.

Ethical Issues in Studying Pornography

Powerful ethical issues are involved in studying pornography and aggression. All subjects in these experimental studies (as well as similar studies) are forewarned of the content of the materials they may view, and only those who are willing to take part are studied. In addition, subjects are carefully debriefed afterward. The procedure is particularly crucial for those who view "positive ending" aggressive erotica. Experimenters must be careful to stress afterward that such depictions are very unrealistic and that women do not really enjoy such humiliation at all. The ethics in conducting and reporting such studies, as well as the effectiveness of the debriefing procedures used, have been carefully weighed within social psychology (C. Sherif, 1980; Donnerstein et al., 1987).

What Can Social Psychology Tell Society?

Although the President's Commission on Obscenity and Pornography (*Report*, 1971) asserted that pornographic materials showed no harmful impact on adult human sexual behavior, the ensuing years of careful research have caused most concerned social scientists to back off from this blanket acceptance. It now appears that male-oriented violent pornography may indeed have a negative social impact, particularly on males who are predisposed to think in terms of possible rape (Malamuth & Check, 1981). Although it would be difficult to identify a direct causal path between viewing violent pornography and subsequent sexual abuse, some relationship is suggested by the results of many laboratory studies. Numerous observers have also pointed out that the degradation of women in such depictions may encourage a prejudicial, condescending view of women even in other nonsexual contexts. Hence, while the elimination of *all* sexually explicit materials does not seem called for, the elimination of materials that include violence (with or without sexual content) or are degrading to either sex might serve a healthy purpose for society.

WAYS OF CONTROLLING AGGRESSION AND VIOLENCE

A number of scientists have turned their attention from the study of factors that increase aggression to factors that may control or reduce aggression. Let us now look at the major processes that have been investigated, most thoroughly by Robert Baron (1983).

Processes That Do Not Work Well: Catharsis and Punishment

Two commonly recommended procedures for reducing aggression are catharsis and punishment. Angry individuals who are allowed to aggress may feel better afterward, but this does not weaken their tendency to engage in further aggression. As social learning theory suggests, they are usually more likely to engage in aggression in the future. The threat of punishment is effective in reducing present aggression or inhibiting later aggression only under very limited conditions. If the potential aggressor is not very angry, the punishment is strong, and there is little to gain from further aggressive actions, punishment may be effective. Punishment is likely to be successful in inhibiting later aggression only when it is viewed as legitimate by the recipient, when it follows the aggressive actions quite swiftly, and when it is administered in a sure and predictable manner. Seldom are all of these conditions met (Baron, 1977).

Factors That May Work but Are Difficult to Control

Additional factors may be effective in reducing aggression, but they demand considerable control of the environment to implement. One could try to change the attitudes and values about aggression that are taught by parents and the mass media (especially television). As noted in Chapter 4, large-scale changes in attitudes and values are not easy to achieve. Nevertheless, if cultural values change so that aggression and violence become less socially acceptable, this should have some impact on the aggressive behavior of society's members. Another step is to modify social conditions that may encourage or reward overt aggression. Our criminal justice system often seems so ineffective that aggressiveness on the part of criminals is punished inconsistently or not at all. If the criminal justice system was streamlined so that rewards and punishments were more directly related to behavior, then its avowed purpose of discouraging aggression and violence might be achieved.

Another step could be to change the environmental factors that may encourage violence. Excessive noise and crowding (Chapter 12), aggressive cues, and frustration all may increase the likelihood of aggressive behavior. Although it would be difficult, some of these factors such as crowding, the presence of aggressive cues, and excessive noise may be controllable.

Tactics That Show Promise

Modifying TV Content or Viewing Habits

Working with children to modify their TV viewing habits or their interpretation of violent events may be a valuable procedure for breaking the viewing violence-aggression cycle. Huesmann and his co-workers (1983) had second- and fourth-graders who were relatively violent write a paragraph on "Why TV violence is unrealistic and why viewing too much of it is bad." The children wrote the paragraphs, received suggestions and rewrote them, were videotaped reading them, and watched a TV tape of themselves and their classmates reading their paragraphs. Four months later the peer-rated aggression scores for these children were significantly lower than for a comparable group of high-violence children who did not undergo this treatment. Other researchers have attempted to teach "critical viewing skills" to children—giving them knowledge of production techniques, information about the purpose of commercials, how TV distorts the real world, and television's possible effects on behavior. But the results of such training on subsequent aggressiveness of the children have thus far been difficult to determine (Eron, 1986; Singer & Singer, 1986).

Another tactic is to try to change the level of violence on television. Although a significant overall reduction of the level of violence on television might lower the level of violence in American society, in 1980 Eron asserted that "trying to get any significant change in television programming would be like tilting at windmills (p. 250)." Nevertheless, national organizations like the National Coalition on Television Violence, the American Medical Association, and various Parent-Teacher Associations (PTAs) are trying to get broadcasters to reduce violence levels. Perhaps it has had an effect—the level of TV violence declined between 1985 and 1990 (NCTV News, January 1990). Also, researchers are working with parents in teaching them how to turn off the television and to monitor the child's watching, as well as sharing the viewing experience and helping the child distinguish real from fantasy figures (Singer & Singer, 1981).

Socializing Children Differently

Another productive direction may be to change the way that young children, particularly boys, are socialized. Traditionally, emphasis has been placed on the "macho" male role, in which aggression and violence are associated with power, masculinity, and success. Just as Western society discourages aggressive behavior in girls very early in life and rewards them for engaging in other kinds of activities, society could also discourage boys from aggression very early in life and reward them, too, for other behaviors. The level of individual aggression in this society will be reduced, Eron (1980) asserted, only when male adolescents and young adults subscribe to the same standards of behavior that have been traditionally encouraged for women. Since there is a tendency to model nonaggressive behavior as well as aggressive behavior (Chapter 7), if nonaggressive models can be provided in people's everyday lives (by teachers, parents, and peers) and through the media (television, movies, books), then the overall levels of aggression might be reduced.

Inducing Responses Incompatible with Aggression

People are incapable of engaging in two incompatible responses at the same time. It follows that if one is feeling an emotion incompatible with aggression, one will not feel aggression. Possible relevant responses include empathy, feelings of amusement, and *mild nonviolent* sexual arousal (Baron, 1977). A number of studies have found that people high in *empathy,* as measured by questionnaire, tend to be less aggressive (Miller & Eisenberg, 1988). Some attempts at training people to be more empathic have produced reduced aggressiveness (Feshbach et al., 1982), but overall the results of training programs are mixed. It appears that training that focuses on empathic *emotions* is more effective than cognitive training where one learns to take the role of the other (Miller & Eisenberg, 1988).

On the surface it might seem inconsistent to say that mild sexual arousal inhibits aggression in angry people, for we have seen that explicit, violent sexual stimuli can increase aggressiveness. Zillmann's excitation-transfer theory provides an explanation for this difference. Erotic stimuli can exert at least two different effects (Baron, 1983). First, they induce positive (pleasure) or negative (disgust) affective reactions. Second, they induce relatively low (nonexplicit stimuli) or high (explicit materials) levels of emotional arousal. A combination of positive affect and low arousal can be expected to reduce aggressiveness (incompatible responses). A combination of negative affect and high arousal, on the other hand, could lead to increased aggression, due to people misattributing the arousal they experience to feelings of anger.

LOOKING TOWARD THE FUTURE

In the 5,600 years of recorded human history there have been more than 14,600 wars: a rate of approximately 2.6 wars per year. Of the roughly 185 generations of human beings who have been born, lived, and died during this same time period, only ten generations seem to have known the blessing of uninterrupted peace (Montagu, 1976). Given this disturbing record of almost continuous violence, you may wonder whether it is possible to modify such a seemingly deep-rooted human tendency.

The answer seems to be yes, we *can* modify it. Just as we have learned so much about factors that increase aggression, so we have begun to learn more about factors that can decrease the incidence of aggression. Scientific study of the causes of aggression and of ways to reduce their prevalence is of critical importance. The development of techniques and expertise applicable to human survival is especially crucial in a world characterized by widespread aggression on both an interpersonal and an international level.

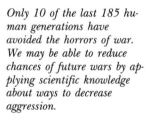

Only 10 of the last 185 human generations have avoided the horrors of war. We may be able to reduce chances of future wars by applying scientific knowledge about ways to decrease aggression.

Summary

Aggression in humans is caused by internal states, learned habits, reduced inhibitions, and situational factors. Moderate or heavy alcohol consumption is related to increased aggression, probably due to a combination of biological effects and the drinker's expectations. People who are angry, frustrated, in pain, or low in self-awareness are more likely to be aggressive. People in a state of high physiological arousal may also become more aggressive if they attribute (or misattribute) the arousal to aggressive feelings. Important situational factors include threat or attack, instigation by others, ingroup-outgroup conflict, environmental stressors, and aggressive stimulus cues.

The Freudian and ethological views suggest that people who view aggression ought to become less aggressive because their aggressive urges are drained off (catharsis). In contrast, social learning theory predicts that observing aggression is likely to increase the viewer's aggressive tendencies due to observational learning and modeling. Numerous laboratory and field studies strongly support the social learning analysis. Recent studies of violent pornography indicate that it may stimulate some men to aggressive behavior toward women and also may foster attitudes that are degrading to women. The major affect seems more due to violent content than to sexual content. If children's viewing habits and general socialization processes can be modified so that children are frustrated less often and are exposed largely to prosocial models, not violent ones, the level of violence in future society might be reduced.

CHAPTER 11
Prejudice and Discrimination

See that man over there?
 Yes.
 Well, I hate him.
 But you don't know him.
 That's why I hate him.
Gordon Allport

Nature intended women to be our slaves . . . they're our property; we're not theirs. They belong to us, just as the tree that bears fruit belongs to a gardener.   Napoleon Bonaparte

Women are more alike than men [are].   Lord Chesterfield ❖

PREVIEW

Having analyzed the factors involved in aggression against our fellow humans, we can now turn our attention to a specific manifestation of aggression—prejudice and discrimination against those of different races, ethnic origin, age, or gender. Our analysis of prejudice will look at how people respond to race and gender as *social categories*. After reviewing the concepts of prejudice, stereotype, racism, and sexism, we will analyze how we perceive people belonging to other groups (outgroups). You will see people prefer their own group (the ingroup), hold biased perceptions and memory for information concerning the outgroup, assume that outgroup members are very similar to each other, and interpret information in ways that confirm their expectations about outgroup members.

We will examine relationships between groups and the causes of ethnic and gender prejudice, focusing on conflict, competition, frustration, and feelings of relative deprivation. We will also look at the impact of perceived and actual differences in attitudes and values, conformity to norms and cues provided by society, institutional racism, and the "prejudiced personality." Turning to techniques for reducing prejudice, you will see that mass-media campaigns and individual and group therapy have limited effectiveness. Research shows that cooperative equal-status contact appears to be the most effective way to reduce ethnic prejudice.

RACIAL PREJUDICE AND RACISM

Racial Prejudice

ethnic group:
Any group defined by nationality, by race, or by common cultural and religious heritage.

People are often treated differently because of their membership in an ethnic group. (An **ethnic group** is any group defined by nationality, by race, or by common cultural and religious heritage, such as Italians, Asians, Jews, and Muslims.) But does differential treatment (discrimination) imply prejudice?

Prejudice and *discrimination* are part of everyday language. Gordon Allport (1954, p. 9) proposed that a prejudiced attitude is one that is based on a "faulty inflexible generalization" that "places the object of the prejudice at some disadvantage not merited by his [or her] own conduct." To extend Allport's definition, **prejudice** can be understood as a negative attitude that is considered to be unjustified by an observer (Brigham & Weissbach, 1972). To determine whether an attitude is unjustified, one could focus on the *process* through which the attitude is acquired (Is it based on faulty reasoning or learned from an unreliable source?), on the *content* of attitude itself (Is it an overgeneralization or too rigid?), or on the *consequences* of that attitude for the attitude target (Does it lead to unfair discrimination?). A prejudiced attitude can serve important functions (Chapter 4) for an individual. It can lend meaning to the world, promote social adjustment, express values, or help externalize personal problems such as frustration, low self-esteem, or perceived threat.

prejudice:
A negative attitude that is considered unjustified by an observer.

Stereotypes

stereotype:
A generalization that is considered unjustified by an observer.

When interacting with someone about whom we know very little, our behavior is guided by whatever person schema (Chapter 3) seems relevant. Our schemas about social groups often contain generalizations, some of which might be labeled stereotypes. A **stereotype** can be defined as a generalizaton that is considered unjustified by an observer (Brigham, 1971). The basic problem with a stereotype, as with prejudice, is its unjustifiable basis.

Does everyone have stereotypes? Probably, because we all have schemas about social groups. Stereotypes do not necessarily represent deficient cognitive functioning but, rather, stem from the information-processing shortcuts and procedures (discussed in Chapter 2) that usually serve us well by making our cognitive tasks easier. In the case of stereotypes, however, these processes lead to undesirable ends, such as overgeneralization, dehumanization, defensive rationalization for discrimination, blaming the victim, and selectively interpreting information to be consistent with one's expectations (Miller, 1982). Three central aspects of stereotyping can be identified (Linville et al., 1989). A stereotype may involve *systematic bias,* the tendency to attribute negative characteristics to outgroup members. It may involve a *lack of differentiation* between outgroup members, as the stereotype-holder does not distinguish between outgroup members even when they differ from each other in the relevant characteristic. And, at a group level, stereotypes may involve a *lack of perceived variability,* as all outgroup members are assumed to be similar to each other.

If stereotypes are unjustified, why do they persist? For one thing, people perceive and remember information in a biased manner that supports their existing schemas, including stereotypic schemas. Moreover, people's stereotypes may guide their social interactions in ways that induce members of the stereotyped group to behave consistently with the stereotypes, creating a behavioral confirmation effect (Snyder, 1981) or a self-fulfilling prophecy. Also, as we will see, general cognitive biases in perception and memory usually operate to support our existing schemas and stereotypes.

Racism

racism:
A racially discriminatory aspect of a culture that is accepted uncritically by many people and leads to competition, power differentials, and mistreatment of outgroup members.

Racism can be defined as a racially discriminatory aspect of a culture that is accepted uncritically by many people and leads to competition, power differentials, and mistreatment of outgroup members (J. Jones, 1983). It can be manifested in individual attitudes—prejudice—or more broadly in societal structures and institutions. Many of the major social institutions and bureaucratic policies of our society—our laws, the education system, welfare, employment practices, immigration policies, religion—are structured to permit or encourage the subjugation or mistreatment of minority groups.

Modern racism, self-interest, or concern for children? Opposition to busing for racial balance may represent a mixture of these motivations.

old-fashioned racists:
People who hold obviously bigoted beliefs about minorities.

modern racism:
Modern racists believe that discrimination is a thing of the past and that minorities are pushing too hard and are getting too much attention and sympathy (also called symbolic racism).

People who hold obviously bigoted beliefs about minorities have been called **old-fashioned racists** (McConahay, 1982). But as race relations in the U.S. have shifted from struggles over basic civil rights in the mid-1900s to struggles over distributing educational, economic, political, and social resources (Bobo, 1988), a more suble form, labeled **modern racism**, has been identified. These whites have antiblack feelings and a commitment to traditional values of individualism, stressing hard work, ambition, self-reliance, delay of gratification, and egalitarianism (Sears, 1988). They are ambivilant toward blacks, resulting from a conflict between negative feelings toward blacks acquired during early socialization and a belief in the "American Creed" which calls for fair play, freedom, and equality (McConahay, 1986).

It would violate the value of egalitarianism to express antiblack feelings openly through old-fashioned racism, so the modern racist vents hostility indirectly, by accusing minorities of not living up to individualistic values, seeing them as lacking ambition, as impulsive, dependent on welfare, and so forth. A modern racist is apt to oppose welfare, affirmative action, and busing to achieve racial balance in schools. In attributional terms, the modern racist makes dispositional attributions as the cause of a minority's less-favored status in society (Pettigrew, 1988). David Duke, a former Ku Klux Klan leader elected to the Louisiana state legislature in 1989 is an extreme

David Duke, former KKK leader and Louisiana legislator: the prototype of the video-friendly racist for the 1990s?

example. A *Newsweek* article labeled him "the prototype of the video-friendly racist for the '90s", as he used "veiled buzzwords" such as concern over welfare payments, crime, and affirmative action to mask his strong antiminority feelings (Turque, 1989).

Though many whites who would score high on a measure of modern racism might protest that they are not prejudiced at all, research reveals that on average such whites are more likely to vote against blacks (McConahay & Hough, 1976), to try and maintain social distance from blacks (Hardee & McConahay, 1981), and to express subtle antiblack feelings (McConahay et al., 1981).

I am not implying that everyone who opposes welfare or busing is a modern racist. Perceived threat, self-interest, and other sociopolitical values also are important determinants of those attitudes. People often oppose a social program when they perceive it as a threat to their accepted practices and life-styles. Bobo (1983) argued that it is the protection of economic advantages and patterns of residential **segregation** that are the crucial features of social relations between blacks and whites, and these are at the heart of why many whites respond to blacks' demands for change as if they stood to lose something valuable.

segregation:
The act or policy of imposing the social separation of races, as in schools, housing, and industry.

GENDER PREJUDICE AND SEXISM

Sexism

Sexism can be defined as any attitude, action, or institutional structure that subordinates a person because of his or her gender. Both sexism and racism involve situations in which people are subordinated because of their membership in a group. *Sexism* is a more general term than *racism* in that it describes both individual cases of prejudice and more general cases of discrimination by groups and institutions.

sexism:
Any attitude, action, or institutional structure that subordinates a person because of his or her gender.

Socialization by Gender and by Race

In some ways, socialization according to gender, **sex-role socialization**, in Western society is similar to socialization according to race. Both women and blacks have high social visibility, are the objects of negative stereotypes, encounter rationalizations for their inferior social status, and are faced with various discriminatory activities. Yet there are also a number of differences in the way that women and minority ethnic groups are treated by society. First, women are not numerically a minority in American culture as other minority groups are. (Should women still be described as members of a minority group? I think so, because they share with other minority groups

sex-role socialization:
The social process by which children are taught and reinforced for behaving in ways seen as appropriate for their gender.

Sex-role socialization. In our culture, most girls and boys learn sex-typed behaviors very early in life.

a lack of access to social, political, and economic power in society.) Second, during their upbringing girls and women have more direct contact with their outgroup (men and boys) than most ethnic minorities have with their outgroup. Third, although majority- and minority- group members often have little contact with each other, men and women constantly interact with each other. Another difference involves the availability and variability of models. Other-sex models are generally more available and less stereotypical than are other-race models during childhood. Finally, most children's information about another race is obtained secondhand from the media or same-race people (parents, friends), but much of a child's information about sex roles comes directly from interactions with the opposite sex. It has been argued that American racism is a uniquely American phenomenon, arising from our heritage of slavery and segregation, whereas sexism is a more general cultural factor, visible in virtually all cultures and time periods (Reid, 1988).

Sexism as an Unconscious Ideology

Sexism may be considerably more subtle than racism. The word *sexism* was not even invented until the mid-1960s, whereas the concept of racism has been around much longer. Bem and Bem (1977) suggested that sexism is taken for granted in our society to such an extent that it is an *unconscious ideology*—the beliefs and values that support it are such a part of society that many people cannot imagine it being different. The unconscious ideology results, in Bem and Bem's opinion, in the *homogenization of women*. "Talent, education, ability, interests, motivation: all irrelevant. In our society, being female uniquely qualifies an individual for domestic work—either by itself or in conjunction with typing, teaching, nursing, or (most often) unskilled labor. It is this homogenization of America's women that is the major consequence of our society's sex-role ideology" (p. 174).

CAUSES OF PREJUDICE

Prejudice can result from a number of different factors. The pattern of interactions between groups, such as competition and aggression, can lead to prejudicial attitudes. On a more cognitive level, making comparisons between the ingroup and outgroup can increase prejudice. If one believes that outgroup members have beliefs and values dissimilar to one's own, prejudice is likely. Societal factors also play a role. Discriminatory social norms, conformity pressures, societal barriers to outgroups, and institutional racism are often associated with prejudice. Finally, prejudice may be related to an individual's personality characteristics, such as authoritarianism.

Natural Ways That We Perceive People in Groups

ingroup:
The group that one belongs to, one's own group.

outgroups:
Groups other than the group to which an individual belongs.

ethnocentrism:
A general tendency to prefer the ingroup over all outgroups.

social competition:
Group members attempt to increase their self-esteem by comparing their group favorably with other social groups.

Throughout recorded history humanity has formed itself into groups: us, the **ingroup**, and them, the **outgroups**. The criteria used for dividing into groups have been diverse: appearance (race), gender, location (nationality), religion, attitudes (political affiliation, clubs), and so forth. A number of cognitive processes operate when groups form.

Preference for the Ingroup
Simply categorizing others in terms of group membership results in a systematic bias: People evaluate ingroup members more favorably than outgroup members (Brewer & Kramer, 1985; Howard & Rothbart, 1980). The general tendency to prefer the ingroup was first labeled by Sumner (1906) as **ethnocentrism.** Membership in a social group can be beneficial to one's self-esteem if the group compares favorably with other social groups through social comparison (Chapter 2). Consequently, people tend to perceive their group as superior to other groups in order to enhance their self-esteem. When groups compete, each group views itself as superior and prejudice is likely to arise. Tajfel and Turner (1986) labeled this process **social competition.**

Ingroup-outgroup distinctions can encourage prejudice and discrimination.
Source: From *Penguin Dreams and Stranger Things: A Bloom County Book* by Berke Breathed. Copyright © 1985 by The Washington Post Company.

When a group's social identity is unsatisfactory, individuals will either leave their existing group or strive to make it more positively distinct from other groups.

Thus, pressure to evaluate one's own group positively leads social groups to differentiate themselves from outgroups. To further protect self-esteem, group members may also differentiate themselves from fellow ingroup members, when those ingroup members are performing poorly. Research shows that group members may be very harsh on undesirable ingroup members, turning against those members who jeopardize the ingroup members' self-esteem (Marques & Yzerbyt, 1988; Marques et al., 1988).

The Illusion of Outgroup Homogeneity

People tend to perceive members of other groups as more similar to each other than they view members of their own group (Quattrone, 1986). There are several reasons why outgroup members are seen as overly homogeneous. First, people are likely to be more familiar with the diversity in their own group than in the lesser-known outgroup. As people become more familiar with a group, they generally perceive more variation within the group. For example, Linville et al. (1989) found that students in a big introductory psychology class perceived much more variability among class members at the end of the semester than they had at the semester's beginning. Second, perceiving an outgroup as homogeneous may make the outgroup seem more predictable and less anxiety provoking. Further, this bias may make it easier to deindividuate and dehumanize the outgroup in preparation for negative actions toward them (Mullen & Hu, 1988).

This tendency has been demonstrated with gender as well as race. Both males (cf., Lord Chesterfield) and females assume greater homogeneity in attitudes on the part of members of the opposite sex than with members of their own sex. Even within the same sex, ingroup/outgroup differences occur. Park and Rothbart (1982) had members of three different sororities indicate how similar, or dissimilar, members of each sorority were to each other. The women in each sorority perceived greater homogeneity among members of the other sororities than among members of their own.

There is a tendency not only to assume that outgroups are similar to each other in attitudes and behaviors, but also to assume that they are highly similar in appearance. Biases in memory contribute to these tendencies. Failure to learn differentiating information about the outgroup perpetuates the view of the outgroup as relatively homogeneous and undifferentiated (Park & Rothbart, 1982). A number of studies have demonstrated that whites are better at distinguishing among white faces than among black faces, and blacks are better at distinguishing among black faces than among white faces (Bothwell, Brigham, & Malpass, 1989; Brigham, 1985). An eyewitness's ability to distinguish among faces in a lineup is a very important step in many criminal investigations. If members of a different race "all look alike" to the average eyewitness, then the likelihood of a witness making an incorrect identification from an other-race lineup may be especially strong (Figure 11-1). This issue will be discussed in more detail in Chapter 13.

FIGURE 11-1

"They All Look Alike": Homogeneity in Appearance of Outgroup Members

The ability of blacks and whites to accurately identify same and other-race faces.

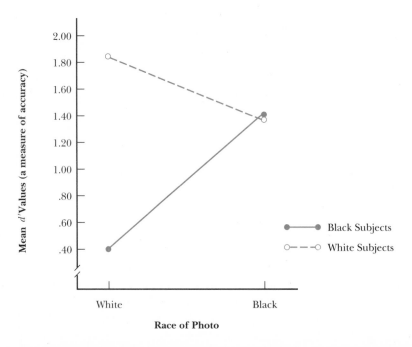

Source: From Brigham, J. C., & Barkowitz, P. B. (1978). Do "they all look alike"? The effect of race, sex, experience, and attitudes on the ability to recognize faces. *Journal of Applied Social Psychology, 8,* 306–318. Copyright © 1978 by V. H. Winston & Sons, Inc. Reprinted by permission.

Extreme Evaluations of Outgroup Members

Individuals tend to evaluate outgroup members more extremely—in a negative or positive direction—than ingroup members (Meindl & Lerner, 1984). Positive or negative information about a group member is likely to have a greater effect on evaluations if the person is a member of the outgroup. Linville (1982) found that young males demonstrated greater complexity in the descriptions of other young males, the ingroup, than of older males, the outgroup. Less complexity in evaluating a group was associated with more extreme evaluations. Later I will discuss the link between prejudice and simplistic cognitive styles.

Overgeneralizing

Individuals tend to make strong generalizations from a person's behavior and apply them to the person's group as a whole. The tendency to overgeneralize from individual to group has been labeled the "law of small numbers" (Tversky & Kahneman, 1974). This tendency can lead to stereotyping because it promotes a homogeneous image of the outgroup. Since research indicates that people consider outgroups to be relatively homogeneous in appearance and in dispositions ("They all look and think alike but we don't"), people are quite willing to generalize about outgroup members based on the behavior of a single member of the group.

For example, Quattrone and Jones (1980) had students at Rutgers and Princeton universities view videotapes of individuals from the two universities in three types of situations. They found, as predicted, that students often were willing to generalize about what "most of the students" at the other school would do based on the one student they saw; in contrast, the students were unwilling to generalize about students at their own school based on seeing one person. The tendency to overgeneralize can be modified, however. Research (Borgida et al., 1981; Nisbett et al., 1981) suggests that the effects of stereotypes on judgment may be radically decreased by providing the perceiver with additional information about the individual, information that individuates (describes in a personal way) the characteristics of the target person (Borgida et al., 1981; Miller, 1982).

Selective Perceptions and Memory

When persons do have prior expectancies or schemas about a group, perceptual and memory processes serve to confirm already-existing beliefs. Stereotype-relevant information may activate negative schemas against outgroups (Greenberg & Pyszczynski, 1985). In contrast, when evidence against a stereotype or schema is encountered, people still tend to cling to the stereotype. Studies show that it may actually strengthen the beliefs on which the stereotype rests and improve memory for evidence supporting the schema's validity (O'Sullivan & Durso, 1984). Or the person may develop images of subtypes (exceptions) while retaining the stereotype for the group as a whole (Weber & Crocker, 1983).

People expect their own group to engage in more favorable behaviors than the outgroup and they show significantly better memory for negative outgroup behaviors than for negative ingroup behaviors (Howard & Rothbart, 1980). Undesirable traits that have been associated with minority groups are remembered better than undesirable traits associated with majority groups (R. Jones & Scott, 1979). Because attitudes toward a group are influenced by memory of the group members' behaviors, this can generate unfavorable attitudes and stereotypes about outgroups.

One of the major ways memory can deceive us is by providing a biased sample of what we know. We are likely to recall unusual and easily available information about a group (recall the availability and representativeness heuristics from Chapter 2), which may not be an accurate portrayal of the group. Further, our implicit theories of personality may influence what we perceive and remember about group members. Memory is a constructive process; when trying to retrieve something from memory we may change what is in memory (Loftus, 1980). Our memories of interactions with members of stereotyped groups are susceptible to this bias. Stereotypes also may lead us to ignore new information that conflicts with the stereotypes and to behave in ways that induce others to conform to our expectations of them, setting in motion a self-fulfilling prophecy.

FIGURE 11-2

Memory for Traits
of Others

*Percentage of desirable and
undesirable traits remembered
by majority-group members.*

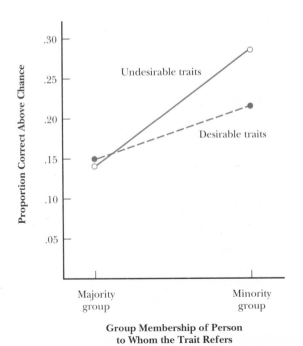

Source: From Jones, R. A., & Scott, J. V. (1979). Availability and the Pollyanna effect in memory for the characteristics of group members. Unpublished manuscript, University of Kentucky. Reprinted by permission of R. A. Jones.

Expectancy Confirmation

Our expectancies about others affect not only our behavior but also the reactions of others to us. Recall the *behavioral confirmation effect* (Chapter 2) where a perceiver's behaviors toward the individual channel the interaction so that expectancy-confirming behaviors are elicited from the other individual. A second process, the *cognitive confirmation effect*, refers to cases where, in the absence of any interaction, perceivers selectively interpret or recall aspects of a target person's actions in ways that are consistent with their expectations.

Although many research subjects are unwilling to make obviously stereotypic trait attributions about group members in recent years (Brigham, 1971; 1972), confirmation effects are often produced when racial, gender, or other negative social labels are implied. Word, Zanna, and Cooper (1974) studied the impact of self-fulfilling prophecies in a job interview setting. White subjects served as interviewers of black and white job applicants (who were accomplices of the experimenter). The interviewers tended to treat the black applicants with less immediacy: they maintained greater physical distance and less eye contact, and leaned forward less toward the applicant. The interviewers also spent considerably less time with the black job applicants and had higher rates of speech errors. A second study used white job applicants, rather than interviewers, as subjects. Half of the applicants were treated as the blacks had been treated in the first study (greater physical distance, more speech errors, shorter interviews) and the other half were treated as whites had been treated in the first study. Videotapes of the job applicants showed that those applicants who were treated as the blacks had been previously treated were judged to be less adequate for the job. These job applicants also liked their interviewer less. The study suggests that poor performance of blacks being interviewed by whites may result not from shortcomings in the job applicant, but may stem instead from the behavior of the white interviewer and the self-fulfilling prophecy that it sets in motion.

For the sake of consistency I have used race in most of the examples, but remember that these tendencies apply to gender as well. The biases in perceiving outgroups — the preference for the ingroup, the illusion that the outgroup is more homogeneous than the ingroup, and the tendency to make more extreme evaluations of the outgroup — apply to gender too. People tend to show a preference for their own sex, to see the other sex as more homogeneous, and to be more extreme in their evaluations of other-sex persons. We also tend to be selective in our perceptions and memories, confirming our expectancies about the way males and females should act by evaluating the evidence in a biased way (cognitive confirmation) or engaging in stereotyped interactions (behavioral confirmation).

Developing and Maintaining Stereotypes

The biases associated with commonly used shortcuts in information processing illuminate how stereotypes and other prejudicial beliefs can be maintained in the face of conflicting evidence. Cultural stereotypes are widely known (the availability heuristic) and stereotypic schemas can produce biased interpretations of ambiguous events. When white college students witnessed an ambiguous shove that concluded in a heated argument, most (73 percent) coded it as "violent behavior" when committed by a black person (outgroup member). Yet only 13 percent of students who saw the same action committed by a white actor (ingroup member) coded it as violent (Duncan, 1976). Duncan argued that because of whites' stereotypes associating blacks with violence, the "violent behavior" category was cognitively more accessible when viewing a black than when viewing a white.

Stereotypes can also be enhanced by biased reconstructive memory for events, as shown by subjects in the Snyder and Uranowitz (1978) study who, when told that a man was homosexual, reinterpreted previous information about him to be consistent with this fact. The **illusory correlation effect**, seeing an expected association between two factors (e.g., being a minority-group member and possessing a disliked trait) where none exists, also supports stereotyping. Hamilton and Trollier (1986) proposed that interactions between majority- and minority-group members are infrequent, and because undesirable behaviors also occur infrequently, people are likely to overestimate the association between minority membership and negative behaviors. Looking at interactions between groups, for a white a negative interaction with a black is a distinctive, memorable event. As a result, even though minority and majority groups might display an equal ratio of positive to nega-

illusory correlation effect:

Seeing an expected association between two factors (e.g., being a minority-group member and possessing a disliked trait) where none exists.

Due to the illusory correlation effect and the shared infrequency effect, a few negative interactions between a black and a white are likely to be remembered as more numerous than they actually were.

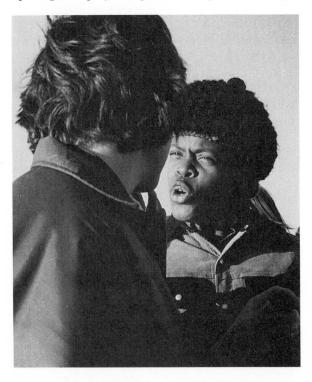

shared infrequency effect:

When interactions between majority and minority-group members are infrequent, negative interactions may seem distinctive and be remembered better.

tive behaviors, this **shared infrequency effect** will lead to a stereotypically unfavorable view of the minority that has no basis in reality (Schaller & Maass, 1989).

Failures in *reality monitoring* (distinguishing memories of real events from memories of imagined events) also contribute to stereotyping. Slusher and Anderson (1987) found that when people were presented with a list of trait-occupation combinations and were also asked to imagine stereotypic trait-occupation combinations, they later incorrectly remembered many of the imagined combinations as real. These results suggest that prejudiced people may imagine stereotyped events and later remember them as real, providing false confirmation for their stereotypic beliefs.

When most majority-group members are aware of the negative cultural stereotype of a minority (even if they do not endorse it), the stereotype is, in the language of social cognition, highly accessible (Chapter 2). Patricia Devine (1989) suggested that such accessible schemas, learned early in childhood, are likely to be activated (primed) automatically in memory whenever a minority-group member is encountered. The stereotype functions much like a bad habit, she argued. The low-prejudice person is likely to make a deliberate attempt to inhibit the negative stereotypic feelings; the highly prejudiced person does not try to inhibit them. Stereotypes, like bad habits, can be unlearned, Devine proposed, but it demands considerable motivation, effort, and time.

One modern development that could contribute to sex-role stereotyping is the rock music video (see also Focus 10-4). Christine Hansen (1989) identified two sex-role stereotypic event schemas or scripts (Chapter 2) common in rock music videos: the "boy-meets-girl" script and the "boy-dumps-girl" script. Hansen found that exposure to such videos primed viewers' sex-role stereotypes—they interpreted a subsequent interaction between a man and a woman more stereotypically than did people who had not seen the videos. The cognition effects of viewing a rock video are probably enhanced, Hansen proposed, by the strong, positive emotions produced by the music itself.

Cultural stereotypes, attitudes, and beliefs are transmitted to children by their parents, other children, and the media (especially television). Another source is the observation of people in social roles. To the extent that children consistently see group members in stereotypic roles (e.g., women as housewives, minorities in low-status jobs), they are likely to make trait attributions that are consistent with these roles. If children observe mostly men in positions of power and influence and women in positions stressing nurturance and sensitivity, as mother/homemaker, they are likely to make general assumptions about men's and women's personalities (Eagly & Wood, in press). If the distribution of people into social roles becomes less sex-typed, we can expect gender stereotypes to weaken.

Gender stereotypes exist worldwide. Surveys by John Williams and his colleagues in 25 countries around the world yielded a remarkable degree of cross-cultural agreement in which traits were seen by adults and by children as more typical of men or of women (Best, 1982; Williams, 1982). Women were seen as "naturally" affectionate, gentle, sympathetic, and sensitive, and men as adventurous, aggressive, courageous, and independent (Table 11-1). Williams (1982) speculated that these stereotypes arose originally from sex-typed role assignments due to biological factors—women bear and nurse young; men are generally bigger, stronger, and more aggressive than women. Societies found it socially efficient to assign child care to women and defense of the group to men. Then it became adaptive to believe that men and women had traits that "naturally" fitted these activities. Once established, these beliefs could become norms for the socialization of future generations.

TABLE 11-1   THE INTERNATIONAL FLAVOR OF ADULTS' SEX STEREOTYPES

Associated with Men[a]	Associated with Women[a]
active	affected
adventurous	affectionate
aggressive	anxious
autocratic	attractive
coarse	complaining
courageous	curious
daring	dependent
dominant	dreamy
enterprising	emotional
forceful	fearful
independent	feminine
inventive	gentle
masculine	mild
progressive	prudish
robust	self-pitying
rude	sensitive
severe	sentimental
stern	sexy
strong	soft-hearted
tough	submissive
	superstitious
	weak
	whiny

[a]*Adjectives associated with men or with women in 23 or more of the 25 countries.*

Source: From William, J. E. (1982). An overview of findings from adult sex sterotype studies in 25 countries. In R. Rath, H. S. Asthana, D. Sinha & J. B. Sinha (Eds.), *Diversity and unity in cross-cultural psychology* (p. 254). Lisse, Netherlands: Swets and Zeitlinger. Reprinted by permission.

Members of the rap group, 2 Live Crew, were unsuccessfully prosecuted for obscenity after a 1990 performance in Florida. The group's sexually explicit lyrics and their performances were seen by many as extremely sexist and degrading to women.

Interactions between Groups

Competition

realistic conflict theory:

Theory focusing on situations in which conflict and competition lead to prejudice, discrimination, and intergroup hostility.

Realistic conflict theory (Sherif, 1966) focuses on situations in which conflict and prejudice go hand in hand. This perspective has been labeled the "power approach" (Giles & Evans, 1986): hostility is seen as the natural consequence of ongoing competition for power, prestige, and privilege. The way in which competition can produce intergroup hostility was vividly demonstrated by the "Robber's Cave study." Sherif and his co-workers (1961) set up a summer camp for a group of boys near Robber's Cave, Oklahoma. After an initial period of harmony, the boys were divided into two groups, housed separately in two cabins, and a series of competitive events between the two cabins was conducted. This arrangement quickly led to conflict, hostility, stereotyping, and ambushes and raids between the two groups. To reduce the hostility, the experimenters set up a series of situations involving

superordinate goals:

Goals that can only be achieved through cooperation and interdependence between groups.

superordinate goals, goals that required cooperation and interdependence between the groups to solve the common problems. Although these activities did not immediately end the hostility, they led to a gradual reduction in unfriendliness and conflict.

On a much larger scale, competition, this time for land, had tragic consequences for the true Native American, the American Indian. The Native American population, estimated at one to three million when Columbus came to America, had been slashed by disease and destruction to a mere 260,000 in 1910. Not until 1924 were Native Americans granted the right to become

Competition and cooperation in the Robber's Cave study. Competitive events such as the tug-of-war increased prejudice and aggression between the two groups of boys, while cooperative endeavors with a superordinate (shared) goal, such as a canoe trip, decreased intergroup hostility.

American citizens. Prejudice and desire for economic gain (land) led to brutal mistreatment of native Americans by early settlers (Brigham & Weissbach, 1972).

Japanese-American families probably embodied the American spirit in the early 1900s as much as any group within our society. Yet when World War II broke out, 112,000 Japanese-Americans (70,000 of whom were American citizens) living on or near the West Coast were forcibly evacuated to ten "relocation centers" stretching from eastern California to Arkansas. Their property was confiscated, their constitutional guarantees suspended. Economic losses averaged nearly ten thousand dollars per family. Yet not a single documented case of sabotage was carried out by a Japanese-American during the entire war! The relocation resulted from fear, prejudice, political expediency, and desire for economic gain by majority-group Americans. One of the byproducts of the civil rights movement was renewed attention to this event (Nakanishi, 1988). Finally, in 1988 a bill was passed by Congress creating a trust fund so that payments of twenty thousand dollars in damages could be made to each of the approximately sixty thousand surviving Japanese-Americans who had been interned. The bill also said that the U. S. Government would issue individual apologies for all violations of civil liberties that occurred (Johnson, 1988). The first payments were made in 1990.

Frustration and Scapegoating

Another result of social competition may be frustration. An individual may experience frustration through actual competition or through worrying about

Wartime fears and prejudices led to the imprisonment of American citizens. Fear of sabotage, political expediency, prejudice, and desire for economic gain all contributed to the forced relocation of 112,000 Japanese-Americans during World War II.

loss of status. As discussed in Chapter 10, frustration-aggression theory predicts that as a result of frustration, aggression may occur—either against the source of the frustration or against a substitute object. In the United States, blacks have often served as scapegoats for frustrated whites. A gruesome example of scapegoating due to economic problems involved lynchings of blacks in the South from 1882 until 1930. Researchers found that whenever the price of cotton decreased, the number of lynchings increased. The economic situation may have created frustrations in the white cotton farmers that were vented on blacks (Hovland & Sears, 1940).

Intergroup Aggression

Research has examined the ways in which race affects the tendency toward aggression. Donnerstein and his co-workers (1972) found that white subjects showed less aggression toward blacks than toward whites when the subjects were visible (Figure 11-3a) or when the victims might have been able to retaliate (Figure 11-3b). When the white subjects were anonymous to the victims or if the victims were unable to retaliate, in contrast, more aggression was shown to blacks than to whites. A similar interaction occurred with censure (Figure 11-3c). When the white subjects' responses were videotaped and easily available to the experimenter (high potential for censure) they behaved more aggressively toward whites than to blacks. Under more private conditions (low potential for censure) the reverse held true—they showed more aggression toward blacks (Donnerstein & Donnerstein, 1973). Finally, Rogers and Prentice-Dunn (1981) found that whites, when insulted, delivered more aggression to a black aggressor than to a white aggressor, whereas the reverse held true when they had not been insulted (Figure 11-3d).

Whites clearly behaved very differently toward blacks depending on whether or not their aggressive behaviors could be detected, punished, or justified. When their behaviors could be detected, or punished, or could not be justified, they engaged in reverse discrimination. To avoid appearing prejudiced, whites treated blacks less aggressively than they treated whites. Further, the findings suggest that antiblack hostility is pervasive but subtle and covert. Whites were very hostile toward blacks when whites' negative behaviors could not be detected or punished; that is, under anonymous, retaliation-free, or censure-free conditions.

Between-Group Comparisons

In situations where group status differences have been legitimized and justified, there is generally little ethnocentrism between the different groups because the subordinate group's self-esteem is so low (Tajfel & Turner, 1979). But whenever a subordinate group begins to question or deny the negative characteristics associated with its low status, it may reawaken previously dormant struggles over resources. The dominant group may react by doing everything possible to maintain and justify the status quo.

relative deprivation:
The condition in which someone is not receiving the outcome that he or she feels entitled to.

Competition can lead to increases in intergroup hostility from minority-group members because of feelings of **relative deprivation,** which exist when someone is not receiving what he or she feels entitled to. With increased intergroup contact and the spread of television in the 1950s and 1960s, minorities in the United States were bombarded with information about the "better life" enjoyed by many Americans. As the expectations of minority-group members rose, the likelihood that they would feel relative deprivation increased.

A person may respond to feelings of deprivation by: (1) changing attitudes toward oneself, resulting in depression, learned helplessness, self-devaluation, or symptoms of stress; (2) devaluing the object one has been deprived of; (3) changing attitudes or behaviors toward the system by feeling anger or perceiving injustice, aggressing, or working for constructive change (Mark & Folger, 1984). Studies of the urban race riots in the United States in the late 1960s suggested that a major contributing factor was feelings of relative deprivation among the rioters. The outbreaks in the black ghettos were attempts to change the system after other less aggressive tactics had failed (Kerner et al., 1968).

Potentially explosive racial differences remain. In the 1980s the median income of black families was 56 percent of the median for whites. The income earned by black college graduates was about the same as that earned by white high school graduates. The unemployment rate was far higher among minority groups (Herbers, 1983). Despite these differences, blacks' perceptions became more positive in some respects. The percentage of blacks who felt they were treated the same as whites rose from 35 percent in 1980

FIGURE 11-3

Race and Direct Aggression in Whites

The impact of anonymity, locus of retaliation, censure, and insult on the tendency of white students to aggress toward white and black victims.

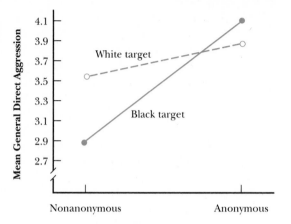

(a) Mean general direct aggression delivered to black and white targets as a function of aggressor anonymity (Donnerstein, Donnerstein, Simon, & Ditrichs, 1972.)

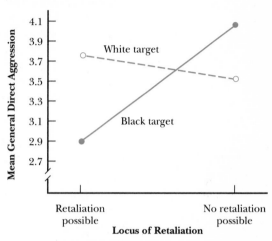

(b) Mean general direct aggression delivered to black and white targets as a function of locus of retaliation instructions (Donnerstein, Donnerstein, Simon, & Ditrichs, 1972.)

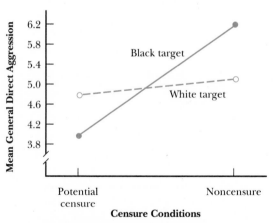

(c) Mean general direct aggression delivered to black and white targets as a function of censure conditions (Donnerstein & Donnerstein, 1973.)

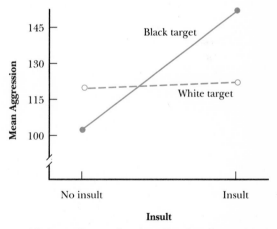

(d) Aggression as a function of insult and race of victim (Rogers & Prentice-Dunn, 1981.)

Panels (a), (b): Copyright 1972 by the American Psychological Association. Panel (c); Copyright 1973 by the American Psychological Association. Panel (d): Copyright 1981 by the American Psychological Association. All panels reprinted by permission of the publisher and authors.

to 44 percent in 1987. However, 44 percent of blacks in 1987 still felt that their community treated blacks "not very well" (Gallup, 1987).

Why Is Conflict Maintained?

In conflict situations, a vicious circle often develops, in which the ingroup expects the worst from the outgroup, looks for the worst, and eventually finds the worst—a self-fulfilling prophecy. As one group arms itself against the potential threat of the other, this reactive arming is seen by the other group as evidence of the first group's extreme aggressive intentions.

Between-group conflict has several additional effects. Conflict or threat from outside actually may produce a beneficial effect within a particular group. The external conflict may provide a safety valve for group members to release internal tension, thereby helping to preserve the group. In addition, heightened intergroup conflict seems to increase within-group cohesiveness (Simmel, 1950). Historians describe many instances where a massive military offensive launched by a more powerful opponent enhances the morale of the weaker country. The heroic resistance in Poland of the Warsaw ghetto Jews against the Nazis in 1943 is a powerful case in point, as was the resistance of the British to German rocket attacks during World War II and the effect of American bombing on the spirit of the North Vietnamese during the Vietnam War.

The complex interplay between conflict and prejudice was exemplified during World War II, when Hitler rode anti-Semitism to power in Germany and later attacked the Soviets partly because of anti-Slavic racism. The Japanese attacked the United States at Pearl Harbor partly because they viewed the Americans as lacking the will to fight, and our own anti-Japanese sentiments flared immediately, and everywhere, even in Walt Disney cartoons. Prejudice and racism feed conflict, and conflict leads to even greater levels of prejudice and racism.

Dissimilarity in Attitudes and Values

People tend to like others who hold attitudes and values similar to their own and to dislike those who don't (Chapter 8). Most people, especially those who are prejudiced, assume that members of outgroups have attitudes and values markedly different from their own (Rokeach, 1960). For noninvolving relationships, perceived similarity in attitudes and values is more important than race in determining people's choices: a *belief effect* (Stein et al., 1965). For more intimate relationships such as close friendship or dating, however, a person will more likely use race as the primary basis for behavior: a *race effect* (Silverman, 1974). As racial attitudes have become more positive in recent years, the overall prevalence of race effects has decreased (Moe et al., 1981).

Perhaps most people do not discriminate in nonintimate situations on the basis of race alone, but on the basis of perceived attitude/value dissimilarity. Yet if people at the same time are *assuming* that any outgroup member will hold different attitudes and values, we are back where we began. The

Interactions between whites and blacks are affected by similarities in attributes and values and by social norms.

situation is complex, but at least this suggests how general levels of discrimination might be reduced. If one can demonstrate to people that the values and attitudes of two groups are not as dissimilar as they have assumed, then the overall level of mistrust and hostility between the groups might be lessened.

Conformity to Social Norms

norms:
Standards for appropriate behavior in one's subculture.

In many cases prejudiced attitudes stem from conforming to the **norms** (standards for appropriate behavior) of one's subculture. Conformity can relate to prejudice in several ways (Pettigrew, 1961). One is the desire to do things as they have always been done. If prejudice and discrimination are enduring elements in one's subculture, then one's prejudicial attitude would serve an understanding function (Chapter 4), providing information about the world. Conformity also may stem from a more emotional commitment to a way of life or to a value system, such as "the Southern way of life" and "black consciousness." Finally, conformity may indicate deep-rooted insecurity, a strong need to belong and be accepted by important groups. Social adjustment and ego-defensive functions of attitudes are relevant in this case.

Norms within the black and white subcultures for appropriate racial attitudes have undergone considerable change since World War II, particularly among Southern whites. Public opinion polls indicated that the percentage of white Southerners who supported school integration rose from a microscopic 2 percent in 1942 to almost 50 percent by 1970. Interestingly, people who had lived in integrated school districts were much more likely to approve of school integration than were people who lived in segregated districts, even when they had no choice as to which type of district to live in (Brigham & Weissbach, 1972). As Figure 11-4 indicates, regional differences in the number of white parents who would object to sending their child to a school where "a few of the children are black" had all but disappeared by 1980.

FIGURE 11-4

Opinions on School
Integration

*Percentages of white parents
who said they would have an
objection to sending their children to a school "where a few
of the children are black".*

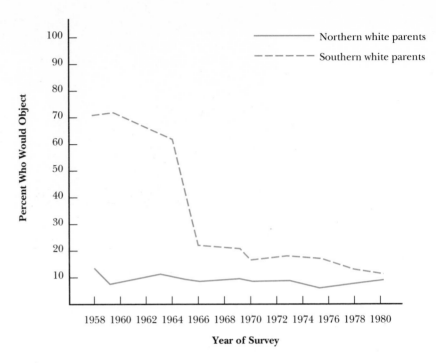

Northern white parents

Southern white parents

Percent Who Would Object

Year of Survey

Source: From the Gallup Poll, February 1982.

Public opinion polls indicate that the greatest positive shift in racial attitudes of whites apparently occurred in the 1960s and early 1970s. Most evidence in the 1980s indicated a return to the slower but steady rate of positive attitude change that had been recorded over the previous four decades, not a reversal of the liberal trend in racial matters as some claimed.

Whites in both the North and the South generally have become more favorably disposed toward racial integration and the ending of legal supports for discrimination and mistreatment. They have also become more positive in their attitudes toward ethnic group members, although this change is perhaps not as great as the change in their policy attitudes. Figure 11-5 illustrates some opinion poll results for recent years.

Though whites' racial attitudes became generally more positive in recent decades, there was still a striking gap between how whites and blacks in 1989 viewed U.S. society's treatment of blacks. Figure 11-6 depicts selected results from a 1989 nationwide Louis Harris opinion poll. Most black respondents felt that, compared to other groups of the same income and education, blacks were less well-off than whites in housing, employment opportunities, treatment by the criminal justice system, and educational opportunities. Most whites, in contrast, believed that blacks were as well-off,

FIGURE 11-5

Changes in Racial Attitudes

The following questions on racial attitudes were administered to a nationwide sample of about 1,350 whites in 1963, 1970, 1972, and 1976. The bars show for each year the percentage of respondents giving what is considered to be a pro-integration response to each question.

1. Do you think white students and black students should go to the same schools or to separate schools?

2. How strongly would you object if a member of your family wanted to bring a black friend home to dinner?

3. White people have a right to keep blacks out of their neighborhoods if they want to, and blacks should respect that right.

4. Do you think there should be laws against marriages between blacks and whites?

5. Blacks shouldn't push themselves where they're not wanted.

1963 1972
1970 1976

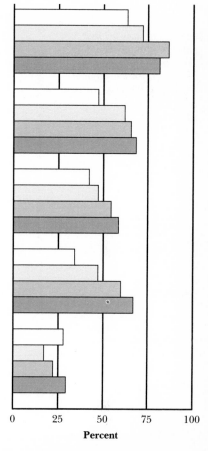

Percent

or better-off than, comparable whites in each of these four areas (Harris, 1989). Further, most whites (70 percent) believed that blacks and whites get equal pay for equal work, but few blacks (29 percent) agreed.

Opinions of whites on two controversial issues, interracial marriage and voting for a black presidential candidate, are portrayed in Figure 11-7. It is interesting that whites' openness to blacks on the nonintimate issue—a black presidential candidate—remained high and constant from 1978 to 1987, but the proportion of whites approving of interracial marriage, though still under half, increased over the same period. Historically, American whites have been less favorably disposed toward interracial marriage than whites in other Western countries have been (Erskine, 1973).

FIGURE 11-6

Are Blacks Less Well-off
Than Whites?

*Percentages of black adults and
white adults who feel that "compared to other groups of the
same income and education,"
blacks were less well-off than
whites in 1989. Data are from
a nationwide Louis Harris
opinion poll.*

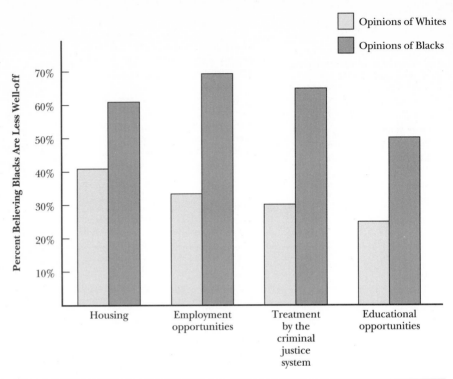

Source: Data from Harris, L.
(1989). *The unfinished agenda
on race in America.* New York:
NAACP Legal Defense and
Education Fund.

The "Prejudiced Personality"

anti-Semitism:
Prejudice or discrimina-
tion against Jews.

**authoritarian
personality:**
A prejudiced, intolerant
personality characterized
by obedience to
authority, prejudice,
loyalty to the ingroup,
and aggression.

Reacting to the rampant racism of World War II, when **anti-Semitism** took
on a tragic aspect in Europe, Adorno and his co-workers (1950) described
a prejudiced, intolerant personality, which they labeled the **authoritarian
personality**. Components of authoritarianism included an emphasis on conventional behavior, generalized loyalty to the ingroup and rejection of outgroups, rigidity, cynicism, support of aggression by authority figures and
of submission to authority, and a preoccupation with power and toughness.
In addition, the authoritarian was thought to be preoccupied with "evil forces"
in the world and with other people's sexual behavior.

Adorno and his co-workers suggested that authoritarian parents are
harsh disciplinarians and will not tolerate misbehavior or aggression from
their child. The harsh upbringing may produce a great deal of aggression
in the child, directed toward the parents but not acted out in childhood.
Instead, in adulthood the hostility is displaced and directed toward minority
groups who cannot fight back. A simpler explanation for the development
of authoritarianism stems from our knowledge of the power of social learning in affecting children's attitudes and behavior (Chapter 10). Authoritarian parents serve as prejudiced models; their children can learn patterns

FIGURE 11-7

Opinions about Black
Presidential Candidacy and
Interracial Marriage

*Percentages of whites who say
they would vote for a generally
well-qualified black man for
president if nominated by their
party, and percent of whites
who say they approve of marriages between whites and non-
whites.*

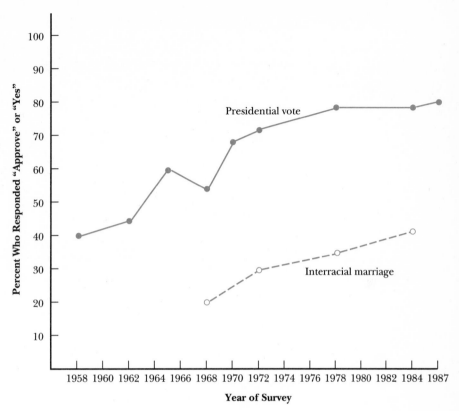

Source: Based upon a series of nationwide Gallup Polls.

of prejudice and discrimination from them. Given the powerful influence
of parents' attitudes on the racial attitudes of their children (Katz & Taylor,
1988; Stephan & Rosenfield, 1978), if parents are discouraged from passing
on prejudicial attitudes, even if they harbor considerable prejudices themselves, then the vicious cycle of prejudice leading to more prejudice might
be weakened.

Concerned that the concept of authoritarianism misses intolerant people who are not politically conservative, Rokeach (1960) developed the concept of **dogmatism**, defined as a relatively closed, intolerant organization
of beliefs. Whatever the sociopolitical position they take, dogmatic people
are rigid in their attitudes and quite resistant to change. Brown (1965) proposed that the single characteristic that would most clearly identify highly
authoritarian or dogmatic persons is the sort of evidence that would be
needed to change their otherwise rigid attitudes. For authoritarian/dogmatic
people, the simple say-so of a respected authority figure should be enough
to cause attitude change.

dogmatism:
A relatively closed,
intolerant organization of
beliefs developed around
the central set of beliefs
about absolute authority.

Authoritarianism at its extreme: American Nazis. These men embody the central characteristics of authoritarianisms: prejudice toward outgroups, a preoccupation with power and toughness, and support of aggression by authority figures.

An Important Caution

Despite the lure of these personality "types," it would be a gross overgeneralization to propose that all people of any type would be prejudiced. As a case in point, one study found that the demographic factors of age, level of education, and the region of the country in which one lives were more powerful predictors of prejudice than were any personality factors (Maykovich, 1975). Our own values can bias our descriptions and schemas of others. For example, in the late 1930s, psychologist E. R. Jaensch reported the identification of two consistent human types. The Anti-type tended to be weak and effeminate, to take childish pleasure in being eccentric, and to think (incorrectly) that environment and education were important determinants of behavior. The J-type, in contrast, showed tough, masculine behavior, made unambiguous perceptual judgments, and believed that human behavior was fixed by blood, soil, and national tradition (Brown, 1965). According to Jaensch, people of North German heritage were likely to make good J-types, while Jews and others of "racially mixed" heredity were Anti-types.

As you have probably guessed, Jaensch was not only a psychologist, but also a German and a Nazi. His J-types no doubt would have made excellent members of the Nazi party. Jaensch's bias is obvious, but be aware that value-related biases may affect how you categorize people as well.

White Prejudice: Less Prevalent or Just More Subtle?

Expressions of old-fashioned racism by whites have become much less prevalent recently. Years ago, Pettigrew (1961) proposed that many Southern whites

latent liberal:

Pettigrew's term for an individual whose prejudices are serving a social adjustment function.

whose present racial attitudes were very negative due to conformity should be called **latent liberals**. These people should readily change their attitudes in the direction of reduced prejudice, he reasoned, if the social norms and patterns of rewards changed. The norms did change somewhat in the next two decades, and many people's attitudes changed with them. If the norms should change back toward greater prejudice, we would expect greater expressions of overt prejudice by conforming people.

Does this mean that the general level of racism has declined? Or is American racism "like a virus that mutates into new forms" (Gaertner & Dovidio, 1986, p. 85)? The answer depends on who is doing the asking and what is being asked. Fewer whites these days will agree with blatantly prejudicial statements. The Harris (1989) poll found a weakening in whites' negative stereotypes of blacks. For example, the number of whites who held the belief that blacks have less ambition than whites, who believed that blacks "breed crime," and who believed that blacks have less native intelligence declined considerably between 1963 and 1988 (Figure 11-8).

FIGURE 11-8

Whites' Stereotypic View of Blacks

Percentages of whites in nationwide surveys in 1963 and 1988 who endorsed negative stereotypic statements about blacks. (Data from Harris surveys.)

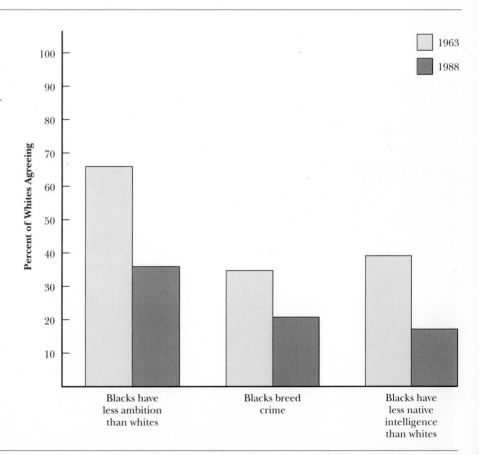

But levels of subtle white racism may remain high when modern racism is measured under conditions in which honest reporting is encouraged (McConahay, 1982). Thus some have argued that only the *style* of expressing one's prejudices has changed. Public opinion poll data indicate less support for institutional policies and laws that discriminate against minorities. Yet a review of many studies that used unobtrusive measures of antiblack sentiments in willingness to help blacks, experimentally induced aggression, and nonverbal communication (voice tone, speech errors, seating distance) suggested that antiblack sentiments in 1980 were much more prevalent among white Americans than survey data would lead one to expect (Crosby et al., 1980). Racist incidents increased at U.S. colleges and universities in the 1980s, with cross-burnings and other ugly racial incidents occurring on a number of campuses. At the same time, black college enrollment declined by one-fifth between 1980 and 1985 as a result of government cutbacks on financial aid to needy minority students (Kantrowitz, 1987). Focus 11-1 depicts a particularly subtle example of discriminatory behavior. Is racial prejudice on the increase or decrease? The jury is still out.

Racism on college campuses. The 1980s saw a troubling increase in ugly racial incidents on many college campuses.

FOCUS 11-1

Subtle Racism in TV Sportscasting

Howard Cosell, a well known and outspoken white TV sportscaster, stirred up much controversy when he referred to a black pro football player as "that little monkey" during the broadcast of a 1983 National Football League game. Cosell protested that the remark had been meant fondly and not as a racial slur. But can patterns of racial prejudice in modern-day sports broadcasting be identified? Unfortunately, yes.

Raymond Rainville, a psychologist who is totally blind, discovered that he seemed to be able to identify the race of NFL players simply by listening to how they were described in the TV broadcasts. To study this apparent racial bias in broadcasting, Rainville and McCormick (1977) created written transcripts of the white TV announcers' comments in reference to players for twelve NFL games on all three networks—with the players' names blanked out. The researchers identified thirty-three pairs of players, one white and one black, who were very similar to each other in ability according to the previous season's statistics: yards gained, touchdowns, and average yards per carry for running backs; number of intercep-

tions and number of tackles for defensive players, and so forth. Ratings of the announcers' comments by persons who did not know the race of the player indicated several significant differences. White players received more praise for their play, more favorable references to their physical and cognitive skills, and were portrayed as more aggressive. Black players received more negative comments about nonprofessional past achievements, such as becoming academically ineligible in college.

The researchers suggested that the announcers might be building a positive reputation for white players as praiseworthy, skillful, and aggressive and a comparatively negative reputation for black players. Probably none of the white announcers would consider themselves highly prejudiced or discriminatory in their announcing. Yet the differences in content were there.

Do you think that the racial patterns may have changed over the past decade, as racial interactions change and more blacks take broadcasting jobs? ❖

Al Campanis, Vice President of the Los Angeles Dodgers, was forced to resign in 1989 after he claimed in a nationwide TV interview that blacks "lacked the necessities" to be major league managers. This photo shows Campanis in earlier days.

Societal Causes

Social Barriers in a "Just World"

Throughout history, legal and illegal barriers have impeded the social and economic advancement of minority groups. Consider the impact of such barriers on the views of majority-group children who look at society, see the barriers, and see people whom they respect helping to maintain the barriers. Most likely, the children will make sense of the world by deciding that the barriers must be justified; the minority groups must deserve the discriminatory treatment. Recall the just world effect (Chapter 3)—people often devalue the victims of misfortune, seeing them as deserving their fate, so that they can maintain their feelings of control in a world seen as just and fair.

Institutional Racism

institutional racism:
Indirect and often unintentional mistreatment of minority groups by major institutions of American society.

Prejudice and discrimination can be an indirect result of how the major institutions in a society are structured. Black activist Stokely Carmichael coined the term **institutional racism** to describe the indirect and often unintentional mistreatment of minority groups in American society. A vivid example of the distinction between individual prejudice and institutional racism was provided by Carmichael and Hamilton (1967, p.4).

> When white terrorists bombed a black church and killed five black children, that was an act of individual racism, widely deplored by most segments of the society. But when in the same city—Birmingham, Alabama—five hundred black babies die each year because of the lack of proper food, shelter, and medical facilities, and thousands more are destroyed and maimed physically, emotionally, and intellectually because of conditions of poverty and discrimination in the black community, this is the operation of institutional racism.

One institutional force that sometimes maintains prejudice is organized religion. Christianity in America once placed strong emphasis on "civilizing the heathen" through performing missionary work and shouldering the "white man's burden" to help "our little brown brothers," implying the superiority of the white Christian American culture. When people try to compare cultures, the doctrine of **Social Darwinism** often arises. Coming into popularity soon after the acceptance of Darwin's theory of biological evolution, this doctrine holds that "survival of the fittest" is applicable to cultures and ethnic groups as well as to species of animals. Therefore, the ethnic group that has "survived best" and gained control of the culture—the dominant group—must be the fittest. In this potentially racist view, the barriers that have been placed in the way of accomplishment for minority groups are ignored, and it is naively assumed that the cream of any culture inevitably will rise to the top.

Social Darwinism:
The naive belief that "survival of the fittest" applies to cultural and ethnic groups and that those groups that gain control of the culture must be the fittest.

Public schools have contributed to the legacy of discrimination, because minority-group members have often been presented in textbooks in a stereotyped, derogatory manner. Traditional histories of American society have often ignored the crucial contributions made by minority-group members and by minority cultures. Such inadequate educational materials, coupled with the use of ability groupings in schools, may lead to within-class segregation by socioeconomic status and hence often by ethnic group, thereby repeating the cycle (Epstein, 1985).

Movies and television, too, have been prime examples of institutional racism. A survey of white elementary school children found that 40 percent of them reported that television was their best source of information about how blacks looked, talked, and dressed (Greenberg, 1972). Minority presence in the media has increased considerably and blacks are more likely to be portrayed in equal-status interactions with whites than in past years (Dovidio & Gaertner, 1986). But differences remain. Most black-white relationships depicted on TV have been in nonintimate job-related situations, whereas intimate behaviors (friendship, romance) were more characteristic of white/white interactions than black/white interactions (Weigel et al., 1980). Many critics praised "The Cosby Show," one of the most popular TV shows of the 1980s, as the first to portray a minority family in a nonstereotypic manner.

United States immigration policies also illustrate institutional racism. After World War I, quotas were established so that large numbers of supposedly "desirable" ethnic groups—Scandinavians, Germans, Irish, and British—were allowed to emigrate to the United States, whereas the immigration of other people—Russians, Poles, Italians, Jews—was drastically limited. Although strict quotas were discontinued in the late 1960s, as recently as 1962 fewer than five percent of the immigrants permitted by the quotas to emigrate were non-European; about 70 percent of those admitted were from just three countries: Great Britain, Germany, and Ireland (Berry, 1965).

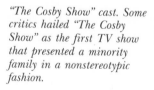

"The Cosby Show" cast. Some critics hailed "The Cosby Show" as the first TV show that presented a minority family in a nonstereotypic fashion.

REDUCING PREJUDICE AND DISCRIMINATION

Three general techniques have been studied as ways to reduce levels of prejudice and between-group hostility: changing people's attitudes, changing group categorizations, and changing behaviors. Changing attitudes might seem the easiest route, but attitude-change techniques have not proven very effective in changing racial attitudes, as the attitudes tend to be strongly held and important to the individual. Changes in behavior can be initiated by making behaviors such as racial, age, or gender discrimination illegal. Behavior changes can also occur as a result of equal-status contact between ingroup and outgroup members.

Translating Social Psychology into Social Policy

Throughout this book we have analyzed the implications of results of laboratory and field studies for social issues. One of the clearest examples of this applicability was the Social Science Brief, written by three social psychologists (Isidor Chein, Kenneth Clark, and Stuart Cook) and evaluated by the U.S. Supreme Court during the momentous 1954 *Brown v. Board of Education* case that outlawed state-supported segregation. The brief argued that segregated schools created low self-esteem in black children. Part of the research basis for this assertion was a series of "doll studies" in which black children and white children were asked questions about a doll with dark brown skin and another with "white" skin. Clark and Clark (1947) found that a majority of both black and white children preferred to play with the white doll and rated the white doll as "good" and the black doll as "bad." The findings were interpreted as an indication of self-rejection and low self-esteem among the black children. Much later, psychologists debated whether the social scientists overgeneralized from the doll studies in their eagerness to provide ammunition to the court for overturning segregation. Were the findings evidence of self-rejection or did the doll preferences simply reflect a general pro-light/anti-dark prejudice that did not involve self-esteem (Cook, 1984; Gerard, 1983)?

Changing Attitudes

Mass-Media Campaigns

In these days of electronic wizardry, persuasive communications can reach millions of people. In the U.S., private organizations and the government have mounted extensive persuasion campaigns to reduce intergroup hostility and prejudice. The campaigns have not been particularly effective, producing only a small amount of attitude change. One difficulty is that racial attitudes are usually important to those who hold them, and important attitudes are least likely to change (Chapter 4). Individuals display a small lati-

Public demonstrations and mass-media campaigns often do not produce a great deal of attitude change.

tude of acceptance for contrary arguments; in addition, such attitudes are apt to be closely interrelated with other important attitudes and values. Hence, it is unlikely that an attitude-change message would fall within the appropriate latitude of acceptance zone and lead to attitude change for large numbers of individuals.

Another factor that hampers mass persuasion is *de facto selective exposure*. Often prejudice-reduction messages fail to reach the intended audience and, even if they do, many people are likely to misinterpret them. A case in point is "All in the Family," the most popular and controversial television program of the 1970s, which focused on previously taboo subjects such as prejudice. Some observers predicted that "All in the Family" would have a beneficial effect on race relations, feeling that viewers would become less prejudiced as they saw bigotry satirized. But others feared that the program would increase the acceptability of bigotry, as Archie Bunker provided an attractive model for viewers (Adler, 1979).

Several in-depth surveys concluded that viewers' perceptions of the program's intent were strongly related to their racial attitudes. Overall, the program seemed to reinforce viewers' existing attitudes. Most nonprejudiced viewers saw the show as a satire that ridiculed bigotry, but most prejudiced viewers saw it as reinforcing their own feelings of superiority and hostility toward minorities (Brigham, 1977; Brigham & Giesbrecht, 1976; Vidmar & Rokeach, 1974).

Changing Individual Attitudes

The growth of T-groups, encounter groups, and sensitivity groups in the 1960s and 1970s suggested to some that racial prejudice might be reduced through increases in self-insight, self-acceptance, and honesty in communication. Some data suggested that sensitivity groups involving both blacks and whites can lead to considerable reduction in interracial prejudice and hostility (Rubin, 1967). However, such findings should be interpreted with caution, as individuals who participate in a sensitivity group may already be quite low in prejudice or may be ready to change. Further, individuals who invest time and energy in such programs may feel the need to report beneficial results (such as prejudice reduction) in order to justify their efforts. Finally, we do not yet know whether such change—if accomplished—is lasting, or whether it disappears over time.

Changing Group Categorizations

differentiation:
The perception of individual differences among people in a social category.

personalization:
Responding to others in terms of their relationship to the self, rather than in terms of social categories.

Just as the categorization of people into distinct groups is sufficient to arouse between-group bias (Stephan, 1985), changes in social structure can reduce that bias. **Differentiation**, making people aware of individual differences within the other group (individuating the outgroup members), can reduce bias, as can **personalization**, responding to others in terms of their relationship to the self, rather than in terms of social categories (Brewer & Miller, 1988). Forming new subgroups that cross-cut the old group distinctions can also reduce hostility (Brewer et al., 1987). Gaertner and his co-workers (1989) showed that encouraging members of both groups to think of them all as one big group (e.g., "the family of man") reduced bias by increasing the perceived attractiveness of former outgroup members, while inducing subjects to think of everyone as separate individuals also reduced bias, this time by reducing the attractiveness of fellow ingroup members.

Changing Behavior

Changes in the Law

People are accustomed to thinking that laws cannot change attitudes. Around the turn of the century, sociologist William Graham Sumner (1906) said, "Stateways cannot change folkways." Sumner was arguing that no matter what behaviors a new law might require, people will continue to feel as they always have—in other words, you can't legislate morality. This position was also reflected in the attitude of American courts, as illustrated in the 1896 Supreme Court decision, *Plessy v. Ferguson*, that set the precedent for the separate-but-equal doctrine. The court said, "Legislation is powerless to eradicate racial instincts or to abolish distinctions based upon physical differences, and the attempt to do so can only result in accentuating the difficulties of the present situation."

We have seen, however, that racial attitudes *have* changed dramatically in recent decades. One major influence has been legal changes such as the 1954 Supreme Court decision that struck down school segregation laws. We saw earlier that cognitive dissonance and self-perception theories suggest that changing behaviors can change attitudes. A new (nondiscriminatory) behavior may be inconsistent with old (prejudiced) attitudes—to reduce the inconsistency, one may change the attitude. Moreover, changes in behavior may produce new and different experiences that themselves lead to attitude change. To some extent, then, you *can* legislate morality by changing people's behavior first.

Equal-Status Contact: Historical Patterns

During World War II the U.S. Army was in part racially segregated and in part integrated. When white soldiers were asked whether they approved of integration in the Armed Forces, their opinions varied depending on their prior experiences. Among white soldiers who had had no experience with integration in the service, only 38 percent favored integration. Among those whose regiment or division was integrated but who had served in a segregated company, 78 percent accepted integration. Finally, among white soldiers who had served in integrated companies, 93 percent approved of integration in the Armed Forces. Since the men had no choice as to which type of company they served in, we can assume that initial attitudes of the three groups toward integration were approximately the same but were changed through interracial contact (Stouffer et al., 1949). Studies of low-cost government housing projects built after World War II, some fully racially integrated, some partly integrated, and some completely segregated, indicated that the opportunity for contact and an approving social climate significantly reduced whites' prejudice (Deutsch & Collins, 1951; Wilner et al., 1955).

Though investigations demonstrated that interracial contact can lead to reduced prejudice, it isn't always the case. In Hitler's Germany, Jews had lived in close contact with Gentiles for almost a century. Three hundred years of relatively close contact between blacks and whites in the United States has not ended racial prejudice. Other variables interact with contact to determine whether a situation will reduce or increase prejudice.

Equal-Status Contact: Important Conditions

The ideal conditions for fostering positive attitude change were outlined by Gordon Allport (1954), Yehuda Amir (1969), and Stuart Cook (1978). This perspective draws from general research on the factors shown to increase friendship and liking (Chapter 7). The most important condition is that the participants in the contact situation be of **equal status** with each other. This has not been the case in many interracial contact situations in America. Intergroup contact can actually increase prejudice when preexisting status differences are large (Triandis, 1988).

The situation should be structured to encourage *mutual interdependence and cooperation.* (Recall how competition increased hostility and cooperation reduced hostility among the boys in the Robber's Cave study.) Moreover, the cooperation should lead to a successful outcome. Here we run into a difficult practical question: How can groups be induced to cooperate after they have experienced a history of conflict? The natural tendency of such groups will be to withdraw and cease communication with each other. The introduc-

equal-status contact: An often effective means of reducing levels of prejudice and hostility between groups.

tion of common goals (remember the Robber's Cave study), a reduction in the "threat potential" of each group, and the spread of positive information about the other group can be utilized to induce cooperation.

On an individual level, the expectation of an unpleasant encounter with an outgroup member generates anxiety. Research shows that this competition-based anxiety interferes with people's ability to appreciate favorable behavior by the outgroup member (Wilder & Shapiro, 1989). Anxiety may also increase participants' tendencies to perceive homogeneity among outgroup members and dehumanize them. These findings indicate that contact will be most beneficial when participants' anxiety has been minimized.

Social norms in the situation should *promote personal relationships* and *authorities should approve* of intergroup contact and tolerance. The situation should encourage communication and development of friendship. The attributes of participants should *contradict any negative stereotypes*. For example, a contact situation is unlikely to work if all of the whites are insensitive racists and the blacks fit the negative stereotypes that many prejudiced whites hold. In this case, each group's negative racial stereotypes would be reinforced.

Finally, the situation should *encourage participants to generalize* their changed attitudes to other situations and ethnic group members (see Focus 11-2). Oftentimes people fail to generalize from an attitude-changing experience. "The problem of generalization is one that has dogged research in this area" (Hewstone & Brown, 1986, p. 16). Here we run into a tricky paradox. On the one hand, we want to encourage people to treat outgroup members as individuals, not as stereotyped group members. But on the other hand, we want people to generalize less-hostile attitudes derived from equal-status contact to all outgroup members, not limiting their positive feelings to the minority individuals they have come to know. Suppose that equal-status contact leads to friendship between Amy, a white woman who previously held antiblack attitudes, and Beth, a black woman. Amy now thinks of Beth not as black, but simply as her friend Beth. This **decategorization** process could be seen as indicative of reduced prejudice by Amy; Beth's race is no longer important to Amy. But we might want Beth's race to *remain* salient to Amy, so that she will generalize her favorable feelings to blacks in general, rather than seeing Beth as an exception.

There are several reasons why equal-status cooperative interactions reduce intergroup hostility. First, the cooperative experience may *destroy negative stereotypes* about members of other groups. Second, it may demonstrate the *similarity in beliefs and values* between the two groups. People also learn about and understand the group differences that do exist (Stephan & Stephan, 1984). Third, people may *reduce* any *cognitive dissonance* stemming from the interracial contact by adopting positive beliefs about outgroup members. Fourth, if participants have been *reinforced* for cooperation (by the relevant authorities or by positive outcomes), then their attitudes toward others in the situation will be positively affected. Fifth, cooperation may encourage *decategorization,* lessening the tendency to categorize people and to focus on ingroup/outgroup distinctions (Messick & Mackie, 1989). Then the various

decategorization:
Lessening the tendency to categorize people and to focus on ingroup/outgroup distinctions.

FOCUS 11-2

Intergroup Contact as a Way of Reducing Prejudice and Discrimination

Ideally, the intergroup contact situation should be one in which:

1. the participants have equal status.
2. there is cooperation leading to a successful outcome.
3. social norms and authorities promote personal relationships and friendship information.
4. participants do not have characteristics that reinforce negative stereotypes the other group holds.
5. the situation encourages participants to generalize changed attitudes to other people and situations.
6. the participants' feelings of anxiety and social competition are minimized.

Reduced prejudice and discrimination may result from:

1. learning about similarities in beliefs and values between groups.
2. learning that the other group is as heterogeneous as one's own group.
3. reinforcement for cooperation by authorities or by a successful outcome.
4. destruction of negative stereotypes about the other group.
5. reducing cognitive dissonance caused by the contact by deciding it was worthwhile.
6. feeling that membership in one's own group is less important.
7. minimizing ingroup/outgroup distinctions. ❖

cognitive biases toward outgroups—biased perceptions and memory, assumptions of outgroup homogeneity, favoritism toward the ingroup, and so forth—will be less prevalent.

Current vs. Historical Status

Black students and white students working toward a common goal in the classroom may have equal status in relation to the present task (equal current status) but they may still have unequal status based on their social, economic, or academic backgrounds (unequal historical status) and they may hold different expectations about each other. Creating equal roles within the classroom will not instantly wipe out all these preexisting differences. Friendships develop more easily during classroom intergroup contact when the students have only small (as opposed to large) differences on socioeconomic status and achievement levels (Rosenfeld et al., 1981).

Many social policies have aimed at balancing historical status. Affirmative action programs try to improve the status of the group that was deprived in the past—for example, through differential admissions or hiring policies—creating an imbalance in current status in favor of the previously deprived group. The creation of an intentional imbalance in current status is often seen by majority-group members as unfair (Focus 11-3). But even when it is seen as unfair, correcting differences in historical status may still increase liking for the previously deprived person. Research suggests that restoration of balance in historical status so that members of previously

FOCUS 11-3

Affirmative Action and the Bakke Case

Like many other students, Allan Bakke wanted to be physician, but had a tough time getting into medical school. He was twice rejected, in 1973 and 1974, by the medical school of the University of California at Davis. He subsequently filed suit against the university claiming that as a white he suffered "reverse discrimination" and was unfairly disqualified because of a special admissions policy that reserved sixteen of the school's one hundred entering slots for disadvantaged minorities, some of whom had scored lower than he on admissions tests. The California Supreme Court found almost unanimously for Bakke and ordered U.C. Davis to admit him to its medical school. The court also forbade the university to use race as an admissions standard. U.C. Davis pursued its case to the U.S. Supreme Court.

In *Regents of the University of California v. Bakke*, a badly split U.S. Supreme Court ruled in favor of Bakke in 1978 and he entered school that fall by the court's order. Bakke, an average student, graduated from medical school in June 1982 at the age of forty-two. In its landmark decision, the Supreme Court outlawed quotas but also ruled that race could be considered as one factor in admissions, along with others, to promote diversity among students.

Following the 1978 decision, U.C. Davis instituted new admissions policies that gave the poor, minorities, and the handicapped extra points in the early stages of selection, but required them to compete equally with others in test scores, recommendations, grades, and interviews. ❖

deprived groups can work more closely with majority group members tends to increase cooperation, which increases intergroup attraction. Hence, even though the interventions may create an imbalance in current status that is perceived as unfair, the end result may still be an increase in attraction toward outgroup members (Norvell & Worchel, 1981).

The "Railroad Game"

Stuart Cook (1970) created a situation that met all of the optimal conditions for repeated equal-status contact between a highly prejudiced female college student and four nonprejudiced persons: a black student, a white student, and two experimenters, one black and one white. The experiment consisted of a complicated three-person "railroad game," which involved filling shipping orders and keeping track of railroad cars in a complex system; the game was played two hours a day for four weeks. The prejudiced student had no idea that the situation had anything to do with changing racial attitudes. The results were encouraging in terms of prejudice reduction. About 40 percent of the prejudiced women changed their racial attitudes significantly on three separate attitude measures, given in a completely different setting a month or more after the experiment apparently had ended. A control group of highly prejudiced women who did not participate in the game showed a prejudice-reduction rate of 12 percent over the same period (Cook, 1985).

Could personality factors predict which women changed their attitudes and which did not? Yes—"changers" had more positive attitudes toward people and were lower in cynicism than were "nonchangers" (Cook & Wrightsman, 1967). Women who became less prejudiced also tended to have lower self-esteem and a higher need for social approval than nonchangers—two measures that probably indicate general *persuasibility* (Chapter 4).

Cooperative Learning Groups

When children of different ethnic backgrounds are placed in the same classroom, preexisting negative attitudes may become more extreme, or they may be modified into liking and respect for one another (Johnson & Johnson, 1989). Cooperative learning methods, where students work together in small, heterogeneous groups to master academic content, have been designed with the goals of reducing prejudice and increasing achievement by all group members.

One procedure, labeled the Teams-Games-Tournament (TGT) technique, divides children into four- or five-person teams. Each team contains children of both sexes, all ethnic groups, and all academic levels. At the end of each week a class tournament is held, involving a set of skill exercise games or quizzes. The team members study together, trying to make sure every team member knows the material, because the team cannot win if some students are not prepared. This technique leads to improved achievement and more

Cooperative learning groups. Multi-racial cooperative learning groups in the classroom can reduce children's racial prejudice and increase their achievement levels.

positive intergroup attitudes (DeVries et al., 1978; Slavin & Madden, 1979). The improved achievement is due mostly to large gains by black students (Slavin & Oickle, 1981). In a similar procedure, "jigsaw groups" (Aronson & Gonzalez, 1988) of students work together on a specific project. Each group member has to master a single part of the lesson and present it to the others. Reduced prejudice should result from increased participation by all members, increased empathic role taking (the ability to understand and take the role of another person in the group), and a stronger tendency to make similar success and failure attributions to others as to oneself (Aronson & Bridgeman, 1979).

Other researchers have varied conditions of cooperative learning situations to assess their effect on prejudice. A series of studies, some with schoolchildren and others with Air Force personnel (Blanchard, Adelman, & Cook, 1975; Blanchard, Weigel, & Cook, 1975; Weigel et al., 1975) found that liking and respect for one's groupmates were enhanced by success on the task, participation in group decisions, having competent groupmates, and the expectation that help is available if needed for one's own performance.

Cooperation and Competition in Sports

Participation on interracial sports teams could be expected to increase liking for teammates because it involves interdependent, cooperative actions toward a superordinate goal (fun, winning), which often has a positive outcome. Studies have indeed found that playing on an interracial team can significantly reduce prejudice for both whites and blacks (McConahay, 1978; Slavin & Madden, 1979). Of course, if the opposing teams are all-white and all-black, then racial prejudice will not decrease and may actually increase.

Contact, Power, and Prejudice

Outcomes of School Integration

Several large-scale studies have traced the progress of school integration and its impact on attitudes and behaviors. One study (Patchen, 1982) found that white students reacted most positively to new black schoolmates in situations where they felt the least threatened by blacks either physically and or in terms of a growing black presence in the school. Getting black students and white students to work together on tasks of common interest toward common goals (such as extracurricular activities) was an especially important tool for building friendship. Studying an integrated middle school, Schofield (1982) discovered that interracial behavior became more positive over the years, but general interracial attitudes did not. She suggested that general racial attitudes didn't change much because they became irrelevant as students based their behaviors on their specific attitudes toward the other students as individuals. The finding implies that changing race-related *behaviors* may be a more realistic and attainable goal than changing general racial attitudes.

The school desegregation studies underscore the importance of the behaviors of those who set the norms: public officials, administrators, principals, teachers. Indeed, administrative support may be the single most critical factor for positive outcomes from desegregation attempts (St. John, 1975). Research also shows that changed attitudes may not generalize to different situations: intergroup relations are domain-specific. Even when students learn new ways of interacting in one situation—e.g., the classroom—these changes may not easily generalize to other situations—e.g., extracurricular activities. Hence, concerned administrators may need to decide which situations they want to focus their energies on.

Summarizing research on cooperative learning groups, McConahay (1981, pp. 50-51) pointed out that "The concept of interracial work groups as a means of reducing prejudice and improving race relations has a great deal of empirical support. It is rare in social science to find such robust results across a wide range of techniques, empirical evaluation methodologies, grade levels, regions of the country. . . . The importance of contact under the conditions specified by the contact hypothesis is truly impressive."

Unfortunately, school desegregation does not usually involve the ideal conditions set up in cooperative learning groups. Because of the widely varying conditions of desegregation, outcomes vary widely too. A comprehensive review of studies conducted during or shortly after desegregation indicated that 13 percent of the studies found that white prejudice decreased after desegregation, 34 percent found no difference in prejudice after desegregation, and 53 percent found that white prejudice actually increased after desegregation (Stephan, 1978). Do these outcomes suggest that integration cannot have beneficial effects on racial attitudes? Not at all. What they *do* show is that integration will not automatically improve race relations; only repeated contact under desirable conditions is likely to have a positive influence on attitudes. Studies of the long-term effects of desegregation generally paint a more positive picture of its affects than do short-term studies (Braddock, 1985; Stephan, 1987).

Social scientists can make their greatest contributions in this area by adopting an innovative orientation, helping to design situations that will improve racial attitudes (Cook, 1985), rather than just studying situations that have already occurred. It is no easy task, but the work reviewed here shows great promise. Often, desegregation attempts are followed by resegregation, perhaps set in motion by "ability groupings" in the classroom; in addition, members of each group may choose to hang out with ingroup members outside the classroom, in the cafeteria or playground (Schofield, 1986). We need to search for ways to increase the likelihood that meaningful intergroup contact will really occur, as well as developing conditions of equal participation where majority-group members do not dominate and expectations of successful performance by minority students are not low.

intergroup interaction anxiety:
Awkwardness that is often felt in initial interracial contacts.

Outcomes of Continued Ethnic Separation
If racial separation is maintained or increased, this may be comfortable for some individuals because **intergroup interaction anxiety** is avoided (Stephan

& Stephan, 1985). However, the social cost of avoiding this discomfort is immense, when one considers the negative effects of continued racial separation. Separation may prevent blacks and whites from learning that their beliefs and values are not really so dissimilar and, moreover, it may lead to wider actual differences in beliefs and values, making future contact more uncomfortable and potentially nonproductive. Separation, too, leads to the growth of vested interests: individuals and institutions that favor separation for their own economic, social, or political gain (Pettigrew, 1971).

Power and Autonomy

Some have argued that because blacks and whites presently are not equal in terms of economic and social power, increased contact may not decrease prejudice until blacks have gained equal power so that contact can be on an equal footing. Taylor (1974) proposed that power is a necessary precondition for equal status—that without the addition of power, giving minorities access to equal education, employment, income, housing, and so forth will never lead to perceived equality in the eyes of whites. Without perceived equality, he claimed, true equal-status contact may not be possible. Taylor asserted that rarely is power shared or transferred without a confrontation and struggle. The white community can help the black community best by enabling the black community to solve its problems the way it wants to, not the way whites think they ought to be solved, Taylor argued.

But minorities may lack the political power and financial clout to go it alone. Black politicians, even when successful, are not likely to have access to a large part of the tax base, and hence they lack the resources needed to build economic strength. And even if they had it, in the time needed to build economic strength, racist institutions would go unchallenged and probably grow stronger. In my judgment, the negative effects of continued separation (increased belief-value dissimilarity, the growth of vested interests that profit by maintaining separation, and so forth) far outweigh the possible benefits for minorities noted by Taylor. Perhaps we can make better use of our accumulated research findings on successful bargaining and negotiation (Chapter 6). As yet, few have tried to apply these findings to issues of race relations and equality (Messick & Mackie, 1989).

Opinions about the Equal Rights Amendment may be closely related to deeply-held values.

REDUCING GENDER-BASED PREJUDICE AND DISCRIMINATION

Sex-Role Attitudes

The same principles that affect racial attitudes can affect gender-based attitudes as well. Like racial attitudes, gender-based attitudes are difficult to change, as they are strongly held and relate to deep-seated values. But despite a long history of male-dominated attempts to rationalize and justify the subjugation of women, gender-related attitudes *have* changed. Studies of sex-role attitudes found large and significant shifts toward egalitarianism in the 1960s and early 1970s. Since that time, survey findings suggest a leveling off in the trend toward acceptance of sex-role equality (Helmreich et al., 1982). As Figure 11-9 illustrates, the percentage of men and women who said in Gallup polls that they would vote for a qualified woman for president rose steadily from 31 percent in 1937 to 82 percent in 1987. The nomination of Geraldine Ferraro as the Democratic vice-presidential candidate in 1984 represented a major breakthrough in American politics. Yet a nationwide survey a month after the election revealed that only 18 percent of the respondents thought having a woman on the ticket helped the Democrats, while 50 percent said it hurt the party (Survey; Woman hurt party, 1984).

FIGURE 11-9

A Woman for President?

Percent of respondents answering yes to the question, "If your party nominated a woman for president, would you vote for her if she were qualified for the job?"

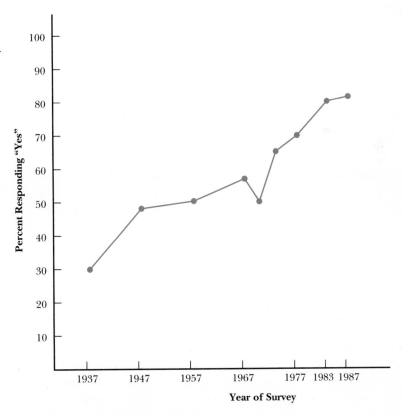

Source: From Gallup Poll findings 1937–1987.

Attacking Discrimination through Legislation

Inasmuch as discrimination according to gender is such a pervasive occurrence, how can it be attacked most effectively? One practical technique, as with race discrimination, is legislation. The Age Discrimination Employment Act of 1967 prohibits government, private employers, government agencies, and unions from discriminating against persons between forty and sixty-five years of age. For women in traditionally female occupations, the act was an important protection because often they could establish a case of age discrimination more easily than sex discrimination (Eastwood, 1978). The Equal Pay Act of 1963 made overt salary discrimination illegal. The Equal Rights Opportunity Act of 1974 outlawed discrimination on the basis of sex or marital status in any aspect of a credit transaction. The 1978 Pregnancy Disability Bill finally made discrimination on the basis of pregnancy illegal (Basow, 1980). But despite such legislation, special restrictions on women's rights continue to exist in many states.

Affirmative Action Programs

Beginning in the late 1960s, many business and government agencies adopted innovative programs to increase their representation of racial minorities and women in an attempt to correct historical inequities that had favored white males. Research reviewed earlier suggests that affirmative action programs that favor minorities in some aspects of the employment process may have a favorable effect on majority-group attitudes and, despite all the political rhetoric to the contrary, the American public apparently supported such programs. A nationwide survey in 1982 found that 69 percent of the respondents favored "federal laws requiring affirmative action programs for women and minorities in employment, provided there are no rigid quotas" (Harris, 1982). In 1988, 65 percent of blacks and 55 percent of whites responded favorably to a similar question (Harris, 1988). But when the issue was framed differently, asking about support for programs that may "favor women and members of minorities over better qualified men and whites in hiring and promoting", 56 percent of blacks but only 25 percent of whites agreed (Gallup, 1987).

The legal status of affirmative action programs was given some support in the 1982 Bakke decision by the U.S. Supreme Court (Focus 11-3). But the court was careful to make its decision applicable only to universities and not to businesses. Studies have found that how an affirmative action program is presented (Is it fair and just? Will it help or hinder productivity?) has a strong impact on whether people, majority- and minority-group members alike, favor it or oppose it (Blanchard & Crosby, 1989). Some blacks have opposed affirmative action programs because they fear it will lead to increased resentment among whites and self-doubt among blacks (Nacoste, 1989). But concerned researchers have argued that improved and strengthened affirmative action programs can be fair and effective in increasing equity in our society (Crosby & Blanchard, 1989).

Observers have argued that improved and strengthened affirmative action programs can be fair and effective ways to increase equity in our society.

OVERVIEW

I have suggested that equal-status contact may lead to attitude change, due to a combination of learning to understand group differences, the realization that ingroup and outgroup members' beliefs and values are often quite similar, decategorization, and rationalizations associated with counterattitudinal behavior. As a case in point, as gender-based restrictions in employment have diminished, equal-status contacts between men and women on the job have increased dramatically in recent years. With regard to race, however, the situation is more complex. Residential racial segregation is widespread and opportunities for racial equal- status contact are often limited. But such opportunities are increasing.

One way to approach the dilemma is to modify the institutions that foster intergroup separation and institutional discrimination (Pettigrew, 1986). If discriminatory aspects of societal institutions were changed, the racism or sexism associated with them might also change. But who is to do the changing? Individuals in the best positions to effect change are those who hold power within those institutions. Ironically, they might be those who are most blind to the ethnic bias or sexism in "their" institutions, having worked within the institutions for so long and having effectively rationalized their discriminatory behavior.

If far-reaching progress is to be made toward a truly egalitarian society, changes must take place on at least two fronts. At the individual level, attitudes, beliefs, and behavioral inclinations of Americans—both minority-

and majority-group members—must undergo major changes, perhaps through cooperative equal-status contact and educational programs. But intergroup contact alone is not a panacea. The broader cultural framework cannot be ignored. Repeated equal-status contact situations will only be possible in societies that have norms of tolerance and do not stress social categorization according to race or gender (Pettigrew, 1986). So institutional changes are necessary to create the atmosphere in which one-on-one contact situations can occur. Continued attention must be given to the ways in which society and its institutions contribute to the oppression of minority group members and measures must be taken to eliminate such societal barriers. Only then will it be possible for the concepts of equal opportunity and justice for all to become a reality in American society.

SUMMARY

Prejudice, racism, and sexism are supported by natural tendencies in the way we perceive people in groups. There is a generalized preference for one's own group and individuals assume that the outgroup is more homogeneous than the ingroup in attitudes and appearance. Biases in processing and remembering social information often provide false support for stereotypes and schemas (cognitive confirmation), or channel interactions in ways that seem to support behavioral expectations (behavioral confirmation). Prejudice is affected by the nature of group interactions, whether competitive or cooperative, and by perceived and actual group differences in beliefs and values. Social norms and conformity pressures may either increase or decrease prejudice. Authoritarian and dogmatic personality styles are often associated with prejudice.

Attempts to reduce prejudice via mass media messages have not been too successful, partially because of de facto selective exposure. The most powerful individual prejudice-reduction technique is cooperative equal-status contact between ingroup and outgroup members. When contact takes place under beneficial conditions, as demonstrated by the "railroad game" study, significant reductions in prejudice can occur. Unfortunately, much interracial contact in our society, especially school integration, has not taken place under these beneficial conditions. Studies of cooperative learning groups in schools provide encouraging examples of techniques for reducing the overall level of ethnic prejudice in our society.

PART FIVE

Applications

CHAPTER 12

The Impact of the Environment on Behavior

Unless man can make new and original adaptations to his environment as rapidly as his science can change the environment, our culture will perish.   Carl Rogers

People often complain of their environment: It is dull, colorless, or even hostile; and it never occurs to them to enliven it or rectify it rather than just endure it. A lamp doesn't complain because it must shine at night.   Antonin G. Sertillanges ❖

PREVIEW

Years ago Kurt Lewin (1951) pointed out that a person's behavior is determined both by internal characteristics, such as attitudes and personality, and by the social system in which the person exists. In Lewin's formulation, $B = f(P, E)$: Behavior is a function of the person and the environment. Most psychologists have focused their attention on factors within the person (P) such as attitudes, personality, needs, and abilities, and have paid relatively little attention to social system or environment (E) factors. However, in recent years increasing numbers of social scientists have turned their attention to factors in the psychological and physical environments. Of course, we've been dealing with those factors all along as we've analyzed situational influences on behavior. But in this chapter I will discuss research designed specifically to assess how several important aspects of the environment affect social behavior.

Three major features of our environment have caught researchers' attention: social density, the design of "built environments", and the effect of environmental stressors. Back in Chapter 1 I described social psychology's *interpersonal focus,* the analysis of individuals' behavior in terms of the social factors and social situations that people deal with. Up to now, we have looked at the effects of the presence of others in particular roles—as bystanders to an emergency, as romantic partners, as an audience, as aggressive models, and so forth. From an environmental psychology perspective, the presence of others can be analyzed in terms of social density—the number of people who are typically in a given area (e.g., a nation, a neighborhood, a dorm room, a prison). Social density can be studied as it affects individuals, such as students forced to share a small dorm room, or from the perspective of worldwide population demographics. We will examine the concepts of crowding, personal space, privacy, and territoriality as they relate to social density. After looking at the impact of social density, we will analyze the ways in which the design of "built environments" (dormitories, apartment complexes, airports, etc.) regulates patterns of social interactions (prosocial or antisocial) that are likely to occur. We will then turn our attention to environmental stressors, those facets of the environment that induce psychological stress, such as excessive noise and heat, insufficient light, and air pollution. I will analyze research on the effects of each of these stressors and will touch upon methods for combating their negative effects.

We are not just helpless pawns at the mercy of our environment. To a large extent we create our environment and people can take steps to improve theirs. I will take a social psychological look at attempts to change attitudes and behavior in two areas that can conserve the world's resources: energy conservation and fighting overpopulation. After reading this chapter you may have a better notion of how our environment affects us and, in turn, how we can change our environment in a positive way.

SOCIAL DENSITY

The Importance of Social Density

social density:
The number of people in a particular area.

The behavioral affects of **social density**, the number of people in a particular area, can be studied on many levels, ranging from the number of people sharing a bedroom to worldwide population trends. Initially I will review research on social density's effects on individuals' personal space, privacy needs, territoriality, perceptions of control, and feelings of crowdedness. Later on, we will see how living areas can be redesigned to minimize the negative effects of high social density. Toward the end of the chapter I will analyze high social density on a worldwide scope, briefly addressing the complex social and scientific issues involved in trying to control population at a national and international level.

An area of high social density. Areas of high social density often have higher levels of pathology (e.g., infant mortality, delinquency, sickness).

Social Density in Cities

It is not news to anyone that population has grown rapidly in recent years. Predictions are that in a few years our country will consist of about twenty-five large urban centers. For example, all of the area from Boston to Washington will be one large sprawling city (Figure 12-1); most of Florida and California will also be citylike (de Blij, 1981).

High population density can have a strong impact on human behavior. Working with census data from Chicago, Winsborough (1965) found that

FIGURE 12-1

Projected Megalopolitan Growth in the United States

It has been estimated that by the year 2000, over half of the approximately 270 million people in the United States will live and work in one of the four giant megapolitical regions (dark areas on the map): the Atlantic Seaboard (Boston–Washington) megapolis, the Lower Great Lakes (Chicago–Pittsburgh–Toronto) megapolis, the California megapolis, and the peninsular Florida megapolis.

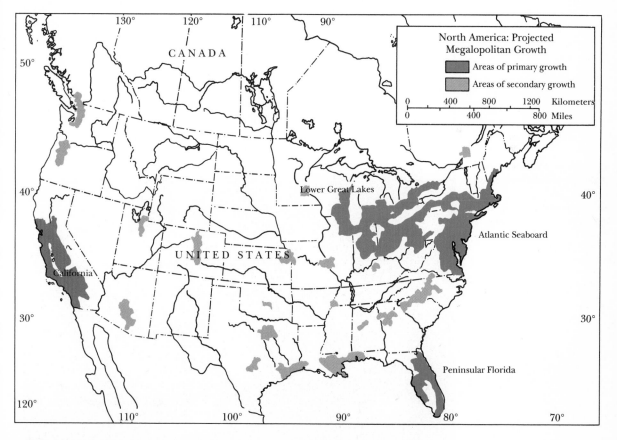

Source: From de Blij, H. J. (1981). *Geography: Regions and concepts* (3rd ed.). New York: Wiley. Copyright © 1971, 1978, 1981 by John Wiley & Sons, Inc. Reprinted by permission of John Wiley & Sons, Inc.

interpersonal density:
The number of people who live in the same room or building in a given area.

subjective crowding:
Feelings of excessive social demands and a lack of privacy stemming from high interpersonal density.

the more people there were in a given area, the greater the infant mortality, delinquency, sickness, and the more welfare systems were needed. Most important is how many people are forced to live in the same room or building in a given area—interpersonal density. Studies in large U.S. cities have indicated that high **interpersonal density** may be related to poor mental health, poor social relationships in the home, poor child care, poor physical health, and poor relationships outside the home (Gove et al., 1979). In fact, Gove and his co-workers concluded that measures of interpersonal density—number of persons per room—and of **subjective crowding**—feelings of excessive social demands and a lack of privacy—together had a stronger effect on the behaviors they measured than did the combined effects of race, gender, education, income, age, and marital status.

Another study involving census data from sixty-five nations, including the United States, found a relationship between interpersonal density and rates of homicide, even after controlling statistically for socioeconomic factors. A similar study in the United States, using data from over 650 cities, found that density of people per room was significantly related to rates of murder, assault, and rape (Booth, 1976). Hence, household density in large cities may be associated with high rates of violent crime, independent of socioeconomic factors. High density may not only increase the likelihood of being a victim of crime, but may also increase fear and anxiety about crime in one's neighborhood. A survey of several U.S. cities found that while not many city dwellers surveyed had been personally victimized by crime (under 6 percent), almost 50 percent expressed fear and anxiety about crime in their neighborhoods (Riger, 1985).

Do these people feel crowded? Although there is high interpersonal density, they may not feel crowded if their social needs are being met.

Although high social density is often associated with pathology, it is not always the case. Other situational factors can moderate its effect. For example, in a situation where the social norms encourage cooperative behavior and positive feelings (e.g., a party), negative effects of social density may not occur. Extremely low social density can have a negative impact too. If communities are built so that contact between residents is very difficult, loneliness and isolation can occur. There is some evidence that this happened in a planned community in Denmark named Albertslund, built in the mid-1960s. Many family disturbances occurred and, among couples who had no children, the suicide rate for wives far exceeded the national norm (Severy et al., 1976). The "right" number of people for any particular situation depends on the design of the environment and the kind of social interactions that are desired. Hence both high and low density can have an undesirable impact on a person's life.

Proxemics: The Social Use of Space

Personal Space

proxemics:
The manner in which people use space as a means of regulating social interactions.

personal space:
The area immediately around people's bodies that is treated as an extension of themselves.

Proxemics describes the manner in which people use space as a means of regulating social interactions (Sommer, 1969). People react to the area immediately around their bodies as though it were an extension of themselves. This **personal space** stays with us wherever we go and sometimes expands or contracts in different situations. Our space "bubble" can act as a buffer to maintain privacy and protect us from too much intimacy and too much stimulation. When one's personal space is violated, flight, discomfort, and negative impressions usually result. Personal space can also affect communications. Hall (1966) defined four distances at which Americans interact: *intimate distance,* 0 to 1 1/2 feet; *personal distance,* such as conversation between friends, 1 1/2 to 4 feet; *social distance,* for impersonal contact, 4 to 12 feet; and *public distance,* such as a speaker addressing an audience.

Very young children maintain very little personal space, but these boundaries expand with age until about age twenty-one (Hayduk, 1983). Sex differences also appear in late childhood: twelve-year-old boys stand farther apart than twelve-year-old girls and mixed-sex pairs stand farther apart than same-sex pairs (Severy et al., 1979). Research results also indicate that: (1) women have more tolerance for invasion of their personal space than men; (2) women stand closer to other women than men do to other men; (3) when men get as close to other men as they normally do to women, the men get upset, thinking the other man is pushy or homosexual; and (4) both men and women tend to stand closer to women than to men (Richmond-Abbott, 1983).

People who like each other tend to stand closer together if they are females (Heskha & Nelson, 1972) or if they are of the opposite sex (Haase & Pepper, 1972). For two males, however, friendship is not associated with reduced interpersonal distances, perhaps because of social taboos. Different ethnic groups may have different-sized personal space bubbles. Arab,

Greek, French, and Latin American persons prefer smaller interpersonal distances than do American, English, Swiss, or Swedish people (Hall, 1966; Sommer, 1969). Within the United States it appears that lower socioeconomic individuals have smaller interaction distances than do those of the middle class (Scherer, 1974). Individuals with a positive self-concept or low social anxiety approach others more closely than do those with negative self-concepts or high anxiety (Karabenick & Meisels, 1972). Further, extroverts keep closer distances that do introverts (Cook, 1970). These studies all suggest that individuals who feel more confident about their environment are more at ease when maintaining close distances with other individuals.

Invasion of Personal Space

People do not like their personal space invaded by others. They tend to move away and avoid eye contact with the invader (Patterson, 1976) or engage in defensive behaviors, such as hostile stares, verbal comments, shifts of body position, and the use of objects to create barriers (Altman & Vinsel, 1977). One study of prisoners showed that violent prisoners needed nearly three times as much area surrounding them as did nonviolent prisoners (Kinzel, 1970). The violent prisoners especially needed more space behind them than in front. The stranger who comes up too closely behind the violent individual may be in for an unpleasant surprise.

Invasion of personal space. Based on his backward lean, it appears that the man on the right feels that his personal space is being invaded by President Lyndon B. Johnson.

Privacy and Territoriality

Privacy is the degree to which individuals can control others' access to them and maintain a desired level of contact with others (Altman, 1975; Kelvin, 1973). If your attempts to regulate the amount of privacy you enjoy are ineffective, this will be unpleasant because you will feel a lack of control over your environment. Access to privacy is not just a luxury; in some situations it may have a major impact on one's well-being. For example, researchers have determined that lack of privacy may interfere with a hospital patient's ability to cope with the stress of disease or illness (Shumaker & Reizenstein, 1982). These researchers suggested that seats in hospital lounges should be movable so that various small group seating arrangements are possible. Curtains surrounding patients' beds should be available and visual access to patients by people in corridors should be limited by making it possible for doors to be kept closed.

Establishing territoriality

Territoriality refers to the behavior by which individuals lay claim to a particular area and defend it against members of their own species. For years ethologists have studied territoriality in animals, but the concept has only recently been studied with reference to human behavior. Population biologists suggest that the primary function of territoriality is to maintain a balance between population size and existing resources in an area (Wynne-Edwards, 1962). If population size exceeds the "carrying capacity" of the area, the survival of all group members is endangered by the scarcity of food, which may lead to mass starvation. When population size begins to increase, animals come in closer contact with each other and territorial infringements are more common, prompting more frequent displays of aggression. The fact that dominant animals have first access to territory, food, and sexual partners increases the likelihood that the strongest and most fit members of the animal community will survive, even during periods of extreme food shortages.

People have multiple territories, such as their homes, offices, and automobiles, some of which are extremely large, for example, one's nation. Many people personalize and demarcate their territories with a variety of social and cultural symbols. The purpose of territorial marking is to distinguish between insiders and outsiders. If you have ever owned a male dog, you know how he goes about marking territories he considers his. Fortunately, human beings do not resort to the same procedure, but make use of physical markers such as fences and symbolic markers such as signs to indicate particular territories. One study found that homeowners who used markers such as fences, hedges, and private property signs tended to have lived in their residence for a longer period of time than homeowners who did not use such indicators (Edney, 1972). The marker's effectiveness in regulating access to a territory ultimately depends on the user's power to defend the territory. A study of territorial behavior in a boys' rehabilitation center found that the most dominant boys maintained control of preferred areas such as the TV room (Sundstrom & Altman, 1974).

A primary function of human territoriality is the regulation of privacy. By establishing personal territory, individuals are able to regulate their contact with others. Humans' territorial distinctions are based on two factors: the degree of control the occupants have, and the relative duration of the user's claim to the space (Altman, 1975). **Primary territories** are those owned and used exclusively by individuals or groups, clearly identified as theirs by others, and controlled on a relatively permanent basis. They would include private property and some other territories, such as business offices, that may not actually be the legal property of the users. **Secondary territories** are only partially controlled by their users. Private clubs, neighborhood bars, and even stretches of a beach may be considered such by particular groups, and they figure prominently in the turf mentality of street gangs and underworld groups. Finally, **public territories** are those that everyone has free access to, at least theoretically. Parks, libraries, sidewalks, streets, and playgrounds are all public territories, although they may also be seen as secondary territories by particular groups.

Home Area Advantage

A sports stadium can be classed as a secondary territory (as seen by the hometown fans) or a public territory. The psychological edge of the home field advantage is well known in competitive sports. Most teams do better at home than away. They are more familiar with the idiosyncrasies of the home field or court, and the cheers of the home fans can be a powerful motivator. But the home area advantage is not limited to sports. In one study, male college students role-played prosecuting and defense attorneys and had to negotiate a jail sentence for a fictitious criminal; the debate took place in the room of one of the students. Results showed that the room's occupant tended to exert more influence on the negotiations, spent more time speaking, and argued more persuasively than the outsider did, so that the "home"

primary territories:
Territories owned and used exclusively by individuals or groups, clearly identified as theirs by others and controlled on a relatively permanent basis.

secondary territories:
Territories that are only partially controlled by their users, such as private clubs, neighborhood bars, and stretches of beach.

public territories:
Territories that everyone has free access to, at least theoretically.

negotiator won the debate 70 percent of the time (Martindale, 1971). This illustrates why attorneys prefer to use their own offices in negotiations with the opposition and also explains why it often takes so long for international negotiators to agree on a site for treaty negotiations.

Once the location of a group meeting is established, the physical arrangements of the meeting place can affect what happens in the group. The Paris peace negotiations in the early 1970s concerning ending American involvement in the Vietnam War were held up for months while negotiators tried to decide on an appropriate shape for the negotiating table. Most people's immediate reaction to this apparent nonsense was to wonder why there was so much fuss about it. What difference could it possibly make if the table was rectangular, circular, square, hexagonal, or whatever? But it well might make a difference: research indicates that seating arrangements can affect social influence (Sommer, 1969). People who sit at the head of a rectangular table usually exert more influence than those sitting at the sides. This does not mean that the negotiators were aware of the psychological research. The initial negotiations probably concerned status—creating the image of a tough bargainer (Chapter 6) and, perhaps, an intuitive application of the foot-in-the-door technique—gaining a trivial concession from the other side early in the negotiations might make it easier to gain other concessions later on.

If you are in a high-status position and want to dominate a conversation, you would do best to choose a square or rectangular table with yourself at the head. In fact, one study of jury deliberations found that jurors from professional or managerial backgrounds (high-status persons) usually took the head seat at the jury table (Strodtbeck & Hook, 1961). If you have high status and want to ease group conversation, you would be wise to use a round table. Legend has it that King Arthur chose a round table because he didn't want status distinctions to affect the meetings of his knights, and this lesson has not been lost on contemporary leaders and their spouses. Mamie Eisenhower enjoyed the role of First Lady and relished the status that the position afforded. Consequently, she used rectangular tables in the White House dining room, with herself and President Eisenhower at the heads. Jacqueline Kennedy, who wanted a more egalitarian atmosphere during dining and more relaxed conversations, moved the rectangular tables out and brought round ones in.

Crowding

The Effect of Crowding on Animals

The best-known animal study of high social density and social pathology was carried out by John Calhoun (1962). Calhoun took an enclosure designed to support forty-eight rats comfortably and allowed the population to grow to eighty rats; after that the young were removed to retain a stable population of eighty. Calhoun structured the habitat to create higher population density in the middle two pens. He deliberately made eating a difficult pro-

behavioral sinks:
Calhoun's term for extreme behavioral disturbances that developed in very overcrowded rat pens.

cess that occurred in areas where rats were likely to meet other rats. Within a year, the rats developed **behavioral sinks** in the two middle pens—Calhoun's term for extreme behavioral disturbances. Many females were not able to perform maternal functions. The males developed abnormal sexual behavior, cannibalism, and severe withdrawal. Infant mortality was abnormally high.

Because of the odd environment he created, Calhoun's study should be interpreted cautiously. With other cage and feeding arrangements, groups of mice bred under standing-room-only conditions have not had major problems (Holahan, 1982). Nevertheless, findings from other animal studies have indicated that high social density can cause abnormalities in physiological functioning involving the adrenal glands, brain, and reproductive processes (Christian, 1975), and can have negative social and behavioral effects, including social disorganization, aggression, learning decrements, and reduced exploratory behavior (Goeckner et al., 1973; Holahan, 1982).

In another animal study on the effects of crowding, Marsden (1972) allowed the mouse population to grow without limits in an environment suited for about 150 adult mice. The mouse population grew to about 2,200, then it began to decline. As the population grew, more and more animals deviated strongly from how a normal mouse should behave. Some females behaved very aggressively and many male mice withdrew and did not participate in sex or compete for territory. Regular mating behavior disappeared and four years and 3 months after the colony began, the last mouse died.

Marsden suggested that many of the factors paralleled those proposed by Toffler (1970) in his provocative book, *Future Shock*. Toffler argued that new behavioral types were emerging in society with terrifying speed. The social dynamics that Toffler described seem to parallel the events observed by Calhoun and Marsden at many points: the acceleration of change, the increasing diversity of types, and the sudden emergence and dropping out of behaviors. This change and increase in diversity could be indicative of a new creative phase in humanity's history, or, if carried too far too fast, might result in mass future shock, social withdrawal, and pathology (Esser, 1972).

The Experience of Crowding in Humans

When do you feel crowded? Some have argued that crowding is in direct proportion to social density, the number of people within a given area (Freedman, 1975). Others have suggested that crowding induces psychological stress (Epstein, 1981), perhaps caused by heightened arousal resulting from the invasion of personal space, which often occurs with high density (Loo, 1977).

two-factor theory of crowding:
The experience of crowding results from arousal caused by violation of personal space that is attributed to the presence of others.

When the distance between persons (interaction distance) is small, one's personal space is likely to be violated. Worchel and Teddlie's (1976) **two-factor theory of crowding** asserted that feeling crowded results from feeling aroused (from the violation of personal space) and a causal attribution that the arousal is caused by the other people in the situation. Worchel and Teddlie found that men whose personal space had been violated felt more crowded and uncomfortable, estimated that the experiment lasted longer, performed more poorly on a task, were more punitive, and attributed more nervous-

FIGURE 12-2

The Rise and Fall of a
Mouse Colony

*Number of mice living in an
enclosure designed for 150
adult mice, when allowed to
breed without limits.*

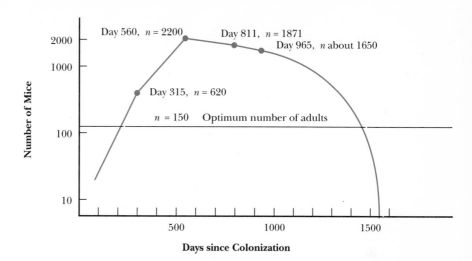

Source: Based on Marsden, H. M. (1972). Crowding and animal behavior. In J. F. Wohlwill &
D. F. Carson (Eds.), *Environment and the social sciences: Perspectives and applications.* Washington,
D. C.: American Psychological Association. Copyright 1972 by the American Psychological
Association. Reprinted by permission of the publisher.

ness and aggressiveness to other group members than did men whose personal space had not been violated. This confirms the arousal portion of the two-factor theory of crowding.

Subsequently, Worchel and Yohai (1979) tested the attribution portion of the two-factor theory. They predicted that people whose personal space had been violated would not feel crowded if they were led to misattribute the source of their arousal to some other factor. Groups of five men worked in crowded conditions and were informed that an inaudible noise causing arousal and stress would be played into the room. Other groups were told that the noise would have a relaxing effect. Actually, there was no noise. As predicted, the men who were led to misattribute their arousal to the noise did not feel crowded (Figure 12-3). Other researchers (Gochman & Keating, 1980) found that students who did not obtain their desired courses during registration felt that the registration room was more crowded than did students who received their desired courses. They proposed that perhaps the students who did not get their desired courses became aroused and attributed this arousal to the crowded conditions.

Crowding and Personal Control

The negative consequences of crowding may also be related to the limitations that high social and spatial density impose on people's freedom. Proshansky et al. (1976) argued that crowding occurs when the number of people in a setting restricts an individual's freedom of choice, as when a noisy

FIGURE 12-3

Attributions and Feelings
of Crowdedness

*Mean scores for how crowded
subjects felt depending upon
personal space violations (interpersonal distance) and the
explanation they were given for
noise that was supposedly
present. Having an explanation for arousal occurring at
close interpersonal distance
reduced feelings of crowdedness and confinement.*

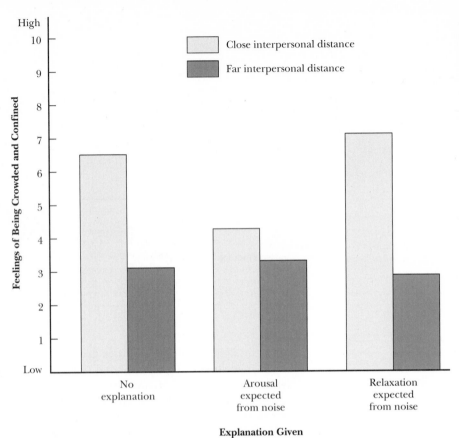

Source: Data from Worchel, S., & Yohai, S. M. L. (1979). The role of attribution in the experience
of crowding. *Journal of Experimental Social Psychology, 15,* 91–104.

conversation makes it impossible to study, or rush-hour traffic makes it impossible to reach an important appointment on time. Recall the theory of
psychological reactance (Chapter 5): When people's freedom of action is threatened they will take steps to restore it. Later we will analyze ways in which
spatial arrangements in group living situations (e.g., dorms, prisons) affect
individuals' freedom to control their interactions.

The concept of *privacy* is crucial here. An individual's effort to achieve
a desired level of privacy is central to the social processes of territoriality,
personal space, and crowding (Altman, 1975). We feel crowded when we experience more contact than we desire. When density interferes with our goal-
directed behavior, we experience crowding stress. Crowding may produce
unwanted social inputs such as conversation from others and interference

with desired goals, making a person feel stressed, aroused, and irritable toward others. In order to cope with this factor, the person may withdraw or intensify his attention on the tasks at hand.

Either the structure of the environment or the presence of too many people can interfere with one's behavioral flexibility. We can distinguish between **personal thwartings** — interference from another person that is seen as deliberately directed against oneself — and **neutral thwartings** — interference from an environmental setting (Stokols, 1976). In general, personal thwartings are more likely to occur in situations involving high social density, and neutral thwartings are more likely with high spatial density. For example, consider the residents of an old, cramped dorm. The situational annoyances will remain neutral thwartings as long as they are attributed to the physical environment, such as poor architectural design. However, if there is social strife between the dorm residents, then these same inconveniences may be perceived as personal thwartings, increasing the individuals' desire to obtain more space as a means of protecting their physical and emotional security. In Stokols' terms, neutral crowding has turned into personal crowding.

A combination of these social and spatial factors was studied in several high-density urban neighborhoods (Fleming et al., 1987). The highest stress levels were found in the neighborhoods that also contained commercial establishments. These businesses caused increased crowding within relatively small spaces, leaving residents of the area with less perceived personal control and privacy and more feelings of crowding and stress. In this situation, the structure and the people within this environment both contributed to psychological feelings of crowdedness.

The negative psychological consequences of high density can be reduced by enhancing people's feeling of personal control. One study found that shoppers who were informed beforehand that the crowded situation might cause them to feel aroused or anxious dealt better with a crowded store than shoppers who were not forewarned (Langer & Saegart, 1977). Another study, this time with students, showed that perceived crowding in both laboratory and field study settings was related to perceived control. Subjects who felt in a high-control position felt less crowded than those in a low-control position (Rodin et al., 1978). Studies of the male inmates of two prisons in Georgia examined the perceived control that inmates had. The prisoners' who felt less control reported more negative physical symptoms and stress (Ruback et al., 1986). Inmates who had been in prison for a longer period of time reported more control than the prisoners who had not been there as long.

The inability to control environmental stressors can also result in learned helplessness. For example, students who were unable to exert behavioral control over the nature, frequency, and duration of social contacts in their dormitories demonstrated the symptoms of learned helplessness (Baum & Valins, 1977). They were less likely than residents who had high control to exercise a choice over the experimental condition in which they

personal thwartings:
Interference from another person that is seen as deliberately directed against oneself.

neutral thwartings:
Interference from an environmental setting.

would participate and were more likely to show withdrawal responses in a laboratory social game. A follow-up study (Baum et al., 1978) demonstrated that the learned helplessness responses of students in the low-control environment became more pronounced as the length of residence in the crowded dormitory increased.

A study of black six- to nine-year-old boys who lived in a low-income housing project provided more evidence of this phenomenon. Rodin (1976) reasoned that increases in inside social density would lead to reduced personal control in one's home. One group of youngsters was asked to solve a problem that was solvable; the other group was given a problem that was unsolvable (a condition that can induce learned helplessness). Both groups were then asked to solve a second problem that was solvable. When the first problem had been solvable, correct solutions to the second problem were alike for youngsters from high- and low-density residential environments. However, when the first problem had been unsolvable, the youngsters from the high-density environments performed more poorly on the second problem than youngsters from the low-density environments, suggesting a pattern of learned helplessness.

Whether or not crowding has a negative effect depends partially on whether the people crowded together are compatible or incompatible. Smith and Haythorn (1972) observed Navy personnel in a simulated undersea laboratory. Those subjects who were incompatible with others withdrew from interaction, but those who were compatible sought group recreational activities such as card playing more often than a control group that did not experience crowding. A person in a roomful of strangers will feel more crowded than when in a room full of friends (Kamal & Mehta, 1987).

The effects of residential crowding may be different across cultures. While a study of crowded residential living in Chicago showed that the higher the density, the greater the pathology (Galle et al., 1972), a study in the Netherlands showed the reverse relationship (Levy & Herzog, 1974), and a study of residential crowding in Hong Kong (perhaps as crowded a residential setting as can be found anywhere) revealed no overall adverse effects of high-density living (Mitchell, 1971). Laboratory studies indicate that personality characteristics such as personal space preferences (Aiello et al., 1977) or locus of control (McCallum et al., 1979) may affect people's reactions to crowding.

Stimulus Overload

stimulus overload:
Inability of a system to process inputs from the environment because they are too numerous to cope with or because they arrive so rapidly that one cannot be processed before the next arrives.

Another factor often associated with crowding is **stimulus overload**. As noted in Chapter 7, overload refers to the inability of a system (such as a person) to process inputs from the environment because they are too numerous to cope with or because they arrive so rapidly that one cannot be processed before the next arrives. In our increasingly crowded world, contacts with other people can be overwhelming. An individual working in a New York suburb might encounter 11,000 people in a ten-minute walk from her office, while an individual working in midtown Manhattan might meet 220,000 people within the same radius of the office (Milgram, 1970). In order to adapt to overload, a person can give less time to each input or interaction; disregard low-priority inputs, reserving time and energy for interactions perceived as important; and utilize "social-screening" devices, such as unlisted phone numbers or an unfriendly expression, that discourage others from initiating contact.

Research has shown that students in high-density dorm settings who used screening as a coping style were more successful in adapting to the crowded environment (Baum et al., 1982). As noted in our analysis of emergency helping, the ultimate adaptation to an overloaded social environment may be to disregard the needs, interests, and demands of those people not seen as relevant to one's own personal need satisfaction, even if they desperately need help.

Explanations of Crowding Effects

To summarize, the effects of crowding on human behavior can be explained by: (1) invasion of personal space and the attribution that the stressed feelings are caused by the presence of others; (2) behavioral constraint, invasion of privacy, and restricted freedom of choice; (3) perceived lack of personal control; and (4) stimulus overload. These positions are briefly summarized in Table 12-1.

TABLE 12-1   SUMMARY OF THEORETICAL PERSPECTIVES ON CROWDING IN HUMANS

Theoretical Perspectives	Critical Antecedents of Crowding	Emotional Concomitants	Primary Adaptive Processes
Attributional	Arousal due to violations of personal space	Attribution that the arousal is caused by the presence of others	Perform poorly on tasks; aggression or nervousness
Behavioral Constraint	Reduced behavioral freedom	Psychological reactance, infringement	Leave situation or improve coordination and relations with others
Personal Control	Feelings of lack of control	Learned helplessness	Stop trying to control apparently uncontrollable stimuli; give up
Stimulus Overload	Excessive stimulation	Confusion, fatigue	Escape stimulation; behavioral or psychological withdrawal; architectural intervention

Source: Stokols, D. (1976). The experience of crowding in many primary and secondary environments. *Environment and Behavior. 8,* 61. Copyright © 1976 by Sage Publications, Inc. Reprinted by permission of Sage Publications, Inc.

Conditions at stimulus overload. It would be impossible for any of these people to interact with all of the others that they meet on the street.

HOW DESIGN AFFECTS SOCIAL INTERACTIONS

The Person-Environment Fit

person-environment fit:

The person-environment fit is good when the structure of the physical environment permits people to achieve the social, cognitive, and behavioral goals that they wish to.

built environment:

The part of the environment that is man made, such as, dorms, houses, and airports.

Upon the reopening of the British House of Commons after its destruction in World War II, Winston Churchill commented, "We shape our buildings and afterwards our buildings shape us" (Michelson, 1970). An architect later suggested that stress results from a misfit between individual needs and environmental attributes (Zimring, 1981). An individual in any situation has a wide range of social, cognitive, and behavioral goals: intimacy or separation, privacy or interaction, task achievement or socializing, and so forth. The design of the physical environment affects the **person-environment fit**, the match between the individual's goals and the types of interactions permitted or encouraged by the design of the environment. It may indirectly influence the person-environment fit by making desired social interactions easier or more difficult to achieve. In addition, the design of the environment affects the coping processes used to resolve problems. One aspect of the **built environment** that affects psychological factors is the layout of group living areas: dorms, barracks, prisons, apartment buildings. These areas can be designed to encourage or discourage interactions among the residents. The quantity and quality of possible social interactions, and the degree to which residents can control them, are strongly related to personal space, privacy, and perceived crowding.

The Design of Multiple-Dwelling Buildings

A good example of the impact of design on usage is the Pruitt-Igoe housing project built in 1954 in St. Louis, Missouri. The complex consisted of forty-three modern eleven-story high-rise apartment buildings containing almost

The Death of Pruitt-Igoe The "person-environment fit" was poor in the Pruitt-Igoe housing project in St. Louis. The project did not fit the needs of the tenants; there was too much "indefensible territory" and too little chance for a sense of community to develop among the tenants. Less than twenty years after its construction the project had to be torn down; it had been so heavily vandalized it was no longer livable.

three thousand apartments and housing nearly twelve thousand people on fifty-seven acres of land. Each apartment had modern facilities and each family was assured ample living space (low inside density). Yet by the 1960s the housing project was in utter disarray and in 1972 demolition of the entire project began.

Several studies indicated that the housing complex, although well designed architecturally, did not fit the needs of the tenants; the person-environment fit was poor. The way the apartments were designed made informal socializing impossible because there were no common terraces, porches, recreation rooms, lobbies, or public spaces, thus preventing the development of any sense of community, which might have motivated the residents to take good care of their surroundings. Tenants were upset because building design did not foster interactions among neighbors and because they could not supervise their children once the children were out of the apartments (Yancey, 1971). There was also too much "indefensible territory" in the project, such as stairwells, elevators, and alleyways, which could not be adequately patrolled and were not open to visual inspection—it was impossible to see who lurked there (Newman, 1972). The sheer size of the complex led to feelings of a lack of control over the environment, which may inhibit people from attempting to improve their environment. The example of Pruitt-Igoe shows that people need structures that simultaneously encourage social relations and allow privacy (Table 12-2).

More recently, designers of public developments have tried to add fences to create individual front yards, provide more attractive lighting, and give residents a sense of ownership or control over their living areas. These factors seem to increase the residents' liking for the projects and to decrease vandalism somewhat (Rubin, 1981).

The Use of Inside Space

Dormitories

Given the same outside dimensions of a building, dormitories can be designed so that many people sleep together in large rooms, or separately in small rooms along long corridors, or in a small number of bedrooms formed around a common lounge or suite. Living in an open dormitory is likely to be anxiety-producing and leads to less feeling of control over one's environment (Knight et al., 1978; D'Atri, 1975).

Some architectural arrangements can make social interactions more common or frequent than the occupants desire. Traditional corridor-style dormitories may have such a drawback (Reichner, 1979). Research has suggested that corridor-style dormitories promote excessive levels of unwanted social interaction among some residents, whereas suite-style dormitories do not. In college dormitories with more public, open space the crime rates were found to be higher than those dormitories with more private, defensible areas (Sommer, 1987). There was one incidence of crime for every five occupants of the large halls as opposed to one crime for every twenty-five occupants in the smaller dorms. Subjects in such smaller "cluster" halls were also more satisfied with their living arrangements and rated the atmosphere around the dorm as friendly and sociable. Overall social interaction was found to be much more favorable in the small dorm condition than in the large "high-rise" type dormitory.

In study after study, Baum and his colleagues (e.g., Baum & Gatchel, 1981) found that people living in long-corridor dorms feel more crowded and forced into unwanted interactions with others. Baum and Davis (1980) were able to institute a simple change that had a considerable impact. They divided one floor of a long-corridor women's dorm into two short-corridor sections by installing unlocked doors in the middle of the floor. For comparison, the floor just above was left undivided. After ten weeks, those living on the divided corridor were more likely to leave their door open (presumably signaling their willingness to interact) than residents of the long-corridor floor. They also reported making more friends and were less likely to view dorm life as hectic, crowded, and uncontrollable. Residents of the long-corridor floor reported more crowding and residential social problems as time passed, whereas divided-corridor residents reported fewer of these problems.

Let us suppose that three college students are assigned as roommates to a dorm room designed for two persons. Because inside social density is relatively high, interaction distance and personal spaces are small and the roommates are likely to feel being crowded. In 1974 during a housing shortage, one of the colleges at Rutgers University randomly assigned freshmen to small dorm rooms that were designed for double occupancy. The students were assigned by lottery—some were tripled, three to a room, others were doubled.

Researchers (Karlin et al., 1978) found that freshmen who were tripled into rooms designed for two people had more difficulties than those who were doubled; their grade point averages were lower and they were less satisfied with their living conditions than were doubled students. Tripled students who had the most experience with crowded conditions in their precollege days adjusted relatively well to tripling. Fortunately for the students, the tripling situation lasted a year or less. A follow-up study (Karlin et al., 1979) found that the negative effects of tripling as a freshman apparently had disappeared by the students' junior year.

TABLE 12-2   THE STRUCTURE OF THE "BUILT ENVIRONMENT"
AFFECTS PSYCHOLOGICAL INTERACTIONS AND
WELL-BEING

Desirable Aspects of the Outside "Built Environment"	Reason
Permits moderate levels of socialization	Otherwise, too much socialization opportunity can lead to feelings of crowding and lack of control; too little can lead to isolation and loneliness
Allows privacy to be maintained	Permits people to regulate the level of interactions they prefer, in order to feel in control of their environment.
Does not have much "indefensible territory"	Indefensible territories (stairwells, alleyways) cannot be easily patrolled or controlled (e.g., Pruitt-Igoe).
Encourages feelings of ownership or control	Increases liking for surroundings, may decrease vandalism.
Low to moderate outside density	High outside density increases feelings of crowding, lack of control, and environmental stressors such as excessive noise.

A suite-style dorm permits greater control of interactions than a corridor-style dorm does.

Why should tripling have such a negative effect, at least for a year? The two-factor theory of crowding suggests that high density should lead to feelings of crowding if a student attributes the negative arousal associated with high density to the fact that he has two roommates. Karlin and his associates suggested that such attributions are likely due to the tripled students' greater difficulty in obtaining desired goals, which in a college dorm probably include studying, relaxation, and positive social interactions.

Three-roommate situations also create a tricky social environment. Between-roommate relationships are unstable and often two of the roommates become better friends (forming a coalition) while the third feels left out. Baum and his co-workers (1979) found that this coalition/isolation developed in 80 percent of the tripled groups they studied over a two-year period. Most of the negative effects of tripling (withdrawal and perceived loss of control) were felt by the "isolate"— the roommate who most often felt left out. The other two roommates did not differ from doubled roommates in perceived loss of control or in other reported problems associated with crowding. Hence, although loss of personal control and withdrawal are often associated with crowding, they may also be attributable to adjustment difficulties within the small group. Tripled roommates had the worst of both worlds: crowdedness and a very difficult social situation.

A crowded dorm room can have a variety of undesirable effects. A meta-analysis of ten studies of tripled roommates at seven universities across the country (Mullen & Felleman, 1990) found that tripling had a negative impact on roommates on several broad areas: affect (general satisfaction), social relationships between roommates, residential perceptions (feelings of crowdedness, satisfaction with the room), and general well-being (estimated by GPA and visits to the student health center). The latter effects were somewhat weaker than the others, but Mullen and Felleman (1990) noted that it was intriguing that tripling had any impact at all on grades or on general health, since they are likely to be influenced by so many other factors such as study habits, diet, course load, and intellectual ability. Men showed larger negative reactions to tripling than women did, reflecting the more general finding that men generally have more adverse reactions to crowding than do women (Epstein & Karlin, 1975).

Even the arrangement of furniture in a room can affect behavior. In a study of a geriatric ward, Osmond (1957) found that furniture arrangement could encourage the development of stable interpersonal relationships, or could separate people and reduce social interaction. Another analysis of a geriatric ward (Sommer & Ross, 1958) showed a similar impact of furniture arrangement. The new furniture had been lined up in long straight rows, so that patients sat shoulder-to-shoulder and back-to-back. Little interaction between the patients occurred. The investigators regrouped the furniture so that four chairs were grouped around small tables. After a few weeks, interaction among the patients had nearly doubled. As further evidence, studies have shown that the location of lounges in university psychology departments substantially affected the quality of the interactions that occurred there (Campbell & Campbell, 1988). The layout of a school playground can significantly affect the type of interactions (cooperative play, fighting, or isolation) that take place (Weinstein & Pinciotti, 1988).

Public Spaces

Sommer (1974) studied the way space is utilized in airports. He noted that most airports were laid out in a manner that discourages or prohibits social interaction between waiting passengers. Such a design may be appropriate for people with a desire for privacy, but not for those who wish to interact with others or who would like to wait in a reassuring and comfortable environment. Sommer pointed out that the typical airport terminal atmosphere did nothing to calm people who may have latent fears about flying because it promoted a sense of loneliness and alienation that would probably intensify their discomfort. Recall Schachter's (1959) work (Chapter 3) showing that fearful people have a greater desire to affiliate with others. The lone business-person may easily adapt to the isolating arrangements, but fearful or gregarious individuals who wish to talk to one another are discouraged from doing so. The only place where one could find chairs not bolted to the floor and lined up in such an antiseptic fashion, Sommer noted, was in the special lounges and club facilities available only to corporation executives and others who can afford luxury. The rest of us simply have to suffer. Sommer commented that the only place where the passenger is (sometimes) made to feel a valued individual is inside the plane itself.

The "friendliness" of the built environment and the degree of social interaction it permits also can affect employee satisfaction on the job. Improving communications can be "good business" within a company by providing a comfortable work atmosphere among the employees. A study by Campbell and Campbell (1988) examined the relationship between environmental supports, spatial organization, and what they called "informal communication," defined as the interaction of employees during the day at times when they did not have to be working (such as lunch or break periods). The researchers made informal communication easier in some situations by varying the lounge locations and what they contained (food, beverages, and aesthetics). They found that the features of the lounge positively affected the amount of lounge use and the degree of interpersonal relations within the lounge setting. People were more likely to visit an attractive lounge, thus permitting more person-to-person contact.

Dormitories, airports, and businesses are not the only situations where crowding may be a problem. Studies in prisons have shown that overcrowding is associated with increased rate of suicides, higher blood pressure, more psychiatric commitments, more reported illnesses, more disciplinary infractions, and a higher death rate (Cox et al., 1984; Paulus et al., 1985). Social interactions in overcrowded prisons, as in overcrowded dorms, allow less control over one's interactions, and permit more unwanted social contact, goal interference, and cognitive overload, leading to cognitive strain, anxiety and fear, frustration, and bodily stress reactions such as high blood pressure and adrenal gland overactivity (Schaeffer et al., 1988).

THE IMPACT OF ENVIRONMENTAL STRESSORS

environmental stressors:
Those facets of the environment that induce stress, such as excessive social density, noise, heat, and air pollution.

Environmental stressors are aspects of the environment that may cause stress or pathology in people exposed to them. The impact of a stressor depends on its excessiveness, its controllability, the personal goals with which it may interfere (e.g., relaxation), and any rewards that may be associated with it (Stokols, 1982). The person's ability to manage the stressor (personal coping skills) is important as well.

Excessive Noise

Noise can be defined as sound that is unpleasant and bothersome to the listener. Prolonged exposure to excessive noise can lead to permanent hear-

Excessive Noise Can Have a Detrimental Impact. Excessive environmental noise from nearby airports, factories, highways, or subways can have a powerful detrimental effect on people's well-being.

ing loss. At a psychological level, excessive noise has the strongest effects when it is uncontrollable and interferes with people's ability to communicate or to accomplish a task (such as studying). It is obvious that a task whose performance requires auditory communication will suffer under high-intensity noise, but noise may also interfere with the reception of subtle auditory feedback cues or with hearing one's own internal speech (Cohen & Weinstein, 1981). Noise that masks parent/child or teacher/child communication may be responsible for the poorer scholastic performance among children living or attending school in noisy neighborhoods. The decreased social interactions may be partly due to one's expectation that communication would be awkward and difficult under the noisy conditions (Appleyard & Lintel, 1972).

Many studies have found that excessive environmental noise (from nearby subways, highways, railroads, factories, airports) has a dramatic impact on children's well-being. Scientists studied schools in Los Angeles that were directly under the approach route to the L.A. International Airport, where there were over three hundred overflights a day, averaging one every two and a half minutes. Children in these noisy schools had higher blood pressure and were more likely to fail on a puzzle task than children from quieter schools (Cohen et al., 1980; Cohen & Weinstein, 1981). Many of the performance deficits continued even after the noisy schools had been insulated to reduce the noise. Studies of a New York school located only 220 feet from an elevated train track found that on the noisy side of the building, where classes were disrupted every four and a half minutes by a passing train, the children had reading scores three to four months behind those whose classes were on the quiet side of the building (Bronzaft & McCarthy, 1975). It is interesting to note that the L.A. airport noise affected children's test performance in much the same way that residential crowding did in Rodin's (1976) study. Both stressors made the children act more helpless on laboratory tests than children not subjected to those stressors.

People are not as responsive to others' needs when they are overloaded with loud noise or other urban stressors. A number of studies have demonstrated that helpfulness decreases as noise increases. In one laboratory study, subjects who had worked on tasks while overloaded with loud noise were less helpful to a fellow student's request for assistance at the conclusion of the experiment than were other subjects (Sherrod & Downs, 1974). Persons who had been overloaded with simultaneous auditory and visual tasks were less responsive to a staged accident victim than were less overloaded people who were not working on the two tasks simultaneously (Weiner, 1976). Similarly, pedestrians were less likely to help a passerby pick up dropped packages or to provide change for the telephone if these incidents took place immediately adjacent to a noisy jackhammer rather than on a quieter part of the street (Page, 1977) . Another field study (Matthews & Cannon, 1975) found that people were more likely to help a person wearing a wrist-to-shoulder cast who dropped a box loaded with books when a nearby power mower was turned off than when it was running full blast without a muffler (Figure 12-4).

Because stimulus overload may lead people to narrow their attentional focus, they may simply be unaware of the social cues that signal that help is needed (Broadbent, 1978). Excessive stimulation demands extra attentional capacity and as a result, our remaining attention is temporarily reduced so that we may not be responsive to inputs encountered just after exposure to stress. You may have had the experience of driving blithely down the super-highway with music blaring; yet when your exit comes up and you have to pull off into heavy street traffic, you turn the music down. The reason may be that you need more attentional capacity than before to handle the additional inputs and decisions required by stop-and-go street traffic.

Perceived lack of control and unpredictability increase the negative impact of noise (Gardner, 1978). Individuals perform better on tasks when

FIGURE 12-4

Noise and Helping

Amount of helping as a function of noise level and of whether the person needing help was wearing a cast. When the power mower was off (Soft Noise), people were more helpful to the person wearing a cast than to the person not wearing a cast. When the mower was running without a muffler (Loud Noise), people tended to be equally unhelpful whether or not the person needing help was wearing a cast.

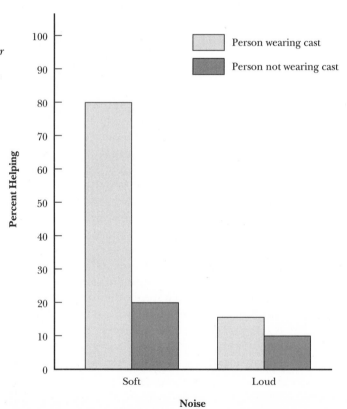

Source: Data from Mathews, K. E., & Canon, L. K. (1975). Environmental noise level as a determinant of helping behavior. *Journal of Personality and Social Psychology, 32,* 571–577.

they think they can control the onset of noise, even if they never test this control (Glass & Singer, 1972). Not only does perceived control alleviate the effects of noise, but the more control people think they have, the better they will do on post-noise tasks, even though the control was not exercised (Sherrod et al., 1977). Noise may make angry people more aggressive, but perceived control reduces this effect (Donnerstein & Wilson, 1976; Geen, 1978).

Although noise has been found to impair learning, increase apathy, and create stress, people who are accustomed to a noisy environment sometimes perform better in a noisy environment than a quieter one. When children were distracted by noise while being tested, the ones who were from noisy households performed better than the children from quiet homes (Heft, 1979). Noise during learning can have a significant effect on free recall, yet noise during recall itself does not seem to affect performance (Bell et al., 1984).

Excessive Heat

> I pray thee, good Mercutio, let's retire;
> The day is hot, the Capulets abroad,
> And, if we meet, we shall not 'scape a brawl,
> For now, these hot days, is the mad blood stirring.
>
> —Shakespeare, *Romeo and Juliet*

Another important environmental stressor is excessive heat. Hippocrates, comparing civilized ancient Greece to the savagery in central Europe, believed that the savagery was due to Europe's harsher climate. Later, the British based their belief in their superior culture partly on England's "ideal climate." Interest in the role of heat grew during the late 1960s when racial riots occurred in many places during summer in the United States, and the phrase "the long, hot summer" took on a new meaning. The U.S. Riot Commission (Kerner et al., 1968) noted that all but one of the riots studied began on days when the temperature was at least 80°F (27°C). There were also reports from police that crime seemed to go up with the temperature. In light of these summertime riots, it seemed reasonable to assume that heat made people both irritable and aggressive, increasing the chances that a riot would break out.

What do the data tell us? The answer depends, in part, on whether one looks at experimental laboratory research or at actual rates of violent crime. Some laboratory research (Baron & Ransberger, 1978; Bell, 1981) found a curvilinear relationship between aggression and temperature. Up to a point, higher temperatures were associated with greater aggression, but in very hot rooms (temperature in the mid-90s) aggression decreased. Baron and Ransberger (1978) suggested that perhaps heat intensifies aggression up to a certain point, but beyond that point people will be more interested in escaping the heat than in being aggressive.

Other researchers (Anderson & Anderson, 1984) suggested that maybe aggression was less in the unreasonably hot rooms because of subjects' suspicions that their possibly aggressive reactions to heat were being evaluated. Outside of the laboratory, the picture looks pretty clear—hotter temperatures are associated with increases in aggressive motives and tendencies. Hotter regions of the world yield more aggression, even within the same country. Hotter years, seasons, months, and days all yield relatively more aggressive behaviors such as murders, rapes, assaults, riots, and wife beatings (Anderson, 1989; Michael & Zumpe, 1986). Anderson and Anderson (1984) studied the rates of violent crime (criminal assault, murder, rape) in Chicago and in Houston (Figure 12-5). Not only was the overall rate of murder and rape highest on the hottest days (a), but so too was the *ratio* (b) of aggressive crimes (number of murders and rapes divided by the number of robberies and arson cases).

Data on seasonal differences in violent crimes are summarized in Figure 12-6, based on several studies conducted over the last one hundred years. Quite clearly, summer is the time for violence. But does this mean that hot temperatures, by themselves, cause violent behavior? That's a tough question to answer, in part because the field studies are correlational; and cause-and-effect information cannot be easily derived. For example, there are more daylight hours during warm months, and when the temperature rises in lower-income areas of the city, where residents are unlikely to have air conditioning, more people will go outside to avoid the oppressive heat in their homes. Hence, they will have more contact with one another, which could lead to aggression. Is there a theoretical explanation for how heat might cause aggressive behavior? Recall Zillmann's excitation-transfer theory outlined in Chapter 10 (see Figure 10-2). He proposed that people who are initially aroused by one source (e.g., excessive heat) may misattribute some of the arousal to another source (e.g., an aggression-producing stimulus) that becomes salient. Hence, excitation (or arousal) by excessive heat may add to the excitation associated with an aggression-producing stimulus that appears on the scene (a disliked person, a potential victim), increasing the likelihood of violent behavior. We also know that uncomfortable conditions by themselves prime aggressive thoughts (Berkowitz, 1984). It seems most likely that some combination of heat and group dynamics (all the people who turn out into the streets when their rooms get too hot) increases the likelihood of aggression and violent crimes. Recent research indicates that several other atmospheric conditions in addition to heat—humidity, wind, barometric pressure—also appear to be linked to violence in a causal fashion (Rotton & Frey, 1985).

Lack of Sufficient Light

Lack of light can also be a significant environmental stressor for some people. In Europe, for example, countries that have less sunshine have higher suicide rates (Thorson & Kasworm, 1984). Bright light has been used to treat

FIGURE 12-5

Crime and Temperature

(a) Aggressive crime (murder and rape) as a function of maximum ambient (outdoor) temperature in Houston, 1980–1982. (b) Aggressive crime ratio (number of murders and rapes divided by the number of robberies and arsons) as a function of maximum ambient temperature in Houston, 1980–1982.

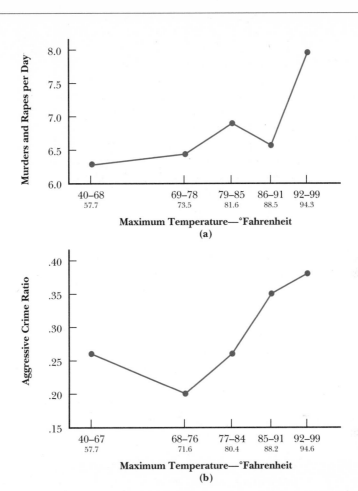

Source: Anderson, C. A., & Anderson, D. C. (1984). Ambient temperature and violent crime: Tests of the linear and curvilinear hypotheses. *Journal of Personality and Social Psychology, 46,* 95, 96. Copyright 1984 by the American Psychological Association. Reprinted by permission of the publisher and author.

seasonal affective disorder:

Severe depression associated with the lack of sunlight during the dark winter months.

individuals suffering from recurring winter depression known as **seasonal affective disorder** (SAD), severe depression associated with the lack of sunlight during the dark winter months. Experiments using "light therapy" (exposure to bright light for one to two hours a day) indicate that this treatment is effective in treating SAD (Byerly et al., 1987; Rosenthal et al., 1985). Many people respond best to treatment right after they wake up, although some do better with light in the evening (Terman & Link, 1989). Exposure to light does not affect other types of depression (Rosenthal et al., 1987).

Lighting level preferences in a room can vary depending upon the activity being done and who is present. Biner and co-workers (1989) had subjects complete visual attention tasks while in a room with a friend, a romantic

FIGURE 12-6

Quarterly and Seasonal
Distribution of Aggressive
Behavior

*Quarterly data are from
Anderson, 1987 (violent
crime), and Leffingwell, 1892
(murder and rape). Seasonal
data are from Lombroso,
1899/1911 (uprisings), Rotton
and Frey, 1985 [family disturbances and assualt (solid
line)], and Chang, 1972
[rape and assualt (diamonds)].*

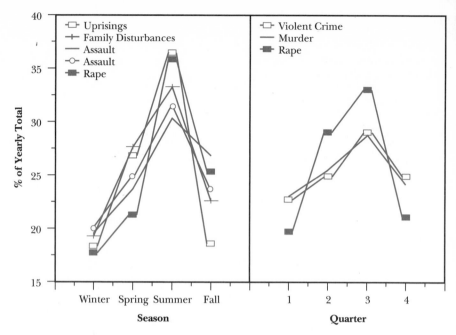

Source: From Anderson, C. A. (1989). Temperature and aggression. *Psychological Bulletin, 106,*
82. Copyright © 1989 by the American Psychological Association. Reprinted by permission.

partner, or a group of friends. No matter what the task, persons in a room
with a romantic partner preferred lower lighting levels. With the more complicated tasks, people in groups preferred lower lighting than when with a
single friend.

Air Pollution

The impact of air pollution on human behavior may be considerable, but
very little research has examined the relationship. In 1976, forty-three major cities, comprising over half the total U.S. population, had poor air quality (Evans & Jacobs, 1981). Two decades ago, scientists focusing on
respiratory-related health studies estimated that at least $200 million a year
would be saved in U.S. health costs if air quality were improved by 50 percent (Lave & Seskin, 1970).

Air pollution affects the amount of time we spend outdoors and the
extent of our physical activity. It may have a large influence on residential
decisions, recreation patterns, task performance, and interpersonal relationships (Evans & Jacobs, 1981) . Air pollution can also be a localized individual
problem, as when a nonsmoker's personal space is invaded by the fumes from

FOCUS 12-1

Negative Ions and Their Effect on Behavior

For thousands of years people have associated weather with human behaviors. For example, in Shakespeare's *King Lear*, the King's madness was accompanied by violent storms. While excessive heat has been the most widely studied weather condition, other types of weather may also be important. Several studies have suggested that the amount of positive and negative ions in the air can have an effect on a person's behavior (Baron, 1987). Various weather conditions such as lightning and wind cause molecules to separate, creating positive and negative ions. Atmospheric electricity, resulting from the concentration of ions in a specific area, has been correlated with higher rates of suicides, crime, and industrial accidents in certain areas (Muecher & Ungeheuer, 1961; Sulman et al., 1964).

To test these effects experimentally, experimenters have used ion generators that create varying amounts of atmospheric electricity. This research indicates that negative ions can be responsible for intensifying whatever dominant mood a person may have at that time. Baron, Russell, and Arms (1985) found a high level of negative ions increased the aggressiveness of people who were already aggressively inclined. They concluded that increased negative ions can only heighten the existing mood and not cause an individual to go from a calm disposition to an aroused state or vice versa.

Increased negative ion levels may also affect liking. Baron (1987) hypothesized that subjects who already liked someone (due to sharing similar opinions) would like them even more when in the presence of negative ions, while subjects who disliked someone (because they held dissimilar opinions) would act even more negatively toward the disliked person. As predicted, when negative ions were present, friendliness increased when the other person had similar opinions, and dislike increased for the other person with contrasting views.

Most people would not have expected that atmospheric electricity could have such distinct effects on our behavior. Nevertheless, some companies have begun using negative ion generators to try to indirectly increase employees' productivity by improving their attitudes while on the job. This could be a positive step in personnel management, yet companies must be aware of the fact that aggressive and negative moods could be increased as well. Although these experiments have had intriguing outcomes, much remains to be learned about atmospheric electricity, the psychological effects it creates, and its impact on human functioning. ❖

someone's cigarette. Researchers have found that nonsmokers feel more irritable, anxious, and fatigued when in close contact with cigarette smokers (J. Jones, 1978). Individuals sitting on a public bench are more likely to leave, and leave faster, when their personal space is invaded by a smoking adult than by a nonsmoking adult (Bleda & Bleda, 1978). Another study reported that exposure to cigarette smoking increased feelings of aggression in nonsmokers (J. Jones & Bogat, 1978).

Researchers have begun to study the effects of air pollution on various types of performance. Carbon monoxide is one air pollutant that has a consistent impact. When subjects are exposed to carbon monoxide in moderate levels while working on tasks that demand alert vigilance, performance suffers (Evans & Jacobs, 1981). People who feel less control over pollutants are likely to be more bothered by them, as is the case with other stressors (Baum et al., 1981). More generally, a study in Dayton, Ohio, found a significant relationship between levels of air pollution and number of psychiatric emergencies. With weather controlled for, when air pollution was high, more emergencies occurred (Rotton & Frey, 1984). While researchers studying the impact of pollution on health have concentrated mostly on drastic physical results such as death or disease, it is also important to examine social outcomes that may by affected by air quality, such as discomfort, irritability, learned helplessness, depression, and anxiety.

CHANGING THE ENVIRONMENT TO CONSERVE RESOURCES

The Commons Dilemma

commons dilemma:
When people recognize that available resources are becoming scarcer, they may "get while the getting is good" and devour as many of the remaining resources as possible.

In the late 1970s, President Carter asserted, "With the exception of preventing war, [energy conservation problems are] the greatest challenge our nation will face during our lifetime" (Becker & Seligman, 1981). Recently social psychologists have rediscovered the **commons dilemma** as a prototype of the conflict between individual gains and the common good. Hundreds of years ago many villages in England and New England had public pastures, the commons, where all citizens could freely graze their livestock. In such a setting, noncooperation with others (adding one's own livestock to the commons in large number) makes good sense at an individual level. Unfortunately, in many cases noncooperation between the villagers—all attempting to graze as many of their own animals in the commons as they could—led to overuse of the pasture, turning it into a muddy, barren field. This represents a *social trap,* if people recognize that available resources (such as the commons) are becoming scarcer, they may rush to "get while the getting is good" and devour as many of the remaining resources as possible. The remaining resources will be gobbled up at an ever-increasing rate until they are all gone: the commons dilemma repeated. The larger message is that uncontrolled population growth coupled with free access to natural resources may inevitably destroy the earth's resources (Hardin, 1968).

Ways of Solving the Commons Dilemma
There are two general types of nontechnical solutions to such social dilemmas (Messick & Brewer, 1983). One solution comes through coordinated, organized *group action,* such as the formation of regulatory agencies and other

FOCUS 12-2

Nuclear Power: A Psychological Stressor?

A new environmental stressor has arisen within the past fifty years—the potential hazards associated with nuclear power. Along with the advent of nuclear energy and its overwhelming capabilities comes the realization that our society could be in a great deal of danger if precautions are not taken to assure the safe operation of nuclear power. If we are not careful, there could be devastating effects like those that occurred in 1979 at the Three Mile Island nuclear power plant in Pennsylvania. Because of a loss of water in the reactor, two-thirds of the nuclear core was uncovered and a portion of that core melted, releasing radioactive gas into the atmosphere. A more recent tragedy was the Chernobyl nuclear accident in the Soviet Union in 1986. These occurrences reinforce many people's fear of the nuclear age and have created a growing tension in communities, especially those closest to the sites of the accidents.

Stress levels for individuals living in close proximity to Three Mile Island (TMI) when the accident occurred were significantly more severe than those people in communities farther away from TMI (Houts et al., 1988). Generally speaking, the degree of stress experienced by residents close to TMI resembled the magnitude of "daily hassles" stress, but this low-level stress persisted seventeen months after the accident (Baum et al., 1983). Stress measured three years after the accident remained higher than normal, thus showing a long-

lasting effect of the disaster. Not only was this distress reflected in fears of the nuclear plant, but the anxiety generalized to other situations as well (Houts et al., 1988).

The most effective way of reducing stress was to reappraise one's emotional states, creating new, less-threatening ways of viewing the situation. This coping method remained effective over a long period of time. People who used denial or problem-oriented modes of coping were less successful in reducing stress, presumably because the stress was chronic and its sources could not be controlled easily. If the stressor lasts for an exceedingly long time, denial can become increasingly difficult to maintain (Collins et al., 1983).

One way to handle anxiety about TMI would be to move away from the area. About 40 percent of the 1983 residents of Middletown, Pennsylvania, the closest town to TMI, had moved out of the area by late 1985. (The reactor was restarted in late 1985, despite widespread community opposition.) TMI-related worries were most related to feelings of loss of control among those who moved and to a loss of faith in nuclear power "experts" among those who stayed (Prince-Embury & Rooney, 1989). These findings indicate that fear caused by nuclear power can generate stress that affects individuals' life-style, mobility, physical condition, and feelings of helplessness within society. ❖

The Three Mile Island nuclear power plant in Pennsylvania.

The outcome of the "commons dilemma." A useless, over-grazed field may be the result when people compete to devour a limited shared resource, in this case, the public pasture.

applications of external control designed to restrict individual choices for the collective good. Studies show that when faced with an overused resource that may become depleted, most people vote to elect a leader and restrict everyone's free access to the resource. In the researchers' words, "Our sub-jects seem to make the sensible choice that regulation is preferable to deple-tion" (Samuelson et al., 1984, p. 102).

For regulation to be effective, some sort of punishment for violations is necessary. But research involving a laboratory simulation of the commons dilemma found that punishment for one selfish behavior may increase an-other. Bell and his co-workers (1989) found that when people were punished for the selfish behavior of overconsumption of a common resource, they turned to a different selfish behavior — stealing from others. When stealing was punished more harshly, overconsumption rose again. While stealing typi-cally is regarded as unethical, people are likely to see overconsumption as unethical only when the size of the resource pool is small. Thus, heavy water-ing to maintain a lush, green lawn may be taken for granted when one lives on the shore of a lake, but the use of water for lawn upkeep in a hot, arid climate could be seen as a blatant example of waste and overconsumption. Bell et al. (1989) noted that our culture seems to value a high probability of punishment for stealing and a low probability of punishment for over-consumption, protecting property rights but allowing exploitation of pub-lic goods (such as water).

A second possible solution is to get people to *consider collective interests* when making decisions. For instance, Brewer (1979) showed that increasing people's feelings of ingroup identification caused them to act with greater concern for the group's collective goals. Further research (Kramer & Brewer, 1984) demonstrated that when two groups were involved (young people and old people), when a *superordinate group identity* was emphasized ("We are studying the residents of this community"), members of each group were more likely to exercise personal restraint in their use of an endangered shared resource than when group differentiations were highlighted ("We are comparing the behavior of young people with the behavior of elderly persons").

Energy Conservation

In the 1980s, for most Americans the energy situation did not appear to be the "crisis" it had seemed a decade earlier when gasoline lines, natural gas shortages, soaring fuel prices, and the accompanying double-digit inflation captured the headlines. But conservation of energy remains an issue of critical importance. U.S. oil reserves continue to decline—down 30 percent since their peak in 1971 (Tanner, 1986). Energy use is increasingly linked to other environmental issues as well, ranging from acid rain and the global "greenhouse effect" to general air and water quality, resource depletion, and wilderness preservation (Kushler, 1989).

Since we can't predict with certainty what energy resources may be unlocked by future technology, the conservation of existing resources seems the best way to bring us safely to the time when additional energy sources may be available (Stobaugh & Yergin, 1979). Much progress has been made. It has been estimated that after 1973, energy efficiency improvements provided more energy than all sources of new fuel supplies combined, saving the U.S. economy $150 billion per year in energy costs by the late 1980s (Schneider, 1986). For example, it is possible to save 50 percent of the energy needed to heat houses by plugging warm air leaks, adding insulation, tuning the furnace, and improving windows (Sinden, 1978). Analysts estimated that 40 percent to 50 percent of energy costs could be saved within the next fifteen to twenty years through economically justified conservation measures in the U.S. (Ross & Williams, 1981).

There are many technological solutions to energy conservation. But psychologically, there's still a major problem. Despite our technical knowledge about how to conserve energy, the vast majority of homeowners haven't complied with the experts' recommendations (Aronson, 1990). Part of the problem is that many have assumed that consumers will respond to energy-conservation messages as rational decision-makers, carefully weighing the information and coming to a logical decision. You should be well aware by now (especially after reading Chapter 2) that this is not how we humans generally proceed. The ways in which we process social information and develop our attitudes and social influence processes are complex and often not entirely rational. Social psychological knowledge of persuasion, techniques of social influence, applications of social power, psychological reactance, and the like can help illuminate what techniques are most likely to influence people to undertake energy-saving behaviors. For example, we know that persuasion via the print media is generally not as effective as modeling for changing behavior. Energy-conservation programs are more effective when they show precisely what people are *doing* to save energy, rather than just stressing that people *should* conserve. The use of models combines both normative and informational social influence (Aronson, 1990).

Social scientists have studied energy conservation by measuring consumer attitudes, designing attitude-change programs, and studying the attitude-behavior link (Chapter 4). They have also served as program evaluators, measuring the effectiveness of energy-efficient programs. However, as I suggested in Chapter 1, it has often proved difficult to get policymakers to pay attention to the evaluation results (Kushler, 1989).

People may fear that cleaning up our environments, finding alternatives to the automobile, or making our homes and buildings energy efficient mean returning to some undesirable time in history, to "the bad old days." Persuasive messages could be developed to show people that that is not necessarily the case, perhaps using the example of Western Europe (Becker & Seligman, 1981).

Conserving Energy in the Home

Use of cash rewards such as rebates on monthly utility bills is one way of encouraging household energy conservation (Cone & Hayes, 1980; Stern & Gardner, 1981). Modest reductions in electricity consumption can be obtained if individuals are paid to conserve. Yet research indicates that the effectiveness of the monetary incentives diminishes over time and disappears once the incentives have been discontinued. This finding, as well as the costliness of this type of treatment, suggests that cash incentives alone cannot be touted as an effective means of encouraging energy conservation.

Accurate feedback is important. If one is trying to lose weight, the bathroom scale plays a vital role in providing feedback about weight loss. Ordinarily, we lack such a convenient feedback system for seeing how we are doing in conserving energy. Attempting to remedy the situation, a number of studies have provided consumers with immediate detailed feedback on energy use. For example, Winett et al. (1979) gave town house residents daily written feedback on energy use. Residents in a self-monitoring condition received additional information—charts to record the daily consumption and a note each day identifying the "expected use" (according to the weather) for the previous day. The feedback group consumed 14 percent less electricity than would have been expected (saving an average of $23 a month per household), whereas the self-monitoring subjects consumed an average of 8 percent less electricity.

More generally, the effectiveness of feedback varies according to energy cost and consumer income. A meta-analysis (Winkler & Winett, 1982) found that feedback was generally not effective when the cost of energy was low and family income was high, making energy costs only a small part of the family's budget. When the energy cost was high and income was relatively low, on the other hand, feedback was quite effective. For instance, written feedback resulted in average reduction of 30 percent in electricity use among low-and middle-level users during the summer (high energy costs) but when the same procedure was used during the spring (lower energy costs), reductions of only 13 percent occurred (Bittle et al., 1980).

Psychological Factors in Energy Conservation

Several possible approaches to encouraging conservation behavior are summarized in Focus 12·3. One can promote proconservation attitudes through persuasive communication or by encouraging conservation actions from people who already have favorable attitudes. Inasmuch as behavior change may often follow attitude change (Chapter 4), changing behaviors by incentives or through modeling may eventually lead to proconservation attitudes as well. But even if people have proconservation attitudes, they may not know how much energy they waste or how to go about changing. Filling this knowledge gap with feedback on energy usage and information on effective conservation techniques can be very helpful. The more vivid and personal (as opposed to statistical) the proconservation information is, the more influential it is likely to be (Chapter 2). Research indicates that people respond more seriously to information about losses than information about gains (Kahneman & Tversky, 1979). Therefore, an effective program should show people how much they're losing each month by not adopting the recommended practices (Yates & Aronson, 1983). At the same time the program could counter anticipated undesirable consequences (such as the idea that 65°F is bad for one's health) with accurate information.

People are most likely to support government-sponsored conservation policies when they: (1) have adequate knowledge or awareness of the overall ecological situation, (2) accept personal responsibility for energy conservation, (3) expect to be personally affected by conservation, and (4) hold favorable attitudes toward the current political administration (Olsen, 1981). Effective programs expose people to conservation information and practices through interpersonal interaction and "hands on" demonstrations, rather than through the impersonal mass media.

We saw in Chapter 4 that attitudes are strengthened by making a public commitment. Researchers have found that public commitment can have a similar impact on conservation behaviors. For example, residents who agreed to have their names publicized as attempting to conserve used less energy in the year following than those who also agreed to conserve but were told that their names would not be mentioned (Pallak et al., 1980).

In order to understand why proconservation attitudes sometimes do not translate into proconservation behaviors, we can review Ajzen's theory of planned behavior discussed in Chapter 4. The three major predictors of behavior in this model are one's *attitude* toward a specific behavior (determined by the anticipated consequences from that action and one's evaluation of those consequences), one's *subjective norm* concerning that action (one's understanding of what others expect one to do and the degree to which one is influenced by those expectations), and one's *perceived control* over the behavior.

From this perspective, we would not expect general attitudes about energy issues to be strongly related to specific acts of energy conservation. The relevant attitudes that are likely to predict behavior and which are, therefore, the most important targets for persuasive communications, are specific attitudes toward particular conserving behaviors. Most important are likely to be people's beliefs about short-term personal consequences for themselves (e.g., cost, inconvenience, discomfort, savings, effect on their general quality of life). Consumers' perceptions of how others feel about energy conservation (friends, neighbors, public figures) will determine their subjective norm. Perceived control can be enhanced by messages or models that convince consumers that they *can* do what it takes to save energy.

Applying Behavioral Science Research to Social Problems

I previewed the central issues and problems in applying research to social problems in Chapter 1. We have encountered these issues at many points, especially with reference to studies of violence in the media. The environmental questions discussed in this chapter are also very relevant to these general research/policy issues.

Determinants of Energy Usage

Although our discussion of energy conservation has focused on changing individuals' attitudes and behaviors, in fact two-thirds of the energy consumed in the United States is in the institutional context: businesses, schools, government. Although changing individuals' behaviors can substantially influence energy usage, an even greater effect could be achieved by changing institutional patterns of usage via legislative or policy changes (such as state laws requiring a deposit on all bottles, maximum and minimum thermostat settings for public buildings, and energy-efficient construction codes). Such changes involve not only individual personalities and attitudes but complex group decision-making processes (as discussed in Chapter 6), plus political, legal, and economic concerns and, often, pressure from powerful political, business, or environmental lobbying groups.

Psychological factors are important in answering two questions. First, is a particular attitude/behavior change technique effective? Second, what psychological factors (e.g., cognitive dissonance, self-presentational concerns, reactance) determine whether or not people will accept or resist change techniques suggested to them? As an example, several researchers (Kantola et al., 1984) reasoned that if people felt dissonance between important proconservation attitudes and nonconserving behaviors, they would resolve the dissonance by bolstering their important attitudes and increasing their conservation behaviors. They told some homeowners that their high level of electricity usage was inconsistent with the pro-environment attitudes they had expressed. As predicted, these homeowners used significantly less electricity in the ensuing two weeks than did other homeowners merely given tips on how to save energy.

FOCUS 12-3

Approaches to Encouraging Conservation Behavior

1. *Promoting conservation by persuasive communications.* Provide information about the negative consequences of shortages of energy, water, farmland, clean air, etc. Need a credible source and the message must fall within the audience's latitude of acceptance (see Chapter 4).

2. *Eliciting pro-conservation behavior from those already holding pro-conservation attitudes.* Direct their attention to conservation actions or make their pro-conservation attitudes more salient to behavior choice. Try to link pro-conservation activities—such as taking a shower instead of a bath—to attitudes.

3. *Inducing conservation behavior with material incentives and disincentives.* Effective in the short run but changed behaviors may not persist when the incentives are removed. May not be cost-effective. The impact of disincentives such as fines is effective only if positive reinforcement is provided for an alternative behavior.

4. *Inducing conservation behavior with social incentives and disincentives.* May provide social recognition and approval for conservation, or seek public commitment to conservation, or involve people in group conservation decisions. More research is needed on the possible effectiveness of these techniques.

5. *Providing models of conservation behavior.* Research on behavior modification and social learning (Chapters 7 and 10) suggests this should be effective. There has been little, if any, use of "prestige figures" to model conservation behavior. A rare exception was the wearing of a sweater by President Carter during his televised speech on energy policy.

6. *Facilitating the implementation of conservation intentions.* Despite pro-conservation inclinations, people may lack knowledge of possible pro-conservation actions and their impact. Providing information on appropriate conservation practices and making conservation alternatives more available can facilitate conservation behavior. Minimizing the anticipated negative consequences (costs) of conservation behaviors may be important, too.

7. *Providing information on the effectiveness of conservation efforts.* Feedback on savings can fill a "knowledge gap" and show consumers how much energy they really use. Detailed feedback may also make the effects of short-term efforts visible; these effects might not be visible in a single monthly bill. A practical disadvantage of many detailed feedback programs is their costliness. ❖

Source: Cook, S. W. & Berrenberg, J. L. (1981). Approaches to encouraging conservation behavior: A review and conceptual framework. *Journal of Social Issues, 37*(2), 73–107.

The Quality and Applicability of Research Findings

For a research finding to be useful it must have *internal validity*—the research must be well designed, executed, and free from confounding variables (Chapter 1). Complicated field studies (such as of those investigating energy use) are sometimes of questionable internal validity because of practical difficulties and compromises (such as inability to randomly assign subjects to conditions) that may be necessary.

Another important facet of a research study is its *external validity,* or the extent to which the findings can be generalized to other situations and other research populations. In areas where we may want to generalize the findings directly to important social policy areas, such as energy conservation, legal issues (Chapter 13), and health care delivery (Chapter 14), these issues are particularly important. For the research findings to be useful to policymakers, they must have clear internal and external validity and should be stable and powerful enough to justify changes in policies.

An innovative suggestion for implementing energy conservation was put forth by Darley and Beniger (1981), who suggested that the government consider providing a local conservation change agent similar to the county agricultural extension agents who played such a large role in modernizing farming practices in this country. Such a "house doctor" would be a trained technician employed by the city or state (not the utility company) and who carries out a series of tests on a person's house and determines which innovations make sense for that particular house. The house doctor would help write the specifications for the work to be done and would check that the work got done to those specifications.

As a step in this direction, many cities now provide free energy audits to homeowners, where the auditor checks out the home and makes recommendations for energy-saving steps. However, most homeowners then fail to follow the recommendations. Why? It's not that the homeowners are irresponsible or uncaring—after all, they invited the auditor out in the first place. The problem may be that most auditors are technical experts who are not trained in attitude-change skills. To see if training could make a difference, Gonzalez et al. (1988) taught a sample of energy auditors four communication strategies: to use vivid, concrete examples, to make their recommendations personally relevant to the homeowner's current situation, to induce commitment from the homeowner, and to frame their recommendations in terms of loss rather than gain, as research suggests that behavior is affected more by threats of loss than by promises of gain (Kahneman et al., 1982). About 50 percent more of the homeowners who were visited by the retrained auditors took the recommended steps (weatherizing their homes) than did those who were visited by auditors who had not been retrained.

Controlling Population Growth

We can now take a brief look at an entirely different route toward conserving resources—limiting the number of people who draw on the resources by controlling overpopulation.

The future of humanity on this planet may depend upon how effectively we can control and limit the growing world population. Estimates of the growth of the U.S. population over the next hundred years. Even if a trend toward a two-child family norm began immediately in the U.S., another 130 million or so people would live in this country a hundred years from now.

Overpopulation is not only an American problem. From the year 6000 B.C.E. to A.D. 1650, the world's population grew from about five million to five hundred million, doubling about every thousand years. There are now four billion people in the world. In the early 1980s the population of India, despite strong government pleas for birth control and family planning, grew by the entire population of Australia every year. If expansion continues at current rates, demographers estimate that it will take only another thirty-five years for the population of the world to double. High social density will continue to be a worldwide problem unless something drastic is done. The earth simply will not be able to provide what is needed to sustain life in future years (Ehrlich, 1968).

It is this worldwide problem that makes the study of proxemics, territoriality, privacy, and crowding so relevant and urgent. In addition to gathering knowledge about the psychological experience of crowding, many scientists have taken an active role in designing and evaluating programs to control overpopulation. In addition to difficult scientific problems, such programs involve complex ethical, moral, and religious issues as well.

The Ethics of Population Control

Many national governments have taken an active role in population control and family planning advocacy, especially in very overpopulated countries such as India and China. Focus 12-4 describes one tragic consequence of such programs — the killing of female infants in China by families who wanted their only child to be a boy. Though the field of family planning is beyond the scope of this book, we can still take a brief look at the applications of social psychological principles to this important problem.

Population control raises highly emotional ethical, moral, nationalistic, religious, and political concerns. The Roman Catholic Church still considers the use of contraceptives a sin, and the issue of legalized abortion has been an emotion-laden topic in the United States for decades. Birth control and family planning are one of the biggest issues faced by young couples. The bombing of abortion clinics in this country in the 1980s provided chilling evidence of the emotionalism of this area. Some ethnic groups and Third World countries have argued that population control is another name for genocide (Cone & Hayes, 1980) or an attempt to limit an oppressed group's population, thereby minimizing their social power.

Why Do People Want Large Families?

A scientific examination of overpopulation might begin by analyzing the reasons why many people want large families. Surveys in many areas of the world have revealed that most parents desire from two to four children, far too many for population stability (George, 1973). Several reasons for these preferences are:

1. *Pleasure.* Many parents find children fun and interesting and enjoy having a large family for this reason.
2. *Religion.* In many religions, "barrenness" is a curse and children are considered a heavenly blessing. Some religions (in America, Catholicism) stress having large families more than others (Rainwater, 1965).
3. *Ingroup growth.* Some nationalities or ethnic groups may want their members to reproduce at a high rate so as to increase their proportion in the general population (Dow, 1967).
4. *Consolidation of the family.* Some parents believe that having children stabilizes a marriage and draws the parents together. There is also a widespread cultural belief that it is not good to be an only child, although research does not support this stereotype (Thompson, 1974).
5. *Monetary value.* In agrarian societies, children provide a ready source of labor for the fields or market. The more children (especially boys) in a family, the more hands to work the land.
6. *Old-age security for the parents.* In cultures where societal support (e.g., Social Security, Medicare) is not available for the elderly, children may be the only viable source of support for aging parents.

FOCUS 12-4

Killing of Female Infants in China Reported Threatening Social Balance

Peking — The killing of unwanted female babies is occurring with such frequency in China that the sex ratio is being upset, an official Chinese report says.

The *China Youth News* said recent letters received from across the nation report drownings and abandonment on the streets of unwanted female babies. It said statistics from communes already indicate an imbalance in the sex ratio in the last two years because of infanticide.

China's tough birth-control policy allows only one child per couple in urban areas and a maximum of two in the countryside. Couples who exceed limitations risk economic penalties and forced abortions.

For young couples clinging to "feudalistic thinking" that favors men over women, the pressure is to have a son, even if it means killing a female baby born first, the newspaper said. The traditional Chinese belief is that a son can provide more labor as he grows up, take better care of his parents when they retire, and carry on the family name.

A daughter is viewed as a finanical burden. ❖

Source: UPI, *St. Petersburg Times*, November 11, 1982, p. 26A. Reprinted with permission of United Press International, Inc.

Types of Family-Planning Programs

Leaving aside for the moment the ethical, moral, and religious questions surrounding this issue, we can examine the general types of family-planning programs that have been developed (Cone & Hayes, 1980). *Informational campaigns* focus on making people aware of population programs, giving them knowledge about family planning, such as methods of contraception, and getting them to accept and practice the desired behaviors. The success of informational campaigns is affected by all of the factors relating to the effectiveness of communications (Chapter 4): the credibility, attractiveness, and power of the source, the audience's existing attitudes, subjective norms and perceived control, whether to try the central or peripheral route to attitude change, and so forth.

Service programs try to deliver a relevant service, such as contraceptives or sterilization, to the people who will benefit from it. Questions revolve around whether people will accept the service and whether they will keep on using it (contraceptives) after the program personnel have left.

Incentive programs are a third possibility. Focus 12-5 describes the incentive program in Singapore; other developing countries have designed

---

FOCUS 12-5

Reduce Your Family Size — or Else!

One of the most successful and comprehensive population control programs is in Singapore. It includes many specific measures that cover the entire population of about 2.3 million.

1. *Hospital fees*. Hospital costs for having a child increase as a woman has more children. Although the fees are low for the first two children, they are quite high after the fourth child.

2. *Income tax*. In many countries, families receive a tax break if they have children, as in the United States, where the more dependents you have, the more tax deductions you are allowed. In Singapore the tax law is reversed. Large families are not allowed tax breaks for additional children.

3. *Education*. Not all eligible children can get an advanced education in Singapore, especially children from large families, who are given low priorities for admission to school.

4. *State housing*. Families with four or more children are given low priorities for admission to state housing projects. Having too many children after you move into a project can lead to eviction.

5. *Maternity leave*. Women can receive paid maternity leaves in Singapore. Consistent with the overall policy, however, they are allowed for the first two children only.

This collection of incentives — or, one might say, disincentives — apparently reduced the birth rate over 50% between the late 1950s and the mid-1970s, from 44 births per thousand to about 21 births per thousand (Fook-Kee & Swee-Hock, 1975; Swee-Hock, 1975). Do you see any ethical issues involved in this program? Is the country likely to be better off because of these regulations? ❖

Source: Cone, J. D., & Hayes, S. C. (1980). *Environmental problems/Behavioral solutions*. Monterey, CA: Brooks/Cole, p. 120. Reprinted by permission of J. D. Cone.

similar programs. Studies have shown that there are problems in using cash incentives for not having children—people do not want to feel that they have sold their future progeny (Enke, 1961). More acceptable incentives might be educational benefits for the family's other children, savings accounts or savings bonds for later use, health care, food, or clothing (Ridker & Muscat, 1983; Rogers, 1971). Drawing on cognitive dissonance theory, Cooper (1974) suggested that the incentives should be just minimally sufficient to elicit the behavior (nonconception). In this case, dissonance caused by the counterattitudinal behaviors (of not having additional children) should be relatively great and the parents' attitudes may change in the direction of the behavior (supporting family planning) in order to reduce the dissonance.

SUMMARY

Early in this chapter I described Kurt Lewin's well-known dictum, $B = f(P, E)$; behavior is a function of the person and the environment. Although the studies described here have focused primarily on Lewin's E (environment) factor, they do not ignore the transactions between individuals and the environments in which they behave. Social density is related to the concepts of personal space, privacy, territoriality, feelings of personal control, stimulus overload, and the experience of crowding. The design of built environments such as apartment complexes, prisons, and dormitories can affect feelings of privacy, control, and isolation which, in turn, strongly influence behaviors. Social density is particularly relevant to the controversial issue of worldwide population control. Environmental stressors such as excessive noise, heat, lack of sufficient light, and air pollution can affect a wide range of behaviors, all the way from the classroom performance of schoolchildren to urban riots.

Perhaps one thing the studies tell us is that a slight modification and expansion of Lewin's formulation is in order (Krupat, 1977). To more fully explain behavior, the formula might better be stated: $B = f(P$ in the E_{SOCIAL} in the $E_{PHYSICAL})$. Understanding the influence of the physical environment (design of living areas) as well as the social environment (social density, personal space, etc.) can lead us toward a deeper understanding of human behavior. In turn, this understanding can be used to modify our environment to make it a safer, more attractive, and better place to live.

CHAPTER 13

Social Psychology and the Legal System

The first thing we do, let's kill all the lawyers.   Shakespeare, King
Henry IV

When I was a young man practicing at the bar, I lost a great many
cases I should have won. As I got along I won a great many cases I
ought to have lost; so on the whole, justice was done.   Lord Justice
Matthews ❖

PREVIEW

Many social psychologists have sought to apply social psychological concepts
to important sectors of contemporary society. In this chapter we focus on
the legal/criminal justice system. We will be concerned with social psychological analyses of the legal system as well as the injection of psychological
research into the legal system, especially the criminal justice system.

I begin by presenting four dilemmas involving basic values that perme-
ate psychological reactions to our legal system. Then attention swings to psychological aspects of pretrial procedures: plea bargaining, setting bail, the
use of eyewitness evidence, lie detection techniques, and hypnosis. At the
trial itself important factors include jury selection (the *voir dire* process) and
a judge's rulings on the admissibility of evidence and the judge's instructions
to the jury as they begin deliberation. Jury deliberations themselves have
been widely studied. Juries have an inherent appeal for social psychologists
because juries are, after all, problem-solving groups that have specific tasks
to carry out.

THE JUSTICE SYSTEM

The Law and Psychology

Throughout this book we have analyzed how people influence each other.
We have studied attitudes and values of individuals and of groups, and the
positive (prosocial) and negative (aggressive) interactions between individuals
and between groups. Nowhere are these factors more visible than in our legal system. The idea of applying psychological findings to the legal system
has been discussed since the beginning of this century. In a 1906 speech to
judges, Sigmund Freud suggested that psychology had some very practical
applications for their field. In a 1908 book Hugo Munsterberg, an experimental psychologist, argued that psychological principles could be applied to
events in the courtroom. The famous behaviorist John B. Watson also ar-

gued in the early 1900s that lawyers and psychologists had many common interests (Horowitz & Willging, 1984). Despite this early enthusiasm, however, little empirical social psychological research of direct relevance to the legal system was carried out in the first half of the century. It is only in the past two decades or so that we have seen a proliferation of studies attempting to answer questions of general legal/psychological interest.

This research is important for two general reasons. First is the scientific goal of increasing our knowledge about socially important behaviors. If we improve our understanding of why people behave as they do within the criminal justice system, we increase our understanding of human behavior in general. The second reason is to gather knowledge that can be valuable in improving the justice process, either by improving the system in general or improving the quality of justice in any particular trial. In order to appreciate the possible applications of social psychology to the criminal and civil justice systems, it is necessary to understand the workings of the systems, the adversarial roles played by prosecution and defense (or plaintiff and defendant), and how the concept of "truth" differs in law and in science. I will begin by discussing four basic dilemmas in the psychological study of the law.

Basic Dilemmas in the Psychological Study of the Law

The legal system of any society codifies certain values that its members have deemed most important. In choosing which values to support, the law struggles to balance individual rights against the good of society and the goals that are seen as most central. Lawrence Wrightsman (1987) identified four basic choices that pervade the law in the United States as it affects each one of us. Each choice creates a dilemma, he proposed, because no decision is going to be completely acceptable and it cannot simultaneously attain two incompatible goals, both of which are valued by our society.

Rights of Individuals versus the "Common Good"
In the next chapter I will review research on ways to encourage automobile passengers to wear seat belts. Recently, states have passed laws mandating the use of seat belts. Are such laws unfair to individuals who prefer not to wear seat belts? An individual might argue that the choice should be his alone, that he is hurting no one other than (possibly) himself if he chooses not to wear a seat belt. But in fact, his choice does have an impact on society. Chances of serious injury or death due to an auto accident are increased and, in the aggregate, societal costs in lost wages and taxes, medical insurance premiums, and welfare payments to children of the deceased will all be higher to the extent that people choose not to wear seat belts.

Many of the civil rights issues touched upon in Chapter 11 also invoke this dilemma. Should you be free to choose whom to sell your home to, even if you refuse to sell it to a minority-group member? Looking back at Chap-

ter 10, should you be free to distribute (or watch) videotapes that depict violence toward women, even if research suggests that there is a greater
likelihood that males may mistreat women after viewing these materials? The
debate about affirmative action programs also invokes this dilemma. These
controversial issues involve basic values of individual rights and the protection of individuals in our society.

Equality versus Discretion

Our legal system assumes that everyone is "equal before the law" and the
Declaration of Independence argues that "all men are created equal." All people, rich or poor, black or white, male or female, are supposed to receive
equal treatment in the legal system. (Although we saw in Chapter 11 that
most blacks in the U.S. today do not believe that this is the case.) But our
legal system depends on judges and juries rather than computers for making decisions. We assume that these people can (and should) use discretion
in applying the law in specific cases—relying on sensitivity, empathy, wisdom, and the like. But decision makers might also rely on other qualities,
such as racism, sexism, political allegiances, and personal prejudices. This
dilemma is most evident in judges' decisions in setting bail and sentencing
convicted defendants. As we will see, there are sometimes great disparities
in the amount of bail or length of sentence given by two judges for the same
crime. Recent "determinate sentencing" legislation places narrow limits on
the sentences that judges can give for particular crimes, stressing equality
over discretion.

To Discover the Truth or To Resolve Conflicts?

If asked the purpose of a trial, one might answer that it is our legal system's
way of discovering the truth about what happened. But most criminal cases
never go to trial; they are settled earlier by a deal between the prosecution
and the defense—a plea bargain. While plea bargains are efficient ways of
resolving conflict, they do not contribute to discovering truth. No trial takes
place, so there will be no public airing of the evidence, no opportunity for
the public to find out what really happened.

Attorneys do not see themselves as objective seekers of "truth" (as social psychologists might); rather, defense attorneys see their duty as zealously
defending their client to the best of their ability, while prosecuting attorneys see themselves as the representatives of "the people." In a criminal case,
the burden of proof is on the prosecution: It must prove the defendant guilty
"beyond a reasonable doubt." In a civil case, unlike criminal cases, the decision can be based on a "preponderance of the evidence."

criminal case:
When the state brings
charges against an
individual for alleged
illegal acts.

The jobs of the attorneys on the two sides of a **criminal case** differ.
The defense lawyer is supposed to do anything ethical to win acquittal for
his or her client. Even if the defense attorney suspects that his client is guilty,
he still owes the client the best possible defense within acceptable legal and
moral grounds. The defense attorney does not have a responsibility to turn

over to the prosecution evidence that might implicate the client. In recognition of the enormous power wielded by the prosecutor against any defendant, the prosecutor is held to a much higher standard. The prosecutor's responsibility is not "victory" but justice (Schwartz & Jackson, 1976). The prosecution has the responsibility of providing the defense with any evidence it uncovers that would point to the defendant's innocence.

Throughout this book, I have been describing "truth" from the scientific perspective—findings resulting from scientific research conducted by scientists who strive to remain objective and unbiased. Truth in our legal system rests on an entirely different base. The clash of perspectives and traditions is one reason why legal authorities often have been reluctant to accept research findings in the courts.

Two psychologists, Loftus and Monahan (1980, p. 281), described concepts of truth aptly:

> Law is an adversary process. The truth is believed to emerge from a brawl in which each participant pulls no punches and gives no quarter. The judge is the referee who watches for rabbit punches and keeps things above the belt. The jury does the scoring. The best man or woman—the one with the most truth—wins, it is hoped. Psychology, on the other hand, likes to think it is above all this. The truth is like a mountain, there for all to see. Research is the guide to help us . . . reach the summit and all rejoice.

Although the clash of these idealized perspectives creates many difficulties, there are still many areas where psychological "truth" can make valuable contributions to legal "truth," as we will see in the pages ahead.

Science versus the Law as a Source of Decisions

Science and the law approach knowledge in a different way. The law is doctrinal, science is empirical. Legal experts rely heavily on precedent—rulings in earlier cases dealing with the same issues—in coming to decisions. The law as established by rulings in earlier cases is called "case law," as differentiated from "statutory law" that results from laws passed by legislatures.

In a trial, the prosecution and defense attorneys may present the jurors with two contrasting versions of "truth" about the defendant's guilt. The jurors' task, psychologically, may be to choose between these two conceptions of truth after they have been bombarded with a confusing, and perhaps contradictory, set of "facts".

An Overview of the United States Justice System

The Criminal Justice System: From Crime to Arrest

The American criminal justice system is very complex. There are many points between the time a crime is committed and when the accused may go to jail at which an individual's discretion (the victim, the police, the prosecutor, the judge) determines whether the case is carried forward or dropped. The beginning of a hypothetical case is described in Focus 13-1; I will refer to this case throughout the chapter.

The first step in the criminal justice process is the lodging of a complaint, usually by the victim (Mrs. Franklin in Focus 13-1). The police record the complaint, investigate it, make arrests if they seem warranted, and decide how far to follow the case. In some large cities, for example, because of the number of crimes, police will take a report but will not investigate further (by dusting for fingerprints, interviewing neighbors, and so forth) any burglary in which the loss is less than a specified amount, say $2,000 (Ellison & Buckhout, 1981). Frequently a police officer may decide to let the accused go with a warning or to try to mediate the issue on the spot, as is likely for disputes among neighbors and family members.

FOCUS 13-1

A Hypothetical Case: *State v. Lang*

Margaret Franklin, a black 24-year old managerial trainee in a publishing firm, returns home in early afternoon to pick up some important papers she had left behind. Finding the front door unlocked, she reminds herself to tell her husband to be more careful about locking the door. As she walks into the kitchen there is a sudden loud noise from the bedroom and a young white man rushes by, knocking her to the floor as he bolts past her and out the front door. Picking herself up, she rushes to the door and sees a white late-model autombile speed away down the street. She gets a glance at the license plate number but later can't remember what it was. Badly shaken, she calls the police, who arrive within ten minutes. She describes the incident and gives the best description she can of the young man, although it all happened so fast that she can't remember as much as she would like. A search of the bedroom shows that the bureau and closet have been ransacked and several valuable pieces of jewelry valued at $500 and a camera worth $325 are missing.

Two days later Mrs. Franklin receives a call from the police, asking her to come down to the police station and look at some pictures. She is shown six photos of young white males who look similar to each other (a photo lineup), and is asked if the man who robbed her house is among them. She hesitantly points to the fourth photo and the police officer smiles, thanks her, and says they'll be in touch.

The man she tentatively identified was, indeed, the police suspect. Mark Lang, a 20-year-old white male, was picked up earlier because he fit the general description given by Mrs. Franklin, and he has been accused (though not convicted) of several similar daytime home burglaries. He did not have a convincing alibi for his whereabouts at the time the crime was committed and he owns a late-model white automobile. Although a search of his home failed to turn up the jewelry or the camera, on the basis of Mrs. Franklin's identification of him from the photograph lineup, Mr. Lang is indicted for burglary and jailed while he awaits a hearing at which his bail will be set. ❖

The first step in the criminal justice process. The burglary victim describes the incident and lodges a complaint with the police.

   If the police decide that the offense is serious enough to warrant arrest, the suspect (Mr. Lang in Focus 13-1) is arrested, advised of his constitutional rights, and taken to the police station to be booked, fingerprinted, and photographed. Mr. Lang's photo might then be put into a photo lineup with five other men's photos and shown to Mrs. Franklin. He would then be taken for an initial court appearance, which must be held "without unnecessary delay," usually within six hours of the arrest, where he enters a plea of guilty or not guilty, and bail is set. If Mr. Lang cannot post bail, he will be transferred to jail to await the next step. In some cases the accused may be "released on his own recognizance" without any bail.

   During the time between the preliminary hearing and the trial, plea bargaining may occur. The defense attorney and prosecutor may meet informally to try to work out a deal in which the defendant will plead guilty to some of the charges while others will be reduced or dropped. The prosecutor might also agree to recommend a lesser sentence for the offenses. If Mr. Lang agrees to such a deal, the prosecutor makes a recommendation to the judge, which the judge usually accepts. Defense attorneys often try to persuade their clients to "plead" (even though the client may be innocent) when they feel that the prosecution has a strong case or (sometimes) because the attorney is overworked and anxious to get on to other matters. A defendant who does not plead must go through the trial process.

The Civil Justice System

civil case:
When an individual brings suit against another individual for noncriminal acts.

In contrast to a criminal case, the primary purpose of a **civil case** is to resolve a dispute between two or more parties. Disputes can include reimbursement for injuries and lost wages due to an accident, a court injunction to get one party to stop harassing the other, disputes over property or financial holdings, divorce proceedings, adoption, lawsuits for libel or slander, and so forth. The person who initiates the civil claim is called the **plaintiff** while the person being sued is the defendant. As with criminal cases, the vast majority of civil cases are settled out of court without going to trial (Miller & Sarat, 1981). In recent years a number of less expensive, more accessible alternatives to the courtroom have emerged. These include neighborhood centers for arbitration, mediation, or dispute resolution. These centers are able to process cases quite rapidly and usually receive favorable evaluations from the participants (McGillis, 1981).

plaintiff:
The person who initiates a case in civil court; one who sues someone else.

PRETRIAL PROCESSES

Before a trial begins there are points at which psychological analyses can be informative. Many criminal cases never go to trial because plea bargaining results in a guilty plea by the defendant. Similarly, in many civil cases the plaintiff and defendant agree to a settlement prior to trial. Some psychologists have sought to understand the negotiating and bargaining techniques that are effective in plea bargaining. In criminal cases, the amount of bail set by the judge is an important factor. Bail is a monetary payment to ensure that the defendant will appear in court for a trial. While the amount of bail is supposedly based on factors such as the prosecutor's recommendation and the defendant's prior record and ties to the community, psychological factors may also influence the amount of bail a judge requires a defendant to post.

Plea Bargaining

Reasons for Plea Bargaining

plea bargaining:
The state makes a deal with the defendant; the defendant agrees to plead guilty to some charges while other charges may be reduced or dropped or the prosecution may ask the judge for a relatively light sentence.

Roughly 10 percent of all criminal cases go to trial; from 75 percent to 90 percent of them are disposed of by **plea bargaining** (Greenberg & Ruback, 1982). It is important that a lawyer be a skilled trial lawyer even though few cases come to trial, for the trial remains the ultimate threat ("If you don't settle, we'll see you in court!"). The threat is effective only if the lawyer has sufficient skills to have a good chance of winning the case.

Why are so many cases settled without a trial? One reason is pressure from the huge number of potential court cases. As the number of cases increases, pressure to avoid costly and time-consuming trials increases. Perhaps because of this, prosecutors may favor plea bargaining more than defense attorneys do (McAllister & Bregman, 1986). In criminal cases it

Plea-bargaining in action. Most criminal cases are settled when the defendant pleads guilty in a plea-bargaining agreement with the prosecution.

resolves the issues quicker than waiting for trial and gives prosecutors impressive conviction rates. It also saves lawyers and clients time, effort, and expense, and allows them to retain control of the case outcomes, which they give up once the decision is in the hands of a judge or jury.

Some observers see plea bargaining as a destructive process (Focus 13-2). In fact, in 1973 the National Advisory Commission on Criminal Justice Standards and Goals recommended the total abolition of plea bargaining (Church, 1976). One could argue that plea bargaining is not bargaining in the usual sense (Chapter 6) because the prosecutor holds all the cards and dictates the terms of the agreement (Gifford, 1983). Defense attorneys are sometimes (perhaps often) in a relationship that is more adversarial with their clients, trying to persuade them to accept a settlement offer, than with their lawyerly adversary. Attorneys realize that they will be interacting with the same sets of attorneys in front of the same judges in many subsequent cases, so there is little to be gained by overly aggressive behavior and much to be gained by negotiation and information sharing. Because of concerns about its effects, some jurisdictions experimented with abolishing plea bargaining in the 1970s and 1980s. Although results were not entirely consistent in different areas, these experiences suggested that plea bargaining could be abolished without major negative effects (such as further overburdening the courts) on the criminal justice system (Church, 1976; Daudistel, 1980; Rubinstein & White, 1980).

Psychological Analyses of Plea Bargaining
After his arrest, Mr. Lang (Focus 13-1) and his attorney might receive offers from the prosecution for a plea bargain. Plea bargaining is difficult to study

FOCUS 13-2

Plea Bargaining in the College Classroom?

The process of plea bargaining is not limited to the courtroom. For example, suppose that Jeff, a classmate of yours, is accused by his professor of cheating on the midterm exam and Jeff vehemently denies it (he pleads not guilty). The professor points out to Jeff that if he is brought before the school's Judicial Board and convicted of cheating, he will receive an F in the course and may be expelled from the university. The professor suggests that, rather than go through this lengthy formal procedure, Jeff admit his guilt to the professor, accept a grade of F on the midterm, and continue with the possibility of passing the course if he does well on the final exam.

What are Jeff's options? He can accept the professor's offer or he can continue to maintain his innocence and be brought before the Judicial Board. Suppose Jeff is innocent—he did not cheat. He may decide to accept the professor's offer anyway, just to avoid the hassle and embarrassment of the Judicial Board hearing and the possibility of more extreme penalties if he is found guilty. Jeff may figure, "Hell, it's the professor's word against mine and who are they going

to believe? The professor, naturally." As you can see, a good deal of pressure can be brought to bear on people to plead guilty in plea-bargaining situations even when they are innocent.

Some observers (Kipnis, 1979; Langbein, 1980) have made a different analogy to the classroom. Imagine a system of "grade bargaining" in which the teacher who had not yet read a student's term paper offered the student a grade of B on the paper. This seems to have some advantages. The professor would save time and effort. Presumably the student would not accept the teacher's offer unless he calculated that the B was as good or better than his expected results from conventional grading. What would be wrong here? First, others who rely on grades in admissions and hiring decisions would be denied accurate information about the quality of your work. Second, it would not be fair to other students obtaining grades in conventional ways. Finally, a grade is meant to inform a student about the comparative quality of performance and a grade achieved by bargaining loses this quality. ❖

scientifically because negotiations and bargaining between opposing attorneys, or between the defense attorney and the defendant, take place in offices, in hallways, or on the phone where it is unlikely that an outsider could observe them. Nevertheless, social psychologists have tried to study this important component of the legal process. Bordens (1984) had students play the role of defendants who were offered plea bargains. He found that subjects were likely to accept the plea bargain when it contained a relatively short sentence, when the likelihood of conviction was high, and when they would receive a relatively long sentence if they refused the plea bargain and were convicted. Mr. Lang would probably consider these same factors in deciding whether to accept the state's offer.

Gregory and his co-workers (1978) conducted a study in which half of the subjects were induced by a confederate to cheat on a test (to gain extra credit). In a complicated scenario, the experimenter later told each subject he suspected that the subject had had prior information about the test because he scored so well. The researcher offered each subject a deal: If he admitted receiving prior information (pled guilty), the subject would not receive credit for participating in the study, but he would not be taken before the Psychology Department Ethics Committee. If he refused to admit the "crime," he would be taken before the Committee. Not one of the innocent subjects (those who had not been induced to cheat) accepted the deal, but 75 percent of the guilty subjects did. This experiment underscores the powerful role of guilt and expectation of conviction in plea bargaining. (The study also raises ethical questions, and as soon as the subject made his decision, he was informed of the nature and purpose of the study and careful steps were taken to make sure no subjects were negatively affected by their participation.)

We are just beginning to see psychological research on plea bargaining in actual cases. Interviews with sixty-seven people who had been charged initially with felonies and who had plea bargained (70 percent were currently on probation) found several general reasons why the plea bargain had been accepted (Bordens & Bassett, 1985). Important reasons included direct external pressure (pressure from the prosecutor, pressure from the defense attorney), other aspects of the case (sentence offered, perceived likelihood of conviction) and the defendant's feelings (remorse, desire to minimize family suffering, desire to be cooperative).

Setting Bail

bail:
A monetary payment made by a defendant or his agent to ensure that the defendant will appear later in court for the trial.

In the typical bail-setting hearing, a judge reviews a short summary of the charges against the defendant, the defendant's economic status, ties to the local community, and prior criminal record. Though the legal object of the **bail** system is to ensure the suspect's reappearance, a number of other factors may enter into a judge's bail decision. Unfortunately, neither social science nor law has yet discovered an effective way of distinguishing high-risk defendants (those likely not to return for trial) from low-risk ones. Hence, there is no solid empirical ground for deciding who should receive high bail. Also, the effects of the monetary bail system are critically dependent on the defendant's finances. It seems to violate the value of equality that a poor person will be jailed even though "presumed innocent until proven guilty" merely because he or she does not have enough money to meet bail, while a wealthier defendant charged with the same offense may remain free on bail.

Social psychologists have attempted to find out whether the factors that are supposed to determine bail are the ones that, in reality, critically affect bail setting. Ebbesen and Konečni (1975) enlisted eighteen judges as subjects in a bail-setting experiment. Each judge was asked to review several model cases and to set bail as though it were a real case. The researchers varied aspects of the cases given the judges. Results indicated that the prosecutor's recommendation had a significant influence on their decisions but, interestingly enough, the defense attorney's recommendation had no influence. Although studies of bail decisions in a laboratory setting had indicated that the prosecutor's recommendations, strength of ties to the local community (a wife, parents, job), and prior record all had an influence (Goldkamp & Gottfredson, 1979; Clark et al., 1976), in actual bail hearings the final bail was directly related only to the prosecutor's recommendation. But we should not necessarily blame the judge for ignoring the other factors. In many cases, the fault may lie with the defense attorney who fails to bring community ties and prior record to the judge's attention when these factors are in favor of the accused (Saks & Hastie, 1978).

Detecting Deception

In our hypothetical case the police have only one solid piece of evidence against Mark Lang: Mrs. Franklin's identification of him from the photo lineup. And as we will see, eyewitness identifications, especially those made under stress, often are incorrect. Other information on Mr. Lang—his being suspected of other similar crimes, owning a white car, and not having a convincing alibi—probably increase police suspicions but would not be convincing evidence in court. Hence, the police will continue to look for more compelling evidence. They may make further attempts to find the stolen goods, or perhaps give Mr. Lang a lie detector test regarding the burglary and his alibi, or possibly hypnotize Mrs. Franklin to see if she could remember the license plate number. Major problems, however, are associated with the techniques of lie detection and hypnosis.

The Controversial Polygraph

The use of physiological cues to detect lying has a long history. Arabian Bedouins required a suspected liar to lick a piece of hot iron; if it burned the subject's tongue, the person was assumed to be lying. In Britain, the test was to swallow a "trial slice" of bread and cheese; inability to swallow the slice was interpreted as a sign of deception. These rituals derive from the notion that one who is lying has a dry mouth.

The polygraph in operation. Research indicates that the widely-used polygraph can yield many "false positive" outcomes, where innocent people are misclassified as guilty.

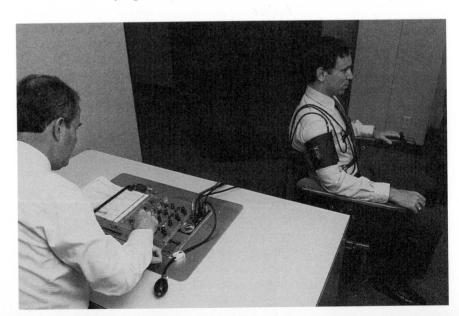

polygraph:
A controversial machine, used as a "lie detector", that reads physiological changes that occur when people are under emotional stress.

In modern times, the **polygraph** has been used as a lie detector. The polygraph does not measure lying; rather, it records physiological changes that occur when people are under emotional stress. The Keeler Polygraph, the most commonly used technique, measures blood volume and pulse rate, respiration rate, and skin conduction (which is affected by sweating).

Experts disagree heatedly about the accuracy of this controversial technique. Critics argue that polygraph results can be easily faked, are often inaccurate, and may overwhelm the jury if used as evidence in court (Lykken, 1979). Supporters argue that when procedures are carefully carried out, polygraph results are valuable for identifying guilty persons, and can also help exonerate wrongly accused people (Horvath, 1984) (but see Focus 13-3). Summarizing data from a number of field studies, the U.S. Office of Technology Assessment (1983) estimated that guilty people were correctly identified 86 percent of the time while innocent people were exonerated 76 percent of the time. A recent meta-analysis of fourteen laboratory studies (Figure 13-1) yielded somewhat lower accuracy rates (Kircher et al., 1988).

Some studies demonstrate that "false positive" errors, misclassifying innocent people as guilty, can be distressingly frequent. Kleinmuntz and Szucko (1984a) were able to obtain records from a leading polygraph firm for a number of theft-related investigations. The researchers selected the polygraph charts of fifty innocent (someone else had later confessed to the theft) and fifty guilty persons (who had later confessed to the theft). These one hundred polygraph charts were shown to six polygraph trainees at the end of

FIGURE 13-1

The Accuracy of the Polygraph as a "Lie Detector"

Overall results of a meta-analysis of fourteen laboratory studies.

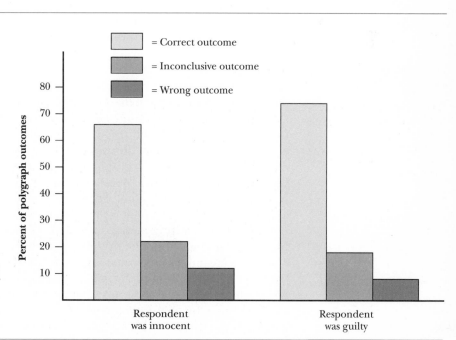

Source: Data from Kircher, J. C., Horowitz, S. W., & Raskin, D. C. (1988). Meta-analysis of mock studies of the control question polygraph technique. *Law and Human Behavior, 12,* 79–90.

their training period. While the trainees were able to classify people as guilty or not guilty at a better than chance rate, still, on the average, the polygraph interpreters misclassified 37 percent of the innocent as guilty. Unfortunately this study had several methodological shortcomings, as polygraphers had to base their decision on one chart per person (the standard is three) and were not allowed to categorize responses as "inconclusive" (Kleinmuntz & Szucko, 1984b; Raskin, 1988). Nevertheless, similar results were found in a large-scale field study of people who were later found to be innocent (someone else confessed) and were tested by experienced police investigators. Only 55 percent of these innocent suspects were correctly classified as innocent based on their polygraph responses (Patrick & Iacono, 1987).

These same investigators (Patrick & Iacono, 1989) used prisoners as subjects in another study. Half of the prisoners were induced to commit a "mock theft" of money. To create an atmosphere of threat and reward, all forty-eight prisoners were told that if the group was able to "beat" the polygraph to the extent that no more than ten of the forty-eight participants failed the polygraph (remember, twenty-four had actually committed the mock theft), then every participant would receive a bonus of twenty dollars, a great deal of money in the prison environment. If more than ten participants failed the polygraph, no one would receive the reward and the names of those who failed would be posted. The polygraph proved effective in identifying guilty persons—87 percent of the "thieves" were identified, not including those classified as "inconclusive." But for the innocent prisoners, the same problem arose as in other studies—only 56 percent of them were correctly classified as innocent, an accuracy rate not significantly greater than chance. Similar findings resulted from a laboratory study (Szucko & Kleinmuntz, 1981) in which some students were induced to commit a theft while others were not. All subjects were given polygraph tests by experienced examiners. The rate of "false positives" (nonthief subject being identified as a thief) ranged from 18 percent to 55 percent, depending on the examiner. The more experienced interpreters did no better than the less experienced interpreters.

The polygraph operator compares responses to critical questions (questions about the crime) with responses to control questions (that concern irrelevant matters). To "beat" this system, there are two types of actions people can take to deceive the polygraph. They can try to suppress their emotionality while reacting to critical questions or try to raise their emotionality while reacting to control questions. To suppress one's physiological reaction to a critical question, one might try to mentally distract himself by doing a monotonous or distracting mental task (such as counting the holes in the ceiling tiles or doing arithmetic problems) or one might rationalize an answer to give it a meaning unlike what is intended. For example, if a thief is asked, "Did you take $50 from the woman?" when he knows that he actually took $51.60, he might be able to answer no and appear truthful.

One may be able to generate false positive (emotional) responses to irrelevant questions by thinking erotic, embarrassing, or painful thoughts, flexing or tensing muscles, or producing pain (say, by putting a thumbtack

FOCUS 13-3

Can the Lie Detector Lie? A Case History

Floyd "Buzz" Fay was identified by Fred Ery, mortally wounded in an Ohio robbery attempt, as the hold-up man. Seveal hours before dying of his wounds, Ery had said, "It looked like Buzz, but it couldn't have been." Ery died about five hours later after losing a great deal of blood and receiving large doses of Demerol. During the five-hour period he became more certain of his assailant, stating numerous times that "Buzz did it."

Arrested the next day, Buzz Fay didn't take his arrest very seriously, thinking the right person would soon be apprehended. Nevertheless, he was charged with aggravated murder. Realizing the weakness of its case—Fred Ery's dying identification was the only evidence against Fay—the prosecution offered Fay a deal. The murder charges would be dropped if he was judged truthful by a polygraph examination administered by the Bureau of Criminal Investigation. If determined to be deceptive, a second, privately administered lie detector exam would be conducted. If the results of the two exams conflicted, the polygraph results would be discarded and the case would go to

trial without them. If both tests indicated deception, Fay would plead guilty to the lesser charge of murder. If he refused to do so, he would be tried on the aggravated murder charge and the polygraph evidence would be used against him in the trial.

Assuming that the polygraph would demonstrate his innocence, Fay accepted the offer. Subsequently he "flunked" both polygraph tests, was convicted of murder at his trial, and given a sentence of life. However, two and one half years later Fred Ery's real assailant was tracked down, apprehended, and convicted, and Buzz Fay was released from prison (Cimmerman, 1981). Ironically, Fay, while he was in prison, became something of an expert on "beating" the polygraph. He coached 27 inmates who freely admitted they were guilty of the offenses charged. Yet, after about 20 minutes of instruction, 23 of the 27 inmates managed to pass a lie detector test (Lykken, 1981). Taken together, these events suggest that the lie detector is not only highly fallible, but may be highly fakeable as well. ❖

in one's shoe or mouth and pressing on it). Recent studies (Honts et al., 1985; 1987) have found that after training, "guilty" students (who had committed a mock crime) were able to deceive the polygraph operator from 50 to 70 percent of the time by biting their tongues and pressing their toes against the floor while responding to control questions.

But it takes considerable training and understanding of the logic of the polygraph to defeat it, as another study (Honts et al., 1988) found that untrained students were unable to deceive the polygraph despite their best efforts to do so. Some have suggested that psychopaths, who are accustomed to lying, would be better able to beat the polygraph, but Patrick and Iacono (1989) found that prisoners who scored high on measures of psychopathy were no better at beating the polygraph than were nonpsychopaths.

What can we make of the widely differing professional opinions about the accuracy of polygraph interpretations? It appears that the polygraph is much more accurate for some kinds of people, and under some testing conditions, than others (Kircher et al., 1988). It may do well in identifying guilty people who are not trained to effectively use countermeasures, but there is a substantial risk of "false positives"—innocent people being classified as guilty. Clearly, much more scientific research is needed before we can draw firm conclusions.

In the meantime, because of uncertainties about the accuracy of lie-detector methods, a federal law that took effect in 1989 banned the routine use of the polygraph in employment situations in most types of jobs (except defense contractors, law enforcement, drug manufacturers). Direct evidence from polygraph records is not *automatically* admissible in any American court, although thirty-six states have admitted polygraph evidence at least once (Raskin, 1981). In twenty-six states it can be admitted if both sides agree before the test is taken, as was the case for Buzz Fay (Iacono & Patrick, 1987).

Detecting Lying in Everyday Interactions

Can lying be detected accurately in everyday interactions? In a review of thirty-five studies on this issue, Zuckerman et al. (1981) concluded that the average rate of detecting lies ranged from 45 percent to 60 percent, where 50 percent would be performing at a chance level. On the average, then, people do only slightly better than chance. Studies suggest that facial expressions are not good indicators of lying because people are conscious of their expressions and control them well. Verbal cues such as speech pitch or hesitations (Krauss et al., 1976; Kraut, 1978) and **body language** (such as jerky, fragmented bodily movements) may be more informative about lying than are facial cues (Manstead et al., 1984; Zuckerman, Kernis, Driver, & Koestner, 1984).

But even nonverbal cues are not always useful indicators of deception. One clever field study (Kraut & Poe, 1980) induced some volunteers waiting at an airport to try smuggling contraband through a mock customs inspection, while other volunteers went through the inspection "clean." The travelers' behavior during the mock inspection was videotaped and shown to a group of experienced U.S. Customs inspectors and to a sample of ordinary citizens who were asked to identify those travelers most likely to be carrying contraband. Both the inspectors and the citizens tended to pick out travelers who were young, lower class, appeared nervous, hesitated before answering, gave short answers, avoided eye contact with their questioner, shifted their posture, and said they were taking a pleasure rather than a business trip. But neither group of judges identified the passengers carrying contraband at better than a chance level. The cues they used for their judgments were not related to actual deception. Another study (DePaulo & Pfeifer, 1986) compared experienced law enforcement officers, law enforcement trainees, and college students. The law enforcement personnel were no better at detecting deception than the students were, although they were more confident of their decisions, even when they were wrong.

A content-analysis technique, labeled **criteria-based statement analysis,** attempts to assess the truthfulness of statements by analyzing their con-

body language:
The subtle communication of thoughts and feelings through body positions and movements.

criterion-based statement analysis:
A technique that attempts to assess the truthfulness of statements by analyzing their contents in terms of specific criteria. Has only preliminary research support.

Can customs officers tell when travelers are lying? One study found that experienced customs officials did no better than ordinary citizens in detecting which travelers were carrying contraband.

tents according to nineteen specific criteria. Used in German courts for years, the procedure has received some recent research support (Steller et al., 1988) but it is too early to know whether it will prove to be an effective and valid technique (Raskin & Yiulle, 1989; Steller & Koehnken, 1989).

Although people generally cannot detect deception at much better than a chance rate, can they be taught to detect deception more accurately? It's not easy: a program that attempted to train police officers to detect deception more accurately yielded disappointing results — the officers did no better than chance after their training (Koehnken, 1987). However, it appears that one may be able to learn to detect deception *in a particular individual* (as parents might learn to detect deception in their child), but the ability does not generalize to detecting deception in other people. Zuckerman, Koestner, and Alton (1984) had subjects watch sixty-four videotaped segments of eight different people giving eight one-minute descriptions of someone they knew. Half of the descriptions were accurate, half were deceptive; after each segment subjects guessed whether the message was truthful or deceptive. Half the subjects were told after each segment whether their guesses were accurate; the other subjects received no feedback. The researchers found that the no-feedback subjects over time became somewhat more accurate in their judgments of the same target person, as accuracy rose from around

50 percent to 61 percent—a practice effect. Subjects given feedback increased their accuracy to 70 percent, showing that learning occurred. When both sets of subjects began observing a new target person, however, their accuracy rates dropped back to about 50 percent. Cues to deception differ widely from person to person, and even though people can learn to detect deception fairly accurately in one person, it doesn't help them in detecting deception from other people—in short, the skill does not generalize.

Hypnosis

Uses of Hypnosis

hypnosis:
A state of heightened suggestibility that may also include posthypnotic amnesia in which the events that occurred during hypnosis may be forgotten.

Hypnosis is used as an investigative tool by police in some jurisdictions. Hypnosis involves a state of heightened suggestibility; it may also include "posthypnotic amnesia" in which, on instruction from the hypnotist, the events that occurred during hypnosis may be forgotten. Hypnosis is currently big business in the American criminal justice system; several thousand criminal justice personnel have had some training in it, usually a three-day seminar (Reiser, 1989). Probably the best-known application of hypnosis was used to help solve the 1976 kidnapping of twenty-six children and their bus driver in Chowchilla, California, by three armed masked men. Under hypnosis, the bus driver, who had escaped, recalled all but one digit of the license plate on the kidnappers' van, and the information assisted in the capture of the three suspects. The Los Angeles Police Department's guidelines for hypnosis interviews appear in Focus 13-4.

FOCUS 13-4

Police Hypnosis Guidelines

The following guidelines have been utilized at the Los Angeles Police Department to help ensure that hypnosis interviews are conducted in a professional and ethical manner (from Reiser, 1989, p. 155):

1. The hypnosis project director screens all requests for investigative hypnosis to determine appropriateness.
2. The hypnosis session is conducted by a qualified hypno-investigator or health professional.
3. Informed consent is obtained from the subject or guardian.
4. The entire hypnosis session is recorded on audiotape or videotape.
5. The person conducting the hypnosis session shall not be otherwise involved in the conduct of the investigation in which the subject was a victim or witness.
6. Hypnosis interviews will be conducted with volunteer witnesses but not with suspects or defendants.
7. The welfare of the hypnosis subject is primary and takes precedence over any other considerations. ❖

Source: From PSYCHOLOGICAL METHODS IN CRIMINAL INVESTIGATION AND EVIDENCE, edited by David C. Raskin (p. 155). Copyright © 1989 by Springer Publishing Company, Inc., New York 10012. Used by permission.

While police departments that regularly use hypnosis report that it is effective in improving the recall of some witnesses or victims (Reiser, 1989), remember that such reports are merely uncontrolled case studies. The crucial question is: What does the scientific research evidence tell us?

Many scientists are skeptical of the validity of the information gathered under hypnosis. Although valid information may emerge from hypnosis, as in the Chowchilla kidnapping case, false information also can occur. The problem is that neither the hypnotist nor the subject can tell the difference. **Confabulation** may occur, a filling of gaps in memory with fantasy. Because a hypnotized person is in a state of heightened suggestibility, any hints or biases suggested (intentionally or unintentionally) by the hypnotist can become incorporated into the subject's memory.

confabulation:
A filling of gaps in memory with fantasy.

Reviews of laboratory studies have concluded that there is no substantial evidence that hypnotized subjects have any better recall than do suitable control subjects (Scheflin & Shapiro, 1989: M. Smith, 1983). Hypnosis may not improve things; indeed, it may make them worse (Putnam, 1979). For example, Sanders and Simmons (1983) exposed a hundred subjects to a twenty-second videotape of a pickpocket stealing a wallet. Leading questions (that suggested an incorrect answer) and nonleading questions were used while interviewing the subject later. In addition, half the subjects were exposed to a lineup that contained the thief, while the other half saw a sug-

The Chowchilla schoolbus kidnapping. Pictured is the driver of the schoolbus (Frank Ray, Jr,.), who escaped and was able under hypnosis to remember the license plate of the kidnappers' van.

gestive lineup that contained a person wearing the same jacket that was seen on the thief in the videotape. Hypnotized subjects were found to be less accurate on both the recall and recognition task than were controls, because of their heightened susceptibility to leading questions and the suggestive lineup. Though they were less likely to be accurate, hypnotized subjects were no less confident than nonhypnotized subjects were.

Memories can actually be *created* under hypnosis by a simple indirect suggestion. To illustrate, Laurence and Perry (1983) gave highly hypnotizable subjects an indirect suggestion for a "pseudomemory" while hypnotized (that they had been awakened one night the week before by a loud noise). While still hypnotized, about half confirmed that they had heard the noise. After hypnosis, half of these people continued to claim that they had really heard the noise, even after the experimental manipulation was explained to them!

It is important to realize that nonhypnotized witnesses can also have their memories distorted by leading questions, can create memories as a result of indirect suggestion (Loftus, 1979), and can confabulate when repeatedly questioned (Eugenio et al., 1982). Hypnosis just enhances suggestive tendencies that are already present in most of us. It appears that hypnotically induced pseudomemories are no more or less resistant to cross-examination than are other incorrect memories (Spanos et al., 1989).

Does Hypnosis Have Value in the Justice System?

On hypnotizing witnesses, Martin Orne commented, "Hypnosis is the worst of both worlds. It decreases reliability while making the witness more compelling" in court because he or she is highly confident of the memory (quoted in Stark, 1984, p. 36). Most jurors seem moderately skeptical of hypnotically induced testimony (Greene et al., 1989). The most appropriate use of hypnosis is probably in the evidence-gathering stage, where promising leads (such as license numbers) turned up by hypnosis can be investigated. If the leads appear true they can be followed up; if they appear false they can be dropped. In this way, no one is hurt if the evidence was a result of confabulation.

But there is a strategic risk to hypnotizing witnesses—in many states witnesses who have been hypnotized may not be allowed to testify at trial about their posthypnosis "memories" (Scheflin & Shapiro, 1989). However, the U.S. Supreme Court appeared to reverse this trend in a 1987 case, *Rock v. Arkansas*, when they ruled that a defendant's "hypnotically refreshed" memory *should* be allowed at trial if the defendant is the only possible witness for the defense because no one else was around when the crime (a murder in this case) was committed. In the case, crucial parts of the defendant's memory (supporting a self-defense scenario) had only appeared after she had been hypnotized. Subsequent analysis had corroborated part of her memory— that the gun was defective and could have gone off even if the trigger was not pulled. The justices stated that "we express no opinion on the larger issue" of whether hypnotically induced memories should be admissible in other types of cases and it remains to be seen how broadly other courts will interpret this decision. Observers noted that "True to its word, the majority opinion was written just carefully enough to make it unclear whether the justices favored or feared hypnosis in the courtroom (Scheflin & Shapiro, 1989, p. 113)." We'll have to wait and see.

An Alternative to Hypnosis: The "Cognitive Interview"

cognitive interview:
Interview technique that focuses on complete reports, reinstating the context of the event, and recounting the event in a different order and from different perspectives. Designed to gain more information without increasing errors.

It would be ideal if we could achieve the focused concentration that characterizes hypnosis without problems caused by confabulation from enhanced suggestibility. The **cognitive interview** technique, developed by Edward Geiselman and Ronald Fisher, shows promise. First, the interviewee is asked to recount the entire incident, without interruption from the interviewer (unlike a typical police interview, which is usually interrupted by questions). Then, reasoning that information not accessible with one retrieval cue (one type of question, one perspective) may be accessible with a different cue, interviewees are asked to mentally reinstate the context that surrounded the event. What time was it, what was the weather like, what were you wearing, what were the surroundings, how were you feeling? They are encouraged to report everything, even details that seem unimportant. Interviewees may be asked to recount the event in a different order (i.e., backwards) or from a different perspective (How would it have looked to someone else?).

Initial studies suggest that the cognitive interview is effective. After watching a realistic, violent police training film, subjects give more accurate information, and less confabulated information, with the cognitive interview than when hypnotized or when given a standard police interview (Geiselman et al., 1985). A further study trained seven experienced Miami police detectives in the cognitive interview technique. In subsequent robbery cases, these officers obtained, on average, 63 percent more information than did untrained detectives in the same types of cases (Fisher et al., 1988).

Eyewitness Evidence

The Accuracy of Eyewitness Evidence

In many cases when the police detain a suspect, they will conduct a lineup to see if the eyewitnesses can identify the suspect. Many people believe that eyewitness evidence ("That's the man—I'll never forget his face!") is accurate and valuable. Yet a number of attorneys and judges have asserted that this is not true; eyewitness evidence is often wrong. The U.S. Supreme Court in a 1967 decision (*U.S. v. Wade*) noted that many judges and lawyers agreed that "mistaken identifications have been responsible for more miscarriages of justice than any other factor—moreso, perhaps, than all other factors combined" (see Focus 13-5).

Our perception and memory processes do not operate like a camera or video recorder, faithfully storing accurate images of what has been perceived. Rather, memory is a *constructive* process where what is remembered is affected by one's needs and values and can be modified by subsequent events (Loftus, 1979). Three stages are involved in perceiving and remem-

FOCUS 13-5

That's the Man! . . . or Is It?

Let's hope none of us has a string of bad luck such as Bob Dillen, age 29, did. In 1979 and 1980 Dillen, a freelance photographer, was arrested thirteen times for armed robberies of Fotomat and Foto Hut booths in Pittsburgh, Pennsylvania. He had to stand trial for five of those cases; each time, fortunately, the jury did not convict him. Nevertheless, stress and the loss of time and money were immense. Finally, in the thirteenth case, a cashier who had been kidnapped and held hostage overnight led police to the cabin where they arrested the real criminal. Dillen's only "crime" was that he looked too much like the real criminal (*Tallahassee Democrat*, December 23, 1980, p. 1).

Although Dillen underwent much undeserved trauma, he was lucky compared to many other victims. For example, Lennel Geter, 26, a black engineer working in Greenville, Texas, was convicted of armed robbery of a fried chicken restaurant and sentenced to life imprisonment, on the basis of an eyewitness identification. Geter's white court-appointed attorney spent more energy trying to convince him to plea bargain than in following up leads, Geter's supporters claimed. Several of Geter's white co-workers asserted that he was at work, fifty miles away from the restaurant, at the time the robbery occurred, but he was convicted nevertheless. Many of his co-workers continued to press for a new trial and TV's "60 Minutes" did a feature story on his case. Eventually, the weight of the publicity motivated the authorities to reopen the case. Finally, in

March 1984 Texas authorities announced that they had located a new suspect and Geter was cleared of all counts against him, after spending more than a year in prison (*New York Times*, March 23, 1984).

William Jackson was unluckier still. Two rape victims picked him out of a police lineup in 1977; he was convicted of rape and sentenced to fourteen to fifty years in prison. Five years later a prominent local internist, Dr. Edward Jackson (no relation), was arrested while burglarizing a house and police identified him as the "Grandville rapist," suspected of nearly 100 assaults in an affluent Ohio neighborhood. They also deduced that he had committed the two rapes for which William Jackson had been in prison for five years. The two men looked remarkably alike: tall slender blacks with short Afros, sparse beards, mustaches, and similar facial features. William Jackson was released from prison seven and one half hours after Dr. Edward Jackson was indicted in September 1982. William Jackson, who was stabbed and repeatedly assaulted during his imprisonment, said he held no grudge against the mistaken eyewitnesses, but he was bitter toward the system of justice that put him behind bars. "They took away part of my life, part of my youth. I spend five years down there, and all they said was 'We're sorry.'" (*Time*, October 4, 1982, p. 45). Sadly, such cases of mistaken identity are not as rare as most of us assume. How many other people are in prison at this moment because of mistaken eyewitness identifications? ❖

acquisition phase:
The first stage involved in perceiving and remembering a crime, which includes the conditions at the time the event occurs.

bering a crime. The **acquisition phase** includes conditions at the time the event occurs. For a crime this would include the length of time it took, lighting, the distance between the witness and the criminal, any disguise the criminal might have been wearing, the witness's state of mind (interested, bored, terrified, angry), and any distractions present in the situation. The second

retention:
The second stage involved in perceiving and remembering. The longer the interval between witnessing the crime and attempting to identify the criminal from a lineup, the greater the chance of error.

retrieval:
The third stage involved in perceiving and remembering a crime, which occurs when the person attempts to "retrieve" the image from memory in order to identify the criminal from a lineup or in the courtroom.

phase, the **retention** interval, refers to the interval between when the crime was committed and when the eyewitness attempts to identify the criminal from a live or photo lineup. The length of the interval can range from a few minutes to several months or even years, and events that occur during this interval can affect and change what is in memory. The third phase, **retrieval**, occurs when the person attempts to "retrieve" the image from memory in order to identify the criminal from the lineup. Important factors at this phase include the fairness of the lineup and any suggestive cues or pressures on the witness to identify one particular person (see Focus 13-6).

The U.S. Supreme Court's Guidelines

Legal authorities have wrestled with ways to protect the accused from erroneous eyewitness identifications while not interfering with the conviction of the guilty. The U.S. Supreme Court made some "educated guesses" and specified five conditions that should be considered in evaluating eyewitness identification evidence (*Neil v. Biggers*, 1972). These factors were: (1) the opportunity of the witness to view the criminal at the time of the crime, (2) the length of time between the crime and the identification, (3) the level of certainty demonstrated by the witness at the identification, (4) the accuracy of the witness's prior description of the criminal, and (5) the witness's degree of attention during the crime. Unfortunately, research carried out in the years since this decision has shown that most of the Court's "educated guesses" were wrong or incomplete.

Research generally has supported the importance and relevance of the first two factors. The closer the witness is to the criminal, the longer the criminal is in view, the better the lighting, the more accurate the witness's later identification is likely to be. Most studies also have concluded that longer retention intervals lead to poorer identifications (as we might expect), though some studies have found no significant decrease in accuracy after longer intervals (Shepherd, 1983). Investigations of the third factor, the witness's certainty about his/her identification, have produced inconsistent findings. A meta-analysis of thirty-five studies found an average correlation between certainty and accuracy of +.25, indicating a fairly small positive relationship (Bothwell, Deffenbacher, & Brigham, 1987). Studies in which the witnessing conditions were poor, (little opportunity to view the target person, long retention interval, high stress, etc.), as in many crime situations, have generally found the weakest relationship between confidence and accuracy. Hence, it cannot be assumed that crime witnesses who are more certain of their identifications are necessarily more accurate. Nevertheless, jurors are typically very impressed by confident witnesses. For example, when mock jurors observed eyewitnesses to a staged crime being questioned by lawyers, they tended to use each witness's confidence as a cue to the witness's likely accuracy. But since witness accuracy was not related to confidence in this study, the mock jurors' evaluations were thrown off—on average they believed 68 percent of the accurate witnesses and 70 percent of the innaccurate witnesses (Lindsay et al., 1989).

FOCUS 13-6

Assessing the Fairness of a Lineup

Several years ago comedian Richard Pryor participated in a skit on the "Saturday Night Live" TV program in which he was placed in a lineup after being accused of a crime. The other members of the lineup were a nun, a refrigerator, and a duck. Not surprisingly, the eyewitness (who had previously described the criminal as a black male) picked out Pryor as the criminal. Although lineups used in present-day criminal cases are not as blatantly unfair as this one was, how can we determine whether a particular lineup is fair to the accused person? Several statistical methods have been proposed (Brigham et al., 1990; Malpass, 1981; Wells et al., 1979). A lineup is defined as fair if all lineup members match the general appearance of the suspect. To study the fairness of a lineup, a sample of people not involved with the crime (often called "mock witnesses") are shown the description of the criminal given by the eyewitness. The lineup is then shown to them and they guess which of the lineup members is the suspect. If a six-person lineup is fair, roughly one-sixth of the mock witnesses should guess each of the six different lineup members. If the lineup is unfair, because the suspect more closely resembles the criminal's description than the other lineup members (foils) do, then a disproportionately high percentage of mock witnesses will pick the suspect.

In the case of Richard Pryor's lineup, the unfairness is obvious and every mock witness would pick Pryor. In actual cases, the distinctions are more subtle. For example, I was asked to evaluate the fairness of a lineup used to identify the suspect in an upcoming murder case. The defense attorneys felt that the lineup was biased. I obtained a large photograph of the live lineup used plus descriptions of the criminal given by three eyewitnesses. I then showed the photo plus one of the three eyewitnesses' descriptions, or no description at all, to different samples of college students. Their task was to guess which one of the lineup members was the suspect.

The results of this study are presented in Figure 13-3. Note that when mock witnesses were given one of the eyewitnesses' descriptions, one-third to one-half of them picked out the real suspect, indicating that the other lineup members did not fit the description as closely as the suspect did. Furthermore, even when given *no* description, more mock witnesses picked the suspect than anyone else. Why? Because the suspect's appearance was *distinctive*, different from the foils. His hair was lighter in color and his uniform was a slightly different shade of blue than everyone else's. In addition, he was the only lineup member with a suntan, as the other men all had been recruited from the jail and had "jailhouse pallor." When I presented these data via expert testimony at a pretrial hearing, the judge ruled in agreement with the prosecuting attorney's assertion that although the research showed the lineup "was not perfect," the lineup was not "impermissibly suggestible." The lineup evidence was allowed to stand and the suspect was later convicted. ❖

The Court's fourth assumption, that witnesses who can describe a suspect accurately will also be likely to identify him positively, has not been supported. In two studies, we found no relationship between accuracy of prior descriptions and accuracy of identifications made from photograph lineups (Pigott & Brigham, 1985; Pigott, Brigham, & Bothwell, 1990). The two skills involved, *recall memory* (the ability to describe someone from memory) and *recognition memory* (the ability to pick someone out of a lineup), are not strongly related to each other.

The amount of arousal or stress that a witness experiences has received some research attention. The venerable **Yerkes-Dodson Law** (Yerkes & Dodson, 1908) asserts that there is an optimal level of arousal for performance on any task. For complex tasks there is a curvilinear relation between arousal and performance (Deffenbacher, 1983). Because trying to recognize a previously seen person is a complex task, it suggests that high levels of arousal (the right-hand portion of Figure 13-2) should lead to poorer performance, namely, poorer recognition on the lineup task. "Weapon focus," where a witness's attention is riveted to the criminal's weapon, rather than his face, can make subsequent identifications even tougher (Tooley et al., 1987; Maass & Koehnken, 1989).

Because many crimes involve very high levels of arousal (fear, anxiety, anger), the question of the impact of arousal on eyewitness accuracy is of great practical significance. Yet for both practical and ethical reasons, researchers cannot terrorize their subjects to the extent that real criminals do: They have to be content with milder procedures. The importance of high arousal and the mixed nature of preliminary research results (e.g., Brigham et al., 1983) suggest that additional research in this area would be extremely valuable.

Yerkes-Dodson law:
The principle that there is an optimal level of arousal for performance in any task; for complex tasks, there will be a curvilinear relationship between arousal and performance, with performance best at moderate levels of arousal.

FIGURE 13-2

The Yerkes-Dodson Law

Performance on a task depends on one's level of arousal and the complexity of the task.

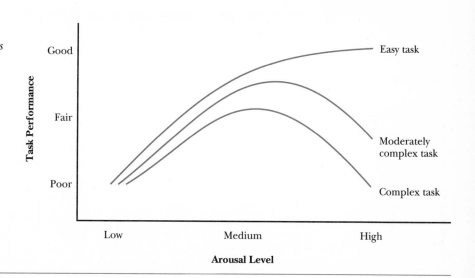

FIGURE 13-3

Analyzing the Fairness of an Actual Lineup

Percentage of "mock witnesses" picking out the suspect from a six-person lineup when given an eyewitness's description or no description at all.

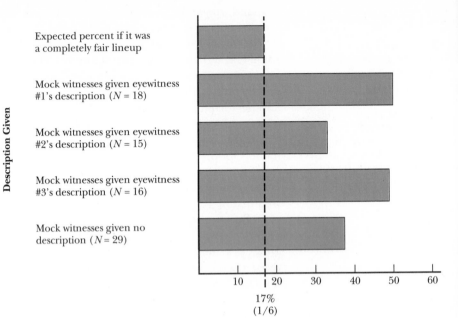

Expected percent if it was a completely fair lineup

Mock witnesses given eyewitness #1's description (*N* = 18)

Mock witnesses given eyewitness #2's description (*N* = 15)

Mock witnesses given eyewitness #3's description (*N* = 16)

Mock witnesses given no description (*N* = 29)

Description Given

10   20   30   40   50   60

17%
(1/6)

Percent Who Chose the Suspect

Source: Based on a Florida murder case.

The Own-Race Bias

To the human cartoonist, all penguins look alike.
Source: From *Penguin Dreams and Stranger Things: A Bloom County Book* by Berke Breathed. Copyright © 1985 by The Washington Post Company.

More than a half-century ago, Feingold (1914, p. 50) suggested that it was "well known that, other things being equal, individuals of a given race are distinguishable from each other in proportion to our familiarity, to our contact with the race as a whole. Thus, to the uninitiated American, all Asiatics look alike, while to the Asiatic all white men look alike." Many present-day

own-race bias:
The tendency for individuals to have difficulty in identifying people from another race in a lineup.

attorneys and law enforcement personnel share this assumption (Brigham & WolfsKeil, 1983). As noted in Chapter 11, a meta-analysis of fourteen studies indicated that an **own-race bias** occurred in laboratory studies for blacks and for whites (Bothwell, Brigham, & Malpass, 1989). Both races have an easier time identifying members of their own race accurately.

FOCUS 13-7

Eyewitness Accuracy in Convenience Stores and Banks

In an attempt to study eyewitness identifications in a realistic setting, several of my students and I have used clerks in Tallahassee convenience stores and bank tellers as subjects. Convenience store clerks and bank tellers are much more likely to be involved as eyewitnesses than are most citizens. We (Brigham, Maass, Snyder, & Spaulding, 1982) organized seventy-three visits to convenience stores by two "customers," one white and one black. Each customer did something unusual. One would ask for cigarettes and then pay in pennies. The other, at a different time, would take a product up to the counter, discover he didn't have enough money, fumble in his pockets, start for the door, then finally find the money and complete the transaction. Each customer also asked directions to the bus station, airport, hospital, or a local shopping mall. Two hours later, two well-dressed male "law interns" approached the counter and asked the clerk to look at two photo lineups, saying, "We have reason to believe that one or both of two people we are interested in may have been in your store within the last twenty-four hours." Each photo lineup contained one of our "customers" and five other males of similar age, race, and general appearance. About one-third (34 percent) of the time the clerks correctly picked out the customer, but over half the time they picked out someone else: They made a mistaken identification.

In another study (Pigott, Brigham, & Bothwell,

1990) at forty-two banks, a young white man attempted to cash a postal money order that had been clumsily altered from $10 to $110. (This scenario had been worked out in secret with the cooperation of the banks' officers.) After arguing with the teller (who, of course, would not cash the altered money order) for about one and one half minutes, the customer angrily stalked out of the bank. Four to five hours later, a female "law intern" came to the bank and asked the teller to describe the customer and then try and identify him from a photo lineup (half the time he was in the lineup, half the time he was not). Overall, the tellers were accurate 55 percent of the time. Most disturbingly, when shown the "blank" lineup in which the customer did not appear, 38 percent of the time the teller positively, but inaccurately, identified someone as the troublesome customer. As an illustration of the fallibility of eyewitness evidence, in one bank an officer who was concerned by our customer's behavior followed him to the door and watched to see where he went. The officer later told the law intern that the customer had talked with a man waiting in a white truck and they had then switched vehicles, with the customer driving off in the truck. Nothing of the sort had actually transpired. Our customer had happened to park next to a white truck, but he never talked to anybody outside and he left in his own car! ❖

Applications to the Legal System

Since eyewitness evidence has a high error rate, what can the criminal justice system do about it? As Figure 13-4 indicates, almost 90 percent of the defense attorneys in our survey believed that judges and juries place too much emphasis on such evidence (Brigham & WolfsKeil, 1983). There are two things we can do: improve the procedures for obtaining identifications, and educate judges and jury members about problems with eyewitness evidence.

Among the ways to improve procedures are minimizing the time delay between the apprehension of the suspect and the identification procedure; creating fair lineups by using foils of generally similar appearance to the suspect (see Focus 13-5); avoiding biased instructions or comments while the identification is being made; eliminating unintentional "nonverbal cue-

Opinions about the Accuracy of Eyewitness Identificaions

Responses of statewide samples of defense attorneys (N = 166), prosecuting attorneys (N = 69), and law enforcement personnel who handle eyewitness evidence (N = 201), about the weight given to eyewitness evidence by judges and juries.

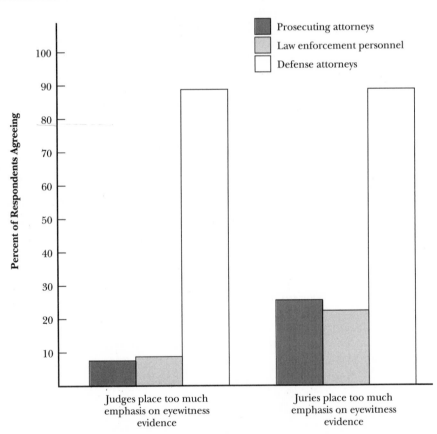

Weight Given

Sources: Data from Brigham, J. C. (1981). The accuracy of eyewitness evidence: How do attorneys see it? *Florida Bar Journal,* 55 (11), 714–721; Brigham, J. C., & WolfsKeil, M. P. (1983). Opinions of attorneys and law enforcement personnel on the accuracy of eyewitness identifications. *Law and Human Behavior, 7,* 337–349.

ing" of witnesses about the investigators' expectations; and minimizing the possibility that witnesses will see a photograph of the suspect before they view the lineup.

Changing the type of lineup may also help. Cutler and Penrod (1988) showed that the rate of false identifications was reduced by using a *sequential lineup,* wherein the witness sees one picture at a time and makes a yes/no decision for each, rather than seeing all the photos at once, as is usually done. The sequential lineup functions like a series of true/false questions, while the usual lineup can be seen as more analogous to a multiple-choice question in which people may be more likely to guess (often incorrectly).

The other route would be to use expert testimony concerning problematical aspects of eyewitness identifications in a particular case. Mr. Lang's attorney (Focus 13-1) might attempt to have a researcher testify about problems with eyewitness accuracy in situations involving high stress, short viewing time, and persons of a different race. It would be up to the trial judge to decide whether to let the researcher testify. Cutler and his co-workers (1989) showed that hearing expert testimony about eyewitness identification research did not make mock jurors uniformly more skeptical about eyewitnesses. Rather, while viewing a videotaped trial, they tended to pay more attention to the witnessing conditions (stress, lighting, viewing time, etc.) and gave less weight to a witness's confidence. These are exactly the effects one would hope for if the goal is an accurate appraisal of this type of evidence.

EVENTS DURING A TRIAL

If the defendant in a criminal trial decides not to plead guilty, then a trial begins. Social psychological factors, such as persuasion and attitude change, social power, prejudice, and the attributions made about the causes of the defendant's behavior, are important throughout the trial. In jury trials, the first step is the selection of jury members, carried out by the judge or by attorneys for both sides. The attorneys strive to act as effective persuasive communicators throughout the trial (Chapter 4), attempting to convince the judge and jury members of the rightness of their position. The judge continues to play a vital role, ruling whether or not evidence is admissible, giving final instructions to the jury before it begins to deliberate and, if the defendant is found guilty, deciding on the sentence to be handed down.

Selection of the Jury

Jury Selection Procedures

A law textbook many years ago contended "Many practitioners maintain that the selection of a jury is the most important step toward the winning of the case" (Brumbaugh, 1917, p. 285). More recently a book describing jury selec-

venire:
The group of people from which a jury is chosen.

voir dire:
The questioning procedure carried out by attorneys or judges through which jury members are selected.

tion techniques asserted that "People who constitute the jury can have as much or more to do with the outcome of the trial as the evidence or arguments" (Kairys et al., 1975, p. 1). In order to select the jury for a trial, the court calls in a large sample of citizens, called the **venire**, as the pool of potential jurors. A questioning procedure, called the **voir dire**, is employed to identify potentially biased jurors, who will then be excused *for cause:* they may know the defendant, or one of the witnesses, or one of the attorneys, or they may have strong feelings about the particular crime that prevent them from responding objectively to the evidence. Additionally, each attorney has a certain number of *peremptory challenges;* that is, he or she can excuse potential jurors without having to give a reason. Usually the defense is permitted more peremptory challenges than the prosecution (often about twelve for the defense as compared to six for the prosecution), but this procedure depends on the specific jurisdiction.

Usually the *voir dire* questioning is carried out in the open courtroom. Psychologists have pointed out that questioning on sensitive issues such as a juror's racial prejudices might yield more honest answers if carried out privately in the judge's chambers (Nietzel & Dillehay, 1982). But questioning in the judge's chambers may not be the answer either, because people may be intimidated by the judge. A study found that jurors are more candid when responding to attorneys than when replying to judges (S. Jones, 1987). Apparently, people are more inclined to tell a judge what they think the judge wants to hear. Might social psychologists be able to devise jury selection procedures that involve fewer demand characteristics?

"Death-Qualified" Juries

In capital cases (those that may result in the death penalty), special problems arise. In some states, after a guilty verdict is reached in a capital case, the jury then must decide whether to recommend a life sentence or the death penalty. During *voir dire,* prospective jurors who state that their opposition to the death penalty would make it impossible to vote for the death penalty if the defendant were convicted, or who say that they would have trouble finding the defendant guilty if conviction would lead to execution, are automatically excluded from the jury in capital cases. Some fifteen research studies have shown that the resulting **"death-qualified" juries** are composed largely of more conservative, authoritarian persons, because the excluded jurors who abhor the death penalty tend also to be the liberal and nonauthoritarian. Research shows that conservative, authoritarian persons are also more likely to convict, in general, than are more liberal persons (Cowan et al., 1984; Moran & Comfort, 1986). In 1986 the U.S. Supreme Court reviewed evidence from the fifteen research studies showing the link between pro-death penalty views and pro-conviction leanings. Many psychologists hoped that this case would be the one in which the majority of the justices would finally pay close attention to psychological research. However, despite these findings the court upheld the "death qualification" procedure in a controversial 5-4 decision, *Lockhart v. McCree* (1986). The majority appeared unim-

"death-qualified" juries:
In capital cases, juries in which all members have said they are comfortable with the death penalty. May be more likely to convict defendants than other juries would be.

pressed by the potential applicability of the research findings. Donald Bersoff, counsel for the American Psychological Association, lamented afterwards that "it is clear that even the most unassailable and methodologically perfect [research] evidence would not have convinced the majority" (Turkington, 1986, p.20). Another psychologist observed that, if this was a test of the Court's receptivity to social science, "the Court failed the test badly" (Thompson, 1989).

Strategies during the Voir Dire Examination

In states where defense attorneys are permitted to question the prospective jurors (in some states the judge does it), there are several strategies that may be used. Some attorneys believe they should pick any twelve people without questioning them very carefully, hoping to impress the jurors with the attorney's likability and sincerity (Brody, 1957). A second strategy is to try to indoctrinate the jury members while questioning them. For example, Mr. Lang's attorney (Focus 13-1) might ask each potential juror, "Are you aware that eyewitness identifications made in stressful conditions are often wrong?" Here the attorney tries to change the attitudes of the prospective jurors about the upcoming eyewitness testimony. Alert to this tactic, many judges have become more cautious about attorneys' *voir dire* techniques than they used to be (Blunk & Sales, 1977).

The third strategy, the most straightforward one, is simply to try and identify prejudices and prevent biased persons from becoming jury members. It is a tough job, for people may not recognize their own biases or they may deliberately conceal them. Further, aggressive questioning about possible prejudices may be resented by the prospective jury members and turn them against the attorney's side.

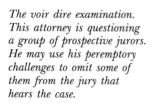

The voir dire examination. This attorney is questioning a group of prospective jurors. He may use his peremptory challenges to omit some of them from the jury that hears the case.

scientific jury selection:

A jury selection technique in which prospective members' opinions and attitudes are predicted from demographic characteristics.

A number of teams of attorneys and social scientists in the 1970s tried to select juries favorable to their cases in widely politicized trials, such as those involving Vietnam War dissenters and Watergate defendants. In addition to monitoring the *voir dire* process, the teams conducted surveys (Focus 13-8), checked out prospective jurors' homes and neighborhoods, asked their neighbors about them, and even checked their cars for bumper stickers that might give hints about their social attitudes. Focus 13-7 describes these tactics in the 1974 trial of John Mitchell, President Nixon's Attorney General, and Maurice Stans, Nixon's reelection campaign chairman.

Scientific jury selection is used in civil as well as criminal trials. One California consulting firm, which evaluated potential jurors for civil cases, claimed in its advertising: "We can help predict and influence what takes place in a juror's mind during a trial" (Andrews, 1982, p. 67). Determining the effect of such "scientific jury selection" procedures is very difficult. One can study what happened in a particular case but there is no way of knowing what would have happened if the techniques had not been used. Some attorneys and social scientists believe the techniques are effective (Glauber, 1984) and others doubt their worth. There have, as yet, been no *controlled* studies from which to make a conclusion about the effectiveness of the social science technique of juror selection (Berman & Sales, 1977; Horowitz & Willging, 1984).

If the techniques are effective, this raises important ethical questions. First, not everyone has access to these techniques. As one observer commented, "It gives rich people and radicals an edge over the rest of us" (Glauber, 1984). Second, the process may be used to bias the jury selection process. Instead of achieving an impartial jury (supposedly the goal in our system), the experts may be aiming for a jury that is strongly biased in favor of their side. In the interest of fair play, should behavioral scientists make the information they gather available to both sides, so that each side can use its peremptory challenges most effectively (Herbsleb et al., 1979)?

Users of the procedures offer two kinds of justification. One is that the techniques really are not much different from standard legal practice (Christie, 1976). But the process *is* different, as we have seen. Ordinarily, attorneys do not use surveys or statistical profiles. A second justification, offered by one of the jury selection teams (Schulman et al., 1973), rests on the social scientists' beliefs that the defendant's rights to presumption of innocence are sometimes seriously threatened in trials where the government goes after citizens holding unpopular positions, as was the case for some trials of Vietnam War protesters in the 1970s.

If the task of scientific jury selection is to demonstrate bias and to remedy that bias by providing a jury that does not exclude any element of the community, then scientific jury selection can help to achieve a representative yet unbiased panel, and can be seen as an ethical procedure. Scientific jury selection is detrimental to the judicial process if it is used solely for the purpose of creating or maximizing prejudice for or against the defen-

FOCUS 13-8

"Scientific Jury Selection" and the Mitchell-Stans Case

Former U.S. Attorney General John Mitchell and Maurice Stans hired a team of social scientists to aid their defense in their 1974 trial for conspiracy to impede a Securities and Exchange Commission investigation of financier Robert Vesco. The research team analyzed survey results to see what demographic characteristics were strongly associated with opinions unfavorable to the defendants. They used results of a public opinion survey conducted among the general population of potential jurors and a more specific, but indirect, survey of the prospective jurors called to court for that particular trial. The second survey was based upon interviews with neighbors, friends, and employers of the prospective jurors. The team concluded that the "worst possible juror" from the defense perspective (that is, a person having negative attitudes toward Mitchell and Stans) was as follows: a liberal Jewish Democrat who read the *New York Times* or *New York Post,* was interested in political affairs, and was well informed about Watergate.

Through skillful use of *voir dire* questioning and peremptory challenges, the defense was able to end up with a jury that contained mostly "good jurors" from their perspective, and they were able to do this even though the judge took an active role in the *voir dire* process. The distribution, by education and occupation, for the actual jury was dramatically different from the original sample of citizens (*venire*) from which the jury was picked. Forty-five percent of the people in the *venire* had some college education; only 8 percent of those finally selected to be on the jury had any. Thirty-two percent of the original panel were well informed about Watergate and only one of the actual jurors was. Thus the team of defense attorneys and their consultants were successful in establishing their goal of a jury that did not have "antidefendant" prejudices.

Mitchell and Stans were acquitted. It is impossible, of course, to know for sure what role, if any, the jury selection procedures played in this "victory," yet it is an intriguing question. As Zeisel and Diamond (1976, p. 151) noted, " . . . since the defense won the case, which many spectators and court reporters thought they should have lost, speculation was rife as to the part played by the survey in this victory." ❖

John Mitchell (center) and Maurice Stans (left) talk with reporters after their trial.

dant. As scientific jury selection continues to increase in frequency, society will have to come to terms with the questions of fairness and impartiality.

Persuasion by Attorneys

Characteristics of the Attorney

During a trial, attorneys act as *persuasive communicators* to the judge and jury members. The greater the lawyer's perceived credibility (recall from Chapter 4 that this includes expertise and trustworthiness), and the greater the lawyer's attractiveness, the more influence he or she will have in the courtroom. Attractiveness includes physical appearance, familiarity, similarity to the audience members, and likability. The greater the attorney's social power (Chapter 5), the greater the influence as well. A study that had people view simulated attorney-client interviews found that clients' perceptions of attorneys were affected more by the attorneys' relational skills (social poise) than their level of legal competence (Feldman & Wilson, 1981).

Attractiveness, status, and expertise can influence the jury member's *attention* to the attorney's message. Well-crafted arguments can influence a jury's *comprehension* of the message, and high credibility and power can help get the jury to *yield* to the message (see Figure 4-3). In terms of Petty and Cacioppo's (1986) elaboration likelihood model, if a person is motivated to process the communication (which unbiased jurors are presumed to be), then the quality of the arguments is crucial. The attorney's social poise and attractiveness, on the other hand, would be more important for getting attitude change via the peripheral route, which does not involve serious consideration of the issues.

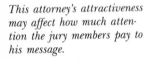

This attorney's attractiveness may affect how much attention the jury members pay to his message.

The Attorney's Message

It is generally more effective to use a one-sided message and to draw a conclusion unless the audience is particularly intelligent, well-educated, or initially opposed to one's side (Chapter 4). It is said that Clarence Darrow (1857–1938), the famous lawyer, employed the tactic of distraction to prevent the jury from hearing his opponent's closing arguments. Darrow would insert a wire inside a cigar. When he smoked the cigar during his opponent's closing statement and the ash grew very long, the jury would become increasingly fascinated and not pay attention to the opponent's arguments. Modern research on the effects of distraction on attitude change shows that extreme distraction does prevent the audience from attending to a message. However, mild distractors may *increase* the persuasive impact of a message because they may interfere with the audience's tendency to argue internally against the message (Zimbardo et al., 1977). Hence, Darrow's tactic, which probably led only to mild distraction, may actually have backfired and increased his opponent's effectiveness.

One important task for an attorney is to provide counterarguments to his adversary's positions, thereby trying to *inoculate* the audience (the judge or jury members) against opposing attitude change messages (McGuire, 1964). Many attorneys may do this during opening arguments when they present their cases and suggest arguments that weaken their opponent's position. Even the length of a lawyer's opening statement may affect the final verdict: A lengthy statement may be more effective (Pyszcynski & Wrightsman, 1981).

The words, pictures, or videotapes that an attorney uses can affect the jury's reaction. For example, damages given by research subjects to the parents of an injured ten-year-old boy in a hypothetical case were greater when color photographs of the boy were shown than when black-and-white photographs or just a verbal description of the boy was given (Whalen & Blanchard, 1982). Another study showed subjects a film of two cars colliding and later asked them whether or not broken glass resulted (it did not). Those who were asked whether broken glass occurred when the cars "smashed together" were more likely to recall seeing broken glass than those who saw the same film but were asked about when the cars "hit each other" (Loftus & Palmer, 1974).

Evaluating the Effectiveness of Persuasion

The ultimate measure of an attorney's effectiveness is the outcome of the case—a win, a loss, or a negotiated settlement. But there also are ways of monitoring an attorney's effectiveness as the trial is in progress. In the late 1970s a panel of twelve jurors was seated to hear a $300 million antitrust suit against IBM. IBM's attorneys thought the case so important that they had a consultant recruit six people with backgrounds and attitudes similar to those of the real jury. Members of this "shadow jury" were paid to sit in the courtroom each day, weigh the evidence, and report their impressions to the consultant each evening. (They did not know which side the consultant was working for.) IBM's lawyers used the shadow jury's reactions to modify and develop the arguments to be made in court the next day (Andrews, 1982). IBM won the suit, though it's impossible to know what role the shadow jury played in this victory. Nowadays, before an important trial, some firms recruit mock juries on which the lawyers practice their arguments while psychologists make suggestions on how to increase persuasiveness.

The Judge's Actions

Telling Jurors to Ignore Evidence or Testimony

The trial judge exerts an enormous influence on any criminal trial. Unless the defendant has waived rights to a jury trial, the judge directs the *voir dire* proceedings during which the trial jury is selected. The judge decides on motions by the lawyers concerning admissibility of evidence, prior statements of witnesses, statements made by witnesses who cannot be present at the trial, expert testimony, and so forth.

One of the judge's tasks is to decide whether or not the jury should pay attention to disputed pieces of evidence. The judge may on occasion instruct the jury to disregard a portion of testimony they have just heard. Are jury members truly able to disregard statements that bear upon the case? Research suggests they are not. Several studies using mock jurors (college student subjects playing the role of jurors) found they were affected by testimony they had heard even when they were instructed to disregard it (Carretta & Moreland, 1983).

Think back to our analysis of social cognition in Chapter 2. As a trial unfolds, jurors form *person schemas* for the various witnesses they hear, and an *event schema* for the crime itself. Once the initial schemas are formed, subsequent information is likely to be remembered and interpreted in ways that fit into the existing schemas. The belief perseverance effect notes that beliefs may continue to be held even when their original basis has been discomfirmed. If a juror hears an important piece of information (about a confession, a wiretap, a polygraph test) that modifies her schema about the event or the defendant, and then is told by the judge to disregard that information, the changed schema may remain. And even though she may try hard to ignore that specific piece of information, her entire orientation toward the trial may have been shifted.

The effect of inadmissible evidence may be different depending on which side the evidence favors. Jurors are better able to ignore inadmissible evidence when it favors the prosecution than when it favors the defendant (Thompson et al., 1981). Also, jurors apparently find it easier to ignore a confession obtained under threat than a confession obtained under a promise of leniency, even though both of these confessions are equally inadmissible in court (Kassin & Wrightsman, 1981).

Final Instructions to the Jury

The last thing that jurors hear before retiring to the jury room to deliberate on a verdict is the judge's verbal instructions on the relevant law in the case and the specific decisions the jury needs to make. These final instructions are often very technical and lengthy, sometimes fifty to a hundred pages long!

Interviews with jurors have shown that, because of length and incomprehensible legal language, less than half of the instructions are remembered. Misunderstandings and forgetting affect the jurors' interpretations of the relevant law, the content of their deliberations, and the verdicts they reach. Elwork et al. (1982) videotaped an actual trial and showed it to volunteer jurors who then deliberated and came to a verdict. Afterward they completed a questionnaire testing their understanding of the judge's instructions. On the average, the jurors answered only 40 percent of the questions correctly. What can be done? One step is to shorten and simplify the instructions, using as little legal jargon as possible. When this was tried, juror comprehension increased greatly (Alfini et al., 1982; Severance et al., 1984). Another aid is to give each juror a copy of the judge's instructions for reference.

We have seen how our schemas guide and channel the way information is processed. Person and event schemas develop quite early in a trial, and influence how the trial information is remembered. A judge's instructions to the jury at the end of the testimony, before they begin deliberations, might not be able to undo the effects of inappropriate schemas that jurors may have developed during the trial. Therefore, it might be valuable for jurors to get instructions from the judge *before* the trial begins, to help them develop trial-relevant schemas that fit the way they are supposed to evaluate the evidence. To assess the impact of such a step, Heuer and Penrod (1989) were able to get judges to give standard preliminary pretrial instructions that discussed the central procedures (the structure of the trial) and concepts (e.g., burden of proof, evaluation of witnesses and evidence) in thirty-four civil and criminal trials. Compared with thirty-three other trials where preliminary instructions were not given, jurors were more satisfied with the trial process and found it easier to follow legal guidelines in their decision making when they had been given the preliminary instructions.

Sentencing

Here is where the equality versus discretion dilemma is most visible. There are sometimes vast differences in sentences given by different judges for similar crimes. One reason for these differences is that there are several different theories regarding the purpose of sentencing. The sentence can be intended: (1) to satisfy the public's need for vengeance on the criminal *(retribution)*; (2) to discourage other potential offenders *(deterrence)*; (3) to protect society from additional crimes by the criminal *(incapacitation)*; and/or (4) to rehabilitate the criminal *(rehabilitation)*. Disparities in sentencing are particularly great in areas where a judge's sociopolitical values strongly influence the sentencing decision, as in sexual abuse, political protest, and drug use cases.

A study within the federal court system in New England provided a clear demonstration of the power of individual judges in setting sentences. Partridge and Eldridge (1974) asked fifty federal judges to impose sentences on twenty different hypothetical defendants. As Table 13-1 indicates, there was enormous disagreement among the judges. For example, for a convic-

The sentencing hearing. The judge evaluates several factors in deciding what sentences to give.

tion of theft and possession of stolen goods the recommended sentences ranged from no prison and four years probation to seven and a half years in prison. The authors of the study concluded "It would appear that absence of consensus is the norm in sentencing." Other researchers concluded that sentence disparities result more from different judges receiving different types of cases than from judges' attitudes (Ebbeson & Konečni, 1981).

Characteristics of the Defendant

In Chapter 8 we saw that physical attractiveness has a powerful influence on how we are treated by others. It is no different in the courtroom. Not only have laboratory studies shown that unattractive defendants are punished more harshly than attractive defendants who have committed the same crime (Efran, 1974; Michelini & Snodgrass, 1980), but an analysis of sixty-seven actual criminal cases found that unattractive defendants were much more likely to receive prison sentences than were attractive defendants (Stewart, 1980). Not only does the attractiveness of the defendant matter, but so does the attractiveness of the victim. On the average, the more attractive the victim, the harsher is the punishment given the criminal (Kerr, 1978; Thornton, 1977).

In what ways does the defendant's race make a difference in sentencing? Stewart (1980) found that nonwhite defendants were more likely to be convicted than were whites for comparable crimes. Further, the convicted were much more likely to be sent to prison if they were nonwhite than if white. Other studies have also shown that jurors tend to be more likely to convict when the defendant is of a different race or when the victim is the same race as the jurors (Dane & Wrightsman, 1982).

TABLE 13-1	DISPARITIES IN JUDGES' SENTENCING FOR HYPOTHETICAL CASES

Second Circuit Sentencing Study. The numbers in the table indicate the federal judges' sentence assignments for seven cases. The range in sentences, the difference between the most and least severe figures for each case, is quite large, implying that disagreement between judges is high even when they review the same cases.

Experimental Case	Most Severe Sentence	Median Sentence	Least Severe Sentence
Extortionate credit transactions; income tax violations	20 years prison, $65,000 fine	10 years prison, $50,000 fine	3 years prison
Bank robbery	18 years prison, $5,000 fine	10 years prison	5 years prison
Sales of heroin	10 years prison, 5 years probation	5 years prison, 3 years probation	1 year prison, 5 years probation
Theft and possession of stolen goods	7.5 years prison	3 years prison	4 years probation
Operating an illegal gambling business	1 year prison, 18 months probation	3 years probation	1 year probation
Mail theft	6 months prison, 18 months probation	3 years probation	1 year probation
Perjury	1 year prison, $1,000 fine	2 years probation, $500 fine	$1,000 fine

Source: Partridge, A., & Eldridge, C. (1974). *The Second Circuit sentencing study: A report to the judges of the Second Circuit.* Washington, D.C: Federal Judicial Center. Reprinted by permission.

Early analyses (Williams, 1969) had suggested pervasive antiblack discrimination in sentences received, but more careful recent analyses found systematic discrimination only in certain circumstances: (1) the death penalty for murder has been imposed in a fashion discriminatory toward blacks in the South but not elsewhere; (2) in the past, for executions imposed for rape, discrimination against black defendants who raped white victims was substantial (the death penalty can no longer be imposed for rape). An archival study of actual trials found that the combination of defendants' and victims' race accounted for twenty-two percent of the variance in capital rape trials (Hagan, 1974); (3) there has been a general pattern of less-severe punishment for crimes with black victims than those with white victims (Kleck, 1985).

Another important factor is the apparent similarity between the defendant's beliefs and the jurors' beliefs. Not surprisingly, defendants who express beliefs similar to those of the jury members are more likely to be acquitted or given light sentences than those who express beliefs quite different from the jury members (Griffitt & Jackson, 1973). Clothing may matter, too. In many jurisdictions poorer defendants who have been awaiting trial in jail, unable to make bail, appear in the courtroom in their prison uniforms. Defense lawyers feared that the failure to allow the defendants to dress in their usual street clothes may prejudice the jurors even further against them (Saks & Hastie, 1978). The just world assumption (Chapter 2) might also come into play. Jurors may assume that if an individual has been confined to jail awaiting trial, the person must have deserved this misfortune and be guilty as charged (Lerner, 1980). An astute defense attorney will pay considerable attention to the appearance of her client.

Jury Decision Making

Characteristics of Jury Members

Folklore abounds as to what personal or demographic characteristics affect jurors. For example, years ago Brumbaugh (1917) suggested that biases are associated with religion, nationality, politics, class, and education. A more recent description of legal folklore asserted, "As a rule, clergymen, schoolteachers, lawyers, and wives of lawyers do not make desirable jurors. They are too often sought out for advice and tend to be too opinionated. Retired businessmen are usually fair but disinclined to render wild verdicts. A reasonably well-educated laboring man is not to be despised" (Simon, 1967, pp. 103–104).

A study of jurors in three Midwestern cities found that education and ethnicity were the only two demographic factors related to a juror's vote (Simon, 1967). Concerning personality, research has shown that, as we would expect, persons high in authoritarianism (Chapter 11) are more likely to be punitive toward defendants and think defendants are guilty (Mitchell & Byrne, 1982), unless the defendant is a police officer (Mitchell, 1979). People high in empathy are more likely to vote for a not-guilty verdict (Mills & Bohannon, 1980).

Jury members listen to a case. There is a lot of folklore among attorneys about which types of people make "good jurors".

For many years, social psychologists have been interested in the group processes that transpire during deliberations. As we saw in Chapter 6, the product of a group process depends upon four factors: (1) the composition of the group, (2) the group structure, (3) the nature of the group process, and (4) the task facing the group. The composition of the jury (the characteristics of its members) is determined when jury members are selected. Group structure includes variables such as group size (six or twelve), spatial arrangements and social organization, whereas process refers to what the group does. The group's task in a criminal trial is usually clear (a guilty/not-guilty verdict) although in civil lawsuits the task may be more complex.

Jury Size

In recent years, as a way to save money and expedite court matters, a number of jurisdictions have allowed six-person as well as twelve-person juries. In 1970, the U.S. Supreme Court was called upon to decide on the constitutionality of juries smaller than twelve (*Williams v. Florida*, 1970). The court held that smaller juries were not prejudicial to defendants and, hence, were constitutional. Yet, as you may already have noted, psychological research questions such an assumption. The Court argued that it is the *ratio* of convict-to-acquit jurors that is important, and that a jury split 5 to 1 (with 83 percent for conviction) will exert the same degree of pressure on the lone minority that a jury split 10 to 2 (83 percent for conviction) will exert on the minority of two. But research on conformity and minority influence (Chapter 5) shows that this is not so. Recall that in Asch's study of conformity, the amount of conformity dropped drastically when there were two dissenters rather than one. A single dissenter will have a much tougher time resisting group pressure than will two dissenters, even if the majority is twice as large in the second case.

Generally, a larger group (a jury of 12 persons) will be more *reliable* and *accurate* in its work than will a smaller group. For example, although the average verdict awarded in damage cases by a small jury might be the same as for large juries, the fluctuations in verdicts will be greater (less reliable) for small juries. In addition, the smaller a jury, the more likely that groups that are in the minority in the population will not be represented at all. According to probability theory, if a minority group comprises 10 percent of a population and the jury is drawn representatively from the population, there is a 72 percent probability that a twelve-person jury will contain at least one member of the minority. For a six-person jury, however, the probability is only 47 percent that the jury will contain at least one member of the minority group (Saks & Hastie, 1978).

In a later decision (*Ballew v. Georgia*, 1978), the U.S. Supreme Court took note of the recent social science research and criticism of its earlier decision on jury size. The court noted that smaller juries had been shown to be less likely to reach "legally correct" decisions, were less likely to foster "effective group deliberation," and were more likely to convict defendants, because in a case where the majority of jurors favor conviction, prodefendant minorities are apt to be smaller or nonexistent. While continuing to allow six-person juries, the Court concluded that a jury of fewer than six persons would not be permitted.

Selection of a Leader

One of the more important processes in jury deliberation is selection of a foreperson. How does this proceed? Seating is one important factor (Chapter 12). Research has shown that persons who sit at either end of a rectangular table are three times as likely to be selected as foreperson of the jury by the other jury members than persons sitting in any other positions (Strodtbeck & Hook, 1961). Persons sitting at the end positions also engage in considerably more communications than those in any other position. The researchers also found that persons from the proprietor and manager classes took the end positions about 15 percent more frequently than would be expected by chance. Hence, people who are accustomed to being in leadership positions are more likely to take the "leadership position" at the table and be picked as forepersons. Additionally, the person who speaks first in the jury room often ends up being selected. Gender and socioeconomic status are also important. Research showed that in the past, males were five times more likely to be selected as forepersons than were females (Strodtbeck, James, & Hawkins, 1957), as were persons with higher socioeconomic status.

Sometimes these research findings are useful. While revising this chapter I was called to serve on a jury in a case involving alleged "acquaintance rape" of a college student. As the case unfolded, I became eager to be selected as foreperson for the jury, hoping to do some persuasion of my own in the jury room. As we approached the jury room to deliberate after four days of trial, I inched in front, poised to slide into the chair at the head of the table—only to find out that it was a round table! Not to be denied, I quickly spoke up first, "Well, who should we pick as foreperson?" As I had hoped, someone responded, "Why don't you be it?" and I humbly assented.

The Polarization Effect

The group polarization effect, the tendency for groups to make more extreme decisions than individuals do (Chapter 6), has also been observed in jury deliberations. Group interaction seems to magnify already-existing tendencies in the individual preferences of group members. In one study, jurors' final ratings of guilt and of recommended punishment became more extreme as the case was discussed—in a high guilt and punishment direction for cases where guilt was already rated as high, and in the opposite direction for cases where guilt was already rated as relatively low (Myers & Kaplan, 1976). Other research (MacCoun & Kerr, 1988) suggests that there is a general "leniency bias"—proacquittal factions are likely to be more persuasive than are proconviction factions.

Although individual differences in personality factors such as dominance and persuasibility may influence the decision-making process, research indicates that by far the strongest predictor of the eventual verdict is the distribution of viewpoints at the beginning of deliberation. Kalven and Zeisel's (1966) analysis of actual trials found that hung juries (juries unable to reach a unanimous verdict) occurred only when there was a substantial split in opinion at the beginning of deliberation. If an initial minority was three persons or less on a twelve-person jury, a hung jury hardly ever resulted. Initial minorities of four or five persons out of twelve were more likely to hold out against the majority. The researchers suggested that the deliberation process can be likened to what the developer does for an exposed film: "It brings out the picture, but the outcome is predetermined" (Kalven & Zeisel, 1966, p. 489). Although the original distribution of beliefs is the most potent predictor of a jury's final verdict, personality characteristics are not irrelevant, as they may have determined those original beliefs in the first place.

The Hindsight Bias

The hindsight bias also may play a crucial role in jury deliberations. In medical malpractice lawsuits, for example, jurors are supposed to base their judgment on the defendant's behavior prior to the occurrence of the harm (e.g., Did the doctor take all due care to avert some bad outcome?), not on how bad the outcome was for the patient. But if the hindsight bias operates (e.g., "You should have known all along what was going to happen"), then we would expect jurors to attribute more responsibility to physicians whose actions happened to result in very bad outcomes than those whose actions led to less disastrous outcomes, even when their prior behaviors were the same (and hence, in legal terms, they should be held equally responsible). Research (Casper et al., 1989) indicates that this bias occurs — the severity of the outcome affects perceptions of prior responsibility.

The hindsight bias, in combination with the just world assumption may affect jurors' evaluation of rape victims, as they unfairly engage in "victim blaming", making the assumption that the event was foreseeable and the victim "should have known better", thereby attributing some of the responsibility for the attack to her (McCaul et al., 1990; Thornton et al., 1988). One study identified two common stereotypes of the rape victim — a young, naive, attractive "flirt" who does not realize the effect she has on men, and the "slut" who dresses and behaves in a provocative manner (Mazelan, 1980). Rape victims themselves may engage in self-blame, again as a consequence of the hindsight bias and the just world assumption. Analysts have suggested that it is more adaptive if the victim blames the incident on her *behavior* ("I should not have walked alone." "I should have locked the windows."), which is modifiable, than on her *character* ("I'm a weak person and can't say no." "I'm the type of person who attracts rapists."), which may be perceived as unchangeable (Abbey, 1987). Her feelings of control and her perceived ability to avoid future attacks will be greater when she has attributed the rape to her prior behavior, rather than to her character. The National Commission on the Causes and Prevention of Violence estimated that fewer than *five percent* of rape victims played any type of responsible role at all in the crime, but jurors and victims alike may be all too willing to place part of the responsibility on the victim's shoulders.

Making Attributions

Perhaps the only place where people consciously and systematically go through attributional processes is in the jury deliberation situation (Shaver, 1975). Here they indirectly observe a behavior (as depicted by the evidence, by the attorneys, and by the witnesses), make judgments of the intentions underlying the behavior, and decide whether to make a dispositional or environmental attribution for the defendant's behavior. The procedure is most clear in a case centering on the defendant's perceived intention (self-defense or aggression). If the jurors make a dispositional attribution in such a case, they will reach a guilty verdict, for they will have decided that the accused's behaviors represent his underlying personality dispositions. Deciding on an environmental attribution, on the other hand, would lead to a not-guilty verdict, for this would assert that the behavior was caused by environmental factors, such as a menacing person from whom the accused was defending himself.

Several of the biases in attributions are relevant here. We saw earlier how schemas and the hindsight bias can affect interpretations of the evidence. The *fundamental attribution error,* wherein people are more likely to make dispositional attributions for others' behaviors than for their own, implies that jurors, being human, will be biased toward underestimating the environmental factors that may have affected a witness's behavior. They will be likely to focus on the dispositional factors of the witness (such as a "criminal mind" or "irresponsibility"). One way to try to reduce the fundamental attribution error might be to encourage the jury to covertly play a role similar to the one the witness played. ("Imagine that you are facing the following situation. What would you do?") As the jury members become "vicarious actors" they are more likely to make situational attributions that favor the witness.

We have seen that the just world assumption also may come into play. Because of the tendency to believe that bad things happen only to bad people who deserve them, the victim of crime or the plaintiff in a civil matter may not receive as much empathy from jury members as would be appropriate or fair, for jury members may assume, "Well, it must have been partly his/her fault."

SOCIAL PSYCHOLOGY IN THE COURTROOM: LEGAL AND PRACTICAL ISSUES

Research Issues: Mundane Realism and External Validity

Although many social scientists have been eager to apply their research findings to the legal system, judges and attorneys often have not been eager to receive them. Some of the legal system's reluctance stems from two concepts introduced in Chapter 1: the *mundane realism* and *external validity* of research results. The mundane realism of a study refers to how closely the research situation reflects the real-world situation to which it is applied. External validity denotes how far one can generalize research findings, based on the heterogeneity of the research sample and the procedures employed. Many psychological studies of potential legal relevance do not do well on either count. Studies that use college students as subjects are of limited external validity because, on the average, students differ from jurors in many ways. Studies that have used six- or twelve-person mock juries have usually exposed the mock jury to a typed summary of a trial or a videotaped portion of a role-played trial segment. This is quite different from watching an actual trial over a period of several hours or days. Finally, knowing that one's verdict will have no real effect on anyone (it's an experiment, no one will go to prison) may affect the way persons behave. Legal authorities quite understandably have questioned the relevance of these laboratory studies for actual courtroom situations.

Attitudinal Issues: Misunderstanding the Scientific Method

The legal system has been generally reluctant to use research findings. One reason may be a general reluctance to let outsiders onto one's home turf (the courtroom). One social scientist, who has attempted to deliver expert testimony on factors affecting eyewitness identifications, asserted that the basic reason he often was rejected by judges was that "nobody loves a smartass" (Buckhout, 1976). The outside expert may be perceived by judges as a "smartass" who just complicates things needlessly.

Another problem is that many court personnel have little understanding of (or interest in) the scientific method and the value of carefully done scientific research (Chapter 1). They do not understand the process of generalizing from a relatively small sample of people studied to the larger group from which the sample was selected. They are unfamiliar with notions of probability and statistical significance. In the U.S. Supreme Court's 1978 *Ballew v. Georgia* decision on jury size reviewed earlier, the majority opinion stated that the use of social science data was justified "because they provide the only basis, besides judicial hunch, for a decision" on the impact of juries of different sizes. Yet three other justices, including Chief Justice Warren Burger, criticized their fellow justices for their "heavy reliance upon numerology derived from statistical studies" (Loftus & Monahan, 1980). Hence, although several of the justices were impressed by the research results, others clearly were not, as was also the case for the 1987 *Lockhart v. McCree* decision on "death-qualified" juries discussed earlier. It appears that many judges are willing to accept and utilize social science research when it supports the conclusion they wanted to reach anyway, as in the 1954 *Brown v. Board of Education* decision that outlawed school segregation (Chapter 11), but are willing to ignore or distort social science findings when they support the "wrong" conclusion (Thompson, 1989).

Nevertheless, as social scientists carry out research that is more directly relevant to the particular perspective of the legal system, their findings may be gradually blended into the law over time, despite the legal system's resistance to accepting scientific data (Acker, 1990). As Yarmey (1979, p. 227) noted, "What one generation of lawyers prefer to understand as 'common sense' often depends upon the theory and findings of the previous generation of [scientific] investigators." By one means or another, scientific research will make a difference in the application of justice.

SUMMARY

Social psychological concepts are highly applicable to legal issues and the justice system. There are four general dilemmas in the psychological study of the law that stem from conflicts between basic values. These include the rights of individuals versus the "common good," equality versus discretion, using law to discover truth or to resolve conflicts, and science versus the law as a source of decisions. During the pretrial phase, bargaining and negotiation skills are important in affecting plea bargaining and bail setting. Controversial methods are often used in gathering evidence: the polygraph, or "lie detector," and hypnosis. Experts disagree strongly as to the worth of these techniques. Eyewitness evidence has been the focus of much recent research because such evidence is very convincing to jurors but often may be incorrect, especially if the witness and the criminal are of different races.

Some attorneys have relied on techniques of "scientific jury selection" as a way to select a jury favorable to their side. This usually involves the identification of demographic characteristics likely to be associated with favorable attitudes. It is difficult to assess the effectiveness of these techniques but they raise important ethical questions. Social psychological analyses also can help us understand the persuasive effectiveness of attorneys and interpret judges' behaviors. Jury decision making has been widely studied. Processes involved in selecting a leader (the jury foreperson), the polarization effect, and biases in making attributions are particularly important. There are a number of basic scientific and attitudinal issues involved in applying social psychology to the courtroom.

CHAPTER 14

The Social Psychology
of Health

Every affection of the mind that is attended with either pain or pleasure, hope or fear, is the cause of an agitation whose influence extends to the heart.   Dr. William Harvey, 1628

The only way to keep your health is to eat what you don't want, drink what you don't like, and do what you druther not.   Mark Twain, Pudd'nhead Wilson ❖

PREVIEW

In recent decades psychologists have shown that an understanding and application of psychological principles can have a major impact on physical health. Many of the concepts discussed in previous chapters — compliance, attitude change, social power, attributions, and so forth — are directly relevant to improving health and health care. In this chapter we will discuss the applications of social psychology to behavioral medicine and health psychology. We will analyze the effectiveness of techniques for getting people to change self-destructive behaviors such as smoking, excessive drinking, overeating, and unsafe sex. Then we will consider the patterns of communication between medical practitioners and patients. The practitioner, to be most effective, must communicate concern and caring to the patient and must persuade the patient to follow specific instructions for healthful behaviors, such as taking medication properly, sticking to a special diet, and making life-style changes. Social psychological findings about social power are particularly important in getting patients to comply with, or adhere to, medical instructions. We will then look more closely at psychological factors that can lead to illness, namely stress, coping style, pessimism, the Type A behavior pattern, and hostility.

THE APPLICATIONS OF SOCIAL PSYCHOLOGY TO MEDICINE

Changes in Medical Problems in Recent Years

The pattern of major health problems in the United States has changed markedly in recent years as new medical discoveries have eradicated many of the killers of earlier centuries. For example, pneumonia, tuberculosis, and gastrointestinal enteritis were the top three causes of death in 1900, but by 1987 these three diseases were no longer among the top five causes of death; diseases of the heart ranked first and cancers second. It has been estimated that one-half of all deaths in the U.S. today are due to unhealthy behavioral life-styles. As a case in point, the U.S. Surgeon General reported that cigarette smoking is the leading preventable cause of death in the United States (Richmond, 1979a). Seven of the ten leading causes of death today are largely behaviorally determined (Table 14-1) and could be drastically reduced if people changed their habits in five areas: stopping smoking, better diet, more exercise, lessening alcohol use, and taking medication for hypertension (high blood pressure) if needed (Richmond, 1979b). As we saw earlier (Chapter 9), AIDS is another cause of death that is critically affected by behavior. Understanding the psychological factors that contribute to the adoption of health-threatening behaviors is of major importance.

Behavioral Medicine and Health Psychology

Although the convergence of interest in medical and psychological processes has received greater attention in recent years, it is not entirely new. Indeed, years ago John B. Watson, later to be known as "the father of behaviorism," commented, "The medical student must be taught that whether he is specializing in surgery, obstetrics, or psychiatry, his subjects are human beings and not merely objects on which he may demonstrate his skill. This shift in his ideas of value will lead him to feel the need of psychologic training and to accept that training" (Watson, 1912, p. 917). The American Psychological Association had sponsored its first symposium on psychology and medical education one year earlier, in 1911.

behavioral medicine:
The development of behavioral science knowledge for understanding physical health and applying this knowledge to the prevention, diagnosis, and treatment of illness.

biopsychological model:
The position that biological, psychological, and social factors are involved in all stages of health and illness.

health psychology:
An area of psychology that focuses on developing techniques to help in the prevention of behaviors that are harmful to health, such as alcohol, and drug abuse and cigarette smoking.

Despite this early interest, the concept of **behavioral medicine** began to receive attention only in the 1970s (Birk, 1973). Behavioral medicine refers to the development of behavioral science knowledge for understanding physical health and applying this knowledge to the prevention, diagnosis, and treatment of illness (Schwartz & Weiss, 1978). Beginning in the 1960s, a number of medical schools created Departments of Behavioral Sciences so that medical students could be informed about the applications of social science knowledge to medical problems. Psychologists are the largest single group of nonphysician behavioral scientists employed in medical schools in the United States (Gentry, 1982). As Peterson (1988, p. 119) put it, "The germ model is dead. Illness is now viewed in terms of the interaction among biological, psychological, and social factors." This position represents the **biopsychological model** (Taylor, 1990).

Behavioral medicine and health psychology became "buzz words of the 1980s" (Pomerleau & Rodin, 1986), as the Division of Health Psychology became one of the larger divisions in the American Psychological Association. A primary focus of **health psychology** is developing techniques to help in the prevention of behaviors harmful to health, such as smoking, excessive drinking, overeating, and drug abuse. Dietary and life-style changes can have a dramatic impact on reducing the chances of some types of disease. Experts estimate that people at age forty-five would have an average life expectancy that is *seven years longer* for women and *eleven years longer* for men if they fol-

TABLE 14-1	LEADING CAUSES OF DEATH IN AMERICA
1900	1987
1. Pneumonia and influenza	*1. Diseases of the heart
2. Tuberculosis	2. Malignant neoplasms (cancers) (*some)
3. Diarrhea, enteritis	*3. Cerebrovascular diseases (stroke)
*4. Diseases of the heart	*4. Accidents
5. Intracranial lesions of vascular origin	*5. Pulmonary diseases (emphysema, bronchitis)
6. Nephritis	6. Pneumonia and influenza
*7. Accidents	*7. Diabetes mellitus
8. Cancer and other malignant tumors (*some)	*8. Suicide
9. Senility	*9. Chronic liver disease and cirrhosis
*10. Bronchitis	10. Atherosclerosis (hardening of the arteries)

* *Causes that can be affected by behavior or life-style changes.*
Source: National Center for Health Statistics (1989b)

lowed at least six of the following health practices, as compared with following fewer than four: (1) getting seven or eight hours of sleep a night, (2) eating breakfast, (3) eating regularly and not between meals, (4) keeping a normal weight in relation to height, (5) refraining from smoking, (6) exercising regularly, and (7) drinking alcohol moderately or not at all (Whalen, 1977).

Science has provided us with knowledge about behaviors that are beneficial or destructive to health. But that is only half the battle. Knowledge without behavior change has no effect. People have to be induced to engage in health-enhancing behaviors. Social psychological concepts such as persuasion, social power, attitude change, social learning, and compliance techniques can play a crucial role in leading to beneficial behavior changes.

PREVENTING SELF-DESTRUCTIVE BEHAVIORS

The Role of Threat in Changing Behavior

For years threats have been used widely in attempts in change self-destructive behaviors as, for example, using the threat of lung cancer and heart disease in messages designed to reduce smoking behavior, using the threat of liver cirrhosis to reduce alcohol consumption, or utilizing the threat of heart disease and stroke to reduce overeating. But threatening messages are not always effective.

If fear serves as the dominant drive that motivates behavior, then one might predict that the relationship between fear and acceptance of a message would be in the form of an inverted U-shaped curve (Figure 14-1a), with the greatest behavior change occurring at a moderate level of fear just before the interfering effects of fear start to overwhelm the facilitating effects (Janis, 1967; McGuire 1968b).

fear-drive model:
Assumes that the relationship between fear and acceptance of a persuasive message will be in the form of an inverted U-shaped curve, with the greatest behavior change occurring at a moderate level of fear.

This **fear-drive model** has intuitive appeal to many people; it may seem reasonable that too much fear would somehow mess up an attitude-change program. But a meta-analysis of thirty-five studies on fear-arousing communications (Sutton, 1982) found little support for a fear-drive model. Significant increases in fear were accompanied only rarely by an inverted U-shaped pattern in responses; generally the relationship was linear—the more fear, the more change. The meta-analysis also indicated that providing specific instructions on how to take the recommended action led to a higher rate of acting in accordance with the recommendation.

danger control:
Coping with the environment and responding to avert the danger.

fear control:
Responding to reduce the unpleasant feeling of fear, guided largely by internal cues.

Fear is not the only possible response to a health-related message. Response to a fear communication may involve two parallel responses: **danger control** and **fear control** (Leventhal, 1970). Danger control involves coping with the environment and aiming responses at averting the danger. Fear control, on the other hand, is guided largely by internal cues and involves responses to reduce the unpleasant feeling of fear. Consider heavy smokers who see ads depicting the dangers of heavy smoking and the risks of lung cancer and heart disease. The most effective danger control response would be to stop smoking. But if the smokers respond primarily in terms of fear control, they may disregard these messages and avoid future messages, develop further rationalizations for smoking, and convince themselves that smoking may harm other people but not them. These behaviors may be effective for fear control, though they are ineffective for danger control.

A high-fear appeal. Will this ad sponsored by the American Cancer Society be effective in convincing people to avoid overexposure to the sun?

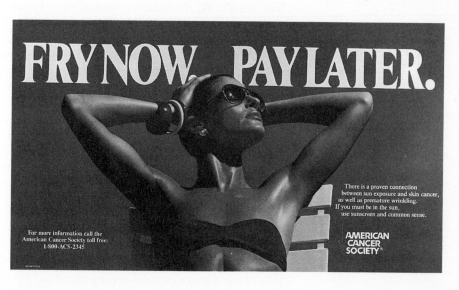

Enhancing feelings of personal vulnerability. This ad is designed to convince young people that the AIDS epidemic is personally relevant to their lives.

If you get the AIDS virus now, you and your license could expire at the same time.

Let's say you don't think you'll get AIDS because you don't know anyone who has it. There is one small thing that you are overlooking.

AIDS is caused by a virus called HIV. And HIV doesn't lead to AIDS right away.

Someone can have HIV for many years without even knowing it. This means that many people in their twenties who have AIDS may have been infected with the virus while they were in their teens.

Don't wait for proof that AIDS exists. It does. So, take precautions now.

If you would like more information about the AIDS virus, how to prevent it, and how to reduce your risks, you can call the National AIDS hotline. 1-800-342-AIDS. The hotline for the hearing impaired is 1-800-AIDS-TTY.

AMERICA RESPONDS TO AIDS

The motivation to protect oneself from impending danger is based on four beliefs: (1) the threat is severe, (2) one is personally vulnerable to the threat, (3) one has the ability to perform the coping response, and (4) the coping response is effective in dealing with the threat (Rogers, 1984). Beliefs in one's ability to perform the coping response are based on judgments of the effectiveness of the response and one's competence, minus any costs of adopting a preventive response (such as inconvenience, expense, unpleasantness, side effects, and the difficulty of changing strong habits). For example, persuading smokers that they *could* stop smoking (Maddux & Rogers, 1983) and persuading nonexercisers that they *could* begin a program of regular exercise (Wurtele, 1982), strengthened their intentions to adopt these activities. If the response is relatively ineffective, however, increasing feelings of danger may actually decrease intentions to adopt a protective response. Smokers may increase their cigarette consumption (Rogers & Mewborn, 1976) and social drinkers increase their alcohol consumption (Kleinot & Rogers, 1982) if they believe that there is nothing they can do to stop their present behavior.

High-threat messages do not lead to changed behavior unless the details of the danger-control coping response are also provided. For example,

FIGURE 14-1

Hypothesized Relations between Fear and Attitude-Behavior Change

(a) Curvilinear relationship between threat and attitude and behavior change suggested by fear-drive models of Janis (1967) and McGuire (1968b). (b) Positive relationships between threat and attitude and behavior change under the conditions suggested by Leventhal's (1970) parallel response model and Rogers's (1984) protection motivation model.

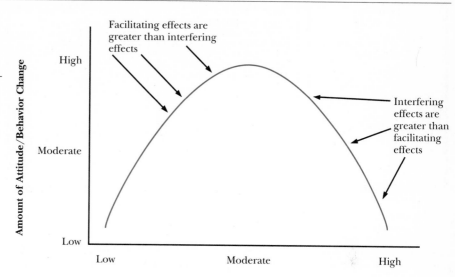

Facilitating effects are greater than interfering effects

Interfering effects are greater than facilitating effects

Amount of Attitude/Behavior Change

High

Moderate

Low

Amount of Threat or Fear Generated by the Message

Low   Moderate   High

(a)

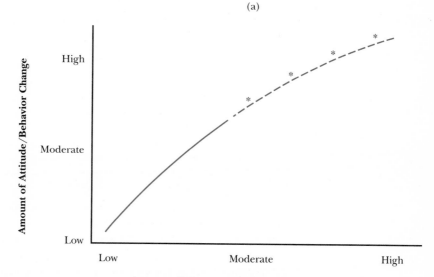

Amount of Attitude/Behavior Change

High

Moderate

Low

Amount of Threat or Fear Generated by the Message

Low   Moderate   High

(b)

*Change will continue to increase with increased fear *if* fear control and danger control (specific recommendations for action) are possible (Leventhal), or the person believes that the threat is severe and also believes that coping reponses are effective and can be competently performed without excessive costs (Rogers).

An anti-smoking campaign: behavior changes coupled with a high-fear appeal.
Source: From *Penguin Dreams and Stranger Things: A Bloom County Book* by Berke Breathed. Copyright © 1985 by The Washington Post Company.

Leventhal (1974) found that subjects who received specific instructions on how to control a smoking habit along with a high- or low-fear message showed significantly reduced levels of smoking in a three-month follow up. When presented without fear messages, the specific action plans had no effects on attitudes or on smoking behavior.

People with relatively low self-esteem are more likely than others to feel incompetent in dealing with threats (Rosen et al., 1982). Low self-esteem people appear to have two problems with the threat communication: One involves internal cues and emotions (fear control) and the other, coping (danger control). Rosen and his co-workers suggested that fear control and lack of competency inhibit compliance in separate stages. Fear has a negative effect on attention or comprehension of the communication, whereas perceived competency affects the persuasion process only *after* intentions have been formed, when the person must translate intentions into actions.

Analyzing Self-Destructive Behaviors

Self-destructive habits may influence not only the development of disease but also general levels of physical and mental well-being. Henderson et al. (1979) estimated that forty to eighty million people in the United States were overweight and lacking in proper nutrition, about fifty million were cigarette smokers, and approximately nine million were alcohol abusers. Self-destructive behaviors can start relatively early in life. A nationwide survey of high school seniors in 1982 found that 70 percent of the students had used alcohol, 30 percent had smoked cigarettes, and 29 percent had used marijuana in the month preceding the survey (Cody, 1984). The AIDS epidemic has added "unsafe sex" to the list of important self-destructive behaviors.

The control of self-destructive behaviors is especially difficult because they are largely outside the scope of traditional medicine. Unfortunately, much self-destructive behavior is not accompanied by unpleasant symptoms and so goes unnoticed by individuals until advanced stages of disease. For example, hypertension (high blood pressure), cigarette smoking, and diets high in saturated fat, cholesterol, and sugar contribute to an individual's risk of coronary heart disease. Obesity, lack of physical activity, various life stresses, and some behavior patterns also increase the likelihood of heart disease. Cigarette smoking has been linked to lung cancer, emphysema, chronic bronchitis, and diseases of the heart and blood vessels. Further, alcohol abuse leads to a number of physical complications such as liver cirrhosis and kidney diseases, as well as social and emotional problems in employment, marital and family relationships, and interaction with the community. The abuse of alcohol while operating a motor vehicle (drinking and driving) is a major societal problem.

Many attempts have been made to change health-related attitudes and behaviors via mass communication. This is no easy task. One method involves programs in school systems, such as the federally funded nationwide program of Health Fairs. These programs may include lectures by the school principal or a physician, posters, teacher participation, threatening films, and student participation. They generally are successful in teaching students about the hazards of smoking and those participating acquire more knowledge than do unexposed students. Still, the behavioral effects (changes in smoking rates) are usually very small or nonexistent (Leventhal & Cleary, 1980). It is clear that public health messages increased public knowledge about sexually transmitted diseases and "safe sex" in the late 1980s.

A number of community studies also have been conducted. Perhaps the single largest community study to date is the Stanford Heart Disease Prevention Program (Meyer et al., 1980), a study of three communities. One community was exposed to a mass-media campaign about heart disease risk factors, including smoking. A second community received a mass media campaign and selected high-risk persons received face-to-face instruction on techniques to stop smoking. The third community served as a control. Two years later there was a 17 percent reduction in the number of smokers in the media plus face-to-face instruction community, a 5 percent reduction in the media only community, and a 12 percent increase in the control community (Figure 14-2). Among people in the second community who were particularly high risks for heart disease, 50 percent of them quit smoking for two years, whereas only 15 percent of those in the control community quit.

Why are mass-media techniques not more effective? There are at least four reasons. First, exposure to the message cannot be controlled and *de facto selective exposure* (Chapter 4) may occur: The message never reaches those people who might be most affected by it. Second, media messages are usually abstract and do not focus on concrete experiences that are meaningful to the audience. Third, messages are often developed on the basis of hunches without prior assessment of their effectiveness and interest to the audience. Fourth, there are many different contexts in which the media message may be received. The audience may be at home alone, among friends, or in school, and this context may interfere with, or be supportive of, acceptance (Leventhal & Cleary, 1980).

FIGURE 14-2

Mass-Media Health
Campaigns

*Effectiveness of two types of
mass-media campaigns (the
Stanford Heart Disease Prevention Program) in affecting
smoking rates two years later
in two communities, compared
with a community where no
campaign occured.*

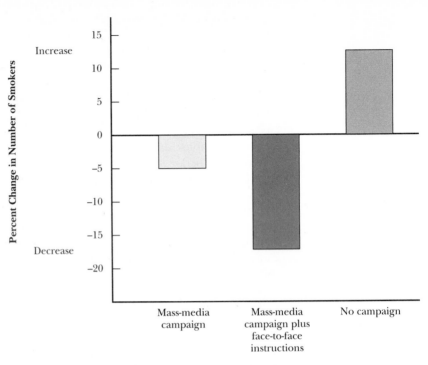

Source: Data from Meyer, A. J., Nash, J. D., McAllister, A. L., Maccoby, N., & Farquhar, J. W. (1980). Skills training in a cardiovascular health education campaign. *Journal of Consulting and Clinical Psychology, 48,* 129–192.

Another approach is to focus on modeling, imitation of the behavior of others, and expectations regarding the consequences of their action. Children can learn harmful (or healthful) dietary, smoking, or alcohol habits by watching and modeling the behavior of adult or peer models. *Disinhibition* occurs when a model engages in an apparently enjoyable behavior that the observer assumes to be socially prohibited (e.g., heavy drinking), but the model receives no negative consequences. Now that you are aware of these general approaches, we can look at what has been tried for specific behaviors—cigarette smoking, problem drinking, and overeating.

Trying to Change Cigarette-Smoking Behavior

The Development of Smoking Behavior
Smoking is considered the major preventable risk in premature death and

An anti-smoking ad that focuses on attractiveness and dissimilarity.

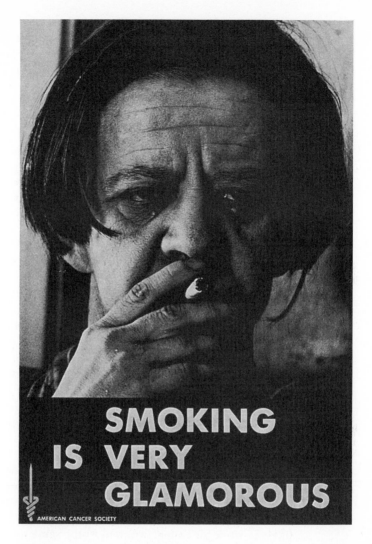

SMOKING
IS VERY
GLAMOROUS

AMERICAN CANCER SOCIETY

disability in the U.S. (U.S. Department of Health and Human Services, 1986). Almost 90 percent of those who smoke more than four cigarettes eventually become regular smokers (Salber et al., 1968). For this reason, antismoking programs have been designed to catch youngsters at important formative ages before they have tried several cigarettes. The sixth grade may be the best time to educate students about smoking, because there appears to be less peer pressure at this level than in other grades (Chen & Winder, 1986). Because there are several different reasons why young people begin to smoke (coping with social pressures and controlling one's internal state are the most common ones), effective antismoking programs may need to have several facets, depending on which path the prospective smoker is likely to take (Hirschman et al., 1984).

Many of the concepts discussed in earlier chapters are directly relevant (Chassin et al., 1990). First, attitudes and beliefs are primary factors in adolescents' decisions to try smoking. The theory of reasoned action (Chapter 4), reviewed below, explains how the process may work. Second, social influence processes (Chapter 5) are crucial, as indicated by the impact of parents and peers who smoke, serving as models (Leventhal et al., 1988). Third, self-concept processes play a major role. We saw in Chapter 3 that people often behave in ways that express or affirm an existing self-image or, via strategic self-presentation, attempt to present a desired impression to others. For many adolescents, smoking may serve as a means of self-verification or self-enhancement. For many teens, smoking carries a social image of toughness, sociability, and interest in the opposite sex (Burton et al., 1989).

Looking first at attitudes and beliefs, we can distinguish between general and personal beliefs (Fishbein, 1982). A person's personal beliefs about his or her *own* behavior are directly relevant to the person's intentions. For example, although individuals may believe that "Smoking increases the chance of lung cancer" (a general belief), it will have little influence on their smoking decisions if they also believe that "*My* smoking is not increasing my chances of getting lung cancer" (a personal belief).

The relative importance of attitudes and of subjective norms (perceived expectations of others and motivation to comply with those expectations) may differ according to age and the situation. For example, Fishbein (1982) showed that grade-school-children's intentions to start smoking were influenced almost as much by expectations of others (normative control) as by attitudinal considerations (because he/she wanted to smoke). In contrast, college women's intentions to smoke were almost entirely under attitudinal control. However, whereas the grade-schoolers' intentions to quit were almost entirely under attitudinal control, young women's intentions to quit were mostly under normative control. These findings suggest that an antismoking campaign based on normative pressure would be an effective way to prevent grade-school students from starting to smoke, but would be less likely to work for college women. At the same time, however, the use of normative pressure to stop should be quite effective for college women, but would be ineffective for getting grade-school students to quit.

A number of large-scale programs have attempted to discourage children from starting to smoke. Richard Evans and his co-workers (Evans, 1980; Evans et al., 1981) focused on social influence processes, including a strategy of inoculation against pressures to smoke (remember our discussion of inoculation theory in Chapter 4), believing that if students could be "nursed" through the period during which they are particularly vulnerable to social influences to smoke (the junior high years), they would be sufficiently fortified so that heavy addictive smoking, which is generally first found in high school, would be less likely to occur. In a demonstration of the *false consensus effect* (Chapter 2), adolescents who smoke grossly overestimate the proportion of adolescents and adults who smoke.

A three-year investigation in thirteen junior high schools in Houston (Evans et al., 1981), tested an antismoking treatment that involved group discussions and antismoking films emphasizing the immediate effects of smoking on the teenager (using teenage narrators). The filmed messages emphasized making a *conscious decision* about smoking, rather than being guided by external (normative) influences. Students were inoculated against social pressures to begin smoking by being shown specific strategies for coping with social pressures to smoke. Those students who received the antismoking program showed lower rates of smoking in the eighth and ninth grades than did those who received no treatment (Figure 14-3).

Several large-scale studies have shown that there is no single technique that consistently works best in preventing smoking. A combination of approaches works best (Chassin et al., 1984). In one study a combination of antismoking information, skills training (learning how to resist social pressures to smoke), decision making (listing the advantages and disadvantages of smoking) and commitment (announcing to the class one's own decisions to smoke or not smoke) were effective in keeping junior high students from beginning to smoke (Best et al., 1984). Still another study found that learning to resist pressure to smoke, awareness of the short-term physiological effects of smoking, and the use of same-age peer discussion leaders was effective (Murray et al., 1984). Contingency management techniques have also proven effective, as when young people are given personal feedback on the physiological effects of smoking by having their pulse rate and the carbon

FIGURE 14-3

An Effective Program to Prevent Young Teenagers from Beginning to Smoke

Percentage of seventh-, eighth-, and ninth-grade students who were frequent cigarette smokers. Comparison of students who received multiple antismoking communications (treatment group) with those who received none (control group).

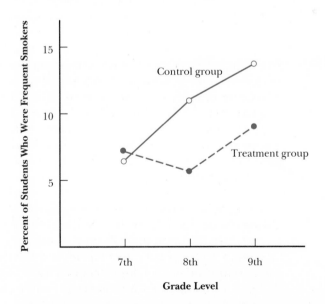

Source: Based on Evans, R. I., Rozell, R. M., Maxwell, S. E., Raines, B. E., Dill, C. A., Guthrie, T. J., Henderson, A. H., & Hill, P. C. (1981). Social modeling films to deter smoking in adolescents: Results of a three-year field investigation. *Journal of Applied Psychology, 66,* 399–414.

monoxide level in their blood measured after smoking a cigarette (Hansen & Evans, 1982), or when prizes are awarded for the best skit depicting ways of resisting peer pressure to smoke (Perry et al., 1980).

Helping Adults to Stop Smoking

Nine out of ten adult smokers either have tried to quit or say they would try if effective methods were available (United States Public Health Service, 1976). Methods used to try to help smokers quit include educational and attitude change strategies, pharmacological strategies, hypnosis, and behavior modification (Best & Bloch, 1979). The reasons for smoking are complex and vary with individuals, so treatment is more apt to be effective if it uses several techniques.

Analyses of smoking cessation studies have suggested four main findings (Leventhal & Cleary, 1980). First, there is often an impressive decrease in smoking during the treatment itself. Some of the most promising change efforts involve behavior therapy techniques, among which are those in which smokers carry a timer that buzzes every time they light up, electrical aversion procedures in which smoking behaviors are paired with electrical shock, and a variety of self-control procedures such as confining smoking to a specific area, gradually avoiding situations in which smoking takes place, and self-administered punishment for smoking (Elliot & Denney, 1978). Another technique, rapid smoking, induces aversion and/or satiation by having a person smoke at two to three times the normal rate until nauseous (Lando, 1977; Lando & McCullough, 1978).

Second, there is frequently a high dropout rate, often up to 50 percent of those included in the initial sample. Thus, many outcome reports are inflated because dropouts from therapy are not counted as failures. Third, therapy works well in helping people to stop smoking but does less well in keeping them stopped; most backsliding occurs within the first six months. Individuals are more likely to maintain change if they are in a supportive physical and social environment and have learned cognitive strategies for dealing with problem urges. The self-attribution of change ("I controlled my behavior and stopped smoking") and the development of effective alternative behaviors that contribute to a new nonsmoking life-style also help. Finally, success rates for different therapies are not markedly different. It is simply better to do something than nothing.

The National Heart, Blood, and Lung Institute carried out a six-year project at twenty locations attempting to lessen the chances of coronary heart disease in men aged thirty-five to fifty-seven who were at high risk for heart disease. One goal of the project was to get the men to stop smoking. After four years in the project, 44 percent of the smokers had stopped. Then a multiple-method antismoking program was designed for the high-risk men who had been unable to quit during the earlier program. Psychological, social, physiological, and behavioral techniques were used in a "cafeteria" approach whereby these men could select the methods that seemed to work for themselves and ignore the others (Powell & Arnold, 1982). A year later half of the men had stopped smoking. The success of this project indicates that multiple treatment methods are likely to be more effective than techniques that use a single method for everyone. People may feel more committed to stopping when given a choice between several treatments.

But not every smoker seeks professional help when trying to quit. What about people who try to stop smoking on their own? A recent study identified several factors that were related to success in quitting over a 6-month period. Kirscht et al. (1989) found that successful quitters, compared to those who were unable to quit, had: (1) begun with stronger beliefs that they would be a nonsmoker a year later; (2) had received more professional advice to quit from doctors and nurses; (3) had a higher level of education (perhaps associated with more social support for quitting or greater exposure to antismoking messages); and (4) were exposed to fewer cues to smoke (e.g., there were no other smokers in the household.)

Heavy drinking is a major problem on today's college campuses.

theory of genetic predisposition:
The controversial theory that there may be an inherited physiological or biochemical imbalance in some individuals that is corrected by the consumption of alcohol.

Social Analyses of Drinking

Heavy drinking is by far the most critical health issue on college campuses, according to a 1990 survey of 200 schools by the American Council on Alcoholism (Esky, 1990). More generally, alcohol abuse is associated with child and spouse abuse, poor job performance, fatal automobile accidents, and crime. The National Council on Alcoholism estimated that alcoholism is one of the three leading causes of death in the United States, along with heart disease and cancer. Heavy drinking by a pregnant woman may have a destructive effect on her unborn child via the fetal alcohol syndrome (Jones et al., 1973).

The treatment of alcoholism involves unusually complex problems in developing effective methods and persuading people to accept the treatment and stay with it. In recent years, there has been controversy over the role of genetics, as some research has indicated that there may be a strong genetic component to alcoholism (Cadoret et al., 1987; Straus, 1986). The **theory of genetic predisposition** implies that there is a physiological or biochemical imbalance in some individuals that is corrected by consumption of alcohol. Considerably more research is needed on this issue before we will be able to draw clear conclusions. Reviews (Nathan, 1983; Quayle, 1983) have indicated frustration and failures in trying to prevent the devastating effects of alcoholism and drug abuse. As is the case with smoking, a social analysis of heavy drinking finds that people use alcohol to avoid problems, to relax, and to experience a modified physiological state. The reasons for drinking most often given by heavy drinkers are boredom, depression, anxiety, letting anger out, and interpersonal conflict (Engstrom, 1984).

In a study of young Canadian men, DiTecco and Schlegel (1982) found that the most important attitudinal factor was reasons for drinking. Excessive drinkers were likely to rate *any* reason for drinking as more important than were moderate drinkers. This suggests that one should be wary of attempting to promote a "positive approach to responsible alcohol use" because it may lead to increased consumption among previously moderate drinkers. For example, it is often said that the Italian culture shows a positive attitude toward moderate drinking but, in fact, Italy has a high national liver cirrhosis disease rate, indicating a major alcohol problem (DeLint & Schmidt, 1971).

A widely accepted view of problem drinking sees alcoholism as a disease that progresses in stages (Jellinek, 1952). Although this view has proven valuable in the treatment of alcoholism, in some ways it may interfere with effective treatment. Think back to attribution theory—the disease model of alcoholism implies little personal responsibility for one's condition. This may work against the helpful attributions that patients could make about their own recoveries if they attributed their behavior to stable, internal, controllable factors (Davies, 1982). In one study of alcoholics, half were told that responsibility for attaining the treatment goals lay in their own hands and were offered no further appointments at the clinic and no medications. The other half were given a far more comprehensive regimen, including introduction to Alcoholics Anonymous, drugs to cover withdrawal, further appointments with a psychiatrist, and extensive social work involvement. After twelve months the alcoholics who were simply encouraged to take responsibility for their condition made as good a recovery as the matched group offered the comprehensive treatment program (Edwards et al., 1977).

Are heavy drinkers a whole different "class" of people than those who drink less? Perhaps not. Some researchers have suggested that heavy drink-

Public censure for drunk drivers. In some jurisdictions, people convicted of driving while intoxicated must place a bumper sticker on their car for a specified length of time.

ing should not be conceived of as pathological behavior, but simply as behavior on the extreme end of the drinking continuum. From this viewpoint, persons with drinking problems are no different from nonproblem drinkers except that they drink more and, hence, suffer more drinking-related problems (Sadava, 1978).

Overeating and Obesity

Chronic overeating has major social consequences (ridicule, social rejection, stereotyping), psychological effects (lowered self-esteem), and physiological impacts (changes in insulin level). At the physiological level, when people overeat for longer than a few days and undergo a period of active weight gain, several hormonal and metabolic changes occur. An increased level of insulin is produced, which may set a circular process in motion, increasing the experience of hunger and thus leading to more eating and promoting greater storage of what is eaten. The higher the basal levels of insulin, the more insulin is released at the sight, thought, and smell of appealing food (Rodin, 1977). Thus, some overweight people, especially those who are already very responsive to environmental food cues, may become physically "primed" to be tempted by tasty foods as a result of chronic overeating (Janis & Rodin, 1979).

Behavioral approaches to diet modifications usually focus on three steps: becoming aware of present eating habits, identifying problem eating habits, and using specific techniques to alter the problem habits (Foreyt et al., 1980). Behavioral techniques include carefully monitoring food intake, eating in the same situation at all times, eating small portions, eating slowly, savoring the food, and rewarding oneself for adhering to the proper eating behavior (Jeffrey et al., 1978). Behavioral regimens typically have produced high initial success in weight control. Unfortunately, as with antismoking treatments, the immediate post-treatment success has seldom been followed by the maintenance of change over the long term (Leventhal et al., 1983).

In designing a weight-loss program, one would want to work with specific diets and physical activities and get the participants to commit themselves publicly to engaging in each of these activities regularly. Recall from research on stopping cigarette smoking that it is important to distinguish between general and personal beliefs. Personal beliefs ("Dieting will help *me* lose weight") are important determinants of intentions and actions.

The Effect of Attributions about Addiction

Whenever the use of a drug or any other compulsive behavior becomes the center of a person's existence, this person has an addiction. There are two characteristics of addiction: *increased tolerance* and *dependency*. As the body adapts to a drug because of long-term use, tolerance increases and the person must consume more of the substance in order for it to be effective. Dependence is the need for a particular substance or activity that is so severe that the person has feelings of loss or unease when the activity is unavailable. Scientists disagree as to whether there is such a thing as an "addictive personality" (Lang, 1983). It is clear, however, that some personality traits such as impulsiveness and inability to delay gratification are associated with a higher probability of substance abuse.

If one makes a self-attribution that he is addicted to a drug or that his behavior represents a "sickness" such as alcoholism, this may have important consequences. Drug users who define themselves as sick or addicted have an explanation that seems both to account for their behavior and release them from personal responsibility for altering it. A self-attribution of addiction may furnish a smoker not only with an explanation for previous failures at quitting, but also (perhaps as a means of dissonance reduction) with a justification for continuing to smoke.

Recall that *perceived behavioral control* is one of the three determinants of behavior in the theory of planned behavior (Figure 4-2). The most important predictor of intention to stop a particular behavior is people's perceptions of their chances of success at stopping (self-efficacy in Bandura's terms, competency in the fear-appeal models. Those who see themselves as addicted have lower expectancies of success and less firm intentions to stop (Eiser, 1982).

Pulling together all of the research findings, it appears that the most effective techniques for changing attitudes toward self-destructive behaviors such as smoking, excessive drinking, or drug use are those that use *credible communicators* (e.g., same-age peers) who stress each audience member's *personal vulnerability* to the threat, emphasize each member's *ability to control* his or her behavior (rather than emphasizing addiction or sickness), and provide *effective ways to deal with the threat.* Social learning techniques and the use of effective peer models may also be important procedures. Maintaining behavior change, once it has been established, is a particularly difficult problem.

Are "Self-Cures" for Self-Destructive Behaviors Common?

Research on treatment of smoking, alcoholism, obesity, and drug abuse paints a pretty dismal picture, suggesting that permanent change is hard to come by. Studies have found that for three target behaviors—withdrawal from smoking, heroin, and alcohol—60 percent of those "successfully" treated had reverted to their prior destructive behavior patterns within three months after therapy. By one year after therapy, 75 percent had reverted to their previous behavior patterns (Hunt & Bespalec, 1974). Yet people's ability to make permanent changes in self-destructive behaviors may actually be considerably greater than these studies suggest. The samples in most studies represent the toughest cases—people who actively sought help because they were unable to change their behaviors on their own. People who successfully stop smoking or overeating on their own are unlikely to appear in these studies. To illustrate this point, Schachter (1982) found in a small survey that 64 percent of adults who had ever attempted to stop smoking had eventually been successful and 63 percent of people who had been obese and tried to lose weight had been successful in losing weight and keeping it off. More recently, though, Cohen and his co-workers (1989) challenged Schachter's conclusions, noting that the results of ten separate "self-quitting" smoking studies yielded long-term quitting rates of only 20 percent to 30 percent. It's hard to get exact percentages of those who succeed in quitting smoking, for quitting is a dynamic process, not a discrete event, and may require many attempts before success. Those who participate in formal programs seem to have about the same quitting rate as those who go it alone. So, although research attention has been focused mainly on persons who have been unsuccessful in changing their behaviors, it is important to keep in mind that many can, and do, change these behaviors on their own. I will now turn to two behaviors that may, on the surface, seem unrelated—using automobile seat belts, and engaging in "safe sex." What these two acts have in common is that both involve attitude and behavior change to lessen the chances of major negative medical consequences.

Using Automobile Safety Belts

The nonuse of automobile seat belts is a controllable behavior that has significant health consequences. Your chances of dying in an auto accident are five times greater if you are not wearing a safety belt (Gruber, 1986). Even beyond individual tragedies, the costs to society are immense. Yet surveys in the mid-1980s indicated that 85 percent of Americans were not in the habit of wearing their safety belts (Rudd & Geller, 1985). The great reduction in death and injury that could be achieved by safety belt use was not occurring.

Mass-media appeals to increase the use of auto safety belts. Despite the cleverness of these ads, research suggests that such mass-media appeals are usually not very effective.

Why don't people use safety belts? It seems to me that there are at least three reasons. Some people mistakenly believe that safety belt use may increase their chances of dying in an accident, perhaps because of stories they have heard about people being trapped in vehicles. Informational programs might be effective for these people, although remember from Chapter 2 that vivid anecdotes (e.g., stories of trapped victims) are generally more powerful in affecting behavior than is statistical information. Other people may simply forget to buckle up. For them, programs that remind them might be effective. We will see below that some pretty creative reminder techniques have been developed. Still other people may resist wearing safety belts because they don't like being told what to do—they feel psychological reactance. Perhaps changes in the law, if enforced, might eventually change their behavior.

Legal Coercion

In the 1980s American states took a legislative route to encouraging safety belt use, passing laws making safety belt use mandatory. In New York, the first state to pass such a law, seat belt use rose from 13 percent to 60 percent (Carter & Ferrari, 1987). However, in Illinois, although 79 percent of the citizens said they favored a seat belt law, only 42 percent were observed wearing seat belts in the months after the new law took effect (Gruber, 1986). While it is too early to evaluate the eventual success of this tactic, our knowledge of cognitive dissonance theory (Chapter 4) would lead to the prediction that if the law were strictly enforced, then those who previously did not use safety belts would feel dissonance while engaging in this counterattitudinal behavior (wearing a safety belt) and might eventually reduce the dissonance by deciding that safety belt use was a good thing after all. However, because it seems unlikely that society will have the means to enforce seat belt wearing consistently, other attitudinal and behavioral methods may also be useful.

Mass-Media Campaigns

The U.S. government has spent millions of dollars for public service messages encouraging people to use safety belts. Sadly, most analyses have found little or no increase in use of seat belts as a result (Bruskin, 1969; Kelley 1979). These negative outcomes do not mean it is impossible to create a mass-media campaign that will increase safety belt use, but they demonstrate again what we saw in Chapter 4—simply exposing people to persuasive messages does not guarantee that the message will have an effect on behavior.

Behavioral Manipulations

A more promising approach is to reward people for using safety belts. In a series of studies, Scott Geller and his colleagues showed that providing incentives for safety belt use (raffle tickets, discounts from local merchants, prizes, etc.) substantially increased the use of safety belts (Geller & Bigelow, 1984). For example, Geller and his co-workers (1983) provided workers leaving an industrial complex at the end of the day with fliers promoting safety belt usage; belt wearers were also given opportunities to win prizes. The incentives worked better among white-collar (salaried) workers (increasing use from 17 percent to 51 percent) than among blue-collar (hourly) workers (use increased from 3 percent to 6 percent). But after a month, when the incentives were not given any longer, most drivers stopped using safety belts consistently. One group of workers continued to buckle up, however. Most of those who had earlier complied enough to get three or more incentives continued to use their safety belts after the incentives were discontinued; for them, safety belt use had apparently become a habit.

Research at other industrial plants (Geller & Hahn, 1984) showed that different compliance techniques may be most effective for different groups of people, such as white-collar or blue-collar workers. These studies demonstrated that active employer involvement, incentives, personal commitment, and peer pressure can all contribute to achieving health-enhancing behavior changes.

Changing AIDS-Related Behaviors

A condom machine in a university dormitory bathroom. Mass-media campaigns dramatically increased young people's awareness of the importance of using condoms for "safe sex" by 1990, but the evidence suggested that their sexual behaviors (e.g., using condoms) changed less than their attitudes had.

We saw in Chapter 9 that knowledge about the dangers of AIDS increased dramatically in the 1980s. However, behavior change came more slowly in the general population. Fisher and Misovich (1989) studied undergraduates in Connecticut in the late 1980s. Although they found substantial increases in students' knowledge about AIDS, favorable attitudes toward safer sexual behaviors, and increased perceptions of personal vulnerability, these did not apparently produce a corresponding increase in the safety of students' sexual behaviors. The average number of sexual partners and unsafe sexual practices actually increased slightly between 1986 and 1988. Student responses suggested that alcohol may play a significant role in their AIDS-risk behavior. Students who drank more, or who paired drinking with sex, were more likely to engage in AIDS-risk behaviors such as unprotected intercourse. Similar results were reported in Rhode Island (Carroll, 1988) and California (Baldwin & Baldwin, 1988).

This problem is not limited to college campuses. Though all of the fourteen to nineteen-year-olds involved in one survey said they believed condoms to be an effective way to prevent sexually transmitted disease, most who were sexually active simply did not use them (Kegeles et al., 1988). Most had more than one sexual partner, but only 2 percent of the females and 8 percent of the males reported using condoms each time they had intercourse. For many people, information alone is not sufficient to induce behavioral change. Recall that the theory of planned behavior (Figure 4-2) describes three central variables that are involved in determining behavior. Behavioral intentions are affected by attitudes toward the behavior, subjective norms (perceived norms of one's subculture and one's motivation to comply with them), and one's perceived control over the behavior. Education can change attitudes toward the behavior. At a group level, education problems may also affect the relevant cultural norms. As society's norms change about the desira-

Public information programs have dramatically changed overall levels of knowledge about sexually-transmitted diseases.

bility of certain types of behavior (e.g., "unsafe" sexual activities), this affects individuals' subsequent behaviors, provided they are motivated to comply with the norms. Finally, the use of alcohol or other drugs may affect one's perceived control over the sexual situation ("I was too drunk to worry about taking precautions").

There is evidence that sexual norms changed dramatically in the homosexual subculture in the 1980s as the gay male community embarked on an intensive sex education campaign. The spread of AIDS in the gay community slowed considerably (Winkelstein et al., 1987), leading some psychologists (Stall et al., 1988, p. 878) to comment that "AIDS education and prevention campaigns have resulted in the most profound modification of personal health-related behaviors ever recorded." Stall and his colleagues noted that feelings of self-sufficiency and social support may be critical for initiating and maintaining changes in sexual behavior patterns. Researchers then set out to identify factors that differentiated gay men who maintained behavioral changes over the long haul from those who did not (Des Jarlais & Freidman, 1988).

Knowledge alone doesn't always do the job. As a case in point, one study of groups of bisexual and homosexual men who demonstrated "extraordinarily high" levels of knowledge about AIDS and its transmission, found that nearly two-thirds reported engaging in highly risky unprotected sexual acts with more than one partner in the previous six months (Valdiserri et al., 1987). As O'Keeffe et al. (1990) recently pointed out, this is hardly surprising to social psychologists, who view behavior as the product of interrelated attitude, knowledge, intentions, and other psychological factors on the one hand, and of environmental factors on the other. Successful programs to reduce the spread of AIDS must do many things: provide information, change attitudes, increase motivation to practice desired behaviors, help people recognize and avoid situations where high-risk behavior is likely, provide people with negotiating skills (e.g., to say "no" or "please wear a condom") to resist influence attempts, and so forth. It's no easy task, but the stakes are enormous. As the 1990s begin, it appears that reactions to the threat of AIDS has produced significant changes in sexual attitudes and behavior in the gay community. Time will tell whether AIDS-prevention programs will eventually cause changes in the nature of sexual relationships in the general population as well.

COMPLIANCE AND ADHERENCE TO MEDICAL RECOMMENDATIONS

The Importance of Compliance and Adherence

In deciding whether to go to a doctor, you must make a series of decisions. You must first choose whether to seek medical treatment and then decide whether to accept the treatment the doctor recommends. After that, you must make a series of decisions, sometimes every day, as to how conscientiously you are going to follow all the rules laid down for you in the recommended medical regimen, such as taking medication, getting exercise, or changing your eating habits. *Adherence* is an important concept in health psychology. Since a physician generally has no direct control over the actions of an individual, the responsibility for adherence is the patient's. If you choose to adhere to the recommended program, you must do it on your own terms.

Why Are Noncompliance and Nonadherence So Frequent?

A major problem in doctor/patient communication is a patient's *noncompliance* with the physician's advice about medication or changes in life-style. The problem is not new: Over two thousand years ago, Hippocrates noted that the physician "should keep aware of the fact that patients often lie when they state that they have taken certain medicines" (quoted in Haynes et al., 1979, p. 3). There are two types of noncompliance (Raven, 1988)— **miscompliance,** where the client misunderstands the requirements of treatment, and **anticompliance,** when the client understands the recommendation but does not follow it. Many physicians are unaware of the extent of noncompliance (Witenberg et al., 1983).

Miscompliance often results from forgetting the doctor's instructions. One series of studies found that, on the average, patients forgot almost half of the statements made by their physicians within two hours of the appointment (Ley, 1977). Patients frequently do not understand what they have been told because the doctor's message is unclear or the language is too techni-

miscompliance:
In physician-client interactions, when the client misunderstands the requirements of treatment.

anticompliance:
In physician-client interactions, when the client understands the recommendation but does not follow it.

cal. Often the difficult terms used in health communication exceed the reading level of the client. For example, the technical term for high blood pressure, hypertension, is widely misunderstood to mean high levels of nervous tension. One set of researchers (Ley et al., 1976) found that about half of the information given patients about diagnosis, etiology, treatment, and prognosis was not understood. About half of the time patients do not take prescribed medications in accordance with instructions (Sackett, 1976). Table 14-2 shows the results of three surveys on the percentage of patients who failed to follow advice about medication. As you can see, the proportion of people not complying with medical advice varied all the way from 6 percent to 95 percent.

Where changes in habitual behaviors are recommended, as in dietary restrictions, stopping smoking, and getting more exercise, there are still greater problems, because anticompliance (deciding not to comply) is added to miscompliance (not understanding). As we saw earlier, many participants drop out of weight-control and smoking-cessation programs, and dietary restrictions are often ignored (Kirscht & Rosenstock, 1979). For control of hypertension, a "one-third rule" seems to apply. One-third of those in whom high blood pressure is detected fail to appear for a second blood pressure reading, one-third of those who do return drop out or fail to enter treatment, and one-third of those who enter treatment do not adequately control their blood pressure (Leventhal & Hirschman, 1982). As a result, about 70 percent of all cases of hypertension are not adequately treated.

Depending on a person's level of comprehension and intentions, different techniques are likely to be most effective to increase compliance. Clearer

TABLE 14-2	FOLLOWING MEDICAL ADVICE		
Frequency with which patients fail to follow advice about medication **(% not complying)**			
	Author of Study		
Type of Medication	**Ley (1972)**	**FDA* (1979)**	**Barofsky (1980)**
Antibiotics	49%	48%	52%
Psychiatric	39%	42%	42%
Antihypertension	—	43%	61%
Antituberculosis	39%	42%	43%
Other medication	48%	54%	46%
Range of percentages not complying	8–92%	11–95%	6–83%

*Food and Drug Administration

Source: Ley, P. (1982). Giving information to patients. In J. R. Eiser (Ed.). *Social psychology and behavioral medicine* (p. 359). Chichester, England: Wiley. Copyright © 1982 John Wiley and Sons Limited. Reprinted by permission.

information will be most effective when knowledge and comprehension are not adequate and miscompliance has occurred. When knowledge and comprehension already are adequate, then persuasive techniques or mechanical aids may be necessary to fight anticompliance. Many persons might respond positively to compliance-improving strategies if *effective* strategies are used. Health practitioners owe patients the same level of effort in achieving understanding and compliance as they do in diagnosis, treatment, and compassionate care.

Models of Compliance and Adherence

medical model of compliance:
Sees the practitioner as an expert acting to benefit an uninformed patient; if the patient does not comply, this implies ignorance, laziness, or willful neglect on the patient's part.

Compliance can be viewed from at least three perspectives: The **medical model** sees the practitioner as an expert acting to benefit an uninformed patient. It is in the patient's best interests to comply with the physician; not complying suggests ignorance, laziness, or willful neglect. Research from this approach would search for characteristics that differentiate the noncompliant person from the compliant person (hence making dispositional attributions to the patient). This approach has not been productive, as investigations have failed to find many personality characteristics that consistently differentiate between compliant and noncompliant patients (Blackwell, 1973; Stunkard, 1979).

behavioral model of compliance:
Looking for ways to increase compliant behaviors; sometimes does not take into account the goal-directed nature of human behavior.

The **behavioral model** searches for ways to increase adherence. Investigators in diet and weight control, for example, have moved away from studies of the personalities of obese persons to studies of how obese persons eat, when, where, and how often. Behavioral approaches have been criticized because they sometimes do not take into account the future-oriented or goal-directed nature of behavior (Leventhal et al., 1983).

Physicians often function as norm-sending communicators to their patients.

self-regulation model of compliance:
Views behavior as pulled toward goals rather than pushed by stimuli; emphasizes that individuals develop their own beliefs about health threats.

The **self-regulation model** views behavior as pulled toward goals rather than pushed by stimuli. This model emphasizes that if individuals develop their own beliefs about health threats, they will usually act in accordance with them. What type of action is taken depends on at least three other factors: (l) the individual's self-esteem or sense of competence; (2) the individual's strategies for problem situations; and (3) the individual's repertoire of specific coping behaviors and beliefs about the effectiveness of these responses (Leventhal et al., 1983). This model predicts that long-term self-regulative action will take place only if a behavioral treatment is learned, is seen as one's own, and makes sense in the individual's total life context.

The most important difference between these models is how they view the behavior of the patient. The medical viewpoint defines a medical goal, and largely ignores the patient's perspective and understanding of the disease process or the means to cure it. The behavioral model looks at situational factors but does not pay much attention to the patient's point of view. The self-regulation model looks at the patient's view of the illness and what the patient views as appropriate steps for intervention.

Techniques for Improving Compliance and Adherence

Improving Medical Messages

Because misunderstanding or forgetting medical recommendations is so common, one important step is to make them clearer and easier for the patient to understand and remember. Effective methods of improving communication include simplification of the instructions, repetition by the clinician, repetition by the patient, using written instructions, and use of specific rather than general statements. Each of these techniques has been shown effective in improving understanding by patients (Ley, 1982).

A number of studies show that increased understanding generally leads to better compliance, although compliance improves more for short-term medication than for long-term (Morris & Halperin, 1979). To help improve understanding, the American Medical Association introduced a program called the Patient Medication Instruction Program (PMI). PMI instruction sheets, available for many commonly prescribed drugs, describe the uses of the medication, conditions to report to the doctor before using it, how to use it properly, and possible side effects (Levine, 1984). Such precise, direct instructions make misunderstanding less likely.

For long-term medications, generating a plan for action is important. The person must learn to integrate the behavior into the daily routine, to identify the cues for action, and rehearse the action so it can be performed smoothly. The medical communicator first must identify those goals toward which the patient is moving and understand the patient's view of the health problem. The next task is to teach the skills needed to reach the defined goals. If the patient learns to view himself as a problem solver who actively searches for new tactics to deal with behavioral setbacks, it promotes feelings of competence that help motivate him to continue the use of effective strategies and behaviors.

Specific knowledge about the behavior required by the regimen is crucial. The more drugs the doctor prescribes, the more difficult is adherence. Also, medication that has to be taken several times a day is more often taken at the wrong times. Tailoring the timing and dosage of medication to habitual events in patients' lives reduces mistakes (Norell, 1979). Physicians should reduce the number of drugs prescribed to a patient to the minimum number consistent with therapeutic goals so that mistakes will be less likely (Hulka, 1979). Labeling on medicine bottles that is clear and descriptive is helpful so that the patient has an easy reference on how to take medication, as well as a reminder.

Interactions between Patient and Practitioner

A productive means of understanding practitioner/patient interactions may be to focus on the interaction itself. In any such discussion, the patient (or client) is in a problem-solving situation. The patient has to discover what sort of information should be volunteered in order to fit in with the professional's event schema of the situation (Hunt & McLeod, 1979). Research indicates that when the expectations of the patient and of the practitioner agree and the patient's expectations are met during the course of the appointment, the patient generally is satisfied and is likely to adhere to the physician's instructions (Leventhal et al., 1983). Patients are more apt to want to see a particular practitioner again if they were satisfied that he listened, took enough time explaining their medical condition, was available by phone, and cared about them as persons.

Many patients are dissatisfied because they do not receive as much information from their doctors as they desire (Ley, 1988). The majority of patients wish to know as much as possible about their illnesses: the causes, treatments, and outcomes. Patients usually want to know more about their medications than the professionals wish to tell them (Fleckenstein, 1977; Joubert & Lasagne, 1975). Many health professionals do not believe that patients should be informed about matters such as a diagnosis of cancer or the risks of a particular treatment. They predict that such information would lead to undesirable emotional reactions, reduced compliance, anxious overconcern, and/or more frequent reporting of side effects of drugs. But research indicates that this does not happen. Most studies have found that giving patients information about side effects of drugs does not increase the frequency with which they experience or report them (Ley, 1982). Greater information exchange improves communication, often with beneficial effects on compliance and recovery.

Allowing patients to participate more actively in decision making with their physicians might result in four specific advantages: (1) more complete communications; (2) more realistic expectations of care, thus reducing the chances of anger due to unfulfilled expectations; (3) improvement of medical decision making; and (4) greater patient adherence and compliance. There is research evidence to support each of these effects (Brody, 1980).

The likelihood that a patient will comply with a recommendation depends on the patient's preexisting attitude, the amount of social support for compliance, and how easy the compliance will be. Research indicates that the degree of *social support* — the degree to which important others provide support for behavior — is critical. People who can get help and approval from others, particularly from family members, are more likely to comply with the regimen (Green, 1979). At this point the research evidence is mixed about whether or not emotional support can inhibit the development of illness (Rodin & Salovey, 1989). What is clear, though, is that social support plays an important positive role in promoting treatment and recovery (Wortman, 1984). Social support can reduce stress, help people adhere to treatment regimens, and increase feelings of control.

Social Power

Often a physician wants to use social influence on a patient in order to get the patient to take medication regularly, to keep appointments, or to change his life-style. The physician must determine which type of social power is the most effective. The most obvious base of social power for a physician is expert power. Legitimate power, based on the prescribed role relation-

---

FOCUS 14-1

Doctor-Patient Communication

To communicate effectively with patients, a physician must do two general things: (1) communicate concern and caring for the patient, and (2) communicate specific instructions for behavior. The following paragraph describes a case in which a doctor clearly failed the first standard when talking to a mother about a genetic problem he had diagnosed in her child. The physician's apparent lack of concern made it less likely that the parents would be strongly motivated to follow *any* instructions he might give them.

He (the physician) could not know the impact his words had on me. I stood there trying to keep my composure amid the myriad feelings of guilt, inferiority, and hopelessness that engulfed me. I desperately needed to see a glimmer of concern in his eyes. I needed to feel that this man who glowed with pride at having made the correct diagnosis cared even a little bit about me as a fellow human being. The almost-smirk on his face made me know otherwise. This doctor within a space of a few minutes had taken it upon himself to play God, genetic counselor, and the deflator of my ego and my pride. It was a long time before the pall that came over my husband and me lifted. Our emotions ran from guilt to shame and self-hatred and then to fear. How could we have done this terrible thing to our child? We were totally irrational. Perhaps if we had had more information on the disease, we could have behaved more rationally, but I doubt it. The attitude of that doctor was what we were reacting to (McKay, 1974, p. 66). ❖

ship (doctor-patient), is also relevant. Both techniques may distance the physician from the patient, however, causing a patient to question the physician's depth of concern. Reward and coercive power are usually less relevant because the physician does not have control over rewards and punishments. Informational power is used by physicians frequently, but (as we have seen) not always effectively. Frequently physicians fail to provide effective evidence for their recommendation, in part because they are unaware of how little the patient knows.

An innovative use of coercive and reward power in health promotion is *contingency contracting* (Raven, 1988). The client who desires to change is asked, upon entering the program, to make a substantial security deposit. The deposit is returned either gradually or all at once when the client has complied with the regimen. This technique has been used with some success with alcoholic patients (Nathan & Briddell, 1976). The technique is likely to be more effective when presented in reward terms ("We will reward you by giving you back all this money") rather than in coercive terms ("If you fail to comply, we will penalize you by keeping your deposit").

As we saw in Chapter 5, social influence based on reward or coercion leads only to compliance, which is dependent on surveillance by those who can reward or punish. Use of referent, informational, legitimate, or expert power, in contrast, can produce *private acceptance* (Table 5-1). Private acceptance is more likely to be long-lasting than is mere compliance that depends on continual surveillance.

Individuals go through three critical phases when they decide to carry out a recommended course of action (Janis, 1983a). First, the practitioner must *acquire motivating power* as a significant reference person. The physician should encourage the patient to disclose personal feelings and should respond with acceptance. In the second phase, the practitioner begins to use his or her motivating power by functioning as a *norm-sending communicator*, encouraging the patient to carry out a necessary course of action. The physician uses social reinforcement without impairing the supportive relationship when making recommendations. Third, the practitioner can encourage patients to *internalize* recommended changes, so that they attribute the behaviors to themselves rather than to the physician's expertise or social power. I will discuss the two most promising types of social power, referent and informational, in more detail below.

Using Referent Power

Some physicians or nurses concentrate so hard on their professional tasks and are so businesslike they do not express any concern about the patient's current plight or future welfare. These practitioners, in effect, appear to rely heavily on their informational, legitimate, or expert power, but neglect the potential increase in their ability to influence patients that could come from acquiring referent power as well.

Referent power is based on the patient's identification with the physician. When used effectively, as pointed out in Chapter 5, referent power leads to feelings of security and trust. But referent power, which may stress similarity, can be inconsistent with expert or legitimate power, which are based on a perception of difference and superiority. People may find it difficult to attribute superior knowledge to physicians and at the same time see physicians as basically similar to themselves.

Physicians who provide social reinforcement can build and maintain a strong bond and become significant reference persons for their patients or clients. There is evidence, for example, that the medical relationship can be facilitated just by having the physician introduce herself on a first-name basis (Raven, 1982). Another step is to emphasize the similarities between oneself and the patient, particularly with regard to beliefs, attitudes, and values. Praise for specific accomplishments or intentions that contribute to the goals of the treatment is helpful. Also beneficial are "acceptance statements," which convey to the client that she is held in high regard as a worthwhile person despite whatever weaknesses and shortcomings may be apparent. An attitude that is not purely businesslike but reflects a willingness to provide help out of a genuine sense of caring is important. Focus 14-1 describes a situation in which a physician apparently did not take advantage of his opportunity to build referent power.

When patients comply solely because of coercive or reward power of the physician, they are likely to attribute their compliance to external factors and are less likely to perceive themselves as having personal responsibility for their health. Hence, when the reward or coercion is no longer there, compliance with the therapeutic regimen is unlikely. By contrast, the use of referent power is more likely to produce *internalization* of the physician's recommendations. For any treatment that requires voluntary action by the patient without constant surveillance, internalization is essential.

Using Informational Power

Informational power is based on the actual content of the physician's communication. If effective, informational power can lead to long-lasting, stable change, because the client has accepted the message and changed her behavior as a result. This behavior change is accompanied by an internal self-attribution: "I changed my behavior because I saw for myself that it was best for me." Informational power is also the only basis of power that leads to socially independent change — change that does not require surveillance or a continual dependent relationship with the influencing agent (as referent power may) (Raven, 1988).

A major limitation of this approach, though, is that often the information in a physician's message is confusing, too technical, too brief, or contradictory. Only when physicians learn to tailor their messages to the understanding level of their audience, and to be sensitive to cues that the patient is not understanding what is being said, will informational power be utilized most effectivly.

Preliminary research supports the idea that physicians who use some types of power will achieve greater private acceptance than will those who use other bases of power. Brown and Raven (1986) had students say how likely they would be to think that a doctor's recommendation to take a medication was a good idea, when they had initially been hesitant because of possible side effects. Each student was given a statement from the doctor representing one of the power bases. As Figure 14-4 indicates, students given a rationale based on the physician's informational, referent, or expert power were most likely to think it was a good recommendation.

Other Ways to Increase Adherence

Making public one's commitment to a treatment is often helpful. If people are induced to announce their intentions to an esteemed person such as a physician, then they are anchored to the decision, not just by anticipated social disapproval but also by anticipated self-disapproval (Kiesler, 1971). *Vigilance*, described by Janis and Mann (1977) as being the most effective coping strategy for stressful situations (Chapter 6) can be enhanced by the "balance sheet procedure," which gives the patient information about the pros and cons of staying with the treatment or breaking it off. Studies have shown that people given a balance sheet were more successful in sticking to doctor-prescribed diets (Colten & Janis, 1982) and prescribed exercise programs (Hoyt & Janis, 1975) than were those who were given the same general information but were not encouraged to consider the pros and cons of the alternative courses of action.

FIGURE 14-4

Physicians' Social Power and Patients' Acceptance of Recommendations

Students were asked, "Even after complying with the doctor's recommendation (to take a medication four times a day), would you think this was a good recommendation or a bad recommendation?" Answers were on a 9-point scale ranging from 1 = "very bad recommendation" to 9 = "very good recommendation."

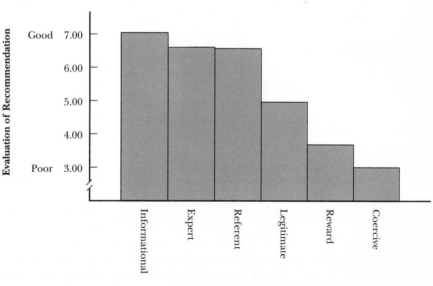

Source: Data from Brown, J. H., & Raven, B. H. (1986). Power and compliance in doctor/patient relationships. Unpublished manuscript, UCLA.

Uses of Social Power in the Hospital: An Example

Of the millions of patients admitted to hospitals in the United States each year, approximately 5 percent of them will acquire a new infection while there. Fifteen thousand U.S. patients per year die from infections acquired in hospitals (Raven & Haley, 1982). It has been estimated that hospital infections can be reduced by 50 percent with extensive infection surveillance and control programs in the hospitals (Bennett, 1978). According to national guidelines, each hospital should have an Infection Control Nurse (ICN), a registered nurse who specializes in epidemiology and infectious diseases and is responsible for detecting and recording hospital infections and taking measures to prevent them.

But will physicians and staff nurses adhere to the ICN's policies? To find out, Raven and Haley (1982) interviewed more than three hundred ICNs and over seven thousand staff nurses in hundreds of hospitals. Of particular interest from a social psychological point of view were the effects of status and social power on the nurses' and doctors' adherence to infection control policies. As you might guess, status made a big difference. The ICNs were more likely to say something to a lower-status person who had violated an infection control practice (head nurse, staff nurse, or laboratory technician) than to a physician. Staff nurses were much more likely to report other staff nurses than a physician for the same violation.

The ICNs and staff nurses also were asked to rate the effectiveness of different types of power in influencing staff nurses to go along with the ICN's recommendations. The ICNs thought that informational power would be the most effective technique but the majority of staff nurses thought that expert power would be the most effective technique. This finding suggests that the ICN could have a greater amount of social influence if she (94 percent of ICNs are women) used expert power more often.

The ICNs said that they used informational and expert power when attempting to influence the behavior of physicians (Table 14-3). Though the ICNs' use of expert power in dealing with physicians may seem surprising, the researchers suggested that the ICNs' choice of expert power came from their perception that other means of influence, especially coercion and reward, were quite ineffective in dealing with physicians; expertise may be one of their few remaining choices. The ICNs felt they had access to a greater variety of influence strategies when dealing with staff nurses.

Review: Ways of Increasing Compliance and Adherence

Important factors in increasing compliance and adherence are summarized in Table 14-4. In general, these include improving the quality of the practitioner-patient relationship, improving the clarity of the message itself, and making the required behaviors as simple and straightforward as possi-

| TABLE 14-3 | USES OF DIFFERENT TYPES OF POWER |

Infection Control Nurses' (ICN's) mean reports of the likelihood that the use of differing power bases will influence staff nurses and physicians.

Power Base	Target Person	
	Physician	**Staff Nurse**
Coercive	0.17[a]	0.71
Reward	0.06	0.57
Legitimate	0.65	0.86
Expert	<u>1.54</u>	0.70
Referent	0.88	0.86
Informational	<u>1.79</u>	<u>1.88</u>

[a]*Scores ranged from 0 = "unlikely," to 2 = "very likely." N = 427.*

Source: Raven, B. H., & Haley, R. W. (1982). Social influence and compliance of hospital nurses with infection control policies. In J. R. Eiser (Ed.), *Social psychology and behavioral medicine* (p. 429). Chichester, England: Wiley. Copyright © 1982 John Wiley and Sons Limited. Reprinted by permission.

ble. Techniques that give clear feedback about drug effects and use reinforcement (such as approval or money) for following the regimen are effective (Epstein & Cluss, 1982).

Taken together, the research findings suggest several general conclusions: (1) In order to mobilize the strengths of particular patients, it is beneficial to *involve patients as responsible participants* in the health care process. The involvement will require some shifts in the role definitions (doctor/patient) that have prevailed during the past hundred years or so. We also need to learn how to distinguish between those patients who will benefit from being given greater responsibility and those who cannot handle it. (2) Health care providers need to understand the *psychological processes* that underlie the behavior of their patients. For example, the personal characteristics of patients and their sociocultural backgrounds may affect which kinds of adherence techniques will work best. (3) Understanding of psychological processes must be linked with interpersonal skills of *communicating information* and *offering support*. Knowledge is of little value unless it can be implemented. The importance of these first three factors cannot be overstated. A meta-analysis of 41 studies by Hall et al. (1988) found that when physicians engaged in "partnership building" with their clients and frequently showed *socioemotional behaviors* (e.g., leaning forward, maintaining eye contact, showing warmth, paying close attention to the client's needs and questions), treatment outcomes were generally more successful. In addition, people feel more satisfied with physicians who have an affiliative style of interaction, rather than a controlling style (Buller & Buller, 1987). (4) Health care providers need

TABLE 14-4   FACTORS THAT ARE LIKELY TO INCREASE COMPLIANCE AND ADHERENCE TO MEDICAL REGIMENS

Source of Regimen (Health Practitioner)	Communication	Compliance/Adherence Behavior
Practitioner has motivating power	Is clear, noncontradictory, comprehensible	Is relatively easy and noncomplex
Practitioner is seen as concerned and caring	Is "personalized" for the patient	Fits patient's preexisting attitudes
Patient in general is satisfied with practitioner	Is repeated by practitioner and/or patient	Is socially supported by important others
Practitioner is a norm-sending communicator	Does not make patient feel deindividuated	Makes patient feel competent to engage in the behavior
Practitioner uses referent and informational power	Makes patient aware of pros and cons of treatment (balance sheet)	"Makes sense" in patient's total life context
Practitioner encourages patient to internalize the recommended changes	Makes patient feel like a responsible participant	Publicly commits patient to the behavior

to *recognize the conditions of cognitive or emotional overload* under which their patients are often operating. High levels of emotional arousal (as when one has just been told that he has a serious illness) may interfere with patients' ability to understand and act on information they are given. Medical people need to make allowances for this state of affairs in communicating information and need also to be sensitive to ways of lightening the pressures on the patient.

Finally, (5) the greater understanding of psychological processes must be used with *sensitivity to ethical problems* that are raised whenever one person attempts to influence the beliefs or behavior of another. People who are important sources of social power for persuasion should use their power with great care and sensitivity. Practitioners also should be very careful that the decisions they reach are the most appropriate ones for each individual. For example, although medical teams have not yet been studied with respect to the possible occurrence of groupthink in their decision making (Chapter 6), there is no reason to believe that groups of medical decision makers would be immune to poor decisions stemming from groupthink. Recognizing the critical importance of all of these factors, medical schools in recent years have developed "interpersonal skills training programs" that teach medical students about the important issues that we have analyzed above (Burchard & Rowland-Morin, 1990).

BEHAVIORAL FACTORS AS CAUSES OF DISEASE

Stress

Stress and Illness

The idea that psychological factors can cause illness is not new. The great physician and pioneering researcher, Dr. William Harvey, was quoted at the beginning of the chapter; the French physician Trousseau suggested in 1882 that anger may aggravate heart disease to such a degree as to cause death. Shortly thereafter, Sir William Osler (1892) attributed coronary disease to "the high pressure at which men live and the habit of working the machine to its maximum capacity." We analyzed the psychological impact of a number of environmental stressors in Chapter 12: crowding, excessive noise, heat, and air pollution. We saw that stress can also result from isolated external stressful events such as the accident at the Three-Mile Island nuclear power plant in Pennsylvania in 1979.

What makes an event stressful? To some extent it's in the eye of the beholder, since an event (e.g., loud rock music) that is seen as stressful to one person (e.g., a parent) may not seem stressful to someone else (e.g., a teenager). **Stress** is felt when an individual's appraisal of the environment indicates that threat and potential harm are high and resources for dealing with it (such as time and attention) are minimal (Lazarus & Folkman, 1984). Stressful events are most likely to have a strong influence on health when they involve a major loss such as the death of a loved one, or when there is an accumulation of diverse life stresses that require readjustment (for instance, graduating from college, getting married, finding a job, and moving to a new city all in the same month), or when an individual is especially likely to interpret ordinary events in a stress-producing way. Stress can lead to disease when coping efforts fail, when the person falls into the generalized emotional state of giving up, when psychological conflicts affect the way events are perceived and coped with, or when personality styles produce negative emotional states (such as depression and anxiety) that lead to ineffective coping behaviors (F. Cohen, 1979; J. Cohen, 1980).

The Schedule of Recent Experience (SRE) developed by Holmes and Rahe (1967) asks people to list how many times in the preceding months each potentially stressful event has occurred (promotion, loss of job, marriage, divorce, arrest, health problems, death of a loved one, etc.). The scale measures both positive and negative events, since there is evidence that both types of life events can result in increased stress due to the necessity of making adjustments to the changed environment. As we might expect, undesirable events are more stressful than positive events (Liem & Liem, 1976). Periods of no change also may be stressful if change has been expected (not

stress:
Occurs when a person feels that threat and potential harm are high and personal resources for dealing with it (such as time and attention) are minimal.

getting a promotion, not going to college as expected, not taking a vacation). Research has shown that the onset of illness is often related to the total number of stressful life events that have occurred during the previous six months (Rahe, 1974; Rahe & Arthur, 1978). Yet much remains to be discovered about *how* people's physical and psychological responses to stressful events affect their general susceptibility to illness.

Stress Inoculation

stress inoculation:
Information that prepares people for upcoming stress by forewarning them of what can be expected and giving realistic reassurances.

Information that prepares people for upcoming stress, forewarning them of what can be expected, and giving realistic reassurances can increase their ability to cope with impending danger or loss. The procedure has been labled **stress inoculation** (Janis, 1983b). A number of experiments with people waiting to undergo surgery or other medical procedures have found that given preoperative information about the stresses of the surgery procedure and ways of coping with these stresses, anxiety, and pain, patients show less subsequent distress and sometimes recover more quickly (Johnson et al., 1978). Such information can help offset the negative impact of feeling that one has no control in the hospital environment (Wells et al., 1986). Patients are not always enthusiastic about these tactics (if they have an avoidant coping style, they may not want to hear about it), but stress inoculation can have beneficial results nevertheless.

Coping Style

Suppose you were told you had a fairly serious illness. How would you react? Coping with serious illness is a difficult task and there are many behavioral paths you could choose: seeking support, seeking information, praying, redefining the situation, trying to avoid thinking about it, problem solving, trying to make yourself feel better (Stone et al., 1988). These might be summarized into three general coping styles: *appraisal-based coping* (trying to define the meaning of the situation); *problem-focused copying* (trying to modify or eliminate the source of stress); and *emotion-focused coping* (managing one's emotions and seeking support) (Moos & Billings, 1982).

psychological hardiness:
Describes people who have a sense of control over their lives, are committed to self, work, and other values, and do not fear change. They may suffer fewer negative health consequences from traumatic events.

Are certain coping responses consistently more effective? It has been proposed that **psychological hardiness** may be associated with resistance to ill health. Hardy people are those who have a sense of control over their lives, are committed to self, work, and other values, and do not fear change, seeing it as a normal and stimulating development (Kobasa et al., 1981). Some theorists believe that hardy people deal with traumatic events in more positive ways and suffer fewer negative health consequences. This concept is intriguing, but research support is only sketchy at this point, though the importance of perceived control seems well supported (Anderson & Arnhoult, 1989).

Looking more generally at coping behaviors, a meta-analysis of forty-three studies (Suls & Fletcher, 1985) found that avoidant coping strategies (e.g., emotion-focused) were effective in the short term while more problem-focused strategies led to better adjustment over the long term. Coping style can affect not only one's psychological state of mind but also the type of care received. A study of cancer patients found that those who coped by complaining and expressing negative feelings survived longest, perhaps because demanding patients may have their complaints acted on more quickly (Jensen, 1987). Below we'll consider a personality factor, optimism/pessimism, that seems related to coping style.

Optimism/Pessimism

The important role of psychological factors in physical health has been clearly demonstrated by Michael Scheier and Charles Carver, who have studied optimists and pessimists. For years writers such as Norman Vincent Peale (1956) have trumpeted the "power of positive thinking." Recent research supports this philosophical view; it seems that optimists suffer fewer medical symptoms in their everyday lives than do pessimists (Scheier & Carver, 1985). Optimists also showed faster recovery from coronary artery bypass surgery—they improved more quickly while in the hospital and also were able to return to their normal life activities sooner (Scheier et al., 1989). Why? Optimists seem to adopt more effective coping strategies for stressful situations. They re-

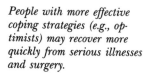

People with more effective coping strategies (e.g., optimists) may recover more quickly from serious illnesses and surgery.

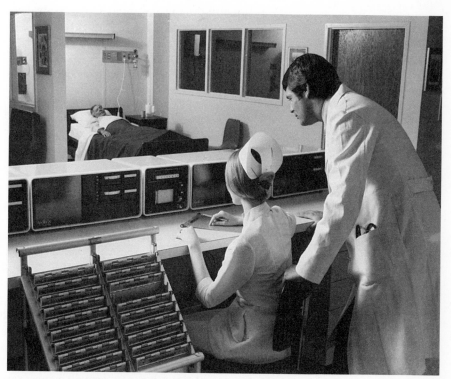

main *problem-focused,* rather than engaging in denial or disengagement from goals (avoidance) as pessimists do. Optimists are also more likeley to *seek social support* and to *emphasize the positive aspects* of the stressful situation, rather than focusing solely on their negative feelings (Scheier et al., 1986). (It's important to remember that because this research is correlational, it cannot prove that coping style *caused* the difference in outcomes. One could speculate that feeling better physically might cause people to adopt a more optimistic viewpoint, for example.)

Another series of recent studies has shown that the way people interpret and explain negative life events can affect physical health. Recall that Weiner's attributional model discussed in Chapter 2 includes three dimensions on which causal attributions may vary: stable/unstable, global/specific, and internal/external locus. A pessimist is likely to react to a negative event with a stable ("It'll happen again"), global ("It affects my whole life"), and internal ("I caused it") attribution. Such an orientation is likely to produce passivity, depression, apathy, hopelessness, low self-esteem, and learned helplessness. Studies show that these reactions are important risk factors in physical illness (Peterson, 1988).

Investigating the lifelong impact of these factors, Peterson et al. (1988) studied ninety-nine men whose explanatory style (optimistic or pessimistic) had been measured back in 1946 when they were twenty-five years old. Those men with pessimistic explanatory styles at age twenty-five had significantly poorer health during ages forty-five to sixty, even when differences in mental and physical health at age twenty-five were controlled for. Hence, a pessimistic cognitive style in early adulthood appears to be a significant risk factor for poor health later in life. Another individual style factor that affects health is the Type A coronary-prone behavior pattern.

The Type A Coronary-Prone Behavior Pattern

Behaviors Associated with Heart Disease

Over 600,000 people in the United States die each year from coronary heart disease (CHD), more than from any other single cause (Table 14-1). Several physicians in the 1700s, 1800s, and early 1900s wrote about the apparent connection between emotional outbursts and heart attacks, but not until the 1950s did researchers begin studying the relationship between behavioral characteristics and coronary heart disease in a systematic fashion. While conducting a large-scale study on the behavior of cardiac patients, Friedman and Rosenman (1974) became disappointed that the traditionally known risk factors (hypertension, serum cholesterol level, systolic blood pressure, smoking) predicted fewer than half of the new cases of coronary heart disease. Therefore, they turned their attention to investigating a collection of behaviors that appeared associated with CHD; they labeled this the **Type A coronary-prone behavior pattern**. The Type A pattern is characterized by excessive hard-driving behavior, job involvement, impatience, competitiveness, a sense of time urgency, aggressiveness, and hostility. It can produce

Type A coronary-prone behavior pattern: A pattern of behavior characterized by excessive hard-driving behavior, job involvement, impatience, competitiveness, desire for control, aggressiveness, and hostility.

anxiety, depression, and interpersonal conflict. Researchers concluded that, coupled with work overload and chronic conflict situations, this behavior pattern might lead to coronary heart disease.

In a large-scale investigation, over three thousand men aged thirty-nine to fifty-nine who were free of clinical symptoms of coronary heart disease when the study began were studied for eight and a half years. Approximately half had been classified as Type A personalities. The Type A men were more than twice as likely as Type B men to develop CHD during the eight-and-a-half-year period. Moreover, the two-to-one risk ratio remained after statistical adjustment for the four traditional risk factors: age, cholesterol level, systolic blood pressure, and smoking (Rosenman et al., 1976; Brand, 1978). As Jenkins (1978) pointed out, this was the first time in medical history that a behavior pattern not directly associated with consummatory behaviors (smoking, heavy drinking) or clinical symptoms successfully and consistently predicted the emergence of a chronic disease. A distinguished panel of scientists under the sponsorship of the National Heart, Lung, and Blood Institute concluded that the Type A pattern increased the risks of CHD "over and above [risks] imposed by age, systolic blood pressure, serum cholesterol, and smoking." The panel estimated that the increase in risk from Type A behavior was about the same as for these other factors (Cooper et al., 1981).

The Type A Behavior Pattern

Hundreds of studies over the past two decades have looked at the psychological correlates of the Type A behavior pattern. When faced with potentially stressful situations, Type As differ from Type Bs in two major ways. First, they *behave differently* (aggression, denial of fatigue, attempts to control the situation) than do Type Bs. Second, Type As show a *stronger internal physiological response* to the challenges of everyday life than do Type Bs. Type As

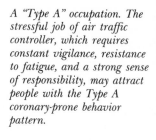

A "Type A" occupation. The stressful job of air traffic controller, which requires constant vigilance, resistance to fatigue, and a strong sense of responsibility, may attract people with the Type A coronary-prone behavior pattern.

show a strong "defensive" physiologic reaction, including increased heart rate and release of hormones such as adrenaline. Although this strong reaction was adaptive in ages past when a person often had to be ready to fight or flee on a moment's notice, it is no longer adaptive in modern society. Many physicians and scientists think this defensive physiologic arousal can be damaging if it is chronic or frequently repeated over time (Dembroski, 1980).

Type A persons respond with greater aggression toward a person who interferes with their performance on an important task than do Type B persons (Carver & Glass, 1978). Type As perform more poorly than Type Bs on tasks that require slow, paced responding in order to achieve the maximum reward (Glass et al., 1974). Type As are more likely to suppress or deny symptoms of fatigue when further effort is required (Weidner & Matthews, 1978).

When under stress, Type As more often elect to work alone than do Type Bs. This preference apparently arises from strong needs to control the work situation and to guard against possible incompetence of co-workers (Dembroski & MacDougall, 1978). In a study of everyday behaviors of college students, Ditto (1982) found that Type A college students spent more time in class, more time studying, more time participating in religious services, and less time socializing with friends than did Type Bs. But Type A individuals were also more likely to be fraternity or sorority members than were Type Bs.

Some research also suggests that uncontrollable stressors encountered in life may have more detrimental effects on Type A than on Type B individuals. Glass (1977) found that Type A subjects responded more vigorously than Type Bs when threatened with failure on an important task, but gave up trying to solve the problems sooner than Bs. This suggests that Type As have a heightened concern with control of the environment, followed by helplessness-prone tendencies. Type As, compared to Type Bs, tend to set high performance goals that they are unlikely to achieve. The unrealistically high performance standard and failure to achieve goals may be what triggers the negative psychological states (depression, hostility, anxiety, dissatisfaction with one's performance) associated with the Type A behavior pattern (Ward & Eisler, 1987).

Explanations for what causes the Type A behavior pattern have focused on three factors: concern with uncontrollability, feedback from parents, and a need for self-appraisal. Perhaps due to an interaction between the constitutional predisposition of some children and parenting styles, some children may grow up with a strong *need to cope with uncontrollable features* of their environment (Glass, 1977). From this perspective, the hard-driving, time-urgent actions of Type As are seen as attempts to maintain or regain control over stressful aspects of their environment. Type As are assumed to desire control more than Type Bs do, and are more threatened by the possibility of a loss of control (Burger, 1985; Dembroski et al., 1984). Type As also show greater psychological reactance (Chapter 5) when their freedom of choice is threatened (Rhodewalt & Davidson, 1983). This tendency toward reactance may cause Type As to be noncompliant to medical recommendations (Rhodewalt & Fairfield, 1990). Type As respond more strongly than Type Bs to uncontrollable events, though they do not exhibit the illusion of control any more than Type Bs do (Strube et al., 1986).

A second causal factor may be *inconsistent feedback from parents.* When a child is strongly encouraged to succeed but is not given consistent parental feedback with which to assess progress toward the lofty goals desired by the parents, the result is a Type-A-to-be child who continuously strives to achieve high but ill-defined goals (Matthews, 1982). This view is supported by research showing that mothers of Type A children actively encouraged them to achieve but provided them with less constructive and consistent feedback than did mothers of Type B children (Matthews et al., 1977).

Type As may also have an especially strong *need for self-appraisal,* according to Strube (1987). He proposed that, because of this need, Type As will respond to uncertainty about their abilities with anxiety and exaggerated attempts to generate relevant diagnostic information (Shalon & Strube, 1988). In the language of social cognition, they have a high need for social comparison. Their hard-driving style may stem from their continual need for diagnostic information to see how they are doing compared to others.

Why Do Type As Give Up?

A consistent but puzzling research finding is that, despite their need for control, Type As are more likely to give up in the face of extensive exposure to uncontrollability or failure than are Type Bs, seeming to show learned helplessness (Chapter 2). At first glance, this doesn't seem to fit in with their competitive personality style. Several interpretations for this finding have been proposed. Some have argued that giving up may not be a helpless response but instead may represent a strategic withholding of effort in an attempt to protect self-esteem (Snyder et al., 1981), as in self-handicapping (Chapter 3). "I could control things if I really wanted to, but it's not worth my time and effort."

A different explanation comes from Strube and his co-workers (1987), who provided a self-appraisal analysis of the apparent learned helplessness response. They found that after repeated failures at an anagram-solving task, Type As did poorly on a new task that supposedly measured the same abilities that the old task had. When presented with a new task that measured a different ability, in contrast, the Type As performed very well. Hence, the researchers argued, giving up on the old task did not represent helplessness, but rather the Type As' conclusion that the task did not provide useful information about their abilities. Type Bs performed at about the same level, regardless of whether or not the new task would provide new diagnostic information.

FIGURE 14-5

Anagram Performance as a Function of Type A Behavior and Similarity of Abilities Tested by the First and Second Tasks

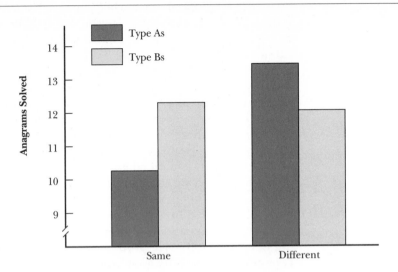

Source: From Strube, M. J., Boland, S. M., Manfredo, P. A., & Al-Falaij, A. (1987). Type A behavior and the self-evaluation of abilities: Empirical tests of the self-appraisal model. *Journal of Personality and Social Psychology, 52,* p. 965. Copyright © 1987 by the American Psychological Association. Reprinted by permission.

Hostility

A recent meta-analysis (Booth-Kewley & Friedman, 1987) found that three chronic emotional reactions seem to be related to CHD—*depression, anxiety,* and *hostility.* The reviewers speculated that perhaps chronic negative emotions in general may be causal factors in CHD. One long-term study (Levenson et al., 1988) found that people who showed high emotionality, a measure of ten factors including hostility, had many more symptoms of psychological distress ten years later. Looking at all the studies carried out thus far on personality factors, the evidence is strongest for the role of hostility as a causal factor in disease. What has been labeled **cynical hostility** seems most strongly related, consisting of anger proneness, resentment, and mistrust of others (Smith & Pope, 1990).

Other studies point to verbal competitiveness and **anger-in**, the suppression of appropriate displays of anger or irritation, as important contributors to CHD. In fact, Dembroski and MacDougall (1985) asserted that the concept of the global Type A Behavior Pattern may have outlived its usefulness. They suggested that the more specific behavioral factors of hostility, verbal competitiveness, and keeping anger in were the important psychological causal factors for CHD. Dembroski and Costa (1987) found that high ratings of potential hostility typify individuals who are described as uncooperative, rude, antagonistic, disagreeable, unsympathetic, and callous—all characteristics of the Type A behavior pattern.

cynical hostility:
Personality style of anger proneness, resentment, and mistrust of others. Appears related to susceptibility to coronary heart disease.

anger-in:
The suppression of appropriate displays of anger or irritation, linked to an increased susceptibility to coronary heart disease.

Hostility, as measured by questionnaire, is strongly related to the Type A behavior pattern (Williams et al., 1985). Several long-term studies have shown that hostility is also related to CHD and to early death. A twenty-year longitudinal study of men working at Western Electric Company in Chicago found that hostility scores measured in 1957–1958 predicted the likelihood of CHD in 1978 and of death from all causes prior to 1978, even when cigarette smoking (another important factor) was taken into account (Shekelle et al., 1983). Men in the highest one-fifth in hostility scores in 1957–1958 were 42 percent more likely to have died in the next twenty years than were men in the lowest one-fifth in hostility. Another long-term study looked at physicians who had taken a hostility scale while in medical school twenty-five years earlier (Barefoot et al., 1983). Again, it was found that the men scoring high on the hostility scale had much higher rates of CHD and higher death rates from all causes than did the less hostile men. Survival rates for men according to their hostility scores are depicted in Figure 14-6. More recently, Barefoot and his co-workers (1987) found that level of *suspiciousness* (closely related to hostility) was related to probability of death from all causes in the ensuing fifteen years in a sample of older adults (average age fifty-nine when suspiciousness was measured) even when other important factors such as age, physicians' ratings of health, smoking, cholesterol level, and alcohol use were taken into account.

Why should hostility be associated with increases in CHD and increases in death from other sources as well? For one thing, hostility tends to produce vigilant behavior, for the hostile person is likely to be cynical and suspicious of others. Chronic vigilance has been shown to cause increased hormonal secretions, which may increase chances of CHD (Zumoff et al. 1983). Researchers speculate that chronic hostility, like stress, also may interfere with the body's immune function (Williams et al., 1985). Further chronic hostility is likely to make interpersonal relationships difficult (Becker & Byrne, 1984) and to reduce the amount of social support one receives when times get tough. People with generally low levels of social support have a higher death rate from all causes (Barefoot et al., 1983; Berkman & Syme,

FIGURE 14-6

Chronic Hostility Can
Kill You

*Percentage of male physicians
who had died prior to each
date, according to their level
of hostility as measured by a
questionnaire when they were
in medical school in the late
1950s.*

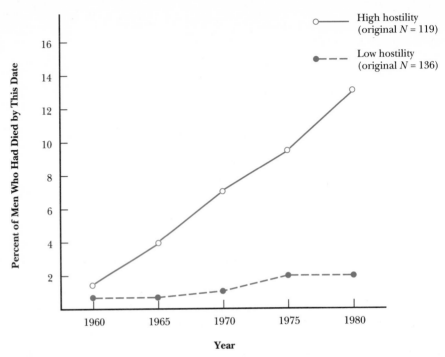

Source: Based on data from Barefoot, J. C., Dahlstrom, W. G., & Williams, R. B., Jr. (1983). Hostility, CHD incidence, and total mortality: A 25-year follow-up study of 255 physicians. *Psychosomatic Medicine, 45,* 59–63.

1979). As psychological and medical research continues in future years, we can anticipate ever more precise information about the psychological and behavioral factors that contribute to CHD. We will also learn more about the most effective ways of changing the behavioral patterns related to CHD.

Changing Type A Behaviors

Concerned by this link between Type A behaviors, hostility, and CHD, some psychologists and physicians have developed programs to modify Type A behaviors and reduce chronic hostility, with the hope of reducing CHD. A meta-analysis of seventeen treatment studies found that, by and large, the studies were successful in reducing the reported prevalence of Type A behaviors (Nunes et al., 1987). Treatments included education (about Type A behaviors, hostility, and CHD), relaxation training (including meditation and yoga), anxiety management training, cognitive therapy (learning to change Type A cognitions), behavior modification (rehearsing Type B coping skills), and emotional support (ventilating painful emotions and experiences in a supportive environment). Treatment programs that used several of these techniques at once were generally the most effective. Two studies (Friedman et al., 1984; Rahe et al., 1979) have documented a reduced probability of CHD in the ensuing three years for people who have undergone such treatment programs. Although the research evidence is still preliminary, there is some evidence that cognitive behavioral strategies are more promising than psychotherapy in creating long-term changes (Kendall & Turk, 1984).

An alternative strategy is to encourage Type A individuals to change their environments (job, type of recreation) so that they are less likely to encounter the uncontrollable, competitive situations that elicit Type A be-

---

FOCUS 14-2

Ways to Develop a "Trusting Heart"

Physician Redford Williams, in his book, *The Trusting Heart: Great News About Type A Behavior* (1989) outlined twelve steps that a person can take to become a more trusting person, reducing the cynicism and hostility characteristic of Type A behavior that can cause bodily responses that lead to heart attacks.

1. *Monitor your cynical and hostile thoughts.* Carry a pocket "hostility log." Note each incident where hostile thoughts occurred, what emotions you felt, and what actions you took. Review your log at the end of each week for common themes.
2. *Confession is good for the soul.* Acknowledge to friends that you have a problem with hostility, put trust in them, and ask for their help.
3. *Stop those thoughts!* As soon as you realize you are having hostile thoughts, yell as loudly as you can (in your mind), "STOP!"
4. *Reason with yourself.* When cynical or hostile thoughts begin, try to develop a noncynical, nonhostile, reasonable explanation for what has happened.
5. *Put yourself in the other person's shoes.* We saw earlier (Chapters 7 and 10) that empathy is a good way to reduce hostility and aggression and increase prosocial behavior.
6. *Learn to laugh at yourself.* We saw also (Chapter 10) that humor is a good way of defusing aggression. Taking yourself less seriously can short-circuit depressive thought patterns.
7. *Learn to relax.* Learning to use deep-relaxation

techniques or meditation may be an effective way of keeping hostile or cynical thoughts away.

8. *Practice trust.* Begin looking for opportunities to trust someone else where, if it doesn't work out, no real harm is done.
9. *Learn to listen.* Being an attentive listener sends the message that you value others and their ideas.
10. *Learn to be assertive.* Learn to calmly tell someone what is bothering you about their behavior and why. Try and suggest a mutually-acceptable solution to the problem. Assertiveness is a constructive alternative to aggression.
11. *Practice forgiving.* Forgiving those who have mistreated or angered you lifts the burden of anger and retribution from your shoulders.
12. *Pretend today is your last.* The steps above may seem more important, and petty annoyances less so, when seen from this perspective. Many times heart patients will comment, "Oh, I used to get angry a lot, but since my heart attack I've realized that all those nitpicking things that used to rile me aren't worth worrying about." ❖

haviors. Focus 14-2 describes several steps that one can take to reduce chronic hostility and, perhaps, increase one's chances for a longer life.

Benefits of Type A Behaviors

Thus far I have focused on the potential negative health aspects (heart disease) and psychological correlates (anxiety, dissatisfaction, hostility) of the Type A Behavior Pattern. But I should also note the other side: these same behaviors can enable a person to be highly productive. Type As work hard, set high standards, get more done under difficult conditions, and are able to focus on essential aspects of a task and ignore distractions (Humphries et al., 1983). Studies of college professors in a wide range of departments found that Type As did more and better research, in general, than did Type B professors (Matthews et al., 1980; Taylor et al., 1984). The Type A professors had higher feelings of self-efficacy, set higher goals for themselves, and were more likely to work on multiple projects at the same time, than were Type B professors (Figure 14-7). This Type A/Type B difference may be particularly applicable to college professors, who have a great deal of freedom to set their own goals and level of work. It is less visible in other occupations that allow less flexibility in work habits (Locke et al., 1981).

The overall message here is that there are advantages and disadvantages to each behavioral style. Type As may accomplish more in the workplace, but sometimes at a high cost to their health or their personal relationships. One solution, as noted earlier, could be to learn to reduce Type A behaviors in general. Another possibility would be to maintain the achievement-oriented aspects of Type A behavior while working to minimize

---

FIGURE 14-7

Type A Behavior in College Professors

College professors who showed the Type A behavior pattern tended to be more productive, earn higher salaries, and feel a higher level of self-efficacy than professors who showed the Type B behavior pattern (Taylor et al., 1984).

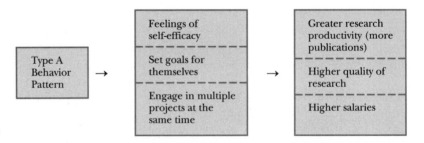

Source: Based upon Taylor, M. S., Locke, E. A., Lee, C., & Gist, M. E. (1984). Type A behavior and faculty research productivity: What are the mechanisms? *Organizational Behavior and Human Performance, 34,* 402–418.

the negative expectations (unrealistic goals, quest for control), and emotions (hostility, frustration, depression) that interfere with physical and psychological health.

SUMMARY

Good health is a matter of great concern to all of us as individuals, as family members, and as people concerned with the welfare of everyone in our society. Although the systematic application of social psychological theory to health-related behaviors is a relatively new field, it holds immense promise. The application of research findings may make it easier for people to avoid or cease self-destructive behaviors such as cigarette smoking, excessive drinking, overeating, and "unsafe sex." Further, the findings provide insights into improving the quality of doctor-patient communication and increase the likelihood that people will follow medical instructions and take medication properly. Finally, research on behaviors that increase the likelihood of illness or interfere with recovery from illness or surgery, such as the Type A behavior pattern, inadequate coping styles, pessimism, and hostility, can be used to change people's life-styles and make it less likely they will be struck down by disease. If concepts and research from psychologists can be employed in developing, evaluating, and implementing programs that modify life-styles, thereby contributing to the prevention of killer diseases such as AIDS, lung cancer, and heart disease, this could become the most important contribution of the behavioral sciences in the latter part of the twentieth century.

Glossary

acquisition phase: The first stage involved in perceiving and remembering which includes the conditions at the time the event a crime occurred.

activist-collaborator role: A scientist advocates social policies and solutions that seem appropriate and tries to influence legislation in order to promote human welfare.

actual similarity: This refers to how similar two people are.

actual reciprocity: This refers to how much someone actually does like us.

adaptive illusions: Three widely-held illusions seem adaptive for mental health: the illusion of control, overly positive self-evaluations, and unrealistic optimism about the future.

affect: Evaluation on a general good-bad dimension. Some theorists have defined attitude as the intensity of positive or negative affect for or against a psychological object.

affirmative action: Programs that attempt to redress historical inequities toward outgroup members by giving them favored treatment in specific situations.

agentic state: When people see themselves as mere agents of an authority figure and deny responsibility for their own actions.

aggression: Behavior intended to bring physical or psychological harm to a person who wishes not to be harmed.

aggressive cognitive script: A program for behavior that is developed early in life and is characterized by violence or aggression.

aggressive pornography: Sexually explicit materials in which women are degraded and the objects of aggression. Research suggests that men's exposure to these materials may increase the likelihood of male assaults on women.

agonistic aggression: The ethological term for within-species aggression which allows the creation of dominance hierarchies and territorial spacing.

altruism: Selfless behavior that has the goal of increasing the recipient's welfare.

altruistic love: Love which is patient, kind, and does not demand reciprocity; very uncommon.

anger-in: The suppression of appropriate displays of anger or irritation, linked to an increased susceptability to coronary heart disease.

angry aggression: Aggression that involves an emotional state of anger; differentiated from instrumental aggression.

angry motivation: Instigation to aggression in which the injury to the victim is an end in itself.

anticipatory polarization effect: When people are forewarned that they will encounter a persuasive message, they tend to develop counterarguments and become more extreme in their preferred position.

anticompliance: In physician-client interactions, when the client understands the recommendation but does not follow it.

anticonformity: An active attempt to contradict group pressures and behave in the opposite manner.

anti-Semitism: Prejudice or discrimination against Jews.

antisocial behavior: Behavior that is not condoned by society, such as aggression, murder, and violence.

anxiety: Feelings of nervousness and dread.

apprehensive subject role: Characteristic of subjects who feel evaluation apprehension and want to present themselves in a socially desirable light.

arousal cost/reward model: An emergency helping model. It proposes that witnesses to an emergency are physiologically and emotionally aroused. Bystanders will generally respond in a way that reduces the arousal as rapidly as possible, with the least possible cost to themselves.

assumed dissimilarity effect: People tend to assume that members of disliked groups have beliefs and values very different from their own.

attachment: According to Rubin, a need for another person. The passionate desire to possess and be fulfilled by another person.

attachment style: Characteristic way of relating to others that develops in infancy and may affect adult romantic relationships. Three major types are: secure, avoidant, and anxious/ambivalent.

attitude: Has been defined as the amount of effect for or against a psychological object or alternatively, as having three components: affect, behavioral tendencies, and cognition.

attractiveness stereotype: The incorrect assumption that all attractive people possess positive traits.

authoritarian personality: A prejudiced, intolerant personality characterized by obedience to authority, prejudice, loyalty to the ingroup and aggression.

audience inhibition effect: People are inhibited from helping by fear of embarrassment and negative evaluations from other bystanders.

authorization: Sanction given by authority figures which allows people to claim little responsibility for their actions.

autokinetic effect: An illusion that occurs when a person looks at a stationary pinpoint of light in an otherwise completely dark room and the point appears to move.

bail: A monetary payment made by a defendant or his agent to ensure that the defendant will appear later in court for the trial.

balance theory: The theory that looks at balance or imbalance between feelings involving a person (P), another person (O) and an issue, object, or third person (X).

"Barnum effect": People are likely to interpret a fake general personality description as a very accurate individual description of their own characteristics.

basking in reflected glory (BIRGing): Through reflection, people attempt to raise their own self-evaluation by pointing out the outstanding accomplishments of others with whom they are associated in some way. The better their performance and the closer the association with the others, the more powerful will this reflection process be.

behavior engulfing the field: The tendency for people to make dispositional attributions to an actor even when the actor's behavior was forced by environmental factors.

behavioral confirmatory bias: When a person's behavior channels an interaction so that behavior that seems to confirm the person's expectancies is elicited from the other individual.

behavioral contagion: Disinhibited behavior; because of lowered self-awareness, individuals engage in previously-inhibited behaviors.

behavioral medicine: The development of behavioral science knowledge for understanding physical health and applying this knowledge to the prevention, diagnosis, and treatment of illness.

behavioral model of compliance: Looking for ways to increase compliant behaviors; it sometimes does not take into account the goal-directed nature of human behavior.

behavioral sinks: Calhoun's term for extreme behavioral disturbances that developed in very overcrowded rat pens.

belief perseverance: The tendency to persevere

in our beliefs even when the original basis for these beliefs has been disconfirmed.

biased sample: A sample of subjects that is not representative of the population from which it was drawn.

biological fitness: It is not just the ability to survive, but rather the ability to get genes like your into the gene pool for future generations.

biopsychological model: The position that biological, psychological, and social factors are involved in all stages of health and illness.

BIRGing: See basking in reflected glory.

blended family: A family resulting from a remarriage bringing together children from one or more former marriages; hence, stepparents and stepchildren are involved.

body language: The subtle communication of thoughts and feelings through body positions and movements.

boomerang effect: If a message is delivered by a highly disliked source, the audience may actually change their attitudes in a direction opposite to what the disliked source advocated.

brainwashing: A popularized term for attitude and behavior change that takes place under extreme authority pressure and control.

built environments: The part of the environment that is man made, such as dorms, houses, and airports.

calibration training: A way of reducing the overconfidence effect by giving people immediate and continuous feedback on the accuracy of their judgments.

caring: The giving of oneself to another person.

caring cluster: One of two clusters of factors that are more typical of love than of friendship; involves championing each other's interests, "giving the utmost".

catharsis: The theory that by acting out or observing others, people are able to release or drain off their pent-up emotions.

causal attributions: The tendency to infer personality characteristics about people based on their behavior.

cause: The condition that produces a particular behavior.

central trait: A trait that is of major importance in determining our reaction to someone, as it affects how they are evaluated on other supposedly related traits.

civil case: When an individual brings suit against another individual for non-criminal acts.

classical conditioning: Learning through association, when a neutral stimulus is consistently associated with a stimulus that produces an emotional response (an unconditioned stimulus).

co-actors: Fellow participants in an activity who are nearby.

coercive power: The ability to force another person to change his or her behavior by threats or punishments.

cognitive confirmation effect: Situations where the perceiver selectively interprets or recalls aspects of another person's actions in a way that is consistent with the perceiver's expectations.

cognitive conservatism: The tendency of the self to resist cognitive change.

cognitive disruption: An interruption in normal thought process which reduces one's ability to cope with difficult situations.

cognitive dissonance theory: Attitude or behavior change is likely when two cognitive elements are in a dissonant relationship to one another.

cognitive interview: Interview technique that focuses on complete reports, reinstating the context of the event, and recounting the event in a different order and from different perspectives. Designed to gain more information without increasing errors.

cognitive overload: The situation in which a person is receiving more input that she or he can handle. Adaptions to overload include giving less time to each input, disregarding low priority inputs, and blocking off inputs.

cohabitation: A premarital relationship that involves a decision to live in the same household without the legal ties of marriage.

collective behavior: Actions of people who, simply because they are in the same place at the same time, behave in a similar manner.

common sense beliefs: Generalizations that are widely shared within a culture, but are often inadequate and inaccurate with describing things as they really are.

commons dilemma: When people recognize that available resources are becoming scarcer, they may "get while the getting is good" and devour as many of the remaining resources as possible.

companionate love: The affection we feel for those with whom our lives are deeply intertwined: similar to very deep friendship.

comparison level: People's judgments as to the kind of outcome they expect to receive from a particular relationship.

comparison level for alternatives: The value of the next best alternative interaction a person could enter into.

competitive marketplace analogy: The idea that if one partner is more attractive than the other, the more attractive partner should more often be the target of the competitive affections of others.

complementarity: The proposition that people with opposite personality characteristics may be attracted to each other. There is not much research support for this proposition.

complementary needs theory: Winch's suggestion that in selecting a partner, individuals look for others who are similar with regard to some factors and then select a partner who best complements their personal needs.

compliance: Changing one's behavior to fit someone's request or order.

concurrence seeking: Trying to get everyone in a group to agree to a decision.

confabulation: A filling of gaps in memory with fantasy.

confirmatory bias: Since our attitudes and schemas guide the processing of social information and our behavior toward others, we tend to interpret and remember information in a biased way that conforms to our preexisting schemata.

conformity: Yielding to perceived group pressure; behaving according to perceived groups norms that are contrary to one's private preferences.

confounding: The degree to which an extraneous variable is unintentionally varied along with the independent variable.

consideration behavior: Leader behavior that includes interpersonal warmth, concern for the feelings of subordinates, and two-way communication.

contingency theory of leadership: The theory that a leader's effectiveness is contingent on the relationship between the leader's style and characteristics of the situation in which the leader functions.

contrast effect: The tendency to support an existing schema by exaggerating its differences with contradictory evidence. A person who is surrounded by "beautiful people" may seem less attractive in comparison due to a contrast effect.

control group: A group that does not receive an experimental treatment. Some experiments use control groups while other experimental designs do not.

Coolidge effect: Named for President Calvin Coolidge, this term describes the results of animal research indicating that novelty of partners can be of importance in instigating sexual behavior.

correlation coefficient: A statistic that describes the strength of a relationship between two variables. The statistic can range from − 1.00 (a perfect inverse relationship) through 0 to + 1.00 (a perfect positive relationship).

correspondent inference theory: A major theory of attribution that analyzes the factors that cause people to make dispositional attributions.

credibility: The credibility of a communication source depends mainly on expertise and trustworthiness.

criminal case: When the state brings charges against an individual for alleged illegal acts.

criterion-based statement analysis: A technique that attempts to assess the truthfulness of statements by analyzing their contents in terms of specific criteria. Has only preliminary research support.

crowding: See subjective crowding and two-factor theory of crowding.

cynical hostility: Personality style of anger proneness, resentment, and mistrust of others. Appears related to susceptibility to coronary heart disease.

danger control: Coping with the environment and responding to avert the danger.

DDD syndrome: Conditions facing prisoners of war (POWs) that make it particularly hard to resist compliance pressures. POWs often face dread, dependency, and debility.

"death-qualified" juries: In capital cases, juries in which all members have said they are comfortable with the death penalty. May be more likely to convict defendants than other juries would be.

debriefing: The experimenter explains to subjects what was done, why it was done, and what it means.

decategorization: Lessening the tendency to categorize people and to focus on in-group/outgroup distinctions.

decision-driven research: Research designed to assess the effect of various policy-related decisions, such as legislation and social programs.

de facto selective exposure: People tend to come into contact mostly with messages that support their existing opinions, because of the subcultures to which they belong and the materials that they encounter.

defensive avoidance: A coping strategy by which people try to avoid information that might stimulate anxiety or reveal the shortcomings of their chosen course of action.

dehumanization: The process through which victims are robbed of their humanity and individuality, making it easier to aggress against them.

deindividuation: The loss of inner restraints that may occur when an individual feels submerged in a group.

demand characteristics: Perceived pressures in a situation that seem to demand certain kinds of behavior; research situations have unique demand characteristics.

dependent love: Love that is characterized by obsession with the loved one and anxiety.

dependent variable: A behavior that is measured in an experiment to see whether it has been affected by the independent variable.

deprogramming: A procedure in which members of unpopular groups are put under intense pressure to recant and reestablish their older and more traditional beliefs.

differential accuracy: The ability to tell where each person stands in relation to others with respect to a particular characteristic.

differentation: The perception of individual differences among people in a social category.

diffusion of responsibility: In emergency situations, the more bystanders present, the less responsibility each individual bystander feels.

discounting: The role of a given factor in producing an effect will be discounted (seen as less important) if other causes are also present (such as status differences, role requirements, or unique outcomes).

discounting cues: In persuasion situations, if a source has low credibility. This is a discounting cue at the time the message is heard, causing the receiving person to reject the message. Over time this discounting cue may be forgotten, leading to the sleeper effect.

disinhibition: The lowering of inhibitions against forbidden behavior. Research suggests that exposure to aggressive pornography may cause some men to disinhibit their aggressive behaviors against women.

dispositional attribution: When a person's behavior is attributed to his or her dispositions, e.g., attitudes, traits, and personality.

dispositions: Internal characteristics such as attitudes, beliefs, values, schemas, and personality traits.

distraction-conflict theory: A theory of social facilitation that suggests that, when observed, people may be in conflict over two competing tendencies—whether to pay attention to the task or to the audience.

distributive justice: A basic component of the equity theory, which describes the balance of rewards and costs for two people involved in a relationship.

diverent thinking: Considering a problem from varying viewpoints, usually resulting in better decision-making.

dogmatism: A relatively closed intolerant organization of beliefs developed around the central set of beliefs about absolute authority.

door-in-the-face effect: If a persons asks first for a very large favor and is refused, and then asks for a smaller favor, compliance with the smaller favor is more likely than if that individual had asked solely for the smaller favor.

downward social comparison: Comparing oneself to others less fortunate in order to enhance one's self-esteem.

egalitarian relationship: A relationship where each partner has equal power.

egocentricity: Greenwald's term for the tendency for judgment and memory to be focused on the self.

elaboration likelihood model: Model describing the central route to attitude change (long-lasting change resulting from thinking about the issue) and the peripheral route (temporary change from non issue relevant factors).

electromyograph (EMG): A machine that measures the tiny electrical output of muscle groups. May be useful in the future as a measure of attitudinal response.

empathy: An emotional state elicited by and congruent with the perceived welfare of someone else.

empirical: Pertaining to facts, experimentation, observation, or data.

empty shell marriage: A marriage that provides little positive satisfaction to the participants but is held together for social or economic reasons. It is considered stable but not satisfying.

entrapment: Entrapment occurs when an individual or group becomes overly committed to a course of action as a result of having invested time, energy, self-esteem, or pride in the action.

environmental forces: From an attribution theory perspective, those characteristics of a situation that "press" for a specific type of behavior. If environmental forces are high, a situational attribution for behavior is likely to be made.

environmental stressors: Those facets of the environment that induce stress, such as excessive social density, noise, heat, and air pollution.

equal-status contact: An often effective means of reducing levels of prejudice and hostility between groups.

egalitarian relationship: A relationship where each partner has equal power.

equitable relationship: A relationship that would lead an observer to believe that the participants were receiving equal relative gains from the relationship.

equity theory: Equity exists when each person in a relationship receives the same relative outcome compared to how much they have invested in the relationship. People are generally happier in equitable relationships than in inequitable ones.

esteem for least preferred co-worker scale: Scale developed by Fiedler on which a leader is asked to rate the individual with whom the leader had the most difficulty accomplishing assigned tasks. A leader who gives a very negative rating to this coworker (low LPC) is seen as a task-motivated leader. A person who gives the least preferred co-worker a relatively positive rating (high LPC) is a relationship-oriented leader.

esteem-oriented individuals: People who tend to be achievement-oriented, assertive, and strive for competence.

ethnic group: Any group defined by nationality, by race, or by common cultural and religious heritage.

ethnocentrism: A general tendency to prefer the in-group over all outgroups.

ethologist: Scientists who study animal behavior.

evaluation apprehension: Apprehension about being evaluated negatively by someone else.

evaluation dimension: One of two major dimensions on which people's views of human nature differ. The degree to which people are seen as trustworthy, rational, altruistic, and independent.

event schema: A schema containing knowledge about typical sequences of events or social occasions.

excitation/transfer theory: The types of excitatory reactions caused by different stimuli may overlap considerably with each other and this can lead to misattribution of excitation to aggression-related stimuli and to feeling higher levels of aggression.

excuses: Explanations designed to maintain a positive self-image and a sense of control.

exemplification: A self-presentational strategy where one attempts to project integrity and moral worthiness.

exit: An active destructive reaction to problems in the relationship as the person leaves the relationship.

expectancy confirmation: The process by which an individual's expectancies bias her or his memories and perceptions of outgroup members or their interactions with outgroup members. (See behavioral confirmation effect and cognitive confirmation effect.)

experiment: Research study in which at least one independent variable is manipulated by the experimenter to evaluate its effect on one or more dependent variables. For a study to be a true experiment, there must have been random assignment of subjects to conditions or levels of the independent variable.

experimenter effects: Changes in a subject's responses unwittingly caused by reactions to the experimenter's behavior or expectations.

experimental realism: The amount of impact that a research situation has on the participants.

expert power: Power deriving from specialized knowledge that one has.

expert witness: A person certified by the trial judge as having expertise in a particular area that is likely to be of relevance and value to the jury.

external validity: The degree to which one can generalize the research findings of a study.

extraneous variables: Variables other than the independent variable that might influence the dependent variable in an experiment.

face: The positive social value claimed for oneself in social interactions.

fact: A logical conclusion based on observation, about which virtually everyone who observes the same situation would agree.

fairness of a lineup: The extent to which other lineup members match the general appearance of the suspect. A lineup is unfair if the other members are quite different in appearance from the suspect, since a witness may identify a suspect simply because he is the only one that looks similar to the criminal.

faithful subject role: Enacted by research subjects who are docile and follow experimental instructions scrupulously.

false consensus bias: People tend to overestimate how typical their own beliefs, judgments, and behaviors are.

favorability bias: People tend to rate favorable self-descriptions as more accurate than unfavorable ones.

fear control: Responding to reduce the unpleasant feeling of fear, guided largely by internal cues.

fear-drive model: Assumes that the relationship between fear and acceptance of a persuasive message will be in the form of an inverted U-shaped curve, with the greatest behavior change occurring at a moderate level of fear.

field studies: Studies that take place in natural settings that are not specifically designed for research.

foot-in-the-door effect: If one complies with a small request, the chances are improved that he or she will later comply with a larger request.

frustration-aggression theory: The theory that frustration instigates aggression and occurrences of aggression presuppose frustration.

functions of attitudes: Theorists have proposed that there are four general functions that an attitude can serve: understanding, social adjustment, ego defense, and expressing values.

fundamental attribution error: The widespread tendency to make dispositional attributions for other people's behaviors but environmental attributions for their own behaviors.

gain/loss theory: The proposition that gain (or loss) of esteem from someone else has a more potent effect on liking (or disliking) than does constant praise or criticism.

galvanic skin response (GSR): A measure of general physiological arousal.

generalization fallacy: The tendency to be heavily influenced by vivid, concrete, easily usable information based on personal experience, and less influenced by statistical base-rate data.

generalized reciprocity: The belief that one will be rewarded in terms of how much one gives to the world.

"Good Samaritan" statute: A statute that protects those who try in good faith to give help in an emergency situation.

good subject role: Enacted when subjects try to give responses that will validate the perceived research hypothesis.

"great person" theory of leadership: The theory that people are effective leaders because of unique personality traits they possess.

GRIT plan: A plan to free ourselves from "psychological vicious circles" of military arms development, wherein one party makes a unilateral conciliatory gesture which may lead to further conciliatory gestures by the other side.

group: Two or more people who interact with and influence each other. The group is held together by the common interests or goals of its members.

group behavior: Group members' responses to the social structure of the group and to the norms it adopts.

group cohesiveness: The degree to which group members like each other, have similar goals, and want to remain in one another's presence.

group polarization effect: Decisions made within a group are likely to be more extreme than decisions made by individuals working separately.

groupthink: The process through which groups faced with an important stressful decision may be more concerned with reaching unanimous agreement than with evaluating the facts of the situation.

halo effect: When we have only a vague, general

impression of someone as good or bad, this may affect our perceptions of many of that person's other more specific traits.

Hawthorne effect: The finding that making people feel special and important may have a more significant impact on their performance than the experimental manipulation that the researchers think is important.

health psychology: An area of psychology that focuses on developing techniques to help in the prevention of behaviors that are harmful to health, such as alcohol and drug abuse and cigarette smoking.

hedonic relevance: The degree to which an action is gratifying or disappointing to the observer of that action.

helping behavior: Behavior designed to help another individual, regardless of the reason.

heuristics: Mental shortcuts and strategies that people use to make sense out of their complex environments.

heuristic value: The degree to which a theory stimulates thought and research and challenges others to develop opposing theories.

hindsight bias: The tendency of people to remember their past judgments as having been much more accurate than they really were, or to assume others should have known what would happen.

hypnosis: A state of heightened suggestability that may also include posthypnotic amnesia in which the events that occurred during hypnosis may be forgotten.

hypothesis: A testable prediction that is derived from a more general theory and can be assessed by research.

ideal self: The self that you would like to be, embodying all your hopes and goals.

ideal self-others: The characteristics that important other people (e.g., your parents) wish you would attain.

identification: Identification occurs when one accepts influence in order to maintain a satis-fying self-defining relationship with another person or group.

idiosyncrasy credits: A person who has demonstrated competence and has achieved status in the group builds up idiosyncrasy credits, and will be permitted (up to a point) to deviate from group standards.

illusion of control: Most people believe that they have more control over their destinies than is actually the case.

illusory correlation effect: Seeing an expected association between two factors (e.g., being a minority-group member and possessing a disliked trait) where none exists.

implicit personality theories: Our implicit and often unrecognized theories about what traits tend to go together in others.

impression-construction: Choosing the particular image one wishes to create and behaving in ways to achieve that goal.

impression management theory: A theory that suggests that people try to rationalize and manage the impressions they create in order to appear as good, consistent people. People are seen as actively changing their self-presentations in order to receive rewards and avoid punishments.

impression-motivation: How motivated you are to control how others see you, to create a particular impression in others' minds.

independence: Behavior that ignores group pressures and norms.

independent variable: A factor that is varied in a study manipulated by the experimenter to assess its effect on a dependent variable.

individuation: The tendency to see people as individuals rather than as group members. Can reduce prejudice and discrimination and aggression.

individualist: A person who resists group pressure to conform.

induced compliance: Situations in which one engages in a counterattitudinal behavior, behavior that goes against one's attitude. This produces cognitive dissonance which, in turn, may cause people to change their attitudes to bring them more in line with their behaviors.

infatuation: In Sternberg's theory, passion without commitment or intimacy.

informational power: Power that exists when an individual has information that others do not have.

informational social influence: Occurs when one changes behavior because of the information that the behavior of others provides.

ingratiation: A self-presentational strategy with the goal of being seen as likable and attractive.

ingroup: The group that one belongs to; one's own group.

initiation of structure: Leader behavior involving directedness goal facilitation, and task-related feedback.

inoculation theory: Training people to defend their position can make them less susceptible to persuasion.

insecure love: Romantic attachment characterized by anxiety and obsession with the loved one.

institutional racism: Indirect and often unintentional mistreatment of minority groups by major institutions of society.

instrumental aggression: Aggression that occurs as a means to an end (as in a robbery).

instrumental motivation: Investigation to aggression in which the violent behavior accomplishes a goal.

instrumental values: Preferences for certain broad modes of conduct such as honesty, courage.

intergroup interaction anxiety: Awkwardness that is often felt in initial interracial contacts.

internal validity: The extent to which a study is well designed and carried out.

internalization: When one accepts influence because the content of the induced behavior is intrinsically rewarding and is congruent with one's value system.

interpersonal attraction: The tendency to evaluate a person or group positively, to approach them, and to behave positively toward them.

interpersonal density: The number of people who live in the same room or building in a given area.

interpersonal focus: Social psychology's focus that analyzes individuals' behavior in terms of the social factors and social situations people often deal with.

interpersonal relationships: The ongoing interactions between two or more people.

interviewer bias: When an interviewer's expectations or preferences for a particular answer influence the respondents reply.

intimidation: A self-presentational tactic of arousing fear and gaining power by convincing someone you are dangerous.

jealousy: An issue common to many relationships, thought to result from the loss of relationship rewards and the loss of self-esteem. Jealousy describes the thoughts and feelings triggered by the loss or anticipated loss of a romantic partner to a rival.

jigsaw groups: Aronson's term for mixed-race cooperative learning groups which work together on a project, resulting in reduced levels of prejudice between group members.

just world assumption: The tendency for people to believe that the world is a just and fair place, and thus victims of misfortune must have done something to deserve their fate.

kin selection: A theory maintaining that the greater the percentage of genes shared by descent between individuals, the more helpful will be the behavior and the greater will be the readiness to sacrifice.

knowledge bias: One of two types of bias, along with reporting bias, that a source may have. Knowledge bias occurs when the source has incorrect information, and relates to the source's expertise.

knowledge-driven research: Basic research that is

designed to increase general knowledge about human social behavior.

known self (sense of me): The characteristic that we believe we possess.

laboratory studies: Studies conducted in designated research areas, often with students as subjects.

laissez-faire: A leadership style characterized by very low levels of activity by the leader.

latent liberal: Pettigrew's term for an individual whose prejudices are serving a social adjustment function.

latitude of acceptance: In M. Sherif's theory, that area centered around one's own position within which attitude-relevant statements are seen as acceptable. Arguments within this latitude will produce attitude change.

latitude of noncommitment: In M. Sherif's theory, the area wherein statements are neither acceptable nor unacceptable to the audience members. The area between the latitude of acceptance and the latitude of rejection.

latitude of rejection: In M. Sherif's theory, the area that includes positions unacceptable to the audience. Arguments that fall in an audience's latitude of rejection will not lead to attitude change.

law of attraction: One's attraction toward a person depends directly on the proportion of positive reinforcement received from that person.

law of small numbers: The common tendency to overgeneralize from an individual to the group to which the individual belongs.

leader: A person who can influence the direction of the group by influencing its attitudes and behaviors, while maintaining the image of having the group's best interests in mind.

leadership effectiveness: Determined by how well a group performs under one's leadership.

leadership emergence: The process by which one gets chosen to be a leader.

learned helplessness: People who fail repeatedly may make a self-attribution to lack of ability, increasing the chance that they will not try hard subsequently even in situations where they would have been effective if they had tried.

legitimate power: Power derived from being in a particular role or position.

locus of control: A personality characteristic describing feelings about what controls one's destinies. People with an external locus of control feel that they do not control their own destinies, while people with an internal locus of control feel that they control their own destinies.

loneliness: Defined by Perlman and Peplau as a painful warning signal that a person's social relations are deficient in some important way. Research indicates that loneliness is less common among married people than among nonmarrieds.

looking glass self: Our sense of self that evolves out of others' opinions of us.

love: Every scientific investigator, poet, and songwriter has a different definition of love. Rubin suggested that romantic love has three characteristics: attachment, caring, and intimacy, while Kelley identified four components: caring, needing, trust, and tolerance for another's faults.

low-balling: Once a person has made a decision to engage in a behavior, the cost of that behavior can be raised and the person may still feel committed to the action and engage in it.

loyalty: A passive constructive reaction to problems in the relationship as the person remains loyal and supportive.

LPC: See Esteem for least preferred co-worker scale.

matching: People tend to pair off with others who are at about the same level of physical attractiveness.

medical model of compliance: Sees the practitioner as an expert acting to benefit an uninformed patient; if the patient does not comply, this implies ignorance, laziness, or a willful neglect on the patient's part.

mere exposure effect: People develop more positive feelings toward objects and individuals they see often.

meta-analysis: A sophisticated way of statistically combining the results of many research studies on the same topic to arrive at a statistical analysis of the findings as a whole.

mindguards: In groupthink situations, group members who try to "protect" the group from adverse information that might shatter their shared complacency about their decision.

mindlessness: The tendency to respond in routinized, unthinking ways.

minimax strategy: The social exchange theory assumption that people attempt to minimize the cost and maximize the rewards of relationships.

minority influence: The process by which a consistent, firm minority may alter the beliefs and behaviors of the majority.

mirror-image wars: Wars in which both sides genuinely believe that the other side is the true aggressor.

misattribution of love: Based upon Schachter's two-factor theory of emotion. The proposition that strong emotional arousal, from whatever cause, linked with the presence of an appropriate romantic partner, may increase perceived feelings of love.

misattribution therapy: A therapeutic technique that changes the focus of a person's attributions in a self-enhancing way.

miscompliance: In physician-client interactions, when the client misunderstands the requirements of treatment.

modeling: The social learning proposition that much of human learning takes place by observing other people (models) behaving. Of particular relevance to the observation of aggressive or prosocial models in the media.

modern racism: Modern racists believe that discrimination is a thing of the past and that minorities are pushing too hard and are getting too much attention and sympathy (also called symbolic racism).

multiplexity dimension: One of two major dimensions on which people's views of human nature differ. The degree to which people are seen as complex and differing widely from each other.

mundane realism: The degree of similarity between the research situation and real world situations to which it is intended to relate.

need complimentarity: The idea that people will like others whose needs are the opposite of their own.

negative reinforcement theory of attraction: The suggestion that people who are associated with the termination or reduction of aversive stimulation (negative reinforcement) will be attractive to others. An alternative explanation for misattribution of love findings.

negative state relief model: A model suggesting that helping others may be a way to relieve the unpleasant state of a bad mood if the perceived reward value for helping is high and costs are low.

negativistic subject role: Enacted when a subject tries to disconfirm the researcher's hypothesis.

neglect: A passive destructive reaction to problems in the relationship as the person takes no actions to improve things.

neutral thwartings: Interference from an environmental setting.

noise: Sound that is unpleasant and bothersome to the listener. Excessive uncontrollable noise is an environmental stressor.

noncommon effects: Unique outcomes of a behavior that could not have been achieved in any other way.

normative social influence: Occurs when one changes behavior in order to gain acceptance and approval from others.

norm of noninvolvement: A social norm often prevalent in urban areas, that people should not involve themselves in other people's affairs.

norm of reciprocity: A standard social idea that we should help those who help us.

norm of social responsibility: A widely shared social norm suggesting that we should help people in need when they are dependent on us.

norms: Standards for appropriate behavior in one's subculture.

obedience: Changing one's behavior to fit someone's order.

observational learning: The process of imitating behaviors that are portrayed by real or animated characters.

obsessive or insecure love: Love that is characterized by obsession with the loved one and anxiety.

offensive aggression: Aggression that is not directly in retaliation to someone else's behavior.

old-fashioned racists: People who hold obviously bigoted beliefs about minorities.

ought self: The characteristics that you feel you ought to have to fit your sense of duty, responsibility, and obligations to others.

ought self-others: The characteristics that important other people feel that you ought to have.

outgroups: Groups other than the group to which an individual belongs.

overconfidence effect: People tend to be more confident in the accuracy of their judgments than they should be.

overjustification effect: This occurs when an external reward leads people to discount the importance of internal factors in their self-attributions.

own-race bias: The tendency of people to recognize people of their own race better than people of another race. This tendency appears equally strong for blacks and for whites.

passion: The drives that lead to romance, physical attraction, and sexual behaviors.

passion cluster: A group of characteristics that are more typical of love than friendship (fascination, sexual desire, and exclusivity).

passionate love: Romantic love that has cognitive behavioral, and emotional components; seems not as directly related to rewards as is liking.

perceived behavioral control: One's beliefs about how difficult it would be to perform a given behavior.

perceived reciprocity: This refers to how much we think someone likes us.

perceived similarity: This refers to how similar two people think they are.

peremptory challenges: During jury selection, each side is permitted a number of peremptory challenges in which they can exclude prospective jurors without having to justify this exclusion. Usually the defense is granted more peremptory challenges than is the prosecution.

personalization: Responding to others in terms of their relationship to the self, rather than in terms of social categories.

person-environment fit: The person-environment fit is good when the structure of the physical environment permits people to achieve the social, cognitive, and behavioral goals that they wish to.

person schema: A schema containing assumptions about typical people and prototypes.

personal force: In Heider's attributional model, the product of ability (or power) and the effort that one exerts. If either ability or effort is lacking, the strength of personal force will be zero.

personal space: The area immediately around people's bodies that is treated as an extension of themselves.

personal thwartings: Interference from another person that is seen as deliberately directed against oneself.

personalism: The degree to which an observer

perceives an action as directed specifically toward her or him.

physical attractiveness stereotype: The widely shared belief that "what is beautiful is good," that physically attractive people also have other desirable characteristics.

plaintiff: The person who initiates a case in civil court; one who sues someone else.

plea bargaining: The state makes a deal with the defendant; the defendant agrees to plead guilty to some charges while other charges may be reduced or dropped or the prosecution may ask the judge for a relatively light sentence.

pluralistic ignorance: Bystanders to an emergency may interpret the situation as a nonemergency due to the apparently calm reaction of other bystanders.

polarization effect: See group polarization effect.

polygraph: A controversial machine used as a "lie detector" that reads physiological changes that occur when people are under emotional stress.

population: The larger group from which a research sample is drawn.

pornography: See aggressive pornography.

position power: In Fiedler's contingency theory, the degree to which the leader has formal authority to reward and punish followers. High position power is favorable for a leader.

power: The capacity to influence others' behavior.

practical love: This refers to couples who are an appropriate match in terms of personality and background. The hope is that they will develop a deeper bond.

prejudice: A negative attitude that is considered unjustified by an observer.

primacy effect: In some persuasion situations, a person who argues first has the most impact on an audience. This occurs most often when the opposing messages are close together and there is a long delay afterwards. (See also recency effect.)

primary territories: Those owned and used exclu-sively by individuals or groups, clearly identified as theirs by others and controlled on a relatively permanent basis.

priming: The effect of prior context on the retrieval of information.

priming effect: The process by which observing a particular kind of behavior, or hearing about it, can activate thoughts related to other incidences of this behavior, making similar behavior more likely.

principle of individualism: An argument against passing laws to require people to help, based on the principle that the law should not interfere with people's freedom to behave as they wish as long as they do not harm anyone.

principle of least interest: The principle that the person who is least interested in continuing a relationship is able to have a greater influence on what happens and is more likely to hold out for the greatest advantage.

prisoner's dilemma: A research method for studying cooperation and competition. If both partners cooperate, they both can receive a positive payoff. However, if one attempts to cooperate while the other competes, the competitive partners wins and the cooperative partner loses. If both partners attempt to compete, they both lose.

privacy: The degree to which individuals can control others' access to them and maintain a desired level of contact with others.

private self-awareness: When attention is focused on relatively private aspects of the self not readily available to outside observers, such as moods, perceptions and feelings.

probability sample: A type of representative sample in which every individual in a population has a known probability, usually an equal probability, of being chosen as a respondent.

propinquity: This refers to an individual's proximity to others.

prosocial behavior: Behavior intended to contribute to the well-being of another person.

prototypes: Sets of features that one associates with members of a category with varying probabilities.

"pro-us" illusion: The general tendency to see people in another country as more friendly to one's own side than they actually are.

proxemics: The manner in which people use space as a means of regulating social interactions.

psychological hardiness: Describes people who have a sense of control over their lives, are committed to self, work, and other values, and do not fear change. They may suffer fewer negative health consequences from traumatic events.

psychological reactance: People who feel that their freedom of choice is under attack will attempt to reestablish freedom directly by performing the threatened behavior, and may aggress toward the influence source.

public self-awareness: Attention directed at aspects of the self that are visible to others, such as social appearance and actions.

public territories: Territories that everyone has free access to, at least theoretically.

racism: A racially discriminatory aspect of a culture that is accepted uncritically by many people and leads to competition, power differentials, and mistreatment of outgroup members.

railroad game: A technique developed by S. Cook for inducing equal-status contact between blacks and whites and reducing levels of prejudice in whites.

random assignment: A crucial part of an experiment wherein each subject is randomly assigned to one condition (or level) of the independent variable.

reactance: See psychological reactance.

realistic conflict theory: Theory focusing on situations in which conflict and competition lead to prejudice, discrimination, and intergroup hostility.

reason: The purposes or goals of a behavior as the actor understands them.

reattribution training: A technique, used especially with children, to change the focus of attribution about failures to a more productive one.

recency effect: In some persuasion situations, the second of two opposing arguments has more effect. This is most likely when the two messages occur far apart and attitudes are measured shortly after the second message is delivered. (See also primacy effect.)

receptive-giving individuals: People who are generally helpful but are especially so when reciprocation or social rewards are forthcoming.

reciprocal altruism: This sociobiological model suggests that it is in your long-term selfish interest to help others because this increases the chance that others will help you in the future.

reciprocity: Social pressure to return a favor.

referent power: Power derived from the degree to which one is admired and liked.

reflection: The way of raising self esteem by pointing out the outstanding accomplishments of others with whom one is associated.

relationship-oriented: Open and participatory leadership style concerned with interpersonal relations.

relative deprivation: The condition in which someone is not receiving outcomes that he or she feels entitled to.

reporting bias: Occurs when the source has correct information but fails to report it.

representative sample: A sample whose members show the same distribution of characteristics as the population from which it was drawn.

research: The means by which scientists test hypotheses derived from theory. Within social psychology the two most widely used research methods are correlational studies and experiments.

research artifact: A research finding that is not what it appears to be, which occurs because of poor research design, e.g., confounding.

retaliatory aggression: Aggression in response to someone else's provocation.

retention: The second stage involved in perceiving and remembering. The longer the interval between witnessing the crime and attempting to identify the criminal from a lineup, the greater the chance of error.

retrieval: The third stage involved in perceiving and remembering a crime, which occurs when the person attempts to "retrieve" the image from memory in order to identify the criminal from a lineup or in the courtroom.

reverse discrimination effect: Occurs when majority-group members behave more favorably to racial minority-group members in terms of helping behavior.

reward level: Degree to which an individual receives positive rewards such as love, status, services, money, and sexuality from a relationship.

reward power: Power gained by giving positive reinforcements such as money, praise, or prestige to others.

risk/benefit ratio: According to the Ethical Standards propounded by the American Psychological Association, all research must be evaluated in terms of the risks to potential subjects and the benefits to society of the research. Research should be carried out only when the benefits substantially outweigh the risks, and if risks are too high, no amount of benefit is sufficient to make the research ethical.

ritualized aggression: A release of violent behavior which is considered socially acceptable, such as a football game.

rivalry: Increased motivation due to competition.

role schema: A schema containing concepts of appropriate norms and behaviors for people in various social categories.

routinization: Transformation of behavior into routine, mechanical operation.

safety-oriented individuals: People who tend to be insecure, anxious, and dependent.

sample: The group of subjects, taken from the population, on which a study is conducted.

sampling error: In opinion polling, the degree to which the sample's responses are likely to differ from the entire population's responses. If probability sampling has been used, this can be calculated exactly. A

representative sample of 1,500 respondents should not miss the true population value by more than 2.5% in either direction.

scapegoating: The tendency to vent frustrations on substitute objects such as relatively powerless minority groups.

scarcity principle: The concept that when a resource is in low supply, desire for it may increase.

schemas: Schemas are cognitive structures that determine how social information is selectively perceived and organized in memory. Schemas are crucial in directing our attention to relevant information, giving us a structure for evaluating information, and providing categories for memory.

"scientific jury selection": A jury selection technique in which prospective members' opinions and attitudes are predicted from demographic characteristics.

scientific method: The method by which scientists make controlled observations, develop theory, specify hypotheses, and test these hypotheses through research. The theories are then revised in light of the research results.

seasonal affective disorder: Severe depression associated with the lack of sunlight during the dark winter months.

secondary territories: Territories that are only partially controlled by their users, such as private clubs, neighborhood bars, and stretches of beach.

segregation: The act of policy of imposing the social separation of races, as in schools, housing and industry.

self-affirmation theory: Steele's theory that people are motivated to take actions to affirm important aspects of their self-concept.

self-awareness: The degree to which attention is directed inward to focus on aspects of the self.

self-centered love: Love that is used as a game. Partners tend to not become too attached while the other person's affection grows.

self-concept: Our assumptions about our personal qualities, organized by self-schemas.

self-consistency theory: The theory that people

prefer social information that confirms their self-concept, providing self-verification.

self-determination theory: The proposition that the way a leader provides feedback to her followers is critical.

self-discrepancies: Differences between one's self-concept and self-guides.

self-discrepency theory: The theory that the amount of emotion inspired by discrepancies between the actual self and self-guides depends upon the magnitude and awareness of discrepancies.

self-enhancement: Increasing one's self-esteem, often by making downward social comparisons with others less fortunate than oneself.

self-enhancement theory: The theory that people seek information that will enhance their self-concepts.

self-evaluation maintenance model: Tesser's model of how people maintain positive self-evaluations by comparing themselves with others who do less well or associating themselves with people who do very well.

self-esteem: The evaluate side of the self-concept.

self-esteem maintenance: Maintaining a positive self-image via processes of reflection and comparison.

self-fulfilling prophecy: A type of behavioral confirmation bias in which one's expectations (the prophecy) set in motion a behavioral sequence that ends up seeming to confirm (fulfill) the expectations.

self-guides: The personal standards that we all possess: the ideal self, the self-others, the "ought self," and the ought self-others.

self-handicapping: Acquiring a handicap before an ego-threatening event so that subsequent failure can be blamed on the handicap.

self-monitoring: The aspect of the self that one typically focuses on. High self-monitors are concerned with the impression they give to others, while low self-monitors pay more attention to their inner feelings.

self-perception theory: Theory that we often infer what our attitudes are by observing our own behavior.

self-promotion: A self-presentational strategy in which one attempts to impress others with one's accomplishments.

self-referent effect: Information processed with reference to the self is more easily recalled than information processed by other means.

self-regulation model of compliance: Views behavior as pulled toward goals rather than pushed by stimuli; emphasizes that individuals develop their own beliefs about health threats and then usually act in accordance with them.

self-schema: A schema containing information about one's own characteristics.

self-serving bias: The general tendency to interpret information in a way that supports a positive self-image.

self-verification: The authentic presentation of the self as one believes it to be.

sex-role socialization: The social process by which children are taught and reinforced for behaving in ways seen as appropriate for their gender.

sex-typed individuals: People for whom gender is a dominant schema which is applied to many situations. They accept and embody most of the traits that sex role socialization has associated with their sex.

sexism: Any attitude, action, or institutional structure that subordinates a person because of his or her gender.

shared infrequency effect: When interactions between majority and minority-group members are infrequent, negative interactions may seem and be remembered better.

sleeper effect: The impact of a communicator's credibility may lessen as time passes and the audience forgets who the source was.

social categorization: When people perceive themselves as members of a group, they distinguish themselves from people outside of the group and adopt the characteristics seen as typical of their group.

social comparison: Comparison with other people in order to allow one to assess the appropriateness or validity of one's thoughts, feelings, and behaviors.

social competition: Group members are likely to attempt to increase their self-esteem by comparing their group favorably with other social groups.

social Darwinism: The naive belief that "survival of the fittest" applies to cultural and ethnic groups and that those groups that gain control of the culture must be the fittest.

social density: The number of people in a particular area.

social dilemma: A situation in which there is a higher individual payoff for the selfish response but lower overall payoffs if both sides consistently make the selfish response.

social exchange theory: A theory that analyzes human interaction in terms of costs and rewards.

social facilitation: Stimulation merely from seeing or hearing the similar movements of other people. This may improve performance in some situations.

social impact theory: The proposition that the impact (social influence for conformity) within a group is a function of the number of influence sources.

social influence: How people attempt to change others' attitudes and behaviors.

social inhibition: When the presence of others interferes with performance due to distraction or anxiety.

social learning: A theory that stresses the impact of observational learning and reinforcement on human social behavior.

social loafing: The finding that although groups may accomplish more than individuals, the members of a group may work less hard than they would individually.

social penetration theory: Theory that focuses on the breadth and depth of self-disclosure in developing relationships.

social power: A person's capacity to alter the actions of others.

social proof: Using other people's behavior as social standards for evaluating one's own behavior.

social psychology: The scientific study of the behavior of an individual (or groups of individuals) as he or she influences, and is influenced by, other persons.

social traps: Situations in which short-run, self-serving behaviors create long-run losses.

socialization: The process of molding an individual's social behavior to fit the expectations of the culture in which he or she lives.

sociobiology: A controversial approach that argues that much of human social behavior is biologically determined.

sociofugal spaces: Furniture arrangements that separate people and reduce social interaction.

sociopetal spaces: Furniture arrangements that encourage the development of stable interpersonal relationships.

source credibility: See credibility.

spontaneous self-concept: Those aspects of your self that are most salient to you.

stereotype: A generalization that is considered unjustified by an observer.

stereotype accuracy: The ability to predict an individual's response based on knowledge of the social category to which the individual belongs.

stigmatization: Occurs when people who deviate noticeably from norms of appearance or behavior are usually avoided or treated in a negative manner.

stimulus overload: Inability of a system to process inputs from the environment because they are too numerous to cope with or because they arrive so rapidly that one cannot be processed before the next arrives.

stimulus-value-role model: Murstein's suggestion

that mate selection occurs in three stages: the stimulus stage, the value stage, and the role stage.

stress: Occurs when a person feels that threat and potential harm for high and personal resources for dealing with it (such as time and attention) are minimal.

stress inoculation: Information that prepares people for upcoming stress by forewarning them of what can be expected and giving realistic assurances.

stylized aggression: Aggression seen as acting or a spoof.

subjects: Individuals whose thoughts, feelings, or behaviors are studied in research.

subject roles: The roles or modes of responses that subjects may choose to enact in a research situation. These include the good subject role, the negativistic subject role, the faithful subject role, and the apprehensive subject role.

subjective crowding: Feelings of excessive social demands and a lack of privacy stemming from high interpersonal density.

subjective norm: In the theory of reasoned action, subjective norm is one's understanding of what others expect one to do and one's willingness to accept these expectations.

suffering-leads-to-liking-effect: People who put forth great effort or endure suffering to join a group may value the group highly in order to justify their behavior.

superordinate goals: Goals that require cooperation and interdependence between groups to solve a common problem. If competing groups cooperate toward superordinate goals, intergroup hostility may be lessened.

supplication: A self-presentational strategy where one advertises one's weakness or dependence in order to solicit help or sympathy.

task-motivated: Leadership style focusing mainly on task achievement, on getting the job done.

task structure: In contingency theory, the degree to which the goals and procedures for ac-

complishing the group's tasks are clearly specified. High task structure is more favorable for the leader.

terminal values: Preferences for certain end states such as equality, freedom, or self-fulfillment.

territoriality: The personalization, ownership, and defense of areas and objects. The behavior by which individuals lay claim to a particular area and defend it against members of their own species.

Thanatos: The "death instinct" or aggressive instinct described by Sigmund Freud. Freud felt that destructive aggressive urges can be released directly in aggressive behavior, released indirectly by observing aggression, or displaced or sublimated in more socially accepted ways.

that's-not-all technique: Inducing compliance by adding a benefit or dropping the price while the customer is considering the deal.

theory: An organized system of ideas that summarizes current knowledge and allows predictions of future occurrences.

theory of genetic predisposition: The controversial theory that there may be an inherited physiological or biochemical imbalance in some individuals that is corrected by the consumption of alcohol.

theory of reasoned action: An attitude change theory developed by Fishbein and Ajzen that proposes that beliefs influence attitudes toward a particular behavior and subjective norms. These two components influence behavioral intentions which in turn influence behavior.

theory of relatedness: Levinger and Shoek's theory that describes long term relationships in five stages: awareness, buildup, continuation, deterioration, and ending.

theory of planned behavior: Beliefs influence: (1) attitudes toward behavior, (2) subjective norms, and (3) perceived behavioral control.

Theory X: McGregor's term describing the beliefs of leaders who assume that most people prefer to be directed, are not interested in assuming responsibility, and want safety above all. It assumes workers are motivated most by money, fringe benefits, and the threat of punishment. Contrasted with Theory Y.

Theory Y: McGregor's term for the beliefs of leaders who assume that others can be self-directed and creative at work if properly motivated, and that it is the task of management to unleash the potential of individuals. Contrasted with Theory X.

threat-to-self-esteem model: Proposes that a negative response to aid is likely when the aid contains a negative self-message for the recipient, conflicts with the recipient's values, or is not effective.

transactional view of leadership: A view that sees leadership as a reciprocal process of social influence between leader and followers.

triangular theory of love: Sternberg's theory that love has three central components; intimacy, passion, and commitment.

two-factor theory of crowding: Asserts that the experience of crowding is a function of an aroused state caused by violation of personal space and an attribution that the cause of the arousal is the presence of others.

two-sided communications: Messages that acknowledge that there are two sides to the issue; effective when the audience is well-educated, involved, intelligent, and initially disagrees.

type A coronary-prone behavior pattern: A pattern of behavior characterized by excessively hard driving behavior, job involvement, impatience, competitiveness, desire for control, aggressiveness, and hostility.

unconscious ideology: An ideology that is taken for granted because the beliefs and values that support it are such a part of society that many people cannot imagine it being any other way. Bem and Bem asserted that sexism is often an unconscious ideology.

value: See instrumental values and terminal values.

value-guided attributions: Actions by one's own country are attributed to altruistic motives while similar actions by other countries are attributed to self-serving motives.

variable: Any factor that changes and can be measured.

venire: The group of people from which a jury is chosen.

voice: An active constructive reaction to problems in the relationship as the person takes action to improve things.

voir dire: The questioning procedure carried out by attorneys or judges through which jury members are selected.

weapon effect: The research finding that aggressive behavior is more prevalent in the presence of aggressive cues (such as weapons) than in the presence of nonaggressive cues. Research findings on this issue have been mixed.

"why me" principle: This principle focuses on the enormous difficulty in creating standards for acceptable behavior in emergencies and in deciding who should be prosecuted for failure to help.

XYY males: Males who have an extra Y (male) chromosome. They tend to be slightly larger than other males, slightly less intelligent, and are more heavily represented in prison populations.

Yerkes-Dodson law: The principle that there is an optimum level of arousal for performance in any task; for complex tasks, there will be curvilinear relationship between arousal and performance, with performance best at moderate levels of arousal.

zeitgeist: The social and political "spirit of the times"; social psychological theories and research directions are heavily influenced by the prevalent zeitgeist.

References

Abbey, A. (1987). Perceptions of personal avoidability versus responsibility: How do they differ? *Basic and Applied Social Psychology, 8,* 3–19.

Abeles, N. (1983). Proceedings of the American Psychological Association, Incorporated, for the year 1982. *American Psychologist, 38,* 649–682.

Abelson, R. P. (1981). Psychological status of the script concept. *American Psychologist, 36,* 717–729.

Abelson, R., & Miller, J. (1967). Negative persuasion via personal insult. *Journal of Experimental Social Psychology, 3,* 321–333.

Abramson, L. Y., Metalsky, G. I., & Alloy, L. B. (in press). The hopelessness theory of depression: Does the research test the theory? In L. Y. Abramson (Ed.), *Social cognition and clinical psychology: A synthesis.* New York: Guilford Press.

Acker, J. R. (1990). Social science in Supreme Court criminal cases and briefs: The actual and potential contributions of social scientists as *amici curiae. Law and Human Behavior, 14,* 25–42.

Acock, A., & Kiecolt, K. (1988). It is family structure or socioeconomic status: Effects of family structure during adolescence on adult adjustment. Paper presented at the annual meeting of the American Sociological Association, Atlanta, Georgia.

Adair, J. G. (1984). The Hawthorne effect: A reconsideration of the methodological artifact. *Journal of Applied Psychology, 69,* 344–345.

Adams, G. R. (1977). Physical attractiveness: Toward a developmental social psychology of beauty. *Human Development, 20,* 217–230.

Adams, G. R. & Huston, T. L. (1975). Social perception of middle-aged persons varying in physical attractiveness. *Developmental Psychology, 11,* 657–658.

Adams, G. R., & LaVoie, J. C. (1977). Teacher expectations: A review of the student characteristics used in expectancy formation. *Journal of Instructional Psychology, 4,* 1–28.

Adams, W. C., & Beatty, J. J. (1977). Dogmatism, need for social approval, and the resistance to persuasion. *Communication Monographs, 44,* 321–325.

Adler, R. P. (Ed.). (1979). *All in the family: A critical appraisal.* New York: Praeger.

Adorno, T., Frenkel-Brunswik, E., Levinson, D., & Sanford, R. N. (1950). *The authoritarian personality.* New York: Harper.

Ahammer, I. M., & Murray, J. P. (1979). Kindness in the kindergarten: The relative influence of role playing and prosocial television in facilitating altruism. *International Journal of Behavioral Development, 2,* 133–157.

Aiello, J. R., DeRisi, D., Epstein, Y. M., & Karlin, R. A. (1977). Crowding and the role of interpersonal distance preference. *Sociometry, 40,* 271–282.

Ajzen, I. (1988). *Attitudes, personality and behavior*. Chicago: Dorsey.

Ajzen, I., & Fishbein, M. (1980). *Understanding attitudes and predicting social behavior*. Englewood Cliffs, NJ: Prentice-Hall.

Ajzen, I., & Madden, T. J. (1986). Prediction of goal-directed behavior: Attitudes, intentions, and perceived behavioral control. *Journal of Experimental Social Psychology, 22,* 453–474.

Ajzen, I., & Timko, C. (1986). Correspondence between health attitudes and behavior. *Basic and Applied Social Psychology, 1,* 259–276.

Alfini, J. J., Sales, B. D., & Elwork, A. (1982). *Making jury instructions understandable*. New York: Michie/Bobbs-Merrill.

Allen, B. P. (1976). Race and physical attractiveness as criteria for white students' dating choices. *Social Behavior and Personality, 4,* 289–296.

Allen, B. P. (1978). *Social behavior: Facts and falsehoods*. Chicago: Nelson Hall.

Allen, J. L., Walker, L. D, Schroeder, D. A., & Johnson, D. E. (1987). Attributions and attribution-behavior relations: The effect of level of cognitive development. *Journal of Personality and Social Psychology, 52,* 1099–1109.

Allen, V. I., & Levine, J. M. (1971). Social support and conformity: The role of independent assessment of reality. *Journal of Experimental Social Psychology, 7,* 48–58.

Alloy, L. B., & Abramson, L. Y. (1982). Learned helplessness, depression, and the illusion of control. *Journal of Personality and Social Psychology, 52,* 1114–1126.

Alloy, L. B., & Ahrens, A. H. (1987). Depression and pessimism for the future: Biased use of statistically relevant information in predictions for self versus others. *Journal of Personality and Social Psychology, 52,* 366–378.

Alloy, L. B., Peterson, C., Abramson, L. Y., & Seligman, M. E. P. (1984). Attributional style and generality of learned helplessness. *Journal of Personality and Social Psychology, 46,* 681–687.

Allport, F. H. (1924). *Social psychology*. Boston: Houghton Mifflin.

Allport, G. W. (1935). Attitudes. In C. Murchison (Ed.), *A handbook of social psychology*. Worcester, MA: Clark University Press.

Allport, G. W. (1954). *The nature of prejudice*. Reading, MA: Addison-Wesley.

Alterman, E. (1987). Inside Ollie's mind. *The New Republic*. February 16, 1987, pp. 12–15.

Altman, I. (1975). *The environment and social behavior*. Monterey, CA: Brooks/Cole.

Altman, I., & Taylor, D. A. (1973). *Social penetration: The development of interpersonal relationships*. New York: Holt, Rinehart & Winston.

Altman, I., & Vinsel, A. M. (1977). Personal space: An analysis of E. T. Hall's proxemics framework. In I. Altman & J. F. Wohlwill (Eds.), *Human behavior and environment: Advances in theory and research* (Vol. 2, pp. 181–259). New York: Plenum Press.

Amato, P. R. (1983). Helping behavior in urban and rural environments: Field studies based on a taxonomic organization of helping episodes. *Journal of Personality and Social Psychology, 45,* 571–586.

American Armed Forces Code of Conduct. (1955). Washington, DC.

American Psychiatric Association (1987). *Diagnostic and statistical manual of mental disorders* (Third edition-revised). Washington, DC: American Psychiatric Association.

American Psychological Association (1982). *Ethical principles in the conduct of research with human participants*. Washington, DC: APA.

Amir, Y. (1969). Contact hypothesis in ethnic relations. *Psychological Bulletin, 71,* 319–341.

Andersen, S. M., & Bem, S. L. (1981). Sex typing and androgyny in dyadic interaction: Individual differences in responsiveness to physical attractiveness. *Journal of Personality and Social Psychology, 41,* 74–86.

Anderson, A. (1982). How the mind heals. *Psychology Today, 16,* 51–56.

Anderson, C. A. (1987). Temperature and aggression: Effects on quarterly, yearly, and city rates of violent and nonviolent crime. *Journal of Personality and Social Psychology, 52,* 1161–1173.

Anderson, C. A. (1989). Temperature and aggression. *Psychological Bulletin, 106,* 74–96.

Anderson, C. A., & Anderson, D. C. (1984). Ambient temperature and violent crime: Tests of the linear and curvilinear hypotheses. *Journal of Personality and Social Psychology, 46,* 91–97.

Anderson, C. A., & Arnhoult, L. H., (1985). Attributional style and everyday problems in living: Depression, loneliness, and shyness. *Social Cognition, 3,* 16–35.

Anderson, C. A., & Arnhoult, L. H. (1989). An examination of perceived control, humor, irrational beliefs, and positive stress as moderators of the relation between negative stress and health. *Basic and Applied Social Psychology, 10,* 101–117.

Anderson, N. H., & Hubert, S. (1963). Effects of concomitant verbal recall on order effects in personality impression formation. *Journal of Verbal Learning and Verbal Behavior, 2,* 379–391.

Andison, F. S. (1977). TV violence and viewer aggression: A cumulation of study results, 1956–1976. *Public Opinion Quarterly, 41,* 314–331.

Andrews, L. B. (1982). Mind control in the courtroom. *Psychology Today,* March, 1982, pp. 66ff.

Appleyard, D., & Lintel, M. (1972). The environmental quality of city streets: The residents' viewpoint. *Journal of the American Institute of Planners, 38,* 84–101.

Ardrey, R. (1966). *The territorial imperative.* New York: Atheneum.

Argyris, C. (1969). The incompleteness of social-psychological theory: Examples from small group, cognitive consistency, and attribution research. *American Psychologist, 24,* 893–908.

Arkin, R. M., Appelbaum, A., & Burger, J. M. (1980). Social anxiety, self-presentation, and the self-serving bias in causal attribution. *Journal of Personality and Social Psychology, 38,* 23–35.

Arkin, R. M., & Baumgardner, A. H. (1985). Self-handicapping. In J. H. Harvey & G. Weary (Eds.), *Basic issues in attribution theory and research* (pp. 169–202). New York: Academic Press.

Arkin, R. M., Lake, E. A., & Baumgardner, A. H. (1986). Shyness and self-presentation. In W. H. Jones, J. M. Cheek, & S. R. Briggs (Eds.), *Shyness: Perspectives on research and treatment* (pp. 189–204). New York: Plenum Press.

Arms, R. L., Russell, G. W., & Sandilands, M. L. (1979). Effects on the hostility of spectators of viewing aggressive sports. *Social Psychology Quarterly, 42,* 275–279.

Aronoff, J., & Wilson, J. P. (1984). *Personality in the social process.* Hillsdale, NJ: Erlbaum.

Aronson, E. (1969). The theory of cognitive dissonance: A current perspective. In L. Berkowitz (Ed.), *Advances in experimental social psychology* (Vol 4). New York: Academic Press.

Aronson, E. (1990). Applying social psychology to desegregation and energy conservation. *Personality and Social Psychology Bulletin, 16,* 118–132.

Aronson, E., & Bridgeman, D. (1979). Jigsaw groups and the desegregated classroom: In pursuit of common goals. *Personality and Social Psychology Bulletin, 5,* 438–446.

Aronson, E., & Carlsmith, J. M. (1963). The effect of the severity of threat on the devaluation of forbidden behavior. *Journal of Abnormal and Social Psychology, 66,* 584–588.

Aronson, E., & Cope, V. (1968). My enemy's enemy is my friend. *Journal of Personality and Social Psychology, 8,* 8–12.

Aronson, E., & Gonzalez, A. (1988). Desegregation, jigsaw, and the Mexican-American experience. In P. A. Katz & D. A. Taylor (Eds.), *Eliminating racism: Profiles in controversy* (pp. 301–314). New York: Plenum.

Aronson, E., & Linder D. (1965). Gain and loss of esteem as determinants of interpersonal attractiveness. *Journal of Experimental Social Psychology, 1,* 156–171.

Aronson, E., & Mills, J. (1959). The effects of severity of initiation on liking for a group. *Journal of Abnormal and Social Psychology, 59,* 177–181.

Aronson, E., Brewer, M., & Carlsmith, J. M. (1985). Experimentation in social psychology. In G. Lindzey and E. Aronson (Eds.), *Handbook of social psychology* (Vol. 1, pp. 441–486). New York: Random House.

Aronson, E., Ellsworth, P. C., Carlsmith, J. M., & Gonzalez, M. H. (1990). *Methods of research in social psychology* (second ed.). New York: McGraw-Hill.

Aronson, E., Turner, J. A., & Carlsmith, J. M. (1963). Communicator credibility and communication discrepancy as determinants of opinion change. *Journal of Abnormal and Social Psychology, 67,* 31–36.

Aronson, E., Willerman, B., & Floyd, J. (1966). The effect of the pratfall on increasing interpersonal attractiveness. *Psychonomic Science, 4,* 227–228.

Asch, S. E. (1946). Forming impressions of personality. *Journal of Abnormal and Social Psychology, 41,* 258–290.

Asch, S. E. (1956). Studies of independence and conformity. A minority of one against a unanimous majority. *Psychological Monographs, 70* (Whole No. 416).

Asch, S. E. (1958). Effects of group pressures upon modification and distortion of judgments. In E. E. Maccoby, T. M. Newcomb, & E. L. Hartley (Eds.). *Readings in social psychology* (3rd ed.). New York: Holt, Rinehart & Winston.

Ashmore, R., Ramchandra, V., & Jones, R. (1971). Censorship as an attitude change induction. Paper presented at meeting of Eastern Psychological Association, New York.

Atkins, A., Deaux, K., & Bieri, J. (1967). Latitude of acceptance and attitude change: Empirical evidence for a reformulation. *Journal of Personality and Social Psychology, 6,* 47–54.

Atkinson, R. (1977). Reflections on psychology's past and concerns about its future. *American Psychologist, 32,* 205–210.

Austrom, D. (1984). *The consequences of being single.* New York: American University Studies.

Axelrod, R., & Dion, D. (1988). The further evolution of cooperation. *Science, 242,* 1385–1390.

Baldwin, J. D. & Baldwin, J. I. (1988). Factors affecting AIDS-related sexual risk-taking behavior among college students. *The Journal of Sex Research, 25,* 181–196.

Bales, R. F., & Slater, P. E. (1955). Role differentiation in small decision-making groups. In T. Parsons & R. F. Bales, *Family socialization and interaction process* (pp. 259–306). New York: Free Press.

Ballew v. Georgia (1978). 435 U.S. 223.

Bandura, A. (1973). *Aggression: A social learning analysis.* Englewood Cliffs, NJ: Prentice-Hall.

Bandura, A. (1974). Behavior theory and the models of man. *American Psychologist, 29,* 859–869.

Bandura, A. (1977). Self-efficacy: Toward a unifying theory of behavioral change. *Psychological Review, 84,* 191–215.

Bandura, A. (1982). The psychology of chance encounters and life paths. *American Psychologist, 37,* 747–755.

Bandura, A. (1983). Psychological mechanisms of aggression. In R. G. Geen & E. I. Donnerstein (Eds.), *Aggression: Theoretical and empirical reviews* (Vol. 1, pp. 1–40). New York: Academic Press.

Bandura A., Ross, D., & Ross, S. A. (1963). Imitation of film-mediated aggressive models. *Journal of Abnormal and Social Psychology, 66,* 3–11.

Bandura, A., Underwood, B., & Fromson, M. E. (1975). Disinhibition of aggression through diffusion of responsibility and dehumanization of victims. *Journal of Research in Personality, 9,* 253–269.

Barber, J. D. (1980). *The pulse of politics: Electing presidents in the media age.* New York: Norton.

Barber, J. D. (1987). *The presidential character.* Englewood Cliffs, NJ: Prentice-Hall.

Barefoot, J. C., Dahlstrom, W. G., & Williams, R. B., Jr. (1983). Hostility, CHD incidence, and total mortality: A 25-year follow-up study of 255 physicians. *Psychosomatic Medicine, 45,* 59–63.

Barefoot, J. C., Siegler, I. C., Nowlin, J. B., Peterson, B. L., Harey, T. L., & Williams, R. B., Jr. (1987). Suspiciousness, health, and mortality: A follow-up study of 500 older adults. *Psychosomatic Medicine, 49,* 450–457.

Bargh, J. A., & Pietromonaco, P. (1985). Automatic information processing and social perception: The influence of trait information presented outside of conscious awareness on impression formation. *Journal of Personality and Social Psychology, 43,* 437–449.

Barnlund, D. C. (1962). Consistency of emergent leadership in groups with changing tasks and members. *Speech Monographs, 29,* 45–52.

Baron, R. A. (1977). *Human aggression.* New York: Plenum Press.

Baron, R. A. (1987). Effects of negative ions on interpersonal attraction: Evidence for intensification. *Journal of Personality and Social Psychology, 52,* 547–553.

Baron, R. A. (1983). The control of human aggression: A strategy based on incompatible responses. In R. G. Geen and E. I. Donnerstein (Eds.), *Aggression: Theoretical and empirical reviews* (Vol. 2, pp. 173–190). New York: Academic Press.

Baron, R. A., & Ransberger, V. M. (1978). Ambient temperature and the occurrence of collective violence: The "long hot summer" revisited. *Journal of Personality and Social Psychology, 36,* 351–360.

Baron, R. A., Russell, G. W., Arms, R. L. (1985). Negative ions and behavior: Impact on mood, and aggression among Type A and Type B persons. *Journal of Personality and Social Psychology, 3,* 746–754.

Baron, R. S., Moore, D. L., & Sanders, G. S. (1978). Distraction as a source of drive in social facilitation research. *Journal of Personality and Social Psychology, 36,* 816–824.

Bar-Tal, D., & Saxe, L. (1976). Perceptions of similarly and dissimilarly attractive couples and individuals. *Journal of Personality and Social Psychology, 33,* 772–781.

Bartis, S., Szymanski, K., & Harkins, S. (1988). Evaluation and performance: A two-edged knife. *Personality and Social Psychology Bulletin, 14,* 242–251.

Basow, S. (1980). *Sex-role stereotypes: Traditions and alternatives.* Monterey, CA: Brooks/Cole.

Bass, A. (1989). Do slasher films foster violence? *Tallahassee Democrat,* Jan. 10, 1989, p. B-1.

Bass, B. M. (1981). *Stogdill's handbook of leadership: A survey of theory and research,* (rev. ed.). New York: Free Press.

Batson, C. D. (1983). Sociobiology and the role of religion in promoting prosocial behavior: An alternative view. *Journal of Personality and Social Psychology, 45,* 1380–1385.

Batson, C. D. (1990). How social an animal? The human capacity for caring. *American Psychologist, 45,* 336–346.

Batson, C. D., & Associates (1988). Five studies testing two new egoistic alternatives to the empathy-altruism hypothesis. *Journal of Personality and Social Psychology, 55,* 52–77.

Batson, C. D., Batson, J. G., Griffitt, C. A., Barrients, J. R., Sprenglemeyer, P., & Bayly, M. J. (1989). Negative-state relief and the empathy-altruism hypothesis. *Journal of Personality and Social Psychology, 56,* 922–933.

Batson, C. D., & Coke, J. S. (1983). Empathic motivation of helping behavior. In J. T. Cacioppo & R. E. Petty (Eds.), *Social psychophysiology: A sourcebook* (pp. 417–433). New York: Guilford Press.

Batson, C. D., Coke, J. S., Chard, F., Smith, D., & Taliaferro, A. (1979). Generality of the "glow of goodwill": Effects of mood on helping and information acquisition. *Social Psychology Quarterly, 42,* 176–179.

Batson, C. D., Harris, A. C., McCaul, K. D., Davis, M., & Schmidt, T. (1979). Compassion or compliance: Alternative dispositional attributions for one's helping behavior. *Social Psychology Quarterly, 42,* 405–409.

Batson, C. D., O'Quin, K., Fultz, J., Vanderplas, M., & Isen, A. M. (1983). Influence of self-reported distress and empathy versus altruistic motivation to help. *Journal of Personality and Social Psychology, 45,* 706–718.

Baum, A., Aiello, J. R., & Calesnick, L. E. (1978). Crowding and personal control: Social density and the development of learned helplessness. *Journal of Personality and Social Psychology, 36,* 1000–1011.

Baum, A., Calesnick, L. E., Davis, G. E., & Gatchel, R. J. (1982). Individual differences in coping with crowding: Stimulus screening and social overload. *Journal of Personality and Social Psychology, 43,* 821–830.

Baum, A., & Davis, G. E. (1980). Reducing the stress of high-density living: An architectural intervention. *Journal of Personality and Social Psychology, 38,* 471–481.

Baum, A., & Gatchel, R. J. (1981). Cognitive elements of reaction to uncontrollable events: Development of reactance and learned helplessness. *Journal of Personality and Social Psychology, 40,* 1078–1089.

Baum, A., Gatchel, R. J., & Schaeffer, M. A. (1983). Emotional, behavioral, and physiological effects of chronic stress at Three Mile Island. *Journal of Consulting and Clinical Psychology, 51,* 565–572.

Baum, A., Shapiro, A., Murray, D., & Wideman, M. (1979). Interpersonal mediation of perceived crowding and control in residential dyads and triads. *Journal of Applied Social Psychology, 9,* 491–507.

Baum, A., Singer, J. E., & Baum, C. S. (1981). Stress and the environment. *Journal of Social Issues, 37*(1), 4–35.

Baum, A., & Valins, S. (1977). *Architecture and social behavior: Psychological studies in social density.* Hilldale, NJ: Erlbaum.

Baumann, D. J., Cialdini, R. B., & Kenrick, D. T. (1981). Altruism as hedonism: Helping and self-gratification as equivalent responses. *Journal of Personality and Social Psychology, 40,* 1039–1046.

Baumeister, R. F., & Tice, D. M. (1984). Role of self-presentation and choice in cognitive dissonance under forced compliance: Necessary or sufficient causes? *Journal of Personality and Social Psychology, 46,* 5–13.

Baumrind, D. (1964). Some thoughts on the ethics of research: After reading Milgram's "Behavioral study of obedience." *American Psychologist, 19,* 421–423.

Baumrind, D. (1985). Research using intentional deception: Ethical issues revisited. *American Psychologist, 40,* 165–174.

Baxter, T. L., & Goldberg, L. R. (1987). Perceived behavioral consistency to oneself and another: An extension of the actor-observer effect. *Personality and Social Psychology Bulletin, 13,* 437–447.

Bazerman, M. H. (1986). Why negotiations go wrong. *Psychology Today,* June, 1986, pp. 54–58.

Beaman, A. L., Barnes, P. J., Klentz, B., & McQuirk, B. (1978). Increasing helping rates through information dissemination: Teaching pays. *Personality and Social Psychology Bulletin, 4,* 406–411.

Beaman, A. L., Cole, C. M., Preston, M., Klentz, B., & Steblay, N. M. (1983). Fifteen years of foot-in-the-door research: A meta-analysis. *Personality and Social Psychology Bulletin, 9,* 181–196.

Beck, A. T., Rush, A. J., Shaw, B. F., & Emery, G. (1979). *Cognitive therapy of depression.* New York: Guilford Press.

Beck, M. (1981). Last hurrah for the ERA? *Newsweek,* June 1, 1981, p. 24.

Becker, C. (1935). Everyman his own historian. *American Historical Review, 40,* 221–236.

Becker, L. J., & Seligman, C. (1981). Welcome to the energy crisis. *Journal of Social Issues, 37*(2), 1–7.

Becker, M. A., & Byrne, D. (1984). Type A behavior and daily activities of young married couples. *Journal of Applied Social Psychology, 14,* 82–88.

Becker, M. H., Maiman, L. A., Kirscht, J. P., Haefner, D. P, Drachman, R. H., & Taylor, D. W. (1979). *Patient perceptions and compliance: Recent studies of the health belief model.* Baltimore, MD: Johns Hopkins University Press.

Belgrave, F. Z. (1984). The effectiveness of strategies for increasing social inter-action with a physically disabled person. *Journal of Applied Social Psychology, 14,* 147–161.

Bell, A. P., & Weinberg, M. S. (1978). *Homosexualities: A study of diversity among men and women.* New York: Simon and Schuster.

Bell, P. A., (1981). Physiological comfort, performance, and social effects of heat stress. *Journal of Social Issues, 37*(1), 71–94.

Bell, P. A., Hess, S., Hill, E., Kukas, S. L., Richards, R. W., & Sargent, D. (1984). Noise and context-dependent memory. *Bulletin of the Psychonomic Society, 22,* 99–100.

Bell, P. A., Peterson, T. R., & Hautaloma, J. E. (1989). The effect of punishment probability on overconsumption and stealing in a simulated commons. *Journal of Applied Social Psychology, 19,* 1483–1495.

Bellah, R. N., Madsen, R., Sullivan, W. N., Swodler, A., & Tipton, S. N. (1985). *Habits of the heart: Individualism and commitment in American life.* Berkeley: University of California Press.

Belson, W. (1978). *Television violence and the adolescent boy.* London: Saxon House.

Bem, D. J. (1972). Self-perception theory. In L. Berkowitz (Ed.), *Advances in experimental social psychology* (Vol. 6). New York: Academic Press.

Bem, D. J., & Allen, A. (1974). On predicting some of the people some of the time: The search for cross-situational consistencies in behavior. *Psychological Review, 81,* 506–520.

Bem, D. J., & Funder, D. C. (1978). Predicting more of the people more of the time: Assessing the personality of situations. *Psychological Review, 85,* 485–501.

Bem, S. L., & Bem, D. J. (1977). Homogenizing the American woman: The power of an unconscious ideology. In J. C. Brigham & L. S. Wrightsman (Eds.), *Contemporary issues in social psychology* (3rd ed.) (pp. 172–185). Monterey, CA: Brooks/Cole.

Bender, I. E., & Hastorf, A. H. (1953). On measuring generalized empathic ability (social sensitivity). *Journal of Abnormal and Social Psychology, 48,* 503–506.

Bennett, J. V. (1978). Human infections: Economic implications and preventions. *Annals of Internal Medicine (Supplement), 89,* 761–763.

Benton, A. A. (1971). Some unexpected consequences of jeopardy. Paper presented at American Psychological Association meetings.

Berg, J. H. (1984). Development of friendship between roommates. *Journal of Personality and Social Psychology, 46,* 346–356.

Berg, J. H., & McQuinn, R. D. (1986). Attraction and exchange in continuing and noncontinuing dating relationships. *Journal of Personality and Social Psychology, 50,* 942–952.

Berg, S., Mellstrom, D., Persson, G., & Saunborg, A. (1981). Loneliness in the Swedish aged. *Journal of Gerontology, 36,* 342–349.

Berglas, S. (1985). Self-handicapping and self-handicappers: A cognitive/attributional model of interpersonal self-protective behavior. In R. Hogan & W. H. Jones (Eds.), *Perspectives in personality, 1,* 235–270.

Berglas, S. (1987). The self-handicapping model of alcohol abuse. In H. T. Blane & K. E. Leonard (Eds.), *Psychological theories of drinking and alcoholism* (pp. 305–345). New York: Guilford.

Berglas, S. (1988). Self-handicapping behavior and the self-defeating personality disorder: Toward a refined clinical perspective. In R. C. Curtis (Ed.), *Self-*

defeating behaviors: experimental research, clinical impressions, and practical implications. New York: Plenum Press.

Berkman, L., & Syme, S. (1979). Social networks, host resistance and mortality: A nine-year follow-up study of Alameda county residents. *American Journal of Epidemiology, 109,* 186–204.

Berkowitz, L. (1969). Simple views of aggression: An essay review. *American Scientist, 57*(3), 372–383.

Berkowitz, L. (1972). Social norms, feelings, and other factors affecting helping and altruism. In L. Berkowitz (Ed.), *Advances in experimental social psychology* (Vol. 6). New York: Academic Press.

Berkowitz, L. (1983). Aversively stimulated aggression: Some parallels and differences in research with animals and humans. *American Psychologist, 38,* 1135–1144.

Berkowitz, L. (1984). Some effects of thoughts on anti- and prosocial influence of media events: A cognitive-neoassociationistic analysis. *Psychological Bulletin, 95,* 410–427.

Berkowitz, L. (1987). Mood, self-awareness, and willingness to help. *Journal of Personality and Social Psychology, 52,* 721–729.

Berkowitz, L. (1989a). Frustration-aggression hypothesis: Examination and reformulation. *Psychological Bulletin, 106,* 59–73.

Berkowitz, L. (1989b). On the formation and regulation of anger and aggression: A cognitive-neoassociationistic analysis. Distinguished Scientist Award Lecture, American Psychological Association meetings, New Orleans.

Berkowitz, L., Cochran, S. T., & Embree, M. C. (1981). Physical pain and the goal of aversively stimulated aggression. *Journal of Personality and Social Psychology, 40,* 687–700.

Berkowitz, L., & Donnerstein, E. (1982). External validity is more than skin deep: Some answers to criticisms of laboratory experiments. *American Psychologist, 37,* 245–257.

Berkowitz, L., & LePage, A. (1967). Weapons as aggression-eliciting stimuli. *Journal of Personality and Social Psychology, 7,* 202–207.

Berkowitz, L., & Thome, P. R. (1987). Pain expectation, negative affect, and angry aggression. *Motivation and Emotion, 11,* 183–193.

Berman, J., & Sales, B. D. (1977). A critical evaluation of the systematic approach to jury selection. *Criminal Justice and Behavior, 4,* (3), 219–240.

Bernstein, W. M., & Davis, M. H. (1982). Perspective-taking, self-consciousness, and accuracy in person perception. *Basic and Applied Social Psychology, 3,* 1–19.

Berry, B. (1965). *Race and ethnic relations* (3rd ed.). Boston: Houghton Mifflin.

Berscheid, E. (1981). An overview of the psychological effects of physical attractiveness. In G. W. Lucher, K. A. Ribbens, & J. A. McNamara, Jr. (Eds.), *Psychological aspects of facial form* (Monograph No. 11). Ann Arbor, MI: Craniofacial Growth Series.

Berscheid, E. (1982). Attraction and emotion in interpersonal relationships. In M. S. Clark & S. T. Fiske (Eds.). *Affect and cognition.* Hillsdale, NJ: Erlbaum.

Berscheid, E. (1983). Emotion. In H. H. Kelley et al. (Eds.), *Close relationships* (pp. 110–167). New York: Freeman.

Berscheid, E. (1988). Some comments on love's anatomy: Or, whatever happened to old-fashioned lust? In R. J. Sternberg & M. L. Barnes (Eds.), *The psychology of love* (pp. 359–374). New Haven, CT: Yale University Press.

Berscheid, E., & Gangestad, S. (1982). The social psychological implications of facial physical attractiveness. *Clinics in Plastic Surgery, 9,* 289–296.

Berscheid, E., Graziano, W., Monson, T., & Dermer, M. (1976). Outcome dependency: Attention, attribution, and attraction. *Journal of Personality and Social Psychology, 34,* 978–989.

Berscheid, E., Snyder, M., & Omoto, A. M. (1989a). Issues in studying close relationships: Conceptualizing and measuring closeness. In C. Hendrick (Ed.), *Close relationships* (pp. 63–91). Newbury Park, CA: Sage.

Berscheid, E., Snyder, M., & Omoto, A. M. (1989b). The relationship closeness inventory: Assessing the closeness of interpersonal relationships. *Journal of Personality and Social Psychology, 57,* 792–807.

Best, D. L. (1982). An overview of findings from children's studies of sex trait stereotypes in 23 countries. In R. Rath, H. S. Asthana, D. Sinha, & J. B. Sinha (Eds.), *Diversity and unity in cross-cultural psychology* (pp. 261–271). Lisse, Netherlands: Swets & Zeitlinger.

Best, J. A., & Bloch, M. (1979). Compliance and the control of cigarette smoking. In R. B. Haynes, D. W. Taylor, & D. L. Sackett (Eds.), *Compliance in health care* (pp. 202–222). Baltimore: Johns Hopkins University Press.

Best, J. A., Flay, B. R., Towson, S. M. J., Ryan, K. B., Perry, C. L., Brown, K. S., Kersell, M. W., & d'Avernas, J. R. (1984). Smoking prevention and the concept of risk. *Journal of Applied Social Psychology, 14,* 257–273.

Bevan, W. (1976). The sound of the wind that's blowing. *American Psychologist, 31,* 779–789.

Bierbrauer, G. (1979). Why did he do it? Attribution of obedience and the phenomenon of dispositional bias. *European Journal of Social Psychology, 9,* 67–84.

Biner, P. M., Butler, D. L., Fischer, A. R., & Westergren, A. J. (1989). An arousal optimization model of lighting level preferences. *Environment and Behavior, 21,* 3–16.

Bird, C. (1979). The best years of a woman's life. *Psychology Today,* June, 1979, pp. 22–26.

Birk, L. (Ed.). (1973). *Biofeedback: Behavioral medicine.* New York: Grune and Stratton.

Bittle, R. G., Valesano, R. M., & Thaler, G. M. (1980). The effects of daily feedback on residential electricity usage as a function of usage level and type of feedback information. *Journal of Environmental Systems, 9,* 275–287.

Bixenstine, V. E., Lowenfeld, B., & Englehart, C. E. (1981). Role enactment versus typology: Another test of the triangle hypothesis. *Journal of Personality and Social Psychology, 41,* 776–788.

Blackburn, R. T., Pellino, G. R., Boberg, A., & O'Connell, C. (1980). Are instructional improvement programs way off? *Current Issues in Higher Education, 1,* 32–48.

Blackman, J., & Hornstein, H. (1977). Newscasts and the social actuary. *Public Opinion Quarterly, 41,* 295–313.

Blackwell, B. (1973). Drug therapy: Patient compliance. *New England Journal of Medicine, 289,* 249–253.

Blanchard, F. A., Adelman, L., & Cook, S. W. (1975). The effect of group success and failure upon interpersonal attraction in cooperating interracial groups. *Journal of Personality and Social Psychology, 31,* 1020–1030.

Blanchard, F. A., & Crosby, F. J. (1989). (Eds.), *Affirmative action in perspective.* New York: Springer-Verlag.

Blanchard, F. A., Weigel, R. H., & Cook, S. W. (1975). The effect of relative competence of group members upon interpersonal attraction in cooperating interracial groups. *Journal of Personality and Social Psychology, 32,* 519–530.

Blascovich, J., Nash, R. P., & Ginsburg, G. P. (1978). Heart rate and competitive decision making. *Personality and Social Psychology Bulletin, 4,* 115–118.

Bleda, P., & Bleda, E. (1978). Effects of sex and smoking on reactions to spatial invasion at a shopping mall. *Journal of Social Psychology, 104,* 311–312.

Blight, J. G. (1987). Toward a policy-relevant psychology of avoiding nuclear war: Lessons for psychologists from the Cuban missile crisis, *American Psychologist, 42,* 12–29.

Block, J., & Lanning, K. (1984). Attribution therapy revisited: A secondary analysis of the Wilson-Linville study. *Journal of Personality and Social Psychology, 46,* 705–708.

Bloom, B. L., Asher, S. J., & White, S. W. (1978). Marital disruption as a stressor: A review and analysis. *Psychological Bulletin, 85,* 867–894.

Blumstein, P., & Schwartz, P. (1983). *American couples: Money, work, sex.* New York: Morrow.

Blunk, R., & Sales, B. D. (1977). Persuasion during *voir dire.* In B. D. Sales (Ed.), *Psychology in the legal process.* New York: Spectrum.

Bobo, L. (1983). Whites' opposition to busing: Symbolic racism or realistic group conflict? *Journal of Personality and Social Psychology, 45,* 1196–1210.

Bobo, L. (1988). Group conflict, prejudice, and the paradox of contemporary racial attitudes. In P. A. Katz & D. A. Taylor (Eds.), *Eliminating racism: Profiles in controversy* (pp. 85–114). New York: Plenum.

Bochner, S., & Insko, C. A. (1966). Communicator discrepancy, source credibility, and opinion change. *Journal of Personality and Social Psychology, 4,* 614–621.

Bohannon, P. (1971). *Divorce and after.* New York: Anchor Books.

Bond, C. F., Jr., & Titus, L. J. (1983). Social facilitation: A meta-analysis of 241 studies. *Psychological Bulletin, 94,* 265–292.

Booth, A. (1976). *Urban crowding and its consequences.* New York: Praeger.

Booth, A., & Johnson, D. (1988). Premarital cohabitation and marital success. *Journal of Family Issues, 9,* 255–271.

Booth-Kewley, S., & Friedman, H. S. (1987). Psychological predictors of heart diseases: A quantitative review. *Psychological Bulletin, 101,* 343–362.

Borden, R. J. (1975). Witnessed aggression: Influence of an observer's sex and values on aggressive responding. *Journal of Personality and Social Psychology, 31,* 567–573.

Bordens, K. S. (1984). The effects of likelihood of conviction, threatened punishment, and assumed role on mock plea bargaining decisions. *Basic and Applied Social Psychology, 5,* 59–74.

Bordens, K. S., & Bassett, J. (1985). The plea bargaining process from the defendant's perspective: A field investigation. *Basic and Applied Social Psychology, 6,* 93–110.

Borgida, E., & Brekke, N. (1981). The base rate fallacy in attribution and prediction. In J. H. Harvey, W. J. Ickes, & R. F. Kidd (Eds.), *New directions in attribution research* (Vol. 3). Hillsdale, NJ: Erlbaum.

Borgida, E., Locksley, A., & Brekke, N. (1981). Social stereotypes and social judg-ment. In N. Cantor & J. F. Kihlstrom (Eds.), *Personality, cognition, and social interaction* (pp. 153–169). Hillsdale, NJ: Erlbaum.

Bornstein F. R. (1989). Exposure and affect: Overview and meta-analysis of re-search, 1968-1987. *Psychological Bulletin, 106,* 265–289.

Bothwell, R. K., Brigham, J. C., & Malpass, R. S. (1989). Cross-racial identifica-tions. *Personality and Social Psychology Bulletin, 15,* 19–25.

Bothwell, R. K., Deffenbacher, K. A., & Brigham, J. C. (1987). Correlation of eye-witness accuracy and confidence: Optimality hypothesis revisited. *Journal of Applied Psychology, 72,* 691–695.

Bradbury, L., & Fincham, F. (1990). Attribution in marriage: Review and cri-tique. *Psychological Bulletin, 107,* 3–33.

Braddock, J. H. (1985). School desegregation and black assimilation. *Journal of So-cial Issues, 41*(3), 9–23.

Bramel, D. (1969). Interpersonal attraction, hostility, and perception. In J. Mills (Ed.), *Experimental social psychology* (pp. 1–120). New York: Macmillan.

Brand, R. J. (1978). Coronary-prone behavior as an independent risk factor for coronary heart disease. In T. M. Dembroski, S. M. Weiss, J. L. Shields, et al. (Eds.), *Coronary-prone behavior.* New York: Springer-Verlag.

Bray, R. M., Johnson, D., & Chilstrom, J. T. (1982). Social influence by group members with minority opinions: A comparison of Hollander and Moscovici. *Journal of Personality and Social Psychology, 43,* 78–88.

Breckler, S. J., & Greenwald, A. G. (1986). Motivational facets of the self. In E.T. Higgins & R. Sorrentino (Eds.), *Handbook of motivation and cognition* (pp. 145–164). New York: Guilford Press.

Brehm, J. W. (1956). Post-decision changes in desirability of alternatives. *Journal of Abnormal and Social Psychology, 52,* 384–389.

Brehm, J. W. (1966). *A theory of psychological reactance.* New York: Academic Press.

Brehm, S. S. (1985). *Intimate relationships.* New York: Random House.

Brehm S. S., & Brehm, J. W. (1981). *Psychological reactance: A theory of freedom and control.* New York: Academic Press.

Brewer, M. B. (1979). In-group bias in the minimal intergroup situation: A cognitive-motivational analysis. *Psychological Bulletin, 86,* 307–324.

Brewer, M. B., Ho, H., Lee, J., & Miller, N. (1987). Social identity and social dis-tance among Hong Kong schoolchildren. *Personality and Social Psychology Bulletin, 13,* 156–165.

Brewer, M. B., & Kramer, R. M. (1985). The psychology of intergroup attitudes and behavior. *Annual Review of Psychology, 36,* 219–243.

Brewer, M. B., & Miller, N. (1988). Contact and cooperation: When do they work? In P. A. Katz & D. A. Taylor (Eds.), *Eliminating racism: Profiles in con-troversy* (pp. 315–328). New York: Plenum.

Briggs, S., & Cheek, J. (1988). On the nature of self-monitoring: Problems with assessment, problems with validity. *Journal of Personality and Social Psychology, 54,* 663–678.

Brigham, J. C. (1971). Ethnic stereotypes. *Psychological Bulletin, 76,* 15–38.

Brigham, J. C. (1972). Racial stereotypes: Measurement variables and the stereotype-attitude relationship. *Journal of Applied Social Psychology, 2,* 63–76.

Brigham, J. C. (1977). Verbal aggression and ethnic humor: What is their effect? In J. C. Brigham & L. S. Wrightsman (Eds.), *Contemporary issues in social psy-chology* (3rd ed.) (pp. 51–57). Monterey, CA: Brooks/Cole.

Brigham, J. C. (1980). Limiting conditions of the "physical attractiveness stereotype": Attributions about divorce. *Journal of Research in Personality, 4,* 365–375.

Brigham, J. C. (1981). The accuracy of eyewitness evidence: How do attorneys see it? *Florida Bar Journal, 55*(11), 714–721.

Brigham, J. C. (1985). Race and eyewitness identifications. In S. Worchel & W. G. Austin (Eds.), *Psychology of intergroup relations* (2nd. ed., pp. 260–282). Chicago: Nelson-Hall.

Brigham, J. C. (1989). Disputed eyewitness identifications: Can experts help? *The Champion, 8*(5), 10–18.

Brigham, J. C., & Barkowitz, P. B. (1978). Do "they all look alike"? The effect of race, sex, experience, and attitudes on the ability to recognize faces. *Journal of Applied Social Psychology, 8,* 306–318.

Brigham, J. C., & Cook, S. W. (1970). The influence of attitude on judgments of plausibility: A replication and extension. *Educational and Psychological Measurement, 30,* 283–292.

Brigham, J. C., & Giesbrecht, L. W. (1976). The effects of viewed bigotry: Racial attitudes and "All in the Family." *Journal of Communication, 26*(4), 69–74.

Brigham, J. C., Maass, A., Martinez, D., & Whittenberger, G. (1983). The effect of arousal on facial recognition. *Basic and Applied Social Psychology, 4,* 279–293.

Brigham, J. C., Maass, A., Snyder, L. S., & Spaulding, K. (1982). The accuracy of eyewitness identifications in a field setting. *Journal of Personality and Social Psychology, 42,* 673–681.

Brigham, J. C., Ready, D. J., & Spier, S. A. (1990). Standards for evaluating the fairness of photograph lineups. *Basic and Applied Social Psychology, 11,* 149–163.

Brigham, J. C., & Richardson, C. B. (1979). Race, sex, and helping in the marketplace. *Journal of Applied Social Psychology, 9,* 314–322.

Brigham, J. C., & Weissbach, T. A. (Eds.), (1972). *Racial attitudes in America: Analyses and findings of social psychology.* New York: Harper and Row.

Brigham, J. C., & WolfsKeil, M. P. (1983). Opinions of attorneys and law enforcement personnel on the accuracy of eyewitness identifications. *Law and Human Behavior, 7,* 337–349.

Brinkley, W. (1953). Valley Forge GIs tell of their brainwashing ordeal. *Life,* May 23, 1953, pp. 108ff.

Briscoe, W. C., & Smith. J. B. (1974). Psychiatric illness—marital units and divorce. *Journal of Nervous and Mental Disease, 158,* 440–445.

Broadbent, D. E. (1978). The current state of noise research: Reply to Poulton. *Psychological Bulletin, 85,* 1052–1067.

Brock, T. C., & Becker, L. A. (1966). Debriefing and susceptibility to subsequent experimental manipulations. *Journal of Experimental Social Psychology, 2,* 314–323.

Brockner, J., Rubin, J. Z., & Lang, E. (1981). Face saving and entrapment. *Journal of Experimental Social Psychology, 17,* 68–79.

Brockner, J., Shaw. M. D., & Rubin, J. Z. (1979). Factors affecting withdrawal from an escalating conflict: Quitting before it's too late. *Journal of Experimental Social Psychology, 15,* 492–503.

Brockner, J., & Swap, W. C. (1983). Resolving the relationships between placebos, misattribution, and insomnia: An individual-differences perspective. *Journal of Personality and Social Psychology, 45,* 32–42.

Brody, D. S. (1980). The patient's role in clinical decision-making. *Annals of Internal Medicine, 93,* 718–722.

Brody, J. (1957). Selecting a jury—Art or blindman's bluff? *Criminal Law Review, 67,* 67–68.

Bromley, D., & Shupe, A. (1981). *Strange gods: The great American cult scare.* Boston: Beacon.

Bronfenbrenner, U. (1961). The mirror image in Soviet-American relations. *Journal of Social Issues, 17*(3), 45–46.

Bronzaft, A. L., & McCarthy, D. P. (1975). The effect of elevated train noise on reading ability. *Environment and Behavior, 7,* 517–529.

Brook, P. (1964). Filming a masterpiece. *Observer Weekend Review,* July 26, 1964.

Brown, J. D. (1988). Self-directed attention, self-esteem, and causal attributions for valenced outcomes. *Personality and Social Psychology Bulletin, 14,* 252–263.

Brown, J. H., & Raven, B. H. (1986). Power and compliance in doctor/patient relationships. Unpublished manuscript, UCLA.

Brown, R. (1965). *Social psychology.* New York: Free Press.

Brown, R. (1974). Further comment on the risky shift. *American Psychologist, 29,* 468–470.

Brown v. Board of Education of Topeka. (1954), 347 U.S. 483.

Browne, A. (1986). Assault and homicide at home: When battered women kill. In M. J. Saks (Ed.), *Advances in Applied Social Psychology.* (Vol. 3, pp. 57–79). Hillsdale, NJ: Erlbaum.

Brumbaugh, L. J. (1917). *Legal reasoning and briefing.* Indianapolis: Bobbs-Merrill.

Bruskin, R. H. (1969). *Seatbelt usage remains at low level despite $51 million ad effort.* New Brunswick, NJ: R. H. Bruskin Associates.

Bryant, J., Comisky, P., & Zillmann, D. (1981). The appeal of rough-and-tumble play in televised professional football. *Communication Quarterly, 29,* 256–262.

Bryant, J., & Zillmann, D. (1983). Sports violence and the media. In J. H. Goldstein (Ed.), *Sports violence* (pp. 195–211). New York: Springer-Verlag.

Buckhout, R. (1976). Nobody likes a smartass. *Social Action and the Law, 3*(4), 41–53.

Buller, M. K., & Buller, D. B. (1987). Physicians' communication style and patient satisfaction. *Journal of Health and Social Behavior, 28,* 375–388.

Burchard, K. W., & Rowland-Morin, P. A. (1990). A new method of assessing the interpersonal skill of surgeons. *Academic Medicine, 65,* 274–276.

Burger, J. M. (1985). Desire for control and achievement-related behaviors. *Journal of Personality and Social Psychology, 48,* 1520–1533.

Burger, J. M. (1986). Increasing compliance by improving the deal: The that's-not-all technique. *Journal of Personality and Social Psychology, 51,* 277–283.

Burger, J. M. (1987). Desire for control and conformity to a perceived norm. *Journal of Personality and Social Psychology, 53,* 355–360.

Burger, J. M., & Petty, R. E. (1981) The low-ball compliance technique: Task or person commitment? *Journal of Personality and Social Psychology, 40,* 492–500.

Burger, J. M., & Rodman, J. L. (1983). Attributions of responsibility for group tasks: The egocentric bias and the actor-observer difference. *Journal of Personality and Social Psychology, 45,* 1232–1242.

Burns, J. M. (1978). *Leadership.* New York: Harper & Row.

Burnstein, E., & Vinokur, A. (1977). Persuasive argumentation and social comparison as determinants of attitude polarization. *Journal of Experimental Social Psychology, 13,* 315–332.

Buss, A. H. (1980). *Self-consciousness and social anxiety.* San Francisco: Freeman.

Buss, A., Booker, A., & Buss, E. (1972). Firing a weapon and aggression. *Journal of Personality and Social Psychology, 22,* 196–302.

Burton, D., Sussman, S., Hansen, W., Johnson, C., & Flay, B. R. (1989). Image attributions and smoking: Intentions among seventh grade students. *Journal of Applied Social Psychology, 19,* 656–666.

Buunk, B. (1982). Anticipated sexual jealousy: Its relationship to self-esteem, dependency, and reciprocity. *Personality and Social Psychology Bulletin, 8,* 310–316.

Byerly, W. F., Brown, J., & Lebeque, B. (1987). Treatment of seasonal affective disorder with morning light. *Journal of Clinical Psychiatry, 48,* 447–448.

Byrne, D. (1971). *The attraction paradigm.* New York: Academic Press.

Byrne, D., Clore, G., & Worchel, P. (1966). The effect of economic similarity-dissimilarity on interpersonal attraction. *Journal of Personality and Social Psychology, 4,* 220–224.

Byrne, D., Griffitt, W., & Stefaniak, D. (1967) Attraction and similarity of personality characteristics. *Journal of Personality and Social Psychology, 5,* 82–90.

Cacioppo, J. T., Martzke, J. S., Petty, R. E., & Tassinary, L. G. (1988). Specific forms of facial EMG response index emotions during an interview: From Darwin to the continuous flow hypothesis of affect-laden information processing. *Journal of Personality and Social Psychology, 54,* 592–604.

Cacioppo, J. T., & Petty, R. E. (1982). The need for cognition. *Journal of Personality and Social Psychology, 42,* 116–131.

Cacioppo, J. T., & Petty, R. E. (1983). *Social psychophysiology: A sourcebook.* New York: Guilford.

Cacioppo, J. T., & Petty, R. E. (1986). Social process. In M. G. H. Coles, E. Donchir, & S. Porges (Eds.), *Psychophysiology: Systems, processes, and applications* (pp. 646–679). New York: Guilford.

Cacioppo, J. T., & Petty, R. E. (1989). Effects of message repetition on argument processing, recall, and persuasion. *Basic and Applied Social Psychology, 10,* 3–12.

Cacioppo, J. T., Petty, R. E., & Geen, T. R. (1989). Attitude structure and function: From the tripartite to the homeostasis model of attitudes. In A. R. Pratkanis, S. J. Breckler, & A. G. Greenwald (Eds.), *Attitudes Structure and Function* (pp.275–309). Hillsdale, NJ: Erlbaum.

Cacioppo, J. T., Petty, R. E., Kao, C. F., & Rodriguez, R. (1986). Central and peripheral routes to persuasion: An individual difference perspective. *Journal of Personality and Social Psychology, 51,* 1032–1043.

Cacioppo, J. T., Petty, R. E., & Losch, M. E. (1986). Attributions of responsibility for helping and doing harm: Evidence for confusion of responsibility. *Journal of Personal and Social Psychology, 50,* 100–105.

Cacioppo, J. T., & Sandman, C. A. (1981). Psychophysiological functioning, cognitive responding, and attitudes. In R. E. Petty, T. M. Ostrom, & T. C. Brock (Eds.), *Cognitive responses in persuasion.* Hillsdale, NJ: Erlbaum.

Cadoret, R. J., Troughton, E., & O'Gorman, T. W. (1987). Genetic and enviromental factors in alcohol abuse and antisocial personality. *Journal of Studies in Alcohol, 48,* 1–8.

Calhoun, J. B. (1962). Population density and social pathology. *Scientific American, 206,* 136–148.

Calley, W. L. (1972). Lieutenant Calley: His own story. In J. W. Baird (Ed.), *From Nuremberg to My Lai.* Boston: D. C. Heath.

Campbell, D. E., & Campbell, T. A. (1988). A new look at informal communication: The role of the physical environment. *Environment and Behavior, 20,* 211–226.

Campbell, D. T. (1963). Social attitudes and other acquired behavior dispositions. In S. Koch (Ed.), *Psychology: A study of a science* (Vol. 6). New York: McGraw-Hill.

Campbell, D. T. (1975). On the conflicts between biological and social evolution and between psychology and moral tradition. *American Psychologist, 30,* 1103–1126.

Campbell, D. T. (1978). On the genetics of altruism and the counter-hedonic components in human culture. In L. Wispé (Ed.), *Altruism, sympathy, and helping: Psychological and sociological principles.* (pp. 39–58). New York: Academic Press.

Campbell, D. T., & Stanley, J. (1966). *Experimental and quasi-experimental designs for research.* Chicago: Rand McNally.

Campbell, J. D., & Fairey, P. J. (1989). Informational and normative routes to conformity: The effect of faction size as a function of norm extremity and attention to the stimulus. *Journal of Personality and Social Psychology, 57,* 457–468.

Campos, J. J., Barrett, K. C., Lamb, M. E., Goldsmith, H. H., & Stenberg, C. (1983). Socioemotional development. In M. M. Haith & J. J. Campos (Eds.), *Handbook of child psychology: Vol. 2. Infancy and psychobiology* (pp. 783–915). New York: Wiley.

Cannon, W. B. (1929). *Bodily changes in pain, hunger, fear, and rage* (2nd ed). New York: Appleton-Century-Crofts.

Cantor, N. (1981). A cognitive-social approach to personality. In N. Cantor & J. F. Kihlstrom (Eds.), *Personality , cognition, and social interaction* (pp. 23–44). Hillsdale, NJ: Erlbaum.

Cantor, N., & Mischel, W. (1979). Prototypes in person perception. In L. Berkowitz (Ed.), *Advances in experimental social psychology* (Vol. 12). New York: Academic Press.

Carlsmith, J. M., Ellsworth, P., & Whiteside, J. (1968). *Guilt, confession and compliance.* Unpublished manuscript, Stanford University.

Carlsmith, J. M., & Gross, A. E. (1969). Some effects of guilt on compliance. *Journal of Personality and Social Psychology, 11,* 232–239.

Carlson, M., Charlin, V., & Miller, N. (1988). Positive mood and helping behavior: A test of six hypotheses. *Journal of Personality and Social Psychology, 55,* 211–299.

Carlson, M., & Miller, N. (1987). Explanation of the relationship between negative mood and helping. *Psychological Bulletin, 102,* 91–108.

Carmichael, J. (1962). *The death of Jesus.* New York: Macmillan.

Carmichael, S., & Hamilton, C. V. (1967). *Black power: The politics of liberation in America.* New York: Random House.

Carnegie, D. (1936). *How to win friends and influence people.* New York: Simon & Schuster.

Carretta, T. R., & Moreland, R. L. (1982). Nixon and Watergate: A field demonstration of belief perseverance. *Personality and Social Psychology Bulletin, 8,* 446–453.

Carretta, T. R., & Moreland, R. L. (1983). The direct and indirect effects of inadmissable evidence. *Journal of Applied Social Psychology, 13,* 291–309.

Carroll, J. L., Volk, K. D., & Hyde, J. S. (1984). Differences between males and females in motives for engaging in sexual intercourse. *Archives of Sexual Behavior, 14*(3), 131–141.

Carroll, L. (1988). Concern with AIDS and the sexual behavior of college students. *Journal of Marriage and the Family, 50,* 405–411.

Carter, A. L., & Ferrari, J. R. (1987). Compliance by young and older drivers to the New York mandatory seatbelt law: Does wisdom come with age? *Psychological Reports, 61,* 697–698.

Cartwright, D. (1979). Contemporary social psychology in historical perspective. *Social Psychology Quarterly, 42,* 82–93.

Carver, C. S., DeGregorio, E., & Gillis, R. (1980). Ego-defensive bias in attribution among two categories of observers. *Personality and Social Psychology Bulletin, 6,* 44–50.

Carver, C. S., & Glass, D. C. (1978). Coronary-prone behavior pattern and interpersonal aggression. *Journal of Personality and Social Psychology, 36,* 361–366.

Carver, C. S., & Scheier, M. F. (1981). *Attention and self-regulation: A control-theory approach to human behavior.* New York: Springer-Verlag.

Carver, C. S., & Scheier, M. F. (1987). The blind men and the elephant: Selective examination of the public-private literature gives rise to a faulty perception. *Journal of Personality, 55,* 525–541.

Cash, T. F., & Derlega, V. J. (1978). The matching hypothesis: Physical attractiveness among same-sexed friends. *Personality and Social Psychology Bulletin, 4,* 240–243.

Casper, J. D., Benedict, K., & Perry, J. L. (1989). Jurors' decision making, attitudes, and the hindsight bias. *Law and Human Behavior, 13,* 291–310.

Cate, R. M., Lloyd, S. A., & Henton, J. M. (1985). The effect of equity, equality, and reward level on the stability of students' premarital relationships. *Journal of Social Psychology, 125,* 715–721.

Cate, R. M. Lloyd, S. A., Henton, J. M., & Larson, J. H. (1982). Premarital abuse: A social psychological perspective. *Journal of Family Issues, 3*(1), 79–90.

Cate, R. M., Lloyd, S. A., & Long, E. (1988). The role of rewards and fairness in developing premarital relationships. *Journal of Marriage and the Family, 50,* 443–452.

Ceci, S. J., & Peters, D. (1984). Letters of reference: A naturalistic study of the effects of confidentiality. *American Psychologist, 39,* 29–31.

Centers for Disease Control (1989). *AIDS/HIV Record, 3*(4), 7.

Centerwell, B. (1989). Exposure to television as a risk factor for violence. *American Journal of Epidemiology, 129,* 643–652.

Cervone, D., & Peake, P. K. (1986). Anchoring, efficacy, and action: The influence of judgemental heuristics on self-efficacy judgements and behavior. *Journal of Personality and Social Psychology, 50,* 492–501.

Chaiken, A. L., & Derlega, V. J. (1974). Liking for the norm-breaker in self-disclosure. *Journal of Personality, 42,* 117–129.

Chaiken, S., & Eagly, A. H. (1976). Communication modality as a determinant of message persuasiveness and message comprehensibility. *Journal of Personality and Social Psychology, 34,* 605–614.

Chaiken, S., & Eagly, A. H. (1983). Communication modality as a determinant of persuasion: The role of communicator salience. *Journal of Personality and Social Psychology, 45,* 241–256.

Chaiken, S., Liberman, A., & Eagly, A. H. (1989). Heuristic and systematic information processing within and beyond the persuasion context. In J. S. Uleman & J. A. Bargh (Eds.), *Unintended thought:* (pp. 141–173). New York: Guilford.

Chaiken, S., & Stangor, C. (1987). Attitudes and attitude change. *Annual Review of Psychology, 38,* 575–630.

Chang, D. H. (1972). Environmental influences on crime in Korea. *Criminology, 10,* 330–352.

Chapman, L. J. & Chapman, J. (1967). Genesis of popular but erroneous psychodiagnostic observations. *Journal of Abnormal Psychology, 72,* 193–204.

Chassin, L., Presson, C. C., Sherman, S. J., Corty, E., & Oleshavsky, R. W. (1984). Predicting the onset of cigarette smoking in adolescents: A longitudinal study. *Journal of Applied Social Psychology, 14,* 224–243.

Chassin, L., Presson, C. C., & Sherman, S. J. (1990). Social psychological contributions to the understanding and prevention of adolescent cigarette smoking. *Personality and Social Psychology Bulletin, 16,* 133–151.

Chemers, M. M. (1983). Leadership theory and research: A systems-process integration. In P. B. Paulus (Ed.), *Basic group processes* (pp. 9–39). New York: Springer-Verlag.

Chemers, M. (1984). The social, organizational, and cultural context of leadership effectiveness. In B. Kellerman (Ed.), *Leadership: Multidisciplinary perspectives* (pp. 91–112). Englewood Cliffs, NJ: Prentice-Hall.

Chen, T. T., & Winder, A. E. (1986). When is the critical moment to provide smoking education at schools? *Journal of Drug Education, 16,* 121–133.

Cherlin, A. (1983). Remarriage as an incomplete institution. In A. Skolnick & J. Skolnick (Eds.), *Family in transition* (4th ed., pp. 388– 402). Boston: Little, Brown.

Christensen, L. (1982). Examination of subject roles: A critique of Carlston and Cohen. *Personality and Social Psychology Bulletin, 8,* 579–583.

Christian, J. J. (1975). Hormonal control of population growth. In B. E. Eleftherion & R. L. Srott (Eds.), *Hormonal correlates of behavior* (Vol. 1). New York: Plenum.

Christie, R. (1976). Probability v. precedence: The social psychology of jury selection. In G. Bermant, C. Nemeth & N. Vidmar (Eds.), *Psychology and the law: Research frontiers.* Lexington, MA: Lexington Books.

Church, G. J. (1982). Copycats are on the prowl. *Time,* November 8, 1982, p. 27.

Church, T., Jr. (1976). Plea bargains, concessions and the courts: Analysis of a quasi-experiment. *Law and Society Review,* 8, 378–401.

Cialdini, R. B. (1988). *Influence: Science and practice,* (2nd Ed.). Glenview, IL: Scott, Foresman.

Cialdini, R. B., Borden, R. J., Thorne, A., Walker, M. R., Freeman, S., & Sloan, L. R. (1976). Basking in reflected glory: Three (football) field studies. *Journal of Personality and Social Psychology, 34,* 366–375.

Cialdini, R. B., Cacioppo, J. T., Bassett, R., & Miller, J. A. (1978). Low-ball procedure for producing compliance: Commitment then cost. *Journal of Personality and Social Psychology, 36,* 463–476.

Cialdini, R. B., & De Nicholas, M. E. (1989). Self-presentation by association. *Journal of Personality and Social Psychology, 57,* 626–631.

Cialdini, R. B., & Fultz, J. (1990). Interpreting the negative-mood helping literature via "mega"-analysis: A contrary view. *Psychological Bulletin, 107,* 210–214.

Cialdini, R. B., & Kenrick, D. T. (1976). Altruism as hedonism: A social development perspective on the relationship of negative mood state and helping. *Journal of Personality and Social Psychology, 34,* 907–914.

Cialdini, R. B., & Petty, R. E. (1981). Anticipatory opinion effects. In R. E. Petty, T. M. Ostrom, & T. C. Brock (Eds.), *Cognitive responses in persuasion.* Hillsdale, NJ: Erlbaum.

Cialdini, R. B., Petty, R. E., & Cacioppo, J. T. (1981). Attitude and attitude change. *Annual Review of Psychology, 32,* 357–404.

Cialdini, R. B., Schaller, M., Houlihan, D., Arps, K., Fultz, J., & Beaman, A. (1987). Empathy-based helping: Is it selflessly or selfishly motivated? *Journal of Personality and Social Psychology, 52,* 749–758.

Cialdini, R. B., & Schroeder, D. A. (1976). Increasing contributions by legitimizing paltry contributions: When even a penny helps. *Journal of Personality and Social Psychology, 34,* 599–604.

Cialdini, R. B., Vincent, J. E., Lewis, S. K., Catalan, J., Wheeler, D., & Darby, B. L. (1975). Reciprocal concessions procedure for inducing compliance: The door-in-the-face technique. *Journal of Personality and Social Psychology, 31,* 206–215.

Cimmerman, A. (1981). The Fay case. *Criminal Defense, 8,* 7.

Clancey, M., & Robinsin, M. J. (1985). General election coverage: Part I. *Public Opinion, 7,* 49–54, 59.

Clark, K. B., & Clark, M. P. (1947). Racial identification and preference in Negro children. In T. M. Newcomb & E. L. Martin (Eds.), *Readings in social psychology.* New York: Holt, Rinehart & Winston.

Clark, L., & Lewis, D. (1977). *Rape: The price of coercive sexuality.* Toronto: Women's Press.

Clark, M. S., Ouellette, R., Powell, M. C., & Milberg, S. (1987). Recipient's mood, relationship type, and helping. *Journal of Personality and Social Psychology, 53,* 94–103.

Clark, R. D., III (1990). The impact of AIDS on gender differences in willingness to engage in casual sex. *Journal of Applied Social Psychology, 20,* 771–782.

Clark, R. D., III. (1971). Group-induced shift toward risk: A critical appraisal. *Psychological Bulletin, 76,* 251–270.

Clark, R. D., III, & Hatfield, E. (1989). Gender differences in receptivity to sexual offers. *Journal of Psychology and Human Sexuality, 2,* 39–55.

Clark, R. D., & Maass, A. (1988). Social categorization in minority influence: The case of homosexuality. *European Journal of Social Psychology, 18,* 347–364.

Clark, R. D., III, & Word, L. E. (1972). Why don't bystanders help? Because of ambiguity? *Journal of Personality and Social Psychology, 24,* 392–400.

Clark, R. D., III, & Word, L. E. (1974). Where is the apathetic bystander? Situational characteristics of the emergency. *Journal of Personality and Social Psychology, 29,* 279–287.

Clark, S. H., Freeman, J. L., & Koch, G. C. (1976). Bail risk: A multivariate analysis. *Journal of Legal Studies, 5,* 341–386.

Clayton, R., & Voss, H. (1977). Shacking up: Cohabitation in the 1970s. *Journal of Marriage and the Family, 39,* 273–283.

Clifford, M. M., & Walster, E. H. (1973). The effect of physical attractiveness on teacher expectation. *Sociology of Education, 46,* 248–258.

Cline, V. P., & Richards, J. M., Jr. (1960). Accuracy of interpersonal perception—a general trait? *Journal of Abnormal and Social Psychology, 60,* 1–7.

Clore, G. L., & Byrne, D. (l974). *A reinforcement-affect model of attraction: Perspectives on interpersonal attraction.* New York: Academic Press.

Clore, G. L., Wiggins, N. H., & Itkin, S. (1975). Gain and loss in attraction: Attributions from nonverbal behavior. *Journal of Personality and Social Psychology, 31,* 706–712.

Coates, B., Pusser, H. E., & Goodman, I. (1976). The influence of "Sesame Street" and "Mister Rogers' Neighborhood" on children's social behavior in the preschool. *Child Development, 47,* 138–144.

Cockrum, J., & White, P. (1985). Influences on the life satisfaction of never-married men and women. *Family Relations Journal of Applied Family and Child Studies, 34*(4), 551–556.

Cody, B. (1984). Alcohol and other drug abuse among adolescents. *Statistical Bulletin, 65*(1), 4–13.

Cohen, F. (1979). Personality, stress, and the development of physical illness. In G. C. Stone, F. Cohen, & N. E. Adler (Eds.), *Health psychology: A handbook* (pp. 77–111). San Francisco: Jossey-Bass.

Cohen, J. (1980). Aftereffects of stress on human performance and social behavior: A review of research and theory. *Psychological Bulletin, 87,* 578–604.

Cohen, J. L., Dowling, N., Bishop, G., & Maney, W. J. (1985). The effect of self-focused attentiveness and self-esteem feedback on causal attributions. *Personality and Social Psychology Bulletin, 11,* 369–378.

Cohen, L. J. (1981). Can human irrationality be experimentally demonstrated? *Behavioral and Brain Sciences, 4,* 317–331.

Cohen R. (1978). Altruism: Human, cultural, or what? In L. Wispé (Ed.), *Altruism, sympathy, and helping: Psychological and sociological principles.* New York: Academic Press.

Cohen, S. and associates (1989). Debunking myths about self-quitting: Evidence from 10 prospective studies of persons who attempt to quit smoking by themselves. *American Psychologist, 44,* 1355–1365.

Cohen S., Evans, G. W., Krantz, D. S., & Stokols, D. (1980). Physiological, motivational, and cognitive effects of aircraft noise on children: Moving from the laboratory to the field. *American Psychologist, 35,* 231–243.

Cohen, S., & Weinstein, N. (1981). Nonauditory effects of noise on behavior and health. *Journal of Social Issues, 37*(1), 36–70.

Collins, D. L., Baum, A., & Singer, J. E. (1983). Coping with chronic stress at Three Mile Island: Psychological and biochemical evidence. *Health Psychology, 2*(2), 149–166.

Colten, M. E., & Janis, I. L. (1982). Effects of self-disclosure and the decisional balance-sheet procedure in a weight reduction clinic. In I. Janis (Ed.), *Counseling on personal decisions: Theory and field research on helping relationships.* New Haven, CT: Yale University Press.

Colvin, B. K. (1981). *Adolescent perceptions of intrafamilial stress in stepfamilies.* Unpublished doctoral dissertation, Florida State University.

Comstock, G. (1988). Television violence and antisocial and aggressive behavior. In S. Apter & A. Goldstein (Eds.), *Youth violence: Programs and prospects.* New York: Pergamon Press.

Comstock, G. (1982). Violence in television content: An overview. In D. Pearl, L. Bouthilet, & J. Lazar (Eds.), *Television and behavior: Ten years of scientific progress and implications for the eighties* (Vol. 2, pp. 108–125). Washington, DC: U.S. Department of Health and Human Services.

Cone, J. D., & Hayes, S. C. (1980). *Environmental problems/behavioral solutions.* Monterey, CA: Brooks/Cole.

Conger, J. C., Conger, A. J., & Brehm, S. (1976). Fear level as a moderator of false feedback effects in snake phobics. *Journal of Consulting and Clinical Psychology, 44,* 135–141.

Conway, M., & Ross, M. (1984). Getting what you want by revising what you had. *Journal of Personality and Social Psychology, 47,* 738–748.

Cook, S. W. (1970). Motives in a conceptual analysis of attitude-related behavior. In W. J. Arnold & D. Levine (Eds.), *Nebraska Symposium on Motivation, 1969.* Lincoln, NE: University of Nebraska Press.

Cook, S. W. (1975). A comment on the ethical issues involved in West, Gunn, and Chernicky's "Ubiquitous Watergate: An attributional analysis." *Journal of Personality and Social Psychology, 32,* 66–68.

Cook, S. W. (1978). Interpersonal and attitudinal outcomes in cooperating interracial groups. *Journal of Research and Development in Education, 12,* 97–113.

Cook, S. W. (1984). The 1954 Social Science Statement and school desegregation: A reply to Gerard. *American Psychologist, 39,* 819–832.

Cook, S. W. (1985). Experimenting on social issues: The case of school desegregation. *American Psychologist, 40,* 452–460.

Cook S. W., & Berrenberg, J. L. (1981). Approaches to encouraging conservation behavior: A review and conceptual framework. *Journal of Social Issues, 37*(2), 73–107.

Cook, S. W., & Wrightsman, L. S. (1967). *The factorial structure of "positive attitudes toward people."* Symposium paper, Southeastern Psychological Association meeting, Atlanta.

Cook T. D., Gruder, C. L., Hennigan, K. M., & Flay, B. R. (1979). History of the sleeper effect: Some logical pitfalls in accepting the null hypothesis. *Psychological Bulletin, 86,* 662–679.

Cooley, C. H. (1902/1964). *Human nature and the social order.* New York: Schocken Books.

Cooper, J. (1974). Population control and the psychology of forced compliance. *Journal of Social Issues, 30*(4), 265–277.

Cooper, J., & Croyle, R. T. (1984). Attitudes and attitude change. *Annual Review of Psychology, 35,* 395–426.

Cooper, J., & Fazio, R. H. (1984). A new look at dissonance theory. In L. Berkowitz (Ed.), *Advances in experimental social psychology* (Vol. 17, pp. 229–266). New York: Academic Press.

Cooper, T., Detre, T., & Weiss, S. M. (1981). Coronary-prone behavior and coronary heart disease: A critical review. *Circulation, 63,* 1199–1215.

Corter, C., Trehub, S., Boukydis, C., Ford, L., Celhoffe, L., & Minde, K. (1978). Nurses' judgments of the attractiveness of premature infants. *Infant Behavior and Development, 1,* 373–380.

Costanini, E., & Craik, K. H., (1980). Personality and politicians: California party leaders, 1960-1976. *Journal of Personality and Social Psychology, 38,* 641–661.

Cotton, J. L. (1981). A review of research on Schachter's theory of emotion and the misattribution of arousal. *European Journal of Social Psychology, 11,* 365–397.

Cottrell, N. B., & Epley, S. W. (1977). Affiliation, social comparison, and socially mediated stress reduction. In J. M. Suls & R. L. Miller (Eds.), *Social comparison processes: Theoretical and empirical perspectives* (pp. 43–68). Washington, DC: Hemisphere.

Cowan, C., Thompson, W., & Ellsworth, P. (1984). The effects of death qualification on jurors' predispositions to convict and on the quality of deliberation. *Law and Human Behavior, 8,* 95–114.

Cox, V. C., Paulus, P. B., & McCain, G. (1984). Prison crowding research: The relevance of prison housing standards and a general approach regarding crowding phenomena. *American Psychologist, 39,* 1148–1160.

Cramer, R. E., McMaster, M. R., Bartell, P. A., & Dragna, M. (1988). Subject competence and minimization of the bystander effect. *Journal of Applied Social Psychology, 18,* 1133–1148.

Crandall, C. S. (1988). Social contagion of binge eating. *Journal of Personality and Social Psychology, 55,* 588–598.

Crimes of Violence (1969). Staff report to the National Commission on the Causes and Prevention of Violence. Washington, DC: U.S. Government Printing Office.

Crocker, J., Hannah, D., & Weber, R. (1983). Person memory and causal attributions. *Journal of Personality and Social Psychology, 44,* 55–66.

Crohan, S. E., & Veroff, J. (1989). Dimensions of marital well-being among white and black newlyweds. *Journal of Marriage and the Family, 51,* 373–383.

Cronbach, L. J. (1955). Processes affecting scores on "understanding of others" and "assumed similarity." *Psychological Bulletin, 52,* 177–193.

Crosby, F., Bromley, S., & Saxe, L. (1980). Recent unobtrusive studies of black and white discrimination and prejudice: A literature review. *Psychological Bulletin, 87,* 546–563.

Crosby, F. J., & Blanchard, F. A. (1989). Introduction: Affirmative action and the question of standards. In F. A. Blanchard & F. J. Crosby (Eds.), *Affirmative action in perspective* (pp. 3–7). New York: Springer-Verlag.

Croxton, J. S., & Morrow, N. (1984). What does it take to reduce observer bias? *Psychological Reports, 55,* 135–138.

Croyle, R. T., & Cooper, J. (1983). Dissonance arousal: Physiological evidence. *Journal of Personality and Social Psychology, 45,* 482–791.

Crutchfield, R. S. (1955). Conformity and character. *American Psychologist, 10,* 191–198.

Csoka, L. S., & Bons, P. M. (1978). Manipulating the situation to fit the leader's style—Two validation studies of LEADER MATCH. *Journal of Applied Psychology, 63,* 295–300.

Cunningham, M. R. (1979). Weather, mood, and helping behavior: Quasi-experiments with the sunshine Samaritan. *Journal of Personality and Social Psychology, 37,* 1947–1956.

Cunningham, M. R. (1981). Sociobiology as a supplementary paradigm for social psychological research. In L. Wheeler (Ed.), *Review of Personality and Social Psychology* (Vol. 2, pp. 69–106). Beverly Hills, CA: Sage.

Cunningham, M. R. (1986). Levites and brother's keepers: A sociobiological perspective on prosocial behavior. *Humboldt Journal of Social Relations, 13,* 35–67.

Cunningham, M. R. (1989). Reactions to heterosexual opening gambits: Female selectivity and male responsiveness. *Personality and Social Psychology Bulletin, 15,* 27–41.

Curran, J. P., & Lippold, S. (1975). The effects of physical attraction and attitude similarity on attraction in dating dyads. *Journal of Personality, 43,* 528–539.

Curtis, R. C., & Miller, K. (1986). Believing another likes or dislikes you: Behaviors making the beliefs come true. *Journal of Personality and Social Psychology, 51,* 284–290.

Cutler, B. L., & Penrod, S. D. (1988). Improving the reliability of eyewitness identification: Lineup construction and presentation. *Journal of Applied Psychology, 73,* 281–290.

Cutler, B. L., Penrod, S. D., & Dexter, H. R. (1989). The eyewitness, the expert psychologist, and the jury. *Law and Human Behavior, 13,* 311–332.

Dane, F. C., & Wrightsman, L. S. (1982). Effects of defendants' and victims' characteristics on jurors' verdicts. In N. L. Kerr & R. M. Bray (Eds.), *The psychology of the courtroom* (pp. 83–115). New York: Academic Press.

Darley, J. M., & Beniger, J. R. (1981). Diffusion of energy-conserving innovations. *Journal of Social Issues, 37*(2), 150–171.

Darley, J. M., & Gross, P. H. (1983). A hypothesis-confirming bias in labeling effects. *Journal of Personality and Social Psychology, 44,* 20–33.

Darley, J. M., & Latané, B. (1968). Bystander intervention in emergencies: Diffusion of responsibility. *Journal of Personality and Social Psychology, 8,* 377–383.

Darwin, C. (1872). *The expression of the emotions in man and animals.* London: Murray.

D'Atri, S. (1975). Psychophysiological responses to crowding. *Environment and Behavior, 7,* 237–252.

Daudistel, H. C. (1980). On the elimination of plea-bargaining: The El Paso experiment. In W. F. McDonald & J. A. Cramer (Eds.), *Plea-bargaining.* Lexington, MA: Lexington Books.

Davidson, A. R., & Jaccard, J. J. (1979). Variables that moderate the attitude-behavior relation: Results of a longitudinal survey. *Journal of Personality and Social Psychology, 37,* 1364–1376.

Davidson, A. R., & Morrison, D. M. (1983). Predicting contraceptive behavior from attitudes: A comparison of within versus across subjects procedures. *Journal of Personality and Social Psychology, 45,* 997–1009.

Davidson, B., Balswick, J., & Halverson, C. (1983). Affective self-disclosure and marital adjustment: A test of equity theory. *Journal of Marriage and the Family, 45,* 93–102.

Davidson, T. (1977). Wifebeating: A recurring phenomenon throughout history. In M. Roy (Ed.), *A psychosociological study of domestic violence.* New York: Van Nostrand.

Davies, D. L. (1979). Defining alcoholism. In M. Grant & P. Gwinner (Eds.), *Alcoholism in perspective*. London: Croom Helm.

Davies, J. B. (1982). Alcoholism, social policy, and intervention. In J. R. Eiser (Ed.), *Social psychology and behavioral medicine* (pp. 235–260). New York: Wiley.

Davis, K. E. (1985). Near and dear: Friendship and love compared. *Psychology Today*, February, 1985, pp. 22–30.

Davison, G., Tsujimoto, R. N., & Glaros, A. G. (1973). Attribution and the maintenance of behavior change in falling asleep. *Journal of Abnormal Psychology, 82*, 124–133.

Deaux, K. (1972). To err is humanizing: But sex makes a difference. *Representative Research in Social Psychology, 3*, 20–28.

de Blij, H. J. (1981). *Geography: Regions and concepts* (3rd ed.). New York: Wiley.

De Bono, K. G. (1987). Investigating the social-adjustive and value-expressive functions of attitudes: Implications for persuasion process. *Journal of Personality and Social Psychology, 52*, 279–287.

Deci, E. L., Connell, J. R., & Ryan, R. M. (1989). Self-determination in a work organization. *Journal of Applied Psychology, 74*, 580–590.

Deci, E. L., & Ryan, R. M. (1985). *Intrinsic motivation and human behavior*. New York: Plenum.

Deci, E. L., & Ryan, R. M. (1987). The support of autonomy and the control of behavior. *Journal of Personality and Social Psychology, 53*, 1024–1037.

Deci, E. L., Schwartz, A. J., Sheinman, L., & Ryan, K. M. (1981). An instrument to assess adults' orientations toward control versus autonomy with children. *Journal of Educational Psychology, 73*, 642–650.

Deerhunter Kills Three More, 37 Dead & 4 Injured. (1985). *NCTV News, 6*(3–4), 3.

Deffenbacher, K. (1983). The influence of arousal on reliability of testimony. In S. M. A. Lloyd-Bostock & B. R. Clifford (Eds.), *Evaluating witness evidence* (pp. 235–251). London: Wiley.

DeGree, C. E., & Snyder, C. R. (1985). Adler's psychology (of use) today: Personal history of traumatic life events as a self-handicapping strategy. *Journal of Personality and Social Psychology, 48*, 1512–1519.

DeJong, W., & Musilli, L. (1982). External pressure to comply: Handicapped versus nonhandicapped requesters and the foot-in-the-door phenomenon. *Personality and Social Psychology Bulletin, 8*, 522–527.

Delint, J., & Schmidt, W. (1971). Consumption averages and alcoholism prevalence: A brief review of epidemiological investigations. *British Journal of Addiction, 66*, 97–107.

DeMaris, A., & Leslie, G. (1985). Cohabitation with the future spouse: Its influence upon marital satisfaction and communication. *Journal of Marriage and the Family, 46*, 77–84.

Dembroski, T. M. (1980). Coronary-prone behavior: An example of a current development in behavioral medicine. *National Forum, 60*, 5–9.

Dembroski, T. M., & Costa, P. T., Jr. (1987). Coronary-prone behavior: Components of the Type A pattern and hostility. *Journal of Personality, 55*, 211–235.

Dembroski, T. M., & MacDougall, J. M. (1978). Stress effects on affiliation preferences among subjects possessing the Type A coronary-prone behavior pattern. *Journal of Personality and Social Psychology, 36*, 23–33.

Dembroski, T. M., & MacDougall, J. M. (1985). Beyond global Type A: Relationships of paralinguistic attributes, hostility, and anger-in to coronary heart disease. In T. Field, P. McCabe, & N. Schneiderman (Eds.), *Stress and coping* (pp. 223–242). Hillsdale, NJ: Erlbaum.

Dembroski, T. M., MacDougall, J. M., & Musante, L. (1984). Desirability of control versus locus of control: Relationship to paralinguistics in the Type A interview. *Health Psychology, 3,* 15–26.

Demo, D., & Acock, A. (1988). The impact of divorce on children. *Journal of Marriage and the Family, 50,* 619–648.

DePaulo, B. M., Dull, W. R., Greenberg, J. M., & Swaim, G. W. (1989). Are shy people reluctant to ask for help? *Journal of Personality and Social Psychology, 56,* 834–844.

DePaulo, B. M., Tango, J., & Stone, J. I. (1987). Physical attractiveness and skill at detecting deception. *Personality and Social Psychology Bulletin, 13,* 177–187.

DePaulo, B. M., & Pfeifer, R. C. (1986). On-the-job experience and skill at detecting deception. *Journal of Applied Social Psychology, 16,* 249–267.

Dermer, M., & Pyszczynski, T. A. (1978). Effects of erotica upon men's loving and liking responses for women they love. *Journal of Personality and Social Psychology, 36,* 1302–1309.

Dermer, M., & Thiel, D. L. (1975). When beauty may fail. *Journal of Personality and Social Psychology, 31,* 1168–1176.

Des Jarlais, D. C., & Freidman, S. R. (1988). The psychology of preventing AIDS among intravenous drug users: A social learning conceptualization. *American Psychologist, 43,* 865–870.

Detmer, D. E., Fryback, D. G., & Gassner, K. (1978). Heuristics and biases in medical decision-making. *Medical Education, 53,* 682–683.

Deutsch, F. M. (1989). The false consensus effect: Is the self-justification hypothesis justified? *Basic and Applied Social Psychology, 10,* 83–99.

Deutsch, F. M., & Lamberti, D. M. (1986). Does social approval increase helping? *Personality and Social Psychology Bulletin, 12,* 149–157.

Deutsch, M. (1960). The effect of motivational orientation upon trust and suspicion. *Human Relations, 13,* 123–139.

Deutsch, M. (1983). The prevention of World War III: A psychological perspective. *Journal of Political Psychology, 4,* 3–31.

Deutsch, M., & Collins, M. E. (1951). *Interracial housing: A psychological evaluation of a social experiment.* Minneapolis: University of Minnesota Press.

Deutsch, M., & Gerard, H. B. (1955). A study of normative and informational social influence upon individual judgment. *Journal of Abnormal and Social Psychology, 51,* 629–636.

Devine, P. G. (1989). Sterotypes and prejudice: Their automatic and controlled components. *Journal of Personality and Social Psychology, 56,* 5–18.

DeVries, D. L., Edwards, K. J., & Slavin, R. E. (1978). Biracial learning teams and race relations in the classroom: Four field experiments using teams-games-tournament. *Journal of Educational Psychology, 70,* 356–362.

Dicks, H. V. (1972). *Licensed mass murder: A socio-psychological study of some S.S. killers.* New York: Basic Books.

Diehl, M., & Stroebe, W. (1987). Productivity loss in brainstorming groups: Toward the solution of a riddle. *Journal of Personality and Social Psychology, 53,* 497–509.

Diener, E. (1980). Deindividuation: The absence of self-awareness and self-regulation in group members. In P. B. Paulus (Ed.), *Psychology of group influence*. Hillside, NJ: Erlbaum.

Diener, E., & DeFour, D. (1978). Does television violence enhance program popularity? *Journal of Personality and Social Psychology, 36*, 333–341.

Diener, E., Fraser, S. C., Beaman, A. L., & Kelem, R. T. (1976). Effects of deindividuation variables on stealing among Halloween trick-or-treaters. *Journal of Personality and Social Psychology, 33*, 178–183.

Diener, E., & Woody, L. W. (1980). *Content factors predicting the popularity of prime-time television programs, 1950–1978*. Unpublished manuscript, University of Illinois.

Diener, E., & Woody, L. W. (1981). Television violence, conflict, realism, and action. *Communication Research, 8*, 281–308.

Dienstbier, R. A. (1977). Sex and violence: Can research have it both ways? *Journal of Communication, 27*(3), 176–188.

Dietz, P. E., Harry, B., & Hazelwood, R. R. (1986). Detective magazines: Pornography for sexual sadists. *Journal of Forensic Sciences, 31*, 197–211.

Dill, C. A., Gilden, E. R., Hill, P. C., & Hanselka, L. L. (1982). Federal human subjects regulations: A methodological artifact? *Personality and Social Psychology Bulletin, 8*, 417–425.

Dillehay, R. C. (1973). On the irrelevance of the classical negative evidence concerning the effect of attitudes on behavior. *American Psychologist, 28*, 887–891.

Dion K. K. (1972). Physical attractiveness and evaluations of children's transgressions. *Journal of Personality and Social Psychology, 24*, 207.

Dion, K. K., Berscheid, E., & Walster, E. (1972). What is beautiful is good. *Journal of Personality and Social Psychology, 24*, 285–290.

Dion, K. K., & Stein, S. (1978). Physical attractiveness and interpersonal influence. *Journal of Experimental Social Psychology, 14*, 97–109.

Dion, K. L., & Dion, K. K. (1973). Correlates of romantic love. *Journal of Consulting and Clinical Psychology, 41*, 51–56.

Dion, K. L., & Dion, K. K. (1987). Being in a just world and physical attractiveness stereotyping. *Journal of Personality and Social Psychology, 52*, 775–780.

DiTecco, D., & Schlegel, R. P. (1982). Alcohol use among young adult males: An application of problem behavior theory. In J. R. Eiser (Ed.), *Social psychology and behavioral medicine* (pp. 199–233). New York: Wiley.

Ditto, W. B. (1982). Daily activities of college students and the construct validity of the Jenkins Activity Survey. *Psychosomatic Medicine, 44*, 537–543.

Doise, W., & Sinclair, A. (1973). The categorization process in intergroup relations. *European Journal of Social Psychology, 3*, 145–157.

Dollard, J., Doob, L., Miller, N., Mowrer, O., & Sears, R. (1939). *Frustration and aggression*. New Haven: Yale University Press.

Dominick, J. R. (1984). Television violence and aggression in teenagers. *Journal of Communication, 34*(2), 136–147.

Donnerstein, E., & Berkowitz, L. (1981). Victim reactions to aggressive erotic films as a factor in violence against women. *Journal of Personality and Social Psychology, 41*, 710–724.

Donnerstein, E., & Donnerstein, M. (1973). Variables in interracial aggression: Potential ingroup censure. *Journal of Personality and Social Psychology, 27*, 143–150.

Donnerstein, E., Donnerstein, M., & Barrett, G. (1976). Where is the facilitation of media violence? The effects of nonexposure and placement of anger arousal. *Journal of Research in Personality, 10,* 386–398.

Donnerstein, E., Donnerstein, M., & Evans, R. (1975). Erotic stimuli and aggression: Facilitation or inhibition? *Journal of Personality and Social Psychology, 32,* 237–244.

Donnerstein, E., Donnerstein, M., & Munger, G. (1975). Helping behavior as a function of pictorially induced mood. *Journal of Social Psychology, 97,* 221–225.

Donnerstein, E., Donnerstein, M., Simon, S., & Ditrichs, R. (1972). Variables in interracial aggression: Anonymity, expected retaliation, and a riot. *Journal of Personality and Social Psychology, 22,* 236–245.

Donnerstein, E., Linz, D., & Penrod, S. (1987). *The question of pornography research findings and policy implications.* New York: Free Press.

Donnerstein, E., & Linz, P. (1986). The question of pornography. *Psychology Today,* December, 1986, pp. 56–59.

Donnerstein, E., & Wilson, D. W. (1976). Effects of noise and perceived control on ongoing and subsequent aggressive behavior. *Journal of Personality and Social Psychology, 34,* 774–781.

Doob, A. N., & Wood, L. (1972). Catharsis and aggression: The effects of annoyance and retaliation on aggressive behavior. *Journal of Personality and Social Psychology, 22,* 156–162.

Dovidio, J. F., & Gaertner, S. L. (1986). Prejudice, discrimination, and racism: Historical trends and contemporary approaches. In J. F. Dovidio & S. L. Gaertner (Eds.), *Prejudice, discrimination, and racism* (pp. 1–34). Orlando, FL: Academic Press.

Dow, T. E. (1967). Family size and family planning in Nairobi. *Demography, 4,* 780–797.

Drabman, R. S., & Thomas, M. H. (1975). Does TV violence breed indifference? *Journal of Communication, 25*(4), 86–89.

Duffy, S. M., & Rusbult, C. E. (1986). Satisfaction and commitment in homosexual and heterosexual relationships. *Journal of Homosexuality, 12*(2), 1–23.

Duncan, B. L. (1976). Differential social perception and attribution of intergroup violence: Testing the lower limits of stereotyping of blacks. *Journal of Personality and Social Psychology, 34,* 590–598.

Dunning, D., Griffin, D. W., Milojkovic, J. D., & Ross, L. (1990). The overconfidence effect in social perception. *Journal of Personality and Social Psychology, 58,* 568–581.

Dutton, D. G. (1971). Reactions of restauranteurs to blacks and whites violating restaurant dress regulations. *Canadian Journal of Behavioral Science, 3,* 298–302.

Dutton, D. G. (1986). Wife assault: Social psychological contributions to criminal justice policy. *Applied Social Psychology Annual* (Vol. 7). Beverly Hills, CA: Sage.

Dutton, D. G., & Aron, A. P. (1974). Some evidence for heightened sexual attraction under conditions of high anxiety. *Journal of Personality and Social Psychology, 30,* 510–517.

Dutton, D. G., & Browning, J. J. (1984). Power struggles and intimacy anxieties as causative factors of violence in intimate relationships. In G. Russell (Ed.), *Violence in intimate relationships.* New York: Spectrum.

Dutton, D. G., & Lake, R. A. (1973). Threat of own prejudice and reverse discrimination in interracial situations. *Journal of Personality and Social Psychology, 28,* 94–100.

Dutton, D. G., & Lennox, V. L. (1974). Effect of prior "token" compliance on subsequent interracial behavior. *Journal of Personality and Social Psychology, 29,* 65–71.

Duval, S., & Wicklund, R. A. (1973). Effects of objective self-awareness on attributions of causality. *Journal of Experimental Social Psychology, 9,* 17–31.

Dweck, C. S. (1975). The role of expectations and attributions in the alleviation of learned helplessness. *Journal of Personality and Social Psychology. 31,* 674–685.

Eagly, A. H. (1981). Recipient characteristics as determinants of responses to persuasion. In R. E. Petty, T. M. Ostrom, & T. C. Brock (Eds.), *Cognitive responses in persuasion.* Hillsdale, NJ: Erlbaum.

Eagly, A. H., & Crowley, M. (1986). Gender and helping behavior: A meta-analytic review of the social psychological literature. *Psychological Bulletin, 100,* 283–308.

Eagly, A. H., & Steffen, V. J. (1986). Gender and aggressive behavior: A meta-analytic review of the social psychological literature. *Psychological Bulletin, 100,* 309–330.

Eagly, A. H., & Wood, W. (in press). Explaining sex differences in social behavior: A meta-analytic perspective. *Personality and Social Psychology Bulletin.*

Eagly, A. H., Wood, W., & Chaiken, S. (1978). Causal inferences about communicators and their effect on opinion change. *Journal of Personality and Social Psychology, 36,* 424–435.

Eastwood, M. (1978). Legal protection against sex discrimination. In A. Stromberg & S. Harkness (Eds.), *Women working: Theories and facts in perspective.* Palo Alto, CA: Mayfield.

Ebbesen, E. B., & Konecni, V. J. (1975). Decision making and information integration in the courts: The setting of bail. *Journal of Personality and Social Psychology, 32,* 805–821.

Ebbesen, E. B., & Konečni, V. J. (1981). The process of sentencing adult felons: A causal analysis of judicial decisions. In B. D. Sales (Ed.), *The trial process* (pp. 413–458). New York: Plenum Press.

Edney, J. J. (1972). Property, possession, and permanence: A field study in human territoriality. *Journal of Applied Social Psychology, 3,* 275–282.

Edwards, G., Orford, J., Egert, S., Guthrie, S., Hawker, A., Hensman, C., Mitcheson, M., Oppenheimer, E., & Taylor, C. (1977). Alcoholism: A controlled trial of "treatment" and "advice." *Journal of Studies on Alcohol, 38,* 1004–1031.

Efran, M. G. (1974). The effect of physical appearance on the judgment of guilt, interpersonal attraction, and severity of recommended punishment in a simulated jury task. *Journal of Research in Personality, 8,* 45–54.

Ehrlich, P. R. (1968). *The population bomb.* New York: Ballantine.

Eisenberg, N., Fabes, R. A., Miller, P. A., Fultz, J., Shell, R., Mathy, R. M., & Reno, R. R. (1989). Relation of sympathy and personal distress to prosocial behavior: A multimethod study. *Journal of Personality and Social Psychology, 57,* 55–66.

Eisenberg, N., & Miller, P. A. (1987). The relation of empathy to prosocial and related behaviors. *Psychological Bulletin, 101,* 91–119.

Eiser, J. R. (1982). Addiction as attribution: Cognitive processes in giving up smoking. In J. R. Eiser (Ed.), *Social psychology and behavioral medicine* (pp. 202–222). New York: Wiley.

Ekman, P., Levenson, R. W., & Friesen, W. V. (1983). Autonomic nervous system activity distinguishes among emotions. *Science, 221,* 1208–1210.

Elgie, D. M., Hollander, E. P., & Rice, R. W. (1988). Appointed and elected leader responses to favorableness of feedback and level of task activity from followers. *Journal of Applied Social Psychology, 18,* 1361–1370.

Elliot, C. H., & Denney, D. R. (1978). A multiple-component treatment approach to smoking reduction. *Journal of Consulting and Clinical Psychology, 46,* 1330–1339.

Ellison, K. W., & Buckhout, R. (1981). *Psychology and criminal justice.* New York: Harper & Row.

Elms. A. C., & Milgram, S. (1966). Personality characteristics associated with obedience and defiance toward authoritative command. *Journal of Experimental Research in Personality, 2,* 282–289.

Elwork, A., Sales, B. D., & Alfini, J. J. (1982). *Making jury instructions understandable.* Charlottesville, VA: Michie.

Engstrom, D. (1984). A psychological perspective on prevention in alcoholism. In J. D. Matarazzo, S. H. M. Weiss, J. A. Herd, N. E. Miller, & S. M. Weiss (Eds.), *Behavioral health* (pp. 1047–1058). New York: Wiley.

Enke, S. (1961). A rejoinder to comments on the superior effectiveness of vasectomy-bonus schemes. *Economic Development and Cultural Change, 9,* 645–647.

Epstein, J. F., O'Neal, E. C., & Jones, K. J. (1980). *Prior experience with firearms can mitigate the weapons effect.* Paper presented at the meetings of the American Psychological Association.

Epstein, J. L. (1985). After the bus arrives: Resegregation in desegregated schools. *Journal of Social Issues, 41*(3), 23–44.

Epstein, L. H., & Cluss, P. A. (1982). A behavioral medicine perspective on adherence to long-term medical regimens. *Journal of Consulting and Clinical Psychology, 50,* 950–971.

Epstein, Y. M. (1981). Crowding stress and human behavior. *Journal of Social Issues, 37*(1), 126–144.

Epstein, Y. M., & Karlin, R. A. (1975). Effects of acute experimental crowding. *Journal of Applied Social Psychology, 58,* 568–581.

Erber, R., & Fiske, S. T. (1984). Outcome dependency and attention to inconsistent information. *Journal of Personality and Social Psychology, 47,* 709–726.

Erickson, E. (1950). *Childhood and society.* New York: Norton.

Erikson, E. (1958). *Young man Luther.* New York: Norton.

Erikson, E. (1969). *Gandhi's truth: On the origins of militant non-violence.* New York: Norton.

Erickson, P. G., Adlaf, E. M., Murray, G. F., & Smart, K. G. (1987). *The steel drug: Cocaine in perspective.* Lexington, MA: Lexington Books.

Eron, L. D. (1963). Relationship of TV viewing habits and aggressive behavior in children. *Journal of Abnormal and Social Psychology, 67,* 193–196.

Eron, L. D. (1980). Prescription for reduction of aggression. *American Psychologist, 35,* 244–252.

Eron, L. D. (1982). Parent-child interaction, television violence, and aggression of children. *American Psychologist, 37,* 197–211.

Eron, L. D. (1986). Interventions to mitigate the psychological effects of media violence on aggressive behavior, *Journal of Social Issues, 42*(3), 155–170.

Eron, L. D., Huesmann, L. R., Brice, P., Fischer, P., & Mermelstein, R. (1983). Age trends in the development of aggression, sex typing, and related television habits. *Developmental Psychology, 19,* 71–77.

Eron, L. D., Huesmann, L. R., Dubow, E., Romanoff, R., & Yarmel, P. W. (1987). Aggression and its correlates over 22 years. In D. H. Crowell, I. M. Evans, & C. P. O'Donnell (Eds.), *Childhood aggression and violence* (pp. 249–262). New York: Plenum.

Eron, L. D., Huesmann, L. R., Lefkowitz, M. M., & Walder, L. O. (1972). Does television violence cause aggression? *American Psychologist, 27,* 253–263.

Erskine, H. (1973). The polls: Interracial socializing. *Public Opinion Quarterly, 37,* 284–294.

Eskey, K. (1990). Demon rum is still No. 1 abuse problem on campus. *Tallahassee Democrat*, May 29, 1990, p. 1.

Esser, A. H. (1972). Crowding from a biosocial perspective. In J. F. Wohlwill & D. H. Carson (Eds.), *Environment and the social sciences: Perspectives and applications*. Washington, DC: American Psychological Association.

Etzioni, A. (1967). The Kennedy experiment. *Western Political Quarterly, 20,* 361–380.

Etzioni, A. (1968). A model of significant research. *International Journal of Psychiatry, 6,* 279–280.

Eugenio, P., Buckhout, R., Kostes, S., & Ellison, K. W. (1982). Hypermnesia in the eyewitness to a crime. *Bulletin of the Psychonomic Society, 19,* 83–86.

Evans, G. W., & Jacobs, S. V. (1981). Air pollution and human behavior. *Journal of Social Issues, 37*(1), 95–125.

Evans, R. I. (1974). A conversation with Konrad Lorenz about aggression, homosexuality, pornography, and the need for a new ethic. *Psychology Today*, November, 1974, pp. 83ff.

Evans, R. I. (1975). *Konrad Lorenz: The man and his ideas.* New York: Harcourt Brace Jovanovich.

Evans, R. I. (1980). Behavioral medicine: A new applied challenge to social psychology. In L. Bickman (Ed.), *Applied Social Psychology Annual* (Vol. I, pp. 279–305). Beverly Hills: Sage.

Evans, R. I., Rozelle, R. M., Maxwell, S. E., Raines, B. E., Dill, C. A., Guthrie, T. J., Henderson, A. H., & Hill, P. C. (1981). Social modeling films to deter smoking in adolescents: Results of a three-year field investigation. *Journal of Applied Psychology, 66,* 399–414.

Falbo, T., & Peplau, L. A. (1980). Power strategies in intimate relationships. *Journal of Personality and Social Psychology, 38,* 618–628.

Farber, I. E., Harlow, H. F., & West, L. J. (1956). Brainwashing, conditioning, and DDD (debility, dependency, and dread). *Sociometry, 20,* 271–285.

Farr, J. L., & Seaver, W. B. (1975). Stress and discomfort in psychological research: Subject perceptions of experimental procedures. *American Psychologist, 30,* 770–773.

Fazio, R. H. (1986). How do attitudes guide behavior? In R. M. Sorrentino & E. T. Higgins (Eds.), *The handbook of motivation and cognition foundations of social behavior* (pp. 204–243). New York: Guilford.

Fazio, R. H., & Cooper, J. (1983). Arousal in the dissonance process. In J. T. Cacioppo & R. E. Petty (Eds.), *Social psychophysiology: A sourcebook* (pp. 122–152). New York: Guilford.

Fazio, R. H., Sherman, S. J., & Herr, P. M. (1982). The feature-positive effect in the self-perception process: Does not doing matter as much as doing? *Journal of Personality and Social Psychology, 42,* 404–411.

Fazio, R. H., & Williams, C. J. (1986). Attitude accessibility as a moderator of the attitude-perception and attitude-behavior relations: An investigation of the 1984 presidential election. *Journal of Personality and Social Psychology, 51,* 505–514.

Fazio, R. H., Zanna. M. P., & Cooper, J. (1977). Dissonance versus self-perception: An integrative view of each theory's proper domain of application. *Journal of Experimental Social Psychology, 13,* 464–479.

Fehr, B. (1988). Prototype analysis of the concepts of love and commitment. *Journal of Personality and Social Psychology, 55,* 557–579.

Feingold, A. (1988). Matching for attractiveness in romantic partners and same-sex friends: A meta-analysis and theoretical critique. *Psychological Bulletin, 104,* 226–235.

Feingold, G. A. (1914). The influence of environment on identification of persons and things. *Journal of Criminal Law and Political Science, 5,* 39–41.

Feldman, S., & Wilson, K. (1981). The value of interpersonal skills in lawyering. *Law and Human Behavior, 5,* 311–324.

Fenigstein, A. (1979). Self-consciousness, self-attention, and social interaction. *Journal of Personality and Social Psychology, 37,* 75–86.

Fenigstein, A. (1987). On the nature of public and private self-consciousness. *Journal of Personality, 55,* 543–553.

Fenigstein, A., & Levine, M. P. (1984). Self-attention, concept activation, and the causal self. *Journal of Experimental Social Psychology, 20,* 231–245.

Feshbach, S., Feshbach, N. D., & Cohen, S. E. (1982). Enhancing children's discrimination in response to television advertising: The effects of psychoeducational training in two elementary school-age groups. *Developmental Review, 2,* 385–403.

Festinger, L. (1954). A theory of social comparison processes. *Human Relations, 7,* 117–140.

Festinger, L. (1957). *A theory of cognitive dissonance.* Stanford, CA: Stanford University Press.

Festinger, L., & Carlsmith, J. M. (1959). Cognitive consequences of forced compliance. *Journal of Abnormal and Social Psychology, 58,* 203–210.

Festinger, L., Pepitone, A., & Newcomb, T. (1952). Some consequences of deindividuation in a group. *Journal of Abnormal and Social Psychology, 47,* 382–389.

Festinger, L., Riecken, H., & Schachter, S. (1956). *When prophecy fails.* Minneapolis: University of Minnesota Press.

Festinger, L., Schachter. S., & Back, K. (1950). *Social pressures in informal groups: A study of a housing community.* New York: Harper & Row.

Feynman, R. P. (1988). *What do you care what other people think?* New York: Norton.

Fiedler, F. E. (1978). The contingency model and the dynamics of the leadership process. In L. Berkowitz (Ed.), *Advances in experimental social psychology* (Vol. 11). New York: Academic Press.

Fiedler, F. E. (1987). When to lead, when to stand back. *Psychology Today*, September, 1987, pp. 26–27.

Fiedler, F. E., Chemers, M. M., & Mahar, L. (1976). *Improving leadership effectiveness: The leader match concept*. New York: Wiley.

Fiedler, F. E., & Mahar, L. (1979). The effectiveness of contingency model training: A review of the validation of leader match. *Personnel Psychology, 32,* 45–62.

Finman, R., & Berkowitz, L.(1989). Some factors influencing the effect of depressed mood on anger and overt hostility toward another. *Journal of Research in Personality, 23,* 70–84.

Fischhoff, B. (1977). Perceived informativeness of facts. *Journal of Experimental Psychology: Human Perception and Performance, 3,* 349–358.

Fischhoff, B. (1982). Debiasing. In D. Kahneman, P. Slovic, & A. Tversky (Eds.), *Judgment under uncertainty: Heuristics and biases* (pp. 422–444). New York: Cambridge University Press.

Fischhoff, B., & Beyth, R. (1975). "I knew it would happen": Remembered probabilities of once-future things. *Organizational Behavior and Human Performance, 13,* 1–16.

Fischhoff, B., Slovic, P., & Lichtenstein, S. (1978). Fault trees: Sensitivity of estimated failure probabilities to problem representation. *Journal of Experimental Psychology: Human Perception and Performance, 23,* 339–359.

Fishbein, M. (1982). Social psychological analysis of smoking behaviors. In J. R. Eiser (Ed.), *Social psychology and behavioral medicine* (pp. 179–197). New York: Wiley.

Fisher, J. D., & Misovich, S. J. (1989). Technical report on undergraduate students: AIDS-prevention behavior, AIDS-knowledge and fear of AIDS. Technical report, University of Connecticut.

Fisher, J. D., & Nadler, A. (1982). Determinants of recipient reactions to aid: Donor-recipient similarity and perceived dimensions of problems. In T. A. Wills (Ed.), *Basic processes in helping relationships*. New York: Academic Press.

Fisher, R. P., Geiselman, R. E., & Amador, M. (1988). Field test of the cognitive interview: Enhancing the recollection of actual victims and witnesses of crime. *Journal of Applied Psychology, 74,* 722–727.

Fiske, S. T., Neuberg, S. L., Beattie, A. E., & Milberg, S. J. (1987). Category-based and attribute-based reactions to others: Some informational conditions of stereotyping and individuating processes. *Journal of Experimental Social Psychology, 23,* 399–427.

Fiske, S. T., & Ruscher, J. B. (1989). On-line processes in category-based and individuating impressions: Some basic principles and methodological reflections. In J. Bassili (Ed.), *On-line cognition in person perception* (pp. 141–173). Hillsdale, NJ: Erlbaum.

Fiske, S. T., & Taylor, S. E. (1984). *Social cognition*. Reading, MA: Addison-Wesley.

Flanagan, T. J., & Jamison, K. M. (Eds.). *Sourcebook of criminal statistics—1987*. Washington, DC: U.S. Department of Justice, Bureau of Justice Statistics.

Fleckenstein, L. (1977). Attitudes towards patient package inserts. *Drug Information Journal, 11,* 23–29.

Fleming, I., Baum, A., & Weiss, L. (1987). Social density and perceived control as mediators of crowd stress in high-density residential neighborhoods. *Journal of Personality and Social Psychology, 52,* 899-906.

Florida Flambeau, April 6, 1976; Dec. 6, 1982.

Flory, B. (1990). 1990 will be the bloodiest year in U.S. history, Senate panel reports. *Tallahassee Democrat,* August 1, 1990, p. 1.

Fodor, E. M. (1985). The power motive, group conflict, and physiological arousal. *Journal of Personality and Social Psychology, 49,* 1408–1415.

Fook-Kee, W., & Swee-Hock, S. (1975). Knowledge, attitudes, and practice of family planning in Singapore. *Studies in Family Planning, 6,* 109–112.

Folkes, V. S., & Sears, D. O. (1977). Does everybody like a liker? *Journal of Experimental Social Psychology, 13,* 505–519.

Foreyt, J. P., Scott, L. W., O'Malley, M. P., & Gotto, A. M. (1980). Diet modification: An example of behavioral medicine. *National Forum, 60,* 9–13.

Forsyth, D. R. (1990). *Group dynamics* (2nd ed.). Pacific Grove, CA: Brooks/Cole.

Foss, R. D., & Dempsey, C. B. (1979). Blood donation and the foot-in-the-door technique: A limiting case. *Journal of Personality and Social Psychology, 37,* 580–590.

Foushee, H. C. (1984). Dyads and triads at 35,000 feet: Factors affecting group process and aircrew performance. *American Psychologist, 39,* 885–893.

Freedman, J. L. (1965). Long-term behavioral effects of cognitive dissonance. *Journal of Experimental Social Psychology, 1,* 145–155.

Freedman, J. L. (1975). *Crowding and behavior.* San Francisco: Freeman.

Freedman, J. L. (1984). Effect of television violence on aggressiveness. *Psychological Bulletin, 96,* 227–246.

Freedman, J. L., & Doob, A. N. (1968). *Deviancy.* New York: Academic Press.

Freedman, J. L., & Fraser, S. (1966). Compliance without pressure: The foot-in-the-door technique. *Journal of Personality and Social Psychology, 4,* 195–202.

Freedman, J. L., Wallington, S. A., & Bless, E. (1967). Compliance without pressure: The effect of guilt. *Journal of Personality and Social Psychology, 7,* 117–124.

French, J. R. P., & Raven, B. H. (1959). The bases of social power. In D. Cartwright (Ed.), *Studies in social power.* Ann Arbor: University of Michigan Press.

Freud, S. (1906/1959). Psycho-analysis and the ascertaining of truth in courts of law. In S. Freud, *Clinical papers and papers on technique, collected papers, Vol. 2* (pp. 13–24). New York: Basic Books. (Originally published in 1906.)

Freud, S. (1920/1959). *Beyond the pleasure principle.* New York: Bantam Books. (Originally published in 1920.)

Friedman, M., & Rosenman, R. H. (1974). *Type A behavior and your heart.* Greenwich, CT: Fawcett.

Friedman, M., Thoresen, C. E., Gill, J. J., Powell, L. H., Ulmer, D., Thompson, L., Price, V. A., Robin, D. D., Breall, W. S., Dixon, T., Levey, R., & Bourg, E. (1984). Alteration of Type A behavior and reduction in cardiac recurrences in post myocardial infarction patients. *American Heart Journal, 108,* 237–248.

Friedrich, L. K., & Stein, A. H. (1973). Aggressive and prosocial television programs and the natural behavior of pre-school children. *Monographs of the Society for Research in Child Development, 38,* (4, Serial No. 151).

Friedrich, L. K., & Stein, A. H. (1975). Prosocial television and young children: The effects of verbal labeling and role playing on learning and behavior. *Child Development, 46,* 27–38.

Friedrich-Cofer, L., & Huston, H. C. (1986). Television violence and aggression: The debate continues. *Psychological Bulletin, 100,* 364–371.

Friedrich-Cofer, L. K., Huston-Stein, A., Kipnis, D. N., Susman, E. J., & Clewitt, A. S. (1979). Environmental enhancement of prosocial television content: Effects on interpersonal behavior, imaginative play, and self-regulation in a natural setting. *Developmental Psychology, 15,* 637–646.

Frodi, A. (1978). Experimental and physiological responses associated with anger and aggression in women and men. *Journal of Research in Personality, 12,* 335–349.

Frodi, A., Macaulay, J., & Thome, P. R. (1977). Are women always less aggressive than men? A review of the experimental literature. *Psychological Bulletin, 84,* 634–660.

Froming, W., & Carver, C. S. (1981). Divergent influences of private and public self-consciousness in a compliance paradigm. *Journal of Research in Personality, 15,* 159–171.

Frost, D. E., Fiedler, F. E., & Anderson, J. W. (1983). The role of personal risk-taking in effective leadership. *Human Relations, 36,* 185–202.

Funder, D. C., & Ozer, D. J. (1983). Behavior as a function of the situation. *Journal of Personality and Social Psychology, 44,* 107–112.

Gaebelein, J. W., & Mander, A. (1978). Consequences for targets of aggression as a function of aggressor and instigator roles: Three experiments. *Personality and Social Psychology Bulletin, 4,* 465–468.

Gaertner, S. L., & Bickman, L. (1971). Effects of race on the elicitation of helping behavior. *Journal of Personality and Social Psychology, 20,* 218–222.

Gaertner, S. L., & Dovidio, J. F. (1977). The subtlety of white racism, arousal, and helping behavior. *Journal of Personality and Social Psychology, 35,* 691–707.

Gaertner, S. L., & Dovidio, J. F. (1986). The aversive form of racism. In J. F. Dovidio & S. L. Gaertner (Eds.), *Prejudice, discrimination, and racism* (pp. 61–89). Orlando, FL: Academic Press.

Gaertner, S. L., Mann, J., Murrell, A., & Dovidio, J. F. (1989). Reducing intergroup bias: The benefits of recategorization. *Journal of Personality and Social Psychology, 57,* 239–249.

Gager, H., & Schurr, C. (1976). *Sexual assault: Confronting rape in America.* New York: Grosset and Dunlap.

Galle, O. R., Gove, W. R., & McPherson, J. M. (1972). Population density and pathology: What are the relationships for man? *Science, 176,* 23–30.

Gallup, G. (1937–1989). *Gallup poll reports.* Princeton, NJ: The Gallup Poll.

Galton, F. (1884). Measurement of character. *Fortnightly Review, 42,* 179–185.

Gamson, W. A., & Modigliani, A. (1971). *Untangling the cold war: A strategy for testing rival theories.* Boston: Little, Brown.

Gandour, M. J. (1984). Bulimia: Clinical description, assessment, etiology, and treatment. *International Journal of Eating Disorders, 3,* 3–38.

Gardner, G. T. (1978). Effects of federal human subject regulations on data obtained in environmental stressor research. *Journal of Personality and Social Psychology, 36,* 628–634.

Geen, R. G. (1978). Effects of attack and uncontrollable noise on aggression. *Journal of Research in Personality, 12,* 15–29.

Geen, R. G., & Stonner, D. (1973). Context effects in observed violence. *Journal of Personality and Social Psychology, 8,* 55–63.

Geen, R. G., & Thomas, S. L. (1986). The immediate effects of media violence on behavior. *Journal of Social Issues, 42*(3), 7–28.

Geiselman, R. E., Fisher, R. P., MacKinnon, D. P., & Holland H. L. (1985). Eyewitness memory enhancement in the police interview: Cognitive retrieval memories versus hypnosis. *Journal of Applied Psychology, 70,* 401–412.

Geiss, S. I., & O'Leary, K. D. (1981). Therapist rating of frequency and severity of marital problems: Implications for research. *Journal of Marital and Family Therapy, 7*(4), 515–520.

Geller, E. S., & Bigelow, B. E. (1984). Development of corporate incentive programs for motivating seat belt use: A review. *Traffic Safety Evaluation Research Review, 3*(5), 21–38.

Geller, E. S., Davis, L., & Spicer, K. (1983). Industry-based incentives for promoting seat belt use: Differential impact on white-collar versus blue-collar employees. *Journal of Organizational Behavior Management, 5*(1), 17–29.

Geller, E. S., & Hahn, H. A. (1984). Promoting safety belt use at industrial sites: An effective program for blue collar employees. *Professional Psychology: Research and Practice, 15,* 553–564.

Gentry, W. D. (1982). What is behavioral medicine? In J. R. Eiser (Ed.), *Social psychology and behavioral medicine* (pp. 3–13). New York: Wiley.

George, E. I. (1973). Research on measurement of family-size norms. In J. T. Fawcett (Ed.), *Psychological perspectives on population.* New York: Basic Books.

Gerard, H. B. (1983). School desegregation: The social science role. *American Psychologist, 38,* 869–877.

Gerard, H. B., & Mathewson, G. C. (1966). The effects of severity of initiation on liking for a group: A replication. *Journal of Experimental Social Psychology, 2,* 278–287.

Gerard, H. B., Wilhelmy, R., & Connolley, E. (1968). Conformity and group size. *Journal of Personality and Social Psychology, 8,* 79–82.

Gerbner, G., Gross, L., Signorielli, N., & Morgan, M. (1980). Television violence, victimization, and power. *American Behavioral Scientist, 23,* 705–716.

Gergen, K. J. (l973). Social psychology as history. *Journal of Personality and Social Psychology, 26,* 309–320.

Gergen, K. J. (1984). Theory of self: Impasse and evolution. In L. Berkowitz (Ed.), *Advances in Experimental Social Psychology* (Vol. 17, pp. 49–115). New York: Academic Press.

Gergen, K. J., & Gergen, M. (1974). Foreign aid that works. *Psychology Today,* June 1974, pp. 53–58.

Gibb, C. A. (1969). Leadership. In G. Lindzey & E. Aronson (Eds.), *Handbook of Social Psychology* (2nd ed.). Reading, MA: Addison-Wesley.

Gibbons, F. X. (1978). Sexual standards and reactions to pornography: Enhancing behavioral consistency through self-focused attention. *Journal of Personality and Social Psychology, 36,* 976–987.

Gibbons, F. X. (1986). Social comparison and depression: Company's effect on misery. *Journal of Personality and Social Psychology, 51,* 140–148.

Gibbons, F. X., Stephan, W. G., Stephenson, B., & Petty, C. R. (1980). Reactions to stigmatized others: Response amplification versus sympathy. *Journal of Experimental Social Psychology, 16,* 591–605.

Gifford, D. G. (1983). Meaningful reform of plea bargaining: The control of prosecutorial discretion. *University of Illinois Law Review,* 37–98.

Gilbert, D. T., Jones, E. E., & Pelham, B. W. (1987). Influence and interference: What the active perceiver overlooks. *Journal of Personality and Social Psychology, 52,* 861–870.

Gilbert, D. T., & Krull, D. S. (1988). Seeing less and knowing more: The benefits of perceptual ignorance. *Journal of Personality and Social Psychology, 54,* 193–202.

Gilbert, D. T., Pelham, B. W., & Krull, D. S. (1988). When person perceiver meets person perceived. *Journal of Personality and Social Psychology, 54,* 733–740.

Gilbert, S. J. (1981). Another look at the Milgram obedience studies: The role of graduated series of shocks. *Personality and Social Psychology Bulletin, 7,* 690–695.

Giles, M. W., & Evans, A. (1986). The power approach to intergroup hostility. *Journal of Conflict Resolution, 30,* 469–486.

Gilley, M. (1975). Don't the girls all get prettier at closing time? In *The Best of Mickey Gilley* (Vol. 2), Columbia. Written by Baker Knight, Singleton Music Company: BMI.

Glass, D. C. (1977). *Behavior patterns, stress, and coronary disease.* Hillsdale, NJ: Erlbaum.

Glass, D. C., & Singer, J. E. (1972). *Urban stress: Experiments on noise and social stressors.* New York: Academic Press.

Glass, D. C., Snyder, M. L., & Hollis, J. F. (1974). Time urgency and the Type A coronary-prone behavior pattern. *Journal of Applied Social Psychology, 4,* 125–140.

Glauber, S. (Producer) (1984). Trial by jury. *60 Minutes* [Television program]. CBS News: Vol. 16, No. 29, April 1, 1984.

Glenn, N. D. (1989). Duration of marriage, family composition, and marital happiness. *National Journal of Sociology, 3,* 3–24.

Glenn, N. D., & Weaver, C. N. (1988). The changing relationship of marital status to reported happiness. *Journal of Marriage and the Family, 50,* 317–324.

Glick, P. C. (1985). Orientations toward relationships: Choosing a situation in which to begin a relationship. *Journal of Experimental Social Psychology, 21,* 544–562.

Glick, P. C. (1989). Remarried families, step-families, and step children: A brief demographic profile. *Family Relations, 38,* 24–27.

Glick, P. C., Gottesman, D., & Jolton, J. (1988). The fault is not in the stars: Susceptibility of skeptics and believers in astrology to the Barnum effect. *Personality and Social Psychology Bulletin, 15,* 572–583.

Glick, P. C., & Norton, A. J. (1977). Marrying, divorcing, and living together in the U.S. today. *Population Bulletin, 32*(5). Washington, DC: Population Reference Bureau.

Glick, P. C., & Snyder, M. (1986). Self-fulfilling prophecy: The psychology of belief in astrology. *The Humanist,* May/June, pp. 20–25, 50.

Glick, P. C., & Spanier, G. B. (1980). Married and unmarried cohabitation in the United States. *Journal of Marriage and the Family, 42,* 19–30.

Gochman, I. R., & Keating, J. P. (1980). Misattributions to crowding: Blaming crowding for non-density-caused events. *Journal of Nonverbal Behavior, 4,* 157–175.

Goeckner, D., Greenough, W., & Mead, W. (1973). Deficit in learning tasks following chronic overcrowding in rats. *Journal of Personality and Social Psychology, 28,* 256–267.

Goethals, G. R. (1986). Social comparison theory: Psychology from the lost and found. *Personality and Social Psychology Bulletin, 12,* 261–278.

Goethals, G. R., Cooper, J., & Nacify, A. (1979). Role of foreseen, foreseeable, and unforeseeable behavioral consequences in the arousal of cognitive dissonance. *Journal of Personality and Social Psychology, 37,* 1179–1185.

Goethals, G. R., & Darley, J. M. (1977). Social comparison theory: An attributional approach. In J. M. Suls & R. L. Miller (Eds.), *Social comparison processes: Theoretical and empirical perspectives,* Washington, DC: Hemisphere.

Goethals, G. R., & Darley, J. M. (1987). Social comparison theory: Self-evaluation and group life. In B. Mullen & G. R. Goethals (Eds.), *Theories of group behavior.* New York: Springer-Verlag.

Goethals, G. R., & Nelson, R. E. (1973). Similarity in the influence process: The belief-value distinction. *Journal of Personality and Social Psychology, 25,* 117–122.

Goffman, E. (1959). *The presentation of self in everyday life.* Garden City, NY: Doubleday.

Goffman, E. (1967). *Interaction ritual: Essays on face-to-face behavior.* Garden City, NY: Doubleday.

Gold, J. A., Ryckman, R. M., & Mosley, N. R. (1984). Romantic mood induction and attraction to a dissimilar other: Is love blind? *Personality and Social Psychology Bulletin, 10,* 358–368.

Golding, W. (1954). *Lord of the flies.* New York: Coward-McCann.

Goldkamp, J. S., & Gottfredson, M. R. (1979). Bail decision making and pretrial detention: Surfacing judicial policy. *Law and Human Behavior, 3,* 227–249.

Goldman, M. (1986). Compliance employing a combined foot-in-the-door and door-in-the-face procedure. *Journal of Social Psychology, 126,* 111–116.

Goldman, W., & Lewis, P. (1977). Beautiful is good: Evidence that the physically attractive are more socially skillful. *Journal of Experimental Social Psychology, 13,* 125–130.

Goldstein, A. P. (1983). Needed: A war on aggression. *Newsletter, The Begun Institute, 8*(1), 1ff.

Goldstein, J. H., & Arms, R. L. (1971). Effects of observing athletic contests on hostility. *Sociometry, 34,* 83–90.

Goldstein, J. H., Davis, R. W., & Herman, D. (1975). Escalation of aggression: Experimental studies. *Journal of Personality and Social Psychology, 31,* 162–170.

Goldstein, M. J., & Kant, H. S. (1973). *Pornography and sexual deviance.* Berkeley: University of California Press.

Goldwyn, R. (Ed.).(1972). *The unfavorable result in plastic surgery.* Boston: Little, Brown.

Gonzalez, M. H., Aronson, E., & Costanzo, M. (1988). Using social cognition and persuasion to promote energy conservation: A quasi-experiment. *Journal of Applied Social Psychology, 18,* 1049–1066.

Gonzales, M. H., Davis, J. M., Loney, G. L., Lukens, C. K., Junghans, C. M. (1983). Interactional approach to interpersonal attraction. *Journal of Personality and Social Psychology, 44,* 1192–1197.

Goranson, R. E. (1970). Media violence and aggressive behavior: A review of experimental research. In L. Berkowitz (Ed.), *Advances in experimental social psychology* (Vol. 5). New York: Academic Press.

Gordon, S. L., & Peplau, L. A. (1982). The intimate relationships of lesbians and gay men. In E. R. Allgier & N. B. McCormick (Eds.), *Gender roles and sexual behavior: The changing boundaries*. Palo Alto, CA: Mayfield.

Gorer, G. (1968). Man has no "killer" instinct. In M. F. A. Montagu (Ed.), *Man and aggression*. New York: Oxford University Press.

Gouldner, A. W. (1960). The notion of reciprocity: A preliminary statement. *American Sociological Review, 25,* 161–178.

Gove, W. R., Hughes, M., & Galle, O. R. (1979). Overcrowding in the home: An empirical investigation of its possible pathological consequences. *American Sociological Review, 44,* 59–80.

Gove, W. R., Hughes, M., & Geerken, M. R. (1980). Playing dumb: A form of impression management with unpleasant side effects. *Social Psychology Quarterly, 43,* 89–102.

Grabitz-Gniech, G. (1971). Some restrictive conditions for the occurrence of psychological reactance. *Journal of Personality and Social Psychology, 19,* 188–196.

Granzberg, C., & Steinbring, J. (1980). *Television and the Canadian Indian.* Technical Report, Department of Anthropology, University of Winnipeg, Canada.

Green, L. W. (1979). Educational strategies to improve compliance with therapeutic and preventive regimens: The recent evidence. In R. B. Haynes, D. W. Taylor, & D. L. Sackett (Eds.), *Compliance in health care* (pp. 157–173). Baltimore: Johns Hopkins University Press.

Green, S. K., Buchanan, D. R., & Hever, S. K. (1984). Winners, losers, and choosers: A field study of dating initiation. *Personality and Social Psychology Bulletin, 20,* 514–530.

Greenberg, B. S. (1972). Children's reactions to TV blacks. *Journalism Quarterly, 49,* 5–14.

Greenberg, D., & Jacobs, M. (1966). *How to make yourself miserable.* New York: Random House.

Greenberg, J., & Pyszczynski, T. (1985). The effect of an overheard ethnic slur on evaluations of the target: How to spread a social disease. *Journal of Experimental Social Psychology, 21,* 61–72.

Greenberg, M. S. (1980). A theory of indebtedness. In K. Gergen, M. S. Greenberg, & R. Willis (Eds.), *Social exchange: Advances in theory and research.* New York: Plenum.

Greenberg, M. S., & Ruback, R. B. (1982). *Social psychology of the criminal justice system.* Monterey, CA: Brooks/Cole.

Greene, E., Wilson, L., & Loftus, E. F. (1989). Impact of hypnotic testimony on the jury. *Law and Human Behavior, 13,* 61–78.

Greenwald, A. G. (1980). The totalitarian ego: Fabrication and revision of personal history. *American Psychologist, 35,* 603–618.

Greenwald, A. G. (1988). A social-cognitive account of the self's development. In D. K. Lapsey & F. C. Powers (Eds.), *Self, ego, and identity: Integrative approaches* (pp. 30–42). New York: Springer-Verlag.

Greenwald, A. G., & Pratkanis, A. R. (1984). The self. In R. S. Wyer & K. Srull (Eds.), *Handbook of social cognition.* Hillsdale, NJ: Erlbaum.

Greenwald, A. G., Pratkanis, A. R., Leippe, M. R., & Baumgardner, M. H. (1985). Under what conditions does theory obstruct research progress? Unpublished manuscript, Ohio State University.

Gregory, W. L., Mower, J. C., & Linder, D. E. (1978). Social psychology and plea bargaining: Applications, methodology, and theory. *Journal of Personality and Social Psychology, 36,* 1521–1530,

Griffin, B. Q., & Rogers, R. W. (1977). Reducing interracial aggression: Inhibiting effects of victim's suffering and power to retaliate. *Journal of Psychology, 95,* 151–157.

Griffitt, W. (1970). Environmental effects on interpersonal affective behavior: Ambient effective temperature and attraction. *Journal of Personality and Social Psychology, 15,* 240–244.

Griffitt, W., & Jackson, T. (1973). Simulated jury decisions: The influence of jury-defendant attitude similarity-dissimilarity. *Social Behavior and Personality, 1,* 1–7.

Gross, A. E., & Fleming, I. (1982). Twenty years of deception in social psychology. *Personality and Social Psychology Bulletin, 8,* 402–408.

Gruber, C. A. (1986). Motivating the public to buckle up. *The Police Chief, 7,* 42.

Gruder, C. L., Cook, T. D., Hennigan, K. M., Flay, B. R., Alessis, C., & Halamaj, J. (1978). Empirical tests of the absolute sleeper effect predicted from the discounting cue hypothesis. *Journal of Personality and Social Psychology, 36,* 1061–1074.

Grush, J. E. (1976). Attitude formation and mere exposure phenomena: A nonartificial explanation of empirical findings. *Journal of Personality and Social Psychology, 33,* 281–290.

Grush, J. E., McKeough, K. L., & Ahlering, R. F. (1978). Extrapolating laboratory exposure research to actual political elections. *Journal of Personality and Social Psychology, 36,* 257–270.

Guisinger, S., Lowan, P., & Schuldberg, R. (1989). Changing parent and spouse relations in the first years of remarriage of divorced fathers. *Journal of Marriage and the Family, 51,* 445–456.

Haase, R. F., & Pepper, D. T., Jr. (1972). Nonverbal components of empathic communication. *Journal of Counseling Psychology, 19,* 417–424.

Hagan, J. (1974). Extra-legal attributes and criminal sentencing: An assessment of a sociological viewpoint. *Law and Society Review, 8,* 357–383.

Hall, E. T. (1966). *The hidden dimension.* Garden City, NY: Doubleday.

Hall, J., Roter, J. L., & Katz, N. R. (1988). Meta-analysis of correlates of provider behavior in medical encounters. *Medical Care, 26,* 657–672.

Hamilton, D. L., & Sherman, S. J. (1989). Illusory correlations: Implications for stereotyping theory and research. In D. Bar-Tal, C. F. Graumann, A. W. Kruglanski, & W. Stroebe (Eds.), *Stereotyping and prejudice: Changing conceptions* (pp. 59–82). New York: Springer-Verlag.

Hamilton, D. L., & Trolier, T. (1986). Stereotypes and stereotyping: An overview of the cognitive approach. In J. F. Dovidio & S. L. Gaertner (Eds.), *Prejudice, discrimination, and racism: Theory and research* (pp.127–164). New York: Academic Press.

Hamilton, J. C., & Baumeister, R. F. (1984). Biasing evaluations to appear unbiased: A self-presentational paradox. *Journal of Experimental Social Psychology, 20,* 552–566.

Hansen, B., & Evans, I. (1982). Feedback versus information concerning carbon monoxide as an early intervention strategy in adolescent smoking. *Adolescence, 17,* 89–98.

Hansen, C. H. (1989). Priming sex-role stereotype event schemes with rock music videos: Effects on impression favorability, trait inferences, and recall of a subsequent male-female interaction. *Basic and Applied Social Psychology, 10,* 371–391.

Hansen, R. D. (1980). Common sense attribution. *Journal of Personality and Social Psychology, 39,* 996–1009.

Hansson, R. O., & Slade, K. M. (1977). Altruism toward a deviant in city and small town. *Journal of Applied Social Psychology, 7,* 272–279.

Harari, H., Mohr, D., & Hosey, K. (1980). Faculty helpfulness to students: A comparison of compliance techniques. *Personality and Social Psychology Bulletin, 6,* 373–377.

Hardee, B. B., & McConahay, J. B. (1981). *Race, racial attitudes, and the perceptions of interpersonal distance.* Unpublished manuscript, Randolph-Macon Women's College.

Hardin, G. (1968). The tragedy of the commons. *Science, 162,* 1243–1248.

Hardyck, J. A., & Braden, M. (1962). Prophecy fails again: A report of a failure to replicate. *Journal of Abnormal and Social Psychology, 65,* 136–141.

Harkins, S. G. (1987). Social loafing and social facilitation. *Journal of Experimental Social Psychology, 23,* 1–18.

Harkins, S. G., & Szymanski, K. (1988). Social loafing and self-evaluation with an objective standard. *Journal of Experimental Social Psychology, 24,* 354–365.

Harkins, S. G., & Szymanski, K. (1989). Social loafing and group evaluation. *Journal of Personality and Social Psychology, 56,* 934–941.

Harlow, H. F. (1932). Social facilitation of feeding in the white rat. *Journal of Genetic Psychology, 41,* 211–221.

Harper, C. R., Kidera, G. J., & Cullen, J. F. (1971). Study of simulated airline pilot incapacitation: Phase II, subtle or partial loss of function. *Aerospace Medicine, 42,* 946–948.

Harris, L. (1989). *The unfinished agenda on race in America.* New York: NAACP Legal Defense and Education Fund.

Harris, M. J., & Rosenthal, R. (1988). Mediation of interpersonal expectancy effects: 31 meta-analyses. *Psychological Bulletin, 97,* 363–386.

Harrison, A. A. (1977). Mere exposure. In L. Berkowitz (Ed.), *Advances in experimental social psychology* (Vol. 10, pp. 39–83). New York: Academic Press.

Hartmann, E. (1973). Sleep requirement: Long sleepers, short sleepers, variable sleepers, and insomniacs. *Psychosomatics, 14,* 95–103.

Harvey, J. H., & Galvin, K. S. (1984). Clinical interpretations of attribution theory and research. *Clinical Psychology Review, 4,* 15–33.

Harvey, J. H., & Weary, G. (1981). *Perspectives on attributional processes.* Dubuque, IA: William C. Brown.

Harvey, J. H., & Weary, G. (1984). Current issues in attribution theory and research. *Annual Review of Psychology, 35,* 427–459.

Hastie, R. (1981). Schematic principles in human memory. In E. T. Higgins, C. P. Herman, & M. P. Zanna (Eds.), *Social cognition: The Ontario Symposium* (Vol. 1, pp. 39–88). Hillsdale, NJ: Erlbaum.

Hastie, R. (1984). Causes and effects of causal attribution. *Journal of Personality and Social Psychology, 46,* 44–56.

Hastie, R., & Kumar, P. A. (1979). Person memory: Personality traits as organizing principles in memory for behavior. *Journal of Personality and Social Psychology, 37,* 25–38.

Hastorf, A. H., Northcraft, G. B., & Picciotto, S. R. (1979). Helping the handicapped: How realistic is the performance feedback received by the physically handicapped? *Personality and Social Psychology Bulletin, 5,* 373–376.

Hatfield, E. (1982). What do women and men want from love and sex? In E. R. Allgier & N. B. McCormick (Eds.), *Changing boundaries: Gender roles and sexual behavior.* Palo Alto, CA: Mayfield.

Hatfield, E., & Rapson, R. (1987). Passionate love/Sexual desire: Can the same paradigm explain both? *Archives of Sexual Behavior, 16,* 259–278.

Hatfield, E., & Sprecher, S. (1986). Measuring passionate love in intimate relationships. *Journal of Adolescence, 9,* 383–410.

Hatfield, E., & Walster, G. W. (1978). *A new look at love.* Reading, MA: Addison-Wesley.

Hatkoff, T. S., & Lasswell, T. E. (1979). Male-female similarities and differences in conceptualizing love. In M. Cook & G. Wilson (Eds.), *Love and attraction.* Elmsford, NY: Pergamon.

Haugtvedt, C., Petty, R. E., Cacioppo, J. T., & Steidley, T. (1988). Personality and ad effectiveness: Exploring the utility of need for cognition. *Advances in Consumer Research, 15,* 209–212.

Hawkins, S. A., & Hastie, R. (1990). Hindsight: Biased judgments of past events after the outcomes are known. *Psychological Bulletin, 107,* 311–327.

Hayduk, L. A. (1983). Personal space: Where we now stand. *Psychological Bulletin, 94,* 293–335.

Haynes, R. B., Taylor, D. W., & Sackett, D. L. (1979). *Compliance in health care.* Baltimore: Johns Hopkins University Press.

Hazen, C., & Shaver, P. (1987). Romantic love conceptualized as an attachment process. *Journal of Personality and Social Psychology, 52,* 511–524.

Hearold, S. (1986). A synthesis of 1043 effects of television on social behavior. In G. Comstock (Ed.), *Public communication and behavior* (Vol. 1, pp. 65–133). New York: Academic Press.

Heberlein, T. A., & Black, J. S. (1976). Attitudinal specificity and the prediction of behavior in a field setting. *Journal of Personality and Social Psychology, 33,* 474–479.

Heft, H. (1979). Background and focal environmental conditions of the home and attention in young children. *Journal of Applied Social Psychology, 9,* 47–69.

Heider, F. (1944). Social perception and phenomenal causality. *Psychological Review, 51,* 358–374.

Heider, F. (1958). *The psychology of interpersonal relations.* New York: Wiley.

Helmreich, R. L., Spence, J. T., & Gibson, R. H. (1982). Sex-role attitudes: 1972–1980. *Personality and Social Psychology Bulletin, 8,* 656–663.

Henderson, J. B., Hall, S. M., & Lipton, H. L. (1979). Changing self-destructive behaviors. In G. C. Stone, F. Cohen, & N. E. Adler (Eds.), *Health psychology: A handbook* (pp. 141–160). San Francisco: Jossey-Bass.

Hendrick, C., & Hendrick, J. (1983). *Liking, loving, and relating.* Monterey, CA: Brooks/Cole.

Hendrick, C., & Hendrick, S. S. (1989). Research on love: Does it measure up? *Journal of Personality and Social Psychology, 56,* 784–794.

Hendrick, C., Hendrick, S., Foote, F. H., & Slapion-Foote, M. J. (1984). Do women and men love differently? *Journal of Personal and Social Relationships, 1,* 177–195.

Hendrick, C., & Page, H. (1970). Self-esteem, attitude similarity, and attraction. *Journal of Personality, 38,* 588–601.

Herbers, J. (1983). Economic equality eludes blacks. *Tallahassee Democrat,* July 24, 1983, pp. 1B, 5B.

Herbsleb, J. D., Sales, B. D., & Berman, J. J. (1979). When psychologists aid in the *voir dire:* Legal and ethical considerations. In L. E. Abt & I. R. Stuart (Eds.), *Social psychology and discretionary law* (pp. 197–217). New York: Van Nostrand Reinhold.

Hersey, P., & Blanchard, K. H. (1982). *Management of organizational behavior: Utilizing human resources* (4th ed.). Englewood Cliffs, NJ: Prentice-Hall.

Heshka, S., & Nelson, Y. (1972). Interpersonal speaking distance as a function of age, sex, and relationship. *Sociometry, 35,* 491–498.

Hess, E. H. (1965). Attitude and pupil size. *Scientific American, 212,* 46–54.

Hess, R. D., & Camara, K. A. (1979). Post-divorce family relationships as mediating factors in the consequences of divorce for children. *Journal of Social Issues, 35*(4), 79–96.

Hessing, D. J., Elffers, H., & Weigel, R. H. (1988). Exploring the limits of self-report and reasoned action: An investigation of psychology and tax evasion behavior. *Journal of Personality and Social Psychology, 54,* 404–413.

Heuer, L., & Penrod, S. D. (1989). Instructing jurors: A field experiment with written and preliminary instructions. *Law and Human Behavior, 13,* 409–430.

Hewstone, M., & Brown, R, (1986). (Eds.), *Contact and conflict on intergroup encounters.* Oxford, England: Basil Blackwell.

Heydecker, J. J., & Leeb, J. (1958). *The Nuremberg trial.* Cleveland: World Publishing Company.

Hicks, L. E. (1985). Is there a disposition to avoid the fundamental attribution error? *Journal of Research in Personality, 19,* 436–456.

Higbee, K. L., Millard, R. J., & Folkmman, J. R. (1982). Social psychology research during the 1970s: Predominance of experimentation and college students. *Personality and Social Psychology Bulletin, 8,* 180–183.

Higgins, E. T. (1989). Self-discrepancy theory: What patterns of self-beliefs cause people to suffer? In L. Berkowitz (Ed.), *Advances in experimental social psychology* (Vol. 22, pp. 93–136). New York: Academic Press.

Higgins, E. T., Bond, R. N., Klein, R., & Strauman, T. (1986). Self-discrepancies and emotional vulnerability: How magnitude, accessibility, and type of discrepancy influence affect. *Journal of Personality and Social Psychology, 51,* 5–15.

Higgins, E. T., & King, G. (1981). Accessibility of social constructs: Information-processing consequences of individual and contextual variability. In N. Cantor & J. F. Kihlstrom (Eds.), *Personality, cognition, and social interaction* (pp. 69–121). Hillsdale, NJ: Erlbaum.

Higgins, E. T., King, G. A., & Mavin, G. H. (1982). Individual construct accessibility and subjective impressions and recall. *Journal of Personality and Social Psychology, 43,* 35–47.

Higgins, E. T., & McCann, C. D. (1984). Social encoding and subsequent attitudes, impressions, and memory: "Context-driven" and motivational aspects of processing. *Journal of Personality and Social Psychology, 47,* 26–39.

Higgins, E. T., Rhodewalt, F., & Zanna, M. P. (1979). Dissonance motivation: Its nature, persistence, and reinstatement. *Journal of Experimental Social Psychology, 15,* 16–34.

Higgins, E. T., & Rholes, W. S. (1978). Saying is believing: Effects of message modification on memory and liking for the person described. *Journal of Experimental Social Psychology, 14,* 363–378.

Hildebrandt, K. A., & Fitzgerald, H. E. (1978). Adults' responses to infants varying in perceived cuteness. *Behavioral Processes, 3,* 159–172.

Hill, A. C. (1987). Affiliation: People who need people . . . But in different ways. *Journal of Personality and Social Psychology, 52,* 1008–1018.

Hill, C. T., Rubin, Z., & Peplau, L. A. (1976). Break-ups before marriage: The end of 103 affairs. *Journal of Social Issues, 32*(1), 147–167.

Hill, C. T., & Stull, D. E. (1981). Sex differences in effects of social and value similarity in same-sex friendship. *Journal of Personality and Social Psychology, 41,* 488–502.

Hill, G. W. (1982). Group versus individual performance: Are N + 1 heads better than one? *Psychological Bulletin, 91,* 517–539.

Hill, T., Smith, N. D., & Lewicki, P. (1989). The development of self-image bias: A real-world demonstration. *Personality and Social Psychology Bulletin, 15,* 205–211.

Himmelfarb, S., & Lickteig, A. (1982). Social desirability and the randomized response techniques. *Journal of Personality and Social Psychology, 43,* 710–717.

Hindy, C. C., Schwarz, J. C., & Brodsky, A. (1989). *If this is love why do I feel so insecure?* New York: Atlantic Monthly Press.

Hinkin, T. R., & Schriesheim, C. A. (1989). Development and application of new scales to measure the French and Raven (1959) bases of social power. *Journal of Applied Psychology, 74,* 561–567.

Hinsz, V. B. (1989). Facial resemblance in engaged and married couples. *Journal of Social and Personal Relationships, 6,* 223–229.

Hirschman, R. S., Leventhal, H., & Glynn, K. (1984). The development of smoking behavior: Conceptualization and supportive cross-sectional data. *Journal of Applied Social Psychology, 14,* 184–206.

Hobart, C. W. (1958). The incidence of romanticism during courtship. *Social Forces, 36,* 364.

Hobart, C. (1988). Family system in remarriage: An explanatory study. *Journal of Marriage and the Family, 50,* 649–661.

Hoch, S. J. (1987). Perceived consensus and predictive accuracy: The pros and cons of projection. *Journal of Personality and Social Psychology, 53,* 221–234.

Hoelter, J. W. (1983). The effects of role evaluation and commitment on identity salience. *Social Psychology Quarterly, 46,* 140–147.

Hoffman, L. R. (1965). Group problem solving. In L. Berkowitz (Ed.), *Advances in experimental social psychology* (Vol. 2, pp. 99–132). New York: Academic Press.

Hoffman, M. L. (1977). Sex differences in empathy and related behaviors. *Psychological Bulletin, 84,* 712–722.

Hoffman, M. L. (1981). Is altruism part of human nature? *Journal of Personality and Social Psychology, 40,* 121–137.

Hogan, R. (1986). What every student should know about personality psychology. In V. P. Makosky (Ed.), *The G. Stanley Hall Lecture Series* (Vol. 6, pp. 43–64). Washington, DC: American Psychological Association.

Hokanson, J. E., & Burgess, M. (1962a). The effects of frustration and anxiety on overt aggression. *Journal of Abnormal and Social Psychology, 65,* 232–237.

Hokanson, J. E., & Burgess, M. (1962b). The effects of three types of aggression on vascular processes. *Journal of Abnormal and Social Psychology, 64,* 446–449.

Hokanson, J. E., Burgess, M., & Cohen, M. F. (1963). Effects of displaced aggression on systolic blood pressure. *Journal of Abnormal and Social Psychology, 67,* 214–218.

Holahan, C. J. (1982). *Environmental psychology.* New York: Random House.

Hollander, E. P. (1964). *Leader, groups and influence.* New York: Oxford University Press.

Hollander, E. P. (1986). On the central role of leadership processes. *International Review of Applied Psychology, 35,* 39–52.

Hollander, E. P., & Offerman, L. R. (1990). Power and leadership in organizations: Relationships in transition. *Journal of Applied Psychology, 45,* 179–189.

Hollander, E. P., & Willis, R. (1967). Some current issues in the psychology of conformity and nonconformity. *Psychological Bulletin, 68,* 62–76.

Holloway, S., Tucker, L., & Hornstein, H. (1977). The effects of social and nonsocial information on interpersonal behavior of males: The news makes news. *Journal of Personality and Social Psychology, 35,* 514–522.

Holmes, J., & Boon, A. (1990). Developments in the field of close relationships. *Personality and Social Psychology Bulletin, 16,* 23–41.

Holmes, T. H., & Rahe, R. H. (1967). The social readjustment rating scale. *Journal of Psychosomatic Research, 11,* 213–218.

Homans, G. C. (1961). *Social behavior: Its elementary forms.* New York: Harcourt, Brace and World.

Honts, C. R., Hodes, R. L., & Raskin, D. C. (1985). Effects of physical countermeasures on the physiological detection of deception. *Journal of Applied Psychology, 70,* 177–187.

Honts, C. R., Raskin, D. C., & Kircher, J. C. (1986). Countermeasures and the detection of deception. Paper presented at the meeting of the American Psychological Association, Washington, DC.

Honts, C. R., Raskin, D. C., & Kircher, J. C. (1987). Effects of physical countermeasures and their electromyographic detection during polygraph tests for deception. *Journal of Psychophysiology, 1,* 241–247.

Honts, C. R., Raskin, D. C., Kircher, J. C., & Hodes, R. L. (1988). Effects of spontaneous countermeasures on the physiological detection of deception. *Journal of Police Science and Administration, 16,* 91–94.

Hornick, J. (1988). Cognitive thoughts mediating compliance in multiple request situations. *Journal of Economic Psychology, 9,* 69.

Horowitz, I. A., & Willging, T. E. (1984). *The psychology of law: Integrations and applications.* Boston: Little, Brown.

Horvath, F. (1984). Detecting deception in eyewitness cases: Problems and prospects in the use of the polygraph. In G. L. Wells & E. F. Loftus (Eds.), *Eyewitness testimony: Psychological perspectives* (pp. 214–255). Cambridge: Cambridge University Press.

House, J. S., & Wolf, S. (1978). Effects of urban residence on interpersonal trust and helping behavior. *Journal of Personality and Social Psychology, 36,* 1029–1043.

Houseknecht, S., Vaughn, S., & Macke, A. (1984). Marital disruption among professional women: The timing of career and family events. *Social Problems, 31,* 273–284.

Houts, P., Cleary, P., & Hu, T. (1988). *The Three Mile Island crisis: Psychological, social and economic impacts on the surrounding population.* University Park, PA: Pennsylvania State University Press.

Hovland, C. I., Harvey, O. J., & Sherif, M. (1957). Assimilation and contrast effects in reactions to communication and attitude change. *Journal of Abnormal and Social Psychology, 55,* 244–252.

Hovland, C., Janis, I., & Kelley, H. H. (1953). *Communication and persuasion.* New Haven, CT: Yale University Press.

Hovland, C. I., & Sears, R. R. (1940). Minor studies in aggression, VI: Correlation of lynchings with economic indices. *Journal of Personality, 9,* 301–310.

Hovland, C. I., & Weiss, W. (1951). The influence of source credibility on communication effectiveness. *Public Opinion Quarterly, 15,* 635–650.

Howard, J. W., & Rothbart, M. (1980). Social categorization and memory for in-group and out-group behavior. *Journal of Personality and Social Psychology, 38,* 301–310.

Howes, C., & Farver, J. (1987). Toddlers' response to the distress of their peers. *Journal of Applied Developmental Psychology, 8,* 441–452.

Hoyt, M. F., & Janis, I. L. (1975). Increasing adherence to a stressful decision via a motivational balance-sheet procedure: A field experiment. *Journal of Personality and Social Psychology, 31,* 833–839.

Huesmann, L. R. (1984). *TV violence and aggression: Long term effects.* Presentation at the Society of Experimental Social Psychology meetings, Snowbird, Utah.

Huesmann, L. R. (1986a). Psychological processes promoting the relation between exposure to media violence and aggressive behavior by the viewer. *Journal of Social Issues, 42,* 125–139.

Huesmann, L. R. (1986b). The effects of film and television violence among children. In S. J. Katz & P. Vesin (Eds.), *Children and the media* (pp. 101–128). Paris: Centre International de l'Enfance.

Huesmann, L. R. (1988). An information processing model for the development of aggression. *Aggressive Behavior, 14,* 13–24.

Huesmann, L. R., Eron, L. D., Klein, R., Bruce, P., & Fischer, P. (1983). Mitigating the imitation of aggressive behavior by changing children's attitudes about media violence. *Journal of Personality and Social Psychology, 44,* 899–910.

Huesmann, L. R., Eron, L. D., Lefkowitz, M. M., & Walder, L. O. (1984). Stability of aggression over time and generations. *Developmental Psychology, 20,* 1120–1134.

Hull, J., Van Trevran, R., Ashford, S., Prompson, P., & Andrus, B. C.(1988). Self-consciousness and the processing of self-relevant information. *Journal of Personality and Social Psychology, 54,* 452–465.

Hulka, B. S. (1979). *Patient-clinician interaction.* Baltimore, MD: Johns Hopkins University Press.

Humphries, C., Carver, C. J., & Neumann, P. C. (1983). Cognitive characteristics of the Type A coronary-prone behavior pattern. *Journal of Personality and Social Psychology, 44,* 117–187.

Hunt, E. B., & McLeod, C. M. (1979). Cognition and information-processing in patient and physician. In G. C. Stone, F. Cohen., & N. E. Adler (Eds.), *Health psychology—A handbook* (pp. 303–332). San Francisco: Jossey-Bass.

Hunt, W. A., & Bespalec, D. A. (1974). An evaluation of current methods of modifying smoking behavior. *Journal of Clinical Psychology, 30,* 431–438.

Hunter, M. A., Ames, E. W. , & Koopman, R. (1983). Effects of stimulus complexity and familiarization time on infant preferences for novel and familiar stimuli. *Developmental Psychology, 19,* 338–352.

Hurwitz, J. I., Zander, A. F., & Hymovitch, B. (1953). Some effects of power on the relations among group members. In D. Cartwright & A. F. Zander (Eds.), *Group dynamics: research and theory* (pp. 483–492). New York: Harper & Row.

Huston, T. L., & Burgess, R. L. (1979). Social exchange in developing relationships: An overview. In R. L. Burgess & T. L. Huston (Eds.), *Social exchange in developing relationships.* New York: Academic Press.

Huston, T. L., & Levinger, G. (1978). Interpersonal attraction and relationships. In M. R. Rosenzweig & L. W. Porter (Eds.), *Annual review of psychology* (Vol. 29). Palo Alto, CA.: Annual Review.

Huston, T. L., McHale, S. M., & Crouter, A. C. (1984). When the honeymoon's over: Changes in the marriage relationship over the first year. In R. Gilmour & S. Duck (Eds.), *Key issues in personal relations.* Hillside, NJ: Erlbaum.

Hyde, J. S. (1984). How large are gender differences in aggression? A developmental meta-analysis. *Developmental Psychology, 20,* 722–736.

Hyman, R. (1981). Cold reading: How to convince strangers that you know all about them. In K. Frazier (Ed.), *Paranormal borderlands of science.* Buffalo, NY: Prometheus Books.

Hynes, M., & Vanmarche, E. (1976). Reliability of embankment performance predictions. *Proceedings of the ASCE Engineering Mechanics Division Specialty Conference.* Waterloo, Ontario: University of Waterloo Press.

Iacono, W. G., & Patrick, C. J. (1987). What psychologists should know about deception. In I. B. Weiner & A. Hess (Eds.), *Handbook of forensic psychology* (pp. 460–489). New York: Wiley.

Intriligator, M. D., & Brito, D. L. (1988). The potential contribution of psychology to nuclear war issues. *American Psychologist, 43,* 318–321.

Isen, A. (1984). Toward understanding the role of affect in cognition. In R. Weyer & T. Srull (Eds.), *Handbook of social cognition* (Vol. 3). Hillsdale, NJ: Erlbaum.

Isen, A. M., Clark, M., & Schwartz, M. F. (1976). Duration of the effect of good mood on helping: Footprints on the sands of time. *Journal of Personality and Social Psychology, 34,* 385–393.

Isen, A. M., & Levin, P. (1972). The effect of feeling good on helping: Cookies and kindness. *Journal of Personality and Social Psychology, 21,* 384–388.

Isen, A. M., Shalker, T. E., Clark, M., & Karp, L. (1978). Affect accessibility of material in memory, and behavior: A cognitive loop. *Journal of Personality and Social Psychology, 36,* 1–12.

Isenberg, D. J. (1986). Group polarization: A critical review and meta-analysis. *Journal of Personality and Social Psychology, 50,* 1141–1151.

Jackson, D. J., & Huston, T. L. (1975). Physical attractiveness and assertiveness. *Journal of Social Psychology, 96,* 79–84.

Jackson, J. (1980). Promoting human welfare through legislative advocacy: A proper role for the science of psychology. In R. Kasschav & F. Kessel (Eds.), *Psychology and society: In search of symbiosis.* New York: Holt, Rinehart & Winston.

Jacoby, A. P., & Williams, J. D. (1985). Effects of premarital sex standards and behavior on dating and marriage desirability. *Journal of Marriage and the Family, 47,* 1059–1067.

Jaffe, Y., Shapir, N., & Yinon, Y. (1981). Aggression and its escalation. *Journal of Cross-Cultural Psychology, 12,* 21–36.

James, W. (1890/1981). *The principles of psychology.* Cambridge, MA: Harvard University Press. (Originally published in 1890.)

Jamieson, D. W., Lydon, J. E., & Zanna, M. P. (1987). Attitude and activity preference similarity: Differential bases of interpersonal attraction for low and high self-monitors. *Journal of Personality and Social Psychology, 53,* 1052–1060.

Janis, I. L. (1967). Effects of peer arousal on attitude change: Recent developments in theory and experimental research. In L. Berkowitz (Ed.), *Advances in Experimental Social Psychology* (Vol. 13). New York: Academic Press.

Janis, I, L. (1982). *Groupthink* (2nd ed.). Boston: Houghton Mifflin.

Janis, I. L. (1983a). The role of social support in adherence to stressful decisions. *American Psychologist, 38,* 143–160.

Janis, I. L. (1983b). Stress inoculation and health care. In D. Meichenbaum & M. E. Jaremko (Eds.), *Stress reduction and prevention* (pp. 67–99). New York: Plenum.

Janis, I. L., & Mann, L. (1977). *Decision-making: A psychological analysis of conflict, choice, and commitment.* New York: Free Press.

Janis, I. L., & Rodin, J. (1979). Attribution, control and decision making: Social psychology and health care. In G. C. Stone, F. Cohen, & N. E. Alder (Eds.), *Health Psychology.* San Francisco: Jossey-Bass.

Janoff-Bulman, R., & Timko, C. (1987). Coping with traumatic events: The role of denial in light of people's assumptive worlds. In C. R. Snyder & C. E. Ford (Eds.), *Coping with negative life events: Clinical and social psychological perspectives* (pp. 135–159). New York: Plenum.

Jeffrey, R. W., Wing, R. D., & Stunkard, A. J. (1978). Behavioral treatment of obesity: The state of the art in 1976. *Behavior Therapy, 9,* 189–199.

Jellinek, E. M. (1952). Phases of alcohol addiction. *Quarterly Journal of Studies on Alcohol, 13,* 673–684.

Jenkins, C. D. (1978). Behavioral risk factors in coronary heart disease. *Annual Review of Medicine, 29,* 543–562.

Jennings, D. L., Amabile, T. M., & Ross, C. (1982). Informal covariation assessment: Data-based versus theory-based judgments. In D. Kahneman, P. Slovic, & A. Tversky (Eds.), *Judgment under uncertainty: Heuristics and biases* (pp. 211–230). New York: Cambridge University Press.

Jensen, M. R. (1987). Psychobiological factors predicting the course of breast cancer. *Journal of Personality, 55,* 317–342.

Johnson, B. T., & Eagly, A. H. (1989). Effects of involvement on persuasion: A meta-analysis. *Psychological Bulletin, 106,* 290–314.

Johnson, D. J., Rusbult, C. E., & Morrow, G. D. (1983). *Responses to dissatisfaction in longstanding relationships: Predictors and consequences.* Paper presented at the meeting of the American Psychological Association, 1983.

Johnson, D. W., & Johnson, R. (1989). *Cooperation and competition: Theory and research.* Edina, MN: Interaction Book Co.

Johnson, D. W., Johnson, R. T., & Maruyama, G. (1984). Goal interdependence and interpersonal attraction in heterogeneous classrooms: A meta-analysis. In N. Miller & M. B. Brewer (Eds.), *Groups in contact: The psychology of desegregation* (pp. 187–212). New York: Academic Press.

Johnson, J. (1988). President signs law to redress wartime wrong. *New York Times,* Aug. 11, 1988, p. A-16.

Johnson, J. E., Rice, V. H., Fuller, J. J., & Endress, M. P. (1978). Sensory information, instruction in a coping strategy and recovery from surgery. *Research in Nursing and Health, 1*(1), 4–17.

Johnson, R. D., & Downing, L. L. (1979). Deindividuation and valence of cues: Effects on prosocial and antisocial behavior. *Journal of Personality and Social Psychology, 37,* 1532–1538.

Jones, C., & Aronson, E. (1973). Attributions of fault to a rape victim as a function of respectability of the victim. *Journal of Personality and Social Psychology, 26,* 415–419.

Jones, E. E. (1965). Conforming as a tactic of ingratiation. *Science, 149,* 144–150.

Jones, E. E. (1979). The rocky road from acts to dispositions. *American Psychologist, 34,* 107–117.

Jones, E. E. (1985). Major developments in social psychology during the past five decades. In G. Lindzey & E. Aronson (Eds.), *Handbook of social psychology* (Vol. 1, pp. 47–107). New York: Random House.

Jones, E. E., & Berglas, S. (1978). Control of attributions about the self through self-handicapping strategies: The appeal of alcohol and the role of underachievement. *Personality and Social Psychology, 4,* 200–206.

Jones, E. E., & Davis, K. E. (1965). A theory of correspondent inferences: From acts to dispositions. In L. Berkowitz (Ed.), *Advances in experimental and social psychology* (Vol. 2). New York: Academic Press.

Jones, E. E., Davis, K. E., & Gergen, K. J. (1961). Role playing variations and their informational value for person perception. *Journal of Abnormal and Social Psychology, 63,* 302–310.

Jones, E. E., Farina, A., Hastorf, A. H., Markus, H., Miller, D., & Scott, R. A. (1984). *Social stigma: The psychology of marked relationships.* New York: Freeman.

Jones, E. E., & Harris, V. A. (1967). The attribution of attitudes. *Journal of Experimental Social Psychology, 3,* 2(24).

Jones, E. E., & McGillis, D. (1976). Correspondent inferences and the attribution cube: A comparative reappraisal. In J. H. Harvey, W. J. Ickes, & R. F. Kidd (Eds.), *New directions in attribution research* (Vol. 1, pp. 389–420). Hillsdale, NJ: Erlbaum.

Jones, E. E., & Nisbett, R. E. (1971). *The actor and the observer: Divergent perceptions on the causes of behavior.* Morristown, NJ: General Learning Press.

Jones, E. E., & Pittman, T. S. (1982). Toward a general theory of strategic self-presentation. In J. Suls (Ed.), *Psychological perspectives on the self* (Vol.1). Hillsdale, NJ: Erlbaum.

Jones, E. E., Rhodewalt, F., Berglas, S., & Skelton, J. A. (1981). Effects of strategic self-esteem. *Journal of Personality and Social Psychology, 41,* 407–421.

Jones, E. E., Rock, L., Shaver, K. G., Goethals, G. R., & Ward, L. M. (1968). Pattern of performance and ability attribution: An unexpected primacy effect. *Journal of Personality and Social Psychology, 10,* 317–340.

Jones, E. E., & Wortman, C. (1973). *Ingratiation: An attributional approach.* Morristown, NJ: General Learning Press.

Jones, J. M. (1983). The concept of race in social psychology: From color to culture. In L. Wheeler & P. Shaver (Eds.), *Review of Personality and Social Psychology* (Vol. 4, pp. 117–150). Beverly Hills, CA: Sage.

Jones, J. W. (1978). Adverse emotional reactions of nonsmokers to secondary cigarette smoke. *Environmental Psychology and Nonverbal Behavior, 3,* 125–127.

Jones, J. W., & Bogat, G. A. (1978). Air pollution and human aggression. *Psychological Reports, 43,* 721–722.

Jones, K. L., Smith, D. W., Ulleland, C. N., & Streissguth, A. P. (1973). Patterns of malformation in offspring of chronic alcoholic mothers. *Lancet, 1,* 1267–1271.

Jones, R. A., & Brehm, J. W. (1970). Persuasiveness of one- and two-sided communications as a function of awareness there are two sides. *Journal of Experimental Social Psychology, 6,* 47–56.

Jones, R. A., & Scott, J. V. (1979). *Availability and the Pollyanna effect in memory for the characteristics of group members.* Unpublished manuscript, University of Kentucky.

Jones, R. A., Scott, J. V., Solernou, J., Noble, A., Fiala, J., & Miller, K. (1977). Availability and formulation of stereotypes. *Perceptual and Motor Skills, 44,* 631–638.

Jones, S. E. (1987). Judge- versus attorney-conducted *voir dire*: An empirical investigation of juror candor. *Law and Human Behavior, 11,* 131–146.

Joseph, J. G., Montgomery, S., Kirscht, J., Kessler, R., Ostrow, D., Wortman, C., Brian, K., Eller, M., & Eshlem, S. (1987). Perceived risk of AIDS: Assessing the behavioral and psychological consequences in a sample of gay men. *Journal of Applied Social Psychology, 17,* 231–250.

Joubert, P., & Lasagne, L. (1975). Patient packet inserts 1: Nature, notion, and needs. *Clinical Pharmacology and Therapeutics, 18,* 507–515.

Jury finds North guilty (1989). *Tallahassee Democrat,* May 5, 1989, p. 1.

Jussim, L. (1989). Teacher expectations: Self-fulfilling prophecies, perceptual biases, and accuracy. *Journal of Personality and Social Psychology, 57,* 469–480.

Kahn, R. L., & Katz, D. (1953). Leadership practices in relation to productivity and morale. In D. Cartwright & A. Zander (Eds.), *Group dynamics: Research and theory* (pp. 612–628). New York: Harper & Row.

Kahneman, D., & Tversky, A. (1979). Prospect theory: An analysis of decision under risk. *Econometrika, 47,* 263–291.

Kahneman, D., Slovic, P., & Tversky, A. (Eds.) (1982). *Judgment under uncertainty: Heuristics and biases.* Cambridge: Cambridge University Press.

Kairys, D., Schulman, J., & Harring, S. (Eds.). (1975). *The jury system: New methods for reducing prejudice.* Philadelphia: National Lawyers Guild.

Kalick, S. M. (1977). *Plastic surgery, physical appearance, and person perception.* Unpublished doctoral dissertation, Harvard University, 1977. Cited in E. Berscheid (1981). An overview of the psychological effects of physical attractiveness and some comments upon the psychological effects of knowledge of the effects of physical attractiveness. In W. Lucker, K. Ribbens, & J. A. McNamera (Eds.), *Logical aspects of facial form* (Craniofacial growth series). Ann Arbor: University of Michigan Press.

Kalick, S. M. (1978). Toward an interdisciplinary psychology of appearances. *Psychiatry, 41*(3), 243-253.

Kalick, S. M., & Hamilton, T. E. (1986). The matching hypothesis reexamined. *Journal of Personality and Social Psychology, 51,* 673-682.

Kalven, H., Jr., & Zeisel, H. (1966). *The American jury.* Boston: Little, Brown.

Kamal, P., & Mehta, M. (1987). Social environment and feeling of crowding. *Indian Psychological Review, 32,* 25-29.

Kanin, E. J., Davidson, D. K. D., & Scheck, S. R. (1970). A research note on male-female differentials in the experience of heterosexual love. *The Journal of Sex Research, 6,* 64-72.

Kantola, S. J., Syme, G. J., & Campbell, E. A. (1984). Cognitive dissonance and energy conservation. *Journal of Applied Psychology, 69,* 416-421.

Kantrowitz, B. (1987). Blacks protest campus racism. *Newsweek,* April 6, 1987, p. 30.

Kaplan, J. (1978). A legal look at prosocial behavior. In L. Wispé (Ed.), *Altruism, sympathy. and helping: Psychological and sociological principles* (pp. 291-302). New York: Academic Press.

Karabenick, S., & Meisels, M. (1972). Effects of performance evaluation on interpersonal distance. *Journal of Personality, 40,* 275-286.

Karlin, R. A., Epstein, Y., & Aiello, J. (1978). Strategies for the investigation of crowding. In A. Esser & B. Greenbie (Eds.), *Design for communality and privacy.* New York: Plenum.

Karlin, R. A., Rosen, L. S., & Epstein, Y. M. (1979). Three into two doesn't go: A follow-up on the effect of overcrowded dormitory rooms. *Personality and Social Psychology Bulletin, 5,* 391-395.

Karnow, S. (1971). Calley, Eichmann both obedient. *St. Petersburg Times,* March 30, 1971.

Kassin, S. M. (1979). Consensus information, prediction and causal attribution: A review of the literature and issues. *Journal of Personality and Social Psychology, 37,* 1966-1981.

Kassin, S. M., & Wrightsman, L. S. (1981). Coerced confessions, judicial instructions, and mock juror verdicts. *Journal of Applied Social Psychology, 11,* 489-506.

Katz, D. (1960). The functional approach to the study of attitudes. *Public Opinion Quarterly, 24,* 163-204.

Katz, D., & Stotland, E. (1959). A preliminary statement to a theory of attitude structure and change. In S. Koch (Ed.), *Psychology: A study of a science* (Vol. 3, pp. 423-475). New York: McGraw-Hill.

Katz, P. A., & Taylor, D. A. (1988). (Eds.). *Eliminating racism: Profiles in controversy.* New York: Plenum.

Kegeles, S. M., Adler, N. E., & Irwin, C. E. (1988). Sexually active adolescents and condoms: Change over one year in knowledge, attitudes, and use. *American Journal of Public Health, 78,* 460-461.

Kelley, A. B. (1979). A media role for public health compliance? In R. B. Haynes, D. W. Taylor, & D. L. Sackett (Eds.), *Compliance in health care* (pp. 193–201). Baltimore: Johns Hopkins University Press.

Kelley, H. H. (1950). The warm-cold variable in first impressions of persons. *Journal of Personality, 18,* 431–439.

Kelley, H. H. (1967). Attribution theory in social psychology. In D. Levine (Ed.), *Nebraska symposium on motivation* (Vol. 15, pp. 192–241). Lincoln, NE: University of Nebraska Press.

Kelley, H. H. (1973). The process of causal attribution. *American Psychologist, 28,* 107–128.

Kelley, H. H. (1983). Love and commitment. In H. H. Kelley et al. (Eds.), *Close relationships* (pp. 265–314). New York: Freeman.

Kelley, H. H. & Michela, J. L. (1980). Attribution theory and research. *Annual Review of Psychology, 31,* 457–501.

Kelley, H. H., & Thibaut, J. W. (1978). *Interpersonal relations: A theory of interdependence.* New York: Wiley-Interscience.

Kelman, H. C. (1958). Compliance, identification, and internalization. *Journal of Conflict Resolution, 2,* 51–60.

Kelman, H. C. (1973). Violence without moral restraint: Reflections on the dehumanization of victims and victimizers. *Journal of Social Issues, 29,* 25–62.

Kelman, H. C. (1974). Further thoughts on the processes of compliance, identification, and internalization. In J. T. Tedeschi (Ed.), *Perspectives on social power* (pp. 125–171). Chicago: Aldine.

Kelman, H. C., & Hamilton, V. L. (1989). *Crimes of obedience.* New Haven, CT: Yale University Press.

Kelman, H. C., & Hovland, C. I. (1953). "Reinstatement" of the communicator in delayed measurement of opinion change. *Journal of Abnormal and Social Psychology, 48,* 327–335.

Kelvin, P. A. (1973). A social-psychological examination of privacy. *British Journal of Social and Clinical Psychology, 12,* 248–261.

Kendall, P. C., & Turk, D. C. (1984). Cognitive-behavioral strategies and health enhancement. In J. D. Matarazzo et al. (Eds.), *Behavioral health: A handbook of health enhancement and disease prevention* (pp. 393–405). New York: Wiley.

Kenny, D. A., & Nasby, W. (1980). Splitting the reciprocity correlation. *Journal of Personality and Social Psychology, 38,* 249–256.

Kenny, D. A., & Zaccaro, S. J. (1983). An estimate of variance due to traits in leadership. *Journal of Applied Psychology, 68,* 678–685.

Kenrick, D. T. (1989). Altruism, Darwinism, and the gift of Josiah Wedgewood. *Behavioral and Brain Sciences, 12,* 531–532.

Kenrick, D. T., & Cialdini, R. B. (1977). Romantic attraction: Misattribution versus reinforcement explanations. *Journal of Personality and Social Psychology, 35,* 381–391.

Kenrick, D. T., Cialdini, R. B., & Linder, D. E. (1979). Misattribution under fear-producing circumstances: Four failures to replicate. *Personality and Social Psychology Bulletin, 5,* 329–334.

Kenrick, D. T., & Gutierres, S. E. (1980). Contrast effects and judgments of physical attractiveness: When beauty becomes a social problem. *Journal of Personality and Social Psychology, 38,* 131–140.

Kephart, W. M. (1967). Some correlates of romantic love. *Journal of Marriage and the Family, 29,* 470–474.

Kerchkoff, A. C., & Davis, K. E. (1962). Value consensus and need complementarity in mate selection. *American Sociological Review, 27,* 295–303.

Kerner, O., & Associates (1968). *Report of the National Advisory Commission on Civil Disorders.* New York: Bantam Books.

Kerns, P., & Wead, D. (1979). *People's temple — People's tomb.* Plainfield, NJ: Logos International Publishers.

Kerr, N. L. (1978). Beautiful and blameless: Effects of victim attractiveness and responsibility on mock jurors' verdicts. *Personality and Social Psychology Bulletin, 4,* 479–482.

Kiesler, C. A. (1971). *The psychology of commitment: Experiments linking behavior to belief.* New York: Academic Press.

Kiesler, C. A., & Kiesler, S. B. (1969). *Conformity.* Reading, MA: Addison-Wesley.

Kihlstrom, J. F., & Cantor, N. (1984). Mental representations of the self. In L. Berkowitz (Ed.), *Advances in experimental social psychology* (Vol.17). New York: Academic Press.

Kinsey, A., Pomeroy, W., & Martin, C. (1948). *Sexual behavior in the human male.* Philadelphia: W. B. Saunders.

Kinzel, A. S. (1970). Body-buffer zone in violent prisoners. *American Journal of Psychiatry, 127,* 59–64.

Kipnis, D. M. (1976). *The powerholders.* Chicago: University of Chicago Press.

Kipnis, K. (1979). Plea bargaining: A critic's rejoinder. *Law and Society Review, 13,* 555–564.

Kircher, J. C., Horowitz, S. W., & Raskin, D. C. (1988). Meta-analysis of mock crime studies of the control of question polygraph technique. *Law and Human Behavior, 12,* 79–90.

Kirscht, J. P., Janz, N. K., & Becker, M. H. (1989). Psychosocial predictors of change in cigarette smoking. *Journal of Applied Social Psychology, 19,* 298–308.

Kirscht, J. P., & Rosenstock, I. M. (1979). Patients' problems in following recommendations of health experts. In G. C. Stone, F. Cohen, & N. E. Adler (Eds.), *Health Psychology: A Handbook.* San Francisco: Jossey-Bass.

Kleck, G. (1985). Life support for ailing hypotheses: Modes of summarizing the evidence for racial discrimination in sentencing. *Law and Human Behavior, 9,* 271–285.

Kleinke, C. L., Meeker, F. B., & Staneki, R. A. (1986). Preference for opening lines: Comparing ratings by men and women. *Sex Roles, 15,* 585–600.

Kleinmuntz, B., & Szucko. J. J. (1984a). A field study of the fallibility of polygraphic lie detection. *Nature, 308,* 449–450.

Kleinmuntz, B., & Szucko, J. J. (1984b). Lie detection in ancient and modern times: A call for contemporary scientific study. *American Psychologist, 39,* 766–776.

Klineberg, O. (1984). Public opinion and nuclear war. *American Psychologist, 39,* 1245–1253.

Kleinot, M. C., & Rogers, R. R. (1982). Identifying effective components of alcohol misuse prevention programs. *Journal of Studies on Alcohol, 43,* 802–811.

Knight, J. A., & Vallacher, R. R. (1981). Interpersonal engagement in social perception: The consequences of getting into the action. *Journal of Personality and Social Psychology, 40,* 990–999.

Knight, R. C., Weitzer, W. H., & Zimring, C. M. (1978). *Opportunity for control and the built environment: The ELEMR Project*. Amherst, MA: University of Massachusetts, Environmental Institute.

Knox, R. E., & Inkster, J. A. (1968). Postdecision dissonance at posttime. *Journal of Personality and Social Psychology, 8,* 319–323.

Kobasa, S. C., Maddi, S. R., & Courington, S. (1981). Personality and constitution as mediators in the stress-illness relationship. *Journal of Health and Social Behavior, 22,* 368–378.

Koehnken, G. (1987). Training police officers to detect deceptive eyewitness statements: Does it work? *Social Behavior, 2,* 1–17.

Koestner, R., Ryan, R. M., Bernieri, F., & Holt, K. (1984). The effects of controlling versus informational limit-setting styles on children's intrinsic motivation and creativity. *Journal of Personality, 52,* 233–248.

Kohlberg, L. (1969). The cognitive-developmental approach to socialization. In D. A. Goslin (Ed.), *Handbook of socialization theory and research*. Chicago: Rand McNally.

Komorita, S. S., & Brenner, A. (1968). Bargaining and concession making under bilateral monopoly. *Journal of Personality and Social Psychology, 9,* 15–20.

Komorita, S. S., & Kravitz, D. A. (1979). The effects of alternatives in bargaining. *Journal of Experimental Social Psychology, 15,* 147–157.

Konečni, V. J. (1975). The mediation of aggressive behavior. Arousal level versus anger and cognitive labeling. *Journal of Personality and Social Psychology, 32,* 706–712.

Korabik, K. (1981). Changes in physical attractiveness and interpersonal attraction. *Basic and Applied Social Psychology, 2,* 59–66.

Koriat, A., Lichtenstein, S., & Fischhoff, B. (1980). Reasons for confidence. *Journal of Experimental Psychology: Human Learning and Memory, 6,* 107–118.

Kramer, R. M., & Brewer, M. B. (1984). Effects of group identity on resource use in a simulated commons dilemma. *Journal of Personality and Social Psychology, 46,* 1044–1057.

Kramer, R. M., McClintock, C. G., & Messick, D. M. (1986). Social values and cooperative response to a simulated resource conservation crisis. *Journal of Psychology, 54,* 576–592.

Krauss, R. M., Geller, V., & Olson, C. (1976). *Modalities and cues in the detection of deception:* Paper presented at the American Psychological Association meetings.

Kraut, R. E. (1978). Verbal and nonverbal cues in the perception of lying. *Journal of Personality and Social Psychology, 36,* 380–391.

Kraut, R. E., & Poe, D. (1980). Behavioral roots of person perception: The deception judgments of customs inspectors and laymen. *Journal of Personality and Social Psychology, 39,* 784–798.

Krebs, D., & Adinolfi, A. A. (1975). Physical attractiveness, social relations, and personality style. *Journal of Personality and Social Psychology, 31,* 245–253.

Krosnick, J. A., & Alwin, D. F. (1989). Aging and susceptibility to attitude change. *Journal of Personality and Social Psychology, 57,* 416–425.

Kruglanski, A. W. (1979). Causal explanation, teleological explanation: On radical particularism in attribution theory. *Journal of Personality and Social Psychology, 37,* 1447–1457.

Kruglanski, A. (1986). Freeze-think and the *Challenger. Psychology Today,* August, 1986, pp. 48–49.

Krupat, E. (1977). Environmental and social psychology—How different must they be? *Personality and Social Psychology Bulletin, 3,* 51–53.

Kulik, J. A. (1983). Confirmatory attribution and the perpetuation of social beliefs. *Journal of Personality and Social Psychology, 44,* 1171–1181.

Kulka, R. A., & Weingarten, H. (1979). The long-term effects of parental divorce in childhood on adult adjustment. *Journal of Social Issues, 35,* 50–78.

Kushler, M. G. (1989). Use of evaluation to improve energy conservation programs: A review and case study. *Journal of Social Issues, 45*(1), 153–168.

Kushner, H. S. (1981). *When bad things happen to good people.* New York: Schocken Books.

Lando, H. A. (1977). Successful treatment of smokers with a broad-spectrum behavioral approach. *Journal of Consulting and Clinical Psychology, 45,* 361–366.

Lando, H. A., & McCullough, J. A. (1978). Clinical application of a broad-spectrum behavioral approach to chronic smokers. *Journal of Consulting and Clinical Psychology, 46,* 583–585.

Laner, M. R., & Thompson, J. (1982). Abuse and aggression in courting couples. *Deviant Behavior: An Interdisciplinary Journal, 3,* 229–244.

Lang, A. R. (1983). Addictive personality: A viable construct? In P. K. Levinson, D. R. Gerstein, & D. R. Maloff (Eds.), *Commonalities in substance abuse and habitual behavior* (pp. 157–235). Lexington, MA: Lexington Books.

Lang, A. R., Goeckner, D. J., Adesso, V. J., & Marlatt, G. A. (1975). Effects of alcohol on aggression in male social drinkers. *Journal of Abnormal Psychology, 84,* 508–518.

Lang, A. R., & Sibrell, P. A. (1989). Psychological perspectives on alcohol consumption and interpersonal aggression. *Criminal Justice and Behavior, 16,* 300–325.

Langbein, J. H. (1980). Torture and plea bargaining. *Public Interest, 55,* 43–61.

Langer, E. J. (1975). The illusion of control. *Journal of Personality and Social Psychology, 32,* 311–328.

Langer, E. J. (1977). The psychology of chance. *Journal for the Theory of Social Behavior, 7,* 185–208.

Langer, E. J. (1982). Automated lives. *Psychology Today,* April, 1982, pp. 60ff.

Langer, E. J. (1989). *Mindfulness.* Reading, MA: Addison-Wesley.

Langer, E. J., Beck, P., Janoff-Bulman, R., & Timko, C. (1984). The relationship between cognitive desperation and longevity in senile and nonsenile elderly populations. *Academic Psychology Bulletin, 6,* 211–226.

Langer, E., & Newman, H. (1981). Post-divorce adaptation and the attribution of responsibility. *Sex Roles, 7,* 223–232.

Langer, E. J., & Saegart, S. (1977). Crowding and cognitive control. *Journal of Personality and Social Psychology, 35,* 175–182.

Langlois, J. H., & Downs, A. C. (1979). Peer relations as a function of physical attractiveness: The eye of the beholder or behavioral reality? *Child Development, 50,* 409–418.

Langlois, J. H., & Stephan, C. W. (1981). Beauty and the beast: The role of physical attractiveness in the development of peer relations and social behavior. In S. S. Brehm, S. M. Kassin, & F. X. Gibbons (Eds.), *Developmental social psychology* (pp. 152–168). New York: Oxford University Press.

LaPiere, R. T. (1934). Attitudes and actions. *Social Forces, 13,* 230–237.

Larson, J. (1988). The marriage quiz: College students' beliefs and selected myths about marriage. *Family Relations, 37*(1), 3–12.

Laski, H. J. (1919). The dangers of obedience. *Harper's Monthly Magazine, 159,* 1–10.

Latane, B. (1981). The psychology of social impact. *American Psychologist, 36,* 343–356.

Latane, B., & Darley, J. M. (1968). Group inhibition of bystander intervention in emergencies. *Journal of Personality and Social Psychology, 10,* 215–221.

Latane, B., & Darley, J. M. (1969). Bystander apathy. *American Scientist, 57,* 224–268.

Latane, B., & Darley, J. M. (1970). *The unresponsive bystander: Why doesn't he help?* New York: Appleton-Century-Crofts.

Latane, B., & Harkins, S. (1976). Cross-modality matches suggest anticipated stage fright as a multiplicative function of audience size and status. *Perception and Psychophysics, 20,* 482–488.

Latane, B., & Nida, S. (1981). Ten years of research on group size and helping. *Psychological Bulletin, 89,* 307–324.

Latane, B., & Rodin, J. (1969). A lady in distress: Inhibiting effects of friends and strangers on bystander intervention. *Journal of Experimental Social Psychology, 5,* 189–202.

Latane, B., Williams, K., & Harkins, S. (1979). Many hands make light the work: The causes and consequences of social loafing. *Journal of Personality and Social Psychology, 37,* 822–832.

Lauer, J., & Lauer, R. (1985). Marriage made to last. *Psychology Today,* June, 1985, pp. 22–27.

Laurence, J., & Perry, C. (1983). Hypnotically created memory among highly hypnotizable subjects. *Science, 222,* 523–524.

Lave, L., & Seskin, E. (1970). Air pollution and human health. *Science, 169,* 723–733.

Lay, C. H., & Jackson, D. N. (1969). Analysis of the generality of trait-inferential relationships. *Journal of Personality and Social Psychology, 12,* 12–21.

Lazarus, A. A. (1985). *Marital myths.* San Luis Obispo, CA: Impact.

Lazarus, R. S., & Folkman, S. (1984). *Stress, appraisal, and coping.* New York: Springer-Verlag.

Leary, M. R. (1982). Hindsight distortion and the 1980 presidential election. *Personality and Social Psychology Bulletin, 8,* 257–263.

Leary, M. R. (in press). Self-presentational process in leadership emergence and effectiveness. In R. A. Giacalone & P. Rosenfeld (Eds.), *Impression management in the organization.* Hillsdale, NJ: Erlbaum.

Leary, M. R., & Kowalski, R. M. (1990). Impression management: A literature review and two-component model. *Psychological Bulletin, 107,* 34–47.

Leary, M. R., & Shepperd, J. A. (1985). *Self-handicapping: A conceptual note.* Unpublished manuscript, Wake Forest University.

LeBon, G. (1895/1960). *The crowd: A study of the popular mind.* New York: Viking Press. (Originally published in 1895.)

Ledeen, M. A. (1988). *Perilous statecraft.* New York: Macmillan.

Lee, G. (1978). *Family structure and interaction: A comparative analysis.* Philadelphia: Lippincott.

Lee, G. R. (1988). Marital satisfaction in later life: The effects of nonmarital roles. *Journal of Marriage and the Family, 50,* 775–783.

Lee, J. A. (1974). The styles of loving. *Psychology Today,* October 1974, pp. 43ff.

Lee, J. A. (1988). Love-styles. In R. J. Sternberg & M. L. Barnes (Eds.), *The psychology of love* (pp. 38–67). New Haven, CT: Yale University Press.

Leffingwell, A. (1892). *Illegitimacy and the influence of the seasons upon conduct.* New York: Scribners.

Lehrman, L. (1981). *Prosecution of spouse abuse: Innovations in criminal justice response.* Center for Women's Policy Studies, Washington, DC.

Leonard, K. E. (1988). *Alcohol and marital violence: Data from a national sample of young men.* Paper presented at Association for the Advancement of Behavioral Therapy meeting, New York City.

Leonard, K. E. (1989). The impact of explicit aggressive and implicit nonaggressive cues on aggression in intoxicated and sober males. *Personality and Social Psychology Bulletin, 15,* 384–394.

Leonard, R. L., Jr. (1975). Self-concept and attraction for similar and dissimilar others. *Journal of Personality and Social Psychology, 31,* 926–929.

Lepper, M. R., Greene, D., & Nisbett, R. E. (1973). Undermining children's intrinsic interest with extrinsic reward: A test for the overjustification hypothesis. *Journal of Personality and Social Psychology, 28,* 129–137.

Lerner, M. J. (1980). *The belief in a just world: A fundamental delusion.* New York: Plenum.

Lerner, R. M., & Lerner, J. V. (1977). The effects of age, sex and physical attractiveness on child-peer relations, academic performance, and elementary school adjustment. *Developmental Psychology, 13,* 585–590.

Levenson, M. R., Aldwin, C. M., Basse, R., & Sprio, A. III. (1988). Emotionality and mental health: Longitudinal findings from the normative aging study. *Journal of Abnormal Psychology, 97,* 94–96.

Leventhal, H. (1970). Findings and theory in the study of fear communications. In L. Berkowitz (Ed.), *Advances in experimental social psychology* (Vol. 5, pp. 119–186). New York: Academic Press.

Leventhal, H. (1974). Attitudes: Their nature, growth, and change. In C. Nemeth (Ed.), *Social Psychology: Classic and contemporary integrations.* Chicago: Rand McNally.

Leventhal, H., & Cleary, P. D. (1980). The smoking problem: A review of the research and theory in behavioral risk modification. *Psychological Bulletin, 88,* 370–405.

Leventhal, H., Fleming, R., & Glynn, K. (1988). A cognitive-developmental approach to smoking intervention. In S. Maes, C. D. Spielberger, P. Defares, & I. G. Sarason (Eds.), *Topics in health psychology* (pp. 79–105). New York: Wiley.

Leventhal, H., & Hirschman, R. S. (1982). Social psychology and prevention. In G. Sanders & J. Suls (Eds.), *Social psychology of health and illness* (pp. 183–226). Hillsdale, NJ: Erlbaum.

Leventhal, H., Zimmerman, R., & Gutmann, M. (1983). Compliance: A self-regulatory perspective. In D. Gentry (Ed.), *A handbook of behavioral medicine.* New York: Guilford.

Levin, P. F., & Isen, A. M. (1975). Further studies on the effect of feeling good on helping. *Sociometry, 38,* 141–147.

Levine, C. (1984). Toward the talking pill. *Psychology Today,* January 1984, p. 11.

Levinger, G. Factors differentiating high and low cohesive marriages. In G. Levinger & O. C. Moles (Eds.) *Divorce and separation: Context causes, and consequences.* New York: Basic Books.

Levinger, G. (1983). Development and change. In H. H. Kelley, E. Berscheid, A. Christensen., J. H. Harvey, T. L. Huston, G. Levinger, E. McClintock, L. A. Peplau & D. R. Peterson (Eds.), *Close Relationships* (pp. 315–359). New York: Freeman.

Levinger, G. & Moles, O. C. (Eds.). *Divorce and separation: Causes and consequences.* New York: Basic Books.

Levinger, G., & Snoek, J. D. (1972). *Attraction in relationship: A new look at interpersonal attraction.* Morristown, NJ: General Learning Press.

Levy, L., & Herzog, A. (1974). Effects of population density and crowding on health and social adaptation in the Netherlands. *Journal of Health and Social Behavior, 15,* 228–240.

Levy, R. I. (1973). *Tahitians.* Chicago: University of Chicago Press.

Lewicki, P. (1983). Self-image bias in person perception. *Journal of Personality and Social Psychology, 45,* 384–393.

Lewin, K. (1951). Formalization and progress in psychology. In D. Cartwright (Ed.), *Field theory and social science.* New York: Harper & Row.

Lewin, K., Lippett, R., & White, R. K. (1939). Patterns of aggressive behavior in experimentally created "social climates." *Journal of Social Psychology, 10,* 271–299.

Ley, P. (1977). Psychological studies of doctor-patient communication. In S. Rochman (Ed.), *Contributions to medical psychology* (Vol. 1). Oxford: Pergamon Press.

Ley, P. (1982). Giving information to patients. In J. R. Eiser (Ed.), *Social psychology and behavioral medicine* (pp. 339–373). New York: Wiley.

Ley, P. (1988). *Communicating with patients: Improving communication, satisfaction, and compliance.* New York: Crown Helm.

Ley, P., Witworth, M. A., Skilbeck, C. E., Woodward, R., Pinsent, R. J., Pike, L. A., Clarkson, M. E., & Clark, P. B. (1976). Improving doctor-patient communications in general practice. *Journal of the Royal College of General Practitioners, 26,* 720–724.

Leyens, J. P., Camino, L., Parke, R. D., & Berkowitz, L. (1975). Effects of movie violence on aggression in a field setting as a function of group dominance and cohesion. *Journal of Personality and Social Psychology, 32,* 346–360.

Leyens, J. P., & Parke, R. D. (1975). Aggressive slides can induce a weapons effect. *European Journal of Social Psychology, 5,* 229–236.

Lichtenstein, S., & Fischhoff, B. (1977). Do those who know more also know more about how much they know? The calibration of probability judgments. *Organizational Behavior and Human Performance, 20,* 159–183.

Liebert, R. M., & Sprafkin, J. (1988). *The early window: Effects of television on children and youth* (3rd ed.). New York: Pergamon Press.

Liem, J. H., & Liem, R. (1976). *Life events, social supports, and physical and psychological well-being.* Paper presented at the meetings of the American Psychological Association, Washington, DC.

Lifton, R. J. (1961). *Thought reform and the psychology of totalism.* New York: Norton.

Linder, D., & Worchel, S. (1970). Opinion change as a result of effortfully drawing a counterattitudinal conclusion. *Journal of Experimental Social Psychology, 6,* 432–448.

Lindsay, R. C. L., Wells, G. L., & O'Connor, F. J. (1989). Mock-juror belief of accurate and inaccurate eyewitnesses: A replication and extension. *Law and Human Behavior, 13,* 333–340.

Lindsey, K. (1978). When battered women strike back: Murder or self defense? *Viva*, September, 1978, pp. 58–59, 66–74.

Lindskold, S., & Aronoff, J. R. (1980). Conciliatory strategies and relative power. *Journal of Experimental Social Psychology, 16,* 187–198.

Lindskold, S., & Finch, M. L. (1981). Styles of announcing conciliation. *Journal of Conflict Resolution, 25,* 145–155.

Linton, R. (1936). *The study of man.* New York: Appleton-Century.

Linville, P. W. (1982). The complexity-extremity effect and age-based stereotyping. *Journal of Personality and Social Psychology, 42,* 193–211.

Linville, P. W., Fischer, G. W., & Salovey, P. (1989). Perceived distribution of the characteristics of in-group and out-group members: Empirical evidence and a computer simulation. *Journal of Personality and Social Psychology, 57,* 165–188.

Linz, D. (1985). *Sexual violence in media: Effects on male viewers and implications for society.* Unpublished doctoral dissertation, University of Wisconson, Madison.

Linz, D. (1989). Exposure to sexually explicit materials and attitudes toward rape: A comparison of study results. *Journal of Sex Research, 26,* 50–84.

Linz, D., & Donnerstein, E. (1989). The effects of counter-information on the acceptance of rape myths. In D. Zillmann & J. Bryant (Eds.), *Pornography: Research advances and policy considerations.* Hillsdale, NJ: Erlbaum.

Linz, D., & Donnerstein, E. (1988). The methods and merits of pornography research. *Journal of Communication, 38,* 180–184.

Linz, D., Donnerstein, E., & Penrod, S. (1984). The effects of multiple exposures to filmed violence against women. *Journal of Communication, 34,* 130–147.

Linz, D., Donnerstein, E., & Penrod, S. (1987). The findings and recommendations of the Attorney General's Commission on pornography: Do the psychological "facts" fit the political fury? *American Psychologist, 42,* 946–953.

Linz, D. G., Donnerstein, E., & Penrod, S. (1988). Effects of long-term exposure to violent and sexually degrading depictions of women. *Journal of Personality and Social Psychology, 55,* 758–768.

Lippmann, W. (1922). *Public opinion.* New York: Harcourt Brace.

Lloyd, S. A., Cate, R. M., & Henton, J. M. (1984). Predicting premarital relationship stability: A methodological refinement. *Journal of Marriage and the Family, 46,* 71–76.

Locke, D., & Pennington, D. (1982). Reasons and other causes: Their role in attribution processes. *Journal of Personality and Social Psychology, 42,* 212–223.

Locke, E. A., Shaw, K. N., Saari, L. M., & Latham, G. P. (1981). Goal setting and task performance: 1969–1980. *Psychological Bulletin, 90,* 125–152.

Lockhart v. McCree (1986). 106 S. Ct. 1758, 54 U.S. L. W. 4449.

Locksley, A., Ortiz, V., & Hepburn, C. (1980). Social categorization and discriminatory behavior: Extinguishing the minimal intergroup discrimination effect. *Journal of Personality and Social Psychology, 39,* 773–783.

Lofland, J., & Stark, R. (1965). Becoming a world-saver: A theory of conversion to a deviant perspective. *American Sociological Review, 30,* 862–875.

Loftus, E. F. (1979). *Eyewitness testimony.* Cambridge: Harvard University Press.

Loftus, E. F. (1980). *Memories are made of this: New insights into the workings of human memory.* Reading, MA: Addison-Wesley.

Loftus, E. F., & Monahan, J. (1980). Trial by data: Psychological research as legal evidence. *American Psychologist, 35,* 270–283.

Loftus, E. F., & Palmer, J. C. (1974). Reconstruction of automobile destruction: An example of the interaction between language and memory. *Journal of Verbal Learning and Verbal Behavior, 13,* 585–589.

Lombroso, C. (1899/1911). *Crime: Its causes and remedies.* Boston: Little, Brown.

London, K. A., & Wilson, B. F. (1988). Divorce. *American Demographics.* October, 1988, pp. 22–26.

Longfellow, C. (1979). Divorce in context: Its impact on children. In G. Levinger & O. Moles (Eds.), *Divorce and separation: Context, courses, and consequences.* New York: Basic Books.

Longley, J., & Pruitt, D. G. (1980). Groupthink: A critique of Janis's theory. In L. Wheeler (Ed.), *Review of Personality and Social Psychology* (Vol. 1, pp. 74–93). Beverly Hills, CA: Sage.

Loo, C. M. (1977). Beyond the effects of crowding: Situational and individual differences. In D. Stokols (Ed.), *Perspectives on environment and behavior.* New York: Plenum.

Lord, C. G. (1980). Schemas and images as memory aids: Two modes of processing social information. *Journal of Personality and Social Psychology, 38,* 257–269.

Lord, R. G. (1977). Functional leadership behavior: Measurement and relation to social power and leadership perceptions. *Administrative Science Quarterly, 22,* 114–133.

Lord, R. G., DeVader, C. L., & Alliger, G. M. (1986). A meta-analysis of the relation between personality traits and leadership perceptions: An application of validity generalization procedures. *Journal of Applied Psychology, 71,* 402–410.

Lord, R. G., Foti, R. J., & DeVader, C. L. (1984). A test of leadership categorization theory: Internal structure, information processing, and leadership perceptions. *Organizational Behavior and Human Performance, 34,* 343–378.

Lorenz, K. (1966). *On aggression.* New York: Harcourt, Brace & World.

Luchins, A. S., & Luchins, E. H. (1942). Mechanization in problem-solving: The effect of einstellung. *Psychological Monographs, 54*(6).

Luchins, A. S., & Luchins, E. H. (1963). Half-views and the autokinetic effect. *Psychological Record, 13,* 415–444.

Lumsdaine, A. A., & Janis, I. L. (1953). Resistance to "counter-propaganda" produced by one-sided and two-sided "propaganda" presentations. *Public Opinion Quarterly, 17,* 311–318.

Lykken, D. T. (1979). The detection of deception. *Psychological Bulletin, 86,* 47–53.

Lykken, D. T. (1981). The lie detector and the law. *Criminal Defense, 8,* 19–27.

Maass, A., & Clark, R. D., III (1983). Internalization versus compliance: Differential processes underlying minority influence and conformity. *European Journal of Social Psychology, 12,* 89–104.

Maass, A., & Clark, R. D., III (1984). Hidden impact of minorities: Fifteen years of minority influence research. *Psychological Bulletin, 95,* 428–450.

Maass, A., & Koehnken, G. (1989). Eyewitness identification: Simulating the weapon effect. *Law and Human Behavior, 13,* 397–408.

Maass, A., Clark, R. D., III, & Haberkorn, G. (1982). The effects of differential ascribed category membership and norms on minority influence. *European Journal of Social Psychology, 12,* 89–104.

MacCoun, R. J., & Kerr, N. L. (1988). Asymmetric influence in mock jury deliberation: Jurors' bias for leniency. *Journal of Personality and Social Psychology, 54,* 21–33.

Mackie, D. M. (1986). Social identification effects in group polarization. *Journal of Personality and Social Psychology, 50,* 720–728.

Macklin, E. D. (1983). Nonmarital heterosexual cohabitation. In A. S. Skolnick & J. H. Skolnick (Eds.), *Family in transition* (4th Ed.). Boston: Little, Brown.

Macklin, E. D. (1983). Nonmarital heterosexual cohabilitation: An overview. In E. D. Macklin & R. H. Rubin (Eds.) *Contemporary families and alternative lifestyles. Handbook on research and theory* (pp. 49–73). Beverly Hills, CA: Sage.

Maddux, J. E., & Rogers, R. W. (1983). Protection motivation and self-efficacy: A revised theory of fear appeals and attitude change. *Journal of Experimental Social Psychology, 19,* 469–479.

Magnuson, E. (1989). Seven deadly days. *Time,* July 17, 1989, pp. 30ff.

Major, B., Carrington, P. I. & Carnevale, P. J. D. (1984). Physical attractiveness and self-esteem: Attributions for praise from an other-sex evaluator. *Personality and Social Psychology Bulletin, 10,* 43–50.

Malamuth, N. M. (1983). Factors associated with rape as predictors of laboratory aggression against women. *Journal of Personality and Social Psychology, 45,* 432–442.

Malamuth, N. M (1984). Aggression against women: Cultural and individual causes. In N. M. Malamuth & E. Donnnerstein (Eds.), *Poronography and sexual aggression* (pp. 19–52). New York: Academic Press.

Malamuth, N. M. (1986). Predictors of naturalistic sexual aggression. *Journal of Personality and Social Psychology, 50,* 953–962.

Malamuth, N. M., & Ceniti, J. (1986). Repeated exposure to violent and nonviolent pornography: Likelihood of raping ratings and laboratory aggression against women. *Aggressive Behavior, 12,* 129–136.

Malamuth, N., & Check, J. V. P. (1981). The effects of mass media exposure on acceptance of violence against women: A field experiment. *Journal of Research in Personality, 15,* 436–446.

Malamuth, N. M., & Check, J. V. P. (1983). Sexual arousal to rape depictions: Individual differences. *Journal of Abnormal Psychology, 92,* 55–67.

Malamuth, N. M., & Check, J. V. P. (1985). The effects of aggressive pornography on beliefs of rape myths: Individual differences. *Journal of Research in Personality, 19,* 299–320.

Malamuth, N. M., & Donnerstein, E. I. (1984).(Eds.) *Pornography and sexual aggression.* New York: Academic Press.

Malamuth, N. M., Heim, M., & Feshbach, S. (1980). Sexual responsiveness of college students to rape depictions: Inhibitory and disinhibitory effects. *Journal of Personality and Social Psychology, 38,* 399–408.

Malpass, R. S. (1981). Effective size and defendant bias in eyewitness identification lineups. *Law and Human Behavior, 5,* 299–309.

Manis, M., Paskewitz, J., & Colter, S. (1986). Stereotypes and social judgement. *Journal of Personality and Social Psychology, 50,* 461–473.

Mann, R. D. (1959). A review of the relationship between personality and performance in small groups. *Psychological Bulletin, 56,* 241–270.

Manstead, A. S. R., Wagner, H. L., & MacDonald, C. J. (1984). Face, body, and speech as channels of communication in the detection of deception. *Basic and Applied Social Psychology, 5,* 317–332.

Manucia, G. K., Baumann, D. J., & Cialdini, R. B. (1984). Mood influences on helping: Direct effects or side effects? *Journal of Personality and Social Psychology, 46,* 357–364.

Maret, E., & Finlay, B. (1984). The distribution of household labor among women in dual-career families. *Journal of Marriage and the Family, 46,* 357–364.

Mark, M. M., & Bryant, F. B. (1984). Potential pitfalls of a more applied social psychology: Review and recommendations. *Basic and Applied Social Psychology, 5,* 231–253.

Mark, M. M., & Folger, R. (1984). Responses to relative deprivation: A conceptual framework. In P. Shaver (Ed.), *Review of personality and social psychology* (Vol. 5, pp. 192–218). Beverly Hills, CA: Sage.

Markey, E. J. (1985). The politics of arms control: A matter of perception. *American Psychologist, 40,* 557–560.

Marks, G., Miller, N., & Maruyama, G. (1981). The effect of physical attractiveness on assumptions of similarity. *Journal of Personality and Social Psychology, 41,* 198–206.

Markus, H. (1980). The self in thought and memory. In D. M. Wegner & R. R. Vallacher (Eds.), *The self in social psychology*. New York: Oxford University Press.

Markus, H., Crane, M., Bernstein, S., & Siladi, M. (1982). Self-schemas and gender. *Journal of Personality and Social Psychology, 42,* 38–50.

Markus, H., Smith, J., & Moreland, R. L. (1985). Role of the self-concept in the perception of others. *Journal of Personality and Social Psychology, 49,* 1494–1512.

Marques, J. M., & Yzerbyt, V. Y. (1988). The "black sheep effect": Judgmental extremity toward ingroup members in inter- and intra-group situations. *European Journal of Social Psychology, 18,* 287–292.

Marques, J. M., Yzerbyt, V. Y., & Leyens, J. P. (1988). The "black sheep effect": Extremity of judgments towards in group-members as a function of group identification. *European Journal of Social Psychology, 18,* 1–16.

Marsden, H. M. (1972). Crowding and animal behavior. In J. F. Wohlwill & D. F Carson (Eds.), *Environment and the social sciences: Perspectives and applications*. Washington, DC: American Psychological Association.

Marshall, G. D., & Zimbardo, P. G. (1979). Affective consequences of inadequately explained physiological arousal. *Journal of Personality and Social Psychology, 37,* 970–988.

Martin, G. B., & Clark, R. D., III. (1982). Distress crying in neonates: Species and peer specificity. *Developmental Psychology, 18,* 3–9.

Martin, J. (1986). The tolerance of injustice. In J. M. Olson, C. P. Herman & M. P. Zanna (Eds.), *Relative deprivation and social comparison: The Ontario Symposium,* (Vol. 4, pp. 217–242). Hillsdale, N.J: Erlbaum.

Martindale, D. (1971). Territorial dominance behavior in dyadic verbal interactions. *Proceedings of the 79th Annual Convention of the A.P.A., 6,* 305–306.

Martz, L. (1989a). The hero's clay feet. *Newsweek,* May 15, 1989, pp. 32–37.

Martz, L. (1989b). Reagan's role and Ollie's trial. *Newsweek,* April 10, 1989, p. 26.

Maruyama, G., & Miller, N. (1981). Physical attractiveness and personality. In A. Maher & W. B. Maher (Eds.), *Progress in experimental personality research*. New York: Academic Press.

Maslach, C. (1979). Negative emotional biasing of unexplained arousal. *Journal of Personality and Social Psychology, 37,* 953–969.

Masters, J. C. (1984). Psychology, research and social policy. *American Psychologist, 39,* 851–862.

Masters, W. H., & Johnson, V. E. (1970). *Human sexual inadequacy.* Boston: Little, Brown.

Masters, W., Johnson, V., & Kolodny, R. (1988). *Crisis: Heterosexual behavior in the age of AIDS.* New York: Grove Press.

Mathes, E. W. (1975). The effects of physical attractiveness and anxiety on heterosexual attraction over a series of five encounters. *Journal of Marriage and Family, 37,* 769–773.

Mathes, E. W., Adams, H. E., & Davis, R. M. (1985). Jealousy: Loss of relationship rewards, loss of self-esteem, depression, anxiety, and anger. *Journal of Personality and Social Psychology, 48,* 1552–1561.

Matthews, C. S., & Clark, R. D. III. (1982). Marital satisfaction: A validation approach. *Basic and Applied Social Psychology, 3,* 169–186.

Matthews, K. A. (1982). Psychological perspectives on the Type A behavior pattern. *Psychological Bulletin, 91,* 293–323.

Matthews, K. A. (1988). Coronary heart disease and Type A behaviors: Update on an alternative to the Booth-Kewley and Friedman (1987) quantitative review. *Psychological Bulletin, 104,* 373–380.

Matthews, K. A., Glass, D. C., Rosenman, R. H., & Bortner, R. W. (1977). Competitive drive, pattern A, and coronary heart disease: A further analysis of some data from the Western Collaborative Group Study. *Journal of Chronic Disease, 30,* 489–498.

Matthews, K. A., Helmreich, R. A., Beane, W. E., & Lucher, G. W. (1980). Pattern A, achievement striving, and scientific merit: Does pattern A help or hinder? *Journal of Personality and Social Psychology, 39,* 962–967.

Matthews, K. A., Rosenfield, D., & Stephan, W. G. (1979). Playing hard-to-get: A two-determinant model. *Journal of Research in Personality, 13,* 234–244.

Matthews, K. A., & Seigel, J. M. (1983). Type A behaviors by children, social comparison, and standards for self-evaluation. *Developmental Psychology, 19,* 135–140.

Matthews, K. E., & Cannon, L. K. (1975). Environmental noise level as a determinant of helping behavior. *Journal of Personality and Social Psychology, 32,* 571–577.

Mausner, B. (1954). The effect of prior reinforcement on the interaction of observer pairs. *Journal of Abnormal and Social Psychology, 49,* 65–68.

May, R. (1971). Letters to the editor. *New York Times Magazine,* April 1971, p. 100.

Maykovich, M. K. (1975). Correlates of racial prejudice. *Journal of Personality and Social Psychology, 32,* 1014–1020.

Mayo, E. (1933). *The human problems of an industrial civilization.* New York: Macmillan.

Mazelan, P. M. (1980). Stereotypes and perceptions of the victims of rape. *Victimology, 5,* 121–132.

Mazis, M. B. (1975). Antipollution measures and psychological reactance theory: A field experiment. *Journal of Personality and Social Psychology, 31,* 654–660.

McAllister, H. A., & Bregman, N. J. (1986). Plea bargaining by prosecutors and defense attorneys: A decision theory approach. *Journal of Applied Psychology, 71,* 585–590.

McAuliffe, W. E., Doerning, S., Breer, P., Silverman, H., Branson, B., & Williams. K. (1987). *An evaluation of using ex-addict outreach workers to educate intravenous drug users about AIDS prevention.* Paper presented at the Third International Conference on AIDS, Washington, DC.

McCallum, D. M., Haring, K., Gilmore, R., Drenan, S., Chase, J. P., Insko, C. A., & Thibaut, J. (1985). Competition and cooperation between groups and between individuals. *Journal of Experimental Social Psychology, 21,* 301–320.

McCallum, R., Rusbult, C., Hong, G. C., Walden, T. A., & Schopler, J. (1979). Effects of resource availability and importance of behavior in the experience of crowding. *Journal of Personality and Social Psychology, 37,* 1304–1313.

McCaul, K. D., Veltum, L. G., Boyechko, V., & Crawford, J. J. (1990). Understanding attributions of victim blame for rape: Sex, violence, and forseeability. *Journal of Applied Social Psychology, 20,* 1–26.

McCauley, C. (1989). The nature of social influence in groupthink: Compliance and internalization. *Journal of Personality and Social Psychology, 57,* 250–260.

McClelland, D. (1975). *Power: The inner experience.* New York: Irvington.

McClintock, C. G., & Allison, S. T. (1989). Social value orientation and helping behavior. *Journal of Applied Social Psychology, 19,* 353–362.

McConahay, J. B. (1978). The effects of school desegregation upon students' racial attitudes and behavior: A critical review of the literature and a prolegomenon to future research. *Law and Contemporary Problems, 42*(3), 77–107.

McConahay, J. B. (1981). Reducing racial prejudice in desegregated schools. In W. D. Hawley (Ed.), *Effective school desegregation: Equity, quality, and feasibility* (pp. 35–53). Beverly Hills, CA: Sage.

McConahay, J. B. (1982). Self-interest versus racial attitudes as correlates of anti-busing in Louisville: Is it the buses or the blacks? *Journal of Politics, 44,* 692–720.

McConahay, J. B. (1986). Modern racism, ambivalence and the modern racism scale. In J. F. Dovidio & S. L. Gaertner, (Eds.), *Prejudice, discrimination, and racism* (pp. 91–126). Orlando, FL: Academic Press.

McConahay, J. B., Hardee, B. B., & Batts, V. (1981). Has racism declined in America? *Journal of Conflict Resolution, 25,* 563–579.

McConahay, J. B., & Hough, J. C., Jr. (1976). Symbolic racism. *Journal of Social Issues, 32*(2), 23–45.

McConnell, M. (1987). *Challenger: A major malfunction.* New York: Doubleday.

McDougall, W. (1908). *An introduction to social psychology.* London: Methuen.

McGillis, D. (1981). Conflict resolution outside the courts. In L. Bickman (Ed.), *Applied social psychology annual* (Vol. 2). Beverly Hills, CA: Sage.

McGregor, D. (1966). *Leadership and motivation.* Boston: MIT Press.

McGuire, W. J. (1964). Inducing resistance to persuasion: Some contemporary approaches. In L. Berkowitz (Ed.), *Advances in experimental social psychology* (Vol. 1). New York: Academic Press.

McGuire, W. J. (1967). Some impending reorientations in social psychology: Some thoughts provoked by Kenneth Ring. *Journal of Experimental Social Psychology, 3,* 124–139.

McGuire, W. J. (1968a). Personality and susceptibility to social influence. In E. F. Borgatta & W. W. Lambert (Eds.), *Handbook of personality theory and research.* Chicago: Rand McNally.

McGuire, W. J. (1968b). Personality and attitude change: An information processing theory. In A. G. Greenwald, T. C. Brock, & T. M. Ostrom (Eds.), *Psychological foundations of attitudes* (pp. 171–196). New York: Academic Press.

McGuire, W. J. (1969). The nature of attitudes and attitude change. In G. Lindzey & E. Aronson (Eds.), *The handbook of social psychology* (2nd ed.) (Vol. 3, pp. 136–314). Reading, MA: Addison-Wesley.

McGuire, W. J. (1989). The structure of individual attitudes and attitude systems. In A. R. Pratkanis, S. J. Brecker, & A. G. Greenwald (Eds.), *Attitude structure and function.* Hillsdale, NJ: Erlbaum.

McGuire, W. J., & McGuire, C. V. (1982). Significant others in self space: Sex differences and developmental trends in the social self. In J. Suls (Ed.), *Psychological perspectives on the self.* Hillsdale, NJ: Erlbaum.

McGuire, W. J., & Papageorgis, D. (1961). The relative efficacy of various types of prior belief-defense in producing immunity against persuasion. *Journal of Abnormal and Social Psychology, 62,* 327–337.

McKay, A. (1974). View on genetic counseling and family planning. In *First International Conference on the Mental Health Aspects of Sickle-Cell Anemia.* DHEW publication no. (HSM) 73–9141. Washington, DC: U.S. Government Printing Office.

McMillen, D. C., Sanders, D. Y., & Solomon, G. S. (1977). Self-esteem, attentiveness, and helping behavior. *Personality and Social Psychology Bulletin, 3,* 257–261.

McNeel, S. P. (1973). Training cooperation in the prisoner's dilemma. *Journal of Experimental Social Psychology, 9,* 335–348.

Mealey, L. (1985). Comment on genetic similarity theory. *Behavior Genetics, 15,* 571–574.

Mednick, S. A., Pollock, V., Volovka, J., & Gabrielli, W. F., Jr. (1982). Biology and violence. In M. E. Wolfgang & N. A. Weiner (Eds.), *Criminal violence.* Beverly Hills, CA: Sage.

Megargee, E. I. (1982). Psychological determinants and correlates of criminal violence. In M. E. Wolfgang & N. A. Weiner (Eds.), *Criminal violence.* Beverly Hills, CA: Sage.

Megargee, E. I. (1984). Aggression and violence. In H. E. Adams & P. B. Suther (Eds), *Comprehensive handbook of psychopathology* (pp. 523–545). New York: Plenum.

Megargee, E. I. (in press). Aggression and violence. In H. E. Adams & P. E. Sutker (Eds.), *Comprehensive handbook of psychopathology* (2nd ed.). New York: Plenum.

Mehlman, R. C., & Snyder, C. R. (1985). Excuse theory: A test of the self-protective role of attributions. *Journal of Personality and Social Psychology, 49,* 994–1001.

Mehrabian, A. (1981). *Silent messages: Implicit communication of emotions and attitudes* (2nd ed.). Belmont, CA: Wadsworth.

Meindl, J. R., & Lerner, M. J. (1984). Exacerbation of extreme responses to an out-group. *Journal of Personality and Social Psychology, 47,* 71–84.

Menaghan, E. (1982). Measuring coping effectiveness: A panel analysis of marital problems and coping efforts. *Journal of Health and Social Behaviors, 23,* 220–234.

Messick, D. M., & Brewer, M. B. (1983). Solving social dilemmas: A review. In L. Wheeler & P. Shaver (Eds.), *Review of personality and social psychology* (Vol. 4, pp. 11–44). Beverly Hills, CA: Sage.

Messick, D. M., & Mackie, D. M. (1989). Intergroup relations. *Annual Review of Psychology, 40,* 45–81.

Messick, D. M., & McClelland, C. L. (1983). Social traps and temporal traps. *Personality and Social Psychology Bulletin, 9,* 105–110.

Mettee, D. R., & Wilkins, P. C. (1972). When similarity "hurts": Effects of perceived ability and a humorous blunder on interpersonal attractiveness. *Journal of Personality and Social Psychology, 22,* 246–258.

Meyer, A. J., Nash, J. D., McAllister, A. L., Maccoby, N., & Farquhar, J. W. (1980). Skills training in a cardiovascular health education campaign. *Journal of Consulting and Clinical Psychology, 48,* 129–192.

Meyer, J. P., & Koelbl, S. L. M. (1982). Dimensionality of students' causal attributions for test performance. *Personality and Social Psychology Bulletin, 8,* 31–36.

Michael, R. P., & Zumpe, D. (1986). An annual rhythm in the battering of women. *American Journal of Psychiatry, 143,* 637–640.

Michaels, J. W., Blommel, J. M., Brokato, R. M., Linkous, R. A., & Rowe, J. S. (1982). Social facilitation and inhibition in a natural setting. *Replications in Social Psychology, 2,* 21–24.

Michelini, R. L., & Snodgrass, S. R. (1980). Defendant characteristics and juridic decisions. *Journal of Research in Personality, 14,* 340–350.

Michelson, W. (1970). *Man and his urban environment.* Reading, MA: Addison-Wesley.

Mikulincer, M., & Nizan, B. (1988). Causal attribution, cognitive interference, and the generalization of learned helplessness. *Journal of Personality and Social Psychology, 55,* 470–478.

Milgram, S. (1963). Behavioral study of obedience. *Journal of Abnormal and Social Psychology, 67,* 371–378.

Milgram, S. (1964). Issues in the study of obedience: A reply to Baumrind. *American Psychologist, 19,* 848–852.

Milgram, S. (1965a). Some conditions of obedience and disobedience to authority, *Human Relations, 18,* 57–76.

Milgram, S. (1965b). Liberating effects of group pressure. *Journal of Personality and Social Psychology, 1,* 127–134.

Milgram, S. (1970). The experience of living in cities: A psychological analysis. In F. F. Korten, S. W. Cook, & J. I. Lacey (Eds.), *Psychology and the problems of society.* Washington, DC: American Psychological Association.

Milgram, S. (1974). *Obedience to authority.* New York: Harper & Row.

Millar, M. G., Millar, K. V., & Tesser, A. (1988). The effects of helping and focus of attention on mood states. *Personality and Social Psychology Bulletin, 14,* 536–543.

Miller, A. G. (1982). Historical and contemporary perspectives on stereotyping. In A. G. Miller (Ed.), *In the eye of the beholder: Contemporary issues in stereotyping* (pp. 1–40). New York: Praeger.

Miller, A. G., & Lawson, T. (1989). The effect of an informational option on the fundamental attribution error. *Personality and Social Psychology Bulletin, 15,* 194–204.

Miller, D. T., & McFarland, C. (1987). Pluralistic ignorance: When similarity is interpreted as dissimilarity. *Journal of Personality and Social Psychology, 53,* 298–305.

Miller, D. T., & Ross, M. (1975). Self-serving biases in the attribution of causality: Fact or fiction? *Psychological Bulletin, 82,* 213–225.

Miller, G. A. (1969). Psychology as a means of promoting human welfare. *American Psychologist, 24,* 1063–1075.

Miller, I., & Norman, W. (1979). Learned helplessness in humans: A review and attribution theory model. *Psychological Bulletin, 86,* 93–118.

Miller, N. E. (1941). The frustration-aggression hypothesis. *Psychological Review, 48,* 337–342.

Miller, N., & Campbell, D. (1959). Recency and primacy in persuasion as a function of the timing of speeches and measurements. *Journal of Abnormal and Social Psychology, 59,* 1–9.

Miller, N., & Carlson, M. (1990). Valid theory-testing meta-analyses further question the negative state relief model of helping. *Psychological Bulletin, 107,* 215–225.

Miller, P. A., & Eisenberg, N. (1988). The relation of empathy to aggressive and externalizing/antisocial behavior. *Psychological Bulletin, 103,* 324–344.

Miller, R. E., & Sarat, A. (1981). Grievances, claims, and disputes: Assessing the adversary culture. *Law and Society Review, 15,* 525–565.

Mills, C. J., & Bohannon, W. E. (1980). Character structure and jury behavior: Conceptual and applied implications. *Journal of Personality and Social Psychology, 38,* 662–667.

Mills, J. (1969). The experimental method. In J. Mills (Ed.), *Experimental social psychology* (pp. 407–448). New York: Macmillan.

Mineka, S., & Kihlstrom, J. (1978). Unpredictable and uncontrollable events: A new perspective on experimental neurosis. *Journal of Abnormal Psychology, 87,* 256–271.

Mita, T. H., Dermer, M., & Knight, J. (1977). Reversed facial images and the mere-exposure hypothesis. *Journal of Personality and Social Psychology, 35,* 597–601.

Mitchell, H. E. (1979). *Informational and affective determinants of juror decision making.* Unpublished doctoral dissertation, Purdue University.

Mitchell, H. E., & Byrne, D. (1982). Minimizing the influence of irrelevant factors in the courtroom: The defendant's character, judge's instructions, and authoritarianism. In K. M. White & J. C. Speisman (Eds.), *Research approaches to personality.* Monterey, CA: Brooks/Cole.

Mitchell, R. (1971). Some social implications of higher density housing. *American Sociological Review, 36,* 18–29.

Moe, J. L., Nacoste, R. W., & Insko, C. A. (1981). Belief versus race as determinants of discrimination: A study of Southern adolescents in 1966 and 1979. *Journal of Personality and Social Psychology, 41,* 1031–1050.

Montagu, A. (1976). *The nature of human aggression.* New York: Oxford University Press.

Moos, R. H., & Billings, A. G. (1982). Conceptualizing and measuring coping resources and processes. In L. Goldberger & S. Breznitz (Eds.), *Handbook of stress* (pp. 212–230). New York: Macmillan.

Moran, G., & Comfort, J. C. (1986). Neither "tentative" nor "fragmentary": Verdict preference of impaneled felony jurors as a function of attitude toward capital punishment. *Journal of Applied Psychology, 71,* 146–155.

Morris, D. (1968). *The naked ape.* New York: McGraw-Hill.

Morris, J. N., & Crawford, M.D. (1958). Coronary heart disease and physical activity of work. *British Medical Journal,* Dec. 20, 1958, pp. 1485–1496.

Morris, J. N., Heady, J. A., Raffle, P. A. B., Roberts, C. G., & Parks, J. W. (1953). Coronary heart disease and physical activity of work. *The Lancet,* Nov. 21, 1953, pp. 1053–1057.

Morris, L. A., & Halperin, J. (1979). Effects of written drug information on patient knowledge and compliance: A literature review. *American Journal of Public Health, 69,* 47–52.

Moscovici, S. (1980). Toward a theory of conversion behavior. In L. Berkowitz (Ed.), *Advances in experimental social psychology* (Vol. 13, pp. 209–239). New York: Academic Press.

Moscovici, S., Lage, E., & Naffrechoux, M. (1969). Influence of a consistent minority on the responses of a majority in a color perception task. *Sociometry, 32,* 365–379.

Moscovici, S., & Nemeth, C. (1974). Social influence: Minority influence. In C. Nemeth (Ed.), *Social psychology: Classic and contemporary integrations.* (pp. 217–249). Chicago: Rand McNally.

Moscovici, S., & Personnaz, B. (1980). Studies in social influence: V. Minority influence and conversion behavior in a perceptual task. *Journal of Experimental Social Psychology, 16,* 270–282.

Moses, H. (Producer), (1983). The devil is a gentleman. *60 Minutes, 15*(21), February 6, 1983.

Mosher, D. L. (1965). Approval motive and acceptance of "fake" personality test interpretations which differ in favorability. *Psychological Reports, 17,* 395–402.

Moss, M. K., & Page. R. A. (1972). Reinforcement and helping behavior. *Journal of Applied Social Psychology, 2,* 360–371.

Muecher, H., & Ungeheuer, H. (1961). Meteorological influence on reaction time, flicker-fusion frequency, job accidents, and medical treatment. *Perceptual and Motor Skills, 12,* 163–168.

Muehlenhard, C. L., & Linton, M.A. (1987). Date rape and sexual aggression in dating situations: Incidence and risk factors. *Journal of Consulting Psychology, 34,* 186–196.

Mueller, C., & Donnerstein, E. (1977). The effects of humor-induced arousal upon aggressive behavior. *Journal of Research in Personality, 11,* 73–82.

Mueller, C., Donnerstein, E., & Hallam, J. (1983). Violent films and prosocial behavior. *Personality and Social Psychology Bulletin, 9,* 83–89.

Mueller, J. H. (1982). Self-awareness and access to material rated as self-descriptive or nondescriptive. *Bulletin of the Psychonomic Society, 19,* 323–326.

Mueser, K. T., Grau, B. W., Sussman, S., & Rosen, A. J. (1984). You're only as pretty as you feel: Facial expression as a determinant of physical attractiveness. *Journal of Personality and Social Psychology, 46,* 469–478.

Mullen, B. (1983). Operationalizing the effect of the group on the individual: A self-attention perspective. *Journal of Experimental Social Psychology, 19,* 295–322.

Mullen, B., & Felleman, B. (1990). Tripling in the dorms: A meta-analytic integration. *Basic and Applied Social Psychology, 11,* 33–44.

Mullen, B., Atkins, J. L., Champion, D. S., Edwards, C., Hardy, D., Story, J. E., & Vanderklok, M. (1985). The false consensus effect: A meta-analysis of 115 hypothesis tests. *Journal of Experimental Social Psychology, 21,* 262–283.

Mullen, B., Futrell, D., Stairs, D., Tice, D., Baumeister, R., Dawson, K., Riordan, C., Radloff, C., Kennedy, J., & Rosenfeld, P. (1986). Newscasters' facial expressions and voting behavior of viewers. *Journal of Personality and Social Psychology, 51,* 291–295.

Mullen, B., & Hu, L. (1988). Social projection as a function of cognitive mechanisms: Two meta-analytic integrations. *British Journal of Social Psychology, 27,* 333–356.

Munsterberg, H. (1908). *On the witness stand.* New York: Doubleday.

Murchinson, C. (Ed.).(1935). H*andbook of social psychology.* Worchester, MA: Clark University Press.

Murray, D. M., Johnson, C. A., Leupker, R. V., & Mittelmark, M. B. (1984). The prevention of cigarette smoking in children: A comparison of four strategies. *Journal of Social Psychology, 14,* 274–288.

Murstein, B. I. (1970). Stimulus-value-role: A theory of marital choice. *Journal of Marriage and the Family, 32,* 465–481.

Murstein, B. I. (1972). Physical attractiveness and marital choice. *Journal of Personality and Social Psychology, 22,* 8–12.

Murstein, B. I. (1976). *Who will marry whom.* New York: Springer.

Murstein, B. I. (1986). *Paths to marriage.* Beverly Hills, CA: Sage.

Murstein, B. I. (1987). A clarification and extension of the SVR Theory of dynamic pairing. *Journal of Marriage and the Family, 49,* 929–933.

Murstein, B. I., & Christy, P. (1976). Physical attractiveness and marriage adjustment in middle-aged couples. *Journal of Personality and Social Psychology, 34,* 537–542.

Myers, D. G. (1978). Polarizing effects of social comparison. *Journal of Experimental Social Psychology, 14,* 554–563.

Myers, D. G., & Kaplan, M. F. (1976). Group-induced polarization in simulated juries. *Personality and Social Psychology Bulletin, 2,* 63–66.

Myrdal, A. (1976). *The game of disarmament: How the United States and the Russians run the arms race.* New York: Pantheon.

Nacoste, R. (1989). Affirmative action and self-evaluation. In F. A. Blanchard & F. J. Crosby (Eds.). *Affirmative action in perspective* (pp. 103–109). New York: Springer-Verlag.

Nadler, A., & Fisher, J. D. (1986). The role of threat to self-esteem and perceived control in recipient reaction to help: Theory development and empirical validation. In L. Berkowitz (Ed.), *Advances in experimental social psychology.* (Vol. 19, pp. 81–122). Orlando, FL: Academic Press.

Nakanishi, D. T. (1988). Seeking convergence in race relations research: Japanese-Americans and the resurrection of internment. In P. A. Katz & D. A. Taylor (Eds.), *Eliminating racism: Profiles in controversy* (pp. 159–180). New York: Plenum.

Nasby, W. (1989a). Private and public self-consciousness and articulation of the self-schema. *Journal of Personality and Social Psychology, 56,* 117–123.

Nasby, W. (1989b). Private self-consciousness, self-awareness, and the reliability of self-reports. *Journal of Personality and Social Psychology, 56,* 950–957.

Nathan, P. E. (1983). Failures in prevention: Why we can't prevent the devastating effect of alcoholism and drug abuse? *American Psychologist, 38,* 459–467.

Nathan, P. E., & Briddell, D. W. (1976). Behavior assessment and treatment of alcoholism. In B. Kissin & H. Begleiter (Eds.), *The biology of treatment and rehabilitation of the chronic alcoholic* (pp. 567–658). New York: Plenum.

National Center for Health Statistics. (1989a). *Study: Wives usually initiate U. S. divorces. Tallahassee Democrat,* June 7, 1989, p. 7A.

National Center for Health Statistics. (1989b). *Monthly vital statistics, 1987. Vol. 38, Supplement no. 5* (Sept. 26, 1989). Washington, DC.: U. S. Government Printing Office.

NCTV News: *National Coalition on Television Violence News,* various dates.

National Transportation Safety Board (NTSB) (1979). *Aircraft accident report* (NTSB-AAR-79-7). Washington, DC: NTSB Bureau of Accident Investigation (NTIS No. N80-11051).

Neil v. Biggers 409 U.S. 188, 93 S. Ct. 375; 34 L. Ed. 2d 401 (1972).

Neisser, U. (1976). *Cognition and reality: Principles and implications of cognitive psychology.* San Francisco: Freeman.

Nemeth, C. J. (1986). Differential contributions of majority and minority influence. *Psychological Review, 93,* 23–32.

Neuberg, S. L., & Fiske, S. T. (1987). Motivational influences in impression formation: Outcome dependency, accuracy-driven attention, and individuating processes. *Journal of Personality and Social Psychology, 53,* 431–444.

Newcomb, T. M. (1958). Attitude development as a function of reference group: The Bennington study. In E. E. Maccoby, T. M. Newcomb, & E. L. Hartley (Eds.), *Readings in social psychology* (3rd ed.). New York: Holt, Rinehart & Winston.

Newcomb, T. M. (1961). *The acquaintance process.* New York: Holt.

Newcomb, T. M., Koenig, K. E., Flacks, R., & Warwick, D. P. (1967). *Persistence and change: Bennington College and its students after 25 years.* New York: Wiley.

Newman, O. (1972). *Defensible space: Crime prevention through urban design.* New York: Macmillan.

New York Times Staff. (1973). *The Watergate hearings: Break-in and cover-up.* New York: Bantam.

Nida, S. A., & Koon, J. (1983). They get better looking at closing time around here, too. *Psychological Reports, 52,* 657–658.

Nietzel, M. T., & Dillehay, R. C. (1982). The effects of variations in *voir dire* procedures in capital murder trials. *Law and Human Behavior, 6,* 1–13.

Nisbett, R. E., Caputo, C., Legant, P., & Marecek, J. (1973). Behavior as seen by the actor and as seen by the observer. *Journal of Personality and Social Psychology, 27,* 154–164.

Nisbett, R. E., & Gordon, A. (1967). Self-esteem and susceptibility to social influence. *Journal of Personality and Social Psychology, 5,* 268–276.

Nisbett, R. E., Krantz, D. H., Jepson, C., & Kunda, Z. (1983). The use of statistical heuristics in everyday inductive reasoning. *Psychological Review, 90,* 339–363.

Nisbett, R. E., & Kunda, Z. (1985). Perception of social distributions. *Journal of Personality and Social Psychology, 48,* 297–311.

Nisbett, R. E., & Ross, L. (1980). *Human inference: Strategies and shortcomings of social judgment.* Englewood Cliffs, NJ: Prentice Hall.

Nisbett, R. E., & Schachter, S. (1966). Cognitive manipulation of pain. *Journal of Experimental Social Psychology, 2,* 227–236.

Nisbett, R. E., & Wilson, T. D. (1977). Telling more than we can know: Verbal report on mental processes. *Psychological Review, 84,* 231–259.

Nisbett, R. E., Zukier, H., & Lemley, R. E. (1981). The dilution effect: Nondiagnostic information weakens the implications of diagnostic information. *Cognitive Psychology, 13,* 248–277.

Nord, W. (1969). Social exchange theory: An integrative approach to social conformity. *Psychological Bulletin, 71,* 174–208.

Norell, S. E. (1979). Improving medication compliance: A randomized clinical trial. *British Medical Journal, 2,* 1031–1033.

Norman, R. (1976). When what is said is important: A comparison of expert and attractive sources. *Journal of Experimental Social Psychology, 12,* 294–300.

Norton, A., & Glick, P. (1986). One parent families: A social and economic profile. *Family Relations, 35,* 9–17.

Norvell, N., & Worchel, S. (1981). A reexamination of the relation between equal status contact and intergroup attraction. *Journal of Personality and Social Psychology, 41,* 902–908.

Nunes, E. V., Frank, K. A., & Kornfeld, D. S. (1987). Psychologic treatment for the Type A behavior pattern and for coronary heart disease: A meta-analysis of the literature. *Psychosomatic Medicine, 48,* 159–173.

O'Connor, C. (1986). Someone is going to die. *Newsweek,* March 31, 1986, p. 23.

O'Dell, J. W. (1972). P. T. Barnum explores the computer. *Journal of Consulting and Clinical Psychology, 38,* 270–273.

Office of Technology Assessment. (1983). *Scientific validity of polygraph testing: A research review and evaluation* (technical memorandum, OTA-TM-H-15). Washington, DC: U. S. Government Printing Office.

O'Keeffe, M. K., Nesselhof-Kendall, S., & Baum, A. (1990). Behavior and prevention of AIDS: Bases of research and intervention. *Personality and Social Psychology Bulletin, 16,* 166–180.

Olsen, M. E. (1981). Consumers' attitudes toward energy conservation. *Journal of Social Issues, 37(2),* 108–131.

Olson, J. M. (1988). Misattribution, preparatory information, and speech anxiety. *Journal of Personality and Social Psychology, 54,* 758–767.

Olson, J. M. (1990). Self-inference processes in emotion. In J. M. Olson & M. P. Zanna (Eds.), *Self-inference processes: The Ontario symposium.* (Vol. 6, pp. 17–41). Hillsdale, NJ: Erlbaum.

Olson, J. M., & Ross, M. (1988). False feedback about placebo effectiveness: Consequences for the misattribution of speech anxiety. *Journal of Experimental Social Psychology, 24,* 275–291.

Orne, M. T. (1962). On the social psychology of the psychological experiment: With particular reference to demand characteristics and their implications. *American Psychologist, 17,* 776–783.

Orne, M. T., & Holland, C. H. (1968). On the ecological validity of laboratory deceptions. *International Journal of Psychiatry, 6,* 282–293.

Osborn, A. F. (1963). *Applied imagination: Principles and procedures of creative problem-solving* (3rd ed.). New York: Scribner.

Osgood, C. E. (1962). *An alternative to war or surrender.* Urbana, IL: University of Illinois Press.

Oskamp, S. (1965). Overconfidence in case-study judgments. *Journal of Consulting Psychology, 29,* 261–265.

Oskamp, S. (1974). Comparison of sequential and simultaneous responding, matrix and strategy variables in a prisoner's dilemma game. *Journal of Conflict Resolution, 18,* 107–116.

Oskamp, S. (1977). *Attitudes and opinions.* Englewood Cliffs, NJ: Prentice-Hall.

Osler, W. (1892). *Lectures on angina pectoris and allied states.* New York: Appleton.

Osmond, H. (1957). Function as a basis of psychiatric ward design. *Mental Hospitals, 8,* 23–29.

O'Sullivan, C. S., & Durso, F. T. (1984). Effect of schema in congruent information on memory for stereotypical attitudes. *Journal of Personality and Social Psychology, 47,* 55–70.

Page, R. A. (1977). Noise and helping behavior. *Environment and Behavior, 9,* 311–335.

Pallak, M. S., Cook, D. A., & Sullivan, J. J. (1980). Commitment and energy conservation. In L. Bickman (Ed.), *Applied social psychology annual* (Vol. 1). Beverly Hills, CA: Sage.

Pantin, H. M., & Carver, C. S. (1982). Induced competence and the bystander effect. *Journal of Applied Social Psychology, 12,* 100–111.

Papadatos, P. (1964). *The Eichmann trial.* New York: Frederick Praeger.

Park, B., & Rothbart, M. (1982). Perception of out-group homogeneity and levels of social categorization: Memory for the subordinate attributes of in-group and out-group members. *Journal of Personality and Social Psychology, 42,* 1051–1068.

Parke, R. D., Berkowitz, L., Leyens, J. P., West, S. G., & Sebastian, J. (1977). Some effects of violent and nonviolent movies on the behavior of juvenile delinquents. In L. Berkowitz (Ed.), *Advances in experimental social psychology* (Vol. 10). New York: Academic Press.

Partridge, A., & Eldridge, C. (1974). *The Second Circuit sentencing study: A report to the judges of the Second Circuit.* Washington, DC: Federal Judicial Center.

Pasahow, R. J., West, S. G., & Boroto, D. R. (1982). Predicting when uncontrollability will produce performance deficits: A refinement of the reformulated learned helplessness hypothesis. *Psychological Review, 89,* 595–598.

Patchen, M. (1982). *Black-white contact in schools: Its social and academic effects.* West Lafayette, IN: Purdue University Press.

Patrick, C. J., & Iacono, W. G. (1987). Reliability and validity of the control question polygraph test: A scientific investigation. *Psychophysiology, 24,* 604–605.

Patrick, C. J., & Iacono, W. G. (1989). Psychopathy, threat, and polygraph test accuracy. *Journal of Applied Psychology, 74,* 347–355.

Patterson, M. L. (1976). An arousal model of interpersonal intimacy. *Psychological Review, 83,* 235–245.

Patterson, T. E. (1980). The role of the mass media in presidential campaigns: The lessons of the 1976 election. *Items, 34,* 25–30.

Paulhus, D. (1982). Individual differences, self-presentation, and cognitive dissonance: Their concurrent operation in forced compliance. *Journal of Personality and Social Psychology, 43,* 838–852.

Paulus, P. B. (1983). Group influence on individual task performance. In P. B. Paulus (Ed.), *Basic group processes* (pp. 97–120). New York: Springer-Verlag.

Paulus, P. B., McCain, G., & Cox, V. (1985). The effects of crowding in prisons and jails. In D. P. Farrington & J. Quinn (Eds.), *Reactions to crime: The public, the police, the courts and prisons*. London: Wiley.

Pavelchak, M. A. (1989). Piecemeal and category-based evaluation: An idiographic analysis. *Journal of Personality and Social Psychology, 56*, 354–360.

Peale, N. V. (1956). *The power of positive thinking*. Englewood Cliffs, NJ: Prentice-Hall.

Pearl, D., Bouthilet, L., & Lazar, J. (Eds.) (1982). *Television and behavior: Ten years of scientific progress and implications for the eighties*. Washington, DC: U.S. Department of Health and Human Services.

Pearlin, L. S., & Johnson, J. S. (1977). Marital status, life strains, and depression. *American Sociological Review, 42*, 704–715.

Pendleton, M. G., & Batson, C. D. (1979). Self-presentation and the door-in-the-face technique for inducing compliance. *Personality and Social Psychology Bulletin, 5*, 77–81.

Pennebaker, J. W., Dyer, M. A., Caulkins, R. S., Litowitz, D. L., Ackerman, P. L., Anderson, D. B., & McGraw, K. M. (1979). Don't the girls all get prettier at closing time: A country and western application to psychology. *Personality and Social Psychology Bulletin, 5*, 122–125.

Pepitone, A. (1981). Lessons from the history of social psychology. *American Psychologist, 36*, 972–985.

Peplau, L. A. (1981). What homosexuals want. *Psychology Today*, March 1981, pp. 28ff.

Peplau, L. A., & Campbell, S. M. (1989). Power in dating and marriage. In J. Freeman (Ed.), *Women: A feminist perspective* (4th edit., pp. 121–137). Mountain View, CA: Mayfield.

Peplau, L. A., & Cochran, S. D. (1980). *Sex differences in values concerning love relationships*. Paper presented at the annual meeting of the American Psychological Association, Montreal.

Peplau, L. A., & Gordon, S. L. (1983). The intimate relationships of lesbians and gay men. In E. R. Allgeier & N. B. McCormick (Eds.), *Gender roles and sexual behavior: The changing boundaries*. Palo Alto, CA: Mayfield.

Perlin, L., & Johnson, J. (1981). Material status, life strains, and depression. In P. Stein (Ed.), *Single life: Unmarried adults in social context* (pp. 165–177). New York: St. Martin's Press.

Perlman, D., & Peplau, L. A. (1982). Loneliness research: Implications for interventions. In L. A. Peplau & S. Goldston (Eds.), *Preventing the harmful consequences of severe and persistent loneliness*. Washington, DC: U.S. Government.

Pernanen, K. (1981). Theoretical aspects of the relationship between alcohol use and crime. In J. Collins (Ed.), *Drinking and crime* (pp. 1–69). New York: Guilford.

Perrin, S., & Spencer, C. (1981). Independence or conformity in the Asch experiment as a reflection of cultural and situational factors. *British Journal of Social Psychology, 20*, 205–209.

Perry, C., Killen, J., Stunkard, L. A., & McAlister, A. L. (1980). Peer teaching and smoking prevention: The relative efficacy of varied treatments and instructor. *Adoloscence, 18*, 561–566.

Peterson, C. (1988). Explanatory style as a risk factor for illness. *Cognitive Therapy and Research, 12*, 119–132.

Peterson, C., Seligman, M. E. P., & Vaillant, G. E. (1988). Pessimistic explanatory style is a risk factor for physical illness: A thirty-five-year longitudinal study. *Journal of Personality and Social Psychology, 55,* 23–27.

Peterson, J. L., & Zill, N. (1986). Marital disruption, parent-child relationships, and behavior problems in children. *Journal of Marriage and the Family, 48,* 295–307.

Pettigrew, T. F. (1961). Social psychology and desegregation research. *American Psychologist, 16,* 105–112.

Pettigrew, T. F. (1971). *Racially separate or together?* New York: McGraw-Hill.

Pettigrew, T. F. (1986). The intergroup contact hypothesis reconsidered. In M. Hewstone & R. Brown (Eds.), *Contact and conflict in intergroup encounters* (pp. 169–195). Oxford, England: Basil Blackwell.

Pettigrew, T. F. (1988). Integration and pluralism. In P. A. Katz & D. A. Taylor (Eds.), *Eliminating racism: Profiles in controversy* (pp. 19–30). New York: Plenum.

Petty, R. E., & Cacioppo, J. T. (1979). Effects of forewarning of persuasive intent and involvement on cognitive response and persuasion. *Personality and Social Psychology Bulletin, 5,* 173–176.

Petty, R. E., & Cacioppo, J. T. (1981). *Attitudes and persuasion: Classic and contemporary approaches.* Dubuque, IA: Wm. C. Brown.

Petty, R. E., & Cacioppo, J. T. (1983). The role of bodily responses in attitude measurement and change. In J. T. Cacioppo & R. E. Petty (Eds.), *Social psychophysiology: A sourcebook* (pp. 51–101). New York: Guilford.

Petty, R. E., & Cacioppo, J. T. (1986). *Communication and persuasion: Central and peripheral routes to attitude change.* New York: Springer-Verlag.

Phillips, D. P. (1974). The influence of suggestion on suicide: Substantive and theoretical implications of the Werther Effect. *American Sociological Review, 39,* 340–354.

Phillips, D. P. (1979). Suicide, motor vehicle fatalities, and the mass media: Evidence toward a theory of suggestion. *American Journal of Sociology, 84,* 1150–1174.

Phillips, D. P. (1982). The impact of fictional television stories on U.S. adult fatalities: New evidence on the effect of the mass media on violence. *American Journal of Sociology, 87,* 1340–1359.

Phillips, D. P. (1983). The impact of mass media violence on U.S. homicides. *American Sociological Review, 48,* 560–568.

Phillips, D. P., & Hensley, J. E. (1984). When violence is rewarded or punished: The impact of mass media stories of homocide. *Journal of Communication, 34,* 101–116.

Pigott, M. A., & Brigham, J. C. (1985). The relationship between accuracy of prior descriptions and facial recognition. *Journal of Applied Psychology, 70,* 547–555.

Pigott, M. A., Brigham, J. C., & Bothwell, R. K. (1990). A field study of the relationship between description accuracy and identification accuracy. *Journal of Police Science and Administration, 17,* 84–88.

Pihl, R. O., & Ross, D. (1987). Research on alcohol related aggression: A review and implications for understanding aggression. *Drugs and Society, 1,* 105–126.

Piliavin, J. A., Dovidio, J., Gaertner, S., & Clark, R. D., III. (1981). *Emergency intervention*. New York: Academic Press.

Piliavin, J. A., & Piliavin, I. M. (1972). The effect of blood on reactions to a victim. *Journal of Personality and Social Psychology, 23,* 253–261.

Pines, M. (1979). Good Samaritans at age two? *Psychology Today*, June 1979, pp. 66ff.

Pink, J., & Wampler, K. (1985). Problem areas in stepfamilies: Cohesion, adaptability, and the stepparent-adolescent relationship. *Journal of Family Relationships, 34,* 327–335.

Pittman, T. S., & Heler, J. F. (1987). Social motivation. *Annual Review of Psychology, 38,* 461–489.

Platt, J. (1973). Social traps. *American Psychologist, 28,* 641–651.

Plessy v. Ferguson (1897), 163 U. S. 537.

Podsakoff, P. M., & Schriesheim, C. A. (1985). Field studies of French and Raven's bases of power: Critique, reanalysis, and suggestions for future research. *Psychological Bulletin, 97,* 387–411.

Pomazal, R. J., & Clore, G. L. (1973). Helping on the highway: The effects of dependency and sex. *Journal of Applied Social Psychology, 3,* 150–164.

Pomerleau, O. F., & Rodin, J. (1986). Behavioral medicine and health psychology. In S. L. Garfield & A. E. Berlin (Eds.), *Handbook of psychotherapy and behavior change* (pp. 483–522). New York: Wiley.

Porier, G. W., & Lott, A. J. (1967). Galvanic skin responses and prejudice. *Journal of Personality and Social Psychology, 5,* 253–259.

Powell, D. R., & Arnold, C. B. (1982). Antismoking program for coronary-prone men. *New York State Journal of Medicine, 82,* 1435–1438.

Powers, T. A., & Zuroff, D. C. (1988). Interpersonal consequences of overt self-criticism: Comparison with neutral and self-enhancing presentations of self. *Journal of Personality and Social Psychology, 54,* 1054–1062.

Pratkanis, A. R., Greenwald, A. G., Leippe, M. R., & Baumgardner, M. H. (1988). In search of reliable persuasion effects: III. The sleeper effect is dead. Long live the sleeper effect. *Journal of Personality and Social Psychology, 54,* 203–218.

Prentice-Dunn, S., & Rogers, R. W. (1980). Effects of deindividuating situational cues and aggressive models on subjective deindividuation and aggression. *Journal of Personality and Social Psychology, 39,* 104–113.

Prentice-Dunn, S., & Rogers, R. W. (1989). Deindividuation and the self-regulation of behavior. In P. B. Paulus (Ed.), *Psychology of group influence* (2nd ed.) (pp. 89–109). Hillsdale, NJ: Erlbaum.

Price, R. A., & Vandenberg, S. G. (1979). Matching for physical attractiveness in married couples. *Personality and Social Psychology Bulletin, 5,* 398–399.

Prince-Embury, S., & Rooney, J. F. (1989). A comparison of residents who moved versus those who remained prior to restart of Three Mile Island. *Journal of Applied Social Psychology, 19,* 959–975.

Proshansky, H. M., Ittelson, W. H., & Rivlin, L. G. (1976). Freedom of choice and behavior in a physical setting. In H. M. Proshansky, W. H. Ittelson, & L. G. Rivlin (Eds.), *Environmental psychology: People and their physical settings*. New York: Holt, Rinehart & Winston.

Pruitt, D. G. (1968). Reciprocity and credit building in a laboratory dyad. *Journal of Personality and Social Psychology, 8,* 143–147.

Pruitt, D. G. (1976). Power and bargaining. In B. Seidenberg & A. Snadowsky (Eds.), *Social psychology: An introduction*. New York: Free Press.

Pruitt, D. G. (1981). *Negotiation behavior*. New York: Academic Press.

Pruitt, D. G., & Rubin, J. Z. (1986). *Social conflict*. New York: Random house.

Pryor, J. B., Gibbons, F. X., Wicklund, R. A., Fazio, R. A., & Hood, R. (1977). Self-focused attention and self-report validity. *Journal of Personality, 45,* 513–527.

Pryor, J. B., & Steinfatt, T. M. (1978). The effects of initial belief level on inoculation theory and its proposed mechanisms. *Human Communications Research, 4,* 217–230.

Pugh, J. (1981). Doomsayers offer apologia to followers. *St. Petersburg Times,* June 27, 1981.

Putnam, W. H. (1979). Hypnosis and distortions in eyewitness memory. *International Journal of Clinical and Experimental Hypnosis, 27,* 437–448.

Pyszczynski, T. A., & Greenberg, J. (1987). Self-regulatory preservation and the depressive self-focusing style: A self-awareness theory of relative depression. *Psychological Bulletin, 102,* 122–138.

Pyszczynski, T. A., & Wrightsman, L. S. (1981). The effects of opening statements on mock jurors' verdicts in a simulated criminal trial. *Journal of Applied Social Psychology, 11,* 301–313.

Quattrone, G. A. (1985). On the congruity between internal states and action. *Psychological Bulletin, 98,* 1–40.

Quattrone, G. A. (1986). On the perception of a group's variability. In S. Worchel & W. G. Austin (Eds.), *Psychology of intergroup relations* (pp. 24–48). Chicago: Nelson Hall.

Quattrone, G. A., & Jones, E. E. (1980). The perception of variability within ingroups and out-groups: Implications for the law of small numbers. *Journal of Personality and Social Psychology, 38,* 141–152.

Quayle, D. (1983). American productivity: The devastating effect of alcoholism and drug abuse. *American Psychologist, 38,* 454–458.

Rahe, R. H. (1974). The pathway between subjects' recent life changes and their near-future illness reports: Representative results and methodological issues. In B. S. Dohrenwend & B. P. Dohrenwend (Eds.), *Stressful life events: Their nature and effects*. New York: Wiley.

Rahe, R. H., & Arthur, R. H. (1978). Life change and illness studies. *Journal of Human Stress, 4*(1), 3–15.

Rahe, R. M., Ward, H. W., & Hayes, V. (1979). Brief group therapy in myocardial infarction rehabilitation: Three to four year follow-up of a controlled trial. *Psychosomatic Medicine, 41,* 229–242.

Rainville, R. E., & McCormick, E. (1977). Extent of covert racial prejudice in pro football announcers' speech. *Journalism Quarterly, 54,* 20–26.

Rainwater, L. (1965). *Family design: Marital sexuality, family size, and contraception*. Chicago: Aldine.

Rajecki, D. W. (1982). *Attitudes: Themes and advances*. Sunderland, MA: Sinauer Associates.

Rajecki, D. W., Kidd, R. F., & Ivins, B. (1976). Social facilitation in chickens: A different level of analysis. *Journal of Experimental Social Psychology, 12,* 233–246.

Rankin, R. E. (1969). Air pollution control and public apathy. *Journal of Air Pollution Control Association, 19,* 565–569.

Raskin, D. C. (1981). Science, competence, and polygraph techniques. *Criminal Defense, 8,* 11–18.

Raskin, D. C. (1988). Does science support polygraph testing? In A. Gale (Ed.), *Lies, truth, and science* (pp. 96–208). London: Sage.

Raskin, D. C., & Yiulle, J. S. (1989). Problems in evaluating interviews of children in sexual abuse cases. In S. J. Ceci, D. F. Ross, & M. P. Toglia (Eds.), *Perspectives on children's testimony* (pp. 184–207). New York: Springer-Verlag.

Raven, B. H. (1974). *The comparative analysis of power and power preference.* Chicago, IL: Aldine-Atherton.

Raven, B. H. (1982). Introduction. In A. W. Johnson, O., Grushky, & B. H. Raven (Eds.), *Contemporary health services: Social science perspectives* (pp. 11–20). Boston: Auburn House.

Raven, B. H. (1988). Social power and compliance in health care. In S. Maes, C. D. Spielberger, P. B. Defares, & I. G. Sarason (Eds.), *Topics in health psychology* (pp. 229–244). New York: Wiley.

Raven, B. H., Centers, R., & Rodrigues, A. (1975). The bases of conjugal power. In R. S. Cromwell & D. H. Olsen (Eds.), *Power in families.* New York: Wiley.

Raven, B. H., & Haley, R. W. (1982). Social influence and compliance of hospital nurses with infection control policies. In J. R. Eiser (Ed.), *Social psychology and behavioral medicine* (pp. 413–438). New York: Wiley.

Raven, B. H., & Kruglanski, A. (1970). Conflict and power. In P. G. Swingle (Ed.), *The nature of conflict.* New York: Academic Press.

Raven, B. H., & Leff, W. F. (1965). The effect of partner's behavior and culture upon strategy in a two-person game. *Scripta Hierosolymitana, 14,* 148–165.

Rehm, L. P., & O'Hara, M. W. (1979). Understanding depression. In I. H. Frieze, D. Bar-Tal, & J. S. Carroll (Eds.), *New approaches to social problems.* San Fransisco: Jossey-Bass.

Reichner, R. (1979). Differential responses to being ignored. *Journal of Applied Social Psychology, 9,* 13–26.

Reid, P. T. (1988). Racism and sexism: Comparisons and conflicts. In P. A. Katz & D. A. Taylor (Eds.), *Eliminating racism: Profiles in controversy* (pp. 203–221). New York: Plenum.

Reik, T. (1944). *A psychologist looks at love.* New York: Farrar & Rinehart.

Reis, H. T., Nezlek, J., & Wheeler, L. (1980). Physical attractiveness in social interaction. *Journal of Personality and Social Psychology, 38,* 604–617.

Reisenzein, R. (1983). The Schachter theory of emotion: Two decades later. *Psychological Review, 94,* 239–264.

Reiser, M. (1989). Investigative hypnosis. In D. C. Raskin (Ed.), *Psychological methods in criminal investigation and evidence* (pp. 151–190). New York: Springer.

Report of the Presidential Commission on Obscenity and Pornography. (1971). Washington, DC: U.S. Government Printing Office.

Resnick, J. M., & Schwartz, T. (1973). Ethical standards as an independent variable in psychological research. *American Psychologist, 28,* 134–139.

Reston, J. (1975). Proxmire on love. *New York Times,* March 14, 1975.

Rhodewalt, F., & Agustsdottir, S. (1986). Effects of self-presentation on the phenomenal self. *Journal of Personality and Social Psychology, 50,* 47–55.

Rhodewalt, F., & Davidson, J., Jr. (1983). Reactance and the coronary-prone behavior pattern: The role of self-attribution in response to reduced behavioral freedom. *Journal of Personality and Social Psychology, 44,* 220–228.

Rhodewalt, F., & Fairfield, M. (1990). An alternative approach to Type A be-havior and health: Psychological reactance and medical noncompliance. *Journal of Social Behavior and Personality, 5,* 323–342.

Rhodewalt, F., Saltzman, A. T., & Wittmer, J. (1984). Self-handicapping among competitive athletes: The role of practice in self-esteem protection. *Basic and Applied Social Psychology, 5,* 197–210.

Rice, B. (1978). The new truth machines. *Psychology Today,* June 1978, pp. 61ff.

Rice, R. W., & Kastenbaum, D. R. (1983). The contingency model of leadership: Some current issues. *Basic and Applied Social Psychology, 4,* 373–392.

Richardson, D. C., Bernstein, S., & Taylor, S. P. (1979). The effect of situational contingencies on female retaliative behavior. *Journal of Personality and Social Psychology, 37,* 2044–2048.

Richmond, J. B. (1979a). *Healthy people: The Surgeon General's report on health promo-tion and disease prevention.* Washington, DC: U.S. Government Printing Office.

Richmond, J. B. (1976b). *Smoking and health: A report of the Surgeon General.* Washington, DC: U.S. Government Printing Office.

Richmond-Abbott, M. (1983). *Masculine and feminine: Sex roles over the life cycle.* Reading, MA: Addison-Wesley.

Ridker, R. G., & Muscat, R. J. (1983). Incentives for family welfare and fertility reduction: An illustration for Malaysia. *Studies in Family Planning, 4,* 1–11.

Ring, K. (1967). Experimental social psychology: Some sober questions about some frivolous values. *Journal of Experimental Social Psychology, 3,* 113–123.

Riger, S. (1985). Crime as an enviromental stressor. *Journal of Community Psychol-ogy, 13,* 270–280.

Riley, D., & Eckenrode, J. (1986). Social ties: Subgroup differences in costs and benefits. *Journal of Personality and Social Psychology, 51,* 770–778.

Rittle, R. H. (1981). Changes in helping behavior: Self versus situational percep-tions as mediators of the foot-in-the-door effect. *Personality and Social Psy-chology Bulletin, 7,* 431–437.

Rock v. Arkansas (1987), 107 S. Ct. 2704, 97 L. Ed. 2d 37.

Rodin, J. (1976). Density, perceived choice, and response to controllable and un-controllable outcomes. *Journal of Experimental Social Psychology, 12,* 564–578.

Rodin, J. (1977). Obesity: Why the losing battle? In *Master Lecture Series on Brain-Behavior Relationships.* Washington, DC: American Psychological Association.

Rodin, J., & Salovey, P. (1989). Health psychology. *Annual Review of Psychology, 40,* 533–579.

Rodin, J., Solomon, S. K., & Metcalf, J. (1978). Role of control in mediating per-ceptions of density. *Journal of Personality and Social Psychology, 36,* 988–999.

Roethlisberger, F. J., & Dickson, W. J. (1939). *Management and the worker.* Cam-bridge: Harvard University Press.

Rogers, E. M. (1971). Incentives in the diffusion of family planning innovations. *Studies in Family Planning, 2,* 241–248.

Rogers, R. W. (1984). Changing health-related attitudes and behavior: The role of preventive health psychology. In J. H. Harvey, J. E. Maddux, R. P. McGlynn, & C. D. Stoltenberg (Eds.), *Social perception in clinical and counsel-ing psychology* (Vol. 2, pp. 91–112). Lubbock, TX: Texas Tech University Press.

Rogers, R. W., & Mewborn, C. R. (1976). Fear appeals and attitude change: Effects of a threat's noxiousness, probability of occurrence, and the efficacy of coping responses. *Journal of Personality and Social Psychology, 34,* 54–61.

Rogers, R. W., & Prentice-Dunn, S. (1981). Deindividuation and anger-mediated interracial aggression: Unmasking regressive racism. *Journal of Personality and Social Psychology, 41,* 63–73.

Rohrer, J. H., Baron, S. H., Hoffman, E. L., & Swander, D. V. (1954). The stability of autokinetic judgments. *Journal of Abnormal and Social Psychology, 49,* 595–597.

Rokeach, M. (1960). *The open and closed mind.* New York: Basic Books.

Rokeach, M. (Ed.). (1979). *Understanding human values: Individual and social.* New York: Free Press.

Rollins, B. C. , & Cannon, K. (1974). Marital satisfaction over the family life cycle: A reevaluation. *Journal of Marriage and the Family, 36,* 271–282.

Rollins, B. C., & Feldman, H. (1970). Marital satisfaction over the family life cycle. *Journal of Marriage and the Family, 32,* 20–28.

Romer, D., Gruder, C. L., & Lizzaro, T. (1986). A person-situation approach to altruistic behavior. *Journal of Personality and Social Psychology, 51,* 1001–1012.

Room, R. (1977). *The scope and definition of alcohol-related problems.* (Working paper F-58, May 1977). University of California, Berkeley: School of Public Health, Social Research Group.

Rosen, T. J., Terry, N. S., & Leventhal, H. (1982). The role of esteem and coping in response to a threat communication. *Journal of Research in Personality, 16,* 90–107.

Rosenbaum, M. E. (1986). The repulsion hypothesis: On the nondevelopment of relationships. *Journal of Personality and Social Psychology, 51,* 1156–1166.

Rosenfeld, D., Sheehan, D. S., Marcus, M. M., & Stephan, W. G. (1981). Classroom structure and prejudice in desegregated schools. *Journal of Educational Psychology, 73,* 17–26.

Rosenfield, D., Folger, R., & Adelman, H. F. (1980). When rewards reflect competence: A qualification of the overjustification effect. *Journal of Personality and Social Psychology, 39,* 368–376.

Rosenfield, D., Greenberg, J., Folger, R., & Borys, R. (1982). Effect of an encounter with a black panhandler on subsequent helping for blacks: Tokenism or confirming a negative stereotype? *Personality and Social Psychology Bulletin, 8,* 664–671.

Rosenman, R. H., Brand, R. J., Sholtz, R. I., & Friedman, M. (1976). Multivariate prediction of coronary heart disease during 8.5 year followup in the Western Collaborative Group Study. *American Journal of Cardiology, 37,* 903–910.

Rosenthal, A. M. (1964). *Thirty-eight witnesses.* New York: McGraw-Hill.

Rosenthal, N., Rotter, A., Jacobsen, F. M., & Skweres, R. G. (1987). No mood-altering effects found after treatment of normal subjects with bright light in the morning. *Psychiatry Research, 22*(1), 1–9.

Rosenthal, N. E., Sack, D. A., Carpenter, C. J., Parry, B. L., Mendelson, W. B., & Wehr, T. A. (1985). Antidepressant effects of light in seasonal affective disorder. *American Journal of Psychiatry, 142,* 163–170.

Rosenthal, R. (1966). *Experimenter effects in behavioral research.* New York: Appleton-Century-Crofts.

Rosenthal, R., & Jacobson, L. (1968). *Pygmalion in the classroom: Teacher expectation and pupils' intellectual development.* New York: Holt, Rinehart & Winston.

Rosenzweig, M., & Spruill, J. (1986). Twenty years after Twiggy: A retrospective investigation of bulimic-like behaviors. *International Journal of Eating Disorders, 6,* 24–31.

Ross, E. A. (1908). *Social psychology: An outline and a source book.* New York: Macmillan.

Ross, H., & Sawhill, I. (1975). *Time of transition. The growth of families headed by women.* Washington, DC: The Urban Institute.

Ross, L. (1977). The intuitive psychologist and his shortcomings: Distortions in the attribution process. In L. Berkowitz (Ed.), *Advances in experimental social psychology* (Vol. 10). New York: Academic Press.

Ross, L., Amabile, T. M., & Steinmetz, J. L. (1977). Social roles, social control, and biases in social-perception processes. *Journal of Personality and Social Psychology, 35,* 485–494.

Ross, L., & Anderson, C. A. (1982). Shortcomings in the attribution process: On the origins and maintenance of erroneous social assessments. In D. Kahneman, P. Slovic, & A. Tversky (Eds.), *Judgment under uncertainty: Heuristics and biases* (pp. 129–152). New York: Cambridge University Press.

Ross, L., Bierbrauer, G., & Hoffman, S. (1976). The role of attribution processes in conformity and dissent: Revisiting the Asch situation. *American Psychologist, 31,* 148–157.

Ross, L., Greene, D., & House, P. (1977). The "false consensus effect": An egocentric bias in social perception and attribution processes. *Journal of Experimental Social Psychology, 13,* 279–301.

Ross, L., Lepper, M. R., Strack, F., & Steinmetz, J. (1977). Social explanation and social expectation: Effects of real and hypothetical explanations on subjective likelihood. *Journal of Personality and Social Psychology, 35,* 817–829.

Ross, M., McFarland, C., & Fletcher, G. J. O. (1981). The effect of attitude on the recall of personal histories. *Journal of Personality and Social Psychology, 40,* 627–634.

Ross, M., & Sicoly, F. (1979). Egocentric biases in availability and attribution. *Journal of Personality and Social Psychology, 37,* 322–336.

Ross, M. H., & Williams, R. H. (1981). *Our energy: Regaining control.* New York: McGraw-Hill.

Rotton, J., Barry, T., Frey, J., & Soler, E. (1978). Air pollution and interpersonal attraction. *Journal of Applied Social Psychology, 8,* 57–71.

Rotton, J., & Frey, J. (1984). Psychological costs of air pollution: Atmospheric conditions, seasonal trends, and psychiatric emergencies. *Population and Environmental Behavior and Social Issues, 7,* 3–16.

Rotton, J., & Frey, J. (1985). Air pollution, weather, and violent crimes: Concomitant time-series analysis of archival data. *Journal of Personality and Social Psychology, 49,* 1207–1220.

Ruback, R. B., Carr, T. S., & Hopper, C. H. (1986). Perceived control in prison: Its relation to reported crowding, stress, and symptoms. *Journal of Applied Social Psychology, 16,* 375–386.

Rubin, H. J. (1981). Rules, collective needs, and individual action: A case study in a townhouse cooperative. *Environment and Behavior, 13,* 165–188.

Rubin, I. M. (1967). Increased self-acceptance: A means of reducing prejudice. *Journal of Personality and Social Psychology, 5,* 233–238.

Rubin, J., & Shaffer, W. F. (1987). Some interpersonal effects of imposing guilt versus eliciting altruism. *Counseling and Values, 31,* 190–193.

Rubin, J. Z. (1981). Psychological traps. *Psychology Today, 15,* 52–63.

Rubin, J. Z., & Brown, B. R. (1975). *The social psychology of bargaining and negotiation.* New York: Academic Press.

Rubin, J. Z., Provenzano, F. J., & Luria, Z. (1974). The eye of the beholder: Parents' views on sex of newborns. *American Journal of Orthopsychiatry, 44,* 512–519 .

Rubin, Z. (1973). *Liking and loving: An invitation to social psychology.* New York: Holt, Rinehart & Winston.

Rubin, Z. (1974). *From liking to loving: Patterns of attraction in dating relationships; Foundations of interpersonal attraction.* New York: Holt, Rinehart & Winston.

Rubin, Z. (1988). Preface. In R. J. Sternberg & M. L. Barnes (Eds.). *The psychology of love* (pp. vii-xii). New Haven, CT: Yale University Press.

Rubin, Z., Hill, C. T., Peplau, L. A., & Dunkel-Schetter, C. (1980). Self-disclosure in dating couples: Sex roles and the ethic of openness. *Journal of Marriage and the Family, 42,* 305–318.

Rubinstein, M. L., & White, T. J. (1980). Alaska's ban on plea-bargaining. In W. F. McDonald & J. A. Cramer (Eds.), *Plea-bargaining.* Lexington, MA: Lexington Books.

Rudd, J. R., & Geller, E. S. (1985). A university-based incentive program to increase safety-belt use: Toward cost-effective institutionalization. *Journal of Applied Behavior Analysis, 18,* 215–226.

Rusbult, C. E. (1980). Commitment and satisfaction in romantic association: A test of the investment model. *Journal of Experimental Social Psychology, 11,* 78–95.

Rusbult, C. E. (1983). A longitudinal test of the investment model: The development (and deterioration) of satisfaction and commitment in heterosexual involvements. *Journal of Personality and Social Psychology, 45,* 101–117.

Rusbult, C. E. (1984). *The constructive/destructive and active/passive dimensions of exit, voice, loyalty, and neglect behaviors.* Paper presented at Society of Southeastern Social Psychologists meeting, Atlanta.

Rusbult, C., Johnson, D., & Morrow, G. (1986). Predicting satisfaction and commitment in adult romantic involvement: An assessment of the generalizability of the investment model. *Social Psychology Quarterly, 49,* 81–89.

Rusbult, C. E., & Zembrodt, I. M. (1983). Responses to dissatisfaction in romantic involvements: A multidemensional scaling analysis. *Journal of Experimental Social Psychology, 19,* 274–293.

Rusbult, C. E., Zembrodt, I. M., & Gunn, L. K. (1982). Exit, voice, loyalty, and neglect responses to dissatisfaction in romantic involvements. *Journal of Personality and Social Psychology, 43,* 1230–1242.

Rushton, J. P. (1982). Television and prosocial behavior. In D. Pearl, L. Bouthilet, & J. Lazar (Eds.), *Television and behavior: Ten years of scientific progress and implications for the eighties* (Vol. 2, pp. 248–258). Washington, DC: U.S. Dept. of Health and Human Services.

Rushton, J. P. (1986). Altruism and aggression: The heredity of individual differences. *Journal of Personality and Social Psychology, 50,* 1192–1198.

Rushton, J. P. (1988). Epigenetic rules in moral development: Distal-proximal approaches to altruism and aggression. *Aggressive Behavior, 14,* 35–50.

Rushton, J. P. (1989). Genetic similarity, human altruism, and group selection. *Behavioral and Brain Sciences, 21,* 503–559.

Russ, R. C., Gold, J. A., & Stone, W. F. (1980). Opportunity for thought as a mediator of attraction to a dissimilar stranger: A further test of an information-seeking interpretation. *Journal of Experimental Social Psychology, 16,* 562–572.

Ryckman, R. M. (1985). *Theories of personality* (3rd ed.). Monterey, CA: Brooks/Cole.

Ryckman, R. M., Robbins, M. A., Kaczor, L. M., & Gold, J. A. (1989). Male and female raters' stereotyping of male and female physiques. *Personality and Social Psychology Bulletin, 15,* 244–251.

Rytting, M. B., & Carr, J. P. (1978). *The effect of gender information on interaction between infants and adults in a general population.* Paper presented at Midwestern Psychological Association meeting, Chicago.

Sackett, D. L. (1976). The magnitude of compliance and noncompliance. In D. L. Sackett & R. B. Haynes (Eds.), *Compliance with therapeutic regimens.* Baltimore: Johns Hopkins University Press.

Sadalla, E. K., Kendrick, D. T., & Vershure, B. (1987). Dominance and heterosexual attraction. *Journal of Personality and Social Psychology, 52,* 730–738.

Sadava, S. W. (1978). Etiology, personality and alcoholism. *Canadian Psychological Review, 19,* 198–214.

Sagar, H. A., & Schofield, J. W. (1980). Racial and behavioral cues in black and white children's perceptions of ambiguously aggressive acts. *Journal of Personality and Social Psychology, 39,* 590–598.

Sahlins, M. (1976). *The use and abuse of biology.* Ann Arbor: University of Michigan Press.

St. John, N. H. (1975). *School desegregation: Outcomes for children.* New York: Wiley.

Saks, M. J., & Hastie, R. (1978). *Social psychology in court.* New York: Van Nostrand Reinhold.

Saks, M. J., Werner, C. M., & Ostrom, T. M. (1975). The presumption of innocence and the American juror. *Journal of Contemporary Law, 2,* 46–54.

Salber, E. J., Freeman, H. E., & Abelin, T. (1968). Aided research on smoking: Lessons from the Newton study. In E. F. Borgatta & R. R. Evans (Eds.), *Smoking, health, and behavior.* Chicago: Aldine.

Salce, J. E. (1981). *Equity and intimate relationships: A comparison of married, cohabiting, and steady dating individuals.* Unpublished doctoral dissertation, Florida State University.

Salovey, P., & Rodin, J. (1985). The heart of jealousy. *Psychology Today,* Sept. 1985, pp. 22–29.

Salovey, P., & Rodin, J. (1986). The differentiation of social-comparison jealousy and romantic jealousy. *Journal of Personality and Social Psychology, 50,* 1100–1112.

Samuelson, C. D., & Messick, D. M. (1986). Inequities in access to and use of shared resources in social dilemmas. *Journal of Personality and Social Psychology, 51,* 960–967.

Samuelson, C. D., Messick, D. M., Rutte, C. G., & Wilke, H. (1984). Individual and structural solutions to resource dilemmas in two cultures. *Journal of Personality and Social Psychology, 47,* 94–104.

Sande, G. N., Goethals, G. R., Ferrari, L., & Worth, L. T. (1989). Value-guided attributions: Maintaining the moral self-image and the diabolical enemy-image. *Journal of Social Issues, 45*(2), 91–118.

Sande, G. N., Goethals, G. R., & Radloff, C. E. (1988). Perceiving one's own traits and others': The multifaceted self. *Journal of Personality and Social Psychology, 54,* 13–20.

Sanders, G. S., & Baron, R. S. (1975). The motivating effects of distraction on task performance. *Journal of Personality and Social Psychology, 32,* 956–963.

Sanders, G. S., & Simmons, W. C. (1983). Use of hypnosis to enhance eyewitness accuracy: Does it work? *Journal of Applied Psychology, 68,* 70–77.

Santee, R. T., & Maslach, C. (1982). To agree or not to agree: Personal dissent and social pressure to conform. *Journal of Personality and Social Psychology, 42,* 690–700.

Sasfy, J., & Okun, M. (1974). Form of evaluation and audience expertness as joint determinants of audience effects. *Journal of Experimental Social Psychology, 10,* 461–467.

Scanzoni, J. (1979). *Sex roles, women's work, and marital conflict.* Boston: D. C. Heath.

Schachter, S. (1951). Deviation, rejection, and communication. *Journal of Abnormal and Social Psychology, 46,* 190–207.

Schachter, S. (1959). *The psychology of affiliation.* Stanford, CA: Stanford University Press.

Schachter, S. (1964). The interaction of cognitive and physiological determinants of emotional state. In L. Berkowitz (Ed.), *Advances in experimental social psychology* (Vol. 1). New York: Academic Press.

Schachter, S. (1982). Recidivism and self-cure of smoking and obesity. *American Psychologist, 37,* 436–444.

Schachter, S., & Singer, J. E. (1962). Cognitive, social and physiological determinants of emotional state. *Psychological Review, 69,* 379–399.

Schaeffer, M. A., Baum, A., Paulus, P. B., & Gaeg, G. G. (1988). Architecturally mediated effects of social density in prison. *Environment and Behavior, 20,* 3–19.

Schaeffer, P. L. (Ed.) (1971). *Sex differences in personality: Readings.* Monterey, CA: Brooks/Cole.

Schafer, R. B., & Keith, P. M. (1980). Equity and depression among married couples. *Social Psychology Quarterly, 43,* 430–435.

Schaffner, P. E., Wandersman, A., & Stang, D. (1981). Candidate name exposure and voting: Two field studies. *Basic and Applied Social Psychology, 2,* 195–203.

Schaller, M., & Cialdini, R. B. (1988). The economics of empathic helping: Support for a mood management motive. *Journal of Experimental Social Psychology, 24,* 163–181.

Schaller, M., & Maass, A. (1989). Illusory correlation and social categorization: Toward an integration of motivational and cognitive factors in stereotype formation. *Journal of Personality and Social Psychology, 56,* 709–721.

Scheflin, A. W., & Shapiro, J. L. (1989). *Trance on trial.* New York: Guilford.

Scheier, M. F., & Carver, C. S. (1977). Self-focused attention and the experience of emotion: Attraction, repulsion, elation, and depression. *Journal of Personality and Social Psychology, 35,* 625–636.

Scheier, M. F., & Carver, C. S. (1985). Optimism, coping, and health: Assessment and implications of generalized outcome expectations on health. *Health Psychology, 4,* 219–247.

Scheier, M. F., Matthews, K. A., Owens, J., Magovern, G. J. Sr., Lefebre, R. C., Abbott, R. A., & Carver, C. S. (1989). Dispositional optimism and recovery from coronary artery bypass surgery: The beneficial effects on physical and psychological well-being. *Journal of Personality and Social Psychology, 57,* 1024–1040.

Scheier, M. F., Weintraub, J. K., & Carver, C. S. (1986). Coping with stress: Divergent strategies of optimists and pessimists. *Journal of Personality and Social Psychology, 51,* 1257–1264.

Schein, E. H. (1956). The Chinese indoctrination program for prisoners of war. *Psychiatry, 19,* 149–172.

Schein, E. H., Schneider, I., & Barker, C. H. (1961). *Coercive persuasion.* New York: Norton.

Schellenberg, J. A. (1970). *An introduction to social psychology.* New York: Random House.

Scher, S. J., & Cooper J. (1989). Motivational basis of dissonance: The singular role of behavioral consequences. *Journal of Personality and Social Psychology, 56,* 899–906.

Scherer, S. E. (1974). Proxemic behavior of primary school children as a function of their socioeconomic class and subculture. *Journal of Personality and Social Psychology, 29,* 800–805.

Schifter, D. B., & Ajzen, I. (1985). Intention, perceived control and weight loss: An application of the theory of planned behavior. *Journal of Personality and Social Psychology, 49,* 843–851.

Schlenker, B. R. (1980). *Impression management: The self-concept, social identity, and interpersonal relations.* Belmont, CA: Brooks/Cole.

Schlenker, B. R. (1985). *The self and social life.* New York: McGraw-Hill.

Schlenker, B. R. (1986). Self-identification: Toward an integration of the private and public self. In R. F. Baumeister (Ed.), *Public self and private self* (pp. 21–62). New York: Springer-Verlag.

Schlenker, B. R., Forsyth, D. R., Leary, M. R., & Miller, R. S. (1980). Self-presentational analysis of the effects of incentives on attitude change following counterattitudinal behavior. *Journal of Personality and Social Psychology, 39,* 553–577.

Schneider, C. (1986). Least-cost utility planning: Providing a competitive edge. *Public Utilities Fortnightly, 116,* 15–21.

Schofield, J. W. (1982). *Black and white in school: Trust, tension, or tolerance?* New York: Praeger.

Schofield, J. W. (1986). Causes and consequences of the colorblind perspective. In J. F. Dovidio & S. L. Gaertner (Eds.), *Prejudice, discrimination, and racism* (pp. 231–254). New York: Academic Press.

Schulman, J., Shaver, P., Colman, R., Emrich, B., & Christie, R. (1973). Recipe for a jury. *Psychology Today,* May 1973, pp. 37ff.

Schutte, N. S., Malouff, J. M., Post-Gorden, J. C., & Rodasta, A. L. (1988). Effects of playing videogames on children's aggressive and other behaviors. *Journal of Applied Social Psychology, 18,* 454–460.

Schwartz, G. E., Fair, P. L., Salt, P., Mandel, M. R., & Klerman, G. L. (1976). Facial muscle patterning to affective imagery in depressed and nondepressed subjects. *Science, 192,* 489–491.

Schwartz, G. E., & Weiss, S. M. (1978). Behavioral medicine revisited: An amended definition. *Journal of Behavioral Medicine, 1,* 249–252.

Schwartz, H., & Jackson, B. (1976). Prosecutor as public enemy. *Harper's*, February, 1976.

Schwartz, S. H. (1978). Temporal instability as a moderator of the attitude-behavior relationship. *Journal of Personality and Social Psychology, 36,* 715–724.

Schwartz, S. H., & Gottlieb, A. (1980). Bystander anonymity and reactions to emergencies. *Journal of Personality and Social Psychology, 39,* 418–430.

Sears, D. O. (1968). The paradox of de facto selective exposure without preference for supportive information. In R. P. Abelson et al. (Eds.), *Theories of cognitive consistency: A sourcebook.* Chicago: Rand McNally.

Sears, D. O. (1988). Symbolic racism. In P. A. Katz & D. A. Taylor (Eds.). *Eliminating racism: Profiles in controversy* (pp. 53–83). New York: Plenum.

Seligman, C., Paschall, N., & Takata, G. (1974). Effects of physical attractiveness on attribution of responsibility. *Canadian Journal of Behavioral Science, 6,* 290–296.

Severance, L. J., Greene, E., & Loftus, E. F. (1984). Toward criminal jury instructions that jurors can understand. *Journal of Criminal Law and Criminology, 75,* 198–233.

Severy, L. J., Brigham, J. C., & Schlenker, B. R. (1976). *A contemporary introduction to social psychology.* New York: McGraw-Hill.

Severy, L. J., Forsyth, D. R., & Wagner, P. J. (1979). A multi-method assessment of personal space development in female and male, black and white children. *Journal of Nonverbal Behavior, 4,* 68–86.

Shalon, M., & Strube, M. J. (1988). Type A behavior and emotional responses to uncertainty: A test of the self-appraisal model. *Motivation and Emotion, 12,* 385–398.

Shanab, M. E., & Isonio, S. A. (1982). The effects of contrast upon compliance with socially undesirable requests in the foot-in-the-door paradigm. *Bulletin of the Psychonomic Society, 20,* 180–182.

Shanab, M. E., & O'Neill, P. (1982). The effects of self-perception and perceptual contrast upon compliance with socially undesirable requests. *Bulletin of the Psychonomic Society, 19,* 279–281.

Shaver, K. G. (1975). *An introduction to attribution processes.* Cambridge, MA: Winthrop.

Shaver, P., Hazan, C., & Bradshaw, D. (1988). Love as attachment: The integration of three behavioral systems. In R. J. Sternberg & M. L. Barnes (Eds.), *The psychology of love* (pp. 68–99). New Haven, CT: Yale University Press.

Shaw, M. (1932). A comparison of individuals and small groups in the rational solution of complex problems. *American Journal of Psychology, 44,* 491–504.

Shaw, M. E. (1981). *Group dynamics: The psychology of small group behavior* (3rd ed.). New York: McGraw-Hill.

Shaw, M. E., & Constanzo, P. R. (1982). *Theories of social psychology* (2nd ed.). New York: McGraw-Hill.

Shekelle, R. B., Gayle, M., Ostfeld, A. M., & Paul, O. (1983). Hostility, risk of coronary heart disease, and mortality. *Psychosomatic Medicine, 45,* 109–114.

Shepherd, J. R. (1983). Identification after long delays. In S. M. A. Lloyd-Bostock & B. R. Clifford (Eds.), *Evaluating witness evidence* (pp. 173–188). New York: Wiley.

Sheppard, B. H. (1983). Third party conflict intervention: A procedural framework. In B. Staw & L. Cummings (Eds.), *Research in Organizational Behavior*, (Vol. 6). Greenwich, CT: JAI Press.

Shepperd, J. A., & Arkin, R. M. (1989). Self-handicapping: The moderating roles of public self-consciousness and task importance. *Personality and Social Psychology Bulletin, 15,* 252–265.

Sherif, C. W. (1980). Comment on ethical issues in Malamuth, Heim, and Feshbach's "Sexual responsiveness of college students to rape depictions: Inhibitory and disinhibitory effects." *Journal of Personality and Social Psychology, 38,* 409–412.

Sherif, C. W., Kelly, M., Rogers, H. L., Jr., Sarup, G., & Tittler, B. I. (1973). Personal involvement, social judgment, and action. *Journal of Personality and Social Psychology, 27,* 311–328.

Sherif, M. (1935). A study of some social factors in perception. *Archiva Psychologia, 27*(187).

Sherif, M. (1966). *In common predicament: Social psychology of intergroup conflict and cooperation.* Boston: Houghton Mifflin.

Sherif, M., Harvey, O. J., White, B. J., Hood, W. R., & Sherif, C. W. (1961). *Intergroup cooperation and competition: The robber's cave experience.* Norman, OK: University Book Exchange.

Sherif, M., & Hovland, C. I. (1961). *Social judgment: Assimilation and contrast effects in communication and attitude change.* New Haven, CT: Yale University Press.

Sherman, B. L., & Dominick, J. R. (1986). Violence and sex in music videos: TV and rock 'n roll. *Journal of Communication, 36,* 79–93.

Sherrod, D. R., & Downs, R. (1974). Environmental determinants of altruism: The effects of stimulus overload and perceived control on helping. *Journal of Experimental Social Psychology, 10,* 468–479.

Sherrod, D. R., Hage, J. N., Halpern, P. L., & Moore, B. S. (1977). Effects of personal causation and perceived control on responses to an aversive environment: The more control, the better. *Journal of Experimental Social Psychology, 13,* 14.

Shotland, R. L., & Heinold, W. D. (1985). Bystander response to arterial bleeding: Helping skills, the decision-making process, and differentiating the helping response. *Journal of Personality and Social Psychology, 49,* 347–356.

Shotland, R. L., & Yankowski, L. D. (1982). The random response method: A valid and ethical indicator of the "truth" in reactive situations. *Personality and Social Psychology Bulletin, 8,* 174–179.

Shrauger, J. S. (1975). Responses to evaluation as a function of initial self-perceptions. *Psychological Bulletin, 82,* 581–596.

Shumaker, S. A., & Reizenstein, J. E. (1982). Environmental factors affecting inpatient stress in acute care hospitals. In G. W. Evans (Ed.), *Environmental stress* (pp. 179–223). Cambridge: Cambridge University Press.

Shupe, A. D., Jr., Spielman, R., & Stigall, S. (1977). Deprogramming: The new exorcism. *American Behavioral Scientist, 20,* 941–956.

Siegel, A. E. (1970). Violence and aggression are not inevitable. In M. Wertheimer (Ed.), *Confrontation: Psychology and the problems of today.* Glenview, IL: Scott, Foresman.

Sigall, H., & Landy, D. (1973). Radiating beauty: Effects of having an attractive partner on person perception. *Journal of Personality and Social Psychology, 28,* 218–224.

Sigelman, C. K., Berry, C. J., & Wiles, K. A. (1984). Violence in college students' dating relationships. *Journal of Applied Social Psychology, 5,* 530–548.

Silverman, B. I. (1974). Consequences, racial discrimination, and the principle of belief congruence. *Journal of Personality and Social Psychology, 29,* 497–508.

Silvern, S. B., & Williamson, P. A. (1987). The effects of videogame play on young children's aggression, fantasy and prosocial behavior. *Journal of Applied Developmental Psychology, 8,* 453–462.

Silverstein, B., & Flamenbaum, C. (1989). Biases in the perception and cognition of the actions of enemies. *Journal of Social Issues, 45*(2), 51–72.

Simmel, G. (1950). *The sociology of Georg Simmel* (K. H. Wolff, trans.). Glencoe, IL: Free Press.

Simon, R. J. (1967). *The jury and the defense of insanity.* Boston: Little, Brown.

Simpson, J. A. (1987). The dissolution of romantic relationships: Factors involved in relationship stability and emotional distress. *Journal of Personality and Social Psychology, 47,* 683–692.

Simpson, J. A., Campbell, B., & Berscheid, E. (1986). The association between romantic love and marriage. *Personality and Social Psychology Bulletin, 12,* 363–372.

Sinden, F. (1978). Two-thirds reduction in the space heat requirements of a Twin Rivers townhouse. In R. Socolow (Ed.), *Saving energy in the home: Princeton's experiments at Twin Rivers.* Cambridge, MA: Ballinger.

Singer, J. L., & Singer, D. G. (1981). *Television, imagination and aggression: A study of preschoolers' play.* Hillsdale, NJ: Erlbaum.

Singer, J. L., & Singer, D. G. (1986). Family experiences and television viewing as predictors of children's imagination, restlessness, and aggression. *Journal of Social Issues, 42*(3), 107–124.

Singer, J. L., Singer, D. G., & Rapaczynski, W. (1984). Family patterns and television viewing as predictors of children's belief and aggression. *Journal of Communication, 34*(2), 73–89.

Sinoway, C. G., Raupp, C. D., & Newman, J. (1985). *Binge eating and bulimia: Comparing incidence and characteristics across universities.* Paper presented at American Psychological Association meetings, Los Angeles.

Sivacek, J., & Crano, W. D. (1982). Vested interest as a moderator of attitude-behavior consistency. *Journal of Personality and Social Psychology, 43,* 210–221.

Skowronski, J. J., & Carlston, D. E. (1989). Negativity and extremity biases in impression formation: A review of explanations. *Psychological Bulletin, 105,* 131–142.

Slavin, R. E., & Madden, N. A. (1979). School practices that improve race relations. *American Educational Research Journal, 16*(2), 169–180.

Slavin, R. E., & Oickle, E. (1981). Effects of cooperative learning teams on student achievement and race relations: Treatment by race interactions. *Sociology of Education, 54,* 174–180.

Slovic, P., & Fischhoff, B. (1977). On the psychology of experimental surprises. *Journal of Experimental Psychology: Human Perception and Performance, 3,* 544–551.

Slovic, P., Fischhoff, B., & Lichtenstein, S. (1982). Facts versus fears: Understanding perceived risks. In D. Kahneman, P. Slovic, & A. Tversky (Eds.), *Judgment under uncertainty: Heuristics and biases* (pp. 463–492). Cambridge: Cambridge University Press.

Slusher, M. P., & Anderson, C. A. (1987). When reality monitoring fails: The role of imagination in stereotype maintenance. *Journal of Personality and Social Psychology, 52,* 653–662.

Smeaton, G., Byrne, D., & Murnen, S. (1989). The repulsion hypothesis revisited: Similarity irrelevance or dissimilarity bias? *Journal of Personality and Social Psychology, 56,* 54–59.

Smith, C. P. (1983). Ethical issues: Research on deception, informed consent, and debriefing. In L. Wheeler & P. Shaver (Eds.), *Review of personality and social psychology* (Vol. 4, pp. 297–328). Beverly Hills, CA: Sage.

Smith, C. P., & Berard, S. P. (1982). Why are human subjects less concerned about ethically problematic research than human subjects committees? *Journal of Applied Social Psychology, 12,* 209–221.

Smith, G. F., & Dorfman, D. D. (1975). The effect of stimulus uncertainty on the relationship between frequency of exposure and liking. *Journal of Personality and Social Psychology, 31,* 150–155.

Smith, M. C. (1983). Hypnotic memory enhancement of witnesses: Does it work? *Psychological Bulletin, 94,* 387–407.

Smith, M. B. (1986). War, peace, and psychology. *Journal of Social Issues, 42*(4), 23–38.

Smith, M. B., Bruner, J. S., & White, R. W. (1956). *Opinions and personality.* New York: Wiley.

Smith, S., & Haythorn, W. W. (1972). The effects of compatibility, crowding, group size, and leadership seniority on stress, anxiety, hostility, and annoyance in isolated groups. *Journal of Personality and Social Psychology, 22,* 67–69.

Smith, S. S., & Richardson, D. (1983). Amelioration of deception and harm in psychological research: The important role of debriefing. *Journal of Personality and Social Psychology, 44,* 1075–1082.

Smith, T. W., & Pope, M. K. (1990). Cynical hostility as a health risk: Current status and future directions. *Journal of Social Behavior and Personality, 5,* 77–88.

Smith, T. W., Snyder, C. R., & Handelsman, M. D. (1982). On the self-serving function of an academic wooden leg: Test anxiety as a self-handicapping strategy. *Journal of Personality and Social Psychology, 42,* 314–321.

Snell, W. E., & Belk, S. S. (1985). On assessing "equity" in intimate relationships. *Representative Research in Social Psychology, 15,* 16–24.

Snow, C. P. (1961). Either-or. *Progressive.* February, 1961.

Snyder, C. R., & Harris, R. N. (1987). The role of similarity/difference information in excuse-making. In C. R. Snyder & C. E. Ford (Eds.), *Coping with negative life events: Clinical and social psychological perpectives* (pp. 347–369). New York: Plenum.

Snyder, C. R., & Higgins, R. L. (1988). Excuses: Their effective role in the negotiation of reality. *Psychological Bulletin, 104,* 23–35.

Snyder, C. R., Higgins, R. L., & Stuckey, R. J. (1983). *Excuses: Masquerades in search of grace.* New York: Wiley/Interscience.

Snyder, C. R., Larsen, D., & Bloom, L. J. (1976). Acceptance of personality interpretations prior to and after receiving feedback supposedly based on psychological, graphological, and astrological assessment procedures. *Journal of Clinical Psychology, 32,* 258–265.

Snyder, C. R., & Larson, G. R. (1972). A further look at student acceptance of general personality interpretations. *Journal of Consulting and Clinical Psychology, 38,* 384–388.

Snyder, C. R., & Shenkel, R. J. (1975). Astrologers, handwriting analysts, and sometimes psychologists use the P. T. Barnum effect. *Psychology Today,* November 1975, pp. 52–54.

Snyder, C. R., Shenkel, R. J., & Lowery, C. R. (1977). Acceptance of personality interpretations: The "Barnum effect" and beyond. *Journal of Consulting and Clinical Psychology, 45,* 104–114.

Snyder, M. (1981). On the influence of individuals on situations. In N. Cantor & J. F. Kihlstrom (Eds.), *Personality, cognition, and social interaction* (pp. 303–329). Hillsdale, NJ: Erlbaum.

Snyder, M. (1987). *Public appearances/private realities: The psychology of self-monitoring.* New York: Freeman.

Snyder, M., Campbell, B., & Preston, E. (1982). Self-monitoring the self in action. In J. Suls (Ed.), *Psychological perspectives on the self.* Hillsdale, NJ: Erlbaum.

Snyder, M., & Cunningham, M. R. (1975). To comply or not to comply: Testing the self-perception explanation of the foot-in-the-door phenomenon. *Journal of Personality and Social Psychology, 31,* 64–67.

Snyder, M., & Kendzierski, D. (1982). Acting on one's attitudes: Procedures for linking attitude and behavior. *Journal of Experimental Social Psychology, 18,* 165–183.

Snyder, M., & Swann, W. B., Jr. (1978). Behavioral confirmation in social interaction: From social perception to social reality. *Journal of Experimental Social Psychology, 14,* 148–162.

Snyder, M., Tanke, E. D., & Berscheid, E. (1977). Social perception and interpersonal behavior: On the self-fulfilling nature of social stereotypes. *Journal of Personality and Social Psychology, 35,* 656–666.

Snyder, M., & Uranowitz, S. W. (1978). Reconstructing the past: Some cognitive consequences of person perception. *Journal of Personality and Social Psychology, 36,* 941–950.

Solomon, M. R., & Schopler, J. (1982). Self-consciousness and clothing. *Personality and Social Psychology Bulletin, 8,* 508–514.

Sommer, R. (1969). *Personal space: The behavioral basis of design.* Englewood Cliffs, NJ: Prentice-Hall.

Sommer, R. (1974). *Tight spaces: Hard architecture and how to humanize it.* Englewood Cliffs, NJ: Prentice-Hall.

Sommer, R. (1987). Crime and vandalism in university residence halls: A confirmation of defensible space theory. *Journal of Environmental Psychology, 7,* 1–12.

Sommer, R., & Ross, H. (1958). Social interaction on a geriatrics ward. *International Journal of Social Psychiatry, 4,* 128–133.

Spanier, G. B. (1983). Married and unmarried cohabitation in the United States: 1980. *Journal of Marriage and the Family, 45,* 277–288.

Spanier, G. B., & Glick, P. C. (1981). Marital instability in the United States: Some correlates and recent changes. *Family Relations, 31,* 329–338.

Spanier, G. B., Lewis, R. A., & Cole, C. L. (1975). Marital adjustment over the family life cycle: The issue of curvilinearity. *Journal of Marriage and the Family, 37,* 263–275.

Spanos, N. P., Gwynn, M. I., Comer, S. L., Baltruweit, W. J., & Perry, J. L. (1989). Are hypnotically-induced pseudomemories resistant to cross-examination? *Law and Human Behavior, 13,* 271–290.

Spivey, C. B., & Prentice-Dunn, S. (1989). *Assessing the directionality of deindividuated behavior: Effects of deindividuation, modeling, and private self-consciousness on aggressive and prosocial responses.* Unpublished manuscript, University of Alabama.

Stall, R. D., Cortes, T. J., & Hoff, C. (1988). Behavioral risk reduction for HIV infection among gay and bisexual men. *American Psychologist, 43,* 878–885.

Stark, E. (1984). Hypnosis on trial. *Psychology Today,* February 1984, pp. 34–36.

Stasser, G., & Titus, W. (1987). Effect of information load and percentage shared information on the dissemination of unshared information during group discussion. *Journal of Personality and Social Psychology, 53,* 81–93.

Staub, E. (1978). *Positive social behavior and morality* (Vol. 1). New York: Academic Press.

Steblay, N. M. (1987). Helping behavior in rural and urban enviroments: A meta-analysis. *Psychological Bulletin, 102,* 346–356.

Steele, C. M. (1988). The psychology of self-affirmation: Sustaining the integrity of the self. In L. Berkowitz (Ed.), *Advances in experimental social psychology* (Vol. 21, pp. 261–302). Orlando, FL. Academic Press.

Steele, C. M., & Liu, T. J. (1981). Making the dissonant act unreflective of self: Dissonance avoidance and the expectancy of a value-affirming response. *Personality and Social Psychology Bulletin, 7,* 393–397.

Steele, C. M., & Southwick, L. (1985). Alcohol and social behavior. I: The psychology of drunken excess. *Journal of Personality and Social Psychology, 48,* 18–34.

Steele, C. M., Southwick, L. L., & Critchlow, B. (1981). Dissonance and alcohol: Drinking your troubles away. *Journal of Personality and Social Psychology, 41,* 831–846.

Stein, A. H., & Friedrich, L. K. (1972). Television content and young children's behavior. In J. P. Murray, E. A. Rubinstein, & G. A. Comstock (Eds.), *Television and social learning.* Washington, DC: U.S. Government Printing Office.

Stein, D. D., Hardyck, J. A., & Smith, M. B. (1965). Race and belief: An open and shut case. *Journal of Personality and Social Psychology, 1,* 281–289.

Steller, M., & Koehnken, G. (1989). Criteria-based statement analysis: Credibility assessment of children's testimonies in sexual abuse cases. In D. C. Raskin (Ed.), *Psychological methods in criminal investigation and evidence* (pp. 217–246). New York: Springer.

Steller, M., Raskin, D. C., Yuille, J., & Esplin, P. (1988). *Sexually abused children: Interview and assessment techniques.* New York: Springer.

Steller, M., Wellershaus, P., & Wolf, T. (1988). *Empirical validation of criteria-based content analysis.* Paper presented at NATO Advanced Study Institute on Credibility Assessment, Maratea, Italy.

Stephan, W. G. (1978). School desegregation: An evaluation of predictions made in *Brown v. Board of Education. Psychological Bulletin, 85,* 217–238.

Stephan, W. G. (1985). Intergroup relations. In G. Lindzey & E. Aronson (Eds.), *Handbook of social psychology* (Vol. 3, pp. 599–658). New York: Prager.

Stephan, W. G. (1987). The contact hypothesis in intergroup relations. In C. Hendrick (Ed.), *Review of Personality and Social Psychology* (Vol. 9, pp. 13–40). Beverly Hills, CA: Sage.

Stephan, W. G., & Rosenfield, D. (1978). Effects of desegregation on racial attitudes. *Journal of Personality and Social Psychology, 36,* 795–804.

Stephan, W. G., & Stephan, C. W. (1984). The role of ignorance in intergroup relations. In M. B. Brewer & N. Miller (Eds.), *Groups in contact: The psychology of desegregation* (pp. 229–257). New York: Academic Press.

Stephan, W. G., & Stephan, C. W. (1985). Intergroup interaction anxiety. *Journal of Social Issues, 41*(3), 157–177.

Stern, L. O., Mars, S., Millar, M. G., & Cole, E. (1984). Processing time and the recall of inconsistent and consistent behaviors of individuals and groups. *Journal of Personality and Social Psychology, 4,* 253–262.

Stern, P. C., & Gardner, G. T. (1981). Psychological research and energy policy. *American Psychologist, 36,* 329–342.

Sternberg, R. J. (1986). A triangular theory of love. *Psychological Review, 93,* 119–135.

Sternberg, R. J. (1987). Liking versus loving: A comparative evaluation of theories. *Psychological Bulletin, 102,* 331–345.

Sternberg, R. J. (1988). Triangulating love. In R. J. Sternberg & M. L. Barnes (Eds.), *The Psychology of Love* (pp. 119–138). New Haven, CT: Yale University Press.

Stewart, J. E., II. (1980). Defendant's attractiveness as a factor in the outcome of criminal trials: An observational study. *Journal of Applied Social Psychology, 10,* 348–361.

Stobaugh, R., & Yergin, D. (Eds.). (1979). *Energy future.* New York: Random House.

Stogdill, R. M. (1948). Personal factors associated with leadership: A survey of the literature. *Journal of Personality, 25,* 35–71.

Stogdill, R. M., & Coons, A. E. (Eds.). (1957). *Leader behavior: Its description and measurement.* [Research monograph No. 88]. Ohio State University, Bureau of Business Research.

Stokols, D. (1976). The experience of crowding in primary and secondary environments. *Environment and Behavior, 8,* 49–86.

Stokols, D. (1982). Environmental psychology: A coming of age. In A. G. Kraft (Ed.), *The G. Stanley Hall Lecture Series* (Vol. 2). Washington, DC: American Psychological Association.

Stone, A. A., Helder, L., & Schneider, M. S. (1988). Coping with stressful events: Coping dimensions and issues. In L. H. Cohen (Ed.), *Research on stressful life events: Theoretical and methodological issues.* New York: Sage.

Storr, A. (1968). *Human aggression.* New York: Atheneum.

Stouffer, S. A., Suchman, E. A., DeVinney, L. C., Star, S. A., & Williams, R. M., Jr. (1949). *The American soldier: Adjustments during army life* (Vol. 1). Princeton, NJ: Princeton University Press.

Straus, M., Gelles, R. J., & Steinmetz, S. (1980). *Behind closed doors: Violence in the American family.* New York: Anchor Press, Doubleday.

Straus, R. (1986). Alcohol and alcohol problems research. *Behavior Journal of Addiction, 81,* 315–325.

Stricker, L. P., Jacobs, P. I., & Kogan, N. (1974). Trait interrelations in implicit personality theories and questionnaire data. *Journal of Personality and Social Psychology, 30,* 198–207.

Strodtbeck, F. L., & Hook, L. H. (1961). The social dimensions of a twelve-man jury table. *Sociometry, 24,* 397–416.

Strodtbeck, F. L., James, R. M., & Hawkins, D. (1957). Social status in jury deliberations. *American Sociological Review, 22,* 713–719.

Strong, S. R., Hills, H. J., Kilmartin, C. T., DeVries, H., Lanier, K., Nelson, B. N., Strickland, D., & Meyer C. W., III. (1988). The dynamic relations among interpersonal behaviors: A test of complementarity and anticomplementarity. *Journal of Personality and Social Psychology, 54,* 798–810.

Strube, M. J. (1987). A self appraisal model of the Type A behavior pattern. In R. Hogan & W. H. Jones (Eds.), *Perspectives in personality* (pp. 201–250.) New York: Wiley.

Strube, M. J., Berry, J. M., Lott, C. L., Fogelman, R., Steinhart, G., Moergen, S., & Davison, L. (1986). Self-schematic representation of the Type A and B behavior patterns. *Journal of Personality and Social Psychology, 51,* 170–180.

Strube, M. J., Boland, S. M., Manfredo, P. A., & Al-Falaij, A. (1987). Type A behavior and the self-evaluation of abilities: Empirical tests of the self-appraisal model. *Journal of Personality and Social Psychology, 52,* 956–974.

Strube, M. J., & Garcia, J. E. (1981). A meta-analytical investigation of Fiedler's contingency model of leadership effectiveness. *Psychological Bulletin, 90,* 307–321.

Stunkard, A. J. (1979). Behavioral medicine and beyond: The example of obesity. In O. F. Pomerleau & J. P. Brady (Eds.), *Behavioral medicine: Theory and practice.* Baltimore: Williams & Wilkins.

Suedfeld, P., & Borrie, R. A. (1978). Sensory deprivation, attitude change, and defense against persuasion. *Canadian Journal of Behavioral Science, 10,* 16–27.

Suedfeld, P., Rank, D., & Borrie, R. (1975). Frequency of exposure and evaluation of candidates and campaign speeches. *Journal of Applied Social Psychology, 5,* 118–126.

Sulman, F. G., Pfeifer, Y., Hirschman, M. (1964). Effects of hot dry desert winds (sharav, hamsin) on the metabolism of hormones and minerals. *Harokeach Haiuri, 10,* 401–404.

Suls, J., & Fletcher, B. (1985). The relative efficacy of avoidant and nonavoidant coping strategies: A meta-analysis. *Health Psychology, 4,* 249–288.

Sumner, W. G. (1906). *Folkways.* New York and Boston: Ginn.

Sundberg, N. D. (1955). The acceptability of "fake" versus "bona fide" personality test interpretations. *Journal of Abnormal and Social Psychology, 50,* 145–147.

Sundstrom, E., & Altman, I. (1974). Field study of dominance and territorial behavior. *Journal of Personality and Social Psychology, 30,* 115–125.

Surgeon General's Scientific Advisory Committee on Television and Social Behavior. (1972). *Television and growing up: The impact of televised violence.* Washington, DC: U.S. Government Printing Office.

Survey: Woman hurt party. (1984). *Tallahassee Democrat,* December, 10, 1984, p. 1.

Sussman, S., Mueser, K. T., Grau, B. W., & Yarnold, P. R. (1983). Stability of females' facial attractiveness during childhood. *Journal of Personality and Social Psychology, 44,* 1231–1233.

Sutton, S. R. (1982). Fear-arousing communications: A critical examination of theory and research. In J. R. Eiser (Ed.), *Social psychology and behavioral medicine* (pp. 303–337). Chichester, England: Wiley.

Svarstad, B. L. (1974). *The doctor-patient encounter.* Unpublished doctoral dissertation, University of Wisconsin.

Svenson, O. (1981). Are we all less risky and more skillful than our fellow drivers? *Acta Psychologica, 47,* 143–148.

Swann, W. B., Jr. (1986). The self as architect of social reality. In B. R. Schlenker (Ed.), *The self and social life* (pp. 100–125). New York: McGraw-Hill.

Swann, W. B., Jr. (1987). Identity negotiation: Where two roads meet. *Journal of Personality and Social Psychology, 53,* 1038–1051.

Swann, W. B., Jr., & Ely, R. J. (1984). A battle of wills: Self-verification versus behavioral confirmation. *Journal of Personality and Social Psychology, 46,* 1287–1302.

Swann, W. B., Jr., Griffin, J. J., Predmore, S. C., & Gaines, B. (1987). The cognitive affective crossfire: When self-consistency confronts self-enhancement. *Journal of Personality and Social Psychology, 52,* 881–889.

Swann, W. B., Jr., & Hill, C. A. (1982). When our identities are mistaken: Reaffirming self-conceptions through social interaction. *Journal of Personality and Social Psychology, 43,* 59–66.

Swee-Hock, S. (1975). Singapore: Resumption of rapid fertility decline in 1973. *Studies in Family Planning, 6,* 166–169.

Synodinos, N. E. (1986). Hindsight distortion: "I knew it all along and I was sure about it." *Journal of Applied Social Psychology, 16,* 107–117.

Szymanski, K., & Harkins, S. G. (1987). Social loafing and self-evaluation with a social standard. *Journal of Personality and Social Psychology, 55,* 891–987.

Szucko, J. J., & Kleinmuntz, B. (1981). Statistical versus clinical lie detection. *American Psychologist, 36,* 488–496.

Tabachnik, N., Crocker, J., & Alloy, L. B. (1983). Depression, social comparison, and the false-consensus effect. *Journal of Personality and Social Psychology, 45,* 688–699.

Tagiuri, R. (1969). Person perception. In G. Lindzey & E. Aronson (Eds.), *Handbook of social psychology* (2nd ed., Vol. 3). Reading, MA: Addison-Wesley.

Tajfel, H. (1982). Social psychology of intergroup relations. *Annual Review of Psychology, 33,* 1–39.

Tajfel, H., & Turner, J. (1979). An integrative theory of intergroup conflict. In W. G. Austin & S. Worchel (Eds.), *The social psychology of intergroup relations.* Monterey, CA: Brooks/Cole.

Tajfel, H., & Turner, J. C. (1986). The social identity theory of intergroup behavior. In S. Worchel & W. G. Austin (Eds.), *Psychology of intergroup relations* (2nd ed., pp. 7–24). Chicago: Nelson-Hall.

Tanfer, K. (1987). Patterns of premarital cohabitation among never-married women in the U.S. *Journal of Marriage and the Family, 49,* 483–497.

Tannenbaum, P. H. (1980). Entertainment as vicarious emotional experience. In P. H. Tannebaum (Ed.), *The entertainment functions of television.* Hillsdale, NJ: Erlbaum.

Tanner, J. (1986). U.S. hopes for energy independence shattering as oil resource base erodes. *Wall Street Journal,* March 17, 1986, pp. 1, 4.

Tavris, C. (1982). *Anger: The misunderstood emotion.* New York: Simon & Schuster.

Tavris, C., & Wade, C. (1984). *The longest war: Sex differences in perspective.* (rev. ed.) New York: Harcourt Brace Jovanovich.

Taylor, D. (1974). Should we integrate organizations? In H. L. Fromkin & J. J. Sherwood (Eds.), *Integrating the organization.* New York: Free Press.

Taylor, D. G., Sheatsley, P. B., & Greeley, A. M. (1978). Attitudes toward racial integration. *Scientific American, 238*(6), 42–49.

Taylor, M. S., Locke, E. A., Lee, C., & Gist, M. E. (1984). Type A behavior and faculty research productivity: What are the mechanisms? *Organizational Behavior and Human Performance, 34,* 402–418.

Taylor, S. E. (1987). The progress and prospects of health psychology: Tasks of a maturing discipline. *Health and Psychology, 6,* 73–87.

Taylor, S. E. (1990). Health psychology: The science and the field. *American Psychologist, 45,* 40–50.

Taylor, S. E., & Brown, J. D. (1988). Illusion and well-being: A social psychological perspective on mental health. *Journal of Personality and Social Psychology, 103,* 193–210.

Taylor, S. E., & Fiske, S. T. (1978). Salience, attention and attribution: Top of the head phenomena. In L. Berkowitz (Ed.), *Advances in experimental social psychology* (Vol. 11). New York: Academic Press.

Taylor, S. E., Fiske, S. T., Etcoff, N. L., & Ruderman, A. J. (1978). Categorical and contextual bases of person memory and stereotyping. *Journal of Personality and Social Psychology, 36,* 778–793.

Taylor, S. P., Gammon, C. B., & Capasso, D. R. (1976). Aggression as a function of alcohol and threat. *Journal of Personality and Social Psychology, 34,* 938–941.

Taylor, S. P., & Leonard, K. E. (1983). Alcohol and human physical aggression. In R. C. Geen & E. I. Donnerstein (Eds.), *Aggression: Theoretical and empirical reviews* (Vol. 2, pp. 77–101). New York: Academic Press.

Taylor, S. P., Schmutte, G. T., Leonard, K. E., & Cranston, J. W. (1979). The effects of alcohol and extreme provocation on the use of highly noxious shock. *Motivation and Emotion, 3,* 73–81.

Taylor, S. P., Vardaris, R. M., Rawtich, A. C., Gammon, C. B., Cranston, J. W., & Lubetkin, A. (1976). The effects of alcohol and Delta-9-Tetrahydrocan-Nabinol on human physical aggression. *Aggressive Behavior, 2*(2), 153–161.

Taylor, T. (1970). *Nuremburg and Vietnam: An American tragedy.* Chicago: Quadrangle Books.

Tedeschi, J. T. (1974). *Perspectives on social power.* Chicago: Aldine.

Tedeschi, J. T., & Rosenfeld, P. (1981). Impression management theory and the forced compliance situation. In J. T. Tedeschi (Ed.), *Impression management theory and social psychological research.* New York: Academic Press.

Tedeschi, J. T., Smith, R. B., III, & Brown, R. C. (1974). A reinterpretation of research on aggression. *Psychological Bulletin, 81,* 540–562.

Teger, A. (1980). *Too much invested to quit.* New York: Pergamon.

Tennen, H., & Eller, S. J. (1977). Attributional components of learned helplessness and facilitation. *Journal of Personality and Social Psychology, 35,* 265–271.

Tennov, D. (1979). *Love and limerance: The experience of being in love.* New York: Stein and Day.

Terman, M., & Link, M. (1989). Fighting the winter blues with bright light. *Psychology Today,* January/February, 1989, pp. 18–20.

Tesser, A. (1988). Toward a self-evaluation maintenance model of social behavior. In L. Berkowitz (Ed.), *Advances in experimental social psychology,* (Vol. 21, pp. 181–227). New York: Academic Press.

Tesser, A., & Brodie, M. (1971). A note on the evaluation of a "computer date." *Psychonomic Science, 23,* 300.

Tesser, A., & Campbell, J. (1982). Self-evaluation maintenance and the perception of friends and strangers. *Journal of Personality, 50,* 261–279.

Tesser, A., & Campbell, J. (1983). Self-definition and self-evaluation maintenance. In J. Suls & A. N. Greenwald (Eds.), *Psychological perspectives on the self* (Vol. 2, pp. 1–31). Hillsdale, NJ: Erlbaum.

Tesser, A., Campbell, J., & Smith, M. (1984). Friendship choice and performance: Self-evaluation maintenance in children. *Journal of Personality and Social Psychology, 46,* 561–574.

Tesser, A., & Paulhus, D. (1983). The definition of self: Private and public self-management strategies. *Journal of Personality and Social Psychology, 44,* 672–682.

Testa, R., Kinder, B., & Sronson, G. (1987). Heterosexual bias in the perception of loving relationships of gay males and lesbians. *Journal of Sex Research, 23*(2), 163–172.

Tetlock, P. E. (1979). Identifying victims of groupthink from public statements of decision makers. *Journal of Personality and Social Psychology, 37,* 1314–1324.

Tetlock, P. E. (1986). Psychological advice on foreign policy: What do we have to contribute? *American Psychologist, 41,* 557–567.

Tetlock, P. E., & Manstead, A. S. R. (1985). Impression management versus intrapsychic explanations in social psychology: A useful dichotomy? *Psychological Review, 92,* 59–77.

Thibaut, J. W., & Kelley, H. H. (1959). *The social psychology of groups.* New York: Wiley.

Thomas, G., & Batson, C. D. (1981). Effect of helping under normative pressure on self-perceived altruism. *Social Psychology Quarterly, 44,* 127–131.

Thomas, G. C., Batson, C. D., & Coke, J. S. (1981). Do Good Samaritans discourage helpfulness? Self-perceived altruism after exposure to highly helpful others. *Journal of Personality and Social Psychology, 40,* 194–200.

Thomas, M. H., & Drabman, R. S. (1978). Effects of television violence on expectations of other's aggression. *Personality and Social Psychology Bulletin, 4,* 73–76.

Thomas, W. I., & Znaniecki, F. (1918). *The Polish peasant in Europe and America* (Vol. 1). Boston: Badger.

Thompson, S. C., & Kelley, H. H. (1981). Judgments of responsibility for activities in closed relationships. *Journal of Personality and Social Psychology, 41,* 469–477.

Thompson, V. D. (1974). Family size: Implicit policies and assumed psychological outcomes. *Journal of Social Issues, 30*(4), 93–124.

Thompson, W. C. (1989). Death qualification after *Wainwright v. Witt* and *Lockhart v. McCree. Law and Human Behavior, 13,* 185–215.

Thompson, W. C., Cowan, C. L., & Rosenhan, D. L. (1980). Focus of attention mediates the impact of negative affect on altruism. *Journal of Personality and Social Psychology, 38,* 291–300.

Thompson, W. C., Fong, G. T., & Rosenhan, D. L. (1981). Inadmissable evidence and juror verdicts. *Journal of Personality and Social Psychology, 40,* 453–463.

Thornton, A., & Freedman, D. (1983). The changing American family. *Population Bulletin, 38*(4), 1–44.

Thornton, B. (1977). Effect of rape victim's attractiveness in a jury simulation. *Personality and Social Psychology Bulletin, 3,* 666–669.

Thornton, B., Ryckman, R. M., Kirchner, G., Jacobs, J., Kaczor, L., & Kuehnel, R. H. (1988). Reaction to self-attributed victim responsibility: A comparative analysis of rape crisis counselors and lay observers. *Journal of Applied Social Psychology, 18,* 409–422.

Thorson, J. A., & Kasworm, C. (1984). Sunshine and suicide: Possible influences of climate on behavior. *Death Education, 8,* 125–136.

Thousands of homicides linked to TV violence (1989). *NCTV News, 10*(5–6), 1.

Thurstone, L. L. (1946). Comment. *American Journal of Sociology, 52,* 39–40.

Tice, D. M., & Baumeister, R. F. (1985). Masculinity inhibits helping in emergencies: Personality does predict the bystander effect. *Journal of Personality and Social Psychology, 49,* 420–428.

Toffler, A. (1970). *Future shock.* New York: Random House.

Toi, M., & Batson, C. D. (1982). More evidence that empathy is a source of altruistic motivation. *Journal of Personality and Social Psychology, 43,* 281–292.

Tomarelli, M. M., & Shaffer, D. R. (1985). What aspects of self do self-monitors monitor? *Bulletin of the Psychonomic Society, 23*(2), 135–138.

Tooley, V., Brigham, J. C., Maass, A., & Bothwell, R. K. (1987). Facial recognition: Weapon effect and attentional focus. *Journal of Applied Social Psychology, 17,* 845–859.

Traupmann, J., Eckels, E., & Hatfield, E. (1982). Intimacy in older women's lives. *The Gerontologist, 22,* 493–498.

Traupmann, J., & Hatfield, E. (1981). Love and its effect on mental and physical health. In J. March, S. Kiesler, R. Fogel, E. Hatfield, & E. Shanas (Eds.), *Aging: Stability and change in the family.* New York: Academic Press.

Traupmann, J., Peterson, R., Utne, M., & Hatfield, E. (1981). Measuring equity in intimate relations. *Applied Psychological Measurement, 5,* 467–480.

Triandis, H. C. (1988). The future of pluralism revisited. In P. A. Katz & D. A. Taylor (Eds.), *Eliminating racism: Profiles in controversy* (pp. 31–50). New York: Plenum.

Triplett, N. E. (1898). The dynamogenic factors in pacemaking and competition. *American Journal of Psychology, 9,* 507–533.

Trivers, R. L. (1971). The evolution of reciprocal altruism. *Quarterly Review of Biology, 46,* 35–57.

Trope, Y. (1986). Self-enhancement and self-assessment in achievement behavior. In R. M. Sorrentino & E. T. Higgins (Eds.), *Handbook of motivation and cognition: Foundations of social behaviors* (pp. 350–378). New York: Guilford.

Trope, Y., & Bassok, M. (1982). Confirmatory and diagnosing strategies in social information gathering. *Journal of Personality and Social Psychology, 43,* 22–34.

Trost, M. R., Cialdini, R. B., & Maass, A. (1989). Effects of an international conflict simulation on perceptions of the Soviet Union: A FIREBREAKS backfire. *Journal of Social Issues, 45*(2), 139–158.

Trousseau, A. (1882). *Clinical medicine.* Philadelphia: P. Blakiston, Son.

Tukey, D. D., & Borgida, E. (1983). An intrasubject approach to causal attribution. *Journal of Personality, 51,* 137–151.

Turkington, C. (1986). Jury selection ruling disregards research. *APA Monitor,* July 1986, p. 20.

Turner, C. W., Hesse, B. W., & Peterson-Lewis, S. (1986). Naturalistic studies of the long-term effects of television violence. *Journal of Social Issues, 42*(3), 51–74.

Turner, C. W., Layton, J. F., & Simons, L. S. (1975). Naturalistic studies of aggressive behavior: Aggressive stimuli, victim visibility, and horn honking. *Journal of Personality and Social Psychology, 31,* 1098–1107.

Turner, J. C. (1987). *Rediscovering the social group: A self-categorization theory.* New York: Basil Blackwell.

Turner, J. C., & Oakes, P. J. (1989). Self-categorization theory and social influence. In P. B. Paulus (Ed.), *Psychology of group influence* (2nd ed., pp. 233–278). Hillsdale, NJ: Erlbaum.

Turque, B. (1989). Duke shows his true colors. *Newsweek,* December 25, 1989, p. 53.

Tversky, A., & Kahneman, D. (1971). Belief in the law of small numbers. *Psychological Bulletin, 76,* 105–110.

Tversky, A., & Kahneman, D. (1974). Judgment under uncertainty: Heuristics and biases. *Science, 185,* 1123–1131.

Tyler, T. R., & Sears, D. O. (1977). Coming to like obnoxious people when we must live with them. *Journal of Personality and Social Psychology, 35,* 200–211.

Ulrich, R. E., Stachnik, D. J., & Stainton, N. R. (1963). Student acceptance of generalized personality interpretations. *Psychological Reports, 13,* 831–834.

Underwood, B., Berensen, J. F., Berensen, R. J., Cheng, K. J., Wilson, W., Kulik, J., Moore, B. S., & Wenzel, G. (1977). Attention, negative affect, and altruism: An ecological validation. *Personality and Social Psychology Bulletin, 3,* 54–58.

Uniform Crime Reports. (1983). *Crime in the United States.* Washington, DC: FBI, U.S. Department of Justice.

Union of Concerned Scientists. (1987). *Nuclear weapons and arms control.* Cambridge, MA: Author.

U.S. Attorney General's Commission on Pornography. (1986). *Final Report.* Washington, DC: U.S. Department of Justice.

U.S. Department of Commerce, Bureau of Census. (1989). *Statistical abstract of the United States, 1989* (109th edition). Washington, DC: U.S. Government Printing Office.

U.S. Department of Health and Human Services. (1986). *Reducing health consequences of smoking: 25 years of progress. A report of the Surgeon General.* Washington, DC: U.S. Government Printing Office.

U.S. Nuclear Regulatory Commission. (1975). *Reactor safety study: An assessment of accident risks in U.S. commercial nuclear powerplants.* (WASH 1400 [NUREG-75/014]). Washington, DC: Nuclear Regulatory Commission.

U.S. Office of Technology Assessment. (1983). *Scientific validity of polygraph testing: A research review and evaluation—a technical memorandum.* Washington, DC: US GPO.

United States Public Health Service. (1976). *Adult uses of tobacco: 1975.* Washington, DC: U.S. Department of Health, Education, and Welfare.

U.S. v. Wade (1967). 388 U.S. 218, 87 S. Ct. 1926, 18 L. Ed. 2d 1149.

Utne, M. K. (1978). *Equity and intimate relations: A test of the theory in marital interaction.* Unpublished doctoral dissertation, University of Wisconsin, Madison.

Valdiserri, R., Lyter, D., Kingsley, L., Leviton, L., Schofield, J., Hoggins, J., Ho, M., & Rinaldo, C. (1987). The effect of group education on improving attitudes about AIDS risk reduction. *New York State Journal of Medicine, 87,* 272–278.

Valins, S. (1966). Cognitive effects of false heart-rate feedback. *Journal of Personality and Social Psychology, 4,* 400–408.

Valins, S. (1967). Emotionality and information concerning internal reactions. *Journal of Personality and Social Psychology, 6,* 458–463.

Valins, S. (1970). The perception and labeling of bodily changes as determinants of emotional behavior. In P. Black (Ed.), *Physiological correlates of emotion.* New York: Academic Press.

Valins, S., & Ray, A. (1967). Effects of cognitive desensitization on avoidance behavior. *Journal of Personality and Social Psychology, 7,* 345–350.

Vallone, R. P., Griffin, D. W., Lin, S., & Ross, L. (1990). Overconfident prediction of future actions and outcomes by self and others. *Journal of Personality and Social Psychology, 58,* 582–592.

Vallone, R. P., Ross, L., & Lepper, M. R. (1985). The hostile media phenomenon: Biased perception and perceptions of media bias in coverage of the "Beirut Massacre." *Journal of Personality and Social Psychology, 49,* 577–585.

van der Plight, J. (1984). Attributions, false consensus and valence: Two field studies. *Journal of Personality and Social Psychology, 46,* 57–68.

Verner, E., Coleman, M., Ganong, L., & Cooper, H. (1989). Marital satisfaction in remarriage: A meta-analysis. *Journal of Marriage and the Family, 51,* 713–725.

Vidmar, N., & Rokeach, M. (1974). Archie Bunker's bigotry: A study in selective perception and exposure. *Journal of Communication, 24,* 36–47.

Vincent, R. C. (1989). Clio's consciousness raised? Portrayals of women in rock videos re-examined. *Journalism Quarterly, 66,* 155–160.

Visher, E., & Visher, J. (1979). *Stepfamilies: A guide to working with stepparents and stepchildren.* New York: Brunner/Mazel.

Vogel, H. H., Scott, J. P., & Marston, M. V. (1950). Social facilitation and allelomimetic behavior in dogs. I. Social facilitation in a noncompetitive situation. *Behavior, 2,* 121.

Vonnegut, K., Jr. (1966). *Mother night.* New York: Dell.

Vreeland, R. (1972). Is it true what they say about Harvard boys? *Psychology Today,* January 1972, pp. 65–68.

Wagner, H. L., MacDonald, C. J., & Manstead, A. S. R. (1986). Communication of individual emotions by spontaneous facial expressions. *Journal of Personality and Social Psychology, 50,* 737–743.

Wagner, R. V. (1985). Psychology and the threat of nuclear war. *American Psychologist, 40,* 531–535.

Walker, T. G., & Main, E. C. (1973). Choice-shifts in political decision making: Federal judges and civil liberties cases. *Journal of Applied Social Psychology, 2,* 39–48.

Waller, W., & Hill, R. (1951). *The family: A dynamic interpretation.* New York: Dryden Press.

Walster, E. (1964). The temporal sequence of post-decision processes. In L. Festinger (Ed.), *Conflict, decision, and dissonance.* Stanford, CA: Stanford University Press.

Walster, E., Aronson, E., & Abrahams, D. (1966). On increasing the persuasiveness of a low prestige communicator. *Journal of Experimental Social Psychology, 2,* 325–342.

Walster, E., Aronson, E., Abrahams, D., & Rottman, L. (1966). Importance of physical attractiveness in dating behavior. *Journal of Personality and Social Psychology, 4,* 508–516.

Walster, E., & Berscheid, E. (1971). Adrenaline makes the heart grow fonder. *Psychology Today,* June 1971, pp. 47–62.

Walster, E., & Festinger, L. (1962). The effectiveness of "overheard" persuasive communications. *Journal of Abnormal and Social Psychology, 65,* 395–402.

Walster, E., Traupmann, J., & Walster, G. W. (1978). Equity and extramarital sex. *Archives of Sexual Behavior, 7,* 127–141.

Walster, E., Walster, G. W., & Berscheid, E. (1978). *Equity: Theory and research.* Boston: Allyn and Bacon.

Walster, E., Walster, G. W., Piliavin, J., & Schmidt, L. (1973). "Playing hard to get": Understanding an elusive phenomenon. *Journal of Personality and Social Psychology, 26,* 113–121.

Ward, C. H., & Eisler, R. M. (1987). Type A behavior, achievement striving, and a dysfunctional self-evaluation system. *Journal of Personality and Social Psychology, 53,* 318–326.

Ward, L., & Wilson, J. P. (1980). Motivation and moral development as determinants of behavioral acquiescence and moral action. *Journal of Social Psychology, 112,* 271–286.

Watson, J. B. (1912). Content of a course in psychology for medical students. *Journal of the American Medical Association, 58,* 916–918.

Watson, R. E. L., & DeMeo, P. W. (1987). Premarital cohabitation vs. traditional courtship and subsequent marital adjustment: A replication and follow-up. *Family Relations, 4,* 193–197.

Watson, R. I., Jr. (1973). Investigation into deindividuation using a cross-cultural survey technique. *Journal of Personality and Social Psychology, 25,* 342–345.

Watts, W. A., & Holt, L. E. (1979). Persistence of opinion change induced under conditions of forewarning and distraction. *Journal of Personality and Social Psychology, 37,* 778–789.

Weary, G. (1980). Examination of affect and egotism as mediators of bias in causal attributions. *Journal of Personality and Social Psychology, 38,* 348–357.

Weary, G., Elbin, S., & Hill, M. G. (1987). Attributional and social comparison processes in depression. *Journal of Personality and Social Psychology, 52,* 605–610.

Weary, G., Harvey, J. H., Schwieger, P., Olson, C. T., Perloff, R., & Pritchard, S. (1982). Self-presentation and the moderation of self-serving attributional biases. *Social Cognition, 1,* 140–159.

Webb, W. M., Marsh, K. L., Schneiderman, W., & Davis, B. (1989). Interaction between self-monitoring and manipulated states of self-awareness. *Journal of Personality and Social Psychology, 56,* 70–80.

Weber, R., & Crocker, J. (1983). Cognitive process in the revision of stereotypic beliefs. *Journal of Personality and Social Psychology, 45,* 961–977.

Weber, S. J., & Cook, T. D. (1972). Subject effects in laboratory research: An examination of subject roles, demand characteristics, and valid inference. *Psychological Bulletin, 77,* 273–295.

Weidner, G., & Matthews, K. A. (1978). Reported physical symptoms elicited by unpredictable events and the Type A coronary-prone behavior pattern. *Journal of Personality and Social Psychology, 36,* 213–220.

Weigel, R. H., Loomis, J. W., & Soja, M. J. (1980). Race relations on prime-time television. *Journal of Personality and Social Psychology, 39,* 884–893.

Weigel, R. H., & Newman, L. S. (1976). Increasing attitude behavior correspondence by broadening the scope of the behavioral measure. *Journal of Personality and Social Psychology, 33,* 793–802.

Weigel, R. H., Wiser, P. L., & Cook, S. W. (1975). The impact of cooperative learning experiences on cross-ethnic relations and attitudes. *Journal of Social Issues, 31*(1), 219–244.

Weiner, B. (1979). A theory of motivation for some classroom experiences. *Journal of Educational Psychology, 71,* 3–25.

Weiner, B. (1980). *Human motivation.* New York: Holt, Rinehart & Winston.

Weiner, B. (1985). An attributional theory of achievement motivation and emotion. *Psychological Review, 92,* 548–573.

Weiner, B., Amirkhan, J., Folkes, V. S., & Verette, J. A. (1987). An attributional analysis of excuse giving: Studies of a naive theory of emotion. *Journal of Personality and Social Psychology, 52,* 316–324.

Weiner, F. H. (1976). Altruism, ambience, and action: The effects of rural and urban rearing on helping behavior. *Journal of Personality and Social Psychology, 34,* 112–124.

Weinstein, C., & Pinciotti, P. (1988). Changing a schoolyard: Intentions, design decisions, and behavioral outcomes. *Environment and Behavior, 20,* 345–371.

Weiss, R. S. (1976). Impact of separation. *Journal of Social Issues, 32*(1), 135–145.

Wells, G. L., Leippe, M. R., & Ostrom, T. M. (1979). Guidelines for empirically assessing the fairness of a lineup. *Law and Human Behavior, 3,* 285–294.

Wells, G. L., & Murray, D. M. (1983). What can psychology say about the *Neil v. Biggers* criteria for judging eyewitness accuracy? *Journal of Applied Psychology, 68,* 347–362.

Wells, G. L., & Petty, R. E. (1980). The effects of overt head movements on persuasion: Compatibility and incompatibility of responses. *Basic and Applied Social Psychology, 1,* 219–230.

Wells, J. K., Howard, G. S., Nowlin, W. F., & Vargas, M. J. (1986). Presurgical anxiety and postsurgical pain and adjustment: Effects of a stress inoculation procedure. *Journal of Consulting and Clinical Psychology, 54,* 831–835.

Welty, J. C. (1934). Experiments in group behavior of fishes. *Physiological Zoology, 7,* 85–128.

Werner, C., & Parmalee, P. (1979). Similarity in activity preferences among friends: Those who play together stay together. *Social Psychology Quarterly, 42,* 620–626.

West, C. (1982). Why can't a woman be more like a man? *Sociology of Work and Occupation, 9,* 5–29.

West, S. G., & Gunn, S. P. (1978). Some issues of ethics and social psychology. *American Psychologist, 30,* 30–38.

West, S. G., Gunn, S. P., & Chernicky, P. (1975). Ubiquitous Watergate: An attributional analysis. *Journal of Personality and Social Psychology, 32,* 55–65.

West, S. G., Whitney, G., & Schnedler, R. (1975) Helping a motorist in distress: The effects of sex, race, and neighborhood. *Journal of Personality and Social Psychology, 31,* 691–698.

West, S. G., & Wicklund, R. A. (1980). *A primer of social psychological theories.* Monterey, CA: Brooks/Cole.

Westie, F. R., & DeFleur, M. L. (1959). Autonomic responses and their relationship to race attitudes. *Journal of Abnormal and Social Psychology, 58,* 340–347.

Weyant, J. M. (1978). Effects of mood states, costs, and benefits on helping. *Journal of Personality and Social Psychology, 36,* 1169–1176.

Weyant, J. M. (1984). Applying social psychology to induce charitable donations. *Journal of Applied Social Psychology, 14,* 441–447.

Weyant, J. M., & Smith, S. L. (1987). Getting more by asking for less: The effects of request size on donations of charity. *Journal of Applied Social Psychology, 17,* 392–400.

Whalen, D. H., & Blanchard, F. A. (1982). Effects of photographic evidence on mock juror judgment. *Journal of Applied Social Psychology, 12*, 30–41.

Whalen, R. R. (1977). Health care begins with I's. *New York Times*, April 17, 1977, Section 4, p. 21.

Wheeler, L. (1966). Toward a theory of behavioral contagion. *Psychological Review, 73*, 179–192.

Wheeler, L., & Koestner, R. (1984). Performance evaluation: On choosing to know the related attributes of others when we know their performance. *Journal of Experimental Social Psychology, 20*, 263–271.

Wheeler, L., Koestner, R., & Driver, R. E. (1982). Related attributes in the choice of comparison others: It is there, but it isn't all there is. *Journal of Experimental Social Psychology, 18*, 489–500.

White, B. (1989). Gender differences in marital communication patterns. *Family Process, 28*, 89–106.

White, G. L. (1980). Physical attractiveness and courtship progress. *Journal of Personality and Social Psychology, 39*, 660–668.

White, G. L., Fishbein, S., & Rutstein, J. (1981). Passionate love and the misattribution of arousal. *Journal of Personality and Social Psychology, 41*, 56–62.

White, J. D., & Carlston, D. E. (1983). Consequences of schemata for attention, impressions, and recall in complex social interactions. *Journal of Personality and Social Psychology, 45*, 538–549.

White, J. W. (1983). Sex and gender issues in aggression research. In R. G. Geen & E. I. Donnerstein (Eds.), *Aggression: Theoretical and empirical reviews* (Vol. 2, pp. 1–26). New York: Academic Press.

White, L., & Booth, A. (1985). The quality and stability of remarriage: The role of stepchildren. *American Sociological Review, 50*, 689–698.

White, R. K. (1969). Three not-so-obvious contributions of psychology to peace. *Journal of Social Issues, 25*(4), 23–39.

White, R. K. (1977). Misperception in the Arab-Israeli conflict. *Journal of Social Issues, 33*(1), 190–221.

White, R. K. (1984). *Fearful warriors: A psychological profile of U.S.-Soviet relations.* New York: Free Press.

White, R. K. (1985). Ten psychological contributions to the prevention of nuclear war. In S. Oskamp (Ed.), *Applied Social Psychology Annual.* (Vol. 6, pp. 45–61). Beverly Hills, CA: Sage.

Whiting, B., & Edwards, C. P. (1973). A cross-cultural analysis of sex differences in the behavior of children aged three through eleven. *Journal of Social Psychology, 91*, 171–188.

Whyte, W. H., Jr. (1956). *The organization man.* New York: Simon & Schuster.

Wicklund, R. A. (1975). Objective self-awareness. In L. Berkowitz (Ed.), *Advances in experimental social psychology* (Vol. 8). New York: Academic Press.

Wicklund, R. A. (1982). Self-focused attention and the validity of self-reports. In M. P. Zanna, E. T. Higgins, & C. P. Herman (Eds.), *Consistency in social behavior: The Ontario Symposium* (Vol. 2). Hillsdale, NJ: Erlbaum.

Wicklund, R. A., & Brehm, J. W. (1976). *Perspectives on cognitive dissonance.* Hillsdale, NJ: Erlbaum.

Wicklund, R. A., & Gollwitzer, P. M. (1987). The fallacy of the private-public self-focus distinction. *Journal of Personality, 55*, 491–523.

Wilder, D. A., & Shapiro, P. N. (1989). Role of competition-induced anxiety in limiting the beneficial impact of positive behavior by an out-group member. *Journal of Personality and Social Psychology, 56*, 60–69.

Williams vs. Florida. (1970). 399 U.S. 78.

Williams, F. H. (1969). Double jeopardy: Black and poor. *Congressional Record, 115,* 3092–3095.

Williams, J. E. (1982). An overview of findings from adult sex stereotype studies in 23 countries. In R. Rath, H. S. Asthana, D. Sinha, & J. B. Sinha (Eds.), *Diversity and unity in cross-cultural psychology* (pp. 250–260). Lisse, Netherlands: Swets and Zeitlinger.

Williams, K. B., & Williams, K. D. (1983). Social inhibition and asking for help: The effects of number, strength, and immediacy of potential help givers. *Journal of Personality and Social Psychology, 44,* 67–77.

Williams, R. B., Jr. (1989). *The trusting heart: Great news about Type A behavior.* New York: Random House.

Williams, R. B., Jr., Barefoot, J. C., & Shekelle, R. B. (1985). The health consequences of hostility. In M. A. Chesney, S. E. Goldston, & R. H. Rosenman (Eds.), *Anger, hostility, and behavioral medicine.* New York: Hemisphere/McGraw Hill.

Williams, T. M. (1986). *The impact of television: A natural experiment in three communities.* Orlando, FL: Academic Press.

Williamson, G. M., & Clark, M. S. (1989). Providing help and desired relationship type as determinants of changes in moods and self-evaluations. *Journal of Personality and Social Psychology, 56,* 722–734.

Williamson, N. E. (1976). *Sons or daughters: A cross-cultural survey of parental preferences.* Beverly Hills, CA: Sage.

Wills, G. (1977). Measuring the impact of erotica. *Psychology Today,* March 1977, pp. 30ff.

Wills, T. A. (1981). Downward comparison principles in social psychology. *Psychological Bulletin, 90,* 245–271.

Wilner, D. M., Walkley, R., & Cook, S. W. (1955). *Human relations in interracial housing: A study of the contact hypothesis.* Minneapolis: University of Minnesota Press.

Wilson, E. O. (1975). *Sociobiology: The new synthesis.* Cambridge, MA: Harvard University Press.

Wilson, E. O. (1978). *On human nature.* Cambridge, MA: Harvard University Press.

Wilson, J. P., & Petruska, R. (1984). Motivation, model attributes, and prosocial behavior. *Journal of Personality and Social Psychology, 46,* 458–468.

Wilson, J. R., Kuehn, R. E., & Beach, F. A. (1963). Modification in the sexual behavior of male rats produced by changing the stimulus female. *Journal of Comparative and Physiological Psychology, 56,* 636–644.

Wilson, T. D., & Linville, P. W. (1982). Improving the academic performance of college freshmen: Attribution theory revisited. *Journal of Personality and Social Psychology, 42,* 367–376.

Wilson, W., & Miller, H. (1968). Repetition, order of presentation, and timing of arguments and measures as determinants of opinion change. *Journal of Personality and Social Psychology, 9,* 184–188.

Winch, R. F. (1958). *Mate selection: A study of complementary needs.* New York: Harper & Row.

Winett, R. A., Neale, M. S., & Grier, H. C. (1979). The effects of self-monitoring and feedback on residential energy consumption. *Journal of Applied Behavior Analysis, 12,* 173–184.

Winett, R. A., Neale, M. S., Williams, K. R., Yockley, J., & Kauder, H. (1979). The effects of individual and group feedback on residential electricity consumption: Three replications. *Journal of Environmental Systems, 8,* 217–233.

Winkelstein, W., Samuel, M., Padian, N., Wiley, J. A., Lang, W., Anderson, R. E., & Levy, J. (1987). Reduction in human immunodeficiency virus transmission among homosexual/bisexual men: 1982–1986. *American Journal of Public Health, 76,* 685–689.

Winkler, R. C., & Winett, R. A. (1982). Behavioral interventions in resource conservation: A systems approach based on behavioral economics. *American Psychologist, 37,* 421–435.

Winsborough, H. (1965). The social consequences of high population density. *Law and Contemporary Problems, 30,* 120–126.

Winter, D. G. (1987a). Enhancement of an enemy's power motivation as a dynamic of conflict escalation. *Journal of Personality and Social Psychology, 52,* 41–46.

Winter, D. G. (1987b). Leader appeal, leader performance, and the motive profiles of leaders and followers: A study of American presidents and elections. *Journal of Personality and Social Psychology, 52,* 196–202.

Wishner, J. (1960). Reanalysis of "Impressions of personality." *Psychological Review, 67,* 96–112.

Wispé, L. G. (1972). Positive forms of social behavior: An overview. *Journal of Social Issues, 28*(3), 1–19.

Witenberg, S. H., Blanchard, E. B., McCoy, G., Suls, J., & McGoldrick, M. D. (1983). Evaluation of compliance in home and center hemodialysis patients. *Health Psychology, 2,* 227–238.

Witkin, H. A., and Associates. (1977). Criminality, aggression and intelligence among XYY and XXY men. In S. A. Mednick & K. O. Christiansen (Eds.), *Biosocial bases of criminal behavior.* New York: Gardner Press.

Woetzel, R. K. (1972). The Eichmann case in international law. In J. W. Baird (Ed.), *From Nuremburg to My Lai.* Boston: D. C. Heath.

Wolfe, R. N., Lennox, R. D., & Cutler, B. L. (1986). Getting along and getting ahead: Empirical support for a theory of protective and acquisitive self-presentation. *Journal of Personality and Social Psychology, 50,* 356–361.

Wong, P. T. P., & Weiner, B. (1981). When people ask "why" questions, and the heuristics of attributional search. *Journal of Personality and Social Psychology, 40,* 650–663.

Wood, J. V. (1989). Theory and research concerning social comparisons of personal attributes. *Psychological Bulletin, 106,* 231–248.

Wood, J. V., Taylor, S. E., & Lichtman, R. R. (1985). Social comparison in adjustment to breast cancer. *Journal of Personality and Social Psychology, 49,* 1169–1183.

Wood, W., Rhodes, N., & Whelan, M. (1989). Sex differences in positive well-being: A consideration of emotional style and marital status. *Psychological Bulletin, 106,* 249–264.

Wooden, K. (1981). *The children of Jonestown.* New York: McGraw-Hill.

Woozley, A. D. (1983). A duty to rescue: Some thoughts on criminal liability. *Virginia Law Review, 69,* 1273–1300.

Worchel, S., Arnold, S., & Baker, M. (1975). The effects of censorship on attitude change: The influence of censor and communication characteristics. *Journal of Applied Social Psychology, 5,* 227–239.

Worchel, S., & Teddlie, C. (1976). The experience of crowding: A two-factor theory. *Journal of Personality and Social Psychology, 34,* 30–40.

Worchel, S., & Yohai, S. M. L. (1979). The role of attribution in the experience of crowding. *Journal of Experimental Social Psychology, 15,* 91–104.

Word, C. O., Zanna, M. P., & Cooper, J. (1974). The nonverbal mediation of self-fulfilling prophecies in interracial interaction. *Journal of Experimental Social Psychology, 10,* 109–120.

Worringham, C. J., & Messick, D. M. (1983). Social facilitation of running: An unobtrusive study. *Journal of Social Psychology, 121,* 23–29.

Wortman, C. B. (1975). Some determinants of perceived control. *Journal of Personality and Social Psychology, 31,* 282–294.

Wortman, C. B. (1984). Social support and the cancer patient: Conceptual and methodological issues. *Cancer, 53,* 2339–2360.

Wortman, C. B., & Dinzer, L. (1978). Is an attributional analysis on the learned helplessness phenomenon viable? A critique of the Abramson-Seligman-Teasdale reformulation. *Journal of Abnormal Psychology, 87,* 75–90.

Wrightsman, L. S. (1974). The most important social psychological research of this generation? *Contemporary Psychology, 19,* 803–805.

Wrightsman, L. S. (1987). *Psychology and the legal system.* Monterey, CA: Brooks/Cole.

Wurtele, S. K. (1982). *The relative contributions of protection motivation theory components in predicting exercise intentions and behavior.* Unpublished doctoral dissertation, University of Alabama.

Wyer, R. S., Jr., & Srull, T. K. (1981). Category accessibility: Some theoretical and empirical issues concerning the processing of social stimulus information. In E. T. Higgins, C. P. Herman, & M. P. Zanna (Eds.), *Social cognition: The Ontario symposium* (Vol. 1). Hillsdale, NJ: Erlbaum.

Wylie, R. C. (1979). *The self-concept (Vol.2): Theory and research on selected topics.* Lincoln, NE: University of Nebraska Press.

Wynne-Edwards, V. C. (1962). *Animal dispersion in relation to social behavior.* New York: Hafner.

Yancey, W. L. (1971). Architecture and social interaction: The case of a large-scale public housing project. *Environment and Behavior, 3,* 3–21.

Yankelovich, D., & Doble, J. (1984). The public mood: Nuclear weapons and the U.S.S.R. *Foreign Affairs, 63,* 33–46.

Yarmey, A. D. (1979). *The psychology of eyewitness testimony.* New York: Free Press.

Yates, S. M., & Aronson, E. (1983). A social psychological perspective on energy conservation in residential buildings. *American Psychologist, 38,* 435–444.

Yerkes, R. M., & Dodson, J. D. (1908). The relation of strength of stimulus to rapidity of habit formation. *Journal of Comparative Neurology and Psychology, 18,* 459–482.

Yinon, & Dovrat, M. (1987). The reciprocity-arousing potential of the requester's occupation, its status, and the cost and urgency of the request as determinants of helping behavior. *Journal of Applied Social Psychology, 17,* 429–435.

Yinon, Y., & Landau, M. O. (1987). On the reinforcing of helping behavior in a positive mood. *Motivation and Emotion, 11,* 83–93.

Yukl, G. (1974). Effects of the opponent's initial offer, concession magnitude, and concession frequency on bargaining behavior. *Journal of Personality and Social Psychology, 30,* 323–335.

Zaccaro, S. J. (1984). Social loafing: The role of task attractiveness. *Personality and Social Psychology Bulletin, 10,* 99–106.

Zahn-Waxler, C., Radke-Yarrow, M., & King, R. A. (1979). Child rearing and children's prosocial initiations toward victims of distress. *Child Development, 50,* 319–330.

Zajonc, R. B. (1965). Social facilitation. *Science, 149,* 269–274.

Zajonc, R. B. (1968). Attitudinal effects of mere exposure. *Journal of Personality and Social Psychology, 9*(2, part 2), 127.

Zajonc, R. B. (1980a). Feeling and thinking: Preferences need no inferences. *American Psychologist, 35,* 151–175.

Zajonc, R. B. (1980b). Compresence. In P. B. Paulus (Ed.), *Psychology of group influence.* Hillsdale, NJ: Erlbaum.

Zanna, M. P., & Cooper, J. (1974). Dissonance and the pill: An attribution approach to studying the arousal properties of dissonance. *Journal of Personality and Social Psychology, 29,* 703–709.

Zanna, M. P., Kiesler, C. A., & Pilkonis, P. A. (1970). Positive and negative attitudinal affect established by classical conditioning. *Journal of Personality and Social Psychology, 14,* 321–328.

Zanna, M. P., Olson, J. M., & Fazio, R. H. (1980). Attitude-behavior consistency: An individual difference perspective. *Journal of Personality and Social Psychology, 38,* 432–440.

Zeichner, A., & Pihl, R. O. (1980). Effects of alcohol and instigator intent on human aggression. *Journal of Studies on Alcohol, 41,* 265–276.

Zeisel, H., & Diamond, S. S. (1976). The jury selection in the Mitchell-Stans conspiracy trial. *American Bar Foundation Research Journal, 1,* 151–174.

Zillmann, D. (1978). Attribution and misattribution of excitatory reactions. In J. H. Harvey, W. J. Ickes, & R. F. Kidd (Eds.), *New directions in attribution research* (Vol. 2.) Hillsdale, NJ: Erlbaum.

Zillmann, D. (1983). Transfer of excitation in emotional behavior. In J. T. Cacioppo & R. E. Petty (Eds.), *Social psychophysiology* (pp. 215–240). New York: Guilford.

Zillmann, D. (1988). Cognition-excitation interdependencies in aggressive behavior. *Aggressive Behavior, 14,* 51–64.

Zillmann, D., & Bryant, J. (1982). Pornography, sexual callousness, and the trivialization of rape. *Journal of Communication, 32,* 10–21.

Zillmann, D., & Bryant, J. (1988). A response by Dolf Zillmann and Jennings Bryant. *Journal of Communications, 38,* 185–192.

Zimbardo, P. G. (1970). The human choice: Individuation, reason, and order versus deindividuation, impulse, and chaos. In W. J. Arnold & D. Levine (Eds.), *Nebraska symposium on motivation, 1969.* Lincoln: University of Nebraska Press.

Zimbardo, P. G., Ebbesen, E. B., & Maslach, C. (1977). *Influencing attitudes and changing behavior.* Reading, MA: Addison-Wesley.

Zimbardo, P. G., Haney, C., Banks, W. C., & Jaffe, D. (1982). The psychology of imprisonment. In J. C. Brigham & L. Wrightsman (Eds.), *Contemporary issues in social psychology* (4th ed., pp. 230–245). Monterey, CA: Brooks/Cole.

Zimring, C. M. (1981). Stress and the designed environment. *Journal of Social Issues, 37*(1), 145–171.

Zuckerman, M. (1975). Belief in a just world and altruistic behavior. *Journal of Personality and Social Psychology, 31,* 972–976.

Zuckerman, M., DePaulo, B. M., & Rosenthal, R. (1981). Verbal and nonverbal communication of deception. In L. Berkowitz (Ed.), *Advances in experimental social psychology* (Vol. 14, pp. 1–59). New York: Academic Press.

Zuckerman, M., & Feldman, L. S. (1984). Actions and occurrences in attribution theory. *Journal of Personality and Social Psychology, 40,* 541–550.

Zuckerman, M., Kernis, M. R., Driver, R., & Koestner, R. (1984). Segmentation of behavior: Effects of actual deception and expected deception. *Journal of Personality and Social Psychology, 46,* 1173–1182.

Zuckerman, M., Koestner, R., & Alton, A. (1984). Learning to detect deception. *Journal of Personality and Social Psychology, 46,* 519–528.

Zuckerman, M., Mann, R. W., & Bernieri, F. J. (1982). Determinants of consensus estimates: Attribution, salience, and representativeness. *Journal of Personality and Social Psychology, 42,* 839–852.

Zumoff, R., Rosenfeld, R. S., Friedman, M., Byers, J., Rosenman, R. H., & Hellman, J. (1983). Elevated daytime urinary excretion of testosterone glucuronide in men with the Type A behavior pattern. *Psychosomatic Medicine, 45.*

Author Index

Subject Index

Photograph Credits

Unless otherwise acknowledged, all photographs are the property of Scott, Foresman. Page abbreviations are as follows: (T)top, (C)center, (B)bottom, (L)left, (R)right, (INS)inset.